D1087982

PREFACE

Mathematics for Management and Finance, sixth edition, is designed for the first course in mathematics for students of business administration. It meets two basic needs, providing (1) mathematical background and (2) methods of solving mathematical problems in management and finance.

The topics are presented with these two needs in mind. Thus, students who have had little or perhaps no algebra in high school, but who have determination in learning, will find that this text is suitable to their capacities. Those who have a strong background in algebra will find challenging material throughout the text. After the completion of this course, the student should be prepared to continue with more advanced work in subjects involving quantitative analysis, such as accounting, statistics, investments, and insurance. This leads the author to believe that for a student of business administration, this text is more adequate and practical than a one-year course in finite mathematics, mathematical analysis, or college algebra. The latter courses traditionally emphasize theoretical mathematics, which is less pertinent to the foreseeable needs of a business student.

This sixth edition has added new problems and topics, updated information, and reorganized text material. The text is divided into four parts. Part One discusses basic and modern mathematics. It presents fundamental arithmetic and algebraic operations, beginning with elementary concepts. Students who have not had sufficient mathematics in high school will thus have an opportunity to strengthen their background. Furthermore, sufficient material has been provided for those students who may have had mathematics some time ago but now need a review in beginning a study of the subject of mathematics for management and finance.

Part Two discusses mathematics in business management. The topics included in this part represent problem areas found in almost every type of business enterprise. These topics are fundamental statistical methods, the income statement, simple interest, and bank discount. Part Three first introduces the applications of calculators and computers and then discusses the basic topics of the mathematics of long-term investment—

compound interest and annuities. Part Four discusses the applications of the mathematics of compound interest and annuity to debt extinction, bonds, depreciation, depletion, perpetuity, capitalization, life annuities, and life insurance.

Experience shows that when students readily know the principles involved in each type of calculation, they usually become better prepared for problem solving and for more advanced work. Throughout this text, the basic principle for each topic in financial problems is illustrated in detail. Special terms are clearly defined and explained before they are applied. Diagrams are frequently employed as aids to illustrate the more complex examples. After the principles have been illustrated, formulas are often used to facilitate computation. However, the number of formulas has been kept to a minimum, and the formulas are presented in a simple manner. Proofs for the more complicated formulas are given in footnotes to the text where they are presented.

Enough number problems (drills) are placed at the beginning of each exercise so that students can quickly learn the mechanics of the new symbols and terms in each new process. In the statement problems that follow, students have the opportunity to exercise their reasoning ability. In addition, ample review problems are provided at the end of certain chapters to give students an opportunity to solve problems independently without referring to the illustrations in the individual sections of the text.

The problems in each exercise are arranged so that either all odd-numbered or all even-numbered problems can be assigned by the instructor without fear of omitting the material that has been illustrated in the examples. Answers to the odd-numbered problems are placed at the end of the book. Detailed solutions to the odd-numbered and even-numbered problems are given in the instructor's manual.

The material presented in this text is sufficient for a one-year course, offered either in two semesters or in three quarters. However, if there is not sufficient time to cover all material, those sections and problems that have been starred (★) may be omitted without interrupting the continuity of the text organization. The text may also be used as a one-semester course under either of the following suggestions:

1. To emphasize general management and financial problems—Chapters 6 through 13 and Chapters 15 and 16.
2. To emphasize investment problems—Chapters 8 through 13 and Chapters 15 through 19.

Each of the two suggestions may easily be adjusted for either a one-quarter or a two-quarter course. More detailed assignment suggestions are given in the instructor's manual.

The tables included in the Appendices have been designed primarily for this textbook. However, coverage in the tables is complete enough for most practical business problems involving logarithms, compound interest, annuities, and life insurance. The tables of logarithms include six-place and seven-place mantissas. The compound interest and annuity tables include the 40 most commonly used periodic interest rates on the investment market today. Other special features of the tables are summarized in the preface to the tables.

I am deeply grateful to my late wife, Betty Outen Shao, for her expert services in editing the manuscript of the first edition of this book. In addition, I am very grateful to our four sons who have participated in the work of recent editions. They are Professors Stephen P. Shao, Jr., at Northern Telecom Company and formerly at University of Baltimore (Ph.D., U. of Maryland), Dale H. Shao at East Carolina University (Ph.D., Georgia State U.), Lawrence P. Shao at Fordham University (Ph.D., U. of Tennessee), and Alan T. Shao at Kennesaw College (Ph.D., U. of Alabama).

Stephen Pinyee Shao
Old Dominion University

CONTENTS

★ The material contained within a section or a chapter preceded by a boldfaced star is optional. The material may be omitted, and the continuity of the series of mathematical operations will not be interrupted.

3 MATHEMATICS IN INVESTMENT—BASIC TOPICS

4 MATHEMATICS IN INVESTMENT—APPLICATIONS

APPENDIX TABLES

PART ONE
BASIC AND MODERN MATHEMATICS

1 REVIEW OF BASIC ARITHMETIC

The arithmetical operations introduced in this chapter are basic to more advanced study in mathematics. The basic operations are addition, subtraction, multiplication, and division. They involve whole numbers, decimal numbers, and fractions. However, in this chapter the emphasis is on fractions. Fractional operations are more complicated in calculation and thus require more attention in illustrations.

In this chapter, the basic aspects of common fractions are first introduced (Section 1.1). Next, the basic operations of addition, subtraction, and multiplication are illustrated (Section 1.2). Third, the detailed operations of division are explained (Section 1.3). Finally, the topics related to common fractions—decimal fractions, aliquot parts, and repetends—are presented (Section 1.4).

1.1 INTRODUCTION TO COMMON FRACTIONS

A. Terminology

A *fraction* is an *indicated division*. It has two *terms*: the *numerator*, which is written above the line, and the *denominator*, which is written below the line. Thus, $\frac{2}{5}$ is a fraction; 2 is the numerator and 5 is the denominator. The numbers 2 and 5 are the terms of the fraction.

When the division is not actually carried out, the written fraction is interpreted as follows. The denominator 5 represents the number of equal parts into which the whole of a thing has been divided. The numerator 2 shows the number of equal parts that have been taken out of the whole. If the whole is an apple, $\frac{2}{5}$ of the apple is 2 parts of the apple, which has been divided into 5 equal parts.

There are three types of *common fractions*:

Proper Fraction. The numerator is less than the denominator, such as $\frac{1}{3}$ and $\frac{15}{21}$.

Improper Fraction. The numerator is equal to or greater than the denominator, such as $\frac{7}{7}$, $\frac{5}{3}$, and $\frac{17}{6}$.

Complex Fraction. One or more fractions are found in either the numerator or denominator, or in both. The line that separates the numerator from the denominator is usually longer than the lines in the numerator or the denominator, such as

$$\frac{\frac{3}{5}}{11}, \quad \frac{9}{\frac{2}{5}}, \quad \text{and} \quad \frac{\frac{2}{3}}{\frac{15}{21}}$$

When the division as indicated by the fraction is carried out, the numerator is divided by the denominator, such as

$$\frac{2}{5} = 2 \div 5 \quad \text{and} \quad \frac{\frac{3}{5}}{11} = \frac{3}{5} \div 11$$

When a number consists of a whole number and a fraction, it is called a *mixed number*. Thus, a mixed number is the sum of a whole number and a fraction, such as the sum of 3 and $\frac{1}{4}$ being written as $3\frac{1}{4}$. A mixed number may be expressed as an improper fraction, such as $3\frac{1}{4}$ being written as $\frac{13}{4}$ in Example 1.

EXAMPLE 1

$$3\frac{1}{4} = 3 + \frac{1}{4} = \frac{3 \times 4}{4} + \frac{1}{4} = \frac{13}{4}; \text{ or simply, } 3\frac{1}{4} = \frac{(3 \times 4) + 1}{4} = \frac{13}{4}$$

An improper fraction, such as $\frac{17}{6}$, may be expressed as a mixed number by writing it as $2\frac{5}{6}$, as in Example 2.

EXAMPLE 2

$$\frac{17}{6} = 17 \div 6 = 2 + \frac{5}{6} = 2\frac{5}{6}$$

B. Converting Fractions to Higher and Lower Terms

The terms of a fraction may be converted to either higher or lower terms without changing the value of the fraction. The process of converting a fraction in this manner is called *reduction*. Thus, the word "reduction" (or reduce) as used in this sense does not mean to reduce a fraction to a smaller or a lower value. In division, multiplying or dividing both the dividend and divisor by the *same number* does not affect the quotient. For example, $6 \div 3 = 2$ and $(6 \times 10) \div (3 \times 10) = 2$; or $(6 \div 3) \div (3 \div 3) = 2$. The principle that multiplying or dividing both the numerator and the denominator by the same number, other than zero, does not affect the value of the fraction is shown in the following illustrations.

EXAMPLE 3

Reduce (or convert) $\frac{2}{3}$ to higher terms.

$$\frac{2}{3} = \frac{2 \times 4}{3 \times 4} = \frac{8}{12}; \qquad \frac{8}{12} = \frac{8 \times 3}{12 \times 3} = \frac{24}{36}$$

There are an unlimited number of higher terms of $\frac{2}{3}$.

EXAMPLE 4 Reduce $\frac{84}{315}$ to lower terms.

$$\frac{84}{315} = \frac{84 \div 3}{315 \div 3} = \frac{28}{105}; \qquad \frac{28}{105} = \frac{28 \div 7}{105 \div 7} = \frac{4}{15}$$

In Example 4, 3 is the common divisor of 84 and 315; 7 is the common divisor of 28 and 105; and there is no common divisor for the terms of the fraction $\frac{4}{15}$. When the numerator and the denominator have no common divisor, the fraction has been reduced to its *simplest form*, also called *lowest terms*. The best way to reduce a fraction to its *lowest terms* is to divide both the numerator and the denominator by their *greatest common divisor*. In Example 4, the product of the two common divisors (3 and 7) equals 21, which is the greatest common divisor of 84 and 315; that is,

$$\frac{84}{315} = \frac{84 \div 21}{315 \div 21} = \frac{4}{15}$$

C. Finding the Greatest Common Divisor

When the *greatest common divisor* (g.c.d.), also called the *highest common factor*, of the numerator and denominator is not apparent, the following procedure is recommended to find the desirable divisor:

STEP (1). Divide the larger number by the smaller number.
STEP (2). If there is a remainder in Step (1), divide the smaller number by the remainder.
STEP (3). If there is a remainder in Step (2), divide the remainder in Step (1) by the remainder in Step (2).
STEP (4). Continue dividing each remainder by its succeeding remainder until the remainder is zero. The last divisor, a nonzero remainder, is the greatest common divisor.

EXAMPLE 5 (a) Find the g.c.d. of 84 and 315.
(b) Reduce the fraction $\frac{84}{315}$ to its lowest terms.

(a) Here 315 is larger than 84. Thus,

```
                          3
                     84)315 ..................Step (1)
                        252    1
                         63 )84...............Step (2)
                              63   3
      Last divisor            21 )63...........Steps (3) and (4)
      The g.c.d. is 21.           63
                                   0 (Remainder)
```

(b) Answer: $\frac{4}{15}$ (See Example 4.)

EXAMPLE 6 (a) Find the g.c.d. of 170 and 9.
(b) Reduce the fraction $\frac{9}{170}$ to its lowest terms.

(a) Here 170 is larger than 9. Thus,

```
       18
    9)170
      9
      80
      72  1
       8 )9
          8  8
Last divisor   1 )8
The g.c.d. is 1.   8
                   0
```

(b) The answer is $\frac{9}{170}$ since the g.c.d. is 1.

In general, the g.c.d. of two or more numbers is the product of all the prime factors *common* to these numbers. A *prime factor* is a number consisting of no other factors but itself and 1, such as 1, 2, 3, 5, 7, and 11. All other integers (whole numbers), called *composite numbers*, may consist of two or more prime factors. Thus, the product of all the prime factors of a number is the number itself. For example, the prime factors of the composite number 6 are 2 and 3, and the product of 2 and 3 is 6.

EXAMPLE 7

Find the g.c.d. of 4, 16, 24, 28, 36.

Since 4 consists of two prime factors, 2 and 2, it may be written: $4 = 2 \times 2$. Hence, the numbers above may be written by their respective prime factors as follows:

$$
\begin{aligned}
4 &= 2 \times 2 \\
16 &= 2 \times 2 \times 2 \times 2 \\
24 &= 2 \times 2 \times 2 \times 3 \\
28 &= 2 \times 2 \times 7 \\
36 &= 2 \times 2 \times 3 \times 3
\end{aligned}
$$

The prime factors common to all of the five numbers are 2 and 2; therefore, the g.c.d. is $2 \times 2 = 4$.

The work is usually done by division and can be conveniently arranged as follows:

```
2)4, 16, 24, 28, 36
2)2,  8, 12, 14, 18
  1,  4,  6,  7,  9
```

The common divisors of the five numbers are 2 and 2; thus, the g.c.d. is $2 \times 2 = 4$.

Note that the method of finding a g.c.d. of more than two numbers is useful in reducing the terms of a ratio to the lowest terms, such as the ratio having five terms $4{:}16{:}24{:}28{:}36 = \frac{4}{4}{:}\frac{16}{4}{:}\frac{24}{4}{:}\frac{28}{4}{:}\frac{36}{4} = 1{:}4{:}6{:}7{:}9$. A more complete discussion on the subject of ratios is presented in Chapter 2.

D. Finding the Lowest Common Denominator

In order to compare one fraction with other fractions, there is a need to find a *common denominator* for all of the fractions.

EXAMPLE 8

Compare the fractions $\frac{2}{3}$ and $\frac{7}{11}$. Which is larger?

By visual inspection, it is difficult to know which one of the two fractions is larger. However, when the two fractions are reduced to the point that they have a common denominator, the comparison becomes a simple operation.

$$\frac{2}{3} = \frac{2 \times 11}{3 \times 11} = \frac{22}{33} \qquad \frac{7}{11} = \frac{7 \times 3}{11 \times 3} = \frac{21}{33}$$

Since $\frac{22}{33}$ is larger than $\frac{21}{33}$, the fraction $\frac{2}{3}$ is found to be the larger one.

However, in the above example, there are an unlimited number of common denominators of the fractions $\frac{2}{3}$ and $\frac{7}{11}$, such as 33, 33×2 or 66, and 33×3 or 99; but 33 is the lowest and the simplest one. In adding and subtracting fractions, the work is greatly simplified if the *lowest common denominator* is used.

The lowest common denominator (l.c.d.) of a group of fractions is the *least common multiple* (l.c.m.) of the denominators of the fractions. The method of finding the least common multiple is presented below.

E. Finding the Least Common Multiple

A multiple of a given number is the product of that number and any multiplier. For example, 18 is a multiple of the given number 6, since 18 is the product of 6 and the multiplier 3. Also, 6 and 12 are multiples of 6, since

$6 \times 1 = 6$
$6 \times 2 = 12$

A common multiple of a group of numbers is a number that is a multiple of each of the numbers in the group. For example, 18 is a common multiple of 18, 9, 6, 3, 2, and 1, since

$18 \times 1 = 18$
$9 \times 2 = 18$
$6 \times 3 = 18$

Every integer is a multiple of 1, such as $6 \times 1 = 6$ and $18 \times 1 = 18$, as illustrated above.

The following methods may be used to find the *least common multiple* (l.c.m.) of a group of numbers:

METHOD A

When there is no common factor in a group of numbers, the product of the numbers in the group is the l.c.m. Thus,

6 is the l.c.m. of 2 and 3, since $2 \times 3 = 6$
33 is the l.c.m. of 3 and 11, since $3 \times 11 = 33$
70 is the l.c.m. of 2, 5, and 7, since $2 \times 5 \times 7 = 70$

There is no common factor in the group of numbers 2 and 3, or 3 and 11, or 2, 5, and 7.

METHOD B

When there are common factors in a group of numbers, the l.c.m. can be determined by division, as shown below. In each step of the division, at least *two* of the numbers are divided by their common *prime* factor. The product of the common prime factors and the final quotients is the l.c.m.

EXAMPLE 9 Find the l.c.m. of 12, 30, and 56.

$$\begin{array}{l} 2\underline{)12,\ 30,\ 56} \\ 2\underline{)\ 6,\ 15,\ 28} \\ 3\underline{)\ 3,\ 15,\ 14} \\ \quad 1,\ \ 5,\ 14 \end{array}$$

The l.c.m. is $2 \times 2 \times 3 \times 1 \times 5 \times 14 = 840$.

NOTE: The first divisor 2 is the common prime factor to all the numbers. However, the second divisor 2 is the common prime factor to 6 and 28 only; the number 15 is not divisible by 2 and remains unchanged. The divisor 3 is the prime factor to 3 and 15 only; the number 14 is not divisible by 3 and remains unchanged.

If a divisor is not a common prime factor, there is danger of obtaining a common multiple that is not the *least* common multiple, such as the result in the following division:

$$\begin{array}{l} 6\underline{)12,\ 30,\ 56} \\ 2\underline{)\ 2,\ \ 5,\ 56} \\ \quad 1,\ \ 5,\ 28 \end{array}$$

Here, $6 \times 2 \times 1 \times 5 \times 28 = 1{,}680$, which is not the l.c.m. The divisor 6 is not a prime factor, since $6 = 2 \times 3$.

Note carefully the distinction between the method used in finding the g.c.d. and the method for finding the l.c.m. when the division method is used. The g.c.d. for a group of numbers is found by multiplying the prime factors which are divisible into *all* of the numbers in the group, whereas the l.c.m. is found by multiplying the prime factors, which are divisible into at least two of the numbers in each step, *and* the quotients of the division. In the preceding example, 2 (the first divisor common to *all* three numbers) is the g.c.d. of the group of numbers 12, 30, and 56, whereas the l.c.m. is 840. The g.c.d. is generally used for reducing a fraction to its lowest terms, whereas the l.c.m. is used for finding the lowest common denominator for a group of fractions.

EXAMPLE 10 Reduce the fractions $\frac{5}{12}$, $\frac{13}{30}$, and $\frac{23}{56}$ to fractions with an l.c.d. Then arrange them in order beginning with the largest.

The l.c.m. of the *denominators* of the three fractions is 840 (see Example 9); or the l.c.d. of the three *fractions* is 840. When the denominator of a fraction is multiplied by a number, the numerator must also be multiplied by the same number if the value of the fraction is to stay unchanged.

$$\text{Since } 840 \div 12 = 70, \quad \text{then} \quad \frac{5}{12} = \frac{5 \times 70}{12 \times 70} = \frac{350}{840}$$

$$840 \div 30 = 28, \quad \frac{13}{30} = \frac{13 \times 28}{30 \times 28} = \frac{364}{840}$$

$$840 \div 56 = 15, \quad \frac{23}{56} = \frac{23 \times 15}{56 \times 15} = \frac{345}{840}$$

The order of the three fractions is as follows:

$$\frac{13}{30}, \frac{5}{12}, \frac{23}{56}$$

When the l.c.m. of a set of numbers is to be found, any number that is a factor of others in the set may be omitted in the computation. For example, the l.c.m. of 6, 12, 30, and 56 should be the same as the l.c.m. of 12, 30, and 56, because 6 is a factor of 12 and 30. Thus, the l.c.m. of 6, 12, 30, and 56 is also 840.

EXERCISE 1-1 REFERENCE: SECTION 1.1

A. Express the following mixed numbers as improper fractions:

1. $4\frac{1}{5}$ 4. $6\frac{4}{15}$ 7. $9\frac{3}{5}$ 10. $26\frac{23}{81}$
2. $8\frac{2}{7}$ 5. $3\frac{11}{12}$ 8. $20\frac{6}{25}$ 11. $124\frac{12}{325}$
3. $11\frac{3}{8}$ 6. $9\frac{5}{7}$ 9. $45\frac{5}{6}$ 12. $453\frac{235}{311}$

B. Express the following improper fractions as mixed numbers:

13. $\frac{9}{2}$ 16. $\frac{17}{4}$ 19. $\frac{42}{5}$ 22. $\frac{357}{46}$
14. $\frac{7}{3}$ 17. $\frac{41}{8}$ 20. $\frac{31}{6}$ 23. $\frac{4,617}{124}$
15. $\frac{11}{8}$ 18. $\frac{38}{5}$ 21. $\frac{214}{31}$ 24. $\frac{3,263}{216}$

C. Find the g.c.d. of the numerator and the denominator in each of the following and then reduce the fraction to its lowest terms:

25. $\frac{5}{10}$ 28. $\frac{16}{64}$ 31. $\frac{847}{1,331}$ 34. $\frac{92}{138}$
26. $\frac{6}{24}$ 29. $\frac{20}{35}$ 32. $\frac{215}{258}$ 35. $\frac{308}{374}$
27. $\frac{10}{15}$ 30. $\frac{42}{28}$ 33. $\frac{78}{208}$ 36. $\frac{2,231}{4,559}$

D. Arrange the fractions in each group in order beginning with the largest:

37. $\frac{1}{4}, \frac{1}{5}$ 41. $\frac{7}{16}, \frac{4}{9}$ 45. $\frac{1}{2}, \frac{2}{7}, \frac{3}{5}$ 49. $\frac{12}{15}, \frac{2}{3}, \frac{3}{5}, \frac{12}{5}, \frac{1}{3}$
38. $\frac{3}{7}, \frac{4}{7}$ 42. $\frac{14}{15}, \frac{22}{25}$ 46. $\frac{7}{8}, \frac{3}{4}, \frac{1}{2}, \frac{2}{3}$ 50. $\frac{25}{48}, \frac{21}{32}, \frac{19}{30}, \frac{23}{40}$
39. $\frac{5}{7}, \frac{3}{4}$ 43. $\frac{3}{4}, \frac{5}{6}, \frac{2}{5}$ 47. $\frac{11}{9}, \frac{9}{7}, \frac{5}{3}, \frac{13}{11}$
40. $\frac{2}{5}, \frac{6}{13}$ 44. $\frac{2}{3}, \frac{8}{9}, \frac{1}{4}$ 48. $\frac{3}{8}, \frac{3}{6}, \frac{3}{7}, \frac{3}{4}, \frac{3}{5}$

1.2 ADDITION, SUBTRACTION, AND MULTIPLICATION OF FRACTIONS

A. Addition of Fractions

When fractions are added, all addends should be reduced to fractions having a *lowest common denominator*. The sum of the numerators of all addends is the numerator of the required sum; the common denominator is unchanged and is the denominator of the required sum. The required sum will be a proper or an improper fraction. If the sum is an improper fraction, it should be reduced to a mixed number. When mixed numbers are added, it is unnecessary to reduce the numbers to improper fractions. It is much easier to add the integers and the fractions separately. The fractional part of an answer should always be reduced to its lowest terms.

EXAMPLE 1 Add $\frac{2}{3}, \frac{3}{8}, \frac{1}{2}$.

Here the least common multiple (l.c.m.) of the denominators 3, 8, and 2 is 24. The three fractions are reduced to fractions with the l.c.m. as the common denominator:

$$\frac{2}{3} = \frac{2 \times 8}{3 \times 8} = \frac{16}{24}; \quad \frac{3}{8} = \frac{3 \times 3}{8 \times 3} = \frac{9}{24}; \quad \frac{1}{2} = \frac{1 \times 12}{2 \times 12} = \frac{12}{24}$$

Thus, $\frac{2}{3} + \frac{3}{8} + \frac{1}{2} = \frac{16}{24} + \frac{9}{24} + \frac{12}{24} = \frac{16 + 9 + 12}{24} = \frac{37}{24} = 1\frac{13}{24}$

EXAMPLE 2

Add $\frac{5}{12}$, $\frac{13}{30}$, and $\frac{23}{56}$.

The l.c.m. of the *denominators* of the three fractions is 840. See Example 10 in Section 1.1.

Thus,

$$\frac{5}{12} + \frac{13}{30} + \frac{23}{56} = \frac{350}{840} + \frac{364}{840} + \frac{345}{840} = \frac{1{,}059}{840} = \frac{353}{280} = 1\frac{73}{280}$$

EXAMPLE 3

Add $5\frac{6}{7}$, $\frac{16}{3}$, $\frac{232}{21}$, and $29\frac{3}{7}$.

The l.c.m. of the denominators 7, 3, 21, and 7 is 21.

$5\frac{6}{7} = 5\frac{18}{21}$; $\qquad \frac{232}{21} = 11\frac{1}{21}$

$\frac{16}{3} = 5\frac{1}{3} = 5\frac{7}{21}$; $\qquad 29\frac{3}{7} = 29\frac{9}{21}$

Thus, $5\frac{6}{7} + \frac{16}{3} + \frac{232}{21} + 29\frac{3}{7} = 5\frac{18}{21} + 5\frac{7}{21} + 11\frac{1}{21} + 29\frac{9}{21}$

$$= 5 + 5 + 11 + 29 + \frac{18 + 7 + 1 + 9}{21}$$

$$= 50 + \frac{35}{21} = 51\frac{14}{21} = 51\frac{2}{3}$$

B. Subtraction of Fractions

When fractions are subtracted, both the subtrahend (the number to be subtracted) and the minuend (the number from which the subtrahend is subtracted) should be reduced to fractions with a lowest common denominator. The difference between the numerators of the minuend and the subtrahend is the numerator of the required remainder; the common denominator is unchanged and is the denominator of the required remainder. Mixed numbers do not need to be reduced to improper fractions before the subtraction is performed unless the fractional part of the minuend is smaller than the fractional part of the subtrahend.

EXAMPLE 4

Subtract $\frac{2}{7}$ (subtrahend) from $\frac{3}{5}$ (minuend).

Here the l.c.m. of the denominators 7 and 5 is 35.

$$\frac{3}{5} - \frac{2}{7} = \frac{21}{35} - \frac{10}{35} = \frac{11}{35}$$

EXAMPLE 5

Subtract $\frac{2}{7}$ from $2\frac{3}{5}$.

$$2\frac{3}{5} - \frac{2}{7} = 2\frac{21}{35} - \frac{10}{35} = 2\frac{11}{35}$$

EXAMPLE 6

Subtract $\frac{4}{9}$ from 3.

$$3 - \frac{4}{9} = 2\frac{9}{9} - \frac{4}{9} = 2\frac{5}{9}$$

EXAMPLE 7

Subtract $\frac{4}{9}$ from $3\frac{1}{3}$.

$$3\frac{1}{3} - \frac{4}{9} = 3\frac{3}{9} - \frac{4}{9} = 2\frac{9+3}{9} - \frac{4}{9} = 2\frac{12}{9} - \frac{4}{9} = 2\frac{8}{9}$$

C. Multiplication of Fractions

When multiplying fractions, there is no need to find a common denominator of the fractions. The product of the numerators is the numerator of the required product, and the product of the denominators is the denominator of the required product.

EXAMPLE 8

Multiply $\frac{6}{11}$ by $\frac{2}{9}$.

$$\frac{6}{11} \times \frac{2}{9} = \frac{6 \times 2}{11 \times 9} = \frac{12}{99} = \frac{4}{33}$$

Since the product of 6×2 is the same as the product of 2×6, the above computation may be written as follows:

$$\frac{6}{11} \times \frac{2}{9} = \frac{2}{11} \times \frac{6}{9} = \frac{2}{11} \times \frac{6 \div 3}{9 \div 3} = \frac{2}{11} \times \frac{2}{3} = \frac{4}{33}$$

For convenience, $\frac{6 \div 3}{9 \div 3} = \frac{2}{3}$ is usually written as $\frac{\not{6}^{2}}{\not{9}_{3}}$. This method of simplifying fractions should be used in multiplication whenever possible. Thus, multiplication for the above example may be simplified in the following manner:

$$\frac{\not{6}^{2}}{11} \times \frac{2}{\not{9}_{3}} = \frac{4}{33}$$

In *multiplication involving mixed numbers*, a simple method is to reduce each mixed number to an improper fraction before multiplying.

EXAMPLE 9

Multiply $\frac{3}{5}$ by $3\frac{3}{4}$.

$$\frac{3}{5} \times 3\frac{3}{4} = \frac{3}{5} \times \frac{(3 \times 4) + 3}{4} = \frac{3}{\not{5}_{1}} \times \frac{\not{15}^{3}}{4} = \frac{9}{4} = 2\frac{1}{4}$$

EXAMPLE 10

Multiply $5\frac{3}{5}$ by $3\frac{3}{4}$.

$$5\frac{3}{5} \times 3\frac{3}{4} = \frac{\not{28}^{7}}{\not{5}_{1}} \times \frac{\not{15}^{3}}{\not{4}_{1}} = 21$$

EXERCISE 1-2 REFERENCE: SECTION 1.2

Perform the following indicated operations and reduce all answers to lowest terms.

A. *Addition:*

1. $\frac{1}{5} + \frac{1}{5}$
2. $\frac{1}{3} + \frac{1}{4}$
3. $\frac{1}{2} + \frac{5}{6}$
4. $\frac{3}{7} + \frac{3}{8}$
5. $\frac{3}{4} + \frac{2}{3}$
6. $\frac{2}{9} + \frac{1}{6}$
7. $\frac{2}{3} + 5\frac{3}{4}$
8. $2\frac{3}{5} + \frac{1}{2}$
9. $2\frac{2}{5} + \frac{1}{8}$

10. $1\frac{3}{7} + 3\frac{2}{5}$
11. $5\frac{1}{4} + 11\frac{7}{8}$
12. $8\frac{1}{12} + 21\frac{4}{5}$
13. $\frac{3}{7} + \frac{1}{3} + \frac{1}{7}$
14. $\frac{7}{12} + \frac{5}{6} + \frac{1}{5}$
15. $\frac{5}{16} + \frac{3}{8} + \frac{3}{4}$
16. $\frac{4}{21} + \frac{2}{3} + \frac{4}{7}$
17. $\frac{3}{20} + \frac{3}{25} + \frac{7}{10}$
18. $7\frac{1}{6} + 4\frac{2}{3} + 1\frac{5}{12}$
19. $\frac{3}{5} + 2\frac{7}{6} + \frac{19}{3} + \frac{4}{3}$
20. $\frac{3}{2} + 2\frac{1}{4} + \frac{16}{9} + \frac{24}{5}$
21. $\frac{65}{11} + 7\frac{14}{33} + \frac{137}{22} + 3\frac{1}{66}$
22. $3\frac{5}{8} + 4\frac{5}{6} + \frac{7}{12} + \frac{211}{12}$
23. $\frac{17}{4} + \frac{130}{3} + \frac{82}{5} + \frac{19}{6}$
24. $64\frac{1}{2} + 15\frac{1}{3} + 11\frac{1}{6} + 8\frac{2}{5}$

B. *Subtraction:*

25. $\frac{4}{5} - \frac{3}{4}$
26. $\frac{5}{12} - \frac{1}{4}$
27. $\frac{3}{7} - \frac{1}{3}$
28. $\frac{6}{13} - \frac{2}{7}$
29. $\frac{21}{50} - \frac{87}{300}$
30. $\frac{16}{25} - \frac{29}{60}$
31. $1 - \frac{4}{7}$
32. $3\frac{5}{8} - \frac{3}{8}$
33. $4\frac{5}{9} - 2\frac{2}{9}$
34. $9\frac{13}{15} - \frac{4}{5}$
35. $8\frac{1}{3} - \frac{2}{3}$
36. $7\frac{1}{5} - \frac{5}{7}$
37. $15\frac{2}{3} - 7\frac{8}{9}$
38. $23\frac{1}{3} - 5\frac{1}{2}$
39. $6\frac{7}{11} - \frac{8}{9}$
40. $6 - \frac{7}{9}$
41. $4 - 1\frac{3}{4}$
42. $10\frac{11}{13} - 4\frac{11}{12}$
43. $7\frac{11}{12} - 7\frac{3}{4}$
44. $4\frac{3}{5} - \frac{6}{7}$
45. $\frac{12}{5} - \frac{9}{4}$
46. $212\frac{1}{4} - \frac{460}{11}$
47. $\frac{436}{45} - 2\frac{4}{9}$
48. $\frac{543}{20} - \frac{104}{15}$

C. *Multiplication:*

49. $\frac{1}{2} \times \frac{1}{6}$
50. $\frac{3}{8} \times \frac{6}{7}$
51. $\frac{8}{13} \times \frac{7}{16}$
52. $\frac{7}{12} \times \frac{6}{11}$
53. $\frac{26}{40} \times \frac{20}{39}$
54. $\frac{21}{25} \times \frac{1}{7}$
55. $\frac{5}{7} \times \frac{5}{12}$
56. $\frac{12}{19} \times \frac{3}{7}$
57. $\frac{14}{25} \times \frac{7}{18}$
58. $\frac{11}{12} \times \frac{4}{3}$
59. $\frac{17}{22} \times \frac{9}{2}$
60. $\frac{124}{17} \times \frac{5}{44}$
61. $\frac{4}{7} \times \frac{14}{19} \times \frac{5}{36}$
62. $\frac{25}{42} \times \frac{3}{5} \times \frac{4}{15}$
63. $\frac{6}{7} \times \frac{2}{3} \times \frac{7}{8} \times \frac{4}{9}$
64. $\frac{13}{25} \times \frac{3}{14} \times \frac{5}{78} \times \frac{2}{27}$
65. $2\frac{1}{5} \times 3\frac{2}{3}$
66. $4\frac{6}{7} \times 7\frac{4}{5}$
67. $11\frac{1}{2} \times 13\frac{2}{7}$
68. $39\frac{5}{9} \times 20\frac{7}{8}$
69. $211\frac{4}{5} \times 16\frac{3}{8}$
70. $250\frac{7}{16} \times 16$
71. $362\frac{1}{7} \times 2\frac{1}{3}$
72. $156\frac{1}{4} \times 111\frac{1}{5}$

1.3 DIVISION OF FRACTIONS

A. Methods of Dividing Fractions

The following three methods are generally used in dividing fractions. Although the first method is relatively popular, it is not superior in every case. Students should be familiar with all the methods in order to perform the division efficiently.

METHOD A

Multiply the dividend by the reciprocal of the divisor. This method may be expressed as follows:

Dividend ÷ Fraction = Dividend × Reciprocal of the Fraction

The reciprocal of a fraction is the fraction inverted. The product of a fraction and its reciprocal is always equal to 1. Thus, the reciprocal of the fraction $\frac{5}{7}$ is $\frac{7}{5}$ and their product is 1; that is, $\frac{5}{7} \times \frac{7}{5} = 1$. The following example is used to illustrate the method.

EXAMPLE 1 Divide 20 by $\frac{3}{4}$.

$$20 \div \frac{3}{4} = 20 \times \frac{4}{3} = \frac{80}{3} = 26\frac{2}{3}$$

The above method is derived from the definition of division, which gives the following equation:

Dividend ÷ Divisor = Quotient, or
Quotient × Divisor = Dividend

Let the dividend be 20 and the divisor be $\frac{3}{4}$; the above equations become

$20 \div \frac{3}{4} =$ Quotient, or
Quotient $\times \frac{3}{4} = 20$

If the left side of the above equation is multiplied by $\frac{4}{3}$, the right side of the equation must be multiplied by the same quantity in order to keep both sides equal. Thus,

Quotient $\times \frac{3}{4} \times \frac{4}{3} = 20 \times \frac{4}{3}$; Quotient $= 20 \times \frac{4}{3}$

Notice that $\frac{4}{3}$ is the reciprocal of the fraction $\frac{3}{4}$, which is the divisor. Thus, *when a number is to be divided by a fraction, invert the terms of the fraction and then multiply. The product obtained is the quotient of the division*. This method is further illustrated by Examples 2 to 7.

Common Fractions.

EXAMPLE 2 Divide $\frac{2}{3}$ by $\frac{5}{7}$.

$$\frac{2}{3} \div \frac{5}{7} = \frac{2}{3} \times \frac{7}{5} = \frac{14}{15}$$

EXAMPLE 3 Divide 1 by $\frac{3}{8}$.

$$1 \div \frac{3}{8} = \frac{1}{1} \times \frac{8}{3} = \frac{8}{3} = 2\frac{2}{3}$$

NOTE: $\frac{8}{3}$ is the reciprocal of $\frac{3}{8}$. When 1 is divided by a given number, the quotient is the reciprocal of the given number.

EXAMPLE 4 Divide $\frac{3}{5}$ by 11.

$$\frac{3}{5} \div 11 = \frac{3}{5} \times \frac{1}{11} = \frac{3}{55}$$

EXAMPLE 5 Simplify $\dfrac{\frac{10}{33}}{\frac{5}{11}}$.

This problem may be interpreted as $\frac{10}{33}$ divided by $\frac{5}{11}$.

$$\frac{10}{33} \div \frac{5}{11} = \frac{\cancel{10}^{2}}{\cancel{33}_{3}} \times \frac{\cancel{11}^{1}}{\cancel{5}_{1}} = \frac{2}{3}$$

Mixed Numbers. A simple method is to reduce the mixed numbers to improper fractions, then divide.

EXAMPLE 6

Divide $26\frac{1}{4}$ by $2\frac{2}{5}$.

$$26\frac{1}{4} \div 2\frac{2}{5} = \frac{105}{4} \div \frac{12}{5} = \frac{\cancel{105}^{35}}{4} \times \frac{5}{\cancel{12}_{4}} = \frac{175}{16} = 10\frac{15}{16}$$

EXAMPLE 7

Divide $27\frac{3}{4}$ by 6.

$$27\frac{3}{4} \div 6 = \frac{111}{4} \div \frac{6}{1} = \frac{\cancel{111}^{37}}{4} \times \frac{1}{\cancel{6}_{2}} = \frac{37}{8} = 4\frac{5}{8}$$

METHOD B

After reducing both the dividend and the divisor to fractions having the lowest common denominator, cancel the common denominators and divide. This method is recommended when the fractions have a common denominator, as in Example 9.

EXAMPLE 8

Divide $\frac{2}{3}$ by $\frac{5}{7}$.

The l.c.m. of the denominators 3 and 7 is 21. This division may be written as a complex fraction and divided as follows:

$$\frac{\frac{2}{3}}{\frac{5}{7}} = \frac{\frac{14}{21}}{\frac{15}{21}} = \frac{\frac{14}{\cancel{21}} \times \cancel{21}}{\frac{15}{\cancel{21}} \times \cancel{21}} = \frac{14}{15}; \quad \text{or it may be written}$$

$$\frac{2}{3} \div \frac{5}{7} = \frac{14}{\cancel{21}} \div \frac{15}{\cancel{21}} = 14 \div 15 = \frac{14}{15}$$

EXAMPLE 9

Divide $2\frac{7}{30}$ by $\frac{11}{30}$.

Here the common denominator is 30.

$$2\frac{7}{30} \div \frac{11}{30} = \frac{67}{\cancel{30}} \div \frac{11}{\cancel{30}} = \frac{67}{11} = 6\frac{1}{11}$$

METHOD C

Divide after reducing both the dividend and the divisor to integers. The reduction may be accomplished by multiplying the dividend and the divisor by the l.c.m. of their denominators. This method is useful when the denominator of one fraction is a factor of the denominator of the other fraction, as in Example 10.

EXAMPLE 10

Divide $6\frac{1}{20}$ by $2\frac{2}{5}$.

Here 5 is a factor of 20, since $5 \times 4 = 20$.

$$6\frac{1}{20} \div 2\frac{2}{5} = \frac{121}{20} \div \frac{12}{5} = \left(\frac{121}{\cancel{20}} \times \cancel{20}\right) \div \left(\frac{12}{\cancel{5}} \times \cancel{20}^{4}\right) = \frac{121}{48} = 2\frac{25}{48}$$

EXAMPLE 11

Divide $\frac{2}{3}$ by $\frac{5}{7}$.

The l.c.m. of the denominators 3 and 7 is 21.

$$\frac{2}{3} \div \frac{5}{7} = \frac{\frac{2}{3}}{\frac{5}{7}} = \frac{\frac{2}{\cancel{3}} \times \cancel{21}^{7}}{\frac{5}{\cancel{7}} \times \cancel{21}^{3}} = \frac{14}{15}; \quad \text{or it may be written}$$

$$\frac{2}{3} \div \frac{5}{7} = \left(\frac{2}{\cancel{3}} \times \cancel{21}^{7}\right) \div \left(\frac{5}{\cancel{7}} \times \cancel{21}^{3}\right) = 14 \div 15 = \frac{14}{15}$$

B. Rounding Decimal Places

When the numerator is divided by the denominator in a given fraction, the quotient obtained will be a decimal number. The decimal number is usually rounded to a desired number of decimal places. There are various methods of rounding decimal places. For example, the rounding method for an engineer is different from the rounding method for a statistician. However, the following rounding method, which is used in this text, does meet most purposes in business.

To round a given number to a desired number of decimal places, the general rule is that *if the portion to be dropped begins with the figure 5* (which is one-half of the unit of the last figure retained) *or above, add 1 to the last figure retained; if the portion to be dropped is less than 5, discard it.*

EXAMPLE 12 The numbers in the left-hand column below have been rounded to two decimal places, as shown in the column on the right:

1.376	1.38
51.2454	51.25
\$ 2.983	\$ 2.98 (rounded to the nearest cent)
\$32.72451	\$32.72 (rounded to the nearest cent)

NOTE: Refer to the number 1.376. Since 6 (thousandths) is more than 5 [or one-half of the unit of the last figure retained, 7 (hundredths)], 1 is added to 7 and the answer is 1.38. Now refer to the number \$32.72451. Since the thousandths digit is 4, the places consisting of 4 and thereafter are discarded.

EXAMPLE 13 Divide $6\frac{1}{20}$ by $2\frac{2}{5}$ and round the quotient to four decimal places.

$$6\frac{1}{20} \div 2\frac{2}{5} = 2\frac{25}{48} \quad \text{(see the quotient in Example 10)}$$

$$= 2.5208333, \quad \text{rounded to } 2.5208$$

EXERCISE 1-3 REFERENCE: SECTION 1.3

Perform the following indicated operations and reduce all answers to lowest terms.

A. Write the reciprocal of each number:

1. $\frac{1}{3}$	3. $\frac{4}{5}$	5. $\frac{15}{18}$	7. $3\frac{9}{110}$
2. 14	4. $\frac{4}{9}$	6. $2\frac{12}{25}$	8. $2\frac{26}{43}$

B. Divide by using the reciprocal:

9. $\frac{5}{6} \div \frac{1}{6}$	13. $25 \div 3\frac{2}{7}$	17. $\frac{8}{15} \div 2$	21. $\frac{108}{25} \div \frac{54}{205}$
10. $\frac{2}{3} \div \frac{5}{12}$	14. $32 \div \frac{4}{5}$	18. $\frac{14}{19} \div \frac{16}{31}$	22. $18\frac{2}{3} \div 6\frac{2}{5}$
11. $\frac{3}{7} \div \frac{10}{13}$	15. $\frac{8}{9} \div 1\frac{1}{7}$	19. $\frac{17}{8} \div \frac{9}{4}$	23. $22\frac{6}{7} \div 3\frac{5}{9}$
12. $18 \div 4\frac{1}{2}$	16. $\frac{11}{12} \div 3\frac{5}{12}$	20. $\frac{26}{9} \div \frac{13}{8}$	24. $104\frac{3}{8} \div 28\frac{7}{11}$

C. Divide after reducing to fractions having a common denominator:

25. $\frac{2}{5} \div \frac{3}{7}$	28. $\frac{11}{12} \div \frac{7}{15}$	31. $\frac{25}{33} \div \frac{14}{11}$	34. $42\frac{11}{12} \div 7\frac{13}{15}$
26. $\frac{2}{3} \div \frac{5}{18}$	29. $\frac{14}{15} \div 3$	32. $\frac{98}{99} \div \frac{22}{9}$	35. $\frac{5}{12} \div 3\frac{1}{3}$
27. $\frac{3}{4} \div \frac{7}{10}$	30. $\frac{7}{42} \div 2$	33. $32\frac{4}{5} \div 6\frac{1}{5}$	36. $12\frac{6}{7} \div 11\frac{5}{14}$

D. Divide after reducing both the dividend and the divisor to integers:

37. $\frac{4}{7} \div \frac{1}{3}$ 40. $\frac{13}{14} \div \frac{7}{8}$ 43. $\frac{24}{33} \div \frac{15}{22}$ 46. $32\frac{12}{17} \div 5\frac{2}{3}$
38. $\frac{3}{5} \div \frac{3}{4}$ 41. $\frac{15}{16} \div 2$ 44. $\frac{69}{88} \div \frac{15}{8}$ 47. $8\frac{4}{9} \div 11\frac{1}{3}$
39. $\frac{6}{11} \div \frac{2}{5}$ 42. $\frac{8}{60} \div 3$ 45. $46\frac{5}{7} \div 5\frac{2}{7}$ 48. $12\frac{7}{9} \div 11\frac{5}{6}$

E. Round the following numbers to two decimal places:

49. 42.7543 53. 1.6723 57. 2.3847
50. 317.6551 54. 0.8246 58. 6.6871
51. 632.438 55. 7,362.0564 59. 43.0051
52. 52.769 56. 8,319.0486 60. 68.0462

1.4 DECIMAL FRACTIONS, ALIQUOT PARTS, AND REPETENDS

A. Decimal Fractions

Common fractions whose denominators are 10 or some power of 10 (that is, the product of 10's, such as 100, 1,000 and 10,000) can be written in a special way by using a decimal point, as follows:

$$\frac{1}{10} = .1, \quad \frac{3}{100} = .03, \quad \frac{57}{1,000} = .057$$

The above equivalents of the common fractions are called *decimal fractions, decimal numbers*, or simply decimals. The relationship between a common fraction and its equivalent decimal fraction is further illustrated as follows.

Changing a Common Fraction to a Decimal Fraction. Any common fraction can be written in decimal fraction form. To change a common fraction to decimal fraction form, simply divide the numerator by the denominator in the given common fraction.

EXAMPLE 1 $\frac{9}{20} = 9 \div 20 = .45$

EXAMPLE 2 $5\frac{3}{15} = 5 + \frac{3}{15} = 5 + .2 = 5.2$

EXAMPLE 3 $12\frac{6}{19} = 12 + \frac{6}{19} = 12.315\frac{15}{19}$

NOTE: When the result in Example 3 is rounded to 3 decimal places, the answer is 12.316, since $\frac{15}{19}$ is more than one-half of the unit of the last figure retained.

Changing a Decimal Fraction to a Common Fraction. When a decimal fraction is written in a common fraction form, the figures are used as the numerator, and 1, with as many zeros annexed as there are decimal places, is used as the denominator. The common fraction is then simplified or reduced to its lowest terms.

EXAMPLE 4 $.0195 = \frac{195}{10,000} = \frac{39}{2,000}$

EXAMPLE 5 $6.52 = 6\frac{52}{100} = 6\frac{13}{25}$

EXAMPLE 6

$$14.641\frac{2}{7} = 14\frac{641\frac{2}{7}}{1,000} = 14\frac{\frac{4,489}{7}}{\frac{1,000}{1}} = 14\frac{4,489}{7,000}$$

NOTE: In Example 6 there are only three decimal places, since $\frac{2}{7}$ is a fraction of the thousandths unit.

B. Aliquot Parts

An *aliquot part* is the part of a number by which the number may be divided leaving no remainder. For example, $1\frac{1}{2}$, 2, and 3 are aliquot parts of 6, because $6 \div 1\frac{1}{2} = 4$, $6 \div 2 = 3$, and $6 \div 3 = 2$. Numbers 50, $33\frac{1}{3}$, and 20 are aliquot parts of 100, because $100 \div 50 = 2$, $100 \div 33\frac{1}{3} = 3$, and $100 \div 20 = 5$. Since percentage (% or $\frac{1}{100}$) problems frequently occur in business computations, the aliquot parts of 100 are of particular interest. In many cases, computation in multiplication and division is greatly simplified when percents with aliquot parts of 100, such as $33\frac{1}{3}\%$ in Example 7, are converted to common fractions before the computation. Of course, if there is to be any practical value to a student, he should memorize the aliquot parts of the numbers that are frequently used by him. The most important aliquot parts of 100 as expressed in hundredths ($\frac{1}{100}$ or %) and their equivalent values in the lowest common fraction form are given in Table 1–1.

Table 1–1 Common Aliquot Parts of 100, as Expressed in Hundredths ($\frac{1}{100}$ or %) and Their Equivalent Values in the Lowest Common Fraction Form

Denominator of Common Fraction	*Numerator of Common Fraction*												
	1	2	3	4	5	6	7	8	9	10	11	12	13
	Unit: $\frac{1}{100}$ *or %*												
2	50												
3	$33\frac{1}{3}$	$66\frac{2}{3}$											
4	25		75										
5	20	40	60	80									
6	$16\frac{2}{3}$				$83\frac{1}{3}$								
7	$14\frac{2}{7}$	$28\frac{4}{7}$	$42\frac{6}{7}$	$57\frac{1}{7}$	$71\frac{3}{7}$	$85\frac{5}{7}$							
8	$12\frac{1}{2}$		$37\frac{1}{2}$		$62\frac{1}{2}$		$87\frac{1}{2}$						
9	$11\frac{1}{9}$	$22\frac{2}{9}$		$44\frac{4}{9}$	$55\frac{5}{9}$		$77\frac{7}{9}$	$88\frac{8}{9}$					
10	10		30				70		90				
11	$9\frac{1}{11}$	$18\frac{2}{11}$	$27\frac{3}{11}$	$36\frac{4}{11}$	$45\frac{5}{11}$	$54\frac{6}{11}$	$63\frac{7}{11}$	$72\frac{8}{11}$	$81\frac{9}{11}$	$90\frac{10}{11}$			
12	$8\frac{1}{3}$				$41\frac{2}{3}$		$58\frac{1}{3}$				$91\frac{2}{3}$		
13	$7\frac{9}{13}$	$15\frac{5}{13}$	$23\frac{1}{13}$	$30\frac{10}{13}$	$38\frac{6}{13}$	$46\frac{2}{13}$	$53\frac{11}{13}$	$61\frac{7}{13}$	$69\frac{3}{13}$	$76\frac{12}{13}$	$84\frac{8}{13}$	$92\frac{4}{13}$	
14	$7\frac{1}{7}$		$21\frac{3}{7}$		$35\frac{5}{7}$				$64\frac{2}{7}$		$78\frac{4}{7}$		$92\frac{6}{7}$
15	$6\frac{2}{3}$	$13\frac{1}{3}$		$26\frac{2}{3}$			$46\frac{2}{3}$	$53\frac{1}{3}$			$73\frac{1}{3}$		$86\frac{2}{3}$
16	$6\frac{1}{4}$		$18\frac{3}{4}$		$31\frac{1}{4}$		$43\frac{3}{4}$		$56\frac{1}{4}$		$68\frac{3}{4}$		$81\frac{1}{4}$
20	5		15				35		45		55		65
25	4	8	12	16		24	28	32	36		44	48	52
30	$3\frac{1}{3}$			$13\frac{1}{3}$			$23\frac{1}{3}$		30		$36\frac{2}{3}$		$43\frac{1}{3}$
40	$2\frac{1}{2}$		$7\frac{1}{2}$				$17\frac{1}{2}$		$22\frac{1}{2}$		$27\frac{1}{2}$		$32\frac{1}{2}$
50	2		6				14		18		22		26

For example: $\frac{1}{2} = 50\%$; $\frac{2}{6} = \frac{1}{3} = 33\frac{1}{3}\%$; $\frac{4}{10} = \frac{2}{5} = 40\%$; $\frac{12}{14} = \frac{6}{7} = 85\frac{5}{7}\%$; $\frac{8}{40} = \frac{4}{20} = \frac{2}{10} = \frac{1}{5} = 20\%$.

The following examples illustrate the use of Table 1–1 in multiplication and division.

EXAMPLE 7 Multiply 21 by $33\frac{1}{3}\%$.

The table shows that $33\frac{1}{3}\% = \frac{1}{3}$. Thus,

$$21 \times 33\frac{1}{3}\% = \cancel{21}^{7} \times \frac{1}{\cancel{3}} = 7$$

EXAMPLE 8 Multiply 21 by $33\frac{1}{3}$.

$33\frac{1}{3} = 33\frac{1}{3}\% \times 100 = \frac{1}{3} \times 100$. Thus,

$$21 \times 33\frac{1}{3} = \cancel{21}^{7} \times \frac{1}{\cancel{3}} \times 100 = 700$$

EXAMPLE 9 Divide 140 by $58\frac{1}{3}\%$.

The table shows that $58\frac{1}{3}\% = \frac{7}{12}$. Thus,

$$140 \div 58\frac{1}{3}\% = 140 \div \frac{7}{12} = \cancel{140}^{20} \times \frac{12}{\cancel{7}} = 240$$

EXAMPLE 10 Divide 140 by $58\frac{1}{3}$.

$58\frac{1}{3} = 58\frac{1}{3}\% \times 100 = \frac{7}{12} \times 100 = \frac{700}{12}$. Thus,

$$140 \div 58\frac{1}{3} = 140 \div \frac{700}{12} = \cancel{140} \times \frac{12}{\cancel{700}_{5}} = \frac{12}{5} = 2\frac{2}{5} \text{ or } 2.40$$

★C. Repetends

When some common fractions are reduced to decimals, it may be found that the remainders do not terminate and the decimals continue repeating. For example, when the fraction $\frac{1}{3}$ is reduced to a decimal, the result is .3333. . . . Decimals that continue to repeat infinitely are called *repetends*. They are also known as *circulating* or *periodic decimals*. A repetend may be expressed by placing a dot ($\dot{}$) or dots above the figure or figures that do the repeating.

When any common fraction is expressed in its lowest terms, it may be reduced to a *finite decimal* if its denominator contains only the prime factors 2's and/or 5's. If the denominator contains other prime factors as well as 2's and/or 5's, the reduced decimal is a mixed one; it is partly finite and partly repeating. If the denominator contains neither 2 nor 5 as a factor, the reduced decimal is a purely repeating one.

Thus, $\frac{1}{4}$ and $\frac{1}{20}$ may be reduced to finite decimals:

$\frac{1}{4} = .25$; the denominator 4 contains the prime factors 2 and 2.

$\frac{1}{20} = .05$; the denominator 20 contains the prime factors 2, 2, and 5.

$\frac{1}{12}$ and $\frac{1}{70}$ may be reduced to partly finite and partly repeating decimals:

$\frac{1}{12} = .083333\ldots = .08\dot{3}$; the denominator 12 contains the prime factors 2, 2, and 3.

$\frac{1}{70} = .0\,142857\,142857\,142857\ldots = .0\dot{1}4285\dot{7}$; the denominator 70 contains the prime factors 2, 5, and 7.

$\frac{2}{3}$ and $\frac{1}{21}$ may be reduced to purely repeating decimals:

$\frac{2}{3} = .666666\ldots = .\dot{6}$

$\frac{1}{21} = .047619\ 047619\ 047619\ldots = .\dot{0}4761\dot{9}$; the denominator 21 contains the prime factors 3 and 7.

A repetend may be reduced to a fraction. Use the repeating figures as the numerator and write as many 9's as the number of repeating figures to form the denominator.

EXAMPLE 11 (a) $.\dot{6} = \frac{6}{9} = \frac{2}{3}$ (b) $.\dot{1}\dot{5} = \frac{15}{99} = \frac{5}{33}$

EXAMPLE 12 $.\dot{9} = \frac{9}{9} = 1$ (Thus, .9999... = 1)[1]

EXAMPLE 13

$$.08\dot{3} = .08\frac{3}{9} = \frac{8\frac{3}{9}}{100} = \frac{\frac{75}{9}}{100} = \frac{75}{900} = \frac{1}{12}$$

EXAMPLE 14

$$.4\dot{1}2\dot{3} = .4\frac{123}{999} = \frac{4\frac{41}{333}}{10} = \frac{1{,}373}{3{,}330}$$

EXAMPLE 15

$$5.8\dot{7} = 5.8\frac{7}{9} = 5\frac{8\frac{7}{9}}{10} = 5\frac{79}{90}$$

A partly finite and partly repeating decimal may be directly reduced to a fraction as follows:

STEP (1). Subtract the finite figures from the overall figures; the remainder is the numerator.
STEP (2). Write as many 9's as there are places in the repeating figures and annex as many zeros as there are finite decimal places to form the denominator.

EXAMPLE 16 $.08\dot{3} = \frac{83 - 8}{900} = \frac{75}{900} = \frac{1}{12}$

EXAMPLE 17 $.4\dot{1}2\dot{3} = \frac{4{,}123 - 4}{9{,}990} = \frac{4{,}119}{9{,}990} = \frac{1{,}373}{3{,}330}$

EXAMPLE 18 $5.8\dot{7} = 5\frac{87 - 8}{90} = 5\frac{79}{90}$

---

[1] This relationship, .9999... = 1, can further be illustrated as follows:

$$
\begin{aligned}
\text{Let } 10x &= 9.9999 \ldots\ldots\ldots\ldots\ldots (1)\\
x &= .9999 \ldots\ldots\ldots\ldots\ldots (2)\\
\hline
9x &= 9.00000 \ldots\ldots\ldots\ldots\ldots (1) - (2)\\
x &= \frac{9}{9} = 1
\end{aligned}
$$

EXERCISE 1-4 REFERENCE: SECTION 1.4

A. Reduce the following common fractions to decimal fractions (round to 3 decimal places):

1. $\frac{2}{10}$
2. $\frac{3}{7}$
3. $\frac{6}{17}$
4. $\frac{8}{23}$
5. $\frac{14}{15}$
6. $\frac{18}{25}$
7. $\frac{21}{38}$
8. $\frac{35}{48}$
9. $\frac{40}{13}$
10. $\frac{56}{11}$
11. $\frac{72}{15}$
12. $\frac{103}{25}$
13. $3\frac{7}{20}$
14. $12\frac{8}{9}$
15. $42\frac{7}{16}$
16. $32\frac{71}{80}$

B. Reduce the following decimals to common fractions in lowest terms:

17. .32
18. .45
19. .68
20. .84
21. .038
22. .0056
23. 1.82
24. 7.035
25. 3.002
26. 1.254
27. 11.035
28. 15.005
29. $4.35\frac{1}{2}$
30. $10.42\frac{2}{3}$
31. $2.875\frac{1}{4}$
32. $4.305\frac{2}{5}$

C. Perform the following indicated operations by the aliquot parts method:

33. $18 \times 66\frac{2}{3}\%$
34. $42 \times 42\frac{6}{7}\%$
35. $36 \times 44\frac{4}{9}\%$
36. $55 \times 27\frac{3}{11}\%$
37. $81 \times 55\frac{5}{9}$
38. $42 \times 71\frac{3}{7}$
39. $52 \times 46\frac{2}{13}$
40. $75 \times 46\frac{2}{3}$
41. $128 \times 43\frac{3}{4}\%$
42. $90 \times 53\frac{1}{3}\%$
43. $440 \times 27\frac{1}{2}\%$
44. $180 \times 43\frac{1}{3}\%$
45. $60 \times 3\frac{1}{3}$
46. $40 \times 2\frac{1}{2}$
47. $20 \times 17\frac{1}{2}$
48. $27 \times 33\frac{1}{3}$
49. $36 \times 83\frac{1}{3}\%$
50. $42 \times 16\frac{2}{3}\%$
51. $77 \times 57\frac{1}{7}\%$
52. $63 \times 28\frac{4}{7}\%$
53. $16 \times 37\frac{1}{2}$
54. $56 \times 12\frac{1}{2}$
55. $18 \times 11\frac{1}{9}$
56. $66 \times 36\frac{4}{11}$
57. $60 \times 8\frac{1}{3}\%$
58. $42 \times 35\frac{5}{7}\%$
59. $48 \times 12\frac{1}{2}\%$
60. $80 \times 17\frac{1}{2}\%$
61. $26 \times 38\frac{6}{13}$
62. $33 \times 66\frac{2}{3}$
63. $21 \times 42\frac{6}{7}$
64. $48 \times 43\frac{3}{4}$
65. $52 \div 33\frac{1}{3}\%$
66. $56.6 \div 28\frac{4}{7}\%$
67. $360 \div 27\frac{3}{11}\%$
68. $55 \div 83\frac{1}{3}\%$
69. $74 \div 22\frac{2}{9}$
70. $78.3 \div 23\frac{1}{13}$
71. $44 \div 26\frac{2}{3}$
72. $85 \div 31\frac{1}{4}$
73. $99 \div 56\frac{1}{4}\%$
74. $121 \div 68\frac{3}{4}\%$
75. $210 \div 23\frac{1}{3}\%$
76. $49.7 \div 53\frac{11}{13}\%$
77. $42 \div 33\frac{1}{3}$
78. $30 \div 16\frac{2}{3}$
79. $500 \div 71\frac{3}{7}$
80. $600 \div 42\frac{6}{7}$
81. $1500 \div 55\frac{5}{9}\%$
82. $55 \div 45\frac{5}{11}\%$
83. $72 \div 46\frac{2}{13}\%$
84. $84 \div 46\frac{2}{3}\%$

★**D.** Reduce the following common fractions to decimal fractions and indicate the repetends by placing a dot or dots above the repeating figures:

85. $\frac{1}{7}$
86. $\frac{4}{9}$
87. $\frac{5}{12}$
88. $\frac{2}{15}$
89. $\frac{7}{18}$
90. $\frac{13}{36}$
91. $\frac{14}{27}$
92. $\frac{17}{90}$
93. $\frac{13}{15}$
94. $\frac{25}{42}$
95. $\frac{17}{150}$
96. $\frac{41}{270}$

★**E.** Reduce the following to common fractions or mixed numbers:

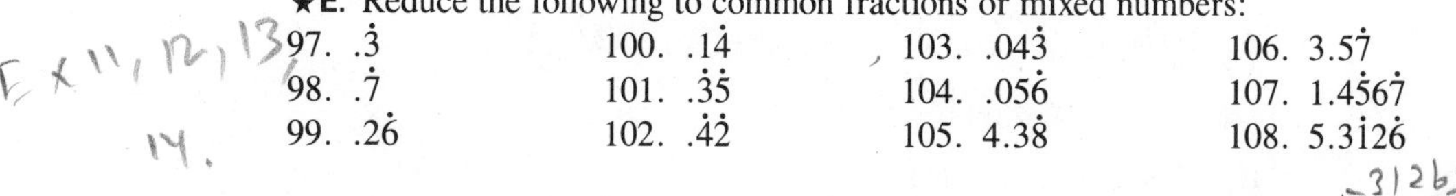

97. $.\dot{3}$
98. $.\dot{7}$
99. $.2\dot{6}$
100. $.1\dot{4}$
101. $.\dot{3}\dot{5}$
102. $.\dot{4}\dot{2}$
103. $.04\dot{3}$
104. $.05\dot{6}$
105. $4.3\dot{8}$
106. $3.5\dot{7}$
107. $1.4\dot{5}6\dot{7}$
108. $5.3\dot{1}2\dot{6}$

2 REVIEW OF BASIC ALGEBRA

This chapter reviews the basic topics of ordinary algebra. After the introduction (Section 2.1), the chapter deals with the fundamental operations of algebra (Sections 2.2 to 2.5), grouping (Section 2.6), factoring (Section 2.7), equations (Section 2.8), ratio and proportion (Section 2.9), and percentages (Sections 2.10 to 2.11).

The above topics are essential for deriving some simple formulas and for enabling students to solve algebraically the problems in the following chapters. The value of algebra should be fully understood and appreciated by those who study mathematics for management and finance. Mathematical operations for numerous problems in this text usually can be greatly simplified when algebraic methods are employed.

2.1 INTRODUCTION TO ALGEBRA

Students who are familiar with arithmetic operations should enjoy learning algebraic operations. The basic principles of the four fundamental operations of algebra—addition, subtraction, multiplication, and division—are the same as those of arithmetic operations. However, algebra is characterized by the use of letters as symbols for numbers and by the relationships among numbers being expressed in the form of equations. The methods presented in the two sections, symbols of grouping and factoring, are frequently used in algebra to facilitate the performance of fundamental operations.

A. Basic Arithmetic Rules as Applied to Algebra

Let a, b, c, and d represent numbers.

If $a = b$ and $c = b$, then $a = c;$
if $a = b$ and $c = d$, then $a + c = b + d;$
if $a = b$ and $c = d$, then $a - c = b - d;$

if $a = b$ and $c = d$, then $a \times c = b \times d$; and
if $a = b$ and $c = d$, then $a/c = b/d$, provided c is a number other than zero.

Other important arithmetic rules which are accepted for algebra are as follows:

$a + b = b + a$

CHECK

Let a and b represent any two numbers.
For example, let $a = 9$ and $b = 7$. Thus,
$9 + 7 = 7 + 9 = 16$

$a + b + c = (a + b) + c = a + (b + c)$

CHECK

Let $a = 9$, $b = 7$, $c = 4$. Thus,
$9 + 7 + 4 = (9 + 7) + 4 = 9 + (7 + 4) = 20$

$a \times b = b \times a$

CHECK

Let $a = 5$, $b = 3$. Thus,
$5 \times 3 = 3 \times 5 = 15$

$a \times b \times c = (a \times b) \times c = a \times (b \times c)$

CHECK

Let $a = 5$, $b = 3$, $c = 2$. Thus,
$5 \times 3 \times 2 = (5 \times 3) \times 2 = 5 \times (3 \times 2) = 30$

Other signs instead of "×" are frequently used in multiplication in algebra. For example, the product of a and c may be written $a \cdot c$, $(a)(c)$, or simply ac. Thus, the two equations above may be written as $ab = ba$, and $abc = (ab)c = a(bc)$, respectively.

Division should be done in the order indicated. Thus,

$$a \div b \div c = (a \div b) \div c, \text{ or } \frac{\frac{a}{b}}{c} = \frac{a}{b} \cdot \frac{1}{c} = \frac{a}{bc},$$

$$\textit{not} = a \div (b \div c), \text{ or } \frac{a}{\frac{b}{c}} = a \cdot \frac{c}{b} = \frac{ac}{b}$$

$48 \div 6 \div 2 = (48 \div 6) \div 2 = 8 \div 2 = 4,$
not $= 48 \div (6 \div 2) = 48 \div 3 = 16$

However, the following order is also permissible:

$$a \div b \div c = (a \div c) \div b, \text{ or } \frac{\frac{a}{c}}{b} = \frac{a}{c} \cdot \frac{1}{b} = \frac{a}{bc};$$

$48 \div 6 \div 2 = (48 \div 2) \div 6 = 24 \div 6 = 4$

Note that in the above division, a is the dividend, and b and c are divisors. The order of divisors may be changed in division.

B. Terminology in Algebra

Algebraic Expression. An *algebraic expression*, or simply an *expression*, is any symbol or combination of symbols that represents a number. When an expression consists of several parts that are connected by plus (+) and minus (−) signs, each of the parts, together with the sign preceding it, is called a *term*. If there is no sign expressed preceding a term, the sign is understood to be plus. An expression consisting of one term is called a *monomial*, whereas an expression having more than one term is called a *multinomial*, or a *polynomial*. An expression of two terms is also called a *binomial*, whereas one of three terms is a *trinomial*. For example, $+4ax$ or $4ax$ is an expression and is a *monomial;* $4ax + 7$ is also an expression but has two terms and is a binomial; and the expression $ax^2 + 4x + 5$ is a trinomial.

Factor and Coefficient. If two or more numbers are multiplied together, each number or the product of any of the numbers is called a *factor*. Any factor of a term is called the *coefficient* of the remaining factors. When a factor is an explicit number, it is called the *numerical coefficient* of the term; other factors are called *literal coefficients*. As an illustration let us examine the term $6xy$. Each number and symbol—6, x, and y—or the product of any of these—$6x$, $6y$, and xy—is called a factor. The coefficient of $6x$ is y, y is the literal coefficient. The coefficient of xy is 6, 6 is the numerical coefficient. If no numerical coefficient is indicated in a term, it is understood that the numerical coefficient is one.

Power. The product of equal factors is called a *power* of the factor. Thus, $a \cdot a \cdot a$ is the third power of a and is written a^3; $2 \cdot 2 \cdot 2 \cdot 2\,(= 16)$ is the fourth power of 2 and is written 2^4. The symbol a is called the *base*, and the number 3, which indicates the number of equal factors, is the *exponent*. The expression of an indicated power of a given symbol or number is called an *exponential*, such as a^3. The exponent for the first power of a base is 1, which is understood and usually not written; that is, $a^1 = a$. A second power is called a *square*, whereas a third power is a *cube*.

+ and − Signs. The plus and minus signs which were used exclusively to indicate addition and subtraction in arithmetic are now also used as the indicators of positive numbers and negative numbers. When the concept of positive or negative numbers is disregarded, the value of any number is then called its *absolute value* and is denoted by the sign $|\ |$. When no sign is written, the number is understood to be a positive one. For example, $+3$ or 3 is a positive number, whereas -3 is a negative number; $|+3|$ and $|-3|$ indicate the absolute value of 3; that is, $|+3| = |-3| = |3|$.

C. Operations with 0 and 1.

The numbers zero and one have certain properties which are explained below:

1. When zero is added to a number, the sum is the number unchanged. Thus, $3 + 0 = 3$; $a + 0 = a$; $0 + 0 = 0$.
2. When zero is subtracted from a number, the remainder is the number unchanged. Thus, $3 - 0 = 3$; $a - 0 = a$; $0 - 0 = 0$. However, when a number is subtracted from zero, the remainder is the absolute value of the number with its sign changed. Thus, $0 - 3$ or $0 - (+3) = -3$; $0 - (-3) = +3$ or 3; $0 - a = -a$; $0 - (-a) = a$.
3. When zero is multiplied by a number, or a number is multiplied by zero, the product is zero. Thus, $3 \times 0 = 0$; $0 \times 3 = 0$; $0 \times 0 = 0$; $a \times 0 = 0$.

4. When zero is divided by any number except zero, the quotient is zero. Thus, $0 \div 3$ or $\frac{0}{3} = 0$; $\frac{0}{a} = 0$
5. Division by zero is undefined, because there is no answer. For example, if $\frac{7}{0} = c$, then by multiplying both sides of the equation by 0, we have $\frac{7}{\not{0}} \times \not{0} = c0$, or $7 = c0 = 0$. We know that $7 \neq 0$, or 7 is not equal to 0. When $\frac{0}{0}$, the quotient is meaningless. (Note that the symbol $\neq$ is read "is not equal to.")
6. When a number is multiplied by one, the product is the number unchanged. Thus, $6 \times 1 = 6$; $a \times 1 = a$.
7. When a number is divided by one, the quotient is the number unchanged. Thus, $\frac{6}{1} = 6$; $\frac{a}{1} = a$

2.2 ADDITION

A. Addition of Signed Numbers

ADDITION OF NUMBERS HAVING THE SAME SIGNS

When adding numbers that have the same signs, first find the sum of their absolute values. Second, prefix the common sign to this sum.

EXAMPLE 1

Add (-5), (-6), and (-3).

The sum of the absolute values is $5 + 6 + 3 = 14$.
The common sign is negative. Thus,

$$(-5) + (-6) + (-3) = -14$$

or, written simply,

$$-5-6-3 = -14$$

EXAMPLE 2

Add $(+9)$, $(+3.45)$, and $(+0.162)$.

The sum of the absolute values is

$$\begin{array}{r} 9 \\ 3.45 \\ +\ 0.162 \\ \hline 12.612 \end{array}$$

The common sign is positive. Thus,

$$(+9) + (+3.45) + (+0.162) = +12.612$$

or, written simply,

$$9 + 3.45 + 0.162 = 12.612$$

ADDITION OF NUMBERS HAVING UNLIKE SIGNS

When adding numbers that have unlike signs, first subtract the smaller absolute value from the larger. Second, prefix the sign of the larger to the remainder.

EXAMPLE 3

Add (-9) and $(+3)$.

The difference between the two absolute values is $9 - 3 = 6$.

The sign of the larger number, 9, is negative. Thus,

$(-9) + (+3) = -6$

To obtain the sum of three or more numbers having unlike signs, we may first add two of the numbers, then add the sum to the third number, and so on.

EXAMPLE 4

$(+14) + (-15) + (+.8179) = (-1) + (+.8179) = -.1821$

Or, first add numbers having the same sign, then combine:

$(+14) + (-15) + (+.8179) = (+14.8179) + (-15) = -.1821$

B. Addition of Algebraic Expressions

ADDITION OF MONOMIALS

Terms whose literal factors are the same are called *like terms*. To add like terms, add the numerical coefficients. The sum thus obtained is the coefficient of the common literal factors.

EXAMPLE 5

Add $5ax$, $9ax$, and $(-20ax)$.

The sum of the numerical coefficients is

$5 + 9 + (-20) = -6$. Thus,

$5ax + 9ax + (-20ax) = -6ax$

The numerical coefficients of *unlike terms*, such as $5a$ and $6b$, cannot be combined; their sum is simply indicated by signs and is written as a polynomial, $5a + 6b$.

EXAMPLE 6

Add $6xy$, $(-5x)$, $(-3xy)$, and $(-4x)$.

$6xy + (-3xy) = 3xy$

$(-5x) + (-4x) = -9x$. Thus,

$6xy + (-5x) + (-3xy) + (-4x) = 3xy + (-9x) = 3xy - 9x$

The process of finding the algebraic sum of like terms and unlike terms is sometimes called *collecting terms*.

ADDITION OF POLYNOMIALS

Like terms should be combined when two or more polynomials are added. Each set of like terms may be arranged in a vertical column before adding.

EXAMPLE 7

Add $(3a + 4b + 6)$, $(-4a - 6b - 3)$, and $(7a + 4b - 9)$.

$$\begin{array}{r} 3a + 4b + 6 \\ -4a - 6b - 3 \\ 7a + 4b - 9 \\ \hline 6a + 2b - 6 \end{array}$$

2.3 SUBTRACTION

A. Subtraction of Signed Numbers

When subtracting signed numbers, first change the sign of the subtrahend. Then add.

EXAMPLE 1 Subtract (-17) from (-8).

$(-8) - (-17) = (-8) + (+17) = 9$

EXAMPLE 2 Subtract (-16) from $(+19)$.

$(+19) - (-16) = 19 + (+16) = 35$

EXAMPLE 3 Subtract $(+17.436)$ from $(+12)$.

$(+12) - (+17.436) = 12 + (-17.436) = -5.436$

or, written simply,

$12 - 17.436 = -5.436$

B. Subtraction of Algebraic Expressions

SUBTRACTION OF MONOMIALS

To subtract like terms, subtract the numerical coefficient of the subtrahend from that of the minuend. The remainder thus obtained is the coefficient of the common literal factors.

EXAMPLE 4 Subtract $5xy$ from $18xy$.

$18xy - 5xy = 13xy$, or
$(18 - 5)xy = 13xy$

EXAMPLE 5 Subtract $-7ab$ from $11ab$.

$11ab - (-7ab) = 11ab + 7ab = 18\,ab$, or
$[11 - (-7)]ab = 18ab$

SUBTRACTION OF POLYNOMIALS

When one polynomial is subtracted from another, change the sign of each term in the subtrahend and then add.

EXAMPLE 6 Subtract:

Subtract:	$5a - 2b + 9$	(Minuend)
	$-2a + 9b - 4$	(Subtrahend)
Minuend	$5a - 2b + 9$	(with the same signs)
Subtrahend	$2a - 9b + 4$	(signs are changed)
	$7a - 11b + 13$	(add)

Or, written in horizontal form,

$(5a - 2b + 9) - (-2a + 9b - 4)$
$= 5a - 2b + 9 + 2a - 9b + 4$
$= 7a - 11b + 13$

EXAMPLE 7 Subtract $(4x - 5y + 7)$ from $(9x + 10y - 4)$.

$$(9x + 10y - 4) - (4x - 5y + 7)$$
$$= 9x + 10y - 4 - 4x + 5y - 7$$
$$= 5x + 15y - 11$$

EXERCISE 2-1 REFERENCE: SECTIONS 2.2 and 2.3

A. Addition of signed numbers:

1. $(-7) + (-5)$
2. $(-18) + (-6)$
3. $(-12) + (-18)$
4. $(-15) + (-17)$
5. $(-23) + (-24)$
6. $(-38) + (-2)$
7. $(-15) + (-16)$
8. $(-26) + (-9)$
9. $(+24) + (+7)$
10. $(+45) + (+16)$
11. $(+32) + (+13)$
12. $(+63) + (+41)$
13. $(+52) + (-30)$
14. $(+47) + (-15)$
15. $(+38) + (-13)$
16. $(+44) + (-15)$
17. $(+25) + (-46.23)$
18. $(+19) + (-60.15)$
19. $(+46) + (-80.37)$
20. $(+38) + (-54.49)$
21. $(-17.264) + (+20)$
22. $(-42.317) + (+36)$
23. $(-40.943) + (+64)$
24. $(-39.174) + (+50)$
25. $(-7) + (-4) + (-12)$
26. $(-18) + (+20) + (+6)$
27. $(+4) + (-8) + (+11)$
28. $(+10) + (-42) + (-41)$
29. $(+6) + (-4) + (-12) + (-15)$
30. $(-2) + (+4) + (-21) + (+2)$
31. $(+4) + (+19) + (+42) + (-58)$
32. $(-41) + (-36) + (-42) + (-6)$

B. Addition of algebraic terms:

33. $42a + (-16a)$
34. $34bc + (-12bc)$
35. $(-23c) + 5c$
36. $(-36t) + (-2t)$
37. $(-65et) + 7et$
38. $(-27d) + 3d$
39. $(-36f) + (-32f)$
40. $(-24g) + 5g$
41. $14h + 46h + (-17h)$
42. $25v + 13v + 40v$
43. $24w + (-3w) + (7w)$
44. $(-36q) + 3q + (-16q)$
45. $8cd + (-6c) + 4c + (-6cd)$
46. $6xy + 3x + (-15xy) + (-2x)$
47. $4ab + (-a) + 7ab + (-2ab)$
48. $7tb + 5t + 16tb + (-3t)$
49. $(3a + 7b + 4) + (2a + 5b - 2) + (5a - 2b + 1)$
50. $(6x + 4y + 3) + (3x - 7y - 2) + (5x + 2y - 6)$
51. $(4xy + 33x + 11y + 1) + (3xy - 5x - 4y - 1)$
52. $(6abc + 4ab - 3bc + 6) + (3abc - 2ab + bc - 2)$

C. Subtraction of signed numbers:

53. $(+23) - (-4)$
54. $(+24) - (-6)$
55. $(+38) - (-7)$
56. $(+46) - (-5)$
57. $(-3) - (-8)$
58. $(-53) - (-17)$
59. $(-38) - (-12)$
60. $(-26) - (-6)$
61. $(-5.36) - (+32.2164)$
62. $(+2.18) - (-23.4759)$
63. $(-6.145) - (+25.216)$
64. $(+8.627) - (-17.354)$
65. $(+5) - (-6) - (+4.21)$
66. $(+9) - (+6) - (-15.46)$
67. $(-10) - (-11) - (-13.83)$
68. $(-16) - (+7) - (+2.59)$

69. $(-32) + (-4) - (+6) - (-10)$
70. $(+46) - (-3) + (-4) - (-10)$
71. $(-43) + (+7) - (-63) - (+4)$
72. $(+39) + (-30) - (+7) + (-4)$

D. Subtraction of algebraic terms:

73. $28xy - 6xy$
74. $16x - (-7x)$
75. $32ab - 6ab$
76. $40t - 2t$
77. $(-9bc) - (-4bc)$
78. $(-6cd) - 7cd$
79. $(-4b) - (-2b)$
80. $(-12ct) - 5ct$
81. $4a - (2a + 7a - 6d)$
82. $(-8t) - (-4t + 3t - 6t)$
83. $(23f - 4f) - (5f + 2f)$
84. $(17g + 4g) - (7g - 3g)$
85. $(14h + 2h) - (3h + 4h)$
86. $(17tb + 2tb) - (-4tb - 7tb)$
87. $(5a + 2b + 7) - (4a + 3b + 6)$
88. $(4xy + 2x + 6) - (2xy - 6x + 4)$

2.4 MULTIPLICATION

A. Multiplication of Signed Numbers

When multiplying two numbers having unlike signs, multiply the numerical values and prefix a negative sign to the product.

EXAMPLE 1 $(+6) \times (-9) = -54$; $(-6) \times (+3) = -18$

If the two numbers have like signs, prefix a positive sign to the product.

EXAMPLE 2 $(-4) \times (-5) = +20$; $(+4) \times (+5) = +20$

B. Multiplication of Algebraic Expressions

MULTIPLICATION OF EXPONENTIALS

When multiplication involves exponentials, the following laws apply.

When exponentials have the same base:

LAW (1) $a^m \cdot a^n = a^{m+n}$

ILLUSTRATION:

$$a^m \cdot a^n = \underbrace{(a \cdot a \cdot a \cdot a \cdot \cdots)}_{m \text{ factors}}\underbrace{(a \cdot a \cdot a \cdot a \cdot \cdots)}_{n \text{ factors}} = a^{m+n}$$

EXAMPLE 3 $2^3 \cdot 2^2 = (2 \cdot 2 \cdot 2)(2 \cdot 2) = 2^5$; or $2^3 \cdot 2^2 = 2^{3+2} = 2^5 = 32$

EXAMPLE 4 $x^3 \cdot x^4 = (x \cdot x \cdot x)(x \cdot x \cdot x \cdot x) = x^7$; or $x^3 \cdot x^4 = x^{3+4} = x^7$

The above law gives the following definitions:

I. $a^0 = 1 \quad (a \neq 0)$

NOTE: "$\neq$" means "not equal to."

ILLUSTRATION:

$$a^m \cdot a^0 = a^{m+0} = a^m$$

$$a^0 = \frac{a^m}{a^m} = 1$$

Thus, $4^0 = 1$; $5^0 = 1$; $126^0 = 1$

II. $\boldsymbol{a^{-m} = \frac{1}{a^m}}$

ILLUSTRATION:

$$a^m \cdot a^{-m} = a^{m+(-m)} = a^0 = 1$$

$$a^{-m} = \frac{1}{a^m}$$

Thus, $4^{-1} = \frac{1}{4}$; $5^{-2} = \frac{1}{5^2} = \frac{1}{25}$; $2^{-4} = \frac{1}{2^4} = \frac{1}{16}$

When exponentials have different bases but have the same exponent:

LAW (2) $\boldsymbol{a^m \cdot b^m = (ab)^m}$

ILLUSTRATION:

$$a^m \cdot b^m = \overbrace{(a \cdot a \cdot a \cdot a \cdot \cdots)}^{m \text{ factors}}\overbrace{(b \cdot b \cdot b \cdot b \cdot \cdots)}^{m \text{ factors}}$$

$$= \overbrace{ab \cdot ab \cdot ab \cdot ab \cdot \cdots}^{m \text{ products}}$$

$$= (ab)^m$$

EXAMPLE 5 $5^2 \cdot 4^2 = 5 \cdot 5 \cdot 4 \cdot 4 = (5 \cdot 4)(5 \cdot 4) = 20^2 = 400$; or
$5^2 \cdot 4^2 = (5 \cdot 4)^2 = 20^2 = 400$

EXAMPLE 6 $x^3 \cdot y^3 = (x \cdot x \cdot x)(y \cdot y \cdot y) = (xy)(xy)(xy) = (xy)^3$; or
$x^3y^3 = (xy)^3$

When the base is an exponential:

LAW (3) $\boldsymbol{(a^m)^n = a^{mn}}$, **or** $\boldsymbol{(a^{1/m})^n = a^{n/m}}$

ILLUSTRATION:

$$(a^m)^n = \overbrace{a^m \cdot a^m \cdot a^m \cdot a^m \cdot \cdots}^{n \text{ exponentials}}$$

$$= a^{\overbrace{m+m+m+m+\cdots}^{n \text{ times}}}$$

$$= a^{mn}$$

EXAMPLE 7 $(3^2)^3 = (3 \cdot 3)(3 \cdot 3)(3 \cdot 3) = 3^6 = 729$, or
$(3^2)^3 = 3^{2 \cdot 3} = 3^6 = 729$

EXAMPLE 8 $(x^3)^2 = (x \cdot x \cdot x)(x \cdot x \cdot x) = x^6$; or
$(x^3)^2 = x^{3 \cdot 2} = x^6$

EXAMPLE 9

$(3^{1/2})^4 = (3^{1/2})(3^{1/2})(3^{1/2})(3^{1/2}) = 3^{(1/2)+(1/2)+(1/2)+(1/2)} = 3^2 = 9$, or
$(3^{1/2})^4 = 3^{4/2} = 3^2 = 9$

EXAMPLE 10

$(x^{1/3})^2 = (x^{1/3})(x^{1/3}) = x^{(1/3)+(1/3)} = x^{2/3}$, or
$(x^{1/3})^2 = x^{2/3}$

MULTIPLICATION OF MONOMIALS

The product of two or more monomials is equal to the product of their numerical coefficients multiplied by the product of their literal factors.

EXAMPLE 11 $5ab \cdot 4c = 20abc$

EXAMPLE 12 $3x^2 \cdot 4x^3y \cdot 5y^2 = (3 \cdot 4 \cdot 5)x^{2+3}y^{1+2} = 60x^5y^3$

MULTIPLYING A POLYNOMIAL BY A MONOMIAL

Multiply each term of the polynomial by the monomial. The algebraic sum of the partial products is the product of the multiplication.

EXAMPLE 13

Multiply $(4a + 7b)$ by $3c$.

$$\begin{array}{r} 4a + 7b \\ 3c \\ \hline 12ac + 21bc \end{array}$$

$12ac + 21bc$, or, as written,

$(4a + 7b)3c = (4a \times 3c) + (7b \times 3c) = 12ac + 21bc$

MULTIPLYING A POLYNOMIAL BY ANOTHER POLYNOMIAL

Multiply each term of the multiplicand by each term of the multiplier. The algebraic sum of the partial products is the product of the multiplication.

EXAMPLE 14

Multiply $(4a + 7b)$ by $(3c + 5d)$.

$$\begin{array}{l} 4a + 7b \\ 3c + 5d \\ \hline 12ac + 21bc \\ \qquad\qquad + 20ad + 35bd \\ \hline 12ac + 21bc + 20ad + 35bd \end{array}$$

$12ac + 21bc + 20ad + 35bd$, or, as written,

$(4a + 7b)(3c + 5d) = 12\,ac + 21bc + 20ad + 35bd$

Notice that $12ac = (4a)(3c)$; $21bc = (7b)(3c)$; $20ad = (4a)(5d)$; and $35bd = (7b)(5d)$.

The following examples are used to illustrate the multiplication of polynomials involving exponentials:

EXAMPLE 15 Multiply: $(3a - 2)(2a + 5)$.

$$\begin{array}{l} 3a - 2 \\ \underline{2a + 5} \\ 6a^2 - 4a \\ \underline{\quad + 15a - 10} \\ 6a^2 + 11a - 10, \text{ or} \end{array}$$

$(3a - 2)(2a + 5) = 6a^2 - 4a + 15a - 10 = 6a^2 + 11a - 10$

Notice that $6a^2 = (3a)(2a)$; $-4a = (-2)(2a)$; $+15a = (3a)(5)$; and $-10 = (-2)(5)$.

EXAMPLE 16 Multiply: $(4bx - 3y)(3b^2 + 2y)$.

$$\begin{array}{l} 4bx - 3y \\ \underline{3b^2 + 2y} \\ 12b^3x - 9b^2y \\ \underline{\qquad\qquad + 8bxy - 6y^2} \\ 12b^3x - 9b^2y + 8bxy - 6y^2, \text{ or} \end{array}$$

$(4bx - 3y)(3b^2 + 2y) = 12b^3x - 9b^2y + 8bxy - 6y^2$

EXERCISE 2-2 REFERENCE: SECTION 2.4

A. Multiply the following signed numbers:

1. $(-7)(-6)$
2. $(+8)(+7)$
3. $(-9)(-10)$
4. $(+6)(+9)$
5. $(-6)(-3)$
6. $(+9)(+4)$
7. $(+5)(+7)$
8. $(-3)(-8)$
9. $(-6)(+4)$
10. $(+5)(-7)$
11. $(-8)(+9)$
12. $(-12)(+11)$
13. $(-7)(+2)$
14. $(+10)(-5)$
15. $(+32)(-71)$
16. $(+15)(-46)$

B. Simplify the following:

17. $2^3 \cdot 2^2$
18. $4^3 \cdot 4^0$
19. $5^2 \cdot 5^4$
20. $6^3 \cdot 6^2$
21. $a^4 \cdot a^2$
22. $b^2 \cdot b^{-5}$
23. $c^4 \cdot c^0$
24. $d^5 \cdot d^2$
25. $3^2 \cdot 4^2$
26. $2^3 \cdot 5^3$
27. $x^3 \cdot y^3$
28. $a^4 \cdot b^4 \cdot c^4$
29. $m^a n^a$
30. $t^{7r} p^{7r}$
31. $(5^2)^3$
32. $(4^3)^2$
33. $(p^5)^2$
34. $(x^4)^3$
35. $(y^a)^b$
36. $(ab^2)^3$
37. $(b^{1/x})^y$
38. $(d^{1/p})^q$
39. $(4^{1/2})^6$
40. $(16^{1/2})^4$

C. Multiply the following algebraic expressions:

41. $(6x)(-3y)$
42. $4ab \cdot 7c$
43. $7xy \cdot 5y$
44. $(-8ab) \cdot 2b$
45. $5x^2 \cdot 2xy \cdot 3y$
46. $9t \cdot (-3t) \cdot (-4tp)$
47. $(-7pq) \cdot 3pq^2 \cdot p^3$
48. $(-6bc) \cdot (-4bcd) \cdot 3b$
49. $2(4a + 3)$
50. $3(2b + 7)$
51. $5(4c - 3)$
52. $-4(3d - b)$
53. $4t(a + b)$
54. $-5c(-4c + 5)$
55. $7b(-3e + 2b)$
56. $3t(-3t - 2p)$
57. $(a + b)(a - b)$
58. $(a + b)(a + b)$
59. $(a - b)(a - b)$
60. $(3m + 2)(4m - 3)$
61. $(-4y + 2)(y - 3)$
62. $(3ab + 2c)(a + 3c)$
63. $(3t^2 - 3a)(2t^3 + 4)$
64. $(-5d^2 + e)(3c^2 - e)$

2.5 DIVISION

A. Division of Signed Numbers

When dividing one number by another with unlike signs, divide the numerical values and prefix a negative sign to the quotient.

EXAMPLE 1

(a) $10 \div (-5) = -2$, or $\frac{10}{-5} = -2$

(b) $(-18) \div (+6) = -3$, or $\frac{-18}{6} = -3$

If two numbers have like signs, the quotient is positive.

EXAMPLE 2

(a) $10 \div 5 = 2$, or $\frac{10}{5} = 2$

(b) $(-18) \div (-6) = 3$, or $\frac{-18}{-6} = 3$

When zero is divided by any number except zero, the quotient is zero.

EXAMPLE 3

$0 \div 4 = \frac{0}{4} = 0$. Also, $0 \div (-4) = \frac{0}{-4} = 0$.

NOTE: Division by zero is *undefined*, because there is no answer.

B. Division of Algebraic Expressions

DIVISION INVOLVING EXPONENTIALS

When division involves exponentials, the following laws apply.

When exponentials have the same base:

LAW (1)

$$a^m \div a^n = \frac{a^m}{a^n} = a^{m-n}$$

EXAMPLE 4

$$2^5 \div 2^3 = \frac{\cancel{2} \cdot \cancel{2} \cdot \cancel{2} \cdot 2 \cdot 2}{\cancel{2} \cdot \cancel{2} \cdot \cancel{2}} = 2^2 = 4, \quad \text{or}$$

$$2^5 \div 2^3 = \frac{2^5}{2^3} = 2^{5-3} = 2^2 = 4$$

EXAMPLE 5

$$2^3 \div 2^5 = \frac{\cancel{2} \cdot \cancel{2} \cdot \cancel{2}}{\cancel{2} \cdot \cancel{2} \cdot \cancel{2} \cdot 2 \cdot 2} = \frac{1}{2 \cdot 2} = \frac{1}{2^2} = \frac{1}{4}, \quad \text{or}$$

$$2^3 \div 2^5 = \frac{2^3}{2^5} = 2^{3-5} = 2^{-2} = \frac{1}{2^2} = \frac{1}{4}$$

NOTE: See Law (1), definition II, on page 28.

EXAMPLE 6

$$x^4 \div x^2 = \frac{x^4}{x^2} = \frac{x \cdot x \cdot \cancel{x} \cdot \cancel{x}}{\cancel{x} \cdot \cancel{x}} = x \cdot x = x^2, \quad \text{or}$$

$$\frac{x^4}{x^2} = x^{4-2} = x^2$$

Similarly,

$$a^m \div a^n = \frac{a^m}{a^n} = a^{m-n}, \quad \text{if} \quad m > n$$

$$\frac{a^m}{a^n} = a^{m-n} = a^{-(n-m)} = \frac{1}{a^{n-m}}, \quad \text{if} \quad m < n$$

$$\frac{a^m}{a^n} = a^{m-n} = a^0 = 1, \quad \text{if} \quad m = n$$

NOTE: The sign "$>$" means greater than; "$m > n$" means m is greater than n. The sign "$<$" means smaller than; "$m < n$" means m is smaller than n.

$a^m \div a^n = a^{m-n}$ may be proved in the following manner:

$$\frac{a^m}{a^n} = a^m \cdot \frac{1}{a^n}$$
$$= a^m \cdot a^{-n}$$
$$= a^{m-n}$$

When exponentials have different bases but have the same exponent:

LAW (2) $\frac{a^m}{b^m} = \left(\frac{a}{b}\right)^m$

ILLUSTRATION:

$$\frac{a^m}{b^m} = \frac{a \cdot a \cdot a \cdot a \cdot \cdots (m \text{ factors})}{b \cdot b \cdot b \cdot b \cdot \cdots (m \text{ factors})}$$

$$= \frac{a}{b} \cdot \frac{a}{b} \cdot \frac{a}{b} \cdot \frac{a}{b} \cdot \cdots (m \text{ factors}) = \left(\frac{a}{b}\right)^m$$

EXAMPLE 7

$$\frac{6^2}{3^2} = \frac{6 \cdot 6}{3 \cdot 3} = \frac{6}{3} \cdot \frac{6}{3} = \left(\frac{6}{3}\right)^2 = 2^2 = 4, \quad \text{or}$$

$$\frac{6^2}{3^2} = \left(\frac{6}{3}\right)^2 = 2^2 = 4$$

EXAMPLE 8

$$x^3 \cdot y^{-3} = \frac{x^3}{y^3} = \left(\frac{x}{y}\right)^3$$

DIVISION INVOLVING MONOMIALS

When dividing a monomial by another monomial, the quotient of the division is found by multiplying the quotient of the numerical coefficients by the quotient of the literal coefficients.

EXAMPLE 9

Divide $-45x^3$ by $5x$.

$$\frac{-45x^3}{5x} = \frac{-45}{5} \cdot \frac{x^3}{x} = -9x^2$$

EXAMPLE 10

Divide $36x^5y^2z^4$ by $9ax^2y^3$.

$$\frac{36x^5y^2z^4}{9ax^2y^3} = \frac{36}{9} \cdot \frac{1}{a} \cdot \frac{x^5}{x^2} \cdot \frac{y^2}{y^3} \cdot \frac{z^4}{1} = \frac{4x^3z^4}{ay}$$

DIVIDING A POLYNOMIAL BY A MONOMIAL

Divide each term of the polynomial by the monomial. The algebraic sum of the partial quotients is the quotient of the division.

EXAMPLE 11

Divide $28a^2b^3 - 7a^3b + 3ab^3$ by $7a^2b^2$.

$\frac{28a^2b^3}{7a^2b^2} = 4b$; $\frac{-7a^3b}{7a^2b^2} = -\frac{a}{b}$; $\frac{3ab^3}{7a^2b^2} = \frac{3b}{7a}$. Thus,

$$\frac{28a^2b^3 - 7a^3b + 3ab^3}{7a^2b^2} = 4b - \frac{a}{b} + \frac{3b}{7a}$$

DIVIDING A POLYNOMIAL BY ANOTHER POLYNOMIAL

The procedure of dividing one polynomial by another is illustrated in the following example:

EXAMPLE 12

Divide $(15x^3 - 3 + 2x^2)$ by $(3x^2 + 5 - 2x)$.

The division is arranged as follows:

$$\begin{array}{lrl|ll}
\text{(Dividend)} & 15x^3 + 2x^2 \qquad - 3 & & 3x^2 - 2x + 5 & \text{(Divisor)} \\
 & \underline{15x^3 - 10x^2 + 25x \quad} & & 5x + 4 & \text{(Quotient)} \\
 & 12x^2 - 25x - 3 & & & \\
 & \underline{12x^2 - 8x + 20} & & & \\
 & -17x - 23 & \text{(Remainder)} & &
\end{array}$$

The division may also be written in the following form:

$$\begin{array}{llrl}
 & & 5x + 4 & \text{(Quotient)} \\
\text{(Divisor)} & 3x^2 - 2x + 5 \,) & 15x^3 + 2x^2 \qquad - 3 & \text{(Dividend)} \\
 & & \underline{15x^3 - 10x^2 + 25x \quad} & \\
 & & 12x^2 - 25x - 3 & \\
 & & \underline{12x^2 - 8x + 20} & \\
 & & -17x - 23 & \text{(Remainder)}
\end{array}$$

Thus, the solution equation is

$$(15x^3 + 2x^2 - 3) \div (3x^2 - 2x + 5) = (5x + 4) + \frac{-17x - 23}{3x^2 - 2x + 5}$$

The steps in the division above are summarized below:

STEP (1). Arrange the terms of both the dividend and the divisor in descending (or ascending) powers of the same letter.

Dividend: $15x^3 - 3 + 2x^2 = 15x^3 + 2x^2 - 3$
Divisor: $3x^2 + 5 - 2x = 3x^2 - 2x + 5$

STEP (2). Divide the first term of the dividend by the first term of the divisor to obtain the first term of the quotient.

$15x^3 \div 3x^2 = 5x$

STEP (3). Multiply the divisor by the quotient term of Step (2).

$(3x^2 - 2x + 5)(5x) = 15x^3 - 10x^2 + 25x$

STEP (4). Subtract the product of Step (3) from the dividend to obtain a remainder. If the remainder is not zero or is not a lower power than the divisor, continue dividing it by the procedure used in Steps (2), (3), and (4).

CHECK

METHOD A. Let $x = 2$ (or any number except 0 or 1).

Substitute the value in the solution equation.

$$\begin{aligned}\text{Left side} &= [15(2)^3 + 2(2)^2 - 3] \div [3(2)^2 - 2(2) + 5]\\ &= (120 + 8 - 3) \div (12 - 4 + 5)\\ &= 125 \div 13 = 9\tfrac{8}{13}\end{aligned}$$

$$\begin{aligned}\text{Right side} &= [5(2) + 4] + \frac{-17(2) - 23}{3(2)^2 - 2(2) + 5} = 14 + \frac{-57}{13}\\ &= 14 - 4\tfrac{5}{13} = 9\tfrac{8}{13}\end{aligned}$$

★**METHOD B.** $\dfrac{\text{Dividend}}{\text{Divisor}} = \text{Quotient} + \dfrac{\text{Remainder}}{\text{Divisor}}$, or

Dividend = Quotient × Divisor + Remainder. Thus,

$$\begin{aligned}\text{Dividend} &= (5x + 4)(3x^2 - 2x + 5) + (-17x - 23)\\ &= 5x(3x^2 - 2x + 5) + 4(3x^2 - 2x + 5) + (-17x - 23)\\ &= 15x^3 - 10x^2 + 25x + 12x^2 - 8x + 20 - 17x - 23\\ &= 15x^3 + 2x^2 - 3, \quad \text{which is correct}\end{aligned}$$

EXERCISE 2-3 REFERENCE: SECTION 2.5

A. Divide:

1. $24 \div (-6)$
2. $21 \div (-7)$
3. $30 \div (-5)$
4. $36 \div (-4)$
5. $(-24) \div 2$
6. $(-45) \div 9$
7. $(-63) \div 3$
8. $(-132) \div 11$
9. $(-36) \div (-2)$
10. $(-44) \div (-11)$
11. $(-92) \div (-4)$
12. $(-48) \div (-12)$
13. $45 \div 3$
14. $104 \div 4$
15. $\dfrac{112}{-8}$
16. $\dfrac{-60}{15}$
17. $\dfrac{-77}{-11}$
18. $\dfrac{27}{(-3)(-3)}$
19. $\dfrac{(-4)(-5)}{-2}$
20. $\dfrac{-32}{(-4)(2)}$
21. $2^5 \div 2^3$
22. $4^5 \div 4^2$
23. $6^3 \div 6^5$
24. $7^4 \div 7^6$
25. $a^5 \div a^2$
26. $b^9 \div b^8$
27. $x^5 \div x^9$
28. $t^3 \div t^7$
29. $15^2 \div 3^2$
30. $4^2 \div 2^2$
31. $8^3 \div 2^3$
32. $26^3 \div 13^3$
33. $a^3 \div b^3$
34. $x^5 \div y^5$
35. $(ab)^4 \div c^4$
36. $(x^2y^2) \div y^2$
37. $52x^2 \div 2x$
38. $36x^3 \div (-2x^2)$
39. $42a^2 \div 2a$
40. $34b^2c \div 17bc$
41. $7ab \div 4a^2b$
42. $(-5x) \div 4x^3$
43. $(-10x) \div 2x^4$
44. $6t^3 \div 12t^5$
45. $(24b^4 - 18b^2) \div 3b$
46. $(8n^3 + 5n^2t) \div 2n^2$
47. $(6a^5 - ab^2) \div (-2a)$
48. $(14t^7 - 4t^3q) \div 2t^2$
49. $(-18m^3n - 4m^2n^8 - 6mn) \div 2mn$
50. $(14p^2q^3 - 21pq^3 - 7q^6) \div (-7q^4)$
51. $(-18a^2b + 8ab - 8b^2) \div 8b$
52. $(2b^3 - 3b^2 + 10b^5cx) \div (-6b^4)$

B. Divide the following and check (let $x = 2$):

53. $(12x^2 + 5x - 25) \div (4x - 5)$
54. $(21x^2 - 5x + 23) \div (7x + 3)$
55. $(24x^3 - x^2 - 2x + 42) \div (8x + 5)$
56. $(36x^3 + 2x^2 + x + 4) \div (9x - 4)$
57. $(25x^3 + 5x^2 + 3x - 2) \div (5x^2 - 2x + 3)$
58. $(20x^3 + 3x^2 - 4x + 5) \div (4x^2 + 3x - 7)$
59. $(28x^3 + 2x + 4) \div (7x^2 - 3)$
60. $(30x^3 + 22x^2 - 6) \div (15x^2 - 4x + 3)$

2.6 SYMBOLS OF GROUPING

Frequently in mathematical problems one has to do a sequence of algebraic operations. In such cases, grouping symbols should be used to indicate the groups of the terms in an expression. The most common grouping symbols are parentheses ( ). The terms inside the symbol ( ) are treated as a single number. When a symbol of grouping is required within another symbol of grouping, different symbols, such as brackets [ ], braces { }, and the vinculum (a horizontal bar over the digits to be grouped) are often used in addition to parentheses in order to avoid confusion. To carry out the indicated operations in an expression including several symbols of grouping, it is often convenient to remove the inside symbol first. When this is being done, the following rules should be observed:

RULE 1 **When a symbol of grouping is preceded by a plus (+) sign, the symbol may be removed without changing the signs of the terms inside the symbol.**

EXAMPLE 1 $24 + [17 + (8 + 3)] = 24 + [17 + 8 + 3] = 24 + 17 + 8 + 3 = 52,$ or
$= 24 + [17 + (11)] = 24 + [28] = 52$

EXAMPLE 2 $20 + [42 + (5 - 30)] = 20 + [42 + 5 - 30] = 20 + [17] = 37,$ or
$= 20 + [42 + (-25)] = 20 + [17] = 37$

EXAMPLE 3 $x + [y + 2(a - b)] = x + [y + (2a - 2b)] = x + [y + 2a - 2b]$
$= x + y + 2a - 2b$

RULE 2 **When a symbol of grouping is preceded by a minus (−) sign, the symbol may be removed only if the signs of the terms inside the symbol are changed; that is, (+) to (−) and (−) to (+).**

EXAMPLE 4 $7 - [23 - (9 + 4)] = 7 - [23 - 9 - 4] = 7 - [10] = -3,$ or
$= 7 - [23 - 13] = 7 - [10] = -3$

EXAMPLE 5 $x - [y - 3(2a - b)] = x - [y - (6a - 3b)] = x - [y - 6a + 3b]$
$= x - y + 6a - 3b$

The following examples illustrate expressions that include three symbols of grouping:

EXAMPLE 6 $10\{4 + 3[5 - \frac{2}{3}(8 - 2) + 7] - 9\} = 10\{4 + 3[5 - 4 + 7] - 9\}$
$= 10\{4 + 3[8] - 9\}$
$= 10\{19\}$
$= 190$

EXAMPLE 7

$$\begin{aligned}
&9x - \{4x + 2[(3x + y) - \tfrac{1}{4}(4x + 12)] - 5y\} + 7\\
&= 9x - \{4x + 2[3x + y - x - 3] - 5y\} + 7\\
&= 9x - \{4x + 2[2x + y - 3] - 5y\} + 7\\
&= 9x - \{4x + 4x + 2y - 6 - 5y\} + 7\\
&= 9x - \{8x - 3y - 6\} + 7\\
&= 9x - 8x + 3y + 6 + 7\\
&= x + 3y + 13
\end{aligned}$$

EXERCISE 2-4 REFERENCE: SECTION 2.6

Perform the indicated operations in each of the following expressions:

1. $(20 \div 5) \times 2$
2. $(66 \div 11) \times 2$
3. $158 \div (7.9 \times 5)$
4. $89.6 \div (4 \times 7)$
5. $(84 \div 3) \div 4$
6. $(126 \div 6) \div 7$
7. $480 \div (5 \div 12)$
8. $252 \div (9 \div 14)$
9. $(5 + 4) \times 2$
10. $(17 - 88) \div 4$
11. $(192 \div 8) \times (4 - 5)$
12. $(252 \div 7) \times (3 + 5)$
13. $62 + [41 + (10 + 5)]$
14. $37 + [30 + (7 + 12)]$
15. $15 + [18 + (9 - 3)]$
16. $42 + [20 + (8 - 15)]$
17. $44 - [29 - (6 + 5)]$
18. $68 - [31 - (22 + 10)]$
19. $82 - [40 - (30 - 7)]$
20. $120 - [67 - (48 - 36)]$
21. $3\{942 - 5[32 + 17(5 + 3)] + 6\} - 15$
22. $40\{87 - 4[45 - 2(8 + 5)] - 9\} - 83$
23. $32 - \{45 + [18 - 6(7 - 2)] + \frac{1}{3}(24 - 3)\}$
24. $86 - \{52 + [47 - 12(10 - 4)] + \frac{2}{5}(80 - 5)\}$
25. $2x + [3x - \frac{1}{2}(4x + 6)]$
26. $8y + (4y - \frac{1}{6}(6y + 18)]$
27. $4x - [2x - (5x - 4)]$
28. $10y - [11y - (8y - 3)]$
29. $14x - [20x + 9(4x - y)]$
30. $11y - [16y + 7(5x - 2y)]$
31. $2x - \{5y + 4x + [7y - 3(2x - y)] - 2x\}$
32. $16y - \{7x + 3y - [4x + 5(x + y - z) - 3y] + 4z\}$

2.7 FACTORING

In arithmetic, the operations of multiplication and division can be greatly simplified when the products of every two of the basic figures from 0 to 9 are memorized. For example, although 5 × 9 means to repeat five 9 times, it does not actually have to be repeated. A student should readily know that the product of 5 and 9 is 45. Also, when one is able to recognize the factors of a number, such as the factors of 45 being 5 and 9, or 5, 3, and 3, a great amount of computation in arithmetic is eliminated. Similarly, if one knows certain frequently occurring algebraic expressions and their factors, much work in algebraic operations is reduced. The process of finding the factors in a given expression is called *factoring*. The most common types of factoring are illustrated below.

A. Monomial Factor

Frequently, each term in an expression contains the same or *common* factor which can easily be detected by inspection. When this occurs, the given expression may be written as the product of the common monomial factor and another factor. The other factor is obtained by dividing the given expression by the common factor. In general, the factors can be expressed as follows:

$$ax + ay = a(x + y).$$

Factor $(x + y)$ is obtained by dividing $(ax + ay)$ by a; a is the common factor. The left side of the equation is the expanded form, and the right side is the factor form.

EXAMPLE 1

Factor $7x + 7y$.

$$7x + 7y = 7(x + y)$$

EXAMPLE 2

Factor $5x - 5y$.

$$5x - 5y = 5(x - y)$$

EXAMPLE 3

Factor $12ax - 18ay + 6az$.

$$12ax - 18ay + 6az = 6a(2x - 3y + z)$$

B. Common Binomial Factors

In general, this type of factor form is expressed as follows:

$$a(x + y) + b(x + y) = (a + b)(x + y)$$

The factor $(a + b)$ on the right side is obtained by dividing $a(x + y) + b(x + y)$ by the common factor $(x + y)$.

EXAMPLE 4

Factor $3ax - ay + 6cx - 2cy$.

$$3ax - ay + 6cx - 2cy = a(3x - y) + 2c(3x - y) = (a + 2c)(3x - y)$$

C. Difference of Two Squares

This type of factor form is generally expressed:

$$x^2 - y^2 = (x + y)(x - y)$$

The above equation is obtained by multiplying the factors on the right side:

$$\begin{array}{rrr}
 & x + y & \\
(\times) & x - y & \\
\hline
 & x^2 + xy & \\
 & - xy & - y^2 \\
\hline
 & x^2 & - y^2
\end{array}$$

EXAMPLE 5

Factor $25x^2 - 9y^2$.

$$25x^2 - 9y^2 = (5x)^2 - (3y)^2 = (5x + 3y)(5x - 3y)$$

D. Trinomials—Perfect Squares

The general forms of this type are written below:

$x^2 + 2xy + y^2 = (x + y)^2$ and
$x^2 - 2xy + y^2 = (x - y)^2$

The above two equations may also be obtained by multiplying the factors on the right side of each equation.

EXAMPLE 6

Factor $9a^2 + 12ab + 4b^2$.

$$9a^2 + 12ab + 4b^2 = (3a)^2 + 2(3a)(2b) + (2b)^2 = (3a + 2b)^2$$

EXAMPLE 7

Factor $16a^2 - 24ab + 9b^2$.

$$16a^2 - 24ab + 9b^2 = (4a)^2 - 2(4a)(3b) + (3b)^2 = (4a - 3b)^2$$

E. Trinomial—General Case

The general form of this type is written as follows:

$$acx^2 + (ad + bc)x + bd = (ax + b)(cx + d)$$

To verify:

$$\begin{array}{rl} & ax + b \\ (\times) & cx + d \\ \hline & acx^2 + bcx \\ & \quad + adx \qquad + bd \\ \hline & acx^2 + (ad + bc)x + bd \end{array}$$

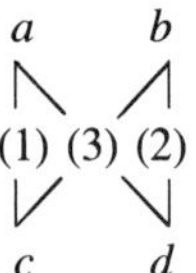

The numerical coefficients of each term in a factor form thus may be determined by the trial-and-error method, as illustrated in the following examples. This method may be conveniently carried out when the required numbers are arranged in columnar form, as shown at the left, so that (1) = ac, (2) = bd, and (3) = $ad + bc$.

EXAMPLE 8

3 1
a b
(1) (3) (2)
c d
2 7

Factor $6x^2 + 23x + 7$.

STEP (1). Find a pair of numbers (a and c) whose product is 6. The factors of 6 are 2 and 3 and also 1 and 6.
STEP (2). Find a pair of numbers (b and d) whose product is 7. The factors of 7 are 1 and 7.
STEP (3). Place the 2 pairs of numbers ($a, c; b, d$) in appropriate positions; that is, the algebraic sum of the products (ad) and (bc) must equal 23.

According to the trial-and-error method, the result is that $a = 3$, $b = 1$, $c = 2$, and $d = 7$. Thus, the desired factors are:

$$6x^2 + 23x + 7 = (3x + 1)(2x + 7)$$

EXAMPLE 9

Factor $10x^2 - 21 + 29x$.

The trinomial should be arranged in the order of descending powers of x. The expression thus obtained is shown below:

$$10x^2 + 29x - 21$$

5		−3
a		b
(1)	(3)	(2)
c		d
2		7

STEP (1). Find a pair of numbers (a and c) whose product is 10. (Factors of 10 are 1 and 10; 2 and 5.)
STEP (2). Find a pair of numbers (b and d) whose product is (-21). (Factors of 21 are 1 and 21; 3 and 7.)
STEP (3). Place the 2 pairs of numbers (a, c; b, d) in proper positions; that is, the algebraic sum of the products (ad) and (bc) must equal 29.

According to the trial-and-error method, the result is that $a = 5$; $b = (-3)$; $c = 2$; and $d = 7$. Thus,

$$10x^2 + 29x - 21 = (5x - 3)(2x + 7)$$

★The following procedure may also be used to factor a trinomial:

STEP (1). Multiply the coefficient of x^2 by the term not containing x.
STEP (2). Find two numbers whose algebraic sum is the coefficient of x and whose product is equal to the one obtained in Step (1).
STEP (3). Use the two numbers to replace the coefficient of x in the trinomial and factor the new expression by grouping the terms.

EXAMPLE 10 Factor $6x^2 + 23x + 7$.

STEP (1). $(6)(7) = 42$
STEP (2). According to the trial-and-error method, $21 + 2 = 23$ and $(21)(2) = 42$.
STEP (3).
$$\begin{aligned} 6x^2 + (21 + 2)x + 7 &= 6x^2 + 21x + 2x + 7 \\ &= 3x(2x + 7) + (2x + 7) \\ &= (3x + 1)(2x + 7) \end{aligned}$$

EXAMPLE 11 Factor $10x^2 + 29x - 21$.

STEP (1). $(10)(-21) = -210$
STEP (2). According to the trial-and-error method, $35 + (-6) = 29$ and $(35)(-6) = -210$.
STEP (3).
$$\begin{aligned} 10x^2 + (35 - 6)x - 21 &= 10x^2 + 35x - 6x - 21 \\ &= 5x(2x + 7) - 3(2x + 7) \\ &= (5x - 3)(2x + 7) \end{aligned}$$

EXERCISE 2-5 REFERENCE: SECTION 2.7

Factor the following:

1. $10a + 5b$
2. $2a - 4b$
3. $6x + 6$
4. $15t - 5$
5. $-18x + 6y - 6z$
6. $24ab + 9ac - 3az$
7. $3ax - ay + 6cx - 2cy$
8. $ax + ay + bx + by$
9. $ax + ay - bx - by$
10. $ax - ay - bx + by$
11. $28ac + 14bc - 4ad - 2bd$
12. $6am - 9an + 4bm - 6bn$
13. $9x^2 - y^4$
14. $x^2 - 1$
15. $25x^2 - 16y^2$
16. $a^2b^2 - 64c^2$
17. $x^4 - 49$
18. $36x^4 - 81y^2$
19. $x^2 + 6x + 9$
20. $x^2 + 8x + 16$
21. $4x^2 + 24x + 36$
22. $9x^2 - 18x + 9$
23. $36y^2 - 60y + 25$
24. $16a^2 - 16a + 4$
25. $9a^2 + 24ab + 16b^2$
26. $25t^2 - 30ts + 9s^2$
27. $x^2 + 3x + 2$
28. $x^2 - 3x + 2$
29. $2y^2 + 5y + 3$
30. $3y^2 + 5y - 2$

31. $2a^2 - a - 3$
32. $12x^2 + 10x + 2$
33. $7x^2 + 20x - 3$
34. $20x^2 + 9x - 18$
35. $21b^2 + 13b - 20$
36. $-15x^2 + 28x - 12$

2.8 LINEAR EQUATIONS IN ONE UNKNOWN

A. Concept of an Equation

An *equation* is a statement that indicates that two algebraic expressions are equal. The two expressions are called the *sides* or *members* of the equation. There are two types of equations: the identical equation, and the conditional equation.

When the two sides of an equation are equal for any value that may be substituted for the letter or letters involved, the equation is called an *identical equation*, or simply an *identity*. For example, $2x + x = 3x$ is an identity because the two sides are equal when x represents any value. Thus, when $x = 1$, the left side becomes $2(1) + 1 = 3$, and the right side becomes $3(1) = 3$.

When the sides of an equation are equal for only definite values of the letters involved, the equation is called a *conditional equation*, or simply an *equation*. For example, $2x + 1 = 7$ is a conditional equation, because only when x represents 3 are the two sides equal to each other. The value, 3, that satisfies the equation is called the *solution* or the *root*. The letter or letters whose value is desired are called the *unknown*. When only one letter occurs in an equation, the root is a number, and when letters other than the unknown are included, the root is usually expressed in terms of those letters.

The number of powers of the single unknown value in an equation indicates the *degree* of an equation. Equations of the *first power* are called *linear equations*. Thus, $2x + 1 = 7$ is a linear equation because $x = x^1$.

B. Solution of Equations

In solving a linear equation in one unknown, the operations are based on the axiom that if the *same* number is added to, subtracted from, multiplied by, or divided into both sides of an equation, the two sides are still equal; that is, the equality of the equation is not destroyed. By applying this axiom, if an equation is obtained in such a way that the unknown is alone on one side, the other side is the desired solution. The procedure for finding the solution of an equation in one unknown is shown below.

STEP (1). Add (or subtract) the same numbers to (or from) both sides so that the resulting equation will have the term that has the unknown on one side and all other terms on the other.

STEP (2). Divide both sides of the new equation by the coefficient of the unknown to obtain the solution.

EXAMPLE 1

Solve $4x + 3 = 6x - 15$.

STEP (1). Subtract $6x$ from both sides to remove $6x$ at the right.

$4x + 3 - 6x = 6x - 15 - 6x$

Collect the like terms on both sides.

$-2x + 3 = -15$

Subtract 3 from both sides to remove 3 at the left.

$-2x + 3 - 3 = -15 - 3$

Collect the like terms on both sides.

$-2x = -18$

STEP (2). Divide both sides by (-2).

$x = 9$

The operations listed above may be simplified by moving the terms from one side of the equation to the other side after changing their signs; that is, from + to −, − to +, × to ÷, and ÷ to ×. Usually, all the terms containing the unknown are moved to the left side and all other terms are moved to the right side until the unknown remains alone on the left side. The above example thus may be simplified as follows:

$$
\begin{aligned}
4x + 3 &= 6x - 15 \\
4x - 6x &= -15 - 3 \\
-2x &= -18, \\
x &= \frac{-18}{-2} \\
x &= 9
\end{aligned}
$$

CHECK

$$
\begin{aligned}
4(9) + 3 &= 6(9) - 15 \\
36 + 3 &= 54 - 15 \\
39 &= 39
\end{aligned}
$$

EXAMPLE 2

Solve $4x - 8 = 2x$.

$$
\begin{aligned}
4x - 2x &= 8 \\
2x &= 8 \\
x &= 4
\end{aligned}
$$

CHECK

$$
\begin{aligned}
4(4) - 8 &= 2(4) \\
16 - 8 &= 8 \\
8 &= 8
\end{aligned}
$$

EXAMPLE 3

Solve $5(x - 2) = x + 18$.

$$
\begin{aligned}
5x - 10 &= x + 18 \\
5x - x &= 10 + 18 \\
4x &= 28 \\
x &= 7
\end{aligned}
$$

CHECK

$$
\begin{aligned}
5[(7) - 2] &= (7) + 18 \\
5[5] &= 7 + 18 \\
25 &= 25
\end{aligned}
$$

EXAMPLE 4

Solve $2ax + b = 3c$ for x.

$$
\begin{aligned}
2ax &= 3c - b \\
x &= \frac{3c - b}{2a}
\end{aligned}
$$

CHECK

$$2a\left(\frac{3c - b}{2a}\right) + b = 3c$$
$$3c - b + b = 3c$$
$$3c = 3c$$

C. Solution of Statement Problems Involving One Unknown

A *statement* or *word problem* may conveniently be solved by the use of a linear equation in one unknown. The steps are:

STEP (1). Represent one of the unknown quantities by a letter, usually x; and express other unknown quantities, if there are any, in terms of the same letter.
STEP (2). Translate the quantities from the statement of the problem into algebraic expressions and set up an equation.
STEP (3). Solve the equation for the unknown that is represented by the letter, and find the other unknowns from the solution.
STEP (4). Check the findings according to the statement in the problem.

EXAMPLE 5 If \$4 is added to 3 times an amount, and the sum is \$19, what is the amount?

STEP (1). Let x = the unknown amount.
STEP (2). Then $4 + 3x = 19$.
STEP (3). Solve the equation: $3x = 19 - 4$

$$3x = 15$$
$$x = 5$$

The unknown amount is \$$x$; that is, \$5.

STEP (4). Check the statement of the problem.

If 4 is added to 3 times 5, the answer is $4 + 3 \cdot 5 = 19$. Thus, the answer is correct.

EXAMPLE 6 A computer sells for \$560. The gross profit is computed as $\frac{3}{4}$ of the cost. Assume that the selling price is equal to the gross profit added to the cost. What are the cost and the gross profit?

STEP (1). Let x = cost. Then, gross profit $= (\frac{3}{4})x$.
STEP (2). According to the statement,

gross profit + cost = selling price; then

$$\left(\tfrac{3}{4}\right)x + x = 560$$

STEP (3). Solve the equation in Step (2).

$$\left(\frac{3}{4} + 1\right)x = 560$$
$$\left(\frac{7}{4}\right)x = 560$$
$$x = 560\left(\frac{4}{7}\right) = 320, \quad \text{or}$$
$$\text{cost} = \$320$$
$$\text{gross profit} = \left(\frac{3}{4}\right)x = \left(\frac{3}{4}\right)(320) = \$240$$

STEP (4). *Check:* Gross profit + cost = selling price:

\$240 + \$320 = \$560

Or the problem may be solved as follows:

STEP (1). Let x = gross profit. Then, $(\frac{3}{4})$ cost = x, or cost = $(\frac{4}{3})x$.

STEP (2). $x + (\frac{4}{3})x = 560$

STEP (3). Solve the equation:

$$\left(1 + \frac{4}{3}\right)x = 560$$

$$\left(\frac{7}{3}\right)x = 560$$

$$x = 560\left(\frac{3}{7}\right) = 240, \quad \text{or}$$

$$\text{gross profit} = \$240$$

$$\text{cost} = \left(\frac{4}{3}\right)x = \left(\frac{4}{3}\right)240 = \$320$$

EXERCISE 2-6 REFERENCE: SECTION 2.8

A. Solve the following equations for x:

1. $2x - 3 = 0$
2. $7x + 6 = 20$
3. $3x - 7 = 8$
4. $x - 9 = 5x$
5. $5x - 13 = 7$
6. $12 - 5x = -18$
7. $4x + 3 = 2x + 11$
8. $6x - 4 = 3x + 29$
9. $3(x - 1) = 2x + 9$
10. $5x - 2(2x - 5) = 15$
11. $4x + 5(3x - 7) = 22$
12. $7(x - 2) = 3x + 26$
13. $3x - 2.4 = -4.2$
14. $8x + 3.6 = 7.8 - 2x$
15. $0.48 + x = 0.26 + 3x$
16. $3x - 0.33 = 0.44 - 4x$
17. $4x = 8a$
18. $4a - 3x = -2a$
19. $2x + 7d = 11d$
20. $7b + 3x = 16b + 6$
21. $3cx + d = 5n$
22. $4y + 2x = 7y$
23. $5(3a - x) - 4(2a - 7x) = -3x$
24. $3(x - 6g) = 5(9x - 2g) - 9g$

B. Statement problems:

25. Ten years ago John's firm was twice as old as Mary's firm. Now the sum of the years in business of the two firms is 41. How many years has John been in business today?
26. Jack and Peter made \$56,000 net profit from their partnership at the end of the year. By agreement, Jack's share was $\frac{2}{5}$ as much as Peter's. How much did Jack receive?
27. Betty and Joan together have \$1,496. If Betty has \$452 more than Joan, how much does Betty have?
28. A man is 4 times as old as his daughter. The difference between their ages is 27 years. What is the man's age?
29. Rita would like to change a \$10 bill into dimes and quarters. She wants to have 12 more quarters than dimes. How many of each should she receive?

30. The sum of three numbers is 86. The second number is five times the first, and the third is 9 more than the first. What are the three numbers?
31. The sum of the digits of a two-digit number is 10. If the digits are reversed, the number is decreased by 18. What is the number?
32. A service station has two kinds of gasoline, one selling for \$1.27 a gallon and the other for \$1.18 a gallon. How many gallons of each must be used to make 90 gallons of a mixture that can be sold for \$1.24 a gallon?
33. A bus that averages 50 miles per hour leaves a station 30 minutes before another bus that averages 60 miles per hour. If both buses take the same route, how long will it take for the second bus to catch up with the first and how far will the buses have traveled?
34. Two planes leave an airport for the East Coast and West Coast, respectively. The westbound plane travels 20 miles per hour faster than the other. At the end of 3 hours they are 900 miles apart. What is the average speed of each plane?
35. A car that travels 45 miles an hour left a city 15 minutes after a truck, and was passing it in 2 hours. What was the average speed of the truck?
36. Two cars left a place at the same time and headed in the same direction. The average hourly speed of one car was $1\frac{1}{4}$ times the speed of the other. At the end of 2 hours they were 26 miles apart. Find the average speed of each car.
37. A washing machine sells for \$336. The gross profit is computed as $\frac{2}{5}$ of the cost. Assume that the selling price is equal to the gross profit plus the cost. What is the cost?
38. The difference between two amounts is \$98 and their sum is \$260. What are the amounts?
39. In a mathematics of finance class, there are 30 students. The number of boys is 4 times the number of girls. How many girls are there?
40. A student made A grades on $\frac{1}{3}$ of a semester's assignments and B grades on $\frac{3}{7}$ of the assignments. The remaining 5 assignments were not handed in. What was the total number of the assignments in the semester?
41. Bill has three times as many dimes as quarters and twice as many half-dollars as dimes. The total value of his money amounts to \$10.65. How many coins of each kind does he have?
42. Maria has 48 dimes and quarters, totaling \$7.05. How many of each does she have?
43. If an amount is added to 2 times the amount, the sum is \$66. Find the amount.
44. If \$5 is subtracted from 3 times an amount, the remainder is \$40. Find the amount.
45. The sum of three amounts is \$85. The largest is \$15 more than the middle one and the smallest is one-half of the largest one. What are the amounts?
46. Divide \$99 into two parts. The difference between the two parts should be \$7.
47. The fixed costs of a factory are \$5,000. The variable costs for producing each unit are \$75. The selling price of each unit is \$125. How many units should the factory produce so that the total costs will be exactly equal to revenues (the total selling price)?
48. A theater sold 40 tickets amounting to \$208.75 in one evening. The tickets were sold to adults for \$5.50 and to children for \$3.25. How many of each were sold?

2.9 RATIO AND PROPORTION

A. Meaning of Ratio

Numbers may be compared in various ways. One convenient way is to express the comparison according to the relative values of the things being compared instead of stating the actual values. For example, in one city there are 220,000 women and 110,000 men. Since $\frac{220{,}000 \text{ women}}{110{,}000 \text{ men}} = \frac{2 \text{ women}}{1 \text{ man}}$, it is more convenient to state that the number of women compared with the number of men is 2 to 1, which are relative values, instead of saying 220,000 to 110,000, which are actual values. *Ratio* is a way of expressing the relative values of things. Thus, the comparison above may also be expressed as "the ratio of the number of women to the number of men in the city is 2 to 1," which may be written 2 : 1.

Generally, when two numbers are expressed in ratio form, the ratio is the quotient of the two numbers. When a number, called the *first term*, is divided by another number, called the *second term*, the quotient is the ratio of the first term to the second term. This relationship may be written as follows:

$$\begin{aligned}\text{Ratio of the first term to the second term} &= \text{The first term} : \text{The second term}\\ &= \frac{\text{The first term}}{\text{The second term}}\end{aligned}$$

Thus, the ratio of a to b is expressed as $a : b$, or $\frac{a}{b}$, or $a \div b$. The ratio of b to a is expressed as $b : a$, or $\frac{b}{a}$, or $b \div a$. The ratio of 2 to 10 is $2 : 10$ or $\frac{2}{10}$; whereas the ratio of 10 to 2 is $10 : 2$, or $\frac{10}{2}$.

Since a ratio may be expressed as a fraction, the rules applying to fractions likewise apply to ratios. For convenience, the fraction may be reduced to its lowest terms. Thus, $\frac{2}{10}$ may be reduced to $\frac{1}{5}$; the ratio of 2 to 10 is equal to the ratio of 1 to 5, or $2 : 10 = 1 : 5$.

When more than two relative values are expressed in ratio form, the ratios of the values may be written in separate form or in combined form. For example, assume that the relative values of three things, A, B, and C are 2, 3, and 4, respectively. If $A = 2$, then $B = 3$ and $C = 4$; if one of them is doubled, then the others are also doubled; if one of them is tripled, then the others are also tripled; and so on. Thus, if $A = 4$ (or 2×2), then $B = 6$ (or 3×2) and $C = 8$ (or 4×2). The relationships may be expressed individually as $A : B = 2 : 3$, $B : C = 3 : 4$, $A : C = 2 : 4$, or written in combined form as $A : B : C = 2 : 3 : 4$, where

$$\begin{aligned}2 : 3 : 4 &= (2 \times 2) : (3 \times 2) : (4 \times 2)\\ &= (2 \times 3) : (3 \times 3) : (4 \times 3) \quad \text{and so on, or}\\ A : B : C = 2 : 3 : 4 &= 4 : 6 : 8 = 6 : 9 : 12 \quad \text{and so on}\end{aligned}$$

In other words, if each term of the ratio in combined form is multiplied (or divided) by the same number, other than zero, the value of the ratio does not change.

When measurements of the same kind are expressed in ratio form, the measurements should be stated in the same unit for comparison.

EXAMPLE 1

Express the ratio of the length of a desk measuring 9 feet to the length of a bookshelf measuring 18 inches.

(a) Let the unit be an inch.
Since 9 feet (the length of the desk) equals 108 inches (or 9×12),

$108 \text{ (inches)} : 18 \text{ (inches)} = \frac{108}{18} = \frac{6}{1}$, or 6

(b) Let the unit be a foot.
Since 18 inches (the length of the bookshelf) equals $1\frac{1}{2}$ feet (or $\frac{18}{12}$),

$9 \text{ (feet)} : 1\frac{1}{2} \text{ (feet)} = \frac{9}{1\frac{1}{2}} = (9)\left(\frac{2}{3}\right) = \frac{18}{3} = \frac{6}{1}$, or 6

The answer indicates that the length of the desk is 6 times the length of the bookshelf. In Example 1 the quantities compared, the lengths, are of the same kind. When numbers of the same kind are compared, the ratio is always abstract.

There are also ratios of different kinds of quantities. For example, if a carpenter makes 10 chairs in 5 days, the ratio of the chairs produced to the time consumed is expressed as 10 chairs : 5 days, which may be written $\frac{10 \text{ chairs}}{5 \text{ days}} = \frac{2 \text{ chairs}}{1 \text{ day}} = 2$ chairs/day, or simply 2. However, when the number 2 is written, it is understood that the ratio indicates the carpenter's average speed; that is, he can make 2 chairs each day during that time.

B. Allocation of a Number According to Ratio

To allocate or divide a number into parts according to a ratio, consider the sum of the terms of the ratio as a unit for dividing.

EXAMPLE 2

Divide \$100 into portions A and B in a ratio of 2 : 3.

The sum of the terms of the ratio = 2 + 3 = 5. For each unit, \$5, A gets \$2 and B gets \$3. \$100 ÷ \$5 = 20 units for dividing.

Thus, A's portion is: 20 × \$2 = \$40
B's portion is: 20 × \$3 = \$60

In general, to allocate or divide a number into parts according to ratio, use the following procedure: To obtain the first part, multiply the number by the fraction whose denominator is the sum of the terms of the ratio and whose numerator is the first term of the ratio. To obtain the second part, use the second term of the ratio as the numerator of the fraction. The following examples further illustrate the problems involved in dividing a number according to ratio.

EXAMPLE 3

Divide 45 into three parts in the ratio 2 : 3 : 4.

$2 + 3 + 4 = 9$

$45 \times \frac{2}{9} = 10$

$45 \times \frac{3}{9} = 15$

$$45 \times \frac{4}{9} = 20$$

The three parts are 10, 15, and 20.

CHECK

$10 + 15 + 20 = 45$

$$10 : 15 : 20 = \frac{10}{5} : \frac{15}{5} : \frac{20}{5} = 2 : 3 : 4$$

EXAMPLE 4 \$510 is to be divided among A, B, and C in the ratio of $\frac{1}{2} : \frac{2}{3} : \frac{1}{4}$, respectively. How much should each receive?

First, reduce each term of the given ratio to have a common denominator. Here the l.c.d. is 12. If each term of the reduced ratio is multiplied by 12, the value of the ratio does not change. Thus,

$$\frac{1}{2} : \frac{2}{3} : \frac{1}{4} = \frac{6}{12} : \frac{8}{12} : \frac{3}{12} = 6 : 8 : 3$$

According to the ratio 6 : 8 : 3, the amount is divided as follows:

$6 + 8 + 3 = 17$

$$\text{A's share} = 510 \times \frac{6}{17} = \$180$$

$$\text{B's share} = 510 \times \frac{8}{17} = \$240$$

$$\text{C's share} = 510 \times \frac{3}{17} = \$\ 90$$

CHECK

$180 + 240 + 90 = 510$

$$180 : 240 : 90 = \frac{180}{30} : \frac{240}{30} : \frac{90}{30} = 6 : 8 : 3$$

Thus, to allocate a number in fractional ratio (such as $\frac{1}{2} : \frac{2}{3} : \frac{1}{4}$), reduce the given fractions to fractions with a lowest common denominator ($\frac{6}{12} : \frac{8}{12} : \frac{3}{12}$); then use the numerators (6 : 8 : 3) as the ratio in allocating the number.

C. Proportion

A *proportion* is a statement of the equality of two ratios. For example, 2 : 10 = 1 : 5, or $\frac{2}{10} = \frac{1}{5}$, is a proportion. Thus, $a : b = c : d$, or $a/b = c/d$, is also a proportion. It is read "*a* is to *b* as *c* is to *d*," or "the ratio of *a* to *b* is equal to the ratio of *c* to *d*." The letters *a*, *b*, *c*, and *d* are the *terms* of the proportion; *a* and *d* are the *extremes*; *b* and *c* are the *means*.

Since proportions are equations, the rules and operations of equations also apply to proportions. For example, if both sides of the proportion $\frac{a}{b} = \frac{c}{d}$ are multiplied by bd, the common denominator, the result is $\frac{a}{\cancel{b}} \cdot \cancel{b}d = \frac{c}{\cancel{d}} \cdot b\cancel{d}$, or $ad = bc$. The answer indicates that when the terms in the proportion are cross-multiplied, the two products are equal. The answer is diagrammed as follows:

$$\frac{a}{b} = \frac{c}{d}; \quad ad = bc$$

Since the proportion may be written in the form $a : b = c : d$, the answer also indicates that the product of the extremes (ad) equals the product of the means (bc). When any three of the four terms in a proportion are given, the other unknown term can always be found by this relationship. Proportion thus may be used in solving many types of problems in business and is referred to frequently in the forthcoming chapters. The following examples illustrate some uses of proportion in various types of problems.

EXAMPLE 5 Solve for x. $13 : 4 = 52 : x$

Multiply the extremes and the means. $13 : 4 = 52 : x$

$$13x = 4 \cdot 52 = 208; \qquad x = \frac{208}{13} = 16$$

EXAMPLE 6 Solve for x. $\frac{28}{7} = \frac{x}{5}$

Use cross multiplication:

$$\frac{28}{7} = \frac{x}{5}; \qquad 7x = 28 \cdot 5 = 140; \qquad x = \frac{140}{7} = 20$$

EXAMPLE 7 Solve for x. $x : \frac{3}{4} = \frac{1}{5} : \frac{9}{11}$

$$\frac{9}{11}x = \left(\frac{3}{4}\right)\left(\frac{1}{5}\right); \qquad x = \frac{\left(\frac{3}{4}\right)\left(\frac{1}{5}\right)}{\frac{9}{11}} = \frac{\frac{3}{20}}{\frac{9}{11}} = \left(\frac{3}{20}\right)\left(\frac{11}{9}\right) = \frac{11}{60}$$

EXAMPLE 8 A grocery store charges \$7.80 for 5 dozen eggs. How much will it charge for 18 dozen eggs?

Let y be the price of 18 dozen eggs. Thus, the problem may be stated in proportional language as follows:

\$7.80 is to 5 dozen as y is to 18 dozen, which may be written

$$\frac{7.80}{5 \text{ dozen}} = \frac{y}{18 \text{ dozen}}, \text{ or simply } \frac{7.80}{5} = \frac{y}{18}; \qquad 5y = (7.80)(18);$$

$$y = \frac{(7.80)(18)}{5} = \$28.08.$$

EXAMPLE 9 When a tree casts a shadow 24 feet long, the shadow of a boy $5\frac{1}{2}$ feet tall is 8 feet long. How high is the tree?

The ratio of the boy's height to his shadow equals the ratio of the tree's height to its shadow. Let x = the height of the tree. Thus,

$$\overbrace{\frac{5\frac{1}{2}}{8}}^{\text{boy}} = \overbrace{\frac{x}{24}}^{\text{tree}}; \qquad 8x = (5\tfrac{1}{2})(24); \qquad x = \frac{(5\frac{1}{2})(24)}{8} = 16\tfrac{1}{2} \text{ (feet)}$$

NOTE: Two things are frequently related in quantitative variation. When the quantity of one thing varies *as* the quantity of another thing changes, the variation is direct. In *direct variation*, the ratio of one thing to another is constant and their changes are proportional to each other. Examples 8 and 9 are direct variation problems. In Example 8, for instance, the total price for a certain number of dozens of eggs varies with the number of dozens of eggs sold. The total price increases as the number of dozens of eggs increases. However, the ratio of the total price to the corresponding number of dozens of eggs sold is constant:

$$\frac{\$7.80}{5\text{ dozen}} = \frac{\$28.08}{18\text{ dozen}} = \$1.56\text{ per dozen}$$

EXERCISE 2-7 REFERENCE: SECTION 2.9

A. Express the ratios of the following in fractional form and reduce them to their lowest terms:

1. 5 to 45
2. 8 to 24
3. 60 to 15
4. 52 to 13
5. $8\frac{2}{3}$ to $5\frac{1}{4}$
6. $6\frac{5}{12}$ to $12\frac{5}{6}$
7. 2.45 to 9.13
8. 6.5 to 2.5
9. 195 miles to 3 hours
10. 18 minutes to 3 hours
11. 150 dollars to 5 days
12. 8 ounces to 2 pounds

B. Solve for x in each of the following proportions:

13. $\frac{x}{6} = \frac{7}{21}$
14. $\frac{20}{x} = \frac{2}{3}$
15. $\frac{x}{6} = \frac{11}{15}$
16. $\frac{3}{7} = \frac{x}{14}$
17. $\frac{18}{x} = \frac{3}{26}$
18. $\frac{36.45}{27} = \frac{x}{5}$
19. $\frac{21.35}{28} = \frac{30.5}{x}$
20. $\frac{60}{73} = \frac{36}{x}$
21. $x : 9 = 4 : 15$
22. $26 : x = 8 : 25$
23. $3 : 15 = x : 32$
24. $x : 6 = 9 : 21$
25. $19 : x = 30 : 65$
26. $\frac{5}{4} : \frac{6}{7} = \frac{5}{6} : x$
27. $x : \frac{3}{7} = \frac{2}{3} : \frac{6}{7}$
28. $15 : 5 = 9 : x$

C. Statement problems:

29. Company A has current assets of \$780,000 and current liabilities of \$420,000. Company B has current assets of \$480,000 and current liabilities of \$360,000. What is the ratio of the current assets to the current liabilities of Company A? of Company B? Which of the two ratios is higher?
30. Last year George's income was \$54,000. There were 6 persons in his family. John's income was \$70,000. There were 10 persons in his family. (a) Find the ratios of their respective annual incomes to the sizes of their families. (b) According to the sizes of the families, whose income per person was larger?
31. A retail store sells an article for \$40. The cost of the article is \$25, the total amount of other expenses is \$5, and the remaining part is the profit. Find the ratios of (a) the cost to the selling price, (b) the total amount of other expenses to the selling price, and (c) the profit to the selling price.
32. Refer to Problem 31. Find the ratios of the following: (a) the total of other expenses to the cost and (b) the profit to the cost.
33. Divide 240 into two numbers in the ratio 1 : 3.
34. Divide 300 into two numbers in the ratio 3 : 5.

35. Divide 648 into three numbers in the ratio 2 : 3 : 7.
36. Divide 680 into three numbers in the ratio 4 : 5 : 8.
37. Divide 1,020 into four numbers in the ratio 2 : 3 : 5 : 7.
38. Divide 720 into four numbers in the ratio 1 : 4 : 5 : 8.
39. Divide 7,688 into three numbers in the ratio $2\frac{3}{4} : \frac{5}{7} : 3\frac{2}{5}$.
40. Divide 2,040 into three numbers in the ratio $\frac{2}{7} : \frac{3}{8} : \frac{1}{4}$.
41. Eleanor divides her estate of $46,200 among her four daughters in the ratio $\frac{1}{2} : \frac{1}{3} : \frac{1}{4} : \frac{1}{5}$. How much does each daughter receive?
42. Four partners, A, B, C, and D, agree to share profits in the ratio $\frac{1}{2} : \frac{2}{3} : \frac{1}{4} : \frac{2}{5}$, respectively. This year the partnership has a profit of $4,360. How much does each partner receive?
43. A car runs 58 miles on 3 gallons of gasoline. How far will it run on 5 gallons?
44. A man can plow 15 acres in 4 days. How much time is needed to plow 74 acres?
45. If 7 yards of cloth cost $25, what will 21 yards cost?
46. If 130 bushels of corn cost $275, what will 220 bushels cost?
47. When a building casts a shadow 45 feet long, the shadow of a man 6 feet tall is $3\frac{1}{2}$ feet long. Find the height of the building.
48. The scale of a map is $1\frac{1}{4}$ inches for 300 miles. How many miles are represented by 5 inches?
49. If a seamstress is paid at the rate of $9.00 per dress completed, how much does she receive after completing 12 dresses?
50. The B. B. Candy Store bought 560 boxes of candy at 90¢ a box. How much is the total cost?
51. If a plane travels 20 miles in 16 minutes, how long will it take to travel 125 miles?
52. If a field containing 35 acres yields 1,071 bushels of wheat, how much will a field containing 100 acres yield?
53. If 25 men can build 1,000 cubic feet of brick wall in one day, how many men will be needed to build 2,560 cubic feet of brick wall in one day?
54. If a pile of wood containing 344 cubic feet costs $160, how much will a pile containing 4,730 cubic feet cost?

2.10 PERCENT—BASIC CONCEPTS AND OPERATIONS

The word "percent" is derived from the Latin words *per* and *centum*, which indicate "in the hundred." The symbol for percent, %, means $\frac{1}{100}$ or .01 (one hundredth). Thus, percent is a form of fraction and is also a type of ratio. For example, 5% may be written as $\frac{5}{100}$, which is the ratio of 5 to 100.

Since percent (%) may be written as a fraction ($\frac{1}{100}$) or a decimal (.01), the following basic operations should be regarded as essential in solving problems involving percent.

A. Reducing a Percent to a Decimal or a Whole Number

To reduce a percent to a decimal or a whole number, move the decimal point in the percent two places to the left and drop the percent sign (%).

or Divide by 100

EXAMPLE 1

$100\% = 1$ $\quad 4{,}700\% = 47$ $\quad 29\frac{1}{4}\% = .29\frac{1}{4}$

$126\% = 1.26$ $\quad 35.52\% = .3552$ $\quad \frac{1}{2}\% = .00\frac{1}{2}$

$2.234\% = .02234$ $\quad 4\% = .04$

B. Reducing a Percent to a Common Fraction

A general way to reduce a percent to a common fraction is to first drop the percent sign and then use the number as the numerator and 100 as the denominator. Next, reduce the fraction to its lowest terms.

EXAMPLE 2

$5\% = \frac{5}{100} = \frac{1}{20}$ $\quad 239\% = \frac{239}{100} = 2\frac{39}{100}$

$71\% = \frac{71}{100}$ $\quad .015\% = \frac{.015}{100} = \frac{15}{100{,}000} = \frac{3}{20{,}000}$

$6.3\% = \frac{6.3}{100} = \frac{63}{1{,}000}$ $\quad .25\% = \frac{.25}{100} = \frac{25}{10{,}000} = \frac{1}{400}$

The reduction may also be done by changing the percent to a decimal and then changing the decimal to a common fraction in its lowest terms.

EXAMPLE 3

$25\% = .25 = \frac{25}{100} = \frac{1}{4}$ $\quad 1.25\% = .0125 = \frac{125}{10{,}000} = \frac{1}{80}$

$.065\% = .00065 = \frac{65}{100{,}000} = \frac{13}{20{,}000}$

To reduce a fractional percent to a common fraction, simply drop the percent sign and then annex two zeros to the denominator.

EXAMPLE 4

$\frac{3}{4}\% = \frac{3}{400}$ $\quad \frac{10}{21}\% = \frac{10}{2100} = \frac{1}{210}$

C. Reducing a Decimal or a Whole Number to a Percent

To reduce a decimal or a whole number to a percent, move the decimal point two places to the right and annex a percent sign.

EXAMPLE 5

$.15 = 15\%$ $\quad .034 = 3.4\%$

$683 = 68{,}300\%$ $\quad 1.2 = 120\%$

$23.4 = 2{,}340\%$ $\quad .0089 = .89\%$

D. Reducing a Common Fraction to a Percent

To reduce a common fraction to a percent, reduce the fraction to a decimal and then reduce the decimal to a percent. Note that the decimals in the illustrations in Example 6 are carried to two places.

EXAMPLE 6

$\frac{2}{5} = .4 = 40\%$

$\frac{7}{25} = .28 = 28\%$

$\frac{25}{4} = 6\frac{1}{4} = 6.25 = 625\%$

$\frac{2}{3} = .66\frac{2}{3} = 66\frac{2}{3}\%$, or rounded to 67%, since $\frac{2}{3}\%$ is more than one-half of the unit to be retained $\left(\text{that is, more than } \frac{1}{2}\%\right)$

$\frac{31}{6} = 5\frac{1}{6} = 5.16\frac{2}{3} = 516\frac{2}{3}\%$, or rounded to 517%

$\frac{1}{14} = .07\frac{2}{14} = 7\frac{2}{14}\%$, or rounded to 7%, since $\frac{2}{14}\% = \frac{1}{7}\%$, which is less than $\frac{1}{2}\%$

However, if the denominator of the fraction is an aliquot part of 100, the fraction may be reduced to a percent without first being changed to a decimal. An *aliquot part* is the part of a number by which the number may be divided leaving no remainder. For example, 5, 10, and 20 are aliquot parts of 100, because $100 \div 5 = 20$, $100 \div 10 = 10$, and $100 \div 20 = 5$.

EXAMPLE 7

$\frac{2}{5} = \frac{(2)(20)}{(5)(20)} = \frac{40}{100} = 40\%$

$\frac{3}{10} = \frac{(3)(10)}{(10)(10)} = \frac{30}{100} = 30\%$

$\frac{7}{20} = \frac{(7)(5)}{(20)(5)} = \frac{35}{100} = 35\%$

NOTE: At this point, a review of the method of reducing a common fraction to a decimal and vice versa, as given in Section 1.4A, page 15, should be helpful. Also, it will be found that computations in multiplication and division are greatly simplified when percentage problems concerning aliquot parts of 100 are converted to common fractions before the computation, such as $30\% = \frac{3}{10}$, $40\% = \frac{2}{5}$, and $35\% = \frac{7}{20}$ shown in Example 7 above. Also see Section 1.4B.

EXERCISE 2-8 REFERENCE: SECTION 2.10

A. Express each of the following as a decimal or a whole number:

1. .31%
2. .72%
3. 4.58%
4. 5.78%
5. 29%
6. 12%
7. 216%
8. 135%
9. 4,500%
10. 3,400%

B. Express each of the following as a common fraction in its lowest terms:

11. 6%
12. 18%
13. 615%
14. 6,025%
15. 1.2%
16. 4.8%
17. .024%
18. .062%
19. .0042%
20. .005%

C. Express each of the following as a percent (in Problems 31 to 40, carry decimals to two places, then reduce the decimals to percents; round the fractional percents, if any):

21. .45
22. .12
23. .047
24. .132
25. .0035
26. .00049
27. 72
28. 62
29. 1.46
30. 2.84
31. $\frac{1}{50}$
32. $\frac{2}{5}$
33. $3\frac{5}{7}$
34. $2\frac{3}{8}$
35. $\frac{12}{13}$
36. $\frac{22}{27}$
37. $16\frac{15}{32}$
38. $23\frac{71}{82}$
39. $\frac{4.5}{8.25}$
40. $\frac{5.62}{6.48}$

2.11 PERCENT—COMPUTATION

A. Finding the Percentage

The term *percentage* has a twofold meaning. It is the name used for calculations in which hundredths or percents are involved. It is also the product of the base and the rate.

The *base* is the number that is regarded as a whole and from which a certain number of hundredths (%) is expressed or taken. The number of hundredths (%) is called the *rate*. *A percent has no meaning if it does not have a base*. For example, 10% standing alone has no meaning, but 10% of 200 has meaning. To solve the problem of finding 10% of 200, regard 200 as a whole (base) or 100%. If 200 is 100%, what is 10%? To answer the question, first find the value of 1%: $\frac{200}{100} = 2$. Then find the value of 10%: $2 \times 10 = 20$. The entire computation may be written as follows:

$$\frac{200}{100} \times 10 = 20, \quad \text{or} \quad 200 \times \frac{10}{100} = 200 \times 10\% = 20$$

Therefore, 20 is 10% of 200. In other words, 200 is the base, 10% is the rate, and 20 is the product, which is called the percentage. The relationship may be expressed as follows:

Percentage = Base × Rate

From the above relationship, the following is derived:

$$\text{Rate} = \frac{\text{Percentage}}{\text{Base}}; \qquad \text{Base} = \frac{\text{Percentage}}{\text{Rate}}$$

The following examples illustrate the uses of the expression
Percentage = Base × Rate.

EXAMPLE 1 What is 25% of $510?

25% is the rate, and $510 is the base from which 25% is taken. Thus,

$$\text{Percentage} = 510 \times 25\% = 510 \times \tfrac{1}{4} = \$127.50$$

CHECK Since $510 is 100% (base), then 1% should be $\frac{\$510}{100} = \$5.10$, and 25% should be $\$5.10 \times 25 = \$127.50$

EXAMPLE 2 Lawrence Shaw sold a truck for Bill Smith for $12,000. If his commission is 8% of the selling price and he paid $250 for advertising expenses, how much should he remit to Smith?

8% is the rate and $12,000 is the base from which 8% is taken. Thus, the amount of commission is the percentage.

12,000 × 8% = 12,000 × .08 = $960 (commission)

12,000 − 960 − 250 = $10,790 (amount he should remit to Smith after the deductions of commission and expenses)

EXERCISE 2-9 REFERENCE: SECTION 2.11A

A. Find the percentage in each of the following (note: some of the problems may be solved by using the aliquot part method, as discussed in Section 2.10D):

	Base	*Rate*		*Base*	*Rate*
1.	700	25%	11.	48	$41\frac{2}{3}\%$
2.	420	16%	12.	56	$14\frac{2}{7}\%$
3.	32.12	75%	13.	42.60	15%
4.	76.44	$16\frac{2}{3}\%$	14.	14.50	22%
5.	40.50	72%	15.	90	$6\frac{2}{3}\%$
6.	152	43%	16.	72	$37\frac{1}{2}\%$
7.	164	$62\frac{1}{2}\%$	17.	612	12%
8.	130.8	$87\frac{1}{2}\%$	18.	835	35%
9.	67.32	18%	19.	66.93	$66\frac{2}{3}\%$
10.	39.12	24%	20.	24.60	$83\frac{1}{3}\%$

B. Statement problems:

21. What is 45% of $425?
22. What is 70% of $560?
23. Rose purchased a dress that was priced at $140. She made a down payment of 20% of the price. (a) How much was the down payment? (b) What percent of the price was the unpaid balance?
24. A retail store sold an article at 25% more than its cost. What was the selling price if the cost of the article was $60?
25. Bob's take-home pay is $2,500 a month. His family expenses for each month are as follows: rent, $500; gas and electricity, $80; telephone, $30; food and clothing, 25% and 10% respectively, of his monthly pay. Other incidental expenses amount to $6,000 a year. How much can he save in a year?
26. James Kelley and Howard Smith are co-owners of a service station. They have agreed that profits should be divided as follows: 55% to Kelley, 40% to Smith, and the remaining part to a local boys' camp. If the profits amount to $90,000 this year, how much will Kelley and Smith each receive? How much will the boys' camp receive? What percent of the profits will the camp receive?

B. Finding the Rate

The following examples are presented to illustrate the uses of the expression

$$\text{Rate} = \frac{\text{Percentage}}{\text{Base}}$$

EXAMPLE 3 What percent of $428 is $64.20?

$428 is the base from which the percent (rate) is taken, and the part taken is $64.20, which is the percentage. Thus,

$$\text{Rate} = \frac{64.20}{428} = .15 = 15\%$$

CHECK

1% of $428 is $4.28. $64.20 contains 15 times $4.28 (or 64.20 ÷ 4.28 = 15). Hence, $64.20 is 15% of $428.

EXAMPLE 4

In 1990 the total sales of a store were $15 million; in 1991 sales were $17.7 million. What was the percent of change in 1991 based on the 1990 sales?

(1) The amount of increase based on the sales of 1990 is

$$\$17.7 \text{ million} - \$15 \text{ million} = \$2.7 \text{ million}$$

The amount of the 1990 sales must also be the base from which the percent of increase is expressed. Thus, the percent of increase is

$$\frac{\$2.7 \text{ million}}{\$15 \text{ million}} = .18 = 18\%$$

The sales of 1991 were 18% more than the sales of 1990.

(2) This problem may be solved in a different way as follows.

First, the following question must be answered: What percent of $15 million is $17.7 million? Here $15 million is the base from which the percent is computed, and $17.7 million is the percentage. Thus,

$$\frac{\$17.7 \text{ million}}{\$15 \text{ million}} = 1.18 = 118\%$$

Then, $17.7 million, the amount of the 1991 sales, is 118% of $15 million, the amount of the 1990 sales. Since a base is always equal to 100%, the percent of increase of 1991 sales over 1990 sales is

$$118\% - 100\% = 18\%$$

CHECK

18% of 1990 sales is $2.7 million (or $15 million × 18%).

$$\$15 \text{ million} + \$2.7 \text{ million} = \$17.7 \text{ million},$$

the sales of 1991.

EXERCISE 2-10 REFERENCE: SECTION 2.11B

(Round all answers to the nearest tenth of one percent. *Example:* 2.34% is rounded to 2.3%.)

A. Find the rate in percent (%) of each of the following:

Rate	*Percentage*	*Base*	*Rate*	*Percentage*	*Base*
1. ?	27	36	6. ?	120	560
2. ?	70	40	7. ?	65	50
3. ?	93	31	8. ?	24	48
4. ?	73.5	175	9. ?	30	75
5. ?	56.4	400	10. ?	28.5	57

B. Statement problems:

11. What percent of \$260 is \$20.80?
12. What percent of \$140 is \$49.28?
13. \$7.50 is what percent of \$45?
14. \$16 is what percent of \$84?
15. \$13 is what percent more than \$10?
16. \$32 is what percent more than \$24?
17. \$45 is what percent less than \$60?
18. \$224 is what percent less than \$320?
19. A radio bought for \$49 is sold for \$64. What percent of the cost is the profit?
20. In the above problem, what percent of the selling price is the profit?
21. Alice pays an employment agency a fee of \$547.50 from her first month's salary of \$1,500. What percent of the salary is the fee?
22. Aron gave \$30 from his week's pay of \$90 to his sister for her birthday party. What percent of his pay did he give?
23. The price of a pound of round steak was \$3.84 in 1989 and \$4.80 in 1990. What was the percent of change in 1990?
24. There were 600 freshmen last year and 800 this year in a small midwestern college. Find the percent of increase.
25. A girl sold her typewriter for 90% of its cost. (a) What percent did she lose? (b) If the cost was \$290, how much did she lose?
26. A retailer has an investment of \$100,000 in his store. His net income for last year was 55% of his investment. His net income for this year is \$44,000. What is the percent of decrease or increase this year?

C. Finding the Base

A base may be found in two ways. Method A: use the expression Base $= \dfrac{\text{Percentage}}{\text{Rate}}$; Method B: let x = the base, and then solve for x in the translated algebraic equation. Of the two methods, Method A is easier to compute if one understands the relationship between the percentage and the rate.

When Method A is applied in finding the base, it is vitally important to know that the base always corresponds to 100% and the percentage always corresponds to the rate. The expression has the same meaning as the proportion $\dfrac{\text{Base}}{100\%} = \dfrac{\text{Percentage}}{\text{Rate}}$, which states that "Base is to 100% as Percentage is to Rate." *The base is always 100% of itself.* The following examples are used to illustrate the problems in finding the base by the two methods.

EXAMPLE 5 If 14% of a number is 112, what is the number?

METHOD A The unknown number is the base, which is equivalent to 100%. Since 14% is equivalent to 112, the value of 100% is $\dfrac{112}{14\%} = 800$.

By examining the division $\dfrac{112}{14\%}$, the following method is derived:

To find a number that is equivalent to 100% (the base), divide a given number (percentage) by its equivalent percent (rate).

CHECK

1% of the number is $\frac{112}{14} = 8$. 100% of the number is $8 \times 100 = 800$. Or, $800 \times 14\% = 112$.

METHOD B

Let x = the number (base). Then

$$x(14\%) = 112$$
$$x = \frac{112}{14\%} = 800$$

EXAMPLE 6

Alberto had $3,348 at the end of last year after losing 7% of his investment. What was the amount of his investment?

METHOD A

The unknown amount is the base (100%) from which 7% has been lost. The remainder, 93% (or 100% − 7%), corresponds to the remaining amount, $3,348. In other words, 93% is equivalent to $3,348. Thus, the value of 100% is computed as follows:

$$\frac{3{,}348}{93\%} = \frac{3{,}348}{.93} = \$3{,}600$$

METHOD B

Let x = the amount of investment. Then

$$x - 7\%x = 3{,}348$$
$$x(1 - 7\%) = 3{,}348$$
$$x = \frac{3{,}348}{93\%} = \$3{,}600$$

CHECK

$$\$3{,}600 \times 7\% = \$252$$
$$\$3{,}600 - \$252 = \$3{,}348$$

EXAMPLE 7

A store manager priced his sugar at $9.01 per sack. The price was 6% more than the cost. What was the cost per sack?

METHOD A

The cost is the base (100%) from which 6% is computed. The price $9.01 is the percentage that corresponds to 106% (or 100% + 6%). In other words, $9.01 is to 106% as the unknown cost is to 100%.

Thus, the value of 100% is $\frac{9.01}{106\%} = \$8.50$ (cost).

METHOD B

Let x = cost. Then

$$x + 6\%x = 9.01$$
$$x(1 + 6\%) = 9.01$$
$$x = \frac{9.01}{106\%} = \$8.50$$

CHECK

$$\$8.50 \times 6\% = \$.51$$
$$\$8.50 + \$.51 = \$9.01 \quad \text{(price)}$$

EXAMPLE 8

If a number decreased by 52% is 364.8, what is the number?

METHOD A

364.8 corresponds to 48% (or 100% − 52%). Thus, the value of 100%, the number (base), is

$$\frac{364.8}{48\%} = 760$$

METHOD B

Let x = the number.

$$x - x \cdot 52\% = 364.8$$
$$x(1 - 52\%) = 364.8$$
$$x = \frac{364.8}{48\%} = 760$$

CHECK

$$760 \cdot 52\% = 395.2$$
$$760 - 395.2 = 364.8$$

EXAMPLE 9 What number increased by 12% of itself is 296.8?

METHOD A

296.8 corresponds to 112% (or 100% + 12%). Thus, the value of 100%, the number (base), is

$$\frac{296.8}{112\%} = 265$$

METHOD B

Let x = the number.

$$x + 12\%x = 296.8$$
$$112\%x = 296.8$$
$$x = \frac{296.8}{112\%} = 265$$

CHECK

$$265 \times 12\% = 31.8$$
$$265 + 31.8 = 296.8$$

EXERCISE 2-11 REFERENCE: SECTION 2.11C

A. Find the base (or 100%) in each of the following:

	Base	*Percentage*	*Rate*		*Base*	*Percentage*	*Rate*
1.	?	368	46%	7.	?	740	148%
2.	?	195	39%	8.	?	1,470	245%
3.	?	575	12.5%	9.	?	89.84	112.3%
4.	?	186	62%	10.	?	17,304	432.6%
5.	?	5,264	75.2%	11.	?	514.65	282%
6.	?	588	2.1%	12.	?	247.39	71.5%

B. Statement problems:

13. Find the number if 34% of the number is 68.
14. Find the number if 6% of the number is 10.2.
15. If 29% of a number is 58, what is the number?
16. If 5% of a number is 7, what is the number?
17. What number decreased by 10% of itself is 193.50?
18. What number decreased by 30% of itself is 302.40?
19. What number increased by $5\frac{1}{2}\%$ of itself is 42.20?

20. What number increased by 9% of itself is 34.88?
21. James Kart received a dividend of $2,500, which is 5% of his investment. What is the size of the investment?
22. Linda West purchased a car and made a down payment of $1,800. After the payment, she owes 85% of the purchase price. What is the price of the car?
23. A piece of jewelry was sold for $5.60, which includes a federal tax of 10% and a state sales tax of 2%. What is the price excluding the taxes?
24. A man sold a washing machine for $370.50. His profit was 30% of his original purchase price. What was his purchase price?
25. A certain cloth will shrink 2% after washing. If 176.4 inches of the cloth are needed, how long should the piece be before washing?
26. A retailer sold an odd lot of ladies' dresses for $465, a loss of 7% on her purchase price. What was her purchase price?

EXERCISE 2-12 REVIEW OF SECTIONS 2.9 to 2.11

1. A field of 12 acres yields 368 bushels of wheat. How much should a field of 42 acres yield?
2. If it costs $28,375 to repair $3\frac{1}{2}$ miles of highway, how much will it cost to repair $\frac{4}{5}$ mile of the same type of highway?
3. If a car runs 315 miles on $20\frac{1}{2}$ gallons of gasoline, how many gallons of gasoline are needed for going 1,200 miles?
4. If 120 pounds of potatoes cost $9.60, what will 88 pounds cost?
5. Divide 76 into two parts in the ratio 3 : 5.
6. Divide 825 into two parts in the ratio 7 : 8.
7. Divide 686 into three parts in the ratio 2 : 5 : 7.
8. Divide 151.2 into three parts in the ratio 1 : 2 : 3.
9. How should Dean and Mesk divide $1,704 if Dean's share is to exceed Mesk's share by 40%?
10. In Problem 9, if Dean's share is to be 40% less than Mesk's, how much should each of them receive?
11. Find 5% of 100, of 200, of 450, of 620.
12. Find 10% of 13.7, of 42.5, of 63.58, and of 65.45.
13. What is 7% of 425?
14. What percent of $260 is $150?
15. 50.60 is 11% of what number?
16. Find 15.5% of 76.
17. 25% of how many dollars is $30?
18. $180 is what percent of $750?
19. What percent of $28 is $42?
20. 180% of $65 is what?
21. How many dollars plus 15% is $414?
22. How many dollars less 20% is $360?
23. A, B, and C started a business as partners. A contributed $15,000; B, $24,000; and C, $32,000. In proportion to their investments, how much should each of the partners receive from a profit of $9,372?

24. In a partnership consisting of three persons, X contributed $23,000; Y, $21,000; and Z, $17,000. At the end of the first year the loss was $7,747. If the partners shared the loss in proportion to their contributions, how much loss did each bear?
25. Leon bought two cows for $525. He sold one cow at an 8% profit and the other at a 3% loss. His net profit was $20. How much did he pay for each?
26. Nancy has an annual income of $111 from her investments. She invested $\frac{1}{6}$ of her total investments at 6%, $\frac{1}{10}$ at 5%, and the remainder at 3%. Find the amount of her total investments.
27. If unroasted coffee, which is purchased at $1.80 a pound, shrinks 10% in weight when roasted, what is the total cost of unroasted coffee needed to secure 15 pounds of roasted coffee?
28. If 85% of the weight of wheat is made into flour, how many pounds of wheat are needed to make $701\frac{1}{4}$ pounds of flour?
29. Based on his experience, a manufacturer found that the change in the quantity sold is approximately proportional to the change in price. His records show that when the price of television sets was $299.99 each, 1,000 were sold in a one-month period; but only 800 were sold when the price was $319.99. How many television sets should the manufacturer expect to sell in a one-month period when the price is $289.99?
30. A grocery store manager found that she could sell 1,200 pounds of apples a day at 75¢ per pound and 1,500 pounds a day when the price was 60¢. If the change in the quantity sold is approximately proportional to the change in price, how many pounds should she expect to sell in a day if the price is 66¢?

3 ★SUPPLEMENTAL ALGEBRAIC OPERATIONS

This chapter presents additional algebraic topics. The topics are: systems of linear equations (Section 3.1), algebraic fractions (Section 3.2), graphs and equations (Section 3.3), radicals (Section 3.4), quadratic equations (Section 3.5), the binomial theorem (Section 3.6), and logarithms (Sections 3.7 and 3.8). Those topics are useful in proving certain complicated formulas (proofs of which are placed in footnotes) and solving many problems in the optional sections (starred material) in this text. They are also useful in preparing the student for advanced studies in the fields of business and economics.

3.1 SYSTEMS OF LINEAR EQUATIONS

A. Concept of a System of Equations

A *system* of equations is a group of two or more equations. A linear equation in *one* unknown has only *one* solution, but a linear equation in *two* unknowns has an *unlimited number* of solutions. For example, $x + 2y = 11$ is satisfied by unlimited pairs of numbers such as $x = 1$, $y = 5$; $x = 3$, $y = 4$; and $x = 7$, $y = 2$. If x represents any particular numerical value, there is a solution for y in the equation. However, in general, if there are two linear equations in two unknowns, there is only one solution for each unknown that satisfies both equations. The two equations are called *independent simultaneous equations*, or simply *independent equations*. If two equations can be reduced to the same form, they are said to be *dependent*. Thus, $x + y = 2$ and $2x + 2y = 4$ are dependent equations because the latter can be reduced to the form of the previous one by dividing by 2; hence there are unlimited pairs of numbers that satisfy the equation. If there is no common solution for two linear equations in two unknowns, they are called *inconsistent equations*. Thus, $x + y = 5$ and $x + y = 7$ are inconsistent equations.

B. Solution by Elimination

To solve two independent linear equations simultaneously, first eliminate one of the two unknowns from the two equations and solve the resulting equation in one unknown. The eliminated unknown is then found by substituting the value obtained in either one of the given equations or their derived equivalents. Two methods of elimination are illustrated by the following example. Method A is the simpler method.

EXAMPLE 1 Solve the two equations:

$3x + y = 5$ (1)
$6x - y = 6$ (2)

METHOD A Elimination by addition or subtraction:

Eliminate y by addition

Add equations (1) and (2):

$3x + 6x = 5 + 6$
$9x = 11, x = \frac{11}{9}$

Substitute $x = \frac{11}{9}$ in (1):

$3(\frac{11}{9}) + y = 5$
$\frac{11}{3} + y = 5$
$y = 5 - \frac{11}{3} = \frac{4}{3}$

Eliminate x by subtraction

Multiply equation (1) by 2	$6x + 2y = 10$	(3)
Rewrite (2)	$6x - y = 6$	(4)
Subtract (3) − (4)	$3y = 4$	(5)
Solve (5) for y	$y = \frac{4}{3}$	
Substitute $y = \frac{4}{3}$ in (2)	$6x - \frac{4}{3} = 6$	(6)
Solve (6) for x	$6x = 6 + \frac{4}{3}$	
	$x = \frac{11}{9}$	

CHECK Substitute $x = \frac{11}{9}$ and $y = \frac{4}{3}$ in (1) and (2).

In (1):

$3(\frac{11}{9}) + \frac{4}{3} = 5, \frac{11}{3} + \frac{4}{3} = 5, \frac{15}{3} = 5, 5 = 5$

In (2):

$6(\frac{11}{9}) - \frac{4}{3} = 6, \frac{22}{3} - \frac{4}{3} = 6, \frac{18}{3} = 6, 6 = 6$

METHOD B Elimination by substitution:

Solve (2) for y in terms of x.

$y = 6x - 6$ (7)

Substitute (7) in (1).

[Note: Do not substitute in (2), since (7) is derived from (2).]

$3x + (6x - 6) = 5$ (8)

Solve (8) for x.

$3x + 6x - 6 = 5, 9x = 11, x = \frac{11}{9}$

Solve for y as in Method A when x is found first. Thus, $y = \frac{4}{3}$.

CHECK As in Method A.

When there are *three* linear equations in *three* unknowns, a solution that satisfies the three equations may be obtained. However, it must be an independent system. The method of solving a system of three linear equations in three unknowns is an extension of the methods used in solving two equations in two unknowns. Similarly, the methods may be extended to n number of linear equations in n number of unknowns.

C. Solution of Statement Problems Involving Two Unknowns

The four steps discussed in Section 2.8C are also applicable in solving statement problems involving two unknowns. However, two letters and two independent equations are set up instead of one letter and one equation.

EXAMPLE 2

The cost of three dozen eggs and two dozen oranges is \$6.96. The cost of two dozen eggs and one dozen oranges is \$4.08. What is the cost per dozen of each item?

STEP (1). Let x = cost in dollars of one dozen eggs
y = cost in dollars of one dozen oranges

STEP (2). Then $3x + 2y = 6.96$ (1)
$2x + y = 4.08$ (2)

STEP (3). Solve the above two equations simultaneously by eliminating x.

Multiply (1) by 2 $\quad 6x + 4y = 13.92$ (3)
Multiply (2) by 3 $\quad 6x + 3y = 12.24$ (4)
(3) − (4) $\quad y = 1.68$

Note that 6, the coefficient of x in (3) and (4), is the *least common multiple* of 3 and 2, which are the coefficients of x in (1) and (2), respectively.

Substitute $y = 1.68$ in (1).

$$3x + 2(1.68) = 6.96$$
$$3x + 3.36 = 6.96$$
$$3x = 6.96 - 3.36 = 3.60$$
$$x = \frac{3.60}{3} = 1.20$$

The cost of one dozen eggs is \$1.20; the cost of one dozen oranges is \$1.68.

STEP (4). According to the statement of the problem, the answer gives the following:

The cost of three dozen eggs and two dozen oranges is

$3(1.20) + 2(1.68) = 3.60 + 3.36 = \$6.96$

The cost of two dozen eggs and one dozen oranges is

$2(1.20) + 1.68 = 2.40 + 1.68 = \$4.08$

EXAMPLE 3

John and Jimmy divided \$500. If John had received \$70 more and Jimmy had spent \$30 of his money, they would have equal amounts. How much did each receive?

Let x = John's share in dollars
y = Jimmy's share in dollars

Then $x + y = 500$
$x + 70 = y - 30$

Solve the two equations.

$x = 200$
$y = 300$

Answer: John received \$200.
Jimmy received \$300.

CHECK

If John had received \$70 more, he would have had (\$200 + \$70) or \$270. If Jimmy had spent \$30 of his money, he would have had (\$300 − \$30) or \$270. Their shares are \$200 and \$300; the sum is (\$200 + \$300) or \$500.

EXAMPLE 4 A computer sells for \$560. The gross profit is computed as $\frac{3}{4}$ of the cost. Assume that the selling price is equal to the gross profit added to the cost. What are the cost and the gross profit? (This problem is the same as that of Example 6, Section 2.8.)

Let x = cost, and y = gross profit. Then

$$x + y = 560$$
$$y = (\tfrac{3}{4})x$$

Solve the two equations.

x = \$320 (cost)
y = \$240 (gross profit)

CHECK Selling price = 320 + 240 = \$560
Gross profit = $\frac{3}{4}(320)$ = \$240

EXERCISE 3-1 REFERENCE: SECTION 3.1

A. Solve for x and y (elimination by addition or subtraction):

1. $2x + 5y = 32$, $3x - 2y = 29$
2. $3x - 4y = 26$, $5x - 8y = 46$
3. $3x - 2y = -13$, $x + 4y = 19$
4. $5x + 4y = 29$, $7x + 6y = 41$
5. $3x + y = 8$, $2x - y = 7$
6. $x - 2y = 18$, $x + 3y = 8$
7. $x + 2y = -4$, $2x + y = 1$
8. $2x + 3y = 11$, $x + 4y = 8$
9. $2x - y = 4$, $2x + y = 16$
10. $3x - 2y = 1$, $2x + y = -4$
11. $4x + 2y = -12$, $x - y = -6$
12. $5x + y = -7$, $x + 4y = 10$
13. $x + 3y = 4$, $x - 4y = 18$
14. $3x - 2y = 1$, $x + 3y = 15$
15. $2x + 3y = 29$, $3x - 2y = 24$
16. $x + y = 11$, $2x - y = 4$
17. $6x + 4y = 34$, $7x + 6y = 41$
18. $3x - 4y = 30$, $5x - 8y = 54$

B. Solve for x and y (elimination by substitution):

19. $5x + 2y = 16$, $2x + y = 7$
20. $3x - 5y = -31$, $x + y = 3$
21. $x + 2y = 5$, $3x + 2y = -1$
22. $x + 5y = -6$, $3x + y = 10$
23. $2x + y = -7$, $3x + 2y = -12$
24. $5x - y = 1$, $4x - 2y = -4$
25. $x + y = 5$, $5x - 2y = 4$
26. $3x - 2y = 7$, $x + 3y = 6$
27. $x + 2y = 3$, $4x - 3y = -10$
28. $3x + 2y = 13$, $x - y = 1$
29. $2x - y = 11$, $4x + y = 13$
30. $2x + 6y = -2$, $6x + 4y = 1$
31. $4x - y = 13$, $2x - 3y = 19$
32. $2x + y = 1$, $5x + 2y = 4$
33. $3x - y = 15$, $x + y = 1$
34. $2x + 5y = 5$, $3x + 2y = -9$
35. $2x + 3y = 4$, $3x + 2y = 11$
36. $3x + 5y = -1$, $6x + 15y = -5$

C. State whether each of the following is a dependent or an inconsistent system of equations:

37. $3x + 4y = 11$
$6x + 8y = 22$

38. $5x - 4y = 20$
$10x - 8y = 40$

39. $4x + y = 6$
$4x + y = 16$

40. $8x - 17y = 15$
$8x - 17y = 19$

41. $2x + 5y = 19$
$6x + 15y = 57$

42. $3x + y = 7$
$15x + 5y = 35$

43. $6x + 4y = 22$
$3x + 2y = 10$

44. $7x + 2y = 14$
$21x + 6y = 9$

D. Statement problems:

45. The cost of a hat and a coat is \$153.50 and the cost of 3 hats and 2 coats is \$328.50. Find the cost of the hat and the cost of the coat.
46. The sum of A and B is 575. The sum of A times $\frac{1}{25}$ and B times $\frac{3}{50}$ is 30. What is the value of A? of B?
47. The sum of two amounts is \$12 and their difference is \$2. What are the amounts?
48. Two students made a total of 185 points in a game. One student made 15 points more than the other student. How many points did each student make?
49. A theater sold 40 tickets amounting to \$208.75 in one evening. The tickets were sold to adults for \$5.50 and to children for \$3.25. How many of each were sold?
50. A druggist wishes to prepare 100 gallons of 45% alcohol. She has two kinds of alcohol solution in stock; one is 55% pure and the other is 30% pure. How many gallons of each kind must be used for the mixture?
51. The sum of the ages of a girl and her brother is 20. Four years ago her age was 3 times the age of her brother then. Find the girl's age and her brother's age.
52. Two cars start at the same place and the same time but travel in opposite directions. After 6 hours, they are 540 miles apart. If one car travels 10 miles per hour slower than the other, what are their speeds per hour?
53. The sum of the digits of a two-digit number is 17. The tens' digit is greater than the units' digit by 1. Find the number.
54. The sum of the digits of a two-digit number is 10. If the digits are reversed, the number is decreased by 18. What is the number?
55. A grocer wishes to make 50 pounds of coffee by mixing two grades of coffee worth \$2.70 and \$3.00 per pound, respectively. If the mixed coffee will be sold at \$2.79 per pound, how many pounds of each grade of coffee should the grocer use?
56. A service station has two kinds of gasoline, one selling for \$1.27 a gallon and the other for \$1.18 a gallon. How many gallons of each must be used to make 90 gallons of a mixture that can be sold for \$1.24 a gallon?

3.2 FRACTIONS AND FRACTIONAL EQUATIONS

A. General Statements

The rules for computing algebraic fractions are the same as those for computing fractions in arithmetic. However, algebraic fractions are more involved because symbols, as well as numbers, are employed in computation. The principle—multiplying or dividing both the numerator and the denominator by the same number, other than zero, does not affect the value of the fraction—is also important to algebraic fractions. Thus, $\frac{2}{5}$ may be reduced to $\frac{2 \times 7}{5 \times 7} = \frac{14}{35}$; likewise, $\frac{a}{b}$ may be reduced to $\frac{ac}{bc}$. Furthermore, if the numerator and the denominator of a fraction can be factored and divided by any common factor, it is possible to reduce the fraction to a simpler form. If the numerator and the denominator have no common factors, the fraction is in its simplest form. Thus,

$$\frac{x^2 - 9}{x^2 - 8x + 15} = \frac{(x + 3)\cancel{(x - 3)}}{(x - 5)\cancel{(x - 3)}} = \frac{x + 3}{x - 5}, \quad \text{and} \quad \frac{x + 3}{x - 5} \text{ is the simplest form.}$$

When a fraction is reduced to its simplest form, the numerator and the denominator in the final answer are usually retained in factored form, as shown in the answer to Example 3 below.

B. Addition and Subtraction of Algebraic Fractions

Algebraic fractions should have a common denominator if the fractions are to be added or subtracted. If the given fractions do not have the same denominator, it is necessary to reduce them to equivalent fractions with the lowest common denominator (l.c.d.) before adding or subtracting. The algebraic sum of the numerators is the numerator of the resulting fraction, and the l.c.d. is its denominator.

EXAMPLE 1

Combine and simplify $\frac{2x}{3} + \frac{x}{5}$.

Here the l.c.d. is $3 \times 5 = 15$.

$$\frac{2x}{3} + \frac{x}{5} = \frac{2x \cdot 5}{3 \cdot 5} + \frac{x \cdot 3}{5 \cdot 3} = \frac{10x + 3x}{15} = \frac{13x}{15}$$

EXAMPLE 2

Combine and simplify $\frac{2}{a} + \frac{5}{b}$.

Here the l.c.d. is ab.

$$\frac{2}{a} + \frac{5}{b} = \frac{2b}{ab} + \frac{5a}{ab} = \frac{2b + 5a}{ab}$$

EXAMPLE 3

Combine and simplify $\frac{10}{a^2 - b^2} + \frac{3}{a - b}$.

Here the l.c.d. is $a^2 - b^2 = (a + b)(a - b)$.

$$\frac{10}{a^2 - b^2} = \frac{10}{(a + b)(a - b)}; \quad \frac{3}{(a - b)} = \frac{3(a + b)}{(a + b)(a - b)}$$

Thus,

$$\frac{10}{a^2 - b^2} + \frac{3}{a - b} = \frac{10}{(a + b)(a - b)} + \frac{3(a + b)}{(a + b)(a - b)} = \frac{10 + 3(a + b)}{(a + b)(a - b)}$$

EXAMPLE 4

Combine and simplify $\frac{a}{a - b} - \frac{b}{a + b}$.

Here the l.c.d. is $(a - b)(a + b)$.

$$\frac{a}{a - b} - \frac{b}{a + b} = \frac{a(a + b)}{(a - b)(a + b)} - \frac{b(a - b)}{(a + b)(a - b)}$$

$$= \frac{a(a+b) - b(a-b)}{(a+b)(a-b)} = \frac{a^2 + ab - ab + b^2}{(a+b)(a-b)}$$

$$= \frac{a^2 + b^2}{(a+b)(a-b)}$$

EXAMPLE 5 Combine and simplify $\frac{2}{x+1} + \frac{3x+1}{2x^2+5x+3}$.

Here the l.c.d. is $(x+1)(2x+3)$ or $2x^2 + 5x + 3$.

$$\frac{2}{x+1} + \frac{3x+1}{2x^2+5x+3} = \frac{2(2x+3)}{(x+1)(2x+3)} + \frac{3x+1}{(x+1)(2x+3)}$$

$$= \frac{4x+6+3x+1}{(x+1)(2x+3)} = \frac{7x+7}{(x+1)(2x+3)}$$

$$= \frac{7\cancel{(x+1)}}{\cancel{(x+1)}(2x+3)} = \frac{7}{2x+3}$$

C. Multiplication and Division of Algebraic Fractions

The rules for multiplication and division used in arithmetic also apply in calculations involving algebraic fractions. In some cases, however, the numerators and the denominators of the given fractions may be factored before multiplying.

EXAMPLE 6 Multiply $\frac{10x}{6y}$ by $\frac{3y}{15x}$.

$$\frac{10x}{6y} \cdot \frac{3y}{15x} = \frac{30xy}{90xy} = \frac{1}{3}$$

EXAMPLE 7 Multiply $\frac{x^2 - y^2}{2x^2}$ by $\frac{3y}{x+y}$.

$$\frac{x^2 - y^2}{2x^2} \cdot \frac{3y}{x+y} = \frac{\cancel{(x+y)}(x-y)}{2x^2} \cdot \frac{3y}{\cancel{x+y}} = \frac{3y(x-y)}{2x^2}$$

EXAMPLE 8 Simplify $\dfrac{\frac{x-1}{x+y}}{\frac{3x+y}{3(x+y)}}$.

The problem can be simplified by various methods, as shown below.

METHOD A Multiply the dividend by the reciprocal of the divisor. This complex fraction may be written as follows:

$$\frac{x-1}{x+y} \div \frac{3x+y}{3(x+y)} = \frac{x-1}{\cancel{x+y}} \cdot \frac{3\cancel{(x+y)}}{3x+y} = \frac{3(x-1)}{3x+y}$$

★METHOD B After reducing both of the simple fractions (the numerator and the denominator of the complex fraction) to have the lowest common denominator (l.c.d.), cancel the l.c.d. and then divide. Here the l.c.d. is $3(x+y)$.

$$\frac{\dfrac{x-1}{x+y}}{\dfrac{3x+y}{3(x+y)}} = \frac{\dfrac{3(x-1)}{\cancel{3(x+y)}}}{\dfrac{3x+y}{\cancel{3(x+y)}}} = \frac{3(x-1)}{3x+y}$$

★**METHOD C** Multiply the numerator and the denominator of the complex fraction by the l.c.d. of the simple fractions. Here the l.c.d. also is $3(x + y)$.

$$\frac{\dfrac{x-1}{x+y}}{\dfrac{3x+y}{3(x+y)}} = \frac{\dfrac{x-1}{\cancel{x+y}} \cdot 3\cancel{(x+y)}}{\dfrac{3x+y}{\cancel{3(x+y)}} \cdot \cancel{3(x+y)}} = \frac{3(x-1)}{3x+y}$$

EXAMPLE 9 Divide $\dfrac{5x+10}{9x-9}$ by $\dfrac{5}{3x-3}$.

Method A is used for this illustration.

$$\frac{5x+10}{9x-9} \div \frac{5}{3x-3} = \frac{5x+10}{9x-9} \cdot \frac{3x-3}{5} = \frac{\cancel{5}(x+2)}{\underset{3}{\cancel{9}}\cancel{(x-1)}} \cdot \frac{\cancel{3(x-1)}}{\cancel{5}}$$

$$= \frac{x+2}{3}$$

D. Operations of Fractional Equations

When solving an equation involving fractions, first multiply both sides by the lowest common denominator to derive an equation that will contain no fractions. This step is called *clearing* an equation of fractions. Next, solve the derived equation for the unknown, as discussed in Section 2.8.

When a fractional equation is being cleared, multiplying by a denominator other than the lowest common denominator may introduce solutions that are not solutions of the original equations. These extra solutions are called *extraneous roots*. When both sides of an equation are multiplied by the same expression containing the unknown, or when both sides of the equation are raised to the same integral power, the resulting equation may also have more solutions than the original equation possessed. The extraneous roots are discarded in solving statement problems. However, when both sides of an equation are divided by an expression containing the unknown, the new equation may have fewer roots than the original equation had. Furthermore, division or multiplication by zero should be excluded.

EXAMPLE 10 Solve $\dfrac{x}{x-6} = 4$.

Clear the equation.

$$\frac{x}{\cancel{x-6}}\cancel{(x-6)} = 4(x-6)$$

$$x = 4(x-6)$$

Solve the derived equation.

$$x = 4x - 24$$
$$x - 4x = -24$$
$$-3x = -24$$
$$x = 8$$

CHECK

$$\frac{x}{x-6} = \frac{8}{8-6} = \frac{8}{2} = 4$$

EXAMPLE 11

Solve $\frac{7}{x+2} = \frac{3}{x-6}$.

Here the l.c.d. is $(x + 2)(x - 6)$.

Clear the equation.

$$\frac{7}{\cancel{x+2}} \cdot \cancel{(x+2)}(x-6) = \frac{3}{\cancel{x-6}} \cdot (x+2)\cancel{(x-6)}$$

$$7(x - 6) = 3(x + 2)$$

Solve the derived equation.

$$7x - 42 = 3x + 6$$
$$7x - 3x = 42 + 6$$
$$4x = 48$$
$$x = 12$$

CHECK

Substitute the x value in the original equation.

Left side: $\frac{7}{x+2} = \frac{7}{12+2} = \frac{7}{14} = \frac{1}{2}$

Right side: $\frac{3}{x-6} = \frac{3}{12-6} = \frac{3}{6} = \frac{1}{2}$

EXAMPLE 12

A gasoline tank can be filled by one pipe in 2 hours and drained by another pipe in 5 hours. How long will it take to fill the tank if the drain is left open?

Let x = the number of hours needed to fill the tank if the drain is left open.

The one pipe can fill $\frac{1}{2}x$ of the tank in x hours because it can fill $\frac{1}{2}$ of the tank each hour (or it can fill the entire tank in 2 hours).

The other pipe can drain $\frac{1}{5}x$ of the tank in x hours because it can drain $\frac{1}{5}$ of the tank each hour (or it can drain the entire tank in 5 hours).

Thus, $\frac{1}{2}x - \frac{1}{5}x = 1$ (the capacity of the tank)

Solve the above equation. Here the l.c.d. is $(2)(5) = 10$.

$\frac{x}{2} - \frac{x}{5} = 1, \qquad 10\left(\frac{x}{2} - \frac{x}{5}\right) = 10(1)$

$5x - 2x = 10, \qquad 3x = 10$

$x = \frac{10}{3} = 3\frac{1}{3}$ hours

CHECK

One pipe will fill $(\frac{1}{2})(3\frac{1}{3})$ tanks of gasoline in $3\frac{1}{3}$ hours, and the other pipe will drain $(\frac{1}{5})(3\frac{1}{3})$ tanks of gasoline in $3\frac{1}{3}$ hours. Thus, the amount that remains in the tank is the difference, or $(\frac{1}{2})(3\frac{1}{3}) - (\frac{1}{5})(3\frac{1}{3}) = \frac{10}{6} - \frac{10}{15} = \frac{50}{30} - \frac{20}{30} = 1$, or one tank full of gasoline.

EXERCISE 3-2 REFERENCE: SECTION 3.2

A. Simplify the following fractions to their lowest terms:

1. $\dfrac{23}{115}$
2. $\dfrac{147}{441}$
3. $\dfrac{3}{6a - 6b}$
4. $\dfrac{2a + 2b}{8a + 8b}$
5. $\dfrac{x + y}{ax + ay + bx + by}$
6. $\dfrac{x^2 - 4}{(x + 2)(x + 1)}$
7. $\dfrac{3x + y^2}{9x^2 - y^4}$
8. $\dfrac{2ab - 16c}{a^2b^2 - 64c^2}$
9. $\dfrac{4x^2 + 28}{x^2 - 49}$
10. $\dfrac{12x - 12}{9x^2 - 18x + 9}$
11. $\dfrac{4x + 12}{x^2 + 6x + 9}$
12. $\dfrac{6a + 8b}{9a^2 + 24ab + 16b^2}$

B. Perform the following indicated operations and simplify:

13. $\dfrac{3x}{4} + \dfrac{x}{5}$
14. $\dfrac{5y}{7} + \dfrac{2y}{3}$
15. $\dfrac{5}{3x} + \dfrac{1}{2x}$
16. $\dfrac{2}{9y} + \dfrac{3}{2xy}$
17. $1 + \dfrac{a}{a + b}$
18. $\dfrac{4}{x + 2} + \dfrac{7}{x^2 + 3x + 2}$
19. $\dfrac{3}{4x + 2} + \dfrac{3x}{12x^2 + 10x + 2}$
20. $\dfrac{4x}{2 - x} + \dfrac{2}{3x - 4}$
21. $\dfrac{2x}{5} - \dfrac{x}{3}$
22. $\dfrac{5y}{4} - \dfrac{3y}{7}$
23. $\dfrac{3}{4x} - \dfrac{8}{6x}$
24. $\dfrac{4}{9y} - \dfrac{5}{3xy}$
25. $1 - \dfrac{a}{a + c}$
26. $\dfrac{15}{4x - 3} - \dfrac{3x}{20x^2 + 9x - 18}$
27. $\dfrac{-4}{5x - 6} - \dfrac{-9x}{-15x^2 + 28x - 12}$
28. $\dfrac{7}{6x^2 + x - 1} - \dfrac{3}{4x^2 - 1}$
29. $\dfrac{2a^3b^4}{3x^2y^4} \cdot \dfrac{9x^3y^2}{8ab}$
30. $\dfrac{6x^2}{7y^2} \cdot \dfrac{5y}{4z} \cdot \dfrac{2z^2}{3x^3}$
31. $\dfrac{24m^2n^3}{36x^2y^3} \cdot \dfrac{12x^2y^2}{6m^4n}$
32. $\dfrac{9}{3x - 12} \cdot \dfrac{x - 4}{3}$
33. $\dfrac{x^2y^3}{x^2 + 2xy + y^2} \cdot \dfrac{x + y}{x^3y^4}$
34. $\dfrac{x^2 - y^2}{y^4} \cdot \dfrac{4y^2}{x - y}$
35. $\dfrac{6x^2 - 18x}{4x^2 - 1} \cdot \dfrac{4x^2 + 8x + 3}{12x^2 - 30x - 18}$
36. $\dfrac{2x - 8}{x^2 - 16} \cdot \dfrac{x^2 + x - 12}{x - 3}$
37. $\dfrac{4x - 10}{8x - 12} \div \dfrac{2x - 5}{2x - 3}$
38. $\dfrac{5x^2y^3}{6x^3y^4} \div \dfrac{4xy}{3xy^3}$
39. $\dfrac{6x^2 + 6xy}{2x - y} \div \dfrac{3x^2 - 3y^2}{6x^2 - y^2}$
40. $\dfrac{4x + 8}{8x - 8} \div \dfrac{8x + 16}{4x - 4}$
41. $\dfrac{10x^2 - 9x + 2}{15x - 6} \div \dfrac{5x^2 + 23x - 10}{3x + 15}$
42. $\dfrac{4 - x^2}{x^2 - 9} \div \dfrac{12 + 6x}{x^2 - 6x + 9}$
43. $\dfrac{x + \dfrac{2}{y^2}}{\dfrac{2 + x}{y^2}}$
44. $1 - \dfrac{1}{3 - \dfrac{1}{2 - \frac{1}{3}}}$

C. Solve for x:

45. $\frac{x}{3} + \frac{x}{6} = 21$

46. $\frac{x}{2} + \frac{2x}{5} = 18$

47. $\frac{2x}{x - 8} = 6$

48. $\frac{x}{x + 5} = \frac{2}{3}$

49. $\frac{x}{x - 8} = 5$

50. $\frac{4}{3 + x} = \frac{5}{8 + x}$

51. $\frac{6x + 3}{3} = \frac{7x - 2}{4}$

52. $\frac{x + 6}{x} = \frac{x - 9}{x - 6}$

53. $\frac{x + 1}{x + 3} = \frac{4}{3}$

54. $\frac{x^2}{x - 4} = x - 2$

55. $\frac{x - 2}{x + 3} = \frac{x - 1}{x + 5}$

56. $\frac{x + 3}{x + 12} = \frac{x - 5}{x - 4}$

57. $\frac{x + 10}{x - 2} = \frac{x - 1}{x - 3}$

58. $\frac{x + 7}{x - 1} = \frac{x + 17}{x + 1}$

59. $S = x(1 + in)$

60. $\frac{a - b}{x} = \frac{b - c}{a + b}$

61. $\frac{4}{3x - 3a} = \frac{a}{x^2 - a^2}$

62. $\frac{2y}{x} = \frac{2 + 4a}{3 - a}$

D. Statement problems:

63. The sum of two amounts is \$80, and one amount is $\frac{7}{9}$ of the other. Find the amounts.
64. If $\frac{1}{5}$ of an amount is added to $\frac{2}{3}$ of the amount, the sum is \$26. What is the amount?
65. If a swimming pool can be filled by one pipe in 10 hours and drained by another pipe in 14 hours, how long will it take to fill the pool if the drain is left open?
66. Steve and Dale together can paint a house in 10 hours. If Dale can paint it by himself in 30 hours, how long would it take Steve to paint it alone?
67. A toy store purchased a shipment of toy guns at \$20 a dozen. The store sold $\frac{5}{8}$ of the shipment at \$2 each and the remainder at 3 for \$5. The total profit was \$25.00. How many of the toy guns were in this shipment?
68. A student answered correctly 80% of the problems in a test. Thirty-seven correct answers were made in the first 41 problems. Five out of every 8 answers were correct in the remaining problems. How many problems were in the test?
69. A bus driver estimated that his gasoline supply would last 10 hours, but it lasted only 8 hours. The actual consumption per hour was $\frac{1}{4}$ gallon more than he had estimated. How many gallons of gasoline did he have?
70. Doris beat Jean by 10 miles and Anna by 20 miles in a 1,000-mile car race. If Jean and Anna kept their respective speeds until Jean finished, by how many miles did Jean beat Anna?

3.3 GRAPHS AND ALGEBRAIC EQUATIONS

The method of graphic presentation of quantitative data is used frequently in analyzing business and economic activities. Details of this method are presented in Chapter 6, which describes statistical methods. In this section the discussion concerning graphs emphasizes their use in solving a system of equations.

A. Rectangular Coordinates

A graph is constructed according to the system of rectangular coordinates. *Rectangular coordinates* are based on two straight reference lines perpendicular to each other in a plane, as shown in Figure 3-1. The horizontal line is usually referred to as the *x-axis*, or

Figure 3–1 Rectangular Coordinates

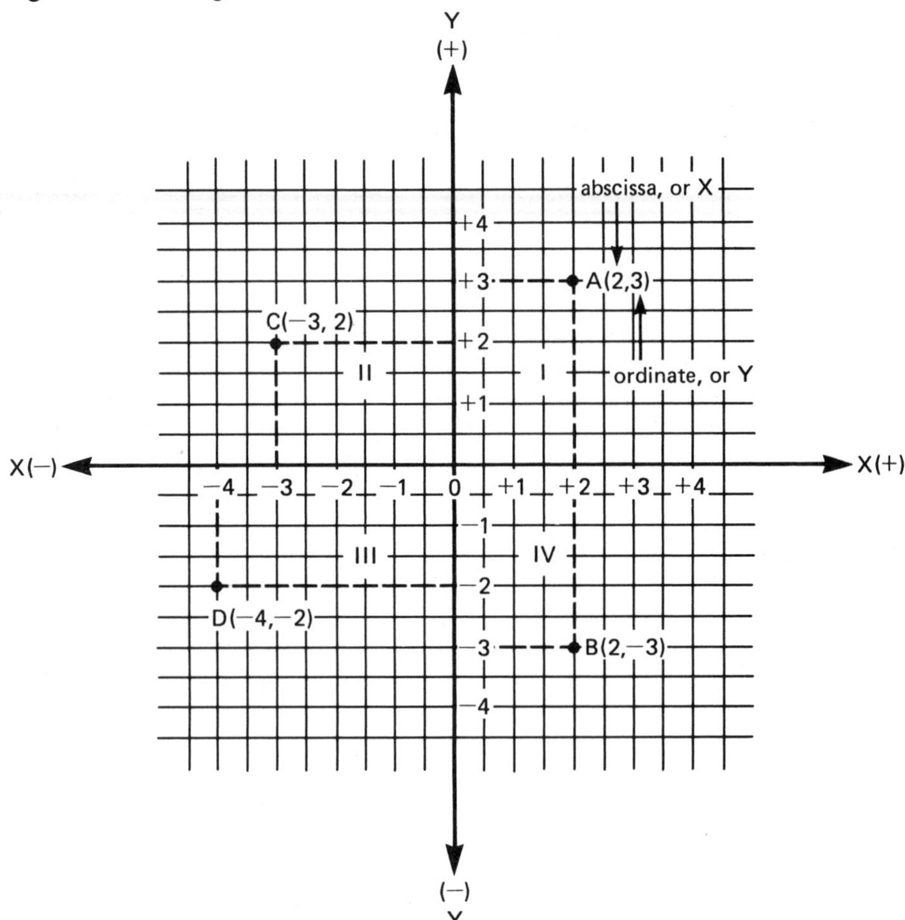

the *abscissa*. The vertical line is referred to as the *y-axis*, or the *ordinate*. The two lines divide the plane into four parts called *quadrants*, which are numbered I, II, III, and IV, as indicated in the figure. The point of intersection of the two lines is called the *origin*, which is usually regarded as the zero point. Scales, which begin at the point of origin, are placed along the horizontal and vertical axes. The scale is not necessarily the same for both axes, although use of the same scale is customarily preferred. The abscissas to the *right* of the origin are conventionally designated as *positive*, whereas those to the *left* of the origin are *negative*. The ordinates *above* the origin are *positive* and those *below* the origin are *negative*.

In the plane it is possible to describe the location of any point that refers to two variables. One is called the *dependent* variable and the other the *independent* variable. The dependent variable is so called because its location depends upon the value of the independent variable; that is, once the value of the independent variable is fixed, the corresponding value of the dependent variable is determined from it according to an equation. The independent variable is usually placed on the x-axis and thus is also called the x-variable (or x). The dependent variable is usually placed on the y-axis and is called the y-variable (or y).

In placing a point on the plane for a set of corresponding x and y values, first draw a line parallel to the y-axis, starting at a distance equal to the x-value (abscissa). Second, draw a line parallel to the x-axis, starting at the y-axis at a distance equal to the y-value (ordinate), until it intersects the first line. The point of intersection is the desired answer. The abscissa and the ordinate of the point of intersection are called the *coordinates* of the point.

For example, in Quadrant I of Figure 3-1 the abscissa of point A is 2, while the ordinate of A is 3. The values of 2 and 3 constitute the coordinates of A. It is customary to write the coordinates in parentheses and to separate them by a comma; the abscissa is written before the ordinate. Thus, (2, 3) means that 2 is the abscissa and 3 is the ordinate of point A. Notice that the coordinates of B, C, and D are also written in the same manner as those of A.

B. Drawing the Graph of an Equation

The following example illustrates the method for drawing the graph of an equation.

EXAMPLE 1

Draw a graph for each of the following two equations:

(a) $x + y = 4$ (b) $2x - y = 14$

(a) In the equation $x + y = 4$, there are unlimited answers for x and y. For example, when $x = 1$, the equation becomes $1 + y = 4$, $y = 4 - 1 = 3$.

Here, only three pairs of answers are shown.

x	y
1	3
−8	12
10	−6

The three pairs of answers are plotted in Figure 3-2. Notice that when the three points are connected, straight line A is formed. Any point on the straight line, in turn, will satisfy the equation. Thus, a first-degree equation in one or two unknowns can be represented by a straight line. A first-degree equation is therefore frequently referred to as a linear equation.

(b) In the equation $2x - y = 14$, there are also unlimited answers for the two unknowns, x and y. For example, when $x = 10$, the equation becomes $2(10) - y = 14$, $y = 20 - 14 = 6$. Theoretically, as illustrated in (a) above, a straight line representing a first-degree equation can be determined by knowing only two points. However, as a checking point, three pairs of answers are listed below.

The three points give the straight line B in Figure 3-2.

x	y
10	6
8	2
1	−12

Figure 3–2 Graphic Solution of Two Linear Equations (Example 1, Section 3.3)

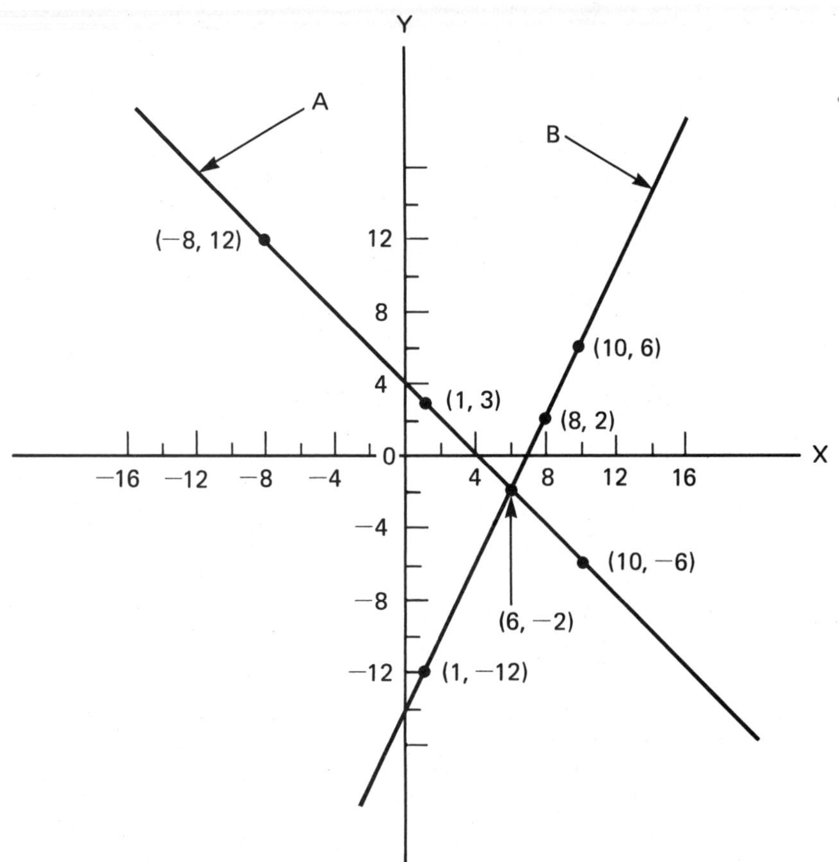

C. Graphic Solution

Observe that in Figure 3-2 lines A and B intersect at the point (6, −2). The values $x = 6$ and $y = -2$ thus satisfy both Equations (a) and (b). Therefore, the graphic method can be used to solve a pair of simultaneous linear equations in two unknowns. The graphic solution of the two equations above is checked as follows:

Substitute $x = 6$ and $y = -2$ in Equations (a) and (b).

Equation (a):

$$\begin{aligned} x + y &= 4 \\ 6 + (-2) &= 4 \\ 4 &= 4 \end{aligned}$$

Equation (b):

$$\begin{aligned} 2x - y &= 14 \\ 2(6) - (-2) &= 14 \\ 14 &= 14 \end{aligned}$$

EXERCISE 3-3 REFERENCE: SECTION 3.3

Solve for x and y graphically:

1. $x + 3y = 4$, $x - 4y = 18$
2. $3x - 2y = 1$, $x + 3y = 15$
3. $2x + 3y = 17$, $3x - 2y = 19$
4. $3x - y = 5$, $x + 4y = 19$
5. $x + 2y = -6$, $2x - y = 8$
6. $x - y = 1$, $x + 2y = 13$
7. $3x + y = 6$, $5x - y = 2$
8. $2x + 3y = 5$, $4x - y = 17$
9. $2x - y = 4$, $3x + y = 11$
10. $x + y = 10$, $x - 3y = -6$
11. $x + y = -5$, $2x - 3y = 5$
12. $x - 2y = 2$, $3x + 2y = -18$
13. $x + y = 8$, $2x - y = 10$
14. $x - 2y = 9$, $x + y = 3$

3.4 RADICALS

A. Introduction

In the previous chapter, Section 2.1B, it was stated that the product of equal factors can be expressed in an exponential form, such as $a \cdot a \cdot a \cdot a = a^4$. One of the equal factors of a quantity is called a *root* of the quantity. Thus, if $a^4 = b$, the base a is the 4th root of b.

A root is usually indicated by the sign $\sqrt{}$, and is called a *radical*. The number written at the upper left of the sign is the *index* of the radical, and the quantity under the sign is called the *radicand*. Thus, the expression "a is the 4th root of b" may be written $a = \sqrt[4]{b}$. In the radical $\sqrt[4]{b}$, b is the radicand and 4 is the index; the radical indicates the 4th root of b. When the index is 2, it is usually omitted and the radical is understood to be the square root. Thus, $\sqrt[2]{9} = \sqrt{9}$.

When the index is an *even* integer, a *positive* radicand has two numerically equal roots; one is positive and the other is negative. For example, 9 has two square roots, ± 3, since $(+3)(+3) = 9$ and $(-3)(-3) = 9$; 16 has two 4th roots, ± 2, since $(+2)(+2)(+2)(+2) = 16$ and $(-2)(-2)(-2)(-2) = 16$.

However, the radical sign $\sqrt{}$ is restricted to represent only the positive root, called the *principal root*. This restriction is necessary because mathematicians always like to have an operation lead to a unique result. Thus,

$\sqrt{9} = +3$, not -3; $\sqrt[4]{16} = +2$, not -2

To indicate a negative root, we place a minus sign before the radical, such as

$-\sqrt{9} = -3$ and $-\sqrt[4]{16} = -2$

When the index is an *odd* integer, a *positive* radicand has only a *positive* root, and a *negative* radicand has only a *negative* root, such as

$$\sqrt[3]{27} = +3, \quad \text{since} \quad (+3)(+3)(+3) = 27$$

$$\sqrt[3]{-27} = -3, \quad \text{since} \quad (-3)(-3)(-3) = -27$$

$$\sqrt[5]{-32} = -2, \quad \text{since} \quad (-2)(-2)(-2)(-2)(-2) = -32, \quad \text{but}$$
$$(+2)(+2)(+2)(+2)(+2) = +32, \quad \textit{not } -32$$

When the index is an *even* integer, a radical with a *negative* radicand, such as $\sqrt{-9}$, represents an imaginary number, since neither $+3$ nor -3 qualifies as a square root of the radicand -9. Since imaginary numbers are rarely used in business and economics, they are excluded in the following discussion.

B. Fractional Exponents

When an exponential has a fractional exponent, the exponential may be changed to the form of a radical according to the following definition:

$$\boldsymbol{a^{n/m} = (\sqrt[m]{a})^n = \sqrt[m]{a^n}}$$

The definition is illustrated as follows:

Let $n = 1$ and $m = 2$: $a^{n/m} = a^{1/2}$. When $a^{1/2}$ is raised to its second power,

$$a^{1/2} \cdot a^{1/2} = a^{(1/2)+(1/2)} = a^1 = a$$

Since $a^{1/2}$ is one of the two equal factors whose product is a, the square root of a should be $a^{1/2}$, or $\sqrt{a} = a^{1/2}$. Similarly, let $n = 4$ and $m = 3$: $a^{n/m} = a^{4/3}$. When $a^{4/3}$ is raised to its third power,

$$a^{4/3} \cdot a^{4/3} \cdot a^{4/3} = (a^{4/3})^3 = a^{(4/3)(3)} = a^4$$

Thus, $a^{4/3}$ is the third root of a^4, or $a^{4/3} = \sqrt[3]{a^4}$. According to the illustrations above, the following occurs:

$a^{n/m} = \sqrt[m]{a^n}$; and $a^{1/m} = \sqrt[m]{a}$
But $a^{n/m} = (a^{1/m})^n = (\sqrt[m]{a})^n$ [see Section 2.4, Law (3)]
Thus, $a^{n/m} = \sqrt[m]{a^n} = (\sqrt[m]{a})^n$

From the above definition, it may be seen that an exponential with a fractional exponent can be changed to its equivalent value in the form of a radical. However, the change must be made in conformity with the laws of exponents, as presented in Section 2.4B.

EXAMPLE 1

Express the exponentials in their radical forms.

$64^{1/3} = \sqrt[3]{64}$, $\quad k^{1/2} = \sqrt[2]{k} = \sqrt{k}$

$84^{3/4} = \sqrt[4]{84^3}$ or $(\sqrt[4]{84})^3$, $\quad x^{2/5} = \sqrt[5]{x^2}$ or $(\sqrt[5]{x})^2$

EXAMPLE 2

Express the radicals in their exponential forms.

$\sqrt{81} = 81^{1/2}$, $\quad \sqrt[3]{x} = x^{1/3}$

$\sqrt[4]{25^5} = 25^{5/4}$, $\quad \sqrt[7]{y^4} = y^{4/7}$

EXAMPLE 3 Express the coefficients of the radicals as part of their respective radicands.

$$a\sqrt{b} = a^{2/2}b^{1/2} = (a^2b^1)^{1/2} = \sqrt{a^2b}$$

$$x \cdot \sqrt[3]{y} = x^{3/3}y^{1/3} = (x^3y^1)^{1/3} = \sqrt[3]{x^3y}$$

$$x^3 \cdot \sqrt{y} = x^{6/2}y^{1/2} = (x^6y^1)^{1/2} = \sqrt{x^6y}$$

In general, the calculations in Example 3 may be made by following two steps:

STEP (1). Raise the coefficient to the power of the index of the radical.
STEP (2). Write the result obtained in Step (1) as a factor of the radicand.

Thus, the illustrations in Example 3 may be simplified as follows:

$a\sqrt{b} = \sqrt{a^2b}$, since the index of the radical is 2.
$x \cdot \sqrt[3]{y} = \sqrt[3]{x^3y}$, since the index of the radical is 3.
$x^3 \cdot \sqrt{y} = \sqrt{x^6y}$; here x^6 is obtained by raising x^3 to the second power, or $(x^3)^2 = x^6$.

The following example further illustrates the applications of the two steps above.

EXAMPLE 4 Express the coefficients of the radicals as part of their respective radicands.

$$3\sqrt{2} = \sqrt{3^2 \cdot 2} = \sqrt{18}$$
$$2 \cdot \sqrt[4]{3} = \sqrt[4]{2^4 \cdot 3} = \sqrt[4]{48}$$
$$3^2 \cdot \sqrt{2} = \sqrt{3^{2 \cdot 2} \cdot 2} = \sqrt{3^4 \cdot 2} = \sqrt{162}$$

C. Computation of Radicals

ADDITION AND SUBTRACTION OF RADICALS

Radicals whose indexes and radicands are the same are called *like radicals*. To add (or to subtract) numbers with like radicals, first add (or subtract) the numerical coefficients. The sum (or remainder) thus obtained is the coefficient of the common radical.

EXAMPLE 5 Combine $7\sqrt{3} + 4\sqrt{3} - 5\sqrt{3}$.

$$7\sqrt{3} + 4\sqrt{3} - 5\sqrt{3} = (7 + 4 - 5)\sqrt{3} = 6\sqrt{3}$$

EXAMPLE 6 Combine $\sqrt{18} - \sqrt{32} + \sqrt{50}$.

Here the three terms have unlike radicals. However, they can be changed to like radicals as follows:

$$\sqrt{18} = \sqrt{3^2 \cdot 2} = 3\sqrt{2}$$
$$\sqrt{32} = \sqrt{4^2 \cdot 2} = 4\sqrt{2}$$
$$\sqrt{50} = \sqrt{5^2 \cdot 2} = 5\sqrt{2}$$

Notice that the procedure for changing a factor of each radicand to the coefficient of the radical is the reverse of the procedure employed in Examples 3 and 4.

Thus, $\sqrt{18} - \sqrt{32} + \sqrt{50} = 3\sqrt{2} - 4\sqrt{2} + 5\sqrt{2}$
$= (3 - 4 + 5)\sqrt{2} = 4\sqrt{2}$

MULTIPLICATION OF RADICALS

In multiplying radicals, when the indexes are the same, observe the following rule:

$\sqrt[n]{a} \cdot \sqrt[n]{b} = \sqrt[n]{ab}$

where a and b are greater than zero.

ILLUSTRATION: $\sqrt[n]{a} \cdot \sqrt[n]{b} = a^{1/n} \cdot b^{1/n} = (ab)^{1/n} = \sqrt[n]{ab}$

EXAMPLE 7 Multiply $(4\sqrt{3})$ by $(2\sqrt{5})$.

$(4\sqrt{3})(2\sqrt{5}) = (4)(2)(\sqrt{3})(\sqrt{5}) = 8\sqrt{(3)(5)} = 8\sqrt{15}$

When the indexes are different, follow the laws of exponents.

EXAMPLE 8 Multiply $\sqrt[3]{2}$ by $\sqrt{5}$.

$\sqrt[3]{2} \cdot \sqrt{5} = 2^{1/3} \cdot 5^{1/2} = 2^{2/6} \cdot 5^{3/6} = (2^2 \cdot 5^3)^{1/6} = \sqrt[6]{500}$

Note that the fractional exponents $\frac{1}{3}$ and $\frac{1}{2}$ above have been reduced to fractions having the lowest common denominator 6.

DIVISION OF RADICALS

In dividing radicals, when the indexes are the same, observe the following rule:

$$\frac{\sqrt[n]{a}}{\sqrt[n]{b}} = \sqrt[n]{\frac{a}{b}}$$

where a and b are greater than zero.

ILLUSTRATION:

$$\frac{\sqrt[n]{a}}{\sqrt[n]{b}} = \frac{a^{1/n}}{b^{1/n}} = \left(\frac{a}{b}\right)^{1/n} = \sqrt[n]{\frac{a}{b}}$$

EXAMPLE 9 Divide $\sqrt{20}$ by $\sqrt{5}$.

$$\sqrt{20} \div \sqrt{5} = \frac{\sqrt{20}}{\sqrt{5}} = \sqrt{\frac{20}{5}} = \sqrt{4} = 2$$

The quotient derived from the division of radicals is frequently expressed in fractional form. Fractions involving radicals are considered to be in their simplest form when the denominators include no radicals.

EXAMPLE 10 Divide $\sqrt{3}$ by $\sqrt{5}$.

$$\frac{\sqrt{3}}{\sqrt{5}} = \frac{\sqrt{3}}{\sqrt{5}} \cdot \frac{\sqrt{5}}{\sqrt{5}} = \frac{\sqrt{15}}{5}$$

When the indexes are different, follow the laws of exponents.

EXAMPLE 11 Divide $\sqrt{3}$ by $\sqrt[3]{2}$.

$$\frac{\sqrt{3}}{\sqrt[3]{2}} = \frac{3^{1/2}}{2^{1/3}} = \frac{3^{3/6}}{2^{2/6}} = \frac{3^{3/6}}{2^{2/6}} \cdot \frac{2^{4/6}}{2^{4/6}} = \frac{(3^3 \cdot 2^4)^{1/6}}{2^{6/6}} = \frac{(432)^{1/6}}{2} = \frac{\sqrt[6]{432}}{2}$$

Note that the fractional exponents of both numerator and denominator in the third fraction have been reduced to have a lowest common denominator 6.

D. Finding the Square Root

The radicals that occur most frequently in business and economics applications are the square roots. The method of finding the square root of a radicand is illustrated by the following examples.

EXAMPLE 12 Find $\sqrt{1{,}049.76}$.

The steps for finding the square root of 1,049.76 are:

STEP 1. The radicand 1,049.76 is divided into groups of two digits each, starting at the decimal point and moving in both directions, or

$\sqrt{\overline{10}\ \overline{49}.\overline{76}}$

Each group will have one digit in the final answer. The three groups will provide a three-digit answer.

STEP 2. Beginning with the first group at the left, 10, find the largest square that is less than or equal to 10. The square found is 9, which has a square root of 3. The square root of 9, or 3, is the first digit of the answer and is positioned on the answer line directly above the 10.

STEP 3. Subtract the square 9 from 10; then bring down the next pair of digits, 49, to form the first remainder, 149.

```
                          3          (Answer line)
                        √10   49.76
3²----------------------- 9(−) ↓
                          1   49
```

STEP 4. The next step involves operating on the first remainder, 149. To begin this step the value of the answer line, 3, must be doubled (or $3 \times 2 = 6$) and placed in a position to the left of 149. This is shown below:

```
                          3       (Answer line)
                        √10 49.76
                          9(−)
3 × 2-----------6__  |    1 49
                     |
```

The 6 is placed to the left of 149. Note that a blank space has been placed to the right of the 6; its use will be described below.

The 149 is operated on by attempting to find a particular single-digit integer (from the 10 possible digits, 0 to 9). The integer, when placed in the blank space, will form a number between 60 and 69. Multiplying the number by the integer should produce the largest product that is less than or equal to 149. If 0 is tried, the result will be $60 \times 0 = 0$, which is less than 149. Use of 1 yields $61 \times 1 = 61$, which is also less than 149 but nearer to it. When 2 is tried, the result is $62 \times 2 = 124$, which again is less than 149 but nearer yet. The integer 3 yields $63 \times 3 = 189$, which exceeds 149. Hence the sought integer is 2, since it yields a product which is as near to 149 as possible without exceeding it.

Having located the particular integer, place it both in the blank space and on the answer line directly above the 49. The 62 is multiplied by the 2 on the answer line and the product, 124, is subtracted from 149. The next pair of digits is brought down and the next remainder of 2,576 is formed.

```
                 3  2          (Answer line)
               √10 49.   76
                 9(−)          |
           6 2 | 1 49          |
62 × 2---------|---1 24(−)     ↓
                 25      76
```

STEP 5. The same procedure established in step 4 is used to operate on the 2,576 remainder. The numbers on the answer line are doubled ($32 \times 2 = 64$) and placed, along with a blank, to the left of 2,576.

```
                 3  2          (Answer line)
               √10 49.   76
                 9(−)
           6 2 | 1 49
               | 1 24(−)
32 × 2--------64__|  25    76
               |
```

Now an attempt is made to find the integer for the blank space to form a number which, when multiplied by the integer, will result in the largest product that is less than or equal to 2,576. When 4 is tried, the result is $644 \times 4 = 2{,}576$, which is exactly equal to the remainder being operated on. Hence, 4 is the sought integer. It is written in the blank space and on the answer line above the 76. The 644 is multiplied by the 4 on the answer line and the product, 2,576, is subtracted from 2,576. The 0 remainder indicates that the computation has been completed. Finally, a decimal point is located on the answer line at a position directly above the decimal point in the radicand. The answer, 32.4, is read directly from the answer line.

```
                 3  2. 4
               √10 49.76
                 9(−)
           6 2 | 1 49
               | 1 24(−)
          64 4 |  25 76
644 × 4--------+--25 76(−)
               |  00 00
```

STEP 6. *Check:* $32.4^2 = 32.4 \times 32.4 = 1{,}049.76$

EXAMPLE 13 Find $\sqrt{104.976}$ to two decimal places.

The steps for finding the square root of 104.976 are basically the same as those used in Example 12. However, there are a few exceptions, as noted below:

1. The radicand 104.976 is divided into groups of two digits each, or $\overline{1}\ \overline{04}.\overline{97}\ \overline{60}\ \overline{00}$

   Observe that zeros are annexed in the radicand in obtaining decimal places in the answer. For each additional decimal place in the answer, two zeros are annexed.

```
                          1  0. 2  4  5
                         √1 04.97 60 00
       1²-------------1(−)
   1 × 2---------2 0 | 0 04
  20 × 0 ---------------0 00 (−)
  10 × 2---------20 2 | 0 04 97
 202 × 2-----------------4 04(−)
 102 × 2---------204 4 |     93 60
2044 × 4 -------------------81 76(−)
1024 × 2---------2048 5 |    11 84 00
20485 × 5-------------------10 24 25(−)
                             .01 59 75
```

which is rounded to two decimal places, 10.25 (answer)

(remainder)

2. The last remainder, 15975, has an actual value of .015975. (The decimal point of the remainder is located directly below the decimal point in the given radicand.) This remainder can be used for further computation and for checking the final answer.

CHECK

$$10.245^2 = 10.245 \times 10.245 = 104.960025$$

$$\begin{array}{r} 104.960025 \\ +\ .015975 \\ \hline 104.976000 \end{array}$$

EXAMPLE 14 Find $\sqrt{256}$.

```
             1  6
            √2 56
     1² -----------1(−)
 1 × 2------2 6   1 56
26 × 6 -----------1 56(−)
                  0 00
```

CHECK $16^2 = 16 \times 16 = 256$

EXERCISE 3-4 REFERENCE: SECTION 3.4

A. Express the following in radical forms:

1. $a^{1/2}$
2. $(bc)^{1/3}$
3. $18^{2/3}$
4. $25^{3/4}$
5. $x^{1/4}$
6. $n^{2/5}$
7. $x^{5/3}$
8. $y^{3/7}$
9. $127^{3/4}$
10. $108^{2/7}$
11. $a^{3/5}$
12. $b^{4/3}$

B. Express the following in exponential forms:

13. $\sqrt[5]{a^3}$
14. $\sqrt[3]{b^4}$
15. $\sqrt[4]{34^5}$
16. $\sqrt[6]{45^2}$
17. $\sqrt{45^3}$
18. $\sqrt{62^5}$
19. $\sqrt[3]{x^5}$
20. $\sqrt[4]{u^3}$
21. $\sqrt[3]{28}$
22. $\sqrt[3]{46}$
23. $\sqrt[6]{b^2}$
24. $\sqrt[8]{t^4}$

C. Express the coefficient of the following radicals as part of the radicand:

25. $x\sqrt{y^3}$
26. $3\sqrt{15}$
27. $2^3 \cdot \sqrt{x}$
28. $6^2 \cdot \sqrt{u}$
29. $c \cdot \sqrt[3]{d^2}$
30. $4 \cdot \sqrt[3]{5}$
31. $5^3 \cdot \sqrt{3}$
32. $2^4 \cdot \sqrt{5}$
33. $3^2 \cdot \sqrt{2t}$
34. $2^3 \cdot \sqrt{4y}$
35. $a^2 \cdot \sqrt{ab}$
36. $n^3 \cdot \sqrt{7mn}$

D. Compute the following:

37. $16\sqrt{2} + 4\sqrt{2} - 3\sqrt{2}$
38. $13\sqrt{5} - 7\sqrt{5} + 12\sqrt{5}$
39. $3\sqrt{48} + \sqrt{12} - \sqrt{3}$
40. $7\sqrt{20} - \sqrt{45} + \sqrt{125}$
41. $\sqrt{112} - \sqrt{28} + \sqrt{63}$
42. $\sqrt{150} + \sqrt{96} - \sqrt{54}$
43. $(3\sqrt{4})(5\sqrt{6})$
44. $(6\sqrt{3})(9\sqrt{2})$
45. $(2\sqrt{5})(4\sqrt{7})(3\sqrt{2})$
46. $(12\sqrt{22})(4\sqrt{9})(3\sqrt{21})$
47. $\sqrt{64} \div \sqrt{16}$
48. $\sqrt{52} \div \sqrt{4}$
49. $\sqrt{5} \div \sqrt{8}$
50. $\sqrt{144} \div \sqrt{7}$
51. $\sqrt{2} \div \sqrt[3]{3}$
52. $\sqrt{5} \div \sqrt[3]{4}$

E. Find the square root of each of the following:

53. $\sqrt{256}$
54. $\sqrt{529}$
55. $\sqrt{1{,}024}$
56. $\sqrt{1{,}681}$
57. $\sqrt{21{,}025}$
58. $\sqrt{45{,}796}$
59. $\sqrt{4{,}542.76}$
60. $\sqrt{1{,}459.24}$
61. $\sqrt{454.276}$ (to two decimal places)
62. $\sqrt{145.924}$ (to two decimal places)
63. $\sqrt{1.024}$ (to three decimal places)
64. $\sqrt{260.1}$ (to three decimal places)

3.5 QUADRATIC EQUATIONS

A *quadratic equation* in one unknown is an equation that contains up to the second power of the unknown. The standard form of the quadratic equation in x, which represents the unknown, is written as follows:

$$ax^2 + bx + c = 0$$

The left side of the equation is arranged in order of descending powers of the unknown x, and a, b, and c are constants. The letter a may have any value other than zero, and the letters b and c may have any values, including zero. If $a = 0$, the equation will reduce to the form $bx + c = 0$, which is not quadratic, but linear. A quadratic equation in one unknown has only two roots. Any of the following three methods may be used to solve a quadratic equation.

A. Solution by Factoring

When the left side of a quadratic equation is readily factored, the roots can be obtained by applying the principle that if a product equals zero, one or more factors of the product equal zero.

EXAMPLE 1

Solve $x^2 - x = 6$.

Transpose: $x^2 - x - 6 = 0$

Factor: $(x - 3)(x + 2) = 0$

Equate each factor to zero and solve for x.

When $x - 3 = 0, \quad x = 3$

When $x + 2 = 0, \quad x = -2$

CHECK

Substitute separately each root in the original equation.

When $x = 3, \quad 3^2 - 3 = 6, \quad 9 - 3 = 6, \quad 6 = 6$

When $x = -2, \quad (-2)^2 - (-2) = 6, \quad 4 + 2 = 6, \quad 6 = 6$

EXAMPLE 2

Solve $49x^2 = 81$.

$49x^2 = 81$ may be written as $(7x)^2 = 9^2$.

Transpose: $(7x)^2 - 9^2 = 0$

Factor: $(7x + 9)(7x - 9) = 0$

Equate each factor to zero and solve for x.

When $7x + 9 = 0, \quad x = \frac{-9}{7}$

When $7x - 9 = 0, \quad x = \frac{9}{7}$

CHECK

Substitute separately each root in the original equation.

When $x = \frac{-9}{7}, \quad 49\left(\frac{-9}{7}\right)^2 = 81, \quad 81 = 81$

When $x = \frac{9}{7}, \quad 49\left(\frac{9}{7}\right)^2 = 81, \quad 81 = 81$

B. Solution by Completing the Squares

This method of solving a quadratic equation applies to all quadratic equations whether or not a solution can be found by the factoring method illustrated above.

EXAMPLE 3

Solve for x: $ax^2 + bx + c = 0$.

Subtract c from both sides of the equation.

$ax^2 + bx = -c$

Divide each side by a.

$$x^2 + \frac{b}{a}x = -\frac{c}{a}$$

Add the square of half the coefficient of x to both sides to make the left side a perfect square.

$$x^2 + \frac{b}{a}x + \left(\frac{b}{2a}\right)^2 = -\frac{c}{a} + \left(\frac{b}{2a}\right)^2; \quad \text{the right side} = \frac{b^2}{4a^2} - \frac{c}{a} = \frac{b^2 - 4ac}{4a^2}$$

Thus, $\left(x + \frac{b}{2a}\right)^2 = \frac{b^2 - 4ac}{4a^2}$

Extract the square root of each side.

$$x + \frac{b}{2a} = \pm\frac{\sqrt{b^2 - 4ac}}{2a}$$

Solve for x.

$$x = \frac{-b \pm \sqrt{b^2 - 4ac}}{2a}$$

C. Solution by the Quadratic Formula

A formula is a general fact, rule, or principle expressed in algebraic symbols. According to the above example, when $ax^2 + bx + c = 0$,

$$\boldsymbol{x = \frac{-b \pm \sqrt{b^2 - 4ac}}{2a}}$$

This is known as the *quadratic formula*, and it can be used to find the roots of any quadratic equation. When the left side of any quadratic equation is written in the order of descending powers of the unknown and the right side of the equation is zero, only the values of a, b, and c need to be substituted in the formula. Here a is the coefficient of the unknown square (x^2), b is the coefficient of the unknown (x), and c is the constant number.

EXAMPLE 4

Solve $x^2 - x = 6$ by the quadratic formula.

Transpose: $x^2 - x - 6 = 0$

Hence $a = 1, b = -1, c = -6$

Substituting in the formula,

$$x = \frac{-(-1) \pm \sqrt{(-1)^2 - 4(1)(-6)}}{2 \cdot 1} = \frac{1 \pm \sqrt{1 + 24}}{2}$$

$$= \frac{1 \pm \sqrt{25}}{2} = \frac{1 \pm 5}{2}$$

$$x = \frac{1 + 5}{2} = 3$$

$$x = \frac{1 - 5}{2} = -2$$

CHECK

Substitute the answers in the given equation.

When $x = 3$, $3^2 - 3 = 6$, $6 = 6$

When $x = -2$, $(-2)^2 - (-2) = 6$, $6 = 6$

EXERCISE 3-5 REFERENCE: SECTION 3.5

A. Solve the following by factoring:

1. $16x^2 - 81 = 0$
2. $25x^2 - 36 = 0$
3. $15x^2 + 11x - 12 = 0$
4. $6x^2 + 13x + 5 = 0$
5. $4x^2 = 25$
6. $9x^2 = 16$
7. $8x^2 + 3 = 14x$
8. $8y^2 + 6y = 9$

9. $3y^2 + 17y - 28 = 0$
10. $12y^2 + 3y = 42$
11. $12y^2 + 5 = -23y$
12. $41x - 10 = 21x^2$
13. $x^2 - 5x = -6$
14. $9x^2 - 1 = 0$
15. $3x^2 - 13x + 4 = 0$
16. $15x^2 - x - 2 = 0$

B. Solve the following by the quadratic formula:

17. $6x^2 - 11x + 4 = 0$
18. $10x^2 + 13x - 3 = 0$
19. $4x^2 - 31x + 21 = 0$
20. $x^2 - 64 = 0$
21. $18x^2 - 14 = 9x$
22. $14x^2 - 11x = 15$
23. $9x^2 - 49 = 0$
24. $20x^2 - 76x + 72 = 0$
25. $7m^2 - 19m - 6 = 0$
26. $35y^2 - y - 12 = 0$
27. $24n^2 - 41n + 12 = 0$
28. $4x^2 + 12x - 40 = 0$
29. $35x^2 - 57x = -18$
30. $18x^2 + 25x = 3$
31. $12x^2 - 9 = -23x$
32. $35x^2 - 32 = 36x$

3.6 THE BINOMIAL THEOREM

Any power of a binomial $(a + b)$ may be expanded by multiplication as follows:

$$(a + b)^1 = a + b$$
$$(a + b)^2 = a^2 + 2ab + b^2$$
$$(a + b)^3 = a^3 + 3a^2b + 3ab^2 + b^3$$
$$(a + b)^4 = a^4 + 4a^3b + 6a^2b^2 + 4ab^3 + b^4$$
$$(a + b)^5 = a^5 + 5a^4b + 10a^3b^2 + 10a^2b^3 + 5ab^4 + b^5$$

If n represents the exponent of $(a + b)$ in any of the preceding expansions, the following properties may be indicated:

1. The first term is a^n, and the second term is $na^{n-1}b$.
2. In each succeeding term, the exponents of a decrease by 1, and those of b increase by 1. The sum of the exponents of a and b in each term is n.
3. If the coefficient of any term is multiplied by the exponent of a and divided by the exponent of b increased by 1, the result is the coefficient of the next term. The exponent of b increased by 1 equals the number of the term.
4. The total number of terms in the expansion is $(n + 1)$.
5. The coefficients of terms equally distant from the ends of the expansion are the same. For example, in the expansion of $(a + b)^5$, the coefficient of the first and the last term is one; the coefficient of the second and next to the last term is 5.

The above properties give us the following formula, which is known as the *binomial theorem.*[1]

[1]The binomial theorem may also be written with the combination notation (see footnote on page 122):

$$(a + b)^n = {}_nC_0a^n + {}_nC_1a^{n-1}b + {}_nC_2a^{n-2}b^2 + \cdots + {}_nC_{n-1}ab^{n-1} + {}_nC_nb^n$$

$$(a + b)^n = a^n + na^{n-1}b + \frac{n(n-1)}{2}a^{n-2}b^2 + \frac{n(n-1)(n-2)}{2 \cdot 3}a^{n-3}b^3 + \cdots + b^n$$

This formula applies for any positive integral value of n. When n is negative or fractional, the binomial theorem is also valid if $\frac{b}{a}$ is numerically less than one; that is, if the absolute value of a is greater than the absolute value of b. However, when n is negative (see Example 4) or fractional (see Example 5), the resulting expansion does not have a last term. Nevertheless, a very close value of $(a + b)^n$ can be approximated if a sufficient number of terms of the expansion are included in the computation.

EXAMPLE 1 Expand $(3x + y)^4$.

$a = 3x$, $b = y$, $n = 4$. Substituting the values in the binomial formula,

$$(3x + y)^4 = (3x)^4 + 4(3x)^3y + \frac{4 \cdot 3}{2}(3x)^2y^2 + \frac{4 \cdot 3 \cdot 2}{2 \cdot 3}(3x)y^3 + \frac{4 \cdot 3 \cdot 2 \cdot 1}{2 \cdot 3 \cdot 4}y^4$$
$$= 81x^4 + 108x^3y + 54x^2y^2 + 12xy^3 + y^4$$

Examples 2 to 5 will be useful in solving problems relating to compound interest and annuities (Chapters 11 to 14) when the interest rates are not given in the tables in the text.

EXAMPLE 2 Expand $(1 + i)^5$.

$a = 1$, $b = i$, $n = 5$. Substituting the values in the binomial formula,

$$(1 + i)^5 = 1^5 + 5 \cdot 1^4i + \frac{5 \cdot 4}{2}1^3i^2 + \frac{5 \cdot 4 \cdot 3}{2 \cdot 3}1^2i^3 + \frac{5 \cdot 4 \cdot 3 \cdot 2}{2 \cdot 3 \cdot 4}1 \cdot i^4 + \frac{5 \cdot 4 \cdot 3 \cdot 2 \cdot 1}{2 \cdot 3 \cdot 4 \cdot 5}i^5$$
$$= 1 + 5i + 10i^2 + 10i^3 + 5i^4 + i^5$$

EXAMPLE 3 Find the value of $(1 + 2\%)^6$.

$a = 1$, $b = .02$, $n = 6$. Substituting the values in the binomial formula,

$$(1 + 2\%)^6 = 1^6 + 6(1)^5(.02) + \frac{6 \cdot 5}{2}(1)^4(.02)^2 + \frac{6 \cdot 5 \cdot 4}{2 \cdot 3}(1)^3(.02)^3 + \frac{6 \cdot 5 \cdot 4 \cdot 3}{2 \cdot 3 \cdot 4}(1)^2(.02)^4$$
$$+ \frac{6 \cdot 5 \cdot 4 \cdot 3 \cdot 2}{2 \cdot 3 \cdot 4 \cdot 5}(1)(.02)^5 + \frac{6 \cdot 5 \cdot 4 \cdot 3 \cdot 2 \cdot 1}{2 \cdot 3 \cdot 4 \cdot 5 \cdot 6}(.02)^6$$
$$= 1 + .12 + (15 \times .0004) + (20 \times .000008) + (15 \times .00000016)$$
$$+ (6 \times .0000000032) + .000000000064$$
$$= 1.126162419264$$

NOTE: If only 8 decimal places are required, the last term may be disregarded in computation. Also, see Table 5 in the Appendix:

$(1 + 2\%)^6 = 1.12616242$

EXAMPLE 4 Evaluate $(1 + .02)^{-3}$ to 3 decimal places.

$a = 1$, $b = .02$, $n = -3$. Substituting the values in the binomial formula,

$$(1 + .02)^{-3} = 1^{(-3)} + (-3)(1)^{-4}(.02) + \frac{(-3)(-4)}{2}(1)^{-5}(.02)^2$$
$$+ \frac{(-3)(-4)(-5)}{2 \cdot 3}(1)^{-6}(.02)^3 + \cdots$$
$$= 1 + (-.06) + 6(.0004) + (-10)(.000008) + \cdots$$

$$= 1 - .06 + .0024 - .00008 + \cdots$$
$$= .94232, \text{ rounded to 3 decimal places}$$
$$= .942$$

NOTE: Since only 3 decimal places are desired, only those terms having values in the first 4 decimal places need be retained in computation. Here, the 4th term $(-10)(.000008)$ or $(-.00008)$ may be omitted in adding. Also, see Table 6 in the Appendix:

$(1 + 2\%)^{-3} = .94232233$

EXAMPLE 5 Expand $(1 + .02)^{1/4}$ to 4 terms and simplify.

$a = 1$, $b = .02$, $n = \frac{1}{4}$. Substituting the values in the binomial formula,

$$(1 + .02)^{1/4} = 1^{1/4} + \tfrac{1}{4}(1)^{(1/4)-1}(.02) + \frac{(\frac{1}{4})(\frac{1}{4} - 1)}{2}(1)^{(1/4)-2}(.02)^2$$
$$+ \frac{(\frac{1}{4})(\frac{1}{4} - 1)(\frac{1}{4} - 2)}{2 \cdot 3}(1)^{(1/4)-3}(.02)^3 + \cdots$$
$$= 1 + \tfrac{1}{4}(.02) + (-\tfrac{3}{32})(.0004) + \tfrac{7}{128}(.000008) + \cdots$$
$$= 1 + .005 - .0000375 + .0000004375 + \cdots$$
$$= 1.0049629375$$

NOTE: When $(1 + .02)^{1/4}$ is expanded to 5 terms, the result is 1.00496293149. Round the result to 8 decimal places: $(1 + .02)^{1/4} = 1.00496293$. Also, see Table 5A in the Appendix:

$(1 + 2\%)^{1/4} = 1.00496293$

Another simple way to learn the binomial coefficients of the terms in the binomial expansion of $(a + b)^n$ is to arrange the coefficients in a triangular array. Such an array, as illustrated below, is known as Pascal's triangle.

Binomial	*Coefficients of the terms in the binomial expansion, according to the order of terms*
$(a + b)^0$	1
$(a + b)^1$	1 1
$(a + b)^2$	1 2 1
$(a + b)^3$	1 3 3 1
$(a + b)^4$	1 4 6 4 1
$(a + b)^5$	1 5 10 10 5 1
$(a + b)^6$	1 6 15 20 15 6 1
$(a + b)^7$	1 7 21 35 35 21 7 1
....	....

Excluding the 1's at the corners of the base of the triangle, each numerical coefficient in the table is the sum of the two numbers in the row above the coefficient. For example, in the fifth row, $4 = 1 + 3$, $6 = 3 + 3$, and $4 = 3 + 1$. Thus,

$$(a + b)^4 = a^4 + 4a^3b + 6a^2b^2 + 4ab^3 + b^4$$

EXERCISE 3-6 REFERENCE: SECTION 3.6

A. Expand each of the following by the binomial formula and simplify:

1. $(x + y)^5$	4. $(5x + 2y)^3$	7. $(x - 2y)^6$	10. $(1 + 0.025)^4$
2. $(2x + 3y)^4$	5. $(1 + i)^7$	8. $(m - n)^5$	11. $(1 + 2\%)^5$
3. $(x + 4y)^6$	6. $(1 - i)^3$	9. $(1 + 0.02)^3$	12. $(1 + 3\%)^6$

B. Find the numerical value of each of the following problems by expanding to 4 terms only (round the answers to 7 decimal places):

13. $(1 + 1\frac{1}{4}\%)^{10}$	17. $(1 + 2\%)^{-5}$	21. $(1 + 4\%)^{1/12}$	23. $(1 + 7\%)^{1/4}$
14. $(1 + 5\%)^{40}$	18. $(1 + 2\frac{1}{2}\%)^{-6}$	22. $(1 + 3\%)^{1/6}$	24. $(1 + 2\frac{1}{4}\%)^{1/3}$
15. $(1 + 1\frac{1}{2}\%)^{36}$	19. $(1 + 4\%)^{-10}$		
16. $(1 + 2\frac{1}{2}\%)^{50}$	20. $(1 + 3\%)^{-20}$		

3.7 LOGARITHMS—BASIC PRINCIPLES

A. General Statement

Logarithms can be used to simplify the operations of multiplication, division, raising to powers, and extracting roots. In mathematics of finance, logarithms are especially useful in solving problems that involve compound interest and annuities when interest rates are not given in the available tables.

B. What is a Logarithm?

A *logarithm* is an exponent. In exponential form, if $b^x = N$, the exponent x is the logarithm of the number N to the base b. Likewise, since

$2^3 = 8$, the exponent 3 is the logarithm of the number 8 to the base 2;
$5^2 = 25$, the exponent 2 is the logarithm of the number 25 to the base 5; and
$10^3 = 1{,}000$, the exponent 3 is the logarithm of the number 1,000 to the base 10.

The above relationship can be written in simpler form as follows:

Since $b^x = N$, then $\log_b N = x$, where *log* represents "the logarithm of."
Since $2^3 = 8$, then $\log_2 8 = 3$.
Since $5^2 = 25$, then $\log_5 25 = 2$.
Since $10^3 = 1{,}000$, then $\log_{10} 1{,}000 = 3$.

Among various bases, 10 is the most convenient base for logarithmic computation, since 10 is also the base in our decimal number system. When the base 10 is used, it is customary to omit the subscript that indicates the base; thus, $\log_{10} 1{,}000$ can be written as log 1,000. The logarithms based on 10 are called the *common* or *Briggsian* (Henry

Briggs, 1560–1631) system of logarithms. In this system, the following corresponding forms may be written:

Logarithmic Form	*Exponential Form*
$\log 100{,}000 = 5$	$10^5 = 100{,}000$
$\log 10{,}000 = 4$	$10^4 = 10{,}000$
$\log 1{,}000 = 3$	$10^3 = 1{,}000$
$\log 100 = 2$	$10^2 = 100$
$\log 10 = 1$	$10^1 = 10$
$\log 1 = 0$	$10^0 = 1$
$\log .1 = -1$	$10^{-1} = \frac{1}{10} = .1$
$\log .01 = -2$	$10^{-2} = \frac{1}{10^2} = \frac{1}{100} = .01$
$\log .001 = -3$	$10^{-3} = \frac{1}{10^3} = \frac{1}{1{,}000} = .001$
In general, $\log N = x$	$10^x = N$

Note that all numbers (N) indicated above have *positive values*.

From the above explanation it may be seen that as a number becomes greater, the logarithm of the number also becomes greater. Thus, if N and M are two positive numbers and N is larger than M, then $\log N$ is also larger than $\log M$. This concept is important in finding the logarithm of a number that is not an exact power of 10. For example, if the number is 249, which is larger than 100 (or 10^2), the logarithm of 249 is larger than the logarithm of 100. Further, since the number 249 is smaller than 1,000 (or 10^3), the logarithm of 249 is smaller than the logarithm of 1,000. The relationships may be written as follows:

$$\log 100 < \log 249 < \log 1{,}000$$

or $2 < \log 249 < 3$

since $\log 100 = 2$ and $\log 1{,}000 = 3$

Thus, $\log 249 = 2 +$ a decimal (since $2 + 1 = 3$), or, in exponential form,

$$10^{2 \ + \text{ a decimal}} = 249$$

Similarly, we may find the logarithm of a positive number that is less than 1, such as .0045.

Since $.001 < .0045 < .01$

or $10^{-3} < .0045 < 10^{-2}$

then $\log .001 < \log .0045 < \log .01$

or $-3 < \log .0045 < -2$

Thus, $\log .0045 = (-3) +$ a decimal [since $(-3) + 1 = (-2)$], or, in exponential form,

$$10^{-3 \ + \text{ a decimal}} = .0045$$

In general, when a number is not an exact power of 10, the logarithm of the number consists of a whole-number part and a decimal part. The whole-number part is called the *characteristic* of the logarithm, and the decimal part is called the *mantissa* of the logarithm.

Logarithm of a positive number = Characteristic + Mantissa

Examples of characteristics of selected numbers are tabulated below:

Number		*Digits in Whole-Number Part (1 and Above)* — *or* — *Zeros Between Decimal Point and First Nonzero Digit (less than 1)*	*Characteristic*
10,000 to 99,999.99	(but less than 100,000)	5	4
1,000 to 9,999.99	(but less than 10,000)	4	3
100 to 999.99	(but less than 1,000)	3	2
10 to 99.99	(but less than 100)	2	1
1 to 9.99	(but less than 10)	1	0
.1 to .99	(but less than 1)	none	−1
.01 to .099	(but less than .1)	1	−2
.001 to .0099	(but less than .01)	2	−3
.0001 to .00099	(but less than .001)	3	−4

This table shows that the characteristic of the logarithm of a number depends only on the position of the decimal point, regardless of the value of the individual digits in the number. The following rules may be used in determining characteristics.

RULE 1 **If a number is greater than or equal to 1, the characteristic of its logarithm is positive and is 1 less than the number of digits to the left of the decimal point.**

RULE 2 **If a number is less than 1, the characteristic of its logarithm is negative and is 1 more than the number of zeros between the decimal point and the first nonzero digit.**

Unlike the characteristic, the mantissa of the logarithm of a number is independent of the position of the decimal point in the number. The mantissa is always positive and is determined by the significant digits of the number. Logarithms of numbers that have the same significant digits arranged in the same order thus have the same mantissas. Here the significant digits in a number are the digits that do not include the zeros to the left of the first nonzero digit in a decimal, or the zeros to the right of the last nonzero digit in a whole number. Thus, the significant digits of the numbers 3,408,000, 34,080, 34.08, and .003408 are 3,4,0,8, and the logarithms of the numbers have the same mantissas, but not the same characteristics.

C. Tables of Mantissas

Tables of mantissas are also called tables of logarithms. The mantissas of the logarithms of most numbers are unending decimal fractions, but they can be computed to any required number of decimal places. Methods of computing most values of mantissas are developed in advanced algebra. Because they are beyond the scope of this text, those methods are not introduced here. However, for practical uses, various tables of mantissas are available; they are known as six-place tables, seven-place tables, and so on, according to the number of digits in the mantissas. It should be noted that, while mantissas are decimal fractions, they are usually given in tables without decimal points. Therefore, a decimal point should always be placed before the first digit in the mantissa when it is used. In this text, a six-place table, which gives the mantissas of numbers from 1 to 9,999, and a seven-place table, which gives the mantissas of numbers from 10,000 to 11,009, are used for computing logarithmic problems.[2] The uses of these two tables are described below.

HOW TO DETERMINE THE LOGARITHM OF A GIVEN NUMBER

In general, three operations are required to determine the logarithm of a given number:

1. Determine the characteristic by the rules given above.
2. In the table, find the mantissa corresponding to the significant digits of the given number. Two steps are necessary to locate the mantissa.
   STEP (A). In Column N, find the first three significant digits of the given number. The mantissa required is in the row horizontal with these digits.
   STEP (B). In this row, locate the required mantissa in the column headed by the fourth significant digit of the given number.
3. Place a decimal point before the first digit of the mantissa, and add the mantissa to the characteristic. The sum is the required logarithm of the given number.

EXAMPLE 1

Find log 82.46.

1. The characteristic is $+1$, since there are two digits to the left of the decimal point.
2. STEP (A). The first three significant digits, 824, are found in Column N of Table 2 of the Appendix.
   STEP (B). The required mantissa is found opposite the digits 824, in the column that has 6 at the top. The mantissa is 916243.[3]
3. The logarithm of 82.46 is $1 + .916243 = 1.916243$, or

$$\log 82.46 = 1.916243$$

[2]See Tables 2 and 3 in the Appendix.

[3]The first two digits of each mantissa are not printed in every column in the tables of mantissas. They are printed only in the columns which have 0 at the top. However, when the mantissas have the same first two digits, only the digits for the line having the smallest mantissa and the line having the largest mantissa of the group are printed in the 0 column. In order to secure a six-place mantissa, the first two digits must be prefixed to each entry on the same line and the lines below it until the two digits change. The first two digits of an entry marked by * are located on the line below the entry in the 0 column. Thus, in Example 1, Step (B), the first two digits 91 are prefixed to 6243, written as 916243. On the same page in the tables, the first two digits 92 must be prefixed to entry *0019, written as 920019.

In exponential form, the logarithm is written as

$10^{1.916243} = 82.46$

EXAMPLE 2

Find log 0.008246.

1. The characteristic is -3, since there are two zeros between the decimal point and the first nonzero digit 8.
2. The mantissa is 916243, because the significant digits of the given number are the same as those in the preceding example.
3. The logarithm of 0.008246 is $-3 + .916243 = -2.083757$.

Thus, $\log 0.008246 = -3 + .916243$, or
$\log 0.008246 = -2.083757$

In exponential form, the logarithm is written as

$10^{-3 + .916243} = 0.008246$, or
$10^{-2.083757} = 0.008246$

When a characteristic is negative, there are other ways to write the logarithm of a number. It can be written by placing the negative sign above the characteristic. Thus, the logarithm in Example 2 may be written as

$\log 0.008246 = \bar{3}.916243$

Or it may be written in a more convenient way by using an equivalent form, such as

$\log 0.008246 = 7.916243 - 10$

because $7 - 10 = -3$. In exponential form the logarithm now is written:

$10^{7.916243 - 10} = 0.008246$

ADDITIONAL ILLUSTRATIONS:

(Use Table 2 for the first five illustrations.)

$\log 8246 = 3.916243$
$\log 1.175 = 0.070038$
$\log 0.0004269 = -4 + .630326 = -3.369674$
$\text{or} = \bar{4}.630326 = 6.630326 - 10$
$\log 732.4 = 2.864748$
$\log 0.7901 = -1 + .897682 = -.102318$
$\text{or} = \bar{1}.897682 = 9.897682 - 10$
$\log 10{,}742 = 4.0310851$ (use Table 3)

HOW TO DETERMINE THE NUMBER FROM A GIVEN LOGARITHM (FINDING THE ANTILOGARITHM)

In general, the process of determining the number from a given logarithm is the inverse of the process used in determining the logarithm of a number. The number found is called the *antilogarithm* (abbreviated *antilog*) of the given logarithm. The steps in this process follow:

1. Find the given mantissa in the table.
2. Determine the significant digits from the location of the mantissa.

3. The required number is determined by placing a decimal point in the significant digits according to the given characteristic.

EXAMPLE 3

If $\log N = 2.072617$, find N.

1. In Table 2 of the Appendix, find the mantissa 072617.
2. The significant digits are 1182.
3. The required number, N, is 118.2 because the characteristic is 2. The solution may be written:

$N = \text{Antilog } 2.072617 = 118.2$

EXAMPLE 4

If $\log N = -1.9609033$, find N.

Since the mantissas in the tables are all positive, first convert the given negative value of the log N to its equivalent form having the positive mantissa 0390967. The conversion may be done by adding 10 to, and subtracting 10 from, the given value as follows:

$$\begin{aligned} -1.9609033 &= -1.9609033 + 10 - 10 \\ &= 10 - 1.9609033 - 10 \\ &= 8.0390967 - 10 \end{aligned}$$

Thus,

$\log N = -1.9609033 = 8.0390967 - 10$

Then proceed with the usual process:

1. In Table 3 of the Appendix, find the mantissa 0390967.
2. The significant digits are 10942.
3. The required number, N, is 0.010942 because the characteristic is $8 - 10 = -2$.

$N = \text{Antilog } (8.0390967 - 10) = 0.010942$

EXERCISE 3-7 REFERENCE: SECTION 3.7 B and C

A. Write the following in logarithmic form:

1. $58 = 10^{1.763428}$
2. $7 = 10^{0.845098}$
3. $0.00325 = 10^{7.511883-10}$
4. $0.02513 = 10^{8.400192-10}$
5. $0.4795 = 10^{9.680789-10}$
6. $5{,}683 = 10^{3.754578}$
7. $136 = 10^{2.133539}$
8. $10{,}253 = 10^{4.0108510}$
9. $0.010492 = 10^{8.0208583-10}$
10. $0.000395 = 10^{6.596597-10}$

B. Write the following in exponential form:

11. $\log 147 = 2.167317$
12. $\log 10.6 = 1.025306$
13. $\log 2{,}452 = 3.389520$
14. $\log 2.603 = 0.415474$
15. $\log 79 = 1.897627$
16. $\log .003559 = 7.551328 - 10$
17. $\log .0634 = 8.802089 - 10$
18. $\log 10{,}356 = 4.0151920$
19. $\log 104.23 = 2.0179927$
20. $\log 5{,}684 = 3.754654$

C. From Tables 2 and 3, determine the logarithm of each number:

21. 285
22. 0.00285
23. 3.823
24. 43.25
25. 4,328
26. 624
27. 0.0003952
28. 0.687
29. 2,374
30. 453.6
31. 10.452
32. 102,830

D. Find N if $\log N$ is:

33. 2.201670
34. 3.176959
35. 0.445604
36. 8.431685 − 10
37. 7.600428 − 10
38. 9.799478 − 10
39. 4.691081
40. 1.700184
41. 0.162564
42. 6.202761 − 10
43. 5.446537 − 10
44. 4.596047 − 10

D. Interpolation Method

Since tables of mantissas provide only a limited number of digits, a mantissa for a number containing more than the provided significant digits cannot be found directly in the tables. The mantissa for such a number thus is approximated by using the interpolation method. When this method is used, it is assumed, although it is not necessarily so, that the differences between numbers and the differences between corresponding mantissas of the numbers in the tables are proportional.

EXAMPLE 5 Find log 584.36.

In Table 2 the *nearest number larger* than and the *nearest number smaller* than the given number 584.36 are 584.40 and 584.30, respectively. The mantissa of 584.40 is 766710 and that of 584.30 is 766636. When the decimal points in the numbers are disregarded, they may be arranged in the following manner:

	Number		*Mantissa*	
	58440		766710	(1)
	58436		x	(2)
	58430		766636	(3)
Subtract line (3) from (2)	6	=	$x -$ 766636	(4)
Subtract line (3) from (1)	10		74	(5)

The differences between the numbers are assumed to be proportional to the differences between the corresponding mantissas, that is, 6 is to ($x -$ 766636) as 10 is to 74.

Solve for x from the proportion formed by the differences on lines (4) and (5).

$$x - 766636 = 74 \cdot \tfrac{6}{10}$$
$$x - 766636 = 44.4, \text{ or } 44$$
$$x = 766636 + 44 = 766680$$

The characterisitic of log 584.36 is 2. Thus,

$$\log 584.36 = 2.766680$$

NOTE: In the above arrangement, the larger number and mantissa are placed on the top line in order to facilitate subtraction. Although there are many other ways of interpolation, the method introduced above is a convenient one. A reader who is familiar with the arrangement can immediately write the value of x as follows:

$$x = 766636 + 74\left(\frac{6}{10}\right) = 766636 + 44.4 = 766680.4$$

The difference, 74, can be derived from the D column of Table 2. (Also see the footnote to Table 2 in defining the values in the D column.)

The interpolation method may also be used in finding the number of a given logarithm when the mantissa is not listed in the tables.

EXAMPLE 6 If $\log N = 3.642682$, find N to five significant digits.

The mantissa 642682 cannot be found in Table 2. Thus, it must be approximated by the interpolation method. The nearest mantissa larger than and that smaller than the given mantissa are 642761 and 642662, which correspond to numbers 43930 and 43920, respectively. The decimal point is disregarded in computing the value of N at first. The numbers and the corresponding mantissas may be arranged as follows:

	Number	*Mantissa*	
	43930	642761	(1)
	x	642682	(2)
	43920	642662	(3)
(2) − (3)	$x - 43920$	20	(4)
(1) − (3)	10	99	(5)

$$\frac{x - 43920}{10} = \frac{20}{99}$$

Solve for x from the proportion formed by the differences on lines (4) and (5).

$$x - 43920 = 10 \cdot \tfrac{20}{99} = 2.02, \text{ or } 2$$
$$x = 43920 + 2 = 43922$$

Since the characteristic is 3, $N = 4{,}392.2$.

NOTE: If six significant digits are required, two zeros may be added to the numbers 4392 and 4393; that is, the required number is between 439200 and 439300. When six-place tables are used, there is usually no need to compute seven or more significant digits, since the values obtained from the interpolation method are approximations. However, when seven-place tables are used, we may interpolate to seven, or sometimes to eight, significant digits to obtain close approximations. See Note 4 to Example 6 of Section 11.3 for an example.

EXERCISE 3-8 REFERENCE: SECTION 3.7 D

A. Using the interpolation method, determine the logarithm of each number:

1. 0.026584	4. 6,523.5	7. 0.78614	10. 371,256
2. 0.0032468	5. 1.3784	8. 531.13	11. 82.564
3. 0.32465	6. 45.375	9. 386.24	12. 503,723

B. Using the interpolation method, find N (Problems 13–20, find N to 5 significant digits; Problems 21–24, find N to 6 significant digits; use Table 3 for Problems 23 and 24) if $\log N$ is:

13. 3.740654	16. 1.760141	19. 4.447211	22. 1.663084
14. 0.536274	17. 7.536274 − 10	20. 2.944895	23. 8.0184568 − 10
15. 2.568254	18. 9.929455 − 10	21. 3.462894	24. 0.0283795

3.8 LOGARITHMS—COMPUTATION

The operations of multiplication, division, raising to powers, and extracting roots by using logarithms are presented in this section. Although logarithms can be used to simplify such operations, there is a disadvantage in their use; except for a few numbers, the results of the operations computed by means of logarithms are approximations. In general, the results in logarithmic computations will be more accurate if the mantissa parts have more places included. Unless otherwise specified, the interpolation process is omitted for simplifying the following illustrations. The nearest value in the tables of mantissas is used in finding an antilog of a computed logarithm.

A. Law for Multiplication

The logarithm of the product of two or more factors equals the sum of their logarithms.

The general form is[4]

$$\log MN = \log M + \log N$$

The above law may be used to simplify computation in multiplication, as shown in the following examples.

EXAMPLE 1

If $MN = (1.67)(.055)$, find the product.

First, take logarithms of both sides of the equation.

$\log (MN) = \log [(1.67)(.055)]$, or

$\log MN = \log 1.67 + \log .055$

$$\begin{aligned} \log 1.67 &= 0.222716 \\ (+)\ \log .055 &= 8.740363 - 10 \\ \hline \log MN &= 8.963079 - 10 \end{aligned}$$

Find the antilog.

$MN = 0.09185$

EXAMPLE 2

Compute $(-1.67)(.055)$.

First, change the negative factor (-1.67) to a positive factor as follows:

$(-1.67)(.055) = -[(1.67)(.055)]$

Then, find the value of $(1.67)(.055)$ by logarithms. In Example 1, $(1.67)(.055) = .09185$. Thus,

$(-1.67)(.055) = -.09185$

EXAMPLE 3

If $MN = (23.57)(5.598)$, find the product.

$\log MN = \log 23.57 + \log 5.598$

---

[4]*Proof:* Let $x = \log M$, or $M = 10^x$
$y = \log N$, or $N = 10^y$

Then $MN = 10^x \cdot 10^y = 10^{x+y}$
$\log MN = x + y = \log M + \log N$

$$\begin{array}{r l}
\log 23.57 &= 1.372360 \\
(+) \log 5.598 &= 0.748033 \\
\hline
\log MN &= 2.120393
\end{array}$$

Find the antilog.

$MN = 131.9$ (approximately)

NOTE: The nearest value to the computed mantissa 120393 in the six-place table (Table 2) is 120245, where the number is 1319.

For a more accurate result, further significant digits in Example 3 may be obtained by the interpolation method. The interpolation shown below is computed to six significant digits.

	Number	*Mantissa*	
	132000	120574	(1)
	x	120393	(2)
	131900	120245	(3)

$$\begin{array}{l c}
(2) - (3) \\
(1) - (3)
\end{array} \quad \frac{x - 131900}{100} = \frac{148}{329} \quad \begin{array}{c} (4) \\ (5) \end{array}$$

Solve for x from the proportion formed by the differences on lines (4) and (5).

$$x - 131900 = 100 \cdot \tfrac{148}{329} = 44.98 \quad \text{or} \quad 45$$

$$x = 131900 + 45 = 131945$$

Thus, $MN = 131.945$ (approximately)

NOTE: The actual product is $(23.57)(5.598) = 131.94486$.

B. Law for Division

The logarithm of a quotient equals the logarithm of the dividend (numerator) minus the logarithm of the divisor (denominator).

The general form is[5]

$$\log \frac{M}{N} = \log M - \log N$$

The above law may be used to simplify computation in division, as shown in the following example.

---

[5]*Proof:* Let $x = \log M$, or $M = 10^x$
$y = \log N$, or $N = 10^y$

Then $\dfrac{M}{N} = \dfrac{10^x}{10^y} = 10^{x-y}$

$\log \dfrac{M}{N} = x - y = \log M - \log N$

EXAMPLE 4

If $\frac{M}{N} = \frac{0.1071}{2.38}$, find the quotient.

First, take logarithms of both sides of the equation.

$$\log\left(\frac{M}{N}\right) = \log\left(\frac{0.1071}{2.38}\right), \quad \text{or}$$

$$\log\frac{M}{N} = \log 0.1071 - \log 2.38$$

$$\begin{aligned} \log 0.1071 &= 9.029789 - 10 \\ (-)\ \log 2.38 &= 0.376577 \\ \hline \log\frac{M}{N} &= 8.653212 - 10 \end{aligned}$$

Find the antilog.

$$\frac{M}{N} = 0.045$$

C. Law for Powers and Roots

The logarithm of an exponential equals the exponent times the logarithm of its base.

The general form is[6]

$$\mathbf{\log M^p = p\,(\log M)}$$

If the exponent is a fraction, the general form may be written as

$$\mathbf{\log M^{1/q} = \frac{1}{q}(\log M)} \quad \text{or}$$

$$\mathbf{\log \sqrt[q]{M} = \frac{1}{q}(\log M)}$$

Applications of the above law are illustrated below.

EXAMPLE 5

Compute $(17)^3$.

Let $N = (17)^3$. Then

$$\begin{aligned} \log N = \log(17)^3 &= 3 \log 17 \\ &= 3(1.230449) = 3.691347 \end{aligned}$$

$$N = \text{antilog } 3.691347 = 4{,}913, \quad \text{or} \quad (17)^3 = 4{,}913$$

EXAMPLE 6

Compute $(-17)^3$.

$$(-17)^3 = [(-1)(17)]^3 = (-1)^3(17)^3 = (-1)(17)^3$$

---

[6]*Proof:* Let $x = \log M$, or $M = 10^x$. When both sides of the equation are raised to the pth power, the following results:

$$\begin{aligned} M^p &= (10^x)^p = 10^{px} \\ \log M^p &= px = p(\log M) \end{aligned}$$

Find the value of $(17)^3$ by logarithms. (See Example 5.)

$(-17)^3 = (-1)(17)^3 = (-1)(4{,}913) = -4{,}913$

EXAMPLE 7 Compute $(1.045)^{32}$.

Let $N = (1.045)^{32}$. Then

$$\log N = \log (1.045)^{32} = 32 \log 1.045$$
$$= 32(0.019116) = 0.611712$$

$$N = \text{antilog } (0.611712) = 4.09, \quad \text{or}$$
$$(1.045)^{32} = 4.09$$

NOTE:

1. The multiplication, $32(0.019116) = 0.611712$, is carried out by the conventional method. It may also be done by using logarithms, as illustrated in Example 1.
2. The nearest value to the computed mantissa 611712 in the six-place table is 611723, where $N = 4{,}090$.
3. The answer may be checked by using Table 5, where $i = 4\frac{1}{2}\%$, $n = 32$, and $(1 + i)^n = (1 + 4\frac{1}{2}\%)^{32} = 4.08998104$

EXAMPLE 8 Find N if $N = \sqrt[7]{2{,}187}$.

Let $N = \sqrt[7]{2{,}187} = 2{,}187^{1/7}$. Then

$\log N = \log (2{,}187)^{1/7} = \frac{1}{7} \log 2{,}187 = \frac{1}{7}(3.339849) = 0.477121$, or

$$\log N = 0.477121$$
$$N = \text{antilog } 0.477121 = 3.000, \text{ or } 3$$

CHECK $3^7 = 2{,}187$.

EXAMPLE 9 Compute $\sqrt{0.6576}$.

Let $N = \sqrt{0.6576} = (0.6576)^{1/2}$. Then

$$\log N = \tfrac{1}{2}\log 0.6576 = \tfrac{1}{2}(-1 + .817962)$$
$$= \tfrac{1}{2}(-.182038) = -.091019$$

There are only positive mantissas in the tables of logarithms. The negative result therefore must be converted to its equivalent form having a positive mantissa before using the table to find the antilog.

$$\text{Since } -.091019 = -.091019 + 10 - 10 = 10 - .091019 - 10$$
$$= 9.908981 - 10$$

$$\log N = -.091019 = 9.908981 - 10, \quad \text{or} \quad -1 + .908981$$
$$N = \text{antilog } (-1 + .908981) = .8109, \quad \text{or} \quad \sqrt{0.6576} = .8109$$

NOTE: The nearest value to the computed mantissa 908981 in the six-place table is 908967, where $N = 8{,}109$.

EXERCISE 3-9 REFERENCE: SECTION 3.8 A, B, and C

Perform each of the following indicated operations by use of logarithms. Compute Problems 1, 2, 3, and 4 to six significant digits. Omit interpolation in the remaining problems.

A. Multiplication:

1. 2.35×0.453
2. 46.25×3.42
3. 743×235
4. $5{,}684 \times 39$
5. 0.03452×236
6. 431.6×35.47
7. $(-4.25) \times 728.6$
8. $56.73 \times (-68.54)$

B. Division:

9. $0.2346 \div 1.46$
10. $4{,}326 \div 26.4$
11. $375.6 \div 0.134$
12. $4.768 \div 2.167$
13. $74.26 \div 2.75$
14. $88 \div 22$
15. $6.543 \div 7{,}428$
16. $3.427 \div 0.01648$

C. Powers and roots:

17. $(1.015)^{27}$
18. $(1.025)^{46}$
19. $(3.752)^{12}$
20. $(23.4)^5$
21. $(-45)^2$
22. $(-26)^2$
23. $(-33.64)^3$
24. $(-12.2)^3$
25. $\sqrt[3]{4{,}913}$
26. $\sqrt[3]{2{,}744}$
27. $\sqrt{15.21}$
28. $\sqrt{84.64}$
29. $\sqrt[6]{583}$
30. $\sqrt[8]{642}$
31. $\sqrt[4]{0.4243}$
32. $\sqrt[5]{0.8736}$

D. Solving Equations

To solve an equation by using logarithms, first equate the logarithms of both sides of the equation; then solve the unknown from the new logarithmic equation.

EXAMPLE 10 If $(1 + i)^{69} = 2.794$, find i.

First, equate the logarithms of both sides.

$$\log (1 + i)^{69} = \log 2.794$$

$$69 \log (1 + i) = 0.446226$$

$$\log (1 + i) = \frac{0.446226}{69} = 0.006467$$

$$1 + i = \text{antilog } 0.006467 = 1.015$$

$$i = 1.015 - 1 = 0.015, \quad \text{or} \quad 1\tfrac{1}{2}\%$$

NOTE:

1. The nearest value to the computed mantissa 006467 in the six-place table is 006466, where $N = 1{,}015$.
2. The answer may be checked by using Table 5, where $i = 1\frac{1}{2}\%$, $n = 69$, and $(1 + i)^n = (1 + 1\frac{1}{2}\%)^{69} = 2.79355300$.

EXAMPLE 11 If $(1 + i)^{-46} = 0.2871$, find i.

First, equate the logarithms of both sides.

$$\log (1 + i)^{-46} = \log 0.2871$$

$$(-46) \log (1 + i) = -1 + .458033 = -.541967$$

$$\log (1 + i) = \frac{-.541967}{-46} = 0.0117819$$

$$1 + i = \text{antilog } 0.0117819 = 1.0275$$

$$i = 1.0275 - 1 = 0.0275 \quad \text{or} \quad 2\tfrac{3}{4}\%$$

NOTE:

1. The nearest value to the computed mantissa 0117819 in the seven-place table is 0117818, where $N = 10{,}275$.
2. The answer may be checked by using Table 6, where $i = 2\frac{3}{4}\%$, $n = 46$, and $(1 + i)^{-n} = (1 + 2\frac{3}{4}\%)^{-46} = 0.28710172$.

EXAMPLE 12

If $(1 + 2\frac{1}{2}\%)^n = 2.15$, find n.

First, equate the logarithms of both sides.

$$\log (1 + 2\tfrac{1}{2}\%)^n = \log 2.15$$

$$n(\log 1.025) = \log 2.15$$

$$n = \frac{\log 2.15}{\log 1.025} = \frac{0.332438}{0.010724} = 31$$

NOTE:

1. The division, 0.332438/0.010724 = 31, is carried out by the conventional method. It may also be done by using logarithms, as illustrated in Example 4.
2. The answer may also be checked by using Table 5, where $i = 2\frac{1}{2}\%$, $n = 31$, and $(1 + i)^n = (1 + 2\frac{1}{2}\%)^{31} = 2.15000677$.

EXERCISE 3-10 REFERENCE: SECTION 3.8 D

Solving equations (omit interpolation):

1. If $(1 + i)^{46} = 1.771$, find i.
2. If $(1 + i)^{25} = 1.45$, find i.
3. If $(1 + i)^{2/5} = 1.008$, find i.
4. If $(1 + i)^{1/6} = 1.0049$, find i. (Hint: Use 7-place table.)
5. If $(1 + i)^{-20} = .3118$, find i.
6. If $(1 + i)^{-4} = .8548$, find i.
7. If $(1 + i)^{-1/4} = .9951$, find i.
8. If $(1 + i)^{-1/2} = .9713$, find i.
9. If $(1 + 1\frac{1}{2}\%)^n = 4.432$, find n.
10. If $(1 + 4\%)^n = 1.9479$, find n.
11. If $(1 + 4\frac{1}{2}\%)^{-n} = .267$, find n. 30
12. If $(1 + 5\%)^{-n} = .0107$, find n.

To be used Later

4 BASIC MODERN ALGEBRA

Chapters 4 and 5 present modern algebraic topics. Those topics are essential in developing many modern decision-making techniques, such as computer programming, operations research, and statistical methods. The techniques have been used very extensively in recent years to solve various complicated business and economic problems.

The topics included in this chapter are sets and subsets (Section 4.1), counting procedures (Section 4.2), and probabilities (Section 4.3). The concept of sets and subsets is basic in modern mathematics. The fundamental theories of many branches of mathematics are now commonly expressed in the language of sets. Probability theory, introduced here, is one of the branches based on set theory. Probabilities are fundamental to statistical decision theory applicable to business problems. The counting procedures are included in this chapter because they are useful in computing probabilities.

4.1 SETS AND SUBSETS

This section introduces the meaning of sets, the methods of specifying sets, and the operations with sets. The algebra of sets is frequently referred to as *Boolean Algebra*, in honor of the English mathematician George Boole (1815–64).

A. The Meaning of Sets

We often use the word *set* to represent a group of things having some common property, such as a set of books, a set of tools, and a set of golf clubs. Similarly, in mathematics a set is used to represent a *well-defined* collection of objects, things, numbers, or symbols. A member of a set is called an *element* of the set. Each element of a set must be well-defined; that is, we must be able to tell without any doubt whether or not a given object belongs to that set. For example, a set may consist of the three numbers (or elements) 5, 7, and 9.

A set may be *finite* or *infinite*. If the number of elements in a set is limited, or can be expressed by a positive number, the set is finite. If the number of elements in a set is unlimited, the set is infinite.

EXAMPLE 1 The following collections are regarded as finite sets:

1. The members of a fraternity (such as 20 members)
2. The students in a mathematics class (such as 30 students)
3. The integers above 1 but less than 5 (namely, 2, 3, and 4)
4. The even numbers larger than 4 but smaller than 12 (namely, 6, 8, and 10)

EXAMPLE 2 The following collections are regarded as infinite sets:

1. The stars in the universe (unlimited stars)
2. The people in the past, present, and future (unlimited people)
3. The integers above 1 (namely, 2, 3, 4, . . .)
4. The numbers below 1 (such as .1, .01, .001, . . .)

A set that has no elements is called an *empty set* or a *null set*, and is denoted by the symbol ϕ (the Greek letter phi, pronounced fī). The role of the empty set in the algebra of sets is similar to that of zero in the decimal number system.

EXAMPLE 3 The following collections are regarded as empty sets:

1. The trees over 50 miles tall
2. The students over 1,000 years old now attending college
3. The even integers above 4 but below 6
4. The odd integers above 1 but below 3

There are also a *universal set* and *subsets*. The universal set, usually denoted by U, is the total collection of all elements under consideration in a given problem. A universal set may have many *subsets*. The relationship between a universal set and its subsets may clearly be shown by a diagram, called a *Venn diagram*, in honor of the English logician John Venn (1834–83).

EXAMPLE 4 Let U = the set of all students in a college
A = the set of all freshmen in the college
B = the set of all sophomores in the college

The Venn diagram is shown below:

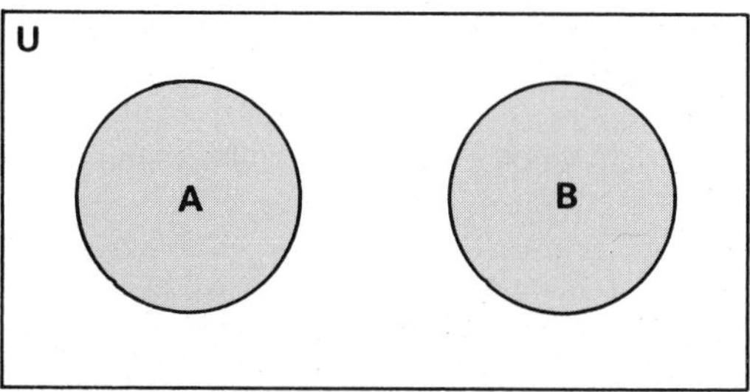

If every element of a set is also an element of another set, we then say that the former is a subset of the latter. Observe the diagram in the preceding example. The total area of the rectangle represents the set of all students in the college, or the universal set. Since every element of set A (a freshman) is also an element of set U (a student in the college), set A is a subset of the universal set U. Also, B is a subset of U. Similarly, we may reason that a set is a subset of itself, such as U is a subset of U. In addition, the empty set ϕ is a subset of every set.

B. Methods of Specifying Sets

It is customary to use a capital letter to indicate a set and to specify all elements within braces. There are two basic methods of specifying the elements of a set:

1. *List* the names of all elements of the set. This method is convenient when the number of elements of the set is not too large.
2. *Describe* a rule by which all elements of the set can be determined.

EXAMPLE 5 The grades of the five students in Professor Minton's class are expressed as set A by the listing method below:

$A = \{80, 85, 88, 90, 95\}$

EXAMPLE 6 The integers above 3 but less than 6,150 are expressed as set B by the description method as follows:

$B = \{x \mid x \text{ is an integer and } 3 < x < 6{,}150\}$

The above expression may be read: "B is the set of all elements x such that x is an integer and x is larger than 3 but less than 6,150."

C. Operations with Sets

There are three basic operations with sets: *union*, *intersection*, and the *complement*. The operations with sets may be performed or reasoned in a manner similar to the basic operations (addition, subtraction, multiplication, and division) in ordinary algebra. Let A and B represent two subsets of the universal set U. The three basic operations may be conveniently illustrated by using a Venn diagram of the subsets and the universal set.

(1) UNION

The union of sets A and B is denoted by the set $A \cup B$ (read: A union B, or A cup B), which contains all elements of U that belong either to A or to B or to both. The set $A \cup B$ is also called the *sum* of sets A and B and written $A + B$. We shall use the symbol $\cup$ in this text. The sum is indicated by the shaded area in each of the following Venn diagrams.

Case (a) Case (b) Case (c)

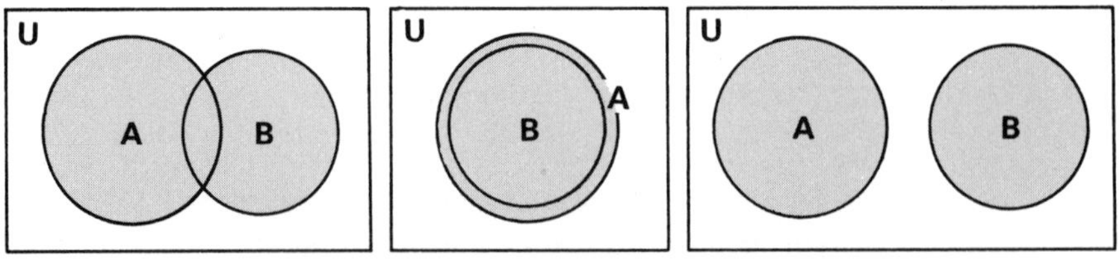

U A B

U B A

U A B

Observe that every element of A belongs to $A \cup B$; also, every element of B belongs to $A \cup B$.

EXAMPLE 7 Let all (8) students in a classroom be the universal set, or

$U = \{\text{Alan, Dale, Larry, Stevie, Peter, Betty, Nancy, Mary}\}$

Also, let all (6) students in the classroom who are majoring in English be set A, or

$A = \{\text{Alan, Dale, Larry, Stevie, Betty, Nancy}\}$

and all (3) girls in the classroom be set B, or

$B = \{\text{Betty, Nancy, Mary}\}$

Then

$A \cup B = \{\text{Alan, Dale, Larry, Stevie, Betty, Nancy, Mary}\}$

$A \cup B$ represents the set of all (7) students in the classroom who either are majoring in English or are girls. Note that Betty and Nancy are not listed twice in the set $A \cup B$ and that Peter does not fit in either set A or B. See Case (a) in the preceding diagram.

EXAMPLE 8 Let $U = \{x \mid x \text{ is an integer and } 5 < x < 20\}$
$A = \{6, 8, 9, 12, 18, 19\}$
$B = \{7, 11\}$

Then

$A \cup B = \{6, 7, 8, 9, 11, 12, 18, 19\}$

[See Case (c) in the preceding diagram.]

Similarly, for any set A, we have $A \cup \phi = A$.

(2) INTERSECTION

The intersection of sets A and B is denoted by the set $A \cap B$ (read: A intersect B, or A cap B), which contains all elements of U that belong to both A and B. The set $A \cap B$ is also called the *product* of sets A and B and written $A \cdot B$. We shall use the symbol $\cap$ in this text. The product is indicated by the shaded area in each of the Venn diagrams below.

Case (a)

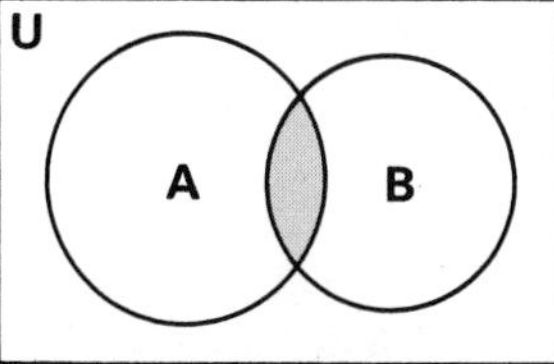

Case (b)

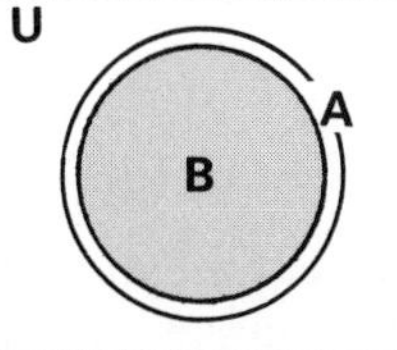

Case (c)

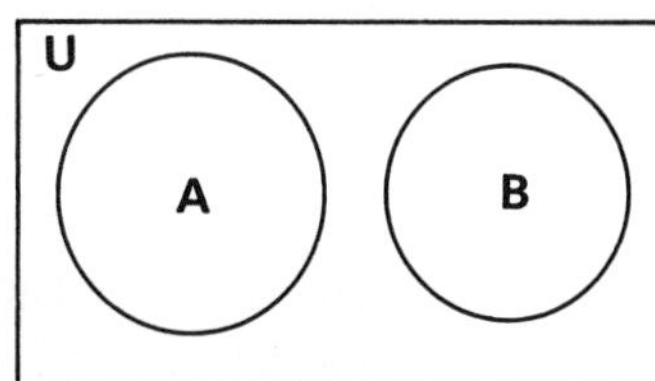

Observe that every element that belongs to both A and B belongs to $A \cap B$. Note that $A \cap B$ is an empty set in Case (c) above, since there are no elements that belong to both A and B. Sets A and B in Case (c) are said to be *disjoint* or *mutually exclusive*.

EXAMPLE 9

Refer to Example 7. Find the set $A \cap B$.

$A \cap B = \{\text{Betty, Nancy}\}$ (see Case (a) in the diagram above)

$A \cap B$ represents the set of all (2) students in the classroom who are majoring in English and are girls.

EXAMPLE 10

Refer to Example 8. Find the set $A \cap B$.

$A \cap B = \phi$ (the empty set) (See Case (c) in the diagram above.)

A and B are disjoint, since their intersection is the empty set. Note that neither 7 nor 11 (elements of set B) is an element of set A.

Similarly, for any set A, we have $A \cap \phi = \phi$.

(3) COMPLEMENT

The complement of set A is denoted by the set A' (read A prime or written $\overline{A}$, $\sim A$, or $\tilde{A}$), which contains all elements of U that do not belong to A. Set A' is indicated by the shaded area in the diagram below:

Complement of A ($= A'$)

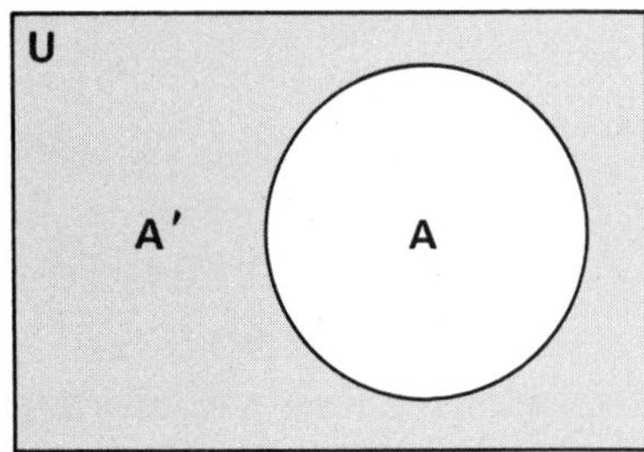

EXAMPLE 11

Refer to Example 7. Find (a) set A' and (b) set B'.

(a) $A' = \{\text{Peter, Mary}\}$
The set A' represents all students in the classroom not majoring in English.

(b) $B' = \{\text{Alan, Dale, Larry, Stevie, Peter}\}$
The set B' represents all students in the classroom who are not girls.

★(4) OTHER OPERATIONS WITH SETS

Operations of Difference (or Subtraction). A set may also be subtracted from another set. In a universal set U, to subtract B from A, denoted by the set $A - B$, is to find the difference between A and B. The difference is obtained by taking all elements that belong both to B and to A away from A. The set $A - B$ is shown by the shaded area in each of the diagrams following. Note the difference between Case (b) and Case (d).

Case (a)

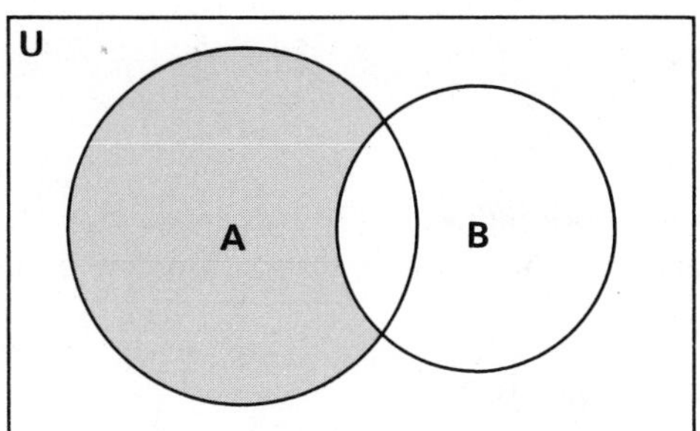

Case (b)

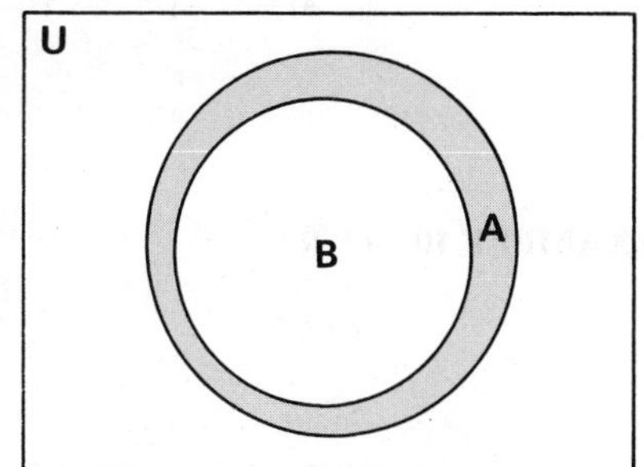

Case (c)

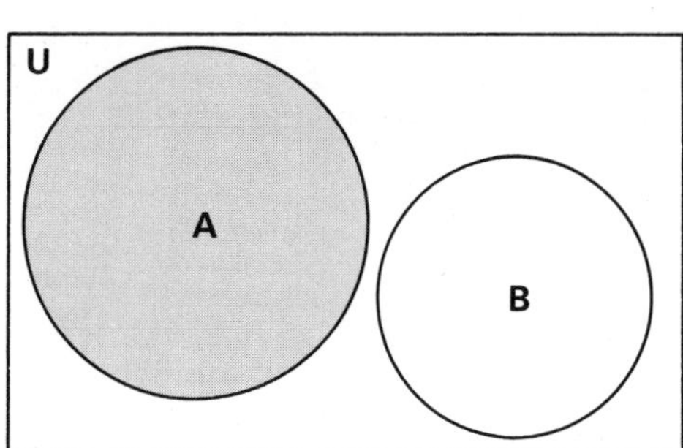

Case (d) $A - B = \phi$

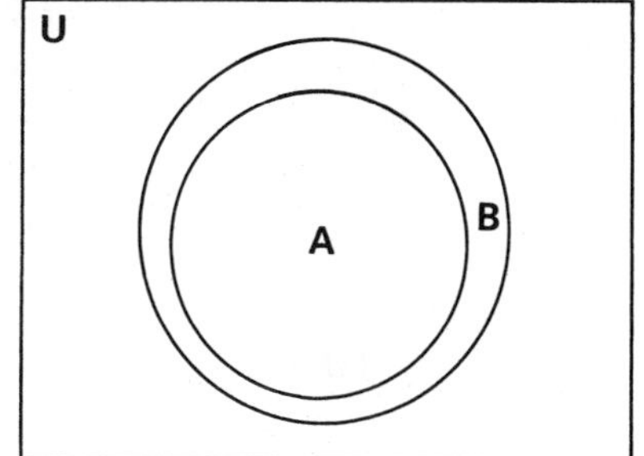

Observe that every element that belongs to $A - B$ belongs to both A and B'. In other words,

set $A - B$ = set $A \cap B'$

Since the subtraction operation $(A - B)$ may be replaced by the combined operations of intersection and complement $(A \cap B')$, it is generally not regarded as a basic operation in the algebra of sets.

EXAMPLE 12 Let

$$U = \{1, 2, 3, 4, 5, 6, 7, 8, 9, 10\}$$
$$A = \{1, 2, 4, 5\}$$
$$B = \{2, 3, 5, 6\}$$

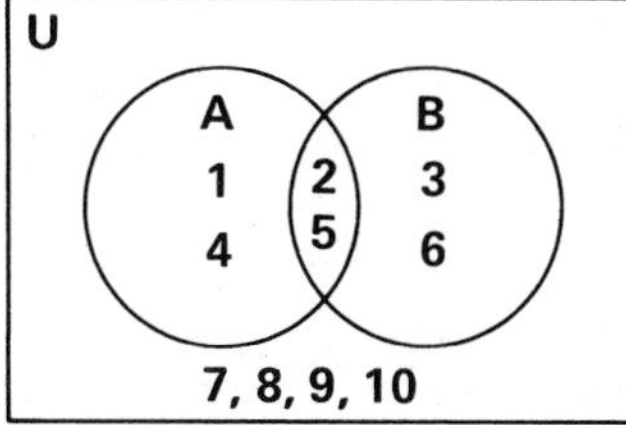

Find (a) $A - B$ and (b) $B - A$.

(a) $A - B = \{1, 4\}$, or
$A - B = A \cap B' = \{1, 4\}$, where $B' = \{1, 4, 7, 8, 9, 10\}$

(b) $B - A = \{3, 6\}$, or
$B - A = B \cap A' = \{3, 6\}$, where $A' = \{3, 6, 7, 8, 9, 10\}$

Operations with Three or More Subsets. The operations with sets or subsets presented above may be expanded for three or more subsets. Observe the diagram below. We may find:

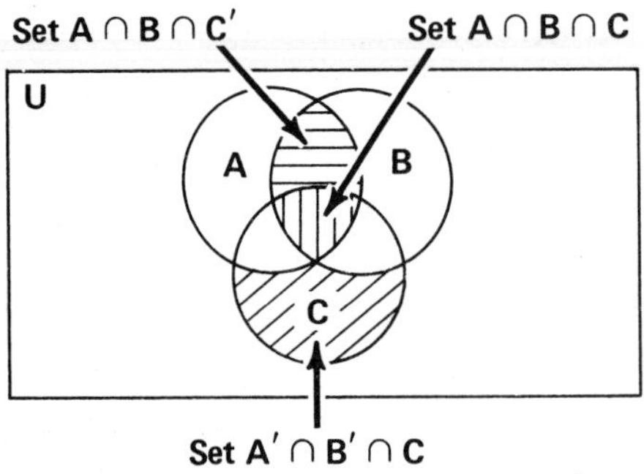

1. The shaded area with vertical lines represents set $A \cap B \cap C$.
2. The shaded area with horizontal lines represents set $A \cap B \cap C'$.
3. The shaded area with diagonal lines represents set $A' \cap B' \cap C$.

EXAMPLE 13 Let $U = \{1, 2, 3, 4, 5, 6, 7, 8, 9, 10\}$
$A = \{1, 2, 4, 5\}$
$B = \{2, 3, 5, 6\}$
$C = \{4, 5, 6, 7, 8\}$

Find the following sets:

(a) $A \cup B \cup C$, (b) $A \cap B \cap C$, (c) $A \cap B \cap C'$, and (d) $A' \cap B' \cap C$.

The elements of each set are written on the diagram below:

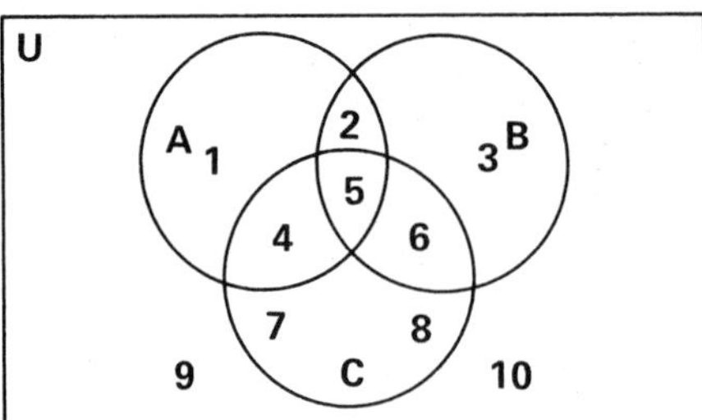

(a) $A \cup B \cup C = \{1, 2, 3, 4, 5, 6, 7, 8\}$
(b) $A \cap B \cap C = \{5\}$
(c) $A \cap B \cap C' = \{2\}$, where $C' = \{1, 2, 3, 9, 10\}$
(d) $A' \cap B' \cap C = \{7, 8\}$, where $A' = \{3, 6, 7, 8, 9, 10\}$ and $B' = \{1, 4, 7, 8, 9, 10\}$

Operations by Postulates. The operations with sets may be performed according to postulates instead of diagrams as illustrated above. Many of the postulates for sets are the same as those for ordinary algebra. Examples are listed below:

1. The commutative laws: $A \cup B = B \cup A$ (or $A + B = B + A$)
   $A \cap B = B \cap A$ (or $A \times B = B \times A$)

2. The associative laws: $(A \cup B) \cup C = A \cup (B \cup C)$ (or $(A + B) + C = A + (B + C)$)
   $(A \cap B) \cap C = A \cap (B \cap C)$ (or $(A \times B) \times C = A \times (B \times C)$)

3. The distributive law: $A \cap (B \cup C) = (A \cap B) \cup (A \cap C)$
   (or $A \times (B + C) = (A \times B) + (A \times C)$)

EXAMPLE 14

Refer to Example 13. Find the set $A \cap (B \cup C)$ by the distributive law.

Since $A \cap B = \{2, 5\}$ and $A \cap C = \{4, 5\}$

then $A \cap (B \cup C) = (A \cap B) \cup (A \cap C) = \{2, 5\} \cup \{4, 5\} = \{2, 4, 5\}$

This answer may be checked by observing the diagram in Example 13.

EXERCISE 4-1 REFERENCE: SECTION 4.1

1. Determine whether each of the following collections is a finite set, an infinite set, or an empty set:

   (a) The living members of your immediate family
   (b) The points on a straight line
   (c) The Martians discovered on the earth
   (d) The integers above 10 but below 100

2. Determine whether each of the following collections is a finite set, an infinite set, or an empty set:

   (a) The chairs in a classroom
   (b) The integers above 520
   (c) The even integers between 30 and 32
   (d) The numbers between 8 and 14

3. Use both the listing method and the description method to specify the sets given below:

   (a) The first ten letters of the alphabet
   (b) The integers from 2 to 8, inclusive

4. Use either the listing method or the description method to specify each set given below; state your reason for selecting the method in each case:

   (a) The integers above 40
   (b) The students whose names are Adams, Clark, Fink, Jones, and Shaw

5. Draw a Venn diagram to show the universal set U and the subsets A and B:
   $U = \{x \mid x \text{ is an integer and } 4 < x < 15\}$
   $A = \{7, 8, 10, 11, 14\}$
   $B = \{5, 6, 12\}$

6. From the information given in Problem 5 above, find the following sets:

   (a) $A \cup B$ (b) $A \cap B$ (c) B' ★(d) $U - B$

7. From the information given in Problem 5 above, find the following sets:

   (a) $A \cup B'$ (b) $A \cap B'$ (c) A' ★(d) $B - A$

8. Draw a Venn diagram to show the universal set U and the subsets A and B:
   $U = \{a, b, c, d, e, f, g, h, i, j, k\}$
   $A = \{a, c, e, g, h, i\}$
   $B = \{a, b, d, e, f\}$

9. From the information given in Problem 8 above, find the following sets:

   (a) $A \cup B$ (b) $A \cap B$ (c) A' (d) $A \cup A'$ ★(e) $A - B$

10. From the information given in Problem 8 above, find the following sets:

   (a) $A \cup U$ (b) $A \cap U$ (c) B' (d) $A \cap A'$ ★(e) $B - A$

★11. Let $U = \{1, 2, 3, 4, 5, 6, 7, 8, 9, 10, 11, 12\}$
   $A = \{1, 2, 3, 5, 6\}$
   $B = \{3, 4, 6, 7\}$
   $C = \{5, 6, 7, 8, 9, 10\}$

   List the elements of each of the following sets:
   (a) $A \cup B$ (c) $A \cap B$ (e) $A \cap B \cap C$ (g) $A' \cap B' \cap C$
   (b) $A - C$ (d) $B \cap C$ (f) $(A \cup B) \cap C$ (h) $A \cap B \cap C'$

★12. From the information given in Problem 11, list the elements of each of the following sets:

   (a) $A \cup C$ (c) $A \cap C$ (e) $(B \cup C) \cap A$ (g) $A \cap B' \cap C'$
   (b) $A - B$ (d) $A \cup B \cup C$ (f) $(A \cup C) \cap B$ (h) $A' \cap B' \cap C'$

★13. Let the area inside the circle be set A; inside the square, set B; and inside the triangle, set C. Shade the area that represents each of the following sets with the type of lines indicated in the parentheses:

   (a) $(A \cap B') \cup C$ (/ / / /)
   (b) $(A - B) - C$ (\ \ \ \)
   (c) $(B - C) \cap A'$ (═══)

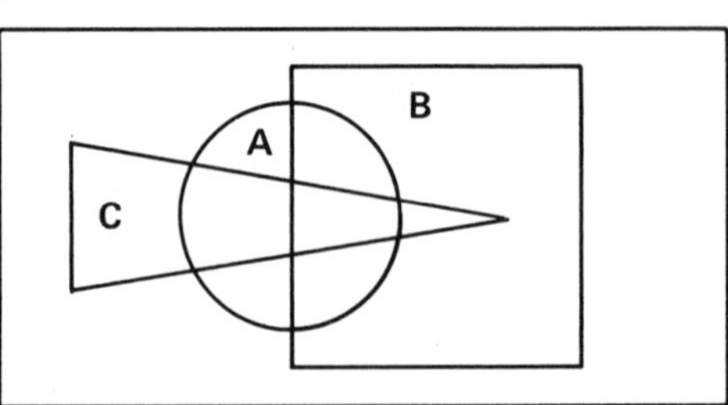

★14. Let the area inside the square be set X; inside the circle, set Y; and inside the triangle, set Z. Shade the area that represents each of the following sets with the type of lines indicated in the parentheses:

(a) $X \cup Y \cup Z$ (/ / / /)
(b) $(Y \cup Z) \cap X$ (\ \ \ \)
(c) $(Z - X) \cap Y'$ ($\equiv$)

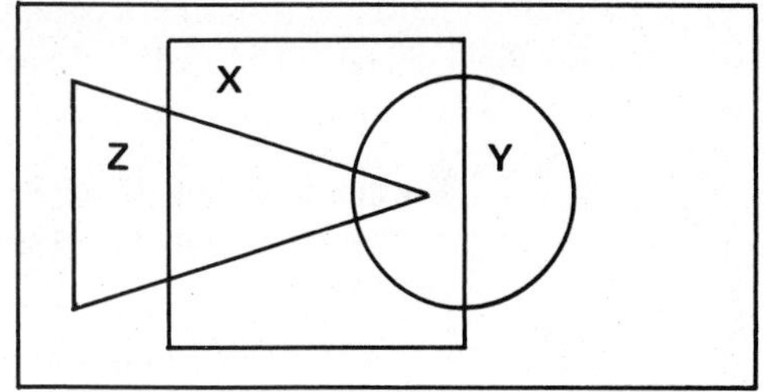

4.2 COUNTING PROCEDURES

This section presents the procedures for counting the number of possible arrangements of the elements (or objects) in a set or sets. The counting procedures may be performed in four ways: the tree diagram, the multiplication principle, permutation, and combination.

A. Tree Diagram

When the number of elements included in a set or sets is small, we can list all the possible arrangements of the elements in the form of a tree, called a *tree diagram*, as shown in the example below.

EXAMPLE 1 A vacationing student wishes to go to Boston from Chicago with a stop in New York City. Assume that he has the following choice of methods of traveling:

Chicago to New York,
represented by set $A = \{\text{plane, train, bus}\}$;

New York to Boston,
represented by set $B = \{\text{plane, bus}\}$.

How many possible ways can the trip be made by the student?

There are six possible ways to make the trip, as shown in the following tree diagram:

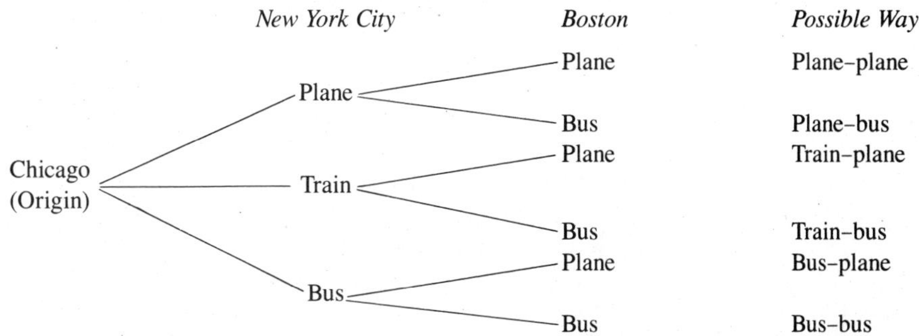

B. The Multiplication Principle

When the number of elements in a set or sets is large, the tree diagram method is not convenient. In such a case, the multiplication principle, which is based on the reasoning method illustrated in Example 1, may be used to compute the number of possible arrangements:

The multiplication principle—If one thing can be performed in *a* ways, a second thing in *b* ways, a third thing in *c* ways, and so on for *n* things, then the *n* things can be performed together in

$a \times b \times c \times \cdots$ (*n* factors) ways.

Example 1 is now computed by the use of the multiplication principle, as follows:

3 (ways from Chicago to New York) × 2 (ways from New York to Boston)
= 6 (ways from Chicago to Boston)

EXAMPLE 2

Let $U = \{a, b, c\}$. What is the total number of possible subsets of U?

According to the multiplication principle, we may use a in 2 ways (*include* it or *do not include* it in the subset); after a we may use b in 2 ways; and after b we may use c in 2 ways. Then, we may use the three letters together in

$2 \times 2 \times 2 = 2^3 = 8$ subsets.

The 8 subsets may also be obtained by the use of a tree diagram:

	First Letter	*Second Letter*	*Third Letter*	*Possible Subsets*
Origin	a	b	c	a, b, c (= universal set)
			0	a, b
		0	c	a, c
			0	a
	0	b	c	b, c
			0	b
		0	c	c
			0	no element (empty set)

0 indicates "do not include the letter in the subset."

C. Permutations

The procedures illustrated in the tree diagram and the multiplication principle provide a general method for counting the number of possible arrangements of elements of a single set or several sets. The formulas developed for permutations and combinations, however, give more convenient counting procedures for the elements of a *single* set.

A permutation is an arrangement of all or part of the elements of a set in a *definite order*. The formulas for computing the total number of permutations of the elements of a set are presented below.

(1) PERMUTATIONS OF DIFFERENT ELEMENTS TAKEN ALL AT A TIME

Let

n = the number of elements in a given set
${}_nP_n$ = the total number of permutations of n elements taken n at a time [It may also be written as $P(n, n)$.]

Then

$$\mathbf{{}_nP_n = n(n-1)(n-2)(n-3)\ldots(2)(1)}$$

or, written simply,

$$\mathbf{{}_nP_n = n!}$$ (Read, "n factorial or factorial n.")

NOTE: When $n = 0$, by definition $0! = 1$.

EXAMPLE 3 What is the total number of permutations of the set of the three letters a, b, and c, taken all at a time?

$n = 3$
${}_nP_n = {}_3P_3 = (3)(2)(1) = 6$

This answer may be checked by the tree diagram, as follows:

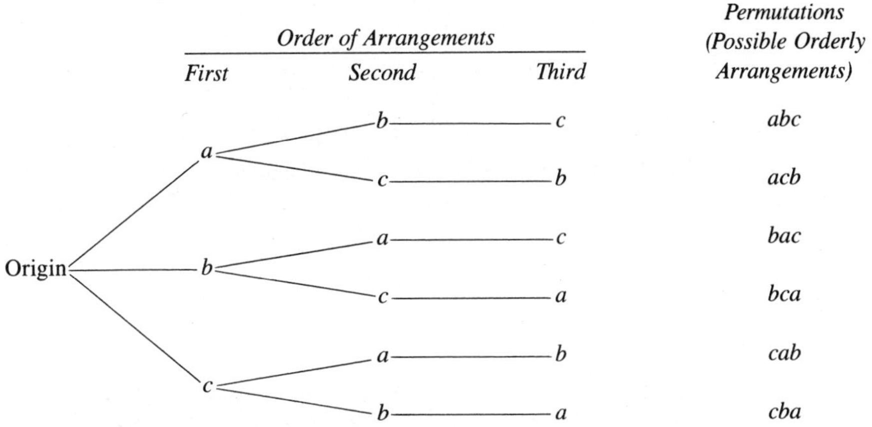

	Order of Arrangements			*Permutations (Possible Orderly Arrangements)*
	First	*Second*	*Third*	
Origin	*a*	*b*	*c*	*abc*
		c	*b*	*acb*
	b	*a*	*c*	*bac*
		c	*a*	*bca*
	c	*a*	*b*	*cab*
		b	*a*	*cba*

The order of each letter in the sequence is important in a permutation. For example, the arrangement *abc* is different from *acb*.

The 6 permutations may also be obtained by the use of the multiplication principle, as follows:

3 (possibilities for the first position) × 2 (possibilities for the second position) × 1 (possibility for the third position) = 6 possible orderly arrangements.

EXAMPLE 4

Additional illustrations:

$_2P_2 = 2! = 2 \times 1 = 2$
$_4P_4 = 4! = 4 \times 3 \times 2 \times 1 = 24$
$_6P_6 = 6! = 6 \times 5 \times 4 \times 3 \times 2 \times 1 = 720$

(2) PERMUTATIONS OF DIFFERENT ELEMENTS TAKEN A PART AT A TIME

Let

$n =$ the number of elements in a given set
$r =$ the number of elements taken at a time for each permutation
$_nP_r =$ the total number of permutations of n elements taken r at a time [It may also be written as $P(n, r)$.]

Then

$$_nP_r = n(n-1)(n-2)(n-3)\ldots(n-r+1) \quad \text{for } r \text{ factors}$$

or, written simply,

$$_nP_r = \frac{n!}{(n-r)!}$$

EXAMPLE 5

What is the total number of permutations of the set of the three letters a, b, and c, taken two at a time?

Here $n = 3$ and $r = 2$.

$_nP_r = {_3P_2} = (3)(2) = 6$, or

$$_nP_r = \frac{n!}{(n-r)!} = \frac{3!}{(3-2)!} = \frac{3 \times 2 \times 1}{1} = 3 \times 2 = 6$$

Also, see the tree diagram in Example 7.

EXAMPLE 6

Three persons enter a car containing five seats. In how many ways can they be seated?

The total number of seating arrangements for five seats taken three at a time is

$_nP_r = {_5P_3} = (5)(4)(3) = 60$, or

$$= \frac{5!}{(5-3)!} = \frac{5 \times 4 \times 3 \times 2 \times 1}{2 \times 1} = 5 \times 4 \times 3 = 60$$

Note that when the multiplication principle is used, this example can be computed in the following manner:

5 (seats available for the first person) $\times$ 4 (seats available for the second person) $\times$ 3 (seats available for the third person) $=$ 60 seating arrangements.

D. Combinations

A combination is a collection of all or part of the elements of a single set *without regard to the order* of the elements. The possible arrangements from the set of letters a and b are ab and ba. The arrangements ab and ba are considered as two different permutations; but they are considered as only one combination. Thus, the total number of possible combinations of a set of elements taken all at a time is always 1.

The total number of possible combinations of a set of n different elements taken r (part of n) at a time, denoted by ${}_nC_r$, may be obtained as follows:

$${}_nC_r = \frac{{}_nP_r}{r!}$$

$$= \frac{n(n-1)(n-2)\ldots\text{for } r \text{ factors}}{r(r-1)(r-2)\ldots 1}, \quad \text{or, written simply,}$$

$${}_nC_r = \frac{n!}{r!(n-r)!}$$

where $r!$ represents the total number of permutations with the same r elements. The $r!$ permutations are considered as one combination.

Note that the symbol ${}_nC_r$ is sometimes written as $C(n, r)$ or $\binom{n}{r}$.

EXAMPLE 7 What is the total number of possible combinations of the set of the three letters a, b, and c, taken two at a time?

Here $n = 3$ and $r = 2$.

$${}_nC_r = {}_3C_2 = \frac{{}_3P_2}{2!} = \frac{3 \times 2}{2 \times 1} = 3, \text{ or}$$

$${}_nC_r = \frac{n!}{r!(n-r)!} = \frac{3!}{2!(3-2)!} = \frac{3 \times 2 \times 1}{2 \times 1 \times 1} = 3$$

Example 7 is diagrammed as follows to illustrate the combination formula:

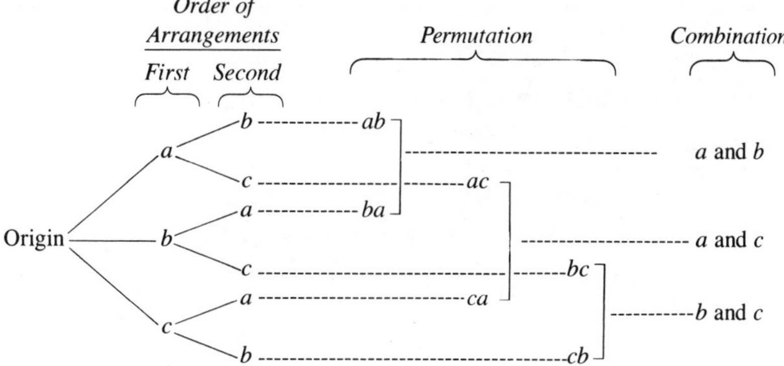

Observe that the total number of permutations of 3 letters taken 2 letters at a time is

$${}_3P_2 = 3 \times 2 = 6$$

The total number of permutations of the *same* 2 letters taken all at a time is

$${}_2P_2 = 2! = 2 \times 1 = 2$$

such as *ab* and *ba* from letters *a* and *b*. Permutations with the same letters are considered as only one combination. Therefore, the total number of combinations is

$$\frac{{}_3P_2}{2!} = \frac{6}{2} = 3$$

EXAMPLE 8 A club has 15 members. (a) Three members are to be chosen to fill the positions of manager, assistant manager, and treasurer. In how many ways can the positions be filled? (b) Three members are to be chosen to form a committee. In how many ways can the committee be formed?

(a) The order of arrangement is taken into consideration in this case. For example, the set of manager A, assistant manager B, and treasurer C is different from the set of manager C, assistant manager A, and treasurer B. Thus, this is a permutation problem:

$${}_{15}P_3 = 15 \times 14 \times 13 = 2{,}730 \text{ ways}$$

(b) The order of arrangement is disregarded in this case. For example, the set of committee members Adams, Brown, and Clark is the same as the set of committee members Clark, Adams, and Brown. Thus, this is a combination problem:

$${}_{15}C_3 = \frac{15 \times 14 \times 13}{3 \times 2 \times 1} = \frac{2{,}730}{6} = 455 \text{ ways}$$

When r is larger than $n - r$, we may use the following expression to simplify the computation for a combination:

$${}_nC_r = {}_nC_{n-r}$$

EXAMPLE 9 Compute (a) ${}_3C_2$ and (b) ${}_{50}C_{47}$.

(a) ${}_3C_2 = {}_3C_{3-2} = {}_3C_1 = \frac{3}{1} = 3$ (Also see the solution of Example 7.)

(b) ${}_{50}C_{47} = {}_{50}C_{50-47} = {}_{50}C_3 = \frac{50 \times 49 \times 48}{3 \times 2 \times 1} = 19{,}600$

EXERCISE 4-2 REFERENCE: SECTION 4.2

1. Calculate:

   (a) ${}_{10}P_3$; ${}_8P_4$; ${}_5P_3$; ${}_6P_6$.
   (b) ${}_5C_3$; ${}_6C_2$; ${}_8C_0$; ${}_{300}C_{298}$.

2. Calculate:

   (a) ${}_{11}P_2$; ${}_7P_3$; ${}_6P_4$; ${}_{15}P_0$.
   (b) ${}_{10}C_3$; ${}_7C_5$; ${}_5C_5$; ${}_{100}C_{97}$.

3. Let the universal set $U = \{k, l, m, n\}$. Find the total number of possible subsets of U.
4. Let the universal set $U = \{a, b, c, d, e\}$. Find the total number of possible subsets of U.
5. A traveling salesperson in city W plans to go to city Z with stops in cities X and Y. There are 3 highways from W to X, 4 highways from X to Y, and 2 highways from Y to Z. In how many ways can the trip be made?
6. How many unique automobile license plates can be produced if two different letters of the alphabet are printed on each plate, followed by a 3-digit number from 100 through 999?

7. Find the total number of possible permutations from the set of letters a, b, c, and d taken (a) all at a time, and (b) two at a time.
8. Find (a) the number of 3-letter groups and (b) the number of 4-letter groups that can be formed from the letters of the word *special*.
9. In how many ways can three different books be placed on a shelf?
10. In how many ways can 5 students be seated in a classroom with 10 chairs?
11. A car containing six seats is being used by six persons for a trip. In how many ways can the persons be seated if only three of them can drive?
12. Find how many 3-digit numbers can be formed from the digits 1, 2, 3, and 4 (a) if no digits may be repeated in the numbers, and (b) if the digits may be repeated in the numbers.
13. In how many ways can we take a sample of the ages of 5 students from a group of 30 students?
14. A bureau of business research wishes to know the average family income in a city of 1,000 families. If a sample of three families is required, how many possible samples can be taken from the families in the city?
15. Find the total number of combinations of the set of letters a, b, c, and d taken (a) all at a time, (b) 3 at a time, and (c) 0 at a time.
16. What is the total number of combinations of the 26 letters of the alphabet taken (a) all at a time, (b) 2 at a time, and (c) 24 at a time?
17. An association was organized by 12 persons. (a) In how many ways can the offices of president, vice-president, and secretary be filled by the 12 persons? (b) In how many ways can a committee of 4 members be formed by the 12 persons?
18. A restaurant offers mayonnaise, tomato, lettuce, cheese, and pickle as toppings for the ham sandwich. How many different ways can a ham sandwich be made by the restaurant?
19. In how many ways can a coach select a team of 5 from a group of 12 players if (a) two certain players must be included in the team, and (b) no restrictions are made on the selection?
20. A bridge deck of 52 cards has 13 different kinds of 4 cards each. In how many ways can we select 5 cards from the deck if (a) 4 of the 5 cards must be of one kind, and (b) there are no restrictions on the selection?

4.3 PROBABILITY

The idea of probability was originated in gambling games during the 17th century in France. However, the theory of probability has now become one of the most important topics in modern mathematics and statistical decision theory.

The subject of probability deals with the chance of success or failure from a trial or experiment. Let

P = the probability of
A = the event of success from a trial
A' (or not A) = the event of a failure
n = the number of possible outcomes from the trial

h = the number of successful outcomes
$n - h$ = the number of unsuccessful (or failure) outcomes

The probabilities of success and failure can be expressed in ratio forms as follows:

$$\text{Probability of success} = P(A) = \frac{h}{n}$$

$$\text{Probability of failure} = P(A') = \frac{n-h}{n} = 1 - \frac{h}{n} = 1 - P(A)$$

The sum of the probability of success and the probability of failure is always equal to 1, or

$$\mathbf{P(A) + P(A') = 1}$$

Probabilities can be computed under two conditions: (1) We can assume that all the possible outcomes from a trial will occur on an *equally likely* basis. The probability computed under this condition is called *theoretical* or *mathematical* probability. (2) We cannot assume, or we are in doubt, that all the possible outcomes will happen on an equally likely basis. The computation of the probability of the event under such a condition thus must be based on our experiences, experiments, or statistical data of what has happened on similar occasions in the past. This type of probability is called *empirical* or *statistical* probability.

A. Computing Theoretical Probability

In a trial, we may wish to compute the probability of a single event or that of two or more events occurring. Also, we may perform repeated trials of a single event. The methods of computing the various theoretical probabilities are presented below.

(1) PROBABILITY OF ONE EVENT OCCURRING

Probabilities may be conveniently computed by the use of the theory of sets.

EXAMPLE 1

One ball is drawn at random from a bag containing 4 red balls and 5 white balls. Compute the probability that it is (a) red, (b) not red, (c) white, and (d) black.

Let the possible outcomes from the trial be the universal set U. The universal set has 4 (red balls) + 5 (white balls) = 9 elements, or

$U = \{R, R, R, R, W, W, W, W, W\}$
$n = 9$

(a) Let A = the event of drawing a red ball. The successful outcomes are the 4 red balls, or set

$A = \{R, R, R, R\}$ (A is a subset of U)
$h = 4$

$$P(A) = \frac{h}{n} = \frac{4}{9}$$

(b) Let A' = the event of not drawing a red ball. Then

$A' = \{W, W, W, W, W\}$
$n - h = 9 - 4 = 5$

$$P(A') = \frac{n-h}{n} = \frac{5}{9}, \quad \text{or}$$

$$P(A') = 1 - P(A) = 1 - \frac{4}{9} = \frac{5}{9}$$

(c) Let B = the event of drawing a white ball. The successful outcomes are the 5 white balls, or set

$$B = \{W, W, W, W, W\}$$

$$P(B) = \frac{h}{n} = \frac{5}{9}$$

(d) Let C = the event of drawing a black ball. Since there are no black balls in the bag, this set is an empty set. Thus, set

$$C = \phi, \quad \text{or} \quad h = 0; \qquad P(C) = \frac{0}{9} = 0$$

(2) PROBABILITY OF TWO OR MORE EVENTS

Two or more events may be (a) mutually exclusive (disjoint), (b) intersected, (c) independent, or (d) dependent.

Mutually Exclusive (or Disjoint) Events. Two or more events are mutually exclusive if the events cannot occur together. In other words, the occurrence of any one of the events precludes the occurrences of the others.

Let A and B be mutually exclusive events, as shown in the following Venn diagram:

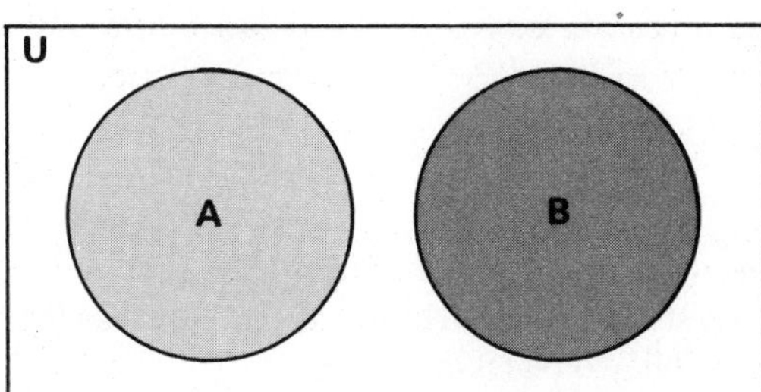

Then, the probability of event A or B is the sum of the probability of A and that of B, or

$$\mathbf{P(A \text{ or } B) = P(A) + P(B)}$$

Observe that events A and B are subsets of the universal set U. The two subsets have no elements in common. Thus they are *disjoint* subsets.

EXAMPLE 2

What is the probability that one throw of a die will yield either 2 or 4?

Let A = the event yielding 2
B = the event yielding 4

The two events are mutually exclusive, since *one* throw of a die cannot yield *both* 2 and 4 on the top.

$U = \{1, 2, 3, 4, 5, 6\}$, or $n = 6$ (sides of a die, or 6 possible outcomes or elements)
$A = \{2\}$, or $h = 1$ (successful outcome or 1 element)

$$P(A) = \frac{h}{n} = \frac{1}{6}$$

$B = \{4\}$, or $h = 1$ (element)

$$P(B) = \frac{h}{n} = \frac{1}{6}$$

Thus, $P(A \text{ or } B) = P(A) + P(B) = \frac{1}{6} + \frac{1}{6} = \frac{2}{6} = \frac{1}{3}$

Intersected Events. Two or more events are intersected if the events have some elements in common. Let A and B be intersected events, as shown in the following Venn diagram:

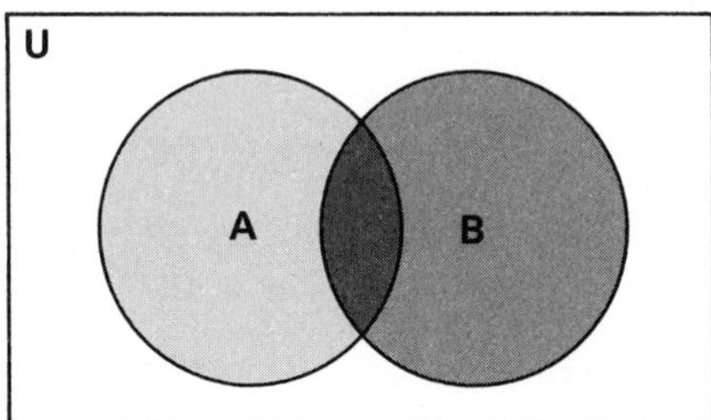

Observe that the area with the darkest shading represents the elements in the intersection of subsets A and B. The probability of the events occurring for the common elements is denoted by $P(A \text{ and } B)$. Since it belongs to $P(A)$ and also to $P(B)$, one $P(A \text{ and } B)$ must be subtracted from the sum of $P(A)$ and $P(B)$ to avoid counting it twice. The probability of the intersected events *A or B* thus is:

$$\mathbf{P(A \text{ or } B) = P(A) + P(B) - P(A \text{ and } B)}$$

EXAMPLE 3 In a group of 15 students, 7 are boys and 8 are girls; 3 of the boys and 2 of the girls are taking algebra. If one student is selected from the group at random, find the probability that the student is a boy or is taking algebra.

This example is diagrammed below:

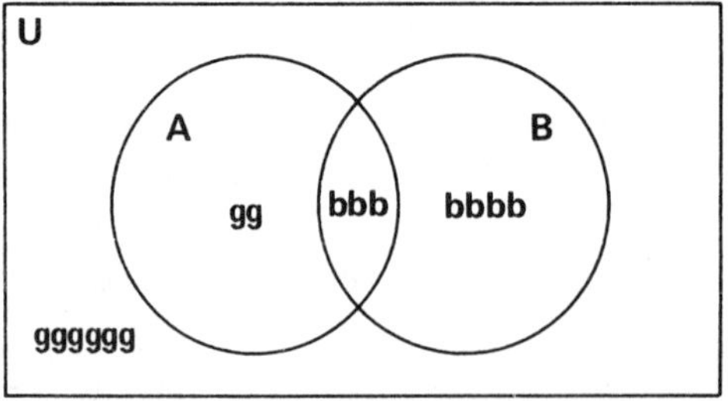

Let $U = \{b, b, b, b, b, b, b, g, g, g, g, g, g, g, g\}$, or 15 elements
A = the event of taking algebra

set $A = \{b, b, b, g, g\}$, or 5 elements
$B =$ the event of selecting a boy
set $B = \{b, b, b, b, b, b, b\}$, or 7 elements

Observe that 3 elements (boys) belong to set A and also to set B. The intersection of sets A and B, denoted by the set $A \cap B$, or set "A and B," is

A and $B = \{b, b, b\}$

Thus

$$P(A \text{ or } B) = P(A) + P(B) - P(A \text{ and } B) = \frac{5}{15} + \frac{7}{15} - \frac{3}{15} = \frac{9}{15} = \frac{3}{5}$$

Independent Events. Two or more events are independent if the happenings of the events in no way affect each other. Thus, if A and B are independent events, the occurrence of event A has no effect on the occurrence of event B. The probability that both independent events A and B will occur is based on the multiplication principle, as follows:

$$\boldsymbol{P(A \text{ and } B) = P(A) \cdot P(B)}$$

EXAMPLE 4 One ball is drawn at random from a bag containing 4 red balls and 5 white balls. A second ball is drawn after the first is replaced into the bag. What is the probability that both balls drawn will be red?

Since the second ball is drawn after the first ball is replaced, the result of the first drawing obviously has nothing to do with the second drawing. Therefore, the two drawings are independent events.

Here, $U = \{R, R, R, R, W, W, W, W, W\}$, or 9 elements.
Let $A =$ the event of the first drawing that will yield a red ball
set $A = \{R, R, R, R\}$, or 4 elements
$B =$ the event of the second drawing that will yield a red ball

Then

set $B = \{R, R, R, R\}$, or 4 elements

$$P(A \text{ and } B) = P(A) \cdot P(B) = \frac{4}{9} \cdot \frac{4}{9} = \frac{16}{81}$$

Dependent Events. If the occurrence of a second event depends on the occurrence of the first event, the two events are called dependent. Thus, A and B are dependent events when the occurrence of B depends on the occurrence of A. The probability of event B depending on the occurrence of event A is called *conditional probability*, which is written:

$P(B \mid A)$ or $P_A(B)$ (Read, "the probability of B, given A.")

The probability that both the dependent events A and B will occur is based on the multiplication principle, as follows:

$$\boldsymbol{P(A \text{ and } B) = P(A) \cdot P(B \mid A)}$$

EXAMPLE 5 Refer to Example 4. Assume that the first ball is not replaced in the bag before the second ball is drawn. What is the probability that in the two drawings both balls will be red?

Since the first ball is not replaced for the second draw, the result of the first drawing affects the result of the second drawing. Thus, the two drawings are dependent events. In the first drawing,

set $U = \{R, R, R, R, W, W, W, W, W\}$, or 9 elements

Let A = the event of the first drawing that will yield a red ball
set $A = \{R, R, R, R\}$, or 4 elements

$$P(A) = \frac{4}{9}$$

In the second drawing,

set $U = \{R, R, R, W, W, W, W, W\}$, or 8 elements, since the first ball, which is red, is not replaced

Let B = the event of the second drawing that will yield a red ball
set $B = \{R, R, R\}$, or 3 elements

$$P(B \mid A) = \frac{3}{8}$$

The probability that both balls of the two drawings are red is

$$P(A \text{ and } B) = P(A) \cdot P(B \mid A) = \frac{4}{9} \times \frac{3}{8} = \frac{12}{72} = \frac{1}{6}$$

NOTE: The above solution may also be obtained by the use of the combination formula, as follows:

The number of successful outcomes from 4 red balls taken 2 at a time is

$${}_4C_2 = \frac{4!}{2!(4-2)!} = \frac{4 \times 3}{2 \times 1} = 6$$

The number of possible outcomes from 9 balls taken 2 at a time is

$${}_9C_2 = \frac{9 \times 8}{2 \times 1} = 36$$

$$P(A \text{ and } B) = \frac{{}_4C_2}{{}_9C_2} = \frac{6}{36} = \frac{1}{6}$$

★(3) REPEATED TRIALS

Let

$p = P(A)$, the probability that event A will happen in a single trial
$q = P(A')$, the probability that event A will *not* happen in the single trial, or
$q = 1 - p$

Then, the probability that event A will happen exactly r times in n repeated trials is[1]

$$\mathbf{P(\text{exactly } r \text{ times})} = {}_nC_r \cdot p^r \cdot q^{n-r}$$

[1]This is the general expression of the $(r + 1)$th term of the binomial theorem. See footnote on page 85.

Note that the outcome of a trial referred to here is not affected by that of any other trial; that is, the *events are independent*.

EXAMPLE 6 A bag contains 4 red balls and 5 white balls. One ball is drawn and is replaced after each drawing. In two repeated drawings, find the probability that the drawings will yield (a) exactly 2 red balls, (b) exactly 1 red ball, and (c) no red ball.

Let A = the event of drawing a red ball in each drawing
A' = the event of not drawing a red ball in each drawing

Then

$$P(A) = p = \frac{4}{9}$$

$$P(A') = q = 1 - p = 1 - \frac{4}{9} = \frac{5}{9}$$

$n = 2$ (repeated drawings)

(a) The probability that event A will occur twice (or $r = 2$ red balls) in the 2 repeated drawings is

$$P(2 \text{ red}) = {}_2C_2 \cdot \left(\frac{4}{9}\right)^2 \cdot \left(\frac{5}{9}\right)^0 = 1 \cdot \left(\frac{16}{81}\right) \cdot 1 = \frac{16}{81} \quad \text{(same as Example 4)}$$

Note that ${}_2C_2 = 1$ represents the number of combinations from 2 (repeated trials) taken 2 (red balls) at a time; that is,

R, R (or the first is red and the second is red)

(b) The probability that event A will occur once (or $r = 1$ red ball) in the 2 repeated drawings is

$$P(1 \text{ red}) = {}_2C_1 \cdot \left(\frac{4}{9}\right)^1 \cdot \left(\frac{5}{9}\right)^1 = 2\left(\frac{20}{81}\right) = \frac{40}{81}$$

Note that ${}_2C_1 = 2$ represents the number of combinations from 2 (repeated trials) taken 1 (red ball) at a time; that is, there are two ways:

R, W (the first is red and the second is white)
W, R (the first is white and the second is red)

(c) The probability that event A will not occur either time, or $r = 0$ (red ball) in the 2 repeated drawings is

$$P(0 \text{ red}) = {}_2C_0 \cdot \left(\frac{4}{9}\right)^0 \cdot \left(\frac{5}{9}\right)^2 = 1 \cdot 1 \cdot \frac{25}{81} = \frac{25}{81}$$

W, W (the first is white, or not red, and the second is also white)

The sum of the probabilities of all possible happenings (2, 1, and 0 red balls) in the 2 repeated trials must be 1.

CHECK

$$P(2 \text{ red}) + P(1 \text{ red}) + P(0 \text{ red}) = \frac{16}{81} + \frac{40}{81} + \frac{25}{81} = \frac{81}{81} = 1$$

★B. Computing Empirical Probability

Computation of empirical probability based on the results of experiments or experiences is illustrated in the following examples.

EXAMPLE 7

A coin is tossed 1,000 times. The results are 497 heads and 503 tails. What is the probability that one toss of the given coin will turn up a head?

Based on the record, the probability that one toss of the coin will turn up a head is

$$P(\text{head}) = \frac{497}{497 + 503} = \frac{497}{1{,}000} = .497$$

The probability based on the theory that the two possible outcomes, head and tail, will occur with equal likelihood is

$$P(\text{head}) = \frac{1}{2} = .5$$

The empirical probability (.497) is very close to the theoretical probability (.5) in this example. In practice, experiments are often used to check the results obtained by theoretical computations.

EXAMPLE 8

Find the probability that a man who is now 30 years old will (a) be alive at age 31, or (b) die before reaching age 31.

In the present case, although we can count exactly the different conditions in which the man will be at age 31, dead or alive, we cannot assume that the two occurrences are *equally likely*. The record concerning similar statistics in the past thus must be used as a basis to compute the probability of a given event.

According to the Commissioners 1958 Standard Ordinary Mortality Table, based on the experience of life insurance companies for the years from 1950 to 1954 (Table 12 in the Appendix), 9,460,165 out of 9,480,358 men now aged 30 will be alive at age 31. Thus,

$$\text{(a) } P(\text{the man will be alive at age 31}) = \frac{9{,}460{,}165}{9{,}480{,}358} = .99787$$

$$\text{(b) } P(\text{the man will die before age 31}) = \frac{9{,}480{,}358 - 9{,}460{,}165}{9{,}480{,}358}$$

$$= \frac{20{,}193}{9{,}480{,}358} = .00213$$

CHECK

(a) + (b) = .99787 + .00213 = 1

The death rate per 1,000 men is .00213 × 1,000 = 2.13 men. The rate is shown in the 4th column of Table 12 in the Appendix.

Note that the empirical probability is usually based on a large number of occurrences or trials in an experiment.

EXERCISE 4-3 REFERENCE: SECTION 4.3

1. A box contains 6 black chips and 17 yellow chips. One chip is drawn at random from the box. Find the probability that it is (a) black, (b) not black, (c) yellow, (d) black or yellow, and (e) red.
2. A group of children consists of 10 boys and 11 girls. One child is selected at random from the group. Find the probability that the person is (a) a boy, (b) not a boy, (c) a girl, (d) a boy or a girl, and (e) an adult.

3. A group of 400 students contains 120 students who read the *New York Times* and 75 students who read the *Wall Street Journal*. Among the readers, 30 students read both the *New York Times* and the *Wall Street Journal*. A student is chosen at random from the group. Find the probability that the student reads either the *New York Times* or the *Wall Street Journal*.
4. A college has 195 teachers. There are 58 teachers who can speak French, 40 who can speak German, and 33 who can speak both French and German. A teacher is chosen at random from the college. What is the probability that the teacher can speak either French or German?
5. In a group of 35 employees, 6 of the 23 women and 7 of the 12 men are working in the business office. If one employee is selected at random from the group, what is the probability that the employee is (a) a woman, (b) a man, (c) working in the business office, (d) a man or a woman, and (e) a man or working in the business office?
6. One card is drawn at random from a bridge deck of 52 cards. (The deck has 13 different values—2, 3, 4, 5, 6, 7, 8, 9, 10, jack, queen, king, and ace—and each value has 4 suits—spade, heart, diamond, and club.) Find the probability of drawing (a) a spade, (b) a diamond, (c) a face card (face cards are jacks, queens, and kings), (d) a spade or diamond, and (e) a spade or face card.
7. A bag contains 6 black balls and 10 red balls. One ball is drawn at random from the bag. A second ball is drawn after the first is replaced. What is the probability that (a) both balls in the two drawings are black, (b) first a black ball is drawn and then a red ball, (c) one ball is black and one is red, and (d) both are red? Also, find the sum of the probabilities found in (a), (c), and (d). Is the sum equal to 1? Explain.
8. Two dice, one white and the other red, are tossed. Find the probability that (a) both dice are 2 or less, (b) the white die is 2 or less and the red die is more than 2, (c) one is 2 or less and the other is more than 2, (d) both dice are more than 2. Also, find the sum of the probabilities found in (a), (c), and (d). Is the sum equal to 1? Explain.
9. Refer to Problem 7. Suppose that the first ball is not replaced before the second ball is drawn. What is the probability that (a) both balls in the two drawings are black and (b) the first ball is black and the second one is red?
10. One card is drawn at random from a bridge deck of 52 cards. A second card is drawn but the first card is not replaced for the second drawing. Find the probability that (a) both cards are hearts and (b) the first card is a heart and the second card is a spade. (See Problem 6 for the description of the deck of cards.)

★11. A box contains 7 red chips and 3 white chips. One chip is drawn at random and is replaced into the box for the next drawing. In three repeated drawings, find the probability that the drawings will yield (a) 3 red chips, (b) 2 red chips, (c) 1 red chip, and (d) 0 red chips. Is the sum of the probabilities equal to 1?

★12. There are 2 girls and 18 boys in a classroom. One student is selected at random and is asked to return to the classroom after each selection. In 5 repeated selections, find the probability that the selections will have (a) exactly 5 girls, (b) exactly 3 girls, and (c) exactly 2 girls.

★13. 125 heads and 875 tails occurred when a coin was tossed 1,000 times. According to the results, find the probability that one toss of the given coin yields a head. Is it a well-balanced coin?

★14. A die is tossed 900 times, of which 150 throws show 4 dots on the top of the die. What is the probability that one toss of the given die will have a 4 based on the above results? Do you think that it is an honest die (that is, the occurrences of the six sides of the die are equally likely)?

★15. What is the probability that a person who is now 20 years old will (a) be alive at age 21, and (b) die before reaching age 21?

★16. Find the probability that a person who is now 40 years old will (a) be alive at age 41, and (b) die before reaching age 41.

★17. Compute the probability that a person who is now 80 years old will (a) be alive at age 81, and (b) die before reaching age 81.

★18. Determine the probability that a person who is now 90 years of age will (a) be alive at age 91, and (b) die before reaching age 91.

5 ★MODERN ALGEBRA—SUPPLEMENTAL TOPICS

The topics included in this chapter are very useful for computer programming in solving many complicated problems by the utilization of modern high-speed electronic computers. They have become increasingly important in recent years. The topics are: the basic concepts and operations related to matrix algebra (Sections 5.1 to 5.5), linear programming (Section 5.6), and the binary number system (Section 5.7). Matrix algebra includes operations with vectors and matrices, evaluating determinants, finding the inverse of a square matrix, and solving linear equations. Linear programming uses inequalities and equations to find optimum solutions for many types of business problems, such as maximizing profits and minimizing costs. The binary number system can be used to represent data within electronic computers. In addition, the metric system (Section 5.8), which is a decimal system of weights and measures, is also included here since it is used more extensively in the United States at the present time.

5.1 VECTORS

A vector is an ordered collection of numbers. The numbers may be arranged either in a row or in a column and enclosed in brackets [ ] or in boldfaced parentheses ( ). In general, vectors are represented by lowercase letters, such as a, b, c, and so on.

For example, vectors a and b are *row vectors*:

$$a = [1, 7]; \qquad b = [6, 4]$$

and c and d are *column vectors*:

$$c = \begin{bmatrix} 2 \\ 5 \\ 9 \end{bmatrix}; \qquad d = \begin{bmatrix} 3 \\ 8 \\ 4 \end{bmatrix}$$

The above vectors may be applied to a practical problem, as follows:

Company *R* has two plants: #1 and #2. Each plant manufactures products *X* and *Y*. The production of the products during a given period by each plant is shown in Table 5–1. (See vectors *a* and *b*.) Each product is made of three different types of raw material, M-1, M-2, and M-3. The material required by each product is shown in Table 5–2. (See vectors *c* and *d*.)

Table 5–1 Company *R*—Production by Plants
(Row vectors *a* and *b*)

Product	*Plant*	
	#1	*#2*
X	1 unit	7 units
Y	6	4
Total	7	11

Table 5–2 Company *R*—Material Requirements by Products
(Column vectors *c* and *d*)

Type of material	*Product*		*Total*
	X	*Y*	
M-1	2 lb	3 lb	5 lb
M-2	5	8	13
M-3	9	4	13

The numbers in the rows or columns are also known as the *components* of the vectors. Thus, *a* and *b* are two-component row vectors, and *c* and *d* are three-component column vectors. The concept of components is important in the basic vector operations: addition, subtraction, and multiplication.

A. Addition

Vectors with the same number of components and the same arrangement may be added. The corresponding components of the vectors are added to obtain the components of the sum. The sum is also a vector with the same arrangement as the given vectors.

EXAMPLE 1

(a) Add the two-component row vectors *a* and *b*.

$$a + b = [1, 7] + [6, 4] = [1 + 6, 7 + 4] = [7, 11] \quad \text{(see the Total row of Table 5–1)}$$

(b) Add the three-component column vectors *c* and *d*.

$$c + d = \begin{bmatrix} 2 \\ 5 \\ 9 \end{bmatrix} + \begin{bmatrix} 3 \\ 8 \\ 4 \end{bmatrix} = \begin{bmatrix} 2+3 \\ 5+8 \\ 9+4 \end{bmatrix} = \begin{bmatrix} 5 \\ 13 \\ 13 \end{bmatrix} \quad \text{(see the Total column of Table 5–2)}$$

B. Subtraction

Vectors with the same number of components and the same arrangement may be subtracted. The corresponding components of the vectors are subtracted to obtain the components of the remainder. The remainder is also a vector with the same arrangement as the given vectors.

EXAMPLE 2

(a) Subtract vector *b* from vector *a*.

$$a - b = [1, 7] - [6, 4] = [1 - 6, 7 - 4] = [-5, 3]$$

(b) Subtract vector *d* from vector *c*.

$$c - d = \begin{bmatrix} 2 \\ 5 \\ 9 \end{bmatrix} - \begin{bmatrix} 3 \\ 8 \\ 4 \end{bmatrix} = \begin{bmatrix} 2 - 3 \\ 5 - 8 \\ 9 - 4 \end{bmatrix} = \begin{bmatrix} -1 \\ -3 \\ 5 \end{bmatrix}$$

C. Multiplication

Multiplication involving vectors is presented in two different cases below.

CASE I. SCALAR MULTIPLICATION

Any real number, called a *scalar* (as opposed to an imaginary number), may be multiplied by a vector. The number must be multiplied by each component of the vector to obtain the components of the product. The product thus is also a vector with the same number of components and the same arrangement as the vector multiplied.

EXAMPLE 3 (a) Multiply 7 by vector $e = \begin{bmatrix} 3 \\ 5 \end{bmatrix}$.

$$7 \cdot e = 7\begin{bmatrix} 3 \\ 5 \end{bmatrix} = \begin{bmatrix} 7 \times 3 \\ 7 \times 5 \end{bmatrix} = \begin{bmatrix} 21 \\ 35 \end{bmatrix}$$

(b) Multiply 2 by vector $f = [1, 3, 7]$.

$$2 \cdot f = 2[1, 3, 7] = [2 \times 1, 2 \times 3, 2 \times 7] = [2, 6, 14]$$

CASE II. MULTIPLICATION OF TWO VECTORS

In multiplying two vectors, a row vector is multiplied by a column vector with the same number of components. Each component of the row vector is multiplied by the corresponding component of the column vector to obtain the partial product. The sum of all partial products, called the *inner product* or *dot product* of the two vectors multiplied, is a *number*, not a vector.

EXAMPLE 4 (a) Multiply the row vector a by the column vector e.

$$a \cdot e = [1, 7]\begin{bmatrix} 3 \\ 5 \end{bmatrix} = (1 \times 3) + (7 \times 5) = 38$$

(b) Multiply the row vector f by the column vector c.

$$f \cdot c = [1, 3, 7]\begin{bmatrix} 2 \\ 5 \\ 9 \end{bmatrix} = (1 \times 2) + (3 \times 5) + (7 \times 9) = 2 + 15 + 63 = 80$$

Note that the row vector is always written first and the column vector second.

Vectors may be shown graphically. A two-component vector, such as $a = [1, 7]$, or its *transposed* column vector $a' = \begin{bmatrix} 1 \\ 7 \end{bmatrix}$, may be represented by a point $(X = 1, Y = 7)$ in a 2-dimensional space based on the system of rectangular coordinates. Figure 5–1, for example, shows the points representing vectors a, b, and $a + b$ on a 2-dimensional space. Likewise, a three-component vector, such as $c = \begin{bmatrix} 2 \\ 5 \\ 9 \end{bmatrix}$, or its transposed row vector $c' = [2, 5, 9]$, may be represented by a point (2, 5, 9) in a 3-dimensional space.

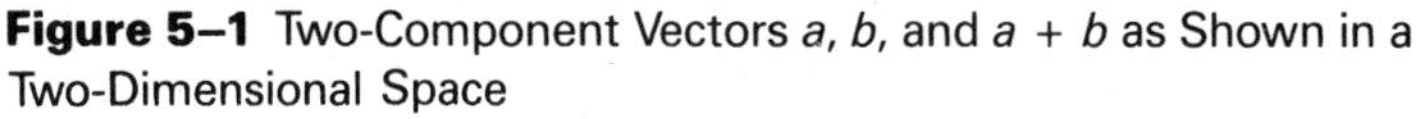

Figure 5–1 Two-Component Vectors a, b, and $a + b$ as Shown in a Two-Dimensional Space

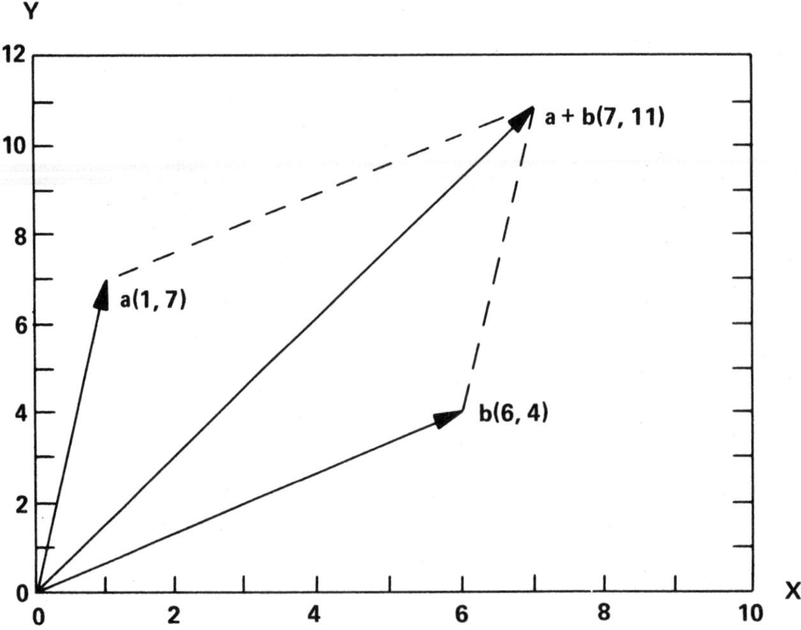

The lines drawn from the origin (0) to the three points (a, b, and $a + b$) show the geometric interpretation of vectors. Vectors may be interpreted as lines representing direction and length.

Note that two vectors are said to be equal if, and only if, both vectors are arranged in the same form (both in rows or both in columns) and their corresponding components are equal. Thus, row vector a is not equal to column vector a', although they are represented by the same point on a graph. This concept is consistent with matrices, presented in the next sections.

ADDITIONAL ILLUSTRATION:

$$a = [1, 7], \qquad a' = \begin{bmatrix} 1 \\ 7 \end{bmatrix}, \qquad g = [7, 1], \qquad h = [1, 7]$$

We have $a = h$, $a \neq a'$, $a \neq g$, $g \neq h$, $a' \neq h$, and $a' \neq g$. (The symbol $\neq$ means "is not equal to.")

5.2 MATRICES

A matrix is a rectangular array of numbers enclosed in brackets or in boldfaced parentheses. In general, matrices are represented by capital letters, such as A, B, C, and D, as shown below:

$$A = \begin{bmatrix} 1 & 7 \\ 6 & 4 \end{bmatrix}, \quad B = \begin{bmatrix} 3 & 2 \\ 5 & 8 \end{bmatrix}, \quad C = \begin{bmatrix} 2 & 3 \\ 5 & 8 \\ 9 & 4 \end{bmatrix}, \quad D = \begin{bmatrix} 6 & 1 \\ 4 & 2 \\ 9 & 7 \end{bmatrix}$$

A matrix is usually described first by its number of rows and then by its number of columns. This type of description is referred to as the *order* of a matrix. In the above illustrations, the order of matrices A and B is 2 by 2, written 2×2, and that of matrices C and D is 3 by 2, written 3×2. In general, let m represent the number of rows and n represent the number of columns of a matrix. Then, the order of a matrix is $m \times n$ and we may call it an $m \times n$ matrix. When $m = n$, it is called a *square matrix*. Thus, A and B are also called square matrices of order 2.

Operations with matrices are basically the same as those with vectors. When a matrix has only one row or only one column, it is identical to a row or a column vector. Thus, in performing the basic operations – addition, subtraction, and multiplication – with matrices, it is convenient to consider a matrix as a collection of vectors of the same number of components.

However, the numbers in the brackets of a matrix are called *elements*. Note that two matrices are equal if, and only if, they are of the same order and they consist of equal elements in corresponding positions. Thus, matrix $\begin{bmatrix} 1 & 7 \\ 6 & 4 \end{bmatrix}$ is not equal to matrix $\begin{bmatrix} 6 & 4 \\ 1 & 7 \end{bmatrix}$, since the corresponding elements are not equal, although the two matrices are of the same order; but $\begin{bmatrix} 1 & 7 \\ 6 & 4 \end{bmatrix} = \begin{bmatrix} 3 - 2 & 8 - 1 \\ 6 \times 1 & 2 + 2 \end{bmatrix}$.

A. Addition

The corresponding elements of two matrices with the same order (the same number of rows and the same number of columns) may be added. The sum is a matrix with the same order as the given matrices.

EXAMPLE 5

(a) Add the 2×2 matrices A and B.

$$A + B = \begin{bmatrix} 1 & 7 \\ 6 & 4 \end{bmatrix} + \begin{bmatrix} 3 & 2 \\ 5 & 8 \end{bmatrix} = \begin{bmatrix} 1 + 3 & 7 + 2 \\ 6 + 5 & 4 + 8 \end{bmatrix} = \begin{bmatrix} 4 & 9 \\ 11 & 12 \end{bmatrix}$$

(b) Add the 3×2 matrices C and D.

$$C + D = \begin{bmatrix} 2 & 3 \\ 5 & 8 \\ 9 & 4 \end{bmatrix} + \begin{bmatrix} 6 & 1 \\ 4 & 2 \\ 9 & 7 \end{bmatrix} = \begin{bmatrix} 2 + 6 & 3 + 1 \\ 5 + 4 & 8 + 2 \\ 9 + 9 & 4 + 7 \end{bmatrix} = \begin{bmatrix} 8 & 4 \\ 9 & 10 \\ 18 & 11 \end{bmatrix}$$

B. Subtraction

The corresponding elements of two matrices of the same order may also be subtracted. The remainder is a matrix with the same order as the given matrices.

EXAMPLE 6

(a) Subtract matrix B from matrix A.

$$A - B = \begin{bmatrix} 1 & 7 \\ 6 & 4 \end{bmatrix} - \begin{bmatrix} 3 & 2 \\ 5 & 8 \end{bmatrix} = \begin{bmatrix} 1-3 & 7-2 \\ 6-5 & 4-8 \end{bmatrix} = \begin{bmatrix} -2 & 5 \\ 1 & -4 \end{bmatrix}$$

(b) Subtract matrix D from matrix C.

$$C - D = \begin{bmatrix} 2 & 3 \\ 5 & 8 \\ 9 & 4 \end{bmatrix} - \begin{bmatrix} 6 & 1 \\ 4 & 2 \\ 9 & 7 \end{bmatrix} = \begin{bmatrix} 2-6 & 3-1 \\ 5-4 & 8-2 \\ 9-9 & 4-7 \end{bmatrix} = \begin{bmatrix} -4 & 2 \\ 1 & 6 \\ 0 & -3 \end{bmatrix}$$

C. Multiplication

Multiplication involving matrices is presented in two different cases below.

CASE I. SCALAR MULTIPLICATION

When a real number (scalar) is multiplied by a matrix, the number must be multiplied by each element of the matrix. The product thus is also a matrix with the same order of the matrix multiplied.

EXAMPLE 7

(a) Multiply 4 by the 2×3 matrix $E = \begin{bmatrix} 1 & 3 & 6 \\ 2 & 5 & 7 \end{bmatrix}$.

$$4 \cdot E = 4\begin{bmatrix} 1 & 3 & 6 \\ 2 & 5 & 7 \end{bmatrix} = \begin{bmatrix} 4 \times 1 & 4 \times 3 & 4 \times 6 \\ 4 \times 2 & 4 \times 5 & 4 \times 7 \end{bmatrix} = \begin{bmatrix} 4 & 12 & 24 \\ 8 & 20 & 28 \end{bmatrix}$$

(b) Multiply $\frac{1}{2}$ by the 2×2 matrix A.

$$\tfrac{1}{2} \cdot A = \tfrac{1}{2}\begin{bmatrix} 1 & 7 \\ 6 & 4 \end{bmatrix} = \begin{bmatrix} \frac{1}{2} \times 1 & \frac{1}{2} \times 7 \\ \frac{1}{2} \times 6 & \frac{1}{2} \times 4 \end{bmatrix} = \begin{bmatrix} \frac{1}{2} & 3\frac{1}{2} \\ 3 & 2 \end{bmatrix}$$

CASE II. MULTIPLICATION OF TWO MATRICES

A matrix may be multiplied by another matrix if, and only if, the number of columns in the first matrix is equal to the number of rows in the second matrix. Thus, an $m \times n$ matrix may be multiplied by an $n \times p$ matrix. The product of the two matrices is an $m \times p$ matrix.

Multiplication of Two Matrices

First matrix		*Second matrix*	
Rows	*Columns*	*Rows*	*Columns*
m	$\times\ n$	n	$\times\ p$

$n = n$

$m \times p$ matrix
(product)

Let A be the first matrix and B be the second matrix. Each row vector of A is multiplied by each column vector of B to obtain the corresponding element of the product matrix $A \cdot B$. Or, more generally, the element in the ith row and jth column in the product is obtained by multiplying the ith row vector in the first matrix by the jth column vector in the second matrix.

EXAMPLE 8 (a) Multiply matrix A by matrix B. The order of each matrix is written directly under the matrix for checking the answer. Since A and B are 2×2 matrices, the product $A \cdot B$ should be a 2×2 matrix also.

$$A \cdot B = \underset{2\times 2}{\begin{bmatrix} 1 & 7 \\ 6 & 4 \end{bmatrix}} \cdot \underset{2\times 2}{\begin{bmatrix} 3 & 2 \\ 5 & 8 \end{bmatrix}} = \begin{bmatrix} [1 \quad 7]\begin{bmatrix} 3 \\ 5 \end{bmatrix} & [1 \quad 7]\begin{bmatrix} 2 \\ 8 \end{bmatrix} \\ [6 \quad 4]\begin{bmatrix} 3 \\ 5 \end{bmatrix} & [6 \quad 4]\begin{bmatrix} 2 \\ 8 \end{bmatrix} \end{bmatrix}$$

$$= \begin{bmatrix} (1 \times 3) + (7 \times 5) & (1 \times 2) + (7 \times 8) \\ (6 \times 3) + (4 \times 5) & (6 \times 2) + (4 \times 8) \end{bmatrix} = \underset{2\times 2}{\begin{bmatrix} 38 & 58 \\ 38 & 44 \end{bmatrix}}$$

NOTE: It can easily be verified that $A \cdot B \neq B \cdot A$.

(b) Multiply matrix C by matrix A.

Since C is a 3×2 matrix and A is a 2×2 matrix, the product $C \cdot A$ will be a 3×2 matrix.

$$C \cdot A = \underset{3\times 2}{\begin{bmatrix} 2 & 3 \\ 5 & 8 \\ 9 & 4 \end{bmatrix}} \cdot \underset{2\times 2}{\begin{bmatrix} 1 & 7 \\ 6 & 4 \end{bmatrix}} = \begin{bmatrix} [2 \quad 3]\begin{bmatrix} 1 \\ 6 \end{bmatrix} & [2 \quad 3]\begin{bmatrix} 7 \\ 4 \end{bmatrix} \\ [5 \quad 8]\begin{bmatrix} 1 \\ 6 \end{bmatrix} & [5 \quad 8]\begin{bmatrix} 7 \\ 4 \end{bmatrix} \\ [9 \quad 4]\begin{bmatrix} 1 \\ 6 \end{bmatrix} & [9 \quad 4]\begin{bmatrix} 7 \\ 4 \end{bmatrix} \end{bmatrix}$$

$$= \begin{bmatrix} (2 \times 1) + (3 \times 6) & (2 \times 7) + (3 \times 4) \\ (5 \times 1) + (8 \times 6) & (5 \times 7) + (8 \times 4) \\ (9 \times 1) + (4 \times 6) & (9 \times 7) + (4 \times 4) \end{bmatrix} = \underset{3\times 2}{\begin{bmatrix} 20 & 26 \\ 53 & 67 \\ 33 & 79 \end{bmatrix}}$$

Note that since the number of columns in A (2 columns) is not equal to the number of rows in C (3 rows), we could not multiply A by C (or $A \cdot C$).

The multiplication shown in Example 8(b) may be applied to a practical problem, as shown in Table 5–3. Table 5–3 is constructed from the information given in Section 5.1 (Tables 5–1 and 5–2). It shows the total amount of each type of raw material required by each plant. The totals shown in the table are the same as the elements in the product matrix $C \cdot A$.

EXERCISE 5-1 REFERENCE: SECTION 5.1 and 5.2

A. Operations with vectors.

Let $u = [1, 6]$; $v = [4, 5]$; $v' = \begin{bmatrix} 4 \\ 5 \end{bmatrix}$; $w = \begin{bmatrix} 2 \\ 9 \end{bmatrix}$;

$x = \begin{bmatrix} 1 \\ 6 \\ 5 \end{bmatrix}$; $y = \begin{bmatrix} 2 \\ 3 \\ 7 \end{bmatrix}$; and $z = [4, 8, 9]$.

Table 5–3 Company *R*—Material Requirements by Plants

	Plant #1							*Plant #2*						
	Product X			*Product Y*				*Product X*			*Product Y*			
Material	*For each unit*	*Units of X*	*Subtotal*	*For each unit*	*Units of Y*	*Subtotal*	*Total*	*For each unit*	*Units of X*	*Subtotal*	*For each unit*	*Units of Y*	*Subtotal*	*Total*
M-1	2 lb	1	2 lb	3 lb	6	18 lb	20 lb	2 lb	7	14 lb	3 lb	4	12 lb	26 lb
M-2	5	1	5	8	6	48	53	5	7	35	8	4	32	67
M-3	9	1	9	4	6	24	33	9	7	63	4	4	16	79

First column vector of matrix $C \cdot A$ (Plant #1 Total column)

Second column vector of matrix $C \cdot A$ (Plant #2 Total column)

Source: Computed from Tables 5–1 and 5–2. See Example 8(b) for matrix $C \cdot A$.

Perform the indicated operations in each of the following expressions:

1. $u + v$
2. $v - u$
3. $u - v$
4. $v' - w$
5. $w - v'$
6. $w + v'$
7. $x + y$
8. $y - x$
9. $12u$
10. $\frac{5}{6}v$
11. $2v'$
12. $3w$
13. $6z$
14. $4x$
15. $\frac{1}{5}y$
16. $v \cdot v'$
17. $u \cdot w$
18. $v \cdot w$
19. $z \cdot x$
20. $z \cdot y$

B. Operations with matrices.

Let $A = \begin{bmatrix} 3 & 9 \\ 2 & 4 \end{bmatrix}$; $B = \begin{bmatrix} 5 & 6 \\ 1 & 7 \end{bmatrix}$; $C = \begin{bmatrix} 1 & 2 \\ 3 & 9 \\ 8 & 4 \end{bmatrix}$; $D = \begin{bmatrix} 5 & 1 \\ 2 & 7 \\ 3 & 6 \end{bmatrix}$;

$E = \begin{bmatrix} 4 & 6 & 3 \\ 1 & 5 & 8 \end{bmatrix}$; and $F = \begin{bmatrix} 2 & 4 & 7 \\ 5 & 3 & 1 \end{bmatrix}$.

Perform the indicated operations in each of the following expressions:

21. $A + B$
22. $C + D$
23. $C - D$
24. $A - B$
25. $3A$
26. $2B$
27. $\frac{1}{4}C$
28. $\frac{1}{3}E$
29. $A \cdot B$
30. $B \cdot A$
31. $A \cdot E$
32. $B \cdot F$
33. $A \cdot F$
34. $B \cdot E$
35. $E \cdot C$
36. $F \cdot D$
37. $C \cdot A$
38. $D \cdot B$
39. $F \cdot C$
40. $E \cdot D$
41. $C \cdot E$
42. $D \cdot F$
43. $C \cdot F$
44. $D \cdot E$
45. $7(C \cdot B)$
46. $\frac{1}{2}(D \cdot A)$

5.3 DETERMINANTS

A *determinant* is a number that determines whether or not there is an *inverse* of a square matrix. The details concerning the inverse of a square matrix are presented in the next section. This section introduces the basic operations with determinants.

A determinant is written in a manner similar to its associated square matrix except that two vertical lines are used instead of brackets. For example, if the 2 × 2 square matrix

$$A = \begin{bmatrix} 2 & 5 \\ 1 & 3 \end{bmatrix}$$

the determinant of A, denoted by $|A|$, is

$$|A| = \begin{vmatrix} 2 & 5 \\ 1 & 3 \end{vmatrix}$$

which is also called a determinant of order 2.

The value of a determinant may be computed in two ways: (1) by cross multiplying the elements, and (2) by finding the minors. Each of these methods is discussed in more detail below.

A. Evaluating Determinants by Cross Multiplication

We shall evaluate only the determinants of orders 2 and 3 by this method.

If the 2 × 2 square matrix

$$A = \begin{bmatrix} a_{11} & a_{12} \\ a_{21} & a_{22} \end{bmatrix}$$

then the determinant of A is

$$|A| = \begin{vmatrix} a_{11} & a_{12} \\ a_{21} & a_{22} \end{vmatrix} = a_{11}a_{22} - a_{12}a_{21}$$

secondary diagonal primary diagonal

Observe that the letter a represents the elements of the matrix A, with the first subscript indicating the location of the row and the second subscript indicating the location of the column. The positive product $(+\ a_{11}a_{22})$ consists of the elements on the primary diagonal and the negative product $(-a_{12}a_{21})$ consists of the elements on the secondary diagonal of the determinant; also, each product has only one element from each row and each column.

EXAMPLE 1

Evaluate the determinant of the matrix A if (a) $A = \begin{bmatrix} 2 & 5 \\ 1 & 3 \end{bmatrix}$, and

(b) $A = \begin{bmatrix} 3 & 1 \\ 6 & -1 \end{bmatrix}$.

(a) $|A| = \begin{vmatrix} 2 & 5 \\ 1 & 3 \end{vmatrix} = (2 \times 3) - (5 \times 1) = 6 - 5 = 1$

(b) $|A| = \begin{vmatrix} 3 & 1 \\ 6 & -1 \end{vmatrix} = (3 \times (-1)) - (1 \times 6) = -3 - 6 = -9$

Likewise, the determinant of order 3 is associated with a 3 × 3 matrix, written:

$$|A| = \begin{vmatrix} a_{11} & a_{12} & a_{13} \\ a_{21} & a_{22} & a_{23} \\ a_{31} & a_{32} & a_{33} \end{vmatrix}$$

$$= a_{11}a_{22}a_{33} + a_{12}a_{23}a_{31} + a_{13}a_{21}a_{32} - a_{13}a_{22}a_{31} - a_{12}a_{21}a_{33} - a_{11}a_{23}a_{32}$$

The three positive products are obtained from the primary diagonals, as shown below:

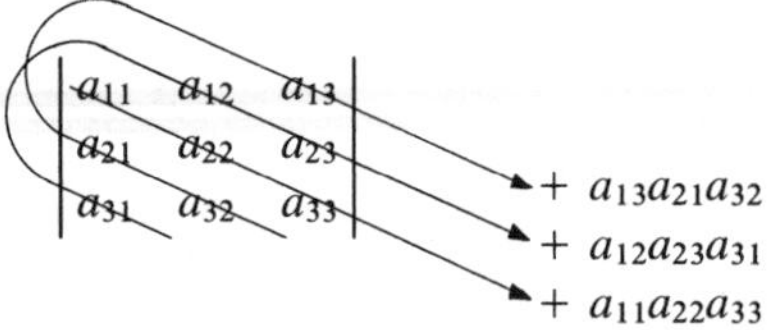

a_{11} a_{12} a_{13}
a_{21} a_{22} a_{23}
a_{31} a_{32} a_{33}
$+ a_{13}a_{21}a_{32}$
$+ a_{12}a_{23}a_{31}$
$+ a_{11}a_{22}a_{33}$

The three negative products are obtained from the secondary diagonals, as shown below:

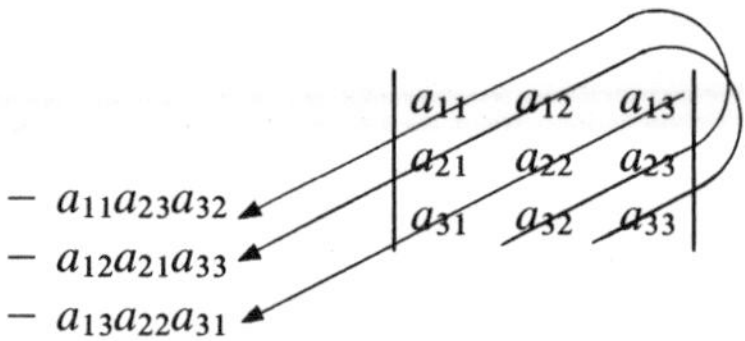

Note that the cross multiplication method as shown above does not work for determinants of order higher than 3. Determinants of higher order should be evaluated by the minors, as shown below.

EXAMPLE 2 Evaluate the determinant $|A|$.

$$|A| = \begin{vmatrix} 2 & -3 & 4 \\ 1 & 5 & -2 \\ 4 & 2 & 6 \end{vmatrix} = (2 \times 5 \times 6) + [(-3) \times (-2) \times 4] + (4 \times 1 \times 2) - (4 \times 5 \times 4) - [(-3) \times 1 \times 6] - [2 \times (-2) \times 2]$$
$$= 60 + 24 + 8 - (80) - (-18) - (-8) = 38$$

The positive and negative products may be computed in the following manner. Note that the first two columns of the determinant are written as the 4th and the 5th columns, respectively, to facilitate the computation.

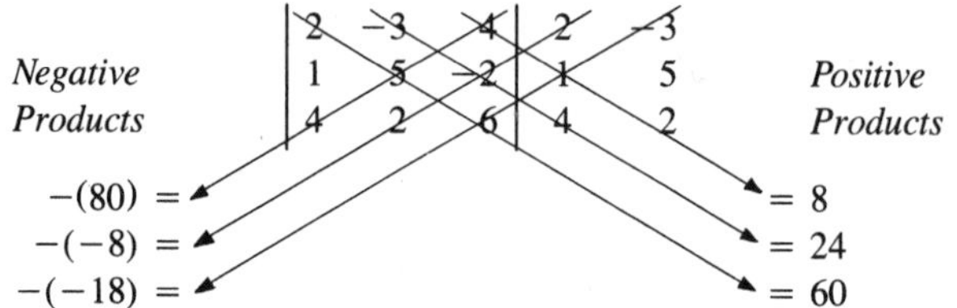

B. Evaluating Determinants by Minors

A *minor* is a determinant of order $(n - 1)$ obtained from a determinant of order n. Thus, in a 3 × 3 determinant, we may have 2 × 2 minors. A minor is specified by an element. The minor of the element a_{ij}, located in the ith row and the jth column in a determinant, is denoted by A_{ij}. Minor A_{ij} is obtained by deleting both the ith row and jth column of the determinant. Thus, in the 2 × 2 determinant

$$|A| = \begin{vmatrix} a_{11} & a_{12} \\ a_{21} & a_{22} \end{vmatrix}, \text{ minor } A_{11} = \begin{vmatrix} \not{a_{11}} & \not{a_{12}} \\ \not{a_{21}} & a_{22} \end{vmatrix} = |a_{22}|$$

and in the 3 × 3 determinant

$$|A| = \begin{vmatrix} a_{11} & a_{12} & a_{13} \\ a_{21} & a_{22} & a_{23} \\ a_{31} & a_{32} & a_{33} \end{vmatrix}, \text{ minor } A_{21} = \begin{vmatrix} a_{11} & a_{12} & a_{13} \\ \textcircled{a_{21}} & a_{22} & a_{23} \\ a_{31} & a_{32} & a_{33} \end{vmatrix} = \begin{vmatrix} a_{12} & a_{13} \\ a_{32} & a_{33} \end{vmatrix}$$

(The element a_{ij} (a_{11} and a_{21}) is circled in each illustration.)

A minor should be prefixed by a sign when it is used for evaluating a determinant. When $i + j$ is an even number, the sign of the minor is positive, or $+A_{ij}$. When $i + j$ is an odd number, the sign is negative, or $-A_{ij}$.

ILLUSTRATIONS: The minor of element a_{11} is $+A_{11}$, since it appears in the first row and first column and $1 + 1 = 2$, an even number.

If $|A| = \begin{vmatrix} 2 & 5 \\ 1 & 3 \end{vmatrix}$, $a_{11} = 2$ and $+A_{11} = \begin{vmatrix} \textcircled{2} & 5 \\ 1 & 3 \end{vmatrix} = +|3|$

The minor of element a_{21} is $-A_{21}$, since it appears in the second row and first column and $2 + 1 = 3$, an odd number.

If $|A| = \begin{vmatrix} 2 & -3 & 4 \\ 1 & 5 & -2 \\ 4 & 2 & 6 \end{vmatrix}$, $a_{21} = 1$ and $-A_{21} = -\begin{vmatrix} 2 & -3 & 4 \\ \textcircled{1} & 5 & -2 \\ 4 & 2 & 6 \end{vmatrix} = -\begin{vmatrix} -3 & 4 \\ 2 & 6 \end{vmatrix}$

NOTE: A signed minor is also called a *cofactor* of the element a_{ij}.

A determinant may be evaluated by signed minors as follows:

STEP (1). Multiply each element of *any* column (or any row) by its signed minor.
STEP (2). Add the n products obtained above. The sum is the value of the determinant.

Thus, for a 2×2 determinant $|A|$, we may express the value in terms of the elements of the *first column* and their signed minors:

$$|A| = a_{11}A_{11} - a_{21}A_{21}$$

EXAMPLE 3 Evaluate the determinants in Example 1 by minors.

(a) $|A| = \begin{vmatrix} 2 & 5 \\ 1 & 3 \end{vmatrix} = 2\begin{vmatrix} \textcircled{2} & 5 \\ 1 & 3 \end{vmatrix} - 1\begin{vmatrix} 2 & 5 \\ \textcircled{1} & 3 \end{vmatrix} = 2|3| - 1|5|$
$= 6 - 5 = 1$

(b) $|A| = \begin{vmatrix} 3 & 1 \\ 6 & -1 \end{vmatrix} = 3\begin{vmatrix} \textcircled{3} & 1 \\ 6 & -1 \end{vmatrix} - 6\begin{vmatrix} 3 & 1 \\ \textcircled{6} & -1 \end{vmatrix} = 3|-1| - 6|1|$
$= (-3) - 6 = -9$

For a 3×3 determinant $|A|$, we may also express the value in terms of the elements of the *first column* and their signed minors:

$$|A| = a_{11}A_{11} - a_{21}A_{21} + a_{31}A_{31}$$

EXAMPLE 4 Evaluate the determinant in Example 2 by minors.

$$|A| = \begin{vmatrix} 2 & -3 & 4 \\ 1 & 5 & -2 \\ 4 & 2 & 6 \end{vmatrix} = 2\begin{vmatrix} \textcircled{2} & -3 & 4 \\ 1 & 5 & -2 \\ 4 & 2 & 6 \end{vmatrix} - 1\begin{vmatrix} 2 & -3 & 4 \\ \textcircled{1} & 5 & -2 \\ 4 & 2 & 6 \end{vmatrix} + 4\begin{vmatrix} 2 & -3 & 4 \\ 1 & 5 & -2 \\ \textcircled{4} & 2 & 6 \end{vmatrix}$$

$$= 2\begin{vmatrix} 5 & -2 \\ 2 & 6 \end{vmatrix} - 1\begin{vmatrix} -3 & 4 \\ 2 & 6 \end{vmatrix} + 4\begin{vmatrix} -3 & 4 \\ 5 & -2 \end{vmatrix}$$
$$= 2[30 - (-4)] - 1[(-18) - 8] + 4(6 - 20)$$
$$= 68 + 26 - 56 = 38$$

Determinants of higher order may be evaluated by repeating the process of finding the products of the elements of the first column and their signed minors, as illustrated in Example 4. For instance, a 4×4 determinant may be evaluated from its 3×3 signed minors. Each of the 3×3 signed minors is then evaluated from its 2×2 signed minors.

EXERCISE 5-2 REFERENCE: SECTION 5.3

A. Evaluate each of the following determinants by (a) the cross multiplication method and (b) finding the signed minors of the first column elements:

1. $\begin{vmatrix} 3 & 8 \\ 5 & 6 \end{vmatrix}$

2. $\begin{vmatrix} 2 & -3 \\ 5 & 4 \end{vmatrix}$

3. $\begin{vmatrix} -2 & 8 \\ 4 & -9 \end{vmatrix}$

4. $\begin{vmatrix} -3 & 12 \\ -7 & 8 \end{vmatrix}$

5. $\begin{vmatrix} 4 & 5 \\ 9 & 7 \end{vmatrix}$

6. $\begin{vmatrix} 1 & -6 \\ 2 & 3 \end{vmatrix}$

7. $\begin{vmatrix} 1 & -2 & 3 \\ 4 & 5 & -6 \\ 7 & 8 & 9 \end{vmatrix}$

8. $\begin{vmatrix} 3 & 5 & -1 \\ 2 & -7 & 8 \\ 4 & 1 & 6 \end{vmatrix}$

9. $\begin{vmatrix} 1 & 2 & 0 \\ -1 & 1 & 2 \\ 2 & 1 & 0 \end{vmatrix}$

10. $\begin{vmatrix} 1 & 3 & 2 \\ 2 & -1 & 0 \\ 3 & 2 & 1 \end{vmatrix}$

B. Evaluate each determinant by the signed minors of the elements of the row or column indicated:

11. The determinant given in Problem 1—use the elements in the first row.
12. The determinant given in Problem 2—use the elements in the first row.
13. The determinant given in Problem 7—use the elements in the second row.
14. The determinant given in Problem 8—use the elements in the second column.

5.4 THE INVERSE OF A SQUARE MATRIX

In algebra, the *inverse* or *reciprocal* of the number a is a^{-1} (or $\frac{1}{a}$); the product of the number and its inverse is always equal to 1, or $a \cdot a^{-1} = 1$. A similar relationship between a matrix and its inverse may be expressed.

Let A = a square matrix
A^{-1} = the inverse of A

Then $A^{-1} \cdot A = A \cdot A^{-1} = I$
where I = an identity matrix of the same order as A and A^{-1}

An *identity matrix* or *unit matrix* is a square matrix with all elements on its *principal diagonal* (the line from the upper left corner to the lower right corner) equal to 1 and all other elements 0, such as

the 2×2 identity matrix $I = \begin{bmatrix} 1 & 0 \\ 0 & 1 \end{bmatrix}$, and

the 3×3 identity matrix $I = \begin{bmatrix} 1 & 0 & 0 \\ 0 & 1 & 0 \\ 0 & 0 & 1 \end{bmatrix}$

An identity matrix acts in matrix algebra in the same way as 1 in the ordinary algebra concerning multiplication. Thus, the expression

$A \cdot I = I \cdot A = A$

is true for all matrices A.

EXAMPLE 1

Let the 2×2 matrix $A = \begin{bmatrix} 2 & 5 \\ 1 & 3 \end{bmatrix}$ and $I = \begin{bmatrix} 1 & 0 \\ 0 & 1 \end{bmatrix}$.

$$A \cdot I = \begin{bmatrix} 2 & 5 \\ 1 & 3 \end{bmatrix} \cdot \begin{bmatrix} 1 & 0 \\ 0 & 1 \end{bmatrix} = \begin{bmatrix} (2 \times 1) + (5 \times 0) & (2 \times 0) + (5 \times 1) \\ (1 \times 1) + (3 \times 0) & (1 \times 0) + (3 \times 1) \end{bmatrix}$$

$$= \begin{bmatrix} 2 & 5 \\ 1 & 3 \end{bmatrix} = A$$

$$I \cdot A = \begin{bmatrix} 1 & 0 \\ 0 & 1 \end{bmatrix} \cdot \begin{bmatrix} 2 & 5 \\ 1 & 3 \end{bmatrix} = \begin{bmatrix} (1 \times 2) + (0 \times 1) & (1 \times 5) + (0 \times 3) \\ (0 \times 2) + (1 \times 1) & (0 \times 5) + (1 \times 3) \end{bmatrix}$$

$$= \begin{bmatrix} 2 & 5 \\ 1 & 3 \end{bmatrix} = A$$

There are various methods of finding the inverse of a square matrix. We shall introduce two methods: (A) the basic method, and (B) the short method by using determinants.

A. Basic Method

This method is illustrated by the following example.

EXAMPLE 2

Find the inverse of the square matrix $A = \begin{bmatrix} 2 & 5 \\ 1 & 3 \end{bmatrix}$. Let $I = \begin{bmatrix} 1 & 0 \\ 0 & 1 \end{bmatrix}$.

If A^{-1}, the inverse of A, exists, then we may write $A \cdot A^{-1} = I$ as

$$\begin{bmatrix} 2 & 5 \\ 1 & 3 \end{bmatrix} \cdot A^{-1} = \begin{bmatrix} 1 & 0 \\ 0 & 1 \end{bmatrix}$$

Since A is a 2×2 square matrix and the product I is a 2×2 square matrix, the unknown matrix A^{-1} must also be a 2×2 square matrix. Let b represent the elements of the matrix A^{-1}, with the first and second subscripts indicating the locations of rows and columns in the matrix respectively, or

$$A^{-1} = \begin{bmatrix} b_{11} & b_{12} \\ b_{21} & b_{22} \end{bmatrix}$$

We then have

$$\begin{bmatrix} 2 & 5 \\ 1 & 3 \end{bmatrix} \cdot \begin{bmatrix} b_{11} & b_{12} \\ b_{21} & b_{22} \end{bmatrix} = \begin{bmatrix} 1 & 0 \\ 0 & 1 \end{bmatrix}$$

Multiply the left side:

$$\begin{bmatrix} (2b_{11} + 5b_{21}) & (2b_{12} + 5b_{22}) \\ (1b_{11} + 3b_{21}) & (1b_{12} + 3b_{22}) \end{bmatrix} = \begin{bmatrix} 1 & 0 \\ 0 & 1 \end{bmatrix}$$

Equate corresponding elements of the matrices on both sides. We have a system of four equations:

$$\begin{cases} 2b_{11} + 5b_{21} = 1 & (1) \\ 1b_{11} + 3b_{21} = 0 & (2) \end{cases}$$

Solve equations (1) and (2) for b_{11} and b_{21}:

(2) × 2: $2b_{11} + 6b_{21} = 0$ (2′)

(2′) − (1): $b_{21} = -1$

Substitute $b_{21} = -1$ in (2):

$$b_{11} + 3(-1) = 0$$
$$b_{11} = 3$$

$$\begin{cases} 2b_{12} + 5b_{22} = 0 & (3) \\ 1b_{12} + 3b_{22} = 1 & (4) \end{cases}$$

Solve equations (3) and (4) for b_{12} and b_{22}:

(4) × 2: $2b_{12} + 6b_{22} = 2$ (4′)

(4′) − (3): $b_{22} = 2$

Substitute $b_{22} = 2$ in (4):

$$b_{12} + 3(2) = 1$$
$$b_{12} = -5$$

Thus,

$$A^{-1} = \begin{bmatrix} b_{11} & b_{12} \\ b_{21} & b_{22} \end{bmatrix} = \begin{bmatrix} 3 & -5 \\ -1 & 2 \end{bmatrix}$$

CHECK

$$A \cdot A^{-1} = \begin{bmatrix} 2 & 5 \\ 1 & 3 \end{bmatrix} \cdot \begin{bmatrix} 3 & -5 \\ -1 & 2 \end{bmatrix} = \begin{bmatrix} 6 + (-5) & (-10) + (10) \\ 3 + (-3) & (-5) + 6 \end{bmatrix} = \begin{bmatrix} 1 & 0 \\ 0 & 1 \end{bmatrix} = I$$

Also,

$$A^{-1} \cdot A = \begin{bmatrix} 3 & -5 \\ -1 & 2 \end{bmatrix} \cdot \begin{bmatrix} 2 & 5 \\ 1 & 3 \end{bmatrix} = \begin{bmatrix} 6 + (-5) & 15 + (-15) \\ (-2) + 2 & (-5) + 6 \end{bmatrix} = \begin{bmatrix} 1 & 0 \\ 0 & 1 \end{bmatrix} = I$$

The results from the checking show that $A^{-1} \cdot A = A \cdot A^{-1} = I$.

B. Short Method

The process of finding the inverse of a square matrix can be simplified when determinants are used. Observe the procedures illustrated in Example 2. Let the 2 × 2 square matrix A be written in a general form, or

$$A = \begin{bmatrix} a_{11} & a_{12} \\ a_{21} & a_{22} \end{bmatrix}$$

If A^{-1} exists, we may write $A \cdot A^{-1} = I$ as

$$\begin{bmatrix} a_{11} & a_{12} \\ a_{21} & a_{22} \end{bmatrix} \cdot \begin{bmatrix} b_{11} & b_{12} \\ b_{21} & b_{22} \end{bmatrix} = \begin{bmatrix} 1 & 0 \\ 0 & 1 \end{bmatrix}$$

After multiplying the matrices on the left side of the above equation, equating corresponding elements to obtain the four equations, and solving the four equations, we have[1]

$$b_{11} = \frac{a_{22}}{|A|}, \qquad b_{12} = \frac{-a_{12}}{|A|}, \qquad b_{21} = \frac{-a_{21}}{|A|}, \qquad b_{22} = \frac{a_{11}}{|A|}; \quad \text{and}$$

$$A^{-1} = \begin{bmatrix} b_{11} & b_{12} \\ b_{21} & b_{22} \end{bmatrix} = \begin{bmatrix} \dfrac{a_{22}}{|A|} & \dfrac{-a_{12}}{|A|} \\ \dfrac{-a_{21}}{|A|} & \dfrac{a_{11}}{|A|} \end{bmatrix} = \frac{1}{|A|}\begin{bmatrix} a_{22} & -a_{12} \\ -a_{21} & a_{11} \end{bmatrix}, \text{ where}$$

$$|A| = \begin{vmatrix} a_{11} & a_{12} \\ a_{21} & a_{22} \end{vmatrix} = a_{11}a_{22} - a_{12}a_{21} \neq 0$$

Thus, the determinant $|A|$ determines the existence of the inverse of a square matrix A. If, and only if, $|A| \neq 0$, the inverse A^{-1} exists.

Example 2 may now be solved by the short method, as follows:

$$A = \begin{bmatrix} a_{11} & a_{12} \\ a_{21} & a_{22} \end{bmatrix} = \begin{bmatrix} 2 & 5 \\ 1 & 3 \end{bmatrix} \qquad |A| = \begin{vmatrix} 2 & 5 \\ 1 & 3 \end{vmatrix} = (2 \times 3) - (5 \times 1) = 1$$

Since $|A| \neq 0$, A has an inverse.

$$A^{-1} = \frac{1}{|A|}\begin{bmatrix} a_{22} & -a_{12} \\ -a_{21} & a_{11} \end{bmatrix} = \frac{1}{1}\begin{bmatrix} 3 & -5 \\ -1 & 2 \end{bmatrix} = \begin{bmatrix} 3 & -5 \\ -1 & 2 \end{bmatrix}$$

In summary, to write the inverse of a 2×2 square matrix A for which $|A| \neq 0$, we may interchange the elements on the principal diagonal, prefix each of the other two elements with a negative sign, and multiply the resulted matrix by $1/|A|$.

The inverse of a 2×2 square matrix may also be written in terms of signed minors, as follows:

---

[1]Multiply the left side.

$$\begin{bmatrix} a_{11}b_{11} + a_{12}b_{21} & a_{11}b_{12} + a_{12}b_{22} \\ a_{21}b_{11} + a_{22}b_{21} & a_{21}b_{12} + a_{22}b_{22} \end{bmatrix} = \begin{bmatrix} 1 & 0 \\ 0 & 1 \end{bmatrix}$$

Equate corresponding elements.

$$\begin{cases} a_{11}b_{11} + a_{12}b_{21} = 1 \ldots (1) \\ a_{21}b_{11} + a_{22}b_{21} = 0 \ldots (2) \end{cases} \quad \begin{cases} a_{11}b_{12} + a_{12}b_{22} = 0 \ldots (3) \\ a_{21}b_{12} + a_{22}b_{22} = 1 \ldots (4) \end{cases}$$

Solve Equations (1) and (2) for b_{11} and b_{21}.

$$\begin{aligned} (1) \times a_{21}&: \quad a_{21}a_{11}b_{11} + a_{21}a_{12}b_{21} = a_{21} \ldots (1') \\ (2) \times a_{11}&: \quad a_{11}a_{21}b_{11} + a_{11}a_{22}b_{21} = 0 \ \ldots (2') \\ (1') - (2')&: \quad a_{21}a_{12}b_{21} - a_{11}a_{22}b_{21} = a_{21} \\ & \quad b_{21}(a_{21}a_{12} - a_{11}a_{22}) = a_{21} \end{aligned}$$

$$b_{21} = \frac{a_{21}}{a_{21}a_{12} - a_{11}a_{22}} = \frac{a_{21}}{-(a_{11}a_{22} - a_{21}a_{12})} = \frac{-a_{21}}{|A|}$$

Substitute b_{21} value in (2).

$$a_{21}b_{11} + a_{22}\left(\frac{a_{21}}{a_{21}a_{12} - a_{11}a_{22}}\right) = 0$$

$$b_{11} = -\frac{a_{22}a_{21}}{a_{21}a_{12} - a_{11}a_{22}} \cdot \frac{1}{a_{21}} = \frac{a_{22}}{|A|}$$

We may solve equations (3) and (4) in a similar manner to obtain the values of b_{12} and b_{22}.

$$A^{-1} = \frac{1}{|A|}\begin{bmatrix} A_{11} & -A_{21} \\ -A_{12} & A_{22} \end{bmatrix}, \quad \text{since} \quad \begin{cases} A_{11} = a_{22}, & -A_{21} = -a_{12}, \\ -A_{12} = -a_{21}, & A_{22} = a_{11}. \end{cases}$$

Observe that the signed minors in the above matrix are in *transposed order*. For example, the subscripts 21 in element a_{21} indicate that the element is in the second *row* and the first *column*. Now, the subscripts 21 in the signed minor $-A_{21}$ indicate that the minor is located in the second *column* and the first *row*.

Similarly, the inverse of a 3 × 3 square matrix may be written in terms of signed minors:

$$\mathbf{A}^{-1} = \frac{\mathbf{1}}{|\mathbf{A}|}\begin{bmatrix} \mathbf{A}_{11} & -\mathbf{A}_{21} & \mathbf{A}_{31} \\ -\mathbf{A}_{12} & \mathbf{A}_{22} & -\mathbf{A}_{32} \\ \mathbf{A}_{13} & -\mathbf{A}_{23} & \mathbf{A}_{33} \end{bmatrix}$$

Again observe the transposed subscripts, such as 31 in the signed minor A_{31}, indicating the location of the minor in the third column and the first row. Note that the minor of element a_{31} is $+A_{31}$ (a positive determinant), since the sum of the subscripts $3 + 1 = 4$ is an even number. The minors A_{12}, A_{21}, A_{23}, and A_{32} have negative signs, since the sums of their subscripts are odd numbers, such as $1 + 2 = 3$, and $2 + 3 = 5$.

EXAMPLE 3

Find the inverse of the 3 × 3 square matrix $A = \begin{bmatrix} 2 & -3 & 4 \\ 1 & 5 & -2 \\ 4 & 2 & 6 \end{bmatrix}$.

$$|A| = \begin{vmatrix} 2 & -3 & 4 \\ 1 & 5 & -2 \\ 4 & 2 & 6 \end{vmatrix} = 38$$ (see Example 4, pages 137–138)

Since $|A| \neq 0$, A^{-1} or the inverse of A exists. Use the A^{-1} formula above; we have

$$A_{11} = \begin{vmatrix} 5 & -2 \\ 2 & 6 \end{vmatrix}, \qquad -A_{21} = -\begin{vmatrix} -3 & 4 \\ 2 & 6 \end{vmatrix}, \quad \text{and so on.}$$

Thus,

$$A^{-1} = \frac{1}{38}\begin{bmatrix} \begin{vmatrix} 5 & -2 \\ 2 & 6 \end{vmatrix} & -\begin{vmatrix} -3 & 4 \\ 2 & 6 \end{vmatrix} & \begin{vmatrix} -3 & 4 \\ 5 & -2 \end{vmatrix} \\ -\begin{vmatrix} 1 & -2 \\ 4 & 6 \end{vmatrix} & \begin{vmatrix} 2 & 4 \\ 4 & 6 \end{vmatrix} & -\begin{vmatrix} 2 & 4 \\ 1 & -2 \end{vmatrix} \\ \begin{vmatrix} 1 & 5 \\ 4 & 2 \end{vmatrix} & -\begin{vmatrix} 2 & -3 \\ 4 & 2 \end{vmatrix} & \begin{vmatrix} 2 & -3 \\ 1 & 5 \end{vmatrix} \end{bmatrix} = \frac{1}{38}\begin{bmatrix} 34 & 26 & -14 \\ -14 & -4 & 8 \\ -18 & -16 & 13 \end{bmatrix}$$

CHECK

$$A^{-1} \cdot A = \frac{1}{38}\begin{bmatrix} 34 & 26 & -14 \\ -14 & -4 & 8 \\ -18 & -16 & 13 \end{bmatrix} \cdot \begin{bmatrix} 2 & -3 & 4 \\ 1 & 5 & -2 \\ 4 & 2 & 6 \end{bmatrix} = \begin{bmatrix} 1 & 0 & 0 \\ 0 & 1 & 0 \\ 0 & 0 & 1 \end{bmatrix}$$

EXERCISE 5-3 REFERENCE: SECTION 5-4

A. Let $A = \begin{bmatrix} 5 & -3 \\ 7 & 1 \end{bmatrix}$, $B = \begin{bmatrix} 1 & 8 \\ 2 & -6 \end{bmatrix}$, and $I = \begin{bmatrix} 1 & 0 \\ 0 & 1 \end{bmatrix}$.

1. Show that $A \cdot I = A$ and $I \cdot A = A$.
2. Show that $B \cdot I = B$ and $I \cdot B = B$.

B. Find the inverse of each matrix A, if the inverse exists, by (a) the basic method and (b) the short method. Also, check your answers by the relationship $A \cdot A^{-1} = I$.

3. $A = \begin{bmatrix} 2 & 2 \\ 9 & 9 \end{bmatrix}$ 4. $A = \begin{bmatrix} -4 & 2 \\ -1 & \frac{1}{2} \end{bmatrix}$ 5. $A = \begin{bmatrix} 4 & 5 \\ 9 & 7 \end{bmatrix}$ 6. $A = \begin{bmatrix} 1 & -6 \\ 2 & 3 \end{bmatrix}$

C. Find the inverse of each matrix A, if the inverse exists, by the short method. Also, check your answers by the relationship $A \cdot A^{-1} = I$.

7. $A = \begin{bmatrix} 1 & -2 & 3 \\ 4 & 5 & -6 \\ 7 & 8 & 9 \end{bmatrix}$, $|A| = 240$. 8. $A = \begin{bmatrix} 3 & 5 & -1 \\ 2 & -7 & 8 \\ 4 & 1 & 6 \end{bmatrix}$, $|A| = -80$.

5.5 SOLVING LINEAR EQUATIONS BY MATRIX ALGEBRA

A system of linear equations may be solved by the usual algebraic operations as presented in Chapter 3. However, the work of solving a system of three or more linear equations becomes increasingly difficult by the ordinary method. Matrix algebra offers a simplified and systematic method of solving the equations. The systematic steps may also be conveniently programmed for electronic computers to speed the calculations.

There are various methods of solving a system of n linear equations in n unknowns by matrix algebra. We shall introduce two methods below: (A) by using the inverse of a square matrix, and (B) by using determinants.

A. Using the Inverse of a Square Matrix in Solving Equations

This method is illustrated by Example 1. Here we use only 2 equations, although the method is also applicable to a system of more than 2 linear equations.

EXAMPLE 1

Solve the following equations simultaneously:

$$\begin{cases} 3x + y = 5 \\ 6x - y = 6 \end{cases}$$

The two equations can be written in matrix form as follows:

$$\begin{bmatrix} 3 & 1 \\ 6 & -1 \end{bmatrix} \cdot \begin{bmatrix} x \\ y \end{bmatrix} = \begin{bmatrix} 5 \\ 6 \end{bmatrix}$$

The first matrix on the left side is formed by the coefficients of unknowns x and y, the second matrix by the unknowns, and the matrix on the right side by the constants.

Let A be the coefficient matrix, or $A = \begin{bmatrix} 3 & 1 \\ 6 & -1 \end{bmatrix}$. Then

$$A \cdot \begin{bmatrix} x \\ y \end{bmatrix} = \begin{bmatrix} 5 \\ 6 \end{bmatrix}$$

Multiply both sides by A^{-1}, the inverse of the 2×2 square matrix A.

$$A^{-1} \cdot A \cdot \begin{bmatrix} x \\ y \end{bmatrix} = A^{-1} \cdot \begin{bmatrix} 5 \\ 6 \end{bmatrix}$$

Since $A^{-1} \cdot A = I$ and $I \cdot \begin{bmatrix} x \\ y \end{bmatrix} = \begin{bmatrix} x \\ y \end{bmatrix}$, we obtain

$$\begin{bmatrix} x \\ y \end{bmatrix} = A^{-1} \cdot \begin{bmatrix} 5 \\ 6 \end{bmatrix}$$

Thus, the problem of solving a system of linear equations now becomes a problem of finding the inverse of the coefficient matrix, A^{-1}. The value of A^{-1} is computed first:

$$|A| = \begin{vmatrix} 3 & 1 \\ 6 & -1 \end{vmatrix} = (3 \times (-1)) - (1 \times 6) = -9$$

Since $|A| \neq 0$, A has an inverse.

$$A^{-1} = \frac{1}{-9}\begin{bmatrix} -1 & -1 \\ -6 & 3 \end{bmatrix}$$

Substitute the value of A^{-1} in the equation obtained above.

$$\begin{bmatrix} x \\ y \end{bmatrix} = \frac{1}{-9}\begin{bmatrix} -1 & -1 \\ -6 & 3 \end{bmatrix} \cdot \begin{bmatrix} 5 \\ 6 \end{bmatrix} = \frac{1}{-9}\begin{bmatrix} (-5) + (-6) \\ (-30) + 18 \end{bmatrix}$$

$$= \begin{bmatrix} -11/-9 \\ -12/-9 \end{bmatrix} = \begin{bmatrix} 11/9 \\ 4/3 \end{bmatrix}$$

Thus, $x = \frac{11}{9} = 1\frac{2}{9}$

$y = \frac{4}{3} = 1\frac{1}{3}$

B. Cramer's Rule: Using Determinants in Solving Equations

Let $|A|$ = the determinant formed by coefficients of unknowns in a system of linear equations. The following rule, called *Cramer's Rule* in honor of Gabriel Cramer of Geneva (1704–52), has been established:

A system of n linear equations in n unknowns has a single solution if, and only if, the determinant formed by the coefficients of the unknowns is not equal to zero; that is, $|A| \neq 0$. Each unknown is equal to the product of $1/|A|$ and the determinant obtained from $|A|$ by replacing the column of coefficients of this unknown by the column of constants.

The application of this rule is illustrated in the following example.

EXAMPLE 2

Solve $\begin{cases} 3x + y = 5, \\ 6x - y = 6. \end{cases}$ (same as Example 1)

Let $|A|$ = the determinant of the coefficients of the unknowns in the two equations, or

$$|A| = \begin{vmatrix} 3 & 1 \\ 6 & -1 \end{vmatrix} = -9$$

The coefficients of x in $|A|$ are replaced by the constants:

$$x = \frac{1}{|A|}\begin{vmatrix} \overset{\downarrow}{5} & 1 \\ 6 & -1 \end{vmatrix} = \frac{1}{-9}[5(-1) - 1(6)] = \frac{11}{9} = 1\frac{2}{9}$$

The coefficients of y in $|A|$ are replaced by the constants:

$$y = \frac{1}{|A|}\begin{vmatrix} 3 & 5 \\ 6 & 6 \end{vmatrix} = \frac{1}{-9}[3(6) - 5(6)] = \frac{12}{9} = \frac{4}{3} = 1\frac{1}{3}$$

EXAMPLE 3

$$\text{Solve: } \begin{cases} 2x - 3y + 4z = -4, \\ x + 5y - 2z = 15, \\ 4x + 2y + 6z = 10. \end{cases}$$

Let $|A|$ = the determinant of the coefficients of the unknowns in the three equations, or

$$|A| = \begin{vmatrix} 2 & -3 & 4 \\ 1 & 5 & -2 \\ 4 & 2 & 6 \end{vmatrix} = 38$$ (see Example 4, pages 137–138)

The coefficients of x in $|A|$ are replaced by the constants:

$$x = \frac{1}{|A|}\begin{vmatrix} -4 & -3 & 4 \\ 15 & 5 & -2 \\ 10 & 2 & 6 \end{vmatrix} = \frac{1}{38}\left(-4\begin{vmatrix} 5 & -2 \\ 2 & 6 \end{vmatrix} - 15\begin{vmatrix} -3 & 4 \\ 2 & 6 \end{vmatrix} + 10\begin{vmatrix} -3 & 4 \\ 5 & -2 \end{vmatrix}\right)$$

$$= \frac{1}{38}(114) = 3$$

The coefficients of y in $|A|$ are replaced by the constants:

$$y = \frac{1}{|A|}\begin{vmatrix} 2 & -4 & 4 \\ 1 & 15 & -2 \\ 4 & 10 & 6 \end{vmatrix} = \frac{1}{38}\left(2\begin{vmatrix} 15 & -2 \\ 10 & 6 \end{vmatrix} - 1\begin{vmatrix} -4 & 4 \\ 10 & 6 \end{vmatrix} + 4\begin{vmatrix} -4 & 4 \\ 15 & -2 \end{vmatrix}\right)$$

$$= \frac{1}{38}(76) = 2$$

The coefficients of z in $|A|$ are replaced by the constants:

$$z = \frac{1}{|A|}\begin{vmatrix} 2 & -3 & -4 \\ 1 & 5 & 15 \\ 4 & 2 & 10 \end{vmatrix} = \frac{1}{38}\left(2\begin{vmatrix} 5 & 15 \\ 2 & 10 \end{vmatrix} - 1\begin{vmatrix} -3 & -4 \\ 2 & 10 \end{vmatrix} + 4\begin{vmatrix} -3 & -4 \\ 5 & 15 \end{vmatrix}\right)$$

$$= \frac{1}{38}(-38) = -1$$

CHECK

Substitute $x = 3$, $y = 2$, and $z = -1$ in the given equations:

$$2x - 3y + 4z = 2(3) - 3(2) + 4(-1) = -4$$
$$x + 5y - 2z = (3) + 5(2) - 2(-1) = 15$$
$$4x + 2y + 6z = 4(3) + 2(2) + 6(-1) = 10$$

NOTE:

1. If there are 3 unknowns, we must have 3 equations in order to have a single solution. If one of the 3 given equations includes only 2 unknowns, we may change it to an equation with 3 unknowns by adding the third unknown with a zero coefficient; for example, $3x + 4y = 17$ is equal to $3x + 4y + 0z = 17$. This addition of a zero coefficient is necessary if we wish to have a square determinant $|A|$.
2. If $|A| = 0$ and $1/|A| = 1/0$ for a system of linear equations, there will be no single

solution. That is, the system either has an infinitely large number of solutions, such as for dependent equations:

$$\begin{cases} x + y = 2, \\ 2x + 2y = 4, \end{cases} \qquad |A| = \begin{vmatrix} 1 & 1 \\ 2 & 2 \end{vmatrix} = 0$$

or has no solution, such as for inconsistent equations:

$$\begin{cases} x + y = 5, \\ x + y = 7, \end{cases} \qquad |A| = \begin{vmatrix} 1 & 1 \\ 1 & 1 \end{vmatrix} = 0$$

3. The symbol $|A|$ used in Cramer's Rule is sometimes written as Δ (delta).

EXERCISE 5-4 REFERENCE: SECTION 5.5

A. Solve each of the following systems of equations by (a) using the inverse of a square matrix and (b) using determinants:

1. $x + 2y = 19$
   $4x + y = -8$
2. $5x + y = -7$
   $x + 4y = 10$
3. $x + y = 8$
   $2x - y = 10$
4. $3x - y = 5$
   $x + 4y = 19$
5. $x + 2y = -4$
   $2x + y = 1$
6. $x + 4y = 11$
   $2x - y = 4$

B. Solve each of the following systems of equations by using determinants:

7. $3x + y + z = 4$
   $2x + 2y + 3z = 1$
   $3x - y - 2z = 7$
8. $3x + 2y - z = 1$
   $2x + z = 13$
   $x + y + 2z = 11$
9. $2x + y + 2z = 3$
   $x - 2y - 3z = 1$
   $3x + 2y + 4z = 5$
10. $x - 3y + 3z = -2$
    $2x + y - 2z = 3$
    $3x - y + z = 2$

5.6 INEQUALITIES AND LINEAR PROGRAMMING

This section introduces the basic concepts of inequalities and linear programming. We shall first present the concept of inequalities, since it is needed in the illustrations of linear programming problems.

A. Inequalities

An inequality is a statement which indicates that one algebraic expression is *greater than* ($>$) or *less than* ($<$) another. Let a, b, and c be real numbers. Then, the statement "a is greater than b" or, written symbolically,

$a > b$

is an inequality. Also, the statement "a is less than c," or

$a < c$

is an inequality. The rules for dealing with inequality operations are as follows:

1. If the same number is added to, or subtracted from, both sides of an inequality, the same inequality sign is used for the new inequality. Thus,

	Let $15 > 2$		Let $15 < 25$
Then	$15 + 8 > 2 + 8$	Then	$15 - 8 < 25 - 8$
	or $23 > 10$		or $7 < 17$

2. If both sides of an inequality are multiplied or divided by the *same positive number*, the same inequality sign is used for the new inequality. Thus,

	Let $6 < 12$		
Then	$6 \times 3 < 12 \times 3$	and	$6 \div 3 < 12 \div 3$
	or $18 < 36$		or $2 < 4$

3. If both sides of an inequality are multiplied or divided by the *same negative number*, the reversed inequality sign is used for the new inequality. Thus,

	Let $8 > 3$		
Then	$8(-4) < 3(-4)$	and	$8 \div (-2) < 3 \div (-2)$
	or $-32 < -12$		or $-4 < -1\frac{1}{2}$

The signs representing equality ($=$) and inequality ($>$ or $<$) may also be written together. The sign $\geq$ represents "is equal to or greater than," and the sign $\leq$ represents "is equal to or less than." Thus,

$X \geq 20$ means that X is equal to 20 or is greater than 20, and
$Y \leq 30$ means that Y is equal to 30 or is less than 30.

Note that the $=$ part of a combined sign indicates the limit of the inequality, such as 20 being the lower limit of the inequality $X \geq 20$ and 30 being the upper limit of the inequality $Y \leq 30$.

Inequalities may be presented graphically according to the system of rectangular coordinates.

EXAMPLE 1

Graph each of the following statements:

(a) $X \geq 0$, (c) $3X + Y \leq 15$, and
(b) $Y \geq 0$, (d) $2X + 4Y \leq 20$

The four graphs are shown in Figure 5–2.

Note the following:

(a) The graph of $X = 0$ is the set of points on the Y-axis. The graph of $X > 0$ is the set of points on the right side of the Y-axis. The graph of $X = 0$ and $X > 0$, or $X \geq 0$, is shown by the shaded area on graph (a) of the figure. *Check:* Point K (in the shaded area) has $X = 3$ and $X > 0$.

(b) The graph of $Y = 0$ is the set of points on the X-axis. The graph of $Y > 0$ is the set of points above the X-axis. The graph of $Y = 0$ and $Y > 0$, or $Y \geq 0$, is shown by the shaded area on graph (b). *Check:* Point K has $Y = 2$ and $Y > 0$.

(c) The graph of equation $3X + Y = 15$ is determined by the points representing the following three pairs of X and Y values:

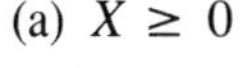

Figure 5–2 (Example 1)

(a) $X \geq 0$

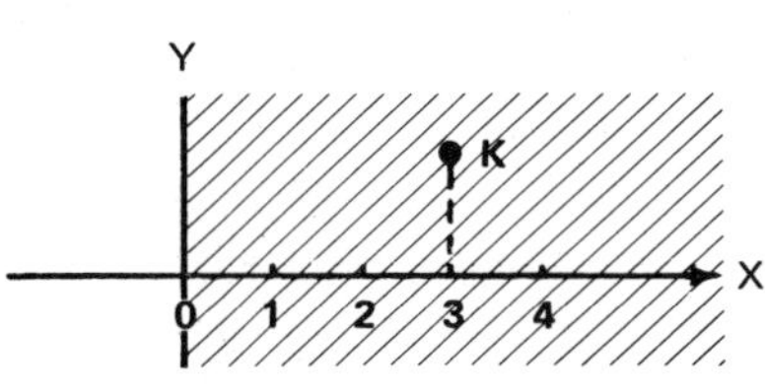

(b) $Y \geq 0$

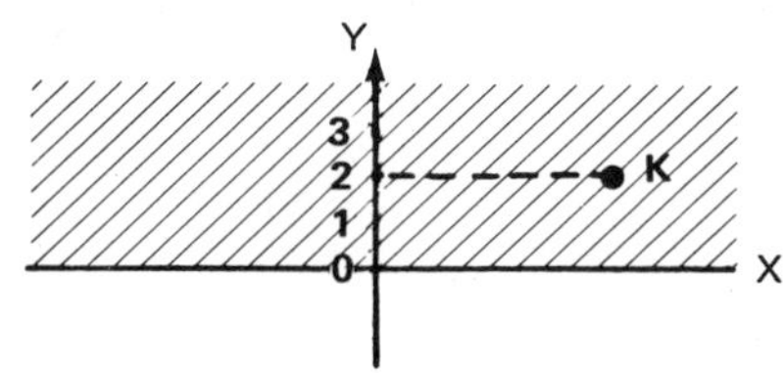

(c) $3X + Y \leq 15$

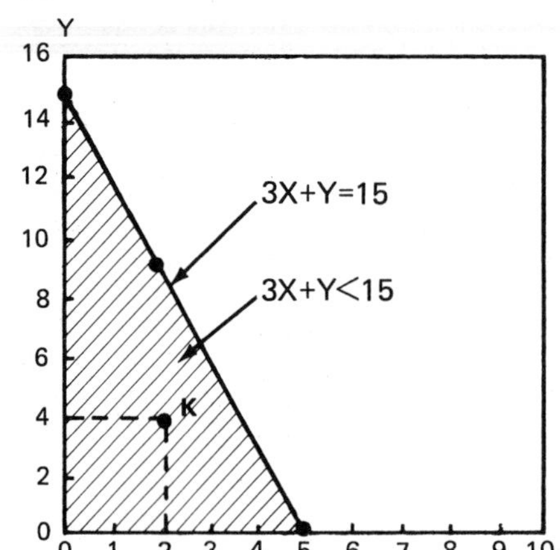

(d) $2X + 4Y \leq 20$

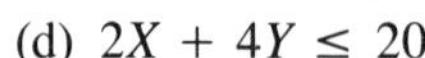

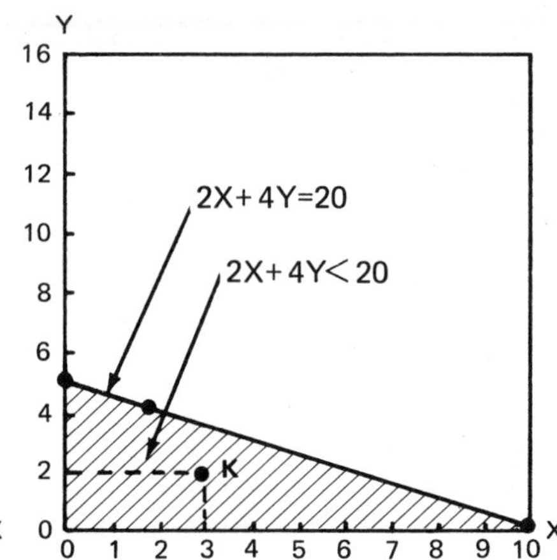

X	Y
0	15
5	0
2	9

The three points are on a straight line, as shown on graph (c). The two points representing ($X = 0, Y = 15$) and ($X = 5, Y = 0$) are called *terminal points*.

The graph of the inequality $3X + Y <$ *15 is the set of points below the straight line, as indicated by the shaded area on graph (c). Check:* Point K on the graph has $X = 2$ and $Y = 4$. $3X + Y = 3(2) + 4 = 10$, which is smaller than 15.

(d) The graph of equation $2X + 4Y = 20$ is determined by the points representing the following three pairs of X and Y values:

X	Y
0	5
10	0
2	4

The three points are on a straight line, as shown on graph (d). The two terminal points represent ($X = 0$, $Y = 5$) and ($X = 10$, $Y = 0$).

The graph of the inequality $2X + 4Y < 20$ is the set of the points below the straight line, as indicated by the shaded area on graph (d). *Check:* Point K on the graph has $X = 3$ and $Y = 2$. $2X + 4Y = 2(3) + 4(2) = 14$, which is smaller than 20.

B. Linear Programming

Linear programming is a mathematical technique for finding the best or *optimum* solution from a set of possible solutions to a given problem. It can be used to solve various complicated business problems, such as maximizing profits and minimizing costs. The basic steps for solving a problem by the linear programming technique are:

1. Derive a group of linear equations and inequalities under certain restraining conditions given by the problem.
2. Solve the group of linear equations and inequalities for an optimum solution.

There are various methods for solving a group of linear equations and inequalities in linear programming. The simplex method, which is derived by the use of matrix algebra, is commonly used. The chief advantage of the simplex method is that its systematic steps in computation can be programmed conveniently on an electronic computer to solve very complicated problems. To illustrate the detailed steps of the simplex method is beyond the scope of this text. We shall use only the graphic method in introducing the basic concept of linear programming techniques.

Note that the example illustrated below involves only two variables (X and Y). Two variables can easily be shown on a two-dimensional space (Figure 5–3). Drawing a three-dimensional space is more difficult but is occasionally used with the graphic method. However, the graphic method becomes impracticable when a linear programming problem involves more than three variables.

EXAMPLE 2

A toy factory is planning to produce two types of toys: boats and cars. Each boat requires 3 hours on machine I and 2 hours on machine II. Each car requires 1 hour on machine I and 4 hours on machine II. Machine I has a maximum of 15 hours available. Machine II has a maximum of 20 hours available.

The profit on each boat is \$7. The profit on each car is \$9. Determine the best combination of boats and cars that should be produced in order to maximize profit.

Let $X =$ the number of boats to be produced
$Y =$ the number of cars to be produced

Then the equation representing the objective of our study, called the *objective function*, is:

Maximize the profits: Profit $= \$7X + \$9Y$ (X boats at \$7 each and Y cars at \$9 each)

The inequalities based on the restraining conditions, called *restraints*, are:

Restraint on machine I:

(1) $3X + 1Y \leq 15$. (Each boat requires 3 hours on the machine and each car requires 1 hour on the machine. The total number of hours on the machine should be equal to or less than 15 hours.)

Restraint on machine II:

(2) $2X + 4Y \leq 20$. (Each boat requires 2 hours on the machine and each car

Figure 5–3 (Example 2)

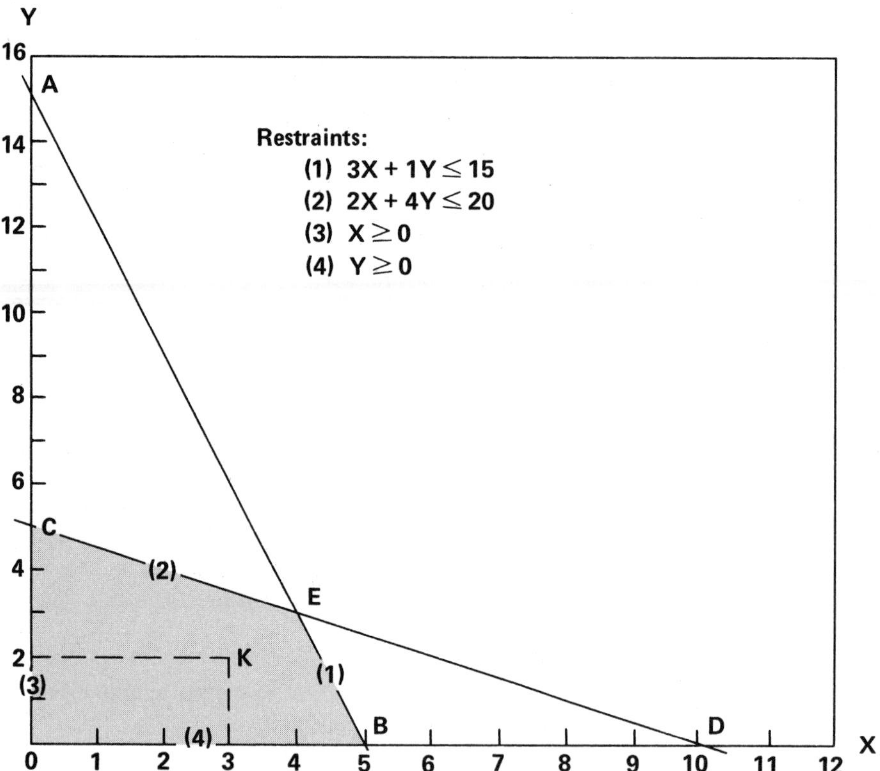

requires 4 hours on the machine. The total number of hours on the machine should be equal to or less than 20 hours.)

Other restraints:

(3) $X \geq 0$, and	(The values of X and Y must be positive. We cannot produce a
(4) $Y \geq 0$.	negative number of boats or cars.)

The four straight lines, (1) *AB*, (2) *CD*, (3) *Y*-axis, and (4) *X*-axis, representing the four equations of the above restraints, respectively, are plotted in Figure 5–3. Lines *AB* and *CD* may be determined by finding the two terminal points for each equation represented. Details concerning the construction of the four lines were presented in Example 1. Observe the four straight lines on the graph. The lines form a four-sided polygon, *OCEB*, the shaded area. The polygon also represents the four inequalities stated above. Any point within the polygon will satisfy the four restraints and thus is a possible solution.

However, our problem is to maximize the objective function, the profit. Thus, we should select a point in the shaded area that will give the highest profit. This point must be located on an extreme far position of the polygon. There are four extreme points on the polygon: O, C, E, and B. The profits based on the four points are computed from the profit equation as follows:

Objective function:	Profit = \$7X + \$9Y
Point O–X = 0 and Y = 0:	Profit = \$7(0) + \$9(0) = \$ 0
Point C–X = 0 and Y = 5:	Profit = \$7(0) + \$9(5) = \$45
Point E–X = 4 and Y = 3:	Profit = \$7(4) + \$9(3) = \$55
Point B–X = 5 and Y = 0:	Profit = \$7(5) + \$9(0) = \$35

Point E, which gives the highest profit (\$55), is the optimum solution, or the best solution from all possible solutions indicated by the points in the shaded area. Thus, the toy factory should produce 4 boats and 3 cars by using the available hours of machines I and II.

CHECK

The four restraints are satisfied by the optimum solution $X = 4$ and $Y = 3$, since

(1) $3X + Y = 3(4) + 1(3) = 15$ (hours available on machine I)
(2) $2X + 4Y = 2(4) + 4(3) = 20$ (hours available on machine II)
(3) $X = 4$, which is larger than 0
(4) $Y = 3$, which is larger than 0

Also, select any point in the shaded area, say point K, which has $X = 3$ and $Y = 2$. Substitute the X and Y values in the profit equation:

Profit = \$7(3) + \$9(2) = 39

which is smaller than the profit based on the optimum solution.

It is possible to have more than one optimum solution. This fact is illustrated in the example below.

EXAMPLE 3

Refer to Example 2. Find the answer if the profit on each boat is \$18 and that on each car is \$6.

Here, the objective function is to maximize: Profit = \$18X + \$6Y.

The profits based on the four points in Figure 5–3 are computed from the new profit equation as follows:

Objective function:	Profit = \$18X + \$6Y
Point O–X = 0 and Y = 0:	Profit = \$18(0) + \$6(0) = \$ 0
Point C–X = 0 and Y = 5:	Profit = \$18(0) + \$6(5) = \$30
Point E–X = 4 and Y = 3:	Profit = \$18(4) + \$6(3) = \$90
Point B–X = 5 and Y = 0:	Profit = \$18(5) + \$6(0) = \$90

Thus, the toy factory may produce either 4 boats and 3 cars (indicated by point E) or 5 boats and 0 cars (indicated by point B) to realize the highest profit, \$90.

Note that when two points give the same maximized profit, the line formed by the two points is the optimum solution. That is, any point on line EB indicates a combination of the number of boats and the number of cars that may be produced to obtain the maximized profit of \$90 under the conditions given in Example 3.

EXERCISE 5-5 REFERENCE: SECTION 5.6

1. Graph each of the following statements (shade the areas representing the statements):
   (a) $X \geq 3$, (b) $Y \geq 4$, (c) $4Y + 3X \leq 12$, (d) $5Y + 2X \leq 10$.
2. Graph each of the following statements (shade the areas representing the statements):
   (a) $X \leq 2$, (b) $Y \leq 5$, (c) $4Y + 5X \geq 20$, (d) $2Y + X \geq 6$.
3. Restraints:

   $$X + Y \leq 7$$
   $$2X + 5Y \leq 20$$
   $$X \geq 0$$
   $$Y \geq 0$$

   Use the graphic method to find the values of X and Y that maximize the objective function F:

   (a) $F = 3X + 8Y$
   (b) $F = 3X + 4Y$
4. Refer to Problem 3. Find the answers if (a) $F = 10X + 8Y$
   (b) $F = 7X + 7Y$
5. Restraints:

   $$X + \tfrac{1}{2}Y \leq 6$$
   $$2X + 3Y \leq 24$$
   $$X \geq 0$$
   $$Y \geq 0$$

   Use the graphic method to find the values of X and Y that maximize the objective function F:

   (a) $F = 8X + 7Y$
   (b) $F = 16X + 6Y$
6. Refer to Problem 5. Find the answers if (a) $F = 8X + 16Y$
   (b) $F = 8X + 4Y$
7. Smith Company makes chairs and tables, among other products. The company can realize a profit of \$5 on each chair and \$10 on each table. Each chair requires 1 hour on the machine and 2 hours of skilled labor. Each table requires 3 hours on the machine and 1 hour of skilled labor. The company has a maximum of 9 hours on the machine available and a maximum of 8 hours of skilled labor available. Determine the units of chairs and tables that should be produced in order to maximize profit. Use the graphic method.
8. Find the answer to Problem 7 if the company can realize a profit of
   (a) \$5 on each chair and \$15 on each table
   (b) \$5 on each chair and \$20 on each table

5.7 BINARY NUMBER SYSTEM

The number systems discussed in this section concern the methods of expressing numbers. A number system usually has a *base*. The base may consist of any fixed number of symbols, such as two (*binary system*), ten (*decimal system*), and twelve (*duodecimal system*).

The decimal system is by far the most popular among the various number systems. Perhaps its popularity is mainly due to the fact that human beings have ten fingers. It is rather convenient for a person to count by tens. The ten symbols used in the decimal system are Arabic figures, or digits 0, 1, 2, 3, 4, 5, 6, 7, 8, and 9. The decimal system was used in the previous sections and will also be used in illustrations throughout this text.

Among the other number systems, the binary system is more frequently mentioned in many areas during recent years. The binary system uses two symbols, 0 and 1. This system can conveniently be used to represent data within modern high-speed electronic computers, although other number systems may also be used. Data within a computer are indicated by electronic signals in two possible conditions, *on* (indicating the presence of the electrical pulse) and *off* (indicating the absence of the electrical pulse). This is the same principle as turning an electric light bulb on or off. We may assign the symbol 1 to indicate *on* and the symbol 0 to indicate *off*.

After a base is selected for a system, the principle of place value is usually employed in expressing numbers larger and smaller than the values of basic symbols. The *principle of place value* states that the value of a symbol varies according to its location in a number. In the decimal system, the value of any digit is *ten* times the value of a *like* digit placed in a position immediately to its right. For example, the value of 9 in the three-digit number 900 is ten times the value of 9 in the two-digit number 90.

Table 5–4 further illustrates the place values of basic symbols in the decimal system.

Note that whole numbers are separated from decimal fractions by a decimal point. For convenience in reading large numbers, the digits are usually divided, by commas or by extra spaces, into groups of three to the left of the decimal point. The number 8,267,943.21 should be read as "eight million, two hundred sixty-seven thousand, nine hundred forty-three, *and* twenty-one hundredths."

Table 5–4 Place Values in the Decimal System (Base 10)

Place Value	$10^6 =$ 1,000,000	$10^5 =$ 100,000	$10^4 =$ 10,000	$10^3 =$ 1,000	$10^2 =$ 100	$10^1 =$ 10	$10^0 =$ 1*	$10^{-1} = \frac{1}{10} = .1$	$10^{-2} = \frac{1}{100} = .01$
Decimal Digit	8 ,	2	6	7 ,	9	4	3 .	2	1
Value of Each Digit	8,000,000	200,000	60,000	7,000	900	40	3	.2	.01

*By definition, any number raised to the zero power is equal to 1 (see page 27).

In the binary system, the principle of place value means that the value of the digit 1 is *two* times the value of the like digit placed in a position immediately to its right. For example, the value of 1 in the three-digit number 100 (equivalent to $1 \times 2^2 + 0 \times 2^1 + 0 \times 2^0 = 4$ with base 10) is two times the value of 1 in the two-digit number 10 (equivalent to $1 \times 2^1 + 0 \times 2^0 = 2$ with base 10). With the understanding of the principle of place value, a binary number can easily be changed to its equivalent decimal number, and vice versa. Also, the fundamental arithmetic operations for binary numbers can be performed in a manner similar to those for decimal numbers.

A. Changing a Binary Number to Its Equivalent Decimal Number

A number with base 2 (a binary number) may be changed to its equivalent number with base 10 (a decimal number) by adding the place values of individual digits of the binary number. The steps of the change are illustrated in Example 1 below.

EXAMPLE 1

Change the number 1010111.11 with base 2 to its equivalent number with base 10.

The place value of each digit of the given binary number is listed in Table 5–5.

Table 5–5 Place Values in the Binary System (Base 2)

Place Value	$2^6 = 64$	$2^5 = 32$	$2^4 = 16$	$2^3 = 8$	$2^2 = 4$	$2^1 = 2$	$2^0 = 1$	$2^{-1} = \frac{1}{2} = .5$	$2^{-2} = \frac{1}{2^2} = .25$
Binary Digit	1	0	1	0	1	1	1	. 1	1
Value of Each Digit	64	0	16	0	4	2	1	.5	.25

Since $64 + 0 + 16 + 0 + 4 + 2 + 1 + .5 + .25 = 87.75$, the number 1010111.11 with base 2 is equivalent to the number 87.75 with base 10.

B. Changing a Decimal Number to Its Equivalent Binary Number

A number with base 10 may be changed to its equivalent number with base 2 by reversing the steps illustrated in Example 1.

EXAMPLE 2

Change the number 53 with base 10 to its equivalent number with base 2.

First, subtract successively the place values as listed in the first row of the table in Example 1 from the given number 53 until the remainder is zero:

$$\begin{array}{r} 53 \\ -32 \\ \hline 21 \\ -16 \\ \hline 5 \\ -4 \\ \hline 1 \\ -1 \\ \hline 0 \end{array}$$

Observe that the first place value in the subtraction, 32, is the largest number that is smaller than the given number, 53. Also, since the remainder after subtracting 16 is only 5 and that after subtracting 4 is only 1, the place values 8 and 2, respectively, are omitted in the successive subtractions.

Next, write 1's under the place values used in the subtractions and 0's under the place values omitted, as follows:

Place value	32	16	8	4	2	1
Binary figure	1	1	0	1	0	1

Thus, the number 53 with base 10 is equivalent to the number 110101 with base 2.

Table 5–6 shows 0 to 16 with base 10 and their equivalent numbers with base 2 for further comparison of the two systems:

Table 5–6 Decimal Numbers 0 to 16 as Compared to Equivalent Binary Numbers

Decimal Number (Base 10)	*Binary Number (Base 2)*	*Decimal Number (Base 10)*	*Binary Number (Base 2)*
0	0	9	1001
1	1	10	1010
$2(=2^1)$	$10(=10^1)$	11	1011
3	11	12	1100
$4(=2^2)$	$100(=10^2)$	13	1101
5	101	14	1110
6	110	15	1111
7	111	$16(=2^4)$	$10000(=10^4)$
$8(=2^3)$	$1000(=10^3)$		

C. Performing Fundamental Arithmetic Operations

The methods of performing the four fundamental operations – addition, subtraction, multiplication, and division – in the binary system are basically the same as those in the decimal system. However, we should remember that the binary system has only two digits, 0 and 1. Keep the place value of the binary digits in mind as you look at the examples below.

EXAMPLE 3 Addition.

(a) Base 2 / Base 10

$$\begin{array}{r} 1 \\ +\ 1 \\ \hline 10 \end{array} \quad = \quad \begin{array}{r} 1 \\ +\ 1 \\ \hline 2 \end{array}$$

(b) Base 2 / Base 10

$$\begin{array}{rcr} 1011 & = & 8+0+2+1=11 \\ +\quad 110 & = & 4+2+0=\ \ 6 \\ \hline 10001 & = & 16+0+0+0+1=17 \end{array}$$

Detailed steps for the addition with base 2 of (b), adding columns from right to left, are:

$$\begin{array}{rll} 1011 & & \\ +\ \ 110 & & \\ \hline 1 & =1+0 & \text{(Add 1st column)} \\ 10\ & =1+1 & \text{(Add 2nd column)} \\ 1\ \ \ & =0+1 & \text{(Add 3rd column)} \\ 1\ \ \ \ & =1 & \text{(Add 4th column)} \\ \hline 01 & & \\ 10\ & & \\ 1\ \ \ & & \\ \hline 10001 & & \end{array}$$

EXAMPLE 4 Subtraction.

(a) Base 2 / Base 10

$$\begin{array}{rcr} 1000 & = & 8+0+0+0=8 \\ -\quad 11 & = & 2+1=3 \\ \hline 101 & = & 4+0+1=5 \end{array}$$

(b) Base 2 / Base 10

$$\begin{array}{rcr} 110111 & = & 32+16+0+4+2+1=55 \\ -\quad 1101 & = & 8+4+0+1=13 \\ \hline 101010 & = & 32+\ \ 0+8+0+2+0=42 \end{array}$$

Detailed steps for each subtraction with base 2 may be illustrated in two ways:

1. *Borrowing Method.* This method may be used when 1 is subtracted from 0 in a column. Since 0 is smaller than 1, the value in a higher place-value column must be

borrowed for the subtraction. The borrowing process can be done in two steps:

First, move to the left of the given 0 in the minuend until a 1 is found.

Second, change the found 1 to 0, each 0 (if any) between the found 1 and the given 0 to 1, and the given 0 to 10 (two).

The detailed steps for (a) and (b) are thus as follows:

(a)
```
   0 1 1 10
   1̸ 0̸ 0̸ 0̸   (Minuend)
 −       1 1   (Subtrahend)
 ___________
       1 0 1   (Remainder)
```

(b)
```
       0 10
   1 1̸ 0̸ 1 1 1   (Minuend)
 −       1 1 0 1   (Subtrahend)
 _______________
   1 0 1 0 1 0     (Remainder)
```

2. *Complementing Method.* The complement of a binary number is obtained by replacing each 0 by 1 and each 1 by 0 in the number. Subtraction by the complementing method involves three steps:

   First, add zeros to the left of the subtrahend until there is the same number of digits as in the minuend and find the complement of the new subtrahend.

   Second, add the minuend, the complement of the new subtrahend, and 1.

   Third, cancel the 1 in the far-left position of the sum obtained in the second step.

   The detailed steps for (a) and (b) by the complementing method are presented below.

(a)
```
     1000   (Minuend)
 +   1100   (Complement of
            subtrahend 0011)
 ________
    10100
 +      1
 ________
    1̸0101   (Answer: 101)
```

(b)
```
    110111   (Minuend)
 +  110010   (Complement of
             subtrahend 001101)
 _________
   1101001
 +       1
 _________
   1̸101010   (Answer: 101010)
```

NOTE:

1. There are 4 digits in the minuend 1000 of (a). The subtrahend 11 is therefore prefixed by two zeros to obtain the 4-digit binary number 0011. There are 6 digits in the minuend 110111 of (b). The subtrahend 1101 is written as the 6-digit binary number 001101.
2. The complementing method is based on the fact that the sum of a binary number, its complement, and 1 is always equal to 1 with as many zeros annexed as there are digits in the binary number, such as

```
    0011   (A binary number)
 +  1100   (Complement of 0011)
 _______
    1111
 +     1
 _______
   10000   (1 with 4 zeros)
```

Subtraction (a) in Example 4 may thus be written in a more complicated form, as shown below:

$$\left.\begin{array}{r} 1000 \\ -\quad 11 \end{array}\right\} = \left\{\begin{array}{rl} +\ 1000 & \text{(Minuend)} \\ -\ 0011 & \text{(Subtrahend)} \\ & \\ +\ 0011 & \text{(Same as the subtrahend)} \\ +\ 1100 & \text{(Complement of 0011)} \\ +\ 1 & \\ -\ 10000 & \\ \hline \not{1}0101 & \end{array}\right. \quad \left.\begin{array}{l} \\ \\ \end{array}\right\} = 0$$

The sum of the two subtrahends (-0011 and $+0011$) is zero. Thus, the complicated form may be simplified as the arrangement presented in the complementing method above.

EXAMPLE 5 Multiplication.

Base 2	Base 10
1101 =	8 + 4 + 0 + 1 = 13
× 111 =	4 + 2 + 1 = 7
1101	21
1101	7
1101	
1011011 =	64 + 0 + 16 + 8 + 0 + 2 + 1 = 91

The multiplication with base 2 may be arranged for ease in addition as follows:

$$\begin{array}{r} 1101 \\ \times\ 111 \\ \hline 1101 \\ +\ 1101 \\ \hline 100111 \\ +\ 1101 \\ \hline 1011011 \end{array}$$

EXAMPLE 6 Division.

(a)

Base 2	Base 10
101 =	4 + 0 + 1 = 5
110)11110	6)30
110	30
110	
110	

Check:

	Base 2	Base 10
Dividend	11110 =	16 + 8 + 4 + 2 + 0 = 30
Divisor	110 =	4 + 2 + 0 = 6
Quotient	101 =	4 + 0 + 1 = 5

(b)

Base 2	Base 10
1101	=13
111)1011011	7)91
111	7
1000	21
111	21
111	
111	

Check: See Example 5.

EXERCISE 5-6 REFERENCE: SECTION 5.7

A. Convert each of the following numbers with base 2 to its equivalent number with base 10:

1. 101	4. 1101	7. 111101	10. 1101101
2. 111	5. 10111	8. 101111	11. 11101111
3. 1010	6. 11011	9. 1111101	12. 11101110

B. Convert each of the following numbers with base 10 to its equivalent number with base 2:

13. 14	16. 30	19. 49	22. 263
14. 18	17. 42	20. 38	23. 336
15. 26	18. 57	21. 125	24. 448

C. The following numbers are expressed with base 2. Perform each indicated operation for the numbers (a) with base 2, and (b) after converting them to base 10:

Addition:

25. $\begin{array}{r} 10 \\ +\ 11 \\ \hline \end{array}$ 27. $\begin{array}{r} 101 \\ +\ 100 \\ \hline \end{array}$ 29. $\begin{array}{r} 1110 \\ +\ 1011 \\ \hline \end{array}$ 31. $\begin{array}{r} 11001 \\ +\ 100111 \\ \hline \end{array}$

26. $\begin{array}{r} 11 \\ +\ 1 \\ \hline \end{array}$ 28. $\begin{array}{r} 110 \\ +\ 111 \\ \hline \end{array}$ 30. $\begin{array}{r} 1101 \\ +\ 1011 \\ \hline \end{array}$ 32. $\begin{array}{r} 1101110 \\ +\ 110101 \\ \hline \end{array}$

Subtraction (use the borrowing method to compute and the complementing method to check your answers for the numbers with base 2):

33. $\begin{array}{r} 1001 \\ -\ 11 \\ \hline \end{array}$ 35. $\begin{array}{r} 1110 \\ -\ 101 \\ \hline \end{array}$ 37. $\begin{array}{r} 111110 \\ -\ 10010 \\ \hline \end{array}$ 39. $\begin{array}{r} 1100011 \\ -\ 1011101 \\ \hline \end{array}$

34. $\begin{array}{r} 110 \\ -\ 100 \\ \hline \end{array}$ 36. $\begin{array}{r} 1100 \\ -\ 111 \\ \hline \end{array}$ 38. $\begin{array}{r} 101101 \\ -\ 11011 \\ \hline \end{array}$ 40. $\begin{array}{r} 1100000 \\ -\ 100010 \\ \hline \end{array}$

Multiplication:

41. $\begin{array}{r} 111 \\ \times\ 110 \\ \hline \end{array}$ 43. $\begin{array}{r} 1100 \\ \times\ 1010 \\ \hline \end{array}$ 45. $\begin{array}{r} 10100 \\ \times\ 1010 \\ \hline \end{array}$ 47. $\begin{array}{r} 11111 \\ \times\ 1100 \\ \hline \end{array}$

42. $\begin{array}{r} 101 \\ \times\ 101 \\ \hline \end{array}$ 44. $\begin{array}{r} 1101 \\ \times\ 1001 \\ \hline \end{array}$ 46. $\begin{array}{r} 11011 \\ \times\ 1101 \\ \hline \end{array}$ 48. $\begin{array}{r} 11111 \\ \times\ 1001 \\ \hline \end{array}$

Division:

49. $10\overline{)110}$	52. $101\overline{)1111}$	55. $110\overline{)111100}$	58. $101\overline{)1100100}$
50. $11\overline{)110}$	53. $111\overline{)100011}$	56. $111\overline{)1000110}$	59. $10100\overline{)1111000}$
51. $11\overline{)1100}$	54. $1001\overline{)110110}$	57. $1000\overline{)1100000}$	60. $1001\overline{)1101100}$

5.8 THE METRIC SYSTEM

The metric system is a decimal system of weights and measures. A distinct advantage of the metric system over the United States system used today is its simplicity. This advantage, plus its popular usage now by most nations, leads us to believe that the United States will gradually join the world in using the metric system.

Under the metric system, the name of each unit has a prefix that indicates the value of the unit based on 10. Thus, it is easy to convert between units. Some of the prefixes and their meanings are listed in Table 5–7.

Table 5–7 Selected Prefixes and Their Meanings in the Metric System

Prefix	*Meaning*
Micro	$10^{-6} = \frac{1}{1{,}000{,}000} = .000001$, one millionth
Milli	$10^{-3} = \frac{1}{1{,}000} = .001$, one thousandth
Centi	$10^{-2} = \frac{1}{100} = .01$, one hundredth
Deci	$10^{-1} = \frac{1}{10} = .1$, one tenth
—	$10^0 = 1$, the basic unit
Deca	$10^1 = 10$, ten times
Hecto	$10^2 = 100$, one hundred times
Kilo	$10^3 = 1{,}000$, one thousand times
Mega	$10^6 = 1{,}000{,}000$, one million times

The basic unit of weight is the *gram*, which is equivalent to 0.0353 ounce. Thus, a centigram is 0.01 gram, a decagram is 10 grams, a hectogram is 100 grams, a kilogram is 1,000 grams, and so on. Notice that the ratio of a larger unit to its smaller unit is always 10 to 1.

The same prefixes are used for length, area, volume, and capacity. The basic unit of length is the *meter* (m). One meter is equivalent to approximately 3.2808 feet (or 39.3701 inches).

The basic unit of area is the *square meter* (m^2). One square meter is equivalent to 10.7639 square feet. However, in measuring land, the basic unit of the metric system is the *are*. One *are* (= 100 square meters) is equivalent to 0.0247 acre.

The basic unit of volume is the *cubic meter* (m^3). One cubic meter is equivalent to 35.3147 cubic feet.

The *liter* (L) is the basic unit of capacity. A liter is equal to 1,000 cubic centimeters, or a volume with each side being 10 centimeters, since $10^3 = 1{,}000$. Converting to U.S. units, one liter is equivalent to 0.9081 quart for dry capacity, or 1.0567 quart for liquid capacity.

More conversion factors between selected metric units and their corresponding U.S. units are given in Tables 5–8 and 5–9. Mathematical operations based on the tables are presented below.

Table 5–8 Conversion Factors from Metric Units to U.S. Units

Metric Unit	*Approximate U.S. Equivalent*
Weight—Basic Unit: Gram (g)	
1 decigram (0.1 g)	1.5432 grains
1 gram (1 g)	0.0353 ounce
1 kilogram (1,000 g)	2.2046 pounds
1 metric ton (1,000,000 g)	1.1023 short tons
Length—Basic Unit: Meter (m)	
1 centimeter (0.01 m)	0.3937 inch
1 meter (1 m)	3.2808 feet
1 kilometer (1,000 m)	0.6214 mile
Area—Basic Unit: Square Meter (m^2)	
1 square centimeter $= (.01\text{ m})^2 = .0001\text{ m}^2$	0.1550 square inch
1 square meter (1 m^2)	10.7639 square feet
1 square decameter $= (10\text{ m})^2 = 100\text{ m}^2 = 1$ are	0.0247 acre
1 square kilometer $= (1{,}000\text{ m})^2 = 1{,}000{,}000\text{ m}^2$	0.3861 square mile
Volume—Basic Unit: Cubic Meter (m^3)	
1 cubic meter (1 m^3)	35.3147 cubic feet
Capacity—Basic Unit: Liter (L) *1 Liter = 1,000 Cubic Centimeters = .001 Cubic Meter*	
A. Dry	
1 deciliter (.1 L)	0.1816 pint
1 liter ($.001\text{ m}^3$)	0.9081 quart
1 hectoliter (100 L)	2.8378 bushels
B. Liquid	
1 deciliter (.1 L)	0.2113 pint
1 liter ($.001\text{ m}^3$)	1.0567 quarts
1 decaliter (10 L)	2.6418 gallons

A. Conversion Between Metric Units

To convert one metric unit to another metric unit, first find the relationship between the two units as defined in Table 5–7. Next, either use the proportional method or move the decimal point to find the answer. In converting a larger unit to a smaller unit, move the decimal point to the right. Conversely, in converting a smaller unit to a larger unit, move the decimal point to the left.

Table 5–9 Conversion Factors from U.S. Units to Metric Units

U.S. Units	*Approximate Metric Equivalent*
Weight	
1 grain	0.0648 gram
1 ounce (=437$\frac{1}{2}$ grains)	28.3495 grams
1 pound (=16 ounces)	453.5924 grams
1 short ton (=2,000 pounds)	0.9072 metric ton
Length	
1 inch	2.5400 centimeters
1 foot (=12 inches)	0.3048 meter
1 mile (=5,280 feet)	1.6093 kilometers
Area	
1 square inch	6.4516 square centimeters
1 square foot (=144 square inches)	0.0929 square meter
1 acre (=43,560 square feet)	4,046.8564 square meters=40.4686 ares
1 square mile (=640 acres)	2.5900 square kilometers
Volume	
1 cubic foot	0.0283 cubic meter
Capacity	
A. Dry	
1 pint	0.5506 liter
1 quart (= 2 pints)	1.1012 liters
1 bushel (= 32 quarts)	35.2381 liters
B. Liquid	
1 pint	0.4732 liter
1 quart (= 2 pints)	0.9463 liter
1 gallon (= 4 quarts)	3.7853 liters

EXAMPLE 1 Convert (a) 2.46 kilograms to grams and (b) 736.5 centimeters to meters.

(a) 1 kilogram = 1,000 grams (Table 5–7)
2.46 kilograms = 2.46(1,000)
= 2,460 grams, or
2.46 kilograms = 2.460. grams

(b) 1 centimeter = .01 meter (Table 5–7)
736.5 centimeters = 736.5(.01)
= 7.365 meters, or
736.5 centimeters = 7.36.5 meters

EXAMPLE 2 Convert (a) 25 meters to millimeters and (b) 36 grams to hectograms.

(a) 1 millimeter = .001 meter (Table 5–7)

Thus,

1 meter = 1,000 millimeters
25 meters = 25.000. or 25,000 millimeters

Or let x = unknown converted millimeters.
Then, by proportional expression,

x is to 25 meters as 1 millimeter is to .001 meter;

$$\frac{x}{1} = \frac{25}{.001}, \qquad x = \frac{25}{.001} = 25{,}000 \text{ millimeters}$$

(b) 1 hectogram = 100 grams (Table 5–7)
Thus,

$$1 \text{ gram} = \frac{1}{100} = .01 \text{ hectogram}$$

36 grams = .36. or .36 hectograms

Or let x = unknown hectograms.
Then, by proportional expression,

x is to 36 grams as 1 hectogram is to 100 grams;

$$\frac{x}{1} = \frac{36}{100}, \qquad x = .36 \text{ hectograms}$$

The above two examples illustrate the methods of converting a metric unit to its basic unit (Example 1) and the basic unit to a smaller or larger unit (Example 2). In the conversion between nonbasic units, it is usually convenient for a beginner to use a basic unit in the intermediate steps. This method is illustrated in Example 3 below.

EXAMPLE 3 Convert (a) 41.76 hectograms to kilograms, (b) 238 decimeters to millimeters, and (c) 65 centimeters to decameters.

(a) 1 hectogram = 100 grams
1 kilogram = 1,000 grams

$$\frac{1 \text{ hectogram}}{1 \text{ kilogram}} = \frac{100}{1{,}000} = .1$$

1 hectogram = .1 kilogram

Thus, 41.76 hectograms = 41.76(.1) = 4.176 kilograms

(b) 1 decimeter = .1 meter
1 millimeter = .001 meter

$$\frac{1 \text{ decimeter}}{1 \text{ millimeter}} = \frac{.1}{.001} = 100$$

1 decimeter = 100 millimeters

Thus, 238 decimeters = 238(100) = 23,800 millimeters

(c) 1 centimeter = .01 meter
1 decameter = 10 meters

$$\frac{1 \text{ centimeter}}{1 \text{ decameter}} = \frac{.01}{10} = .001$$

1 centimeter = .001 decameter

Thus, 65 centimeters = 65(.001) = .065 decameter

B. Conversion from Metric Units to U.S. Units, and Vice Versa

The following illustrations are based on the conversion factors between metric units and U.S. units shown in Tables 5–8 and 5–9.

EXAMPLE 4 Convert (a) 7 meters to feet, (b) 4 square meters to square feet, and (c) 5 cubic meters to cubic feet.

(a) 1 meter = 3.2808 feet
7 meters = 3.2808(7) = 22.9656 feet

(b) 1 square meter = 10.7639 square feet
4 square meters = 10.7639(4) = 40.0556 square feet

(c) 1 cubic meter = 35.3147 cubic feet
5 cubic meters = 35.3147(5) = 176.5735 cubic feet

EXAMPLE 5 Convert (a) 10 pounds to kilograms, (b) 6 feet 2 inches to centimeters, and (c) 6 gallons to liters.

(a) 1 pound = 453.5924 grams
10 pounds = 453.5924(10) = 4,535.924 grams
= 4.535924 kilograms

(b) 1 inch = 2.54 centimeters
6 feet 2 inches = 6(12) + 2 = 74 inches
= 74(2.54) = 187.96 centimeters

(c) 1 gallon = 3.7853 liters
6 gallons = 3.7853(6) = 22.7118 liters

★EXERCISE 5-7 REFERENCE: SECTION 5.8

A. Convert the following between metric units:

1. Convert 120 meters to (a) decimeters, (b) centimeters, (c) decameters, and (d) millimeters.
2. Convert 85.2 meters to (a) millimeters, (b) decimeters, and (c) hectometers.
3. Convert 14.3 decagrams to (a) decigrams, (b) centigrams, and (c) kilograms.
4. Convert 213.7 decimeters to (a) millimeters, (b) hectometers, and (c) megameters.
5. Convert 3.58 kilograms to (a) grams, (b) decigrams, and (c) decagrams.
6. Convert 31.5 kilograms to (a) grams, (b) milligrams, (c) hectograms, and (d) decagrams.
7. Convert 136.4 grams to (a) centigrams, (b) micrograms, and (c) decagrams.
8. Convert 1 cubic meter to (a) cubic decimeters and (b) cubic hectometers.
9. Convert 5 liters to (a) deciliters and (b) kiloliters.
10. Convert 35 decaliters to (a) centiliters and (b) hectoliters.

11. Convert 1,254 centimeters to (a) meters, (b) millimeters, and (c) hectometers.
12. Convert 1 square meter to (a) square centimeters and (b) square decameters.

B. Convert the following from metric units to U.S. units, and vice versa (round your final answers to two decimal places):

13. Convert 15 meters to (a) feet and (b) yards (1 yard = 3 feet).
14. Convert 42.6 meters to (a) feet, (b) inches, and (c) yards.
15. Convert 500 decigrams to (a) grains and (b) ounces (1 ounce = 437.5 grains).
16. Convert 1,000 kilograms to (a) pounds and (b) short tons (1 short ton = 2,000 pounds).
17. Convert 10,000 square meters to (a) square feet and (b) acres (1 acre = 43,560 square feet).
18. Convert 5,000 square meters to (a) square feet, (b) acres, and (c) square miles.
19. Convert 238 centimeters to (a) inches and (b) feet (1 foot = 12 inches).
20. Convert 20 kilometers to (a) miles, (b) yards, and (c) feet (1 mile = 1,760 yards = 5,280 feet).
21. Convert 600 grams to (a) ounces and (b) pounds (1 pound = 16 ounces).
22. Convert 10 square kilometers to (a) square miles and (b) acres (1 square mile = 640 acres).
23. Convert 10 cubic meters to (a) cubic feet and (b) cubic yards (1 cubic yard = 27 cubic feet).
24. Convert 10 dry liters to (a) quarts and (b) pints (1 quart = 2 pints).
25. Convert 5 dry hectoliters to (a) bushels, (b) pecks, and (c) quarts (1 bushel = 4 pecks, 1 peck = 8 quarts).
26. Convert 10 liquid liters to (a) quarts, (b) pints, (c) ounces, (d) gallons, and (e) barrels (1 quart = 2 pints, 1 pint = 16 ounces, 1 gallon = 4 quarts, and 1 barrel = 31.5 gallons).
27. Convert to dry liters from (a) 100 pints, (b) 200 quarts, and (c) 10 bushels.
28. Convert to liquid liters from (a) 500 pints, (b) 300 quarts, and (c) 100 gallons.
29. A company sold 3,000 pounds of sugar to a dealer in France. How many kilograms should the company put on the invoice for the sale?
30. An American wishes to purchase 100 feet of silk material in Taiwan. How many meters of the material is this?
31. The measurements of a room are 10 feet wide and 20 feet long. What is the room size in square meters?
32. Johnson Company plans to build a 20,000-cubic-foot warehouse in its Italian branch. Express the size of the warehouse in cubic meters.
33. An American car averages 25 miles per gallon of gasoline. The average would be advertised as how many kilometers per liter of gasoline in the European market?
34. A company shipped 4,000 yards of clothing material to Japan. The shipping company charges 5¢ per meter of material. How much is the shipping cost?

PART TWO MATHEMATICS IN BUSINESS MANAGEMENT

6 INTRODUCTION TO STATISTICAL METHODS

The subject of statistics may involve complicated mathematical operations. However, this chapter introduces only selected fundamental statistical topics that are particularly useful in solving business management problems. The topics are: the meaning of statistics (Section 6.1), presentation of data (Section 6.2), averages (Section 6.3), dispersion (Section 6.4), and frequency distribution (Section 6.5).

6.1 THE MEANING OF STATISTICS

There are vast amounts of quantitative information, or numerical data, as a result of daily activities such as sales, purchases, wages, and school enrollments. The field of statistics was developed to help us deal with this abundance of quantitative information. The word *statistics* has been broadly used to mean either the information itself or the methods of dealing with the information. However, statisticians prefer to call the quantitative information *statistical data* and the methods of dealing with the information *statistical methods*. Statistical methods include the techniques used in collecting, organizing, presenting, analyzing, and interpreting statistical data. The techniques can be used not only in business and economic studies, but also in such fields as education, psychology, agriculture, and biology.

Techniques used in the various statistical methods are numerous. In this chapter, we shall limit our discussion to the following techniques:

1. Presentation of data—Presenting the statistical data tabularly and graphically.
2. Averages—Finding a single value that can be used as a representative value of a series of data.
3. Dispersion—Measuring the deviation from an average of a given series of data.
4. Frequency distribution—Organizing the data into groups in order to facilitate statistical analysis and interpretation.

6.2 PRESENTATION OF DATA

The first step in statistical work is to collect data. Not all quantitative information is regarded as statistical data. Statistical data are the numbers that represent some measurable or countable things and show significant relationships. The so-called "statistics" of a customer as measured by a tailor are not statistical data because the individual measurements, such as height, weight, and waist size, show no significant relationship to each other. However, information regarding the heights of all the tailor's customers within a certain period of time is statistical, since the measurements can be compared, analyzed, and interpreted according to their relationships.

Statistical data may be obtained from various sources, such as government units, corporations, magazines, books or other publications, and firsthand collections. Data collected from sources other than firsthand collections may be in organized or unorganized form. Firsthand collections in the original form usually need organization. The process of complete organization involves editing, classifying, and tabulating the collected data. Although statistical data can be presented in paragraphs without formal organization, an organized presentation is usually appreciated by most readers. A formal statistical presentation may be in the form of tables or graphs.

A. Tables

When statistical data are presented in tabulated form, the data are systematically arranged in columns and rows. The major parts of a table are as follows:

1. Title—The title is a description of the contents of the table. It should be compact and complete. When more than one table is presented, each table should be numbered.
2. Headnote—The headnote usually concerns the whole body of the table. It is written below the title.
3. Captions—Captions are the headings of the columns.
4. Stubs—Stubs are the descriptions of the rows.
5. Body—The body is the content of the statistical data.
6. Footnotes—Footnotes are used to clarify certain items or some part of the table. They are placed below the stub.
7. Source—The source is the place from which the data were obtained. It is usually written below the footnotes. If the data were not collected originally by the one who presents them, the source should be stated to enable the reader to check the data or to obtain additional information from the source.

Table 6–1 is presented as an illustration.

B. Graphs

A *graph* or a *chart* is a pictorial device for presenting certain statistical data or for showing the relationships among several classes of quantities. It is an effective visual aid for management personnel, policymakers, researchers, and other readers. A person

TITLE → **Table 6–1** Composition of Budget Outlays, 1980 and 1989

HEADNOTE → (in billions of 1982 dollars)

CAPTIONS

Type of Outlay	*Year*	
	1980	*1989*
National defense	164.0	241.6
Net interest	62.0	119.5
Payments for individuals	324.7	415.3
Low-income benefits	61.5	76.7
Elderly and retirees	213.9	296.5
Other	49.3	42.1
Basic government functions	21.4	23.7
Other administration priorities	12.3	18.5
Grants to state and local government*	68.0	41.4
Remaining programs	47.6	9.3
Total outlays	700.0	869.3

STUB → BODY

FOOTNOTE → *Excludes grants for payments for individuals.

SOURCE → **Source:** Executive Office of the President, *Budget of the United States Government, 1989,* page 2a–3.

using graphs can acquire certain types of information much more quickly than by studying the figures in tabulated form or reading the same information in paragraph form.

Nearly all types of quantitative data may be expressed in the form of graphs. A graph should be presented in an interesting and effective manner. A well-organized and vivid graphical presentation can help readers acquire much knowledge in a short period of time. However, a graph gives a reader only an approximate representation of the facts. If precision is desired, the tabulated figures or the original source of the graph should be consulted.

Generally, graphs are drawn according to a coordinate system (see Section 3.3, page 71). The types of graphs that are most commonly used by statisticians are the line chart, the bar chart, and the component-part chart.

LINE CHART

A chart that consists of lines or broken lines is called a *line chart.* To construct a line chart, first plot the data by points according to the scales on the two reference lines. Then connect the points by straight lines. The scales used on the two reference lines may or may not be equal. They may be arithmetic or logarithmic. When one line is arithmetic and the other is logarithmic, the chart is called a *semilogarithmic* chart or a *ratio* chart.

The logarithmic scale is usually placed on the vertical line in a semilogarithmic chart. A logarithmic scale is rarely used for both reference lines.

On an arithmetic scale, equal distances represent equal amounts. On a logarithmic scale, the distance between two numbers represents the difference between the logarithms of the two numbers; it does not represent the difference between the actual numbers. In other words, equal distances on a logarithmic scale represent the equal ratios of the numbers. Therefore, a logarithmic scale cannot have zero as the origin.

EXAMPLE 1

The annual net income of the Walton Hardware Store from 1982 to 1990 is listed in Table 6–2. Using these data, construct (a) an arithmetic line chart and (b) a semilogarithmic line chart.

Table 6–2 Net Income of Walton Hardware Store, 1982–1990

Year	*Net Income*	*Year*	*Net Income*
1982	$ 300	1987	$ 6,800
1983	600	1988	8,800
1984	1,200	1989	10,800
1985	2,400	1990	12,800
1986	4,800		

Source: Hypothetical.

SOLUTION:

(a) See Figure 6–1.
(b) See Figure 6–2.

A semilogarithmic chart can be constructed either by plotting the numbers in a series on a logarithmic scale or by plotting the logarithms of the numbers in a series on an arithmetic scale. The former method is usually preferred because it does not require finding the logarithms, and plotting the numbers on a logarithmic scale is as easy as plotting the numbers on an arithmetic scale. This method has been used in constructing Figure 6–2.

On printed semilogarithmic paper, the value at the top of a cycle on the logarithmic scale is always ten times the value at the bottom of the cycle. Notice the logarithmic scale in Figure 6–2. The value at the top of the first cycle is 2,000 ($200 \times 10 = 2{,}000$) and the value at the top of the second cycle is 20,000 ($2{,}000 \times 10 = 20{,}000$). When the ratio of two numbers is equal to the ratio of two other numbers, the distances between the points representing the numbers are the same. For example, the ratio of 600 to 300 (=2) is the same as the ratio of 1,200 to 600 (=2). Thus, the distance between 600 and 300 is the same as the distance between 1,200 and 600. Further, when the ratio is constant, the points are on a straight line. For example, all the ratios of 4,800 to 2,400, 2,400 to 1,200, 1,200 to 600, and 600 to 300 are 2. Thus, the points representing the net income for the years from 1982 to 1986 are on a straight line when the logarithmic scale is used. This is not true in Figure 6–1, where the arithmetic scale is used.

Figure 6–1 Arithmetic Line Chart
Net Income of Walton Hardware Store, 1982–1990

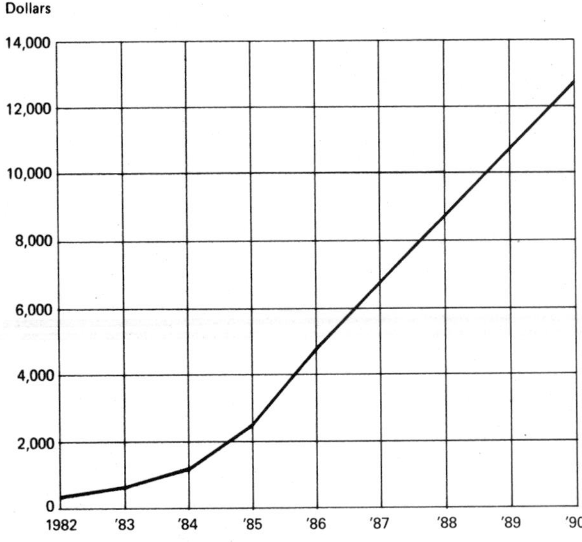

The points for the years 1986, 1987, 1988, 1989, and 1990 are not on a straight line in Figure 6–2, but are on a straight line in Figure 6–1. When a series of numbers increases by a constant *amount* ($2,000 each year from 1986 to 1990 in the present case), the points representing the numbers are on a straight line on an arithmetic scale, as in Figure 6–1.

Source of data: Table 6–2.

NOTE: Time is always regarded as the independent variable in time series and is placed on the horizontal reference line.

Figure 6–2 Semilogarithmic Line Chart
Net Income of Walton Hardware Store, 1982–1990

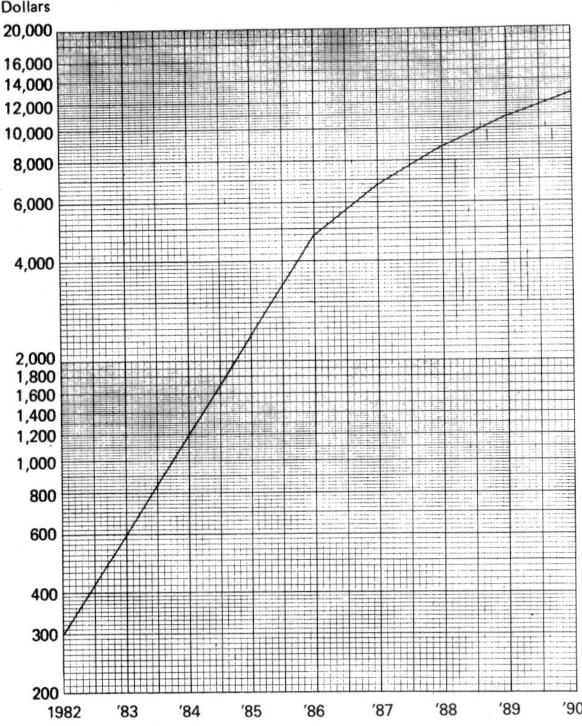

Source of data: Table 6–2.

BAR CHART

A *bar chart* is a graph that consists of a number of rectangular bars which may be arranged vertically or horizontally. The width of the bars is usually equal. The length of the bars represents the values of the data.

EXAMPLE 2 The number of houses constructed by the Aron Company during each year from 1980 to 1990 is given in Table 6–3. Use the information to draw a vertical bar chart.

Table 6–3 Number of Houses Constructed by Aron Company, 1980–1990

Year	*Number of Houses*	*Year*	*Number of Houses*
1980	75	1986	240
1981	110	1987	270
1982	130	1988	290
1983	180	1989	325
1984	190	1990	390
1985	220		

Source: Hypothetical.

SOLUTION: See Figure 6–3.

Figure 6–3 Vertical Bar Chart
Number of Houses Constructed by Aron Company, 1980–1990

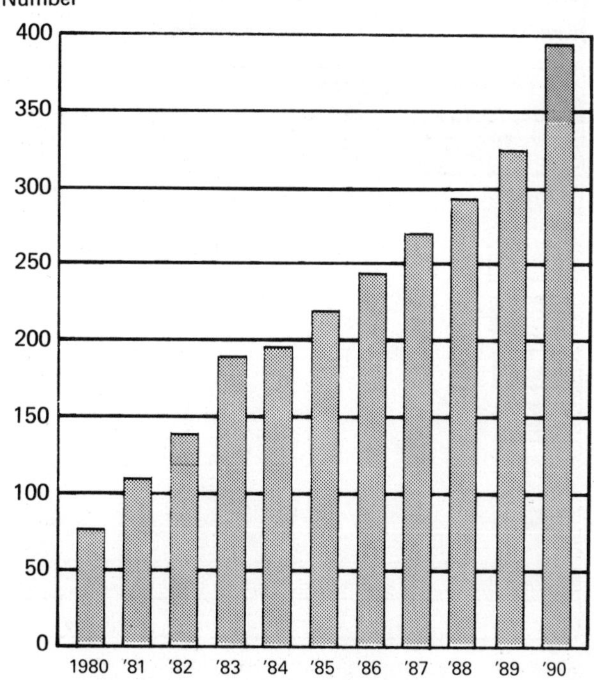

Source of data: Table 6–3.

EXAMPLE 3 The world production of crude oil in 1988 is listed in Table 6–4. Draw a horizontal bar chart for this data.

Table 6–4 World Production of Crude Oil, 1988

Nation	*Production (Millions of Barrels per Day)*
USSR	11.83
United States	8.24
Saudi Arabia	4.46
China	2.71
Iraq	2.62
Mexico	2.53
United Kingdom	2.40
Iran	2.14
Venezuela	1.78
Canada	1.59
Other nations	16.74
Total	57.04

Source: U. S. Department of Energy, *Monthly Energy Review,* July 1988.

SOLUTION: See Figure 6–4.

Figure 6–4 Horizontal Bar Chart
World Production of Crude Oil, 1988 (Millions of Barrels per Day)

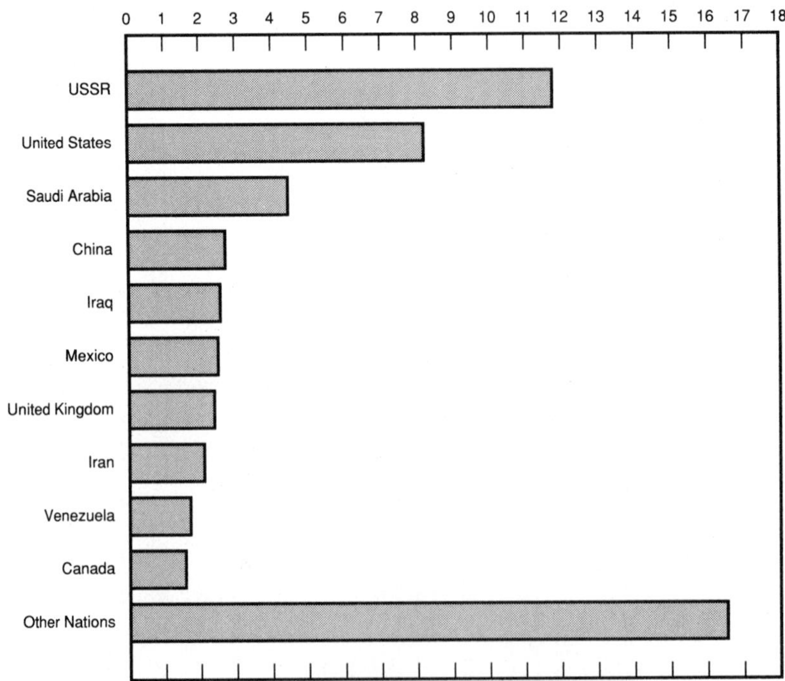

Source of data: Table 6–4.

COMPONENT-PART CHART

A *component-part chart* is used to show the relationships among the individual items of a total or of a series of totals. It is frequently constructed by using bars, lines, or segments of a circle (pie diagram). The following three examples illustrate the various ways to construct component-part charts.

EXAMPLE 4 Use the information in Table 6–5 to construct a component-part bar chart showing the number of employees in each educational group for each year.

Table 6–5 Employees in Waxen Company by Education Level, 1985 and 1990

Education	*Number of Employees*	
	1985	*1990*
3 years high school or less	1,570	2,804
4 years high school	2,750	3,130
1 to 3 years college	1,540	2,587
4 years college or more	2,420	3,566
Not classified by education	350	403
Total	8,630	12,490

Source: Hypothetical.

SOLUTION: See Figure 6–5.

Figure 6–5 Component-Part Bar Chart
Employees in Waxen Company by Education Level, 1985 and 1990

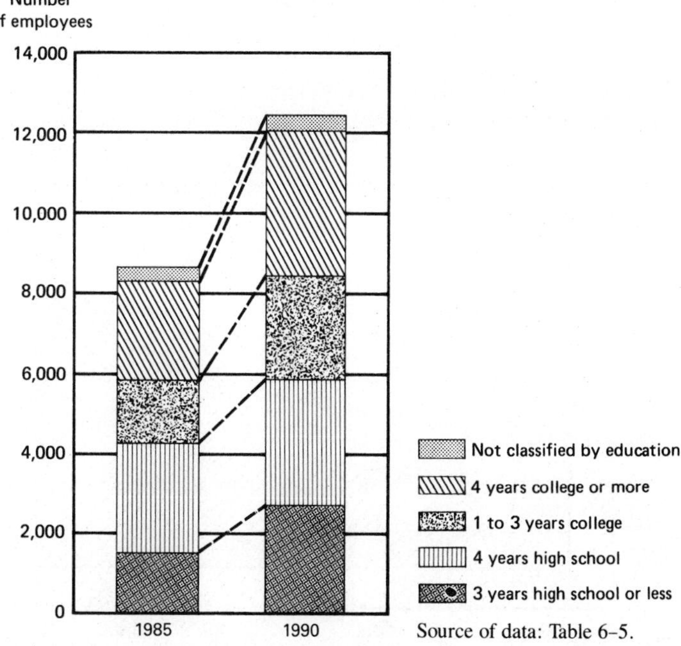

Source of data: Table 6–5.

In Figure 6–5, the length of each part of a bar is made according to the size of each educational group. For example, the part representing employees with 4 years of high school in 1985 is placed on the scale between 1,570 and 4,320, since 1,570 + 2,750 = 4,320. The individual parts are shaded in different ways to show distinctively the number represented.

EXAMPLE 5 Use the facts in Table 6–6 to construct a component-part line chart.

Table 6–6 Selling, Administrative, and Other Expenses Paid by Jackston Company, 1984–1991
(Thousands of Dollars)

Year	*Selling Expenses*	*Administrative Expenses*	*Other Expenses*	*Total*
1984	600	252	106	958
1985	532	270	118	920
1986	589	309	128	1,026
1987	641	301	241	1,183
1988	730	321	245	1,296
1989	773	358	250	1,381
1990	818	396	261	1,475
1991	986	416	280	1,682

Source: Hypothetical.

SOLUTION: See Figure 6–6.

Note that in Figure 6–6 the changes in the component parts are again shown by different shades. Figures 6–5 and 6–6 show the actual numbers of each distribution. However, the two types of component-part charts may also be used in showing percent distributions. A total is usually expressed as 100% when a percent distribution is shown.

Figure 6–6 Component-Part Line Chart
Selling, Administrative, and Other Expenses Paid by Jackston Company, 1984–1991

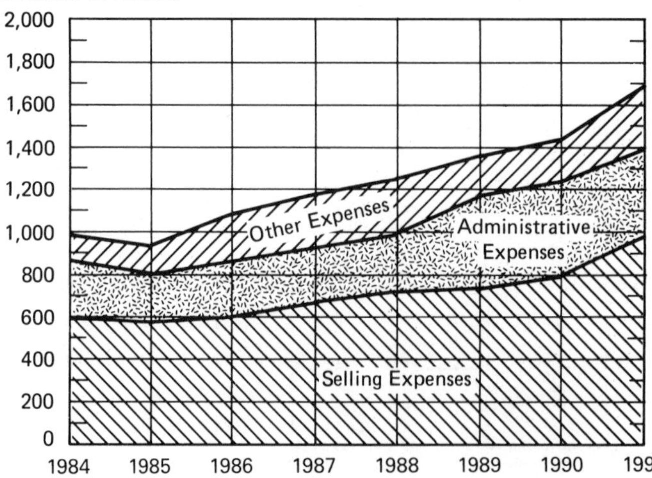

Source of data: Table 6–6.

A percent distribution may also be shown by means of a pie chart. A *pie chart* is a circle divided proportionally into component parts according to the sizes of the individual items that make up the total. The circle may be conveniently divided into either 360 degrees or 100 equal parts by means of a printed form or a protractor. However, if a 360-degree protractor is used, the percent distribution should be multiplied by 3.6 before the data are plotted.

EXAMPLE 6 Use the data provided in Table 6–7 to construct a pie chart for the year 1991.

Table 6–7 Percent Distribution of Selling, Administrative, and Other Expenses Paid by Jackston Company, 1991

Type of Payment	*1991*
Selling expenses	58.62%
Administrative expenses	24.73%
Other expenses	16.65%
Total	100.00%

Source: Computed from Example 5. For example, 986 ÷ 1,682 = 58.62%, the first figure of the 1991 column.

SOLUTION: See Figure 6–7.

Figure 6–7 Pie Chart
Percent Distribution of Selling, Administrative, and Other Expenses Paid by Jackston Company, 1991

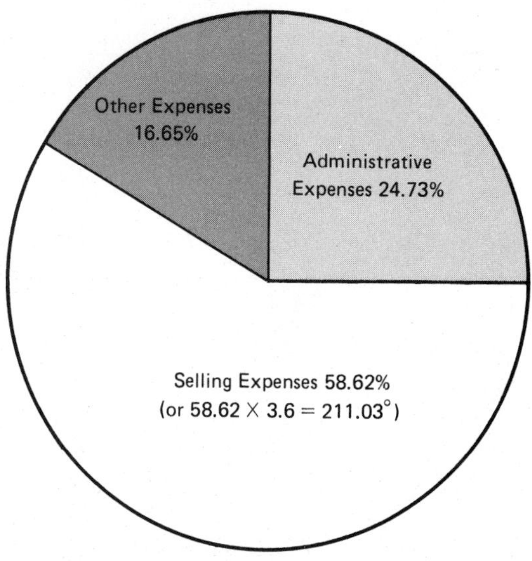

Source of data: Table 6–7.

EXERCISE 6–1 REFERENCE: SECTION 6.2

1. The *Survey of Current Business*, issued by the United States Department of Commerce, contains in the July 1988 issue the following information concerning personal income by sources:

   Wage and salary disbursements were $2,425.0 billion in 1988, $176.7 billion more than in 1987; other labor income rose to $217.4 billion in 1988, $9.5 billion more than in 1987; proprietors' income increased to $323.0 billion in 1988, $10 billion higher than in 1987; rental income was $18.2 billion in 1988, $0.2 billion lower than in 1987; dividends totaled $95.4 billion in 1988, $6.8 billion more than in 1987; personal interest income advanced to $573.2 billion in 1988, $46.2 billion higher than in 1987; and net transfer payments amounted to $389.6 billion in 1988, up $12.8 billion from 1987.

   Construct a table showing the above information and the totals of personal income for 1987 and 1988.

2. The *Federal Reserve Bulletin*, issued by the Board of Governors of the Federal Reserve System, has the following facts in the July 1977 and September 1988 issues concerning personal consumption expenditures:

   Total personal consumption expenditures in the United States were $192.0 billion in 1950 and $3,186.8 billion in 1988. The 1988 total includes expenditures for durable goods in the amount of $446.9 billion, which is $416.1 billion more than in 1950; nondurable goods, $1,030.3 billion, which is $932.1 billion more than in 1950; and services, $1,709.6 billion, which is $1,646.6 billion higher than in 1950.

   Construct a table showing the above facts.

3. The number of units shipped yearly by Fox Distributors from 1984 to 1991 is given below. Construct (a) an arithmetic line chart and (b) a semilogarithmic line chart depicting this time series.

Year	*No. of Units*	*Year*	*No. of Units*
1984	1,500	1988	3,900
1985	2,100	1989	4,500
1986	2,700	1990	4,000
1987	3,300	1991	3,500

4. The total deposits of a bank from 1984 to 1991 are listed in the following table. Construct (a) an arithmetic line chart and (b) a semilogarithmic line chart showing the total deposits for each year.

Year	*Total Deposits*	*Year*	*Total Deposits*
1984	$ 2,000	1988	$20,500
1985	4,000	1989	12,400
1986	8,000	1990	9,300
1987	10,900	1991	18,000

5. Use the data in Problem 3 to draw a vertical bar chart.

6. The total number of transactions during a month for each of the four branches of a company is listed below. Draw a horizontal bar chart illustrating these data.

Branch	*Total Transactions*
East	2,300
South	1,900
West	2,700
North	1,600

7. Use the data given in the following table to construct a component-part bar chart showing the actual amount of stocks of each type for the years 1985 and 1991:

Types of Common Stocks Owned by Bagge Investment Company
(Thousands of Dollars)

Type	*1985*	*1991*
Railroad	39	49
Public utility	815	1,217
Industrial and miscellaneous	2,329	4,666
Total	3,183	5,932

Source: Hypothetical.

8. Use the information in the following table to construct a component-part line chart showing the actual income for each item for 1985 to 1991.

Gross Income of Griffin Department Store, 1985–1991
(Thousands of Dollars)

Year	*Income from Clothing Department*	*Income from Shoe Department*	*Income from Other Departments*	*Total Income*
1985	324	50	84	458
1986	341	51	90	482
1987	366	52	100	518
1988	394	57	111	562
1989	436	59	122	617
1990	470	58	122	650
1991	498	60	128	686

Source: Hypothetical.

9. Use the data provided in Problem 7 to construct a pie chart for 1991.
10. Refer to the data provided in Problem 8. Compute the percent of total income for each item, and construct (a) a component-part bar chart showing the percents for the years 1985, 1987, 1989, and 1991; (b) a component-part line chart showing the percents for the years from 1985 to 1991; and (c) a pie chart for the year 1991.

6.3 AVERAGES

Since statistical data usually include a large number of items, it is rather difficult for a person to describe simultaneously the characteristics of all items included in the data or to compare one group of data with another. However, if a single value can be determined that can be used as the representative value of the given data, the task of description or comparison becomes simpler.

Statisticians have developed various methods of finding the representative value, called the *average*. Each type of average has its particular characteristics, which should be understood thoroughly before that method is chosen. The three types of averages that are most commonly used by statisticians are described in this section. They are (1) the arithmetic mean, (2) the median, and (3) the mode.

A. Arithmetic Mean

Of all types of averages, the *arithmetic mean*, generally referred to as the *mean*, is used most frequently by both statisticians and nonstatisticians. The arithmetic mean of a group of values is obtained by dividing the sum of the values by the number of items in the group, as follows:

$$\text{Mean} = \frac{\text{Sum of values}}{\text{Number of items}}$$

EXAMPLE 1

Find the arithmetic mean of the values 3, 4, 8, 2, 5, 8, and 12.

Sum of the values $= 3 + 4 + 8 + 2 + 5 + 8 + 12 = 42$
Number of items $= 7$

Arithmetic mean $= \frac{42}{7} = 6$

The chief characteristics of an arithmetic mean are:

1. The mean is rigidly defined by the above formula and it can be treated algebraically. Thus, if any two of the three elements in the expression (mean, sum of values, and number of items) are known, the third one can be determined. For example, if the mean is 6 and the number of items is 7, the sum of the values in the series of data can be determined, or $6 \times 7 = 42$.
2. Every value in the series is taken into consideration in computing the mean. The mean thus obtained lies at the point at which the deviations of the individual values from the mean are in balance. In other words, the sum of the positive deviations is equal to the sum of the negative deviations. The algebraic sum of the deviations is equal to zero.

NOTE:

The deviations are computed as follows:

$2 - 6 = -4$
$3 - 6 = -3$

and so on. (See Example 1.)

Value	*Deviation from the Mean (6)*	
2	−4	
3	−3	= −10
4	−2	
5	−1	
8	+2	
8	+2	= +10
12	+6	
Total		0

3. The arithmetic mean is sensitive to extreme values, since the value of each item in the series affects the mean. Thus, the mean becomes less representative of the group of data when the group includes extreme values. For example, the mean of the values 2, 2, 3, 4, and 89 is 20, or $(2 + 2 + 3 + 4 + 89)/5 = 20$. It is obvious that the mean does not represent very well any one of the five values.

B. Median

The *median* of a group of values is the middle item when the values are arranged according to their magnitude. The number of items above the median is the same as the number of items below the median. If there is an even number of items, the median is the midpoint of the two central items.

EXAMPLE 2 Find the median of the values 3, 4, 8, 2, 5, 8, and 12.

The values in the series are first arranged in order according to their magnitudes.

2
3
4
5(*median*) The median is 5, since it is the middle item in the orderly arrangement.
8 There are three values (2, 3, 4) below 5 and three values (8, 8, 12)
8 above 5.
12

EXAMPLE 3 Find the median of the values 3, 4, 6, 8, 9, and 10.

The given values are already in the proper order. The median is the midpoint of the two central items 6 and 8, or

$$\text{Median} = \frac{6 + 8}{2} = 7$$

The chief characteristics of a median are:

1. The median is determined according to position. It is not defined algebraically as is the arithmetic mean. For example, if the median is 5 and the number of items is 7, the sum of the values in the series is not necessarily 35 (or 5×7). Note that the sum of the values in Example 2 is 42.
2. The median is not affected by the values of other items. However, since the median is

centrally located, the absolute sum (disregarding positive and negative signs) of the deviations of the individual values from the median is at a minimum. For example, the absolute sum of the deviations from median 5 in Example 2 is 19 (see below), whereas the absolute sum of the deviations from mean 6 in Example 1 is 20 (= 10 + 10).

Value	*Deviation from the Median (5)*
2	3(= 2 − 5)
3	2
4	1
5	0
8	3
8	3
12	7
Total	19 (absolute sum, disregarding signs)

3. Unlike the mean, the median is not sensitive to extreme values, since the median is not computed from all values. For example, the median of the values 2, 2, 3, 4, and 89 is 3. Here the median is more representative of the group of data than is the mean, 20.

C. Mode

The *mode* of a group of values is obtained by finding the value that occurs most frequently in the series. It is the value of greatest density in a given set of data.

EXAMPLE 4

Find the mode of the values 2, 3, 4, 5, 8, 8, and 12.

The mode is 8, since it occurs two times; the other numbers occur only once.

The chief characteristics of a mode are:

1. The mode is determined according to the frequencies of the values in the series. Unlike the mean, it is not defined algebraically. For example, if the mode is 8 and the number of items is 7, the sum of the values in the series is not necessarily 56 (or 7 × 8). Note that the sum of the values in Example 4 is 42.
2. The mode is generally regarded as the most typical value in a series. If an item is selected at random, a modal item is the most likely item to be selected, since the modal item occurs more times than any other item. Frequently, however, a mode is not determinable. For example, there is no mode in the values 2, 3, 4, and 7, since each value appears only once. On the other hand, in some cases there is more than one mode, such as in a series of values 2, 2, 3, 3, 6, and 8, which has two modes. The arithmetic mean and the median can easily be determined under such circumstances.
3. The mode, unlike the mean, is not sensitive to extreme values, since the mode is not computed from all values. For example, the mode of the values 2, 2, 3, 4, and 89 is 2. Here the mode is more representative of the group of data than is the mean, 20. However, in this case, the median is the superior method according to the absolute sums of the deviations from the averages, as follows:

Value	Deviations		
	From Mean (20)	From Median (3)	From Mode (2)
2	18	1	0
2	18	1	0
3	17	0	1
4	16	1	2
89	69	86	87
Absolute sum	138	89 (smallest)	90

EXERCISE 6–2 REFERENCE: SECTION 6.3

1. Find (a) the arithmetic mean, (b) the median, and (c) the mode of the following values, which represent the consumption of cigarettes for a group of 9 workers during one week:

   2, 3, 4, 8, 7, 11, 5, 4, 10 (packages)

   Which one of the averages may be regarded as most representative for the given data?
2. Find (a) the arithmetic mean, (b) the median, and (c) the mode of the following values, which represent numbers of visits to a doctor by a group of five families during one month:

   1, 12, 3, 6, 30

   Which one of the averages may be regarded as the most typical number of visits for the group of families?
3. Find (a) the median and (b) the mode of the following values:

   3, 5, 11, 15, 19, 19
4. Find (a) the median, and (b) the mode of the following values:

   3, 18, 12, 12, 12, 24, 24, 24

6.4 DISPERSION

An average alone cannot give a complete description of the characteristics of the items included in a group of data. More measures are needed for a complete description. For example, the mean of numbers 1, 10, and 19 is 10 or [(1 + 10 + 19)/3 = 10], and the mean of numbers 9, 10, and 11 is also 10 or [(9 + 10 + 11)/3 = 10]. Since 10 is not as close to values 1 and 19 as to values 9 and 11, the mean is less representative of the first group of numbers than of the latter group. A very common method for supplementing the usefulness of averages is to find a *measure of dispersion*, which indicates how the items included in the data disperse (deviate or scatter) from the average. When the value of the measure of dispersion is high, the average thus becomes of little or no significance. On the other hand, if the value of the measure is low, the value of the average becomes increasingly significant; that is, the average is a highly representative figure.

A measure of dispersion is commonly expressed in absolute numbers as follows: (1) range, (2) quartile deviation, (3) average deviation, and (4) standard deviation. Although the range and the quartile deviation are not based on an average, they are discussed here because they may also be used as measures of dispersion.

A. Range

The *range* of a group of data is the difference between the lowest and the highest values. It is easy to compute. Although the range is the simplest measure of dispersion, it has the disadvantage of being based on only two items. Thus, the manner of dispersion of the other items about the central value is ignored.

EXAMPLE 1

Find the range of the following data: 3, 4, 5, 10, and 13.

The highest value is 13, and the lowest value is 3. The range is

$13 - 3 = 10$

Notice that the items with values between 3 and 13 have no effect on the range.

B. Quartile Deviation

To find the *quartile deviation* of a group of data, first divide the items into 4 equal parts according to their values. The first quartile (Q_1) is the point on the scale of value below which there are $\frac{1}{4}$ of the items. The second quartile (Q_2) is the point below or above which there are $\frac{1}{2}$ of the items. Thus, Q_2 corresponds to the median. The third quartile (Q_3) is the point below which there are $\frac{3}{4}$ of the items. The distance between the first quartile and the third quartile is called the *interquartile range*. When this distance is divided by 2, the quotient is the quartile deviation (QD), or

$$QD = \frac{Q_3 - Q_1}{2}$$

EXAMPLE 2

Find (a) Q_1, (b) Q_2, (c) Q_3, and (d) QD of the following data:

2, 5, 4, 8, 7, 18, 13, 11

First, arrange the data in ascending order according to their values. (See below.)

2
4
———$(Q_1) = (4 + 5)/2 = 4.5$
5
7
———$(Q_2) = (7 + 8)/2 = 7.5$
8
11
———$(Q_3) = (11 + 13)/2 = 12$
13
18

(a) Q_1 is defined as the point on the scale of values below which $\frac{1}{4}$ of the items lie. There are 8 items in the group. One-fourth of the 8 items is 2 items. The point must be above values 2 and 4 but below 5. Thus, Q_1 is determined to be 4.5, the halfway point between 4 and 5.

(b) Q_2 = the median, above or below which there must be $\frac{1}{2}$ (or 50%) of the items ($8 \times \frac{1}{2} = 4$). Thus, the value of Q_2 must be between the two central values, 7 and 8. The halfway point between the two values is 7.5.

(c) Q_3 = the point below which there are $\frac{3}{4}$ of the items ($8 \times \frac{3}{4} = 6$). The point must be between the 6th and 7th items, or between values 11 and 13. Thus, Q_3 is determined to be 12, the halfway point between 11 and 13.

(d) $QD = \dfrac{Q_3 - Q_1}{2} = \dfrac{12 - 4.5}{2} = 3.75$

Frequently the number of items in a series is not divisible by 4. In such cases, the following rules are generally used in finding the *approximate* values of Q_1 and Q_3:

1. If the number of items in a series is even, such as 10 or 14 items, Q_1 is the median obtained from the lower 50% of the values.
2. If the number of items in a given series is odd, such as 7 or 9 items, disregard the middle item (Q_2); then locate Q_1 as in rule 1.

The method of locating the value of Q_3 is the same as that for Q_1, except that the higher 50% of the values in the series is used.

EXAMPLE 3

Find the QD of values in each of the following groups:

(a) 3, 7, 8, 10, 13, 17, 19, 20, 25, 30

(b) 1, 3, 4, 6, 8, 11, 13

(a) The group has 10 items.

Use rule 1:

Lower 50% values: 3, 7, $8-Q_1$, 10, 13

Upper 50% values: 17, 19, $20-Q_3$, 25, 30

$QD = \dfrac{20 - 8}{2} = 6$

(b) The group has 7 items.

Use rule 2:

Lower 50% values: 1, $3-Q_1$, 4

Disregarded in locating Q_1 and Q_3: $6-Q_2$

Upper 50% values: 8, $11-Q_3$, 13

$QD = \dfrac{11 - 3}{2} = 4$

Extending this idea further, a series of data may be divided into 10 groups, thus obtaining a decile; or into 100 groups, thus obtaining a percentile.

C. Average Deviation

When statisticians wish to consider the effects of all items in measuring the dispersion around the average, they generally use two methods—the average deviation and the standard deviation.

The *average deviation* (*AD*) is the arithmetic mean of the deviations of the individual items from the average of the given data. The average that is frequently used is either the median or the arithmetic mean. However, only the arithmetic mean will be used here for illustration purposes. In computing the average deviation, the absolute values of the deviations are used; that is, the positive or negative signs of the deviations are ignored.

EXAMPLE 4 Compute the average deviation of each group:

(a) 3, 4, 5, 10, 13
(b) 1, 2, 4, 13, 15

(a) The *AD* is 3.6. The following procedure should be used for the computation:

	(1) Item	*(2) Deviation: (1) − Mean, 7*	*(3) Absolute Value of Deviation*
	3	−4	4
	4	−3	3
	5	−2	2
	10	3	3
	13	6	6
Total	35	0	18

$$\text{Mean} = \frac{35}{5} = 7 \qquad AD = \frac{18}{5} = 3.6$$

(b) The *AD* is 5.6. It is computed in the following table:

	(1) Item	*(2) Deviation: (1) − Mean, 7 (Absolute Values)*
	1	6
	2	5
	4	3
	13	6
	15	8
Total	35	28

$$\text{Mean} = \frac{35}{5} = 7 \qquad AD = \frac{28}{5} = 5.6$$

D. Standard Deviation

The *standard deviation* (commonly represented by the lowercase Greek letter sigma, σ) is computed in the same manner as the average deviation, except that the signs (either positive or negative) of the individual deviations from the mean are considered. Each type of deviation is squared, and thus all become positive. All the squared numbers are added; then the sum is divided by the number of items included. The standard deviation is then found by taking the square root of that quotient. The standard deviation has a mathematical advantage over the average deviation, although its calculation requires considerably more work than that of the average deviation. The standard deviation is widely used for further statistical analysis. (See Example 1 in Section 6.5 for an example of the use of a standard deviation.)

EXAMPLE 5

Refer to Example 4. Compute the standard deviation of each group.

(a) The standard deviation is 3.85. It is computed as follows:

	(1) Item	*(2) Deviation: (1) − Mean, 7*	*(3) Square of (2)*
	3	−4	16
	4	−3	9
	5	−2	4
	10	3	9
	13	6	36
Total	35	0	74

$$\text{Mean} = \frac{35}{5} = 7 \qquad \text{Standard deviation} = \sqrt{\frac{74}{5}} = \sqrt{14.8} = 3.85$$

(b) The standard deviation is 5.83. It is computed as follows:

	(1) Item	*(2) Deviation: (1) − Mean, 7*	*(3) Square of (2)*
	1	−6	36
	2	−5	25
	4	−3	9
	13	6	36
	15	8	64
Total	35	0	170

$$\text{Mean} = \frac{35}{5} = 7 \qquad \text{Standard deviation} = \sqrt{\frac{170}{5}} = \sqrt{34} = 5.83$$

Note that the measures of dispersion about the mean are smaller in group (a) than those in group (b) in both Examples 4 and 5, although the means of the two groups (7) are the same. Thus, the mean is regarded as a more representative figure for group (a) than for group (b).

EXERCISE 6–3 REFERENCE: SECTION 6.4

1. The following numbers are the years of employment for a group of eight drivers at the K. W. Boston Taxicab Co. Find (a) the range and (b) the quartile deviation.

   6, 12, 8, 2, 18, 16, 19, 15

2. The weights in pounds of eight soldiers are listed below. What are (a) the range and (b) the quartile deviation?

   140, 174, 176, 146, 184, 130, 180, 230

3. The weekly earnings of a group of nine workers in a manufacturing company are given below. Find the quartile deviation.

   $380, $393, $390, $382, $395, $389, $410, $400, $375

4. The grade points of 14 students in an English class are as follows:

   78, 74, 80, 73, 84, 85, 65, 90, 62, 92, 70, 58, 96, 75

   What is the quartile deviation?
5. Refer to Problem 1. Compute (a) the average deviation and (b) the standard deviation.
6. Refer to Problem 2. Compute (a) the average deviation and (b) the standard deviation.

6.5 FREQUENCY DISTRIBUTION

When statistical data include a large number of items, the values of the items should be organized in order to facilitate statistical analysis. The values are usually arranged in ascending order. Data so arranged are called an *array*. Thus, the values 12, 6, 3, 12, 8, 3, 6, 8, 8, and 11 may be arranged as an array: 3, 3, 6, 6, 8, 8, 8, 11, 12, 12. Here, as in many cases, there are repeating values in the array. If the number of times that a certain value repeats in an array is indicated, the arrangement of the data is shortened by such an indication. This arrangement is known as a *frequency array*, and the number indicating the times a value is repeated is called the *frequency*. Thus, the above illustration may be arranged as a frequency array:

Value	*Frequency*
3	2
6	2
8	3
11	1
12	2
Total	10 (items)

When the values are grouped into several classes and the number of values within each class is indicated in the arrangement, a more compact presentation is provided. Such an arrangement showing grouped data is called a *frequency distribution*. The size of the class, called the *class interval*, is preferred to be the same for each class. The number of classes depends upon the number of items to be grouped and the type of information that the arranger wishes to have. Thus, the above illustration may be further grouped into the following frequency distribution:

Class Interval	*Frequency*
1–4	2
5–8	5
9–12	3
Total	10 (items)

Basically, the procedures of various statistical methods applied to grouped data are the same as those applied to ungrouped data in Sections 6.3 and 6.4. However, certain details are involved in applying these methods to grouped data. The following example illustrates the methods of finding the arithmetic mean and two types of deviation from the mean – the average deviation and the standard deviation – from a frequency distribution.

EXAMPLE 1

The hourly wages of 18 workers in a construction company are classified in the following frequency distribution table:

Wages (Class Interval)	*Number of Workers (Frequency)*
$1–3	1
4–6	2
7–9	3
10–12	8
13–15	4

Find (a) the arithmetic mean, (b) the average deviation, and (c) the standard deviation.

(a) The following table is arranged to find the mean:

(1) Wages (Class Interval)	*(2) Average Wages (Midpoint)*	*(3) Number of Workers (Class Frequency)*	*(4) Total Wages (2) × (3)*
$ 1–$ 3	$ 2	1	$ 2
4– 6	5	2	10
7– 9	8	3	24
10– 12	11	8	88
13– 15	14	4	56
Total	. . .	18	180

$$\text{Mean} = \frac{\text{Total wages}}{\text{Number of workers}} = \frac{180}{18} = \$10$$

The midpoint value of each class is obtained by dividing the sum of the lower limit and the upper limit in the class by 2. The midpoint of each class is assumed to be the average value of the items included in the class and is used as a base for computing the value of the class. For example, in the class $7–$9, the lower limit is $7, the upper limit is $9, and the midpoint is $8 [or (7 + 9)/2 = 8]. The total wages for the class are $24 (or $8 × 3). The actual values included in the class may vary from \$7 to \$9. Thus, each of the actual values may lose its identity in a frequency distribution.

(b) The following table is arranged to find the average deviation:

(1) Wages (Class Interval)	*(2) Average Wages (Midpoint)*	*(3) Number of Workers (Class Frequency)*	*(4) Deviation from Mean: (2) −10*	*(5) Total Deviation: (3) × (4) (Disregard signs)*
\$ 1–\$ 3	\$ 2	1	−8	8
4– 6	5	2	−5	10
7– 9	8	3	−2	6
10– 12	11	8	1	8
13– 15	14	4	4	16
Total	. . .	18	. . .	48

$$\text{Average deviation} = \frac{48}{18} = 2.67$$

Again the midpoint of each class is used to represent the value of the class. First, deviation of each midpoint from the mean is found [column (4)]. Next, each deviation is multiplied by the class frequency [column (5)]. The sum of the products, regardless of positive or negative signs, is then divided by the total number of workers.

(c) The following table is arranged to find the standard deviation:

(1) Wages (Class Interval)	*(2) Average Wages (Midpoint)*	*(3) Number of Workers (Class Frequency)*	*(4) Deviation from Mean: (2) − 10*	*(5) Square of Deviation: $(4)^2$*	*(6) Total Squared Deviation: (3) × (5)*
\$ 1–\$ 3	\$ 2	1	−8	64	64
4– 6	5	2	−5	25	50
7– 9	8	3	−2	4	12
10– 12	11	8	1	1	8
13– 15	14	4	4	16	64
Total	. . .	18	. . .	. . .	198

$$\text{Standard deviation} = \sqrt{\frac{198}{18}} = \sqrt{11} = 3.32$$

The method for computing the standard deviation involving a frequency distribution is the same as that used for ungrouped data except that each of the deviations is squared and multiplied by the class frequency to obtain the total squared deviation for each class [see column (6)]. Notice that the first 4 columns above are the same as the first 4 columns in solution (b) for the average deviation. In computing the standard deviation, however, the sign for each deviation is considered.

NOTE: There are various shortcut methods for computing the arithmetic mean, the average deviation, and the standard deviation. Students may consult any standard statistics textbook for further study.

When the values in a large set are *normally distributed*, the values in the set are theoretically expected to fall within the ranges as follows:

68.268% of the values will be within the mean $\pm$one standard deviation

95.45% of the values will be within the mean $\pm$two standard deviations

99.73% of the values will be within the mean $\pm$three standard deviations

Observe the values in the frequency distribution of Example 1 that fall within the one standard deviation. There are 11 or more items (3 in the class \$7–\$9, 8 in the class \$10–\$12, and an undetermined number of items in the class \$13–\$15) out of the total of 18 items, or 61% (=11/18) or more of the values in the distribution, within the range:

\$10 ± \$3.32 = \$6.68 to \$13.32

There are 17 items (except the 1 item in the class \$1–\$3) out of the total of 18 items, or 94% (=17/18) of the values in the distribution, within the range:

\$10 ± 2(\$3.32) = \$3.36 to \$16.64

All of the 18 items, or 100% of the values, are within the range:

\$10 ± 3(\$3.32) = \$0.04 to \$19.96

Thus, the values in the set of Example 1 are close to a normal distribution.

EXERCISE 6–4 REFERENCE: SECTION 6.5

1. From the following frequency distribution table, compute (a) the arithmetic mean, (b) the average deviation, and (c) the standard deviation.

Class Interval	*Class Frequency*
\$3–\$5	2
6–8	3
9–11	4
12–14	10
15–17	2

2. From the following frequency distribution table, find (a) the arithmetic mean, (b) the average deviation, and (c) the standard deviation.

Class Interval	*Class Frequency*
2–6	1
7–11	3
12–16	5
17–21	5
22–26	3
27–31	1

3. The amounts of sales for 32 transactions in a retail store are given below. What are (a) the average deviation and (b) the standard deviation?

Sales	*Number of Transactions*
\$2 and under \$4	1
\$4 and under \$6	4
\$6 and under \$8	6
\$8 and under \$10	9
\$10 and under \$12	8
\$12 and under \$14	3
\$14 and under \$16	1
	32

4. The grades of twenty students in a mathematics of finance class are given below:

38	41	45	51	53	57	58	59	61	62
63	65	67	69	70	73	75	81	85	95

(a) Use the following class intervals to construct a frequency distribution table, and compute the standard deviation.

Class Interval (Grades)
26–40
41–55
56–70
71–85
86–100

(b) Indicate the number of grades that fall within the following ranges:

(1) the mean $\pm$ one standard deviation
(2) the mean $\pm$ two standard deviations
(3) the mean $\pm$ three standard deviations

What percent of the total number of grades is within each range?

7 THE INCOME STATEMENT

This chapter presents the concepts and the mathematical operations of the items listed in the income statement. The concepts of the individual items are first introduced (Section 7.1). Next, the relationships among major items are analyzed (Section 7.2). Other related topics to be discussed in this chapter are: trade discount (Section 7.3), cash discount (Section 7.4), commissions and fees (Section 7.5), sales taxes (Section 7.6), excise taxes (Section 7.7), property taxes (Section 7.8), payroll taxes (Section 7.9), and income taxes (Section 7.10).

7.1 INTRODUCTION TO THE INCOME STATEMENT

The income statement, sometimes called the *profit and loss statement*, is one of the most important types of financial reports of a business. The profit or loss is obtained as a result of comparison between the revenue and the expenses listed in the statement for a designated period of operation. When the total revenue exceeds the total expenses, there is a profit; otherwise, there is a loss. The period of operation may be a month, a year, or any other unit of time, depending on the intention of the management or the accounting system of the business. Since the income statement shows the result of operation, the arrangement of the items listed in the statement provides a logical order in discussing the mathematical operations, especially percentages, applying to common problems in business.

The income statement of a trading business, whose major activities are purchasing and selling merchandise, is given in Figure 7–1 as an illustrative example. In this income statement, the total of the revenue is the net sales of $100,000, and the total of the expenses is $90,000, which includes the cost of goods sold, $53,000, and the total operating expenses, $37,000. Thus, the net income from operations before income tax is $10,000. The income tax is not treated by an accountant as an operating expense but is considered to be a share of profit.

Because of their simplicity, not all of the income statement items need a detailed mathematical discussion. A brief explanation of the items and the plan for discussing them are presented below.

Figure 7–1 Income Statement of a Trading Business

PETER GIFT SHOP
Income Statement
For the Month Ended June, 19–

Revenue from sales:		
Sales (or selling price)		$102,000
Less: Sales discount (or cash discount)		2,000
Net sales		$100,000
Cost of goods sold (or cost)		53,000
Gross profit on sales (or gross profit)		$ 47,000
Operating expenses:		
Delivery expenses	$ 4,000	
Store supplies expenses	2,000	
Store rent expense	4,500	
Salespersons' salaries	18,000	
Sales commissions and fees	4,000	
Taxes expense (other than income tax)	3,000	
Interest expense	500	
Depreciation expense–office furniture and equipment	1,000	
Total operating expenses		37,000
Net income from operations (net profit)		$ 10,000
Estimated income tax		2,800
Net income after income tax		$ 7,200

A. Sales (Selling Price)

In a trading business, the transactions that involve the delivery of merchandise in exchange for cash or promises to pay are called *sales*. The amount recorded by an accountant under this title is the actual selling price at which the seller agrees to sell and the buyer agrees to buy. Thus, the selling price is the buyer's purchase price.

Sometimes a trade discount may be involved in determining the selling price. In this case, the selling price is the amount remaining after the trade discount has been deducted from the list price (the price listed in the sales catalog). For example, a portion of the selling price in the above income statement may have been derived as follows:

List price	$100	
Less: trade discount	20	(= 20% of the list price)
Selling price	$ 80	

A detailed method of computing trade discounts is discussed in Section 7.3.

B. Sales Discounts (or Cash Discounts)

Sales discounts are also called *cash discounts*. A cash discount is called a sales discount by the seller and a purchase discount by the buyer. Details concerning cash discounts are discussed in Section 7.4.

The difference between the selling price and the sales discount is the *net sales*. The seller collects the net sales as revenue.

C. Cost of Goods Sold (or Cost)

The *cost of goods sold* is the total cost of purchase of the merchandise that has been sold. The cost of purchases includes not only the net purchase price but also the incidental costs relating to merchandise acquisition, preparation, and placement for sale. Examples of the incidental costs are transportation charges, duties, taxes, insurance, and storage.

D. Gross Profit on Sales (or Gross Profit)

As shown in the income statement, the *gross profit on sales*, or *gross profit*, is the excess of the net sales over the cost of goods sold. It is called gross profit because the operating expenses of the business must be deducted from gross profit before the net income from operations is obtained.

E. Operating Expenses

In a large business, the various types of operating expenses may be classified into a number of groups. As shown in the income statement, Figure 7–1, however, only the common types of operating expenses are listed and these have been classified in a single group in order to simplify the discussion. The mathematical operations required to determine the delivery expenses, store supplies expenses, store rent, and salespersons' salaries are not discussed because their calculation is relatively simple. Other operating expenses are discussed as follows:

Sales commissions and fees are discussed in Section 7.5.

Taxes expense (other than income tax) is discussed in Sections 7.6 through 7.9. Only the taxes that frequently affect every business are discussed in these sections. These taxes are: *sales taxes* (7.6), *excise taxes* (7.7), *property taxes* (7.8), and *payroll taxes* (7.9). If a tax is imposed upon the business, the tax payment is classified as an operating expense. However, if the business is required by law to collect the tax and to transfer the tax collected to a government agency at a later date, the amount is not listed as an income statement item.

The calculations necessary to determine *interest expense* require a detailed discussion. From Chapter 8 to the end of this text, almost all of the discussion is devoted to the mathematics of interest computation.

Depreciation expense can be computed in various ways. Some of the methods of computing depreciation expense require a knowledge of compound interest and annuity. For convenience and uniformity, the discussion of methods of computing depreciation expense is deferred until Chapter 17.

F. Net Income from Operations (Net Profit)

As shown in the income statement, the excess of the gross profit on sales over the total operating expenses is the *net income from operations*, or, as it is commonly called, *net profit*.

G. Estimated Income Tax

Income taxes are levied on a taxpayer's annual income by the federal government, by many states, and by some cities. Net income from business operations is subject to tax under income tax laws. The tax rate usually increases as the taxable income increases. In the preceding income statement, it is assumed that the net income from operations, \$10,000, is a portion of the business owner's taxable income of the year and that the tax rate applied to the portion is 28%. The method of computing income taxes is discussed in Section 7.10.

H. Net Income After Income Tax

The *net income after income tax* is the actual income that the owner of a business may use as he or she wishes.

The income statement items mentioned above, from *sales* through *net income after income tax*, give complete financial information about the business operations. However, if the information is further analyzed, the use of the statement can be increased and thus a more intelligent business policy may be achieved. An analysis of the relationships among the individual income statement items is presented in Section 7.2.

7.2 ANALYZING MAJOR INCOME STATEMENT ITEMS WITH PERCENTS

This section discusses the methods of analyzing the relationships among the five major items with percents. The major items are: selling price, cost, gross profit, operating expenses, and net profit. This type of analysis will give important information to the business concern in reviewing its operations during a given period and thus assists management in making policies for the future.

Buying and selling are basic activities. A business person usually buys merchandise at a lower cost but sells it at a higher price. The difference between the *buying cost* and *selling price* is called *gross profit on sales*. From the gross profit, the *operating expenses*, such as store supplies and rents, are deducted to obtain the *net profit* or *net loss*.

ILLUSTRATION: If the selling price of an article is \$125, the cost of the good is \$100, and the operating expenses are \$15, the gross profit and the net profit may be obtained as follows:

Selling price		\$125
Cost	−	100
Gross profit		\$ 25
Operating expenses	−	15
Net profit		\$ 10

To express in percents the relationships among the items, a base (or 100%) must first be selected. Theoretically, any one of the items may be selected as the base. However, in most business concerns, either the cost or the selling price is used as the base. Many businesses, such as manufacturers, that keep inventory records at cost, usually find that the cost is a convenient figure to use as a basis for computing selling price, gross profit, operating expenses, and net profit. On the other hand, some business concerns find that the selling price is the most convenient figure to use as a basis for computing cost, gross profit, operating expenses, and net profit. In these firms, sales commissions and bonuses are often expressed as a certain percent of the selling price instead of the cost.

The relative values in percent form for the preceding illustration are computed as shown in the table below.

		Relative Values	
Actual Value		*Selling Price as the Base*	*Cost as the Base*
Selling price	$125	100% (or $\frac{125}{125}$)	125% (or $\frac{125}{100}$)
Cost	100	80% (or $\frac{100}{125}$)	100% (or $\frac{100}{100}$)
Gross profit	$ 25	20% (or $\frac{25}{125}$)	25% (or $\frac{25}{100}$)
Operating expenses	15	12% (or $\frac{15}{125}$)	15% (or $\frac{15}{100}$)
Net profit	$ 10	8% (or $\frac{10}{125}$)	10% (or $\frac{10}{100}$)

The rates (in percent form) for the above computation are calculated from the formula Rate $= \frac{\text{Percentage}}{\text{Base}}$. The base is always 100% of itself. Thus, when the selling price is the base, the selling price is 100% of itself. The cost is 80% of the base, gross profit is 20%, operating expenses are 12%, and net profit is 8% of the base. These percentages may be proved as follows:

Cost = 125 (selling price) × 80% = $100
Gross profit = 125 × 20% = $25
Operating expenses = 125 × 12% = $15
Net profit = 125 × 8% = $10

When the cost is the base, the cost is 100% of itself. The selling price is 125% of the base, gross profit is 25%, operating expenses are 15%, and net profit is 10% of the base. These percentages may be proved as follows:

Selling price = 100 (cost) × 125% = $125
Gross profit = 100 × 25% = $25
Operating expenses = 100 × 15% = $15
Net profit = 100 × 10% = $10

When the dollar amounts are reduced to relative values, preferably in percent form, the relationships among the income statement items may easily be analyzed. Thus, the "reduced" statement may serve as a more powerful guide to management. For example, it should be an easier task in pricing various articles if the relative values, in percents, of the gross profit and the base cost are known. Also, management would be more alert if it were informed that operating expenses were 25% of the selling price this year and the rate was only 10% last year.

The following examples illustrate additional problems that involve the use of cost and selling price as the basis for computation.

A. Finding the Selling Price from the Cost, and Vice Versa

(1) THE VALUE OF A BASE IS GIVEN

The base may be the selling price or the cost. When the value of a base is given, the required item can easily be computed by the formula: Percentage = Base × Rate.

EXAMPLE 1 If the cost of an item is $350 and the gross profit is 18% of the cost, what is the selling price?

The cost is the base (from which the gross profit, 18%, is computed) and is given as $350.

Gross profit = 350 × 18% = $63

Selling price = Cost + Gross profit
= 350 + 63 = $413

EXAMPLE 2 The selling price of an item is $90, the operating expenses are 30% of the selling price, and the net profit is 10% of the selling price. What is the cost?

The selling price is the base and is given as $90.

Operating expenses = 90 × 30% = $27
Net profit = 90 × 10% = $ 9(+)

Gross profit = 90 × 40% = $36

Cost = Selling price − Gross profit
= 90 − 36 = $54

(2) THE VALUE OF A BASE IS NOT GIVEN

Under this condition, the value of an item related to the base and the percent rate representing the item must be given or can be determined. When a given value and its percent rate are known, the base can be obtained by dividing the given value by its corresponding percent rate, or

$$\text{Base} = \frac{\text{Percentage}}{\text{Rate}}$$ (see Section 2.11C.)

EXAMPLE 3 If the cost of an item is $13.75 and the gross profit is 45% of the selling price, what should the selling price be?

The selling price is the base (100%), from which the gross profit (45%) is computed. The given cost ($13.75) is not the base.

Cost = Selling price − Gross profit
= 100% − 45% = 55% (of selling price), or

Selling price × 55% = Cost = $13.75

Since \$13.75 is 55% of the selling price, the selling price should be

$$\frac{13.75}{55\%} = \frac{13.75}{.55} = \$25$$

NOTE: Example 3 may also be solved in either of the following two ways:

1. By proportional expression.

   Let x = the selling price. Then

	\$ Value	*% of Selling Price*
Selling price	x	100%
Gross profit		45% (−)
Cost	\$13.75	55%

   Thus, x is to 100% as \$13.75 is to 55%, or

$$\frac{x}{13.75} = \frac{100\%}{55\%}$$

   By cross multiplication, $x(55\%) = 13.75(100\%)$

$$x = \frac{13.75}{55\%} = \$25$$

2. By using algebra.

   Let x = the selling price. Then

$$x = 13.75 + 45\%x$$
$$x - 45\%x = 13.75$$
$$x(1 - 45\%) = 13.75$$
$$x = \frac{13.75}{55\%} = \$25$$

EXAMPLE 4 The selling price of an item is \$29.28 and the gross profit is 15% of the cost. What is the cost?

The cost is the base (100%), from which the gross profit (15%) is computed. The given selling price (\$29.28) is not the base.

$$\text{Selling price} = \text{Cost} + \text{Gross profit}$$
$$= 100\% + 15\% = 115\% \text{ (of cost)}, \quad \text{or}$$

$$\text{Cost} \times 115\% = \text{Selling price} = \$29.28$$

Since \$29.28 is 115% of the cost, the cost should be

$$\frac{29.28}{115\%} = \$25.46$$

CHECK

$25.46 \times 15\% = 3.82$

$25.46 + 3.82 = \$29.28$ (selling price)

NOTE: Example 4 may also be solved in either of the following two ways:

1. By proportional expression.

Let x = the cost. Then

	$ Value	*% of Cost*
Cost	x	100%
Gross profit		15% (+)
Selling price	$29.28	115%

Thus, x is to 100% as $29.28 is to 115%, or

$$\frac{x}{29.28} = \frac{100\%}{115\%}$$

By cross multiplication, $x(115\%) = 29.28(100\%)$

$$x = \frac{29.28}{115\%} = \$25.46$$

2. By using algebra.

Let x = cost. Then

$$x + 15\%x = 29.28$$
$$x(1 + 15\%) = 29.28$$
$$x = \frac{29.28}{115\%} = \$25.46$$

EXERCISE 7-1 REFERENCE: SECTION 7.2A

A. Find the selling price in each of the following problems:

	Cost	*Gross Profit Based on Cost*		*Cost*	*Gross Profit Based on Selling Price*
1.	$35.00	16%	7.	$ 63.00	10%
2.	8.25	14%	8.	22.00	12%
3.	15.40	5%	9.	41.73	22%
4.	43.60	15%	10.	42.00	25%
5.	75.30	6%	11.	227.15	30%
6.	86.50	8%	12.	204.96	20%

B. Find the cost in each of the following problems:

	Selling Price	*Gross Profit Based on Cost*		*Selling Price*	*Gross Profit Based on Selling Price*
13.	$ 45.44	42%	19.	$ 24.00	40%
14.	94.50	26%	20.	30.00	25%
15.	493.68	32%	21.	46.50	38%
16.	784.32	52%	22.	53.40	26%
17.	1,691.16	36%	23.	267.42	55%
18.	2,461.69	15%	24.	654.14	45%

C. Statement problems:

25. The gross profit of a furniture store, as figured on cost, is 45%. What is (a) the gross profit and (b) the selling price of a table that costs $65?

26. A jewelry store wishes to price a watch that costs $125 to yield a gross profit of 36% of the cost. What should the selling price be?
27. The cost of a mattress is $95, the operating expenses are 20% of the cost, and the net profit is 5% of the cost. What should be the selling price?
28. The cost of a comb and brush set is $18.50, the operating expenses are 15% of the cost, and the retailer wishes to gain 25% net profit of the cost. What should be the selling price of the set?
29. The gross profit of a shoe store is 35% based on the selling price. What are (a) the selling price and (b) the gross profit of a pair of shoes that costs $55.64?
30. A department store bought 250 scarves for $975.00. At what price should the store sell each scarf if it is to have a gross profit of 22% of the selling price?
31. A retail store owner purchased men's dress slacks at $22.75 per pair. He knows from past experience that the operating expenses are 20% of the selling price. If he wishes to gain 15% of the selling price as the net profit, what is the lowest price at which he should sell each pair of slacks?
32. The cost of a dozen pairs of socks is $18, the operating expenses are 18% of the selling price, and the net profit is 7% of the selling price. What is the selling price for each pair of socks?
33. The gross profit of a hardware store is 30% of cost. How much are (a) the cost and (b) the gross profit of a shovel that sells for $9.50?
34. A shop figures its gross profit at 45% of cost. What are (a) the cost and (b) the gross profit of a blouse that sells for $13.95?
35. The selling price of a watch is $75.60, the operating expenses are 20% of the cost, and the net profit is 15% of the cost. What is the cost?
36. The selling price of a fan is $49, the operating expenses are 28% of the cost, and the retailer wishes to have a net profit of 12% of the cost. What is the cost?
37. The gross profit of a women's apparel store is 45% of the selling price. What are (a) the gross profit and (b) the cost of a coat that sells for $49.98?
38. A garden store owner plans to buy garden hoses for a line that sells for $8.50 per hose. What is the highest price that she can afford to pay for this line if her gross profit must be 38% of the selling price?
39. A dealer needs a camera that sells for $96. He knows from past experience that the operating expenses are 35% of the selling price. If he wishes to gain 20% of the selling price as the net profit from the sale, what is the highest price that he can afford to pay for the purchase of the camera?
40. A clothier sells a dozen sweaters for $450. If her operating expenses are 32% of the selling price and her net profit is 16% of the selling price, what is the cost of each sweater?

B. Finding the Gross Profit Rates from the Selling Price and the Cost, and Vice Versa

(1) FINDING THE GROSS PROFIT RATES

Example 5 indicates how the gross profit rate based on the selling price (also called *margin rate*) and the gross profit rate based on cost (also called *markup rate*) are determined when the selling price and the cost are given.

EXAMPLE 5

The selling price of an item is \$90 and the cost is \$54. What is the gross profit and its rate (a) based on the selling price and (b) based on the cost?

Gross profit = Selling price − Cost
= 90 − 54 = \$36

(a) Gross profit rate on selling price $= \dfrac{\text{Gross profit}}{\text{Selling price}} = \dfrac{36}{90} = \dfrac{2}{5} = 40\%$

(b) Gross profit rate on cost $= \dfrac{\text{Gross profit}}{\text{Cost}} = \dfrac{36}{54} = \dfrac{2}{3} = 66\frac{2}{3}\%$

(2) FINDING THE SELLING PRICE AND THE COST

Examples 6 and 7 illustrate how the selling price and the cost are determined when the gross profit and its rate on the selling price and on the cost are given.

EXAMPLE 6

The gross profit of an item is \$35 and the gross profit rate is 7% of the selling price. What are the selling price and the cost?

The selling price is the base, 100%. Since \$35 is equivalent to 7% of the selling price, or

the selling price × 7% = 35

the selling price $= \dfrac{35}{7\%} = \$500$

The cost = the selling price − the gross profit
= 500 − 35 = \$465

CHECK

The cost = 100% − 7% = 93% (of the selling price)
The cost = 500 × 93% = \$465

EXAMPLE 7

The gross profit of an item is \$25 and the gross profit rate is 20% of the cost. What are the selling price and the cost?

The cost is the base, 100%. Since \$25 is equivalent to 20% of the cost, or

the cost × 20% = 25

the cost $= \dfrac{25}{20\%} = \$125$

The selling price = the cost + the gross profit
= 125 + 25 = \$150

CHECK

The selling price = 100% + 20% = 120% (of the cost)
The selling price = 125 × 120% = \$150

EXERCISE 7-2 REFERENCE: SECTION 7.2B

A. In each of the following problems, find (a) the gross profit, (b) the gross profit rate on the selling price, and (c) the gross profit rate on the cost:

	Selling Price	*Cost*		*Selling Price*	*Cost*
1.	\$50.00	\$40.00	3.	\$46.25	\$30.15
2.	35.00	25.00	4.	98.50	86.50

	Selling Price	Cost		Selling Price	Cost
5.	$ 8.20	$ 7.40	8.	$ 76.24	$ 55.40
6.	9.45	8.30	9.	128.50	86.20
7.	88.20	65.10	10.	236.43	186.00

B. In each of the following problems, find (a) the selling price, and (b) the cost:

	Gross Profit	Gross Profit Rate on Cost	Gross Profit Rate on Selling Price
11.	$ 60.00	15%	
12.	99.00		18%
13.	56.00		35%
14.	43.80	12%	
15.	16.80	32%	
16.	18.99		45%
17.	12.71		50%
18.	15.26	35%	
19.	761.42	55%	
20.	313.45		25%
21.	987.51		30%
22.	529.06	20%	

C. Statement problems:

23. A dealer bought a piano for $1,200 and sold it for $1,800. (a) What was the gross profit? (b) What was the gross profit rate on the cost? (c) What was the gross profit rate on the selling price?
24. A furniture store bought a chair for $250 less 20% and sold it for $260. (a) What was the gross profit? (b) What was the gross profit rate on the cost? (c) What was the gross profit rate on the selling price?
25. A jewelry store buys a dozen watches for $540 less 12%, and sells them at $52 each. What is the gross profit rate (a) on the cost? (b) on the selling price?
26. A grocery store sold 3 pounds of peaches for $1.80. The cost of the fruit was $20.00 per box containing 40 pounds. What was the gross profit rate (a) on the cost? (b) on the selling price?
27. The gross profit of a furniture store for last year was $5,600. The store manager figured the gross profit rate on all pieces of furniture at 40% of cost. What was (a) the total cost of sales? (b) the amount of the sales?
28. A department store made a gross profit of 32% of the selling price on all merchandise sold. The gross profit for last month was $39,580. What was (a) the total amount of the sales? (b) the cost of the sales?
29. On March 1, a shoe store had merchandise on hand worth $1,400 at cost. Merchandise worth $2,200 had been purchased during March. The net sales at selling price during the month amounted to $1,000. The gross profit was estimated to be 40% of the selling price. At the end of the month, the store was destroyed by fire. At the time of the fire, what was the value of the inventory at cost?

30. On June 1, a hardware store had merchandise worth $1,200 at cost. The selling price of the merchandise was $2,000. Later the store sold part of it for $750. What is the value of the remaining merchandise at cost?

C. Converting One Base to Another Base

In converting the base on cost to the base on selling price or vice versa, first set up the Selling price–Cost–Gross profit relationship according to the base (100%) of the gross profit rate. Then find the desired answer from the relationship, as illustrated in the examples below.

EXAMPLE 8

The gross profit rate of an item is $66\frac{2}{3}\%$ of the cost. What is the gross profit rate based on the selling price?

Since the known rate is based on the cost, the cost is the original base and is 100% of itself. Thus,

Cost	100%	of cost
Gross profit	(+) $66\frac{2}{3}\%$	of cost
Selling price	$166\frac{2}{3}\%$	of cost

Since the gross profit rate on selling price $= \dfrac{\text{Gross profit (or Rate)}}{\text{Selling price (or Rate)}}$, the new converted gross profit rate on selling price is

$$\frac{66\frac{2}{3}\%}{166\frac{2}{3}\%} = \frac{66\frac{2}{3}}{166\frac{2}{3}} = 40\%$$

CHECK

Let the cost be any amount, such as $300.

Then the gross profit is $300 \times 66\frac{2}{3}\% = \$200$.

The selling price is $300 + 200 = \$500$.

When the gross profit rate on the selling price is 40%, the gross profit should be

$500 \times 40\% = \$200$

EXAMPLE 9

The gross profit rate of an item is 20% of the selling price. What is the gross profit rate based on cost?

The selling price is the original base and is 100% of itself, since the given rate is based on the selling price. Thus,

Selling price	100%	of selling price
Gross profit	(−) 20%	of selling price
Cost	80%	of selling price

Gross profit rate on cost $= \dfrac{\text{Gross profit}}{\text{Cost}}$. Hence, the new converted gross profit rate on cost is

$$\frac{20\%}{80\%} = \frac{1}{4} = 25\%$$

CHECK

Let the selling price be any amount, such as $200.

Then the gross profit on selling price is $200 \times 20\% = \$40$.

The cost is 200 − 40 = $160.

The gross profit on the cost is 160 × 25% = $40.

EXAMPLE 10

The gross profit rate of an item is 10% of the selling price and the operating expenses are 7.2% of the selling price. What percent of the cost are the operating expenses?

The selling price is the original base and is 100% of itself, since the given gross profit rate is based on the selling price. Thus,

Selling price	100%	of selling price
Gross profit	(−) 10%	of selling price
Cost	90%	of selling price
Operating expenses	7.2%	of selling price

Since the operating expenses are also based on the selling price and the operating expenses rate on cost $= \frac{\text{Operating expenses}}{\text{Cost}}$, the new converted operating expenses rate on cost is

$$\frac{7.2\%}{90\%} = \frac{7.2}{90} = .08 = 8\%$$

CHECK

Let the selling price be any amount, such as $200.

Then the gross profit is 200 × 10% = $20.

The cost is 200 − 20 = $180.

The operating expenses based on the selling price are

200 × 7.2% = $14.40

The operating expenses based on the cost are

180 × 8% = $14.40

EXAMPLE 11

What percent of the selling price is equal to 34% of the cost if the gross profit is 26% of the selling price?

The selling price is the base and is 100% of itself, since the known profit rate is based on the selling price. Thus,

Selling price	100%	of selling price
Gross profit	(−) 26%	of selling price
Cost	74%	of selling price

34% of the cost	= 34% of 74%	of selling price
	= 34% × 74%	of selling price
	= 25.16%	of selling price

CHECK

Let the selling price be any amount, such as $200.

Then the gross profit is 200 × 26% = $52.

The cost is 200 − 52 = $148.

The value of 34% of the cost is

148 × 34% = $50.32

The value of 25.16% of the selling price is

200 × 25.16% = $50.32

EXERCISE 7-3 REFERENCE: SECTION 7.2C

A. Convert each of the following gross profit rates based on cost to the rate based on selling price:

1. 15%	4. 40%	7. 65%	10. 140%
2. 24%	5. 48%	8. 70%	11. 150%
3. 32%	6. 56%	9. 80%	12. 200%

B. Convert each of the following gross profit rates based on selling price to the rate based on cost:

13. 12%	16. 42%	19. 75%	22. 45%
14. 25%	17. 58%	20. 85%	23. 10%
15. 34%	18. 60%	21. 90%	24. 50%

C. Statement problems:

25. If the gross profit rate on the sale of a watch is 35% of the cost, what is the gross profit rate based on the selling price?
26. If the gross profit rate on the sale of a radio is 30% of the selling price, what is the gross profit rate based on the cost?
27. The gross profit rate on the sale of a table is 55% of the selling price and the operating expenses are 15% of the selling price. What percent of the cost are the operating expenses?
28. For the sale of a typewriter, the operating expenses are 22% of the selling price and the gross profit is 40% of the selling price. What percent of the cost are the operating expenses?
29. If the gross profit rate is 65% of the selling price, what percent of the selling price is equal to 30% of the cost?
30. What percent of the selling price is equal to 38% of the cost if the gross profit is 48% of the cost?
31. When the gross profit is 65% of the selling price, what percent of the selling price is equal to 54% of the cost?
32. What percent of the selling price is equal to 36% of the cost if the gross profit rate based on cost is 25%?
33. If the gross profit is 75% of the cost, what percent of the cost is equal to 42% of the selling price?
34. What percent of the cost is equal to 26% of the selling price if the gross profit is 32% of the cost?
35. If the gross profit rate on the sale of a television set is 36% of the cost, what is the gross profit rate based on the selling price?
36. When the gross profit is 52% of the selling price, what percent of the cost is 35% of the selling price?
37. If the gross profit rate on the sale of a book is 45% of the selling price, what is the gross profit rate based on the cost?
38. The gross profit rate on the sale of a fan is 25% of the cost and the operating expenses are 12% of the cost. What percent of the selling price are the operating expenses?

EXERCISE 7-4 REVIEW OF SECTION 7.2

1. If the cost of an item is $25 and the gross profit is 20% of the cost, what is the selling price?
2. Carla bought a chair for $125. If she wishes to sell it and to realize a gross profit equal to 15% of the cost, what should the selling price be?
3. The cost of an electric drill is $36. If the operating expenses are 16% of the cost and the net profit is 12% of the cost, find the selling price.
4. The cost of a refrigerator is $350. The company wants to sell it so as to cover 28% of the cost as the operating expenses and to earn 15% of the cost as the net profit. What should the selling price be?
5. The cost of a table is $103.20 and the gross profit is 14% of the selling price. What is the selling price?
6. The cost of a radio is $70.40 and the gross profit is 12% of the selling price. What is the selling price?
7. The cost of a trailer is $1,925, the operating expenses are 35% of the selling price, and the net profit is 10% of the selling price. Find the selling price.
8. What is the selling price of a pair of shoes that costs $43.92 if the operating expenses are 24% of the selling price and the net profit is 15% of the selling price?
9. The selling price of a pound of beef is $3.75 and the gross profit is 30% of the cost. What is the cost?
10. The selling price of a box of candy is $4.35 and the gross profit is 45% of the cost. Find the cost.
11. An electric sewing machine is sold for $260. The gross profit is 30% of the selling price. What is the cost of the machine?
12. A bottle of perfume sells at a price to give a gross profit of $15, which is also $33\frac{1}{3}$% of cost. What is the selling price?
13. A shoe store manager figures that her operating expenses are 34% of cost and that she needs a net profit of 13% of cost. What is the cost of a pair of shoes that sells for $60?
14. An office equipment store manager buys some typewriters for $272 each. Her operating expenses are 33% of the selling price and her net profit is 22% of the selling price. At what price should she mark the typewriters?
15. The selling price of a bag of sugar is $7.37, the operating expenses are 14% of the cost, and the net profit is 20% of the cost. What is the cost of the bag of sugar?
16. In a retail store, the manager computed the operating expenses at 22% of the cost and the net profit at 15% of the cost. What is the cost of a handbag that sells for $20.55?
17. A pair of scissors sells for $5 and the gross profit is 40% of the selling price. What is the cost?
18. The selling price of an electric coffee maker is $36 and the gross profit is 45% of the selling price. What is the cost?
19. The selling price of a box of cookies is $4.80 and the cost is $3.60. What is the amount of gross profit and its rate (a) based on the selling price and (b) based on the cost?

20. The cost of a portable typewriter is $300 and it sells for $360. Find the amount of gross profit and the gross profit rate based on (a) the cost and (b) the selling price.
21. The gross profit on the sale of a clock is $6, which is 40% of the cost. What are (a) the cost and (b) the selling price?
22. A company computed its gross profit rate as 25% of cost. If the gross profit on the sale of a cabinet is $50, find (a) the cost and (b) the selling price of the cabinet.
23. The gross profit on the sale of a book is $4.20, which is 35% of the selling price. What are (a) the selling price and (b) the cost?
24. A company computed its gross profit as 42% of the selling price. Find (a) the cost and (b) the selling price of a boy's jacket if the gross profit on the sale of the jacket is $16.80.
25. The gross profit rate on the sale of a bag of potatoes is 35% of the cost. What is the gross profit rate based on the selling price?
26. The gross profit rate on the sale of a set of tools is 55% of the cost. What is the gross profit rate based on the selling price?
27. The gross profit rate on the sale of a machine is 30% of the cost and the operating expenses are 26% of the cost. What percent of the selling price are the operating expenses?
28. On the sale of a handsaw, the operating expenses are figured at 30% of the cost and the gross profit rate is 42% of the cost. What percent of the selling price are the operating expenses?
29. What percent of the selling price is 65% of the cost if the gross profit is 30% of the selling price?
30. What percent of the selling price is 52% of the cost if the gross profit is 35% of the selling price?
31. If the gross profit rate on the sale of an item is 38% of the selling price, what is the gross profit rate based on cost?
32. If the gross profit rate on the sale of a truck is 28% of the selling price, what is the gross profit rate based on the cost of the truck?
33. The gross profit rate on the sale of a mirror is 15% of the selling price and the operating expenses are 6% of the selling price. What percent of the cost are the operating expenses?
34. The operating expenses are 14% of the selling price for a desk and the gross profit rate is 24% of the selling price. Find the operating expense rate based on the cost.
35. What percent of the cost is 42% of the selling price if the gross profit is 35% of the cost?
36. What percent of the cost is 58% of the selling price if the gross profit is 30% of the cost?

7.3 TRADE DISCOUNT

A. General Concept and Computation

Generally speaking, there are two types of merchants in the trading business: the wholesaler and the retailer. The *wholesale merchant* usually purchases goods from manufacturers and producers and sells them to retailers and large consumers. The *retail merchant* purchases goods from several sources, including wholesalers, producers, manufacturers, and agent middlemen such as brokers and manufacturer's agents. The retailer mainly sells the goods to ultimate consumers.

Wholesalers normally tend to buy in larger amounts than retailers, and retailers tend to buy in larger amounts than consumers. Manufacturers, wholesalers, or other types of sellers therefore frequently grant substantial reductions from the list price quoted in their catalogs to allow for price differentials among different classes of customers. Such reductions, usually based on list price, are called *trade discounts*. For example, a manufacturer may offer the following selling prices:

Type of Customer	*Selling Price*
Ultimate consumer	list (as quoted in catalog)
Retailer	10% off list
Wholesaler	10% and 5% off list

Trade discounts are sometimes used to make a revision in list prices without reprinting the catalog. As prices fluctuate, new schedules of trade discounts are issued. For example, as market prices decrease, a manufacturer may offer a 5% discount from all prices listed in the catalog for the purpose of establishing new prices for the consumer. When market prices increase, the discounts might be reduced or dropped. Other reasons for granting trade discounts are: the location of the customer, the size of the order, and the customer's credit rating.

If there are two or more trade discounts applying to a list price, the discounts are known as a *discount series* or as *chain discounts*. When chain discounts are allowed, each succeeding discount is deducted from the remainder of the preceding discount.

EXAMPLE 1

The price of a ring listed in a catalog is $600. This list price is subject to a discount of 20%. What are the trade discount and the selling price?

Trade discount = List price × Discount rate
= 600 × 20% = $120

Selling price = List price − Trade discount
= 600 − 120 = $480

EXAMPLE 2

The list price of $400 for a television set is subject to discounts of 10%, 5%, and 2%. What is the selling price?

This problem may be computed in the following two ways:

(a)		(b)	
$400.00	List price	$400.00	
− 40.00	10% of $400	× .90	100% − 10% = 90%
$360.00	1st remainder	$360.00	
− 18.00	5% of $360	× .95	100% − 5% = 95%
$342.00	2d remainder	$342.00	
− 6.84	2% of $342	× .98	100% − 2% = 98%
$335.16	Selling price	$335.16	

Chain discounts may be converted to a single equivalent discount. In Example 2, the total amount of trade discounts is

$400.00 - 335.16 = \$64.84$

If the amount $64.84 is considered as a single trade discount, since

$$\begin{aligned} \text{List price} \times \text{Discount rate} &= \text{Trade discount, then} \\ 400 \times \text{Discount rate} &= 64.84 \end{aligned}$$

$$\text{Discount rate} = \frac{64.84}{400} = .1621, \text{ or } 16.21\%$$

The answer indicates that the single discount rate 16.21% is equivalent to the discounts 10%, 5%, and 2%. The single discount rate is *not* equal to the sum of the chain discounts, since 10% + 5% + 2% = 17%. The result is used to check the answer in Example 2 as follows:

$$\begin{aligned} 400 \times 16.21\% &= 64.84 \\ 400 - 64.84 &= \$335.16 \end{aligned}$$

EXERCISE 7-5 REFERENCE: SECTION 7.3A

A. Find (a) the selling price, (b) the total amount of the trade discount, and (c) the single equivalent discount rate in Problems 1–10:

	List Price	*Discount Rates*
1.	$700	5%, 10%, 20%
2.	$450	$12\frac{1}{2}$%, 8%, 4%
3.	$150	10%, $12\frac{1}{2}$%, 15%
4.	$200	20%, 10%, 5%
5.	$1,000	25%, 20%, $16\frac{2}{3}$%
6.	$2,500	15%, 30%, 20%
7.	$30	40%, 40%, 40%
8.	$80	50%, 50%, 50%
9.	$35.50	5%, 3%
10.	$60.80	2%, 1%

B. Statement problems:

11. The list price of an electric clock is $25.50 and the trade discount rate is 26%. Find the net price (selling price).
12. If the list price of a chair is $101.60 and the trade discount is 5%, what is the selling price?
13. The list price of a fountain pen is $12, and the discount rate listed on the discount sheet for this item is 15%. Find the selling price.
14. If the list price of an electric fan is $45 and the discount rate is 12%, what is the selling price?
15. A wholesaler ordered a dozen kitchen ranges listed at $250 each less discounts of 10%, 5%, and 2%. What is the net price of the entire order?
16. What is the net price of a sewing machine listed at $340, less discounts of 20%, 12%, and 10%?

B. Calculation by Formulas

The computation of the solution in Example 2(b), page 207, may be written in the following manner:

$$\begin{aligned}\text{Selling price} &= 400(100\% - 10\%)(100\% - 5\%)(100\% - 2\%)\\ &= 400(90\%)(95\%)(98\%)\\ &= 400 \times .8379\\ &= \$335.16\end{aligned}$$

According to this method, the following formula may be developed in computing chain discounts:

$$\begin{aligned}\text{Selling price} = {} & \text{List price } (1 - \text{First discount rate})\\ & (1 - \text{Second discount rate})(1 - \text{Third discount rate})(\ldots)\end{aligned}$$

NOTE: $1 = 100\%$

Let S = Selling price	r_2 = 2d discount rate
L = List price	r_3 = 3d discount rate
r_1 = 1st discount rate	r_n = nth discount rate

The above formula can be simplified as follows:

$$S = L(1 - r_1)(1 - r_2)(1 - r_3)\ldots(1 - r_n) \tag{7–1}$$

NOTE: The order in which the individual discount rates in a chain are multiplied does not affect the results. For example, the result of 400(90%)(95%)(98%) is the same as the result of 400(95%)(98%)(90%) or 400(98%)(90%)(95%). In other words, the result of any one of the calculations equals 335.16.

EXAMPLE 3 The list price of $1,200 for a refrigerator is subject to discounts of $33\frac{1}{3}\%$, 25%, and 10%. Find (a) the selling price and (b) the total amount of trade discount.

(a) $L = \$1{,}200,\ r_1 = 33\frac{1}{3}\%,\ r_2 = 25\%,\ r_3 = 10\%$

Substituting the values in formula (7–1),

$$\begin{aligned}S &= 1{,}200(1 - 33\tfrac{1}{3}\%)(1 - 25\%)(1 - 10\%)\\ &= 1{,}200(1 - \tfrac{1}{3})(1 - \tfrac{1}{4})(1 - \tfrac{1}{10})\\ &= 1{,}200(\tfrac{2}{3})(\tfrac{3}{4})(\tfrac{9}{10})\\ &= \$540\end{aligned}$$

(b) Trade discount = 1,200 − 540 = $660

When the selling price and the trade discounts are known, the list price may be found by formula (7–1), as shown in the following example.

EXAMPLE 4 The selling price of a radio is $27.36. At what price should the radio be listed if a series of discounts of 20%, 10%, and 5% is allowed?

$S = \$27.36,\quad r_1 = 20\%,\quad r_2 = 10\%,\quad r_3 = 5\%$

Substituting the values in formula (7–1),

$$27.36 = L(1 - 20\%)(1 - 10\%)(1 - 5\%)$$
$$27.36 = L(.8)(.9)(.95) = L(.684)$$

$$L = \frac{27.36}{.684} = \$40$$

CHECK

$40.00	
− 8.00	20% of $40
$32.00	
− 3.20	10% of $32
$28.80	
− 1.44	5% of $28.80
$27.36	Selling price

Or

$$S = 40(1 - 20\%)(1 - 10\%)(1 - 5\%)$$
$$= 40(.8)(.9)(.95) = 40(.684)$$
$$= \$27.36$$

Chain discounts may be converted to a single equivalent discount rate by formula (7–2), as shown below, without referring to the list price or the selling price.

Let r = the single discount rate that is equivalent to a series of discounts, $r_1, r_2, r_3 \ldots$

Formula (7–1) becomes $S = L(1 - r)$.

Equate the right sides of the above equation and formula (7–1). The following equation is obtained:

$$L(1 - r) = L(1 - r_1)(1 - r_2)(1 - r_3)\ldots(1 - r_n)$$

Divide both sides by L and solve for r. Then

$$\mathbf{r = 1 - (1 - r_1)(1 - r_2)(1 - r_3)\ldots(1 - r_n)} \quad \textbf{(7–2)}$$

EXAMPLE 5

What is the single trade discount rate that is equivalent to chain discounts of 10%, 5%, and 2%?

$r_1 = 10\%, \quad r_2 = 5\%, \quad r_3 = 2\%$

Substituting the values in formula (7–2), the single equivalent discount rate r is computed as follows:

$$r = 1 - (1 - 10\%)(1 - 5\%)(1 - 2\%)$$
$$= 1 - (90\%)(95\%)(98\%)$$
$$= 1 - (.9)(.95)(.98)$$
$$= 1 - .8379$$
$$= .1621, \text{ or } 16.21\%$$

The answer may be used to check the solution in Example 2, page 207, as shown below:

Selling price, $S = L(1 - r) = 400(1 - 16.21\%) = 400 \times .8379$
$= \$335.16$

EXERCISE 7-6 REFERENCE: SECTION 7.3B

A. Find (a) the selling price and (b) the total amount of trade discount in Problems 1–6:

	List Price	*Rates of Trade Discounts*
1.	\$48	10%, 7%, 5%
2.	\$25	12%, 15%, 18%
3.	\$96	15%, 20%, 45%
4.	\$150	20%, 22%, 35%
5.	\$125.70	$33\frac{1}{3}\%$, $37\frac{1}{2}\%$, $88\frac{8}{9}\%$
6.	\$434	$66\frac{2}{3}\%$, 75%, $28\frac{4}{7}\%$

B. Find the list price in Problems 7–12:

	Selling Price	*Rates of Trade Discounts*
7.	\$27.72	10%, 20%, 30%
8.	\$828.75	15%, 25%, 35%
9.	\$237.00	30%, 40%, 50%, 60%
10.	\$1,365.00	20%, 25%, 30%, 35%
11.	\$500.65	5%, 15%
12.	\$132.30	2%, 10%

C. Find the single equivalent rate of trade discount in Problems 13–18:

13. 20%, 10%, 2%
14. 25%, 20%, 10%
15. 5%, 10%, 20%
16. 10%, 12%, 15%
17. 25%, $28\frac{4}{7}\%$, $37\frac{1}{2}\%$
18. $12\frac{1}{2}\%$, $18\frac{2}{11}\%$, $8\frac{1}{3}\%$

D. Statement problems:

19. A dealer can buy a chair from manufacturer X for \$120 less discounts of 15% and 10%, or from manufacturer Y for \$150 less discounts of 20%, 5%, and 15%. (a) Which manufacturer has offered the lower price? (b) What is the difference between the two prices?
20. Company A offers a retailer trade discounts of $33\frac{1}{3}\%$, 25%, 5%, and 1%. Company B offers the retailer trade discounts of 30%, 20%, and 15%. Which company offers the lower price on an article if the list price is the same at both companies?
21. A manufacturer of hosiery offers to ship 500 pairs of ladies' hose to a retailer at \$3 per pair less discounts of 10%, 5%, and 2%. If the 2% discount is later removed, by what amount will the retailer's cost be affected?
22. Two television manufacturers offer similar products at prices as follows: Manufacturer C offers a list price less 20%, 8%, and 2%. Manufacturer D offers a list price less 15%, 10%, and 5%. Which manufacturer has the lower net price on the item if the list price is the same for both manufacturers?
23. A refrigerator that sold for \$581.40 net has been subject to discounts of 5%, 10%, and 15%. What is the list price?
24. A wholesaler paid \$54 in cash for an electric sander that was bought at trade discounts of 20%, 25%, and 10%. What was the list price?
25. The selling price of a washing machine is \$327.60. At what price should the machine be listed if a series of discounts of 10%, 20%, and 30% is allowed?

26. The selling price of a car is \$9,690. At what price should the car be listed if the list price is subject to discounts of 25%, 15%, and 5%?
27. A manufacturer can cover his expenses and make a fair profit if he sells his tape recorder for \$136.89. What should the list price of the item be in his catalog so that his customers can be allowed a series of discounts of 35% and 22%?
28. An invoice shows that the net price of an electric saw is \$106.19 after discounts of 30% and 18% have been taken. Find the list price.
29. The list price of an electric fan is \$28.80 less a discount of 10%. The wholesaler later allowed an additional discount to make the selling price of \$19.44. (a) What was the additional discount rate? (b) What single discount rate will give the same new selling price?
30. The list price of an electric coffeepot is \$50 less discounts of 15% and 12%. Because of rising costs, the company changed the 12% discount to 10%. (a) What is the net change in the selling price? (b) What single discount rate will give the same new selling price?

7.4 CASH DISCOUNT

There is considerable variation in the methods of payment among different types of businesses. Some firms require immediate payment, but others allow their customers to pay their bills within a specified period of time known as the *credit period*. Many companies offer their customers a discount from the selling price called a *cash discount*. A cash discount is also called a *sales discount* by the seller, and a *purchase discount* by the buyer. Such a discount, which is usually stated on the invoice, is generally used to induce an early payment before the expiration of the credit period. For example, the seller may offer his debtor cash discount terms of "2/10, *n*/30." These terms mean that if payment is made within 10 days from the date of the invoice, a 2% cash discount is allowed, although the debtor is permitted a period of 30 days to pay the bill. However, if the bill is paid after the end of 10 days but on or before the end of the 30-day period, the *net amount* of the invoice must be paid. After 30 days, the bill will be considered overdue and may be subject to an interest charge.

When an invoice states credit terms in a form such as 2/10, 1/20, *n*/30, the number at the left in each term is the discount rate in percent; the number at the right is the allowed credit period in number of days; and *n* indicates the net amount in the invoice, or the selling price.

The amount of cash discount is determined as follows:

Cash discount = Invoice amount (or selling price) × Cash discount rate (%)

EXAMPLE 1

An invoice for \$600 was dated May 1 with credit terms of 2/10, 1/20, *n*/30. What amount should the buyer pay if he pays in full on (a) May 8? (b) May 15? (c) May 31?

(a) It is 7 days from May 1 to May 8. Thus, 2% cash discount is allowed.

$$600 \times 2\% = 12$$
$$600 - 12 = \$588$$

(b) It is 14 days from May 1 to May 15. Thus, 1% cash discount is allowed.

$600 \times 1\% = 6$
$600 - 6 = \$594$

(c) It is 30 days from May 1 to May 31. Thus, no cash discount is allowed. The debtor must pay the entire bill of $600.

EXAMPLE 2 An invoice dated April 6 states that the selling price for merchandise is $620.50, the freight charge is $12.60, and the terms are 2/10, *n*/30. Find the total payment if the bill is paid on (a) April 12, (b) April 20.

(a) It is 6 days from April 6 to April 12. Thus, a discount of 2% of the selling price is allowed. However, discount is not taken on the freight charges.

$620.50 \times 2\% = 12.41$
$620.50 - 12.41 + 12.60 = \$620.69$

(b) It is 14 days from April 6 to April 20. Thus, no cash discount is allowed. The total amount of the payment for the invoice is the selling price plus the freight charge.

$620.50 + 12.60 = \$633.10$

Although the credit period generally begins with the date of the invoice, it may begin on the day of receipt of goods (*ROG*). The ROG dating is particularly useful when a considerable amount of time is required for transportation. Or, it may begin at the end of the month (*EOM*) following the date of the invoice, such as "2/10 EOM."

"2/10 EOM" means that if the invoice is paid during the first ten days following the end of the month of the invoice date, the buyer is entitled to a 2% cash discount. If the invoice is not paid during the cash discount period, an additional 20-day period is usually allowed to pay the net amount.

Sometimes the buyer makes a partial payment on the invoice. If the partial payment is made within the discount period, the purchaser is entitled to a discount on the portion of the amount paid.

EXAMPLE 3 An invoice for $400 dated September 25 with credit terms of 2/10 EOM was issued to G. D. Miller. He paid $245 on the invoice on October 7. What is: (a) the amount credited to Miller's account by the seller? (b) the cash discount? (c) the balance due?

(a) The credit period begins at the end of September. It is 7 days from the end of September to October 7. Thus, Miller is entitled to a 2% cash discount on the amount he pays. Since $245 is equivalent to 98% (or 100% − 2%), the base (100%) must be

$245 \div 98\% = \$250$

The amount credited to Miller's account is $250, which is the partial payment before the 2% discount is taken.

(b) Cash discount is

$250 - 245 = \$5$ *Check:* $250 \times 2\% = \$5$

(c) Balance due is

$400 - 250 = \$150$

EXERCISE 7-7 REFERENCE: SECTION 7.4

A. In each of the following cases, find (a) the amount of cash discount, and (b) the amount paid. Assume that the invoice date and the date of payment are for the same year.

	Invoice Amount	*Invoice Date*	*Terms*	*Payment Date*
1.	$600	Jan. 6	2/10, *n*/30	Jan. 16
2.	$480	Feb. 2	2/10, *n*/30	Feb. 12
3.	$520.60	March 10	4/10, 2/30, *n*/60	March 26
4.	$836.50	April 7	4/10, 2/30, *n*/60	April 20
5.	$72.84	May 20	3/10, 2/20, *n*/30	May 24
6.	$28.36	June 3	3/10, 2/20, *n*/30	June 9
7.	$126.42	July 5	5/10, 2/30, *n*/60	Aug. 10
8.	$185.37	Aug. 4	5/10, 2/30, *n*/60	Sept. 29
9.	$29.65	Sept. 21	2/10 EOM	Oct. 8
10.	$62.28	Oct. 26	3/10 EOM	Nov. 7

B. Statement problems:

11. The Metro Company received a check from a customer who took the company's usual 2% cash discount on an invoice for $1,582. What was the amount received?
12. What is the amount of the check sent in payment of an invoice for $236.40; terms 3/10, *n*/30; dated November 16; and paid November 21?
13. An invoice for $850 was issued on September 10 with credit terms of 3/10, 2/20, *n*/30. What amount should a buyer pay if she makes the payment in full on (a) September 15? (b) September 22? (c) October 6?
14. An invoice for $522.40 dated October 16 has the terms 2/10, 1/15, *n*/30. Find the amount of payment if the bill is paid on (a) October 20, (b) October 28, and (c) November 10.
15. Billy Meyer, a wholesaler, made a sale of merchandise having a list price of $750 and a trade discount of 25%. He prepared the sales invoice on February 16 and included a freight charge of $16.50. The credit terms are 2/10, *n*/20. How much should the customer pay if the bill is paid on (a) February 24? (b) February 28?
16. Sue Parker, a retailer, received an invoice that gives the following information:

    Date of invoice–June 16, 19–.
    Item 1–2 kitchen ranges; list price, $375 each, less trade discounts of 5% and 10%.
    Item 2–12 radios; list price, $44 each, less trade discounts of 15% and 8%.
    Freight charges–$65.60.
    Credit terms–2/10 EOM.

    Determine (a) the last day on which the cash discount may be taken, and (b) the total amount of the payment for the bill if it is paid on that day.
17. An invoice for $500 dated June 2 with credit terms of 2/10, *n*/30 was received by George Sanders. He paid $196 on June 6 and $162 on June 15. (a) What was the total cash discount on the two payments? (b) What was the balance due after the payments were made?

18. On an invoice for \$650 with credit terms of 5/10, 2/20, *n*/30, dated May 24, the partial payments were made as follows: \$285 cash on June 1; \$260 cash on June 5. Find (a) the total cash discount on the two payments, and (b) the balance due after the payments were made.

7.5 COMMISSIONS AND FEES

Wholesalers and retailers are merchant middlemen who take title to the goods they handle and assume complete responsibility for the risks involved in their trade. Their profits, if any, are obtained by subtracting the cost of goods sold and the operating expenses from the net sales. However, there are other types of middlemen, known as agents or agent middlemen, who do not actually buy, sell, or take title to goods themselves. They only negotiate or assist in purchasing or selling for people, called *principals*, who wish to buy or sell merchandise. Agent middlemen generally receive their remuneration in the form of commissions or fees. The most important types of agent middlemen are brokers, commission merchants, manufacturers' agents, sales agents, purchasing agents, auction companies, and resident buyers.

Commissions and fees are usually expressed as a certain percent of the selling price if the agents represent sellers. If the agents represent buyers, the commissions and fees are usually expressed as a certain percent of the purchase price, known as the *prime cost*. The prime cost includes the price paid to a seller but excludes the amount that is paid for other incidental costs of the purchase, such as the cost of assembling and shipping. As explained below, the computation of commissions and fees is the same as that of percentage problems.

Commission for selling = Selling price × Commission rate

Commission for buying = Prime cost × Commission rate

Selling price − Commission − Expenses = Net proceeds (the amount received by the principal from the agent who sells for the principal)

Prime cost + Commission + Expenses = Net purchase cost (the amount paid by the principal to the agent who buys for the principal)

EXAMPLE 1

Betty Kramer, a farmer, shipped a carload of tomatoes to Harry Baum, a commission merchant. Baum sold the shipment for \$350 and paid \$15 for freight charges. If Baum charges 4% commission, how much will Kramer receive from the shipment?

Commission for the sale is

350 × 4% = \$14

Net proceeds that Kramer will receive are

350 (selling price) − 14 (commission) − 15 (expenses) = \$321

EXAMPLE 2

George Larson, a purchasing agent for Mary Rice, bought 200 crates of apples. He paid $12.25 per crate and $165 for shipping costs. If he charged 5% commission, how much should Larson receive from Rice?

Commission for the purchase is computed below:

12.25 × 200 = $2,450 (prime cost)
2,450 × 5% = $122.50 (commission)

The total amount that Larson should receive from Rice is

$2,450.00	Prime cost
122.50	Commission
+ 165.00	Expenses
$2,737.50	Total amount

EXERCISE 7-8 REFERENCE: SECTION 7.5

1. John Hanson, a commission merchant, received a shipment of 300 cases of bananas from Jane Todd. He stored the entire shipment in a warehouse for 3 days at a cost of 5 cents per case per day. He then sold the shipment for $12 per case. If he charged 10% of the selling price as his commission, how much did Todd receive?
2. The Farmers' House, a sales agent, sold 50 cases of corned beef for $25 per case. The House paid freight charges of $18. If the commission was 8%, how much did the principal receive?
3. Dee Kerr, a purchasing agent, purchased 400 pounds of margarine at 52 cents per pound. Kerr charged a 5% commission and paid $15 for shipping costs. How much did her principal pay?
4. Helen Berman purchased 250 dozen eggs at 55¢ per dozen and 460 dozen eggs at 52¢ per dozen for Be-Rite Super Market. The cost of crating and shipping was $12.50 for the two purchases. If Berman received a check for $426.87, what rate of percent was the commission?
5. The Food Market, a sales agent, received a shipment of 600 cases of eggs. Each case contained 30 dozen eggs, but some of them were broken. They were sorted and repacked at a cost of 7¢ per case. The remaining 575 cases and 2 dozen were sold at $.85 per dozen. If the commission charged was 6% of the selling price, what amount did the principal receive?
6. Cathy Winston, an auctioneer, sold some goods amounting to $5,678.50 for R. G. Paddler and charged 12% commission. How much did Winston receive?
7. Edward Kent sent his agent a shipment of potatoes for sale. The shipment was sold for $55. If the commission was figured at $4\frac{1}{2}$% and Kent received $47, what was the amount of the other expenses?
8. A broker negotiated the sale of 540 cases of B-N baby food for $9.20 per case. His commission was 3% of the selling price. (a) What was the broker's fee? (b) What was the net amount received by the seller?
9. George Martin, a salesman in a shoe store, made sales as follows: $25,000 in January, $43,000 in February, and $36,500 in March. His monthly salary is $1,500 plus 6% commission on the amount of sales exceeding $20,000 each month. How much did he receive for each of the three months?

10. Alice Simons has asked a real estate agent to sell her home. She wishes to realize a net amount of $143,375. If the agent charges 7.5% commission, what should be the selling price of the house?
11. A collection agent remitted $522.50 to her principal after deducting her 5% fee. What was the amount collected by the agent?
12. A collection agent collected 85% of a debt of $700. If his commission was 8% of the amount collected, how much did he remit to his principal?
13. Dorothy Clinton sold a lot through a real estate agent who charged $4\frac{1}{2}$% commission. Clinton's net proceeds were $21,010 after she had paid the agent's commission. What was the selling price of the lot?
14. A sales agent receives a commission of 7% on his sales. In order to receive $507.50 commission in a month, what should be the amount of his sales in the month?
15. A sales agent receives a salary of $700 a month plus 6% commission on all sales. What must the amount of her sales be each month in order to have a total monthly income of $4,000?
16. A sales agent receives a salary of $750 a month plus 8% commission on all sales over $20,000 to $25,000 during the month. He also receives 10% commission on all sales over $25,000 during the month. What must be the amount of his sales each month in order to earn a total monthly income of $5,000?

7.6 SALES TAXES

Many states and cities look upon the sales tax as one of their main sources of revenue. Sales taxes are usually levied on retail sales, although in some states they may apply to general sales and other receipts. *Retail sales* are sales of tangible personal property at retail prices to the consumer. Retail sales also include the sales of specified services, such as amusements, restaurant meals, hotel rooms, and public utility services. *General sales* include both wholesale and retail sales of tangible personal property and, in some cases, specified services. The rate of retail sales taxes, which ranges from 2% to 7.5%, varies among states. The tax is calculated as follows:

Sales tax = Selling price × Sales tax rate

However, when the selling price is less than one dollar, or exceeds a whole number of dollars, the tax on the fraction of a dollar is usually based on a published list or guide.

EXAMPLE 1

The sales tax schedule used in a certain state is shown below:

Amount of Sale	*Amount of Tax*
1¢ to 10¢	none
11¢ to 40¢	1¢
41¢ to 70¢	2¢
71¢ to $1	3¢
$1 and up	3¢ on each dollar (whole dollars)

Find the amount of tax that a furniture store should charge on the sale of a book priced at $10.50.

Tax on $10.00	30¢	(10 × 3¢)
Tax on $ .50	2¢	(per schedule, 41¢ to 70¢)
Tax on $10.50	32¢	

Generally the sales tax law levies the tax upon the purchaser but requires the seller to collect the tax. Some companies may not maintain a separate record of the sales tax on each sale. In such cases, the combined amount of the sale and the sales tax is recorded for each sale. At the end of each accounting period, the tax liability is then computed from the total amount of sales.

EXAMPLE 2

During the month of May, a store collected $53,040, which included sales and sales taxes. If the sales tax rate is 4%, what is the amount of (a) the sales? (b) the sales tax?

(a) The sales tax is 4% of the sales. Therefore, the sales are the base (100%). The amount $53,040 is equivalent to

100% + 4% = 104% (of the sales)

Thus, the amount of the sales during the month is

$53,040 ÷ 104% = $51,000

(b) The tax is

$53,040 − $51,000 = $2,040

CHECK

	$51,000	Sales
$51,000 × 4% =	$ 2,040	Tax
	$53,040	Total amount collected

7.7 EXCISE TAXES

The term *excise tax* has been broadly used to refer to taxes that are levied upon the manufacture, sale, or consumption of commodities within this country, or are in the form of exactions for a license for permission to practice or to conduct certain sports, trades, or occupations. Excise taxes have been most widely used by the federal government, although they have also been used by some state and local governments.

The tax is calculated in a manner similar to that for sales tax, or

Excise tax = Selling price × Excise tax rate

Excise tax rates are frequently changed by the government. The following examples of federal excise taxes are selected for illustration.

Article	*Tax Rate*
Manfuacturers' Excise Taxes (Based on Manufacturers' Selling Price)	
Sport fishing equipment	10%
Pistols and revolvers	10%
Shells and cartridges	11%
Electric outboard motors	3%
Retail Excise Taxes	
Truck chassis and bodies	12%
Trailer chassis and bodies	12%
Tractors	12%

Other Excise Taxes	*Tax Rate*
Gasoline (per gallon)	9¢
Transportation of persons by air	8%
Telephone service	3%

EXERCISE 7-9 REFERENCE: SECTIONS 7.6 and 7.7

A. Use the schedule in Section 7.6 to compute the amount of sales tax for each of the following sales:

1. $0.40	4. $1.27	7. $3.75	10. $1.06
2. $0.50	5. $2.30	8. $5.82	11. $3.12
3. $1.75	6. $2.65	9. $6.60	12. $1.56

13. Bill Becker purchased the following articles at Gray's Department Store: A pair of socks for $2.50, a handkerchief for $1.10, and a sweatband for $3.69. (a) How much sales tax must he pay on the total amount? (b) What is the total cost of the purchase?
14. Mary Jennings bought a brush for $.78, a mirror for $1.20, and a comb for $4.39. (a) How much is the sales tax? (b) What is the total amount that she had to pay?
15. A retail store received $14.42 in cash from a sale that included 3% sales tax. (a) What is the price of the article sold? (b) How much is the sales tax?
16. A department store received $26 in cash, which included a sales tax of 4%, from the sale of a dress. (a) What is the price of the dress? (b) How much is the sales tax?

B. Find the amount of excise tax in each of the following cases. Use the rates given in Section 7.7.

	Article	*Price*
17.	(a) Fishing rods and reels	$ 35.20 (tax included)
	(b) Tractor	$ 9,520.00 (tax included)
18.	(a) Electric outboard motor	$ 2,360.00 (plus tax)
	(b) 18 gallons of gasoline	$ 1.10 per gallon (plus tax)
19.	(a) Airline passenger ticket	$148.61 (plus tax)
	(b) Pistol	$ 82.50 (plus tax)
20.	(a) Shells	$ 32.19 (tax included)
	(b) Revolver	$ 61.82 (tax included)

★7.8 PROPERTY TAXES

Property taxes are commonly looked upon as a chief source of revenue by local governmental units, such as the city, town, and county. Any object, tangible or intangible, capable of being reduced to exclusive possession is considered as *property*.

Generally, property is classified as either real or personal. *Real property*, also referred to as realty or real estate, includes land or anything permanently attached to the land, such as buildings. All other property is thought of as *personal property*. The value of real property that is subject to tax is usually determined by a tax assessor appointed by the governmental unit. The value determined by the assessor is called the *assessed value*, which is generally lower than the fair market value of the property. Personal property may also be appraised by an assessor, although in some cases the property owner may be required to declare the value of the property. The governmental unit determines the property tax rate by dividing the total revenue to be raised from the tax by the total taxable assessed value of the property within the jurisdiction of the governmental unit.

EXAMPLE 1

If the estimated revenue of County X from the property tax amounts to $2,578,400 and the taxable property in the county has an assessed value of $100,000,000, what is the tax rate of the property if all of the assessed value is taxable?

$$\text{Tax rate} = \frac{\text{Estimated revenue from the tax}}{\text{Taxable assessed value}} = \frac{2{,}578{,}400}{100{,}000{,}000}$$

$$= .025784, \quad \text{or } \$.025784 \text{ per dollar of the assessed value}$$

The tax rate may also be expressed as 25.784 mills per dollar, or 2.5784% of the assessed value of the property. ($1 = 1,000 mills.) Note that the tax rate is usually rounded to the next higher figure so that there is assurance of no shortage of revenue. The above tax rate may be rounded to 25.79 mills or 2.58% if only two decimal places are to be retained.

EXAMPLE 2

In Example 1, if only 80% of the assessed value is taxable, what should the tax rate be? Assume that the same amount of revenue is to be raised from the property tax.

$$\text{Tax rate} = \frac{\text{Estimated revenue from the tax}}{\text{Taxable assessed value}} = \frac{2{,}578{,}400}{100{,}000{,}000 \times 80\%}$$

$$= .03223, \quad \text{or } \$.03223 \text{ per dollar of } 80\% \text{ of the assessed value}$$

The tax rate may also be expressed as 32.23 mills per dollar, or 3.223% of 80% of the assessed value.

In Example 2, the computed tax rate (0.03223 or 3.223%) is also called the *nominal rate*. When the nominal rate is multiplied by the taxable percent rate (80%) of the assessed value, the product is called the *effective tax rate*.

$$\begin{aligned}\text{Effective tax rate} &= \text{Nominal rate} \times \text{Taxable assessed value } (\%) \\ &= 0.03223 \times 80\% \\ &= .025784, \text{ or } 2.5784\% \text{ (Example 2)}\end{aligned}$$

which is the same as the tax rate obtained in Example 1. The effective rates are useful in comparing the actual charges by different governmental units, such as the comparison of the property tax rates by rank in 12 selected large cities in the table below.

EXAMPLE 3

If Cornelia has property assessed at $50,000 in County X, how much is her tax on the property?

According to the tax rate in Example 1,

$$\begin{aligned}\text{Tax} &= \text{Taxable value} \times \text{Tax rate} \\ &= 50{,}000 \times .025784 = \$1{,}289.20\end{aligned}$$

According to the tax rate in Example 2,

$$\text{Tax} = 50{,}000 \times 80\% \times .03223 = \$1{,}289.20$$

The taxable value is $50,000 × 80% = $40,000.

Residential Property Tax Rates by Rank in Selected Large Cities, 1985

City	*Nominal Rate %*	*Taxable Assessed Value, %*	*Effective Tax Rate %*
Newark (NJ)	11.93	45.8	5.46*
Wilmington (DE)	4.63	92.0	4.26
Bridgeport	6.60	63.8	4.21
Detroit	8.32	50.0	4.16
Indianapolis	9.96	33.3	3.32
Milwaukee	3.24	99.3	3.22
Providence	7.25	44.3	3.21
Des Moines	3.76	72.5	2.73
Baltimore	6.21	43.5	2.70
Philadelphia	7.48	35.0	2.62
Portland (OR)	2.57	100.0	2.57
Manchester	7.93	30.0	2.38

*11.93% × 45.8% = .1193 × .458 = .054639, or 5.46%.

Source: *Information Please Almanac* (Boston: Houghton Mifflin Company, 1988), p. 84.

EXAMPLE 4

Paul Hopkins has a house assessed at $150,000 in Johnson City. The property tax rate of the city is 8.5% on 60% of the assessed value. How much is his property tax for the year?

Taxable value = 150,000 × 60% = $90,000
Tax = 90,000 × .085 = $7,650

EXERCISE 7-10 REFERENCE: SECTION 7.8

A. Find (a) the property tax rate in % (to 3 decimal places) and (b) the tax on the property owned by an individual in Problems 1–8:

	Revenue to Be Raised by the Tax	*Total Assessed Value in a County*	*Assessed Value of an Individual's Property*	*Taxable Assessed Value*
1.	$ 3,000,000	$ 40,000,000	$ 45,000	100%
2.	5,000,000	350,000,000	400,000	70%
3.	7,500,000	250,000,000	32,500	80%
4.	7,600,000	480,000,000	70,000	100%
5.	1,200,000	60,000,000	30,000	60%
6.	8,340,000	652,000,000	100,000	90%
7.	18,500,000	870,000,000	50,000	85%
8.	45,000,000	1,000,000,000	180,000	65%

B. Statement problems:

9. The required revenue of a city for the coming year is $258,520,000. Miscellaneous income is estimated at $42,620,000. The difference is to be raised by a property tax on the total assessed value of $12,000,000,000. What is the tax rate in % (to 3 decimal places)?
10. The taxable property in a town is assessed at $50,000,000. The amount required to meet the expenses during the coming year is $3,750,000. The amount estimated for receipts from other sources is $250,000. The estimate of the surplus at the end of this year is $160,000. What is the tax rate in percents (%)?
11. Sam Quine owns a house that has an assessed value of $20,000. If the property tax rate is 6.158% on 80% of the assessed value, what is his property tax for the year?
12. The real property in one county is assessed at $4,500,000, and the personal property is assessed at $850,000. The revenue to be raised from the property tax for the coming year is $250,000. The tax will be levied on 100% of the assessed value of the real property, but will be on only 80% of the personal property. What should be the tax rate in % (to 3 decimal places) for the real property and the personal property?
13. The assessed value of taxable property of a school district is $9,000,000,000. The cost of maintaining the schools for the coming year is $150,000,000, of which $25,000,000 will be paid by the state and by tuition fees. (a) What should the tax rate be? (b) If a woman owns property having an assessed value of $50,000, how much is her property tax?
14. The assessed value of the taxable property in one county is $35,000,000. The county needs $320,000 for the coming year. However, 10% of the property tax must be turned over to the state government. (a) What should the tax rate be in order for the county to meet its needs and to pay the state government its stated share? (b) If a person has $65,000 in property at its assessed value, how much property tax must he pay?

★7.9 PAYROLL TAXES

A *payroll* is a schedule that gives information regarding the earnings of employees for a certain period of time. When a payroll is made, payroll taxes are imposed upon either the employees or the employer or, in some instances, upon both the employees and the employer. In general, the payroll taxes imposed upon employees are those levied under the Federal Insurance Contributions Act and the federal income tax laws. The payroll taxes imposed upon employers are levied under the Federal Insurance Contributions Act, the Federal Unemployment Tax Act, and the state unemployment compensation laws.

A. Employees' Payroll Taxes

FICA TAX

The Federal Insurance Contributions Act, which was enacted in 1937 and amended in later years, provides a federal program of old-age and survivors' insurance. The tax levied under this program is frequently referred to as the FICA tax, or the Social Security tax. The program insures almost every kind of employment and self-employment against loss of earnings because of old age, death, or prolonged disability. Some occupations, such as farming and household workers, however, are covered only if certain conditions are met. Beginning July 1, 1966, millions of persons 65 and over became eligible for two kinds of health insurance protection: hospital insurance and medical insurance, often called "Medicare." The persons who are entitled to social security benefits are automatically eligible for hospital insurance. The medical insurance, on the other hand, is only for those who choose to take it. Premiums for the medical insurance are paid monthly by the subscriber, with the federal government matching the amount.

The following table gives the hospital insurance rate, the social security rates under the Federal Insurance Contributions Act and the Self-Employment Contributions Act, and the combined rate.

Calendar Year	*Maximum Taxable Wage Base*	*For Hospital Insurance*	*For Retirement, Survivors, and Disability Insurance*	*Tax Rate*	
				Employee (Also Employer)	*Self-employed*
		(a)	*(b)*	*(a) + (b)*	
1985	$39,600	1.35%	5.70%	7.05%	14.10%
1986	42,000	1.45	5.70	7.15	14.30
1987	43,800	1.45	5.70	7.15	14.30
1988	45,000	1.45	6.06	7.51	15.02
1989	48,000	1.45	6.06	7.51	15.02
1990 and after	Automatic cost-of-living adjustments in wage base	1.45	6.20	7.65	15.30

Source: U.S. Department of Health and Human Services, Social Security Administration.

The tax contributed by an employee is not paid directly by the employee to the federal tax collector but is paid through the employer, who withholds the tax from wages paid to its employees. The employer sends the withheld tax, with an equal amount as its own share of the contribution, to the District Director of the Internal Revenue Service. The contributions are used to pay the benefits and administrative expenses for the program and are administered by the Social Security Administration of the Department of Health and Human Services.

The tax rates are frequently changed by Congress, as shown in the table. In this text we shall use the 1988 FICA tax rate: 7.51% of the first $45,000 paid to each employee during the calendar year. The rate is applied equally to the FICA tax contributions from both employees and employers. Self-employed persons, who do not have an employer to contribute an equal amount, are taxed at a higher rate than are employees, 15.02% in the tax rate table for 1988.

EXAMPLE 1

The Webb Company prepares a monthly payroll. The total amount of wages earned by Alan Taylor, an employee, during August is $4,000. The record of employees' earnings for the current year shows that Alan Taylor has cumulative earnings of $5,600 prior to August. How much FICA tax should the employer (The Webb Company) withhold from Taylor's August wages?

The sum of $5,600 and $4,000 is $9,600, which is less than the maximum taxable amount, $45,000. Thus, all of the $4,000 is taxable.

FICA tax = 4,000 × 7.51% = $300.40

EXAMPLE 2

In Example 1, assume that Alan Taylor's total earnings of this year prior to August were $43,200. How much FICA tax should be withheld from his wages in August?

The amount of his wages subject to withholding tax in August is $1,800. The computation is as follows:

$45,000 − $43,200 = $1,800

$45,000 is the maximum taxable amount.

The other portion of his wages, $2,200 (= 4,000 − 1,800), is not taxable under the FICA tax law.

FICA tax = 1,800 × 7.51% = $135.18

FEDERAL INCOME TAX

Since 1943, the federal income tax for individuals has been collected at the time the income is earned instead of during the following year. Under the "pay-as-you-go" plan as provided by law, employers are required to withhold income taxes from wages paid to their employees. The amount to be withheld may be determined either by reference to withholding tables provided by the government or by exact computation. Under both methods, the amount of tax to be withheld is based on the length of the payroll period, the amount of wages, the number of exemptions claimed by the employee, and the marital status of the employee.

Withholding tables are provided for weekly, biweekly, semimonthly, monthly, and daily or miscellaneous payroll periods. A portion of the income tax withholding table based on a monthly payroll period for married persons is presented on page 225.

Exact computation of the income tax to be withheld is based on the percentage method. This method requires a set of tables with progressive tax rates. The tables can be obtained from the *Employer's Tax Guide*, issued by the Internal Revenue Service. Exact computation is required for quarterly, semiannual, or annual payroll periods although it is not required for the periods already provided on the withholding tables. The percentage method is not illustrated here, since the method involves only simple mathematical operations.

EXAMPLE 3

Refer to Example 1. The employee, Alan Taylor, is married. He claims four exemptions. How much income tax should be withheld from his wages by the employer?

The monthly income tax withholding table for married persons shows that $4,000 is in the "$4,000–$4,040" bracket of the table. When the number of withholding exemptions claimed is 4, the amount of tax to be withheld as shown on the line of the bracket is $550.

Income Tax Withholding Table
Monthly Payroll Period—Married Persons

If the wages are–		*And the number of withholding exemptions claimed is–*						
		0	1	2	3	4	. . .	10
At least	*But less than*	*The amount of income tax to be withheld shall be–*						
$ 0	$ 260	$ 0	$ 0	$ 0	$ 0	$ 0	. . .	$ 0
260	270	2	0	0	0	0		0
270	280	3	0	0	0	0		0
. . .	. . .							
1,000	1,040	115	91	66	42	17		0
1,040	1,080	121	97	72	48	23		0
1,080	1,120	127	103	78	54	29		0
1,120	1,160	133	109	84	60	35		0
. . .	. . .							
2,000	2,040	265	241	216	192	167		21
2,040	2,080	271	247	222	198	173		27
2,080	2,120	277	253	228	204	179		33
2,120	2,160	283	259	234	210	185		39
. . .	. . .							
3,000	3,040	452	407	366	342	317		171
3,040	3,080	463	418	372	348	323		177
3,080	3,120	475	429	384	354	329		183
3,120	3,160	486	440	395	360	335		189
. . .	. . .							
4,000	4,040	732	687	641	596	550		321
4,040	4,080	743	698	652	607	561		327
4,080	4,120	755	709	664	618	573		333
4,120	4,160	766	720	675	629	584		339
. . .	. . .							
5,000	5,040	1,012	967	921	876	830		557
5,040	5,080	1,023	978	932	887	841		568
5,080	5,120	1,035	989	944	898	853		580
5,120	5,160	1,046	1,000	955	909	864		591
5,160	5,200	1,057	1,011	966	920	875		602
$5,200 and over		Use the tables for percentage method of withholding						

Source: U.S. Internal Revenue Service, *Employer's Tax Guide* (1988).

B. Employer's Payroll Taxes

FICA TAX

The nature and requirements of the FICA tax for an employer are the same as those for an employee. The law levies an equal amount of FICA tax upon employee and employer in 1988.

EXAMPLE 4 Refer to Example 1. For what amount of FICA taxes is the employer liable to the government for Taylor's employment in August?

(a) The employer must pay its share of the FICA tax, $300.40, the same as Taylor's tax.

(b) The employer is liable to the government for its own tax and for the tax withheld from Taylor's wages. The total amount of the FICA taxes for which the employer is liable for the employment period is $600.80, or

300.40 + 300.40 = $600.80

FUTA TAX

The Federal Unemployment Tax Act provides a state–federal program that is designed to protect wage earners and their families from wage losses through involuntary unemployment. Under the program, unemployed workers are referred to suitable jobs, but if no such jobs are available, weekly benefits are paid for a certain period of time.

Under the Act and its subsequent amendments, the federal government levies a tax of 6% on the first $7,000 paid by eligible employers to every employee during the calendar year. The provisions of the Act are applicable to those employers who (a) paid a certain amount of wages in any calendar quarter (the amount during 1988 was $1,500 or more), or (b) had one or more employees at any time in each of 20 calendar weeks of the year. No unemployment tax is levied on the employee by the federal government. The employer is allowed a specified credit (not in excess of 5.4% of the first $7,000 of wages) against the tax for contributions he or she makes to state unemployment compensation funds, including credits under merit rating plans of the state.

EXAMPLE 5 Refer to Example 1. Assume that the employer's FUTA tax rate is .6% after the employer made the contribution to state unemployment funds. How much FUTA tax should the employer pay for Taylor's employment during August?

Wages (from $4,000) subject to FUTA tax = 7,000 − 5,600 = $1,400

FUTA tax = 1,400 × .6% = 1,400 × .006 = $8.40

STATE UNEMPLOYMENT TAX

Benefits paid to unemployed workers are financed by state taxes paid by employers under the state unemployment compensation laws. In most states only employers are required to pay the unemployment tax, but in a few states employees are also required to contribute. The tax rates are not the same in all states. The maximum rate that states may credit toward the federal unemployment tax is 90% of a 6% FUTA tax rate, or 5.4% (90% × 6% = 5.4%), of the first $7,000 of wages paid to each eligible employee. A state may provide a merit rating plan under which employers who have stable employment records are taxed at lower rates. Savings under the state merit-rating plan are allowed as a credit in the calculation of the federal contribution made by the employers.

EXAMPLE 6 Refer to Example 1. Compute the state unemployment tax for the employer. Assume that the state unemployment tax rate is (a) 5.4% and (b) 3.2%.

(a) 1,400 × 5.4% = 1,400 × .054 = $75.60 (Also see Example 5.)

(b) 1,400 × 3.2% = 1,400 × .032 = $44.80

The illustrations in Example 1 and the related examples, Examples 3, 4, 5, and 6(a), based on Alan Taylor's cumulative earnings of $5,600 prior to August, are summarized below.

(a) The amount of Taylor's take-home pay:

Wages		$4,000.00
Less: Withholding FICA tax	$300.40	
Withholding income tax	550.00	850.40
Take-home pay		$3,149.60

(b) The total cost to the Webb Company for the employment of Taylor during August:

Employee's wages		$4,000.00
Add: Employer's payroll taxes—		
FICA tax	$300.40	
FUTA tax	8.40	
State unemployment tax	75.60	384.40
Total cost		$4,384.40

(c) The distribution of the employer's cost:

Taylor's take-home pay		$3,149.60
Liability to federal government—		
Withholding FICA tax	$300.40	
Withholding income tax	550.00	
Employer's FICA tax	300.40	
FUTA tax	8.40	1,159.20
Liability to state government		75.60
Total cost		$4,384.40

To summarize, under the 1988 laws and regulations, the payroll taxes in a calendar year for eligible employers and employees were as follows:

Payroll Tax	*Imposed upon Employers*	*Imposed upon Employees*
FICA	7.51% of first $45,000 paid	Same as employers
FUTA	.6% (or 6%–5.4%) of first $7,000 paid	None
State unemployment tax	Varies from state to state	Generally none
Federal income tax	None for the payroll	Based on earnings, payroll period, exemptions claimed, and marital status

★ **EXERCISE 7–11** REFERENCE: SECTION 7.9

Assume that the following rates apply: FICA, 7.51% of the first $45,000; FUTA, .6% of the first $7,000; and state unemployment, 5.4% (or less if it is specified in a problem) of the first $7,000 paid to each employee.

A. In Problems 1–10, find:

(a) The employee's payroll taxes:
  (1) Federal income tax (if it is not given in the problem)
  (2) FICA tax
(b) The employee's take-home pay
(c) The employer's payroll taxes:
  (1) FICA tax
  (2) FUTA tax
  (3) State unemployment tax
(d) The employer's total cost for the employment during the current period
(e) The distribution of the employer's cost

	Employee (Married or Single)	*Earnings in the Current Period*	*Payroll Period*	*Cumulative Earnings Prior to Current Period*	*Number of Exemptions Claimed*	*Federal Income Tax*[1]
1.	A(*M*)	$ 2,050	Monthly	$ 6,900	2	$?
2.	B(*M*)	370	Weekly	8,000	3	31.00
3.	C(*S*)	1,540	Biweekly	9,000	4	249.00
4.	D(*S*)	1,230	Semimonthly	5,500	5	122.00
5.	E(*M*)	10,000	Quarterly	1,500	2	1,347.00
6.	F(*M*)	25,000	Semiannually	0	3	3,820.25
7.	G(*S*)	100,000	Annually	0	4	25,601.50
8.	H(*S*)	100	Daily	7,000	2	13.75
9.	I(*M*)	3,060	Monthly	35,500	3	?
10.	J(*M*)	5,100	Monthly	68,000	4	?

B. Statement problems:

11. The total amount of J. D. Kener's wages for this year up to July 31 was $6,900. He earned $5,060 in August. Assume that the employer prepares the monthly payroll on August 31 and that Kener, married, claims 2 exemptions. How much FICA tax and federal income tax should the employer withhold from Kener's wages for the month of August?
12. Refer to Problem 11. For how much payroll tax is the employer liable? Assume that the tax rate for state unemployment is only 3.2% of the first $7,000 paid to the employee.
13. The earnings record for the current week shows that C. T. Olson worked 42 hours at the rate of $25 per hour for the first 40 hours and at $1\frac{1}{2}$ times $25 for all additional hours. His FICA tax withheld prior to the current week is $3,367.50. He is single and claims 4 exemptions. Find (a) Olson's earnings for the current week, (b) the FICA tax to be withheld, and (c) Olson's take-home pay. (His federal income tax withheld is $189.00.)

[1]The given taxes are obtained from the 1988 *Employer's Tax Guide*, issued by the Internal Revenue Service.

14. Refer to Problem 13. Find the payroll taxes imposed upon the employer. Assume that the tax rate for state unemployment is only 4.6% of the first $7,000 paid to the employee.
15. The total salary and wage expense of a retail store for a year was $160,000. The payroll taxes imposed upon the store were FICA, $9,012; FUTA, $252; and state unemployment tax, $2,268. (a) How much of the total salary and wages was exempt from the FICA taxes? (b) from the state and federal unemployment taxes?
16. The November monthly payroll of Fuller's Department Store indicated that the total salary and wage expense was $50,000. During that month, $2,000 was exempt from the FICA tax and $6,000 was exempt from the state and federal unemployment taxes. Find the employer's payroll taxes in November. Assume that the tax rate for state unemployment is only 3.4%.

★7.10 INCOME TAXES

A. Introduction

Income taxes are levied by the federal government, by most of the states, and by some cities. The states and cities generally follow the federal income tax pattern, although the income tax rates and the details of the methods of computing the tax vary from state to state and city to city. In order to illustrate the principles of income taxation, only the most important and representative tax system—the federal system—is discussed here.

The 16th Amendment to the Constitution of the United States gave Congress the power to lay and collect taxes on income. The first revenue act was passed in 1913 and since that date, revenue acts and other laws containing tax provisions have been enacted in almost every year. The methods of computing individual and corporation income taxes illustrated in the following material are based on the instructions for 1988 income tax returns issued by the Internal Revenue Service.

B. Individual Income Tax Returns

Generally speaking, the method of computing an individual's income tax may be outlined in the following manner [see Examples 1 and 6(a)]:

1. Gross income		$48,000
2. Deductions I—Adjustments to income		650
3. Adjusted gross income		$47,350
4. Deductions from adjusted gross income:		
Deductions II—Itemized or Standard	$7,600	
Deductions III—Personal exemptions	9,750	
		17,350
5. Taxable income		$30,000
6. Tax: Based on Tax Table		$ 4,540
7. Prepaid tax payments		4,600
8. Net tax payable to government (or refundable to taxpayer)		($ 60)

GROSS INCOME

Gross income is the income that must be reported in an income tax return. The tax law states that all kinds of income, other than a return of capital, in whatever form received, are subject to tax unless the income is specifically excluded by law and by the Constitution. The following examples are types of gross income that must be reported in tax returns: wages, salaries, bonuses, commissions, tips, profits from business, rents, royalties, taxpayer's share of partnership profits, estate or trust income, and contest awards and prizes.

The amount of a person's gross income is the decisive factor for whether or not a person must file an income tax return. For example, in 1988 a person was required to file a return if single and under 65 and gross income was $4,950 or more. A person with less income had to file a return to get a refund if tax was withheld by an employer.

DEDUCTIONS I—FOR ADJUSTED GROSS INCOME

Deductions for adjusted gross income are also called the *adjustments to income*. The deductions are subtracted from the gross income to obtain the adjusted gross income. Examples of such deductions are reimbursed employee business expenses, payments to an Individual Retirement Arrangement (IRA), payments to a Keogh Retirement Plan, and penalty on early withdrawal of savings.

ADJUSTED GROSS INCOME

The amount of the adjusted gross income is computed because it is useful in determining the taxable income and other items, such as the right to take the earned income credit and to take certain medical expenses as itemized deductions.

DEDUCTIONS II—ITEMIZED OR STANDARD

Itemized or standard deductions are deductible from adjusted gross income. If the total amount of the itemized deductions is more than the allowed standard deduction, it would be to the taxpayer's advantage to take the itemized deductions so as to pay less tax.

Itemized deductions are generally personal expenses. Examples of deductible personal expenses are: charitable contributions, interest paid on personal loans, state and local income taxes, medical and dental expenses, union dues, casualty or theft losses, and employment fees paid to agencies.

Instead of itemizing deductions, the taxpayer may take a standard deduction for personal expenses. Standard deductions for most people (not for 65 or older or blind or if someone can claim the taxpayer as a dependent) are given below.

Filing Status	*Standard Deduction*
Single	$3,000
Married filing joint return or Qualifying widow(er) with dependent child	5,000
Married filing separate return	2,500
Head of household	4,400

DEDUCTIONS III—PERSONAL EXEMPTIONS

A taxpayer is entitled to one exemption for self unless someone else (such as a parent) can claim him or her as a dependent. If you file a joint return and your spouse cannot be claimed as a dependent on another person's return, you may take an exemption for your spouse. A taxpayer can also claim one exemption for each qualified dependent. According to the 1988 law, each exemption is entitled to a $1,950 deduction.

TAXABLE INCOME

Taxable income is the base to which the tax table and the tax rate schedules are applied in computing tax. Taxable income is determined by subtracting (a) the itemized or standard deduction and (b) personal exemption deductions from the adjusted gross income, or

Taxable income = Adjusted gross income − Itemized or Standard deduction − Personal exemption deductions

where

(a) Itemized or standard deduction, whichever is larger, is taken.
(b) Personal exemption deductions = Total number of exemptions × $1,950.

TAX COMPUTATION

Since income tax rates and regulations are subject to change by the federal government from year to year, the following illustrations are used to present principles rather than to be of practical use. The tax rates in the following examples represent those used in computing the 1988 federal income tax. It is important to consult the current tax regulations when computing taxes in any particular year.

Two tax computation methods are illustrated here:

(A) Using the Tax Table—illustrated in Examples 1 and 2.
(B) Using tax rate schedules (Schedules X, Y, and Z)—illustrated in Examples 3, 4 and 5.

METHOD A—USING THE TAX TABLE

This method is illustrated in the following two examples.

EXAMPLE 1 David Zachary had a salary of $48,000 in 1988. His deductions for the adjusted gross income are $650. His itemized deductions are $7,600. He is married and claims 5 personal exemptions. How much is his tax for 1988 if he files a joint return with his wife?

First, find his taxable income, $30,000, as follows (also see item 5, page 229):

Adjusted gross income = 48,000 − 650 = $47,350

Itemized deductions	= $ 7,600	
(+)Personal exemption deductions	= 9,750	(= $1,950 × 5)
Total deductions	= $17,350	

Note: The itemized deductions ($7,600) are larger than the standard deduction ($5,000).

Tax Table—Based on Taxable Income
Use if your taxable income is less than $50,000.
If $50,000 or more, use the Tax Rate Schedules.

If Taxable Income Is:		*And You Are:*			
		(1)	(2)*	(3)	(4)
At least	*But less than*	*Single*	*Married filing jointly*	*Married filing sepa-rately*	*Head of a house-hold*
		Your Tax Is:			
$0	$5	$0	$0	$0	$0
5	15	2	2	2	2
15	25	3	3	3	3
...	...				
1,000	1,025	152	152	152	152
1,025	1,050	156	156	156	156
1,050	1,075	159	159	159	159
...	...				
2,000	2,025	302	302	302	302
2,025	2,050	306	306	306	306
2,050	2,075	309	309	309	309
...	...				
10,000	10,050	1,504	1,504	1,504	1,504
10,050	10,100	1,511	1,511	1,511	1,511
10,100	10,150	1,519	1,519	1,519	1,519
10,150	10,200	1,526	1,526	1,526	1,526
...	...				
20,000	20,050	3,287	3,004	3,673	3,004
20,050	20,100	3,301	3,011	3,687	3,011
20,100	20,150	3,315	3,019	3,701	3,019
20,150	20,200	3,329	3,026	3,715	3,026
...	...				
30,000	30,050	6,087	4,540	6,473	5,300
30,050	30,100	6,101	4,554	6,487	5,314
30,100	30,150	6,115	4,568	6,501	5,328
30,150	30,200	6,129	4,582	6,515	5,342
...	...				
40,000	40,050	8,887	7,340	9,477	8,100
40,050	40,100	8,901	7,354	9,494	8,114
40,100	40,150	8,915	7,368	9,510	8,128
40,150	40,200	8,929	7,382	9,527	8,142
...	...				
49,800	49,850	11,964	10,084	12,711	10,844
49,850	49,900	11,981	10,098	12,728	10,858
49,900	49,950	11,997	10,112	12,744	10,872
49,950	50,000	12,014	10,126	12,761	10,886

$50,000 or over—use tax rate schedules

*This column must also be used by a qualifying widow(er).

Source: U.S. Internal Revenue Service, *1040 Federal Income Tax Forms and Instructions* (1988).

Taxable income = 47,350 − 17,350 = $30,000

Next, find the tax from the Tax Table based on the taxable income.

The computed taxable income, $30,000, is on the "30,000–30,050" line or the "at least $30,000 but less than $30,050" line in the Tax Table. His tax on that line and in column (2), married filing jointly, is found to be $4,540.

Note that filing a joint return usually results in a lower amount of tax than with a separate return.

EXAMPLE 2

Assume that the facts are the same as in Example 1, except that Zachary is unmarried and qualifies as head of a household. His 5 personal exemptions include himself and his 3 brothers and one sister. How much is his tax?

His taxable income is the same, $30,000.

The taxable income is on the line "30,000–30,050" and in column (4), head of a household. His tax is $5,300.

METHOD B—USING TAX RATE SCHEDULES

A taxpayer must use the tax rate schedules to figure the tax instead of using the Tax Table if the taxable income is $50,000 or more. Uses of the Tax Rate Schedules X, Y(1), Y(2), and Z are illustrated below.

EXAMPLE 3

Sharon Eastwood had an income of $72,000 in 1988. Her adjustments to income are $1,000. Her itemized deductions are $2,500. She is single and claims one personal exemption. How much is her tax?

First, find her taxable income:

Adjusted gross income = 72,000 − 1,000 = $71,000

Standard deduction	=	$ 3,000
(+)Personal exemption deduction	=	1,950
Total deductions	=	$ 4,950

Note: The standard deduction ($3,000) is larger than the itemized deductions ($2,500).

Taxable income = 71,000 − 4,950 = $66,050

Next, compute the tax from the tax rate schedules based on the taxable income.

In Schedule X for single taxpayers, the computed taxable income, $66,050, is on the line "over $43,150 but not over 89,560," and the tax rate is $9,761.50 plus 33% of the amount over $43,150.

Income tax = 9,761.50 + (66,050 − 43,150)33%
= 9,761.50 + (22,900)33%
= 9,761.50 + 7,557.00
= $17,318.50

EXAMPLE 4 Assume that the facts are the same as in Example 3 except that Eastwood is married but files a separate return (and still claims one personal exemption). How much is her tax now?

First, find her taxable income.

Taxable income = $66,050 (see Example 3 above)

Next, compute the tax from the tax rate schedules.

In Schedule Y(2) for married persons filing separate returns, the computed taxable income, $66,050, is on the line "over 35,950 but not over 113,300," and the tax rate is $8,132.25 plus 33% of the amount over $35,950.

$$\begin{aligned}\text{Income tax} &= 8{,}132.25 + (66{,}050 - 35{,}950)33\% \\ &= 8{,}132.25 + (30{,}100)33\% \\ &= 8{,}132.25 + 9{,}933 \\ &= \$18{,}065.25\end{aligned}$$

Tax Rate Schedules
Use ONLY if your taxable income is $50,000 or more. If less, use the **Tax Table**.

Schedule X—Use if your filing status is **Single**

If Taxable Income Is: *Over*	*But Not Over*	*The Tax Is:*	*Of the Amount Over*
$ 0	$17,850	......15%	$ 0
17,850	43,150	$ 2,677.50 + 28%	17,850
43,150	89,560	9,761.50 + 33%	43,150
89,560		(a) 25,076.80 + 28%	89,560
		(b) 5%	89,560
		(c) $546 × (number of exemptions)	
		TAX = (a) + [(b) or (c) whichever is smaller]	

Schedule Y-1—Use if your filing status is **Married filing jointly or Qualifying widow(er)** *

If Taxable Income Is: *Over*	*But Not Over*	*The Tax Is:*	*Of the Amount Over*
$ 0	$ 29,750	......15%	$ 0
29,750	71,900	$ 4,462.50 + 28%	29,750
71,900	149,250	16,264.50 + 33%	71,900
149,250		(a) 41,790.00 + 28%	149,250
		(b) 5%	149,250
		(c) $546 × (number of exemptions)	
		TAX = (a) + [(b) or (c) whichever is smaller]	

*Certain widows and widowers with dependent children may compute the tax as if a joint return had been filed for the first two taxable years after the taxable year in which the spouse died.

Schedule Y-2—Use if your filing status is **Married filing separately**

If Taxable Income Is: Over	But Not Over	The Tax Is:	Of the Amount Over
$ 0	$ 14,875	......15%	$ 0
14,875	35,950	$ 2,231.25 + 28%	14,875
35,950	113,300	8,132.25 + 33%	35,950
113,300		(a) 33,657.75 + 28%	113,300
		(b) 5%	113,300
		(c) $546 × (number of exemptions)	

TAX = (a) + [(b) or (c) whichever is smaller]

Schedule Z—Use if your filing status is **Head of household**

If Taxable Income Is: Over	But Not Over	The Tax Is:	Of the Amount Over
$ 0	$ 23,900	......15%	$ 0
23,900	61,650	$ 3,585 + 28%	23,900
61,650	123,790	14,155 + 33%	61,650
123,790		(a) 34,661.20 + 28%	123,790
		(b) 5%	123,790
		(c) $546 × (number of exemptions)	

TAX = (a) + [(b) or (c) whichever is smaller]

Source: U.S. Internal Revenue Service, *1040 Federal Income Tax Forms and Instructions* (1988).

EXAMPLE 5 Find the tax for a male taxpayer who is single, claims one personal exemption, and has a taxable income of $200,000.

Refer to Tax Rate Schedule X. His taxable income is on the line "over 89,560." His tax is computed as follows:

(a) 25,076.80 + (200,000 − 89,560)28%
= 25,076.80 + (110,440)28%
= 25,076.80 + 30,923,20
= $56,000

(b) (200,000 − 89,560)5%
= (110,440)5%
= $5,522

(c) 546 × 1 = $546 [smaller than $5,522 in (b)]

Tax = 56,000 + 546 = $56,546

NET TAX PAYABLE TO GOVERNMENT (OR REFUNDABLE TO THE TAXPAYER)

There are amounts prepaid by taxpayers to the government before filing tax returns. The amounts that occur most frequently are the tax withheld from the taxpayer's wages by an employer and the taxpayer's prepayment of estimated tax. If the tax indicated on the return is larger than the prepaid payment, the difference must be paid to the government with the return. On the other hand, if the tax on the return is smaller than the prepaid payment, the difference will be refunded to the taxpayer at a later date.

EXAMPLE 6

If the tax withheld from David Zachary's salary for the taxable year was $4,600, what is the net tax payable or refundable in (a) Example 1? (b) Example 2?

(a) Example 1:

Total tax in the return.......	$4,540
Less: tax withheld	4,600
Tax refundable	($ 60)

(b) Example 2:

Total tax in the return.......	$5,300
Less: tax withheld	4,600
Tax payable	$ 700

C. Corporation Taxes

As a general rule, the taxable income of a corporation is computed in much the same manner as that of an individual. However, the tax rates are different and there are a number of variations in terminology and deductions.

The taxable income is the difference between the total income and the total deductions. The total income includes gross profit from sales, dividends, interest, rent, and receipts from other income.

Since there is no provision in the tax law for an adjusted gross income in the case of a corporation, there is no division of deductions between those for adjusted gross income and other itemized deductions. Corporations are generally entitled to the same itemized business deductions as individuals. Examples of the itemized deductions are salaries and wages, rent, repairs, interest, advertising, bad debts, and net operating loss. Deductions of a purely personal nature, such as medical expenses, alimony payments, the standard deduction, and deductions for personal exemptions, are excluded. However, corporations are entitled to special deductions not available to individuals. For example, corporations are allowed a deduction equal to 80% of dividends received from taxable domestic corporations.

The 1988 tax rate for an ordinary business corporation is as follows:

If Taxable Income Is: Over	*But Not Over*	*The Tax Is:*	*Of the Amount Over*
$ 0	$50,000	15%	$ 0
50,000	75,000	$ 7,500 + 25%	50,000
75,000		13,750 + 34%	75,000

EXAMPLE 7

The following pattern is used to compute the income tax for a corporation:

Total income		$5,000,000
Less: Itemized deductions	$3,500,000	
Special deductions	40,000	
Total deductions		3,540,000
Taxable income		$1,460,000

The taxable income, \$1,460,000, is on the line "over \$75,000" in the tax rate table, and the tax rate is \$13,750 plus 34% of the amount over \$75,000.

$$\begin{aligned} \text{Income tax} &= 13{,}750 + (1{,}460{,}000 - 75{,}000)34\% \\ &= 13{,}750 + (1{,}385{,}000)34\% \\ &= 13{,}750 + 470{,}900 \\ &= \$484{,}650 \end{aligned}$$

★EXERCISE 7–12 REFERENCE: SECTION 7.10

A. Compute the tax in Problems 1–14 for each type of return as indicated in the last column. The letters in the last column represent returns as follows: (a) single, (b) joint, (c) married, filing separately, and (d) head of household. (Round to the nearest dollar figure.)

	Gross Income	*Adjustments to Income*	*Deductions– Itemized*	*Deductions– Number of Personal Exemptions*	*Type of Return*
1.	\$ 14,950	None	Not itemized	1	(a)
2.	18,900	None	Not itemized	2	(b)
3.	14,590	None	Not itemized	1	(c)
4.	18,380	None	Not itemized	2	(d)
5.	32,160	\$1,300	\$ 5,000	3	(a)
6.	32,160	1,300	5,000	3	(d)
7.	29,990	1,000	4,700	2	(b)
8.	28,520	2,000	1,500	2	(c)
9.	40,680	400	Not itemized	3	(d)
10.	37,140	2,100	Not itemized	1	(a)
11.	56,470	4,000	8,500	2	(a)
12.	66,710	3,800	7,200	3	(d)
13.	300,000	None	10,000	4	(b)
14.	500,000	None	20,000	5	(c)

B. Statement problems:

15. A married couple who file a joint return had a gross income of \$53,910 in 1988. The payment to the husband's IRA account was \$2,000. Their itemized deductions were \$6,000, and they claimed three exemptions. The tax withheld from their wages for the year was \$7,100. Find (a) the tax and (b) the net tax payable or refundable.
16. Refer to Problem 15. Suppose the couple file separate returns and the information concerning the husband's tax is as follows: gross income, \$53,900; IRA, \$2,000; itemized deductions, \$5,980; exemptions, 3. (a) What is his tax? (b) Compare the total amount of their taxes (the wife's tax is \$0) with the tax computed in Problem 15. Which amount is larger? [Note: If husband and wife (not legally separated) file separate returns and one itemizes deductions, the other must also itemize deductions].

17. Joe Hanson had a salary of $49,350 in 1988. His deductions for adjusted gross income were $420, and his itemized deductions were $5,000. He is head of a household and claims two exemptions. (a) What is the amount of his tax for the year? (b) If the tax withheld was $11,000, what is the net tax payable or refundable?
18. In Problem 17, if Hanson were a married man and claimed 2 exemptions, what would his tax be on a joint return?
19. During the year a corporation has a total income of $3,000,000, itemized deductions of $2,600,000, and special deductions of $4,500. Find the tax.
20. Corporation M has a total income of $1,000,000, itemized deductions of $470,000, and special deductions of $5,000. (a) How much is the tax? (b) If the income and the itemized deductions (excluding the special deductions) applied to married persons who claim two exemptions and file a joint return, how much would the tax be?

8 SIMPLE INTEREST AND SIMPLE DISCOUNT

In this chapter, first, the basic concepts and operations of simple interest (Sections 8.1 and 8.2) and simple discount (Section 8.3) are introduced. These topics are essential for understanding the material to be presented in the following chapters, such as bank discount, compound interest, annuities, and life insurance premiums. Next, the general applications of the simple interest and simple discount methods for debt payments are illustrated (Sections 8.4 to 8.6).

8.1 SIMPLE INTEREST

A. Computation

A person who borrows money usually pays *interest* as a fee for the use of the money. The money borrowed is called the *principal*. The sum of the principal and the interest due is called the *amount*. The *rate of interest* is usually expressed as a percent of the principal for a specified period of time, which is generally one year. Interest paid only on the principal borrowed is called *simple interest*. When the interest for each period is added to the principal in computing the interest for the next period, it is called *compound interest*. Simple interest is usually charged for short-term borrowing, whereas compound interest is commonly employed in long-term obligations. In this chapter, only simple interest is discussed. Compound interest problems are discussed in Part 3.

The basic formula for computing simple interest is:

$$\text{Interest} = \text{Principal} \times \begin{pmatrix}\text{Interest rate} \\ \text{per period}\end{pmatrix} \times \begin{pmatrix}\text{Number of interest} \\ \text{periods (or Time)}\end{pmatrix}$$

The formula may be written simply:

$$I = Pin \qquad \textbf{(8–1)}$$

The values of rate and time must correspond to each other. If the rate is an annual rate, the time must be expressed in years; whereas, if the rate is a quarterly rate, the time must be stated in quarters. Hereafter, unless otherwise specified, the annual interest rate will be used in computing simple interest problems. When the unit of time is one year, the formula is explained as follows:

$I = Pin,$ where I = interest
P = principal
i = interest rate per year
n = number of *years*, or a fraction of *one year*

EXAMPLE 1

What is the simple interest on \$200 at 12% (a) for three years and (b) for two months?

(a) $P = 200$, $i = 12\%$ (per year), $n = 3$ (years)
Substituting these values in formula (8–1),

$$I = Pin = 200 \times 12\% \times 3 = \$72$$

(b) $n = \frac{2}{12}$, since 2 months $= \frac{2}{12}$ years

$$I = Pin = 200 \times 12\% \times \frac{2}{12} = \$4$$

B. Determining the Number of Days

Since time may be expressed in days, the number of days in a year must be determined before computing the interest. There are two methods used in determining the number of days in a year—the *exact method* and the *approximate method*. Under the exact method, as shown in Table 1 of the Appendix, each year has 365 days except leap years, which have 366 days. When the approximate method is used, it is assumed that each of the 12 months in a year has 30 days, and thus there are 360 days in a year. In finding the number of days between two given dates, count either the beginning date or the ending date, but not both. In this text, the practice of counting the ending date will be followed.

EXAMPLE 2

Find (a) the exact time and (b) the approximate time from June 24, 1990, to September 27, 1990.

(a) The exact time:

June	6 days	(remainder, or 30 − 24 = 6)
July	31 days	
Aug	31 days	
Sept	27 days	
	95 days	

Or, according to Table 1, which shows the exact number of days, June 24 is the 175th day of the year and September 27 is the 270th day. 270 − 175 = 95 days.

(b) The approximate time:

First, write the two given dates in the following form, arranging the months to the left of the days, and then subtract:

Month	*Day*
9 (Sept.)	27
6 (June)	24
3 months	3 days

Since there are 30 days in each month by the approximate method, the number of days between the two given dates is $3 \times 30 + 3 = 93$ days.

EXAMPLE 3 Find (a) the exact time and (b) the approximate time from November 14, 1992 to April 24, 1993.

(a) The exact time:

1992	November	16 days	(remainder, or $30 - 14 = 16$)
	December	31 days	
1993	January	31 days	
	February	28 days	
	March	31 days	
	April	24 days	
	Total	161 days	

Or, according to Table 1 in the Appendix, which shows the exact number of days, November 14 is the 319th day of year 1992. The number of days remaining in 1992 is $366 - 319 = 47$ days. April 24 is the 114th day of the year 1993. Thus, the total number of days between the two given dates is $47 + 114 = 161$ days. (1992 is a leap year.)

(b) The approximate time:

Arrange the two given dates in the following form by the order of year, month, and day, and then subtract:

	Year	*Month*	*Day*
Ending date	199~~3~~^{2}	~~4~~^{16}	24
Beginning date	1992	11	14
	0	5	10

In the month column, since 11 months is larger than 4 months, borrow 1 year or 12 months from the year column to make a total of 16 months before subtracting.

The approximate time $= 5 \times 30 + 10 = 160$ days

Leap years are those years evenly divisible by 4, such as 1988, 1992, and 1996, in which the month of February has 29 days instead of 28 days as in other years. But the last year of any century, although it is divisible by 4, is not a leap year unless it is divisible by 400. Thus, 1700, 1800, and 1900 were not leap years, but 2000 will be a leap year.

EXAMPLE 4 Find the exact time from January 22, 1992, to March 12, 1992.

January	9 days	(remainder, or $31 - 22 = 9$)
February	29 days	(leap year)
March	12 days	
	50 days	

EXERCISE 8–1 REFERENCE: SECTION 8.1 A and B

A. Find the simple interest in each of the following problems:

	Principal	*Interest Rate*	*Time*
1.	$458.50	18%	4 months
2.	682.40	21%	5 months
3.	274.10	8%	1 year
4.	395.00	6%	$\frac{1}{2}$ year
5.	126.60	9%	6 months
6.	235.20	10%	3 months
7.	35.00	12%	18 months
8.	78.00	18%	15 months
9.	268.80	15%	1 year, 5 months
10.	346.40	14%	1 year, 7 months

B. Determine the number of days in each of the following problems by (a) the exact time method and (b) the approximate time method:

11. September 19, 1990, to October 28, 1990.
12. June 16, 1990, to August 15, 1990.
13. July 5, 1991, to December 12, 1991.
14. August 13, 1991, to November 20, 1991.
15. April 30, 1992, to July 6, 1992.
16. May 16, 1992, to September 7, 1992.
17. January 6, 1992, to January 30, 1993.
18. February 17, 1992, to March 10, 1993.
19. December 16, 1993, to April 9, 1994.
20. October 10, 1993, to May 7, 1994.

C. Ordinary and Exact Interest

The exact and approximate methods of determining the number of days provide four possible ways to express a number of days as a fraction of a year:

1. $\frac{\text{Exact time}}{360}$ (Banker's Rule)
2. $\frac{\text{Approximate time}}{360}$

} for computing ordinary interest;

3. $\frac{\text{Exact time}}{365}$
4. $\frac{\text{Approximate time}}{365}$

} for computing exact interest.

The value of interest computed by using 360 as the divisor in the time factor is called *ordinary interest*. The first time fraction, which is used in the *Banker's Rule*, is much more commonly used in commercial practice than the second time fraction. Unless otherwise specified, hereafter the Banker's Rule will be used in this text in computing ordinary interest. Also, the unqualified term "simple interest" will mean "ordinary interest" when a number of days is given in a problem.

When 365 is used as the divisor, the result is called *exact interest*. The third time fraction is usually used in calculating interest payments on government obligations, in foreign trade, and in rediscounting notes for member banks by the Federal Reserve Banks. The fourth time fraction is seldom used. Hereafter, only the third time fraction will be used in illustrations and problems in this text for computing exact interest.

EXAMPLE 5 Express the time from June 24, 1990, to September 27, 1990, in years for computing (a) ordinary interest and (b) exact interest.

The exact time between the two dates is 95 days (see Example 2 on page 240). Thus,

(a) $\frac{95}{360}$ (b) $\frac{95}{365}$

CALCULATING ORDINARY INTEREST

Ordinary interest may be calculated by formula or by the 6% for 60 days method.

By Formula. When the number of days is given, the days should be expressed as a fraction of a year. Let t denote the *time* in exact number of days. In computing ordinary simple interest (I) by the Banker's Rule, formula (8–1) becomes

$$I = Pi\left(\frac{t}{360}\right) = \frac{Pit}{360} \tag{8–2}$$

EXAMPLE 6 Find the ordinary interest on $500 at 18% for 30 days.

$P = 500$, $i = 18\%$, $t = 30$ (days). Substituting these values in formula (8–2),

$$I = 500 \times 18\% \times \frac{30}{360} = \$7.50$$

EXAMPLE 7 Find the ordinary interest on $1 at 6% ($= \frac{6}{100}$) for 60 days.

$$I = 1 \times \frac{6}{100} \times \frac{60}{360} = \frac{1}{100} = \$0.01$$

By 6% for 60 Days Method. Example 7 indicates that the ordinary interest on $1 at 6% for 60 days is $.01. A shortcut method of computing ordinary simple interest can thus be derived: *The interest on any amount at 6% for 60 days is determined by moving the decimal point in the principal two places to the left.*

EXAMPLE 8 Find the ordinary interest on $139.20 at 6% for 60 days.

The ordinary interest is $1.39.20 or $1.3920, rounded to $1.39.

When the above idea is extended, the ordinary interest on a principal at any rate and for any number of days may be found by the shortcut method. The following examples are used to illustrate how ordinary interest is computed for a certain period other than 60 days or at a rate other than 6%.

EXAMPLE 9 Find the ordinary interest on $1,392 at 6% for 70 days.

Interest at 6% for 60 days	$13.92	
(+) Interest at 6% for 10 days	2.32	(= 13.92 × $\frac{1}{6}$, since 10 days is $\frac{1}{6}$ of 60 days)
Interest at 6% for 70 days	$16.24	

EXAMPLE 10 Find the ordinary interest on $1,392 at 9% for 70 days.

Interest at 6% for 70 days	$16.24	(see Example 9)
(+) Interest at 3% for 70 days	8.12	$(= 16.24 \times \frac{1}{2}$, since $3\% = \frac{1}{2}$ of $6\%)$
Interest at 9% for 70 days	$24.36	

CHECK $1{,}392 \times 9\% \times \frac{70}{360} = \$24.36$

EXAMPLE 11 Find the ordinary interest on $324 at 5% for 40 days.

Interest at 6% for 60 days	$3.24	
(−) Interest at 1% for 60 days	.54	$(= 3.24 \times \frac{1}{6}$, since 1% is $\frac{1}{6}$ of $6\%)$
Interest at 5% for 60 days	$2.70	
(−) Interest at 5% for 20 days	.90	$(= 2.70 \times \frac{1}{3}$, since 20 days is $\frac{1}{3}$ of 60 days)
Interest at 5% for 40 days	$1.80	

CHECK $324 \times 5\% \times \dfrac{40}{360} = \$1.80$

Note that the 6% for 60 days method may also be used in computing the simple interest when the time is given in a number of months. The interest on $1 at 6% for two months is also $.01, since $I = 1 \times 6\% \times \frac{2}{12} = \$.01$.

CALCULATING EXACT INTEREST

Let I_e denote the exact simple interest. When the number of days is given, formula (8–1) is written in the following manner:

$$I_e = Pi\left(\frac{t}{365}\right) = \frac{Pit}{365} \tag{8–3}$$

EXAMPLE 12 Find the exact interest on $500 at 18% for 30 days.

$500 \times \dfrac{18}{100} \times \dfrac{30}{365} = 7.397$, or $7.40

★THE RELATIONSHIP BETWEEN I AND I_e

Use of the ordinary interest method always gives a larger interest value than does the exact interest method. When the answer in Example 6 is compared with the answer in Example 12, the ordinary interest is found to be larger than the exact interest by $0.10 (or $7.50 − $7.40). The relationship between I and I_e is expressed as follows:

$\dfrac{I}{I_e} = \dfrac{73}{72}$, which means that "the ratio of I to I_e is $\dfrac{73}{72}$."[1] Or

$\dfrac{I_e}{I} = \dfrac{72}{73}$

---

[1]*Proof:*

$$\frac{I}{I_e} = \frac{\dfrac{Pit}{360}}{\dfrac{Pit}{365}} = \frac{Pit}{360} \times \frac{365}{Pit} = \frac{365}{360} = \frac{73}{72}$$

Using the method described above, the ordinary interest for Example 6 may be computed from the exact interest as follows:

Since $I_e = 7.397$ (Example 12)

$$\frac{I}{7.397} = \frac{73}{72}$$

$$I = 7.397\left(\frac{73}{72}\right) = \$7.50$$

Or, written in a more detailed way,

$$I = 7.397\left(1 + \frac{1}{72}\right)$$

$$= 7.397 + 7.397\left(\frac{1}{72}\right) = 7.397 + 0.103 = \$7.50$$

Thus, I is $\frac{1}{72}$ more than I_e, or $I = I_e + I_e\left(\frac{1}{72}\right)$.

The exact interest for Example 12 may be computed from the ordinary interest as shown below:

Since $I = 7.50$ (Example 6)

$$\frac{I_e}{7.50} = \frac{72}{73}$$

$$I_e = 7.50\left(\frac{72}{73}\right) = 7.40$$

Or, written in a more detailed way,

$$I_e = 7.50\left(1 - \frac{1}{73}\right)$$

$$= 7.50 - 7.50\left(\frac{1}{73}\right) = 7.50 - 0.103 = \$7.397, \quad \text{or} \quad \$7.40$$

Thus, I_e is $\frac{1}{73}$ less than I, or $I_e = I - I\left(\frac{1}{73}\right)$.

EXERCISE 8–2 REFERENCE: SECTION 8.1C

A. Express the time in years in each of the following problems for computing (a) ordinary interest, and (b) exact interest.

1. June 6 to September 30.
2. July 10 to November 7.
3. May 21 to July 5.
4. April 15 to June 22.
5. January 4 to February 3.
6. August 17 to December 8.

B. In each of the following cases, find (a) the ordinary interest by the formula method, and (b) the exact interest:

	Principal	*Interest Rate*	*Time*
7.	$ 450	18%	90 days
8.	680	10%	60 days
9.	42,200	15%	30 days
10.	14,400	12%	70 days

	Principal	*Interest Rate*	*Time*
11.	2,192	9%	45 days
12.	2,970	8%	80 days

C. In each of the following cases, find the ordinary interest by the 6% for 60 days method:

	Principal	*Interest Rate*	*Time*
13.	$ 365	7%	120 days
14.	216	6%	36 days
15.	2,880	$5\frac{1}{2}$%	40 days
16.	360	$4\frac{1}{2}$%	66 days

★**D.** For each of the following exact interests (I_e), find the ordinary interest (I):

17. $28.80
18. $43.20
19. $5.04
20. $1.44
21. $6.48
22. $4.32

★**E.** For each of the following ordinary interests (I), find the exact interest (I_e):

23. $36.50
24. $58.40
25. $2.92
26. $2.19
27. $3.65
28. $5.84

8.2 AMOUNT, RATE, AND TIME

A. Finding the Amount

The *amount* is the sum of the principal and the interest, or

Amount = Principal + Interest

Let S denote the amount (or the sum). The formula below is based on this definition:

$S = P + I$, or
$S = P + Pin$, or, factoring P,

$$\mathbf{S = P(1 + in)} \tag{8–4}$$

EXAMPLE 1

(a) What is the simple interest on $700 for 125 days at 10%?
(b) What is the amount? (Use the Banker's Rule.)

(a) Since the number of days is given in the problem, the simple interest is computed by formula (8–2) as follows:

$$I = Pi\left(\frac{t}{360}\right) = 700 \times 10\% \times \frac{125}{360} = \$24.31$$

(b) Substituting the interest and the principal in formula (8–4),

$$\begin{aligned} S &= P + I \\ &= 700 + 24.31 = \$724.31 \end{aligned}$$

EXAMPLE 2

A man borrows $500 for four months at 9%. How much must he repay?

Since the number of months is given in the problem, the simple interest is computed by expressing four months as $\frac{4}{12}$ or $\frac{1}{3}$ of a year and by substituting the given values in formula (8–4) as follows:

$I = 500 \times 9\% \times \frac{1}{3} = 15$

$S = P + I = 500 + 15 = \$515$, or

$S = P(1 + in) = 500(1 + 9\% \times \frac{1}{3}) = 500(1.03) = \$515$

EXAMPLE 3

On May 24, 1991, Joan Harrison borrowed $650 and agreed to repay the loan together with interest at 12% in 90 days. What amount must she repay? On what date?

$I = 650 \times 12\% \times \frac{90}{360} = \$19.50$

$S = 650 + 19.50 = \$669.50$

May. . . . . 7 days (31 − 24 = 7)
June. . . . . .30 days
July . . . . .31 days
68 days

August . . . . .22 days
90 days

The amount, $669.50, must be repaid on August 22, 1991.

B. Finding the Rate

An *interest rate* (*i*) is obtained by dividing the interest by the product of the principal and the time. This is based on formula (8–1). When both sides of the formula $I = Pin$ are divided by Pn, the following result is obtained:

$$i = \frac{I}{Pn} = \frac{\text{Interest}}{\text{Principal} \times \text{Time}}$$

Note that the interest rate and the time must correspond to each other. In other words, when the given time is expressed in months, the interest rate found is expressed in a monthly rate; when the time is expressed in years, the rate found is a yearly rate. In computing simple interest, the time should be expressed in years, since the rate is usually expressed in a yearly rate in such a problem.

EXAMPLE 4

At what interest rate will $450 yield $236.25 in five years?

Substituting $P = 450$, $I = 236.25$, and $n = 5$ (years) in the formula $I = Pin$,

$236.25 = 450(i)(5)$

Solving for i,

$$i = \frac{236.25}{(450)(5)} = \frac{236.25}{2{,}250} = .105 \text{ or } 10\tfrac{1}{2}\% \quad \text{(yearly)}$$

EXAMPLE 5

A payment of $1,567.50 was made for discharging a four-month loan of $1,500. What was the interest rate charged?

When the principal and the amount are given, the interest should be found first. This is done by using formula (8–4): $I = S - P$, since $S = P + I$. Substituting the values $S = 1{,}567.50$ and $P = 1{,}500$ in the formula:

$I = 1{,}567.50 - 1{,}500.00 = \$67.50$

Substituting $I = 67.50$, $n = \frac{4}{12} = \frac{1}{3}$ (year), and $P = 1{,}500$,

$$i = \frac{I}{Pn} = \frac{67.50}{1{,}500(\frac{1}{3})} = \frac{67.50}{500} = .135, \quad \text{or} \quad 13.5\%$$

EXAMPLE 6 A man who borrowed \$1,350 paid \$1,363.50 as the total amount at the end of 30 days. What was the interest rate he paid?

$I = 1{,}363.50 - 1{,}350 = \$13.50$

$$i = \frac{13.50}{1{,}350(\frac{30}{360})} = \frac{13.50}{1{,}350(\frac{1}{12})} = \frac{1}{100(\frac{1}{12})} = \frac{12}{100}, \quad \text{or} \quad 12\%$$

C. Finding the Time

The *time* (n) of a loan is obtained by dividing the interest by the product of the principal and the interest rate. This is also based on formula (8–1). When both sides of the formula $I = Pin$ are divided by Pi, the following result is obtained:

$$n = \frac{I}{Pi} = \frac{\text{Interest}}{\text{Principal} \times \text{Rate}}$$

EXAMPLE 7 How long will it take \$1,000 to yield \$100 interest at 8%?

Substituting $I = 100$, $P = 1{,}000$, and $i = 8\%$ in the formula $I = Pin$,

$100 = 1{,}000(8\%)(n)$

Solving for n,

$$n = \frac{100}{1{,}000 \times .08} = \frac{100}{80} = 1.25 \quad \text{(years)}$$

The answer may be converted to months as $1.25 \times 12 = 15$ (months). It may also be converted to days, if it is an exact time, as $1.25 \times 365 = 456.25$ days; or if it is an approximate time, as $1.25 \times 360 = 450$ days.

EXERCISE 8–3 REFERENCE: SECTION 8.2

A. In each of the following cases, find the unknown values:

	Principal	*Annual Interest Rate*	*Time*	*Interest*	*Amount*
1.	\$2,800	12%	30 days	?	?
2.	5,000	?	45 days	?	\$5,025.00
3.	4,500	6%	? days	\$ 56.25	?
4.	3,600	?	120 days	96.00	?
5.	720	8%	? months	?	739.20
6.	640	?	6 months	16.00	?
7.	570	?	4 months	?	589.00
8.	1,500	15%	? months	150.00	?
9.	2,000	18%	? years	720.00	?
10.	2,250	?	$2\frac{1}{2}$ years	?	2,587.50

	Principal	Annual Interest Rate	Time	Interest	Amount
11.	3,460	?	3 years	519.00	?
12.	5,800	21%	? years	?	7,627.00

B. Statement problems:

13. (a) Find the simple interest on $5,400 at 7% for 45 days. (b) What is the amount?
14. (a) Find the simple interest on $425 at 5% for two years. (b) What is the amount?
15. A man borrowed $1,000 at 10% for five months. How much must he repay?
16. A man borrowed $500 at 12% for 66 days. How much must he repay?
17. If $540 is borrowed for three years at 8%, what is the amount due at the end of the third year?
18. If $820 is borrowed for eight months at 9%, what is the amount due at the end of the period?
19. On July 10, 1991, Jim Tedd borrowed $950 and agreed to repay it with interest at 15% in 120 days. (a) What amount must he repay and (b) on what date?
20. On May 21, 1992, Jane Herbert borrowed $1,200 at 9% interest for 45 days. (a) What amount must she repay and (b) when?
21. At what interest rate will $260 yield $3.90 interest in 60 days?
22. At what interest rate will $450 yield $9.00 interest in (a) three months? (b) one year?
23. A man borrowed $1,350 and paid $1,372.50 after four months. What was the interest rate charged for the debt?
24. A note for $2,400 was repaid after 120 days in the amount of $2,432. What was the interest rate on the note?
25. The Taylor Hardware Store received an invoice for the purchase of handsaws costing $500. The terms were 2/10, *n*/30. If the store were to borrow money to pay the bill in 10 days and repay the loan in 30 days from the date of invoice, what is the highest interest rate at which the store could afford to borrow?
26. The Moore Drug Store received an invoice of $250, terms 3/10, 1/20, *n*/30. If the store borrows money in 10 days to pay the bill and repays the loan in 20 days from the date of invoice, what is the highest interest rate at which the store can afford to borrow?
27. How many months are required for $260 to yield $3.90 interest at 6%?
28. How many years will be required for $55 to yield $11 interest at 10%?
29. How many days are necessary for $240 to yield $1.60 interest at 8%?
30. How many days are needed for $380 to (a) amount to $389.50 at 5%? (b) yield $1.90 interest at 3%?
31. A woman has part of her money invested at 10% and the remainder at 12%. Her annual income from the investment is $480.00. If she had received 1% less interest on both of her two investments, her income would have been $438.00 annually. How much did she invest at each interest rate?
32. A woman borrows $2,000 and agrees to pay $500 on the principal plus the simple interest at 10% on the principal outstanding at the end of each six-month period. Find the total amount that must be paid to discharge the debt.

8.3 PRINCIPAL, PRESENT VALUE, AND SIMPLE DISCOUNT

A. Finding the Principal

The principal may be obtained in the following two ways:

First Way. By the formula $I = Pin$:

When both sides of the formula $I = Pin$ are divided by in, the following result is obtained:

$$P = \frac{I}{in}$$

EXAMPLE 1

A woman receives \$300 interest in three months from an investment that pays 12% interest. What is the principal that she has invested?

Substituting $I = 300$, $i = 12\%$, $n = \frac{3}{12} = \frac{1}{4}$ (year), in $I = Pin$:

$300 = P(12\%)(\frac{1}{4})$

Solving for P,

$$P = \frac{300}{(12\% \times 1/4)} = \frac{300}{(\frac{12}{100} \times \frac{1}{4})} = 300 \times \frac{100}{3} = \$10{,}000$$

Second Way. By the formula $S = P + I = P + Pin = P(1 + in)$:

EXAMPLE 2

A man paid a debt with a \$280 check, which included \$30 interest. Find the principal.

Substituting $S = 280$ and $I = 30$ in the formula $P = S - I$, since $S = P + I$,

$P = 280 - 30 = \$250$

When both sides of the formula $S = P(1 + in)$ are divided by $(1 + in)$, the following result is obtained:

$$P = \frac{S}{1 + in} = \frac{S}{\text{Amount of 1}}$$

The numerator, S, is the total amount, while the denominator is the amount of 1 unit; that is, when the principal is \$1 and is invested at i for n periods, the amount is $\$(1 + in)$.

EXAMPLE 3

How much money must Jones invest today at 12% simple interest if he is to receive \$1,416, the amount, in $1\frac{1}{2}$ years?

Substituting $S = 1{,}416$, $i = 12\%$, and $n = 1.5$ (years) in the formula $S = P(1 + in)$,

$1{,}416 = P[1 + 12\%(1.5)]$

Solving for P,

$$P = \frac{1{,}416}{1 + 12\%(1.5)} = \frac{1{,}416}{1.18} = \$1{,}200$$

In the above example, 1.18 is the amount of a principal of 1 (dollar) plus its interest at 12% for $1\frac{1}{2}$ years.

B. Present Value

Present value is the value at the time of investment, such as the principal, or at any time before the maturity date (due date). Example 3 indicates that if Jones invests \$1,200 today at 12% simple interest, he will have \$1,416 in $1\frac{1}{2}$ years. In other words, the present value of \$1,416 that is due in $1\frac{1}{2}$ years and includes 12% interest is \$1,200. Thus, the method of finding the present value of a given amount that is due in the future is the same as the method used in Example 3 for finding the principal.

C. Simple Discount

The process of finding the present value of a given amount that is due on a future date and includes a simple interest is called *discounting at simple interest*, or commonly, the *simple discount method*. In other words, to discount an amount by the simple interest process is to find its present value.

When interest is involved, the amount must be larger than its present value. The difference between the amount and its present value is called the *simple discount*. Thus, the simple discount on the amount is the same as the simple interest on the principal or the present value. There are numerous occasions in business when it becomes necessary to discount an amount that is due on a future date. The principle of simple discount is important to compound discount problems dealing with long-term investments (Part 3), although the bank discount method (Section 9.1) is used widely in discounting short-term loans.

DISCOUNTING A NON-INTEREST-BEARING DEBT

The following examples are given to illustrate the discounting of a non-interest-bearing debt.

EXAMPLE 4

What is the present value of \$3,248 that is due at the end of two months if the interest rate is 9%? What is the simple discount?

Here, the amount at maturity (due in two months) is \$3,248, which bears no interest, as stated in the problem. The 9% interest rate is used for discounting the maturity amount. Thus,

$S = 3{,}248$, $i = 9\%$, and $n = \frac{2}{12}$ or $\frac{1}{6}$ (year), the discount period.

Substituting the values in $S = P(1 + in)$, or $P = \dfrac{S}{1 + in}$,

$$P = \frac{3{,}248}{1 + (\frac{9}{100})(\frac{1}{6})} = \frac{3{,}248}{1 + .015} = \$3{,}200 \quad \text{(Present value)}$$

$$I = 3{,}248 - 3{,}200 = \$48 \quad \text{(Simple discount)}$$

CHECK

According to the answer, the amount due at the end of two months should be

$$S = P(1 + in) = 3{,}200[1 + (.09)(\tfrac{1}{6})] = 3{,}200(1.015) = \$3{,}248$$

NOTE:

The simple discount on the amount, \$3,248, is the same as the simple interest on the present value, \$3,200. In other words, I has a twofold meaning: It is the simple interest on the principal or the present value; it is also the simple discount on the amount.

EXAMPLE 5

Discount \$3,248 for two months at the simple interest rate 9%. What is the present value and the simple discount?

The answer in this example is the same as that in Example 4, since the two examples have the same meaning.

EXAMPLE 6

A debt of \$875.50 is due in six months. If the debt is settled now and the simple interest rate of 6% is allowed, what is the present value and the simple discount?

Substituting $S = 875.50$, $n = \frac{6}{12} = \frac{1}{2}$, and $i = 6\%$ in

$P = \dfrac{S}{1 + in}$, the present value is

$$P = \frac{875.50}{1 + 6\%(\frac{1}{2})} = \frac{875.50}{1.03} = \$850$$

The simple discount is

$$I = S - P = 875.50 - 850.00 = \$25.50$$

CHECK $850 \times 6\% \times \frac{1}{2} = \$25.50$

DISCOUNTING AN INTEREST-BEARING DEBT

To find the present value of an interest-bearing debt (or to discount the amount by the simple discount method), take the following steps:

STEP (1). Find the maturity value (the amount) according to the original interest rate and the time stipulated for the debt. Use the formula $S = P(1 + in)$, where S is the maturity value and P is the original debt.

STEP (2). Find the present value (the value on the date of discount) of the maturity value according to the interest rate for discounting and the discount period. The discount period is the period from the date of discount to the maturity date. Use the formula in the form $P = \dfrac{S}{1 + in}$, where P is the present value and S is the maturity value. However, the values of i and n in this step are often different from the values of i and n in Step (1).

EXAMPLE 7

A man borrowed \$1,000 on May 1, 1991, and agreed to repay the money plus 8% interest in six months. Two months after the money was borrowed, the creditor agreed to settle the debt by discounting it at the simple interest rate of 9%. How much did the creditor receive when he discounted the debt?

STEP (1). Find the maturity value of the debt according to the original stipulation of the debt. $P = 1{,}000$, $i = 8\%$, $n = \frac{6}{12} = \frac{1}{2}$ (year).

Substituting these values in the formula,

$$S = P(1 + in) = 1{,}000(1 + 8\% \times \tfrac{1}{2})$$
$$= 1{,}000(1.04) = \$1{,}040 \quad \text{(amount on November 1, 1991)}$$

STEP (2). Find the present value of the maturity value according to the discounting terms. $S = 1{,}040$, $i = 9\%$, $n = \frac{4}{12} = \frac{1}{3}$ (year), or $6 - 2 = 4$ (months).

Substituting these values in the formula,

$$P = \frac{S}{1 + in} = \frac{1{,}040}{1 + 9\%(\frac{1}{3})} = \frac{1{,}040}{1.030} = \$1{,}009.71 \quad \text{(value on July 1, 1991)}$$

The example may be diagrammed as follows:

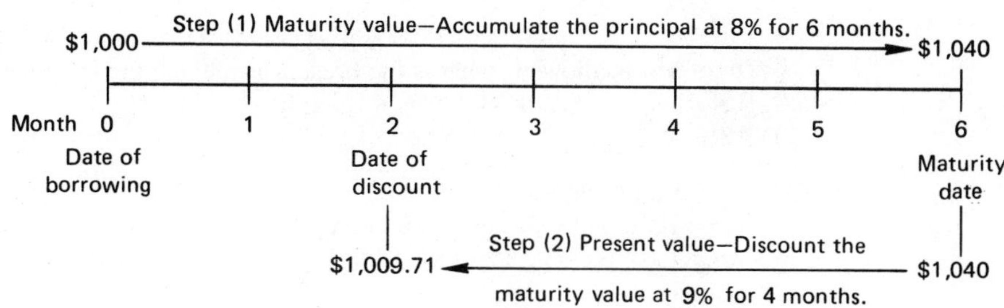

EXAMPLE 8 In Example 7, assume that the simple interest rate for discounting is also 8%. How much would the creditor receive when discounting the debt?

STEP (1). The maturity value is the same, $1,040.
STEP (2). The present value of the maturity value is found as follows:

$S = 1{,}040, \quad i = 8\%, \quad n = \frac{1}{3}$ (year)

$$P = \frac{S}{1 + in} = \frac{1{,}040}{1 + 8\%(\frac{1}{3})} = \frac{1{,}040}{\frac{308}{300}} = \$1{,}012.99$$

NOTE:

1. The fraction $\frac{308}{300}$ in Example 8 is not changed to a decimal in computing the final answer, since it is a repetend, $\frac{308}{300} = 1.02666\ldots = 1.02\dot{6}$. If the repetend is rounded to a decimal in the computation, the final answer might be different from the answer obtained above, such as

   $$\frac{1{,}040}{1.0267} = 1{,}012.95, \quad \text{but} \quad \frac{1{,}040 \times 300}{308} = 1{,}012.99$$

2. Even when the interest rate for computing the maturity value is the same as the interest rate for discounting, the two steps are still required. Refer to Example 8. The sum of the principal and the interest for two months (the period between the date of borrowing and the date of discounting) at a rate of 8% is

   $S = P + Pin = 1{,}000 + (1{,}000 \times 8\% \times \frac{2}{12}) = \$1{,}013.33$

   The sum is not the same as the present value $1,012.99 obtained by the method used in Example 8.

EXERCISE 8–4 REFERENCE: SECTION 8.3

A. In each of the following cases, find the principal:

	Interest Rate	*Time*	*Interest*	*Amount*
1.	...	...	$156.00	$ 676.00
2.	16%	2 years	240.00	...

3. 21%	6 months	. . .	6,077.50
4. 12%	4 months	400.00	. . .
5. 8%	$2\frac{1}{2}$ years	. . .	270.00
6. 9%	120 days	. . .	499.55
7. 5%	90 days	42.50	. . .
8. . . .	. . .	24.38	487.00
9. 15%	60 days	75.00	. . .
10. 18%	90 days	. . .	4,180.00

B. Statement problems:

11. What principal will yield $25 interest in two months at 10%?
12. What principal will yield (a) $67.20 in three years at 8%, and (b) $14 in 180 days at 5%?
13. What principal will accumulate to $644.00 in two years at 20% simple interest?
14. What principal will amount to $974.40 in eight months at 24% simple interest?
15. How much money must J. D. Gooch invest at 16% interest for two years in order to receive $4,620 at the end of the second year?
16. B. C. Dodge will receive $543.60 on June 30. How much can he borrow at 9% on May 1, if he uses his receipts to repay the loan?
17. (a) What is the present value of $1,000 due in two years if the money is worth 7%? (b) How much is the simple discount?
18. (a) What is the present value of $640 due at the end of four months if the money is worth 8%? (b) What is the simple discount?
19. A debt of $1,800 is due in $1\frac{1}{2}$ years. If the debt is settled now and the simple interest rate of 8% is allowed, what are: (a) the present value and (b) the simple discount?
20. A debt of $2,500 is due eight months from now. (a) What is the present value of the debt if 9% simple interest is allowed? (b) What is the simple discount on the debt if it is settled now?
21. Mrs. J. A. Outen purchased a refrigerator and made a down payment of $300. She agreed to pay $100 after one month and $150 after two months. If the rate of interest is 18%, what is the cash price of the refrigerator?
22. Ms. W. R. Wages plans to purchase a television set. She is offered the option of paying $400 down and $400 in five months, or of paying $500 down and $300 in four months. If the rate of interest is 21%, which option would be a better offer for her?
23. Mr. Green borrowed $500 on June 1 of this year and agreed to repay the principal plus 9% interest in four months. He wishes to pay the loan on July 1 by discounting it at the simple interest rate of 8%. How much should he pay according to the discount?
24. Refer to Problem 23. If the debt is discounted at the simple interest rate of 10%, how much should he pay?
25. On May 1, J. D. Taylor borrowed $1,000 from J. C. Bennett and agreed to pay the debt plus 6% simple interest in 90 days. If the debt is settled on May 31 at 8% simple interest, how much did J. C. Bennett receive?
26. In Problem 25, if the debt is settled at an interest rate of 12%, how much did J. C. Bennett receive?

8.4 PARTIAL PAYMENTS

If partial payments are made on a debt before it is due, there should be an agreement between the creditor and the borrower regarding the interest on each partial payment. Some creditors may agree to reduce the interest when partial payments on the debt are made. In general, the two methods used by a creditor in reducing the interest are the Merchants' Rule and the United States Rule. The Merchants' Rule is simpler and is preferred by most business people, whereas use of the United States Rule results from a decision made by the United States Supreme Court.

A. Merchants' Rule

Under the *Merchants' Rule*, the principal and all partial payments are treated as if they earn interest from the time they are made to the date of final settlement. The following steps may be employed:

STEP (1). Find the sum of the principal and its interest for the period from the date of borrowing to the date of final settlement.
STEP (2). Find the sum of the partial payments and the interest on each partial payment from the date of payment to the date of final settlement. This sum is the debtor's credit against the sum in Step (1).
STEP (3). Subtract the result in Step (2) from the result in Step (1). The difference is the balance to be discharged on the date of final settlement.

EXAMPLE 1 On July 1, a man borrowed $2,000 at 6%. He paid $500 on August 30 and $600 on September 29. Find the balance on October 29 of the same year, by the Merchants' Rule.

The Merchants' Rule:

Original debt (7/1)			$2,000
Add: interest on $2,000 for 120 days (7/1–10/29)			40
Amount on 10/29			$2,040
Deduct: partial payments and their interest			
First payment (8/30)	$500		
Add: interest on $500 for 60 days (8/30–10/29)	5	$505	
Second payment (9/29)	$600		
Add: interest on $600 for 30 days (9/29–10/29)	3	$603	
Total partial payments and their interest			$1,108
Balance on 10/29			$ 932

This method is diagrammed as follows:

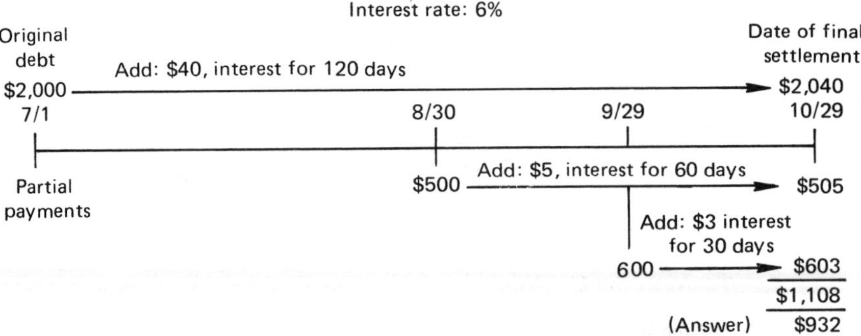

B. United States Rule

Under the *United States Rule*, each partial payment must first be applied to the accumulated interest up to the date of the payment. Any remainder is then credited as a deduction from the principal. Therefore, when the United States Rule is applied, the successive interest is computed from a declining balance each time a payment is made. A debtor may thus know the actual amount of unpaid balance immediately after each payment. The following steps may be employed:

STEP (1). Find the interest on the principal for the period from the date of borrowing to the date of the first partial payment.
STEP (2). Subtract the interest from the first payment. If there is a remainder, subtract the remainder from the principal to obtain the unpaid balance. If the partial payment is not sufficient to cover the interest due, the partial payment is then held and is included in the next payment.
STEP (3). If there are further partial payments, the processes in Steps (1) and (2) are repeated, but the interest is computed on the declining unpaid balance. Each payment must be first applied to the interest that has accumulated up to the date of each payment. The final balance is the sum of the unpaid principal and the accumulated interest up to the date of the final settlement.

EXAMPLE 2 Refer to Example 1. Find the balance on October 29 by the United States Rule.

The United States Rule:

Original debt (7/1)		$2,000.00
Deduct:		
First payment (8/30)	$500.00	
Deduct: interest on $2,000 for 60 days (7/1–8/30)	20.00	
Remainder applied to principal		480.00
Balance on 8/30		$1,520.00

Deduct:
  Second payment (9/29) $600.00
  Deduct: interest on $1,520 for
    30 days (8/30–9/29) 7.60
  Remainder applied to principal 592.40
Balance on 9/29 . . . .$ 927.60

Add: interest on $927.60 for 30 days (9/29–10/29) 4.64
  Balance on 10/29 . . . .$ 932.24

This method may be diagrammed as follows:

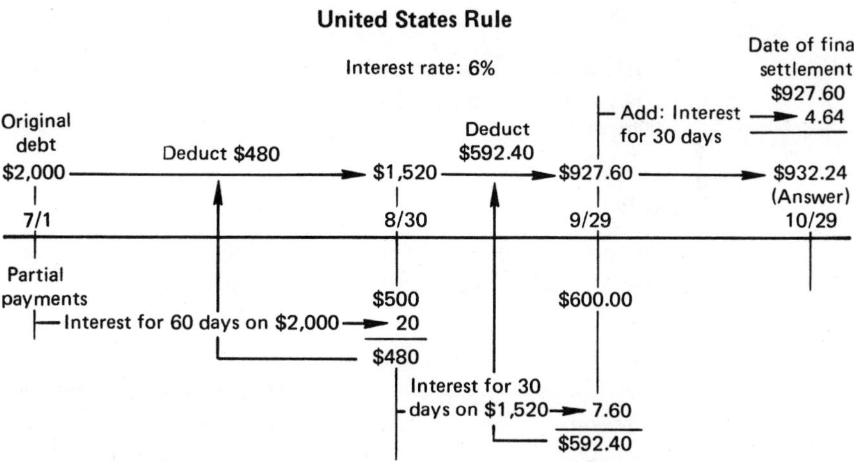

NOTE: The balance on the date of final settlement as calculated by the United States Rule is slightly greater than that by the Merchants' Rule, because compound interest is involved in the United States Rule method. Hence, it is better for a debtor to use the Merchants' Rule in reducing a debt by partial payments.

EXAMPLE 3 On July 1, a man borrowed $1,000 at 12%. He paid $300 on July 31, $6 on September 29, and $400 on October 14. Find the balance due November 13 of the same year by the United States Rule.

Original debt (7/1) $1,000.00

Deduct:
  First payment (7/31) $300.00
  Deduct: interest on $1,000.00 for 30 days
    (7/1–7/31) 10.00
  Remainder applied to principal 290.00
  Balance on 7/31 . . . .$ 710.00

Deduct:

Second payment (9/29) . . . . $ 6.00*
Third payment (10/14) 400.00

Total payment as of 10/14. . . . . $406.00
Deduct: interest on $710 for 75 days (7/31–10/14) 17.75

Remainder applied to principal 388.25

Balance on 10/14 . . . . $ 321.75

Add: interest on $321.75 for 30 days (10/14–11/13) 3.22

Balance on 11/13 . . . . $ 324.97

*Interest on $710 for 60 days (7/31–9/29) is $14.20, which is larger than the partial payment, $6. Thus, the payment is held and is included in the third payment on 10/14.

EXERCISE 8–5 REFERENCE: SECTION 8.4

A. In each of the following problems, find the unpaid balance on the indicated date by (a) the Merchants' Rule and (b) the United States Rule:

	Date of Loan	*Principal*	*Rate of Interest*	*First Partial Payment*		*Second Partial Payment*		*Date of Unpaid Balance*
				Date	*Amount*	*Date*	*Amount*	
1.	4/1/90	$1,000	18%	5/1	$ 300	6/30	$ 500	7/30/90
2.	6/10/90	2,500	8%	8/9	500	10/8	800	12/7/90
3.	1/19/91	560	$4\frac{1}{2}$%	2/8	200	. . .	. . .	3/20/91
4.	9/24/91	840	7%	11/3	300	. . .	. . .	12/23/91
5.	8/15/92	1,600	6%	9/14	200	11/13	1,000	1/12/93
6.	7/6/92	2,800	10%	7/21	1,000	8/20	1,200	9/19/92
7.	11/15/93	4,200	5%	1/14	3,000	. . .	. . .	4/4/94
8.	10/2/93	3,500	9%	12/1	2,000	. . .	. . .	1/10/94
9.	3/25/94	3,700	12%	6/23	1,000	8/22	2,000	10/21/94
10.	5/6/94	4,800	18%	6/5	2,400	11/2	1,800	1/31/95

B. Statement problems:

11. On January 12, 1991, Jack Southerland purchases a lot for $48,000. He makes a partial payment of $10,000 once every 30 days, beginning February 11. On June 11 he plans to make the last payment plus the interest. If the rate of interest is 18%, what is the amount due? Use the Merchants' Rule.
12. A note for $6,000 with an interest rate of 8%, dated March 18, 1991, has the following partial payments: May 17, $2,000; July 1, $2,000, and September 14, $1,000. Find the balance due on December 13, 1991, by using the Merchants' Rule.
13. Find the amount due in Problem 11 by using the United States Rule.

14. Find the balance due in Problem 12 by using the United States Rule.
15. On April 25, 1992, Gloria South borrowed \$4,000 at 4% interest. She paid \$1,000 on June 24, \$500 on July 24, \$5 on August 23, and \$2,000 on September 22. Find the balance due November 21, 1992, by the United States Rule.
16. Mohammed Farr borrowed \$3,000 on May 7, 1993. Partial payments were made as follows: \$500 on June 6, \$15 on July 21, \$1,000 on September 4, and \$800 on November 3. On December 3, 1993, he wishes to settle his obligation. If the interest charged is 6%, what is the total amount due by the United States Method?
17. Find the balance due in Problem 15 by the Merchants' Rule.
18. Find the amount due in Problem 16 by the Merchants' Rule.

8.5 EQUIVALENT VALUES INVOLVING SIMPLE INTEREST

Occasionally there arises the need to replace a single debt or a set of debts by another single debt or another set of debts due at different times. In order to satisfy both the creditor and the debtor, the values of the new debts should be equivalent to the values of the original ones. For example, if a debt of \$100 due now is to be replaced by a new debt due in one year and the money is worth 6%, the new debt is computed as follows:

$$S = P(1 + in) = 100(1 + 6\% \times 1) = \$106$$

The computation indicates that \$100 due now is *equivalent* to \$106 due in one year if the money is worth 6%. Thus, the creditor may allow the debtor to repay \$100 now or \$106 in a year. On the other hand, if a debt of \$212 due in a year is to be replaced by a new debt due now, and the interest rate agreed upon by the creditor and the debtor is 6%, the new debt is computed as follows:

$$P = \frac{S}{1 + in} = \frac{212}{1 + 6\% \times 1} = 212 \div 1.06 = \$200$$

The computation indicates that \$212 due in a year is equivalent to \$200 due now if the rate of interest is 6%. Thus, the creditor and the debtor may agree to settle the debt now by the debtor's payment of only \$200.

When interest is involved, a sum of money has different values at various times. For convenience, a *comparison date*, also called a *focal date*, should first be chosen in comparing the values of old debts with the values of new debts. An *equation of value*, which gives the equivalent values of original debts and new debts on the comparison date at the specified interest rate, should then be arranged for obtaining the required equivalent values. The answer for a required equivalent value may vary slightly in simple interest problems, depending on the selection of the comparion date, but it does not vary in compound interest problems. The following examples are used to illustrate problems in equivalent values involving simple interest.

EXAMPLE 1

A debt of \$200 is due in six months. If the rate of interest is 15%, what is the value of the debt if it is paid (a) two months hence? (b) six months hence? (c) nine months hence?

According to the problem, \$200 is the maturity value or the amount due at the end of six months, and the interest rate agreed upon by both creditor and debtor for settlement of the debt is 15%.

(a) If the \$200 debt is paid two months hence, which is four months before the original due date, the required equivalent value is less than \$200. Thus, the present value formula $P = S/(1 + in)$ should be used to compute the required value. In other words, the value is obtained by discounting the maturity value at a simple interest rate for the advance time of the payment.

$S = 200$, $i = 15\%$, $n = \frac{4}{12} = \frac{1}{3}$ (year)

Substituting the values in the formula,

$$P = \frac{200}{1 + (15\%)(\frac{1}{3})} = \frac{200}{1.05} = \$190.48$$

If the debt is paid two months hence, the payment is \$190.48.

(b) If the debt is paid in six months, at which time the debt is due, the payment is \$200, unchanged.

(c) If the debt of \$200 is paid nine months from now, which is three months after the due date, the required equivalent value is more than \$200. Thus, the amount formula $S = P(1 + in)$ should be used to compute the required value. In other words, the value is obtained by accumulating the original debt, \$200, for the extended time.

$P = 200$, $i = 15\%$, $n = \frac{3}{12} = \frac{1}{4}$ (year)

Substituting the values in the formula,

$$S = 200(1 + 15\% \times \tfrac{1}{4}) = 200(1.0375) = \$207.50$$

When the debt is paid at the end of nine months, the payment is \$207.50.

The example may be diagrammed as follows:

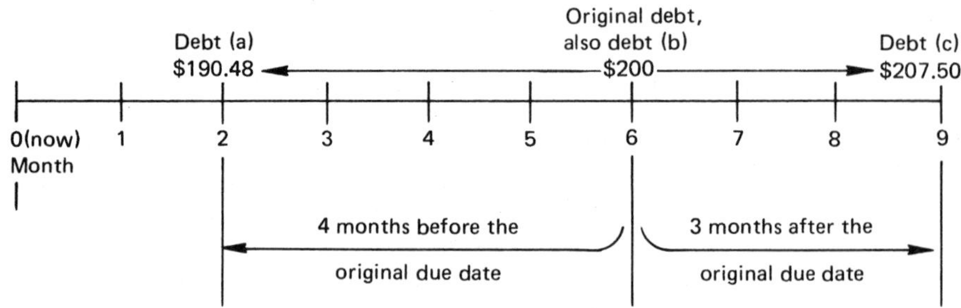

EXAMPLE 2 A man owes (1) \$100 due in two months and (2) \$400 due in eight months. His creditor has agreed to settle the debts by 2 equal payments in four months and ten months, respectively. Find the size of each payment if the rate of interest is 6% and the comparison date is four months hence.

Let x represent each equal payment. The values as of the comparison date are computed as follows:

(a) The value of the old debt of $100 becomes $101 on the comparison date. The value is computed as follows:

$P = 100$, $i = 6\%$, $n = \frac{2}{12} = \frac{1}{6}$ (year), since the comparison date is two months after the due date.

$$S = 100[1 + (6\%)(\tfrac{1}{6})] = 100(1.01) = \$101$$

(b) The value of the old debt of $400 becomes $392.16 on the comparison date. The value is computed as follows:

$S = 400$, $i = 6\%$, $n = \frac{4}{12} = \frac{1}{3}$ (year), since the comparison date is four months before the due date.

$$P = \frac{400}{1 + (6\%)(\frac{1}{3})} = \frac{400}{1.02} = \$392.16$$

(c) The value of the first new debt, which is due in four months, does not change and is x, since the comparison date is also in four months.

(d) The value of the second new debt, which is due in ten months, becomes $x/(1.03)$ on the comparison date. It is computed as follows:

$S = x$, $i = 6\%$, $n = \frac{6}{12} = \frac{1}{2}$ (year), since the comparison date is six months before the due date.

$$P = \frac{x}{1 + (6\%)(\frac{1}{2})} = \frac{x}{1.03}$$

The values are diagrammed in the following manner:

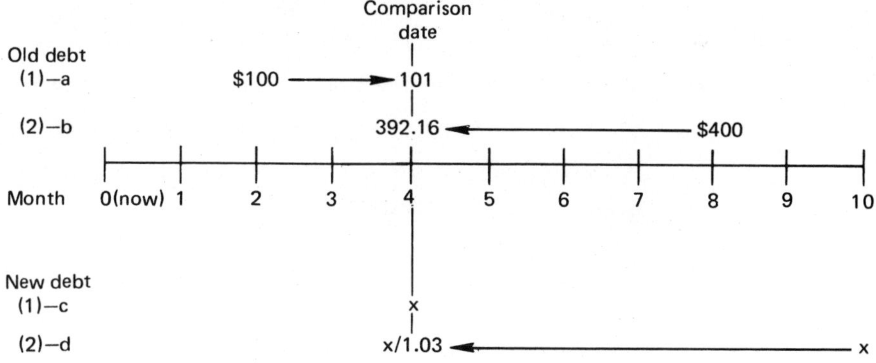

The equation of value based on the comparison date is given below:

$$\overbrace{\underset{(c)}{x} + \underset{(d)}{\frac{x}{1.03}}}^{\textit{New Debts}} = \overbrace{\underset{(a)}{101} + \underset{(b)}{392.16}}^{\textit{Old Debts}}$$

Solve for x.

$$x\left(1 + \frac{1}{1.03}\right) = 493.16$$

$$x\left(\frac{1.03}{1.03} + \frac{1}{1.03}\right) = 493.16$$

$$x\left(\frac{2.03}{1.03}\right) = 493.16$$

$$x = 493.16\left(\frac{1.03}{2.03}\right) = \$250.22$$

The two original debts may be discharged by paying $250.22 in four months and $250.22 in ten months.

CHECK

On the comparison date,

$$\text{New debts} = 250.22 + \frac{250.22}{1 + 6\%(\frac{1}{2})} = 250.22 + 242.94 = \$493.16$$

$$= \text{Old debts}$$

EXAMPLE 3

In the above example, what is the size of each equal payment if the comparison date is set ten months hence?

Let x represent each payment. The values as of the comparison date are computed as follows:

(a) The value of the old debt (1), $100, becomes

$S = 100[1 + (6\%)(\frac{8}{12})] = 104$ (eight months after due date)

(b) The value of the old debt (2), $400, becomes

$S = 400[1 + (6\%)(\frac{2}{12})] = 404$ (two months after due date)

(c) The value of the first new debt, which is due in four months, becomes

$S = x[1 + (6\%)(\frac{6}{12})] = 1.03x$ (six months after due date)

(d) The value of the second new debt, which is due in ten months, does not change and is x, since the comparison date is also in ten months.

Example 3 is diagrammed in the following manner:

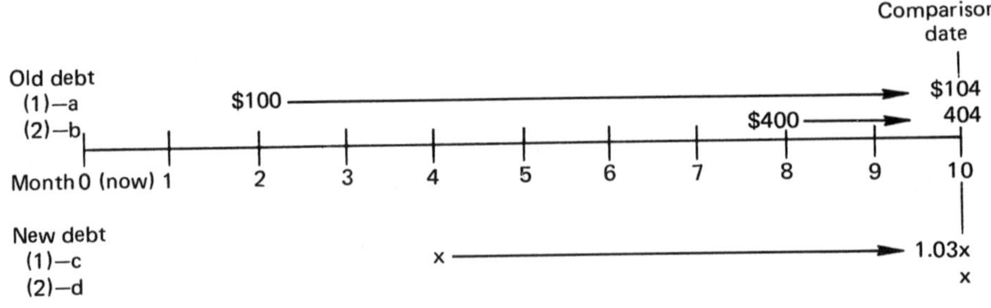

The equation of value based on the comparison date is given below:

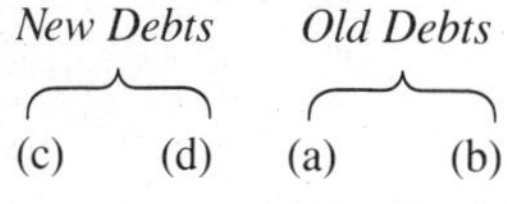

$1.03x + x = 104 + 404$

Solve for x.

$$(1.03 + 1)x = 508$$
$$2.03x = 508$$
$$x = \frac{508}{2.03} = \$250.25$$

This answer may be compared with that obtained in Example 2. The difference is only \$.03 (or \$250.25 − \$250.22), which is due to the selection of the comparison date.

NOTE: When the due date of the last new debt is selected as the comparison date, division in the discounting process may be avoided.

EXAMPLE 4 Donna owes (a) \$500 due in six months and (b) \$1,000 plus 8% interest due in three months. If money is worth 6%, what single payment nine months hence will be equivalent to the two original debts?

Let x represent the unknown single payment. The comparison date is nine months hence. Since debt (b) is interest bearing, its maturity value, having an 8% interest rate for three months, should be computed first. The maturity value plus 6% interest for six months is the value of debt (b) on the comparison date.

The maturity value of debt (b) is

$1{,}000[1 + (8\%)(\frac{3}{12})] = 1{,}000(1.02) = \$1{,}020$

and its value on the comparison date becomes

$1{,}020[1 + (6\%)(\frac{6}{12})] = 1{,}020(1.03) = \$1.050.60$

The value of debt (a), \$500, becomes

$S = 500[1 + 6\%(\frac{1}{4})]$

on the comparison date, which is three months (or $\frac{3}{12} = \frac{1}{4}$ year) after the due date.

The entire problem is diagrammed in the following manner:

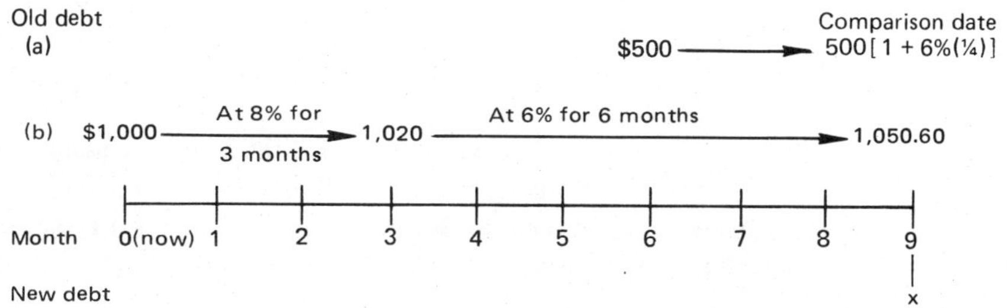

The equation of value based on the comparison date is written below:

$$x = 1{,}050.60 + 500[1 + (6\%)(\tfrac{1}{4})]$$
$$= 1{,}050.60 + 507.50$$
$$= \$1{,}558.10$$

The single payment at the end of nine months is $1,558.10.

EXERCISE 8–6 REFERENCE: SECTION 8.5

A. Find the value of the new obligations in each of the following problems:

	Original Debt	*Value of Money (%)*	*New Debt and Comparison Date*
1.	$4,000 due in 2 months	24%	All in 5 months
2.	$5,150 due in 3 months	18%	All in 1 month
3.	$3,990 due in 6 months	15%	All in 2 months
4.	$6,400 due in 4 months	21%	All in 6 months
5.	(a) $5,000 due in 4 months (b) $2,400 due in 1 month	8%	All in 6 months
6.	(a) $2,200 due in 1 month (b) $4,600 due in 9 months	10%	All in 4 months
7.	(a) $1,000 in 5 months (b) $1,800 in 8 months	6%	Two equal payments: one in 3 months, the other in 10 months. Comparison date, 3 months hence.
8.	(a) $1,000 in 5 months (b) $1,800 in 8 months	6%	Same as Problem 7, except the comparison date is 10 months hence.

B. Statement problems:

9. A debt of $2,000 is due in four months. If money is worth 20%, what is the value of the debt if it is paid (a) one month hence, (b) four months hence, and (c) six months hence?
10. A debt of $5,000 is due at the end of six months. If money is worth 18%, what is the value of the debt (a) at the end of five months, (b) at the end of six months, and (c) at the end of ten months?
11. A man owes (a) $1,000 due in three months and (b) $2,000 due in seven months. He and his creditor agree to settle the obligations by 2 equal payments, one in five months and the other in 11 months. Find the size of each payment if money is worth 6% and the comparison date is five months hence.
12. Answer the questions in Problem 11 if the comparison date is 11 months hence.
13. A debt of $2,400 due in two months is to be paid by 3 equal payments due three, five, and seven months hence. Money is worth 10%. What is the size of each payment? Let the comparison date be seven months hence.

14. Answer the questions in Problem 13 if the comparison date is two months hence.
15. A woman owes (a) \$1,000 due in four months and (b) \$3,000 plus interest at 5% due in six months. If money is worth 8%, what single payment ten months hence will be equivalent to the two original debts?
16. In Problem 15, if money is worth 8%, what single payment three months hence will be equivalent to the two original debts?
17. Jack Simpson owes Dale Peterson (a) \$1,000 which is four months overdue, (b) \$2,000 which is three months overdue, and (c) \$1,500 which is due today. Simpson now wishes to sign a three-month non-interest-bearing note to cover all the debts. If a 6% interest rate is used to compute the obligations, what should be the face value of the note?
18. In Problem 17, assume that Simpson wishes to sign two non-interest-bearing notes of equal amounts with one note due in one month and the other due in two months. The 6% interest rate is used throughout. What should be the face value for each note if the comparison date is (a) now, and (b) two months hence?

★8.6 EQUIVALENT TIME

In the preceding section, the unknown in an equation of value is the value of each new debt. In this section, the value of each new debt in the equation is known, but the equivalent time at which the new debt is due is unknown.

EXAMPLE 1

When will a single payment of \$1,010 discharge the debts of (a) \$400, (b) \$500, and (c) \$100, due in 30 days, 60 days, and 90 days, respectively? Assume that the rate of interest is 6%.

Let the last due date, which is 90 days from now, be the comparison date. The total value of the three original debts is \$1,006.50 on the comparison date. The computation is shown below:

Original Debts	*Value on Comparison Date*	
(a) \$ 400	$400[1 + (\frac{60}{360})(6\%)] =$	\$ 404.00
(b) \$ 500	$500[1 + (\frac{30}{360})(6\%)] =$	502.50
(c) \$ 100		100.00
Total \$1,000		\$1,006.50

Since the single payment of \$1,010 is larger than the total value of \$1,006.50, the single payment is considered as the amount S and the total value as the principal P. The due date for the amount, denoted by t (or t days from now), must come later than 90 days from now. Thus, \$1,010 is discounted to the value of \$1,006.50 for $(t - 90)$ days.

The entire problem is diagrammed as follows:

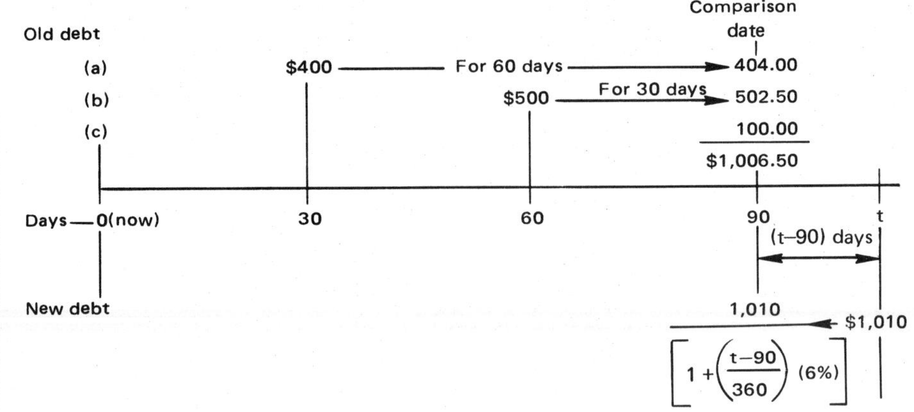

The equation of value based on the comparison date is shown below:

$$\frac{1{,}010}{1 + \left(\frac{t - 90}{360}\right)(6\%)} = 1{,}006.50$$

Solve for t.

$$\frac{1{,}010}{1{,}006.50} = 1 + \left(\frac{t - 90}{6{,}000}\right)$$

$$\frac{1{,}010}{1{,}006.5} - 1 = \frac{t - 90}{6{,}000}$$

$$\frac{3.5}{1{,}006.5}\left(6{,}000\right) = t - 90$$

$$20.86 = t - 90$$

$$t = 90 + 20.86 = 110.86, \quad \text{or } 111 \text{ days}$$

A single payment of $1,010 may be made in 111 days to discharge the three original debts.

NOTE: When the comparison date is set on the last due date of the old debts, division, which is a necessary operation in a discounting process, may be avoided in finding the new value of each old debt. Here again note that the selection of a different comparison date does affect the answer slightly.

In the computation above, when a set of debts is discharged by a single payment or a new set of debts, the sum of the old debts may not be equal to the sum of the new debts. For example, in the above illustration, the old debts totaling $1,000 were discharged by the new debt of $1,010. In Example 4, page 263, the sum of the old debts is $1,520, whereas the new single debt is $1,558.10. In the following examples, the single payment that discharges the old debts is assumed to be *equal* to the sum of the old debts. The date on which the single payment is made is called the *equated date* or the *average due date*. It is found by using the equation of value or a formula as derived below.

EXAMPLE 2 When will a single payment of $1,000 discharge the debts in Example 1?

The single payment of $1,000 equals the three debts: $400, $500, and $100. Assume that the single payment is to be made in t days. The number that t represents must be less than 90, the last due date, because if there are 90 or more days, the payment must include additional interest and thus be larger than $1,000.

The example is diagrammed as follows:

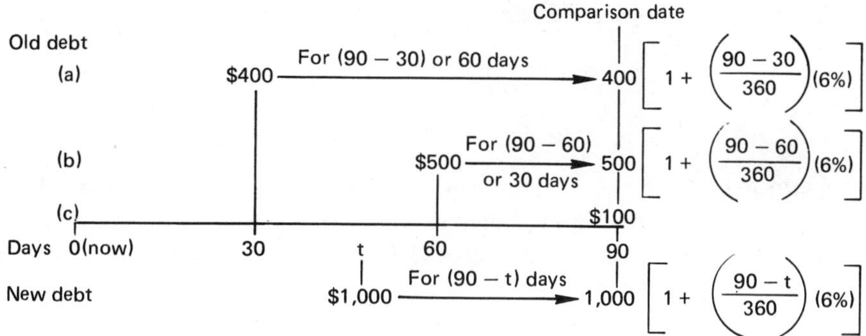

The equation of value based on the comparison date is written below:

$$1{,}000\left[1 + \left(\frac{90 - t}{360}\right)(6\%)\right] = 400\left[1 + \left(\frac{90 - 30}{360}\right)(6\%)\right]$$

$$+ 500\left[1 + \left(\frac{90 - 60}{360}\right)(6\%)\right] + 100 = 1{,}006.50 \quad \text{(see Example 1)}$$

Solve for t.

$t = 51$ days

A single payment of $1,000 may be made in 51 days to discharge the three debts.

In Example 2, $ 400 = the first debt due in 30 days
500 = the second debt due in 60 days
100 = the third debt due in 90 days
$1,000 = the sum of the three debts

In general, let D_1 = the first debt due in t_1 days
D_2 = the second debt due in t_2 days
D_3 = the third debt due in t_3 days
$D = D_1 + D_2 + D_3$, and D will be due in t days

The following formula[2] is obtained:

$$t = \frac{D_1t_1 + D_2t_2 + D_3t_3}{D} \qquad \textbf{(8–5)}$$

By applying this formula, Example 2 is computed as follows:

$$t = \frac{400 \cdot 30 + 500 \cdot 60 + 100 \cdot 90}{1{,}000} = 51$$

In formula (8–5), t is derived after the interest rate (which is not equal to zero) has been canceled. Thus, an interest rate need not be included in computing an equated date. Furthermore, the values of the t's may also represent the number of months or years or other units of time. The equality of formula (8–5) does not change if both sides of the formula are divided by 30 or 360 or other numbers in order to convert the unit of time. However, the unit of time represented by t's in the formula should be consistent throughout. The formula may be extended to include any number of D's, and is written in the following manner:

$$t = \frac{D_1t_1 + D_2t_2 + D_3t_3 + \cdots}{D} \quad \text{where}$$

$D = D_1 + D_2 + D_3 + \cdots$ (that is, D may equal any number of debts)

EXAMPLE 3

A store purchased merchandise in the following amounts: \$200, due in three months; \$500, due in four months; and \$100, due in six months. What will the equated date be if a single payment of \$800 discharges the three debts? Assume that the rate of interest is 18%.

Since the sum of the three debts, \$200, \$500, and \$100, equals \$800, formula (8–5) may be applied to compute the equated date. The interest rate need not be included in the computation.

$D_1 = \$200,\ t_1 = 3$ (months), $D_2 = \$500,\ t_2 = 4$ (months),
$D_3 = \$100,\ t_3 = 6$ (months), $D = \$800$

$$t = \frac{200 \cdot 3 + 500 \cdot 4 + 100 \cdot 6}{800} = \frac{600 + 2{,}000 + 600}{800} = \frac{3{,}200}{800}$$

$= 4$ months, since the unit of time throughout this problem is one month.

NOTE: If there is no interest ($i = 0$), the balance, \$800, probably can be paid at any time; that is, there is no equated date.

---

[2]*Proof–Formula (8–5):*

Substitute the symbols in the equation of value in Example 2. Then

$$D\left[1 + \left(\frac{t_3 - t}{360}\right)(6\%)\right] = D_1\left[1 + \left(\frac{t_3 - t_1}{360}\right)(6\%)\right] + D_2\left[1 + \left(\frac{t_3 - t_2}{360}\right)(6\%)\right] + D_3$$

Extend and subtract $D(= D_1 + D_2 + D_3)$ from both sides, and then divide by 6% and multiply by 360:

$$D(t_3 - t) = D_1(t_3 - t_1) + D_2(t_3 - t_2)$$

Extend:

$$\begin{aligned} Dt_3 - Dt &= D_1t_3 - D_1t_1 + D_2t_3 - D_2t_2 \\ Dt &= Dt_3 - D_1t_3 + D_1t_1 - D_2t_3 + D_2t_2 = (D - D_1 - D_2)t_3 + D_1t_1 + D_2t_2 \\ &= D_3t_3 + D_1t_1 + D_2t_2. \quad \text{Thus,} \\ t &= \frac{D_1t_1 + D_2t_2 + D_3t_3}{D} \end{aligned}$$

EXAMPLE 4

The debts \$200, \$300, and \$500 are due in 11 days, 20 days, and 30 days, respectively. If the payment plans are changed to pay \$100, \$200, and \$300 in 10 days, 20 days, and 30 days, when will a single payment of \$400 discharge the balance?

According to formula (8–5), the equated date of the original debts is

$$t = \frac{200 \cdot 11 + 300 \cdot 20 + 500 \cdot 30}{1{,}000}$$

Assume that the new fourth payment of \$400 is paid in T_4 days. According to formula (8–5), the equated date of the new payment is

$$t = \frac{100 \cdot 10 + 200 \cdot 20 + 300 \cdot 30 + 400 \cdot T_4}{1{,}000}$$

Equate the values of t, and solve for T_4. Then

$$T_4 = \frac{200 \cdot 11 + 300 \cdot 20 + 500 \cdot 30 - (100 \cdot 10 + 200 \cdot 20 + 300 \cdot 30)}{400}$$

$$= 23 \text{ days}$$

CHECK

Let the comparison date be in 30 days, and 6% (or any rate other than zero) be the rate of interest. The values of the old debts on the comparison date are as follows:

$$\text{(a)}\ 200\left[1 + \left(\frac{30 - 11}{360}\right)(6\%)\right] = 200(1.00317) = 200.63$$

$$\text{(b)}\ 300\left[1 + \left(\frac{30 - 20}{360}\right)(6\%)\right] = 300(1.00167) = 300.50$$

$$\text{(c)}\ 500\left[1 + \left(\frac{30 - 30}{360}\right)(6\%)\right] = 500(1) \qquad = \underline{500.00}$$

$$\$1{,}001.13$$

The values of the new debts on the comparison date are computed as follows:

$$\text{(a)}\ 100\left[1 + \left(\frac{30 - 10}{360}\right)(6\%)\right] = 100(1.00333) = 100.33$$

$$\text{(b)}\ 200\left[1 + \left(\frac{30 - 20}{360}\right)(6\%)\right] = 200(1.00167) = 200.33$$

$$\text{(c)}\ 300\left[1 + \left(\frac{30 - 30}{360}\right)(6\%)\right] = 300(1) \qquad = 300.00$$

$$\text{(d)}\ 400\left[1 + \left(\frac{30 - 23}{360}\right)(6\%)\right] = 400(1.00117) = \underline{400.47}$$

$$\$1{,}001.13$$

The total value of the old debts is equal to the total value of the new debts, \$1,001.13, on the comparison date. Thus, the answer is correct. The single payment of \$400 in 23 days will discharge the balance.

Let D_1, D_2, and D_3 be the original debts due in t_1, t_2, and t_3 days, respectively, and P_1, P_2, P_3, and P_4 be the new payments to be made in T_1, T_2, T_3, and T_4 days, respectively, where $D_1 + D_2 + D_3 = P_1 + P_2 + P_3 + P_4$. In a manner similar to that followed in determining the solution for Example 4, the following formula is derived in finding the value of T_4:

$$T_4 = \frac{D_1t_1 + D_2t_2 + D_3t_3 - (P_1T_1 + P_2T_2 + P_3T_3)}{P_4} \qquad \textbf{(8–6)}$$

Formula (8–6) may be extended to any number of *D*'s and *P*'s. Also, the values of *t*'s and *T*'s may represent the number of months, years, or other units of time.

EXAMPLE 5

A man made the following purchases at the Harrow Hardware Co.: September 25, \$400; October 25, \$300; and December 4, \$500. He made the following payments: October 19, \$200, and November 5, \$100. What is the equated date on which he may make a single payment of \$900 to discharge the balance?

Let September 25 be the *present*. Then

D_1 = \$400, t_1 = 0 (due at present)
D_2 = \$300, t_2 = 30 days (from 9/25 to 10/25)
D_3 = \$500, t_3 = 70 days (from 9/25 to 12/4)
P_1 = \$200, T_1 = 24 days (from 9/25 to 10/19)
P_2 = \$100, T_2 = 41 days (from 9/25 to 11/5)
D = 400 + 300 + 500 = \$1,200
$P_3 = D - (P_1 + P_2)$ = 1,200 − (200 + 100) = 1,200 − 300 = \$900, which equals the single payment.

Apply formula (8–6) by using the above values.

$$T_3 = \frac{(400 \cdot 0) + (300 \cdot 30) + (500 \cdot 70) - [(200 \cdot 24) + (100 \cdot 41)]}{900}$$

$$= \frac{0 + 9{,}000 + 35{,}000 - (4{,}800 + 4{,}100)}{900}$$

$$= \frac{35{,}100}{900} = 39 \text{ days from September 25, or on November 3}$$

In such a case as the above, the debt is probably settled after December 4, the last purchase date. The final amount will then include the balance, \$900, and the interest on the balance for the period from November 3 to the date of settlement. For example, if the debt is paid on December 23 (or 50 days after November 3) and the interest rate is 12%, the amount due is

$$I = 900 \times \frac{50}{360} \times 12\% = 15$$

$$S = 900 + 15 = \$915$$

★EXERCISE 8–7 REFERENCE: SECTION 8.6

A. In the following problems, assume that the interest rate is not equal to 0, that is, $i \neq 0$. Find the equated date t or T in each problem:

	Original Debts	*Payment Plan*
1.	(a) $1,000 in 20 days (b) $3,000 in 40 days (c) $6,000 in 60 days	$10,000 in t days
2.	(a) $1,500 in 22 days (b) $2,600 in 35 days (c) $1,900 in 40 days	$6,000 in t days
3.	(a) $200 in 2 months (b) $400 in 3 months (c) $600 in 4 months	$1,200 in t months
4.	(a) $1,200 in 5 months (b) $2,500 in 6 months (c) $4,300 in 10 months	$8,000 in t months
5.	(a) $200 in 1 month (b) $200 in 2 months (c) $200 in 3 months (d) $200 in 4 months	$800 in t months
6.	(a) $500 in 90 days (b) $1,000 in 120 days	$1,500 in t days
7.	(a) $600 in 60 days (b) $800 in 90 days (c) $1,000 in 120 days	(a) $400 in 29 days (b) $700 in 77 days (c) $1,300 in T days
8.	(a) $1,000 in 2 months (b) $1,500 in 4 months (c) $3,000 in 6 months	(a) $500 in 3 months (b) $2,000 in 7 months (c) $3,000 in T months
9.	$4,000 in 6 months	(a) $400 in 2 months (b) $800 in 4 months (c) $1,000 in 11 months (d) $1,800 in T months
10.	$2,500 due now	(a) $800 in 20 days (b) $500 in 50 days (c) $200 in 70 days (d) $1,000 in T days

B. Statement problems:

11. When will a single payment of $2,200 discharge the debts of (a) $500 due in four months, (b) $1,000 due in six months, and (c) $650 due in eight months? Assume that money is worth 9%.

12. How many days are needed for a single payment of $1,702 to discharge the debts of (a) $300 due in 20 days, (b) $600 due in 40 days, and (c) $800 due in 60 days? Assume that money is worth 6%.
13. How many months are required for a single payment of $2,500 to discharge the debts of (a) $500 due in two months, (b) $1,200 due in six months, and (c) $800 due in eight months?
14. A retailer purchased merchandise for $300 due in 10 days, $600 due in 22 days, and $900 due in 30 days. How many days are needed for a single payment of $1,800 to discharge the three purchases?
15. If the three debts in Problem 13 were paid by partial payments of $400 in three months and $600 in seven months, what is the equated date on which a single payment of $1,500 will discharge the balance?
16. If the retailer in Problem 14 had made payments of $400 in 15 days and $200 in 25 days, what is the equated date on which a single payment of $1,200 will discharge the balance?
17. A shoe store purchased merchandise as follows: June 10, $560, terms *n*/20; July 20, $240, terms *n*/10; August 26, $400, terms *n*/15. Find the equated date on which a single payment of $1,200 will discharge the three debts. If the single payment is made on September 28, how much is the payment? Interest is charged at 6%.
18. A retailer bought merchandise from a wholesaler as follows: April 10, $600; May 13, $400; June 9, $800. What is the equated date on which a single payment of $1,800 will discharge the three debts? If the single payment is made on June 13, and money is worth 9%, how much should be paid?

8.7 SUMMARY OF SIMPLE INTEREST AND SIMPLE DISCOUNT FORMULAS

Application	*Formula*	*Formula Number*	*Reference Page*
Simple Interest			
Computation in general	$I = Pin$	(8–1)	239
Calculating ordinary interest (the Banker's Rule)	$I = Pi\left(\frac{t}{360}\right) = \frac{Pit}{360}$	(8–2)	243
Calculating exact interest	$I_e = Pi\left(\frac{t}{365}\right) = \frac{Pit}{365}$	(8–3)	244
Amount, Rate, and Time			
Finding the amount	$S = P + I$ $= P(1 + in)$	(8–4)	246
★ Finding the equated date	$t = \frac{D_1t_1 + D_2t_2 + D_3t_3}{D}$	(8–5)	267
	$T_4 = \frac{D_1t_1 + D_2t_2 + D_3t_3 - (P_1T_1 + P_2T_2 + P_3T_3)}{P_4}$	(8–6)	270

EXERCISE 8–8 REVIEW OF CHAPTER 8

1. What is the simple interest on $500 at 10% for (a) four years? (b) three months?
2. Find the simple interest on $650 at 12% for (a) two years; (b) five months.
3. What are (a) the exact time and (b) the approximate time from April 10 to July 24?
4. Find (a) the exact time and (b) the approximate time from August 2 to December 25.
5. Determine the number of days by (a) the exact time method and (b) the approximate time method from January 14, 1991, to June 10, 1992.
6. Find the number of days by (a) the exact time method and (b) the approximate time method from July 8, 1992, to February 15, 1993.
7. Find (a) the ordinary interest and (b) the exact interest on $2,000 at 8% for 45 days.
8. What are (a) the ordinary interest and (b) the exact interest on $3,500 at 6% for 60 days?
9. What are (a) the ordinary interest and (b) the exact interest on $145 at 9% for 120 days?
10. Find (a) the ordinary interest and (b) the exact interest on $396 at 7% for 78 days.
11. What is the amount of $440 loaned for nine months at 20%?
12. What is the amount of $600 invested for five months at 18%?
13. What is the amount if $630 is borrowed for 120 days at 14%?
14. Find the amount if $1,500 is invested for 95 days at 12%.
15. On June 30, 1991, Jack Horner borrowed $600 and agreed to repay the loan in 60 days. The interest rate is 12%. (a) What is the simple interest? (b) What amount must he repay? (c) On what date?
16. If $800 is borrowed at $5\frac{1}{2}$% simple interest for two years, what will be the amount due?
17. At what interest rate will $360 yield $27 in $2\frac{1}{2}$ years?
18. Mary borrowed $320 four years ago. She paid $384 today to discharge the loan. What was the interest rate charged?
19. Bill borrowed $240 sixty days ago. He has to pay $241.60 now to settle the debt. What is the interest rate?
20. A payment of $676 was made to discharge a six-month loan of $650. What was the interest rate?
21. How many months will it take $1,500 to yield $37.50 interest at 10% simple interest?
22. How many days are required for $2,000 to yield $45 interest at 18% simple interest?
23. How many days are needed for $420 to yield (a) $2.80 interest at 8%? (b) $1.40 interest at 6%?
24. How many months are necessary for $500 to yield $15 interest at 12% simple interest?
25. Cathy receives $150 every two months from an investment that pays 15% interest. What is the principal that she has invested?
26. Denton paid $650 for discharging a debt that includes $60 interest. What is the principal?

27. How much money should Eaton invest now at 14% simple interest if she is to receive $6,400 in two years?
28. What is the present value of $6,300 that is due at the end of ten months? The interest rate is 6%.
29. Discount $840 for three months at the simple interest rate of 20%. What are (a) the present value and (b) the simple discount?
30. Fred promised to pay Jack $750 nine months from now. (a) If the debt is settled now and the simple interest rate of 12% is allowed, how much should Fred pay now? (b) What is the simple discount?
31. Gray borrowed $800 and agreed to repay the loan plus 5% interest at the end of one year. Four months after the loan had been made, his creditor agreed to settle the debt by discounting it at the simple interest rate of 4%. (a) How much should Gray pay? (b) What is the simple discount?
32. On April 10, Hilda borrowed $1,200 and agreed to pay the loan plus 5% simple interest in 60 days. If the debt is settled on May 25 at 6% simple interest, how much should she pay?
33. Sherwood borrowed $4,500 on February 6, 1993, at 4%. He paid $600 on February 21 and $1,400 on March 23. Find the balance on April 22, 1993, by (a) the Merchants' Rule and (b) the United States Rule.
34. On May 2, 1992, Martha borrowed $2,400 at 6%. She paid $800 on June 1, $8 on July 1, and $1,000 on July 16. Find the balance due August 15, 1992, by (a) the Merchants' Rule and (b) the United States Rule.
35. A debt of $600 is due in eight months. If the rate of interest is 12%, what is the value of the debt if it is paid (a) three months hence? (b) eight months hence? (c) ten months hence?
36. A debt of $1,500 is due at the end of five months. If money is worth 6%, what will be the value of the debt if it is settled at the end of (a) three months, (b) five months, (c) nine months?
37. A man owes $600 due in three months and $900 due in nine months. His creditor has offered to settle the debts by two equal payments in five months and in 11 months, respectively. If the man were to accept the offer, what would be the size of each payment, assuming the interest rate is 4% and the comparison date is five months from now?
38. Refer to Problem 37. If the comparison date were set 11 months from now, what would be the size of each payment?
39. Debbie owes $700 due in eight months and $1,200 plus 5% interest due in two months. If money is worth 7% now, what single payment ten months hence will be equivalent to the two original debts?
40. Eleanor owes $300 due in four months and $500 plus 7% interest due in six months. If money is worth 6% now, what single payment one year from now will be equivalent to the two original debts?
★41. When will a single payment of $2,410 discharge the debts of $600, $1,400, and $400 due in 30 days, 45 days, and 60 days, respectively? Assume that the rate of interest is 3%.

★42. When will a single payment of $2,950 discharge the debts of $800, $1,000, and $1,120 due in 15 days, 30 days, and 90 days, respectively? Assume that the rate of interest is 6%.

★43. Refer to Problem 41. When will a single payment of $2,400 discharge the three debts?

★44. Refer to Problem 42. When will a single payment of $2,920 discharge the three original debts?

★45. A store purchased merchandise for the following amounts: $300, due in two months; $40, due in five months; and $150, due in six months. What will the equated date be if a single payment of $490 can discharge the three debts? Assume that the rate of interest is 12%.

★46. Debts of $500, $100, and $60 are due in 15 days, 30 days, and 60 days, respectively. If the payment plans are changed to have $200, $250, and $80 paid in 10 days, 25 days, and 45 days, when will a single payment of $130 discharge the balance?

★47. Robert made the following purchases at the Jenkins Hardware Store in 1993: April 10, $500; July 9, $600; October 7, $800. He made the following payments: June 9, $300; August 8, $250. What is the equated date on which he may make a single payment of $1,350 to discharge the balance?

★48. Taylor made the following purchases at the Kent Retail Store in 1994: March 16, $200; June 14, $700; August 23, $900. He made the following payments: April 15, $100; June 24, $500. What is the equated date on which he may make a single payment of $1,200 to discharge the balance?

9 BANK DISCOUNT AND NEGOTIABLE INSTRUMENTS

The bank discount method is used by a bank to charge a fee for discounting services. The idea of charging a fee by the bank discount method is basically the same as that by the simple discount method. However, the procedures of computing the two types of discounts are different. In this chapter, first, the bank discount method (Section 9.1) and the applications of the method in discounting negotiable instruments (Sections 9.2 and 9.3) are presented. Next, the relationship between the bank discount and the simple discount is discussed (Section 9.4).

9.1 BANK DISCOUNT—INTEREST DEDUCTED IN ADVANCE

A. Terminology

When a bank loan is made, the interest is usually computed on the basis of the *maturity value*, the final amount of the loan on the due date. The interest rate used in computing the loan is called the *bank discount rate*, or simply the *discount rate*. The time used in computing is called the *period of discount*, which is the period from the date of discount to the maturity date. The interest thus computed is deducted immediately from the maturity value of the loan. This deduction is known as the *bank discount*, or *interest deducted in advance*. The value received by the borrower after the deduction is called the *proceeds*.

B. General Computation

In general, bank discount and proceeds may be expressed as follows:

$$\text{Bank discount} = \text{Maturity value} \times \text{Discount rate} \times \text{Period of discount}$$
$$\text{Proceeds} = \text{Maturity value} - \text{Bank discount}$$

In computing bank discount, the rate and the time must correspond to each other. The discount rate is usually stated as a yearly rate. Since the bank discount method is generally used for short-term borrowing, the period of discount normally is a fraction of a year. When a fraction is expressed, the ordinary interest method, discussed on pages 242–244, is again followed. In other words, when the period is stated in days, the exact time is used as the numerator and 360 is used as the denominator. When the period is given in months, the numerator is the number of months and the denominator is 12.

Let P' = proceeds
S = maturity value
I' = bank discount or the interest in advance
d = annual discount rate
n = period of discount expressed in years

The above expressions may be written as follows:

$$I' = Sdn \qquad \textbf{(9–1)}$$

$$P' = S - I' \quad \text{or}$$
$$= S - Sdn \quad \text{or, factoring } S,$$
$$= S(1 - dn) \qquad \textbf{(9–2)}$$

FINDING THE VALUE OF BANK DISCOUNT AND PROCEEDS

To find the value of bank discount and proceeds, formulas (9–1) and (9–2) are used, as illustrated in Examples 1 and 2 below:

EXAMPLE 1

Adell promises to repay a bank loan of $700 at the end of 60 days.

(a) If the bank charges 18% interest in advance, what is the discount?
(b) How much does Adell receive?

(a) Substituting $S = 700$, $d = 18\%$, and $n = \frac{60}{360} = \frac{1}{6}$ (year) in formula (9–1),

$I' = Sdn = 700 \times 18\% \times \frac{1}{6} = \$21$ (bank discount)

(b) Substituting $S = 700$ and $I' = 21$ in formula (9–2),

$P' = S - I' = 700 - 21 = \$679$ (proceeds received by Adell)

EXAMPLE 2

A man borrows $300 for three months from a bank that charges a discount rate of 15%. Find the proceeds.

Substituting $S = 300$, $d = 15\%$, and $n = \frac{3}{12} = \frac{1}{4}$ (year) in formula (9–2),

$P' = S(1 - dn) = 300(1 - .15 \times \frac{1}{4}) = 300(1 - .0375)$
$= 300 \times .9625 = \$288.75$

FINDING THE MATURITY VALUE

To find the maturity value, select either formula (9–1) or (9–2). Examples 3, 4, and 5 are used to illustrate this selection.

EXAMPLE 3

What is the final amount of a loan if a bank charges $2 interest in advance for three months at 8%?

$I' = 2, \qquad d = 8\%, \qquad n = \frac{3}{12} = \frac{1}{4}$ (year)

Substituting the values in formula (9–1),

$$I' = Sdn$$
$$2 = S(8\%)(\tfrac{1}{4})$$
$$S = \frac{2}{(8\%)(\frac{1}{4})} = \frac{2}{(\frac{2}{100})} = \$100$$

EXAMPLE 4 If a man receives $98 from a bank as the proceeds and the discount was $2, what is the total amount of the loan?

$P' = 98, \quad I' = 2$

Substituting the values in formula (9–2),

$$P' = S - I'$$
$$98 = S - 2$$
$$S = 98 + 2 = \$100$$

EXAMPLE 5 Johnson wants $5,000 in cash as the proceeds of a 90-day loan from a bank that charges 16% discount. What is the loan that Johnson must pay on the maturity date?

$P' = 5{,}000 \quad d = 16\%, \quad \text{and} \quad n = \frac{90}{360} = \frac{1}{4}$ (year)

Substituting the values in formula (9–2),

$$P' = S(1 - dn)$$
$$5{,}000 = S\left[1 - (16\%)\left(\frac{1}{4}\right)\right] = S[1 - 4\%]$$
$$S = \frac{5{,}000}{.96} = \$5{,}208.33$$

NOTE: When both sides of the formula $P' = S(1 - dn)$ are divided by $(1 - dn)$, the following result is obtained:

$$S = \frac{P'}{1 - dn}$$

The above result may be used directly in finding the maturity value for Example 5.

FINDING THE ANNUAL DISCOUNT RATE

To find the annual discount rate d, or the rate of interest charged in advance, divide the discount I' by the product of the final amount S and the discount period n. This is based on formula (9–1). When both sides of the formula $I' = Sdn$ are divided by Sn, the following result is obtained:

$$d = \frac{I'}{Sn}$$

EXAMPLE 6 A man received a 30-day loan of $550 from a bank. The proceeds were $544.50. What is the discount rate?

$S = 550, \quad P' = 544.50, \quad n = \frac{30}{360} = \frac{1}{12}$ (year)

$I' = S - P' = 550 - 544.50 = \$5.50$

Substituting the values in formula (9–1),

$$I' = Sdn$$
$$5.5 = 550(d)(\tfrac{1}{12})$$
$$d = \frac{5.5}{550(\frac{1}{12})} = \frac{1}{100 \times \frac{1}{12}} = \frac{12}{100} = 12\%$$

FINDING THE PERIOD OF DISCOUNT

To find the period of discount n (in years), divide the discount I' by the product of the final amount S and the discount rate d. This is also based on formula (9–1). When both sides of the formula $I' = Sdn$ are divided by Sd, the following result is obtained:

$$n = \frac{I'}{Sd}$$

EXAMPLE 7 A man borrowed \$800 from a bank that charged 15% interest in advance. He received \$770 from the loan. When will the loan be due?

$S = 800, \quad P' = 770, \quad d = 15\%$

$I' = S - P' = 800 - 770 = 30$

Substituting the values in formula (9–1),

$$I' = Sdn$$
$$30 = (800)(15\%)n$$
$$n = \frac{30}{(800)(15\%)} = \frac{30}{120} = \frac{1}{4} \text{ (year), or}$$

$\frac{1}{4} \times 360 = 90$ days after the date of borrowing

EXERCISE 9–1 REFERENCE: SECTION 9.1

A. In each of the following cases, find the unknown values:

	Maturity Value (S)	*Discount Rate (d)*	*Period of Discount (n)*	*Bank Discount (I')*	*Proceeds (P')*
1.	\$3,000	14%	2 months	?	?
2.	5,000	18%	? months	\$ 75.00	?
3.	?	?	3 months	12.00	\$ 788.00
4.	150	?	60 days	2.00	?
5.	2,400	10%	? days	?	2,370.00
6.	?	12%	? days	120.00	3,880.00
7.	9,000	?	75 days	112.50	?
8.	1,800	?	4 months	?	1,773.00
9.	?	$10\frac{1}{2}\%$	6 months	?	758.00
10.	?	15%	? days	50.00	950.00

B. Statement problems:

11. Brady Company borrowed $40,000 for 90 days from a bank that charged 9% interest in advance. What was the discount and how much did the company receive?
12. A bank loaned $420 to a man for 120 days. The charge was 10% in advance. How much did the bank charge? What were the proceeds?
13. On July 15, K. C. King received a loan from a bank and agreed to pay $3,500 for the loan on October 16. If the bank charged 18% interest in advance, find the proceeds.
14. On April 1, James Timer obtained a 60-day loan of $4,200 from a bank that charged 7% interest in advance. How much did Timer receive from the loan? On what date does he have to pay his loan?
15. Teresa needs $2,940 in cash for 45 days. If a bank lends her the money and charges 16% interest in advance, how much must Teresa pay after 45 days?
16. Tina desires $3,650 in cash as the proceeds of a 150-day loan from a bank that charges 8% discount. What is the loan that Tina must pay on the maturity date?
17. George Company borrowed $70,000 from a bank for four months. The proceeds were $67,900. What was the discount rate?
18. Shaw received $1,200 in cash as the proceeds from a bank for a 120-day loan of $1,224. What was the interest rate charged by the bank in advance?
19. A man borrowed $3,600 from a bank that charged 18% interest in advance. The proceeds were $3,384. In how many months after the borrowing must he pay the loan?
20. Jackie received $2,632 in cash as the proceeds from a bank for a loan of $2,800. The discount rate was 12%. Find the discount period in years.

9.2 NATURE OF NEGOTIABLE INSTRUMENTS

Negotiable instruments are written promises or orders to pay money. They are transferable or salable by one person to another person or to a bank. Frequently, negotiable instruments are discounted by the bank discount method. Generally speaking, there are two types of negotiable instruments—*promissory notes* and *bills of exchange*.

Promissory notes, or simply notes, have two parties: the *maker*, who makes the promise to pay, and the *payee*, to whom the promise is made (see Figure 9–1).

The following information is found in this promissory note:

Face Value: $500
Date of the Note: November 15, 1991
Term of the Note: 90 days
Interest Rate: 12%
Maturity Date: 90 days after November 15, 1991, or February 13, 1992
Maturity Value: $500(12\%)(\frac{90}{360}) = \$15$
$500 + 15 = \$515$

A bill of exchange has three parties: the *drawer*, the person who draws the bill; the *drawee*, the person to whom the bill is addressed and who is ordered to pay the bill; and the *payee*, the person to whom the payment is made. The drawee is not bound to pay the

Figure 9–1 A Promissory Note

$ 500.00 New York City, New York, November 15, 19 91

90 days AFTER DATE I PROMISE TO PAY TO

THE ORDER OF Charles L. Benson **(Payee)**

PAYABLE AT *Merchants Bank*

Five hundred and 00/100-- DOLLARS

VALUE RECEIVED WITH INTEREST AT 12%

No. 16 DUE February 13, 1992

Sue Webb **(Maker)**

bill unless he or she accepts the order of payment from the drawer. When the bill is accepted by the drawee, he or she immediately becomes the *acceptor* and is liable for the bill.

The most frequently used bills of exchange in commercial practice are *checks* and *drafts*. A check is always drawn upon a bank as the drawee and is always payable upon demand. Drafts are classified as *sight drafts* or *time drafts*. A draft that is payable at sight is called a sight draft. Checks and sight drafts are demand bills of exchange; that is, they are payable as soon as they are presented for payment. There is no need for a discount process in making payments with demand bills. A time draft, however, is payable at a future time, either within a certain number of days *after sight* (see Figure 9–2) or *after date* (see Figure 9–3), or on a *specified date* (see Figure 9–4). The maturity date (or due date) of an after-sight draft is determined by counting the days after the date on which the drawee accepts the draft. The maturity date of an after-date draft is determined by counting the days after the date on which the draft is drawn. If the draft is negotiated or sold before the maturity date, a discount process is involved in determining the selling price.

Figure 9–2 An After-Sight Time Draft

$ 1,000.00 Norfolk, Virginia, August 28, 19 91

Ninety days after sight PAY TO THE

ORDER OF Donald J. Waters **(Payee)**

One thousand and 00/100-- DOLLARS

VALUE RECEIVED AND CHARGE TO ACCOUNT OF

TO Mary Outen **(Drawee)**

No. Bluefield, Virginia

accepted Mary Outen Aug. 30, 1991

Betty Shaw **(Drawer)**

The following information is found in this after-sight time draft:

Face Value: $1,000
Date of the Draft: August 28, 1991
Accepted Date: August 30, 1991
Term of the Draft: 90 days after sight (accepted date)
Interest Rate: None
Maturity Date: 90 days after August 30, 1991, or November 28, 1991
Maturity Value: $1,000

Figure 9–3 An After-Date Time Draft

$ 3,000.00 Chicago, Illinois, June 17, 1991
Thirty days after date Pay to
the order of First National Bank of Chicago (Payee)
Three Thousand and no/100 ---------------- Dollars
Value received and charge the same to account of
To D.C. Jones (Drawee) Bob Tafton (Drawer)
No. Chicago, Illinois
Accepted D. Jones

The following information is found in this after-date time draft:

Face Value: $3,000.00
Date of the Draft: June 17, 1991
Term of the Draft: 30 days after date
Interest Rate: None
Maturity Date: 30 days after June 17, 1991, or July 17, 1991
Maturity Value: $3,000.00

Figure 9–4 A Trade Acceptance (a Type of Draft)

TRADE ACCEPTANCE

No. 36 St. Louis October 12, 1991
To S. P. Simpson Dallas, Texas
On December 2, 1991 Pay to the order of Ourselves
Three hundred eighty and no/100----------- Dollars, ($ 380.00)
The obligation of the acceptor hereof arises out of the purchase of goods from the drawer. The drawee may accept this bill payable at any bank, banker, or trust company in the United States which such drawee may designate.
Accepted at Dallas, Texas on Oct. 18, 1991
Payable at The First National Bank — The Horton Co.
Bank Location Dallas, Texas
Buyers Signature S.P. Simpson
By Agent or Officer — By Alan Branch Manager

The following information is found in this trade acceptance:

Face Value: \$380
Date of the Draft: October 12, 1991
Accepted Date: October 18, 1991
Term of the Draft: 45 days (from October 18, 1991, to December 2, 1991)
Interest Rate: None
Maturity Date: December 2, 1991
Maturity Value: \$380

A promissory note may or may not bear interest, but a draft generally bears none. If no interest is mentioned in the note, it is assumed to be non-interest-bearing, and the face value is the maturity value. However, the omission of a stated interest rate does not necessarily indicate that the original debt bears no interest. The interest, if any, might have been added to the original debt when the face value was determined.

9.3 DISCOUNTING NEGOTIABLE INSTRUMENTS

The basic principles of discounting a note or a draft at a bank are the same as those of obtaining a loan from a bank that deducts interest in advance. The following examples are used to illustrate the problems involved in discounting negotiable instruments by the bank discount method. Observe that when the term of a note or a draft is stated in *days*, the *exact time* is used in determining the maturity date and the period of discount (see Example 1 below). However, when the term is stated in *months*, the corresponding date in the due *month* is used in determining the maturity date, although the exact time is still used in counting the period of discount (see Example 2).

A. Discounting Non-Interest-Bearing Notes

EXAMPLE 1

After D. C. Jones had accepted the draft for \$3,000 (see Figure 9–3), Bob Tafton discounted the draft at the First National Bank of Chicago on June 17. How much did Tafton receive if the draft was discounted at 15%?

The maturity value of the note: $S = 3{,}000$.
The discount rate: $d = 15\%$.
The period of discount: $n = 30$ days (from June 17, date of discount, to July 17, maturity date), or $n = \frac{30}{360} = \frac{1}{12}$ (year).
Substituting these values in the formula $I' = Sdn$,

$$I' = 3{,}000 \times \frac{15}{100} \times \frac{1}{12} = \$37.50$$

Substituting the values of S and I' in the formula $P' = S - I'$,

$$P' = 3{,}000 - 37.50 = \$2{,}962.50$$

EXAMPLE 2

A three-month, non-interest-bearing note dated on March 2, 1991 was discounted in a bank on April 3 at 12%. The proceeds were \$1,470. Find the face value of the note.

The face value of the non-interest-bearing note is the maturity value S on the due date.

The due date is June 2, or on the corresponding date three months from March 2. The period of discount is 60 days, from April 3 to June 2.

$P' = 1{,}470, \quad d = 12\%, \quad n = \frac{60}{360} = \frac{1}{6}$ (year). Thus,

$$S = \frac{P'}{1 - dn} = \frac{1{,}470}{1 - (12\%)(\frac{1}{6})} = \frac{1{,}470}{1 - (\frac{2}{100})} = \frac{1{,}470}{\frac{98}{100}} = 1{,}470 \times \frac{100}{98} = \$1{,}500$$

B. Discounting Interest-Bearing Notes

In Example 1, the discount is computed from the maturity value, which is given. However, the maturity value is usually not given on an interest-bearing note. Thus, in discounting an interest-bearing note, take the following two steps:

STEP (1). Find the maturity value:
Add the interest to the face value of the note. Compute the interest according to the rate and the time stipulated on the note. (Use the formula $S = P(1 + in)$, where S is the maturity value and P is the face value.)

STEP (2). Find the proceeds:
Discount the maturity value. Compute the interest in advance (or the discount) according to the discount rate charged by the buyer (or the bank) and the period of discount, which is from the date of discount to the maturity date. (Use the formula $P' = S - I' = S - Sdn$.)

EXAMPLE 3

Charles L. Benson had a note for $500 with an interest rate of 12%. The note was dated November 15, 1991, and the maturity date was 90 days after date (see Figure 9–1). On November 30, 1991, he took the note to his bank, which discounted it at a discount rate of 14%. How much did he receive from the bank?

STEP (1). Find the maturity value according to the face value, the rate, and the time stipulated on the note.

$P = 500, \quad i = 12\%, \quad n = \frac{90}{360} = \frac{1}{4}$ (year)

Substituting the values in the formula $S = P(1 + in)$,

$S = 500[1 + (12\%)(\frac{1}{4})] = \$515$

STEP (2). Find the proceeds:

Discount the maturity value according to the discount rate and the period of discount.

$S = \$515$ (the maturity value of the note)
$d = 14\%$ (the discount rate charged by the bank)
$n = 75$ days (from November 30, 1991, the date of discount, to February 13, 1992, the maturity date, which is 90 days after November 15, 1991)

Substituting these values in the formula $I' = Sdn$,

$$I' = 515 \times .14 \times \frac{75}{360} = \$15.02$$

Substituting the values of S and I' in the formula $P' = S - I'$,

$P' = 515 - 15.02 = \$499.98$ (Benson received)

This computation may be tabulated as follows:

Face value of note	$500.00
Add: Interest on note (90 days at 12%)	15.00
Maturity value of note	$515.00
Less: Discount on the maturity value (75 days at 14%)	15.02
Proceeds of note discounted	$499.98

Example 3 is diagrammed as follows:

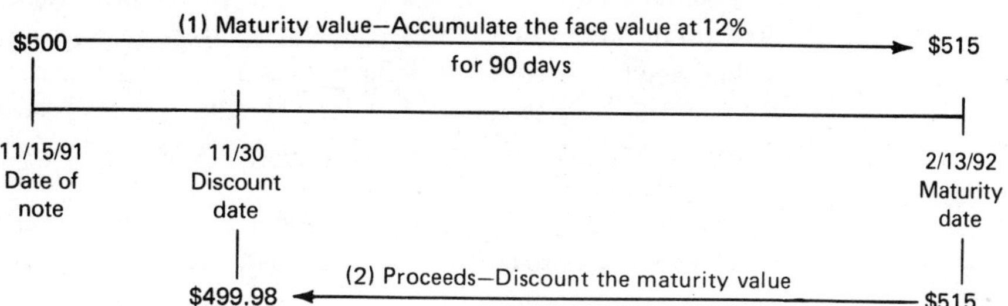

EXERCISE 9–2 REFERENCE: SECTIONS 9.2 and 9.3

A. For each of the following promissory notes, find the (a) maturity date, (b) maturity value, (c) discount period, (d) discount, and (e) proceeds.

	Date of Note	*Face Value*	*Interest Rate on Note*	*Term*	*Date of Discount*	*Bank Discount Rate*
1.	8/5/91	$4,000	21%	90 days	9/4/91	18%
2.	9/16/91	5,000	12%	3 months	11/16/91	20%
3.	4/18/92	1,800	None	2 months	4/29/92	6%
4.	6/14/92	570	8%	120 days	7/14/92	6%
5.	1/6/93	3,600	15%	30 days	1/16/93	16%
6.	2/10/93	2,400	18%	45 days	2/25/93	24%
7.	10/1/94	2,500	9%	2 months	11/1/94	7%
8.	1/15/94	880	7%	180 days	5/15/94	6%
9.	3/24/95	1,620	8%	150 days	6/7/95	9%
10.	4/12/95	630	None	4 months	7/2/95	10%

B. Statement problems:

11. Herbert signs a promissory note for $250 due in 90 days to a bank that charges 12% interest in advance. What is the discount? What should Herbert receive as the proceeds from the loan?
12. On September 29, 1991 the draft in Figure 9–2 was discounted at 18% by Donald J. Waters. What are the discount and the proceeds?
13. Johnson needs $4,387.50 in cash as the proceeds of a three-month, non-interest-bearing note from a bank that charges 10% discount. What should be the face value of the note?

14. A non-interest-bearing note is discounted at 7% at a bank 180 days before the date of maturity. The proceeds are $3,600. Find the face value of the note.
15. On November 2, 1991 the trade acceptance in Figure 9–4 was discounted by The Horton Co. at a local bank that charged a discount of 21%. What are the discount and the proceeds?
16. J. K. Osburn has a three-month, non-interest-bearing note for $2,800. When should she discount it at 7% so that she can receive $2,770.60 as the proceeds?
17. A. C. Tent received a 90-day, 15% note dated March 6 for $2,400 from B. F. Rice. Tent discounted the note at 14% at a bank on March 16. What are the (a) maturity date, (b) maturity value, (c) discount period, (d) discount, and (e) proceeds?
18. A four-month, 6%-interest-bearing note of $1,500 is discounted at 8% one month before maturity. What are the (a) maturity value, (b) discount, and (c) proceeds?
19. A note for $2,100 at 6% for 180 days is discounted at 5% in a bank 120 days before maturity. What is the discount? What are the proceeds?
20. E. F. Smith has a 60-day note for $8,000 at 21% interest. The maturity date is May 6. If the note is discounted on March 17 at 18%, how much will Smith receive?
21. A 120-day note bearing 6% interest is discounted at $4\frac{1}{2}$% 90 days before maturity. If the discount is $573.75, what is the face value?
22. Johnson signed a 60-day, non-interest-bearing note for $2,000 and discounted it at 9% at the First National Bank. If the note was immediately rediscounted by the bank at 7% at a Federal Reserve Bank, what is the profit of the First National Bank? (Note: Federal Reserve Banks use 365 days as a year in rediscounting notes for member banks. The previous discounts have no effect on the rediscount.)

9.4 RELATIONSHIP BETWEEN BANK DISCOUNT AND SIMPLE DISCOUNT

When the simple interest rate (i) and the bank discount rate (d) are the same, the discount computed by the bank discount method is greater than that computed by the simple discount method; that is,

when $i = d, \quad I' > I$

EXAMPLE 1 Discount $1,000 for 60 days at 6% by using (a) the bank discount method and (b) the simple discount method. What are the discount and the proceeds by method (a)? What are the present value and the discount by method (b)? How much is the difference between the two types of discounts? Indicate which discount is larger.

(a) *Bank Discount Method:*

$$\text{Discount} = I' = Sdn = 1{,}000\left(\frac{6}{100}\right)\left(\frac{60}{360}\right) = \$10$$

$$\text{Proceeds} = P' = S - I' = 1{,}000 - 10 = \$990$$

(b) *Simple Discount Method:*

$$\text{Present value} = P = \frac{S}{(1 + in)} = \frac{1{,}000}{1 + (\frac{6}{100})(\frac{60}{360})} = \frac{1{,}000}{1 + .01} = \$990.10$$

Discount $= I = S - P = 1{,}000 - 990.10 = \$9.90$

The difference between the discounts by methods (a) and (b) is

$I' - I = 10.00 - 9.90 = \$.10$

The bank discount is larger than the discount calculated by the simple discount method.

When the simple discount I and the bank discount I' are the same, the interest rate computed by the simple discount method is greater than that computed by the bank discount method; that is,

when $I = I'$, $\quad i > d$

EXAMPLE 2 A man who borrowed \$990 paid \$1,000 at the end of 60 days. (a) Consider the difference as the interest deducted in advance from the maturity value, \$1,000. What is the bank discount rate? (b) Consider the difference as the interest added to the borrowed principal, \$990. What is the simple interest rate? Which rate is larger?

(a) $S = 1{,}000$, $I' = 1{,}000 - 990 = \$10$, $n = \frac{60}{360} = \frac{1}{6}$ (year)

Substituting the values in $d = \dfrac{I'}{Sn}$,

$$d = \frac{10}{1{,}000(\frac{1}{6})} = 6\% \quad \text{(bank discount rate)}$$

(b) $P = 990$, $I = 1{,}000 - 990 = 10$, $n = \frac{1}{6}$ (year)

Substituting the values in $i = \dfrac{I}{Pn}$,

$$i = \frac{10}{990(\frac{1}{6})} = \frac{\overset{2}{\cancel{10}}}{\underset{33}{\cancel{165}}} = 6.06\% \quad \text{(simple interest rate)}$$

The simple interest rate is larger than the bank discount rate by

$6.06\% - 6\% = .06\%$

From the above illustration, it may be seen that the bank discount rate of 6% is equivalent to the simple interest rate of 6.06% in the transaction. In general, if $P = P'$, the relationship between a simple interest rate and a bank discount rate may be expressed by the following formulas:

$$i = \frac{d}{1 - dn} \qquad \textbf{(9–3)}^1$$

---

[1] *Proof–Formula (9–3):*

If $P = P'$, the formula $S = P(1 + in)$ may be written as

$S = P'(1 + in)$; but from formula (9–2), $S = P'/(1 - dn)$.

Thus, $P'(1 + in) = P'/(1 - dn)$; divide both sides by P': $(1 + in) = 1/(1 - dn)$.

(Continued on p. 288)

$$d = \frac{i}{1 + in} \qquad \textbf{(9–4)}^{2}$$

By applying formulas (9–3) and (9–4), Example 2 is computed as follows:

(a) $i = 6.06\% = \frac{2}{33}$ [see solution (b) above], $n = \frac{1}{6}$ (year)

Substituting the values in formula (9–4),

$$d = \frac{i}{1 + in} = \frac{\frac{2}{33}}{1 + (\frac{2}{33})(\frac{1}{6})} = \frac{6}{100} = 6\%$$

(b) $d = 6\%$ [see solution (a) in Example 2], $n = \frac{1}{6}$ (year)

Substituting the values in formula (9–3),

$$i = \frac{d}{1 - dn} = \frac{6\%}{1 - (6\%)(\frac{1}{6})} = \frac{\overset{2}{\cancel{6}}}{\underset{33}{\cancel{99}}} = 6.06\%$$

The answers are the same as those in the original computation. Note that formulas (9–3) and (9–4) do not make use of the amount S nor the proceeds P'. Therefore, in finding the simple interest rate that is equivalent to a bank discount rate, or vice versa, knowledge of the amount and the proceeds is unnecessary.

EXAMPLE 3

A bank discounts a 75-day note at 9%. What is the equivalent simple interest rate earned by the bank?

$d = 9\%, \qquad n = \frac{75}{360} = \frac{5}{24}$ (year)

Substituting the values in formula (9–3),

$$i = \frac{9\%}{1 - (9\%)(\frac{5}{24})} = \frac{9\%}{1 - \frac{15}{800}} = \frac{9}{100} \cdot \frac{800}{785} = \frac{72}{785} = .0917197, \text{ or rounded to } 9.17\%$$

---

[1] *Proof (continued):*

Subtract 1 from both sides and simplify as below:

$$in = \frac{1}{1 - dn} - 1 = \frac{1 - (1 - dn)}{1 - dn} = \frac{dn}{1 - dn}$$

Divide both sides by n: $i = \frac{d}{1 - dn}$.

[2] *Proof—Formula (9–4):*

Multiply both sides of formula (9–3) by $(1 - dn)$; then

$i(1 - dn) = d$, and

$i - idn = d$. Add idn to both sides:

$$i = d + idn = d(1 + in)$$

Divide both sides by $1 + in$: $d = \frac{i}{1 + in}$

EXAMPLE 4

At what rate should a bank discount a 60-day note if the bank is to earn simple interest equivalent to 8%?

$i = 8\%,\qquad n = \frac{60}{360} = \frac{1}{6}$ (year)

Substituting the values in formula (9–4),

$$d = \frac{8\%}{1 + (8\%)(\frac{1}{6})} = \frac{8\%}{1 + \frac{1}{75}} = \frac{\frac{8}{100}}{\frac{76}{75}} = \frac{3}{38} = .078947, \text{ or rounded to } 7.89\%$$

EXERCISE 9–3 REFERENCE: SECTION 9.4

A. In each of the following problems, find the corresponding unknown rate:

	Discount Period	*Discount Rate*	*Simple Interest Rate*
1.	3 months	?	12%
2.	4 months	?	15%
3.	120 days	?	18%
4.	150 days	?	24%
5.	$\frac{1}{2}$ year	?	16%
6.	3 months	9%	?
7.	4 months	10%	?
8.	120 days	7%	?
9.	150 days	8%	?
10.	$\frac{1}{2}$ year	6%	?

B. Statement problems:

11. A bank discounts a 90-day note at 12%. What is the equivalent simple interest rate earned by the bank?
12. What is the corresponding simple interest rate earned by a bank if it discounts a four-month note at $7\frac{1}{2}$%?
13. If a bank's policy is to earn 5% simple interest, what discount rate should be charged on a 60-day note?
14. At what rate should a bank discount a 180-day note if the bank is to earn 7% simple interest?
15. A woman received a 90-day loan of $2,500 from a bank that charged 8% interest in advance. What are the proceeds? What is the simple interest rate of the advanced interest?
16. Johnson signs a three-month note for $1,200. The bank charges 6% interest in advance. How much does Johnson receive as the proceeds? If she borrows the proceeds at simple interest and repays $1,200 at the end of a three-month period, what is the simple interest rate that she must pay?
17. Jackson signs a 60-day note for $3,600 at a bank that deducts 5% interest in advance. What is the value that Jackson receives from the bank? At what simple interest rate is he paying the advanced interest?

18. A retailer received an invoice for \$1,000 with the terms 2/10, *n*/30. In order to take advantage of the cash discount, he plans to borrow money. (a) How long should the loan period be? (b) What is the highest interest rate that he can afford to pay (1) if he pays the interest in advance and (2) if he pays the interest at the end of the period?
19. Frank signs a 120-day note for \$840. He receives \$826 as the proceeds. (a) What is the bank discount rate? (b) What is the simple interest rate if the present value is \$826?
20. Stevenson received \$3,450 in cash from a bank on April 1 and agreed to pay \$3,600 on August 29 for the loan. What is the bank discount? What is the equivalent simple interest rate?

9.5 SUMMARY OF BANK DISCOUNT FORMULAS

Application	*Formula*	*Formula Number*	*Reference Page*
Finding the bank discount – interest deducted in advance	$I' = Sdn$	(9–1)	277
Finding the proceeds	$P' = S(1 - dn)$	(9–2)	277
Finding the simple interest rate	$i = \dfrac{d}{1 - dn}$	(9–3)	287
Finding the bank discount rate	$d = \dfrac{i}{1 + in}$	(9–4)	288

EXERCISE 9–4 REVIEW OF CHAPTER 9

1. Ivan promised to pay a bank \$630 at the end of 30 days for a loan. If the bank charges 12% interest in advance (a) what is the discount? (b) how much does Ivan receive now?
2. Jimmy borrows \$500 for four months from a bank that charges a discount rate of 24%. What are the proceeds?
3. Karl wishes to borrow money and will pay \$700 at the end of eight months. Find (a) the proceeds if the creditor charges 6% interest in advance, (b) the present value if the creditor charges 6% simple interest.
4. Refer to Problem 1. What are the answers if the interest is charged at 12% simple interest?
5. What is the final amount of a loan if a bank charges \$5 interest in advance for 120 days at 5%?
6. If a bank charges \$12 interest in advance for a ten-month loan at 18%, find the total amount of the loan.
7. A man received a 90-day loan of \$600 from a bank. The proceeds were \$580. What is the discount rate?
8. Find the bank discount rate if the amount is \$300, the discount is \$2, and discount time is 60 days.

9. Lynn borrowed $1,000 from a bank that charged 10% interest in advance. He received $980 from the loan. For how long did he borrow the money?
10. Margaret received $712.50 in cash as the proceeds from a bank loan of $750. The discount rate was 15%. Find the discount period in months.
11. A non-interest-bearing note was discounted in a bank 45 days before maturity at 4%. The proceeds were $597. What was the face value of the note?
12. A non-interest-bearing note is discounted in a bank 90 days before maturity at 18%. Find the face value of the note if the proceeds are $191.00.
13. Nancy had a note for $800 with an interest rate of 5%. It was dated April 7, 1991 and the maturity date was 60 days after date. On April 22, 1991, the note was discounted at a discount rate of 6%. How much did Nancy receive as the proceeds from the discounting?
14. A 90-day note bearing 4% interest is discounted 30 days before it is due at 5%. If the discount is $8.20, what is the face value of the note? What are the proceeds?
15. Discount $2,000 for 90 days at 5% by using (a) the bank discount method and (b) the simple interest method. What are the discount and the proceeds by method (a)? What are the present value and the discount by method (b)? How much is the difference between the two types of discounts?
16. Otis borrowed $800 in cash but paid $805 at the end of 45 days to the lender. (a) Consider the difference of $5 as the interest deducted in advance from the maturity value of $805. Find the bank discount rate. (b) Consider the $5 as the interest added to the principal of $800. Find the simple interest rate.
17. A bank discounts a 60-day note at 12%. What is the equivalent simple interest rate earned by the bank?
18. What is the corresponding simple interest rate earned by a bank if it discounts a two-month note at 6%?
19. At what rate should a bank discount a 75-day note if the bank is to earn an 18% simple interest equivalent?
20. If a bank desires to earn 12% simple interest, what discount rate should be charged by the bank on a 45-day note?

PART THREE MATHEMATICS IN INVESTMENT–BASIC TOPICS

10 ★ INTRODUCTION TO CALCULATORS AND COMPUTERS

The material presented in this chapter is optional. This chapter is designed primarily for students who wish to use calculators or computers to compute the investment problems in subsequent chapters. There are numerous types of calculators and computers available in the market today. Here we will introduce only four common types of machines:

1. Simple calculator (Section 10.1)
2. Business analyst calculator (Section 10.2)
3. Computers by time-sharing terminal (Section 10.3)
4. Personal computer (microcomputer) (Section 10.4)

We will first describe the general functions of the machines, then discuss the details of operating them. BASIC programs will be used in the illustrations for operating the computers. The method of writing BASIC programs is explained in a separate section (Section 10.5). In addition, the recently developed electronic spreadsheets are also presented (Section 10.6). Applications to investment problems, however, will be dealt with in later chapters.

10.1 A SIMPLE CALCULATOR

This type of calculator usually has two major parts: (A) a display with solar cell, and (B) a set of basic keys, as shown in Figure 10–1.

A. Display with Solar Cell

The *display* shows a maximum of eight digits (including whole numbers and decimal fractions) and three symbols. The three symbols are:

M *Memory.* This symbol indicates that the displayed number is stored in the memory.

Figure 10–1 A Simple Calculator

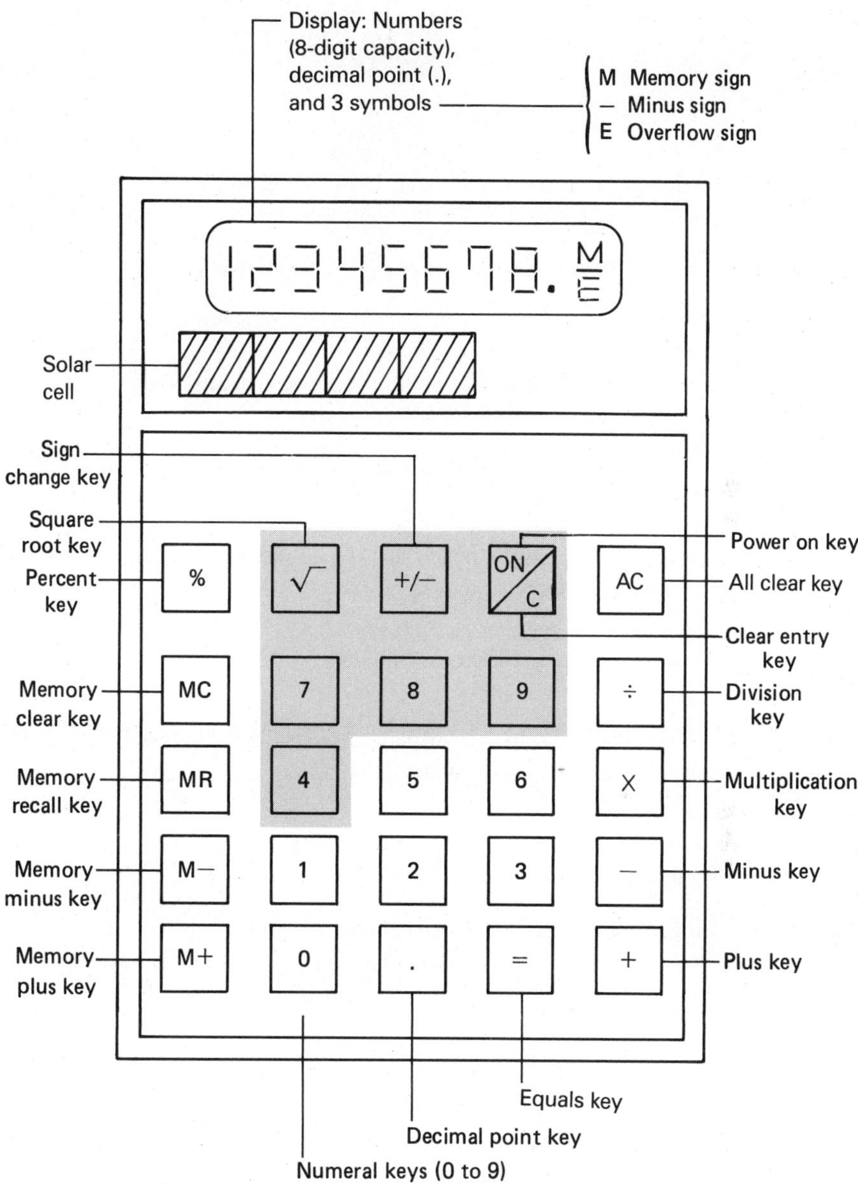

ILLUSTRATION: The display

8.^{M}

indicates that the number 8. is stored in the memory.

— *Minus.* This symbol indicates that the displayed number is a negative number.

ILLUSTRATION: $2 - 7 = -5$

The display

5. −

indicates that the number 5. is negative, or −5.

E *Overflow.* This symbol indicates that the calculation result exceeds eight digits in the integer (the whole number). In this case, we can approximate the exact answer by shifting the decimal point eight places to the right based on the displayed result.

ILLUSTRATION: 123,456 × 23,456 = 2,895,783,936 (by exact computation)

But the display shows only

28.957839 E

By shifting the decimal point in the displayed number

28.957839

eight places to the right

28.95783900.

we have the approximated answer based on the displayed number. The answer is 2,895,783,900.

Note that the number of digits to the left of the decimal point in the display (28.) is the number of zeros (00) to add for the approximated answer (that is, the two zeros after 9 [or 900] in the answer).

The *solar cell* below the display converts light energy to electrical energy. It provides a power source for the calculator to operate.

B. Keys

Numbers and operational instructions are entered into the calculator by pressing the keys on the keyboard (Figure 10–1). The *keys* (shown inside boxes, [ ]) and their functions are explained below.

(1) POWER ON AND OFF KEYS

[ON] Turns power on.

[OFF] Turns power off. However, the calculator shown in Figure 10-1 has no power off key. This calculator is equipped with a solar cell and thus it is totally light powered. It turns off automatically when the solar cell panel is not exposed to enough light. It also turns off automatically after several minutes of nonuse.

(2) CLEAR KEYS

[AC] The *all clear* key clears the display and any pending calculation. Note that with some calculators the AC key does not clear the memory.

[C] The *clear entry* key clears only the display that represents the number just entered. It is used to correct a wrong entry without clearing the previous entries.

[MC] *Memory clear.* This key clears the memory. (Note that pressing the OFF key also clears the memory.)

(3) ARITHMETIC OPERATION AND DECIMAL POINT KEYS

[÷] *Division.* In the sequence 6 [÷] 3, this key divides the displayed number (6) by the next entered number (3).

[×] *Multiplication.* In the sequence 5 [×] 4, this key multiplies the displayed number (5) and the next entered number (4).

[−] *Subtraction.* In the sequence 7 [−] 2, this key subtracts the next entered number (2) from the displayed number (7).

[+] *Addition.* In the sequence 8 [+] 1, this key adds the displayed number (8) and the next entered number (1).

[=] *Equals.* In the sequence 2 × 3 × 4 [=], this key completes all entered operations (2 × 3 × 4) and displays the final result (24).

[.] *Decimal point.* This key indicates decimal places. The decimal point "floats" to the left for each entered decimal place.

(4) NUMERAL KEYS

[0] to [9] There are ten *numeral* keys: 0, 1, 2, 3, 4, 5, 6, 7, 8, and 9.

(5) MEMORY KEYS

[M+] *Memory plus.* This key adds the displayed number to the memory.

[M−] *Memory minus.* This key subtracts the displayed number from the memory.

[MR] *Memory recall.* This key recalls the memory number to the display.

[MC] *Memory clear.* This key clears the memory, as explained in the *clear keys*.

(6) SPECIAL FUNCTION KEYS

[+/−] *Sign change.* This key changes the sign of a number in the display, such as from +8 to −8 or −8 to +8. Thus, to enter a negative number, first enter the number and then press the [+/−] key.

[√] *Square root.* This key finds the square root of the displayed number. If the displayed number is 2, by pressing the [√] key we find that the square root of 2 (or $\sqrt{2}$) is 1.4142135.

[%] *Percent.* This key indicates "one hundredth."

EXAMPLE 1

Find	15% of 400.
Press	400 [×] 15 [%]
Display shows	60 (Answer)

Calculations with the simple calculator are illustrated in the following examples.

EXAMPLE 2

Fundamental calculations

Problem	*Key Pressing Sequence*	*Display (Answer)*
1. 12 + 34 = ?	12 [+] 34 [=]	46.
2. 50 − 23 = ?	50 [−] 23 [=]	27.
3. 12.4 × 3.2 = ?	12.4 [×] 3.2 [=]	39.68
4. 68.9 ÷ 2.4 = ?	68.9 [÷] 2.4 [=]	28.708333

EXAMPLE 3

Combined calculations

Problem	*Key Pressing Sequence*	*Display (Answer)*
1. 10 + 4 − 3 = ?	10 [+] 4 [−] 3 [=]	11.
2. 4 × 6 ÷ 8 = ?	4 [×] 6 [÷] 8 [=]	3.
3. 12 ÷ 2 × 3 = ?	12 [÷] 2 [×] 3 [=]	18.
4. $\frac{5 \times (15 - 7)}{8} = ?$	15 [−] 7 [×] 5 [÷] 8 [=]	5.

EXAMPLE 4

Constant calculations

A calculator that has the *constant* feature can simplify arithmetic operations. Observe that 3 is used as the constant number in each of the four problems below. The constant is the *second* number entered when adding (Problem 1), subtracting (Problem 2), and dividing (Problem 3), and is the *first* number entered when multiplying (Problem 4).

Problem	*Key Pressing Sequence*	*Display (Answer)*
1. 15 + 3 = ?	15 [+] 3 [=]	18.
4 + 3 = ?	4 [=]	7.
8 + 3 = ?	8 [=]	11.
2. 15 − 3 = ?	15 [−] 3 [=]	12.
8 − 3 = ?	8 [=]	5.
3. 15 ÷ 3 = ?	15 [÷] 3 [=]	5.
8 ÷ 3 = ?	8 [=]	2.6666666
4. 3 × 15 = ?	3 [×] 15 [=]	45.
3 × 4 = ?	4 [=]	12.
3 × 8 = ?	8 [=]	24.

EXAMPLE 5

Reciprocal and power calculations

Problem	*Key Pressing Sequence*	*Display (Answer)*
1. Find the reciprocal of the number 4, or $\frac{1}{4} = ?$	4 [÷] [=]	0.25
2. Find the 5th power of the number 2, or $2^5 = ?$	2 [×] [=] [=] [=] [=] (Press 4 [=] keys for the 5th power.)	32.

EXAMPLE 6

Memory calculations

Problem	*Key Pressing Sequence*	*Display*
1. $(12 \times 2.5) + (4 \times 6) - (18 \div 3) = ?$	12 [×] 2.5 [M+]	$30.^{M}$
	4 [×] 6 [M+]	$24.^{M}$
	18 [÷] 3 [M−]	$6.^{M}$
(*Answer:* ? = 48)	[MR]	$48.^{M}$
2. $\frac{24}{15 - 7} = ?$	15 [−] 7 [M+]	$8.^{M}$
(*Answer:* ? = 3)	24 [÷] [MR] [=]	$3.^{M}$
3. $\frac{42 - 6}{15 + 3} - 1.5 = ?$	15 [+] 3 [M+]	$18.^{M}$
(*Answer:* ? = 0.5)	42 [−] 6 [÷] [MR] [−] 1.5 [=]	0.5^{M}
4. $6\sqrt{1.5^2 + 23.4^2} = ?$	1.5 [×] [=] [M+]	2.25^{M}
	23.4 [×] [=] [M+]	547.56^{M}
	[MR]	549.81^{M}
	[√]	23.448027^{M}
(*Answer:* ? = 140.68816)	[×] 6 [=]	140.68816^{M}

EXERCISE 10–1 REFERENCE: SECTION 10.1

Perform the indicated operations in each of the following expressions, using a simple calculator:

1. 5 + 17
2. 18 + 34
3. 25.75 + 15.93
4. 46.82 + 65.14
5. 73 − 52
6. 86 − 49
7. 125.15 − 57.86
8. 257.18 − 61.32

9. 27×18.45
10. 38×64.35
11. 53.24×125.68
12. 123.41×236.15
13. $68.15 \div 14.28$
14. $57.24 \div 26.19$
15. $148.12 \div 56.35$
16. $258.34 \div 35.72$
17. $82 + 41 - 37$
18. $95 - 18 + 43$
19. $12.45 + 36.27 - 18.32$
20. $98.23 + 163.28 - 48.53$
21. $46.12 - 6.27 + 146.90$
22. $78.35 - 13.28 + 256.37$
23. $18 \div 3 \times 5$
24. $28 \div 7 \times 6$
25. $12 \times 4 \div 8$
26. $36 \times 5 \div 9$
27. $\dfrac{3 \times (18 - 5)}{4}$
28. $\dfrac{8 \times (25 - 6)}{5}$
29. $\dfrac{(45 - 13) \times 12}{16}$
30. $\dfrac{(126 - 28) \times 35}{14}$
31. (a) $18 + 5$
    (b) $27 + 5$
    (c) $45 + 5$
32. (a) $26 + 12$
    (b) $38 + 12$
    (c) $54 + 12$
33. (a) $30 - 6$
    (b) $25 - 6$
    (c) $16 - 6$
34. (a) $120 - 30$
    (b) $158 - 30$
    (c) $240 - 30$
35. (a) $40 \div 4$
    (b) $56 \div 4$
    (c) $48 \div 4$
36. (a) $150 \div 50$
    (b) $250 \div 50$
    (c) $160 \div 50$
37. (a) 8×6
    (b) 8×10
    (c) 8×25
38. (a) 12×7
    (b) 12×10
    (c) 12×25
39. $\dfrac{1}{5}$
40. $\dfrac{1}{12}$
41. 3^4
42. 5^6
43. $(15 \times 3.4) + (3 \times 8) - (20 \div 4)$
44. $(4.5 \times 26) - (2.7 \times 15) + (60 \div 12)$
45. $\dfrac{50}{28 - 8}$
46. $\dfrac{78}{36 - 24}$
47. $\dfrac{56 - 8}{19 - 7}$
48. $\dfrac{123 - 3}{46 - 16}$
49. $12\sqrt{1.3^2 + 25.6^2}$
50. $24\sqrt{2.7^2 + 14.8^2}$

10.2 A BUSINESS ANALYST CALCULATOR

A business analyst calculator is designed especially for business students. An example is the Student Business Analyst, BA-35, manufactured by Texas Instruments Incorporated. Just as with the simple calculator, it also has two major parts: (A) a display, and (B) a set of keys, as shown in Figure 10–2.

Figure 10–2 A Business Analyst Calculator

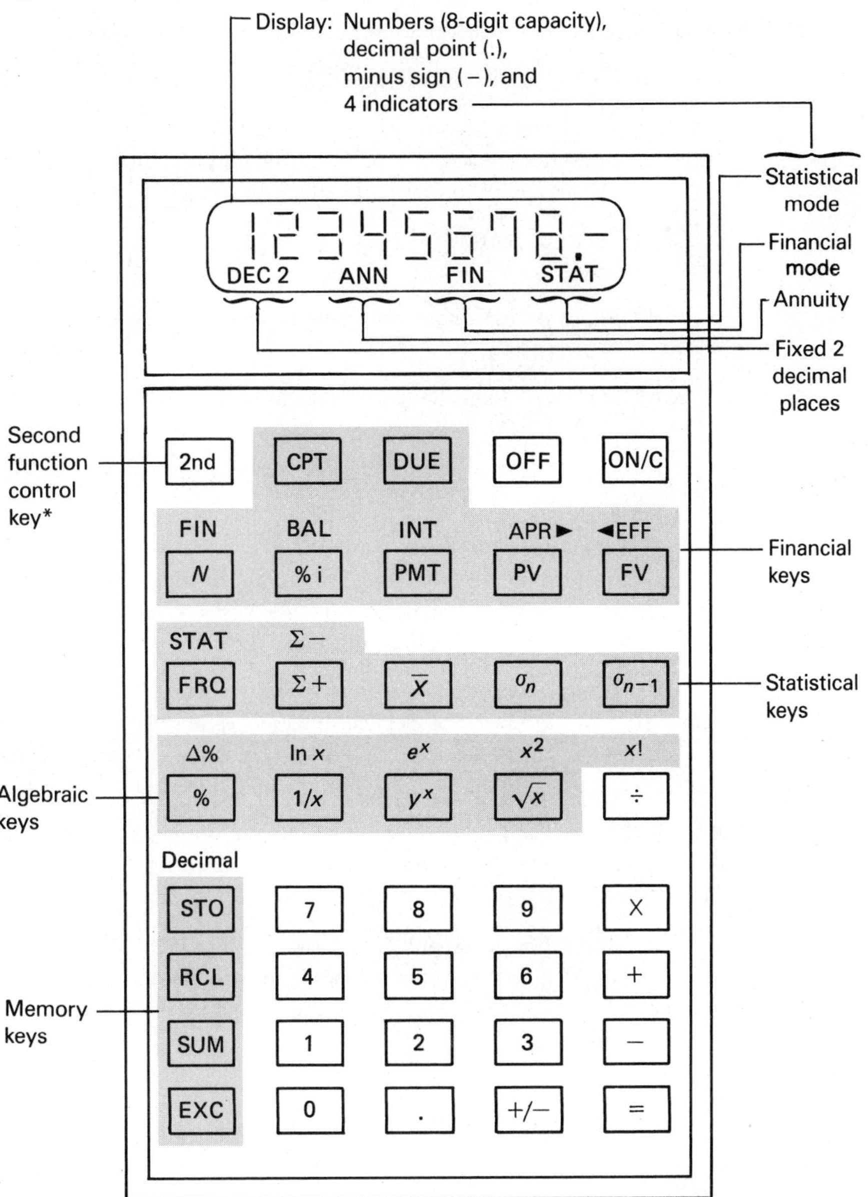

*Some of the keys on the keyboard have two different functions:

The first function is indicated *on the key*, such as [÷]. To use the first function, just press the key.

The second function is indicated *directly above the key*, such as "x!". To use the second function, press the control key [2nd] and then the function key. Keys within a heavier box indicate second functions in all illustrations, such as [x!].

A. Display

The display shows a maximum of eight digits and five symbols. The five symbols are:

— *Minus.* Indicates that the displayed number is a negative number.

DEC 2 *Two decimal places.* Indicates that the decimal point is fixed at two places. The calculator also operates with a floating decimal point. To change from one decimal point format to the other, press [2nd] [Decimal].

ANN *Annuity.* Indicates that the regular payment value in an annuity calculation is not zero.

FIN *Finance.* Indicates the financial mode. To enter the financial mode, press [2nd] [FIN].

STAT *Statistics.* Indicates the statistical mode. To enter the statistical mode, press [2nd] [STAT].

B. Keys

The keys on the keyboard may have only one function, called the *first function*, or two functions, called the *first function* and *second function*, respectively.

The first function is indicated on the key itself, such as the division function [÷]. To use the first function, just press the key.

The second function is indicated *directly above the key*, such as the x factorial function, "x!". To use the second function, press the second function control key [2nd] and then the function key. The second function keys are indicated by heavier boxes in all illustrations in this section. For example, the x! key is shown as [x!].

The keys on the keyboard are arranged into groups as follows.

(1) POWER AND CLEAR KEYS

[ON/C] Turns power on and clears the display. Press this key once to turn on the calculator. Press after a function or operation key to clear the display and any pending calculation. Pressing this key does not affect the memory and mode registers.

[OFF] Turns power off. Press this key to turn off the calculator and clear any incomplete calculation. Pressing this key does not affect the memory and mode registers.

(2) BASIC OPERATION KEYS

The following keys have the same functions as the keys in the simple calculator.

(a) The five *arithmetic operation* keys:
[÷] [×] [−] [+] [=]

(b) The ten *numeral* keys:
[0] [1] [2] [3] [4] [5] [6] [7] [8] [9]

(c) The *decimal point* key:
[.]

(d) The *sign change* key:
[+/−]

(3) MEMORY KEYS

[STO] *Storage.* This key stores the displayed number in memory without removing it from the display. However, any number previously stored in memory is lost. To clear the memory, press [ON/C] [STO].

[RCL] *Recall.* This key recalls a number that is stored in memory and makes it appear on the display. The number then can be used in calculations. The number also remains in the memory after pressing the [RCL] key and can be recalled as often as needed.

[SUM] *Sum.* This key allows us to add the number in the display and the value in the memory without affecting any calculation in progress. Thus, to add 6 + 5, press [6] [STO] [5] [SUM] [RCL]. The answer, 11, is shown in the display.

[EXC] *Exchange.* This key exchanges the value stored in memory with the number in the display.

(4) FINANCIAL KEYS

[FIN] *Finance.* Press [2nd] [FIN] to enter the financial mode. Then the "FIN" indicator appears in the display.

[CPT] *Computation.* This key is used to compute an ordinary annuity (end-of-period payments).

[DUE] *Due.* This key is used to compute an annuity due (beginning-of-period payments).

[BAL] *Balance.* This key is used to calculate the balance of an ordinary annuity or the balance of an annuity due.

[INT] *Interest.* This key is used to compute the interest amount of an ordinary annuity or an annuity due.

[APR] *Annual percentage rate.* This key converts annual percentage rates to annual effective rates.

[EFF] *Annual effective rate.* This key converts annual effective rates to annual percentage rates.

[N] *Number.* Press this key to enter the total number of compounding periods or the total number of payment periods.

[%i] *Percent interest.* Press this key to enter the percent interest per compounding period or the percent interest per payment period.

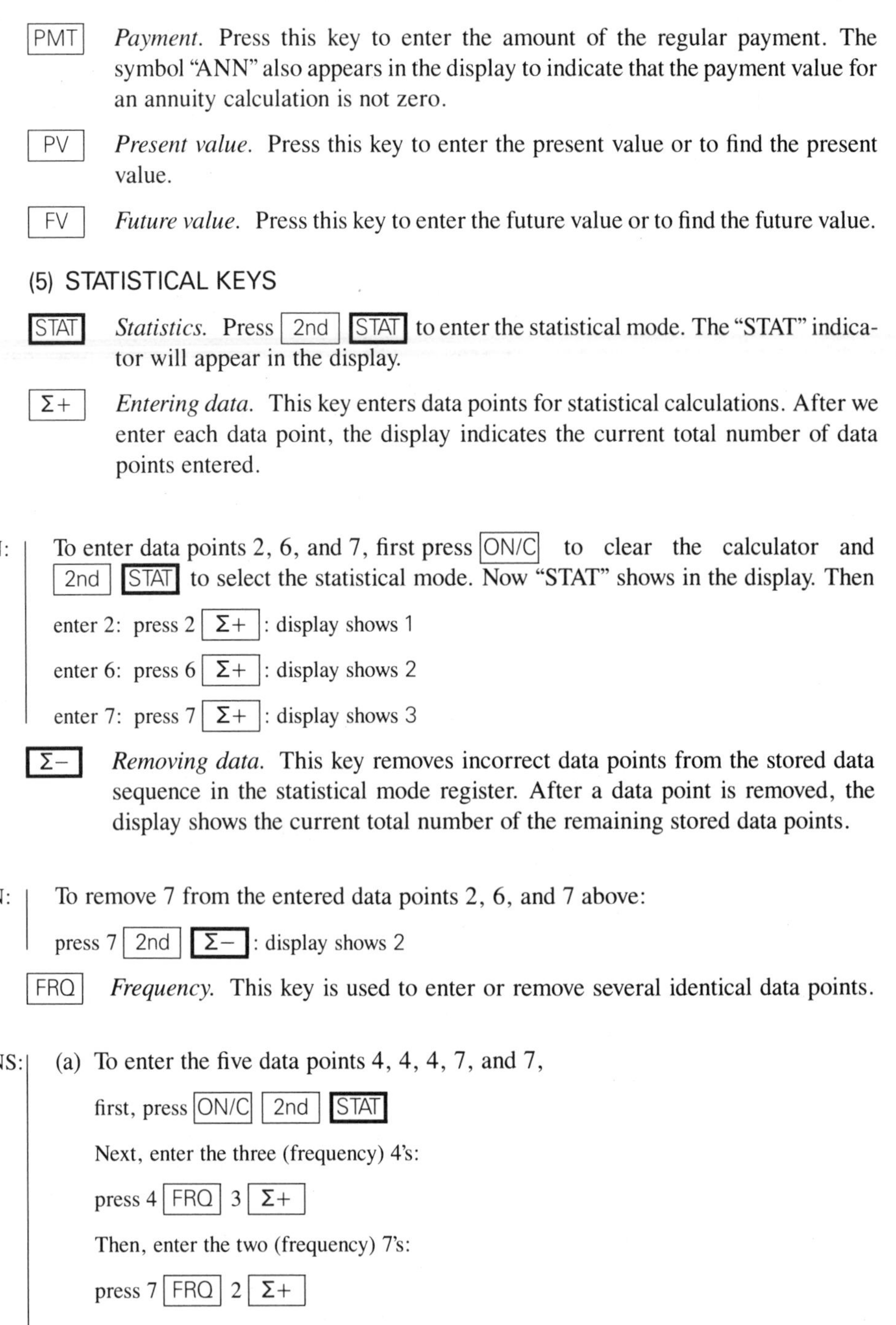

PMT *Payment.* Press this key to enter the amount of the regular payment. The symbol "ANN" also appears in the display to indicate that the payment value for an annuity calculation is not zero.

PV *Present value.* Press this key to enter the present value or to find the present value.

FV *Future value.* Press this key to enter the future value or to find the future value.

(5) STATISTICAL KEYS

STAT *Statistics.* Press 2nd STAT to enter the statistical mode. The "STAT" indicator will appear in the display.

Σ+ *Entering data.* This key enters data points for statistical calculations. After we enter each data point, the display indicates the current total number of data points entered.

ILLUSTRATION: To enter data points 2, 6, and 7, first press ON/C to clear the calculator and 2nd STAT to select the statistical mode. Now "STAT" shows in the display. Then

enter 2: press 2 Σ+ : display shows 1

enter 6: press 6 Σ+ : display shows 2

enter 7: press 7 Σ+ : display shows 3

Σ− *Removing data.* This key removes incorrect data points from the stored data sequence in the statistical mode register. After a data point is removed, the display shows the current total number of the remaining stored data points.

ILLUSTRATION: To remove 7 from the entered data points 2, 6, and 7 above:

press 7 2nd Σ− : display shows 2

FRQ *Frequency.* This key is used to enter or remove several identical data points.

ILLUSTRATIONS: (a) To enter the five data points 4, 4, 4, 7, and 7,

first, press ON/C 2nd STAT

Next, enter the three (frequency) 4's:

press 4 FRQ 3 Σ+

Then, enter the two (frequency) 7's:

press 7 FRQ 2 Σ+

Display shows 5 (total number of data points)

(b) To remove "7, 7" from the entered data points "4, 4, 4, 7, and 7" above,

press 7 [FRQ] 2 [2nd] [Σ−]

Display shows 3 (total number of remaining data points)

[$\overline{x}$] *Mean.* This key computes the arithmetic mean (average) of the entered data points.

[σ_n] *Standard deviation.* This key computes the standard deviation when the number of data points (n) is used as the divisor (for population data).

[σ_{n-1}] *Standard deviation.* This key computes the standard deviation when the number of data points minus one ($n - 1$) is used as the divisor (for sample data).

Applications of the statistical keys are demonstrated in the following examples.

EXAMPLE 1 Compute the mean and standard deviation for a group of individual values: 3, 4, 5, 10, and 13.

Step	*Key Pressing Sequence*	*Display*
1. Clear calculator	[ON/C]	0
2. Select statistical mode	[2nd] [STAT]	0 STAT
3. Enter the given data points	3 [Σ+], 4 [Σ+], 5 [Σ+], 10 [Σ+], 13 [Σ+]	5
4. Compute the mean	[$\overline{x}$]	7
5. Compute the standard deviation	[σ_n]	3.8470768
6. Compute the standard deviation	[σ_{n-1}]	4.3011626

Also see the detailed computation for $\overline{x} = 7$ and $\sigma_n = 3.85$ in Section 6.4 (Dispersion), Example 5.

EXAMPLE 2 Compute the mean and standard deviation for the following frequency distribution.

Wages	*Number of Workers (Frequency)*
\$ 2	1
5	2
8	3
11	8
14	4
Total	18

Solution:

Step	*Key Pressing Sequence*	*Display*
1. Clear calculator	[ON/C]	0
2. Select statistical mode	[2nd] [STAT]	0 STAT
3. Enter the given data	2 [FRQ] 1 [Σ+], 5 [FRQ] 2 [Σ+], 8 [FRQ] 3 [Σ+], 11 [FRQ] 8 [Σ+], 14 [FRQ] 4 [Σ+]	18
4. Compute the mean	[$\overline{x}$]	10
5. Compute the standard deviation	[σ_n]	3.3166248
6. Compute the standard deviation	[σ_{n-1}]	3.4127788

Also see the detailed computation for $\overline{x} = 10$ and $\sigma_n = 3.32$ in Section 6.5 (Frequency Distribution), Example 1.

(6) ALGEBRAIC KEYS

[Δ%] *Percent change.* This key computes the percent change (increase or decrease) of a number (P) based on another number (B).

EXAMPLE 3 In 1990, the total sales of a store were \$28,000; in 1991, sales were \$34,440. Find the percent change of 1991 sales based on 1990 sales.

Press [ON/C] 34440 [2nd] [Δ%] 28000 [=]

Display: 23

Answer: 23% increase.

The above computation is equivalent to:

$$\frac{P - B}{B} = \frac{34{,}440 - 28{,}000}{28{,}000} = .23 = 23\%$$

Also see the other illustration in Example 4, Section 2.11.

EXAMPLE 4 In 1991, the sales of a store were \$34,440; in 1992, sales were \$30,996. Find the percent change of 1992 sales based on 1991 sales.

Press [ON/C] 30996 [2nd] [Δ%] 34440 [=]

Display: −10

Answer: 10% decrease.

[ln x] *Natural logarithm.* This key computes the natural logarithm of the number x to base e. The symbol $ln\ x$ can also be written $log_e\ x$. (x cannot be negative or zero.)

EXAMPLE 5

Find ln 235.

Press [ON/C] 235 [2nd] [lnx]

Display: 5.4595855

Answer: ln 235 = 5.4595855.

The above answer can also be written

$e^{5.4595855} = 235$

$e = 2.7182818$, approximately.

NOTE:

$\ln x = \log_e x = 2.302826(\log_{10} x)$.

Thus, if $x = 235$, the value of ln 235 can be obtained from Table 2 as follows:

$$\begin{aligned}\ln 235 &= 2.302826(\log_{10} 235)\\ &= 2.302826(2.371068)\\ &= 5.460157 \text{ (approximately).}\end{aligned}$$

[e^x] *e to the power x.* This key is used to find the value of e^x.

EXAMPLE 6

Find e^2.

Press [ON/C] 2 [2nd] [e^x]

Display: 7.3890561

Answer: $e^2 = 7.3890561$.

EXAMPLE 7

Find $e^{5.4595855}$.

Press [ON/C] 5.4595855 [2nd] [e^x]

Display: 235

Answer: $e^{5.4595855} = 235$.

Thus, if $\ln x = 5.4595855$, $x = 235$. In other words, we find the "natural antilogarithm" of the value 5.4595855 to be the number 235.

[x^2] *x squared.* This key multiplies the displayed number by itself.

EXAMPLE 8

Find 15^2.

Press [ON/C] 15 [2nd] [x^2]

Display: 225

Answer: $15^2 = 225$.

[x!] *x factorial.* This key finds the factorial of the displayed number.

EXAMPLE 9

Find 5!

Press [ON/C] 5 [2nd] [x!]

Display: 120

Answer: $5! = 5 \times 4 \times 3 \times 2 \times 1 = 120$.

[%] *Percent.* This key divides the displayed number by 100.

EXAMPLE 10 Find the value of 25.8%.

Press [ON/C] 25.8 [%]

Display: 0.258 (Answer)

EXAMPLE 11 Find 15% of 400.

Press [ON/C] 400 [×] 15 [%] [=]

Display: 60 (Answer)

[1/x] *Reciprocal of x.* This key divides the displayed number into 1. The displayed number (x) cannot be zero.

EXAMPLE 12 Find 1/20.

Press [ON/C] 20 [1/x]

Display: 0.05 (Answer)

[y^x] *y to the power x.* This key can (1) raise a positive number y to a power x and (2) take the xth root of the number y.

EXAMPLE 13 Find 2^5.

Step	*Press*	*Display*
1. Clear calculator	[ON/C]	0
2. Enter y	2 [y^x]	2
3. Enter x	5	5
4. Find the answer	[=]	32

EXAMPLE 14 Find $\sqrt[7]{2,187}$.

Step	*Press*	*Display*
1. Clear calculator	[ON/C]	0
2. Enter y	2187 [y^x]	2187
3. Enter root x	7 [1/x]	0.1428571
4. Find the answer	[=]	3

[$\sqrt{x}$] *Square root of x.* This key is used to find the square root of the displayed number (x). The displayed number cannot be negative.

EXAMPLE 15 Find $\sqrt{144}$.

Press [ON/C] 144 [$\sqrt{x}$]

Display: 12 (Answer)

More applications of the business analyst calculator to financial problems will be discussed individually in later chapters.

EXERCISE 10–2 REFERENCE: SECTION 10.2

Find the values by using a business analyst calculator:

1. Compute (a) the mean ($\overline{X}$) and (b) the standard deviations (σ_n and σ_{n-1}) from: 8, 6, 12, 2, 18, 16, 15, 19.
2. Compute (a) the mean ($\overline{X}$) and (b) the standard deviations (σ_n and σ_{n-1}) from: 140, 174, 176, 146, 184, 130, 180, 230.
3. Compute (a) the mean ($\overline{X}$) and (b) the standard deviations (σ_n and σ_{n-1}) from the following frequency distribution:

Wages	*Number of Workers (Frequency)*
$ 4	2
7	3
10	4
13	10
16	2
Total	21

4. Compute (a) the mean ($\overline{X}$) and (b) the standard deviations (σ_n and σ_{n-1}) from the following frequency distribution:

Miles to School	*Number of Students (Frequency)*
3	1
8	3
13	5
18	5
23	3
28	1
Total	18

5. The price of a pound of beef was $3.84 in 1991 and $4.80 in 1992. What was the percent of change in 1992?
6. There were 1,200 girls last year and 1,560 this year in an elementary school. Find the percent of increase.
7. The price of a radio was $160 in 1991 and $152 in 1992. What was the percent of change in 1992?
8. There were 900 workers last year and 765 this year in a factory. Find the percent of decrease.
9. (a) ln 52 (b) ln 5.2
10. (a) ln 186 (b) ln 0.749
11. (a) e^3 (b) $e^{.16}$
12. (a) e^4 (b) $e^{.81}$
13. (a) 18^2 (b) 25^2
14. (a) 32^2 (b) 134^2
15. (a) 7! (b) 10!
16. (a) 12! (b) 9!
17. (a) 14.6% (b) 26.3% of $250

18. (a) 35.27% (b) 125.12% of \$650.24
19. (a) 1/25 (b) 1/15
20. (a) 1/125 (b) 1/250
21. (a) 3^4 (b) 8^5
22. (a) 10^3 (b) 2.3^8
23. (a) $\sqrt[3]{1{,}000}$ (b) $\sqrt[5]{1{,}024}$
24. (a) $\sqrt[4]{16}$ (b) $\sqrt[6]{15{,}625}$
25. (a) $\sqrt{256}$ (b) $\sqrt{20{,}164}$
26. (a) $\sqrt{625}$ (b) $\sqrt{158.4326}$

10.3 COMPUTERS BY TIME-SHARING TERMINALS—USING BASIC PROGRAMS

BASIC (Beginner's All-purpose Symbolic Instruction Code) is a type of computer language that can be used for giving instructions to a computer. An individual instruction is called a *statement* or *command*. A set of related statements one gives to a computer is called a *program*. The process of determining the statements in a program for a computer to execute a desired operation is called *programming*.

BASIC is simple and easy to learn. It was initially developed for computer users at time-sharing terminals in the mid-1960s. Time-sharing is a method of using a computer by terminals that serve many persons at the same time. A terminal has a keyboard device similar to a typewriter and a visual display device or printer. Each user of the terminal may input data to the computer by the keyboard and receive output from the computer by the display or printer. A computer center with time-sharing terminals is shown in Figure 10–3.

There are various types of computers manufactured by many different companies. To describe the details of the physical appearances, speeds, memory capacities, and operation-related matters of the numerous types of computers is impractical for this book. Here we will concentrate on explaining the general procedures required to (1) operate a computer—to get access to the computer for solving problems by using BASIC, and (2) write various types of BASIC programs—to instruct the computer in executing desired operations. First, we will describe the procedure for operating a computer from a time-sharing terminal. Other procedures will be presented in the next two sections.

PROCEDURE FOR OPERATING A COMPUTER FROM A TIME-SHARING TERMINAL

STEP (1). *Turn on the power to connect the terminal to the computer.* This may also involve dialing a phone number through a communication device called a *modem* to make a connection with the computer.

STEP (2). *Log on the computer.* The computer generally requires you to log on (or sign on) with your previously and specially assigned information:

Figure 10–3 A Computer Center with Time-Sharing Terminals

Photo courtesy of Xerox Corporation

(a) Identification number and/or name
(b) Password

Type the input requested by the computer, such as:

Identification number: 31206, 61001
Password: ABETIN (not shown on the display for security reasons).

STEP (3). *Select the programming language.* After the log-on information is accepted, the computer is ready to respond to your commands. Some computers provide multiple languages. You must thus indicate the programming language that you will use. If you select BASIC, the first command will be:

BASIC

The computer will respond after each step with a message or a word, such as

READY

STEP (4). *Indicate the type of program: NEW, OLD, LIB.* After the language is selected, the computer may need to know whether this is a new program to be entered, an old program previously stored, or a request for an existing program from its library. Accordingly, you may wish to enter a new program and type the command:

NEW

STEP (5). *Give a file name to your new program.* If the name "PATSUE" is appropriate, type:

PATSUE

STEP (6). *Enter your new BASIC program.* You may now type the program, statement by statement, on separate lines, as follows:

Line	Statement	RETURN key
10	LET A = 2	RETURN
20	LET B = 3	RETURN
30	LET C = A + B	RETURN
40	PRINT C	RETURN
50	END	RETURN

NOTE:

(a) Every BASIC statement entered must have a number. No two statements will ever have the same number. If two statements have the same number entered, such as

10 LET A = 1
10 LET A = 2

then the second statement will replace the first statement in the memory. In other words,

10 LET A = 1

will be eliminated from the program.

(b) The lines must be numbered in the order they are to be run by the computer. Lines are normally numbered by 10's or 100's. This is done so that the programmer can add lines in the middle of the program later if needed, such as inserting line 15 between lines 10 and 20.

(c) On most computers it is necessary to press the

RETURN

key at the end of each line of input. Otherwise, the computer may fail to respond to your input.

STEP (7). *List your program, if you desire.* If there are replacements or corrections, or your typed statement lines are not arranged in the proper numeric order, such as

10 LET A = 1
10 LET A = 2 (replacement)

20 LG←ET B + ← = 3 (correction)

40 PRINT C
30 LET C = A + B } (not in numeric order)

50 END

you may wish to view the entire program in a simple and orderly form. Then type the command:

LIST

The computer now shows the following in the display:

```
10 LET A=2
20 LET B=3
30 LET C=A+B
40 PRINT C
50 END
```

STEP (8). *Execute your program.* When you have your entire program entered into the computer storage, you may order the computer to execute your program by typing the command:

RUN

The result of the execution for the program listed in Steps 6 and 7 will be shown in the display or in printed form:

5

Thus, C = A + B = 2 + 3 = 5

STEP (9). *Save the program.* If you wish to save the program for later use, type the command SAVE and the name of your program:

SAVE PATSUE

This program is then saved on a diskette or tape and can be loaded again at any time by requesting:

OLD, PATSUE

STEP (10). *Log off (or sign off) the computer.* When you have finished with your program execution and wish to sign off the computer, type the command:

BYE

The computer will then print or show in the display your usage statistics and terminate your connection to the computer.

The ten steps of the procedure for operating a computer terminal given above are not specific to any particular computer system. These steps only demonstrate in a general way how a user usually enters and runs a BASIC program on a time-sharing terminal. For a particular computer system, the user should consult a manual, other written instructions, or knowledgeable persons from the local computer center for detailed operational procedures in order to use the system efficiently.

10.4 PERSONAL COMPUTERS—USING BASIC PROGRAMS

A personal computer (or *microcomputer*), like a time-sharing terminal, also has a keyboard for input and a display device or printer for output. In addition, a personal computer may have a disk drive for reading and writing information on a magnetic diskette for repeated use or a cassette tape recorder for input and output. A personal computer system is shown in Figure 10–4.

Since the BASIC language is simple and easy to learn, it has now become the primary language used by personal computers. To enter and run a BASIC program on a personal computer is a relatively simple task. The procedure for operating a personal computer illustrated here is based on the Apple® IIe system with a disk drive, manufactured by Apple Computer, Inc.[1]

Figure 10–4 A Personal Computer System. Left: Printer. Right: Display screen (top); disk drives (middle); computer, including processor and main memory (bottom back); and keyboard (bottom front).

PROCEDURE FOR OPERATING A PERSONAL COMPUTER

STEP (1). *Start up the system.*

(a) Gently insert the "startup disk" into the slot of the disk drive. The startup disk to use

[1]Apple II Plus, Apple IIe, Apple IIc, Apple IIGS, Applesoft, and the Apple logo are registered trademarks of Apple Computer, Inc.

for our illustration is called the "DOS (Disk Operating System) 3.3 SYSTEM MASTER disk."

(b) Turn on the TV set or video monitor and let it warm up for a few moments.

(c) Turn on the computer. The disk drive's IN USE light will come on, and the drive will make whirring and clicking sounds for a while as the disk is read. When the operating instructions on the disk have been loaded into main memory, the disk drive will stop, and a *prompt* and a *cursor* will appear on the display screen.

] □ ←The cursor.

↑ The prompt. It indicates that we are conversing with the Applesoft BASIC interpreter. (An interpreter is a translator that translates the entered program into computer machine language.)

STEP (2). *Enter your new BASIC program.* When the prompt] and cursor □ appear on the screen, the display indicates that the DOS is in memory and is ready for your BASIC commands. Type your program, statement by statement, on separate lines, pressing the RETURN key after each line, as stated in Step 6 of the procedure for a time-sharing terminal in Section 10.3. Your typed program will look like this on the display screen:

```
]10 LET A=2

]20 LET B=3

]30 LET C=A+B

]40 PRINT C

]50 END
```

STEP (3). *List your program, if you desire.* Type the command (also see Step 7 for the time-sharing terminal):

LIST

The display screen will show:

```
10 LET A=2
20 LET B=3
30 LET C=A+B
40 PRINT C
50 END
```

Notice that the prompt sign] has disappeared from each line.

STEP (4). *Execute your program.* Type the command:

RUN

The display screen will show:

5

(Same as in Step 8 for the time-sharing terminal.)

STEP (5). *Sign off the computer.* Turn off the power and TV or video monitor. Remember, however, that all your current work in memory will be lost.

Basically, the five steps of the procedure for operating the Apple® IIe personal computer system should also be applicable to other types of personal computers, such as IBM® and Tandy® personal computers.[2] Nevertheless, the user should consult a manual, or other written instructions, and the local computer dealer for detailed operational procedures in order to use the particular personal computer system effectively.

10.5 WRITING BASIC STATEMENTS (PROGRAMMING)

BASIC statements consist of various specific symbols, expressions, words, and abbreviations. The common ones used in this book are listed below.

A. Operation Symbols

BASIC Symbol	Operation	Application Example	
		BASIC Statement	Arithmetic and Algebraic Equivalent
+	Addition	A + B 1 + 2	A + B 1 + 2
–	Subtraction	C – D 4 – 3	C – D 4 – 3
* (asterisk)	Multiplication	E * F 5 * 6	E × F 5 × 6
/ (slash)	Division	G/H 7/8	G ÷ H 7 ÷ 8
∧ or ↑	Exponentiation	X∧2 9∧3	X^2 9^3
( )	Grouping	(2 + 3) * 7	(2 + 3) × 7 = 35

In performing BASIC arithmetic operations, the computer first performs any operations enclosed in parentheses ( ).

Thus,

(2 + 3) * 6 = 5 * 6 = 30
12/(2 * 3) = 12/6 = 2
(25 – 15)/5 = 10/5 = 2

In general, if there is no grouping symbol, the computer performs multiplications and divisions before additions and subtractions.

Thus,

2 + 3 * 6 = 2 + 18 = 20
3 * 4/2 * 3 = 12/2 * 3 = 6 * 3 = 18
25 – 15/5 = 25 – 3 = 22

[2]IBM is a registered trademark of International Business Machines Corporation.
Tandy is a registered trademark of the Radio Shack Division of Tandy Corporation.

B. Relation Symbols

BASIC Symbol	Relation	Application Example
=	Equal to	A = B (A is equal to B)
<	Less than	C < D (C is less than D)
>	Greater than	E > F (E is greater than F)
< =	Less than or equal to	G < = 3 (G is less than or equal to 3)
> =	Greater than or equal to	H > = 2 (H is greater than or equal to 2)
< >	Not equal to	K < > 0 (K is not equal to 0)

C. Function Abbreviations

BASIC Abbreviation	Function	Application Example	
		BASIC Statement	Algebraic Equivalent
EXP(X)	e^x (Base e = 2.718281, with exponent x)	EXP(2)	$e^2 = 7.38905610$
LOG(X)	Natural logarithm of x $[\log_e x = 2.302826(\log_{10} x)]$	LOG(1.05)	$\log_e 1.05 = 0.0488$
SQR(X)	Square root of x ($\sqrt{x}$)	SQR(9)	$\sqrt{9} = 3$

D. Command Words

ILLUSTRATION 1: Using the words: LET, PRINT, and END.

EXAMPLE 1

$2 + 3 = ?$

$? = 5$

BASIC Program	Computer Display
10 LET A=2	5
20 LET B=3	
30 LET C=A+B	
40 PRINT C	
50 END	

Solution: C = 5

This is the same program as the one presented on page 315. The statements in the program are executed (RUN) by the computer in sequence from the top line (10) to the bottom line (50). First, the word LET commands the computer to assign value 2 to storage location A in statement 10. Likewise, value 3 is assigned to location B in statement 20. Then statement 30 performs the desired calculation (A + B) and assigns the result to location C. The word PRINT in statement 40 commands the computer to print the information stored in C. The very last statement, 50, commands the computer to END the program.

NOTE: Each statement in a BASIC program begins with a line number. The line numbers may range from 1 to 63,999. However, it is generally desirable to number the statements in increments of 10, since we may wish to insert some additional instructions or modifications at a later time.

ILLUSTRATION 2: Using the words: READ and DATA.

EXAMPLE 2

The program given in Example 1 could have been written in the following manner by using the READ and DATA statements:

BASIC Program

```
10 READ A, B
20 DATA 2, 3
30 LET C=A+B
40 PRINT C
50 END
```

Computer Display

```
5
```

Solution: C = 5

The computer implements the READ command by assigning the values listed in the DATA statements to the variables listed in the READ statements, in their respective order. Thus, if READ statements are used in a BASIC program, there must be one or more DATA statements.

Here, the computer reads A and B in statement 10 and assigns the value 2 to A and the value 3 to B from DATA statement 20.

NOTE: The letters A and B were used as variable names in statement 10 above. In general, single letters (A to Z) or single letters followed by one digit (0 to 9) may be used to denote variables, such as A, B, C, D1, S5, Z3, and so on.

The values in a DATA statement and the variables in a READ statement are separated by commas.

ILLUSTRATION 3: Using the words: GO TO.

EXAMPLE 3

$$15 \times 3 = ?$$
$$? = 45$$
$$20 \times 10 = ?$$
$$? = 200$$

BASIC Program

```
┌10 READ A, B
│20 LET C=A*B
│30 PRINT "PRODUCT IS"; C
└40 GOTO 10
 50 DATA 15, 3, 20, 10
 60 END
```

Computer Display

```
PRODUCT IS 45
PRODUCT IS 200
? OUT OF DATA
```

Solution: C = 45
C = 200

In reading statement 10, the computer first assigns values 15 and 3 in the DATA statement 50 to A and B, respectively. When it reaches line 40, the GOTO 10 statement will cause the computer to go back to line 10 and repeat the calculation for additional numbers. The READ statement then assigns values 20 and 10 to A and B, respectively. The computer will continue to *loop* back through the program until the numbers given in the DATA statement are exhausted. The computer then prints an error message, such as OUT OF DATA, as shown in the display above.

NOTE: In a PRINT statement, such as "PRODUCT IS" in statement 30, everything within quotation marks is printed exactly as typed.

The DATA statement in this program is placed on line 50. If the DATA statement is moved to line 15, or to any line after the READ statement, the result of the program is not affected by the changed location.

ILLUSTRATION 4: Using the words: IF. . . THEN. . . .

EXAMPLE 4

15 ÷ 3 = ? 20 ÷ 10 = ?
? = 5 ? = 2
5 ÷ 0 = ?
? = none

BASIC Program

```
┌10 READ A, B
│15 IF B=0 THEN 10
│20 LET C=A/B
│30 PRINT "QUOTIENT IS"; C
└40 GOTO 10
 50 DATA 15, 3, 5, 0, 20, 10
 60 END
```

Computer Display

```
QUOTIENT IS 5
QUOTIENT IS 2
? OUT OF DATA
```

Solution: C = 5
C = none
C = 2

The general form of the IF. . . THEN. . . statement is:

IF (condition occurs) THEN (statement number),

such as statement 15: IF (B = 0) THEN (10).

This statement will cause the computer to jump out of the normal program sequence if the stated condition occurs. Notice that in reading statement 10 on the second time through the loop in the program, variables A and B assume the values 5 and 0, respectively. When statement 15 is then executed, the fact that B = 0 will cause the computer to jump to statement 10 again. The division A/B = 5/0 is not carried out by the computer.

ILLUSTRATION 5: Using the word: REM.

EXAMPLE 5

70 + 82 + 90 + 93 + 65 = ? 400 ÷ 5 = ?
? = 400 ? = 80

BASIC Program

```
   5 REM—STUDENT GRADES
  10 LET S=0
  20 LET C=0
 ┌30 READ G
 │40 IF G=0 THEN 80
 │50 LET S=S+G
 │60 LET C=C+1
 └70 GOTO 30
  80 PRINT "SUM OF GRADES=";
     S,"NUMBER OF GRADES=";
     C, "AVERAGE="; S/C
  90 DATA 70, 82, 90, 93, 65
 100 DATA 0
 110 END
```

Computer Display

```
SUM OF GRADES=400
NUMBER OF GRADES=5
AVERAGE=80
```

Solution: S = 400
S/C = 80, while C = 5

Note: If more spaces are desired after the = signs in the display or print, the spaces should be provided between the = and " signs in the statement, line 80, such as "SUM OF GRADES =   "; S,.

The word REM represents "remark." The REM statement in a BASIC program is not executed by the computer. We may insert a REM statement in any location of a program to explain or remark on some other statement, such as using statement 5 to remark that the program concerns student grades.

The variable S is used to accumulate the sum of the grades. S is initially set equal to zero in statement 10. The computer then reads a data item G in statement 30. The first value for G is 70. Statement 40 checks to see if G is equal to zero. The indication G = 0, also called a *sentinel*, tells the computer that the sequence of numbers to be read in the program has reached the end. Since at first G has the value 70, statement 50 is executed. Here the sum S = S + G = 0 + 70 = 70. Then the computer goes back to statement 30 to repeat the process. The loop repeats the process for values 82, 90, 93, and 65, the remaining four values. Finally, the computer reads a data value G equal to zero. The fact that G = 0 will cause the computer to execute statement 40 and jump to statement 80, which will print the information as requested.

The variable C is used as a counter to count the number of values or grades. C also is initially set equal to zero in statement 20. By adding statement 60, we can add 1 to C each time through the loop. Finally, C = 5, which represents the number of grades.

NOTE: If a particular number value is to serve as a sentinel, such as zero or G = 0 in the above program, then the selected value must be outside the range of the data. In our program, zero is outside the range of 65 to 93.

In the PRINT statement 80, both commas and semicolons are used to separate the listed items. Semicolons instruct the computer to print the items closer than do the commas.

ILLUSTRATION 6: Using the words: FOR and NEXT.

EXAMPLE 6 Find the squares and square roots of values 1 to 6.

BASIC Program

```
 5 REM—SQUARES AND SQUARE ROOTS
┌10 FOR X=1 TO 6
│20 PRINT X, X∧2, SQR(X)
└30 NEXT X
 40 END
```

Computer Display

1	1	1
2	4	1.41421356
3	9	1.73205081
4	16	2
5	25	2.23606798
6	36	2.44948974
↑	↑	↑
X	X^2	$\sqrt{X}$

(Solution)

The FOR and NEXT statements must be used together to form a loop. The FOR statement is used to open the loop and is placed at the beginning of the loop, while the NEXT statement is used to close the loop and is located at the end of the loop. The statement or statements that are between the FOR and NEXT statements are executed repeatedly.

Statement 10 in the above program requests the computer to print the values in statement 20 for every X value from 1 to 6, as shown in the display. If we change statement 10 to:

```
10 FOR X=1 TO 6 STEP 2
```

the computer calculation will begin with X = 1 and then repeat for X = 3 (or 1 + 2) and X = 5 (or 3 + 2). When no STEP is specified, the computer will automatically use the step size of +1, as in the original program.

ILLUSTRATION 7: Using the word: INPUT.

EXAMPLE 7

A + B = C

(1) A = 2
B = 3
C = ?

(2) A = 7
B = 9
C = ?

BASIC Program

```
10 INPUT A, B
20 LET C=A+B
30 PRINT C
40 END
```

Computer Display

(1)		(2)	
?	2	?	7
?	3	?	9
5		16	

Solution: (1) C = 5
(2) C = 16

The program shown in Example 2 is rewritten for this example. The old READ and DATA statements are replaced by the new INPUT statement 10. With the INPUT statement, the data is furnished externally, by the user, at appropriate times during the running of the program. In display (1), the typed values 2 and 3 are the user's responses to the computer's inquiries: the first "?" for A and the second "?" for B, respectively. Likewise, in display (2), the typed values 7 and 9 are the user's responses to the first "?" for A and the second "?" for B, respectively.

Through the use of the INPUT statement, a program can be constructed for repeated calculations for different input, such as data (1) and (2) in Example 7.

EXERCISE 10–3 REFERENCE: SECTIONS 10.3 to 10.5

Write BASIC programs, using the given command words, for Problems 1–14:

Problem	*Required Command Words*
1. 4 + 7 = ?	LET, PRINT, END
2. 6 + 9 + 21 = ?	LET, PRINT, END
3. 68 + 124 = ?	READ, DATA
4. 2 + 13 + 75 = ?	READ, DATA

Problem	*Required Command Words*
5. (a) $5 \times 16 = ?$ (b) $7 \times 25 = ?$ (c) $8 \times 30 = ?$	GOTO
6. (a) $2 \times 14 \times 42 = ?$ (b) $6 \times 12 \times 56 = ?$	GOTO
7. (a) $20 \div 4 = ?$ (b) $35 \div 0 = ?$ (c) $60 \div 12 = ?$	IF. . .THEN. . .
8. (a) $10 \div 2 = ?$ (b) $25 \div 0 = ?$ (c) $48 \div 6 = ?$ (d) $120 \div 20 = ?$	IF. . .THEN. . .
9. Find (a) sum of wages, (b) number of wages, and (c) average wage from the following data. Wages: \$5.20, \$4.10, \$6.50, \$12.30, \$15.25, and \$24.81.	REM
10. Find (a) sum of miles, (b) number of employees, and (c) average miles traveled from the following data. Miles traveled by employees: 13.5, 17.2, 18.3, 20.1, 22.8, 25.6, 26.3, and 28.2.	REM
11. Find the squares and square roots of values 4 to 8.	FOR, NEXT
12. Find the cubes and square roots of values 1, 3, 5, and 7.	FOR, NEXT
13. $A + B = C$ (a) $A = 5$ and $B = 6$. $C = ?$ (b) $A = 9$ and $B = 12$. $C = ?$	INPUT
14. $A + B + C = D$ (a) $A = 7$, $B = 10$, and $C = 18$. $D = ?$ (b) $A = 3$, $B = 8$, and $C = 30$. $D = ?$	INPUT

15. Use a time-sharing terminal and your BASIC programs to find the answers for Problems 1–14.
16. Use a personal computer and your BASIC programs to find the answers for Problems 1–14.

10.6 APPLICATIONS OF ELECTRONIC SPREADSHEETS

A large sheet of paper, printed with column and row lines, is frequently used by an accountant for preparing or analyzing financial information. This idea is used in developing electronic spreadsheets to be used by microcomputers and larger computers.

Basically, the spreadsheet program is represented electronically in the computer's memory by reading the disk of the program. (See Step (1)—start up the system, in the procedure for operating a personal computer, page 314.) A typical spreadsheet on a computer screen is shown in Figure 10-5. The intersections of the columns and rows are called *cells*, such as Cell E4 located in the column E and row 4 intersection. The computer user places numeric data or text information in these cells. Then the user can manipulate the information and perform mathematical operations, without studying computer languages and programming.

Figure 10–5 A Typical Spreadsheet Seen on a Microcomputer Screen

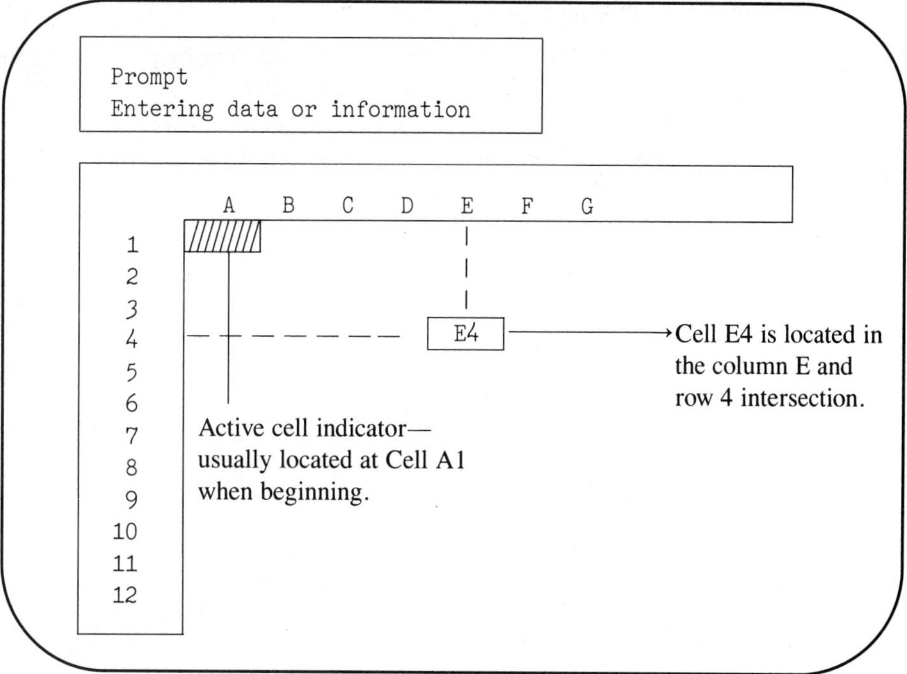

Our interest in introducing spreadsheets here is to find another effective way to compute the investment problems in this book. Today, hundreds of spreadsheet packages appear on the market, such as *VisiCalc*, *Lotus 1-2-3*, and *Excel*. The examples illustrated below are used to show the use of spreadsheets for computation in a general way.

EXAMPLE 1

Find the amount S from the formula $S = P(1 + i)^n$.

Let P = Principal = \$10,000
i = Interest rate = 1%
n = Number of periods = 3

(Also see example 1 of Section 11.7.)

Solution:

First, gently insert the spreadsheet disk into the slot of the disk drive as illustrated in Step (1) of the *Procedure for Operating a Personal Computer*, page 314. Follow the instructions shown on the computer screen to locate the spreadsheet (Figure 10-5). Then, press keys on the keyboard to enter data or instructions into the computer. In each step of entry, we need to press three types of keys:

(a) An arrow key (↑ up, ↓ down, → right, ← left) to move the cell indicator (a screen bar [//////]) to a selected location. For example, move the indicator from cell A1 to cell A2 by pressing the down key ↓.

(b) Enter the data or instructions. For example, enter $10,000 by pressing the 1, 0, 0, 0, 0 keys.

(c) Place the entered data inside the indicator by pressing the RETURN key. Now [10000] is shown on the computer screen.

The order of pressing the keys to obtain the final answer to this problem is shown below. The final answer as shown in cell A5 is $10,303.01.

Solution by Spreadsheet:

Step	*Press Key(s)*		*Computer Display* A	B	C
		1	[//////]	Cell indicator at the beginning location: cell A1.	
1. Enter $10,000 (Principal)	(a) ↓ (b) 10000 (c) Return	2	10000		
2. Enter 1% (Interest rate)	(a) ↓ (b) .01 (c) Return	3	.01		
3. Enter 3 (Periods)	(a) ↓ (b) 3 (c) Return	4	3		
4. Enter the formula: $10{,}000(1 + 1\%)^3$	(a) ↓ (b) +A2 * (1 + A3)^A4 (c) Return	5	10303.01		

NOTE: The formula in Step 4 may also be written: +A2 * A3 * A3 * A3, if the spreadsheet has no "raising to powers" capability. Here, the original A3 (=.01) and A4 (=3) must be replaced by the new A3 (=1.01 or 1 + 1%).

EXAMPLE 2 Find the amount S_n from the formula $S_n = R.\ \frac{(1+i)^n - 1}{i}$.

Let R = Payment = $100
i = Interest rate = 1%
n = Number of periods or payments = 4

(Also see Example 1 of Section 13.8.)

Solution:

The basic procedure for using the spreadsheet in this problem is the same as that for Example 1 above. The order of pressing the keys to obtain the final answer to this problem is shown below. The final answer as shown in cell B4 is \$406.04.

Observe that the cells in the B column are used here to compute this problem. If we wish, we can easily enter the corresponding terms into column A for describing the numbers in column B (i.e., payment to A1, interest to A2, periods to A3, and amount to A4).

Solution by Spreadsheet:

Step	*Press Key(s)*	*Computer Display*			
			A	B	C
1. Enter \$100 (Payment)	(a) → (b) 100 (c) Return	1	//////	100	
2. Enter 1% (Interest rate)	(a) ↓ (b) .01 (c) Return	2		.01	
3. Enter 4 (Periods and Payments)	(a) ↓ (b) 4 (c) Return	3		4	
4. Enter the formula: $100 \cdot \frac{(1 + 1\%)^4 - 1}{1\%}$	(a) ↓ (b) +B1 * ((1 + B2)^B3 − 1)/B2 (c) Return	4		406.04	

NOTE: The formula in Step 4 may also be written as

+B2 * B2 * B2 * B2−1/.01 * B1

if the spreadsheet has no "raising to powers" capability. Here, the original B2 (=.01) and B3 (=4) must be replaced by the new B2 (=1.01 or 1 + 1%).

EXERCISE 10–4 REFERENCE: SECTION 10.6

Use a personal computer and spreadsheet program disk to find the answers to the following problems (use the BASIC symbols +, −, * (×), / (÷), ^ (raising to powers), and ( ), for the mathematical operations):

1. $5 + 16$
2. $8 + 20 - 14$
3. $45 - 18 + 27$
4. $124 + 268 - 57$
5. 4×18
6. 120×324
7. $246 \div 12$
8. $638 \div 125$
9. $15(24 + 56)$
10. $27(11 + 24)$
11. $560(1 + 5\%)^6$
12. $248(1 + 12\%)^4$
13. $150 \cdot \frac{(1 + 2\%)^3 - 1}{2\%}$
14. $600 \cdot \frac{(1 + 6\%)^5 - 1}{6\%}$

11 COMPOUND INTEREST—COMPUTING BASIC VALUES

The term *compound interest* was introduced in Chapter 8. It was stated that when the interest for each period is added to the principal in computing the interest for the next period, it is called compound interest. This chapter first introduces the general terms and the basic method of computing compound interest (Sections 11.1 and 11.2). It then introduces the methods of finding the compound amount (Section 11.3), the present value and compound discount (Section 11.4), the interest rate (Section 11.5), and the number of conversion periods (Section 11.6). In addition, this chapter illustrates, as supplemental material, the method of computing the formulas in the chapter by calculators and computers (Section 11.7).

11.1 BASIC CONCEPT AND TERMINOLOGY

This chapter introduces the method of computing interest and related values based on the concept of *compounding* interest. The compound interest method is generally used in long-term borrowing. There is usually more than one period for computing interest during the borrowing time. The interest for each period is added (compounded or converted) to the principal before the interest for the next period is computed. The final sum at the end of the period of borrowing is called the *compound amount*.

The process of accumulating a principal to obtain a compound amount is called *compound accumulation*. *Compound interest* is the difference between the original principal and the compound amount. The period for computing interest, usually at regularly stated intervals such as annually, semiannually, quarterly, or monthly, is called the *conversion period*, or the *interest period*. The interest rate per conversion period is equal to the stated annual interest rate divided by the number of conversion periods in one year. The stated annual interest rate is called the *nominal annual rate*, or simply the *nominal rate*. Thus, if the nominal rate is 12%, the interest rate for the annual conversion period is also 12%; but, if the conversion period is semiannual, the interest rate for a period of six months is 12%/2, or 6%.

11.2 BASIC METHOD OF COMPUTING COMPOUND INTEREST

The basic method of computing compound interest for *each* conversion period is the same as the method of computing simple interest. Thus, if there is only one conversion period, compound interest is the same as simple interest. The following example illustrates the method of computing compound interest in general.

EXAMPLE 1

What are the compound amount and the compound interest at the end of nine months if $10,000 is borrowed at 4% compounded quarterly?

The original principal is $10,000.

The conversion period is one quarter, or three months.

The number of conversion periods in nine months is $\frac{9 \text{ months}}{3 \text{ months}} = 3$.

The interest rate per conversion period is

$$\frac{\text{Annual interest rate}}{\text{Number of conversion periods in one year}} = \frac{4\%}{4} = 1\%$$

The computation is written as follows:

Original principal	$10,000.00	
Add: Interest for the 1st quarter..........	100.00	= $10,000 × 1%
Principal at the end of 1st quarter..........	$10,100.00	
Add: Interest for the 2d quarter	101.00	= $10,100 × 1%
Principal at the end of 2d quarter	$10,201.00	
Add: Interest for the 3d quarter	102.01	= $10,201 × 1%
Principal at the end of 3d quarter, or the compound amount................	$10,303.01	

Compound interest = Compound amount − Original principal

= 10,303.01 − 10,000 = $303.01

The simple interest at 4% on $10,000 for nine months is

$10,000 \times 4\% \times \frac{9}{12} = \$300$

In Example 1 the compound interest is greater than the simple interest by

$303.01 - 300 = \$3.01$

EXERCISE 11–1 REFERENCE: SECTION 11.2

A. Find the compound amount and the compound interest in each of the following problems:

1. $200 for one year at 10% compounded semiannually.
2. $500 for two years at 16% compounded annually.
3. $3,000 for six months at 12% compounded quarterly.
4. $2,000 for two months at 6% compounded monthly.
5. $1,000 for three years at 20% compounded annually.
6. $5,000 for one year at 8% compounded quarterly.

7. $15,000 for three months at 12% compounded monthly.
8. $40,000 for $1\frac{1}{2}$ years at 8% compounded semiannually.

B. Statement problems:

9. (a) Find the simple interest on $200 for one year at 10%. (b) What is the difference between the simple interest and the answer in Problem 1?
10. (a) What is the simple interest on $500 for two years at 16% interest rate? (b) Compare the simple interest with the compound interest in Problem 2, and find the difference.
11. (a) What is the simple interest on $3,000 for six months at a simple interest rate of 12%? (b) Compare the simple interest with the compound interest in Problem 3, and find the difference.
12. (a) Find the simple interest on $2,000 for two months at 6%. (b) What is the difference between the simple interest and the answer in Problem 4?

11.3 FINDING THE COMPOUND AMOUNT BY FORMULA

To find the compound amount by formula, we shall use the following symbols:

Let P = original principal
i = interest rate per conversion period
n = number of conversion periods
S = compound amount, or the principal at the end of the nth period

The compound amount formula is

$$S = P(1 + i)^n \qquad \textbf{(11–1)}$$ [1]

---

[1] *Proof–Formula (11–1):*

In Example 1 of Section 11.2, let

the original principal $10,000 = P
the interest rate per quarter (conversion period) = i

The computation in Example 1 may be written symbolically as follows:

Original principal	P
Add: Interest (1st quarter)	$(+)\ Pi$
Principal (1st quarter end).	$P(1 + i)$
Add: Interest (2d quarter).	$(+)\ P(1 + i)i$
Principal (2d quarter end)	$P(1 + i)(1 + i) = P(1 + i)^2$
Add: Interest (3d quarter).	$(+)P(1 + i)^2 i$
Principal (3d quarter, end)	$P(1 + i)^2(1 + i) = P(1 + i)^3$

When this idea is extended, the compound amount at the end of the nth period may be expressed as

$S = P(1 + i)^n$

EXAMPLE 1 What is the compound amount at the end of nine months if \$10,000 is borrowed at 4% compounded quarterly?

$P = 10{,}000$, $i = 1\%$ (per quarter), and $n = 3$ (quarters)

Substituting these values in the compound amount formula,

$$\begin{aligned} S = P(1 + i)^n &= 10{,}000(1 + 1\%)^3 \\ &= 10{,}000(1.01)(1.01)(1.01) \\ &= 10{,}000(1.030301) \\ &= \$10{,}303.01 \end{aligned}$$

The answer may be compared with the answer in Example 1 of the preceding section.

When the value of n in formula (11–1) becomes large, considerable time is required in calculating the value of the factor $(1 + i)^n$. For convenience, the most common values of $(1 + i)^n$ are tabulated in Tables 5 and 5A in the Appendix. In Table 5, the numbers of the conversion periods are whole numbers; that is, n is a round number, such as 1, 2, 3, and so on. In Table 5A, the numbers of the conversion periods are fractional numbers; that is, n is a fraction, such as $\frac{1}{2}$, $\frac{1}{3}$, $\frac{1}{4}$, and is generally represented by $1/m$. Each of the values (entries) in the tables is the compound amount when the principal is 1.

Symbolically, let s = the compound amount S when the principal is 1. Then the formula becomes

$$s = S = P(1 + i)^n = 1(1 + i)^n, \quad \text{or} \quad s = (1 + i)^n$$

The unit value of each entry may best be represented by a dollar, although it may be represented by any other unit. Thus, each entry in the tables becomes the compound amount in dollars when the principal is \$1. The factor $(1 + i)^n$ is also frequently referred to as the *accumulation factor* in computing a compound amount.

The methods of computing a compound amount by using the compound amount formula and the tables are illustrated below.

A. Use of Table 5

When Table 5 is used, formula (11–1) may be written as follows:

Compound amount (S) = Principal (P) × An entry in Table 5

(The entry is at the interest rate i per conversion period for n conversion periods.)

Tables 5 through 11 (the compound interest and annuity tables) provide 8 decimal places for each entry. It is obvious that it would be a waste of time if all 8 places were employed in multiplying a multiplicand of a small value. In most financial problems, the answers are required to contain dollars and cents. In order to avoid unnecessary multiplication and at the same time to obtain a result close enough to the exact value, a simple rule is used in this text:

If an answer is to be computed to the nearest cent, the minimum number of decimal places to be multiplied is equal to the number of digits in the multiplicand, including dollars and cents.

For example, in finding a compound amount if the principal is \$250.10, which has three dollar-digits (250) and two cent-digits (.10), an entry in Table 5 containing five decimal places is employed in multiplication.

Hereafter, unless otherwise specified, the words "interest" and "amount" mean compound interest and compound amount, respectively, and the interest rate expressed by % means the nominal annual rate.

EXAMPLE 2 Find the amount of \$1,500 invested at 12% compounded quarterly and due at the end of $4\frac{1}{4}$ years.

The principal (P) is \$1,500.00, which has six digits.

The interest rate (i) per conversion period (3 months) is $12\%/4 = 3\%$.

The number of conversion periods (n) is $4\frac{1}{4} \times 4 = 17$ (quarterly periods).

The value of the factor $(1 + i)^n = (1 + 3\%)^{17}$ is found to be 1.65284763 in the 3% column opposite $n = 17$ in Table 5.

Since the principal in dollars and cents has 6 digits, only 6 decimal places of the factor are needed in multiplication. Thus, the factor 1.65284763 is rounded to 1.652848.

$$\begin{aligned}\text{The compounded amount } (S) &= 1{,}500(1 + 3\%)^{17} \\ &= 1{,}500(1.652848) \\ &= \$2{,}479.272, \quad \text{rounded to} \quad \$2{,}479.27\end{aligned}$$

NOTE: The multiplication $1{,}500(1 + 3\%)^{17}$ may also be performed by using logarithms. Detailed computation is presented in Example 1 of Section 12.1.

EXAMPLE 3 A note having a face value of \$1,000 and bearing interest at 16% compounded quarterly will mature in $10\frac{1}{2}$ years. What is the maturity value?

$P = 1{,}000$, $i = 16\%/4 = 4\%$ (per quarter), and $n = 10\frac{1}{2} \times 4 = 42$ (quarters)

The value of the factor $(1 + 4\%)^{42}$ is found to be 5.19278391 in Table 5.

Thus, the compound amount (or the maturity value) is

$$\begin{aligned}S = P(1 + i)^n &= 1{,}000(1 + 4\%)^{42} \\ &= 1{,}000(5.192784) = \$5{,}192.784 \quad \text{rounded to} \quad \$5{,}192.78\end{aligned}$$

B. The Number of Conversion Periods (n) Is Greater than the Highest Number in Table 5

When the number of conversion periods is greater than that given in Table 5, the number of conversion periods may be divided into several smaller numbers which are listed in the table. The product of the corresponding entries of the smaller numbers is the desired accumulation factor. For example,

$$(1 + 4\%)^{239} = (1 + 4\%)^{100}(1 + 4\%)^{100}(1 + 4\%)^{39}$$
$$(1 + 3\%)^{126} = (1 + 3\%)^{100}(1 + 3\%)^{26}$$

Although the values on the left sides of the equations are not listed in the table, the values of the expanded factors on the right sides of the equations are included in the table. Thus, the entries in the table may be used in computing the accumulation factor $(1 + i)^n$ when the value of n is greater than the highest number in the table.

EXAMPLE 4

Find the compound amount when the principal is $1,000, the interest rate is 24% compounded monthly, and the term is 10 years.

$P = \$1{,}000$, $i = 24\%/12 = 2\%$ (monthly), and $n = 10 \times 12 = 120$ (months)

The factor $(1 + i)^n = (1 + 2\%)^{120} = (1 + 2\%)^{100}(1 + 2\%)^{20}$

According to Table 5,

$(1 + 2\%)^{100} = 7.24464612$, and
$(1 + 2\%)^{20} = 1.48594740$

Thus, $(1 + 2\%)^{120} = 7.24464612 \times 1.48594740 = 10.765163$

$S = 1{,}000(1 + 2\%)^{120} = 1{,}000 \times 10.765163 = \$10{,}765.16$

NOTE: The above computation may also be performed by using logarithms. See Example 2 of Section 12.1.

EXERCISE 11–2 REFERENCE: SECTION 11.3A and B

A. Find the compound amount in each of the following problems:

	Principal (P)	*Interest Rate (i)*	*Time (n)*
1.	$ 500	24% compounded quarterly	10 years
2.	600	21% compounded monthly	$1\frac{1}{2}$ years
3.	7,000	10% compounded annually	25 years
4.	8,000	15% compounded semiannually	9 years
5.	10,000	$6\frac{1}{2}$% compounded monthly	20 years
6.	10,000	8% compounded quarterly	30 years
7.	800	7% compounded semiannually	6 years
8.	2,000	$8\frac{1}{2}$% compounded annually	15 years
9.	1,000	6% compounded every 2 months	1 year
10.	5,000	9% compounded every 4 months	2 years

B. Statement problems:

11. Accumulate $3,000 for eight years at 7% compounded quarterly. How much is the interest?
12. Carl Johnson deposits $4,000 in the First National Bank which pays 20% compounded semiannually. What amount will he have at the end of 11 years?
13. What will the amount be after one year if $1,000 is invested at 6% compounded (a) monthly? (b) quarterly? (c) semiannually? (d) annually?
14. What will the amount be after ten years if $500 is invested at 7% compounded (a) monthly? (b) quarterly? (c) semiannually? (d) annually?
15. Find the amount and the interest on $1,000 at 6% compounded semiannually for (a) 10 years, (b) 20 years, (c) 30 years.
16. Accumulate $600 at 8% compounded quarterly for (a) nine months, (b) five years, (c) ten years. What are the amount and the interest in each case?
17. A note having a face value of $1,650 and bearing interest at 8% compounded monthly will mature in three years. What is the maturity value?

18. Find the maturity value of a five-year note with a face value of \$2,500 and interest at 9% compounded quarterly.
19. Find the difference between investments (a) and (b): (a) \$1,500 is invested for five years at 8% compounded monthly; (b) \$1,500 is invested for five years at 8% simple interest.
20. James Moore deposited \$10,000 in the Home Savings Bank, which pays 6% compounded quarterly. At the same time he deposited another \$10,000 in the Bank of Commerce, which pays $6\frac{1}{2}$% compounded annually. Compare the interest received from the two banks at the end of ten years. (a) Which bank pays more interest? (b) What is the difference?

C. The Interest Rate Changes During Compound Accumulation

If the interest rate changes during compound accumulation, the compound amount is the product of the principal and the several accumulation factors which are at different interest rates for respective given periods.

EXAMPLE 5

If the principal is \$500 and the interest rate is 6% compounded semiannually for the first five years and 8% compounded quarterly for the next six years, what is the compound amount at the end of the 11th year?

The values for computing the amount at the end of the first five years are:

$P = 500$, $i = 6\%/2 = 3\%$ (per six months), and
$n = 5 \times 2 = 10$ (semiannual periods)

$S = 500(1 + 3\%)^{10} = 500(1.34392) = \$671.96$

The values for computing the amount at the end of the 11th year for the remaining six-year period are: $P = \$671.96$ (the new principal at the end of the fifth year), $i = 8\%/4 = 2\%$ (per quarter), $n = 6 \times 4 = 24$ (quarters).

Thus, the compound amount at the end of the 11th year is

$S = 671.96(1 + 2\%)^{24} = 671.96(1.60844) = \$1{,}080.81$, or
$S = 500(1 + 3\%)^{10}(1 + 2\%)^{24} = 500(1.34392)(1.60844) = \$1{,}080.81$

The example is diagrammed as follows:

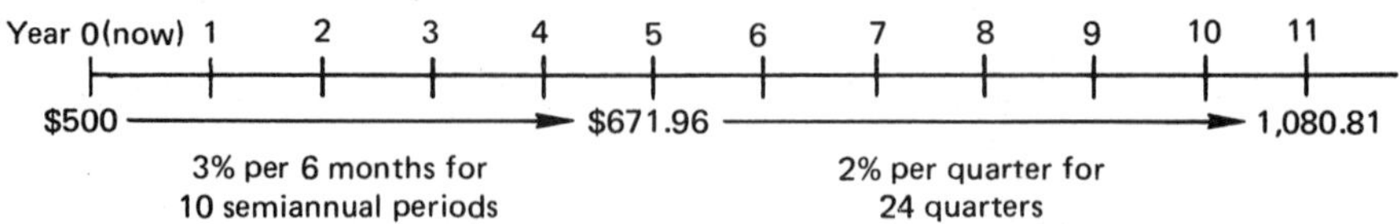

D. The Interest Rate Per Conversion Period (*i*) Is Not Given in the Table

When the interest rate is not given in the table, the interpolation method may be used to obtain an approximate entry that is accurate enough for most purposes.

EXAMPLE 6

Find the compound amount if \$1,000 is invested at $8\frac{1}{2}$% compounded quarterly for $2\frac{1}{2}$ years.

$P = \$1{,}000$, $i = 8\frac{1}{2}\%/4 = 2\frac{1}{8}\%$ (per quarter), and $n = 2\frac{1}{2} \times 4 = 10$ (quarters)

There is no $2\frac{1}{8}\%$ column in Table 5. However, the rate that is just above and that which is just below the rate $2\frac{1}{8}\%$ may be found in the table, and the accumulation factor for $2\frac{1}{8}\%$ may be obtained through interpolation. When the interpolation method is used, it is assumed that the differences between the values of $(1 + i)^n$ are proportional to the differences between the values of i in the table.

The factor $(1 + 2\frac{1}{8}\%)^{10}$ is obtained by the interpolation method as follows:

	i		$(1+i)^{10}$	
	$2\frac{1}{4}\%$		1.24920343	(1)
	$2\frac{1}{8}\%$		x	(2)
	2%		1.21899442	(3)
(2) − (3)	$\frac{1}{8}\%$ 1	=	$x - 1.21899442$	(4)
(1) − (3)	$\frac{1}{4}\%$ 2		0.03020901	(5)

The differences on line (4) are obtained by subtracting the values on line (3) from the corresponding values on line (2), or (2) − (3).

$\frac{1}{8}\% = 2\frac{1}{8}\% - 2\%$, and $x - 1.21899442$ (= unknown)

The differences on line (5) are obtained in a similar manner, or (1) − (3).

$\frac{1}{4}\% = 2\frac{1}{4}\% - 2\%$, and $0.03020901 = 1.24920343 - 1.21899442$

The differences on lines (4) and (5) give the proportion which indicates that $\frac{1}{8}\%$ is to $(x - 1.21899442)$ as $\frac{1}{4}\%$ is to 0.03020901. The proportion is also expressed in equation form on these two lines.

Solve for x in the equation. First, the fraction at the left side of the equation is simplified by multiplying both numerator and denominator by 800, or

$$\frac{\frac{1}{8}\% \times 800}{\frac{1}{4}\% \times 800} = \frac{1}{2}, \quad \text{and} \quad \frac{1}{2} = \frac{x - 1.21899442}{0.03020901}$$

Then $x - 1.21899442 = 0.03020901 \cdot \frac{1}{2}$

$$x = 1.21899442 + 0.015104505 = 1.234098925, \quad \text{or}$$

$$(1 + 2\tfrac{1}{8}\%)^{10} = 1.234098925$$

Thus, $S = 1{,}000(1 + 2\frac{1}{8}\%)^{10} = 1{,}000(1.234099) = \$1{,}234.10$

NOTE:

1. In the above arrangement, the larger values are placed on the top line in order to facilitate subtraction.
2. The order of the subtraction, either by first subtracting line (3) from line (2) or by first subtracting line (3) from line (1), does not affect the answer. The value of x in the proportion

   $$\frac{\frac{1}{8}\%}{\frac{1}{4}\%} = \frac{x - 1.21899442}{0.03020901}$$ is the same as in the reversed-term proportion

   $$\frac{\frac{1}{4}\%}{\frac{1}{8}\%} = \frac{0.03020901}{x - 1.21899442}$$

   However, the former proportion does simplify the operation in solving for x.
3. According to the rule of the number of decimal places in a multiplier, only 6 decimal places are required in multiplying the 6-digit number 1,000.00. Thus, the result in the above interpolation would be a satisfactory one if the value of $(1 + i)^n$

included only 7 decimal places. The one extra place provides for safety in rounding to the 6-place requirement.

4. The value of $(1 + 2\frac{1}{8}\%)^{10}$ may also be obtained by using logarithms or the binomial theorem. (See Problems 11 and 12 of Exercise 12–1, page 359, for instruction.) The value obtained by using the binomial theorem is the most accurate and is 1.234015729. The value obtained by using logarithms (7-place table) is 1.234015625 (see Example 3, Section 12.1), which is very close to the value obtained by using the binomial theorem. Notice that the first seven digits, 1.234015, are the same by both methods; the eighth digits, 7 and 6, respectively, by the two methods, are very close to each other.

EXERCISE 11–3 REFERENCE: SECTION 11.3C and D

A. Statement problems:

1. A man invested \$400 for ten years. The interest rate is 8% compounded annually for the first six years and 10% compounded semiannually for the next four years. What is the amount at the end of ten years?
2. Hank invested \$600 for eight years. The interest rate is 7% compounded quarterly for the first five years and 5% compounded monthly for the next three years. What is the amount at the end of eight years?
3. Accumulate \$600 for 15 years if the interest rate is 8% compounded semiannually for the first ten years and 9% compounded monthly for the remaining five years. Find the amount at the end of 15 years.
4. Accumulate \$500 for 18 years if the interest rate is 5% compounded quarterly for the first six years and 6% compounded annually for the remaining 12 years. Find the amount at the end of 18 years.
5. Find the amount at the end of seven years if \$400 is invested at 6% compounded monthly for the first two years and at $6\frac{1}{2}\%$ compounded annually for the last five years.
6. Find the amount at the end of 12 years if \$1,000 is invested at 20% compounded semiannually for the first five years and at 24% compounded quarterly for the last seven years.

B. Find the compound amount in each of the following problems. (Use the interpolation method to find each accumulation factor.)

	Principal (P)	*Interest Rate (i)*	*Time (n)*
7.	\$1,000	$15\frac{3}{4}\%$ compounded monthly	1 year
8.	1,500	$7\frac{3}{4}\%$ compounded annually	20 years
9.	900	$4\frac{1}{2}\%$ compounded monthly	7 months
10.	850	$8\frac{1}{2}\%$ compounded semiannually	12 years
11.	2,200	$6\frac{1}{4}\%$ compounded quarterly	6 years
12.	2,400	$8\frac{1}{4}\%$ compounded monthly	10 months

E. The Conversion Periods Include a Fractional Part

When the conversion periods include a fractional part, either of the following two methods may be used in computing the compound amount:

METHOD A Use the formula $S = P(1 + i)^n$, where n is a whole number representing the total number of whole conversion periods. (Use Table 5.) The computed value, S, is further computed by the simple interest method for the remaining fractional period.

★METHOD B Use the formula $S = P(1 + i)^n$, where n is a mixed number that equals the entire time. (Use Tables 5 and 5A.)

Theoretically, Method B is more reasonable than the other because the compound method is used throughout. However, Method A is widely employed in practice because its computation is less complicated than that of Method B.

EXAMPLE 7 Find the compound amount and the compound interest when $1,000 is invested for three years and two months at 6% compounded semiannually.

METHOD A $P = 1{,}000$, $i = 6\%/2 = 3\%$ (per six months),

$n = 3 \times 2 = 6$ (semiannual periods)

Thus, the compound amount at the end of the sixth conversion period is

$S = 1{,}000(1 + 3\%)^6 = 1{,}000(1.194052) = \$1{,}194.05.$

The simple interest for the remaining period (two months) is

$1{,}194.05 \times 6\% \times 2/12 = \$11.94$

The final compound amount is

$1{,}194.05 + 11.94 = \$1{,}205.99$

The compound interest $= 1{,}205.99 - 1{,}000.00 = \$205.99$

Method A is diagrammed as follows:

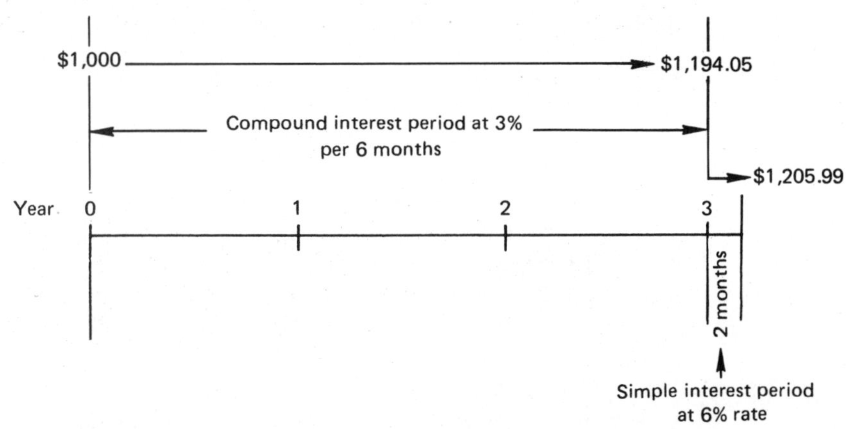

★ **METHOD B** $P = 1{,}000$, $i = 6\%/2 = 3\%$ (per six months),

$n = 3\frac{2}{12} \times 2 = 6\frac{1}{3}$ (semiannual periods)

Thus,

$$S = P(1 + i)^n = 1{,}000(1 + 3\%)^{6\ 1/3} = 1{,}000(1 + 3\%)^6(1 + 3\%)^{1/3}$$
$$= 1{,}000(1.194052)(1.009902)$$
$$= \$1{,}205.88 \quad \text{(Tables 5 and 5A)}$$

The compound interest $= S - P = 1{,}205.88 - 1{,}000.00 = \$205.88$

Notice that the interest obtained in Method A is greater than that calculated in Method B. When the investment time is a fraction of the conversion period, use of the compound interest method always gives less interest than the simple interest method.

NOTE: The multiplication $1{,}000(1 + 3\%)^6(1 + 3\%)^{1/3}$ may be performed by using logarithms. See Example 4 of Section 12.1.

EXERCISE 11–4 REFERENCE: SECTION 11.3E

A. Find the compound amount in each of the following problems. Use Method A in Problems 1–6 and ★Method B in Problems 7–10.

	Principal (P)	*Interest Rate (i)*	*Time (n)*
1.	$ 500	18% compounded monthly	$10\frac{1}{2}$ months
2.	600	7% compounded quarterly	6 years, 2 months
3.	2,400	5% compounded semiannually	15 years, 4 months
4.	3,600	10% compounded annually	20 years, 5 months
5.	1,700	8% compounded quarterly	4 years, 2 months
6.	1,200	8% compounded monthly	2 years, $\frac{1}{2}$ month
7.	3,000	6% compounded quarterly	3 years, 1 month
8.	10,000	21% compounded monthly	$8\frac{1}{2}$ months
9.	1,500	7% compounded annually	12 years, 4 months
10.	1,800	9% compounded semiannually	5 years, 3 months

B. Statement problems:

11. What are the amount and the interest if $16,000 is borrowed at 6% compounded semiannually for nine years and 11 months? Use Method A.
12. What are the amount and the interest if $10,000 is borrowed at $5\frac{1}{2}\%$ compounded annually for ten years and eight months? Use Method A.
★ 13. Find the amount and the interest if $5,000 is invested at 9% compounded monthly for five years and $7\frac{1}{3}$ months. Use Method B.
★ 14. Find the amount and the interest if $2,500 is invested at 10% compounded quarterly for seven years and four months. Use Method B.

11.4 FINDING THE PRESENT VALUE AND COMPOUND DISCOUNT

As stated in Chapters 8 and 9, there are numerous occasions in business when it becomes necessary to discount an amount that is due on a future date. "To discount a given compound amount due in the future" means to find its present value on the date of discount. The difference between the value of the compound amount and its present value is called *compound discount*. Therefore, the compound discount on the compound amount is the same as the compound interest on the present value.

For instance, in Example 2, Section 11.3, the amount of \$1,500 invested at 12% compounded quarterly and due at the end of $4\frac{1}{4}$ years is \$2,479.27. The compound interest is \$2,479.27 − \$1,500 = \$979.27. This example may be stated in a different way. The present value of \$2,479.27 due at the end of $4\frac{1}{4}$ years at 12% compounded quarterly is \$1,500, and the compound discount is \$979.27. In other words, \$1,500 is equivalent to \$2,479.27 after $4\frac{1}{4}$ years according to the compound interest rate. The amount is found by applying the formula $S = P(1 + i)^n$. From the relationship, the present value (P) is obtained as follows:

$$\mathbf{P = S(1 + i)^{-n}} \tag{11–2}$$

or

$$\mathbf{P = \frac{S}{(1 + i)^n}} \tag{11–2A}$$

For convenience, the most common values of $(1 + i)^{-n}$ are tabulated in Table 6 of the Appendix. The values (entries) in the table may best be considered as the present values in dollars when the compound amount is \$1, although each entry may be considered as the value in a unit other than a dollar.

Let p = the present value P when the compound amount is 1. Then the formula becomes

$$p = P = S(1 + i)^{-n} = 1(1 + i)^{-n}, \quad \text{or} \quad p = (1 + i)^{-n}$$

The factor $(1 + i)^{-n}$ is frequently referred to as the *discount factor* in discounting a compound amount. The methods of finding the present value of a given amount that is due on a future date are presented below.

A. Use of Table 6

When Table 6 is used, formula (11–2) may be expressed as follows:

Present value (P) = Compound amount (S) × An entry in Table 6

(The entry is at the interest rate i per conversion period and for n conversion periods.)

EXAMPLE 1

Find the present value of \$2,479.27 due at the end of $4\frac{1}{4}$ years if money is worth 12% compounded quarterly.

The amount (S) = \$2,479.27, the interest rate per quarter (i) = 12%/4 = 3%, and the number of conversion periods (n) = $4\frac{1}{4} \times 4 = 17$ (quarters). The discount factor $(1 + i)^{-n} = (1 + 3\%)^{-17}$ = .60501645 (Table 6).

Substituting these values in formula (11–2),

$$P = S(1 + i)^{-n} = 2{,}479.27(1 + 3\%)^{-17} = 2{,}479.27(.605016) = \$1{,}500$$

NOTE: The multiplication $2{,}479.27(1 + 3\%)^{-17}$ may also be performed by using logarithms. Detailed computation is presented in Example 5 of Section 12.1.

EXAMPLE 2 If \$1,000 is due five years from now and money is worth 4% compounded quarterly, find its present value and the compound discount.

The given amount (S) = \$1,000, $i = 4\%/4 = 1\%$ (per quarter), $n = 5 \times 4 = 20$ (quarters), and the factor $(1 + 1\%)^{-20} = .81954447$ (Table 6).

$$\text{Present value } P = 1{,}000(1 + 1\%)^{-20}$$
$$= 1{,}000(.819544) = \$819.54$$

$$\text{Compound discount} = \text{Compound amount} - \text{Present value}$$
$$= 1{,}000 - 819.54$$
$$= \$180.46$$

The value of P may be obtained by using formula (11–2A), but division is involved.

$$P = \frac{S}{(1+i)^n} = \frac{1{,}000}{(1+1\%)^{20}} = \frac{1{,}000}{1.22019} = \$819.54 \quad \text{(Table 5)}$$

The solution may also be stated as follows:

If \$819.54 is invested now at 4% compounded quarterly for five years, the compound amount at the end of the fifth year is \$1,000.

CHECK

$$S = P(1+i)^n = 819.54(1 + 1\%)^{20} = 819.54(1.22019)$$
$$= \$999.99, \quad \text{or rounded to} \quad \$1{,}000$$

The example is diagrammed as follows:

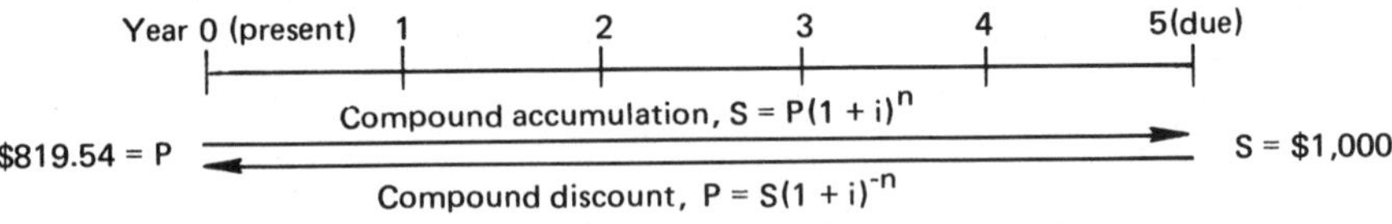

NOTE: The compound amount (S) is always larger than the present value (P). Here the present value (P) may also be thought of as the principal of the investment.

EXERCISE 11–5 REFERENCE: SECTION 11.4A

A. Find the present value in each of the following problems:

	Amount (S)	*Interest Rate (i)*	*Time (n)*
1.	\$2,000	20% compounded quarterly	5 years
2.	5,000	15% compounded monthly	2 years
3.	600	6% compounded annually	10 years
4.	3,500	9% compounded semiannually	7 years
5.	1,500	18% compounded monthly	4 years
6.	800	7% compounded quarterly	6 years
7.	4,000	6% compounded semiannually	20 years
8.	700	$9\frac{1}{2}$% compounded annually	15 years

B. Statement problems:

9. Find the present value of $1,400 due at the end of nine years if money is worth (a) 5% compounded quarterly, and (b) 7% compounded semiannually. How much is the compound discount in each case?
10. Find the present value of $2,500 due at the end of three years if money is worth (a) 6% compounded monthly, and (b) 7% compounded annually. How much is the compounded discount in each case?
11. Jane Harrison has $10,000 at the end of three years in her savings account. The interest rate is 24% compounded monthly. How much did she deposit in the account three years ago?
12. How much money does R. T. White need if she can invest the money at 20% compounded quarterly for six years and wants to receive $6,000 at the end of the period?
13. If $3,600 is due seven years from now and money is worth 5% compounded annually, find the present value and the compound discount.
14. Find the present value and the compound discount if $1,800 is due ten years from now and money is worth 12% compounded semiannually.
15. What principal will accumulate to $3,200 in four years at 4% compounded quarterly?
16. What principal will accumulate to $4,300 in 12 years at 6% compounded annually?
17. A man paid a two-year debt with $1,690.74. The interest charged was at 6% compounded monthly. What was the principal?
18. A man borrowed some money for five years. When the debt was due, he paid $5,200 for the money borrowed and the interest charged. The interest rate was 7% compounded quarterly. How much did he borrow?

B. Compound Discount on Notes

If a note is non-interest-bearing, the present value of its face value is the proceeds. Here, the word "proceeds" represents the value, which is discounted at a compound interest rate, received by the seller of the note. The method of finding the present value of a note is the same as that explained above. However, the word "present" usually is referred to here as the date of discount. Example 2 above may be stated in the following manner:

A non-interest-bearing note of $1,000 is due five years from now. If the note is now discounted at 4% compounded quarterly, what are the proceeds and the compound discount? The answers: proceeds = $819.54, and compound discount = $180.46.

If a note is interest bearing, the proceeds is the present value on the date of discount computed from the maturity value of the note. The maturity value includes the face value of the note and the interest. Thus, two steps are required in finding the proceeds:

STEP (1). Find the compound amount of the face value of the note according to the rate and the time stipulated on the note. The compound amount is the maturity value. [Use the formula $S = P(1 + i)^n$.]

STEP (2). Find the present value (on the date of discount) of the maturity value, according to the rate and the time of discount. [Use the formula $P = S(1 + i)^{-n}$.]

EXAMPLE 3

A note of $1,000 dated January 1, 1987, at 6% compounded quarterly for ten years, was discounted on January 1, 1991. What are the proceeds and the compounded discount if the note was discounted at 8% compounded semiannually?

STEP (1). Find the maturity value on January 1, 1997, according to the rate and the time stipulated on the note.

$P = \$1{,}000$ (face value), $i = 6\%/4 = 1\frac{1}{2}\%$ (per quarter), $n = 10 \times 4 = 40$ (quarters)

$$\text{Maturity value } (S) = P(1 + i)^n = 1{,}000(1 + 1\tfrac{1}{2}\%)^{40}$$
$$= 1{,}000(1.814018) = \$1{,}814.02$$

STEP (2). Find the present value (as of January 1, 1991, the date of discount, or six years before the maturity date).

$S = \$1{,}814.02$, $i = 8\%/2 = 4\%$ (per semiannual period), $n = 6 \times 2 = 12$ (semiannual periods)

$$\text{Proceeds (or present value } P) = S(1 + i)^{-n} = 1{,}814.02(1 + 4\%)^{-12}$$
$$= 1{,}814.02(.624597) = \$1{,}133.03$$

$$\text{Compound discount} = 1{,}814.02 - 1{,}133.03 = \$680.99$$

The example is diagrammed as follows:

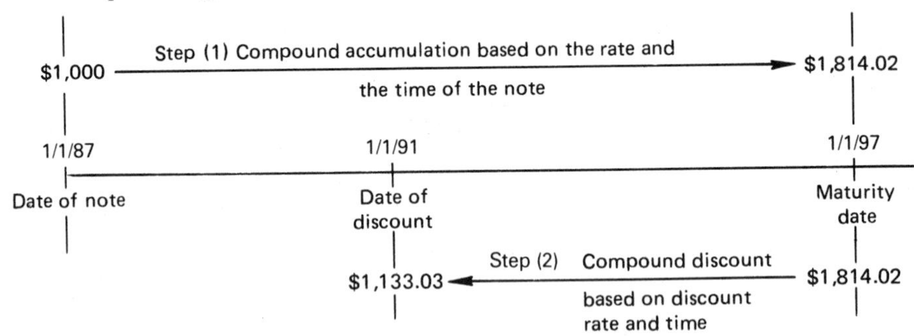

C. The Discount Time Includes a Fraction of a Conversion Period

When the discount time includes a fraction of a conversion period, the proceeds may be computed by either of the following methods:

METHOD A

Use the formula $P = S(1 + i)^{-n}$, where n is a whole number representing the total number of *whole* conversion periods plus 1. (Use Table 6.) The computed value P is then accumulated by the simple interest method for the extra fractional period included in n to obtain the proceeds.

★METHOD B

Use the formula $P = S(1 + i)^{-n}$, where n is a mixed number that equals the entire discount time. (Use Tables 6 and 5A.)

Theoretically, Method B is more reasonable than the other because the compound discount method is used throughout. However, Method A is widely employed in practice because its computation is less complicated than that of Method B.

EXAMPLE 4

A non-interest-bearing note of $1,000 is discounted at 6% compounded semiannually for three years and two months. Find the proceeds and the compound discount.

METHOD A

$S = 1{,}000$
$i = 6\%/2 = 3\%$ (per semiannual period)
$n = 6 + 1 = 7$ (semiannual periods)

$$P = S(1 + i)^{-n} = 1{,}000(1 + 3\%)^{-7} = 1{,}000(.813092) = \$813.09$$

By the simple interest method, accumulate P for the extra fractional period of four months (7 semiannual periods, or $3\frac{1}{2}$ years, minus three years and two months) at 6% as follows:

Simple interest = 813.09 × 6% × 4/12 = $16.26

The proceeds = 813.09 + 16.26 = $829.35

Compound discount = 1,000 − 829.35 = $170.65

Method A is diagrammed as follows:

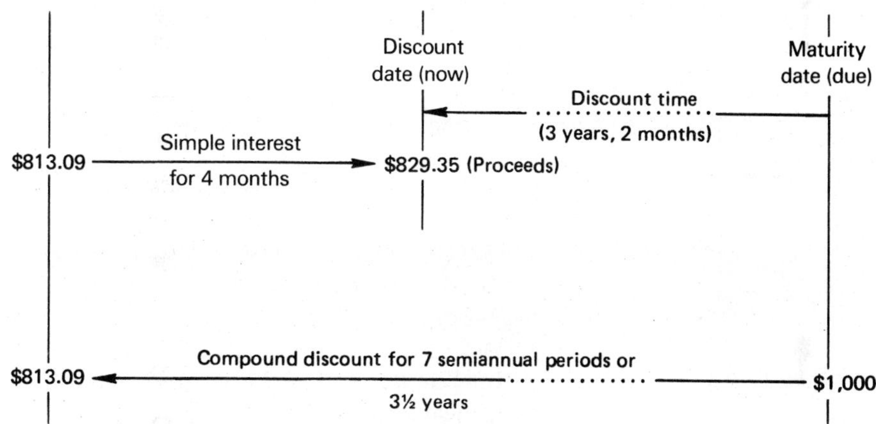

★METHOD B

$S = 1{,}000$
$i = 6\%/2 = 3\%$ (per semiannual period)
$n = 3\frac{2}{12} \times 2 = 6\frac{1}{3}$ (semiannual periods)

$$P = S(1 + i)^{-n} = 1{,}000(1 + 3\%)^{-6\,1/3} = 1{,}000(1 + 3\%)^{-6}(1 + 3\%)^{-1/3}$$

$$= 1{,}000 \times \frac{(1 + 3\%)^{-6} \quad \text{(Table 6)}}{(1 + 3\%)^{1/3} \quad \text{(Table 5A)}}$$

$$= 1{,}000 \times \frac{.837484}{1.009902} = \$829.27$$

Compound discount = 1,000.00 − 829.27 = $170.73

NOTE: The proceeds in Method A are larger than those in Method B. Such a condition is always true when the discount time includes a fraction of the conversion period.

EXERCISE 11–6 REFERENCE: SECTION 11.4B and C

A. Find (a) the proceeds and (b) the compound discount in each of the following problems:

	Date of Note	*Face Value*	*Compound Interest Rate of Note*	*Term of Note*	*Date of Discount*	*Discount Rate*
1.	7/1/91	$ 600	none	4 years	7/1/92	18%, monthly
2.	8/1/91	400	none	12 years	2/1/94	16%, quarterly
3.	5/1/92	6,000	none	7 years	5/1/95	8%, annually
4.	4/1/92	7,000	none	$5\frac{1}{2}$ years	10/1/95	11%, semi-annually
5.	1/2/93	1,500	5%, semi-annually	10 years	1/2/96	4%, quarterly
6.	2/1/93	1,200	9%, monthly	5 years	2/1/94	6%, annually
7.	3/1/94	2,400	4%, quarterly	6 years	3/1/97	5%, semi-annually
8.	5/1/94	8,000	6%, annually	8 years	5/1/99	7%, monthly

B. Statement problems:

9. A non-interest-bearing note of $1,800 is discounted at 24% compounded monthly for $7\frac{1}{2}$ years. Find the proceeds.
10. A non-interest-bearing note of $5,500 is discounted at 7% compounded quarterly five years before it is due. Find the proceeds.
11. A note of $3,000 dated June 1, 1991, at 20% compounded quarterly for $6\frac{1}{2}$ years, is discounted on October 1, 1993. Find the proceeds if the note is discounted at 18% compounded monthly.
12. A note of $400 dated May 1, 1991, at 5% compounded monthly for four years, is discounted on February 1, 1994. Find the proceeds if the note is discounted at 6% compounded quarterly.
13. B. C. Power received a seven-year, $5\frac{1}{2}$% compounded annually, $5,000 note dated April 1, 1991. Power discounted the note at 6% compounded semiannually on February 1, 1992. Find the proceeds. Use Method A.
14. F. W. Bondson has a $4\frac{1}{2}$-year note of $3,600 at 7% compounded monthly. The maturity date is February 1, 1994. If the note is discounted on January 1, 1992, at 5% compounded annually, how much will Bondson receive? Use Method A.
15. A nine-year note bearing interest at 4% compounded semiannually is discounted at 5% compounded quarterly. The face value of the note is $7,200, and the discount period is five years and two months. Find the proceeds. Use Method A.
16. Jack H. Kelly received a non-interest-bearing note for $4,200. He discounted the note at 10% compounded semiannually three years and two months before it was due. How much proceeds did he receive? Use Method A.
17. ★ Mary Dolton signs a note for $7,000 due in $3\frac{1}{2}$ years to a bank that charges $5\frac{1}{2}$% compounded annually. What should Dolton receive as the proceeds from the bank? Use Method B.

★ 18. John Edwards has a note that will pay him \$2,000 at the end of $5\frac{1}{2}$ years. He sells the note three years and one month before it is due at 7% compounded quarterly. How much proceeds does he receive from the sale? Use Method B.

11.5 FINDING THE INTEREST RATE

When finding the interest rate, Table 5 in the Appendix may be used as explained in Section A.

A. Use of Table 5

Solve $(1 + i)^n$ from the formula $S = P(1 + i)^n$. Thus,

$$(1 + i)^n = \frac{S}{P} \qquad \textbf{(11–3)}$$

Formula (11–3) may be expressed as follows:

$$\text{An entry in Table 5} = \frac{\text{Compound amount}}{\text{Principal}}$$

Formula (11–3) contains four values. If the values of S, P, and n are known, an entry that is equal to $\frac{S}{P}$ may be found in the n row of Table 5. The value of the interest rate (i) is thus found in the column containing the entry. If the exact entry cannot be found in the table, the interpolation method may be used to find an approximate value of i.

EXAMPLE 1

If \$1,000 will accumulate to \$5,054.47 in 17 years, what is the interest rate compounded annually?

$P = 1{,}000$, $S = 5{,}054.47$, $n = 17$ (years)

Substituting these values in formula (11–3),

$$(1 + i)^{17} = \frac{5{,}054.47}{1{,}000} = 5.05447$$

In the $n = 17$ row of Table 5, the entry 5.05447 is found in the 10% column. Thus, $i = 10\%$.

EXAMPLE 2

At what nominal interest rate compounded semiannually for ten years will \$300 accumulate to \$890?

$P = 300$, $S = 890$, $n = 10 \times 2 = 20$ (semiannual periods)

Substituting these values in formula (11–3),

$$(1 + i)^{20} = \frac{890}{300} = 2.9667$$

There is no entry 2.9667 in the row where $n = 20$ in Table 5. However, an entry that is just above and one that is just below the value of 2.9667 may be found in the table and the interest rate may be obtained through interpolation. When the interpolation method is used, it is assumed that the differences between the values of i are proportional to the differences between the values of $(1 + i)^n$ in the table. The findings are arranged for interpolation as follows:

	i	$(1 + i)^{20}$	
	6%	3.2071	(1)
	x	2.9667	(2)
	$5\frac{1}{2}\%$	2.9178	(3)
(2) − (3)	$x - 5\frac{1}{2}\%$	0.0489	(4)
(1) − (3)	$\frac{1}{2}\%$	0.2893	(5)

$$\frac{x - 5\frac{1}{2}\%}{\frac{1}{2}\%} = \frac{0.0489}{0.2893}$$

Solve for x from the proportion formed by the differences on lines (4) and (5).

$$x - 5\tfrac{1}{2}\% = \tfrac{1}{2}\%\left(\frac{0.0489}{0.2893}\right) = \frac{1}{200} \cdot \frac{489}{2893} = .000845$$

$$x = 5\tfrac{1}{2}\% + .000845 = .055 + .000845 = .055845, \quad \text{or}$$

$$i = .055845 \quad \text{(interest rate per semiannual period)}$$

The nominal interest rate is

$$.055845 \times 2 = .111690$$
$$= 11.169\%, \quad \text{or rounded to} \quad 11.17\%$$

NOTE:

1. The values of $(1 + i)^n$ include four decimal places in the above interpolation. This practice may be followed in solving the problems in the following exercises. In most cases, the accuracy of the result of an interpolation will not be any greater if the values include more than four decimal places.
2. The time unit of n should always agree with the time unit of i in computing compound interest problems. For instance, in the above example, n represents the number of *semiannual* periods and i represents the interest rate per *semiannual* period.
3. The i value may also be solved by using logarithms as presented in Example 6 of Section 12.1.

B. Effective Annual Interest Rate

The effective annual interest rate is commonly abbreviated as the *effective rate*. If the principal is \$1, the value of the compound interest for a one-year period is the effective rate. In general, the effective rate is the ratio of the compound interest earned for a one-year period to the principal, as shown below:

$$\text{Effective rate} = \frac{\text{Compound interest for a one-year period}}{\text{Principal}}$$

In other words, an effective rate is an interest rate compounded annually.

EXAMPLE 3 If \$1 is invested at 6% compounded quarterly for one year, what is the effective rate?

$P = 1$, $i = 6\%/4 = 1\frac{1}{2}\%$ (per quarter), $n = 4$ (quarters)

The compound amount is computed as follows:

$$S = P(1 + i)^n = 1(1 + 1\tfrac{1}{2}\%)^4 = 1(1.06136355) = 1.06136355$$

The compound interest is

$$1.06136355 - 1 = .06136355$$

The effective rate is .06136355, which may be rounded to 6.14%.

Thus, 6.14% compounded annually is equivalent to an interest rate of 6% compounded quarterly.

Normally, the effective rate is greater than the nominal rate (stated annual rate). In Example 3, the effective rate is greater than the nominal rate by .14% (or 6.14% − 6%).

To obtain a formula for the effective rate, the following assumptions are made:

Let j = nominal rate
m = number of conversion periods for *one* year
$i = j/m$ (per conversion period)
f = effective rate

These values are then substituted in the compound amount formula (11–1). Thus, in a one-year period:

According to the nominal rate, $S = P(1 + j/m)^m$
According to the effective rate, $S = P(1 + f)$

The right sides of the two equations above are equated as follows:

$P(1 + f) = P(1 + j/m)^m$, or $1 + f = (1 + j/m)^m$

$$\boldsymbol{f = \left(1 + \frac{j}{m}\right)^m - 1} \quad \text{or} \qquad \textbf{(11–4)}$$

$$\boldsymbol{f = (1 + i)^m - 1}$$

EXAMPLE 4 Find the effective rate if money is worth 6% compounded quarterly on the investment market.

$j = 6\%, m = 4.$

Substituting the values in formula (11–4),

$$f = \left(1 + \frac{6\%}{4}\right)^4 - 1 = (1 + 1\tfrac{1}{2}\%)^4 - 1 = 1.06136355 - 1$$

$$= .06136355, \quad \text{or} \quad 6.14\%$$

NOTE: The above effective rate, 6.14%, is computed from formula (11–4) without mentioning the values of S and P. The answer may be compared with that in Example 3.

The effective rate is frequently used as a device to compare one interest rate with another rate compounded at different time intervals. It is especially useful to those who invest or borrow money from various sources. By comparing the effective rates of the various sources, a person may select the one having the lowest effective rate for borrowing and the one having the highest effective rate for investing.

EXAMPLE 5 Bank A offers its depositors an interest rate of 6% compounded monthly, while Bank B gives its depositors an interest rate of $6\frac{1}{2}$% compounded semiannually. Which of the two banks makes the better offer?

The effective rate based on the interest rate of Bank A is

$$f = (1 + 6\%/12)^{12} - 1 = (1 + \tfrac{1}{2}\%)^{12} - 1$$
$$= 1.0617 - 1 = .0617, \quad \text{or} \quad 6.17\%$$

The effective rate based on the interest rate of Bank B is

$f = (1 + 6\frac{1}{2}\%/2)^2 - 1 = (1 + 3\frac{1}{4}\%)^2 - 1$
$= 1.0661 - 1 = .0661, \quad \text{or} \quad 6.61\%$

The effective rate of Bank B is greater than that of Bank A by .44% (or 6.61% − 6.17%); that is, Bank B offers a better interest rate to its depositors.

NOTE:

1. If there is only one conversion period in *one* year ($m = 1$), the value of f in formula (11–4) becomes

   $f = (1 + j/1)^1 - 1 = j$

   Also, when $m = 1$, $i = j/m = j/1 = j$, and $f = j = i$.

   The relationships may be stated as follows:

   If there is only *one* conversion period in *one* year, the effective rate equals the nominal rate, which in turn equals the interest rate per conversion period.
2. If the number of conversion periods per year (m) is increased while the value of the nominal rate (j) remains constant, the value of the effective rate (f) also is increased. For example, the effective rates for the nominal rate 6% compounded annually, semiannually, quarterly, monthly, semimonthly, weekly, and daily are shown below. The values of f are computed by substituting the respective values of m in formula (11–4), as illustrated in Example 4.

	Annually	*Semiannually*	*Quarterly*	*Monthly*	*Semimonthly*	*Weekly*	*Daily*
$m =$	1	2	4	12	24	52	365
$f =$	6%	6.09%	6.13636%	6.16778%	6.17570%	6.17998%	6.18313%

The table indicates that the effective rate (f) increases as the number of conversion periods (m) increases. However, the increases of the rate are rather moderate.

EXERCISE 11–7 REFERENCE: SECTION 11.5

A. Find the interest rate per conversion period in each of the following problems:

	Principal	*Amount*	*Term*	*Interest Rate Compounded*
1.	$10,000	$22,972.00	$3\frac{1}{2}$ years	monthly
2.	20,000	45,840.00	$4\frac{1}{4}$ years	quarterly
3.	5,000	30,579.50	$9\frac{1}{2}$ years	semiannually
4.	6,000	17,118.60	11 years	annually
5.	2,500	2,960.00	4 years	quarterly
6.	5,000	7,800	6 years	semiannually
7.	200	700	30 years	annually
8.	3,600	5,600	7 years	monthly

B. Statement problems:

9. At what nominal interest rate compounded quarterly for $5\frac{1}{2}$ years will $1,200 accumulate to the amount of $1,700?

10. If \$2,800 amounts to \$4,200 in eight years with interest compounded semiannually, what is the nominal interest rate?
11. What is the effective rate if \$1 is invested for one year at 4% compounded (a) annually? (b) semiannually? (c) quarterly? (d) monthly?
12. What is the effective rate if money is worth 5% compounded (a) annually? (b) semiannually? (c) quarterly? (d) monthly?
13. Harry invested his money at 18% compounded monthly, while Betty invested her money at 20% compounded semiannually. Who receives the better interest rate?
14. Which is the higher interest rate in the following cases: (a) 7% compounded quarterly, (b) $7\frac{1}{4}\%$ compounded annually?

11.6 FINDING THE NUMBER OF CONVERSION PERIODS

In formula (11–3), $(1 + i)^n = S/P$, if the values of S, P, and i are known, an entry that is equal to the value of S/P may be found in the i column in Table 5. The value of n, the number of conversion periods, is thus found in the row containing the entry. If the value of S/P cannot be found in the table, the interpolation method may be used for finding the value of n. However, most long-term investors are not interested in a fraction of a conversion period. Therefore, it is generally unnecessary to carry out the interpolation.

EXAMPLE 1 How long will it take \$1,000 to accumulate to the amount of \$1,105 at 24% compounded monthly?

$S = 1{,}105$, $P = 1{,}000$, $i = 24\%/12 = 2\%$ (per month)

Substituting the values in formula (11–3),

$$(1 + i)^n = \frac{S}{P}$$

$$(1 + 2\%)^n = \frac{1{,}105}{1{,}000} = 1.105$$

$$n = 6 \text{ months}$$

In the 2% column in Table 5, the value 1.105 is between the entries 1.10408080 (where $n = 5$) and 1.12616242 (where $n = 6$). Since the nearest value to 1.105 is 1.10408080, the required time is slightly over 5 conversion periods, or 5 months. The finding may be written:

$$5 < n < 6$$

that is, n is greater than 5 but is smaller than 6. However, the sixth conversion period is necessary for the principal to accumulate to at least \$1,105. For simplicity in this text, the larger value of n is hereafter regarded as the answer to this type of problem.

CHECK $1{,}000(1 + 2\%)^5 = 1{,}000(1.104081) = \$1{,}104.08$, which is \$.92 less than the required amount.

$1{,}000(1 + 2\%)^6 = 1{,}000(1.126162) = \$1{,}126.16$, which is \$21.16 more than the required amount.

NOTE: The n value may also be found by using logarithms, as presented in Example 7 of Section 12.1.

EXERCISE 11–8 REFERENCE: SECTION 11.6

A. Find the number of conversion periods in each of the following problems:

	Principal	*Amount*	*Interest Rate*	*Compounded*
1.	\$1,000	\$ 1,563	18%	monthly
2.	1,000	1,741	8%	quarterly
3.	8,000	10,500	6%	semiannually
4.	4,500	7,800	$5\frac{1}{2}$%	annually
5.	2,000	3,238	14%	quarterly
6.	7,500	12,000	7%	semiannually
7.	4,000	9,000	9%	annually
8.	6,000	8,637	21%	monthly

B. Statement problems:

9. How long will it take \$1,000 to accumulate to the amount of \$1,100 at 12% compounded monthly?
10. How much time is required for \$1,500 to yield \$1,000 interest if the interest rate is 5% compounded quarterly?
11. How many years are needed for \$4,000 to yield \$1,375.66 interest if the interest rate is 6% compounded semiannually?
12. How long will it take \$3,000 to amount to \$8,753.27 at a $5\frac{1}{2}$% effective rate?
13. On January 1, 1991, Judy Horton borrowed \$1,200 and agreed to repay it with \$465.07 interest. If the interest is at 6% compounded quarterly, what amount must she repay and on what date?
14. On July 1, 1991, Albert Todd borrowed \$2,800 at 15% compounded semiannually. He repaid \$8,906.24 on the due date. Find the due date.

★11.7 COMPUTING FORMULAS BY CALCULATORS AND COMPUTERS

Tables 5 and 6 can be used to save time in computing compound interest problems, as presented in the previous sections. In addition, this section illustrates the methods of computing the formulas by using electronic calculators and computers. The examples are based on the instructions in Chapter 10.

A. Computing Formula (11–1): $S = P(1 + i)^n$

The examples used in this section are obtained from Section 11.3.

EXAMPLE 1

Compute Example 1, Section 11.3:

$S = 10{,}000(1 + 1\%)^3 = 10{,}303.01$

(a) SIMPLE CALCULATOR

Problem	*Step*	*Key Pressing Sequence*	*Display*
$10{,}000(1.01)^3 = ?$	1	1.01 [×] [=] [=]	1.030301
	2	[×] 10000 [=]	10303.01

(b) BUSINESS ANALYST CALCULATOR

Problem	*Step*	*Key Pressing Sequence*	*Display*
Compute future value:	1	ON/C 2nd FIN	0
Number of compounding periods, $n = 3$	2	3 N	3
Percent interest rate per compounding period, $i = 1(\%)$	3	1 %i	1
Present value, $P = 10{,}000$	4	10000 PV	10000
	5	CPT FV	10303.01

(c) COMPUTER WITH BASIC

BASIC Program

```
10 INPUT "P";P
20 INPUT "I";I
30 INPUT "N";N
40 S = P*(1 + I)∧N
50 PRINT "AMOUNT = ";S
60 END
```

Computer Display (RUN)

```
P ? 10000
I ? .01
N ? 3
AMOUNT = 10303.01
```

The numbers after the question marks (?) are typed input.

The same BASIC program given in Example 1 can be used repeatedly for other examples in Section 11.3, as follows:

Computer Display (RUN)—Examples 2 to 7 of Section 11.3

Example 2	*Example 3*	*Example 4*
P ? 1500 I ? .03 N ? 17 AMOUNT = 2479.27	P ? 1000 I ? .04 N ? 42 AMOUNT = 5192.78	P ? 1000 I ? .02 N ? 120 AMOUNT = 10,765.16

Example 5	*Example 6*	*Example 7*
P ? 500 I ? .03 N ? 10 AMOUNT = 671.96	P ? 1000 I ? .02125 N ? 10 AMOUNT = 1234.02	P ? 1000 I ? .03 N ? 6.33333 AMOUNT = 1205.88
P ? 671.96 I ? .02 N ? 24 AMOUNT = 1080.81		

B. Computing Formula (11–2): $P = S(1 + i)^{-n}$ or $P = \dfrac{S}{(1 + i)^n}$

The examples used in this section are obtained from Section 11.4.

EXAMPLE 2

Compute Example 1, Section 11.4:

$$P = 2{,}479.27(1 + 3\%)^{-17} = 1{,}500.00$$

(a) SIMPLE CALCULATOR

Problem	Step	Key Pressing Sequence	Display
$2{,}479.27 \times \frac{1}{1.03^{17}} = ?$	1	1.03 [×] [=] (16 times) [M+]	1.6528468 M
	2	1 [÷] [MR] [×] 2479.27 [=]	1499.9997 M

(b) BUSINESS ANALYST CALCULATOR

Problem	Step	Key Pressing Sequence	Display
Compute present value:	1	[ON/C] [2nd] [FIN]	0
Number of compounding periods, $n = 4.25 \times 4 = 17$	2	4.25 [×] 4 [=] [N]	17
Percent interest rate per compounding period, $i = 12\%/4 = 3\%$	3	12 [÷] 4 [=] [%i]	3
Future value, $S = 2{,}479.27$	4	2479.27 [FV]	2479.27
	5	[CPT] [PV]	1499.9991

(c) COMPUTER WITH BASIC

BASIC Program

```
10 INPUT "S";S
20 INPUT "I";I
30 INPUT "N";N
40 P = S*(1 + I)∧(− N)
50 PRINT "PRESENT VALUE = ";P
60 END
```

Computer Display (RUN)

```
S ? 2479.27
I ? .03
N ? 17
PRESENT VALUE = 1500
```

The numbers after the question marks (?) are typed input.

EXAMPLE 3 Compute Example 2, Section 11.4:

$P = 1{,}000(1 + 1\%)^{-20} = 819.54$

Use the BASIC program given in Example 2:

Computer Display (RUN)

```
S ? 1000
I ? .01
N ? 20
PRESENT VALUE = 819.54
```

The numbers after the question marks (?) are typed input.

C. Computing Formula (11–3): $(1 + i)^n = \frac{S}{P}$

The examples used in this section are obtained from Sections 11.5 and 11.6.

(1) CASE I—FIND THE INTEREST RATE, i

Solve for i from the formula:

$$i = \sqrt[n]{\frac{S}{P}} - 1 = \frac{S^{1/n}}{P^{1/n}} - 1$$

EXAMPLE 4

Compute Example 1, Section 11.5:

$$(1 + i)^{17} = \frac{5{,}054.47}{1{,}000}; \qquad i = 10\%$$

(a) SIMPLE CALCULATOR

Not capable of finding the 17th root of $\frac{5{,}054.47}{1{,}000}$, or $\sqrt[17]{5.05447}$.

(b) BUSINESS ANALYST CALCULATOR

Problem	*Step*	*Key Pressing Sequence*	*Display*
Compute interest rate:	1	[ON/C] [2nd] [FIN]	0
Number of compounding periods, $n = 17$	2	17 [N]	17
Present value, $P = 1{,}000$	3	1000 [PV]	1000
Future value, $S = 5{,}054.47$	4	5054.47 [FV]	5054.47
	5	[CPT] [%i]	9.9999993

(c) COMPUTER WITH BASIC

BASIC Program

```
10 INPUT "S";S
20 INPUT "P";P
30 INPUT "N";N
40 I = S∧(1/N)/P∧(1/N) – 1
50 PRINT "RATE = ";I
60 END
```

Computer Display (RUN)

```
S ? 5054.47
P ? 1000
N ? 17
RATE = 0.1
```

The numbers after the question marks (?) are typed input.

EXAMPLE 5

Compute Example 2, Section 11.5:

$$(1 + i)^{20} = \frac{890}{300}; \qquad i = .055845, \quad \text{or} \quad 5.5845\%$$

Use the BASIC program given in Example 4:

Computer Display (RUN)

```
S ? 890
P ? 300
N ? 20
RATE = 5.58773E – 2
```

The numbers after the question marks (?) are typed input.

NOTE: The number 5.58773E − 2 shown in the display represents the value 0.0558773. The notation E − 2 indicates that the decimal point should be moved two places to the left. Note that E with a positive number indicates that the decimal point should be moved to the right. For example, in

123,456 × 23,456 = 2.89578394E + 09

we should move the decimal point in the product 9 places to the right:

2.89578394E + 09 to 2.895783940. = 2,895,783,940

(2) CASE II—FIND THE NUMBER OF CONVERSION PERIODS, n

Solve for n from the formula:

$$n = \frac{\log S - \log P}{\log (1 + i)}$$

EXAMPLE 6 Compute Example 1, Section 11.6:

$$(1 + 2\%)^n = \frac{1{,}105}{1{,}000}; \qquad n = 5.042$$

(a) SIMPLE CALCULATOR

Not capable of computing with logarithms.

(b) BUSINESS ANALYST CALCULATOR

Problem	*Step*	*Key Pressing Sequence*	*Display*
Compute number of conversion periods:	1	[ON/C] [2nd] [FIN]	0
Present value, $P = 1{,}000$	2	1000 [PV]	1000
Future value, $S = 1{,}105$	3	1105 [FV]	1105
Percent interest rate per compounding period, $i = 2\%$	4	24 ÷ 12 = [%i]	2
	5	[CPT] [N]	5.042

(c) COMPUTER WITH BASIC

BASIC Program

```
10 INPUT "S";S
20 INPUT "P";P
30 INPUT "I";I
40 N = (LOG(S) - LOG(P))/LOG(1 + I)
50 PRINT "# PERIODS = ";N
60 END
```

Computer Display (RUN)

```
S ? 1105
P ? 1000
I ? .02
# PERIODS = 5.04204
```

The numbers after the question marks (?) are typed input.

The methods of computing formula (11–4), finding the effective rate f, by calculators and computers are similar to those for formula (11–1). (See Example 1.)

11.8 SUMMARY OF COMPOUND INTEREST FORMULAS

Application	*Formula*	*Formula Number*	*Reference Page*
Finding the compound amount	$S = P(1 + i)^n$	(11-1)	328
Finding the present value	$P = S(1 + i)^{-n}$	(11-2)	337
	or		
	$P = \dfrac{S}{(1 + i)^n}$	(11-2A)	337
Finding the interest rate (i) and the number of conversion periods (n)	$(1 + i)^n = \dfrac{S}{P}$	(11-3)	343
Finding the effective rate	$f = \left(1 + \dfrac{j}{m}\right)^m - 1$	(11-4)	345

EXERCISE 11–9 REVIEW OF CHAPTER 11

1. What are the compound amount and the compound interest at the end of ten years if $4,000 is borrowed at 16% compounded quarterly?
2. Find the compound amount and the compound interest at the end of six years if $5,000 is invested at 18% compounded monthly.
3. (a) What is the simple interest on $1,000 for five years at 12%? (b) What is the compound interest on $1,000 for five years at 12% compounded monthly?
4. What is the interest on $2,500 for $4\frac{1}{2}$ years at (a) $4\frac{1}{2}$% simple interest? (b) $4\frac{1}{2}$% compounded quarterly?
5. A note having a face value of $2,500 will mature in six years. The interest charged is 6% compounded monthly. Find the maturity value.
6. Find the compound amount if $3,000 is invested at 5% compounded monthly for 20 years.
7. The principal is $600 and the interest rate is 8% compounded monthly for the first seven years and 10% compounded semiannually for the next three years. Find the compound amount at the end of the tenth year.
8. What is the amount at the end of nine years if $1,000 is invested at 4% compounded quarterly for the first five years and at $5\frac{1}{2}$% compounded semiannually for the next four years?
9. Find the amount if $2,000 is invested at $5\frac{1}{4}$% compounded quarterly for seven years.
10. What is the amount if $4,000 is borrowed at $6\frac{1}{4}$% compounded monthly for ten years?
11. What are the amount and the interest if $5,000 is invested for five years and two months at 7% compounded annually?
12. Find the amount and the interest if $300 is borrowed for ten years and one month at 5% compounded quarterly.

13. (a) Find the present value if \$650 is due at the end of $5\frac{1}{2}$ years and money is worth 20% compounded quarterly. (b) What is the compound discount?
14. (a) What is the present value if \$2,000 is due at the end of four years and money is worth 24% compounded monthly? (b) What is the compound discount?
15. A note of \$500, dated April 1, 1988, plus 5% interest compounded quarterly was due in eight years. It was discounted at $5\frac{1}{2}$% compounded monthly on April 1, 1991. Find the proceeds and compound discount.
16. Carl had a note that would pay him \$400 plus 5% interest compounded quarterly at the end of six years. He sold the note two years before it was due at 6% compounded monthly. How much proceeds did he receive?
17. A non-interest-bearing note of \$800 is discounted at 5% compounded quarterly for five years and two months. Find the proceeds and the compound discount.
18. Tina received a note that would pay her \$700 on the due date. She discounted the note at 4% compounded semiannually four years and one month before it was due. Find the proceeds and the compound discount.
19. If \$900 will accumulate to \$1,500 in ten years, what is the interest rate compounded quarterly?
20. What is the nominal interest rate compounded monthly that will enable \$1,000 to amount to \$1,800 in eight years?
21. What is the effective rate if \$1 is invested for one year at 5% compounded (a) annually? (b) semiannually? (c) quarterly? (d) monthly?
22. What is the effective rate if money is worth 18% compounded monthly?
23. Alan invested his money at $5\frac{1}{2}$% compounded quarterly and Paula invested her money at 6% compounded annually. Which one of the two rates is higher?
24. Which is the higher rate: 4% compounded monthly or $4\frac{1}{2}$% compounded semiannually?
25. How long will it take \$200 to accumulate to the amount of \$300 at 12% compounded monthly?
26. How much time is needed for \$400 to yield \$136 interest if the interest rate is 10% compounded semiannually?

12 ★COMPOUND INTEREST—ADDITIONAL PROBLEMS

The additional compound interest problems presented in this chapter are: applications of logarithms using Tables 2 and 3 (Section 12.1), equivalent values (Section 12.2), equated date (Section 12.3), equivalent rates (Section 12.4), and continuously compounded interest (Section 12.5).

Under some conditions, the logarithmic method provides an effective way to compute compound interest and annuity problems. These conditions are listed in Section 12.1A.

In finding equivalent values and equated date, the equation of value must be used. An understanding of the concept of the equation of value is important in derivations and applications of formulas regarding interest problems. The equation of value involving simple interest problems was presented in Chapter 8. The equation of value involving compound interest problems is discussed in this chapter.

The subjects of equivalent rates and continuously compounded interest are closely related to the subject of effective annual interest rate. It is suggested that students review the material in Section 11.5B before studying the two subjects.

12.1 APPLICATIONS OF LOGARITHMS IN COMPOUND INTEREST PROBLEMS

A. Conditions for Using Logarithms

Logarithms can be used to compute compound interest and annuity problems (Chapters 13 to 20) under three different conditions:

1. *The available compound interest tables, such as Tables 5 through 11 in this book, do not provide enough information.* Example 3 in this section illustrates a problem under this condition. This example demonstrates the fact that instead of using the interpolation method as discussed in Chapter 11, we may use the logarithmic method to obtain a more accurate calculation for various rates.
2. *The compound interest tables, advanced calculators, or computers are not available.*

Under this condition the logarithmic method is frequently useful, since logarithmic tables, such as Table 2 with six-place mantissas, are printed in many mathematical, statistical, and other scientific books which can easily be obtained. Examples 6 and 7 are used to illustrate this method by using only Table 2 in the computations.

3. *Logarithms can be used to simplify the operations of multiplication, division, raising to powers, and extracting roots.* The logarithmic method is not always the best way to find the answers in multiplication and division. In some cases, the conventional method is simpler. The student should decide which one of the two methods is the most convenient way for solving a given problem. In general, the choice is not too difficult to make if a student is familiar with logarithmic operations. For instance, it is obvious that the conventional method should be employed in finding the answer for multiplying 2.35678 by 1,000, since the multiplication process can be completed simply by moving the decimal point three places to the right, or

   $2.35678 \times 1{,}000 = 2{,}356.78$

   However, in finding the answer for expression

   $S = 1{,}000(1 + 2\%)^{120}$

   the logarithmic method is the better one. (See Example 2.)

Note that the results of the mathematical operations using logarithms are approximations. However, if the interpolation method is properly applied to the tables of logarithms, the results usually are very close to the actual answers.

B. Applications of Logarithms

The logarithmic method may be used to solve any unknown value if any three of the four values in formula (11–1), $S = P(1 + i)^n$, are known. To obtain a more accurate answer, the use of seven-place mantissa tables, if applicable, is preferred to that of six-place tables.

EXAMPLE 1

Find the value of S when $S = 1{,}500(1 + 3\%)^{17}$.

By applying logarithms,

$$
\begin{array}{rlll}
 & \log 1{,}500 & = 3.176\ 0910 & \text{(Table 2)} \\
(+)\ \log(1 + 3\%)^{17} & = 17\ (\log 1.03) & & \\
 & = 17\ (0.0128372) & = 0.218\ 2324 & \text{(Table 3)} \\
\hline
 & \log S & = 3.394\ 3234 &
\end{array}
$$

Find antilog 3.394 3234 by the interpolation method from Table 2. The number of significant digits (x) is determined by adding 4 to the value of the characteristic, or

Number	*Mantissa*	
2480 000	394 4520	(1)
x	394 3234	(2)
2479 000	394 2770	(3)

$$x = 2479\ 000 + \frac{464}{1750}(1{,}000) = 2479\ 265$$

$$\frac{x - 2479\ 000}{1\ 000} = \frac{464}{1750} \quad \frac{(2) - (3)}{(1) - (3)}$$

$S = 2{,}479.265$, or rounded to 2,479.27

4 + 3 = 7 digits. This number will assure enough decimal places so that the answer may be rounded to the nearest cent.

The answer, $2,479.27, may be compared with that of Example 2 in Section 11.3, page 330.

EXAMPLE 2 Find the value of S when $S = 1{,}000(1 + 2\%)^{120}$.

$$\begin{aligned} \log 1{,}000 &= 3.0000000 \quad \text{(Table 3)} \\ (+)\log(1+2\%)^{120} &= 120\,(\log 1.02) \\ &= 120\,(0.0086002) = 1.0320240 \quad \text{(Table 3)} \\ \hline \log S &= 4.0320240 \end{aligned}$$

Find antilog 4.0320240 by the interpolation method from Table 3. The rule stated in Example 1 requires 4 + 4 = 8 significant digits, since the characteristic is 4. However, we shall use only 7 digits as the maximum number, since the accuracy of the answer would not increase if 8 digits were used in the interpolation. (See the note on page 334.)

Number	*Mantissa*	
1076 600	032 0544	(1)
x	032 0240	(2)
1076 500	032 0140	(3)

$$\frac{x - 1076\ 500}{100} = \frac{100}{404} \quad \begin{matrix}(2)-(3)\\(1)-(3)\end{matrix}$$

$$x = 1076\ 500 + \frac{100}{404}(100)$$
$$= 1076\ 525$$
$$S = 10{,}765.25$$

The answer, $10,765.25, may be compared with that of Example 4 in Section 11.3, page 331.

EXAMPLE 3 Find the value of S when $S = 1{,}000(1 + 2\tfrac{1}{8}\%)^{10}$.

$$\begin{aligned} \log 1{,}000 &= 3.0000000 \quad \text{(Table 3)} \\ (+)\log(1+2\tfrac{1}{8}\%)^{10} = 10 \times \log 1.02125 &= 0.0913205 \quad \text{(Table 3, by interpolation)} \\ \hline \log S &= 3.0913205 \end{aligned}$$

Find the antilog by interpolation from Table 2.

$S = 1{,}234.015625$, or rounded to 1,234.02

The answer, $1,234.02, may be compared with that of Example 6 in Section 11.3, page 334 (also see Note 4 on that page).

EXAMPLE 4 Find the value of S when $S = 1{,}000(1 + 3\%)^{6\ 1/3}$.

$$\begin{aligned} \log 1{,}000 &= 3.0000000 \quad \text{(Table 3)} \\ (+)\log(1+3\%)^{6\ 1/3} &= (6\tfrac{1}{3})(\log 1.03) \\ &= (\tfrac{19}{3})(0.0128372) = 0.0813022 \quad \text{(Table 3)} \\ \hline \log S &= 3.0813022 \end{aligned}$$

Find the antilog by interpolation from Table 2.

$S = \$1{,}205.876$, or round to $1,205.88

The answer, $1,205.88, may be compared with that of Example 7 in Section 11.3, page 336.

EXAMPLE 5 Find the value of P when $P = 2{,}479.27(1 + 3\%)^{-17}$.

$$
\begin{aligned}
\log 2{,}479.27 &= 3.3943243 \quad \text{(Table 2, by interpolation)} \\
(+)\ \log (1 + 3\%)^{-17} &= (-17)(\log 1.03) \\
&= (-17)(0.0128372) \\
&= -0.2182324 = 9.7817676 - 10 \quad \text{(Table 3)} \\
\hline
\log P &= 13.1760919 - 10 \\
&= 3.1760919
\end{aligned}
$$

Find the antilog by interpolation from Table 2. $P = 1{,}500.00$.

The answer, \$1,500, may be compared with that of Example 1 in Section 11.4, page 337.

EXAMPLE 6 Find the value of i when $S = 890$, $P = 300$, and $n = 20$.

Substituting the known values in formula (11–3), $(1 + i)^n = \dfrac{S}{P}$:

$$(1 + i)^{20} = \frac{890}{300}$$

By applying logarithms,

$$\log (1 + i)^{20} = \log \left(\frac{890}{300}\right)$$

$$20 \times \log (1 + i) = \log 890 - \log 300$$

$$
\begin{aligned}
\log 890 &= 2.949390 \\
(-)\ \log 300 &= 2.477121 \quad \text{(Table 2)} \\
\hline
20 \times \log (1 + i) &= 0.472269
\end{aligned}
$$

$$\log (1 + i) = \frac{0.472269}{20} = 0.023613$$

Find the antilog.

$(1 + i) = 1.055857$ (by interpolation)
$i = .055857$, or 5.5857%

The answer may be compared with that of Example 2 in Section 11.5, page 343.

EXAMPLE 7 Find the value of n when $S = 1{,}105$, $P = 1{,}000$, and $i = 2\%$. Substituting the known values in formula (11–3):

$$(1 + 2\%)^n = \frac{S}{P} = \frac{1{,}105}{1{,}000}$$

By applying logarithms,

$$\log (1 + 2\%)^n = \log \left(\frac{1{,}105}{1{,}000}\right)$$

$$n \times \log 1.02 = \log 1{,}105 - \log 1{,}000$$

$$n = \frac{\log 1{,}105 - \log 1{,}000}{\log 1.02} = \frac{3.043362 - 3}{.0086002} = 5.042 \quad \text{(Table 2)}$$

The answer may be compared with that of Example 1 in Section 11.6, page 347.

EXERCISE 12–1 REFERENCE: SECTION 12.1

A. Use the logarithmic method to find the unknown value in each of the following problems:

	S	P	i	n
1.	\$?	\$4,000	3%	10
2.	250	?	$1\frac{1}{4}$%	42
3.	1,140	1,000	?	40
4.	2,930	2,500	1%	?
5.	640	?	4%	30
6.	?	300	$5\frac{1}{2}$%	20
7.	5,470	3,600	$\frac{1}{2}$%	?
8.	4,160	2,800	?	16
9.	?	5,000	$3\frac{1}{2}$%	12
10.	1,665	?	$1\frac{1}{2}$%	22

B. Statement problems:

11. Compute $(1 + 7\frac{1}{4}\%)^3$ by the following methods: (a) binomial theorem (see page 85), (b) interpolation (from Table 5), and (c) logarithmic (carry your answer to seven decimal places). Which method gives the most accurate answer? the next accurate? the least accurate?
12. Compute $(1 + 4\frac{1}{4}\%)^4$ by the methods indicated in Problem 11. Which method gives the most accurate answer? the next accurate? the least accurate?

12.2 EQUIVALENT VALUES INVOLVING COMPOUND INTEREST

It was stated in Chapter 8 that a single obligation or a set of obligations may be replaced by another single obligation or set of obligations due at different times. In order to satisfy both the creditors and the debtors, the values of the new obligations should be equivalent to the values of the original ones. An *equation of value* is usually arranged in order to obtain the required equivalent values. The equation gives the equivalent values of the original obligations and the new obligations on a *comparison date*, sometimes called the *focal date*, at the agreed or present investment market interest rate. The answer for a required equivalent value may vary slightly in simple interest problems, depending on the selection of the comparison date. However, in compound interest problems the selection of the comparison date does not affect the answer.

The formula $S = P(1 + i)^n$ is an equation of value, since the value of S is equivalent to the value of P after n periods with a compound interest rate i per period. Thus, if $P = \$1$, $i = 6\%$ compounded annually, and $n = 3$ (years), then $S = 1(1 + 6\%)^3 = \$1.19$. The illustration may be stated as follows: If money is worth 6% compounded annually (the value on the present investment market), \$1 now is equivalent to \$1.19 in three years.

Likewise, the formula $P = S(1 + i)^{-n}$ is an equation of value, since the value of P is equivalent to the value of S for n periods *before* it is due when the interest rate i per period is involved. Thus, if $S = \$1$, $i = 6\%$ compounded annually, and $n = 3$ (years), then $P = 1(1 + 6\%)^{-3} = \$.84$. Therefore, \$1 due in three years at 6% compounded annually is equivalent to \$.84 now.

Note that a sum of money has different values at different times if interest is involved, and the amount due in the future is normally larger than its equivalent value at the present time. A person may borrow \$1 now and repay \$1.19 after three years. On the other hand, a creditor may agree to discharge a debt of \$1 that is due in three years by having the debtor pay only \$.84 now. The values in the two transactions are equivalent to each other under the compound interest method. The following examples illustrate further problems in equivalent values involving compound interest.

EXAMPLE 1

A debt of \$200 is due at the end of four years. If money is worth 6% compounded quarterly, what is the value of the debt when it is paid (a) at the end of one year? (b) at the end of six years?

According to the problem, \$200 is the maturity value, or the amount due at the end of four years. The interest rate, which is agreed upon by both lender and borrower to settle the debt, is 6% compounded quarterly.

(a) If the debt of \$200 is paid at the end of one year, which is three years (or 12 quarters) before the due date, the required equivalent value is less than \$200. Thus, the compound discount formula $P = S(1 + i)^{-n}$ is used to compute the required value. In other words, the value is obtained by discounting the maturity value (or the amount on the due date) by the compound discount method for the advanced time of three years.

$S = 200$, $i = 6\%/4 = 1\frac{1}{2}\%$ (per quarter), $n = 12$ (quarters)

Substituting the values in the compound discount formula,

$P = 200(1 + 1\frac{1}{2}\%)^{-12} = 200(0.83639) = \$167.28$

If the debt is paid at the end of the first year, the payment is \$167.28.

(b) If the debt of \$200 is paid at the end of six years, which is two years (or eight quarters) after the due date, the required equivalent value is more than \$200. Thus, the compound amount formula $S = P(1 + i)^n$ is used to compute the required value. In other words, the value is obtained by accumulating the amount on the due date for the extended time of two years.

$P = 200$, $i = 1\frac{1}{2}\%$ (per quarter), $n = 8$ (quarters)

Substituting the values in the compound amount formula,

$S = 200(1 + 1\frac{1}{2}\%)^8 = 200(1.12649) = \$225.30$

When the debt is paid at the end of the sixth year, the payment is \$225.30.

The example may be diagrammed as follows:

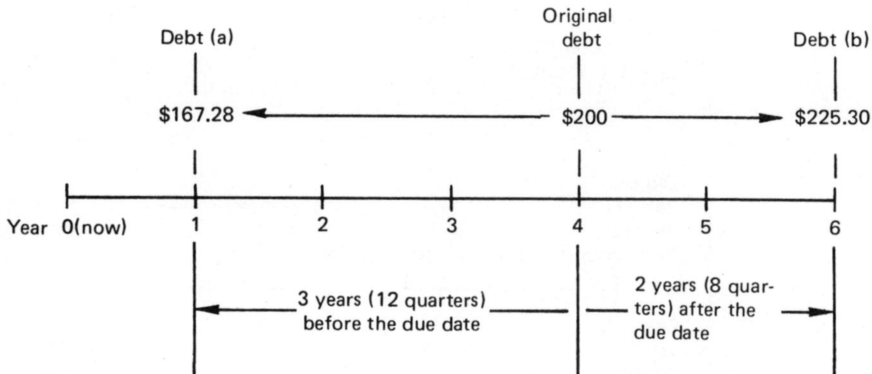

EXAMPLE 2 A man owes (a) \$300 due in three years and (b) \$400 due in eight years. He and his creditor have agreed to settle the debts by two equal payments in five and six years, respectively. Find the size of each payment if money is worth 6% compounded semiannually.

Let x be each payment and the comparison date be six years from now. The values on the comparison date are computed below.

(1) The value of the old debt of \$300 becomes \$358.22 on the comparison date and is computed as follows:

P = 300, $i = 6\%/2 = 3\%$, $n = (6 - 3) \times 2 = 6$ (semiannual periods, from the due date to the comparison date)

Substituting the values in the formula $S = P(1 + i)^n$,

$$S = 300(1 + 3\%)^6$$
$$= 300(1.19405) = \$358.22$$

(2) The value of the old debt of \$400 becomes \$355.40 on the comparison date and is computed as follows:

$S = 400, i = 3\%, n = (8 - 6) \times 2 = 4$ (semiannual periods from the comparison date to the due date)

Substituting the values in the formula $P = S(1 + i)^{-n}$,

$$P = 400(1 + 3\%)^{-4}$$
$$= 400(.88849) = \$355.40$$

(3) The value of the new debt, which is the first payment due in five years, becomes $x(1.03)^2$ on the comparison date and is computed as follows:

$P = x, i = 3\%, n = (6 - 5) \times 2 = 2$ (semiannual periods from the due date to the comparison date)

Substituting the values in the formula $S = P(1 + i)^n$,

$$S = x(1 + 3\%)^2 = x(1.03)^2$$

(4) The value of the second payment due in six years does not change and is x, since the comparison date is also in six years.

The values in Example 2 are diagrammed in the following manner:

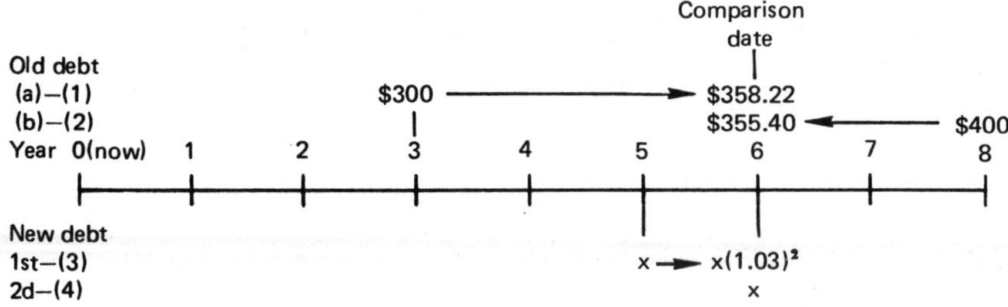

The equation of value based on the comparison date is given below:

$$\overbrace{x + x(1.03)^2}^{\textit{New Debts}} = \overbrace{355.40 + 358.22}^{\textit{Old Debts}}$$

Solve for x.

$$x + x(1.0609) = 713.62$$
$$2.0609x = 713.62$$
$$x = \$346.27$$

EXAMPLE 3 A man owes (a) \$700 due in three years and (b) \$1,000 due in eight years. His creditor has agreed for him to pay the debts with a payment of \$800 in one year and the remainder in five years. If money is worth 4% compounded annually, what size must the second payment be?

Let x be the second payment, which is to be made on the comparison date, or five years hence. The following diagram indicates the equivalent values on the comparison date of the given values.

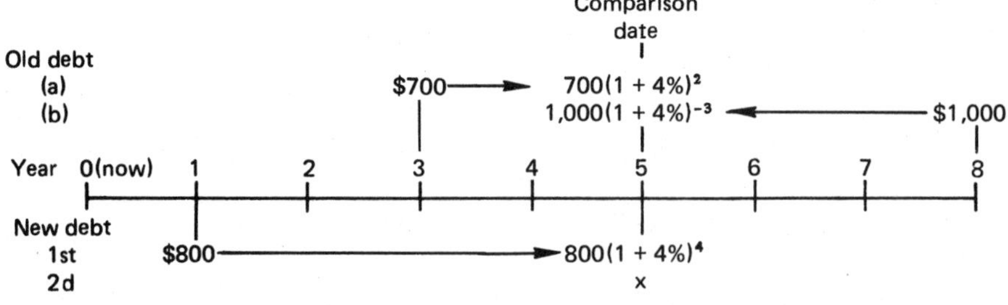

The equation of value based on the comparison date follows:

New Debts *Old Debts*

$$x + 800(1 + 4\%)^4 = 1{,}000(1 + 4\%)^{-3} + 700(1 + 4\%)^2$$
$$x = 1{,}000(0.888996) + 700(1.0816) - 800(1.16986)$$
$$= 888.996 + 757.120 - 935.888$$
$$= \$710.23$$

EXAMPLE 4 A man owes (a) \$500 due in two years, and (b) \$1,000 with interest at 16% compounded quarterly due in three years. If money is worth 18% compounded semiannually, what single payment seven years hence will be equivalent to the two original obligations?

Let x be the unknown single payment and let the comparison date be seven years hence.

(a) The value of the old debt of \$500 on the comparison date is

$$500(1 + 18\%/2)^{10} = 500(1 + 9\%)^{10}$$

(b) Since \$1,000 is an interest-bearing debt, the maturity value based on a 16% interest rate compounded quarterly for three years (or 12 quarters) should be computed first. The maturity value is then accumulated at 18% compounded semiannually for four years (or eight semiannual periods) from the due date to the comparison date.

The maturity value at the end of three years is

$$\$1{,}000(1 + 16\%/4)^{12} = 1{,}000(1 + 4\%)^{12}$$
$$= 1{,}000(1.601032) = \$1{,}601.03$$

and its value on the comparison date becomes

$$\$1{,}601.03(1 + 18\%/2)^8 = 1{,}601.03(1 + 9\%)^8 = \$3{,}190.15$$

The entire problem is diagrammed in the following manner:

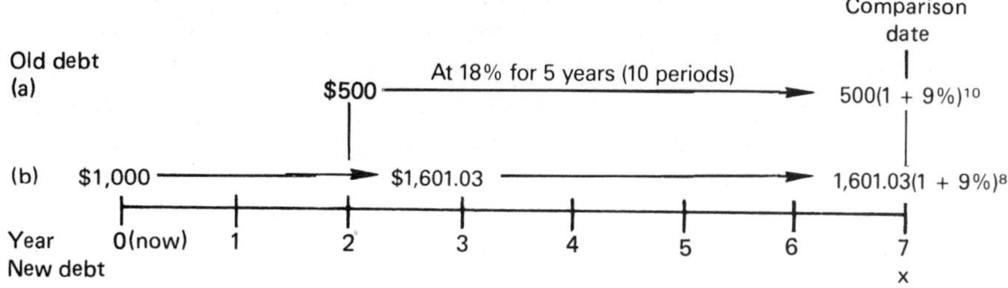

The equation of value based on the comparison date is written below:

New Debts *Old Debts*

$$x = 500(1 + 9\%)^{10} + 1{,}601.03(1 + 9\%)^8$$
$$= 500(2.36736) + 1{,}601.03(1.992563)$$
$$= 1{,}183.68 + 3{,}190.15$$
$$= \$4{,}373.83$$

EXERCISE 12–2 REFERENCE: SECTION 12.2

A. Find the value of the new obligations in each of the following problems:

Original Debt	Interest Rate, Compounded	New Debt and Comparison Date
1. $800 due in 2 years	16%, quarterly	All in 6 years
2. $300 due in 3 years	18%, monthly	All in 5 years
3. (a) $5,000 due in 4 years (b) $2,000 due in 12 years	6%, quarterly	Two equal payments: one in 6 years, the other in 9 years. Comparison date: 9 years hence.
4. (a) $2,400 due in 3 years (b) $4,700 due in 14 years	4%, annually	Two equal payments: one in 7 years, the other in 16 years. Comparison date: 7 years hence.
5. (a) $1,000 due in 5 years (b) $1,600 due in 10 years	7%, semiannually	$600 in 1 year, the remainder in 8 years.
6. (a) $3,400 due in 4 years (b) $4,500 due in 9 years	5%, monthly	$3,000 in 5 years, the remainder in 7 years.
7. (a) $1,800 due in 6 years (b) $2,500 due in 11 years	4%, annually	All in 18 years
8. (a) $1,500 due in 7 years (b) $4,000 due in 10 years	5%, semiannually	All in 8 years

B. Statement problems:

9. A debt of $4,200 is due in seven years. If money is worth 6% compounded monthly, what is the value of the debt if it is paid: (a) five years hence, (b) seven years hence, (c) ten years hence?
10. A debt of $5,200 is due in eight years. If money is worth 5% compounded quarterly, what is the value of the debt if it is paid: (a) at the end of four years, (b) at the end of eight years, (c) at the end of 11 years?
11. A man owes (a) $2,800 due in three years and (b) $3,600 due in ten years. He and his creditor agree to settle the obligations by two equal payments, one in five years and the other in 15 years. Find the size of each payment if money is worth 4% compounded semiannually and the comparison date is 15 years hence.
12. Find the size of each payment in Problem 11 if the comparison date is five years hence.
13. A man owes (a) $2,000 due in four years and (b) $1,700 due in six years. His creditor has agreed for him to pay the debts with a payment of $1,500 in three years and the remainder in eight years. If money is worth 7% compounded quarterly, what size must the second payment be?
14. Refer to Problem 13. If the remainder of the debt is to be paid in five years, what is the size of the second payment?

15. A woman owes (a) \$300 due in one year and (b) \$700 due in four years, plus interest at 6% compounded semiannually. If money is worth 5% compounded monthly, what single payment three years from now will be equivalent to the two debts?
16. Refer to Problem 15. What single payment made six years from now will be equivalent to the two debts?

12.3 EQUATED DATE

The equated date is generally defined as the date on which a single payment equal to the sum of a set of obligations is made to discharge the obligations. Nevertheless, the idea may be extended to a situation where the single payment is not equal to the sum of a set of old obligations.

The basic principle for computing an equated date is the same as the one used in Section 12.2. However, as shown in the following examples, the amount of the payment for discharging the old debts in an equation of value is known, but the equated date is unknown.

EXAMPLE 1

John borrowed some money from Mary as follows: (a) \$100 due in one year, (b) \$300 due in two years, and (c) \$400 due in two and one-half years. If money is worth 4% compounded semiannually, when can John discharge all of his debts by a single payment of \$800?

Let "now" be the comparison date. The problem may be diagrammed as follows:

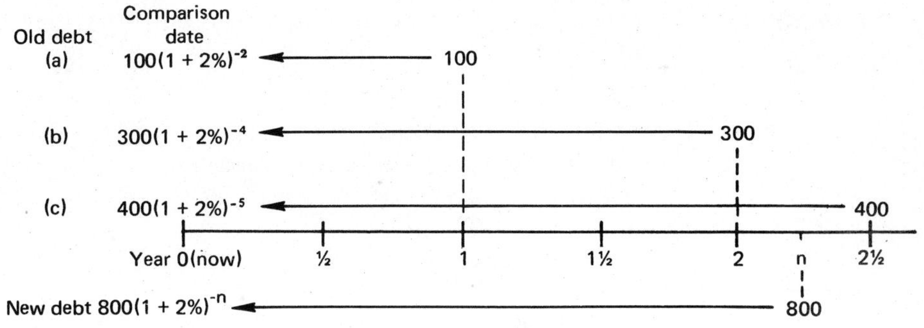

From the above diagram, the following equation of value may be written:

$$\begin{aligned} 800(1 + 2\%)^{-n} &= 100(1 + 2\%)^{-2} + 300(1 + 2\%)^{-4} + 400(1 + 2\%)^{-5} \\ &= 100(.96117) + 300(.92385) + 400(.90573) \\ &= 96.117 + 277.155 + 362.292 \\ &= 735.564 \end{aligned}$$

$$(1 + 2\%)^{-n} = \frac{735.564}{800} = .9195$$

The n value is interpolated from Table 6 as follows: (Write the larger numbers, which are in the column of values all known, on the top lines.)

	n	$(1+2\%)^{-n}$	
	4	.9238	(1)
	x	.9195	(2)
	5	.9057	(3)
(2) − (3)	$x-5$	.0138	(4)
(1) − (3)	−1	.0181	(5)

$$\frac{x-5}{-1} = \frac{.0138}{.0181}$$

Solve for x from the proportion formed by the differences on lines (4) and (5).

$$x - 5 = (-1)\left(\frac{.0138}{.0181}\right) = (-1)\left(\frac{138}{181}\right) = -.7624$$

$$x = 5 - .7624 = 4.2376$$

Thus, $n = 4.2376$ (semiannual periods), or two years and 43 days (.2376 × 180 days = 43 days).

NOTE: The value of n may be obtained by the use of logarithms as follows:

$(1+2\%)^{-n} = .9195, \qquad -n \log 1.02 = \log .9195$

$$-n = \frac{\log .9195}{\log 1.02} = \frac{9.963552-10}{0.0086} = \frac{-.036448}{0.0086} = -4.2381$$

$$n = 4.2381$$

This answer is more accurate than that obtained by the interpolation method.

EXAMPLE 2 Refer to Example 1. If the single payment is \$810, when can John discharge all of his debts?

Again let "now" be the comparison date. Then

$810(1+2\%)^{-n} = 735.564$ (Notice that the right side of the equation of value is identical to that of Example 1.)

$$(1+2\%)^{-n} = \frac{735.564}{810} = .9081$$

By interpolation from Table 6,

$n = 4.8674$ (semiannual periods), or two years and 156 days (.8674 × 180 days = 156 days)

EXAMPLE 3 Refer to Example 1. If the debt of \$400 due in $2\frac{1}{2}$ years is charged with interest at 3% compounded quarterly, when can John discharge his entire debt by a single payment of \$800?

Let "now" be the comparison date. The maturity value of the \$400 debt at the end of $2\frac{1}{2}$ years will be

$400(1+\frac{3}{4}\%)^{10}$

Thus, the equation of value is

$$800(1 + 2\%)^{-n} = 100(1 + 2\%)^{-2} + 300(1 + 2\%)^{-4} + 400(1 + \tfrac{3}{4}\%)^{10}(1 + 2\%)^{-5}$$
$$= 96.117 + 277.155 + 400(1.07758)(.90573)$$
$$= 96.117 + 277.155 + 390.399$$
$$= 763.671$$

$$(1 + 2\%)^{-n} = \frac{763.671}{800} = .9546$$

By interpolation from Table 6,

$n = 2.3492$ (semiannual periods), or one year and 63 days (.3492 × 180 days = 63 days)

EXERCISE 12–3 REFERENCE: SECTION 12.3

A. Find the equated date in each of the following problems:

	Original Debt	*Interest Rate, Compounded*	*Single Payment Used to Discharge the Original Debt*
1.	(a) \$5,000 due in 4 years	6%, quarterly	\$7,000
	(b) \$2,000 due in 12 years		
2.	(a) \$2,400 due in 3 years	4%, annually	7,100
	(b) \$4,700 due in 14 years		
3.	(a) \$1,000 due in 5 years	7%, semiannually	2,600
	(b) \$1,600 due in 10 years		
4.	(a) \$2,000 due in 2 years	9%, monthly	2,500
	(b) \$500 due in $3\frac{1}{2}$ years		
5.	(a) \$180 due in 6 years	4%, annually	530
	(b) \$200 due in 4 years		
	(c) \$150 due in 8 years		
6.	(a) \$150 due in 7 years	5%, semiannually	750
	(b) \$200 due in 8 years		
	(c) \$400 due in 10 years		

B. Statement problems:

7. When will the two debts in Problem 1 be discharged if the single payment is (a) \$6,800? (b) \$7,200?
8. When will the two debts in Problem 2 be discharged if the single payment is (a) \$6,700? (b) \$7,400?
9. Find the date on which the two debts in Problem 3 can be settled by a single payment of \$2,500.
10. Find the date on which the two debts in Problem 4 can be settled by a single payment of \$2,700.
11. Larry owes Steve (a) \$200 due in two years, (b) \$300 with interest at 3% compounded semiannually due in three years, and (c) \$700 with interest at 4% compounded quarterly due in four years. If money now is worth $5\frac{1}{2}$% (effective rate), when will a single amount of \$1,200 repay the three debts?

12. Patricia owes Christina (a) \$400 due in four years, (b) \$500 with interest at 4% compounded monthly due in five years, and (c) \$800 with interest at 5% compounded annually due in seven years. If money now is worth 6% compounded semiannually, when will a single amount of \$1,700 repay the three debts?
13. Refer to Problem 11. If Larry pays Steve \$500 now, when should he pay another \$700 to settle the entire debt?
14. Refer to Problem 12. If Patricia pays Christina \$900 now, when should she pay another \$800 to settle the entire debt?

12.4 EQUIVALENT RATES

If a principal invested at various interest rates will accumulate to the same compound amount in a certain period of time, the rates are said to be equivalent to each other. The various interest rates are thus called *equivalent rates*. Equivalent rates may be obtained by the use of the effective rate method based on a one-year period, as illustrated in the following examples.

EXAMPLE 1

At what nominal rate compounded quarterly will a principal yield an interest that is equivalent to an effective rate of 7%?

$m = 4$ (quarters), $f = 7\%$

Substituting the values in formula (11–4), $f = \left(1 + \frac{j}{m}\right)^m - 1$,

$$7\% = \left(1 + \frac{j}{4}\right)^4 - 1, \left(1 + \frac{j}{4}\right)^4 = 1 + 7\%$$

Extract the fourth root of each side of the above equations; then

$$\left(1 + \frac{j}{4}\right) = (1 + 7\%)^{1/4} = 1.01706 \quad \text{(Table 5A)}$$

Thus, $\frac{j}{4} = 1.01706 - 1 = .01706$

$j = .01706 \times 4 = .06824$, or the nominal rate is 6.824%, which is rounded to 6.82%.

The nominal rate 6.82% compounded quarterly is equivalent to an effective rate of 7%.

A more accurate answer for Example 1 may be obtained from Table 11. Table 11 gives the values of j_m (nominal rate j compounded m times a year) and their equivalent values of f (effective rate).[1]

[1]The formula for the value of j_m may be derived from the effective rate formula (11–4) as follows:

$$\left(1 + \frac{j}{m}\right)^m = 1 + f$$

Extract the mth root of each side of the above equation; then

$$1 + \frac{j}{m} = (1 + f)^{1/m}$$

$$j = m[(1 + f)^{1/m} - 1]$$

When $f = 7\%$, and $m = 4$, the value shown in Table 11 is

$j = .06823410, \quad \text{or} \quad 6.82341\%$

EXAMPLE 2 At what nominal rate compounded monthly will a principal accumulate to the same amount as at 8% compounded quarterly?

Let the unknown nominal rate be j; then $i = j/12$ (per month). The effective rate in the first case is

$$f = \left(1 + \frac{j}{12}\right)^{12} - 1$$

In the latter case, $i = 8\%/4 = 2\%$ (per quarter). The effective rate is

$$f = (1 + 2\%)^4 - 1$$

Since the accumulated amount in the first case is the same as the amount in the latter case, the effective rates must be the same in both cases. Thus,

$$\left(1 + \frac{j}{12}\right)^{12} - 1 = (1 + 2\%)^4 - 1, \quad \text{or}$$

$$\left(1 + \frac{j}{12}\right)^{12} = (1 + 2\%)^4$$

Extract the 12th root on each side of the above equation; then

$$\left(1 + \frac{j}{12}\right) = (1 + 2\%)^{4/12} = (1 + 2\%)^{1/3} = 1.006623 \quad \text{(Table 5A)}$$

$$\frac{j}{12} = 1.006623 - 1 = .006623$$

$$j = .006623 \times 12 = .079476, \quad \text{or rounded to} \quad 7.95\%$$

It may be stated that 7.95% compounded monthly is equivalent to 8% compounded quarterly. This statement holds true for any principal and for any number of periods of investment.

From Example 2, note that the nominal rate of 7.95% is computed from the equation

$$\left(1 + \frac{j}{12}\right) = (1 + 2\%)^{1/3}$$

which does not contain the values of S and P. Furthermore, both sides of the equation are the accumulation factor for a one-month period, which is also the conversion period of the unknown nominal rate. Thus, computation of equivalent rate problems may be simplified by using an equation that contains only the accumulation factors of a length equal to *one conversion period* for the unknown nominal rate.

EXAMPLE 3 If a principal P, invested at 6% compounded quarterly for three years, will accumulate to the compound amount S, at what nominal rate compounded semiannually will the principal accumulate to the same amount in the same period?

Let the unknown nominal rate be j; then $i = j/2$ (per semiannual period). The accumulation factor for one conversion period (six months) is $(1 + j/2)$.

In the first case, $i = 6\%/4 = 1\frac{1}{2}\%$ (per quarter). The accumulation factor for a six-month period (the conversion period for the unknown rate j) or two quarters is $(1 + 1\frac{1}{2}\%)^2$. The equation may be written as follows:

$$\left(1 + \frac{j}{2}\right) = (1 + 1\tfrac{1}{2}\%)^2$$

Since $(1 + 1\frac{1}{2}\%)^2 = 1.030225$ (Table 5)

$$1 + \frac{j}{2} = 1.030225$$

$$\frac{j}{2} = 1.030225 - 1$$

$$j = .030225 \times 2 = .06045, \quad \text{or} \quad 6.05\%$$

Thus, a principal P invested at 6% compounded quarterly will accumulate to the same amount as if invested at 6.05% compounded semiannually during a period of three years. The values of P, S, and n (three years) need not be included in the computation.

12.5 CONTINUOUSLY COMPOUNDED INTEREST

Although compound interest is usually computed at regularly stated intervals such as annually, semiannually, quarterly, or monthly, it may be computed more frequently such as every minute, every second, or continuously. Continuous compounding is not commonly used in the actual investment market. However, the concept is theoretically important in analyzing financial problems.

To compute interest at a nominal rate compounded continuously, first find the equivalent effective rate, then compute the compound interest based on the effective rate. The formula for finding the effective rate of the nominal rate j compounded continuously can be derived from formula (11–4), which is

$$f = \left(1 + \frac{j}{m}\right)^m - 1$$

where f = effective rate
j = nominal rate
m = number of conversion periods for one year

The derivation is presented below.

Let $k = \frac{m}{j}$ and $\frac{1}{k} = \frac{j}{m}$. Then the term

$$\left(1 + \frac{j}{m}\right)^m = \left[\left(1 + \frac{j}{m}\right)^{m/j}\right]^j = \left[\left(1 + \frac{1}{k}\right)^k\right]^j$$

The values of $\left(1 + \frac{1}{k}\right)^k$ can be computed as shown on page 371.

When k approaches an infinitely large value ($k \to \infty$), the limit of $(1 + 1/k)^k$, usually denoted by the letter e, is an irrational number and is approximately 2.71828. It is written

$$e = \lim_{k \to \infty} \left(1 + \frac{1}{k}\right)^k = 2.71828, \quad \text{approximately}$$

When k is	*The value of* $\left(1 + \frac{1}{k}\right)^k$ *is*
1	$\left(1 + \frac{1}{1}\right)^1 = 2$
2	$\left(1 + \frac{1}{2}\right)^2 = (1.5)^2 = 2.25$
10	$\left(1 + \frac{1}{10}\right)^{10} = (1.1)^{10} = 2.594$
100	$\left(1 + \frac{1}{100}\right)^{100} = (1.01)^{100} = 2.705$
1,000	$\left(1 + \frac{1}{1,000}\right)^{1,000} = (1.001)^{1,000} = 2.716$
10,000	$\left(1 + \frac{1}{10,000}\right)^{10,000} = (1.0001)^{10,000} = 2.7164$
. . .	. . . (Use Tables 2 and 3.)

(An irrational number is a number that cannot be written as a fraction with integers for numerator and denominator—it is a never-ending decimal.)

When j is compounded continuously, m becomes infinitely large; the value of $k = m/j$ also becomes infinitely large, and the term $(1 + j/m)^m$ equals e^j, or

$$\left(1 + \frac{j}{m}\right)^m = \left[\left(1 + \frac{1}{k}\right)^k\right]^j = e^j$$

When e^j is substituted into formula (11–4), the effective rate of the nominal rate j compounded continuously is

$$\mathbf{f = e^j - 1} \qquad \textbf{(12–1)}$$

The value of e^j can be approximated by using logarithms, as illustrated in Example 1(a) or by a table, as illustrated in the following examples. Table 12–1 shows the values of e^j for selected values of j computed to eight decimal places. The value of e^j for other values of j may also be obtained from the table after applying the laws of exponents, as illustrated in Example 2.

EXAMPLE 1

Find the effective rate if money is worth 6% compounded continuously. Here $j = 6\% = .06$.

(a) Use logarithms:

$$e^j = 2.71828^{.06}$$

$$\log e^j = \log(2.71828^{.06}) = .06(\log 2.71828)$$
$$= .06(0.434294) = 0.026058$$

$$e^j = 1.061837 \quad \text{(by interpolation from Table 2)}$$

Substituting the e^j value in formula (12–1),

$$f = 1.061837 - 1 = 0.061837, \quad \text{or} \quad 6.1837\%$$

(b) Use Table 12–1.

$$e^j = 1.06183655 \quad \text{at} \quad j = .06 \quad \text{or} \quad 6\%$$
$$f = 1.06183655 - 1 = 0.06183655 \quad \text{or} \quad 6.183655\%$$

(Also see page 346 for the comparison table of f values by different periods of compounding.)

The value of f is more accurate when we use Table 12–1.

Table 12–1 Values of e^j for Selected Values of j

j	e^j	j	e^j	j	e^j
.000	1.0000 0000				
.001	1.0010 0050	.01	1.0100 5017	.1	1.1051 7092
.002	1.0020 0200	.02	1.0202 0134	.2	1.2214 0276
.003	1.0030 0450	.03	1.0304 5453	.3	1.3498 5881
.004	1.0040 0801	.04	1.0408 1077	.4	1.4918 2470
.005	1.0050 1252	.05	1.0512 7110	.5	1.6487 2127
.006	1.0060 1804	.06	1.0618 3655	.6	1.8221 1880
.007	1.0070 2456	.07	1.0725 0818	.7	2.0137 5271
.008	1.0080 3209	.08	1.0832 8707	.8	2.2255 4093
.009	1.0090 4062	.09	1.0941 7428	.9	2.4596 0311
				1.0	2.7182 8183

EXAMPLE 2

Find the effective rate if money is worth $7\frac{1}{2}\%$ compounded continuously.

Here $j = 7\frac{1}{2}\% = .075$.

$$e^j = e^{.075} = e^{.07}(e^{.005}) = 1.07250818(1.00501252)$$
$$= 1.07788415 \quad \text{(Table 12–1)}$$

Substituting e^j value in formula (12–1),

$$f = 1.07788415 - 1 = 0.07788415, \quad \text{or} \quad 7.788415\%$$

By substituting the effective rate for continuous compounding f (formula 12–1) for i in the compound amount formula S, we have

$$S = P(1 + i)^n = P(1 + f)^n = P(1 + [e^j - 1])^n$$
$$= P(e^j)^n = P(e^{jn})$$

Thus, the formula for finding the compound amount (S) of the principal (P) at the nominal rate j compounded continuously for n years is

$$\mathbf{S = P(e^{jn})} \qquad \textbf{(12–2)}$$

EXAMPLE 3

Find the compound amount and the compound interest when \$10,000 is invested at 5% compounded continuously for (a) one year and (b) two years.

$P = \$10{,}000,\ j = 5\% = .05$

Use formula (12–2).

(a) $n = 1$ year and $jn = .05(1) = .05$

$$S = 10{,}000(e^{.05}) = 10{,}000(1.05127110)$$
$$= \$10{,}512.71 \quad \text{(Compound amount)}$$

Compound interest = 10,512.71 − 10,000.00
= \$512.71

(b) $n = 2$ years and $jn = .05(2) = .10$

$S = 10{,}000(e^{.1}) = 10{,}000(1.10517092)$
= \$11,051.71 (Compound amount)

Compound interest = 11,051.71 − 10,000.00
= \$1,051.71

EXERCISE 12–4 REFERENCE: SECTIONS 12.4 and 12.5

1. At what nominal rate compounded semiannually will a principal yield interest that is equivalent to an effective rate of $6\frac{1}{2}$%?
2. What nominal rate compounded monthly is equivalent to an effective rate of 4%?
3. At what nominal rate compounded semiannually will a principal yield interest that is equivalent to 18% compounded monthly?
4. What nominal rate compounded quarterly is equivalent to 5% compounded monthly?
5. Find the nominal rate compounded quarterly that is equivalent to 7% compounded semiannually.
6. Find the nominal rate compounded monthly that is equivalent to 6% compounded semiannually.
7. Find the effective rate if money is worth (a) 5% and (b) 20% compounded continuously.
8. Find the effective rate if money is worth (a) 8% and (b) 50% compounded continuously.
9. What is the effective rate if money is invested at $4\frac{1}{2}$% compounded continuously?
10. What is the effective rate if money is invested at $6\frac{1}{2}$% compounded continuously?
11. Find the compound amount and the compound interest if \$1,000 is invested at 4% compounded continuously for (a) one year and (b) two years.
12. Find the compound amount and the compound interest if \$1,000 is invested at 20% compounded continuously for (a) one year and (b) four years.

★12.6 COMPUTING FORMULAS BY CALCULATORS AND COMPUTERS

Computations illustrated for the examples in Sections 12.1 to 12.5 are based on the formulas presented in Chapter 11. The methods of computing the Chapter 11 formulas by calculators and computers were explained in Section 11.7. Here we illustrate the methods for the two new formulas: (12–1) and (12–2).

A. Computing Formula (12–1): $f = e^{j} - 1$

The examples used in this section are obtained from Section 12.5.

EXAMPLE 1 Compute Example 1, Section 12.5:

$f = e^{.06} - 1 = 6.183655\%$

(a) SIMPLE CALCULATOR

Not capable of raising the number e (= 2.71828) to the fractional power (.06), or $e^{.06}$.

(b) BUSINESS ANALYST CALCULATOR

Problem	*Step*	*Key Pressing Sequence*	*Display*
Compute $e^{.06}$	1	[ON/C] .06 [2nd] [e^x]	1.0618365
Compute f	2	[−] 1 [=]	0.0618365

(c) COMPUTER WITH BASIC

BASIC Program

```
10 INPUT "J";J
20 F = EXP(J) - 1
30 PRINT "EFFECTIVE RATE = ";F
40 END
```

Computer Display (RUN)

```
J ? 0.06
EFFECTIVE RATE = .0618365468
```

The number 0.06 after the question mark (?) is typed input.

EXAMPLE 2 Compute Example 2, Section 12.5:

$f = e^{.075} - 1 = 7.788415\%$

Use the BASIC program given in Example 1:

Computer Display (RUN)

```
J ? 0.075
EFFECTIVE RATE = .0778841511
```

The number 0.075 after the question mark (?) is typed input.

B. Computing Formula (12–2): $S = P(e^{in})$

The examples used in this section are also obtained from Section 12.5.

EXAMPLE 3 Compute Example 3, Section 12.5:

(1) $S = 10{,}000(e^{.05(1)}) = 10{,}000(e^{.05})$
$= 10{,}512.71$

(a) SIMPLE CALCULATOR

Not capable of raising the number e to the fractional power (.05), or $e^{.05}$.

(b) BUSINESS ANALYST CALCULATOR

Problem	*Step*	*Key Pressing Sequence*	*Display*
Compute $e^{.05}$	1	[ON/C] .05 [2nd] [e^x]	1.0512711
Store $e^{.05}$ in memory	2	[STO]	1.0512711
Compute S	3	10000 [×] [RCL] [=]	10512.711

(c) COMPUTER WITH BASIC

BASIC Program

```
10 INPUT "P";P
20 INPUT "J";J
30 INPUT "N";N
40 S = P * EXP(J * N)
50 PRINT "COMPOUND AMOUNT = ";S
60 END
```

Computer Display (RUN)

```
P ? 10000
J ? 0.05
N ? 1
COMPOUND AMOUNT = 10512.711
```

The numbers after the question marks (?) are typed input.

(2) $S = 10{,}000(e^{.05(2)}) = 10{,}000(e^{.1})$
$= 11{,}051.71$

Use the BASIC program given in (1):

Computer Display (RUN)

```
P ? 10000
J ? 0.05
N ? 2
COMPOUND AMOUNT = 11051.7092
```

The numbers after the question marks (?) are typed input.

12.7 SUMMARY OF CONTINUOUSLY COMPOUNDED INTEREST FORMULAS

Application	*Formula*	*Formula Number*	*Reference Page*
Finding the effective rate	$f = e^j - 1$	(12–1)	371
Finding the amount	$S = P(e^{jn})$	(12–2)	372

EXERCISE 12–5 REVIEW OF CHAPTER 12

1. Use the logarithmic method to find each of the following unknown values:
   (a) $S = 2{,}000(1 + 5\%)^{18}$
   (b) $P = 500/(1 + 6\%)^6$
   (c) $(1 + i)^{25} = 1{,}400/370$
   (d) $(1 + 4\%)^n = 1{,}980/920$
2. Use the logarithmic method to find each of the following unknown values:
   (a) $S = 4{,}500(1 + 6\%)^{32}$
   (b) $P = 750/(1 + 3\%)^{40}$
   (c) $(1 + i)^{30} = 1{,}620/590$
   (d) $(1 + 5\%)^n = 4{,}200/1{,}180$
3. A debt of \$300 is due at the end of six years. If money is worth 5% compounded monthly, what is the value of the debt when it is paid at the end of (a) two years? (b) nine years?
4. A debt of \$700 is due in three years. If interest is 6% compounded quarterly, what is the value of the debt when it is paid at the end of (a) one year? (b) $5\frac{1}{2}$ years?
5. Bob owes John \$300 due in four years and \$800 due in ten years. Assume that the two debts are to be discharged by 2 equal payments in three years and eight years, respectively. What is the size of each payment if money is worth 4% compounded quarterly? Let eight years from now be the comparison date.

6. Compute Problem 5 by letting three years hence be the comparison date.
7. Carl owes Dean $900 due in two years and $1,500 due in seven years. Assume that the two debts are to be discharged by a payment of $700 in three years and the remainder in six years. What is the size of the second payment if money is worth 6% compounded semiannually?
8. Refer to Problem 7. (a) If the two debts are to be discharged by 2 equal payments in three years and five years, respectively, what is the size of each payment? (b) What single payment would discharge the two debts ten years hence?
9. Mary owes Jack $400 due in one year and $950 with interest at 5% compounded monthly due in eight years. If money is worth 7% compounded annually, what is the single payment ten years from now that will discharge the two debts?
10. Refer to Problem 9. If the two debts are to be discharged by a payment of $500 in two years and the remainder in five years, what is the size of the second payment?
11. Susan borrowed some money from Janet as follows: $50 due in one year, $200 due in three years, and $300 due in five years. If money is worth 6% compounded monthly, when can Susan discharge all her debts by a single payment of $550?
12. Dorothy promised to pay Bob the following amounts: $100 due in two years, $400 due in five years, and $500 plus interest at 4% compounded semiannually due in six years. If money is worth 6% compounded quarterly, when can Dorothy repay her debts by a single payment of $1,000?
13. What nominal rate compounded quarterly is equivalent to a 5% effective rate?
14. Find the nominal rate compounded semiannually that is equivalent to an effective rate of 10%.
15. What nominal rate compounded monthly is equivalent to 7% compounded semiannually?
16. Find the nominal rate compounded semiannually that is equivalent to 5% compounded quarterly.
17. Find the effective rate if money is invested at (a) 7% and (b) $5\frac{1}{2}$% compounded continuously.
18. What is the effective rate if money is invested at (a) 4% and (b) $8\frac{1}{2}$% compounded continuously.
19. Find the compound amount and the compound interest if $10,000 is invested at 10% compounded continuously for (a) one year and (b) two years.
20. Find the compound amount and the compound interest if $10,000 is invested at 20% compounded continuously for (a) one year and (b) four years.

13 ORDINARY ANNUITIES

In this chapter, we first introduce the concept and classifications of annuities (Section 13.1). We then present the topics involving ordinary annuities: amount (Sections 13.2 and 13.4), present value (Sections 13.3 and 13.4), periodic payment (Section 13.5), interest rate (Section 13.6), and term (Section 13.7). Finally, we explain the methods of computing formulas by calculators and computers as supplemental material.

13.1 CLASSIFICATIONS OF ANNUITIES

Generally speaking, an *annuity* is a series of periodic payments, usually made in equal amounts. The payments are computed by the compound interest method and are made at equal intervals of time, such as annually, semiannually, quarterly, or monthly. The word annuity originally referred only to annual payments, but it now applies to payment intervals of any length of time.

There are numerous types of annuity problems. Financing the huge social security system, for example, is a type of annuity problem. Additional examples of annuities are periodic savings; rental payments; purchases of cars, houses, or home appliances on installment payment plans; life insurance premiums; and interest payments on bonds. From the above examples, we can see that the subject of annuities affects business firms as well as practically every family in the United States.

Annuities may be classified in the following three ways.

A. Annuities Classified by Term

The period of time between two successive payment dates is called the *payment interval*. The time between the beginning of the first payment interval and the end of the last payment interval is called the *term* of the annuity.

According to their terms, annuities may be classified into three groups:

1. *Annuity Certain.* The term of an annuity certain begins and ends on definite dates, such as a five-year term from January 1, 1991, to January 1, 1996.
2. *Perpetuity.* The term of a perpetuity begins on a definite date but never ends, such as a principal that remains forever untouched, drawing interest. The length of the term is infinite.
3. *Contingent Annuity.* The term of a contingent annuity begins on a definite date, but the ending date is not fixed in advance. Instead, the ending date depends on some condition happening in the future. For example, life insurance premiums are paid only so long as the insured is living; the length of time is therefore uncertain.

B. Annuities Classified by Dates of Payment

According to the dates of payment, annuities may be classified into three groups:

1. *Ordinary Annuity.* Periodic payments are made at the *end* of each payment interval. For example, if the term of an annuity is one year, which begins on January 1, and the payment interval is one quarter, the first payment should be made three months later, or on April 1, the end of the first quarter; the second payment should be made on July 1, the end of the second quarter; and so on.
2. *Annuity Due.* Periodic payments are made at the *beginning* of each payment interval. For instance, in the above example the first payment would be made on January 1, the beginning of the first quarter; the second payment would be made on April 1, the beginning of the second quarter; and so on.
3. *Deferred Annuity.* Periodic payments are made at the *end* of each payment interval. However, the term of the annuity does not begin until *after* a designated period of time. For example, a man borrows $100 on April 15, 1991, and agrees to repay the loan by making a series of three equal annual payments, but the first payment is not due until two years from the date of the loan.

C. Annuities Classified by Length of Payment Interval and Interest Conversion Period

According to the *length* of payment interval and interest conversion period, annuities may be divided into two groups:

1. *Simple Annuity.* The payment interval coincides with the interest conversion period. In other words, the payment date is the interest computing date. For example, when the payment interval is one month, the interest is compounded monthly. When each of the payments of an annuity is made at the end of each month, the interest is also computed and compounded at the end of each month.
2. *Complex Annuity (General Annuity).* The payment interval does not coincide with the interest conversion period. For example, the payment interval is one month, and the interest is compounded quarterly; or the payment interval is one quarter, and the interest is compounded monthly. The formulas for a complex annuity may also be used for solving simple annuity problems. Thus, the complex annuity is considered as a general case of annuity and is also called a *general annuity*.

Hereafter, unless otherwise specified, the word *annuity* means an *ordinary annuity*, which is also an *annuity certain*. Only ordinary annuities of the simple annuity type are discussed in this chapter. Other types of annuities are presented in Chapter 14.

13.2 AMOUNT OF AN ANNUITY

The *amount* of an annuity is the final value at the end of the term of the annuity. The amount includes all of the periodic payments and the compound interest.

A. Computation in General

The amount of an annuity is obtained by totaling the compound amounts of the individual periodic payments. Each of the compound amounts is computed by the formula $S = P(1 + i)^n$.

EXAMPLE 1 What is the amount of an annuity if the size of each payment is $100, payable at the end of each quarter for one year at an interest rate of 4% compounded quarterly?

The first payment is made at the end of the first quarter, which is three quarters before the end of the term of the annuity. Thus, interest is accumulated on the first payment for three interest periods; on the second payment, for two interest periods; and on the third payment, for one interest period. The fourth payment is not entitled to interest, since it is paid at the end of the term.

The entire computation is diagrammed as follows:

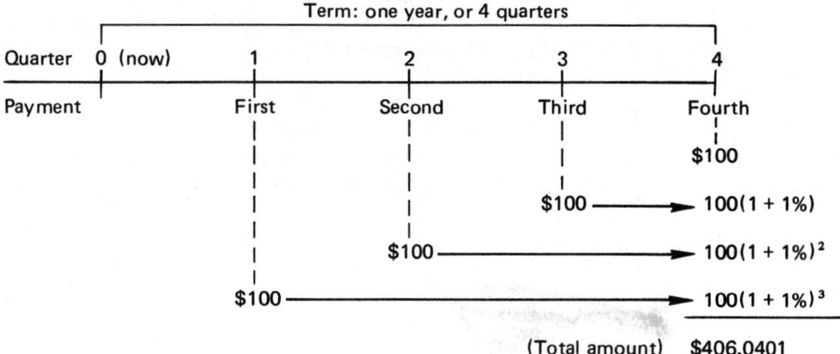

The amount of the annuity, $406.0401, which is the final value at the end of the fourth quarter, is computed as follows (use Table 5):

$$\begin{aligned}
100 &= 100(1) \\
100(1 + 1\%) &= 100(1.01) \\
100(1 + 1\%)^2 &= 100(1.0201) \\
100(1 + 1\%)^3 &= 100(1.030301)
\end{aligned}$$

(Total amount) $100(4.060401) = \$406.0401$, or $406.04

The total of the compound interest on the four payments is

$\$406.04 - (100 \times 4) = \$6.04$

The preceding example may be applied in the following case:

A man deposits $100 in a bank at the end of each quarter for one year. If the money earns interest at 4% compounded quarterly, how much does he have in his account at the end of the year after the last payment is made? Answer: He has $406.04.

EXERCISE 13–1 REFERENCE: SECTION 13.2A

A. Using the method employed in Example 1, find the amount of each annuity and the total interest on the payments in each of the following cases. (Assume that each payment is made at the end of each payment interval.)

	Each Payment	*Payment Interval*	*Term*	*Compound Interest Rate*
1.	$2,000	1 month	4 months	6%, monthly
2.	5,000	1 quarter	9 months	20%, quarterly
3.	800	6 months	1 year	18%, semiannually
4.	700	1 year	2 years	10%, annually
5.	3,000	1 quarter	1 year	8%, quarterly
6.	400	6 months	$1\frac{1}{2}$ years	6%, semiannually

B. Statement problems:

7. What is the amount of an annuity if the size of each payment is $2,000, payable at the end of each year for three years at an interest rate of 9% compounded annually?
8. Find the amount of an annuity if the size of each payment is $80, payable at the end of each month for four months, at an interest rate of 12% compounded monthly.

B. Computation by Formula (13–1)

Let R = size of each regular payment (or periodic rent)
i = interest rate per conversion period
n = number of payments during the term of an annuity (it is also the number of payment intervals, or the number of conversion periods)
S_n = the amount of an ordinary annuity

The formula[1] for the amount of an ordinary annuity is

$$S_n = R \cdot \frac{(1+i)^n - 1}{i} \qquad \textbf{(13–1)}$$

Formula (13–1) is obtained by using the method employed in Example 1. When formula (13–1) is used, the answer to Example 1 may be computed as follows:

R = $100 (per quarter), $i = 4\%/4 = 1\%$ (per quarter), $n = 4$ (quarterly payments)

Substituting the values in formula (13–1),

---

[1]*Proof—Formula (13–1), the amount of an ordinary annuity:*

In Example 1, since R = $100, $i = 1\%$, and $n = 4$ (quarterly payments), a diagram may be drawn with symbols as shown on page 381. *(Continued)*

$$S_n = S_4 = 100 \cdot \frac{(1 + 1\%)^4 - 1}{1\%} = 100 \cdot \frac{1.04060401 - 1}{.01}$$

$$= 100 \cdot \frac{.04060401}{.01} = 100(4.060401) = \$406.0401, \quad \text{or} \quad \$406.04$$

The value of $(1 + 1\%)^4$ is obtained from Table 5. The answer here is the same as that obtained in Example 1.

For convenience, the value of $\frac{(1 + i)^n - 1}{i}$ is usually represented by the symbol $s_{\overline{n}|i}$ (which is read, "*s* angle *n* at *i*"). The values of $s_{\overline{n}|i}$ for various interest rates (i) and numbers of payments (n) are provided in Table 7. The unit value of each entry in the table is best represented by one dollar, although it may be represented by any other unit. Therefore, each entry in the table becomes the amount of the annuity in dollars when each payment is \$1, or when $R = \$1$.

When Table 7 is employed, the computation of the amount of an annuity is simplified. In general, formula (13–1) is written in the following form:

$$\boldsymbol{S_n = Rs_{\overline{n}|i}} \qquad \textbf{(13–1)}$$

or $\left(\begin{array}{c}\text{Amount of an}\\ \text{ordinary annuity } S_n\end{array}\right) = \left(\begin{array}{c}\text{Size of each}\\ \text{payment } R\end{array}\right) \times \left(\begin{array}{c}\text{An entry}\\ \text{in Table 7}\end{array}\right)$

(The entry is at the interest rate i per conversion period for n conversion periods or payments.)

Example 1 may now be computed in the following manner:

$$S_n = Rs_{\overline{n}|i} = 100s_{\overline{4}|1\%} = 100(4.060401) = \$406.0401, \quad \text{or} \quad \$406.04$$

The answer is the same as that found in Example 1.

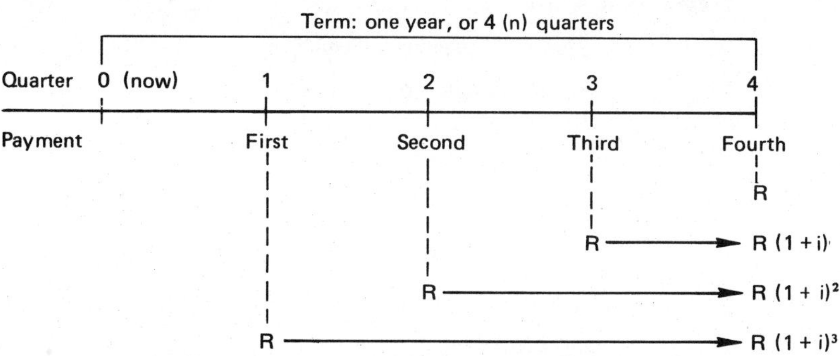

Notice that the number of interest conversion periods for the first payment is 3, which is 1 less than 4, or $(n - 1)$; the number for the second payment is 2, which is 2 less than 4, or $(n - 2)$; and so on. On the other hand, the number of interest conversion periods for the last payment, the fourth or nth payment, is zero; the number for the next to the last, the third or $(n - 1)$th payment, is 1; the number for the second or $(n - 2)$th payment is 2; and so on. Extend this idea and let n = any number of payments. The following results may be obtained: *(Continued)*

EXAMPLE 2 Find the amount of an annuity of $2,000 payable at the end of each year for 45 years, if the interest rate is 10% compounded annually.

R = $2,000 (per year), i = 10% (per year), n = 45 (annual payments)

Substituting the values in formula (13–1), the amount of the annuity is

$S_n = 2{,}000 s_{\overline{45}|10\%} = 2{,}000(718.904837) = \$1{,}437{,}809.67$ (Table 7)

Thus, if a person, aged 20, made an initial deposit of $2,000 in an IRA (Individual Retirement Arrangement) account that pays 10% compounded annually, after 45 equal annual deposits he or she will have $1,437,809.67 at age 65.

Total deposits = $2,000 × 45 = $90,000
Total interest = 1,437,809.67 − 90,000.00
= $1,347,809.67

Note that under certain conditions, income tax on IRA interest income can be deferred until retirement.

EXAMPLE 3 If $20 is deposited at the end of each month for three years in a fund that earns 6%

---

[1]*Proof (continued):*

The compound amount of the 1st payment	$= R(1 + i)^{n-1}$
The compound amount of the 2d payment	$= R(1 + i)^{n-2}$
. . .	= . . .
The compound amount of the $(n - 2)$th payment	$= R(1 + i)^2$
The compound amount of the $(n - 1)$th payment	$= R(1 + i)$
The compound amount of the nth (the last) payment	$= R$

There are n compound amounts.

Let S_n = the sum of n compound amounts (or the amount of the annuity)

Thus, $S_n = R + R(1 + i) + R(1 + i)^2 + \cdots + R(1 + i)^{n-2} + R(1 + i)^{n-1}$ Step (1)

Multiply both sides of the equation in Step (1) by $(1 + i)$.

Then $S_n(1 + i) = R(1 + i) + R(1 + i)^2 + R(1 + i)^3 + \cdots$
$+ R(1 + i)^{n-1} + R(1 + i)^n$ Step (2)

Subtract the equation in Step (2) from the equation in Step (1).

Then $S_n - S_n(1 + i) = R - R(1 + i)^n$ Step (3)

Factor:

$S_n[1 - (1 + i)] = R[1 - (1 + i)^n]$, $S_n(-i) = R[1 - (1 + i)^n]$

$$S_n = \frac{R[1 - (1 + i)^n]}{-i} = \frac{R[1 - (1 + i)^n]}{-i} \cdot \frac{-1}{-1}$$

$$S_n = R \cdot \frac{(1 + i)^n - 1}{i}$$

Note: The right side of the equation in Step (1) is a geometric progression with the common ratio $(1 + i)$.

interest compounded monthly, what will be the final value at the end of the three-year term? What is the total interest?

$R = \$20$ (per month), $i = 6\%/12 = \frac{1}{2}\%$ (per month), $n = 3 \times 12 = 36$ (monthly payments)

Substituting the values in formula (13–1),

$$\text{Final value} = S_n = Rs_{\overline{n}|i} = 20s_{\overline{36}|1/2\%} = 20(39.3361) = \$786.72$$

Total deposits $= 20 \times 36 = \$720$
Total interest $= 786.72 - 720 = \$66.72$

EXAMPLE 4 In Example 3, what will the amount be two years after the last deposit is made?

The final value at the end of the three years now becomes the principal, which is accumulated for two years.

Substituting $P = \$786.72$, $i = \frac{1}{2}\%$, $n = 2 \times 12 = 24$ (months) in the formula $S = P(1 + i)^n$,

$$S = 786.72(1 + \tfrac{1}{2}\%)^{24} = 786.72(1.12715978) = \$886.76$$

EXERCISE 13–2 REFERENCE: SECTION 13.2B

A. Find the amount of the ordinary annuity in each of the following problems:

	Payment (R)	Payment Interval	Term	Compound Interest Rate
1.	$ 700	1 month	2 years	18%, monthly
2.	900	1 quarter	10 years	20%, quarterly
3.	3,000	6 months	$8\frac{1}{2}$ years	15%, semiannually
4.	5,000	1 year	30 years	10%, annually
5.	400	1 quarter	15 years, 6 months	6%, quarterly
6.	500	1 month	4 years, 3 months	4%, monthly
7.	300	1 year	20 years	$5\frac{1}{2}$%, annually
8.	800	6 months	12 years	8%, semiannually

B. Statement problems:

9. What is the amount of an annuity if the size of each payment is $250, payable at the end of each quarter for five years at an interest rate of 16% compounded quarterly?
10. Ana Perez deposits $450 in a bank at the end of each month for three years and nine months. If the money earns interest at 12% compounded monthly, how much money does she have in her account at the end of the period?
11. Find the amount of an annuity of $56 payable at the end of every six months for $4\frac{1}{2}$ years, if the interest rate is 6% compounded semiannually.
12. Find the amount of an annuity of $80 payable at the end of each year for 25 years, if money is worth 7% compounded annually.
13. Frieda Grant deposits $45 monthly at an interest rate of 12% compounded monthly. How much will she have in her account at the end of two years and four months?
14. At the end of each quarter, a company placed $1,500 in a sinking fund. The fund was invested at 7% compounded quarterly. (a) What will be the final value at the end of five years? (b) What will be the total interest?

15. At the end of each month during a three-year period, a hospital business manager invested one-sixth of his monthly bonus of $900. How much will the amount be four years after the last investment is made if the interest rate is 15% compounded monthly?
16. Bill Morton deposited $50 every six months in a fund earning interest at 5% compounded semiannually. The first deposit was made when he was 20 years of age and the last deposit was made when he was 25. If he leaves the fund intact, how much will he have in the fund when he is 28?

13.3 PRESENT VALUE OF AN ANNUITY

The present value of an annuity is the value at the beginning of the term of the annuity. The methods for computing the present value are based on either of the following two different interpretations of the value:

1. It is the sum of the present values of the periodic payments of an annuity.
2. It is the single principal which, at a given compound interest rate, will accumulate to the amount of an annuity by the end of the term of the annuity.

A. Computation in General

EXAMPLE 1 What is the present value of an annuity if the size of each payment is $100 payable at the end of each quarter for one year and the interest rate is 4% compounded quarterly?

METHOD A When the present value of an annuity is considered as the *sum of the present values* of the periodic payments, each of the present values (P) is computed by the compound discount formula $P = S(1 + i)^{-n}$. In the present case, S is the payment, or $S = \$100$.

The first payment is made at the end of the first quarter, which is one quarter after the beginning of the term of the annuity. Thus, the present value of the first payment is obtained by discounting the payment for one quarter, or one interest period. The present value of the second payment is obtained by discounting the payment for two periods, and so on.

The computation is diagrammed as follows:

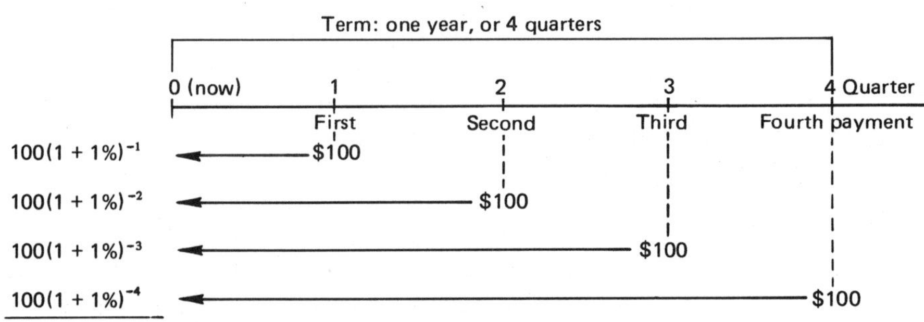

The present value of the annuity, \$390.20, is computed by using Table 6 as follows:

$$100(1 + 1\%)^{-1} = 100(0.99009901)$$
$$100(1 + 1\%)^{-2} = 100(0.98029605)$$
$$100(1 + 1\%)^{-3} = 100(0.97059015)$$
$$100(1 + 1\%)^{-4} = \underline{100(0.96098034)}$$
$$100(3.90196555) = \$390.196555, \quad \text{or} \quad \$390.20$$

METHOD B

When the present value of an annuity is considered as the *single principal* of the amount of the annuity, the principal (P) is obtained by the compound discount formula $P = S(1 + i)^{-n}$. In the present case, S is equal to the amount of the annuity, S_n. The computation is as follows (also see Example 1, Section 13.2):

STEP (1). To obtain the value of S_n, use formula (13–1):

$R = 100, i = 4\%/4 = 1\%, n = 4$

$$S_n = Rs_{\overline{n}|i} = 100s_{\overline{4}|1\%} = 100(4.060401)$$
$$= \$406.0401. \quad \text{(Table 7)}$$

STEP (2). The single principal $P = 406.0401(1 + 1\%)^{-4}$
$= 406.0401(0.96098034)$
$= \$390.19655, \quad \text{or} \quad \$390.20$ (Table 6)

The computation in the above example may also be applied in solving problems such as the following:

A man would like to borrow money from a bank that charges interest at 4% compounded quarterly. If he agrees to pay \$100 at the end of each quarter for one year, how much money should he receive from the bank at the time of borrowing? Answer: He should receive \$390.20.

The sum of compound discounts on the four payments is

$(100 \times 4) - \$390.20 = \$9.80$

EXERCISE 13–3 REFERENCE: SECTION 13.3A

A. Find the present value of the annuity in each of the following problems. Use the methods presented in Example 1, pages 384 and 385. Use Method A for Problems 1–4 and Method B for Problems 5–8.

	Payment	*Payment Interval*	*Term*	*Compound Interest Rate*
1.	\$2,000	1 month	4 months	6%, monthly
2.	1,000	1 quarter	9 months	14%, quarterly
3.	300	6 months	1 year	20%, semiannually
4.	800	1 year	2 years	10%, annually
5.	600	1 quarter	1 year	8%, quarterly
6.	3,000	6 months	$1\frac{1}{2}$ years	6%, semiannually

B. Statement problems:

7. What is the present value of an annuity if the size of each payment is $2,000 payable at the end of each year for three years and the interest rate is 9% compounded annually?
8. Find the present value of an annuity if the size of each payment is $800 payable at the end of each month for four months at an interest rate of 12% compounded monthly.

B. Computation by Formula (13–2)

Let R = size of each regular payment (or periodic rent)
i = interest rate per conversion period
n = number of payments during the term of an annuity (it is also the number of payment intervals, or the number of conversion periods)
A_n = the present value of an ordinary annuity

The formula[2] for the present value of an ordinary annuity is

$$A_n = R \cdot \frac{1 - (1 + i)^{-n}}{i} \qquad \textbf{(13–2)}$$

Formula (13–2) is obtained by using the methods employed in Example 1, pages 384 and 385. When formula (13–2) is used, the answer to Example 1 may be computed as follows:

---

[2]*Proof–Formula (13–2), the present value of an annuity:*

The following diagram shows that the present value of an annuity of R payable at the end of each period for four periods at interest rate i per period is A_4, and the amount of the annuity is S_4.

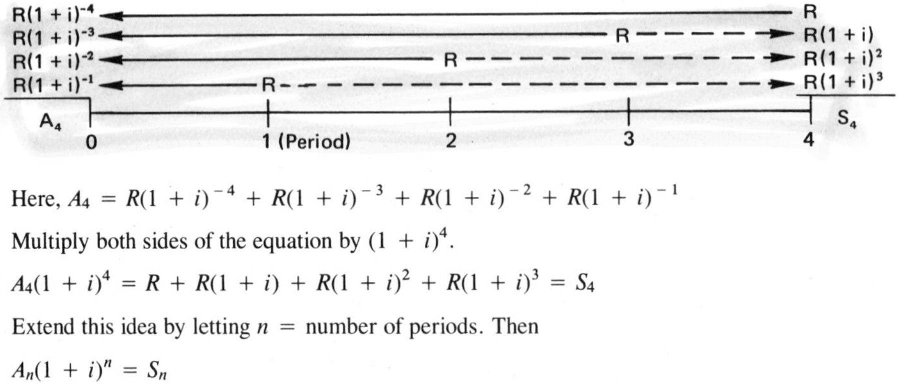

R(1 + i)^-4 ←——————————————— R
R(1 + i)^-3 ←————————— R – – – → R(1 + i)
R(1 + i)^-2 ←—————— R – – – – – → R(1 + i)^2
R(1 + i)^-1 ←—— R – – – – – – – – → R(1 + i)^3
A4 | 0 | 1 (Period) | 2 | 3 | 4 | S4

Here, $A_4 = R(1 + i)^{-4} + R(1 + i)^{-3} + R(1 + i)^{-2} + R(1 + i)^{-1}$

Multiply both sides of the equation by $(1 + i)^4$.

$A_4(1 + i)^4 = R + R(1 + i) + R(1 + i)^2 + R(1 + i)^3 = S_4$

Extend this idea by letting n = number of periods. Then

$A_n(1 + i)^n = S_n$

$$A_n = S_n(1 + i)^{-n} = R \cdot \frac{(1 + i)^n - 1}{i} \cdot (1 + i)^{-n}$$

$$A_n = R \cdot \frac{1 - (1 + i)^{-n}}{i} = Ra_{\overline{n}|i}$$

The proof also indicates that:

1. The present value of an annuity is the sum of the present values of the periodic payments.
2. The present value of an annuity is the single principal of the amount of the annuity.

$R = \$100$ (per quarter), $i = 4\%/4 = 1\%$ (per quarter), $n = 4$ (quarterly payments)

Substituting the values in formula (13–2),

$$A_n = A_4 = 100 \cdot \frac{1 - (1 + 1\%)^{-4}}{1\%} = 100 \cdot \frac{1 - 0.96098034}{.01}$$

$$= 100 \cdot \frac{0.03901966}{.01} = 100(3.901966) = \$390.1966, \quad \text{or} \quad \$390.20$$

The value of $(1 + 1\%)^{-4}$ is found in Table 6. The answer here is the same as that obtained in Example 1.

For convenience, the value of $\frac{1 - (1 + i)^{-n}}{i}$ is usually represented by the symbol $a_{\overline{n}|i}$ (which is read "*a* angle *n* at *i*"). The values of $a_{\overline{n}|i}$ for various interest rates (i) and numbers of payments (n) are provided in Table 8. The unit value of each entry in the table is best represented by one dollar, although it may be represented by any other unit. Therefore, each entry in the table becomes the present value of an annuity in dollars when each payment is \$1, or when $R = \$1$.

When Table 8 is employed, the computation of the present value of an annuity is simplified. In general, formula (13–2) is written in the following form:

$$\mathbf{A_n = Ra_{\overline{n}|i}} \qquad \textbf{(13–2)}$$

or $\begin{pmatrix}\text{Present value of an}\\ \text{ordinary annuity } A_n\end{pmatrix} = \begin{pmatrix}\text{Size of each}\\ \text{payment } R\end{pmatrix} \times \begin{pmatrix}\text{An entry}\\ \text{in Table 8}\end{pmatrix}$

(The entry is at the interest rate i per conversion period for n conversion periods or payments.)

Example 1 may now be computed in the following manner:

$$A_n = Ra_{\overline{n}|i} = 100a_{\overline{4}|1\%} = 100(3.90196555) = \$390.196555, \quad \text{or} \quad \$390.20$$

EXAMPLE 2

If a man wishes to receive \$20 at the end of each month for three years from a bank that pays interest at 6% compounded monthly, how much must he deposit in the bank now?

The monthly payment by the bank is \$20, or $R = \$20$; $i = 6\%/12 = \frac{1}{2}\%$ (per month), $n = 3 \times 12 = 36$ (monthly payments).

Substituting the above values in formula (13–2),

$$A_n = Ra_{\overline{n}|i} = 20a_{\overline{36}|1/2\%} = 20(32.871) = \$657.42$$

The present value of the annuity is \$657.42. Thus, the man must deposit \$657.42 in the bank now. The sum of the compound interest paid by the bank on the 36 payments is computed as follows:

Payments $= 20 \times 36 = \$720$
Compound interest $= 720 - 657.42 = \$62.58$

EXAMPLE 3

What is the cash value of a car that can be bought for \$1,000 down and \$500 a month for 36 months if money is worth 12% compounded monthly?

Since a down payment has been made, the first of the regular payments should be made at the end of the month following the date of purchase. Thus, this is an ordinary annuity problem.

R = \$500 (per month), i = 12%/12 = 1% (per month), n = 36 (months or payments)

Substituting the above values in formula (13–2),

$A_n = 500a_{\overline{36}|1\%} = 500(30.10751) = \$15{,}053.76$

The cash price of the car = 1,000 + 15,053.76 = \$16,053.76

EXAMPLE 4 Find the present value of an annuity of \$150 payable at the end of each year for 15 years if the interest rate is 5% compounded annually.

R = \$150 (per year), i = 5% (per year), n = 15 (yearly payments)

Substituting the values in formula (13–2),

$A_n = 150a_{\overline{15}|5\%} = 150(10.37966) = \$1{,}556.95$

NOTE: The relationship of magnitude among the present value, the sum of actual payments, and the amount of an annuity may be expressed as follows:

Present value < Actual payments < Amount

Using the data given in Example 4, the above expression may be illustrated in the following manner:

Present value = \$1,556.95; Actual payments = 150 × 15 = \$2,250
Amount = $150s_{\overline{15}|5\%} = 150(21.57856) = \$3{,}236.78$

\$1,556.95 < \$2,250 < \$3,236.78

EXERCISE 13–4 REFERENCE: SECTION 13.3B

A. Find the present value of the ordinary annuity in each of the following problems:

	Payment (R)	*Payment Interval*	*Term*	*Compound Interest Rate*
1.	\$3,000	1 month	2 years	18%, monthly
2.	4,500	1 quarter	10 years	16%, quarterly
3.	2,000	6 months	$8\frac{1}{2}$ years	7%, semiannually
4.	5,800	1 year	30 years	10%, annually
5.	800	1 quarter	15 years, 6 months	6%, quarterly
6.	400	1 month	4 years, 3 months	12%, monthly
7.	500	1 year	20 years	$5\frac{1}{2}$%, annually
8.	600	6 months	12 years	8%, semiannually

B. Statement problems:

9. What is the present value of an annuity if the size of each payment is \$200 payable at the end of each quarter for eight years at an interest rate of 7% compounded quarterly?

10. A man wishes to withdraw \$350 at the end of every six months for ten years. If the money earns interest at 11% compounded semiannually, how much must he deposit now?
11. Find the present value of an annuity of \$70 payable at the end of each month for four and one-half years if the interest is at 15% compounded monthly.
12. Find the present value of an annuity of \$95 payable at the end of each year for 15 years if money is worth 10% compounded annually.
13. K. G. Griffin purchased a refrigerator and made a down payment of \$250. She agreed to pay \$30 per month thereafter for one year. If the interest was at 7% compounded monthly, what was the cash price of the refrigerator?
14. Fred Johnson wants to buy a television set. Store A offered him a payment plan of \$70 down and \$50 per quarter thereafter for six payments. Store B offered him a payment plan of \$80 down and \$25 per quarter thereafter for 12 payments. Which store offered him the better plan? Why? Assume that the interest rate charged by both stores is 8% compounded quarterly.
15. A boat sold for \$1,000 cash and \$60 per month for ten years. Find the equivalent cash price if interest was at 5% compounded monthly.
16. Clare Griffith borrowed some money from her employer and agreed to repay the loan by paying \$150 at the end of every six months for three years. If money was worth 14% compounded semiannually, how much did she receive from her employer?

13.4 ADDITIONAL PROBLEMS IN COMPUTING AMOUNT AND PRESENT VALUE OF AN ANNUITY

A. The Interest Rate (i) Is Not Given in the Tables

If an interest rate (i) is not given in the tables, the values of $s_{\overline{n}|i}$ and $a_{\overline{n}|i}$ may be found by either of the following two methods: (a) the interpolation method, or (b) the use of logarithms.

The interpolation method was used in Chapter 11, page 335, to obtain an *approximate* entry from the compound amount table. However, if the method is used in interpolating an entry from the annuity tables, the answer is even less accurate than that obtained from the compound interest tables. Therefore, the use of logarithms is preferred in finding the values.

EXAMPLE 1 Find (a) the amount and (b) the present value of an annuity of \$200 payable at the end of each year for 20 years, if money is worth 5.2% compounded annually.

$R = \$200$ (per year), $i = 5.2\%$ (per year), $n = 20$ (years)

METHOD A *Interpolation*

(a) Finding the amount.

$$S_n = Rs_{\overline{n}|i} = 200s_{\overline{20}|5.2\%}$$

The following interpolation is made according to the values obtained from Table 7:

	i	$s_{\overline{20}\mid i}$	
	$5\frac{1}{2}\% = 5.5\%$	34.868318	(1)
	5.2%	x	(2)
	5.0%	33.065954	(3)
(2) − (3)	.2%	$x - 33.065954$	(4)
(1) − (3)	.5%	1.802364	(5)

$$\frac{.2\%}{.5\%} = \frac{x - 33.065954}{1.802364}$$

The values of $s_{\overline{20}\mid i}$ include six decimal places. The one extra place provides for safety in rounding to the five-place requirement.

Solve for x from the proportion formed by the differences on lines (4) and (5).

$$x - 33.065954 = 1.802364\left(\frac{.2\%}{.5\%}\right) = 1.802364\left(\frac{2}{5}\right) = 0.720946$$

$$x = 33.065954 + 0.720946 = 33.786900, \text{ or } s_{\overline{20}\mid 5.2\%} = 33.786900$$

$$S_n = 200(33.7869) = \$6,757.38$$

(b) Finding the present value.

$$A_n = Ra_{\overline{n}\mid i} = 200a_{\overline{20}\mid 5.2\%}$$

The following interpolation is made according to the values obtained from Table 8 (write the larger numbers, which are in the column of values all known, on the top lines):

	i	$a_{\overline{20}\mid i}$	
	$5\frac{1}{2}\% = 5.5\%$	11.950382	(1)
	5.2%	x	(2)
	5.0%	12.462210	(3)
(2) − (3)	.2%	$x - 12.462210$	(4)
(1) − (3)	.5%	−.511828	(5)

$$\frac{.2\%}{.5\%} = \frac{x - 12.462210}{-.511828}$$

Solve for x from the proportion formed by the differences on lines (4) and (5).

$$x - 12.462210 = (-.511828)(\tfrac{2}{5}) = -.2047312$$

$$x = 12.462210 - .2047312 = 12.2574788, \quad \text{or} \quad a_{\overline{20}\mid 5.2\%} = 12.2574788$$

$$A_n = 200(12.25748) = \$2,451.50$$

★METHOD B *Using Logarithms*

(a) Finding the amount.

$$S_n = R \cdot \frac{(1 + i)^n - 1}{i}$$

$$= 200 \cdot \frac{(1 + 5.2\%)^{20} - 1}{5.2\%}$$

Compute $(1 + 5.2\%)^{20}$ by logarithms.

$$\log (1 + 5.2\%)^{20} = 20 \cdot \log 1.052$$
$$= 20(0.0220157) = 0.440314$$

Find the antilog (to six significant digits).

$$(1 + 5.2\%)^{20} = 2.75622$$

$$S_n = 200 \cdot \frac{2.75622 - 1}{.052} = 200(33.77346) = \$6,754.69$$

(b) Finding the present value.

$$A_n = R \cdot \frac{1 - (1 + i)^{-n}}{i}$$

$$= 200 \cdot \frac{1 - (1 + 5.2\%)^{-20}}{5.2\%}$$

Compute $(1 + 5.2\%)^{-20}$ by logarithms.

$$\log (1 + 5.2\%)^{-20} = (-20) \log 1.052 = (-20)(0.0220157)$$
$$= -0.440314 = 9.559686 - 10$$

Find the antilog (to six significant digits).

$$(1 + 5.2\%)^{-20} = 0.362816$$

$$A_n = 200 \cdot \frac{1 - 0.362816}{.052} = 200(12.25354) = \$2{,}450.71.$$

NOTE: The values of $(1 + 5.2\%)^{20}$ and $(1 + 5.2\%)^{-20}$ may also be obtained by using the binomial theorem, as discussed in Chapter 3, page 85. Also see Problems 11 and 12, Exercise 12–1, for the accuracy of the different methods in finding the value of $(1 + i)^n$.

B. The Number of Payments (*n*) Is Greater Than the Highest Number in the Tables

If the number of payments (n) is greater than the highest number in the tables, the values of $s_{\overline{n}|i}$ and $a_{\overline{n}|i}$ may be found as follows.

EXAMPLE 2 What is the amount of an annuity of \$100 payable at the end of each month for 25 years if money is worth 6% compounded monthly?

R = \$100 (per month), $i = 6\%/12 = \frac{1}{2}\%$ (per month), and $n = 25 \times 12 = 300$ (monthly payments). The value of n is greater than the highest number given for the interest rate $\frac{1}{2}\%$ in both Tables 5 and 7. In such cases, either of two methods may be used to solve the problem.

METHOD A Use formulas $S_n = Rs_{\overline{n}|i}$ and $S = P(1 + i)^n$.

In this method, the annuity is divided into two equal parts of 150 payments each. The total amount of the first 150 payments on the 150th payment date is computed as follows:

$S_n = S_{150} = Rs_{\overline{150}|1/2\%} = 100(222.6095) = 22{,}260.95$ (Table 7)

The amount of the partial annuity is further accumulated to the end of the term of the annuity by using the compound amount formula for 150 periods, as follows:

$S = 22{,}260.95(1 + \frac{1}{2}\%)^{150} = 22{,}260.95(2.1130475) = \$47{,}038.44$

The amount of the second 150 payments (151st to 300th payment, inclusive) at the end of the term of the annuity is also \$22,260.95. The total amount of the annuity is

$47{,}038.44 + 22{,}260.95 = \$69{,}299.39$

Method A is diagrammed as follows:

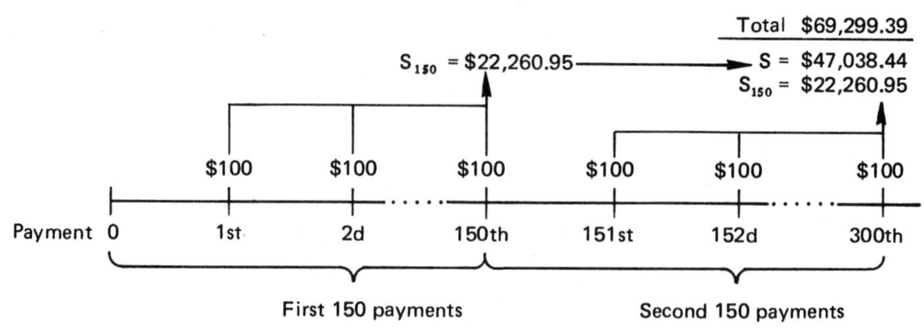

★METHOD B Use the formula $S_n = R \cdot \dfrac{(1+i)^n - 1}{i}$.

$n = 300$, the total number of monthly payments

$$\begin{aligned} S_n = S_{300} &= 100 \cdot \frac{(1+\frac{1}{2}\%)^{300} - 1}{\frac{1}{2}\%} \\ &= 100 \cdot \frac{(1+\frac{1}{2}\%)^{150}(1+\frac{1}{2}\%)^{150} - 1}{\frac{1}{2}\%} \\ &= 100 \cdot \frac{(2.1130475)(2.1130475) - 1}{.005} \\ &= 100 \cdot \frac{4.4649697 - 1}{.005} \\ &= \$69{,}299.39 \end{aligned}$$

(The value of $(1 + \frac{1}{2}\%)^{150}$ is found in Table 5.)

NOTE: The value of $(1 + \frac{1}{2}\%)^{300}$ may also be obtained by using logarithms, as follows:

$\log (1 + \frac{1}{2}\%)^{300} = 300(\log 1.005) = 300(.0021661) = .64983$

Thus, $(1 + \frac{1}{2}\%)^{300} = 4.46509$ (Table 3)

EXAMPLE 3 What is the present value of an annuity of $100 payable at the end of each month for 25 years if money is worth 6% compounded monthly?

$R = \$100$ (per month), $i = 6\%/12 = \frac{1}{2}\%$ (per month), $n = 25 \times 12 = 300$ (monthly payments)

The value of n is greater than the highest number given for an interest rate of $\frac{1}{2}\%$ in both Tables 6 and 8. In such cases, either of two methods may be used to solve the problem.

METHOD A Use formulas $A_n = Ra_{\overline{n}|i}$ and $P = S(1 + i)^{-n}$.

In this method, the annuity is divided into two equal parts of 150 payments each. The present value of the first 150 payments is computed as follows:

$A_{150} = Ra_{\overline{150}|1/2\%} = 100(105.34998) = \$10{,}534.998$, or $10,535

The present value of the second 150 payments (151st to 300th payment, inclusive) is computed by using two steps:

STEP (1). Find the value of the 150 payments at the beginning of the 151st payment interval. The value should also be \$10,535.

STEP (2). Discount the value found in Step (1) at compound interest for 150 periods:

$P = 10{,}535(1 + \frac{1}{2}\%)^{-150} = 10{,}535(0.4732501) = \$4{,}985.69$

The total present value of the annuity is

$10{,}535 + 4{,}985.69 = \$15{,}520.69$

Method A is diagrammed as follows:

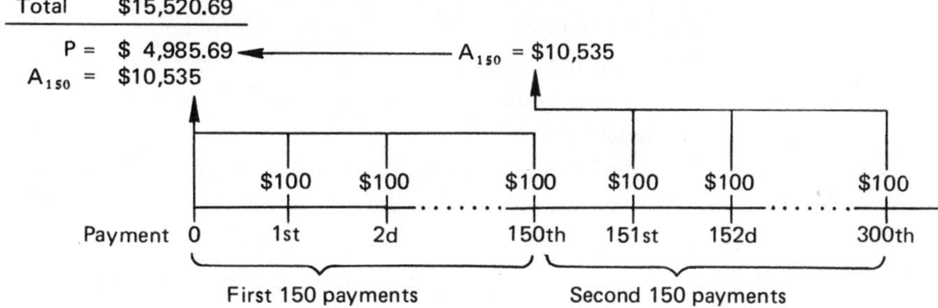

★METHOD B Use the formula $A_n = R \cdot \dfrac{1 - (1 + i)^{-n}}{i}$.

$n = 300$, the total number of monthly payments

$$A_n = A_{300} = 100 \cdot \frac{1 - (1 + \frac{1}{2}\%)^{-300}}{\frac{1}{2}\%}$$

$$= 100 \cdot \frac{1 - (1 + \frac{1}{2}\%)^{-150}(1 + \frac{1}{2}\%)^{-150}}{\frac{1}{2}\%}$$

$$= 100 \cdot \frac{1 - (0.47325012)(0.47325012)}{.005}$$

$$= 100 \cdot \frac{1 - 0.22396568}{.005} = \frac{77.603432}{.005} = \$15{,}520.69$$

(The value of $(1 + \frac{1}{2}\%)^{-150}$ is found in Table 6.)

NOTE: The value of $(1 + \frac{1}{2}\%)^{-300}$ may also be obtained by using logarithms, as follows:

$\log (1 + \frac{1}{2}\%)^{-300} = (-300) \log 1.005 = (-300)(.0021661) = -.64983$ (Table 3)

$= 9.35017 - 10$

Thus, $(1 + \frac{1}{2}\%)^{-300} = 0.22396$

EXERCISE 13–5 REFERENCE: SECTION 13.4

Statement problems:

1. What are the amount and the present value of an annuity of \$2,000 payable at the end of each year for five years if money is worth 4.3% compounded annually?
2. What are the amount and the present value of an annuity if the size of each payment is \$400 payable at the end of every six months for ten years at an interest rate of 6.8% compounded semiannually?

3. Find the amount and the present value of an annuity of $200 payable at the end of each quarter for eight years if the interest rate is 6.4% compounded quarterly.
4. Find the amount and the present value of an annuity of $250 payable at the end of each month for three years if money is worth 7.2% compounded monthly.
5. What is the amount of an annuity of $500 payable at the end of each month for 30 years if money is worth 7% compounded monthly?
6. Find the amount of an annuity of $30 payable at the end of each quarter for 35 years if interest is 12% compounded quarterly.
7. What is the present value of the annuity in Problem 5?
8. Find the present value of the annuity in Problem 6.
9. What are the amount and the present value of an annuity of $10 payable at the end of every six months for 60 years if the interest rate is 13% compounded semiannually?
10. Find the amount and the present value of an annuity of $100 payable at the end of each year for 120 years if the interest rate is 6% compounded annually.

13.5 FINDING THE SIZE OF EACH PERIODIC PAYMENT (R)

Frequently the size of each periodic payment must be determined when the amount or the present value of an annuity is known. In this type of problem the interest rate and the term of the annuity are usually given.

A. The Present Value Is Known

To find the size of each periodic payment when the present value is known, use the formula $A_n = Ra_{\overline{n}|i}$ in either of the following two forms:

$$R = \frac{A_n}{a_{\overline{n}|i}} \quad \text{(use Table 8)} \qquad \text{or} \qquad R = A_n\left(\frac{1}{a_{\overline{n}|i}}\right) \quad \text{(use Table 9)}$$

Certain values of $\frac{1}{a_{\overline{n}|i}}$ are tabulated in Table 9. Each value in the table is the size of the payment when the present value of an annuity is $1.

EXAMPLE 1

The present value of an annuity for ten years is $10,000. Find the size of the quarterly payment if the interest rate is 8% compounded quarterly.

$A_n = \$10{,}000$, $i = 8\%/4 = 2\%$ (per quarter), $n = 10 \times 4 = 40$ (quarterly payments)

Substituting the values in the above formula,

$$R = 10{,}000\left(\frac{1}{a_{\overline{40}|2\%}}\right) = 10{,}000(0.0365558)$$

$$= \$365.558, \quad \text{or} \quad \$365.56 \quad \text{(Table 9)}$$

Or, using Table 8, the problem can be solved as follows:

$$R = \frac{10{,}000}{a_{\overline{40}|2\%}} = \frac{10{,}000}{27.35548} = \$365.56$$

NOTE: Since the operations in division are more complicated than those in multiplication, the use of Table 9 is preferred in finding the size of each periodic payment.

EXAMPLE 2 A man purchased a house for \$120,000. He made a down payment of \$20,000 and agreed to make equal payments at the end of each month for 20 years. If the interest is 12% compounded monthly, what is the size of the monthly payment?

$A_n = 120{,}000 - 20{,}000 = \$100{,}000$, $i = 12\%/12 = 1\%$ (per month), $n = 20 \times 12 = 240$ (monthly payments)

Substituting the values in the above formula,

$$R = 100{,}000\left(\frac{1}{a_{\overline{240}|1\%}}\right) = 100{,}000(0.01101086) = \$1{,}101.086,$$

or rounded to \$1,101.09 (Table 9)

NOTE: Finance companies usually round a monthly payment to the next higher value, even when the digit to be rounded off is less than 5; thus, 1,101.084 is also rounded to 1,101.09.

B. The Amount Is Known

To find the size of each periodic payment when the amount is known, use the formula $S_n = Rs_{\overline{n}|i}$ in either of the following two forms:

$$R = \frac{S_n}{s_{\overline{n}|i}} \text{ (use Table 7)} \quad \text{or} \quad R = S_n \cdot \frac{1}{s_{\overline{n}|i}} = S_n\left(\frac{1}{a_{\overline{n}|i}} - i\right) \text{ (use Table 9)}^3$$

EXAMPLE 3 The amount of an annuity for ten years is \$10,000. Find the size of the quarterly payment if the interest rate is 8% compounded quarterly.

$S_n = \$10{,}000$, $i = 8\%/4 = 2\%$ (per quarter), $n = 10 \times 4 = 40$ (quarterly payments)

---

[3]*Proof–for* $\frac{1}{a_{\overline{n}|i}} - i = \frac{1}{s_{\overline{n}|i}}$:

Since $a_{\overline{n}|i} = \frac{1-(1+i)^{-n}}{i}$, the reciprocals of both sides of the equation must also be equal.

Then,

$$\frac{1}{a_{\overline{n}|i}} = \frac{i}{1-(1+i)^{-n}}$$

Thus

$$\frac{1}{a_{\overline{n}|i}} - i = \frac{i}{1-(1+i)^{-n}} - i = \frac{i - i[1-(1+i)^{-n}]}{1-(1+i)^{-n}} = \frac{i(1+i)^{-n}}{1-(1+i)^{-n}}$$

$$= \frac{i(1+i)^{-n}}{1-(1+i)^{-n}} \cdot \frac{(1+i)^n}{(1+i)^n} = \frac{i}{(1+i)^n - 1} = \frac{1}{\frac{(1+i)^n - 1}{i}} = \frac{1}{s_{\overline{n}|i}}$$

Substituting the values in the preceding formula and using Table 9,

$$R = 10{,}000\left(\frac{1}{a_{\overline{40}|2\%}} - 2\%\right) = 10{,}000(0.0365558 - .02)$$

$$= 10{,}000(0.0165558) = \$165.558, \quad \text{or} \quad \$165.56$$

Or, if Table 7 is used,

$$R = \frac{10{,}000}{s_{\overline{40}|2\%}} = \frac{10{,}000}{60.40198} = \$165.56$$

NOTE: It is more convenient to use Table 9 than Table 7 in finding the value of R, since division may be avoided when the former table is used.

EXAMPLE 4 A man desires to have a $12,000 fund at the end of 20 years. If his savings can be invested at 6% compounded monthly, how much must he invest at the end of each month for 20 years?

$S_n = 12{,}000$, $i = 6\%/12 = \frac{1}{2}\%$ (per month), $n = 20 \times 12 = 240$ (months)

Substituting the values in the above formula and using Table 9,

$$R = 12{,}000\left(\frac{1}{a_{\overline{240}|1/2\%}} - \tfrac{1}{2}\%\right) = 12{,}000(.0071643 - .005)$$

$$= 12{,}000(.0021643) = \$25.9716, \quad \text{or} \quad \$25.97 \text{ (per month)}$$

EXERCISE 13–6 REFERENCE: SECTION 13.5

A. Find the size of the payment in each of the following ordinary annuities:

	Amount (S_n)	*Present Value (A_n)*	*Payment Interval*	*Term*	*Compound Interest Rate*
1.	$ 5,000		1 year	5 years	10%, annually
2.		$3,000	6 months	8 years	8%, semiannually
3.		2,000	1 month	7 years, 1 month	18%, monthly
4.	40,000		1 quarter	10 years, 6 months	7%, quarterly
5.		6,000	1 quarter	3 years	14%, quarterly
6.	10,000		1 month	4 years, 3 months	5%, monthly
7.	500		6 months	$2\frac{1}{2}$ years	12%, semiannually
8.		800	1 year	6 years	$4\frac{1}{2}$%, annually

B. Statement problems:

9. The amount of an annuity for nine years is $5,000. What is the size of the annual payment if the interest rate is 9% compounded annually?
10. The present value of an annuity for 12 years is $4,200. Find the size of the semiannual payment if the interest rate is 7% compounded semiannually.
11. Bill Sanders bought a truck for $12,500. He made a down payment of $500 and agreed to pay the balance in 24 equal monthly payments. If the interest charged was 8% compounded monthly, how much should Sanders pay each month?
12. Doris Hicks bought a machine for $560. She paid $50 down and agreed to pay the

balance plus interest at 6% compounded quarterly in equal quarterly payments for three years. What is the quarterly payment?

13. A debt of $2,500 was repaid in ten equal quarterly payments. If the rate of interest was 7% compounded quarterly, what was the size of each payment?
14. A man wishes to have a $5,000 fund at the end of five years. If his money can be invested at $13\frac{1}{2}$% compounded monthly, how much must he invest at the end of each month during the period?
15. A store manager plans to exchange his old car at the end of four years for a newer one worth $15,000. The trade-in value of the old car at that time is estimated to be $400. If money can be invested at 12% compounded quarterly, how much must the manager invest at the end of each quarter in order to make the exchange?
16. Ed Merrick wishes to provide a college education fund for his daughter, who is now eight years old. If the fund can earn 6% interest compounded semiannually and is to be used when she reaches 18 years of age, what must be the size of each semiannual deposit in order to provide a fund of $10,000? Assume that Merrick wishes to make the first deposit six months from now and the last deposit on his daughter's eighteenth birthday.

13.6 FINDING THE INTEREST RATE PER CONVERSION PERIOD (*i*) AND THE NOMINAL (ANNUAL) INTEREST RATE

Sometimes an investor or borrower desires to know the interest rate of an annuity. In this type of problem, the size of each periodic payment, the term, and the amount or the present value of the annuity are usually given.

A. The Amount Is Known

To find the interest rate when the amount is known, use the formula $S_n = Rs_{\overline{n}|i}$.

EXAMPLE 1

At what nominal rate compounded quarterly will an annuity of $150 payable at the end of each quarter amount to $6,600 in eight years?

$S_n = \$6{,}600$, $R = \$150$ (per quarter), $n = 8 \times 4 = 32$ (quarterly payments), $i = ?$ (per quarter)

Substituting the values in the above formula,

$$6{,}600 = 150s_{\overline{32}|i}, \qquad s_{\overline{32}|i} = \frac{6{,}600}{150} = 44$$

Follow the line for $n = 32$ in Table 7 to find the value of 44 or the two values closest to 44. It is found that the first value greater than 44 is 44.22702961, which is located in the 2% column, and the first value smaller than 44 is 43.30793563, which is located in the $1\frac{7}{8}$% column. Therefore, the desired value of i is greater than $1\frac{7}{8}$% and is smaller than 2%, or

$$1\tfrac{7}{8}\% < i < 2\%$$

When a more accurate value of i is needed, the interpolation method may be employed as follows:

	i	$s_{\overline{32}\vert i}$	
	2%	44.2270	(1)
	x	44.0000	(2)
	$1\frac{7}{8}\%$	43.3079	(3)
(2) − (3)	$x - 1\frac{7}{8}\%$	.6921	(4)
(1) − (3)	$\frac{1}{8}\%$	.9191	(5)

$$\frac{x - 1\frac{7}{8}\%}{\frac{1}{8}\%} = \frac{.6921}{.9191}$$

Solve for x from the proportion formed by the differences on lines (4) and (5).

$$x - 1\tfrac{7}{8}\% = \tfrac{1}{8}\%\left(\frac{.6921}{.9191}\right) = \frac{1}{800} \cdot \frac{6921}{9191} = .00094$$

$$x = 1\tfrac{7}{8}\% + .00094 = .01875 + .00094 = .01969$$

The desired value of i is .01969, or 1.969% per quarter.

The nominal interest rate = .01969 × 4 = .07876, or 7.88%

EXAMPLE 2

T. R. Ford signed a ten-month non-interest-bearing note for $5,000. He was offered the privilege of discharging the obligation by making 10 equal monthly payments of $488 payable at the end of each month. If he can invest his money at $5\frac{1}{2}\%$ compounded monthly, should he accept the offer?

S_n = $5,000, R = $488 (per month), n = 10 (monthly payments), i = ?

Substituting the values in the formula,

$$5{,}000 = 488 s_{\overline{10}\vert i}$$

$$s_{\overline{10}\vert i} = \frac{5{,}000}{488} = 10.2459$$

Follow the line for $n = 10$ in Table 7 to find the value of 10.2459 or the two values closest to it. The first value greater than 10.2459 is 10.2473, which is located in the $\frac{13}{24}\%$ column, and the first value smaller than 10.2459 is 10.2280, which is located in the $\frac{1}{2}\%$ column. Thus, the desired value of i is between $\frac{1}{2}\%$ and $\frac{13}{24}\%$, or

$$\tfrac{1}{2}\% < i < \tfrac{13}{24}\%$$

The nominal rate = $i \times 12$, which must be greater than ($\frac{1}{2}\% \times 12$) or 6%, but smaller than ($\frac{13}{24}\% \times 12$) or $6\frac{1}{2}\%$. Since Ford can invest his money at only $5\frac{1}{2}\%$ compounded monthly, he should accept the offer to discharge his obligation by making the monthly payment. In this type of problem, use of the interpolation method is not required.

B. The Present Value Is Known

To find the interest rate when the present value is known, use the formula $A_n = Ra_{\overline{n}\vert i}$.

EXAMPLE 3

The present value of an annuity of $200 payable at the end of every six months for 10 years is $3,000. What is the nominal rate compounded semiannually?

A_n = $3,000, R = $200 (per six months), $n = 10 \times 2 = 20$ (semiannual periods or payments), i = ? (per semiannual period)

Substituting the values in the above formula,

$$3{,}000 = 200a_{\overline{20}|i}, \qquad a_{\overline{20}|i} = \frac{3{,}000}{200} = 15$$

Follow the line for $n = 20$ in Table 8 to find the value of 15 or the two values closest to it. The first value greater than 15 is 15.22725213, which is located in the $2\frac{3}{4}\%$ column, and the first value smaller than 15 is 14.87747486, which is located in the 3% column. Thus, the desired value of i is

$2\frac{3}{4}\% < i < 3\%$

When a more accurate value of i is needed, the interpolation method may be employed as follows (write the larger numbers, which are in the column of values all known, on the top lines):

	i		$a_{\overline{20}\vert i}$	
	$2\frac{3}{4}\%$		15.2273	(1)
	x		15.0000	(2)
	3%		14.8775	(3)
(2) − (3)	$x - 3\%$	=	.1225	(4)
(1) − (3)	$-\frac{1}{4}\%$		.3498	(5)

Solve for x from the proportion formed by the differences on lines (4) and (5).

$$x - 3\% = (-\tfrac{1}{4}\%)\left(\frac{.1225}{.3498}\right) = -\left(\frac{1}{400}\right)\left(\frac{1225}{3498}\right) = -.0009$$

$$x = 3\% - .0009 = .03 - .0009 = .0291$$

The desired value of i is .0291, or 2.91% per semiannual period.
The nominal interest rate = $.0291 \times 2 = .0582$, or 5.82%

EXAMPLE 4

Anna B. Kello bought a car and paid $3,000 down plus $400 at the end of each month for three years. The cash price of the car was $15,043. What rate of interest did she pay?

A_n = 15,043 − 3,000 = $12,043, R = $400 (per month), $n = 3 \times 12 = 36$ (payments or months), i = ? (per month)

Substituting the values in the formula,

$$12{,}043 = 400a_{\overline{36}|i}$$

$$a_{\overline{36}|i} = \frac{12{,}043}{400} = 30.1075$$

Follow the line for $n = 36$ in Table 8 to find the value of 30.1075 or the two values closest to it. Since 30.1075 appears in the 1% column, no interpolation is needed. The desired value of i is 1%. The nominal interest rate is

$i \times 12 = 1\% \times 12 = 12\%$

EXERCISE 13–7 REFERENCE: SECTION 13.6

A. Find the interest rate per conversion period (i) and the nominal interest rate in each of the following problems. (Omit interpolation for Problems 1–6; use the interpolation method to find the answers for Problems 7–14.)

	Amount (S_n)	*Present Value* (A_n)	*Payment*	*Term*	*Interest Conversion Period*
1.	$4,740		$300 annually	10 years	1 year
2.		$6,060	600 semiannually	10 years	6 months
3.		14,715	450 monthly	3 years	1 month
4.	1,480		80 quarterly	4 years	1 quarter
5.		6,642	270 quarterly	7 years	1 quarter
6.	2,520		100 monthly	2 years	1 month
7.	700		65 semiannually	5 years	6 months
8.		530	80 annually	8 years	1 year

B. Statement problems:

9. At what nominal interest rate compounded semiannually will an annuity of $220 payable at the end of every six months amount to $2,530 in five years?
10. A man deposited $80 each month in a financial association. He received $1,000 immediately after the 12th deposit was made. If the nominal interest rate was compounded monthly, what was the rate?
11. The present value of an annuity of $50 payable at the end of each quarter for $9\frac{1}{2}$ years is $1,380. What is the nominal interest rate compounded quarterly?
12. Mario borrowed $600 from his employer and agreed to repay it in 10 equal monthly payments of $65. The first payment is to be made at the end of one month after the borrowing. The monthly payment plan results in the interest rate being compounded monthly. What is the nominal interest rate?
13. Janet Davis signed a six-year non-interest-bearing note for $520. She is allowed to discharge the debt by making six equal annual payments of $75 payable at the end of each year. If she can invest her money at 5% compounded annually, should she invest the money instead of paying the debt? Why?
14. The cash price of a washing machine is $370. If it can be bought by paying $25 down and $20 at the end of each month for $1\frac{1}{2}$ years, what is the nominal interest rate compounded monthly?

13.7 FINDING THE TERM OF AN ANNUITY (*n*)

Before the term of an annuity can be found, the size of the periodic payment, the interest rate per conversion period, and the amount or the present value of the annuity must be given.

A. The Amount Is Known

To find the term of an annuity when the amount is known, use the formula $S_n = Rs_{\overline{n}|i}$.

EXAMPLE 1

If \$30 is deposited at the end of each month, how many months will be required for the deposits to amount to \$1,220, if the interest rate is 6% compounded monthly?

$S_n = \$1{,}220$, $R = \$30$ (per month), $i = 6\%/12 = \frac{1}{2}\%$ (per month), $n = ?$ (monthly payments)

Substituting the values in the above formula,

$$1{,}220 = 30s_{\overline{n}|1/2\%}, \qquad s_{\overline{n}|1/2\%} = \frac{1{,}220}{30} = 40.6667$$

In the $\frac{1}{2}\%$ column of Table 7, find the two values closest to 40.6667. The findings are as follows:

When $n = 37$, the entry $= 40.53278549$

When $n = 38$, the entry $= 41.73544942$

Since 40.6667 is between the two entries above, the desired value of n is greater than 37 but smaller than 38. Thus, the amount will be less than \$1,220 immediately after the 37th deposit is made, but will be larger than \$1,220 after the 38th deposit. This statement is supported by the following computation:

$$S_n = 30s_{\overline{37}|1/2\%} = 30(40.5328) = \$1{,}215.98$$

$$S_n = 30s_{\overline{38}|1/2\%} = 30(41.7354) = \$1{,}252.06$$

Thus, in order to provide the amount of \$1,220, the 38th deposit is required. However, the size of the last deposit is less than the regular deposit of \$30. The answer to this problem is therefore 38 deposits or 38 months, which is three years and two months. The interpolation method is not used in the present case, since in practice, payments of an annuity are made at equal payment intervals.

B. The Present Value Is Known

To find the term of an annuity when the present value is known, use the formula $A_n = Ra_{\overline{n}|i}$.

EXAMPLE 2

A man borrows \$4,000 and agrees to repay it by paying \$200 at the end of each quarter. If the interest charged is 8% compounded quarterly, how long will he have to pay?

$A_n = \$4{,}000$, $R = \$200$ (per quarter), $i = 8\%/4 = 2\%$ (per quarter), $n = ?$ (quarters or payments)

Substituting the values in the above formula,

$$4{,}000 = 200a_{\overline{n}|2\%}, \qquad a_{\overline{n}|2\%} = \frac{4{,}000}{200} = 20$$

In the 2% column of Table 8, find the two values closest to 20. The findings are as follows:

When $n = 25$, the entry $= 19.52345647$

When $n = 26$, the entry $= 20.12104376$

Since 20 is between the two entries above, the desired value of n is greater than 25 but smaller than 26. In other words, as computed below, the present value of 25 payments is smaller than \$4,000, and the present value of 26 payments is larger than \$4,000.

$A_{25} = 200a_{\overline{25}|2\%} = 200(19.52346) = \$3{,}904.69$

$A_{26} = 200a_{\overline{26}|2\%} = 200(20.12104) = \$4{,}024.21$

Thus, in order to repay $4,000 (the present value of the annuity), the 26th payment is required. However, the last payment will be less than the regular $200 payment (see Note 1 below). The answer to this problem is therefore 26 payments or 26 quarters, which are equal to six years and six months. Use of the interpolation method is unnecessary in problems such as this.

NOTE:

1. The exact size of the final payment is $159.49 in Example 2. (Also see Problem 1, Exercise 15–2.) The method of finding the final payment and the use of the fractional part of the n value are discussed in Chapter 15, Section 15.1B(2).
2. In each of the two examples above, the greater value of n (38 in Example 1 and 26 in Example 2) is used as the answer to the problem.

This practice should be followed in solving the problems in the following exercises in the text.

EXERCISE 13–8 REFERENCE: SECTION 13.7

A. Find the term in each of the following ordinary annuities:

	Amount (S_n)	*Present Value (A_n)*	*Payment*	*Compound Interest Rate*
1.	$3,750		$ 300 annually	10%, annually
2.		$ 4,310	500 semiannually	16%, semiannually
3.		6,000	300 monthly	18%, monthly
4.	936		60 quarterly	7%, quarterly
5.		4,092	120 quarterly	5%, quarterly
6.	1,025		50 monthly	4%, monthly
7.	5,520		300 semiannually	7%, semiannually
8.		18,400	2,000 annually	$8\frac{1}{2}$%, annually

B. Statement problems:

9. If $150 was deposited at the end of every six months, how much time was required for the deposits to amount to $6,000 if the interest rate was 15% compounded semiannually?
10. The price of a small house was $55,000. The buyer made a down payment of $6,000 and agreed to pay $700 at the end of each month. If money was worth 12% compounded monthly, how long did it take the buyer to pay the balance and the interest?
11. A man borrowed $7,500 and agreed to repay it by paying $800 at the end of each year. If the interest rate was 9% compounded annually, how many payments was he required to make?
12. On January 1, 1991, Norma decided to deposit $250 in a savings account at the end of each quarter, with the first deposit to be made on April 1. The interest rate is 14% compounded quarterly. When will $5,000 be on deposit in Norma's account?

★13.8 COMPUTING FORMULAS BY CALCULATORS AND COMPUTERS

Tables 7, 8, and 9 can be used to save time in computing ordinary annuity problems, as presented in the previous sections. In addition, this section illustrates the methods of computing the formulas covered in this chapter by using calculators and computers. The illustrations are based on the instructions in Chapter 10.

A. Computing Formula (13–1): $S_n = R \cdot \frac{(1 + i)^n - 1}{i}$

The examples used in this section are obtained from Sections 13.2 and 13.4.

EXAMPLE 1 Compute Example 1, Section 13.2:

$$S_n = 100 \cdot \frac{(1 + 1\%)^4 - 1}{1\%} = 406.04$$

(a) SIMPLE CALCULATOR

Problem	*Step*	*Key Pressing Sequence*	*Display*
$100 \times \frac{1.01^4 - 1}{.01} = ?$	1	1.01 [×] [=] [=] [=]	1.040604
	2	[−] 1 [÷] .01 [×]	4.0604
	3	100 [=]	406.04

(b) BUSINESS ANALYST CALCULATOR

Problem	*Step*	*Key Pressing Sequence*	*Display*
Compute future value:	1	[ON/C] [2nd] [FIN]	0
Number of payments, $n = 1 \times 4$	2	1 [×] 4 [=] [N]	4
Percent interest rate per payment period, $i = 1\% \; (= 4\%/4)$	3*	1 [% *i*]	1
Payment size, $R = 100$ (must be negative)	4	100 [+/−] [PMT]	−100
Compute future value	5	[CPT] [FV]	406.0401

*Alternate sequence for Step 3: 4 [÷] 4 [=] [% *i*]

(c) COMPUTER WITH BASIC

BASIC Program

```
10 INPUT "R";R
20 INPUT "I";I
30 INPUT "N";N
40 S1 = R*((1 + I)∧N − 1)/I
50 PRINT "AMOUNT = ";S1
60 END
```

Computer Display (RUN)

```
R ? 100
I ? .01
N ? 4
AMOUNT = 406.04
```

The numbers after the question marks (?) are typed input.

In BASIC programs, only single letters or single letters followed by one digit (0 to 9) may be used to denote variables, such as A, B, C, . . . ,Z; A1, S1, Y6, . . . ; and so on. Since we cannot use the two letters SN as a variable, we will use S1 to denote S_n, the amount of an ordinary annuity.

The same BASIC program given in Example 1 can be used repeatedly for other examples in Sections 13.2 and 13.4, as follows:

Computer Display (RUN)

Example 2, Section 13.2	*Example 3, Section 13.2*
R ? 2000	R ? 20
I ? .10	I ? .005
N ? 45	N ? 36
AMOUNT = 1437809.71	AMOUNT = 786.722093

Example 1(a), Section 13.4	*Example 2, Section 13.4*
R ? 200	R ? 100
I ? .052	I ? .005
N ? 20	N ? 300
AMOUNT = 6754.71473	AMOUNT = 69299.3953

B. Computing Formula (13–2): $A_n = R \cdot \dfrac{1 - (1 + i)^{-n}}{i}$

The examples used in this section are obtained from Sections 13.3 and 13.4.

EXAMPLE 2

Compute Example 1, Section 13.3:

$$A_n = 100 \cdot \frac{1 - (1 + 1\%)^{-4}}{1\%} = 390.20$$

(a) SIMPLE CALCULATOR

Problem	*Step*	*Key Pressing Sequence*	*Display*
$100 \times \dfrac{1 - 1.01^{-4}}{.01} = ?$	1	1.01 [×] [=] [=] [=] [M+]	1.040604M
	2	1 [÷] [MR] [=]	0.9609803M
	3	[+/−] [+] 1 [=]	0.0390197M
	4	[÷] .01 [=]	3.90197M
	5	[×] 100 [=]	390.197M

(b) BUSINESS ANALYST CALCULATOR

Problem	*Step*	*Key Pressing Sequence*	*Display*
Compute present value:	1	[ON/C] [2nd] [FIN]	0
Number of payments, $n = 1 \times 4$	2	1 [×] 4 [=] [N]	4

Problem	*Step*	*Key Pressing Sequence*	*Display*
Percent interest rate per payment period, $i = 1\%$ $(= 4\%/4)$	3*	1 [% i]	1
Payment size, $R = 100$	4	100 [PMT]	100
Compute present value	5	[CPT] [PV]	390.19656

*Alternate sequence for Step 3: 4 [÷] 4 [=] [% i]

(c) COMPUTER WITH BASIC

BASIC Program

```
10 INPUT "R";R
20 INPUT "I";I
30 INPUT "N";N
40 A = R*(1 - (1 + I) ∧ (- N))/I
50 PRINT "PRESENT VALUE =";A
60 END
```

Computer Display (RUN)

```
R ? 100
I ? .01
N ? 4
PRESENT VALUE = 390.196549
```

The numbers after the question marks (?) are typed input.

We will use A to denote A_n, the present value of an ordinary annuity, in BASIC programs.

The same BASIC program given in Example 2 can be used repeatedly for other examples, as follows:

Computer Display (RUN)

Example 2, Section 13.3	*Example 3, Section 13.3*	*Example 4, Section 13.3*
R ? 20	R ? 500	R ? 150
I ? .005	I ? .01	I ? .05
N ? 36	N ? 36	N ? 15
PRESENT VALUE = 657.42032	PRESENT VALUE = 15053.7523	PRESENT VALUE = 1556.94871

Example 1(b), Section 13.4	*Example 3, Section 13.4*
R ? 200	R ? 100
I ? .052	I ? .005
N ? 20	N ? 300
PRESENT VALUE = 2450.71164	PRESENT VALUE = 15520.6864

C. Finding the Size of Each Periodic Payment, *R*

The examples used in this section are obtained from Section 13.5.

(1) THE PRESENT VALUE IS KNOWN

Use the formula derived from formula (13–2):

$$R = A_n \cdot \frac{i}{1 - (1 + i)^{-n}}$$

EXAMPLE 3

Compute Example 1, Section 13.5:

$$R = 10{,}000 \cdot \frac{2\%}{1 - (1 + 2\%)^{-40}} \doteq 365.56$$

(a) SIMPLE CALCULATOR

Problem	*Step*	*Key Pressing Sequence*	*Display*
$10{,}000 \times \frac{.02}{1 - \frac{1}{1.02^{40}}} = ?$	1	1.02 [×] [=] (39 times) [M+]	2.2080373M
	2	1 [÷] [MR] [=]	0.4528908M
	3	[+/−] [+] 1 [=]	0.5471092M
	4	[MC] [M+]	0.5471092M
	5	10,000 [×] .02 [÷] [MR] [=]	365.55773

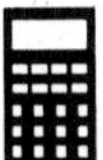

(b) BUSINESS ANALYST CALCULATOR

Problem	*Step*	*Key Pressing Sequence*	*Display*
Compute payment size:	1	[ON/C] [2nd] [FIN]	0
Number of payments, $n = 10 \times 4$	2	10 [×] 4 [=] [N]	40
Percent interest rate per payment period, $i = 8\%/4 = 2\%$	3	8 [÷] 4 [=] [% i]	2
Present value, $A_n = 10{,}000$	4	10000 [PV]	10000
Compute payment size	5	[CPT] [PMT]	365.55748

(c) COMPUTER WITH BASIC

BASIC Program

```
10 INPUT "A";A
20 INPUT "I";I
30 INPUT "N";N
40 R = A*I/(1 - (1 + I) ∧ (- N))
50 PRINT "PAYMENT SIZE =";R
60 END
```

Computer Display (RUN)

```
A ? 10000
I ? .02
N ? 40
PAYMENT SIZE = 365.557471
```

The numbers after the question marks (?) are typed input.

EXAMPLE 4

Compute Example 2, Section 13.5:

$A_n = 100{,}000$

$i = 1\%$

$n = 240$

$R = ? = 1{,}101.086$

Use the BASIC program given in Example 3:

Computer Display (RUN)

```
A ? 100000
I ? .01
N ? 240
PAYMENT SIZE = 1101.08614
```

(2) THE AMOUNT IS KNOWN

Use the formula derived from formula (13–1):

$$R = S_n \cdot \frac{i}{(1 + i)^n - 1}$$

EXAMPLE 5 Compute Example 3, Section 13.5:

$$R = 10{,}000 \cdot \frac{2\%}{(1 + 2\%)^{40} - 1} = 165.56$$

(a) SIMPLE CALCULATOR

Problem	Step	Key Pressing Sequence	Display
$10{,}000 \times \frac{.02}{1.02^{40} - 1} = ?$	1	1.02 [×] [=] (39 times)	2.2080373
	2	[−] 1 [=] [M+]	1.2080373M
	3	10000 [×] .02 [÷] [MR] [=]	165.5578M

(b) BUSINESS ANALYST CALCULATOR

Problem	Step	Key Pressing Sequence	Display
Compute payment size:	1	[ON/C] [2nd] [FIN]	0
Number of payments, $n = 10 \times 4$	2	10 [×] 4 [=] [N]	40
Percent interest rate per payment period, $i = 8\%/4 = 2\%$	3	8 [÷] 4 [=] [% i]	2
Future value, $S_n = 10{,}000$	4	10000 [FV]	10000
Compute payment size	5	[CPT] [PMT] [+/−]	165.55748

(c) COMPUTER WITH BASIC

BASIC Program

```
10 INPUT "S1";S1
20 INPUT "I";I
30 INPUT "N";N
40 R = S1*I/((1 + I) ∧ N − 1)
50 PRINT "PAYMENT SIZE =";R
60 END
```

Computer Display (RUN)

```
S1 ? 10000
I ? .02
N ? 40
PAYMENT SIZE = 165.557471
```

The numbers after the question marks (?) are typed input.

EXAMPLE 6

Compute Example 4, Section 13.5:

$S_n = 12,000$
$i = \frac{1}{2}\%$
$n = 240$
$R = ? = 25.97$

Use the BASIC program given in Example 5:

Computer Display (RUN)

```
S1 ? 12000
I ? .005
N ? 240
PAYMENT SIZE = 25.9717273
```

D. Finding the Interest Rate per Conversion Period, *i*

The examples used in this section are obtained from Section 13.6.

(1) THE AMOUNT IS KNOWN

Use the formula derived from formula (13–1):

$$\frac{(1 + i)^n - 1}{i} = \frac{S_n}{R}$$

EXAMPLE 7

Compute Example 1, Section 13.6:

$S_n = 6,600$
$R = 150$
$n = 8 \times 4 = 32$
$i = ? = .01969$

(a) SIMPLE CALCULATOR

A direct equation representing the i value is not available. However, we may find an approximate value of i by the interpolation method; based on a table showing (S_n/R) values, such as Table 7. See the interpolation method in Section 13.6.

(b) BUSINESS ANALYST CALCULATOR

Problem	*Step*	*Key Pressing Sequence*	*Display*
Compute percent interest rate per conversion period:	1	[ON/C] [2nd] [FIN]	0
Number of payments, $n = 8 \times 4$	2	8 [×] 4 [=] [N]	32
Payment size, $R = 150$	3	150 [+/−] [PMT]	−150
Future value, $S_n = 6,600$	4	6600 [FV]	6600
Compute interest rate	5	[CPT] [% i]	1.9694215

(c) COMPUTER WITH BASIC

BASIC Program

```
10 INPUT "S1";S1
20 INPUT "R";R
30 INPUT "H1";H1
40 INPUT "L1";L1
50 INPUT "H";H
60 INPUT "L";L
70 I = L + (H - L)*(S1/R - L1)/(H1 - L1)
80 PRINT "INTEREST RATE =";I
90 END
```

Computer Display (RUN)

```
S1 ? 6600
R ? 150
H1 ? 44.2270
L1 ? 43.3079
H ? .02
L ? .01875
INTEREST RATE = .0196912741
```

The numbers after the question marks (?) are typed input.

The following i formula is derived by the interpolation method, as illustrated in Section 13.6:

$$i = L + (H - L)(S1/R - L1)/(H1 - L1)$$

where i = interest rate per conversion period,
$S1 = S_n$ = the amount of an ordinary annuity, or the future value
R = payment size

Other values in the formula are obtained from Table 7, based on $n = 32$ and $S_n/R = 6600/150 = 44$:

$H1$ = the entry higher than 44 = 44.2270
$L1$ = the entry lower than 44 = 43.3079
H = percent rate located in $H1$ column = 2%
L = percent rate located in $L1$ column = $1\frac{7}{8}$%

EXAMPLE 8 Compute Example 2, Section 13.6:

$S_n = 5{,}000$
$R = 488$, ($S_n/R = 5{,}000/488 = 10.2459$)
$n = 10$
$i = ? = 0.00539$

Use the BASIC program given in Example 7:

Computer Display (RUN)

```
S1 ? 5000
R ? 488
H1 ? 10.2473
L1 ? 10.2280
H ? .005416667
L ? .005
INTEREST RATE = 5.38647789E - 03*
```

*Or 0.00538647789

(2) THE PRESENT VALUE IS KNOWN

Use the formula derived from formula (13–2):

$$\frac{1-(1+i)^{-n}}{i}=\frac{A_n}{R}$$

EXAMPLE 9

Compute Example 3, Section 13.6:

$A_n = 3{,}000$
$R = 200$
$n = 10 \times 2 = 20$
$i = ? = .0291$

(a) SIMPLE CALCULATOR

A direct equation representing the i value is not available. However, we may find an approximate value of i by the interpolation method, based on a table showing (A_n/R) values, such as Table 8. The interpolation method is illustrated in Section 13.6.

(b) BUSINESS ANALYST CALCULATOR

Problem	*Step*	*Key Pressing Sequence*	*Display*
Compute percent interest rate per conversion period:	1	[ON/C] [2nd] [FIN]	0
Number of payments, $n = 10 \times 2$	2	10 [×] 2 [=] [N]	20
Payment size, $R = 200$	3	200 [PMT]	200
Present value, $A_n = 3{,}000$	4	3000 [PV]	3000
Compute interest rate	5	[CPT] [% i]	2.9114566

(c) COMPUTER WITH BASIC

BASIC Program

```
10 INPUT "A";A
20 INPUT "R";R
30 INPUT "H1";H1
40 INPUT "L1";L1
50 INPUT "H";H
60 INPUT "L";L
70 I = L + (H - L)*(A/R - L1)/(H1 - L1)
80 PRINT "INTEREST RATE =";I
90 END
```

Computer Display (RUN)

```
A ? 3000
R ? 200
H1 ? 15.2273
L1 ? 14.8775
H ? .0275
L ? .03
INTEREST RATE = .0291244997
```

The numbers after the question marks (?) are typed input.

The following i formula is derived by the interpolation method, as illustrated in Section 13.6:

$i = L + (H - L)(A/R - L1)/(H1 - L1)$

where i = interest rate per conversion period
$A = A_n$ = the present value of an ordinary annuity
R = payment size

Other values in the formula are obtained from Table 8, based on $n = 20$ and $A_n/R = 3{,}000/200 = 15$:

$H1$ = the entry higher than 15 = 15.2273
$L1$ = the entry lower than 15 = 14.8775
H = percent rate located in $H1$ column = $2\frac{3}{4}\%$
L = percent rate located in $L1$ column = 3%

The same BASIC program given in Example 9 can be used for other interest rate problems if the interpolation method is required. Note that the solution for Example 4, Section 13.6, requires no interpolation.

E. Finding the Term, *n*

The examples used in this section are obtained from Section 13.7.

(1) THE AMOUNT IS KNOWN

Solve for n from formula (13–1):

$$n = \frac{\log (1 + S_n i/R)}{\log (1 + i)}$$

EXAMPLE 10 Compute Example 1, Section 13.7:

$S_n = 1{,}220$
$R = 30$
$i = \frac{1}{2}\%$
n = ? = greater than 37, but smaller than 38

(a) SIMPLE CALCULATOR

Not capable of computing with logarithms. However, we may find an approximate value of n by the interpolation method, based on a table showing (S_n/R) values, such as Table 7. See Section 13.7.

(b) BUSINESS ANALYST CALCULATOR

Problem	*Step*	*Key Pressing Sequence*	*Display*
Compute number of payments:	1	[ON/C] [2nd] [FIN]	0
Percent interest rate per payment period, $i = \frac{1}{2}\%$	2	.5 [% i]	0.5
Payment size, $R = 30$	3	30 [+/−] [PMT]	−30
Future value, $S_n = 1{,}220$	4	1220 [FV]	1220
Compute number of payments	5	[CPT] [N]	37.11

(c) COMPUTER WITH BASIC

BASIC Program	Computer Display (RUN)

```
10 INPUT "S1";S1
20 INPUT "R";R
30 INPUT "I";I
40 N = LOG(1 + S1*I/R)/LOG(1 + I)
50 PRINT "NUMBER OF PAYMENTS = ";N
60 END
```

Computer Display (RUN)

```
S1 ? 1220
R ? 30
I ? .005
NUMBER OF PAYMENTS = 37.1115678
```

The numbers after the question marks (?) are typed input.

(2) THE PRESENT VALUE IS KNOWN

Solve for n from formula (13–2):

$$n = -\frac{\log(1 - A_n i/R)}{\log(1 + i)}$$

EXAMPLE 11 Compute Example 2, Section 13.7:

$A_n = 4{,}000$
$R = 200$
$i = 2\%$
$n = ? =$ greater than 25, but smaller than 26

(a) SIMPLE CALCULATOR

Not capable of computing with logarithms. However, we may find an approximate value of n by the interpolation method, based on a table showing (A_n/R) values, such as Table 8. See Section 13.7.

(b) BUSINESS ANALYST CALCULATOR

Problem	*Step*	*Key Pressing Sequence*	*Display*
Compute number of payments:	1	[ON/C] [2nd] [FIN]	0
Percent interest rate per payment period, $i = 2\%$	2	2 [% i]	2
Payment size, $R = 200$	3	200 [PMT]	200
Present value, $A_n = 4{,}000$	4	4000 [PV]	4000
Compute number of payments	5	[CPT] [N]	25.8

(c) COMPUTER WITH BASIC

BASIC Program

```
10 INPUT "A";A
20 INPUT "R";R
30 INPUT "I";I
40 N = -(LOG(1 - A*I/R)/LOG(1 + I))
50 PRINT "NUMBER OF PAYMENTS = ";N
60 END
```

Computer Display (RUN)

```
A ? 4000
R ? 200
I ? .02
NUMBER OF PAYMENTS = 25.7958515
```

The numbers after the question marks (?) are typed input.

13.9 SUMMARY OF ORDINARY ANNUITY FORMULAS

Application	*Formula*	*Formula Number*	*Reference Pages*
Finding the amount	$S_n = R \cdot \frac{(1+i)^n - 1}{i} = Rs_{\overline{n}\rceil i}$	(13–1)	380 and 381
Finding the present value	$A_n = R \cdot \frac{1-(1+i)^{-n}}{i} = Ra_{\overline{n}\rceil i}$	(13–2)	386 and 387

EXERCISE 13–9 REVIEW OF CHAPTER 13

1. What is the amount of an annuity if the payment is $50 payable at the end of every six months for 20 years at 18% compounded semiannually?
2. Find the amount of an annuity of $80 payable at the end of each month for five years if the interest rate is 21% compounded monthly.
3. (a) If $40 is deposited at the end of each quarter for 10 years in a bank that pays 10% interest compounded quarterly, what will be the final value at the end of 10 years? (b) What is the total interest at the end of 12 years?
4. (a) If $90 is deposited at the end of each year for six years in a fund that earns 6% interest compounded annually, what will be the value of the fund at the end of nine years? (b) What is the total interest earned?
5. What is the present value of an annuity if the payment is $65 payable at the end of each month for eight years and the interest rate is 6% compounded monthly?
6. If Jerome Wilson wishes to receive $80 at the end of each quarter for seven years from a financial company that pays 12% interest compounded quarterly, how much must he deposit in the company now?
7. What was the cash price of a house bought for $18,000 down and $600 a month for 8 years, if the interest rate was 15% compounded monthly?
8. Find the present value of an annuity of $700 payable at the end of every six months for 30 years if the interest rate is 10% compounded semiannually.
9. What are the amount and the present value of an annuity of $25 payable at the end of each month for four years if the interest rate is 6% compounded monthly?
10. Find the amount and the present value of an annuity that will pay $40 each quarter for 35 quarters with the first payment to be made three months from now. Assume that the interest rate is 11% compounded quarterly.
11. What are the amount and the present value of an annuity of $50 payable at the end of each quarter for 20 years if money is worth $6\frac{1}{4}$% compounded quarterly.
12. Find the amount and the present value of an annuity of $150 payable at the end of every six months for five years if interest is $5\frac{1}{4}$% compounded semiannually.
13. What are the amount and the present value of an annuity of $40 payable at the end of each month for 30 years if the interest rate is 5% compounded monthly?
14. Find the amount and the present value of an annuity of $100 payable at the end of each quarter for 40 years if the interest rate is 6% compounded quarterly.
15. The present value of an annuity payable semiannually for 15 years is $7,500. What is the size of the semiannual payment if the interest rate is 9% compounded semiannually?

16. The price of a small building was $220,000. The buyer made a down payment of $20,000. The balance was to be paid in monthly installments for ten years. If the interest rate charged was 12% compounded monthly, how much did the buyer pay each month?
17. The amount of an annuity payable quarterly for 12 years is $8,500. What is the size of the quarterly payment if the interest rate is 13% compounded quarterly?
18. Yuan Shen wishes to have $4,000 at the end of five years. If his savings can be invested at $13\frac{1}{2}$% compounded monthly, how much must he save at the end of each month for five years?
19. At what nominal interest rate compounded monthly will an annuity of $120 payable at the end of each month amount to $10,000 in six years?
20. At what nominal interest rate compounded quarterly will an annuity of $70 payable at the end of each quarter amount to $8,000 in 25 years?
21. Judy Reese figures that she will have $2,790.80 in her savings account at the end of five years. She deposits $40 one month from now and $40 thereafter at the end of each month. At what nominal interest rate compounded monthly has she figured the interest?
22. Steven Kyle plans to invest $100 each month with the first investment to be made one month from now. He expects $3,993.01 at the end of three years. What must be the nominal interest rate compounded monthly?
23. At what nominal interest rate compounded semiannually will an annuity of $500 payable at the end of every six months for $6\frac{1}{2}$ years have a present value of $5,500?
24. The present value of an annuity of $350 payable at the end of each quarter for six years is $6,500. What is the nominal interest rate compounded quarterly?
25. Robert Oaks bought a used car for $300 down with monthly payments of $50 for 20 months. The cash price was $1,225.40. What was the nominal interest rate charged?
26. Jane Allen bought a color television set. The cash price was $423.32. Under the terms of her installment purchase, she made 24 monthly payments of $20 each, with the first payment beginning on the date of purchase. What was the nominal interest rate charged?
27. If $50 is deposited at the end of each quarter, how many quarterly deposits will be needed for the deposits to amount to $1,000 if the interest rate is 5% compounded quarterly?
28. Johnson plans to invest $150 each month starting one month from now. He wishes to have at least $4,500 as the final value. If he can earn 6% interest compounded monthly on his investment, how many monthly deposits are required for the final value?
29. A company is considering the purchase of a new machine that will increase operating efficiency and thus save $2,000 each year in labor costs. It is estimated that the machine will be used for ten years and it can then be sold for $1,000. If money is worth 6%, how much can the company afford to pay for this machine?
30. A piece of land is available at a price of $100,000. Company G is considering its purchase for future plant expansion. If the land will not be needed for 20 years and the annual taxes will be 2% of the purchase price, what must the prospective price of the land be in 20 years to make it worthwhile for the company to buy the land now? Assume that money is worth 10%.

14 OTHER ANNUITIES CERTAIN

Classifications of various types of annuities certain were presented in Section 13.1 of the previous chapter. This chapter will explain in detail the other types of annuities certain. They are: annuity due (Section 14.1), deferred annuity (Section 14.2), and complex (or general) annuity (Section 14.3). This chapter also explains the methods of computing formulas by calculators and computers as supplemental material.

14.1 ANNUITY DUE

An *annuity due* is an annuity for which the periodic payments are made at the *beginning* of each payment interval. The term of an annuity due begins on the date of the first payment and ends one payment interval after the last payment is made.

A. Amount of an Annuity Due, S_n(due)

The *amount* of an annuity due is the value at the end of the term of the annuity. It includes all the periodic payments plus the compound interest. By a method similar to that used in finding the amount of an ordinary annuity, the amount of an annuity due may be found by totaling the individual compound amounts of the periodic payments (see Section 13.2). Each of the compound amounts is computed by the formula $S = P(1 + i)^n$. However, a simpler method of finding the amount of an annuity due is to use the formula for finding the amount of an ordinary annuity, $S_n = Rs_{\overline{n}|i}$. When this formula is used, the amount of an annuity due may be found in either of two ways.

METHOD A

First, find the amount of the ordinary annuity of $(n + 1)$ payments. Then, subtract the additional payment from the amount obtained.

$$\mathbf{S_n(due) = Rs_{\overline{n+1}|i} - R} \quad \text{or}$$

$$\mathbf{S_n(due) = R(s_{\overline{n+1}|i} - 1)} \qquad \textbf{(14–1)}$$

EXAMPLE 1 What is the amount of an annuity due for one year if each payment is $100 payable at the beginning of each quarter and the interest rate is 4% compounded quarterly?

R = $100 (per quarter), $i = 4\%/4 = 1\%$ (per quarter), $n = 4$ (quarterly payments)

Substituting the values in formula (14–1),

$$S_4(\text{due}) = 100s_{\overline{4+1}|1\%} - 100 = 100s_{\overline{5}|1\%} - 100$$
$$= 100(5.10101) - 100 = \$410.10 \quad (\text{Table 7}, n = 5)$$

The example is diagrammed as follows:

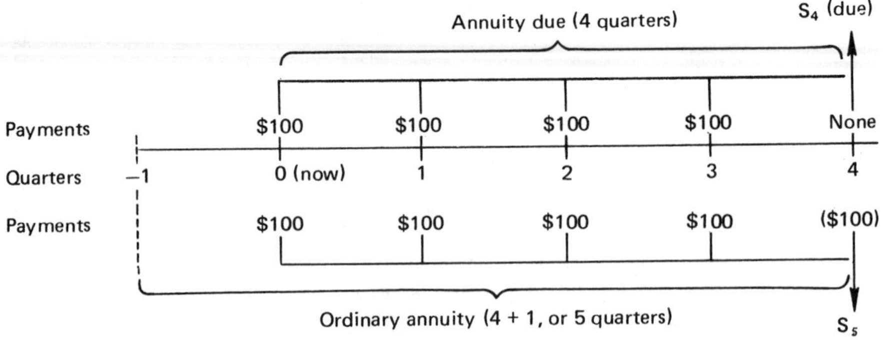

The diagram shows that if an additional payment ($100) is made at the end of the fourth quarter, the 5 (or 4 + 1) payments form an ordinary annuity. The amount of the ordinary annuity is S_5 (or S_{4+1}). The difference between the amount of the ordinary annuity of five payments and the amount of the annuity due of four payments is the additional payment ($100). Thus,

$$S_4(\text{due}) = S_{4+1} - 100 = 100s_{\overline{4+1}|1\%} - 100$$

Extending this idea, let

n = number of payments (or number of interest conversion periods)
R = size of each regular payment

Then

$$S_n(\text{due}) = Rs_{\overline{n+1}|i} - R$$

EXAMPLE 2 If $20 is deposited at the beginning of each month in a fund that earns interest at 18% compounded monthly, what is the final value at the end of three years?

R = $20 (per month), $i = 18\%/12 = 1\frac{1}{2}\%$ (per month), $n = 3 \times 12 = 36$ (months or payments)

Substituting the values in formula (14–1),

$$S_{36}(\text{due}) = 20s_{\overline{36+1}|1\ 1/2\%} - 20 = 20(48.9851 - 1) = \$959.70$$
(Table 7: $n = 36 + 1 = 37$)

★METHOD B First, find the amount as if it were an ordinary annuity. Then, accumulate the amount obtained for one interest period.

$$\mathbf{S_n(due) = Rs_{\overline{n}|i} \cdot (1 + i)} \qquad \textbf{(14–2)}$$

Solution of Example 1 by formula (14–2) (see also page 416):

$R = \$100$, $i = 1\%$, $n = 4$ (quarterly payments)

$S_n(\text{due}) = 100s_{\overline{4}|1\%}(1 + 1\%) = 100(4.060401)(1.01) = \$410.10$

The example is diagrammed as follows:

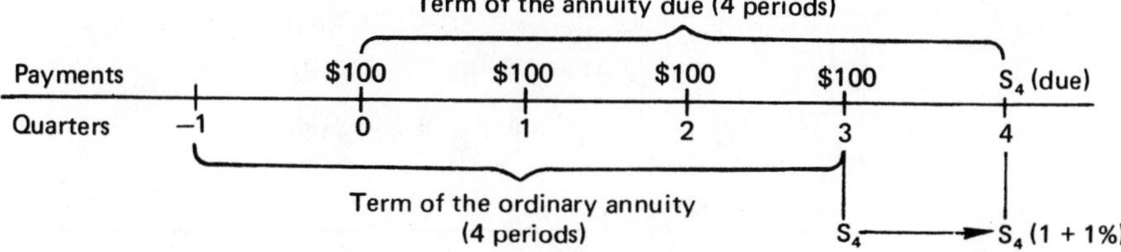

The diagram shows that the annuity due is first converted to an ordinary annuity. The amount of the ordinary annuity (S_4) is the value at the end of the third quarter. The required amount of the annuity due is the value at the end of the fourth quarter. Thus, S_4 is accumulated for one interest period, or

$S_4(\text{due}) = S_4(1 + i) = 100s_{\overline{4}|1\%} \cdot (1 + 1\%)$

Extending this idea,

$S_n(\text{due}) = S_n(1 + i) = Rs_{\overline{n}|i} \cdot (1 + i)$

Solution of Example 2 by formula (14–2) (see also page 416):

$R = \$20$, $i = 1\frac{1}{2}\%$, $n = 36$

$S_{36}(\text{due}) = 20s_{\overline{36}|1\ 1/2\%} \cdot (1 + 1\frac{1}{2}\%) = 20(47.2760)(1.015) = \$959.70$

It is important to master the methods rather than to merely memorize the formulas. Method A is preferred in most cases, since the computation is simpler than that in Method B.

B. Present Value of an Annuity Due, A_n(due)

The *present value* of an annuity due is the value at the beginning of the term of the annuity. By a method similar to that of finding the present value of an ordinary annuity, the present value of an annuity due may be found by totaling the individual present values of the periodic payments (see Section 13.3). Each of the present values is computed by the formula $P = S(1 + i)^{-n}$. However, a simpler method of finding the present value of an annuity due is to use the formula for finding the present value of an ordinary annuity, $A_n = Ra_{\overline{n}|i}$. When this formula is used, the present value may be found in either of two ways.

METHOD A

First, find the present value of the ordinary annuity of $(n - 1)$ payments. Then, add the excluded payment to the present value obtained.

$$\mathbf{A_n(\text{due}) = Ra_{\overline{n-1}|i} + R} \quad \text{or}$$

$$\mathbf{A_n(\text{due}) = R(a_{\overline{n-1}|i} + 1)} \qquad \mathbf{(14\text{–}3)}$$

EXAMPLE 3 What is the present value of an annuity due if the size of each payment is \$100 payable at the beginning of each quarter for one year and the interest rate is 4% compounded quarterly?

R = \$100 (per quarter), $i = 4\%/4 = 1\%$ (per quarter), $n = 4$ (quarterly payments)

Substituting the values in formula (14–3),

$$A_n(\text{due}) = 100a_{\overline{4-1}|1\%} + 100 = 100a_{\overline{3}|1\%} + 100$$
$$= 100(2.94099) + 100 = \$394.10 \quad (\text{Table 8: } n = 4 - 1 = 3)$$

The example is diagrammed as follows:

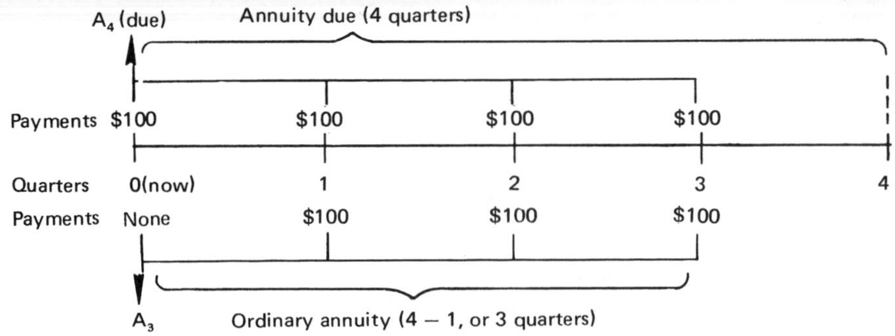

The diagram shows that if the \$100 payment at the beginning of the first quarter is excluded, the remaining three (or 4 − 1) payments form an ordinary annuity. The present value of the ordinary annuity is A_3 (or A_{4-1}). The difference between the present value of the ordinary annuity of three payments and the present value of the annuity due of four payments is the excluded payment of \$100. Thus,

$$A_4(\text{due}) = A_{4-1} + 100 = 100a_{\overline{4-1}|1\%} + 100$$

Extending this idea, let

n = number of payments (or number of interest conversion periods)
R = size of each regular payment

Then

$$A_n(\text{due}) = Ra_{\overline{n-1}|i} + R$$

EXAMPLE 4 What is the selling price of a television set that can be bought for \$50 a month for 10 months beginning now, if money is worth 12% compounded monthly?

This is an annuity due problem, since the first payment starts now, the beginning of the first payment interval.

R = \$50 (per month), $i = 12\%/12 = 1\%$ (per month), $n = 10$ (months or payments)

Substituting the values in formula (14–3),

$$A_n(\text{due}) = 50a_{\overline{10-1}|1\%} + 50 = 50(8.5660 + 1) = \$478.30 \quad (\text{Table 8: } n = 10 - 1 = 9)$$

★METHOD B First, find the present value as if it were an ordinary annuity. Then, accumulate the present value obtained for one interest period.

$$A_n(\text{due}) = Ra_{\overline{n}|i} \cdot (1 + i) \qquad \textbf{(14–4)}$$

Solution of Example 3 by formula (14–4) (see also page 418):

$R = \$100$, $i = 1\%$, $n = 4$ (quarterly payments)

$$A_n(\text{due}) = 100a_{\overline{4}|1\%} \cdot (1 + 1\%) = 100(3.90197)(1.01) = \$394.10$$

The example is diagrammed as follows:

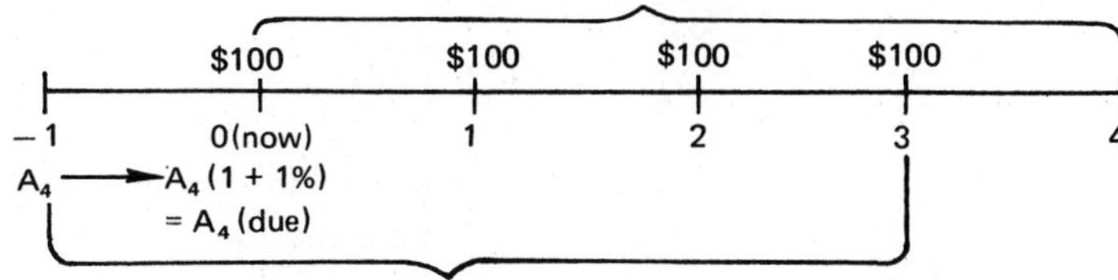

The diagram shows that the annuity due is first converted to an ordinary annuity. The present value of the ordinary annuity (A_4) is the value at the beginning of one quarter before the beginning of the first quarter. The required present value of the annuity due is the value at the beginning of the first quarter. Thus, A_4 is accumulated for one interest period, or

$$A_4(\text{due}) = A_4(1 + i) = 100a_{\overline{4}|1\%} \cdot (1 + 1\%)$$

Extending this idea,

$$A_n(\text{due}) = A_n \cdot (1 + i) = Ra_{\overline{n}|i} \cdot (1 + i)$$

Solution of Example 4 by formula (14–4) (see also page 418):

$$A_{10}(\text{due}) = 50a_{\overline{10}|1\%} \cdot (1 + 1\%) = 50(9.4713)(1.01) = \$478.30$$

C. Relationship Between the Amount and the Present Value of an Annuity Due

The present value of an annuity due is also the single principal which, invested at a given compound interest rate, will accumulate to the amount of the annuity due by the end of the term. The relationship between the amount and the present value may be expressed by using the compound interest formula $S = P(1 + i)^n$ and the compound discount formula $P = S(1 + i)^{-n}$. Here, P is the present value, A_n(due), and S is the amount of the annuity due, S_n(due). The formulas may be written in the following manner:

$$S_n(\text{due}) = A_n(\text{due})(1 + i)^n$$

$$A_n(\text{due}) = S_n(\text{due})(1 + i)^{-n}$$

When the amount of an annuity due is known, for instance, the present value of the annuity due of Example 3 can be computed by using the A_n(due) formula, as shown below:

$S_4(\text{due}) = \$410.10$ (see Example 1), $i = 1\%$, $n = 4$

$$A_4(\text{due}) = S_4(\text{due})(1 + 1\%)^{-4} = 410.10(.96098) = \$394.10$$

EXERCISE 14–1 REFERENCE: SECTION 14.1A, B, and C

A. Find the amount and the present value of the annuity due in each of the following:

	Payment (R)	*Payment Interval*	*Term*	*Compound Interest Rate*
1.	\$ 100	1 month	3 years	18%, monthly
2.	80	1 quarter	9 years	16%, quarterly
3.	640	6 months	$4\frac{1}{2}$ years	7%, semiannually
4.	850	1 year	20 years	10%, annually
5.	500	1 quarter	$12\frac{1}{2}$ years	5%, quarterly
6.	220	1 month	$2\frac{1}{2}$ years	4%, monthly
7.	1,000	1 year	25 years	$5\frac{1}{2}$%, annually
8.	1,200	6 months	10 years	8%, semiannually

B. Statement problems:

9. Find the amount of an annuity due of \$700 payable at the beginning of each quarter for six years if the interest rate is 14% compounded quarterly.
10. What is the amount of an annuity due for two years and five months if each payment is \$450 payable at the beginning of each month and the interest rate is $10\frac{1}{2}$% compounded monthly?
11. Find the present value of the annuity due in Problem 9.
12. What is the present value of the annuity due in Problem 10?
13. If \$600 is deposited at the beginning of each month in a bank that pays 12% interest compounded monthly, what is the final value at the end of three years and four months?
14. On July 1, 1991, a man deposits \$150 in a savings and loan association that pays 8% compounded quarterly. The man continues to deposit \$150 every quarter thereafter. How much will be in his account on July 1, 1996, immediately before the deposit on this date is made?
15. What is the cash price of a freezer that can be bought for \$75 a quarter for $2\frac{1}{2}$ years if the first payment is made now and the interest rate is 7% compounded quarterly?
16. A house was rented for \$800 per month, each month's rent payable in advance. If money was worth 6% compounded monthly, what was the cash value of the rent for one year?

D. Other Types of Problems in an Annuity Due

In formula (14–1), $S_n(\text{due}) = R(s_{\overline{n+1}|i} - 1)$, there are four quantities: S_n(due), R, n, and i. If any three of them are known, the one unknown may be determined by using the formula. Likewise, in formula (14–3), $A_n(\text{due}) = R(a_{\overline{n-1}|i} + 1)$, there are four quantities: A_n(due), R, n, and i. If any three of them are known, the one unknown may be determined by using the formula. The methods used in finding the values of S_n(due) and A_n(due) have already been discussed in this section. In the remaining portion of the section, the methods of finding the values of R, i, and n are given.

(1) FINDING THE VALUE OF R WHEN S_n(due) IS KNOWN

EXAMPLE 5

A man wishes to receive \$2,000 five years from now. How much must he invest at the beginning of each year if the first payment starts now and the interest is 10% compounded annually?

$S_n(\text{due}) = \$2{,}000,\ i = 10\%$ (per year), $n = 5$ (years or payments),
$R = ?$ (per year)

Substituting the values in the formula $S_n(\text{due}) = R(s_{\overline{n+1}|i} - 1)$,

$2{,}000 = R(s_{\overline{5+1}|10\%} - 1) = R\,(7.715610 - 1)$

$$R = \frac{2{,}000}{6.71561} = \$297.81 \quad (\text{Table 7, } n = 6)$$

(2) FINDING THE VALUE OF R WHEN A_n(due) IS KNOWN

EXAMPLE 6

A washing machine that sells for \$600 can be bought under terms of 20 equal monthly payments, starting now. If money is worth 21% compounded monthly, what is the size of each payment?

$A_n(\text{due}) = \$600,\ i = 21\%/12 = 1\tfrac{3}{4}\%$ (per month), $n = 20$ (months or payments),
$R = ?$ (per month)

Substituting the values in the formula $A_n(\text{due}) = R(a_{\overline{n-1}|i} + 1)$,

$600 = R(a_{\overline{20-1}|1\,3/4\%} + 1) = R(16.04606 + 1)$

$$R = \frac{600}{17.04606} = \$35.20$$

(3) FINDING THE VALUE OF i WHEN S_n(due) IS KNOWN

EXAMPLE 7

At what nominal rate compounded annually will an annuity due of \$1,000, payable at the beginning of each year for four years, amount to \$5,000?

$S_n(\text{due}) = \$5{,}000,\ R = \$1{,}000$ (per year), $n = 4$ (years or payments),
$i = ?$ (annual)

Substituting the values in the formula $S_n(\text{due}) = Rs_{\overline{n+1}|i} - R$,

$5{,}000 = 1{,}000s_{\overline{4+1}|i} - 1{,}000$

$$s_{\overline{5}|i} = \frac{5{,}000 + 1{,}000}{1{,}000} = 6.0$$

In Table 7, $s_{\overline{5}|9\%} = 5.9847$ and $s_{\overline{5}|9\,1/2\%} = 6.0446$.

Thus, the value of i is greater than 9% but smaller than $9\tfrac{1}{2}\%$. It may be written:

$9\% < i < 9\tfrac{1}{2}\%$

(4) FINDING THE VALUE OF i WHEN A_n(due) IS KNOWN

EXAMPLE 8

What is the nominal rate compounded quarterly if the present value of an annuity of \$300 payable at the beginning of each quarter for six years is \$5,800?

A_n(due) $= \$5{,}800$, $R = \$300$ (per quarter), $n = 6 \times 4 = 24$ (quarterly payments), $i = ?$ (per quarter)

Substituting the values in the formula $A_n(\text{due}) = Ra_{\overline{n-1}|i} + R$,

$5{,}800 = 300a_{\overline{24-1}|i} + 300$

$$a_{\overline{23}|i} = \frac{5{,}800 - 300}{300} = 18.3333$$

In Table 8, $a_{\overline{23}|1\,7/8\%} = 18.5442$, and $a_{\overline{23}|2\%} = 18.2922$.

Thus, the value of i is greater than $1\frac{7}{8}\%$ but smaller than 2%. It may be written:

$1\frac{7}{8}\% < i < 2\%$

Since $1\frac{7}{8}\% \times 4 = 7\frac{1}{2}\%$, and $2\% \times 4 = 8\%$, the value of the nominal rate is between $7\frac{1}{2}\%$ and 8%. It may be written:

$7\frac{1}{2}\% <$ nominal rate $< 8\%$

NOTE: When a more accurate value of i, such as in $s_{\overline{5}|i}$ of Example 7 and in $a_{\overline{23}|i}$ of Example 8, is needed, the interpolation method explained in Section 13.6 may be used.

(5) FINDING THE VALUE OF n WHEN S_n(due) IS KNOWN

EXAMPLE 9 If \$100 is deposited at the beginning of each month at an interest rate of 9% compounded monthly, how many months will be required for the deposits to amount to at least \$7,600?

S_n(due) $= \$7{,}600$, $R = \$100$ (per month), $i = 9\%/12 = \frac{3}{4}\%$ (per month), $n = ?$ (months or payments)

Substituting the values in the formula $S_n(\text{due}) = Rs_{\overline{n+1}|i} - R$,

$$7{,}600 = 100s_{\overline{n+1}|3/4\%} - 100$$

$$s_{\overline{n+1}|3/4\%} = \frac{7{,}600 + 100}{100} = 77$$

In the $\frac{3}{4}\%$ column of Table 7, find the two entries with values closest to 77.

The entries are as follows:

The entry for $s_{\overline{61}|3/4\%}$ is 76.9898.

The entry for $s_{\overline{62}|3/4\%}$ is 78.5672.

Since 77 is between the two entries above, the desired value of $(n + 1)$ is greater than 61 but smaller than 62. However, the amount in the example is at least \$7,600. Therefore, 62, the larger number, is employed.

$n + 1 = 62$, $n = 62 - 1 = 61$ months, or 5 years 1 month

(6) FINDING THE VALUE OF n WHEN A_n(due) IS KNOWN

EXAMPLE 10 A man bought a \$4,250 boat and agreed to pay for it in installments of \$500 at the beginning of every six months, starting on the date of purchase. If the interest charged is 12% compounded semiannually, how long will it take the man to pay for the boat?

$A_n(\text{due}) = \$4{,}250, R = \$500$ (per six months), $i = 12\%/2 = 6\%$ (per six months), $n = ?$ (semiannual periods or payments)

Substituting the values in the formula $A_n(\text{due}) = Ra_{\overline{n-1}|i} + R$,

$$4{,}250 = 500a_{\overline{n-1}|6\%} + 500$$

$$a_{\overline{n-1}|6\%} = \frac{4{,}250 - 500}{500} = 7.5$$

In the 6% column of Table 8, find the two entries with values closest to 7.5. The entries are as follows:

The entry for $a_{\overline{10}|6\%}$ is 7.3601.

The entry for $a_{\overline{11}|6\%}$ is 7.8869.

Since 7.5 is between the two entries above, the desired value of $(n - 1)$ is greater than 10 but less than 11. The interpolation method is unnecessary in this case. In order to repay the entire debt, the greater number, 11, is considered as the value of $(n - 1)$. Thus,

$$n - 1 = 11, \qquad n = 11 + 1 = 12 \text{ semiannual periods or six years}$$

EXERCISE 14–2 REFERENCE: SECTION 14.1D

A. Find the unknown value in each annuity due (omit interpolation):

	Amount	*Present Value*	*Payment*	*Term (n)*	*Compound Interest Rate*
1.	$ 2,900		$100, monthly	2 years	?, monthly
2.	1,140		60, semiannually	?	18%, semiannually
3.		$ 900	60, quarterly	5 years	?, quarterly
4.		800	?, annually	12 years	10%, annually
5.		3,800	250, semiannually	?	6%, semiannually
6.	12,500		450, quarterly	6 years	?, quarterly
7.		20,000	?, annually	15 years	$8\frac{1}{2}$%, annually
8.		1,600	40, monthly	?	24%, monthly
9.	6,000		?, semiannually	$7\frac{1}{2}$ years	4%, semiannually
10.	3,000		?, quarterly	$4\frac{1}{2}$ years	6%, quarterly
11.	3,200		120, monthly	?	7%, monthly
12.		2,400	340, annually	9 years	?, annually

B. Statement problems:

13. How much money must Adam invest at the beginning of each quarter if he wishes to receive $1,500 six years from now? Assume that the first payment starts now and the interest rate is 7% compounded quarterly.

14. H. K. Jackson wishes to have $500 on December 1 for Christmas shopping. Starting on January 1 of this year, she will make regular monthly investments that will earn 6% interest compounded monthly. However, she does not plan to invest on December 1. What must be the size of each monthly investment in order to accomplish this goal?

15. A house that sells for $90,000 can be purchased under terms requiring 100 monthly payments. Assume that the first payment begins now and the interest is 12% compounded monthly. What is the size of each monthly payment?
16. Jack Newton purchased a mobile home on March 1, 1991, and agreed to pay for it in equal quarterly payments. The first payment was made on the date of purchase. The last payment will be made on March 1, 1996. The cash price of the home was $30,000. If money is worth 16% compounded quarterly, how much should Newton pay each quarter?
17. At what nominal rate compounded semiannually will an annuity due of $500, payable at the beginning of every six months for ten years, amount to $12,772?
18. Alice Williams invested $200 at the beginning of each quarter for 20 quarters. At the end of the 20th quarter, she received $6,200, including principal and interest. If the interest rate was compounded quarterly, what was the interest rate?
19. What is the nominal rate compounded annually if the present value of an annuity due of $80, payable at the beginning of each year for eight years, is $530?
20. Betty Hunt bought a used car for $600 from her cousin on January 1, 1991. She agreed to pay for it by making payments of $60 each month until the last payment on November 1, 1991. The first payment was made on the date of purchase. If the interest was compounded monthly, what was the interest rate?
21. If $60 is deposited at the beginning of each month at 9% compounded monthly, how many months will be needed for the deposits to amount to at least $3,000?
22. Joe Kelly signed a note to his employer on March 1, 1991. The face value of $800 is to be paid in full when it is due. Assume that the note may be discharged by equal monthly payments of $50 each starting now and the interest is computed at 12% compounded monthly. When should the last payment be made?
23. If the present value of an annuity due of $200 payable semiannually is $2,800 and interest is computed at 6% compounded semiannually, what is the number of payments?
24. John buys a $54,000 farm and agrees to pay $2,000 at the beginning of each quarter until he completes his payments. The first payment is due on the date of purchase. How long will it take him to pay for the farm if the interest rate is 14% compounded quarterly?

14.2 DEFERRED ANNUITY

When the term of an annuity starts on a future date, the annuity is called a *deferred annuity*. The period between now and the beginning of the term of the annuity is called the *period of deferment*. The computation of a deferred annuity may be conveniently carried out if the ordinary annuity formulas are used. Hereafter, the name "deferred annuity" actually means "deferred ordinary annuity." It should be recalled that the first payment of an ordinary annuity is always made at the end of the first payment period. Thus, an annuity of $100 payable quarterly for six payments with the first payment to be made at the end of the *third* quarter is a deferred annuity. The period of deferment consists of *two* quarters, and the term of the ordinary annuity is six quarters, starting at the beginning of the third quarter and continuing to the end of the eighth quarter. (See the diagram in Example 2, page 426.)

A. The Amount of a Deferred Annuity

The *amount* of a deferred annuity is the final value at the end of the term of the annuity. The amount includes all the periodic payments plus the accumulated interest. Thus, the amount of the deferred annuity is the same as the amount of the ordinary annuity. Let $S_n(\text{defer.})$ = the amount of a deferred annuity. It follows that

$$\mathbf{S_n(defer.) = S_n = Rs_{\overline{n}|i}} \qquad \textbf{(14–5)}$$

EXAMPLE 1

Find the amount of an annuity of $100 payable at the end of each quarter for six payments. The interest rate is 6% compounded quarterly. The first payment is due at the end of nine months.

This example is identical to the diagram on page 426, which shows that there are no payments during the period of deferment. Therefore, in computing the amount of the annuity, the portion of deferment may be disregarded.

R = \$100 (per quarter), $i = 6\%/4 = 1\frac{1}{2}\%$ (per quarter), $n = 6$ (payments or quarters)

Substituting the above values in the formula $S_n(\text{defer.}) = Rs_{\overline{n}|i}$,

$S_6(\text{defer.}) = 100s_{\overline{6}|1\,1/2\%} = 100(6.22955) = \$622.96$

B. The Present Value of a Deferred Annuity

The *present value* of a deferred annuity is the value at the beginning of the period of deferment, *not* at the beginning of the term of the ordinary annuity. Let d = the number of the deferred payment intervals. The present value of a deferred annuity, denoted by $A_n(\text{defer.})$, may be found by either of the following two methods.

METHOD A

First, consider that the payments were made during the period of deferment. Second, consider that there were two ordinary annuities: one consists of d payments, while the other consists of $d + n$ payments. Third, subtract the present value of the annuity consisting of d payments from the present value of the annuity consisting of $d + n$ payments. The remainder is the present value of the deferred annuity. These steps may be accomplished by the formula:

$$\mathbf{A_n(defer.) = A_{d+n} - A_d = Ra_{\overline{d+n}|i} - Ra_{\overline{d}|i}} \quad \text{or}$$

$$\mathbf{A_n(defer.) = R(a_{\overline{d+n}|i} - a_{\overline{d}|i})} \qquad \textbf{(14–6)}$$

EXAMPLE 2

Find the present value of an annuity of $100 payable at the end of each quarter for six payments. The interest rate is 6% compounded quarterly. The first payment is due at the end of nine months.

R = \$100, $i = 6\%/4 = 1\frac{1}{2}\%$, $n = 6$, $d = 2$ (2 quarters or 6 months)

Substituting the preceding values in formula (14–6),

$$A_{d+n} = A_{2+6} = A_8 = Ra_{\overline{8}|1\ 1/2\%} = 100a_{\overline{8}|1\ 1/2\%}$$

$$A_d = A_2 = Ra_{\overline{2}|1\ 1/2\%} = 100a_{\overline{2}|1\ 1/2\%}$$

$$A_6(\text{defer.}) = A_8 - A_2 = 100a_{\overline{8}|1\ 1/2\%} - 100a_{\overline{2}|1\ 1/2\%}$$

$$= 100(7.48592) - 100(1.95588) = 748.592 - 195.588 \quad \text{(Table 8)}$$

$$= \$553.004, \text{ or } \$553$$

Example 2 is diagrammed as follows to illustrate Method A:

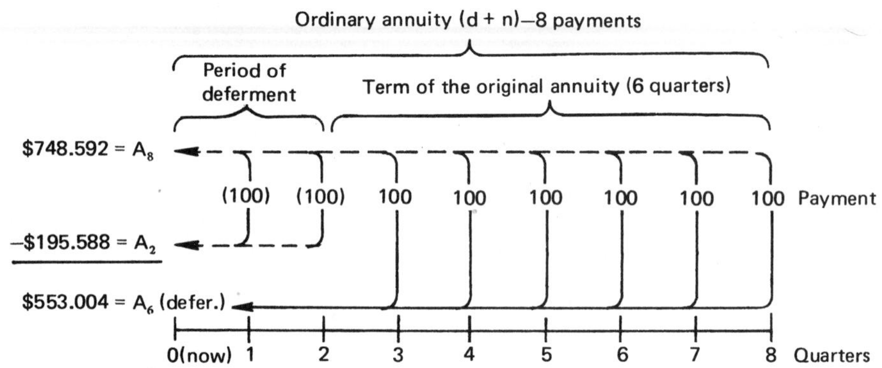

EXAMPLE 3 Find the present value of an ordinary annuity of \$500 each year for 15 years if the first payment is due at the end of five years and money is worth $5\frac{1}{2}\%$ compounded annually.

R = \$500 (per year), $i = 5\frac{1}{2}\%$ (per year), $n = 15$ (years or payments), and $d = 4$. (The payment made at the end of the fifth year covers the payment interval from the end of the fourth year to the end of the fifth year. Thus, the period of deferment is four years, or four payments.)

Substituting the values in the formula $A_n(\text{defer.}) = R(a_{\overline{d+n}|i} - a_{\overline{d}|i})$,

$$A_n(\text{defer.}) = 500(a_{\overline{4+15}|5\ 1/2\%} - a_{\overline{4}|5\ 1/2\%}) = 500(11.60765 - 3.50515)$$

$$= 500(8.1025) = \$4{,}051.25 \quad \text{(Table 8)}$$

★METHOD B Discount the present value of the ordinary annuity for the period of deferment. This may be computed by use of the following formula:

$$\mathbf{A_n(defer.) = A_n(1 + i)^{-d} = Ra_{\overline{n}|i} \cdot (1 + i)^{-d}} \qquad \textbf{(14–7)}$$

Solution of Example 2 by Method B (see also pages 425 and 426):

$$A_n = A_6 = 100a_{\overline{6}|1\ 1/2\%} = 100(5.69719) = \$569.72 \quad \text{(Table 8)}$$

$$A_n(\text{defer.}) = A_n(1 + i)^{-d} = 569.72(1 + 1\tfrac{1}{2}\%)^{-2}$$

$$= 569.72(.97066) = \$553 \quad \text{(Table 6)}$$

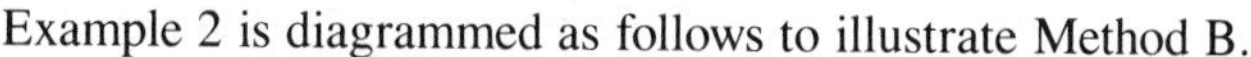

Example 2 is diagrammed as follows to illustrate Method B.

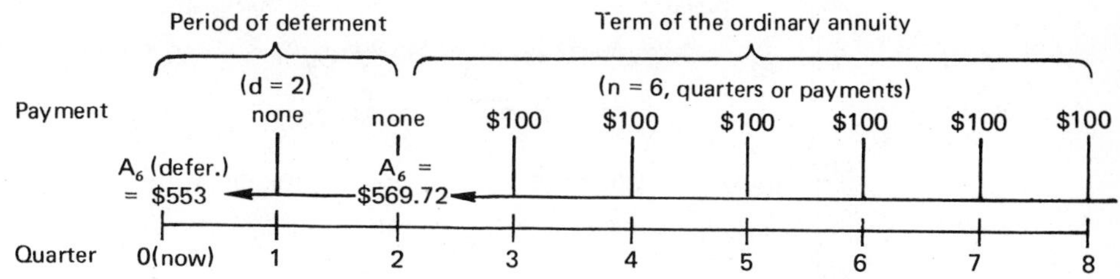

Solution of Example 3 by Method B (see also page 426):

Substituting the values in the formula $A_n(\text{defer.}) = Ra_{\overline{n}|i} \cdot (1 + i)^{-d}$,

$$A_n(\text{defer.}) = 500a_{\overline{15}|5\ 1/2\%} \cdot (1 + 5\tfrac{1}{2}\%)^{-4}$$

$$= 500(10.03758)(0.807217) = \$4{,}051.25$$

The use of Method A, rather than Method B, is recommended. Observe the calculations in the above two examples. Only Table 8 is needed in Method A, while both Tables 6 and 8 are needed in Method B. Therefore, Method A will be used in the following discussion.

C. Other Types of Deferred Annuity Problems

(1) FINDING THE PAYMENT OF A DEFERRED ANNUITY

EXAMPLE 4 A man borrows $10,000 at 14% compounded semiannually and agrees to repay it in 14 equal semiannual payments. Find the size of each payment if the first payment is due at the end of $3\frac{1}{2}$ years.

$A_n(\text{defer.}) = \$10{,}000$, $i = 14\%/2 = 7\%$ (per six months), $n = 14$ (payments or semiannual periods), $d = 3 \times 2 = 6$ (payments or semiannual periods), $R = ?$

Substituting the values in formula (14–6),

$$10{,}000 = R(a_{\overline{6+14}|7\%} - a_{\overline{6}|7\%}) = R(10.594014 - 4.766540)$$

$$= R(5.827474)$$

$$R = \frac{10{,}000}{5.827474} = \$1{,}716.01 \text{ (per six months)}$$

(2) FINDING THE TERM OF A DEFERRED ANNUITY

EXAMPLE 5 If $50 is deposited at the end of each month and the interest rate is 6% compounded monthly, how many months will be required for the deposits to equal a present value of $4,500? The first deposit is made at the end of six months.

$A_n(\text{defer.}) = \$4{,}500$, $R = \$50$ (per month), $i = 6\%/12 = \frac{1}{2}\%$ (per month), $d = 5$ (months or payments), $n = ?$ (months or payments)

Substituting the values in the formula $A_n(\text{defer.}) = Ra_{\overline{d+n}|i} - Ra_{\overline{d}|i}$,

$$4{,}500 = 50a_{\overline{5+n}|1/2\%} - 50a_{\overline{5}|1/2\%} = 50a_{\overline{5+n}|1/2\%} - 50(4.9259)$$

$$= 50a_{\overline{5+n}|1/2\%} - 246.295$$

$$a_{\overline{5+n}|1/2\%} = \frac{4{,}500 + 246.295}{50} = 94.9259$$

In the $\frac{1}{2}\%$ column of Table 8, find the first entry greater than 94.9259:

$a_{\overline{130}|1/2\%} = 95.4216$

Thus,

$5 + n = 130, \quad n = 130 - 5 = 125$ (payments or months)

The first payment is due at the end of six months. There are 125 monthly payments.

EXERCISE 14–3 REFERENCE: SECTION 14.2

A. Find the unknown value of the deferred annuity in each of the following problems:

	Amount S_n(defer.)	*Present Value A_n(defer.)*	*Payment (R)*	*Number of Payments (n)*	*Period of Deferment (d)*	*Compound Interest Rate*
1.	?	?	$500, semi-annually	15	5	7%, semi-annually
2.		$ 940	100, monthly	?	4	12%, monthly
3.		2,000	?, annually	10	3	10%, annually
4.	?	?	500, quarterly	7	10	6%, quarterly
5.		1,600	125, quarterly	?	7	14%, quarterly
6.	?	?	400, annually	18	8	9%, annually
7.	?	?	600, monthly	14	12	18%, monthly
8.		5,000	?, semi-annually	20	6	11%, semi-annually

B. Statement problems:

9. Find the amount and the present value of an annuity of $150 payable at the end of every three months for 30 payments. The first payment is due at the end of seven years. The interest rate is 11% compounded quarterly.
10. Find the amount and the present value of 40 monthly payments of $75 each. The first payment is due in two years. The interest rate is 6% compounded monthly.
11. Janice Berman purchased a theater for $80,000 on January 2, 1991. She paid $10,000 cash and agreed to pay the balance plus interest at $9\frac{1}{2}\%$ compounded annually in 14 annual payments, with the first payment due on January 2, 1994. What is the size of each payment?
12. If $400 is to be paid at the end of every six months, the first payment is to be made at the end of three years, and the interest rate is 13% compounded semiannually, how many payments will be needed to discharge a debt whose present value is $2,900?
13. A man borrowed $6,500 at 7% interest compounded quarterly and agreed to repay

the loan in quarterly payments of $500 each. The first payment is due in two years. Find the number of payments.

14. A student borrowed $250 and agreed to repay the principal and the interest at 15% compounded monthly in 20 equal monthly payments. The first payment is due in $1\frac{1}{2}$ years. How large is each payment?
15. If money is worth $5\frac{1}{2}\%$ compounded annually, what single payment now is equivalent to 45 annual payments of $350 each with the first payment due in five years?
16. Carla Duncan purchases a farm on April 1, 1991. She agrees to pay for it in 30 semiannual payments of $3,000 each. If the first payment is to be made on October 1, 1992, and the interest rate is 6% compounded semiannually, what is the cash price of the farm?

14.3 COMPLEX (OR GENERAL) ANNUITY

When the length of the payment interval of an annuity is not the same as the length of the interest conversion period, the annuity is called a *complex annuity*. Thus, if each of the *payments* of an annuity is made *monthly* and the *interest* is compounded or converted *quarterly*, or if each of the *payments* is made *quarterly* and the *interest* is compounded *monthly*, the annuity is called a complex annuity. On the preceding pages, n represents the number of payments of an annuity, and also the number of interest periods of an annuity. In the remaining portion of this chapter, in order to avoid confusion in a complex annuity problem, *n represents only the number of payments of an annuity*. The letter c will be used to represent the number of interest periods in one payment interval. Thus, the number of the total interest periods of a complex annuity is the product of n and c, or nc.

For example, assume that the payment of an annuity is made quarterly and the interest is compounded monthly. A one-year term of this annuity consists of four payments (or $n = 4$), each payment interval consists of three interest periods (or $c = 3$), and there are 12 interest periods ($nc = 4 \times 3 = 12$) during the year.

The diagram below shows the quarterly payment of an annuity with interest compounded monthly. In this illustration, # denotes the date for computing the interest.

			R			R			R			R	
•	#	#	#	#	#	#	#	#	#	#	#	#	
0(now)	1	2	3	4	5	6	7	8	9	10	11	12	Month
			1			2			3			4	Quarter

If the payment of an annuity is made monthly and the interest is compounded quarterly, a one-year term of an annuity consists of 12 payments (or $n = 12$), each payment interval consists of $\frac{1}{3}$ interest periods (or $c = \frac{1}{3}$), and there are four interest periods (or $nc = 12 \times \frac{1}{3} = 4$) during the year. This type of payment is diagrammed as follows:

			#			#			#			#	
•	R	R	R	R	R	R	R	R	R	R	R	R	
0(now)	1	2	3	4	5	6	7	8	9	10	11	12	Month
			1			2			3			4	Quarter

Additional illustrations of complex annuities are presented in the following table:

Payment Interval	*Interest Conversion Period*	*Term of Annuity*	*Total Number of Payments: (n)*	*Number of Interest Periods in One Payment Interval: (c)*	*Total Interest Periods: (n × c)*
1 quarter	1 month	2 years	8	3	24
1 month	1 quarter	2 years	24	$\frac{1}{3}$	8
6 months	1 month	1 year	2	6	12
1 year	1 quarter	1 year	1	4	4
1 quarter	6 months	1 year	4	$\frac{1}{2}$	2
1 month	1 year	1 year	12	$\frac{1}{12}$	1
1 quarter	1 quarter	1 year	4	1	4
1 month	1 month	1 year	12	1	12

When $c = 1$, the number of payments (n) is the same as the number of interest periods [$nc = n(1) = n$]. The formulas developed below may apply in any case, including simple annuity problems. Therefore, complex annuity is also referred to simply as a general case in annuity problems or as a *general annuity*.

A. The Amount and the Present Value of an Ordinary Complex Annuity

The terms that have been used in the previous sections and in Chapter 13 are also used here with the same meanings. Thus, the word *ordinary* is used to indicate that the periodic payment of a complex annuity is made at the end of each payment interval. The *amount* of a complex annuity (S_{nc}) is defined as the final value at the end of the term of the annuity. The *present value* of a complex annuity (A_{nc}) is the value at the beginning of the term of the annuity.

Basically, as discussed in the previous sections and in Chapter 13, the amount and the present value of an annuity may be found by using the following two compound interest formulas:

$S = P(1 + i)^n$ and $P = S(1 + i)^{-n}$

However, the two principal annuity formulas below, which are derived from the two formulas above, offer a more convenient way to solve any type of *simple* annuity problem (see Chapter 13, pages 380–381 and 386–387):

$$S_n = Rs_{\overline{n}|i} = R \cdot \frac{(1 + i)^n - 1}{i} \qquad \textbf{(13–1)}$$

$$A_n = Ra_{\overline{n}|i} = R \cdot \frac{1 - (1 + i)^{-n}}{i} \qquad \textbf{(13–2)}$$

Two methods will be presented in which the complex annuities are first converted into simple annuities and then computed as ordinary simple annuities by applying the formulas cited above.

METHOD A *Using the Formulas* $S_n = Rs_{\overline{n}|i}$ *and* $A_n = Ra_{\overline{n}|i}$. In applying these two formulas, each of the original periodic payments is first converted into a new periodic *equivalent payment*, which is assumed to be made at the end of each interest conversion period.

EXAMPLE 1 Find the amount and the present value of an annuity of $100 payable at the end of each quarter for 10 years if the interest rate is 6% compounded monthly.

Each of the original quarterly payments of $100 is first converted into a new equivalent monthly payment, E. The original payment, $100, thus is the amount of an annuity of E payable at the end of each month for three months at 6% compounded monthly. That is,

S_n = $100 (in one quarter or 3 months)
$i = 6\%/12 = \frac{1}{2}\%$ (per month)
n = 3 (payments of $$E$ per month)

Substituting the values in formula $S_n = Es_{\overline{n}|i}$,

$100 = Es_{\overline{3}|1/2\%}$

Solve for E.

$$E = \frac{100}{s_{\overline{3}|1/2\%}} = 100\left(\frac{1}{a_{\overline{3}|1/2\%}} - \frac{1}{2}\%\right) = 100(.336672 - \frac{1}{2}\%)$$

$$= 100(.331672) = \$33.1672 \quad \text{(Table 9)}$$

The payment of $100 at the end of each quarter is equivalent to the payment of $33.1672 at the end of each *month*. Therefore, the amount of an annuity of $100 payable at the end of each quarter should equal the amount of an annuity of $33.1672 payable at the end of each month. Here the term is 10 years and the number of quarterly payments is 40 (or 10 × 4). Each payment interval consists of three interest periods.

The number of total monthly interest periods is 120 (or 40 × 3). The amount of an ordinary annuity of 120 payments of E each month at 6% compounded monthly is computed as follows:

$S_{120} = Es_{\overline{120}|1/2\%} = 33.1672(163.8793) = \$5,435.42$

The present value of the ordinary annuity would be

$A_{120} = Ea_{\overline{120}|1/2\%} = 33.1672(90.07345) = \$2,987.48$

Example 1 is diagrammed as follows:

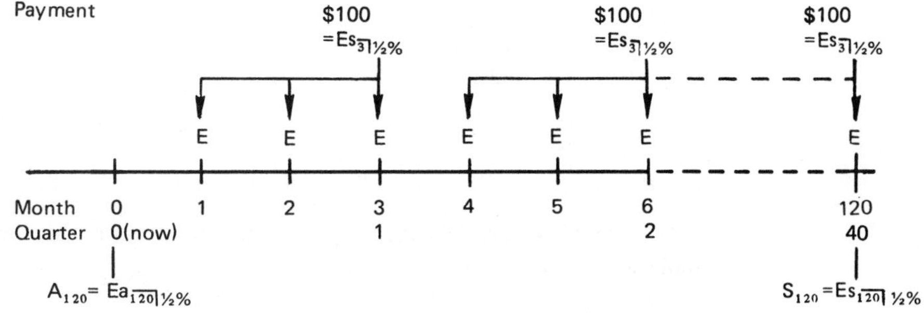

The above calculations may be expanded by letting

R = size of actual periodic payment
E = new equivalent payment at the end of each interest period
i = given interest rate per conversion period
c = number of interest periods in one payment interval
$= \dfrac{\text{payment interval}}{\text{interest period}}$
n = number of actual payments

Then

$$R = Es_{\overline{c}|i}$$

$$E = \frac{R}{s_{\overline{c}|i}}$$

The *formula for the amount of an ordinary complex annuity, S_{nc}*, may be obtained as follows:

$$S_{nc} = Es_{\overline{nc}|i} = \frac{R}{s_{\overline{c}|i}} \cdot s_{\overline{nc}|i}, \quad \text{or it may be written as}$$

$$\mathbf{S_{nc} = Rs_{\overline{nc}|i} \cdot \frac{1}{s_{\overline{c}|i}}} \qquad \textbf{(14–8)}$$

The *formula for the present value of an ordinary complex annuity, A_{nc}*, may be obtained as follows:

$$A_{nc} = Ea_{\overline{nc}|i} = \frac{R}{s_{\overline{c}|i}} \cdot a_{\overline{nc}|i}, \quad \text{or it may be written as}$$

$$\mathbf{A_{nc} = Ra_{\overline{nc}|i} \cdot \frac{1}{s_{\overline{c}|i}}} \qquad \textbf{(14–9)}$$

It should be observed that when $c = 1$ (interest interval = payment interval), the value of $\frac{1}{s_{\overline{c}|i}}$ becomes $\frac{1}{s_{\overline{1}|i}} = \frac{1}{1} = 1$. Thus,

$$S_{nc} = Rs_{\overline{n(1)}|i} \cdot \frac{1}{s_{\overline{1}|i}} = Rs_{\overline{n}|i}, \quad \text{and} \quad A_{nc} = Ra_{\overline{n(1)}|i} \cdot \frac{1}{s_{\overline{1}|i}} = Ra_{\overline{n}|i}$$

These facts indicate that the complex annuity formulas are identical to the simple annuity formulas when the interest conversion period coincides with the payment interval.

NOTE: The values of $s_{\overline{nc}|i}$ and $s_{\overline{c}|i}$ may be found in Table 7. If c is fractional, the value of $s_{\overline{c}|i}$ may be found in Table 7A, where $c = 1/m$. (m = the number of payments in one given interest period.) The value of $\frac{1}{s_{\overline{c}|i}}$ may be found in Table 9 by the use of the formula $\frac{1}{s_{\overline{c}|i}} = \frac{1}{a_{\overline{c}|i}} - i$. However, if c is fractional, its value may be found in Table 10, where $c = 1/m$. The value of $a_{\overline{nc}|i}$ may be found in Table 8.

Application of formulas (14–8) and (14–9) to Example 1:

R = \$100 (per quarter), $i = 6\%/12 = \frac{1}{2}\%$ (monthly), $n = 10 \times 4 = 40$ (quarterly payments), and $c = 3$ (interest periods in one quarter, the payment interval), which is computed as follows:

$$c = \frac{\text{payment interval}}{\text{interest interval}} = \frac{1 \text{ quarter}}{1 \text{ month}} = \frac{3 \text{ months}}{1 \text{ month}} = 3$$

Substituting the above values in formulas 14–8 and 14–9, respectively,

$$\begin{aligned} S_{nc} &= S_{40(3)} = 100 s_{\overline{40 \times 3}|1/2\%} \cdot \frac{1}{s_{\overline{3}|1/2\%}} \\ &= 100(163.87935)(.336672 - \tfrac{1}{2}\%) \\ &= 100(163.87935)(.331672) = \$5{,}435.42 \quad \text{(Tables 7 and 9)} \end{aligned}$$

$$\begin{aligned} A_{nc} &= A_{40(3)} = 100 a_{\overline{40 \times 3}|1/2\%} \cdot \frac{1}{s_{\overline{3}|1/2\%}} = 100(90.07345)(.331672) \\ &= \$2{,}987.48 \quad \text{(Tables 8 and 9)} \end{aligned}$$

The above results obtained for Example 1 may be checked by using the formula $S = P(1 + i)^n$.

$P = A_{nc} = \$2{,}987.48$, $i = \frac{1}{2}\%$, $n = 120$

$S = 2{,}987.48(1 + \frac{1}{2}\%)^{120} = 2{,}987.48(1.8193967) = \$5{,}435.42$

Or the results may be checked by using the formula $P = S(1 + i)^{-n}$.

$S = S_{nc} = \$5{,}435.42$
$P = 5{,}435.42(1 + \frac{1}{2}\%)^{-120} = 5{,}435.42(.5496327) = \$2{,}987.48$

EXAMPLE 2 Find the amount and the present value of an annuity of \$100 payable at the end of each month for six years if the interest rate is 10% compounded semiannually.

R = \$100 (monthly payment), $i = 10\%/2 = 5\%$ (per six months), $n = 6 \times 12 = 72$ (monthly payments), and $c = \frac{1}{6}$ (interest conversion periods in one month, the payment interval), or

$$c = \frac{1 \text{ month}}{6 \text{ months}} = \frac{1}{6}$$

Substituting the values in formulas 14–8 and 14–9, respectively,

$$\begin{aligned} S_{nc} &= S_{72(1/6)} = 100 s_{\overline{72(1/6)}|5\%} \cdot \frac{1}{s_{\overline{1/6}|5\%}} \\ &= 100 s_{\overline{12}|5\%} \cdot 6.123814 = 100(15.91713)(6.123814) \\ &= 1{,}591.713(6.123814) \\ &= \$9{,}747.35 \quad \text{(Tables 7 and 10)} \end{aligned}$$

$$\begin{aligned} A_{nc} &= A_{72(1/6)} = 100 a_{\overline{72(1/6)}|5\%} \cdot \frac{1}{s_{\overline{1/6}|5\%}} \\ &= 100 a_{\overline{12}|5\%} \cdot 6.123814 = 100(8.86325)(6.123814) \\ &= \$5{,}427.69 \quad \text{(Tables 8 and 10)} \end{aligned}$$

EXERCISE 14–4 REFERENCE: SECTION 14.3A

A. Find the amount and the present value of the complex annuity in each of the following problems:

	Payment (R)	*Payment Interval*	*Term*	*Interest Rate Compounded*
1.	\$ 550	1 month	$3\frac{1}{2}$ years	6%, quarterly
2.	420	1 quarter	2 years	10%, semiannually
3.	80	6 months	5 years	12%, monthly
4.	60	1 year	10 years	6%, quarterly
5.	300	1 quarter	12 years	9%, annually
6.	460	1 month	$1\frac{1}{2}$ years	7%, semiannually
7.	1,000	1 year	4 years	12%, monthly
8.	2,500	6 months	20 years.	$8\frac{1}{2}$%, annually

B. Statement problems:

9. Find the amount and the present value of an annuity of \$350 payable at the end of each month for three years if the interest rate is (a) 5% compounded annually, and (b) 5% compounded monthly.
10. What are the amount and the present value of an annuity of \$500 payable at the end of each quarter for six years if the interest rate is (a) 4% compounded annually and (b) 4% compounded quarterly?
11. A man bought a store and agreed to pay \$10,000 at the end of every six months for seven years. What is the equivalent cash price of the store if the interest rate is 5% compounded quarterly?
12. A company deposits \$800 at the end of every nine months in a bank that pays 3% interest compounded monthly. Find the amount of the company's account at the end of $4\frac{1}{2}$ years.
13. What is the present value of the annuity in Problem 12?
14. What is the present value of a series of \$600 payments made at the end of every four months for five years if the interest rate is 18% compounded monthly?

★METHOD B *Using the Formulas* $S_n = R \cdot \frac{(1+r)^n - 1}{r}$ *and* $A_n = R \cdot \frac{1-(1+r)^{-n}}{r}$.

In applying formulas (13–1) and (13–2), let $r =$ the interest rate per payment interval. Then convert the value of r into the given interest rate i. This method is illustrated by the following solutions of Examples 1 and 2.

Solution of Example 1, page 431:

$R = \$100$ (quarterly payment), $n = 40$ (quarterly payments), $i = \frac{1}{2}\%$ (monthly rate), $c = 3$ (interest periods in one payment interval), or $\frac{3 \text{ months}}{1 \text{ month}} = 3$,
$r =$ interest rate per quarter

In one payment interval, one quarter or three months, the compound amount on \$1 at rate r per quarter is $1 + r$ and at rate $\frac{1}{2}\%$ per month is $(1 + \frac{1}{2}\%)^3$.

The two amounts are equal. Thus,

$1 + r = (1 + \frac{1}{2}\%)^3$ and $r = (1 + \frac{1}{2}\%)^3 - 1$

Let S_{40} = the amount of the annuity of 40 quarterly payments at the quarterly rate r.

$$\text{Then}\quad S_{40} = Rs_{\overline{40}|r} = 100 \cdot \frac{(1 + r)^{40} - 1}{r} = 100 \cdot \frac{[(1 + \frac{1}{2}\%)^3]^{40} - 1}{(1 + \frac{1}{2}\%)^3 - 1}$$

$$= 100 \cdot \frac{(1 + \frac{1}{2}\%)^{120} - 1}{\frac{1}{2}\%} \cdot \frac{\frac{1}{2}\%}{(1 + \frac{1}{2}\%)^3 - 1}$$

$$= 100 s_{\overline{120}|1/2\%} \cdot \frac{\frac{1}{2}\%}{(1 + \frac{1}{2}\%)^3 - 1} = 100 s_{\overline{120}|1/2\%} \cdot \frac{1}{s_{\overline{3}|1/2\%}}$$

$$= 100(163.87935)(.331672) = \$5{,}435.42$$

Let A_{40} = the present value of the annuity of 40 quarterly payments at the quarterly rate r

$$\text{Then}\quad A_{40} = Ra_{\overline{40}|r} = 100 \cdot \frac{1 - (1 + r)^{-40}}{r} = 100 \cdot \frac{1 - [(1 + \frac{1}{2}\%)^3]^{-40}}{(1 + \frac{1}{2}\%)^3 - 1}$$

$$= 100 \cdot \frac{1 - (1 + \frac{1}{2}\%)^{-120}}{(1 + \frac{1}{2}\%)^3 - 1}$$

$$= 100 \cdot \frac{1 - (1 + \frac{1}{2}\%)^{-120}}{\frac{1}{2}\%} \cdot \frac{\frac{1}{2}\%}{(1 + \frac{1}{2}\%)^3 - 1}$$

$$= 100 a_{\overline{120}|1/2\%} \cdot \frac{1}{s_{\overline{3}|1/2\%}} = 100(90.07345)(.331672) = \$2{,}987.48$$

Solution for Example 2, page 433:

R = \$100 (monthly payment), $n = 72$ (monthly payments), $i = 5\%$ (per 6 months), $c = \frac{1}{6}$ (interest conversion periods in one payment interval) or $\frac{1 \text{ month}}{6 \text{ months}} = \frac{1}{6}$, r = interest rate per month

In one payment interval (one month), the compound amount of \$1 at rate r per month is $1 + r$, and at 5% per six months is $(1 + 5\%)^{1/6}$.

Thus,

$1 + r = (1 + 5\%)^{1/6}$ and $r = (1 + 5\%)^{1/6} - 1$

$$S_{72} = Rs_{\overline{72}|r} = 100 \cdot \frac{(1 + r)^{72} - 1}{r} = 100 \cdot \frac{[(1 + 5\%)^{1/6}]^{72} - 1}{(1 + 5\%)^{1/6} - 1}$$

$$= 100 \cdot \frac{(1 + 5\%)^{12} - 1}{(1 + 5\%)^{1/6} - 1}$$

$$= 100 \cdot \frac{(1 + 5\%)^{12} - 1}{5\%} \cdot \frac{5\%}{(1 + 5\%)^{1/6} - 1}$$

$$= 100 s_{\overline{12}|5\%} \cdot \frac{1}{s_{\overline{1/6}|5\%}}$$

$$= 100(15.91713)(6.123814) = \$9{,}747.35$$

Similarly,

$$A_{72} = Ra_{\overline{72}|r} = 100 \cdot \frac{1 - (1 + r)^{-72}}{r} = 100 \cdot \frac{1 - [(1 + 5\%)^{1/6}]^{-72}}{(1 + 5\%)^{1/6} - 1}$$

$$= 100 \cdot \frac{1 - (1 + 5\%)^{-12}}{(1 + 5\%)^{1/6} - 1}$$

$$= 100 \cdot \frac{1 - (1 + 5\%)^{-12}}{5\%} \cdot \frac{5\%}{(1 + 5\%)^{1/6} - 1}$$

$$= 100a_{\overline{12}|5\%} \cdot \frac{1}{s_{\overline{1/6}|5\%}}$$

$$= 100(8.86325)(6.123814) = \$5{,}427.69$$

The method used in the above illustration provides another way to prove formulas (14–8) and (14–9). The proofs are presented below.

$1 + r = (1 + i)^c$, and $r = (1 + i)^c - 1$

$$S_n = Rs_{\overline{n}|r} = R \cdot \frac{(1 + r)^n - 1}{r} = R \cdot \frac{[(1 + i)^c]^n - 1}{(1 + i)^c - 1}$$

$$= R \cdot \frac{(1 + i)^{nc} - 1}{i} \cdot \frac{i}{(1 + i)^c - 1}$$

$$= Rs_{\overline{nc}|i} \cdot \frac{i}{(1 + i)^c - 1}$$

$$= Rs_{\overline{nc}|i} \cdot \frac{1}{s_{\overline{c}|i}}$$

Here the value of S_n is the same as the value of S_{nc} obtained by Method A.

Thus,

$$\mathbf{S_{nc} = Rs_{\overline{nc}|i} \cdot \frac{1}{s_{\overline{c}|i}}} \qquad \textbf{(14–8)}$$

Similarly,

$$A_n = Ra_{\overline{n}|r} = R \cdot \frac{1 - (1 + r)^{-n}}{r} = R \cdot \frac{1 - [(1 + i)^c]^{-n}}{(1 + i)^c - 1}$$

$$= R \cdot \frac{1 - (1 + i)^{-nc}}{i} \cdot \frac{i}{(1 + i)^c - 1}$$

$$= Ra_{\overline{nc}|i} \cdot \frac{i}{(1 + i)^c - 1} = Ra_{\overline{nc}|i} \cdot \frac{1}{s_{\overline{c}|i}}$$

Here the value of A_n is the same as the value of A_{nc} obtained by Method A.

Thus,

$$\mathbf{A_{nc} = Ra_{\overline{nc}|i} \cdot \frac{1}{s_{\overline{c}|i}}} \qquad \textbf{(14–9)}$$

The value of the third factor, $\frac{i}{(1+i)^c - 1}$, may be obtained by using Table 5 (when c is a whole number) or Table 5A (when c is a fraction). However, it is more convenient to find the value of $\frac{1}{s_{\overline{c}|i}}$ from Tables 9 and 10, as noted in Method A.

★ EXERCISE 14–5 REFERENCE: SECTION 14.3A

Compute Problems 1 to 8 of Exercise 14–4 by using Method B, as described on pages 434–436.

★ B. The Size of Payment of an Ordinary Complex Annuity

In finding the size of payment of an ordinary complex annuity, use formula (14–8) when the amount of the annuity is known, and formula (14–9) when the present value of the annuity is known.

EXAMPLE 3 A man wishes to receive $20,000 five years from now. How much must he invest at the end of each year if the first payment starts one year from now and he can get 12% interest compounded semiannually?

S_{nc} = $20,000, $i = 12\%/2 = 6\%$ (per six months), $n = 5$ (annual payments), $c = 2$ (interest periods in one year), $R = ?$ (per year)

Substituting the above values in formula (14–8),

$$20{,}000 = Rs_{\overline{5\times 2}|6\%} \cdot \frac{1}{s_{\overline{2}|6\%}}$$

$$\begin{aligned} R &= 20{,}000 s_{\overline{2}|6\%} \cdot \frac{1}{s_{\overline{10}|6\%}} \\ &= 20{,}000(2.06)(.1358680 - .06) \\ &= \$3{,}125.76 \quad \text{(Tables 7 and 9)} \end{aligned}$$

EXAMPLE 4 A lot that sells for $54,000 can be bought for $4,000 down with the balance payable in 24 equal monthly payments. If the interest rate is 10% compounded annually, what is the size of the monthly payment?

$A_{nc} = 54{,}000 - 4{,}000 = \$50{,}000$, $i = 10\%$ (per year), $c = 1/12$ (interest periods in one month), $n = 24$ (monthly payments), $R = ?$ (per month)

Substituting the above values in formula (14–9),

$$50{,}000 = Ra_{\overline{24(1/12)}|10\%} \cdot \frac{1}{s_{\overline{1/12}|10\%}}$$

$$\begin{aligned} R &= 50{,}000 s_{\overline{1/12}|10\%} \cdot \frac{1}{a_{\overline{2}|10\%}} \\ &= 50{,}000(.0797414)(.576190) \\ &= 3{,}987.07(.576190) \\ &= \$2{,}297.31 \quad \text{(Tables 7A and 9)} \end{aligned}$$

★C. The Amount and the Present Value of a Complex Annuity Due

An annuity due has been defined previously as an annuity with periodic payments made at the beginning of each payment interval. In the following diagram, R represents the payment and # represents the date for computing interest. Assume that the term of the annuity is one year, the payments are made quarterly, and the interest is compounded monthly. Notice that when each payment, R, accumulates for three interest periods (or one payment interval, quarter), R becomes $R(1 + i)^3$. In other words, the value of R at the beginning of each payment interval is equivalent to the value of $R(1 + i)^3$ at the end of each payment interval. The values of $R(1 + i)^3$ form an ordinary complex annuity. The amount of the ordinary annuity according to formula (14–8) is

$$S_{nc} = \frac{R(1 + i)^3}{s_{\overline{3}|i}} \cdot s_{\overline{4 \times 3}|i}$$

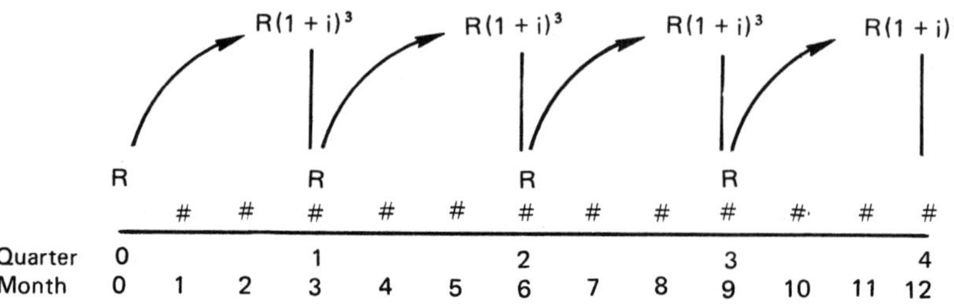

Similarly, let c = the number of interest periods in one payment interval and n = the number of payments. The amount of the complex annuity due, S_{nc}(due), therefore may be obtained from formula (14–8) by replacing R by $R(1 + i)^c$ as follows:

$$S_{nc}(\text{due}) = \frac{R(1 + i)^c}{s_{\overline{c}|i}} \cdot s_{\overline{nc}|i} = \frac{R}{s_{\overline{c}|i} \cdot (1 + i)^{-c}} \cdot s_{\overline{nc}|i}$$

Since $s_{\overline{c}|i} \cdot (1 + i)^{-c} = \dfrac{(1 + i)^c - 1}{i}(1 + i)^{-c} = \dfrac{1 - (1 + i)^{-c}}{i} = a_{\overline{c}|i}$

the above may be written

$$S_{nc}(\text{due}) = \frac{R}{a_{\overline{c}|i}} \cdot s_{\overline{nc}|i}, \quad \text{or}$$

$$\mathbf{S_{nc}(due) = Rs_{\overline{nc}|i} \cdot \frac{1}{a_{\overline{c}|i}}} \qquad \textbf{(14–10)}$$

The present value of the complex annuity due, A_{nc}(due), may be obtained from formula (14–9) by a method similar to that used in developing formula (14–10), and is written as follows:

$$A_{nc}(\text{due}) = \frac{R(1 + i)^c}{s_{\overline{c}|i}} \cdot a_{\overline{nc}|i} = \frac{R}{a_{\overline{c}|i}} \cdot a_{\overline{nc}|i}, \quad \text{or}$$

$$\mathbf{A_{nc}(due) = Ra_{\overline{nc}|i} \cdot \frac{1}{a_{\overline{c}|i}}} \qquad \textbf{(14–11)}$$

EXAMPLE 5 If the interest rate is 6% compounded monthly, what is the amount and the present value of an annuity of $150 payable at the beginning of each quarter for one year?

$R = \$150$ (per quarter), $n = 4$ (quarterly payments), $i = 6\%/12 = \frac{1}{2}\%$ (per month), $c = 3$ (interest periods in one quarter)

Substituting the values in formulas (14–10) and (14–11), respectively,

$$S_{4(3)}(\text{due}) = 150 \cdot s_{\overline{4 \times 3}|1/2\%} \cdot \frac{1}{a_{\overline{3}|1/2\%}} = 150(12.33556)(.33667) = \$622.95$$

(Tables 7 and 9)

$$A_{4(3)}(\text{due}) = 150 \cdot a_{\overline{4 \times 3}|1/2\%} \cdot \frac{1}{a_{\overline{3}|1/2\%}} = 150(11.61893)(.33667) = \$586.76$$

(Tables 8 and 9)

EXAMPLE 6 Find the amount and the present value of an annuity of $100 payable at the beginning of each month for two years. Assume that the interest rate is 12% compounded quarterly.

$R = \$100$ (per month), $n = 2 \times 12 = 24$ (monthly payments), $i = 12\%/4 = 3\%$ (per quarter), $c = \frac{1}{3}$ (interest periods in one month), $nc = 24 \times \frac{1}{3} = 8$ (interest periods in two years)

$$S_{nc}(\text{due}) = S_{24(1/3)}(\text{due}) = 100 \cdot s_{\overline{8}|3\%} \cdot \frac{1}{a_{\overline{1/3}|3\%}}$$

$$= 100(8.892336)(3.029803 + .03) = \$2{,}720.88$$

(Tables 7 and 10)

$$A_{nc}(\text{due}) = A_{24(1/3)}(\text{due}) = 100 \cdot a_{\overline{8}|3\%} \cdot \frac{1}{a_{\overline{1/3}|3\%}}$$

$$= 100(7.019692)(3.029803 + .03) = \$2{,}147.89$$

(Tables 8 and 10)

Notice that $\frac{1}{a_{\overline{1/3}|3\%}} = \frac{1}{s_{\overline{1/3}|3\%}} + 3\% = 3.029803 + .03$ (Table 10)

★D. The Amount and the Present Value of a Deferred Complex Annuity

The amount of a deferred complex annuity is the final value at the end of the term of the annuity. Therefore, the amount of a deferred complex annuity, S_{nc}(defer.), is the same as the amount of the ordinary complex annuity, or

$$\mathbf{S_{nc}(defer.) = S_{nc} = R s_{\overline{nc}|i} \cdot \frac{1}{s_{\overline{c}|i}}} \qquad \textbf{(14–12)}$$

The present value of a deferred complex annuity, A_{nc}(defer.), is the value at the beginning of the period of deferment and may be obtained by either of the two methods described below.

Let d = the number of deferred payment intervals
c = the number of interest periods per payment interval

The period of deferment should include cd interest periods, and the term of the deferred annuity should include nc interest periods.

METHOD A

First, consider that the payments were made during the period of deferment. Second, consider that there are two ordinary annuities; one consists of d payments (or cd interest periods), while the other consists of $d + n$ payments [or $cd + nc = c(d + n)$ interest periods]. Third, subtract the present value of the annuity consisting of d payments from the present value of the annuity consisting of $(d + n)$ payments. The remainder is the answer. This value may be obtained by formula as follows:

$$A_{nc}(\text{defer.}) = A_{cd+nc} - A_{cd} = \frac{R}{s_{\overline{c}|i}} \cdot a_{\overline{c(d+n)}|i} - \frac{R}{s_{\overline{c}|i}} a_{\overline{cd}|i}$$

or

$$\mathbf{A_{nc}(defer.) = \frac{R}{s_{\overline{c}|i}}(a_{\overline{c(d+n)}|i} - a_{\overline{cd}|i})} \qquad \textbf{(14–13)}$$

METHOD B

Discount the present value of the ordinary complex annuity for the period of deferment. This may be done by formula as shown below:

$$\mathbf{A_{nc}(defer.) = A_{nc}(1 + i)^{-cd}} \qquad \textbf{(14–14)}$$

or

$$\mathbf{A_{nc}(defer.) = \frac{R}{s_{\overline{c}|i}} \cdot a_{\overline{nc}|i} \cdot (1 + i)^{-cd}}$$

Methods A and B are diagrammed as follows (also see the diagrams on pages 426 and 427):

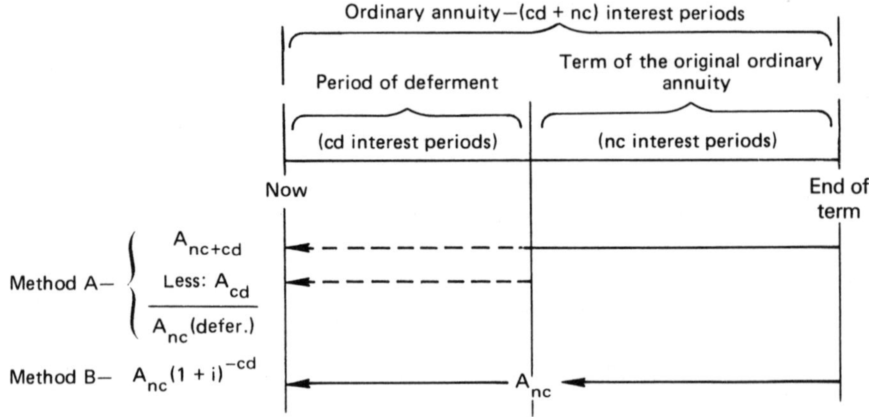

EXAMPLE 7

Find (a) the amount and (b) the present value of an annuity of $150 payable quarterly for 20 payments if the first payment is due at the end of 15 months and money is worth 6% compounded semiannually.

R = \$150 (per quarter), n = 20 (quarterly payments), i = 6%/2 = 3% (per six months), $c = \frac{1}{2}$ (interest periods in one quarter), d = 4 (quarters or 12 months, since the first payment covers the payment interval from the end of the 12th month to the end of the 15th month)

(a) Substituting the above values in formula (14–12),

$$S_{nc}(\text{defer.}) = 150 s_{\overline{20 \times 1/2}|3\%} \cdot \frac{1}{s_{\overline{1/2}|3\%}}$$
$$= 150(11.46388)(2.01489)$$
$$= \$3{,}464.77$$

(b) Substituting the values in formula (14–13),

$$A_{nc}(\text{defer.}) = \frac{150}{s_{\overline{1/2}|3\%}} \cdot (a_{\overline{1/2(20+4)}|3\%} - a_{\overline{4 \times 1/2}|3\%})$$
$$= 150(2.01489)(9.954004 - 1.913470)$$
$$= 302.2335(8.040534)$$
$$= \$2{,}430.12$$

Or substituting the values in formula (14–14),

$$A_{nc}(\text{defer.}) = \frac{150}{s_{\overline{1/2}|3\%}} \cdot a_{\overline{20 \times 1/2}|3\%} \cdot (1 + 3\%)^{-(4 \times 1/2)}$$
$$= 150(2.01489)(8.530203)(.942596)$$
$$= \$2{,}430.12$$

The present value may be checked by the use of the formula $P = S(1 + i)^{-n}$ as follows.

S = \$3,464.77, i = 3% (semiannually), n = 12 (semiannual periods or 20 + 4 = 24 quarters)

$A_{nc}(\text{defer.}) = P = 3{,}464.77(1 + 3\%)^{-12} = 3{,}464.77(0.70137988) = \$2{,}430.12$

★EXERCISE 14–6 REFERENCE: SECTION 14.3B, C, and D

A. Find the payment of the ordinary complex annuity in each of the following problems:

	Amount (S_{nc})	*Present Value (A_{nc})*	*Number of Payments (n)*	*Compound Interest Rate*
1.	\$2,000		5 annual payments	6%, semiannually
2.	6,000		12 semiannual payments	9%, monthly
3.		\$3,500	24 monthly payments	12%, quarterly
4.		4,800	28 quarterly payments	8%, annually
5.	360		3 semiannual payments	6%, monthly
6.		270	9 monthly payments	10%, quarterly

B. Find the amount and the present value of the complex annuity due in each of the following problems:

	Payment (R)	Payment Interval	Term	Compound Interest Rate
7.	$2,500	1 month	$3\frac{1}{2}$ years	6%, quarterly
8.	1,200	1 quarter	2 years	10%, semiannually
9.	80	6 months	5 years	12%, monthly
10.	60	1 year	8 years	7%, quarterly
11.	450	1 quarter	15 years	$5\frac{1}{2}$%, annually
12.	620	1 month	2 years	14%, semiannually

C. Find the amount and the present value of the deferred complex annuity in each of the following problems:

	Payment (R)	Number of Payments (n)	Number of Payment Intervals Deferred (d)	Compound Interest Rate
13.	$200, annually	20	3 (years)	16%, quarterly
14.	460, monthly	15	6 (months)	6%, quarterly
15.	75, semiannually	18	9 ($4\frac{1}{2}$ years)	7%, monthly
16.	80, quarterly	12	8 (quarters)	13%, semiannually
17.	350, quarterly	36	4 (quarters)	8%, annually
18.	500, annually	5	2 (years)	6%, monthly

D. Statement problems:

19. The amount of an annuity at the end of ten years is $8,000, the payments are made at the end of each year, and the interest rate is 11% compounded semiannually. What is the size of each annual payment?
20. Don Emerson wishes to receive $6,000 four years from now. How much must he invest at the end of each quarter during the four-year period? Assume that he will make his first investment three months from now and he can earn $5\frac{1}{2}$% interest compounded annually.
21. The present value of an annuity for three years is $500, the payments are made at the end of every six months, and the interest rate is 6% compounded monthly. How large is each payment?
22. Anna Parker wishes to receive $2,000 in cash now. She agrees to repay it by making 15 equal monthly payments with the first payment to be made one month from now. The interest rate is 15% compounded quarterly. What is the size of each payment?
23. Find the amount and the present value of an annuity of $1,200 payable at the beginning of each year for six years with interest at 5% compounded monthly.
24. What are the amount and the present value of an annuity of $2,800 payable at the end of every six months for 18 years with interest at $8\frac{1}{2}$% compounded annually?
25. What are the amount and the present value of an annuity of $130 payable monthly for 30 payments, with the first payment at the end of 19 months from the present time with interest at 12% compounded semiannually?

26. Find the amount and the present value of an annuity of \$180 payable semiannually, for eight payments, with the first payment in $5\frac{1}{2}$ years with interest at 5% compounded quarterly.

★14.4 COMPUTING FORMULAS BY CALCULATORS AND COMPUTERS

Tables 7, 8, 9, and 10 can be used to save time in computing annuity problems, as presented in Chapter 13 and in the previous sections of this chapter. In addition, this section illustrates the methods of computing the formulas covered in this chapter by using calculators and computers. The illustrations are based on the instructions in Chapter 10.

A. Computing Formulas (14–1) and (14–2): $S_n(\text{due}) = R(1 + i)\frac{(1 + i)^n - 1}{i}$

The examples used in this section are obtained from Section 14.1A.

EXAMPLE 1 Compute Example 1, Section 14.1:

$$S_4(\text{due}) = 100(1 + 1\%)\frac{(1 + 1\%)^4 - 1}{1\%} = 410.10$$

(a) SIMPLE CALCULATOR

Problem	*Step*	*Key Pressing Sequence*	*Display*
$100(1.01) \times \frac{1.01^4 - 1}{.01} = ?$	1	1.01 [×] [=] [=] [=]	1.040604
	2	[−] 1 [÷] .01 [×]	4.0604
	3	100 [×] 1.01 [=]	410.1004

(b) BUSINESS ANALYST CALCULATOR

Problem	*Step*	*Key Pressing Sequence*	*Display*
Compute future value of annuity due:	1	[ON/C] [2nd] [FIN]	0
Number of payments, $n = 1 \times 4$	2	1 [×] 4 [=] [N]	4
Percent interest rate per payment period, $i = 4\%/4 = 1\%$	3	4 [÷] 4 [=] [%i]	1
Payment size, $R = 100$ (must be negative)	4	100 [+/−] [PMT]	−100
Compute future value	5	[DUE] [FV]	410.1005

(c) COMPUTER WITH BASIC

BASIC Program

```
10 INPUT "R";R
20 INPUT "I";I
30 INPUT "N";N
40 S2 = R*(1 + I)*((1 + I)^N – 1)/I
50 PRINT "AMOUNT = ";S2
60 END
```

Computer Display (RUN)

```
R ? 100
I ? .01
N ? 4
AMOUNT = 410.100494
```

The numbers after the question marks (?) are typed input.

We will use S2 to denote S_n(due), the amount or future value of an annuity due, in BASIC programs.

EXAMPLE 2 Use a computer to work Example 2, Section 14.1:

$$R = 20$$
$$i = 1\tfrac{1}{2}\%$$
$$n = 36$$
$$S_{36}(\text{due}) = ? = 959.70$$

Use the BASIC program given in Example 1:

Computer Display (RUN)

```
R ? 20
I ? .015
N ? 36
AMOUNT = 959.702219
```

B. Computing Formulas (14–3) and (14–4): $A_n(\text{due}) = R(1 + i)\dfrac{1 - (1 + i)^{-n}}{i}$

The examples used in this section are obtained from Section 14.1B.

EXAMPLE 3 Compute Example 3, Section 14.1:

$$A_4(\text{due}) = 100(1 + 1\%)\frac{1 - (1 + 1\%)^{-4}}{1\%} = 394.10$$

(a) SIMPLE CALCULATOR

Problem	*Step*	*Key Pressing Sequence*	*Display*
$100(1.01) \times \dfrac{1 - 1.01^{-4}}{.01} = ?$	1	1.01 [×] [=] [=] [=] [M+]	1.040604M
	2	1 [÷] [MR] [=]	0.9609803M
	3	[+/–] [+] 1 [=]	0.0390197M
	4	[÷] .01 [=]	3.90197M
	5	[×] 100 [×] 1.01 [=]	394.09897M

(b) BUSINESS ANALYST CALCULATOR

Problem	*Step*	*Key Pressing Sequence*	*Display*
Compute present value of annuity due:	1	[ON/C] [2nd] [FIN]	0
Number of payments, $n = 1 \times 4$	2	1 [×] 4 [=] [N]	4
Percent interest rate per payment period, $i = 4\%/4 = 1\%$	3	4 [÷] 4 [=] [%i]	1
Payment size, $R = 100$	4	100 [PMT]	100
Compute present value	5	[DUE] [PV]	394.09852

(c) COMPUTER WITH BASIC

BASIC Program

```
10 INPUT "R";R
20 INPUT "I";I
30 INPUT "N";N
40 A2 = R*(1 + I)*(1 - (1 + I)^( - N))/I
50 PRINT "PRESENT VALUE = ";A2
60 END
```

Computer Display (RUN)

```
R ? 100
I ? .01
N ? 4
PRESENT VALUE = 394.098515
```

The numbers after the question marks (?) are typed input.

We will use A2 to denote A_n(due), the present value of an annuity due, in BASIC programs.

EXAMPLE 4 Use a computer to work Example 4, Section 14.1:

$$R = 50$$
$$i = 1\%$$
$$n = 10$$
$$A_{10}(\text{due}) = ? = 478.30$$

Use the BASIC program given in Example 3:

Computer Display (RUN)

```
R ? 50
I ? .01
N ? 10
PRESENT VALUE = 478.300872
```

C. Computing Formula (14–5): S_n(defer.) = S_n

The quantity S_n is defined by formula (13–1). See Section 13.8A for computing S_n by calculators and computers.

D. Computing Formulas (14–6) and (14–7):

$$A_n(\text{defer.}) = Ra_{\overline{n}|i} \cdot (1 + i)^{-d} = R\frac{(1 + i)^n - 1}{i(1 + i)^{n+d}}$$

The examples used in this section are obtained from Section 14.2.

EXAMPLE 5

Compute Example 2, Section 14.2:

$R = 100, i = 1\frac{1}{2}\%, n = 6, d = 2$

$$A_n(\text{defer.}) = 100\frac{(1 + 1\frac{1}{2}\%)^6 - 1}{1\frac{1}{2}\%(1 + 1\frac{1}{2}\%)^{6+2}} = 553.00$$

(a) SIMPLE CALCULATOR

Problem	*Step*	*Key Pressing Sequence*	*Display*
$100 \times \frac{1.015^6 - 1}{.015(1.015)^8} = ?$	1	1.015 [×] [=] (7 times)	1.1264922
	2	[×] .015 [=] [M +]	0.0168973M
	3	1.015 [×] [=] (5 times)	1.093443M
	4	[−] 1 [=]	0.093443M
	5	[÷] [MR] [=] [×] 100 [=]	553.0055M

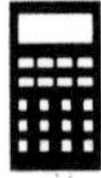

(b) BUSINESS ANALYST CALCULATOR

Problem	*Step*	*Key Pressing Sequence*	*Display*
Part I. Compute $A_n = Ra_{\overline{n}|i}$:	1	[ON/C] [2nd] [FIN]	0
Number of payments, n	2	6 [N]	6
Percent interest rate, i	3	1.5 [%i]	1.5
Payment size, R	4	100 [PMT]	100
Compute present value, A_n	5	[CPT] [PV]	569.7187
Part II. Compute $P = S(1 + i)^{-d}$:	1	[ON/C] [2nd] [FIN]	0
Number of interest periods, d	2	2 [N]	2
Percent interest rate, i	3	1.5 [%i]	1.5
Future value, S = 569.7187	4	569.7187 [FV]	569.7187
Compute present value, P	5	[CPT] [PV]	553.00415

(c) COMPUTER WITH BASIC

BASIC Program

```
10 INPUT "R";R
20 INPUT "I";I
30 INPUT "N";N
40 INPUT "D";D
50 A3 = R*((1 + I)^N − 1)/(I*(1 + I)^ (N + D))
60 PRINT "PRESENT VALUE = ";A3
70 END
```

Computer Display (RUN)

```
R ? 100
I ? .015
N ? 6
D ? 2
PRESENT VALUE = 553.004185
```

The numbers after the question marks (?) are typed input.

We will use A3 to denote A_n(defer.), the present value of a deferred annuity, in BASIC programs.

EXAMPLE 6 Compute Example 3, Section 14.2:

$$R = 500$$
$$i = 5\tfrac{1}{2}\%$$
$$n = 15$$
$$d = 4$$
$$A_{15}(\text{defer.}) = ? = 4{,}051.25$$

Use the BASIC program given in Example 5:

Computer Display (RUN)

```
R ? 500
I ? .055
N ? 15
D ? 4
PRESENT VALUE = 4051.25172
```

E. Computing Complex Annuity Formulas (14–8) to (14–14)

In computing complex annuity formulas, calculators are helpful, but less effective than computers. Therefore, only the method using computers is discussed in the following examples of complex annuity problems. The examples are obtained from Section 14.3.

(1) COMPUTING FORMULAS (14–8) AND (14–12): $S_{nc}(\text{defer.}) = S_{nc} = R\dfrac{(1+i)^{nc}-1}{(1+i)^c-1}$

EXAMPLE 7 Compute S_{nc} (Example 1, Section 14.3):

$R = 100,\ i = 6\%/12 = \tfrac{1}{2}\%,\ n = 10 \times 4 = 40,\ c = 3$

$$S_{nc} = \text{S4} = 100\frac{(1 + \frac{1}{2}\%)^{120} - 1}{(1 + \frac{1}{2}\%)^3 - 1} = 5{,}435.42$$

Here, we use S4 to denote S_{nc} in the BASIC program.

COMPUTER WITH BASIC

BASIC Program

```
10 INPUT "R";R
20 INPUT "I";I
30 INPUT "N";N
40 INPUT "C";C
50 S4 = R*((1 + I)^(N*C) – 1)/((1 – I)^C – 1)
60 PRINT "AMOUNT = ";S4
70 END
```

Computer Display (RUN)

```
R ? 100
I ? .005
N ? 40
C ? 3
AMOUNT = 5435.42251
```

The numbers after the question marks (?) are typed input.

The same BASIC program given in Example 7 can be used for Examples 2 and 7(a) of Section 14.3, as follows:

Computer Display (RUN)

Example 2, Section 14.3– Compute S_{nc}	*Example 7(a), Section 14.3– Compute S_{nc}(defer.)*
R ? 100	R ? 150
I ? .05	I ? .03
N ? 72	N ? 20
C ? .166667	C ? .5
AMOUNT = 9747.35844	AMOUNT = 3464.76694

(2) COMPUTING FORMULA (14–9): $A_{nc} = R\dfrac{1-(1+i)^{-nc}}{(1+i)^c - 1}$

EXAMPLE 8

Compute A_{nc} (Example 1, Section 14.3):

$R = 100, i = \frac{1}{2}\%, n = 40, c = 3$

$$A_{nc} = \text{A4} = 100\frac{1-(1+\frac{1}{2}\%)^{-120}}{(1+\frac{1}{2}\%)^3 - 1} = 2{,}987.48$$

Here, we use A4 to denote A_{nc} in the BASIC program.

COMPUTER WITH BASIC

BASIC Program

```
10 INPUT "R";R
20 INPUT "I";I
30 INPUT "N";N
40 INPUT "C";C
50 A4 = R*(1 – (1 + I)^( – N*C))/((1 + I)^C – 1)
60 PRINT "PRESENT VALUE = ";A4
70 END
```

Computer Display (RUN)

```
R ? 100
I ? .005
N ? 40
C ? 3
PRESENT VALUE = 2987.48614
```

The numbers after the question marks (?) are typed input.

EXAMPLE 9

Compute A_{nc} (Example 2, Section 14.3):

$R = 100$
$i = 5\%$
$n = 72$
$c = \frac{1}{6}$
$A_{72(1/6)} = ? = 5427.69$

Use the BASIC program given in Example 8:

Computer Display (RUN)

```
R ? 100
I ? .05
N ? 72
C ? .166667
PRESENT VALUE = 5427.68756
```

(3) COMPUTING FORMULA (14–10): $S_{nc}(\text{due}) = R\dfrac{(1+i)^{nc} - 1}{1-(1+i)^{-c}}$

EXAMPLE 10

Compute S_{nc}(due) (Example 5, Section 14.3):

$R = 150, i = \frac{1}{2}\%, n = 4, c = 3$

$$S_{nc}(\text{due}) = 100\frac{(1 + \frac{1}{2}\%)^{12} - 1}{1 - (1 + \frac{1}{2}\%)^{-3}} = 622.95$$

Here, we use S5 to denote S_{nc}(due) in the BASIC program.

COMPUTER WITH BASIC

BASIC Program

```
10 INPUT "R";R
20 INPUT "I";I
30 INPUT "N";N
40 INPUT "C";C
50 S5 = R*((1 + I)^(N*C) - 1)/(1 - (1 + I) ^( - C))
60 PRINT "AMOUNT = ";S5
70 END
```

Computer Display (RUN)

```
R ? 150
I ? .005
N ? 4
C ? 3
AMOUNT = 622.95616
```

The numbers after the question marks (?) are typed input.

EXAMPLE 11

Compute S_{nc}(due) (Example 6, Section 14.3):

$$R = 100$$
$$i = 3\%$$
$$n = 24$$
$$c = \tfrac{1}{3}$$
$$S_{24(1/3)}(\text{due}) = ? = 2720.88$$

Use the BASIC program given in Example 10:

Computer Display (RUN)

```
R ? 100
I ? .03
N ? 24
C ? .333333
AMOUNT = 2720.87926
```

(4) COMPUTING FORMULA (14–11): $A_{nc}(\text{due}) = R\frac{1 - (1 + i)^{-nc}}{1 - (1 + i)^{-c}}$

EXAMPLE 12

Compute A_{nc}(due) (Example 5, Section 14.3):

$$R = 150$$
$$i = \tfrac{1}{2}\%$$
$$n = 4$$
$$c = 3$$
$$A_{nc}(\text{due}) = 150\frac{1 - (1 + \frac{1}{2}\%)^{-12}}{1 - (1 + \frac{1}{2}\%)^{-3}} = ? = 586.76$$

Here, we use A5 to denote A_{nc}(due) in the BASIC program.

COMPUTER WITH BASIC

BASIC Program

```
10 INPUT "R";R
20 INPUT "I";I
30 INPUT "N";N
40 INPUT "C";C
50 A5 = R*(1 - (1 + I)^(- N*C))/(1 - (1 + I) ^(- C))
60 PRINT "PRESENT VALUE = ";A5
70 END
```

Computer Display (RUN)

```
R ? 150
I ? .005
N ? 4
C ? 3
PRESENT VALUE = 586.765731
```

The numbers after the question marks (?) are typed input.

EXAMPLE 13 Compute A_{nc}(due) (Example 6, Section 14.3):

$$R = 100$$
$$i = 3\%$$
$$n = 24$$
$$c = \tfrac{1}{3}$$
$$A_{24(1/3)}(\text{due}) = ? = 2147.89$$

Use the BASIC program given in Example 12:

Computer Display (RUN)

```
R ? 100
I ? .03
N ? 24
C ? .333333
PRESENT VALUE = 2147.88772
```

(5) COMPUTING FORMULAS (14–13) AND (14–14):

$$A_{nc}(\text{defer.}) = R\frac{1 - (1 + i)^{-nc}}{(1 + i)^{c} - 1}(1 + i)^{-cd}$$

EXAMPLE 14 Compute A_{nc}(defer.) (Example 7(b), Section 14.3):

$R = 150,\ i = 3\%,\ n = 20,\ c = \tfrac{1}{2},\ d = 4$

$$A_{nc}(\text{defer.}) = 150\frac{1 - (1 + 3\%)^{-10}}{(1 + 3\%)^{1/2} - 1}(1 + 3\%)^{-2} = ? = 2{,}430.12$$

Here, we use A6 to denote A_{nc}(defer.) in the BASIC program.

COMPUTER WITH BASIC

BASIC Program

```
10 INPUT "R";R
20 INPUT "I";I
30 INPUT "N";N
40 INPUT "C";C
50 INPUT "D";D
60 A6 = R*(1 - (1 + I)^(- N*C))*((1 + I) ^(- C*D))/
   ((1 + I)^C - 1)
70 PRINT "PRESENT VALUE = ";A6
80 END
```

Computer Display (RUN)

```
R ? 150
I ? .03
N ? 20
C ? .5
D ? 4
PRESENT VALUE = 2430.11782
```

The numbers after the question marks (?) are typed input.

14.5 SUMMARY OF ANNUITY CERTAIN FORMULAS

Symbols: R = size of equal payments of an annuity
n = number of payments
i = interest rate per conversion period
c = number of interest periods in one payment interval, or
= payment interval/interest period
d = number of deferred payment intervals

Application		*Formula*	*Formula Number*	*Reference Page*
Simple Annuity				
Annuity due	Amount	$S_n(\text{due}) = Rs_{\overline{n+1}\mid i} - R$	(14–1)	415
		or		
		$S_n(\text{due}) = Rs_{\overline{n}\mid i} \cdot (1 + i)$	(14–2)	416
	Present value	$A_n(\text{due}) = Ra_{\overline{n-1}\mid i} + R$	(14–3)	417
		or		
		$A_n(\text{due}) = Ra_{\overline{n}\mid i} \cdot (1 + i)$	(14–4)	419
Deferred annuity	Amount	$S_n(\text{defer.}) = S_n = Rs_{\overline{n}\mid i}$	(14–5)	425
	Present value	$A_n(\text{defer.}) = Ra_{\overline{d+n}\mid i} - Ra_{\overline{d}\mid i}$	(14–6)	425
		or		
		$A_n(\text{defer.}) = Ra_{\overline{n}\mid i} \cdot (1 + i)^{-d}$	(14–7)	426
Complex Annuity				
Ordinary annuity	Amount	$S_{nc} = Rs_{\overline{nc}\mid i} \cdot \dfrac{1}{s_{\overline{c}\mid i}}$	(14–8)	432 and 436
	Present value	$A_{nc} = Ra_{\overline{nc}\mid i} \cdot \dfrac{1}{s_{\overline{c}\mid i}}$	(14–9)	432 and 436
Annuity due	Amount	$S_{nc}(\text{due}) = Rs_{\overline{nc}\mid i} \cdot \dfrac{1}{a_{\overline{c}\mid i}}$	(14–10)	438
	Present value	$A_{nc}(\text{due}) = Ra_{\overline{nc}\mid i} \cdot \dfrac{1}{a_{\overline{c}\mid i}}$	(14–11)	438
Deferred annuity	Amount	$S_{nc}(\text{defer.}) = S_{nc} = Rs_{\overline{nc}\mid i} \cdot \dfrac{1}{s_{\overline{c}\mid i}}$	(14–12)	439
	Present value	$A_{nc}(\text{defer.}) = \dfrac{R}{s_{\overline{c}\mid i}}(a_{\overline{c(d+n)}\mid i} - a_{\overline{cd}\mid i})$	(14–13)	440
		or		
		$A_{nc}(\text{defer.}) = A_{nc}(1 + i)^{-cd}$	(14–14)	440

EXERCISE 14–7 REVIEW OF CHAPTERS 13 and 14

1. What are the amount and the present value of an annuity of $140 payable at the beginning of each quarter for 30 quarters if the interest rate is 12% compounded quarterly?
2. What are the amount and the present value of an annuity of $60 payable at the beginning of every six months for 20 years if the interest rate is 15% compounded semiannually?
3. In Problem 1, if payments are payable at the end of each quarter, what are the amount and the present value?
4. Find the amount and the present value in Problem 2 if the payments of $60 each are payable at the end of every six months.
5. Refer to Problem 1. What are the amount and the present value if the payments of the annuity are payable at the end of each quarter and the interest rate is 12% compounded (a) monthly, (b) semiannually?
6. Refer to Problem 2. What are the amount and the present value if the payments are payable at the end of each semiannual period and the interest rate is 10% compounded (a) quarterly, (b) annually?
7. ★ Refer to Problem 1. What are the amount and the present value if the interest rate is 8% compounded (a) monthly, (b) semiannually?
8. ★ Refer to Problem 2. Find the amount and the present value if the itnerest rate is 8% compounded (a) quarterly, (b) annually.
9. Tom plans to deposit $30 now and $30 hereafter every month for a total of 36 deposits. If his deposits can earn 9% interest compounded monthly, what is the final value at the end of three years?
10. Assume that $80 is deposited now and hereafter for 26 additional quarterly deposits of $80 each. What is the final value if the interest rate is 6% compounded quarterly?
11. Refer to Problem 9. What is the present value of the annuity?
12. Refer to Problem 10. What is the present value of the annuity?
13. On April 1, 1991, Jane Taylor deposits $120 in a bank that pays 6% interest compounded quarterly. She plans to deposit the same amount every three months thereafter until the last deposit on April 1, 1995. How much money will be in her account on July 1, 1995?
14. A suite of living room furniture can be bought for $40 per month for 12 monthly payments with the first payment due now. If money is worth 7% compounded monthly, what is the cash price of the suite?
15. A house can be bought for $11,200 down plus $1,200 per month payable at the end of each month. The last monthly payment will be 14 years and 11 months from the date of purchase. The payment plan is computed at 12% interest compounded monthly. What is the cash price of the house?
16. Refer to Problem 15. If the house can be rented for $850 per month payable in advance each month and the house is expected to have a value of $220,000 at the end of 15 years, should someone, who wishes to occupy the house for 15 years

only, buy or rent the house? Assume that the money can be invested at (a) 12% compounded monthly, (b) $10\frac{1}{2}$% compounded monthly. (Do not consider any other expenses or costs in making the decision to buy or rent.)

17. What are the amount and the present value of an annuity of $40 payable at the end of each month for five years if the interest rate is 6% compounded quarterly?
18. Find the amount and the present value of an annuity of $75 payable at the end of each year for 24 years if the interest rate is 6% compounded quarterly.
19. Johnson wishes to have $3,000 six years from now. How much must he invest each year if the first investment starts now and the interest is 5% compounded annually? He will not make an investment at the end of the six years.
20. Davy's father wishes to have $5,000 when Davy reaches 18 years of age. How much must the father invest now and each quarter thereafter at a 12% interest rate compounded quarterly? Davy is six years old now. His father does not wish to make an investment on Davy's 18th birthday.

★21. Gregorio wants to have $3,000 at the end of six years. His investment can earn 5% interest compounded monthly. How much must he invest each year if the first investment starts (a) now? (b) at the end of one year?

★22. Compute Problem 20 assuming the interest rate is 12% compounded semiannually. Also, find the size of the quarterly investment if Davy's father makes the first investment three months from now and the last investment on Davy's 18th birthday. The interest rate is 12% compounded semiannually.

23. A washing machine can be bought for 18 equal monthly payments with the first payment due now. If the cash price is $400 and the interest rate is 6% compounded monthly, what is the size of each payment?
24. Mrs. Rogers purchased a truck on May 1, 1991, and promised to pay for it in equal quarterly installments. The cash price of the truck was $7,000. The first payment was made on the purchase date and the last payment is to be made on May 1, 1996. What is the size of each quarterly payment if the interest rate is 8% compounded quarterly?

★25. What is the answer in Problem 23 if the interest rate is 6% compounded semiannually?

★26. What is the answer in Problem 24 if the interest rate is 8% compounded monthly?

27. At what nominal rate compounded quarterly will an annuity of $300 payable at the beginning of each quarter for eight years amount to $12,000?
28. What is the nominal rate compounded monthly if the amount of an annuity of $60 payable at the beginning of each month for three years is $2,500?
29. At what nominal rate compounded quarterly does an annuity of $80 payable at the beginning of each quarter for nine years have a present value of $2,300?
30. What is the nominal rate compounded semiannually if the present value of an annuity of $150 payable at the beginning of every six months for 10 years is $2,500?
31. If $80 is deposited at the beginning of each quarter at 6% compounded quarterly, how many payments will be required for the deposits to amount to at least $3,000?

32. On March 1, 1991, Bobson plans to invest \$120 each month with the first investment starting then. She wishes to have at least \$5,000 as the final value. If she can earn 6% interest compounded monthly on her investment, on what date will she have the final value?
33. Carlson purchased a \$6,000 car and agreed to pay for it with monthly installments of \$180 each, starting on the date of purchase. If the interest rate is 12% compounded monthly, how many monthly payments are required?
34. The present value of an annuity of \$60 payable at the beginning of each quarter is \$2,500. What is the number of payments of the annuity if the interest rate is 8% compounded quarterly?
35. What are the amount and the present value of an annuity of \$120 payable at the end of every six months for 15 payments, with the first payment to be made two years from now? Assume that the interest rate is 10% compounded semiannually.
36. Find the amount and the present value of an annuity of \$50 per quarter for 30 payments if the first payment is due four years from now and money is worth 8% compounded quarterly.
37. Smith borrows \$8,000 at 6% interest compounded quarterly and agrees to repay it in 20 equal quarterly payments. What is the size of each payment if the first payment is due at the end of five years?
38. Thomas borrows \$600 at 8% compounded monthly and agrees to repay it in 16 monthly payments. Find the size of each monthly payment if the first payment is due at the end of one year.
39. If \$100 is deposited at the end of each quarter and the interest rate is 12% compounded quarterly, how many quarterly payments will be needed for the deposits to have a present value of \$2,000? Assume that the first deposit is made at the end of two years.
40. If \$25 is deposited at the end of ten months from now and \$25 every month thereafter, how many monthly deposits will be required for a value which now is equivalent to \$800? Assume that the interest rate is 12% compounded monthly.
41. Mrs. Smith deposited \$1,000 on each of the following dates: 1/1/91, 4/1/91, 7/1/91, 10/1/91, 1/1/92. What is the single value on each of the following dates that is equivalent to the five deposits above? (a) 1/1/92? (b) 1/1/91? (c) 10/1/90? (d) 1/1/90? Assume that money is worth 4% compounded quarterly.
42. Let 1/1/92 be the comparison date. Find the value on the comparison date for each of the single values obtained in Problem 41.

PART FOUR MATHEMATICS IN INVESTMENT-APPLICATIONS

15 EXTINCTION OF DEBTS

The methods used in ordinary annuity computations are frequently applied in reducing debt problems. The applications included in this chapter are: debt extinction by amortization (Section 15.1), amortization by the add-on interest method (Section 15.2), amortization of callable bonds (Section 15.3), and debt extinction by sinking fund (Section 15.4). In addition, this chapter explains the methods of computing selected examples by calculators and computers as supplemental material (Section 15.5).

15.1 DEBT EXTINCTION BY AMORTIZATION

The word "debt" in this chapter refers to a long-term obligation. Long-term debts are normally in the form of long-term notes or bonds with a maturity date that is more than one year. Generally, notes are issued to a *single source* from which a loan is obtained, whereas bonds are issued to a *group* of creditors. Long-term debts usually involve large sums of money. A borrower may promise to discharge the debt either by making periodic partial payments under the *amortization* method or by establishing a *sinking fund* into which periodic deposits are made in order to pay a single sum on the date of maturity.

The amortization method broadly refers to the discharging of a debt by means of a set of regular or irregular and equal or unequal payments. The methods for irregular and unequal payments were presented in Chapter 8 (Section 8.4, Partial Payments: the Merchants' Rule and the United States Rule). In this chapter only a debt discharged by a sequence of *equal* payments at *equal* intervals of time is considered. *The original principal of the debt, therefore, is the present value of an annuity of the equal payments.* In order to discharge a debt, each payment must be greater than the periodic interest, so that a part of the payment applies to the interest and the remainder applies to the principal until the principal becomes zero.

The following discussion first treats long-term debts other than bonds. Amortization of bonded debts is discussed later in this chapter.

A. Finding the Size of the Periodic Payment

The size of the periodic payment for amortizing a debt may be found by using the method discussed in Section 13.5 of Chapter 13. The method shows how to find the size of each periodic payment of an ordinary annuity when the present value is known. In applying this method, consider the value of the debt as the present value of the annuity.

EXAMPLE 1

A man purchased a $120,000 house and made a $20,000 down payment. He agreed to pay the balance by making equal payments at the end of each month for 15 years. If the interest charged is 12% compounded monthly, what is the size of the monthly payment?

The unpaid balance is the present value, or $A_n = 120{,}000 - 20{,}000 = 100{,}000$, $i = 12\%/12 = 1\%$ (per month), and $n = 15 \times 12 = 180$ (monthly payments).

Substituting the values in the formula $A_n = Ra_{\overline{n}|i}$,

$$100{,}000 = Ra_{\overline{180}|1\%}$$

$$R = \frac{100{,}000}{a_{\overline{180}|1\%}}$$

$$R = 100{,}000(.01200168) = \$1{,}200.17 \quad \text{(Table 9)}$$

B. Finding the Outstanding Principal

Often both the creditor and the borrower must know the amount of the *outstanding principal* or the *unpaid balance* on a certain date. The information may be needed for various reasons: it may be necessary for accounting purposes; the creditor may want to sell the unpaid balance; the borrower may wish to know his or her equity from an investment (such as house purchase price minus unpaid balance); or the creditor and the borrower may agree to settle the balance on an earlier date. The outstanding principal may be determined under two types of arrangements: (a) all periodic payments are equal, or (b) all periodic payments, except the final payment, are equal.

(1) ALL PERIODIC PAYMENTS ARE EQUAL

When it is necessary for all the periodic payments to be the same size, the method given in Example 1 should be used to find the size of the payments. The outstanding principal on a certain date is the present value of an annuity formed by the remaining unpaid payments, as shown below.

EXAMPLE 2

Refer to Example 1. Find the outstanding principal after the man made the monthly payments for 10 years.

$R = \$1{,}200.17$ (per month), $i = 1\%$ (per month), n (remaining payments) $= 180$ (total) $- 120$ (paid, or 10×12) $= 60$ (monthly payments)

Substituting the values in formula $A_n = Ra_{\overline{n}|i}$

$$A_n = 1{,}200.17a_{\overline{60}|1\%} = 1{,}200.17(44.955038) = \$53{,}953.69 \quad \text{(Table 8)}$$

The above computation is diagrammed as follows:

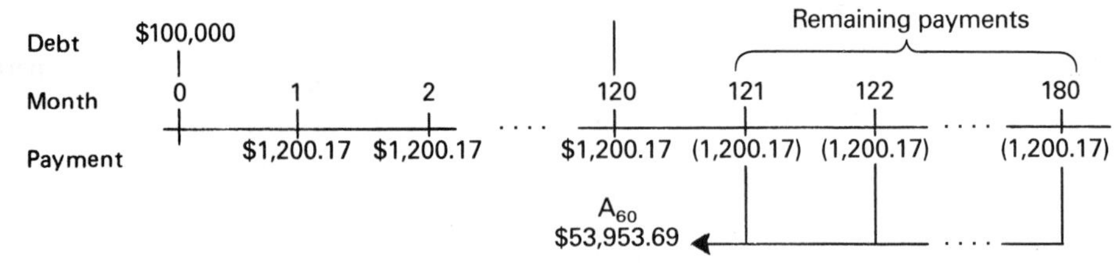

Instead of using the formula method as presented in Example 2, the outstanding principal on a certain date may be obtained by constructing an amortization schedule such as that shown in the following example.

EXAMPLE 3 A debt of $4,000 is to be amortized by equal payments at the end of every quarter for $1\frac{1}{2}$ years. If the interest charged is 12% compounded quarterly, find the outstanding principal after each payment is made.

STEP (1). Find the size of the periodic payment.

$A_n = \$4{,}000,\ i = 12\%/4 = 3\%$ (per quarter), $n = 1\frac{1}{2} \times 4 = 6$ (quarters)

$4{,}000 = Ra_{\overline{6}|3\%}$

$$R = \frac{4{,}000}{a_{\overline{6}|3\%}} = 4{,}000(.1845975) = \$738.39 \quad \text{(Table 9)}$$

STEP (2). Find the outstanding principals by constructing the amortization schedule shown below.

Amortization Schedule (Example 3)

(1) Period (3-Month Interval)	*(2) Outstanding Principal at Beginning of Each Period: (2) − (5)**	*(3) Interest Due at End of Period: (2) × 3%*	*(4) Equal Payment at End of Each Period*	*(5) Portion of Principal Reduced by Each Payment: (4) − (3)*
1	$4,000.00	$120.00	$ 738.39	$ 618.39
2	3,381.61	101.45	738.39	636.94
3	2,744.67	82.34	738.39	656.05
4	2,088.62	62.66	738.39	675.73
5	1,412.89	42.39	738.39	696.00
6	716.89	21.51	738.40	716.89
Total		$430.35	$4,430.35	$4,000.00

* Of the previous period. For example, $3,381.61 = $4,000 − $618.39.

Observe the amortization schedule of Example 3. Column (2) shows the outstanding principal after each payment is made. For example, the outstanding principal after the fourth payment is $1,412.89. The fourth payment is made at the end of the fourth period.

Thus, \$1,412.89 is also the principal at the beginning of the fifth period. The discharged portion of the original principal after the fourth period is \$2,587.11 [= \$4,000 − \$1,412.89, or = \$618.39 + \$636.94 + \$656.05 + \$675.73; see column (5) of the schedule].

Each outstanding principal shown in Column (2) may be checked by using the formula method, $A_n = Ra_{\overline{n}|i}$. For example, the outstanding principal after the fourth payment is made is the present value of an annuity formed by the two remaining unpaid payments.

$A_n = ?$, $R = 738.39$, $i = 3\%$, $n = 2$ (the number of the remaining quarterly payments)

Substituting the values in the formula,

$$A_n = 738.39a_{\overline{2}|3\%} = 738.39(1.91347) = \$1{,}412.89$$

The last figures in Columns (2) and (5) should be the same. The total for Column (5) should be equal to the original principal, \$4,000. Theoretically, all the payments should be equal. However, the schedule shows that the sixth payment is \$738.40. The discrepancy of one cent results from rounding all computations to the nearest cent. For example, interest due at the end of the sixth period is computed as follows:

$$716.89 \times 3\% = \$21.5067, \quad \text{which is rounded to} \quad \$21.51$$

The size of the sixth payment, therefore, is \$716.89 + 21.51 = \$738.40. The final payment covers the outstanding principal at the beginning of the last payment interval and the interest due thereon.

Here, the interest for each period is computed by the simple interest method. It should be observed that *when a debtor makes each of the simple interest payments on the interest date, the simple interest method is actually a compound interest method.* Also, note that as the principal is gradually reduced, the periodic interest becomes smaller after each payment is made. Thus, a greater portion of each equal payment is used in reducing the principal.

EXERCISE 15–1 REFERENCE: SECTION 15.1A and B1

A. Find the size of the periodic payment and the outstanding principal at the indicated time in each of the following problems, without constructing an amortization schedule. Payments are assumed to be made at the end of each period.

	Debt	*Number of Payments by Amortization*	*Compound Interest Rate*	*Required Outstanding Principal*
1.	\$ 2,500	18, monthly	12%, monthly	after 10th payment
2.	1,800	12, semiannual	10%, semiannually	after 5th payment
3.	4,000	4, quarterly	16%, quarterly	after 3rd payment
4.	6,000	8, annual	9%, annually	after 1st payment
5.	8,000	20, semiannual	7%, semiannually	after 7th payment
6.	20,000	45, monthly	18%, monthly	after 18th payment
7.	200	5, annual	8%, annually	after 2nd payment
8.	500	10, quarterly	7%, quarterly	after 6th payment

B. Statement problems:

9. A debt of \$6,000 is to be amortized with four equal semiannual payments. If the interest rate is 6% compounded semiannually, what is the size of each payment? Construct an amortization schedule.

10. A loan of \$2,000 is to be amortized with five equal semiannual payments. The interest rate is 8% compounded semiannually. Find the semiannual payment and construct an amortization schedule.

11. A man bought an \$8,000 truck and made a \$1,000 down payment. He agreed to pay the balance by making equal payments at the end of every three months for a period of two years. The interest charged was 8% compounded quarterly. Find the outstanding principal after the fourth payment by constructing a partial amortization schedule.

12. A \$15,000 boat was purchased with a down payment of \$2,000 and monthly payments for 15 years. The interest rate was 6% compounded monthly. (a) Find the size of the monthly payment. (b) Construct a partial amortization schedule to find the outstanding principal after the third payment.

(2) ALL PERIODIC PAYMENTS EXCEPT THE FINAL PAYMENT ARE EQUAL

Sometimes the size of each payment is not obtained by the method explained in Section A. Instead, it is specified by the agreement between the creditor and the debtor, and a more convenient or rounded figure, such as \$50 or \$100, is decided upon as the size of each payment. The exact size of the final payment is not known. It may or may not equal the size of other payments. Under such a condition, when an amortization schedule is not constructed, the outstanding principal on a certain date is computed by a method different from that discussed above. The following example is used to illustrate the methods of computation for this type of problem.

EXAMPLE 4 A debt of \$6,000 is to be discharged by payments of \$1,000 at the end of every month. Interest charged is 12% compounded monthly. Find (a) the number of payments, (b) the outstanding principal after each payment is made, (c) the interest included in each payment, (d) the principal included in each payment, and (e) the size of the final payment and the total of the payments.

METHOD A *Constructing an Amortization Schedule.* After an amortization schedule has been constructed, the answers may be found in the respective columns, as shown below:

Amortization Schedule (Example 4)

(1) Period (1-Month Interval)	*(2) Outstanding Principal at Beginning of Each Period: (2) − (5)*		*(3) Interest Due at End of Period: (2) × 1%*		*(4) Payment at End of Each Period*	*(5) Portion of Principal Reduced by Each Payment: (4) − (3)*
1	$6,000.00		$ 60.00		$1,000.00	$ 940.00
2	5,060.00		50.60		1,000.00	949.40
3	4,110.60		41.11		1,000.00	958.89
4	3,151.71		31.52		1,000.00	968.48
5	2,183.23		21.83		1,000.00	978.17
6	1,205.06		12.05		1,000.00	987.95
7	217.11	+	2.17	=	219.28	217.11
Total			$219.28		$6,219.28	$6,000.00

METHOD B

Without Constructing an Amortization Schedule. When a schedule is not constructed, the answers in the schedule above may be obtained directly as follows.

Column (1)—The number of payments. Use the formula $a_{\overline{n}|i} = \frac{A_n}{R}$.

A_n = \$6,000, R = \$1,000 (per month), i = 12%/12 = 1% (per month), n = ? (months).

$$a_{\overline{n}|1\%} = \frac{6,000}{1,000} = 6$$

From Table 8, we have

n	$a_{\overline{n}|1\%}$
6	5.79547647
?	6.00000000
7	6.72819453

Thus, n must be between 6 and 7. However, the debt of \$6,000 cannot be completely discharged by six payments of \$1,000 each. The seventh payment is necessary, although the payment may be smaller than each of the first six payments. (Note: By interpolation, n = ? = 6.2192769.)

Column (2)—The outstanding principal after each payment is made. Only the outstanding principal after the fifth payment (or at the beginning of the sixth payment interval) is computed here for illustration.

STEP (1). Find the value of the original debt on the date of the fifth payment as if no payments were made previously. Use the formula $S = P(1 + i)^n$.

P = 6,000, i = 1%, n = 5

$$S = 6,000(1 + 1\%)^5 = 6,000(1.051010) = \$6,306.06$$

STEP (2). Find the value of the five payments up to that date as if the payments were invested. Use the formula $S_n = Rs_{\overline{n}|i}$.

$S_n = 1{,}000s_{\overline{5}|1\%} = 1{,}000(5.10100) = \$5{,}101.00$

STEP (3). Find the difference between the results of Steps (1) and (2).

$6,306.06 − $5,101.00 = $1,205.06

The computation is diagrammed as follows:

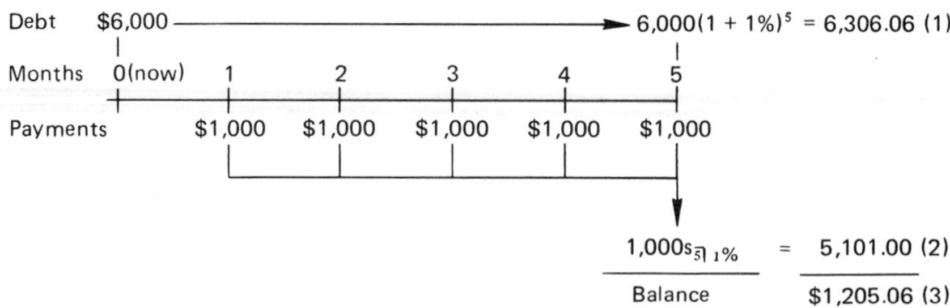

Columns (3) and (5)—The interest and the principal included in each payment. Only the sixth payment is computed here for illustration. Interest for the sixth payment period = Outstanding principal after the fifth payment is made multiplied by 1% = 1,205.06(1%) = $12.05.

Principal included in the sixth payment = sixth payment − interest for the sixth payment period = 1,000 − 12.05 = $987.95.

Column (4)—The final payment of $219.28 and the total payments of $6,219.28. They may be obtained by any one of the following three methods without constructing a schedule:

METHOD (1). Assume that the debtor paid $1,000 (which is the same amount as the other payments) on the seventh payment date. The overpayment after the seventh payment is $780.72 and is computed as follows [see the method used for Column (2) above]:

$S_7 = 1{,}000s_{\overline{7}|1\%}$	$= 1{,}000(7.213535)$	= $7,213.535	(Amount of payments on the seventh payment date)
$S = 6{,}000(1 + 1\%)^7$	$= 6{,}000(1.0721354)$	= $6,432.812	(Amount of the debt on the seventh payment date)
	Overpayment	= $ 780.723,	rounded to $780.72

The overpayment should be recovered. Thus,

the final payment = $1,000.00 − $780.72 = $219.28

The total of the seven payments is the sum of the six equal payments of $1,000 each and the final small payment, or

the total of the payments = 1,000(6) + 219.28 = $6,219.28

★METHOD (2). Find the outstanding principal after the sixth payment (the last of the equal payments of $1,000) and then add the interest on the outstanding principal to obtain the final payment.

$S = 6{,}000(1 + 1\%)^6 = 6{,}000(1.0615202) = \$6{,}369.121$ (Amount of the debt)

$S_6 = 1{,}000 s_{\overline{6}|1\%} = 1{,}000(6.152015) = \$6{,}152.015$ (Amount of payments)

$\$\ 217.106$, or $217.11 (Outstanding principal after the sixth payment)

[See the method used for Column (2) above.]

The interest for the seventh period = 217.11(1%) = $2.17

The final payment = 217.11 + 2.17 = $219.28

★METHOD (3). This method is based on the theoretical expression:

Total of payments = number of payments (n) × the size of each payment (R)

First, find the total of the seven payments as follows:

By interpolation, the actual value of n (number of payments) is 6.2192769. [See solution for Column (1) for $a_{\overline{n}|i}$ values.]

Thus,

total of payments = nR = 6.2192769(1,000) = $6,219.2769, or $6,219.28

Then subtract the sum of the six equal payments from the total.

The final payment = 6,219.28 − 1,000(6) = $219.28

EXERCISE 15–2 REFERENCE: SECTION 15.1B(2)

A. In each of the following problems, find (a) the number of payments, (b) the outstanding principal at the indicated time, (c) the interest and the principal included in the next payment after the indicated time in (b), and (d) the size of the final payment and the total of the cash payments. Do not construct an amortization schedule in finding your answers.

	Debt	*Payment (Made at End of Each Period)*	*Compound Interest Rate*	*Required Outstanding Principal*
1.	$ 4,000	$200 every 3 months	8%, quarterly	after 20th payment
2.	6,000	$600 every 3 months	6%, quarterly	after 7th payment
3.	5,000	$1,000 every month	24%, monthly	after 3rd payment
4.	800	$100 every year	5%, annually	after 4th payment
5.	1,400	$50 every month	12%, monthly	after 6th payment
6.	25,000	$2,000 every 6 months	7%, semiannually	after 11th payment

B. Statement problems:

7. A debt of $8,000 is to be amortized with $2,500 being paid at the end of every six months. The interest rate is 6% compounded semiannually. Construct an amortization schedule.
8. A debt of $4,000 is to be amortized with $800 being paid at the end of each quarter. The interest rate is 16% compounded quarterly. Construct an amortization schedule.

15.2 AMORTIZATION BY THE ADD-ON INTEREST METHOD

The add-on interest method is frequently used by finance companies and banks in computing the equal periodic payments for amortizing a personal loan. In this method, interest charged is added on to the amount of the original loan. The length of borrowing time is usually limited to a range from a few months to about 18 months, although a longer period may also be used for such loans. Under this method, the periodic payments are computed as follows:

1. Compute the interest (I) on the principal (P) by the simple interest method. Use the formula $I = Pin$ where i = the *stated* annual interest rate and n = the borrowing time expressed in the units of years.
2. Divide the sum of the simple interest and the principal ($S = P + I$) by the number of payments to obtain the size of each payment.

The size of the periodic payment computed by the add-on interest method is usually larger than the size computed by the annuity formula $A_n = Ra_{\overline{n}|i}$. Thus, the annual interest rate charged by using the add-on interest method is actually larger than the stated rate. A moneylender should investigate carefully the actual interest rate charged to avoid a situation constituting usury under state laws.

EXAMPLE 1

A man borrowed $1,200 from a bank and agreed to make 12 equal monthly payments, the first installment being payable one month from the date of borrowing. The bank computed the monthly payments by the "add-on interest method" at the advertised interest rate of 6% per year. Find (a) the size of each payment, and (b) the actual annual interest rate charged by the bank.

(a) Under the add-on interest method, the simple interest computed at 6% per year is immediately added to the principal in computing the monthly payments.

$$I\text{ (interest)} = Pin = 1{,}200 \times 6\% \times 1 = \$72 \qquad (n = 1\text{ year})$$
$$S\text{ (amount)} = P + I = 1{,}200 + 72 = \$1{,}272$$
$$\text{Size of payment} = 1{,}272 \div 12 = \$106\text{ (per month)}$$

(b) Since the equal payments are paid in regular intervals, this loan payment plan constitutes an ordinary annuity problem.

$A_n = \$1{,}200$, $R = \$106$ (per month), $n = 12$ (monthly payments), $i = ?$ (per month)

Substituting the values in formula $A_n = Ra_{\overline{n}|i}$,

$$a_{\overline{n}|i} = \frac{A_n}{R} = \frac{1{,}200}{106} = 11.3208$$

By interpolation from Table 8, the actual interest rate is found to be 10.92% compounded monthly. The interpolation is shown below. (Write the larger numbers, which are in the column of values all known, on the top lines.)

	i	$a_{\overline{12}\rvert i}$	
	$\frac{7}{8}\%$	11.3445	(1)
	x	11.3208	(2)
	1%	11.2551	(3)

$$\frac{(2)-(3)}{(1)-(3)} \quad \frac{x - 1\%}{-\frac{1}{8}\%} = \frac{.0657}{.0894}$$

$$x = 1\% + (-\tfrac{1}{8}\%)\left(\frac{.0657}{.0894}\right) = .01 - \left(\frac{1}{800}\right)\left(\frac{657}{894}\right) = .0091, \text{ or}$$

$i = .91\%$ per month

The nominal rate $= i \times 12 = .91\% \times 12 = 10.92\%$ compounded monthly

NOTE:

1. If the periodic payments are computed by the annuity formula, the size of each monthly payment is only $103.28, or

$$R = \frac{1{,}200}{a_{\overline{12}\rvert 1/2\%}} = 1{,}200(.086066) = \$103.28$$

which is smaller than $106, the amount by the add-on interest method.

2. If the effective annual interest rate is desired, the formula $f = (1 + i)^m - 1$, as presented in Section 11.5, may be used. For the above example,

$$f = \left(1 + \frac{10.92\%}{12}\right)^{12} - 1 = (1 + .91\%)^{12} - 1$$

$$= 1.115 - 1 = .115 = 11.5\% \text{ (the effective rate).}$$

The factor $(1 + .91\%)^{12} = (1.0091)^{12}$ is computed by using logarithms:

$12(\log 1.0091) = 12(.0039342) = .0472104$

Find the antilog.

$(1.0091)^{12} = 1.115$

3. If the stated annual interest rate and the payment interval are constant, an amortization plan based on the add-on interest method with a *longer* period of repayment will give a *lower* actual interest rate charged. In the above example, the amortization plan of 1 year (or 12 monthly payments) gives the actual rate of .91% per month, or i is larger than $\frac{7}{8}\%$. However, with the same stated interest rate of 6% and monthly payment interval, the amortization plan of 8 years (or $8 \times 12 = 96$ monthly payments) will give a lower actual rate, or i is smaller than $\frac{7}{8}\%$. The 8-year plan is computed as follows:

$I = 1{,}200 \times 6\% \times 8 = \$576$
$S = 1{,}200 + 576 = \$1{,}776$
$R = 1{,}776 \div 96 = \$18.50$ per month

$$a_{\overline{n}\rvert i} = \frac{A_n}{R} = \frac{1{,}200}{18.50} = 64.8649$$

From Table 8: $\frac{3}{4}\% < i < \frac{7}{8}\%$ $\quad (n = 96)$

★15.3 AMORTIZATION OF CALLABLE BONDS

A *bond* is a type of promissory note issued by corporations or government units for the purpose of borrowing money from a group of creditors, rather than from an individual. Most bonds are redeemable on their maturity date. However, some bonds are redeemable prior to the maturity date if the issuer calls for them. Bonds with such provisions are known as *callable bonds*.

When a company redeems, or retires, a bond, the principal is often reduced by a multiple of the face value that appears on the bond. Since bonds are usually issued in fixed denominations, such as $100, $500, and $1,000, equal periodic payments, which include the interest and the principal for bond retirement, very often are impossible to achieve. The following example illustrates the method of equalizing each of the periodic payments, insofar as possible, in retiring a bonded debt.

EXAMPLE 1

A company issued $200,000 of bonds at 8% interest payable quarterly. The face value of each bond is $1,000. The bonds are to be retired within a $1\frac{1}{2}$-year period. Construct a schedule to equalize each quarterly payment, including interest payment and principal retirement.

There are six interest payment periods. The ideal size of the payment, interest and principal included, on each interest date is an equal figure, which may be computed by using the formula $A_n = Ra_{\overline{n}|i}$.

$A_n = \$200{,}000$, $n = 6$ (payments), $i = 8\%/4 = 2\%$ (per 3 months)

Substituting the values in the above formula,

$$200{,}000 = Ra_{\overline{6}|2\%}$$

$$R = 200{,}000\left(\frac{1}{a_{\overline{6}|2\%}}\right) = 200{,}000(.17852581) = \$35{,}705.16$$

When the ideal size of each payment is used as a guide [see Column (4)], the following schedule may be constructed:

Amortization Schedule for a Callable Bond Debt (Example 1)

(1) Period (3-Month Interval)	*(2) Outstanding Principal at Beginning of Each Period: (2) − (5)*	*(3) Interest Due at End of Period: (2) × 2%*	*(4) Ideal Payment on Principal: $35,705.16 − (3)*	*(5) Bond Value Retired, Multiple of $1,000* Closest to (4)*	*(6) Total Periodic Payment: (3) + (5)*
1	$200,000	$ 4,000	$ 31,705.16	$ 32,000	$ 36,000
2	168,000	3,360	32,345.16	32,000	35,360
3	136,000	2,720	32,985.16	33,000	35,720
4	103,000	2,060	33,645.16	34,000	36,060
5	69,000	1,380	34,325.16	34,000	35,380
6	35,000	700	35,005.16	35,000	35,700
Total		$14,220	$200,010.96	$200,000	$214,220

* The face value of each bond.

EXERCISE 15–3 REFERENCE: SECTIONS 15.2 and 15.3

1. Assume that a bank's stated nominal interest rate is 6%. Find the monthly payments that a bank requires on an $800 personal loan to be repaid in 16 equal monthly installments by (a) the add-on interest method and (b) the annuity formula method as presented in Section 15.1. Which one of the two methods gives higher monthly payments?
2. A man borrowed $1,500 from a finance company and agreed to repay the loan in 8 equal monthly payments, the first payment due in one month. Assume that the company's stated nominal interest rate is 15%. Find the monthly payments by (a) the add-on interest method and (b) the annuity formula method (see Section 15.1). Which one of the two methods requires higher payments?
3. Refer to Problem 1(a). What is the actual annual interest rate charged by the bank?
4. Refer to Problem 2(a). What is the actual annual interest rate charged by the finance company?
★5. A company issued $150,000 of bonds at 10% interest payable semiannually. The face value of each bond is $500. The bonds are to be retired within $2\frac{1}{2}$ years. Construct a schedule to equalize each semiannual payment, including interest payment and principal retirement.
★6. The J. P. Tylon Company issued $100,000 of bonds, each with a face value of $100. The bonds are to be retired within $1\frac{1}{2}$ years. Construct a schedule to equalize each quarterly payment, including 8% interest payable quarterly and principal retirement.

15.4 DEBT EXTINCTION BY SINKING FUND

In some cases, the principal of a long-term investment may be repaid on the maturity date, but the interest is paid periodically when it is due. Since a long-term debt is usually for a large amount, debtors often periodically deposit a sum of money in a fund, known as a *sinking fund*, in order to retire the principal on the maturity date. The periodic deposits need not be of equal amount nor be made at equal intervals of time. However, in this chapter, only examples of periodic deposits made at equal intervals and in equal amounts are considered. The deposits may be made either at the end of or at the beginning of each period. The deposits thus form an annuity problem, and *the amount of the annuity is the value of the principal of the debt on the maturity date*. The size of the periodic deposit can be obtained from the ordinary annuity formula $S_n = Rs_{\overline{n}|i}$ if the periodic deposit (R) is made at the end of each period.

Since the sinking fund is established for the purpose of paying the principal of the debt at maturity, the periodic interest on the debt should not be paid out of the fund. The interest rate on the debt may or may not equal the rate used for the sinking fund investment. The interest on the debt is called interest *expense*, whereas the interest from the sinking fund investment is called sinking fund interest *income*. It should be emphasized here that in the following discussion *the interest date is also regarded as the date for making the periodic deposit to the fund*. The debtor thus is making two payments on each payment date—one for interest on the debt and the other as a deposit in the fund.

EXAMPLE 1

A \$4,000 debt is to be repaid at the end of $1\frac{1}{2}$ years. Interest charged is 15% payable at the end of every 3 months. The debtor establishes a sinking fund that earns 12% interest compounded quarterly. (a) Find the interest payment on the debt for each 3-month period. (b) Construct a sinking fund accumulation schedule.

(a) The quarterly interest payment for the debt is

$4{,}000\ (15\%)(\frac{1}{4}) = \$150$

(b) The sinking fund accumulation schedule is constructed as follows.

First, the size of each quarterly deposit in the sinking fund should be found. Here, we have the problem of finding the periodic payment of an ordinary annuity when the amount is known.

$S_n = \$4{,}000$, $i = 12\%/4 = 3\%$ (per quarter), $n = 1\frac{1}{2} \times 4 = 6$ (quarterly periods), $R = ?$ (per quarter)

Thus,

$$R = S_n \cdot \frac{1}{s_{\overline{n|}i}} = 4{,}000 \cdot \frac{1}{s_{\overline{6|}3\%}} = 4{,}000(.1845975 - .03)$$

$$= 4{,}000(.1545975) = \$618.39 \quad \text{(Table 9)}$$

Sinking Fund Accumulation Schedule (Example 1)

(1) At End of Period (3-Month Interval)	*(2) Interest Income on Sinking Fund 3% × (5)**	*(3) Periodic Deposit in Fund*	*(4) Periodic Increase in Fund: (2) + (3)*	*(5) Sinking Fund Accumulated: (4) + (5)**	*(6) Book Value: \$4,000 − (5)*
1	. . .	\$ 618.39	\$ 618.39	\$ 618.39	\$3,381.61
2	\$ 18.55	618.39	636.94	1,255.33	2,744.67
3	37.66	618.39	656.05	1,911.38	2,088.62
4	57.34	618.39	675.73	2,587.11	1,412.89
5	77.61	618.39	696.00	3,283.11	716.89
6	98.49	618.40**	716.89	4,000.00	. . .
Total	\$289.65	\$3,710.35	\$4,000.00		

* Of the previous period. For example, 18.55 = 618.39(3%); and 37.66 = 1,255.33(3%).
** Correction for 1¢ discrepancy.

The information in the columns of the sinking fund schedule can be obtained directly, as illustrated in the following example.

EXAMPLE 2 Refer to Example 1. Find (a) the amount in the sinking fund at the end of the fourth period, (b) the sinking fund interest income for the fifth payment period, and (c) the book value of the debt at the end of the fourth period, without constructing a schedule.

(a) The amount in the sinking fund at the end of the fourth period.

It is the amount of an annuity of $618.39 payable quarterly at 12% compounded quarterly for four periods.

$R = 618.39, i = 3\%, n = 4$

$S_4 = 618.39s_{\overline{4}|3\%} = 618.39(4.183627) = \$2{,}587.11$

(b) The sinking fund interest income for the fifth payment period.

The principal at the beginning of the fifth payment period is the amount in the sinking fund at the end of the fourth period, $2,587.11.

$I = 2{,}587.11(3\%) = \$77.61$

(c) The book value of the debt at the end of the fourth period.

The *book value* is the net obligation, which equals the original debt less the accumulated amount in the fund at that time.

$4{,}000 - 2{,}587.11 = \$1{,}412.89$

EXAMPLE 3 Refer to Example 1. Assume that the debt bears 12% interest. What is the total cost to the debtor at the end of every 3 months?

The periodic (quarterly) interest for the debt is $4{,}000(12\%)(\frac{1}{4}) = \$120$.

The periodic deposit in the sinking fund is the same as that in Example 1, $618.39, since the interest rate on the debt does not affect the interest rate of the sinking fund.

The total cost $= 618.39 + 120.00 = \$738.39$

Note that the cost is the same as the size of the periodic payment by the amortization method in Example 3, page 458.

In Example 1, the rate of interest is assumed to be unchanged throughout the three-year period. However, in practice, the interest rate on the sinking fund investment does sometimes change. When it changes, the periodic deposits are adjusted for the difference between the scheduled interest income and the actual interest income.

EXAMPLE 4 In Example 1 assume that the interest rate on the sinking fund was 3% per 3-month period during the first and second periods, $3\frac{1}{2}\%$ during the third and fourth periods, and $2\frac{1}{2}\%$ during the fifth and sixth periods. Construct a sinking fund accumulation schedule as a guide for the periodic deposits.

Adjusted Periodic Deposits Schedule (Example 4)

(1) At End of Period (3 Months)	*(2) Scheduled Interest Income (See Example 1*	*(3) Actual Interest Income (See Below)*	*(4) Interest Discrepancy: (2) − (3)*	*(5) Adjusted Deposit Schedule: $618.39 + (4)*	*(6) Periodic Increase in Fund: (3) + (5)*
1	...	...	...	$ 618.39	$ 618.39
2	$ 18.55	$ 18.55	...	618.39	636.94
3	37.66	43.94	−6.28	612.11	656.05
4	57.34	66.90	−9.56	608.83	675.73
5	77.61	64.68	12.93	631.32	696.00
6	98.49	82.08	16.41	634.81*	716.89
Total	$289.65	$276.15	13.50	$3,723.85	$4,000.00

* Corrected for 1¢ discrepancy.

The interest in Column (3) is based on the following expression:

Actual interest income = Sinking fund accumulated × Interest rate
[See Column (5) of Example 1]

Thus, the interest for each period is computed as follows:

$$
\begin{aligned}
\text{First period} &= 0(3\%) = 0\\
\text{Second period} &= 618.39(3\%) = \$18.55\\
\text{Third period} &= 1{,}255.33(3\tfrac{1}{2}\%) = \$43.94\\
\text{Fourth period} &= 1{,}911.38(3\tfrac{1}{2}\%) = \$66.90\\
\text{Fifth period} &= 2{,}587.11(2\tfrac{1}{2}\%) = \$64.68\\
\text{Sixth period} &= 3{,}283.11(2\tfrac{1}{2}\%) = \$82.08
\end{aligned}
$$

Notice that the values in Column (6), periodic increase in fund, of the above schedule are the same as the values in Column (4) of the sinking fund accumulation schedule of Example 1. The sum of the periodic increases in the fund equals the sum of the actual interest income plus the sum of the adjusted (actual) deposits: 276.15 + 3,723.85 = $4,000.

EXERCISE 15–4 REFERENCE: SECTION 15.4

A. In Problems 1–6, find (a) the interest payment on the debt for each interest period, (b) the size of deposits to the sinking fund, (c) the amount in the sinking fund at the end of the nth period, (d) the book value of the debt at the end of the nth period, and (e) the sinking fund interest income for the $(n + 1)$th payment period. Do not construct a sinking fund accumulation schedule in finding your answers.

	Debt	Interest Rate on the Debt	Number of Deposits in Sinking Fund	Interest Rate on Sinking Fund	nth Period
1.	$ 6,000	24%, monthly	20, monthly	18%, monthly	6th
2.	4,000	8%, annually	15, annually	4%, annually	12th
3.	10,000	6%, semiannually	8, semiannually	5%, semiannually	5th
4.	30,000	12%, monthly	40, monthly	5%, monthly	34th
5.	450	7%, annually	5, annually	10%, annually	3rd
6.	800	6%, quarterly	10, quarterly	6%, quarterly	7th

B. Statement problems:

7. A $5,000 debt is to be repaid at the end of one year. The debtor establishes a sinking fund that earns 8% interest compounded quarterly. Construct a sinking fund accumulation schedule.
8. A man borrows $8,000 for $2\frac{1}{2}$ years. The interest rate on the loan is 12% payable at the end of each $\frac{1}{2}$ year. He makes semiannual deposits in a sinking fund earning 8% interest compounded semiannually. Find the semiannual interest payment on the loan and construct a sinking fund accumulation schedule.
9. Refer to Problem 7. Assume that the interest rate on the sinking fund was 8% compounded quarterly during the first $\frac{1}{2}$ year and 12% compounded quarterly during the second $\frac{1}{2}$ year. Construct a sinking fund accumulation schedule as a guide for the periodic deposits.
10. Refer to Problem 8. Assume that the interest rate (compounded semiannually) on the sinking fund was 8% during the first $1\frac{1}{2}$ years and 10% during the last one year. Construct a sinking fund accumulation schedule as a guide for the periodic deposits.

★15.5 COMPUTING EXAMPLES BY CALCULATORS AND COMPUTERS

The examples presented in the previous sections are basically ordinary annuity problems. Students should review Section 13.8 for computing the ordinary annuity formulas in Chapter 13 by calculators and computers. The following examples are selected only for those problems in this chapter requiring special BASIC programs.

A. Constructing an Amortization Schedule

(1) ALL PERIODIC PAYMENTS ARE EQUAL

The method of finding the size of each periodic payment, R, when the present value is known was presented in Section 13.8C(1).

EXAMPLE 1

Compute Example 3, Section 15.1:

A_n (debt to be amortized) = A = \$4,000, i = 3% (per quarter), n = 6 (quarters)

COMPUTER WITH BASIC

BASIC Program (LIST)

```
5 REM—AMORTIZATION SCHEDULE
10 INPUT "A ? ";A
20 INPUT "I ? ";I
30 INPUT "N ? ";N
40 R = A*I/(1 – (1 + I)^( – N))
45 PRINT "(1)PERIOD","(2) O.P.","(3)INTEREST","(4)PAYMENT", "(5) RED."
50 FOR X = 1 TO N
60 A = A – D
70 E = A*I
80 D = R – E
90 PRINT X,A,E,R,D
100 NEXT X
110 END
```

Computer Display (RUN)

```
A ? 4000
I ? .03
N ? 6
```

(1)PERIOD	(2) O.P.	(3)INTEREST	(4)PAYMENT	(5) RED.
1	4000	120	738.390001	618.390001
2	3381.61	101.4483	738.390001	636.941701
3	2744.6683	82.340049	738.390001	656.049951
4	2088.61835	62.6585505	738.390001	675.73145
5	1412.8869	42.3866069	738.390001	696.003394
6	716.883503	21.5065051	738.390001	716.883496

Note: See the amortization schedule on page 458 for detailed interpretation of the above computer display.

(2) ALL PERIODIC PAYMENTS EXCEPT THE FINAL PAYMENT ARE EQUAL

The method of finding the term, n, when the present value is known was presented in Section 13.8E(2).

EXAMPLE 2 Compute Example 4, Section 15.1:

A_n (debt to be amortized) = A = \$6,000, i = 1% (per month), R = \$1,000 (per month)

COMPUTER WITH BASIC

BASIC Program (LIST)

```
5 REM—AMORTIZATION SCHEDULE
10 INPUT "A ? ";A
20 INPUT "I ? ";I
30 INPUT "R ? ";R
40 N = – ( LOG (1 – A*I/R)/ LOG (1 + I))
45 PRINT "(1)PERIOD","(2) O.P.","(3)INTEREST","(4)PAYMENT", "(5) RED."
50 FOR X = 1 TO (N + 1)
60 A = A – D
```

```
70 E = A*I
80 D = R - E
90 PRINT X,A,E,R,D
100 NEXT X
110 END
```

Computer Display (RUN)

```
A ? 6000
I ? .01
R ? 1000
```

(1)PERIOD	(2) O.P.	(3)INTEREST	(4)PAYMENT	(5) RED.
1	6000	60	1000	940
2	5060	50.6	1000	949.4
3	4110.6	41.106	1000	958.894
4	3151.706	31.51706	1000	968.48294
5	2183.22306	21.8322306	1000	978.16777
6	1205.05529	12.0505529	1000	987.949447
7	217.105844	2.17105844	1000	997.828942

Note: 1. For the 7th period:

$$\text{Final payment} = \text{Outstanding principal} + \text{Interest}$$
$$= 217.11 + 2.17 = 219.28$$

which is not the equal payment of 1,000 as in the computer display.

2. See the amortization schedule on page 461 for a detailed interpretation of the above computer display.

B. Constructing a Sinking Fund Accumulation Schedule

The method of finding the size of each periodic payment, R, when the amount is known was presented in Section 13.8C(2).

EXAMPLE 3 Compute Example 1, Section 15.4:

S_n (fund to be accumulated) = S1 = \$4,000, $i = 3\%$ (per quarter), $n = 6$ (quarters)

COMPUTER WITH BASIC

BASIC Program (LIST)

```
5 REM—SINKING FUND ACCUMULATION SCHEDULE
10 INPUT "S1 ?  ";S1
20 INPUT "I ?  ";I
30 INPUT "N ?  ";N
40 R = S1*I/((1 + I)^N - 1)
45 PRINT "(1)PERIOD","(2)INTEREST","(3)DEPOSIT","(4)INCREASE", "(5)FUND","(6)BOOK"
50 FOR X = 1 TO N
65 E = F*I
70 G = E + R
80 F = F + G
85 H = S1 - F
90 PRINT X,E,R,G,F,H
100 NEXT X
110 END
```

Computer Display (RUN)

S1 ? 4000
I ? .03
N ? 6

(1)PERIOD	(2)INTEREST	(3)DEPOSIT	(4)INCREASE	(5)FUND	(6)BOOK
1	0	618.39	618.39	618.39	3381.61
2	18.5517	618.39	636.9417	1255.3317	2744.6683
3	37.659951	618.39	656.049951	1911.38165	2088.61835
4	57.3414496	618.39	675.731449	2587.1131	1412.8869
5	77.6133931	618.39	696.003393	3283.11649	716.883507
6	98.4934948	618.39	716.883495	3999.99999	1.23977661E – 05

Note: See the sinking fund accumulation schedule on page 468 for a detailed interpretation of the above computer display.

EXERCISE 15–5 REVIEW OF CHAPTER 15

1. Patricia Sue bought a $90,000 store and made a down payment of $60,000. The balance will be paid by equal quarterly payments for six years with the first payment due three months from the date of purchase. (a) Find the size of the quarterly payments if the interest rate is 18% compounded quarterly. (b) What is the outstanding principal after the tenth payment is made?
2. A debt of $6,000 is to be amortized by equal payments at the end of each month for five years. (a) If the interest charged is 24% compounded monthly, what is the size of each monthly payment? (b) What is the outstanding principal after the 35th payment is made?
3. Reynolds borrowed $3,000. He agreed to discharge the loan together with the interest by making four equal monthly payments, with the first payment to be made one month from the date of borrowing. Assume that the interest charged is 12% compounded monthly. Construct an amortization schedule.
4. A debt of $7,000 is to be amortized in five equal semiannual payments. Construct an amortization schedule assuming 6% interest compounded semiannually for the debt.
5. A loan of $10,000 is to be discharged by paying $2,000 at the end of every $\frac{1}{2}$ year. The interest rate is 10% compounded semiannually. Construct an amortization schedule.
6. A debt of $6,000 is to be amortized with payments of $1,500 at the end of every 3 months. The interest rate is 8% compounded quarterly. Construct an amortization schedule.
7. White bought a car for $15,000 and made a down payment of $3,000. The balance is to be amortized with payments of $100 at the end of each month. The interest rate is 6% compounded monthly. What is the outstanding principal after the 55th payment?
8. A debt of $30,000 is to be repaid by making a $1,500 payment at the end of each quarter. The interest rate is 8% compounded quarterly. What is the outstanding principal after the 12th payment?

9. In Problem 7, what are the interest and the principal included in the 56th monthly payment?
10. In Problem 8, find the interest and the principal included in the 13th quarterly payment.
11. Mrs. Booker borrowed \$1,000 from a finance company. She agreed to repay the loan by making 10 equal monthly payments, the first installment being payable in one month from the date of borrowing. The company computed the monthly payments by the add-on interest method at 6% per year. Find (a) the size of each payment, and (b) the actual annual interest rate charged by the company.
12. Mrs. Adams borrowed \$900 from a bank at the stated nominal interest rate of 12% per year. The bank requires that the loan must be repaid in 18 equal monthly installments based on the add-on interest method, the first payment being due in one month. What are (a) the size of each payment, and (b) the actual annual interest rate charged by the bank?
★13. Johnson & Co. issued \$300,000 of bonds each with a face value of \$1,000. The bonds are to be retired at the end of every year over a five-year period. Construct an amortization schedule to equalize each annual payment, including 10% interest payable annually and the retirement of the principal.
★14. T. H. White & Co. issued \$400,000 of 4% bonds. The interest is payable semiannually and the face value of each bond is \$500. The bonds are to be retired at the end of every six months over a two-year period. Construct an amortization schedule to equalize the semiannual payment, including the interest and the principal.
15. A debt of \$5,000 is to be repaid at the end of $1\frac{1}{4}$ years under the sinking fund plan with the fund earning 8% interest compounded quarterly. The interest rate on the debt is 12% payable quarterly. (a) Find the value of each interest payment on the debt, and (b) construct a sinking fund schedule.
16. A \$7,000 loan will be repaid at the end of four years by a sinking fund which earns 6% compounded annually. The interest on the loan is payable annually at 9%. (a) Find the interest payment on the loan for each year, and (b) construct a sinking fund schedule.
17. In Problem 15, assume that the debt bears 8% interest compounded quarterly. (a) What is the total of the interest payment and the sinking fund deposit that must be made by the debtor at the end of every 3 months? (b) If the debt is to be amortized by equal quarterly payments at 8% compounded quarterly, what is the size of each payment?
18. In Problem 16, assume that the interest on the loan is 6% payable annually. (a) What is the total payment, including the interest on the loan and the deposit in the sinking fund, made by the borrower at the end of every year? (b) If the loan is to be amortized by equal annual payments at 6% compounded annually, what is the size of each payment?
19. In Problem 15, assume that the interest rate on the sinking fund was 2% per quarter during the first $\frac{1}{2}$ year, 3% per quarter during the second $\frac{1}{2}$ year, and 4% for the last quarter of the borrowing time. Construct a sinking fund accumulation schedule.

20. In Problem 16, assume that the interest rate on the sinking fund was 6% for the first year, 5% for the second year, and 7% for the remaining two years during the loan period. Construct a sinking fund accumulation schedule.
21. A $15,000 debt is to be discharged at the end of ten years by a sinking fund which is invested at 18% compounded quarterly. Find (a) the amount in the sinking fund and the book value of the debt at the end of six years, and (b) the sinking fund interest income for the first quarter of the seventh year.
22. Sumio borrowed $5,000 and agreed to repay the principal at the end of three years but to pay interest periodically. He established a sinking fund which earns 12% compounded monthly. Find (a) the amount in the sinking fund and the book value of the debt at the end of two years, and (b) the sinking fund interest income for the first month of the third year.

16 INVESTMENT IN BONDS

The topics of investment in bonds involving compound interest and ordinary annuity computations are presented in this chapter. The topics are: introduction to stocks and bonds (Section 16.1), computing the purchase price of a bond (Section 16.2), bond premium and discount (Section 16.3), approximate yield rate on bond investment (Section 16.4), bond tables (16.5), annuity bonds and serial bonds (Section 16.6). In addition, the methods of computing the chapter's formulas by calculators and computers are explained (Section 16.7).

16.1 STOCKS AND BONDS

Stocks and bonds are frequently purchased and sold by investors in an investment market to make profits. *Stock*, also called *capital stock*, represents ownership in a corporation and is divided into shares. Those who purchase a share of stock acquire not only a share of the ownership of the corporation but also the right to receive income in the form of dividends. Unlike stocks, *bonds* are generally issued by corporations or governmental units for the purpose of *borrowing* funds from a group of creditors. Those who purchase bonds expect the issuing party to repay the principal on a future date, as well as to provide a periodic income in the form of interest during the life of the investment.

The prices of both stocks and bonds fluctuate frequently on the investment market, although the price of bonds fluctuates within a much smaller range than that of stocks. An investor should have the ability to investigate the possibility of making a fair profit and the safety of such investments. An extensive study of stocks and bonds requires special volumes and is beyond the scope of this text. The following studies are limited to the mathematical operations peculiar to the investment in bonds.

Note that an investor who purchases or sells stocks through a broker usually has to pay a commission or brokerage fee for the broker's services. On the New York Stock Exchange, for example, the charges for the commissions and fees are based on the market value of each stock, but the rate is different for 100-share lots than for a lot consisting of less than 100 shares. The method of computing the charges is basically the same as the method of computing the commissions and fees for buying and selling merchandise presented in Section 7.5.

16.2 COMPUTING THE PURCHASE PRICE OF A BOND

Certain terms frequently used in computing various problems concerning the investment in bonds are explained below:

1. *Face value* or *par value*. The value stated on the bond, usually called the denomination, such as $1,000.
2. *Redemption value*. The value that the issuing party pays to the bondholder when the bond is surrendered. A bond is usually redeemed at the maturity date and is paid according to the face value, or is said to be redeemable at par. However, some bonds may be called prior to the date of maturity. The redemption values of some bonds may also be set above par to make the bonds more attractive.
3. *Bond rate* or *contract rate*. The interest rate stated on the bond. This rate is used as a basis for computing the interest payment.
4. *Yield rate* or *investor's rate*. The actual interest rate that is expected by the purchaser of the bond. The yield rate is usually the prevailing rate on the investment market when the bond is purchased and is often not equal to the bond rate.
5. *Interest dates*. The interest on most bonds is payable semiannually on the first day of the payable month. Sometimes the interest payment dates are indicated by the initial letters of the months. Thus, if the interest is payable semiannually on January 1 and July 1, the dates may be abbreviated as J-J; if on February 1 and August 1, the initials F-A may be used; and so on.
6. *Purchase price* or *flat price*. The purchase price is computed at the yield rate. The purchase price is also the value quoted on the bond market plus accrued interest on the bond, if any. Thus, the quoted price is also called the "and interest" price.
7. *Bond abbreviations*. The name of the issuing party, the bond rate, and the redemption date of a bond are usually abbreviated in publications. Thus, Chryslr 10.4 s 99 means that the bond was issued by Chrysler Corporation, it bears 10.4% interest payable semiannually, and the date of maturity is 1999.

An investor may purchase bonds on the interest payment dates or between the interest payment dates. The methods of computing the purchase prices at different times are presented below.

A. Purchase Price on Interest Date

A bond investor has acquired two items:

1. The redemption value, which will be realized at a future date; that is, at the redemption or maturity date.
2. The periodic interest payment according to the interest rate contracted on the bond.

Therefore, the purchase price of a bond is the sum of the present values of the two items above. The first item, the redemption value, is computed by use of the compound discount formula $P = S(1 + i)^{-n}$, where P is the present value of the redemption value, S is the redemption value, i is the yield rate (or investor's interest rate), and n is the number of interest periods between the date of purchase and the date of redemption.

The second item, the periodic interest payment, is computed by use of the formula $A_n = Ra_{\overline{n}|i}$, where A_n = the present value of all interest payments, n and i mean the same as n and i in the first item above, and R = the periodic interest payment according to the bond contract.

The interest conversion period for the yield rate (investor's rate) is assumed to coincide with the interest payment period for the bond. When the purchase is made on an interest date, the bond interest payment on that date is not included in the purchase price. In summary,

$$\textbf{Purchase price} = P + A_n, \quad \text{or}$$
$$= S(1 + i)^{-n} + Ra_{\overline{n}|i} \qquad \textbf{(16–1)}$$

EXAMPLE 1

A $1,000, 14% bond will be redeemed on March 1, 2007. Interest is payable semiannually on March 1 and September 1. Find the purchase price of the bond if the date of purchase is March 1, 1991, the yield rate is 12% compounded semiannually, and the bond is redeemable (a) at par, and (b) at 105%.

(a) The present value of the redemption value is computed as follows:

The redemption value is at par, $1,000, which is due in 16 years (from March 1, 1991, to March 1, 2007).

$S = \$1{,}000$, $i = 12\%/2 = 6\%$ (yield rate per six months), $n = 16 \times 2 = 32$ (semiannual interest periods)

$$P = 1{,}000(1 + 6\%)^{-32}$$
$$= 1{,}000(.154957)$$
$$= \$154.96$$

The present value of the interest payments is computed as follows:

The periodic interest payment according to the bond (or contract) rate is

$R = 1{,}000(14\%)(\tfrac{1}{2}) = \$70$ (per six months)

Thus, $A_n = 70a_{\overline{32}|6\%} = 70(14.0840) = \$985.88$

The purchase price is

$P + A_n = 154.96 + 985.88 = \$1{,}140.84$

The solution to Example 1 may be diagrammed as follows:

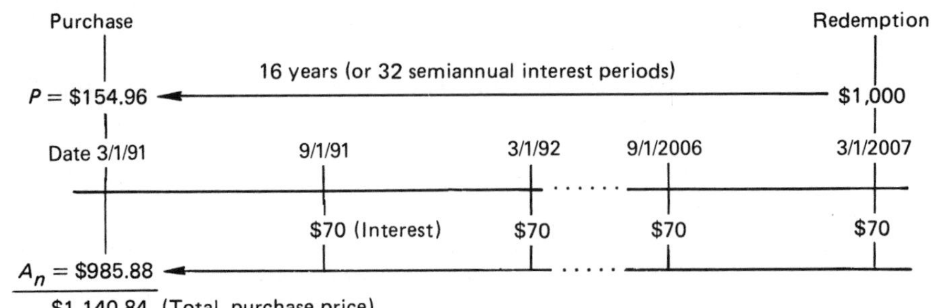

(b) The present value of the redemption value is computed as follows:

The redemption value is 105% of the face value, or $S = 1{,}000(105\%) = \$1{,}050$. The other values are the same as above.

$P = 1{,}050(1 + 6\%)^{-32} = 1{,}050(.154957) = \$162.70$

The present value of the interest payments is also the same as above. Thus, the purchase price is

$162.70 + 985.88 = \$1{,}148.58$

EXAMPLE 2 The investor's interest rate is 12% compounded semiannually. Find the purchase price of a $1,500 bond with 10% interest payable semiannually, and redeemable in six years (a) at par, and (b) at 98%.

(a) $S = \$1{,}500$ (at par), $i = 12\%/2 = 6\%$ (investor's rate per six months), $n = 6 \times 2 = 12$ (semiannual periods), $R = 1{,}500(10\%)(\frac{1}{2}) = \$75$

$$\begin{aligned}\text{The purchase price} &= 1{,}500(1 + 6\%)^{-12} + 75a_{\overline{12}|6\%}\\ &= 1{,}500(.496969) + 75(8.3838)\\ &= 745.45 + 628.79\\ &= \$1{,}374.24\end{aligned}$$

(b) $S = 1{,}500(98\%) = \$1{,}470$

$$\begin{aligned}\text{The purchase price} &= 1{,}470(1 + 6\%)^{-12} + 75a_{\overline{12}|6\%}\\ &= 1{,}470(.496969) + 75(8.3838)\\ &= 730.54 + 628.79\\ &= \$1{,}359.33\end{aligned}$$

EXERCISE 16–1 REFERENCE: SECTION 16.2A

A. Find the purchase price of the bond in each of the following problems:

	Par Value	*Redemption Value*	*Bond Rate*	*Bond Interest Dates*	*Time Before Redemption*	*Yield (Investor's) Rate, Compounded Semiannually*
1.	$ 500	at par	16%	J-J	5 years	15%
2.	3,000	110%	4%	F-A	$4\frac{1}{2}$ years	3%
3.	2,000	95%	5%	M-S	6 years	7%
4.	4,000	at par	13%	A-O	8 years	16%

	Par Value	*Redemption Value*	*Bond Rate*	*Bond Interest Dates*	*Time Before Redemption*	*Yield (Investor's) Rate, Compounded Semiannually*
5.	600	105%	7%	M-N	$7\frac{1}{2}$ years	4%
6.	5,000	98%	6%	J-D	10 years	5%
7.	6,000	at par	4%	A-O	12 years	6%
8.	400	at par	5%	M-N	7 years	4%

B. Statement problems:

9. A $10,000, 14% bond will be redeemed on January 1, 2009. Interest is payable semiannually on January 1 and July 1. Find the purchase price of the bond if the date of purchase is July 1, 1991, the yield rate is 12% compounded semiannually, and the bond is redeemable (a) at par, and (b) at 108%.
10. Find the purchase price of a $1,000, 3% bond, if it is bought to yield 4% compounded semiannually. The bond interest is payable semiannually, and the bond is redeemable at par in (a) 3 years, (b) 15 years.
11. The investor's interest rate is 5% compounded semiannually. Find the purchase price of a $2,000 bond with 3% interest payable semiannually, and redeemable at par in (a) 4 years, and (b) 9 years.
12. An $8,000, 6% bond will be redeemed on April 1, 1999. Interest is payable semiannually on April 1 and October 1. Find the purchase price of the bond if the date of purchase is April 1, 1992, the yield rate is $5\frac{1}{2}$% compounded semiannually, and the bond is redeemable (a) at par, and (b) at 95%.

B. Purchase Price Between Interest Dates

When a bond is purchased between interest dates, the purchase price on the interest date that immediately precedes the purchase date is first computed. The interest at the yield rate for the period between the interest date and the purchase date is then added to obtain the purchase price on the purchase date. *Hereafter, unless otherwise specified, the bond is assumed to be redeemable at par, the face value.* This assumption is made in order to simplify the computation and to meet most practical situations.

EXAMPLE 3

Refer to Example 1(a). If the bond is bought on April 30, 1991, what is the purchase price of the bond?

The purchase price on the interest date, March 1, 1991, which immediately precedes the purchase date, is $1,140.84. See the solution for Example 1(a).

The interest at the yield rate for the period between the interest date (March 1, 1991) and the purchase date (April 30, 1991) is computed as follows:

The period is 60 days, yield rate is 12%, and the principal for computing the interest is $1,140.84. Thus,

$I = 1{,}140.84(12\%)(\frac{60}{360}) = \$22.82$

The purchase price on April 30, 1991, is

$1{,}140.84 + 22.82 = \$1{,}163.66$

On the other hand, the purchase price is the bondholder's selling price. The price should include the incurred, yet not paid, bond interest, called *accrued interest*, for the period from March 1, 1991, to the purchase date (or for 60 days). The accrued interest at the bond rate is computed as follows:

$1{,}000(14\%)(\frac{60}{360}) = \$23.33$

The accrued interest is the seller's income, since he or she owns the bond during the 60 days. Thus, the selling price of $1,163.66 may be considered to include two items: (1) the accrued interest at the bond rate, $23.33, and (2) the net price for the bond, $1,140.33 (or $1,163.66 − $23.33).

The purchase price (or the bondholder's selling price) of $1,163.66 is frequently referred to by a bond house as the *flat price*, and the net price of the bond, $1,140.33, without including the accrued interest, as the *quoted price*.

The above illustration is diagrammed as follows:

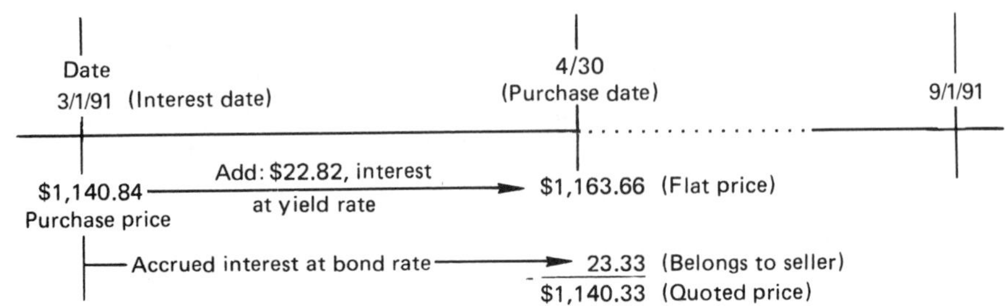

Thus, in general,

Flat price (purchase price) = Quoted price + Accrued interest on a bond

However, if the bond is purchased on an interest date, there is no accrued interest. Thus,

Flat price (purchase price on the interest date) = Quoted price

EXAMPLE 4 A $1,000, 12% bond, redeemable in six years and two months, interest payable semiannually, is bought to yield 13% compounded semiannually. What are (a) the purchase price, (b) the accrued interest on the bond, and (c) the quoted price?

(a) The interest date immediately preceding the purchase date is six years and six months (or 13 semiannual periods) before redemption. The purchase price on the interest date is computed as follows:

$$\text{Yield rate } (i) = 13\%/2 = 6\tfrac{1}{2}\% \text{ (per six months)}$$
$$R = 1{,}000 \times 12\% \times \tfrac{1}{2} = \$60$$
$$n = 6\tfrac{1}{2} \times 2 = 13 \text{ (semiannual periods)}$$

$$\begin{aligned}\text{The purchase price} &= 1{,}000(1 + 6\tfrac{1}{2}\%)^{-13} + 60\, a_{\overline{13}|6\,1/2\%} \\ &= 1{,}000(.441017) + 60(8.5997) \\ &= 441.017 + 515.982 \\ &= 956.999, \quad \text{rounded to} \quad \$957.00\end{aligned}$$

For the four months after the last interest date, the interest on the purchase price based on the yield rate is

$957.00(13\%)(\frac{4}{12}) = \$41.47$

The purchase price on the purchase date, six years and two months before redemption, is

957.00 + 41.47 = \$998.47

(b) According to the bond contract, the accrued interest for the four-month period is

$1{,}000(12\%)(\frac{4}{12}) = \$40$

(c) The quoted price = the purchase price − the accrued interest on the bond =

998.47 − 40 = \$958.47

NOTE: Quoted prices are usually listed in bond tables. A sample bond table is given on page 496. The bond table values are computed by using the compound interest method throughout. However, the difference between the results obtained by using the simple interest method and the compound interest method is small. When the compound interest method is used, the answer to Example 4(c) is \$958.46, a 1¢ difference (or 958.47 − 958.46), and is computed as follows:

$n = 6$ years and two months $= 6\frac{2}{12}$ years $= 6\frac{2}{12} \times 2 = 12\frac{1}{3}$ semiannual interest periods

$$\text{Purchase price} = 1{,}000(1 + 6\tfrac{1}{2}\%)^{-12\ 1/3} + 60a_{\overline{12\ 1/3}|6\ 1/2\%}$$

$$= 1{,}000(.4599262) + 60\left(\frac{1 - (1 + 6\frac{1}{2}\%)^{-12\ 1/3}}{6\frac{1}{2}\%}\right)$$

$$= 459.9262 + 60\left(\frac{1 - .4599262}{.065}\right)$$

$$= 459.9262 + 498.52966$$

$$= 958.45586, \text{ or rounded to } 958.46 \quad \text{(Tables 5A, 6, and 8)}$$

EXAMPLE 5 On February 9, 1992, a man acquired \$10,000 worth of $13\frac{1}{2}\%$ bonds, which were quoted on the market on that date at $92\frac{1}{4}\%$. Interest on the bonds was payable on May 1 and November 1. Find (a) the quoted price, (b) the accrued interest on the bonds, and (c) the purchase price (or flat price).

(a) The quoted price is at $92\frac{1}{4}\%$ of the face value. Thus,

$$\begin{aligned}\text{the quoted price} &= 10{,}000(92\tfrac{1}{4}\%)\\ &= 10{,}000(.9225)\\ &= \$9{,}225\end{aligned}$$

(b) The accrued interest on the bonds at the bond rate for the period from November 1, 1991, to February 9, 1992, or 100 days (during which time the seller owns the bonds), is computed as follows:

$10{,}000(13\frac{1}{2}\%)(\frac{100}{360}) = \$375$

(c) The purchase price = the quoted price + the accrued interest
= 9,225 + 375 = \$9,600

EXERCISE 16–2 REFERENCE: SECTION 16.2B

A. In each of the following problems, find (a) the purchase price, (b) the accrued interest on the bond, and (c) the quoted price:

	Par Value	*Bond Rate Payable Semiannually*	*Time Before Redemption*	*Yield Rate, Compounded Semiannually*
1.	$ 4,000	6%	5 years and 1 month	5%
2.	2,000	14%	4 years and 9 months	13%
3.	5,000	5%	6 years and 4 months	7%
4.	6,000	3%	8 years and 2 months	6%
5.	900	13%	7 years and 5 months	12%
6.	700	10%	10 years and 4 months	9%
7.	10,000	13%	12 years and 3 months	15%
8.	25,000	7%	3 years and 5 months	5%

B. Statement problems:

9. A $3,000, 5% bond, redeemable in five years and three months, interest payable semiannually, is bought to yield 6% compounded semiannually. What are (a) the purchase price, and (b) the quoted price?
10. A $4,000, 12% bond will be redeemed on May 1, 2001. Interest is payable semiannually on May 1 and November 1. Find the purchase price of the bond if the date of purchase is July 1, 1991, and the yield rate is 10% compounded semiannually.
11. A $7,000, 6% bond, interest payable semiannually on March 1 and September 1, redeemable on March 1, 1996, is bought to yield 4% compounded semiannually on November 15, 1992. Find the purchase price.
12. Refer to Problem 11. What would be the purchase price of the bond if the yield rate were 7% compounded semiannually?
13. On May 31, a man purchased a $2,500 bond. The interest rate on the bond was 13% payable semiannually on April 1 and October 1. The bond was quoted on the market at 80%. Find (a) the quoted price, (b) the accrued interest, and (c) the purchase price of the bond.
14. Refer to Problem 13. If the bond were quoted on the market on May 31 at 110%, what are the new answers to (a), (b), and (c)?

16.3 BOND PREMIUM AND DISCOUNT

A. General Computation

In Example 1(a) of Section 16.2, it was found that a $1,000, 14% bond, interest payable semiannually, redeemable on March 1, 2007, was sold on March 1, 1991 at $1,140.84 to give the purchaser a yield rate of 12% compounded semiannually. The purchase price is $140.84 larger than the face value (which is now assumed to be equal to the redemption value) as shown below:

1,140.84 − 1,000 = $140.84 (premium)

When the purchase price of a bond is larger than its face value, the excess amount is called the *premium* on the bond. In the above example, the premium is $140.84. Premium on a bond is paid by the investor when the bond interest rate exceeds the yield rate. The premium can be recovered periodically through bond interest payments, which are greater than the interest based on the yield rate. The excess income of the purchaser in the above example is computed as follows:

Periodic bond interest payment
= bond face value × bond interest rate per interest period
= 1,000(14%)($\frac{1}{2}$) = \$70

Periodic bond interest based on yield rate (expected interest income of bond purchaser)
= bond face value × yield rate per interest period
= 1,000(12%)($\frac{1}{2}$) = \$60

The excess income per interest period = 70 − 60 = \$10

There are 32 interest payments from March 1, 1991, to March 1, 2007, or 32 excess payments of \$10 each. The present value of 32 semiannual payments of \$10 each at 12% compounded semiannually (yield rate) is computed by the use of the formula

$A_n = Ra_{\overline{n}|i}$, where R = \$10 (the excess income)
$i = 12\%/2 = 6\%$
n = 32 (payments)

The premium on the bond = $A_{32} = 10a_{\overline{32}|6\%}$
= 10(14.0840) = \$140.84

Thus, *the premium on a bond is the present value of an annuity that is formed by the periodic excess income.*

When the bond face value and the premium are known, the purchase price may be obtained as follows:

Purchase price = Face value + Premium = 1,000 + 140.84 = \$1,140.84

On the other hand, it was found that a \$1,500, 10% bond, interest payable semiannually, redeemable in six years, was sold at \$1,374.24 to give the purchaser a yield rate of 12% compounded semiannually. [See Example 2(a) in Section 16.2.] When the purchase price is smaller than the face value, the difference is called the *discount* on the bond. A bond is purchased at a discount when the bond interest rate is smaller than the yield rate. The deficit interest for the above example is computed as follows:

Periodic bond interest payment
= bond face value × bond interest rate per interest period
= 1,500(10%)($\frac{1}{2}$) = \$75

Periodic bond interest based on yield rate
= bond face value × yield rate per interest period
= 1,500(12%)($\frac{1}{2}$) = \$90

The deficit per interest period = 90 − 75 = \$15

According to the face value, the investor will sustain a \$15 loss each interest period for six years, or a total of 12 losses of \$15 each. The present value of the annuity that is formed by the periodic deficits is computed by use of the formula

$A_n = Ra_{\overline{n}|i}$, where $R = \$15$ (the periodic deficit)
$i = 12\%/2 = 6\%$ (at yield rate)
$n = 6 \times 2 = 12$ (losses)

$A_{12} = 15a_{\overline{12}|6\%} = 15(8.3838) = \$125.76$

Thus, *the discount is the present value of an annuity that is formed by the periodic deficit income.* The discount must be subtracted from the face value to obtain the purchase price, as shown below:

Purchase price = Face value − Discount = 1,500 − 125.76 = \$1,374.24

In summary, let i = yield rate per interest period
b = bond rate per interest period
F = face value of bond

When b is greater than i:

$$\textbf{Premium} = (Fb - Fi)a_{\overline{n}|i} = F(b - i)a_{\overline{n}|i} \qquad \textbf{(16–2)}$$

When b is smaller than i:

$$\textbf{Discount} = (Fi - Fb)a_{\overline{n}|i} = F(i - b)a_{\overline{n}|i} \qquad \textbf{(16–3)}$$

When b is equal to i, there is no premium or discount, and the purchase price = the face value.

EXAMPLE 1 A \$10,000, 13% bond, redeemable in 10 years, interest payable semiannually, is bought to yield 12% interest compounded semiannually. Find (a) the premium, and (b) the purchase price.

$b = 13\%/2 = 6\frac{1}{2}\%$ (per six months)
$i = 12\%/2 = 6\%$ (per six months)
$n = 10 \times 2 = 20$ (semiannual payments)
$F = \$10,000$

Since the bond rate is greater than the yield rate, there must be a premium.

(a) Premium $= 10,000\,(6\frac{1}{2}\% - 6\%)a_{\overline{20}|6\%}$
$= 10,000(\frac{1}{2}\%)a_{\overline{20}|6\%} = 50(11.4699) = \$573.50$

(b) Purchase price = 10,000 + 573.50 = \$10,573.50

EXAMPLE 2 A \$10,000, $3\frac{1}{2}\%$ bond, redeemable in 10 years, interest payable semiannually, is bought to yield 8% interest compounded semiannually. Find (a) the discount, and (b) the purchase price.

$b = 3\frac{1}{2}\%/2 = 1\frac{3}{4}\%$, $i = 8\%/2 = 4\%$, $n = 10 \times 2 = 20$, $F = \$10,000$

Since the bond rate is smaller than the yield rate, there must be a discount.

(a) Discount $= 10,000(4\% - 1\frac{3}{4}\%)a_{\overline{20}|4\%}$
$= 10,000(2\frac{1}{4}\%)a_{\overline{20}|4\%} = 225(13.5903) = \$3,057.82$

(b) Purchase price = 10,000 − 3,057.82 = \$6,942.18

EXAMPLE 3 Refer to Example 2. If the bond is bought to yield $3\frac{1}{2}\%$ interest compounded semiannually, find (a) the premium or the discount, and (b) the purchase price.

(a) $b = 1\frac{3}{4}\%$ and $i = 1\frac{3}{4}\%$. Since the bond rate is equal to the yield rate, there is no premium or discount.

(b) The purchase price is the face value, \$10,000.

★NOTE: When the redemption value is not at par, the following expressions may be obtained by a method of reasoning similar to that in the illustrations above:

Premium = [(Face value × b) − (Redemption value × i)]$a_{\overline{n}|i}$ **(16–4)**

Purchase price = Redemption value + premium

The premium may be thought of as a positive figure, whereas the discount may be thought of as a negative premium. In other words, when the premium becomes a negative figure, it is a discount; that is,

− Premium = Discount

Example 1(b) of Section 16.2 may be computed as follows:

$$\text{Premium} = [1{,}000(14\%)(\tfrac{1}{2}) - 1{,}050(12\%)(\tfrac{1}{2})]a_{\overline{32}|6\%}$$
$$= (70 - 63)a_{\overline{32}|6\%} = 7(14.084) = 98.588, \quad \text{rounded to} \quad \$98.59$$

Purchase price = 1,050 + 98.59 = \$1,148.59

(The 1¢ discrepancy from the answer \$1,148.58 is due to rounding.)

Example 2(b) of Section 16.2 may be computed as follows:

$$\text{Premium} = [1{,}500(10\%)(\tfrac{1}{2}) - 1{,}470(12\%)(\tfrac{1}{2})]a_{\overline{12}|6\%}$$
$$= (75 - 88.20)a_{\overline{12}|6\%}$$
$$= -13.20(8.3838) = -\$110.66616, \quad \text{rounded to} \quad -\$110.67$$

Purchase price = 1,470 − 110.67 = \$1,359.33

EXERCISE 16–3 REFERENCE: SECTION 16.3A

A. Find (a) the premium or the discount, and (b) the purchase price in each of the following problems:

	Par Value	*Bond Rate Payable Semiannually*	*Time Before Redemption*	*Yield Rate, Compounded Semiannually*
1.	\$ 8,000	12%	5 years	10%
2.	1,000	13%	$4\frac{1}{2}$ years	11%
3.	5,000	5%	6 years	7%
4.	6,000	11%	8 years	14%
5.	900	4%	7 years	3%
6.	700	5%	10 years	4%
7.	10,000	8%	12 years	10%
8.	25,000	7%	3 years	5%

B. Statement problems:

9. A \$3,000, 4% bond, redeemable in eight years, interest payable semiannually, is bought to yield 5% interest compounded semiannually. Find (a) the premium or the discount, and (b) the purchase price.
10. Refer to Problem 9. If the yield rate is 3% compounded semiannually, find the answers to (a) and (b).
11. Refer to Problem 9. If the yield rate is 4% compounded semiannually, find the answers to (a) and (b).
12. ★ Compute Problems 2, 3, 5, and 6 of Exercise 16–1 by the method used in Section 16.3A, page 487 [formula (16–4)].

B. Amortization of Premium

An investor who purchases a bond at premium should be aware that the premium is not redeemable on the maturity date of the bond. The premium is recovered periodically through the interest receipts on the bond. Thus, the book value of the bond investment should be reduced accordingly in the investor's record, until the premium becomes zero on the maturity date. The process of reducing the book value of a bond investment to par by periodic deductions is called *amortization of the bond premium.*

EXAMPLE 4

A \$10,000, 12% bond, interest payable semiannually, redeemable in $3\frac{1}{2}$ years, is bought to yield 11% interest compounded semiannually. Find the purchase price and construct a schedule for amortization of the premium.

$b = 12\%/2 = 6\%$, $i = 11\%/2 = 5\frac{1}{2}\%$, b is greater than i, $n = 3\frac{1}{2} \times 2 = 7$ (semiannual payments)

Amortization Schedule for Bond Premium

(1) At End of Interest Period	*(2) Interest Receipt from Bond: \$10,000 × 6% = \$600*	*(3) Yield (Investor's Interest): (5) × 5½%*	*(4) Premium Amortization: (2) − (3)*	*(5) Book Value of Bond: (5) − (4)*
				\$10,284.15
1	\$ 600	\$ 565.63	\$ 34.37	10,249,78
2	600	563.74	36.26	10,213.52
3	600	561.74	38.26	10,175.26
4	600	559.64	40.36	10,134.90
5	600	557.42	42.58	10,092.32
6	600	555.08	44.92	10,047.40
7	600	552.60*	47.40	10,000.00
Total	\$4,200	\$3,915.85	\$284.15	

*Correction for 1¢ discrepancy. The amount should be \$552.61 (or $10{,}047.40 \times 5\frac{1}{2}\% = 552.607$).

Premium $= 10{,}000(6\% - 5\tfrac{1}{2}\%)a_{\overline{7}|5\ 1/2\%} = 50a_{\overline{7}|5\ 1/2\%}$
$= 50(5.6830) = \$284.15$

Purchase price $= 10{,}000 + 284.15 = \$10{,}284.15$

The schedule on page 488 shows that the periodic premium amortization is the excess of the interest receipt from the bond over the investor's yield. Investors are willing to purchase a bond at a premium because they can recover the premium through the high periodic interest receipts from the bond.

NOTE:

1. The investor receives:

The investor receives:	$ 4,200.00	(interest)
	+ 10,000.00	(redemption value)
	14,200.00	
The investor paid:	− 10,284.15	(purchase price)
The investor's net gain:	$ 3,915.85	[see Column (3)]

2. According to the purchase price and the yield rate, the excess income of the first period is $34.37. It is computed as follows:

   The investor's expected interest for the first period is

   $10{,}284.15 \times 5\tfrac{1}{2}\% = 565.62825$, rounded to $565.63

   However, the actual interest receipt for the first period from the bond is

   $10{,}000 \times 6\% = \$600$

   The first period excess income is

   $600 - 565.63 = \$34.37$

3. The excess income is subtracted from the original purchase price to obtain the book value of the bond at the end of the first period.

   $10{,}284.15 - 34.37 = \$10{,}249.78$

C. Accumulation of Discount

An investor who purchases a bond at discount should know that the entire face value of the bond is redeemable to the bondholder on the maturity date. Investors receive a smaller periodic interest from the bond than they would receive if the interest rate on the bond were equal to the current market interest rate. However, the periodic deficits are recovered through receipt of the full redemption value. Each of the periodic deficits is added to the original purchase price listed in the investor's records. The book value increases periodically and will be equal to par on the maturity date. The process of increasing the book value of a bond investment to par by periodic additions is called *accumulation* of the bond discount.

EXAMPLE 5

A $10,000, 6% bond, interest payable semiannually, redeemable in $3\frac{1}{2}$ years, is bought to yield 7% interest compounded semiannually. Find the purchase price, and construct a schedule for accumulation of the discount.

$i = 7\%/2 = 3\frac{1}{2}\%$, $b = 6\%/2 = 3\%$, i is greater than b, $n = 3\frac{1}{2} \times 2 = 7$ (semiannual interest periods)

$$\text{Discount} = 10{,}000(3\tfrac{1}{2}\% - 3\%)a_{\overline{7}|3\ 1/2\%}$$
$$= 50(6.114544) = \$305.7272, \quad \text{rounded to} \quad \$305.73$$

Purchase price = 10,000 − 305.73 = $9,694.27

Accumulation Schedule for Bond Discount

(1) At End of Interest Period	*(2) Interest Receipt from Bond: \$10,000 × 3% = \$300*	*(3) Yield (Investor's Expected Interest): (5) × $3\frac{1}{2}$%*	*(4) Discount Accumulation: (3) − (2)*	*(5) Book Value of Bond: (5) + (4)*
				$ 9,694.27
1	$ 300	$ 339.30	$ 39.30	9,733.57
2	300	340.67	40.67	9,774.24
3	300	342.10	42.10	9,816.34
4	300	343.57	43.57	9,859.91
5	300	345.10	45.10	9,905.01
6	300	346.68	46.68	9,951.69
7	300	348.31	48.31	10,000.00
Total	$2,100	$2,405.73	$305.73	

NOTE:

1. According to the purchase price and the yield rate, the deficit of the first period is $39.30. It is computed as follows:

   The investor's expected interest for the first period is

   $9{,}694.27 \times 3\frac{1}{2}\% = \$339.30$

   However, the actual interest receipt for the first period from the bond is only

   $10{,}000 \times 3\% = \$300$

   The first period deficit is

   $339.30 - 300.00 = \$39.30$

   The deficit is added to the original purchase price to obtain the book value of the bond at the end of the first period:

   $9{,}694.27 + 39.30 = \$9{,}733.57$

2. The book value of a bond on any interest date is the purchase price of the bond on that date. Thus, the book value may be checked by the method used in finding the purchase price. (See Section 16.2A or 16.3A.) For example, the book value at the

end of the 5th period in Example 5 may be computed as follows:

$n = 2$, which represents the number of interest periods from the end of the 5th period to the redemption date.

Discount $= 10{,}000(3\frac{1}{2}\% - 3\%)a_{\overline{2}|3\ 1/2\%} = 50(1.8997) = \$94.99$

Book value (= Purchase price) $= 10{,}000 - 94.99 = \$9{,}905.01$

It can be determined from the above schedule that the periodic discount accumulation is the deficit of the interest receipt from the bond in relation to the investor's yield. Investors are willing to purchase a bond that offers smaller periodic interest payments than those offered on the prevailing investment market, because they know that the deficits may be accumulated to an amount equal to the discount and may be recovered through redemption of the bond on the maturity date.

EXERCISE 16–4 REFERENCE: SECTION 16.3B and C

1. A \$4,000 bond, interest at 5% payable semiannually, redeemable in $2\frac{1}{2}$ years, is purchased to yield 4% interest compounded semiannually. Find the purchase price, and construct a schedule for amortization of the premium.
2. A \$3,000 bond, interest at 4% payable semiannually, redeemable in three years, is bought to yield 3% interest compounded semiannually. Find the purchase price, and construct a schedule for amortization of the premium.
3. Refer to Problem 1. If the yield rate is 7% compounded semiannually, find the purchase price and construct a schedule for accumulation of the discount.
4. Refer to Problem 2. If the yield rate is 5% compounded semiannually, find the purchase price and construct a schedule for accumulation of the discount.
5. An \$8,000, 6% bond will be redeemed on April 1, 2001. Interest is payable semiannually on April 1 and October 1. The bond was bought on April 1, 1991, to yield an interest rate of $5\frac{1}{2}\%$ compounded semiannually. Find the book value of the bond on April 1, 1994. (A schedule is not required.)
6. Refer to Problem 5. If the yield rate were 10% compounded semiannually, what would be the book value of the bond on April 1, 1999? (A schedule is not required.)

16.4 APPROXIMATE YIELD RATE ON BOND INVESTMENT

When an investor purchases a bond on the market, the bond is usually listed at a quoted price. If the yield rate is not indicated, it should be determined by the investor so that it is possible to decide which one of several bonds is the best investment, or know if the interest payment is what was expected. This information may be found *approximately* by either Method A or Method B as discussed below.

A. Average Investment Method

Under the *average investment method*, the yield rate is obtained by dividing the annual income by the average annual investment.

$$\text{Yield rate (approximate)} = \frac{\text{Annual income}}{\text{Average annual investment}}$$

Here,

$$\text{Average annual investment} = \frac{\text{Beginning investment} + \text{Ending investment}}{2}, \quad \text{or}$$

$$= \frac{\text{Quoted price} + \text{Face value}}{2}$$

Annual income = Annual interest receipts − Annual premium amortization, or
Annual income = Annual interest receipts + Annual discount accumulation

The annual premium amortization and the annual discount accumulation are computed by the following respective expressions:

$$\text{Annual premium amortized} = \frac{\text{Total premium}}{\text{Number of years of the investment}}$$

$$\text{Annual discount accumulated} = \frac{\text{Total discount}}{\text{Numbers of years of the investment}}$$

EXAMPLE 1

A $1,000, 4% bond, redeemable in five years, interest payable semiannually, is bought at the quoted price of $1,060. What is the nominal yield rate?

The annual income is computed first:

Annual interest receipts = 1,000(4%) = $40 (a gain)
Annual premium amortization = (1,060 − 1,000)/5 = $12 (a loss)

The annual income = 40 − 12 = $28 (net gain)

The average annual investment = (1,060 + 1,000)/2 = $1,030

$$\text{The nominal yield rate} = \frac{28}{1{,}030} = .02718, \quad \text{or} \quad 2.718\%$$

NOTE: The average annual investment may be computed as follows:

(1,060 + 1,048 + 1,036 + 1,024 + 1,012 + 1,000)/6 = 6,180/6 = $1,030

The annual investments form an arithmetic progression, whose common difference is the annual premium amortization, $12.

EXAMPLE 2

A $1,000, 5% bond, redeemable in eight years, interest payable semiannually, is bought at the quoted price of $970. What is the nominal yield rate?

The annual income is computed first.

Annual interest receipts = 1,000(5%) = $50 (a gain)
Annual discount accumulation = (1,000 − 970)/8 = $3.75 (a gain)

The annual income = 50 + 3.75 = $53.75 (net gain)

The average annual investment = (970 + 1,000)/2 = $985

$$\text{The nominal yield rate} = \frac{53.75}{985} = .05457, \quad \text{or} \quad 5.457\%$$

★B. Interpolation Method

The *interpolation method* is based on the available interest rates given in Table 8. By one or several trial operations (beginning with the bond interest rate), two purchase prices are found. One is greater than the quoted price and the other one is smaller than the quoted price. Then, through interpolation, the desired interest rate is found. The number of trial operations can be reduced if the average investment method, described above, is used before the interpolation process.

Solution of Example 1 by the interpolation method:

Since the quoted price is at a premium, the yield rate must be smaller than the bond rate, 4%. According to the solution by Method A, the nominal yield rate is .02718. The interest rate per six months is .02718/2 = .01359. The two interest rates closest to .01359 in Table 8 are .01375, or $1\frac{3}{8}\%$, and .0125, or $1\frac{1}{4}\%$. The two rates are then tried to find the purchase prices closest to the quoted price of the bond:

$b = 4\%/2 = 2\%$ (per six months)

When $i = 1\frac{1}{4}\%$,

$$\begin{aligned}\text{Purchase price} &= 1{,}000 + 1{,}000(2\% - 1\tfrac{1}{4}\%)a_{\overline{10}|1\ 1/4\%}\\ &= 1{,}000 + 1{,}000(.0075)(9.3455)\\ &= 1{,}000 + 70.09 = \$1{,}070.09\end{aligned}$$

When $i = 1\frac{3}{8}\%$,

$$\begin{aligned}\text{Purchase price} &= 1{,}000 + 1{,}000(2\% - 1\tfrac{3}{8}\%)a_{\overline{10}|1\ 3/8\%}\\ &= 1{,}000 + 1{,}000(.00625)(9.2836)\\ &= 1{,}000 + 58.02 = \$1{,}058.02\end{aligned}$$

NOTE: When the yield rate becomes greater, the purchase price becomes smaller. When the yield rate becomes smaller, the purchase price becomes greater.

The interpolation method is then carried out as follows (the larger numbers, which are in the column of values all known, are written on the top lines):

	i	*Purchase Price*	
	$1\frac{1}{4}\%$	1,070.09	(1)
	x	1,060.00	(2)
	$1\frac{3}{8}\%$	1,058.02	(3)
(2) − (3)	$x - 1\frac{3}{8}\%$	1.98	(4)
(1) − (3)	$-\frac{1}{8}\%$	12.07	(5)

$$\frac{x - 1\frac{3}{8}\%}{-\frac{1}{8}\%} = \frac{1.98}{12.07}$$

Solve for x from the proportion formed by the differences on lines (4) and (5).

$$x - 1\frac{3}{8}\% = \left(-\frac{1}{8}\%\right)\left(\frac{1.98}{12.07}\right) = -\left(\frac{1}{800}\right)\left(\frac{198}{1{,}207}\right) = -.000205$$

$$x = 1\tfrac{3}{8}\% - .000205 = .01375 - .000205 = .013545, \quad \text{or}$$

$$= 1.3545\% \text{ (per six months)}$$

The nominal yield rate = 1.3545% × 2 = 2.709%

Solution of Example 2 by the interpolation method:

Since the quoted price is at a discount, the yield rate must be greater than the bond rate, 5%. However, according to the solution by Method A, the nominal yield rate is found to be approximately 5.457%. The interest rate per six months is 5.457%/2 = 2.7285%. The two interest rates closest to 2.7285% in Table 8 are $2\frac{1}{2}\%$ and $2\frac{3}{4}\%$. The two rates are tried to find the purchase prices closest to the quoted price of the bond:

$b = 5\%/2 = 2\frac{1}{2}\%$ (per six months)

When $i = 2\frac{1}{2}\%$,
Purchase price = quoted price = \$1,000, because $i = b$

When $i = 2\frac{3}{4}\%$,

$$\begin{aligned}\text{Purchase price} &= 1{,}000 - 1{,}000(2\tfrac{3}{4}\% - 2\tfrac{1}{2}\%)a_{\overline{16}|2\ 3/4\%} \\ &= 1{,}000 - 1{,}000(\tfrac{1}{4}\%)(12.8046) \\ &= 1{,}000 - 32.01 = \$967.99\end{aligned}$$

The interpolation method is then carried out as follows:

	i	*Purchase Price*	
	$2\frac{1}{2}\%$	1,000.00	(1)
	x	970.00	(2)
	$2\frac{3}{4}\%$	967.99	(3)
(2) − (3)	$x - 2\frac{3}{4}\%$	2.01	(4)
(1) − (3)	$-\frac{1}{4}\%$	32.01	(5)

$$\frac{x - 2\frac{3}{4}\%}{-\frac{1}{4}\%} = \frac{2.01}{32.01}$$

Solve for x from the proportion formed by the differences on lines (4) and (5).

$$x - 2\frac{3}{4}\% = \left(-\frac{1}{4}\%\right)\left(\frac{2.01}{32.01}\right) = -\left(\frac{1}{400}\right)\left(\frac{201}{3{,}201}\right) = -.000157$$

$$x = 2\tfrac{3}{4}\% - .000157 = .0275 - .000157 = .027343 \text{ (per six months)}$$

The nominal yield rate = .027343 × 2 = .054686, rounded to 5.469%

EXERCISE 16–5 REFERENCE: SECTION 16.4

A. Find the approximate nominal yield rate in each of the following problems. Use Method A for Problems 1–6. ★Use Method B for Problems 7 and 8.

	Par Value	*Bond Rate Payable Semiannually*	*Time Before Redemption*	*Quoted Price*
1.	\$ 600	15%	15 years	\$ 744
2.	800	4%	10 years	900
3.	2,500	12%	7 years	2,360
4.	3,000	5%	6 years	2,820
5.	4,000	$5\frac{1}{2}\%$	14 years	4,350
6.	5,000	10%	5 years	4,780
7.	3,500	4%	4 years	3,380
8.	500	6%	12 years	560

B. Statement problems:

9. A \$1,000, 5% bond, interest payable semiannually, redeemable on August 1, 1999, is bought at the quoted price of \$920 on August 1, 1991. What is the nominal yield rate? (Use Method A.)
10. A \$2,000, $3\frac{1}{2}$% bond, is to be redeemed on September 1, 2001. Interest is payable semiannually on March 1 and September 1. If the bond is quoted at 96(%) on March 1, 1991, what is the nominal yield rate? (Use Method A.)
11. Refer to Problem 9. If the bond were bought at the quoted price of \$1,080 on August 1, 1991, what would be the nominal yield rate compounded semiannually? (★Use Method B.)
12. Refer to Problem 10. If the bond were quoted at 104(%) on March 1, 1991, what would be the nominal yield rate compounded semiannually? (★Use Method B.)

16.5 BOND TABLES

For convenience, companies that buy and sell bonds commonly use prepared bond tables to compute the purchase price of a bond and the approximate yield rate. These tables include the most frequently used bond rates and yield rates, as well as the purchase prices on a variety of time lengths before the date of bond maturity. Some of the values of a \$100 bond in such tables are given on page 496.

A. Finding the Purchase Price

EXAMPLE 1

A \$10,000, 13% bond, redeemable in 10 years, interest payable semiannually, is bought to yield 12% interest compounded semiannually. Find the purchase price.

Since the bond is bought on an interest date, the purchase price is the quoted price in the bond table. The entry in the above table for the bond rate 13%, 10 years before redemption, yield rate 12.00%, is \$105.735. Since the value of the entry is for a \$100 bond, the value of a \$10,000 bond is

$$105.735\left(\frac{10{,}000}{100}\right) = 105.735(100) = \$10{,}573.50$$

NOTE: This answer may be checked against that given in Example 1(b) in Section 16.3.

EXAMPLE 2

If a \$1,000, 12% bond, redeemable in six years and two months, interest payable semiannually, is bought to yield 13% compounded semiannually, what is the (a) quoted price, (b) accrued interest on the bond, and (c) purchase price?

(a) According to the bond table above, the quoted price for the bond is

$$95.846\left(\frac{1{,}000}{100}\right) = \$958.46$$

Selected "and Interest" Prices (Quoted Prices) of a $100 Bond Interest Payable Semiannually

Nominal Yield Rate in %	*Nominal Bond Interest Rate*					
	12%			*13%*		
	Time Before Redemption			*Time Before Redemption*		
	6 Years	*6 Years, 1 Month*	*6 Years, 2 Months*	*9 Years*	*9½ Years*	*10 Years*
12.00%	$100.000	$100.000	$100.000	$105.414	$105.579	$105.735
12.10%	99.582	99.578	99.574	104.854	105.002	105.141
12.20%	99.166	99.158	99.150	104.299	104.429	104.551
12.30%	98.753	98.741	98.729	103.747	103.860	103.966
12.40%	98.341	98.326	98.310	103.200	103.296	103.386
12.50%	97.932	97.913	97.894	102.657	102.736	102.810
12.60%	97.526	97.503	97.480	102.118	102.180	102.239
12.70%	97.121	97.094	97.068	101.582	101.629	101.673
12.80%	96.719	96.688	96.658	101.051	101.082	101.111
12.90%	96.319	96.284	96.251	100.524	100.539	100.553
13.00%	95.921	95.883	95.846	100.000	100.000	100.000
13.10%	95.525	95.484	95.443	99.480	99.465	99.451
13.20%	95.131	95.086	95.042	98.964	98.935	98.907
13.30%	94.740	94.691	94.644	98.452	98.408	98.367
13.40%	94.350	94.299	94.248	97.944	97.886	97.831
13.50%	93.963	93.908	93.854	97.439	97.367	97.299
13.60%	93.578	93.519	93.462	96.938	96.852	96.772
13.70%	93.194	93.133	93.072	96.441	96.341	96.248
13.80%	92.813	92.749	92.685	95.947	95.835	95.729
13.90%	92.434	92.366	92.299	95.457	95.331	95.214
14.00%	92.057	91.986	91.916	94.970	94.832	94.703

(b) Since the bond is redeemable in six years and two months and interest is payable semiannually, the last interest payment date must be six years and six months before redemption. Thus, there is accrued interest for four months on the bond.

The accrued interest on the bond is

$1{,}000(12\%)(4/12) = \$40$

(c) The purchase price = the quoted price + the accrued interest
= 958.46 + 40 = $998.46

NOTE: These answers may be checked against those given in Example 4 in Section 16.2B, where the simple interest method is used in computing the interest for the fractional interest period.

B. Finding the Approximate Yield Rate

EXAMPLE 3

A $100, 13% bond, redeemable in $9\frac{1}{2}$ years, interest payable semiannually, is quoted at $96.50. What is the approximate nominal yield rate?

The quoted price is between the two entries, 96.852 and 96.341, in the $9\frac{1}{2}$ years column of the 13% bond section of the bond table. Thus, the yield rate is between 3.60% and 3.70%. If a more accurate answer is desired, the interpolation method may be used, as shown below.

The larger numbers, which are in the column of values all known, are written on the top lines.

	Yield Rate	*Quoted Price*	
	13.60%	96.852	(1)
	x	96.500	(2)
	13.70%	96.341	(3)

$$\begin{array}{lrcrl} (2)-(3) & x - 13.70\% & = & 0.159 & (4) \\ (1)-(3) & -.10\% & & 0.511 & (5) \end{array}$$

Solve for x from the proportion formed by the differences on lines (4) and (5).

$$x - 13.70\% = (-.10\%)\left(\frac{0.159}{0.511}\right) = (-.0010)\left(\frac{159}{511}\right)$$
$$= (-.0010)(0.31)$$
$$= -0.00031$$
$$x = 0.1370 - 0.00031$$
$$= 0.13669, \quad \text{or} \quad 13.67\%$$

EXERCISE 16–6 REFERENCE: SECTION 16.5

A. Find the unknown value (?) of the bond in each of the following problems. The bond interest is payable semiannually. (Omit interpolation in Problems 7–10.)

	Bond Face Value	*Time Before Redpemption*	*Bond Interest Rate*	*Yield Rate (Compounded Semiannually)*	*Quoted Price*
1.	$ 200	9 years	13%	13.20%	?
2.	700	$9\frac{1}{2}$ years	13%	13.30%	?
3.	3,000	6 years	12%	12.50%	?
4.	4,000	6 years, 1 month	12%	12.70%	?
5.	500	6 years, 2 months	12%	12.90%	?
6.	600	10 years	13%	12.50%	?
7.	100	$9\frac{1}{2}$ years	13%	?	$102.26
8.	100	10 years	13%	?	99.80
9.	1,000	6 years	12%	?	976.45
10.	600	9 years	13%	?	617.40

B. Statement problems:

11. A \$2,000, 12% bond, redeemable in six years, interest payable semiannually, is purchased to yield 12.6% compounded semiannually. Find the purchase price.
12. A \$3,000, 13% bond, redeemable in $9\frac{1}{2}$ years, interest payable semiannually, is bought to yield 13.2% compounded semiannually. Find the purchase price.
13. If a \$4,000, 12% bond, redeemable in six years and one month, interest payable semiannually, is bought to yield 12.30% compounded semiannually, what are the (a) quoted price, (b) accrued interest on the bond, and (c) purchase price?
14. If a \$2,500, 12% bond, redeemable in six years and two months, interest payable semiannually, is bought to yield 12.7% compounded semiannually, what are the (a) quoted price, (b) accrued interest on the bond, and (c) purchase price?
15. A \$1,000, 12% bond, redeemable in six years, interest payable semiannually, is quoted at \$957.50. What is the approximate nominal yield rate? (Use the interpolation method to find the answer.)
16. A \$1,000, 13% bond, redeemable in 10 years, interest payable semiannually, is quoted at \$1,027. What is the approximate nominal yield rate? (Use the interpolation method to find the answer.)

★16.6 OTHER TYPES OF BONDS

A. Annuity Bonds

An *annuity bond* is a contract in which the issuer promises to pay both the principal and the interest periodically until the entire debt is paid.

EXAMPLE 1

An annuity bond of \$10,000 is to be repaid in 10 equal semiannual payments, principal and interest included. The bond interest rate is 10% compounded semiannually. Assume that the yield rate is 12% compounded semiannually. Find the purchase price (a) now, and (b) after the sixth payment is made.

(a) First, the size of the 10 semiannual payments should be determined. The method to follow is the same as the one used in finding the size of the payments in an ordinary annuity problem when the present value (\$10,000 in this example) is known. (See Section 13.5A.)

$A_n = \$10{,}000$, $b = 10\%/2 = 5\%$ (*bond interest rate* per six months), $n = 10$ (semiannual payments), and $R = ?$ (per six months)

Substituting the values in the formula $A_n = Ra_{\overline{n}|b}$,

$10{,}000 = Ra_{\overline{10}|5\%}$,

$$R = \frac{10{,}000}{a_{\overline{10}|5\%}} = 10{,}000(0.1295046) = \$1{,}295.05 \quad \text{(Table 9)}$$

Second, find the present value of an annuity of \$1,295.05 payable (to the purchaser) at the end of every six months, for 10 payments, at the *yield rate* of 12% compounded semiannually.

$A_n = ?$, $R = 1{,}295.05$, $i = 12\%/2 = 6\%$ (*yield rate* per six months), $n = 10$ (semiannual payments)

Substituting the above values in the formula $A_n = Ra_{\overline{n}|i}$,

$A_{10} = 1{,}295.05a_{\overline{10}|6\%} = 1{,}295.05(7.360087) = \$9{,}531.68$ (Table 8)

(b) Since the bond is purchased after the sixth payment, the annuity is formed by the remaining four semiannual payments of \$1,295.05 each. The present value of the annuity is computed as follows:

$n = 4$, $i = 6\%$ (yield rate)

$A_4 = 1{,}295.05a_{\overline{4}|6\%} = 1{,}295.05(3.465106) = \$4{,}487.49$ (Table 8)

B. Serial Bonds

When the bonds in an issue are redeemable periodically on a series of specified due dates, the bonds are called *serial bonds*. According to the different due dates, a serial bond may be thought of as several groups of bonds combined in one issue. Thus, the purchase price of a serial bond is obtained by totaling the purchase prices of the individual groups of bonds.

EXAMPLE 2 A three-year, 4% bond for \$15,000 provides that the bond is to be redeemed at the end of each year by payments of \$5,000 each and that the interest is to be paid semiannually. If the bond is purchased now to yield 3% compounded semiannually, what is the purchase price?

$b = 4\%/2 = 2\%$, $i = 3\%/2 = 1\frac{1}{2}\%$ (per six months)

Since b is greater than i, there must be a premium. The excess of the periodic bond interest payment over the semiannual yield for a \$5,000 bond is

$$\begin{aligned} 5{,}000(2\%) - 5{,}000(1\tfrac{1}{2}\%) &= 5{,}000(2\% - 1\tfrac{1}{2}\%) \\ &= 5{,}000(\tfrac{1}{2}\%) \\ &= \$25 \text{ (per six months)} \end{aligned}$$

Use the premium method, formula (16–2), as follows:

The purchase price for the \$5,000 bond that is due in one year is

$$\begin{aligned} 5{,}000 + 25a_{\overline{2}|1\,1/2\%} &= 5{,}000 + 25(1.9559) \\ &= 5{,}000 + 48.90 = \$5{,}048.90 \end{aligned}$$

The purchase price for the \$5,000 bond that is due in two years is

$$\begin{aligned} 5{,}000 + 25a_{\overline{4}|1\,1/2\%} &= 5{,}000 + 25(3.8544) \\ &= 5{,}000 + 96.36 = \$5{,}096.36 \end{aligned}$$

The purchase price for the \$5,000 bond that is due in three years is

$$\begin{aligned} 5{,}000 + 25a_{\overline{6}|1\,1/2\%} &= 5{,}000 + 25(5.6972) \\ &= 5{,}000 + 142.43 = \$5{,}142.43 \end{aligned}$$

The total purchase price is

$5{,}048.90 + 5{,}096.36 + 5{,}142{,}43 = \$15{,}287.69$

★EXERCISE 16–7 REFERENCE: SECTION 16.6

1. A $10,000 annuity bond is to be repaid in eight equal semiannual payments, principal and interest included. The bond rate is 14% compounded semiannually. Find the purchase price (a) now, and (b) after the fifth payment is made. Assume that the yield rate is 16% compounded semiannually.
2. A $4,000 annuity bond is to be repaid by 12 equal semiannual payments, principal and interest included. The bond rate is 5% compounded semiannually. Assume that the yield rate is $6\frac{1}{2}$%. Find the purchase price (a) now, and (b) after the ninth payment is made.
3. Refer to Problem 1. Assume that the yield rate is 12% compounded semiannually. What are the answers to (a) and (b)?
4. Refer to Problem 2. Assume that the yield rate is 4% compounded semiannually. What are the answers to (a) and (b)?
5. A 3% serial bond of $18,000, interest payable semiannually, is to be redeemed in three annual installments of $6,000 each. The bond is bought on the interest date, which is one year before the first redemption date. If the yield rate is 5% compounded semiannually, what is the purchase price?
6. A 5% bond for $16,000 is to be redeemed by a series of four annual payments of $4,000 each. The first redemption date is April 1, 1992. The bond interest is payable on April 1 and October 1 each year. If the bond is purchased to yield 4% compounded semiannually, what is the purchase price on April 1, 1991?
7. In Problem 5, if the bond is bought on the interest date, which is seven years before the first annual redemption date, what is the purchase price?
8. In Problem 6, if the first redemption date is October 1, 2000, what is the purchase price on April 1, 1991?

★16.7 COMPUTING FORMULAS BY CALCULATORS AND COMPUTERS

The purchase prices [formula (16–1)], premiums [formulas (16–2) and (16–4)], and discounts [formulas (16–3) and (16–4)] of bonds presented in the previous sections are basically compound interest and annuity problems. Students should review Sections 11.7 (for compound interest), 13.8 (for ordinary annuity), and 15.5 (for constructing schedules) for computing the formulas in this chapter by calculators and computers.

16.8 SUMMARY OF BOND INVESTMENT FORMULAS

Symbols: S = redemption value of bond
R = periodic bond interest payment
i = yield rate per interest period
b = bond rate per interest payment period
n = number of interest periods or payments
F = face value of bond

Application	*Formula*	*Formula Number*	*Reference Page*
Finding the purchase price of a bond on the interest date	Purchase price $= S(1+i)^{-n} + Ra_{\overline{n}\rvert i}$	(16–1)	479
Finding the premium (or discount)	*When face value = redemption value,*		
	Premium $= F(b-i)a_{\overline{n}\rvert i}$	(16–2)	486
	Discount $= F(i-b)a_{\overline{n}\rvert i}$	(16–3)	486
	Purchase price = Face value + Premium, or Purchase price = Face Value − Discount		
	In general, Premium = [(Face value × b) − (Redemption value × i)]$a_{\overline{n}\rvert i}$	(16–4)	487
	Purchase price = Redemption value + Premium		
	Here, −Premium = Discount		

EXERCISE 16–8 REVIEW OF CHAPTER 16

1. A \$1,000, 4% bond is bought five years before redemption to yield 5% compounded semiannually. The interest on the bond is payable semiannually. Find the purchase price if the bond is redeemable at (a) par, (b) 103(%), and (c) 97(%).
2. A \$500, 6% bond is purchased on February 1, 1992, to yield 4% compounded semiannually. The interest on the bond is payable on February 1 and August 1 each year. Find the purchase price by assuming that the bond is redeemable on August 1, 2001, at (a) par, (b) 104(%), and (c) 96(%).
3. Refer to Problem 1(a). If the bond is bought four years and 10 months before redemption, what is (a) the purchase price? (b) the accrued interest on the bond? and (c) the quoted price?
4. Refer to Problem 2(a). Assuming that the bond is purchased on May 1, 1992, what is (a) the purchase price? (b) the accrued interest on the bond? and (c) the quoted price?
5. On April 30, 1991, a man purchased \$2,000 of 4% bonds. Bonds were quoted on the market on that date at 96(%). Interest on the bonds was payable on March 1 and September 1. Find (a) the quoted price, (b) the accrued interest on the bonds, and (c) the purchase price.
6. A $5\frac{1}{2}$% bond of \$5,000 was quoted on the market at $96\frac{1}{2}$(%) on April 21, 1992. Interest on the bond was payable semiannually on April 1 and October 1. Find (a) the quoted price, (b) the accrued interest on the bond, and (c) the purchase price.

7. A $7,000, 5% bond, redeemable in eight years, interest payable semiannually, is purchased to yield 4% interest compounded semiannually. Find (a) the premium and (b) the purchase price.
8. A $5,000, 3% bond, redeemable in 10 years, interest payable semiannually, is bought to yield $4\frac{1}{2}$% interest compounded semiannually. Find (a) the discount and (b) the purchase price.
9. Refer to Problem 7. What is the purchase price if the yield rate is (a) 6% compounded semiannually? (b) 5% compounded semiannually?
10. Refer to Problem 8. What is the purchase price if the yield rate is (a) $2\frac{1}{2}$% compounded semiannually? (b) 3% compounded semiannually?
11. A $6,000, 5% bond, interest payable semiannually, is bought two years before the redemption date to yield 6% compounded semiannually. (a) Find the purchase price. (b) Construct a schedule showing the periodic changes of the book value to par.
12. A $2,000, 6% bond, interest payable semiannually, redeemable in $2\frac{1}{2}$ years, is purchased to yield 4% compounded semiannually. (a) Find the purchase price. (b) Construct a schedule showing the periodic changes of the book value to par.
13. Work Problem 11, using a yield rate of 3% compounded semiannually.
14. Work Problem 12, using a yield rate of 8% compounded semiannually.
15. A $3,000, 6% bond, redeemable in seven years, interest payable semiannually, is bought at the quoted price of $3,420. What is the approximate nominal yield rate? (Use the average investment method.)
16. A $5,000, $4\frac{1}{2}$% bond, redeemable in 12 years, interest payable semiannually, is bought at the quoted price of $4,640. What is the approximate nominal yield rate? (Use the average investment method.)
17. ★ Work Problem 15, using a quoted price of $2,720. (Use the interpolation method.)
18. ★ Work Problem 16, using a quoted price of $5,240. (Use the interpolation method.)
19. An $8,000, 13% bond, redeemable in nine years, interest payable semiannually, is bought to yield 13.40% interest compounded semiannually. Find the purchase price by using the bond table.
20. A $10,000, 12% bond, redeemable in six years, interest payable semiannually, is bought to yield 12.60% interest compounded semiannually. Find the purchase price by using the bond table.
21. If a $10,000, 12% bond, redeemable in six years and two months, interest payable semiannually, is bought to yield 12.20% compounded semiannually, what is the purchase price? (Use the bond table.)
22. A $5,000, 12% bond, redeemable in six years and one month, interest payable semiannually, is bought to yield 12.80% compounded semiannually. What is the purchase price? (Use the bond table.)
23. A $2,000, 13% bond, redeemable in 10 years with interest payable semiannually, is quoted at $2,040. Find the approximate nominal yield rate by using the bond table.

24. A \$100, 12% bond, redeemable in six years, interest payable semiannually, is quoted at \$96.45. Find the approximate nominal yield rate by using the bond table.

★25. An annuity bond of \$10,000 is to be retired in eight semiannual payments, including principal and interest. The bond interest rate is 5% and the yield rate is 6%, both compounded semiannually. What is the purchase price (a) now, and (b) after the fifth payment is made?

★26. A 16% annuity bond of \$5,000 is to be repaid in 12 semiannual payments, principal and interest included. Assume that the yield rate is 14% compounded semiannually. Find the purchase price (a) now, and (b) after the eighth semiannual payment.

★27. A 5% bond of \$21,000 is to be redeemed by three payments of \$7,000 each at the end of every two years. The interest on the bond is payable semiannually. If the bond is purchased now to yield 6% compounded semiannually, what is the purchase price?

★28. A 4% bond of \$12,000 is to be redeemed by a series of four annual payments of \$3,000 each with the first payment on August 1, 1992. Interest on the bond is payable on February 1 and August 1 each year. If the bond is bought to yield 3% compounded semiannually, find the purchase price on August 1, 1991.

17 DEPRECIATION AND DEPLETION

The topics of depreciation (Sections 17.1 to 17.5) and depletion (Section 17.6) are presented in detail in this chapter. Some of the methods of computing depreciations and depletions also involve compound interest and ordinary annuity formulas. In addition, references for the methods of computing chapter formulas by calculators and computers are listed (Section 17.7).

17.1 INTRODUCTION TO DEPRECIATION

The tangible assets of a business, excluding land, usually have limited useful lives. Buildings, machines, and various types of equipment, after being used for a number of years, eventually come to the end of their lives. They must be retired from the business regardless of efforts to maintain and repair them. At the time of retirement, the assets may have a small trade-in or scrap value, or may be worthless. In either case, there is a loss in the value of the property. This loss is called *depreciation expense*, or simply *depreciation*.

Depreciation expense should be periodically charged to business operating expenses or to the cost of goods manufactured during the useful life of the asset. The total of the periodic depreciation charges is limited to the cost of the property. Thus, the computation of the periodic depreciation is actually a process of allocating the cost of the property as an expense or a cost of goods manufactured to the proper business operating periods. The allocation is necessary in order to calculate the periodic net income from business operations. The placement of depreciation expense on an income statement is explained in Chapter 7.

An account, which generally bears the name *accumulated depreciation*, or *allowance for depreciation*, is often used by accountants to record the amount of accumulated depreciation. The difference between the original cost of an asset and its total amount in the accumulated depreciation account is its book value. The book value is not necessarily the same as the market value or the resale value. Rather, it indicates the unallocated cost of the asset.

Retirement of assets is caused by various factors, such as wear and tear, decay, damage, inadequacy, and obsolescence. These factors may operate gradually at one time and drastically at another time. Thus, the value of property may decrease more at one time than at another. However, the allocation of the cost of property is usually gradual and is done in a systematic and rational manner.

There are many methods of estimating the depreciation charges for each business operation period. The methods listed below are generally known and are illustrated in this chapter:

1. *Methods of Averages* (Section 17.2)
   A. Straight line method
   B. Service hours method
   C. Product units method
2. *Reducing Charge Methods* (Section 17.3)
   A. Diminishing rate on fixed depreciation—sum of the years-digits method
   B. Fixed rate on diminishing book value
3. *Compound Interest Methods* (Section 17.4)
   A. Annuity
   B. Sinking fund
4. *Composite Rate Method* (Section 17.5)

The following symbols are used in illustrating the depreciation methods listed above:

C = original cost of an asset
T = estimated trade-in value or scrap value
$C - T$ = total depreciation charges or expenses
n = useful life of the asset estimated in years, service-hours, or product-units
r = rate of depreciation expense per year, per service-hour, per product-unit, or per dollar

17.2 DEPRECIATION—METHODS OF AVERAGES

A. Straight Line Method

The *straight line method* is based on the assumption that the depreciation charges are equal for each year. In other words, the depreciable asset contributes its services equally to each year's operation. The formula for this method is

$$r = \frac{C - T}{n} \tag{17–1}$$

(r = depreciation expense per year, and n = number of years)

EXAMPLE 1 A machine that was purchased for $1,100 has an estimated useful life of five years and a trade-in value of $120. Use the straight line method to find the depreciation charges for each year, and construct a depreciation schedule.

$C = 1{,}100$, $T = 120$, $n = 5$ (years)

Substituting the values in formula (17–1),

$$r = \frac{C - T}{n} = \frac{1{,}100 - 120}{5} = \frac{980}{5} = \$196 \text{ (per year)}$$

Depreciation Schedule—Straight Line Method (Example 1)

(1) End of Year	*(2) Annual Depreciation Expense*	*(3) Accumulated Depreciation from (2)*	*(4) Book Value of Machine: \$1,100 − (3)*
0	. . .	. . .	\$1,100
1	\$196	\$196	904
2	196	392	708
3	196	588	512
4	196	784	316
5	196	980	120
Total	\$980		

NOTE: The annual depreciation expense is a constant amount, \$196. If the above data are plotted on graph paper, the accumulated depreciation forms a straight line. Thus, this method is known as a "straight line" method.

B. Service Hours Method

The *service hours method* relates depreciation to estimated productive capacity of the asset in terms of its hours of useful service. Under this method, first the depreciation rate per service hour (r) is found by using formula (17–1), $r = \frac{C - T}{n}$. For this method, n = number of service hours. Next, the depreciation charges for a given year are determined by multiplying the actual number of service hours used in the year by r.

EXAMPLE 2 Refer to Example 1. Assume that the useful life of the machine is estimated to be 20,000 service hours and the actual number of hours spent in production each year is as follows:

1st year: 5,000 service hours
2d year: 4,500 service hours
3d year: 4,200 service hours
4th year: 3,400 service hours
5th year: 2,900 service hours

Use the service hours method to find the depreciation charges for each year. Construct a depreciation schedule.

$C = 1{,}100$, $T = 120$, $n = 20{,}000$ (service hours)

Substituting the values in formula (17–1),

$$r = \frac{1{,}100 - 120}{20{,}000} = \$.049 \text{ (per service hour)}$$

The annual depreciation charges are computed as follows:

1st year: 5,000 × .049 = \$245.00
2d year: 4,500 × .049 = \$220.50
3d year: 4,200 × .049 = \$205.80
4th year: 3,400 × .049 = \$166.60
5th year: 2,900 × .049 = \$142.10

Depreciation Schedule—Service Hours Method (Example 2)

(1) *End of Year*	*(2)* *Annual Depreciation Expense*	*(3)* *Accumulated Depreciation*	*(4)* *Book Value of Machine: \$1,100 − (3)*
0	. . .	. . .	\$1,100.00
1	\$245.00	\$245.00	855.00
2	220.50	465.50	634.50
3	205.80	671.30	428.70
4	166.60	837.90	262.10
5	142.10	980.00	120.00
Total	\$980.00		

C. Product Units Method

Under the *product units method*, depreciation is related to the estimated number of units that will be produced by each asset during its useful life. To determine the amount of depreciation, first the depreciation rate per unit of product (r) is found by using formula (17–1), $r = \frac{C - T}{n}$. For this method, n = number of product units. Then, the depreciation charges for a given period are determined by multiplying the number of units produced in the period by r.

EXAMPLE 3 Refer to Example 1. Assume that the useful life of the machine is estimated to be 70,000 product units and the number of units produced each year is estimated as follows:

1st year: 14,000 units
2d year: 15,000 units
3d year: 16,500 units
4th year: 17,000 units
5th year: 7,500 units

Use the product units method to find the depreciation charges for each year. Construct a depreciation schedule.

C = 1,100, T = 120, n = 70,000 (units)

Substituting the values in formula (17–1),

$$r = \frac{1{,}100 - 120}{70{,}000} = \$.014 \text{ (per unit)}$$

The annual depreciation charges are computed as follows:

1st year: 14,000 × .014 = $196
2d year: 15,000 × .014 = $210
3d year: 16,500 × .014 = $231
4th year: 17,000 × .014 = $238
5th year: 7,500 × .014 = $105

Depreciation Schedule—Product Units Method (Example 3)

(1) *End of Year*	*(2)* *Annual Depreciation Expense*	*(3)* *Accumulated Depreciation*	*(4)* *Book Value of Machine: $1,100 − (3)*
0	. . .	. . .	$1,100
1	$196	$196	904
2	210	406	694
3	231	637	463
4	238	875	225
5	105	980	120
Total	$980		

EXERCISE 17–1 REFERENCE: SECTION 17.2

1. A building that was constructed for $6,000,000 has an estimated useful life of 20 years and a salvage value of $10,000. Use the straight line method to find the depreciation charges for each year.
2. A piece of equipment that was purchased for $4,700 has an estimated useful life of seven years and a scrap value of $500. Use the straight line method to compute the depreciation charges for each year.
3. The cost of a machine purchased by the Gordon Company is $2,650. It is estimated that the machine will have a $250 trade-in value at the end of its useful life, which is estimated at five years. Use the straight line method to find the depreciation charges for each year, and construct a depreciation schedule.
4. The Kent Company has a machine costing $5,400 with an estimated useful life of six years and a trade-in value of $300. Use the straight line method to find the depreciation charges for each year, and construct a depreciation schedule.
5. Refer to Problem 3. Assume that the useful life of the machine is estimated to be 30,000 service hours and that the actual number of hours spent in production for each year is as follows:

1st year: 5,500 hours
2d year: 7,400 hours
3d year: 6,200 hours
4th year: 5,800 hours
5th year: 5,100 hours

Use the service hours method to find the depreciation charges for each year. Construct a depreciation schedule.

6. Refer to Problem 3. Assume that the useful life of the machine is estimated to be 100,000 units of production, and that the number of units produced each year is estimated as follows:

   1st year: 24,000 units
   2d year: 23,000 units
   3d year: 19,000 units
   4th year: 18,000 units
   5th year: 16,000 units

   Use the product units method to find the depreciation charges for each year. Construct a depreciation schedule.

7. Refer to Problem 4. Assume that the useful life of the machine is estimated to be 17,000 service hours and the actual number of hours spent in production for the first year is 2,800 hours. Use the service hours method to compute the depreciation charges for the first year.

8. Refer to Problem 4. Assume that the useful life of the machine is estimated to be 50,000 units of production and the number of units produced during the first year is 8,500 units. Use the product units method to compute the depreciation charges for the first year.

17.3 DEPRECIATION—REDUCING CHARGE METHODS

Generally, the maintenance and repair expenses for new equipment are less than those for older equipment. Therefore, larger amounts of depreciation are often charged to the earlier years of the useful life of certain equipment than are charged to the later years. When this is done, the sum of the depreciation expenses and the maintenance and repair costs for each year during the useful life are equalized.

A. Diminishing Rate on Fixed Depreciation—Sum of the Years-Digits Method

Under the *sum of the years-digits method*, the depreciation expense for the earlier years is greater than that of later years. The total depreciation is fixed and is the difference between the original cost and the trade-in or scrap value ($C - T$). The rate of depreciation is expressed in a changing fraction which becomes smaller each year. In this changing fraction, the numerator is the number of remaining years of life. The denominator is the sum of the digits that represent the years of life.

EXAMPLE 1

A machine that was purchased for $1,100 has an estimated useful life of five years and a trade-in value of $120. (The information is the same as that in Example 1 of Section 17.2, page 505.) Use the sum of the years-digits method to find the depreciation charges for each year and construct a depreciation schedule.

The sum[1] of the five years-digits is

$1 + 2 + 3 + 4 + 5 = 15$

The total depreciation charge is 1,100 − 120 = $980. The annual depreciation charges are computed as follows:

1st year: $980 \times \frac{5}{15} =$ $326.67
2d year: $980 \times \frac{4}{15} =$ 261.33
3d year: $980 \times \frac{3}{15} =$ 196.00
4th year: $980 \times \frac{2}{15} =$ 130.67
5th year: $980 \times \frac{1}{15} =$ 65.33
Total: $980.00

Depreciation Schedule—Sum of the Years-Digits Method (Example 1)

(1) *End of Year*	(2) *Annual Depreciation Expense*	(3) *Accumulated Depreciation*	(4) *Book Value of Machine: $1,100 − (3)*
0	. . .	. . .	$1,100.00
1	$326.67	$326.67	773.33
2	261.33	588.00	512.00
3	196.00	784.00	316.00
4	130.67	914.67	185.33
5	65.33	980.00	120.00
Total	$980.00		

When the rates based on the sum of the years-digits method are considered too extreme, the rates may be modified by adding the same number to each of the numbers of the years.

EXAMPLE 2 Refer to Example 1. Find the annual depreciation charges by adding 7 to each of the numbers of the years.

[1] The sum of the years-digits may be obtained by using the sum of the arithmetic progression formula:

$$S_n = \frac{n}{2}(a + L)$$

where S_n is the sum, n is the number of years in the life of the asset, a is the first number in the series of numbers, and L is the last number in the series. In Example 1, $n = 5$, $a = 1$, and $L = 5$

The sum of the years-digits $= \frac{5}{2}(1 + 5) = 2.5 \times 6 = 15$

In Example 2, $n = 5$, $a = 8$, and $L = 12$

The sum of the years-digits $= \frac{5}{2}(8 + 12) = 2.5 \times 20 = 50$

The sum of the five years-digits becomes

$(1 + 7) + (2 + 7) + (3 + 7) + (4 + 7) + (5 + 7) = 8 + 9 + 10 + 11 + 12 = 50$

Thus, the annual depreciation charges are as follows:

1st year: $980 \times \frac{12}{50}$ =	\$235.20
2d year: $980 \times \frac{11}{50}$ =	215.60
3d year: $980 \times \frac{10}{50}$ =	196.00
4th year: $980 \times \frac{9}{50}$ =	176.40
5th year: $980 \times \frac{8}{50}$ =	156.80
Total:	\$980.00

The difference between each year and the next in Example 2 is $980 \times \frac{1}{50}$, or \$19.60; whereas the difference between each year and the next in Example 1 is $980 \times \frac{1}{15}$, or \$65.33. Thus, the rates in Example 2 are more moderate than those in Example 1.

B. Fixed Rate on Diminishing Book Value

Under this method, the depreciation expense for earlier years is higher than that of later years. The depreciation expense for each year is obtained by multiplying the fixed (or constant) annual rate by the diminishing book value of an asset as of the beginning of each year. As shown below, there are two ways to compute the fixed annual depreciation rate.

ACCORDING TO FEDERAL TAX REGULATIONS

This method was specifically mentioned in the Internal Revenue Code of 1954 as the *declining balance method*. The declining balance method provides a steadily declining depreciation charge over the estimated life of the asset. The annual rate of depreciation must not exceed twice the straight line rate for the depreciable asset. The maximum rate may be obtained as follows:

1. Find the annual depreciation rate by dividing 100% by the number of years of useful life of the property (straight line method).
2. Find the maximum annual depreciation rate by multiplying the annual depreciation rate obtained above by 2.

The scrap value or the trade-in value under this method is not deducted from the cost of the property prior to the rate application. As shown in the following example, the scrap value often is not equal to the original estimation when using this maximum rate.

EXAMPLE 3 Refer to Example 1. Use the declining balance method to find the maximum depreciation charges for each year, and construct a depreciation schedule.

The annual depreciation rate based on the straight line method is

$100\%/5 = 20\%$ (per year)

The maximum annual depreciation rate is

$20\% \times 2 = 40\%$

The annual depreciation charges are computed in the following schedule:

Depreciation Schedule—Declining Balance Method (Example 3)

(1) End of Year	*(2) Annual Depreciation Expense: (4)* × 40%*	*(3) Accumulated Depreciation*	*(4) Book Value of Machine: $1,100 − (3)*
0	. . .	. . .	$1,100.00
1	$ 440.00	$ 440.00	660.00
2	264.00	704.00	396.00
3	158.40	862.40	237.60
4	95.04	957.44	142.56
5	57.02	1,014.46	85.54
Total	$1,014.46		

* The diminishing book value as of the beginning of each year, which is also the value at the end of each preceding year. For example, the book value as of the beginning of the third year is $396, which is also the book value at the end of the second year. The depreciation charges for the third year are computed as follows:

$396 \times 40\% = \$158.40$

Note that the book value at the end of the fifth year is $85.54, which is not equal to the original estimated amount of $120.[2]

★ACCORDING TO THE FIXED RATE FORMULA

When the following fixed rate formula is used, the book value at the end of the life of the asset is equal to the scrap or trade-in value. The formula for the rate of annual depreciation charges (r) is as follows:

$$r = 1 - \sqrt[n]{\frac{T}{C}} \qquad \textbf{(17–2)}^3$$

EXAMPLE 4 Refer to Example 1. Use the fixed rate formula to find the depreciation charges for each year, and construct a depreciation schedule.

---

[2] The book value at the end of the fifth year can be checked by using the nth term formula of a geometric progression as follows:

$$L = ar^{(n-1)} = 1{,}100(1 - 40\%)^{6-1} = 1{,}100(.6)^5 = 1{,}100(.07776) = 85.536 \quad \text{or} \quad \$85.54$$

[3] *Proof–Formula (17–2):*

C = the original cost
T = the trade-in value or scrap value
n = the number of years of useful life
r = the annual depreciation rate based on the original cost, or declining book value

The depreciation charges and the book value at the end of each year are as follows:

$C = 1{,}100$, $T = 120$, $n = 5$ (years)

Substituting the values in formula (17–2),

$$r = 1 - \sqrt[5]{\frac{120}{1{,}100}}$$

$$= 1 - \sqrt[5]{0.1090909}$$

$$= 1 - 0.6420335$$

$$= 0.3579665, \quad \text{or rounded to } 35.7967\%$$

(See Example 14, Section 10.2, page 308, for the use of the y^x key to find $\sqrt[5]{0.1090909}$.)

Note that the value of $\sqrt[5]{\frac{120}{1{,}100}}$ may also be obtained by using logarithms as follows:

$$\log \sqrt[5]{\frac{120}{1{,}100}} = (1/5) \log \left(\frac{120}{1{,}100}\right)$$

$$= (1/5)(\log 120 - \log 1{,}100)$$

$$= (1/5)(2.079181 - 3.041393)$$

$$= (1/5)(-.962212)$$

$$= -.1924424 = 9.8075576 - 10$$

---

[3]*Proof (continued)*

	Depreciation Charges	*Book Value*
At the end of the 1st year:	Cr	$C - Cr = C(1 - r)$
At the end of the 2d year:	$Cr(1 - r)$	$C(1 - r) - Cr(1 - r)$ $= C(1 - r)(1 - r)$ $= C(1 - r)^2$
At the end of the 3d year:	$Cr(1 - r)^2$	$C(1 - r)^2 - Cr(1 - r)^2$ $= C(1 - r)^2(1 - r)$ $= C(1 - r)^3$
⋮	⋮	⋮
At the end of the nth year:	$Cr(1 - r)^{n-1}$	$C(1 - r)^n$

Since the book value at the end of the nth year is also the trade-in or scrap value (T), then

$$C(1 - r)^n = T$$

Divide both sides by C.

$$(1 - r)^n = \frac{T}{C}$$

Extract the nth root of each side.

$$1 - r = \sqrt[n]{\frac{T}{C}}$$

Then

$$r = 1 - \sqrt[n]{\frac{T}{C}}$$

Find the antilog:

$$\sqrt[5]{\frac{120}{1{,}100}} = 0.642033$$

The annual depreciation charges are computed in the following schedule:

Depreciation Schedule—Based on the Fixed Rate Formula (Example 4)

(1) *End of Year*	*(2)* *Annual Depreciation Expense (4)* × .357967*	*(3)* *Accumulated Depreciation*	*(4)* *Book Value of Machine: $1,100 − (3)*
0	. . .	. . .	$1,100.00
1	$393.76	$393.76	706.24
2	252.81	646.57	453.43
3	162.31	808.88	291.12
4	104.21	913.09	186.91
5	66.91	980.00	120.00
Total	$980.00		

* Of the preceding year. For example, 393.76 = 1,100.00 × .357967
252.81 = 706.24 × .357967

EXERCISE 17–2 REFERENCE: SECTION 17.3

1. A computer, which was bought for $3,350, has an estimated useful life of six years and a trade-in value of $200. Use the sum of the years-digits method to find the depreciation charges for each year, and construct a depreciation schedule.
2. The Johnson Steel Company has a machine costing $2,800 with an estimated useful life of five years and a scrap value of $100. Use the sum of the years-digits method to find the depreciation charges for each year, and construct a depreciation schedule.
3. Refer to Problem 1. Find the annual depreciation charges if 8 is added to each of the numbers of the six years.
4. Refer to Problem 2. What are the annual depreciation charges if 6 is added to each of the numbers of the five years?
5. Refer to Problem 1. Construct a depreciation schedule using the two fixed rate methods: (a) according to federal tax regulations and ★(b) according to the fixed rate formula.
6. Refer to Problem 2. Construct a depreciation schedule using the two fixed rate methods: (a) according to federal tax regulations, and ★(b) according to the fixed rate formula.

★17.4 DEPRECIATION—COMPOUND INTEREST METHODS

In the previous methods, no consideration is given to the interest on either the original cost or its diminishing book value. The following two methods are used in finding the depreciation charges when interest is involved. Both methods will give the same *net* annual depreciation charges.

A. Annuity Method

The annuity method resembles the method of amortizing a debt. Under the annuity method, the periodic depreciation charges are equal and include not only a part of the cost of the asset but also the interest on the book value for each operating period. The periodic book value is assumed to be earning the same interest as the amount would earn if it were invested elsewhere.

Before computing the periodic depreciation charges, find the present value of the total depreciation charges. Let

i = the interest rate per period (year)
n = the estimated number of years of the useful life of the asset

The present value of the trade-in value is $P = T(1 + i)^{-n}$, which is obtained by using the compound discount formula. The present value of the total depreciation charges is the difference between the original cost (C) and the present value of the estimated trade-in or scrap value (P). It may be expressed as follows:

Present value of total depreciation charges $= C - P = C - T(1 + i)^{-n}$

The annual depreciation charges are required to be equal. Thus, the present value may be thought of as the present value of an annuity (A_n) with payments consisting of equal depreciation charges, or

$$C - T(1 + i)^{-n} = A_n = Ra_{\overline{n}|i}$$

Here, R represents the annual depreciation charges. Thus, the annual depreciation charges (R) may be obtained as follows:

$$R = \frac{A_n}{a_{\overline{n}|i}} = \frac{C - T(1 + i)^{-n}}{a_{\overline{n}|i}} \qquad \textbf{(17–3)}$$

EXAMPLE 1

A machine that was purchased for $1,100 has an estimated useful life of five years and a trade-in value of $120. (The information is the same as that in Example 1 of Section 17.2, page 505.) Use the annuity method to find the depreciation charges for each year and construct a depreciation schedule. Assume that the effective interest rate is 6%.

$C = 1{,}100$, $T = 120$, $i = 6\%$, $n = 5$ (years)

The present value of the trade-in or scrap value is

$$P = 120(1 + 6\%)^{-5} = 120(.74726) = \$89.67$$

The present value of the total depreciation charges is

$$A_n = C - P = 1{,}100 - 89.67 = \$1{,}010.33$$

The annual depreciation charges are

$$R = \frac{A_n}{a_{\overline{n}|i}} = \frac{1{,}010.33}{a_{\overline{5}|6\%}} = 1{,}010.33 \times .237396 = \$239.85 \quad \text{(Table 9)}$$

Depreciation Schedule—Annuity Method (Example 1)

(1) End of Year	*(2) Annual Depreciation Charges (R)*	*(3) Interest Income: (6) × 6%*	*(4) Net Depreciation Charges to Be Accumulated: (2) − (3)*	*(5) Accumulated Depreciation from (4)*	*(6) Book Value: $1,100 − (5)*
0	. . .	. . .	. . .	. . .	$1,100.00
1	$ 239.85	$ 66.00	$173.85	$173.85	926.15
2	239.85	55.57	184.28	358.13	741.87
3	239.85	44.51	195.34	553.47	546.53
4	239.85	32.79	207.06	760.53	339.47
5	239.84*	20.37	219.47	980.00	120.00
Total	$1,199.24	$219.24	$980.00		

* Corrected for 1¢ discrepancy.

An accountant using the annuity method in computing annual depreciation charges keeps two accounts:

1. Depreciation charges (or expense) [See Column (2).]
2. Interest income [See Column (3).]

Only the difference between the annual depreciation charges and the interest income is used in reducing the book value of the investment. For example, although the total depreciation charges for the operation of the asset during the first year are $239.85, the net loss is only $173.85 (or $239.85 − $66.00). Thus, the book value at the end of the first year is reduced by $173.85 to obtain a new book value of $926.15 (= $1,100 − $173.85).

B. Sinking Fund Method

Under the sinking fund method, it is assumed that a sinking fund is established for the purpose of replacing an asset at the end of its useful life. The periodic depreciation charges are exactly the same as the periodic increases (including the periodic deposit and the interest) in the sinking fund. Thus, the depreciation charges for each year are not equal. However, the total of the depreciation charges is equal to the amount in the sinking fund (S_n) at the end of the useful life of the asset. The size of each deposit (R) made in the sinking fund can be obtained by using the annuity formula

$$S_n = Rs_{\overline{n}|i}, \quad \text{or} \quad R = \frac{S_n}{s_{\overline{n}|i}} = \frac{C - T}{s_{\overline{n}|i}} \qquad \textbf{(17–4)}$$

EXAMPLE 2 Assume that the effective interest rate is 6%. Use the data in Example 1 to find the annual depreciation charges by the sinking fund method. Construct a depreciation schedule.

$C = 1{,}100,\ T = 120,\ i = 6\%,\ n = 5$ (years)

The total depreciation at the end of the fifth year is

$C - T = 1{,}100 - 120 = \$980$

which should be equal to the final amount in the sinking fund. Thus,

$S_n = \$980$

Substituting the values in formula (17–4),

$$\text{The annual deposit } R = \frac{980}{s_{\overline{5}|6\%}} = 980\left(\frac{1}{a_{\overline{5}|6\%}} - 6\%\right)$$

$$= 980(0.2374 - .06) = \$173.85 \quad \text{(Table 9)}$$

The annual depreciation charges are shown in column (4) in the following depreciation schedule:

Depreciation Schedule—Sinking Fund Method (Example 2)

(1) End of Year	*(2) Period Deposit in Fund (R)*	*(3) Interest Income from Sinking Fund: (5) × 6%*	*(4) Periodic Increase in Fund = Annual Depreciation Charges: (2) + (3)*	*(5) Accumulated Sinking Fund = Accumulated Depreciation from (4)*	*(6) Book Value: $1,100 − (5)*
0	. . .	. . .	. . .	. . .	$1,100.00
1	$173.85	. . .	$173.85	$173.85	926.15
2	173.85	$ 10.43	184.28	358.13	741.87
3	173.85	21.49	195.34	553.47	546.53
4	173.85	33.21	207.06	760.53	339.47
5	173.84*	45.63	219.47	980.00	120.00
Total	$869.24	$110.76	$980.00		

* Corrected for 1¢ discrepancy.

Note that the values in Columns (4), (5), and (6) are the same as the values in the same columns of the depreciation schedule in Example 1 by the annuity method. Also, the actual establishment of a sinking fund for replacement purposes is unnecessary. The depreciation schedule may be used as a standard or a guide for charging the periodic depreciation expense, regardless of whether or not a sinking fund has been established.

★EXERCISE 17–3 REFERENCE: SECTION 17.4

1. A piece of equipment that was bought for $2,400 has an estimated useful life of four years and a scrap value of $300. Use the annuity method to find the annual depreciation charges, and construct a depreciation schedule. Assume that the effective interest rate is 5%.

2. The Boston Sales Company has a machine costing $5,000 with an estimated useful life of six years and a scrap value of $800. Use the annuity method to find the annual depreciation charges, and construct a depreciation schedule. Assume that the effective interest rate is 4%.
3. Refer to Problem 1. Use the sinking fund method to find the depreciation charges for each year, and construct a depreciation schedule.
4. Refer to Problem 2. Use the sinking fund method to find the depreciation charges for each year, and construct a depreciation schedule.
5. Find the book value at the end of the third year in Problem 1 without referring to a depreciation schedule.
6. Find the book value at the end of the fourth year in Problem 2 without referring to a depreciation schedule.

★17.5 DEPRECIATION—COMPOSITE RATE METHOD

The preceding methods of computing depreciation expense are based on a single piece of property. The *composite rate method* is used for computing the depreciation charges of a group of assets.

A. Finding the Composite Rate

The *composite rate* is obtained by dividing the total annual depreciation charges by the total cost of the group of assets. The individual annual depreciation charges of each asset are obtained by the *straight line method.*

EXAMPLE 1

Find the composite rate of the group of assets in the table below:

Asset	*Original Cost*	*Scrap Value*	*Total Depreciation*	*Estimated Life*	*Annual Depreciation Charges*
A	$10,000	$1,000	$ 9,000	10 years	$ 900
B	5,000	200	4,800	12 years	400
C	4,500	275	4,225	5 years	845
	$19,500	$1,475	$18,025		$2,145

$$\text{Composite rate} = \frac{\text{Total annual depreciation charges}}{\text{Total cost}}$$

$$= \frac{2{,}145}{19{,}500} = .11, \quad \text{or} \quad 11\%$$

The composite rate may be used to compute depreciation charges during the later years of a group of assets if there are no significant changes in the values and useful lives of the assets due to replacement, retirement, or addition. Thus, the work of computing the depreciation expense for each item of the group may be avoided. For example, if the total cost of the above group of assets in the next year were $19,600, which would be regarded as a minor change from the cost of this year, the depreciation charge for the next year would be computed as follows:

$\$19{,}600 \times 11\% = \$2{,}156$

B. Finding the Composite Life

The *composite life* of a group of assets is the average life of the group. Composite life is a useful value to management. For example, in obtaining a loan by pledging a group of assets as security, the creditor generally wants to know the average life of the assets. In computing the composite life, the annual depreciation charges of the group of assets may be obtained by using (1) the composite rate as discussed above, or (2) the sinking fund method as discussed in Section 17.4B.

When the composite rate is used, the depreciation charges are assumed to be *equal* for each year. The composite life is obtained by dividing the total depreciation charges by the total annual depreciation charges of the group of assets.

EXAMPLE 2 Find the composite life of the group of assets in Example 1.

$$\text{Composite life} = \frac{\text{Total depreciation charges}}{\text{Total annual depreciation charges}}$$

$$= \frac{18{,}025}{2{,}145} = 8.4 \text{ years}$$

When the sinking fund method is used in computing the annual depreciation charges, the charges for each asset are *not equal* for each year. Thus, a fixed composite rate cannot be obtained. A sinking fund schedule is necessary in this case in order to compute the annual depreciation charges for the group of assets. However, the annual deposits in the fund for each asset are equal during the life of the asset. (See Example 2 of Section 17.4, pages 516 and 517.) The composite life by this method, therefore, is the time necessary for the total annual deposits at the given interest rate to accumulate to the total depreciation charges of the group of assets.

EXAMPLE 3 Use the data in Example 1. Find the composite life of the group of assets based on the sinking fund method. Assume that the effective interest rate is 6%.

The size of the annual deposit for each asset in the fund is computed by using the formula $R = \frac{S_n}{s_{\overline{n}|i}}$ (use Table 9).

$$\text{ASSET A: } R = 9{,}000/s_{\overline{10}|6\%} = 9{,}000(.135868 - .06) = \$\ \ 682.81$$
$$\text{ASSET B: } R = 4{,}800/s_{\overline{12}|6\%} = 4{,}800(.119277 - .06) = \ \ 284.53$$
$$\text{ASSET C: } R = 4{,}255/s_{\overline{5}|6\%} = 4{,}225(.237396 - .06) = \ \ \underline{749.50}$$
$$\text{Total annual deposit} = \$1{,}716.84$$

The composite life, which is the time necessary for the total annual deposits of $1,716.84 to accumulate to the total depreciation charges of $18,025 at 6%, is computed by using the amount of the annuity formula as follows:

$S_n = \$18{,}025$, $R = \$1{,}716.84$ (per year), $i = 6\%$ (per year), $n = ?$ (years)

Substituting the values in the formula $S_n = Rs_{\overline{n}|i}$,

$$18{,}025 = 1{,}716.84 s_{\overline{n}|6\%}$$

$$s_{\overline{n}|6\%} = \frac{18{,}025}{1{,}716.84} = 10.49894$$

In the 6% column of Table 7, the value 10.49894 is between 9.89747 ($n = 8$) and 11.49132 ($n = 9$). By interpolation, $n = 8.38$, the composite life in years.

EXERCISE 17–4 REFERENCE: SECTION 17.5

A. In each of the following problems, use the straight line method to find (a) the composite rate, and (b) the composite life:

	Asset	*Original Cost*	*Scrap Value*	*Estimated Life*
1.	A	\$ 5,000	\$200	8 years
	B	2,300	100	11 years
	C	800	60	20 years
2.	X	6,400	100	15 years
	Y	4,500	300	7 years
	Z	3,600	400	16 years
3.	L	11,900	700	10 years
	M	2,000	500	5 years
	N	550	none	5 years
4.	E	620	20	12 years
	F	2,400	100	4 years
	G	300	none	6 years

B. Statement problems:

5. Refer to Problem 1. Use the sinking fund method to find the composite life. Assume that the effective interest rate is 5%.
6. Refer to Problem 2. Use the sinking fund method to find the composite life. Assume that the effective interest rate is 3%.

★17.6 DEPLETION

A. Introduction

After a period of removal operations, some natural resources, such as minerals, oil, gas, and timber, are eventually exhausted in the areas of the deposits and cannot be replaced in the near future. Such natural resources are frequently called *wasting assets*. The reduction in the value of such a wasting asset resulting from exhaustion is called *depletion*.

B. Method of Computing Depletion

In general, *total depletion* is the difference between the cost and the salvage value of the property. The *annual depletion deduction* is obtained by multiplying the number of units sold during the year by the depletion rate per unit. The depletion rate per unit is derived by dividing the total depletion by the number of units estimated to be in the reserve of the property.

EXAMPLE 1

Jameson invested \$200,000 in a coal mine. The mine is estimated to have a reserve of 264,000 tons of coal. The land can be salvaged for \$2,000. Assume that during the first year $\frac{1}{5}$ of the reserve, or 52,800 tons of coal, was mined and sold. Find the total depletion and the depletion deduction for the first year of operation.

Total depletion = 200,000 − 2,000 = \$198,000
Depletion rate per unit = 198,000 ÷ 264,000 = \$0.75 (per ton)
Depletion deduction for the first year = 0.75 × 52,800 = \$39,600

EXAMPLE 2

Refer to Example 1. Assume that Jameson receives \$50,000 as his income before depletion at the end of the first year. What is his profit from mine operation?

Profit from operation = Income before depletion − Depletion
= 50,000 − 39,600 = \$10,400

C. Sinking Fund for Depletion

Investors generally expect to receive periodic interest on their investment, but may wish to withdraw their original contributions at the end of the terms of the investment rather than through periodic recovery. Thus, the owner of a wasting asset may deposit a portion of his or her annual receipt (income before depletion) at the end of each year in a sinking fund, which will eventually accumulate to an amount equal to the total depletion. Then, net annual income from the property is the difference between the income before depletion and the annual deposit in the sinking fund.

$$\begin{pmatrix}\text{Annual net income}\\ \text{from investment}\end{pmatrix} = \begin{pmatrix}\text{Income before}\\ \text{depletion}\end{pmatrix} - \begin{pmatrix}\text{Annual deposit in}\\ \text{sinking fund}\end{pmatrix}$$

The amounts of the annual deposits in the sinking fund are all equal and the size of each annual deposit can be obtained by using the formula

$$R = \frac{S_n}{s_{\overline{n}|i}}, \quad \text{where}$$

R = annual deposit in the sinking fund
S_n = total depletion (or cost − salvage value)
n = number of interest periods (or deposits)
i = interest rate per period for sinking fund

EXAMPLE 3

Use the information given in Examples 1 and 2. Assume that annual sales and annual income before depletion are expected to be equal each year and the mine is estimated to be exhausted at the end of the five years. If Jameson wishes to withdraw his original investment (\$200,000) at the end of the fifth year and he can invest a portion of his annual income in a sinking fund earning 6% effective interest, what are (a) the size of each annual deposit? (b) the net income from the investment for each year? and (c) the rate of the annual net income on the investment?

(a) Jameson's original investment, \$200,000, may be recovered at the end of five years from two sources: the salvage value of the mine (\$2,000); and the savings from the annual receipts in the sinking fund, which will accumulate to \$198,000 in five years. Since the fund earns 6% interest annually, the annual deposit (R) should be

$$R = \frac{S_n}{s_{\overline{n}|i}} = \frac{198{,}000}{s_{\overline{5}|6\%}} = \frac{198{,}000}{5.63709296} = \$35{,}124.49$$

Thus, if Jameson receives \$50,000 income annually for five years, he should deposit \$35,124.49 in the sinking fund each year in order to draw \$198,000 at the end of the fifth year.

(b) The net income from the investment after the deposit in the sinking fund is the same for each year.

Annual net income = 50,000 − 35,124.49 = \$14,875.51

(c) The rate of the annual net income on the investment is

$$\frac{14{,}875.51}{200{,}000} = .07437755, \quad \text{rounded to} \quad 7.44\%$$

NOTE:

1. The accumulated sinking fund at the end of the operating period is the same as the total depletion. However, the periodic increase in the sinking fund is *not* intended to be a guide for the periodic depletion deduction from income. The periodic depletion deductions should be based on the actual quantities that are sold. In our example, the units sold each year are assumed to be equal during the five-year period. The depletion deduction for each year is a constant amount of \$39,600 (see Example 1), but the periodic increases in the sinking fund are not the same each year (see the sinking fund schedule below). The periodic depletion deductions and the periodic increases in the sinking fund are separate transactions.

   The sinking fund schedule is constructed as follows:

Sinking Fund Schedule
[Example 3(a)]

(1) End of Year	*(2) Deposit in Sinking Fund*	*(3) Sinking Fund Interest Income: (5) × 6%*	*(4) Periodic Increase: (2) + (3)*	*(5) Accumulated Sinking Fund from (4)*	*(6) To Be Recovered: \$200,000 − (5)*
0	. . .	. . .	. . .	. . .	\$200,000.00
1	\$ 35,124.49	. . .	\$ 35,124.49	\$ 35,124.49	164,875.51
2	35,124.49	\$ 2,107.47	37,231.96	72,356.45	127,643.55
3	35,124.49	4,341.39	39,465.88	111,822.33	88,177.67
4	35,124.49	6,709.34	41,833.83	153,656.16	46,343.84
5	35,124.47*	9,219.37	44,343.84	198,000.00	2,000.00
Total	\$175,622.43	\$22,377.57	\$198,000.00		

* Corrected for 2¢ discrepancy.

2. In Example 3, since the units sold each year are assumed to be equal, the amount of \$10,400 (see Example 2) is the annual profit (after depletion) from the mine

operation during the five years. The amount of $14,875.51 is the average annual net income when the profit from mine operation and the sinking fund interest income are included. The actual annual net income is not the same for each year during the five years and may be computed as follows [see column (4)]:

(1) End of Year	*(2) Profit from Operation after Depletion*	*(3) Interest Income from Sinking Fund*	*(4) Total Net Income: (2) + (3)*
1	$10,400	. . .	$10,400.00
2	10,400	$ 2,107.47	12,507.47
3	10,400	4,341.39	14,741.39
4	10,400	6,709.34	17,109.34
5	10,400	9,219.37	19,619.37
Total	$52,000	$22,377.57	$74,377.57

The average annual net income $= \dfrac{74{,}377.57}{5} =$ $14,875.51, which is the same as the answer in Solution (b).

In summary, let

D = annual income before depletion (or dividend)
C = cost of original investment (or purchase price of the wasting asset)
T = salvage value (or trade-in value)
R = annual deposit to sinking fund
I = annual net income after sinking fund deposit
r = rate of the annual net income on the cost of the original investment, or I/C
i = interest rate per period for sinking fund
n = number of years of the life of depletion

Then,

$$\boldsymbol{D = I + R, \quad \text{or} \quad D = Cr + \frac{C - T}{s_{\overline{n}|i}}} \qquad \textbf{(17–5)}$$

Here, $Cr = I$, since
$r = I/C$; and
$C - T = S_n =$ Total depletion

If there is no salvage value (T), the formula becomes

$$\boldsymbol{D = Cr + \frac{C}{s_{\overline{n}|i}} = C\left(r + \frac{1}{s_{\overline{n}|i}}\right)} \qquad \textbf{(17–6)}$$

Any quantity in the above formulas may be solved if the other quantities are known.

Example 3 may be computed by using formula (17–5) in the following manner:

$C = 200{,}000$, $T = 2{,}000$, $D = 50{,}000$, $n = 5$ (years), $i = 6\%$ (per year)
(a) $R = ?$, (b) $I = ?$, (c) $r = ?$

The computations are shown as follows:

(a) $R = \frac{C - T}{s_{\overline{n}|i}} = \frac{(200{,}000 - 2{,}000)}{s_{\overline{5}|6\%}} = \frac{198{,}000}{5.63709296} = \$35{,}124.49$

(b) $I = D - R = 50{,}000.00 - 35{,}124.49 = \$14{,}875.51$

(c) $r = \frac{I}{C} = \frac{14{,}875.51}{200{,}000} = .07437755,$ rounded to 7.44%

EXAMPLE 4 A timberland is estimated to yield an annual income before depletion of \$30,000 for the next 30 years. At the end of that time, the land can be sold for \$1,000. What is the purchase price of the timberland if the purchaser wants to secure a yield of 7% on his investment and if he can invest the sinking fund at 4%?

$D = 30{,}000,\ T = 1{,}000,\ r = 7\%,\ i = 4\%,\ n = 30,\ C = ?$

Substituting the values in formula (17–5),

$$D = Cr + \frac{C - T}{s_{\overline{n}|i}}$$

$$30{,}000 = C(7\%) + \frac{(C - 1{,}000)}{s_{\overline{30}|4\%}}$$

$$= .07C + (C - 1{,}000)(.0178301) \quad \text{(Table 9)}$$
$$= .07C + .0178301C - (.0178301)(1{,}000)$$
$$= .0878301C - 17.8301$$
$$.0878301C = 30{,}000 + 17.8301 = 30{,}017.8301$$

$$C = \frac{30{,}017.8301}{.0878301} = \$341{,}771.56 \text{ (purchase price)}$$

EXAMPLE 5 Refer to Example 4. Assume that the land at the end of the 30th year will be worthless. What is the purchase price of the timberland?

$T = 0$. Substituting the other values (in Example 4) in formula (17–6),

$$D = C\left(r + \frac{1}{s_{\overline{n}|i}}\right)$$

$$30{,}000 = C\left(7\% + \frac{1}{s_{\overline{30}|4\%}}\right) = C(.07 + .0178301) = .0878301C$$

$$C = \frac{30{,}000}{.0878301} = \$341{,}568.55 \text{ (purchase price)}$$

★EXERCISE 17–5 REFERENCE: SECTION 17.6

1. Baxter bought a mine for \$30,000 and expected to operate it for four years. At the end of the period, the mine will be exhausted and the salvage property can be sold for \$2,000. Assume that the mine is estimated to have a reserve of 400,000 units and that during the first year of operation, $\frac{1}{4}$ of the reserve was mined and sold. The income before depletion is \$9,000 for this year. Find (a) the total depletion, (b) the depletion rate per unit, (c) the depletion deduction for the first year, and (d) the profit from the first year of operation.

2. A company purchased a piece of land containing oil wells for $100,000. The total reserves of crude oil in the wells are estimated at 200,000 barrels and are expected to be removed in 10 years. The salvage land can be sold for $4,000 at the end of the operation. Assume that during the first year of operation, $\frac{1}{10}$ of the reserve was removed and sold, and the income before depletion was $14,000. Find (a) the total depletion, (b) the depletion rate per barrel, (c) the depletion deduction for the first year, and (d) the profit from the first year of operation.
3. Refer to Problem 1. Assume that the annual sales and income before depletion are equal for each year during the four years. Baxter wishes to keep his cost of investment intact until the end of the period, and he can invest part of the income in a sinking fund at 3%. Find (a) the size of each deposit in the sinking fund, (b) his net income for each year, and (c) the rate of the annual net income on his cost of investment.
4. Refer to Problem 2. Assume that the sales and income before depletion are equal every year during the 10 years. The company wants to have the cost of investment recovered when the wells become completely exhausted in 10 years so that the company may use the fund to purchase new wells. If the company can invest a part of its income in a sinking fund earning 4% effective interest, what are (a) the size of each annual deposit in the sinking fund? (b) the net annual income for each year? and (c) the rate of the annual net income on the cost of investment?
5. Refer to Problem 3. What are answers to (a), (b), and (c) if the salvage property would be worthless at the end of four years?
6. Refer to Problem 4. What are answers to (a), (b), and (c) if the salvage land would be worthless at the end of 10 years?
7. A piece of land with natural resources is estimated to yield an annual income before depletion of $6,000 for the next 15 years. At the end of that time, the land can be sold for $300. What should be the purchase price of the land if the purchaser wants a yield of 6% on her investment and she can invest the sinking fund at $4\frac{1}{2}$% effective interest?
8. A silver mine is estimated to yield an annual income before depletion of $25,000 for the next 20 years. The salvage land is expected to be worth $900 at the end of the period. If the purchaser wishes a yield of 8% on her investment and she can invest the sinking fund at 5% effective interest, what should be the purchase price of the mine?
9. Refer to Problem 7. If the land were worthless at the end of 15 years, what should be the purchase price?
10. Refer to Problem 8. Find the purchase price if the mine were worthless at the end of 20 years.

★17.7 COMPUTING FORMULAS BY CALCULATORS AND COMPUTERS

The following list shows the formula numbers and corresponding references for computing the formulas by calculators and computers:

Formula Number	*Reference*
17–1	Chapter 10
17–2	Chapter 10
17–3 to 17–6	Sections 11.7 and 13.8
Constructing schedules based on the formulas	Section 15.5

17.8 SUMMARY OF FORMULAS

Application	*Symbols*	*Formula*	*Formula Number*	*Reference Page*
Depreciation				
	C = original cost of asset T = estimated trade-in or scrap value			
Methods of averages		$r = \frac{C - T}{n}$	(17–1)	505
	r = rate of depreciation expense per year, per service-hour, per product-unit, or per dollar n = useful life of the asset estimated in number of years, service-hours, or product-units			
Fixed rate method		$r = 1 - \sqrt[n]{T/C}$	(17–2)	512
	r = rate of depreciation per year based on diminishing book value of asset n = number of years of the estimated life			
Annuity method		$R = \frac{C - T(1 + i)^{-n}}{a_{\overline{n}\vert i}}$	(17–3)	515
	R = annual total depreciation expense i = interest rate per period (year) n = number of years of the estimated life Net annual depreciation = R − interest income			
Sinking fund method		$R = \frac{C - T}{s_{\overline{n}\vert i}}$	(17–4)	516
	R = annual deposit in sinking fund i and n mean the same as in formula (17–3) Net annual depreciation = R + interest income			
Depletion				
Establishment of sinking fund (with salvage value)		$D = Cr + \frac{C - T}{s_{\overline{n}\vert i}}$	(17–5)	523
Establishment of sinking fund (without salvage value)		$D = C\left(r + \frac{1}{s_{\overline{n}\vert i}}\right)$	(17–6)	523
	D = annual income before depletion C = cost of original investment (or purchase price of the wasting asset)			

T = salvage value (or trade-in value)
r = rate of annual net income on investment
i = interest rate per period for sinking fund
n = number of years of the life of depletion

EXERCISE 17–6 REVIEW OF CHAPTER 17

1. A garage that was constructed for $3,000 has an estimated scrap value of $300 at the end of five years. Use the following methods to find the depreciation charges for each year and construct depreciation schedules for methods (d) and (e):

   (a) Straight line method
   (b) Sum of the years-digits method
   (c) Fixed rate – 1. Tax method
   ★2. Formula method (use percent rate including three decimals)
   ★(d) Annuity method (based on 6% effective interest)
   ★(e) Sinking fund method (based on 6% effective interest)

2. A typewriter that was bought for $320 has an estimated useful life of four years and a trade-in value of $20. Use the following methods to find the depreciation charges for each year and construct depreciation schedules for methods (d) and (e):

   (a) Straight line method
   (b) Sum of the years-digits method
   (c) Fixed rate – 1. Tax method
   ★2. Formula method
   ★(d) Annuity method (based on 4% effective interest)
   ★(e) Sinking fund method (based on 4% effective interest)

3. The cost of a bookbinding machine is $1,500. It is estimated that the machine will have a $500 trade-in value at the end of its useful life. Assume that the useful life of the machine is estimated to be 25,000 service-hours and the actual number of hours spent in production for the first year is 2,200, and for the second year, 2,000. Find the depreciation expense for each of the two years.
4. Refer to Problem 3. Assume that the useful life of the machine is estimated to be 300,000 copies of books, and the number of copies bound for the first year is 25,000 and for the second year, 24,000. What is the depreciation expense for each of the two years?

★5. Find the composite rate of the group of assets in the following table:

Asset	*Original Cost*	*Scrap Value*	*Estimated Life*
Tables	$90,000	$2,000	11 years
Chairs	8,000	600	8 years
Cabinets	5,000	500	15 years

★6. Refer to Problem 5. Find the composite life of the group of assets by (a) the straight line method, and (b) the sinking fund method, based on 5% effective interest.

★7. Wanda Barker invested $500,000 in a zinc mine. The mine is estimated to have a reserve of 10,000 tons of zinc. The salvage land can be sold for $4,000. Assume that during the first year $\frac{1}{4}$ of the estimated reserve was mined and sold. Find (a) the total depletion and the depletion deduction for the first year of operation, and (b) the profit if Wanda receives $165,000 as the income before depletion at the end of the first year.

★8. A man invested $800,000 in land containing wasting assets. It is estimated to have a reserve of 5 million units. The salvage land can be sold for $2,500. Assume that during the first year, 600,000 units were mined and sold. (a) What are the total depletion and the depletion deduction for the first year of operation? (b) What is the profit if the man receives $180,000 as the income before depletion at the end of the first year?

★9. Refer to Problem 7. Assume that the mine is estimated to be exhausted at the end of four years and that the sales and the income before depletion in each year are expected to be equal. If Wanda wishes to invest a portion of her annual income in a sinking fund that will earn 5% compounded annually so that she may recover her original investment at the end of the fourth year of operation, find (a) the size of each annual deposit in the fund, (b) the net income from the investment in the mine, and (c) the rate of the annual net income on the original investment.

★10. A $200,000 mine is scheduled for 15 years of operation. Assume that the operation for each year is the same, the income before depletion for each year is $30,000, and the salvage land of the mine can be sold for $2,000 at the end of operation. The owners wish to recover their original investment by means of a sinking fund earning 6% annually. Find (a) the annual deposit in the sinking fund, (b) the net income from the mine investment, and (c) the rate of the annual net income to the original mine investment.

★11. A copper mine is estimated to yield an annual income before depletion of $50,000 for 20 years. The salvage land can be sold for $1,500 at the end of 20 years. Find the purchase price of the mine if the purchaser wishes a 6% yield on his investment and he can invest the sinking fund at 5% compounded annually.

★12. Some land containing oil wells is estimated to yield an annual income before depletion of $600,000 for 10 years. The land can be sold for $2,000 at the end of the tenth year. What is the purchase price of the land if the investor wants a 5% yield on her investment and she can invest part of the annual income in a sinking fund earning 3% annually?

★13. Refer to Problem 11. If the land becomes worthless at the end of 20 years, what should the purchase price be?

★14. Refer to Problem 12. If the land becomes worthless at the end of 10 years, what should the purchase price of the land be?

18 PERPETUITY AND CAPITALIZATION

The basic concepts and applications of perpetuity (Section 18.1) and capitalization (Sections 18.2 and 18.3) are introduced in this chapter. A perpetuity is a type of annuity, as stated in Section 13.1. The method of computing a perpetuity can be used in solving capitalization problems.

18.1 PERPETUITY

When the term of an annuity begins on a definite date but never ends, the annuity is called a *perpetuity*. In other words, the payments of a perpetuity continue forever. Since there is no end to a perpetuity, it is impossible to determine its final value. However, as will be shown in the examples below, the present value of a perpetuity can be determined.

Perpetuities may be divided into two groups: (a) simple and (b) complex (general). Since a perpetuity is a type of annuity, the qualifying words such as ordinary, due, deferred, simple, complex, and general, used previously in annuity problems, are also used within this chapter.

A. Simple Perpetuities

When the payments of a perpetuity are made at the *end* of each interest period, the perpetuity is called a *simple ordinary perpetuity*. It will be recalled that in the method used to find the simple interest on an investment, the simple interest (I) is obtained by using the formula $I = Pin$. When $n = 1$, and i represents the rate per period, the formula becomes $I = Pi$. The formula indicates that if P is invested now at the interest rate of i per period, the periodic interest is the value of Pi. The interest may be drawn periodically as long as the principal (P) is invested. Thus, if \$100 is invested now at the interest rate of 2% per quarter, the quarterly interest is \$2 (or \$100 $\times$ 2%), which may be drawn by the investor at the end of each quarter as long as the \$100 principal is left in the investment. The size of the investment is found by dividing both sides of the formula $I = Pi$ by i. Thus,

$$P = \frac{I}{i}$$

This idea is used in a similar manner in the case of simple perpetuities. Let A_∞ denote the present value of a simple ordinary perpetuity. Then

$$A_\infty = P = \frac{I}{i}, \quad \text{or} \quad A_\infty = \frac{I}{i} \qquad \textbf{(18–1)}$$

NOTE: The symbol "∞" represents "infinity." I is the periodic payment (or receipt, whichever the case may be) of the perpetuity made at the end of each period, and i is the interest rate per period.

EXAMPLE 1

Find the present value of a simple perpetuity of $500 payable at the end of each quarter if the interest rate is 2% per quarter (or 8% compounded quarterly).

$I = 500$, $i = 2\%$

Substituting the values in formula (18–1),

$$A_\infty = \frac{I}{i} = \frac{500}{.02} = \$25{,}000$$

The answer indicates that if $25,000 is invested now at 2% per quarter, the investor can draw $500 at the end of each quarter forever; that is, if the principal remains intact and the interest rate does not change. In other words, $25,000 is the cash equivalent of a perpetuity of $500 payable at the end of each quarter when the given interest rate is involved.

EXAMPLE 2

Find the present value of a simple annuity of $500 payable at the end of each quarter for (a) 20 years, (b) 25 years, and (c) 50 years. The interest rate is 2% per quarter.

(a) $R = 500,\ i = 2\%,\ n = 20 \times 4 = 80$ (quarters)
$A_{80} = 500a_{\overline{80}|2\%} = 500(39.74451) = \$19{,}872.26$

(b) $n = 25 \times 4 = 100$ (quarters)
$A_{100} = 500a_{\overline{100}|2\%} = 500(43.09835) = \$21{,}549.18$

(c) $n = 50 \times 4 = 200$ (quarters)

First, the annuity is divided into two parts with each part consisting of 100 quarterly payments. (See page 391.)

The present value of the first part consisting of 100 payments is $21,549.18 [See (b) above.]

The present value of the second part consisting of 100 payments is

$P = 21{,}549.18(1 + 2\%)^{-100} = 21{,}549.18(.138033) = \$2{,}974.50$

Then the present value of the 200 payments is computed as follows:

$A_{200} = 21{,}549.18 + 2{,}974.50 = \$24{,}523.68$

These answers may be compared with that given in Example 1.

n (Quarters)	*Present Value*
80	\$19,872.26
100	21,549.18
200	24,523.68
∞	25,000.00

The comparison indicates that as the length of the term of an annuity increases, its present value gets closer to the present value of a perpetuity.

When the payments of a perpetuity are made at the *beginning* of each interest period, the perpetuity is called a *simple perpetuity due*.

EXAMPLE 3

Find the present value of a simple perpetuity of \$400 payable at the beginning of each month if the interest rate is 12% compounded monthly.

First, the present value of a simple perpetuity of \$400 payable at the *end* of each month is computed as follows:

$I = 400$, $i = 12\%/12 = 1\%$ (per month)

Substituting the values in formula (18–1),

$$A_{\infty} = \frac{I}{i} = \frac{400}{1\%} = \frac{400}{.01} = \$40{,}000$$

The present value of a simple perpetuity of \$400 payable at the *beginning* of each month is

$40{,}000 + 400 = \$40{,}400$

Note that \$400 is the first payment, whose present value is the value of the payment unchanged.

B. Complex (General) Perpetuities

When each of the periodic payments of a perpetuity is made at the end of several interest periods, the perpetuity is called a *complex* (or *general*) *perpetuity*.

EXAMPLE 4

A man invests \$1,000 now at an interest rate of 16% compounded quarterly and wants to draw interest at the end of each year forever. How much interest will he receive annually?

The compound amount of \$1,000 at the end of every fourth quarter (or every year) is

$1{,}000(1 + 4\%)^4 = 1{,}000(1.169859) = \$1{,}169.86$

The compound interest at the end of each year is

$1{,}169.86 - 1{,}000.00 = \$169.86$

Example 4 is a complex perpetuity problem and may be stated in the following manner:

If the present value of a perpetuity is \$1,000 and the interest rate is 16% compounded quarterly, the periodic payment at the end of every four interest periods (quarters) is \$169.86.

Similarly, let

R = the size of the periodic payment (or periodic interest)
i = interest rate per interest conversion period
c = interest conversion periods per payment interval
A_∞ = present value of a perpetuity, with payments of R made at the end of every c interest periods

The value of R is computed as follows:

$$R = A_\infty(1 + i)^c - A_\infty = A_\infty[(1 + i)^c - 1]$$

Thus,

$$A_\infty = \frac{R}{(1 + i)^c - 1}, \quad \text{or} \quad A_\infty = \frac{R}{i} \cdot \frac{1}{s_{\overline{c}|i}} \qquad \textbf{(18–2)}[1]$$

NOTE: When $c = 1$, the value of $s_{\overline{c}|i} = 1$. Then $A_\infty = \frac{R}{i}$ and $R = I$.

Formula (18–2) becomes identical to formula (18–1).

Thus, formula (18–2) is a general formula for ordinary perpetuities.

The following diagram supports the above illustrations in Example 4 and formula (18–2).

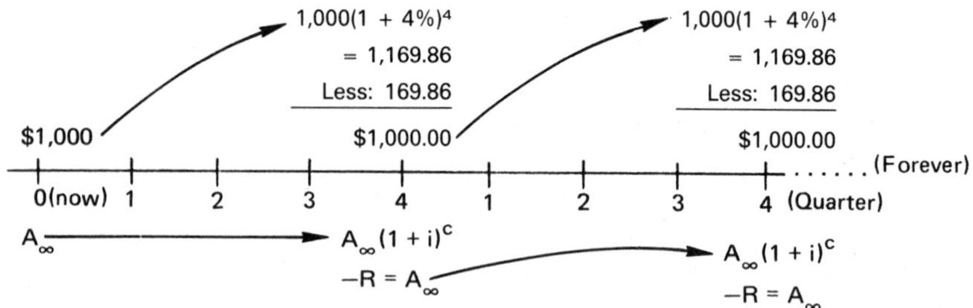

EXAMPLE 5 Find the present value of a perpetuity of \$500 payable semiannually if money is worth 6% compounded monthly, and (a) the first payment is due six months hence, (b) the first payment is due now.

(a) R = \$500 (per six months), $i = 6\%/12 = \frac{1}{2}\%$ (monthly), $c = 6$ (interest periods in one payment interval). Substituting the values in formula (18–2),

$$A_\infty = \frac{R}{i} \cdot \frac{1}{s_{\overline{c}|i}} = \frac{500}{\frac{1}{2}\%} \cdot \frac{1}{s_{\overline{6}|1/2\%}} = \frac{500}{1/200}\left(\frac{1}{a_{\overline{6}|1/2\%}} - \tfrac{1}{2}\%\right)$$

$$= 100{,}000(.16959546 - .005) = \$16{,}459.55 \quad \text{(Table 9)}$$

---

[1] *Proof–Formula (18–2):*

$$A_\infty = \frac{R}{(1 + i)^c - 1} = \frac{i}{i} \cdot \frac{R}{(1 + i)^c - 1} = \frac{R}{i} \cdot \frac{i}{(1 + i)^c - 1}$$

$$= \frac{R}{i} \cdot \frac{1}{s_{\overline{c}|i}}$$

NOTE: The present value of the perpetuity may also be computed by using Table 5, as follows:

$$A_\infty = \frac{R}{(1+i)^c - 1} = \frac{500}{(1+\frac{1}{2}\%)^6 - 1} = \frac{500}{1.03037751 - 1}$$

$$= \$16,459.55$$

Either the method given in (a) or that presented above may be employed. However, in order to avoid long division, the former method is preferred.

(b) The present value of a complex perpetuity *due* is obtained by adding one payment to the answer in (a) as follows:

$500 + 16,459.55 = \$16,959.55$

Note that \$500 is the first payment, whose present value is the value of the payment unchanged.

EXERCISE 18–1 REFERENCE: SECTION 18.1

A. Find the present value of the perpetuity in each of the following problems:

	Payment	*Interest Rate*
1.	\$800 quarterly, at the end of each quarter	4% per quarter
2.	\$900 semiannually, at the end of every six months	10% per six months
3.	\$200 semiannually, at the end of every six months	12% compounded monthly
4.	\$500 annually, at the end of each year	20% compounded quarterly
5.	\$350 quarterly, at the beginning of each quarter	2% per quarter
6.	\$700 monthly, at the beginning of each month	$\frac{1}{2}$% per month
7.	\$800 annually, at the beginning of each year	4% compounded monthly
8.	\$100 semiannually, at the beginning of each six months	5% compounded quarterly

B. Statement problems:

9. Find the present value of a simple perpetuity of \$1,000 payable semiannually if the interest rate is 2% per six months and the first payment is due (a) six months from now, and (b) now.
10. What is the present value of a simple perpetuity of \$1,200 payable quarterly if the interest rate is $1\frac{1}{2}$% per quarter and the first payment is due (a) three months from now, and (b) now?
11. Refer to Problem 9. If the interest rate is 4% compounded quarterly, find the answers to (a) and (b).
12. Refer to Problem 10. If the interest rate is 6% compounded monthly, find the answers to (a) and (b).
13. The alumni of a college want to provide a scholarship fund that will permanently give \$1,000 at the end of each year. If the effective interest rate is 6%, how large must the fund be?
14. A foundation is to be established for the purpose of awarding \$2,000 to an outstanding scientist at the end of each year. If money can be invested by the foundation at 5% compounded annually, how large should the fund be?
15. Find the answer to Problem 13 if the interest is 6% compounded monthly.
16. Find the answer to Problem 14 if the interest is 5% compounded semiannually.

18.2 CAPITALIZATION

Capitalization is the process of converting an unlimited number of periodic payments into a single present value or cash equivalent. In other words, if the single sum were invested now at a given interest rate, the periodic interest would be payable forever. Thus, the single sum is the present value of a perpetuity that is formed by the periodic payments.

A. Asset and Liability Valuations

Capitalization is a very useful method for evaluating assets and liabilities. Income-producing properties (tangible or intangible) and liabilities are often capitalized as standards for estimating their values.

EXAMPLE 1 What is the cash equivalent of one acre of land if the land yields a net rental of \$200 per year and money is worth (a) 10% effective interest rate, and (b) 10% compounded quarterly?

(a) $I = \$200$ (per year), $i = 10\%$ (per year)

Substituting the values in formula (18–1),

$$A_\infty = \frac{I}{i} = \frac{200}{10\%} = \frac{200}{.10} = \$2{,}000 \text{ (land value)}$$

(b) $R = \$200$ (per year), $i = 10\%/4 = 2\frac{1}{2}\%$ (per quarter), $c = 4$ (quarters in a yearly payment interval)

Substituting the values in formula (18–2),

$$A_\infty = \frac{R}{i} \cdot \frac{1}{s_{\overline{c}|i}} = \frac{200}{2\frac{1}{2}\%} \cdot \frac{1}{s_{\overline{4}|2\ 1/2\%}} = 8{,}000(.265818 - .025)$$

$$= 8{,}000(.240818) = \$1{,}926.54 \text{ (land value)}$$

EXAMPLE 2 Capitalize an obligation of \$1,500 payable at the end of each year forever if the effective interest rate is 15%.

$I = \$1{,}500$ (per year), $i = 15\%$ (per year)

$$A_\infty = \frac{1{,}500}{15\%} = \$10{,}000 \text{ (present value of the obligation)}$$

Thus a debtor who has \$10,000 now may use the money to pay off his or her obligation.

B. Capitalized Cost

An asset, such as a building, a machine, or a piece of equipment, often needs to be renewed or replaced periodically after it is constructed or bought. The cost of the asset may be capitalized so that a sufficient sum of money can be invested now and the accumulated interest will become available for an unlimited number of future renewals or replacements. The *capitalized cost* is generally defined as the sum of the original cost and the present value of the future renewals. The future renewals form a perpetuity.

Let K = capitalized cost
F = first (or original) cost
i = interest rate per interest conversion period
c = number of interest periods in one renewal interval
R = each renewal cost if $c > 1$
I = each renewal cost if $c = 1$

The computations for capitalized cost (K) are as follows.

If the *interest period coincides with the renewal interval* (or $c = 1$), the value of K is the sum of the first cost and the present value of the simple ordinary perpetuity, or

$$K = F + \frac{I}{i} \tag{18-3}$$

EXAMPLE 3 The first cost of a new car is $20,000. Thereafter, the purchaser wants to trade his car for a new one every year. Assume that he has to pay $5,000 for each trade-in. If interest is 12.5%, find the capitalized cost for the car.

$F = \$20{,}000$, $I = \$5{,}000$ (per year), $i = 12.5\%$ (per year)

$$K = 20{,}000 + \frac{5{,}000}{12.5\%} = 20{,}000 + \$40{,}000 = \$60{,}000$$

If the *number of interest periods in one renewal interval is more than 1 (or $c > 1$)*, the value of K is the sum of the first cost and the present value of the complex ordinary perpetuity. In general,

$$K = F + \frac{R}{i} \cdot \frac{1}{s_{\overline{c}|i}} \tag{18-4}$$

EXAMPLE 4 The original cost of a warehouse was $30,000. The warehouse must be completely rebuilt every 25 years. If money can be invested at 6% compounded quarterly, what is the capitalized cost of the warehouse? Assume that the cost of each replacement will be $27,000.

$F = \$30{,}000$, $R = \$27{,}000$ (every 25 years), $i = 6\%/4 = 1\frac{1}{2}\%$ (per quarter), $c = 25 \times 4 = 100$ (quarters in a 25-year payment interval)

The capitalized cost of the warehouse is equal to the first cost added to the present value of the future replacement costs.

$$K = 30{,}000 + \frac{27{,}000}{1\frac{1}{2}\%} \cdot \frac{1}{s_{\overline{100}|1\ 1/2\%}}$$

$$= 30{,}000 + \frac{27{,}000}{.015}(0.01937057 - 0.015)$$
$$= 30{,}000 + (1{,}800{,}000)(0.00437057)$$
$$= 30{,}000 + 7{,}867.026 = \$37{,}867.026, \quad \text{or } \$37{,}867.03$$

However, when the *cost of replacement (R) is the same as the first cost (F)*, the value of K may be computed by using the following formula:

$$K = \frac{R}{i} \cdot \frac{1}{a_{\overline{c}|i}} \qquad \textbf{(18–5)}^2$$

EXAMPLE 5 In Example 4, assume that the cost of replacement will be \$30,000, the same as the original cost. What is the capitalized cost of the warehouse?

$F = \$30{,}000$, $R = F = \$30{,}000$, $i = 1\frac{1}{2}\%$, $c = 100$ (quarters)

$$K = \frac{30{,}000}{1\frac{1}{2}\%} \cdot \frac{1}{a_{\overline{100}|1\,1/2\%}}$$
$$= 2{,}000{,}000(0.01937057) = \$38{,}741.14$$

CHECK The present value of the investment is \$38,741.14. After the original cost of \$30,000 has been used, the remaining principal is \$8,741.14. The principal, \$8,741.14, is invested at 6% compounded quarterly. At the end of 25 years, when the warehouse will be replaced for the first time, the compound amount will be as follows.

$P = \$8{,}741.14$, $i = \dfrac{6\%}{4} = 1\frac{1}{2}\%$ (per quarter), $n = 25 \times 4 = 100$ (quarters)

$$S = 8{,}741.14(1 + 1\tfrac{1}{2}\%)^{100} = 8{,}741.14(4.432046)$$
$$= \$38{,}741.1346, \quad \text{rounded to} \quad \$38{,}741.14 \quad \text{to agree with the answer to Example 5.}$$

Therefore, another \$30,000 is available for the first replacement. The remaining part is intact and becomes the new principal to be invested for the next 25 years.

★EXAMPLE 6 Refer to Example 5. Assume that 20 years after the warehouse was built, there is a need for a major repair that will prolong the useful life for three years; that is, the warehouse will become useless and must be replaced at the end of 28 years. How much of the capitalized cost can the owner afford to pay for repair costs?

At the end of 20 years, the remaining capitalized cost, \$8,741.14, will have accumulated to the following amount ($n = 20 \times 4 = 80$ quarters):

$$S = 8{,}741.14(1 + 1\tfrac{1}{2}\%)^{80}$$
$$= 8{,}741.14(3.290663) = \$28{,}764.15$$

At the end of 28 years, the required capitalized cost is \$38,741.14, the same as the cost when the first warehouse was constructed. The principal, which is required to accumulate to the amount of \$38,741.14 from the end of the 20th to the end of the 28th year (eight years, or 32 quarters) is computed as follows:

$$P = 38{,}741.14(1 + 1\tfrac{1}{2}\%)^{-32}$$
$$= 38{,}741.14(.6209929) = \$24{,}057.97$$

---

[2] *Proof–Formula (18–5):*

When $F = R$, formula (18–4) may be written as follows:

$$K = R + \frac{R}{i} \cdot \frac{1}{s_{\overline{c}|i}} = R\left(1 + \frac{1}{i} \cdot \frac{1}{s_{\overline{c}|i}}\right) = R\left[1 + \frac{1}{i}\left(\frac{1}{a_{\overline{c}|i}} - i\right)\right]$$
$$= R\left(1 + \frac{1}{ia_{\overline{c}|i}} - 1\right) = \frac{R}{i} \cdot \frac{1}{a_{\overline{c}|i}}$$

After deducting the required principal, the remaining portion of the capitalized cost investment at the end of the 20th year may be used for the major repair, as shown below:

The repair cost = 28,764.15 − 24,057.97 = $4,706.18

Example 6 is diagrammed as follows:

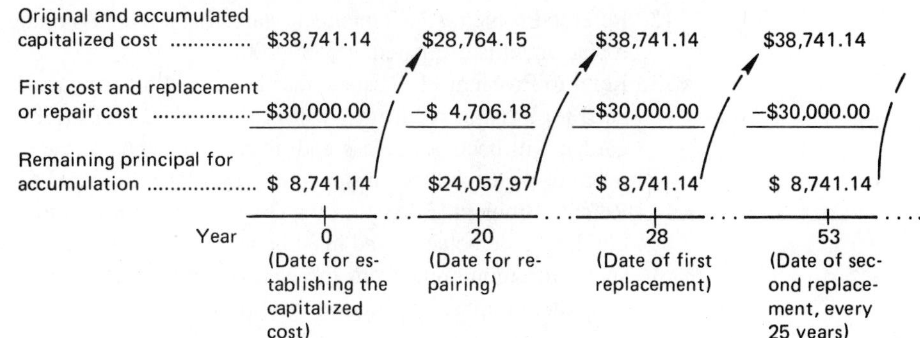

EXERCISE 18–2 REFERENCE: SECTION 18.2

1. What is the cash equivalent of a lot if the lot can be rented for $300 per year and money is worth (a) 15%, (b) 18%, compounded monthly?
2. Capitalize an obligation of $500 payable at the end of each quarter forever if interest is (a) 16% compounded quarterly, (b) 12% compounded monthly.
3. The annual income from a piece of property is $20,000 a year. If someone wishes a return on an investment of 5% compounded semiannually, what should be the purchase price of the property?
4. The annual future earnings of a store are conservatively estimated at $10,000. (a) At what price will a person purchase the store if he or she wishes a return of 4% compounded quarterly on the investment? (b) Assume that the net assets of the store are valued at $225,000. What is the price of goodwill (the excess payment over the value of the net assets)?
5. A factory bought a machine for $2,400. The machine is to be exchanged every year. The net cost of each exchange is estimated to be $700. If interest is 7%, what is the capitalized cost of the machine?
6. A truck was purchased for $15,000. The truck will be traded in for a new one every year. Assume that it is necessary to pay $3,000 for each trade-in. If interest is 15%, find the capitalized cost of the truck.
7. Refer to Problem 5. Compute the capitalized cost of the machine if the interest is 7% compounded quarterly.
8. Refer to Problem 6. Compute the capitalized cost of the truck if the interest is 15% compounded semiannually.
9. The original cost of a garage was $20,000. The garage must be rebuilt every 20 years. If money can be invested at 4% compounded semiannually, what is the capitalized cost of the garage? Assume that the cost of each replacement will be $18,000.

10. A library building for the School of Business Administration in a college was constructed at a cost of \$550,000. The building must be replaced every 40 years and the cost of each replacement is estimated to be \$570,000. Compute the capitalized cost if the interest rate is 5%.
11. Refer to Problem 9. Assume that the cost of replacement will be \$20,000, the same as the original cost. What is the capitalized cost of the garage?
12. Refer to Problem 10. Compute the capitalized cost, assuming that the cost of each replacement is estimated at \$550,000.
★ 13. Refer to Problem 11. Assume that 15 years after the garage was built, there is a need for a major repair that will prolong the useful life for 4 years; that is, the garage will become useless and must be replaced at the end of 24 years. How much of the capitalized cost can the owner afford to pay for repair costs?
★ 14. Refer to Problem 12. Assume that 30 years after the building was constructed, the building is demolished and must be rebuilt. How much can the college afford to spend for rebuilding from the capitalized cost investment if the new type of construction must be replaced thereafter at the same cost every 30 years?

★18.3 COMPARISON OF BUYING COSTS

The method for determining capitalized cost is also useful in selecting equipment (or service) from a number of different types or brands. If the various types of equipment give the same service, the buyer can choose the type with the lowest capitalized cost and thus save money. (See Example 1 below.) The method is also useful in figuring the replacement cost for a different grade or type of equipment (or service) from the same capitalized cost. (See Examples 2 and 3.)

EXAMPLE 1

The cost of machine A is \$200 and must be replaced every 10 years at the same cost. The cost of machine B is \$190 and must be replaced every eight years at a cost of \$180. If money is worth 5% compounded annually, which machine is the better buy?

The capitalized cost of machine A is

$$K = \frac{200}{5\%} \cdot \frac{1}{a_{\overline{10}|5\%}} = 4{,}000(0.129505) = \$518.02$$

The capitalized cost of machine B is

$$K = 190 + \frac{180}{5\%} \cdot \frac{1}{s_{\overline{8}|5\%}} = 190 + 3{,}600(0.154722 - .05)$$

$$= 190 + 377 = \$567$$

Since machine A has a lower capitalized cost, it is the better buy.

EXAMPLE 2

A piece of equipment that now needs to be replaced was purchased for \$150 with a guaranteed life of 10 years. If new equipment is guaranteed for a useful life of 12 years, how much can the buyer afford to pay with the same capitalized cost that is invested at 5%?

Since no replacement costs are stated for either piece of equipment, the replacement costs are considered the same as the original costs in computing the value of the capitalized costs of both items.

The capitalized cost of the old equipment is

$$K = \frac{150}{5\%} \cdot \frac{1}{a_{\overline{10}|5\%}}$$

Let R = the cost of the new equipment.

The capitalized cost of the new equipment is

$$K = \frac{R}{5\%} \cdot \frac{1}{a_{\overline{12}|5\%}}$$

Equate the right sides of the two equations above, since the capitalized cost is the same. Then solve for R as follows:

$$\frac{R}{5\%} \cdot \frac{1}{a_{\overline{12}|5\%}} = \frac{150}{5\%} \cdot \frac{1}{a_{\overline{10}|5\%}}; \qquad \frac{R}{a_{\overline{12}|5\%}} = \frac{150}{a_{\overline{10}|5\%}}$$

$$R = \frac{150}{a_{\overline{10}|5\%}} \cdot a_{\overline{12}|5\%} = 150(.129505)(8.86325) = \$172.18$$

EXAMPLE 3 Refer to Example 2. Assume that the cost of the new piece of equipment is the same as the cost of the old piece. If an attachment had been added to the new equipment to prolong the guaranteed life to 12 years, how much money can the buyer afford to pay for the additional attachment from the same capitalized cost?

R = the entire cost of the replacement, or
R = the cost of the new equipment + the cost of the attachment
= \$172.18

Since the cost of the new equipment is the same as that of the old, or \$150, the cost of the attachment = 172.18 − 150 = \$22.18.

★EXERCISE 18–3 REFERENCE: SECTION 18.3

1. The cost of one type of garage is \$15,000. It has to be replaced every eight years at the same cost. The cost of another type of garage is \$17,500. It has to be replaced every 10 years at the same cost. If money is worth 10% compounded annually, which type of garage is less expensive?
2. A typewriter worth \$250 has to be replaced every five years. Another typewriter, worth \$210, has to be replaced every four years. If money is worth 5%, which typewriter is the better buy?
3. Refer to Problem 1. If the \$17,500 garage must be replaced every 10 years at a cost of \$16,500, which type of garage is less expensive?
4. Refer to Problem 2. If the typewriter worth \$210 can be replaced every four years at a net cost of \$200, which typewriter is the better buy?

5. A machine that now needs to be replaced was purchased for $1,000 with a guaranteed life of 15 years. If a new machine is guaranteed for a useful life of 18 years, how much can the buyer afford to pay with the same capitalized cost that is invested at 5%?
6. A house that was painted three years ago for $70 now needs to be repainted. If a better type of paint is used, it will last four years. How much can the owner afford to pay for the better paint with the same capitalized cost that is invested at $3\frac{1}{2}\%$?
7. Refer to Problem 5. Assume that the price of the new machine is the same as that of the old machine. However, the purchaser wishes to buy a special service so that the new machine will last 20 years. How much can the purchaser afford to pay for the service from the same capitalized cost?
8. Refer to Problem 6. (a) If a type of paint that will last five years is used for the repainting job, how much can the owner afford to pay? (b) What is the difference between the prices of the three-year paint and the five-year paint?

18.4 SUMMARY OF FORMULAS

Symbols: A_∞ = present value of an ordinary perpetuity
I = periodic payment (or renewal cost) if $c = 1$
R = periodic payment (or renewal cost) if $c > 1$
K = capitalized cost
F = first cost from the capitalized cost
i = interest rate per interest period
c = number of interest conversion periods in one payment (or renewal) interval

Application	*Formula*	*Formula Number*	*Reference Page*
Simple ordinary perpetuity	$A_\infty = \frac{I}{i}$	(18–1)	530
Complex (ordinary) perpetuity	$A_\infty = \frac{R}{i} \cdot \frac{1}{s_{\overline{c}\rvert i}}$	(18–2)	532
Capitalized cost	*When* $c = 1$,		
	$K = F + \frac{I}{i}$	(18–3)	535
	When $c > 1$,		
	$K = F + \frac{R}{i} \cdot \frac{1}{s_{\overline{c}\rvert i}}$	(18–4)	535
	When $F = R$,		
	$K = \frac{R}{i} \cdot \frac{1}{a_{\overline{c}\rvert i}}$	(18–5)	536

NOTE: Review Section 13.8 for computing annuity formulas by calculators and computers.

EXERCISE 18–4 REVIEW OF CHAPTER 18

1. Find the present value of a perpetuity of $150 payable at the end of each month if the interest rate is 18% compounded monthly.
2. What is the present value of a perpetuity of $5,000 payable at the end of each quarter if the interest rate is 20% compounded quarterly?
3. Refer to Problem 1. If the first payment of the perpetuity is due now, what is the present value?
4. Refer to Problem 2. If the first payment of the perpetuity is due now, what is the present value?
5. Find the present value of a perpetuity of $50 payable at the end of each quarter if the interest rate is 6% compounded monthly.
6. What is the present value of a perpetuity of $200 payable at the end of each year if money is worth 4% compounded semiannually?
7. Refer to Problem 5. What is the present value of the perpetuity if the first payment is due now?
8. Refer to Problem 6. Find the present value of the perpetuity, assuming that the first payment is due now.
9. What is the cash equivalent of a piece of property if the income from it for every six months is $500 and money is worth (a) 6% compounded semiannually, and (b) 4% compounded quarterly?
10. Capitalize a debt of $100 payable at the end of each year forever if interest is (a) 4% compounded annually, (b) 5% compounded monthly.
11. A bridge is constructed at a cost of $100,000. The bridge must be rebuilt every 30 years. If money can be invested at 5% compounded semiannually, find the capitalized cost of the bridge. Assume that the cost of each rebuilding will be $90,000.
12. The original cost of a photo station is estimated at $50,000. Thereafter, it should be reconstructed every 15 years, and the reconstruction cost is estimated to be $30,000 each time. If money can be invested at 4% compounded monthly, what is the capitalized cost of the station?
13. Refer to Problem 11. Assume that the cost of each rebuilding is $100,000. What is the capitalized cost?
14. Refer to Problem 12. Assume that the remodeling cost is estimated at $50,000 each time. Find the capitalization cost.
15. ★ Refer to Problem 13. Assume that 22 years after the bridge was constructed, a major repair is needed and the bridge will have a useful life of another 15 years after the repair. At the end of the life of the bridge, it is to be rebuilt and will be rebuilt thereafter every 30 years. How much of the capitalized cost is available for the repair?

★16. Refer to Problem 14. Assume that 12 years after the station was built, a major repair is necessary. It is estimated that eight years after the repair, the station will be in need of reconstruction, and will require reconstruction thereafter every 15 years. How much of the capitalized cost can be spent for the repair?

★17. The cost of television set X is $400, and it must be replaced every eight years at a cost of $390. The cost of television set Y is $360, and it must be replaced every six years at the same cost. If money is worth 6% compounded semiannually, which of the two sets is the cheaper one?

★18. The cost of washing machine G is $300, and it must be replaced every 10 years at a cost of $280. The cost of washing machine F is $350, and it must be replaced every 12 years at a cost of $315. If money is worth 7% compounded annually, which machine is comparatively lower in cost?

★19. A machine that now needs to be replaced was bought for $800 with a guaranteed life of six years. If a new machine is guaranteed for a useful life of eight years, how much can the buyer afford to pay with the same capitalized cost that earns $5\frac{1}{2}$% interest compounded quarterly?

★20. A computer was purchased five years ago for $3,500. The capitalized cost of the computer was established for replacement every 5 years at the same cost and invested at 6% compounded quarterly. If a new computer has an estimated useful life of six years, how much can the owner afford to pay for the new computer from the capitalized cost?

★21. Refer to Problem 19. Assume that the cost of the new machine, which has a useful life of eight years, is also $800, the same as the cost of the old one. How much can the buyer afford to pay from the capitalized cost for an attachment to the new machine?

★22. Refer to Problem 20. Assume that the cost of the new computer with a useful life of six years is $3,500, the same as the cost of the old computer. How much can the owner afford to pay from the capitalized cost for an extra piece of equipment?

19 LIFE ANNUITIES

Life annuities and life insurances are different types of contracts. This chapter introduces only life annuities. The next chapter will present life insurances. The basic concepts of life annuity and life insurance are first explained (Section 19.1). Next, the uses of mortality tables are discussed (Section 19.2). The life annuity contracts included in this chapter are: pure endowment contracts (Section 19.3), whole life annuities (Section 19.4), and temporary life annuities (Section 19.5).

19.1 INTRODUCTION

Over the years the life insurance business has come to be one of the most important industries in the nation. According to a report made by the American Council of Life Insurance, the insurance companies of the United States had assets worth $771 million in 1890, but this amount had increased to more than $1,044 billion in 1987.[1] Most of these dollars are earmarked to meet the life insurance companies' future obligations to policyholders. One such obligation is the life annuity, which will be discussed in this chapter.

The basic idea of a *life annuity* is simple. People generally find it rather difficult to save enough money during their working years to support themselves in their old age. Furthermore, individuals themselves would not need their savings should they die before reaching retirement age. With a life annuity, each person within an age group contributes an equal amount of money to an agent, such as an insurance company, for the purpose of sharing in the total amount at a future date, provided that person is still alive. Survivors can later enjoy an amount larger than their original contributions, since some of the contributors will not be alive then and interest is paid by the insurance company for use of the contributions. Since no one knows if he or she will be alive on a particular future date

[1]American Council of Life Insurance, *Life Insurance Fact Book 1988* (Washington, D.C.), p. 73.

and the annuity is payable depending on a future occurrence, a life annuity is a type of contingent annuity.

The basic idea of *life insurance* is the same as that of life annuity. Both life insurance and life annuity contracts are designed for protection against the contingency of future life. However, a life annuity is provided for the purchaser of the annuity (the *annuitant*) to use the money in old age, whereas the purchaser of life insurance (the *insured*) is not usually the one who receives the benefits provided by the life insurance contract (the *policy*). A life annuity is payable to the annuitant by the insurance company if the annuitant is still *alive* on an indicated date, according to the annuity contract. Life insurance is payable to the beneficiary of the insured if the insured *dies* within the indicated time stated in the insurance policy. Thus, the life annuity is not a life insurance contract. However, since the mathematics of a life annuity, or actuarial calculation, is based on a concept similar to that used in life insurance, life annuities have always been considered as part of the life insurance business and are among the oldest types of insurance contracts.

The cost, which is used to provide funds for the payment of the benefit according to a life annuity or an insurance contract, is called the *net premium*. In addition to the net premium, other amounts of money that are charged by an insurance company are called *loading costs*, which include the profit element and the operating expenses of the company, such as salaries, rent, and depreciation. The sum of the net premium and the loading costs is called the *gross premium*. Since both the operating expenses and the profit rates differ among insurance companies, for the sake of simplicity, *only the net premium is computed in this and the following chapter*.

The fundamental relationship between the net premium and the future benefits under any type of annuity contract or insurance policy may be expressed *on the purchase date* as follows:

Present value of net premium = Present value of future benefit(s)

The net premium may be paid in a single amount, called the *net single premium*, on the purchase date. It may also be paid in equal annual payments, called the *net annual premiums*. Net single premiums are generally paid for annuity contracts, while net annual premiums are usually paid for life insurance policies. However, a knowledge of the net single premium is necessary in computing a set of net annual premiums for an insurance policy.

Insurance companies usually invest their collected premiums in various fields to earn interest at rates that fluctuate on the money market. The interest income is first used as a portion of the reserve for the benefit of policyholders. (See Section 20.7B, Uses of the Terminal Reserve.) If the interest income and the collected premiums exceed the reserve requirements, payments of claims, and administrative expenses, the insurance company may use the excess as a dividend payable to policyholders. In order to simplify the mathematical illustrations, *unless otherwise specified, net premiums are computed at a nominal interest rate of* $2\frac{1}{2}\%$ *in all problems in this text*.

Generally, the age of a purchaser on his or her last birthday is taken in computing the purchase price of an insurance contract, but a pro rata allowance is sometimes made for each month that has elapsed since the last birthday. In simplifying the computation in this and the following chapter, it is assumed that *all annuity contracts and insurance policies are made on the purchaser's birthday*. Thus, the expression "a person aged 25" means that the person reaches his 25th birthday on the purchase date.

19.2 MORTALITY TABLES

The computation of life annuity and life insurance net premiums is primarily based on a mortality table. A *mortality table* is a statistical table showing the death rate of people of every age group. Although nobody can predict how long a certain individual will live or when that individual will die, studies of the mortality of people based on years of experience enable insurance companies to make a reasonably accurate prediction of the death rate of any particular age group. A large representative group of people, usually policyholders, is included in each study. The number of people living and dying in each age group is recorded and the findings are tabulated. For example, the American Experience Table was calculated from the mortality experience of the Mutual Life Insurance Company of New York. As a result of the development of actuarial science, medical discoveries, and a higher standard of living that prolongs the life of individuals, new mortality tables have become necessary and have been constructed to meet the current needs of the life insurance business. The best-known mortality tables used in recent years by life insurance companies are as follows:

American Experience Table of Mortality—First published as a part of New York law in 1868. Covered experience, 1843–58.

American Men Ultimate Mortality Table—Published in 1918. Covered experience, 1900–15.

The 1937 Standard Annuity Mortality Table—Published in 1938. Based primarily on experience, 1932–36.

Commissioners' 1941 Standard Ordinary Table of Mortality—Based on experience, 1930–40.

Commissioners' 1958 Standard Ordinary Table of Mortality—Based on experience, 1950–54.

Commissioners' 1980 Standard Ordinary Table of Mortality—Based on experience, 1970–75.

The 1983 Individual Annuity Table—Based on experience, 1971–76.

United States Total Population Mortality Table—Based on experience, 1979–81.

The basic principle involved in the computation of life annuity and life insurance problems is not affected by the use of a particular mortality table. For the sake of simplicity, only the Commissioners' 1958 Standard Ordinary Table of Mortality, commonly referred to as the 1958 CSO Table (Table 12 in the Appendix), and the Table of Commutation Columns, interest at $2\frac{1}{2}\%$, computed by the Society of Actuaries based on the 1958 CSO Table (Table 13), will be used in this text.

Note that the Table of Commutation Columns based on the 1980 CSO Table (Table 15 in the Appendix) is not provided by the Society of Actuaries. Rather than provide numerous tables at different interest rates, the Society has prepared a report that allows the use of different mortality tables. To discuss the use of the report is beyond the scope of this text. We thus use the 1958 CSO Table and its related Table of Commutation Columns for illustrating the basic methods of computing the life annuity and life insurance problems in this chapter and the next. However, the 1980 CSO Table is provided in the Appendix (Table 15) to give the updated information.

From the 1958 CSO Table, the symbols that are used frequently in this chapter are l_x and d_x.[2] The number of people living at age x is represented by l_x, and the number of people who will die between the ages x and $x + 1$ is represented by d_x. The table is based on a study of 10 million people starting at the age of 0. Thus, the expression $l_{30} = 9{,}480{,}358$ means that there are 9,480,358 persons alive at the age of 30 out of a group of 10 million people. A total of 20,193 persons from the group will die between the ages of 30 and 31. The number of deaths at that age is written as

$$d_{30} = 20{,}193$$

Thus, the number of people living at age 31 is

$$l_{31} = l_{30} - d_{30} = 9{,}480{,}358 - 20{,}193 = 9{,}460{,}165$$

The death rate for people aged 30 (or written as q_{30}) is as follows:

$$q_{30} = \frac{d_{30}}{l_{30}} = \frac{20{,}193}{9{,}480{,}358} = .00213 \text{ (per person)}$$

The value of q_{30} can be obtained directly from the deaths per 1,000 column of the 1958 CSO Table (Table 12). The table shows that the death rate per 1,000 at age 30 is 2.13. Thus,

$$q_{30} = \frac{2.13}{1{,}000} = .00213$$

EXERCISE 19–1 REFERENCE: SECTION 19.2

A. Find the number of people in each of the following expressions (use Table 12):

1. (a) l_3 (b) l_{20} (c) l_{32} (d) l_{46} (e) l_{78} (f) l_{99}
2. (a) l_{12} (b) l_{28} (c) l_{41} (d) l_{52} (e) l_{69} (f) l_{88}
3. (a) d_3 (b) d_{20} (c) d_{32} (d) d_{47} (e) d_{68} (f) d_{99}
4. (a) d_{12} (b) d_{28} (c) d_{41} (d) d_{56} (e) d_{72} (f) d_{85}

B. Statement problems (use Table 12):

5. Find the death rate per thousand for persons aged (a) 8, (b) 20, (c) 56, (d) 70.
6. Find the death rate per thousand for persons aged (a) 10, (b) 25, (c) 61, (d) 86.
7. From a group of 50,000 now age 18, how many will probably (a) be alive at age 50, and (b) die after reaching age 50 but before reaching age 51?

[2]The symbols used in the 1958 CSO Table, along with the other symbols used in this chapter and the next, except for a few additional symbols, are based on the statement of the "International Actuarial Notation," printed in *Transactions of the Actuarial Society of America*, Volume XLVIII (1947), pp. 166–76.

8. From a group of 80,000 now age 25, how many are predicted (a) to be alive at age 65, and (b) to die after reaching age 65 but before reaching age 66?

19.3 PURE ENDOWMENT CONTRACTS

A *pure endowment* contract provides that the face value of the contract will be paid if the purchaser of the pure endowment survives to the end of the contract term. However, no payment is made to him or her if the purchaser dies during the period. Although pure endowment contracts are rarely issued by an insurance company, a study of this type of contract is a good starting point to learn the value of a mortality table.

EXAMPLE 1

A person is 30 years of age and wishes to purchase a pure endowment policy that will pay $1,000 when age 65 is reached. Find the net single premium of the policy.

According to the 1958 CSO Mortality Table (Table 12) there are 9,480,358 persons alive at age 30 and 6,800,531 persons alive at age 65. If each one of the group of 9,480,358 persons, aged 30, wants to buy a pure endowment of $1 that will be payable at age 65 if that person is still living then, the required payments to be made by a life insurance company, at age 65, will be $6,800,531.

Assume that the insurance company can invest its money at an interest rate of $2\frac{1}{2}\%$ compounded annually. The present value of the required payments is obtained by the compound discount formula $P = S(1 + i)^{-n}$ as follows:

$S = 6{,}800{,}531$, $i = 2\frac{1}{2}\%$, $n = 35$ (there are 35 years between age 30 and age 65)

Thus

$P = 6{,}800{,}531(1 + 2\frac{1}{2}\%)^{-35} = 6{,}800{,}531(.42137107) = \$2{,}865{,}547.02$ (Table 6)

Example 1 is diagrammed as follows:

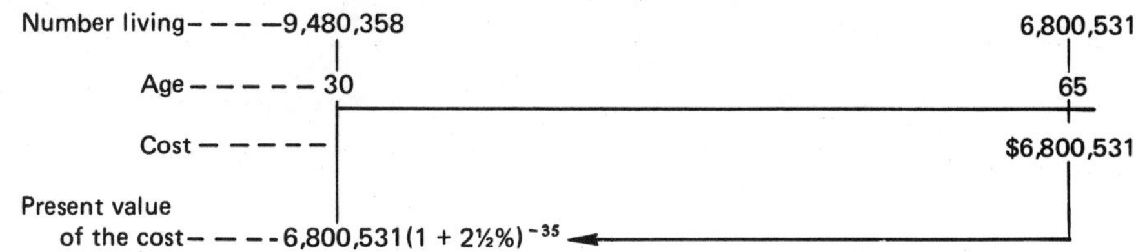

The present value (at age 30) is divided among the group of 9,480,358 persons. The net single premium for each person aged 30 is

$$\frac{2{,}865{,}547.02}{9{,}480{,}358} = \$0.30226$$

For a $1,000 pure endowment policy, the net single premium is

$0.30226 \times 1{,}000 = \$302.26$

A simpler way to compute the net single premium of a pure endowment policy is to apply the following formula:

$$_{n}E_{x} = \frac{D_{x+n}}{D_{x}} \qquad \textbf{(19–1)}^{3}$$

$_{n}E_{x}$ is the net single premium of a \$1, n year, pure endowment contract issued at age x. The contract promises to pay the annuitant the endowment at the end of n years or at age $x + n$ if the annuitant is then still alive.

D_x and D_{x+n} are symbols whose values are listed in Table 13 in the Appendix.

---

[3] *Proof—Formula (19–1):*

Let l_x represent the number of persons at age x. Each of them wants to buy a pure endowment policy of \$1 payable at age $x + n$ if he or she is then alive. The diagram, which is similar to that of Example 1, may be arranged symbolically as follows:

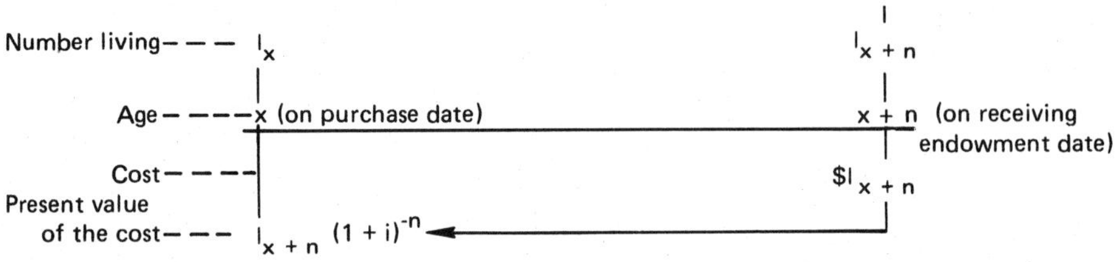

Number living— — — l_x — l_{x+n}

Age — — — — x (on purchase date) — x + n (on receiving endowment date)

Cost — — — — \$$l_{x+n}$

Present value of the cost — — — $l_{x+n}(1 + i)^{-n}$ ←

Let $_{n}E_{x}$ = the net single premium of a \$1, n year, pure endowment contract for each annuitant at age x. The contract will pay \$1 to each annuitant at the end of n years or at age $x + n$ if the annuitant is still living.

Then

$$_{n}E_{x} = \frac{l_{x+n}(1+i)^{-n}}{l_x}$$

Let $v = (1 + i)^{-1}$, or $v^n = (1 + i)^{-n}$ [In Table 6, $v^n = p = (1 + i)^{-n}$]

Then

$$_{n}E_{x} = \frac{v^{n}l_{x+n}}{l_x}$$ Multiply both the numerator and the denominator by v^x.

$$_{n}E_{x} = \frac{v^{x+n}l_{x+n}}{v^{x}l_x}, \text{ or}$$

$$_{n}E_{x} = \frac{D_{x+n}}{D_{x}} \qquad (19\text{–}1)$$

D_x represents the value of $v^x l_x$ for convenience in writing.

The values of D_{65} and D_{30} are obtained by using Table 6 as follows (see Example 1):

$$D_{65} = v^{65}l_{65} = (1 + 2\tfrac{1}{2}\%)^{-65}(6{,}800{,}531) = .20088557(6{,}800{,}531) = 1{,}366{,}128.5462$$
$$D_{30} = v^{30}l_{30} = (1 + 2\tfrac{1}{2}\%)^{-30}(9{,}480{,}358) = .47674269(9{,}480{,}358) = 4{,}519{,}691.3751$$

For convenience, the values of D_x are tabulated in Table 13. Note that the values in Table 13 are computed at an interest rate of $2\frac{1}{2}\%$ compounded annually.

Solution of Example 1 using formula (19–1):

$x = 30, n = 35$

The net single premium for a \$1 payment to each annuitant at age 65 is

$${}_nE_x = {}_{35}E_{30} = \frac{D_{x+n}}{D_x} = \frac{D_{30+35}}{D_{30}} = \frac{D_{65}}{D_{30}} = \frac{1{,}366{,}128.5462}{4{,}519{,}691.3751} = .30226$$

For a \$1,000 payment, the net single premium is

$.30226 \times 1{,}000 = \$302.26$

NOTE: The division D_{65}/D_{30} may also be performed by using logarithms, as follows:

$$\begin{array}{lll} \log D_{65} = 6.135\ 4916 = & 16.135\ 4916 - 10 & \text{(Table 14)} \\ (-)\log D_{30} = & 6.655\ 1088 & \\ \hline \log {}_nE_x = & 9.480\ 3828 - 10 & \end{array}$$

Find the antilog by interpolation from Table 2.

${}_nE_x = .30226$

EXAMPLE 2 Find the net single premium of a \$2,000 pure endowment policy payable in 10 years to a person now aged 18.

$x = 18, n = 10$

$${}_nE_x = {}_{10}E_{18} = \frac{D_{18+10}}{D_{18}} = \frac{D_{28}}{D_{18}} = \frac{4{,}768{,}076.98}{6{,}218{,}174.46} = .7667969 \quad \text{(Table 13)}$$

For a \$2,000 pure endowment policy, the net single payment is

$0.7667969 \times 2{,}000 = \$1{,}533.59$

NOTE: ***In order to simplify mathematical operations, round the decimals of the values in the commutation columns (Table 13) when computing the problems in the exercises in this chapter.*** Examples:

$D_{65} = 1{,}366{,}128.5462$, rounded to 1,366,129

$N_{96} = 11{,}610.1087$, rounded to 11,610

EXERCISE 19–2 REFERENCE: SECTION 19.3

A. Find the net single premium of the pure endowment contract in each of the following problems:

	Contract Amount	*Age on Purchase Date*	*Age on Payment Date*
1.	\$1,000	25	30
2.	1,000	20	28
3.	2,000	35	45
4.	2,000	40	65
5.	4,000	30	55
6.	4,000	45	70
7.	5,000	24	32
8.	5,000	50	80

B. Statement problems:

9. Find the net single premium of a pure endowment contract of $1,000 payable in 15 years to a person now aged 22.
10. What is the net single premium of a 25-year pure endowment contract of $3,000 to a person now aged 34?
11. What is the net single premium of a pure endowment contract of $1,000 payable in 15 years to a person now aged 42?
12. Find the net single premium of a 25-year pure endowment contract of $3,000 to a person now aged 54.
13. How much should a person aged 36 pay an insurance company in order to receive $1,500 at age 60, if then living?
14. How much should a life insurance company collect from a person aged 28 if the company will pay $5,000 to the person at age 40 if he or she is then alive?
15. A person aged 26 pays $300 to a life insurance company for a 30-year pure endowment contract. How much will that person receive at age 56 if then alive?
16. A mother paid $800 for a pure endowment contract for her son, now aged four. The endowment will be payable to her son if and when he reaches age 20. How much will the son receive if he is then alive?

19.4 WHOLE LIFE ANNUITIES

Life annuities are generally classified into two major groups: *whole* life annuities and *temporary* life annuities.

A *whole life annuity* is a contract under which an insurance company will pay the annuitant a given sum periodically for life, ceasing with the last payment preceding the annuitant's death. The purchase price of a whole life annuity depends on the *age* of the annuitant and the *time* of the first payment made to the annuitant.

When the first annual payment is made one year after the date of purchase, the annuity is called an *ordinary whole life annuity*, or an *immediate whole life annuity*. When the first annual payment is made at the time of purchase, it is called a *whole life annuity due*. If the first payment begins after a period of more than one year has elapsed, it is called a *deferred whole life annuity*. The purchase price for each type of whole life annuity is computed below.

A. Ordinary Whole Life Annuity (Immediate Whole Life Annuity)

EXAMPLE 1 Find the net single premium of an ordinary whole life annuity of $1 payable at the end of each year for a person aged 95 years. The first payment will be made one year later (or when the age of 96 is reached). Assume that the 1958 CSO Table is used and the interest rate is $2\frac{1}{2}\%$.

The net single premium is $1.25. The findings from the 1958 CSO Table (Table 12) and the computation are diagrammed below:

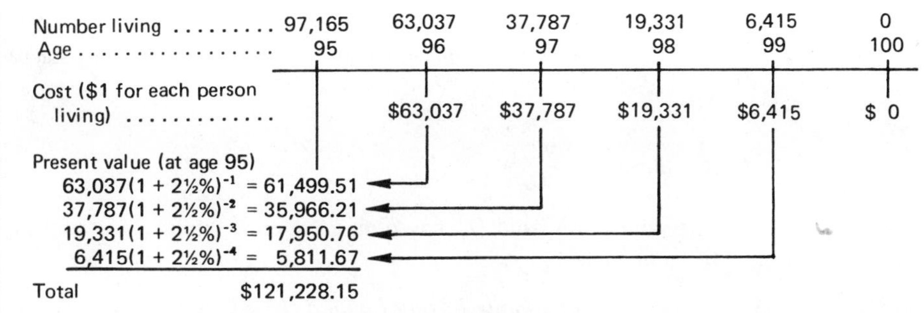

The term "cost" applies to the costs of both the insurance company and the group of annuitants. In other words, the cost to an insurance company is equal to the cost to the group of annuitants. When only the net single premium is computed, the insurance company may be thought of as an agent that collects premiums on the purchase date and pays benefits during later years. The total cost to an insurance company on the purchase date should be divided by the number of annuitants living at that time. Thus, the net single premium for each annuitant is

$$\frac{121{,}228.15}{97{,}165} = \$1.24765, \quad \text{or} \quad \$1.25$$

In general,

let a_x = the net single premium, or the present value, of an ordinary whole life annuity of $1 payable at the end of each year for a person whose age now is x years

Then

$$a_x = \frac{N_{x+1}}{D_x} \qquad \textbf{(19–2)}^4$$

---

[4]*Proof—Formula (19–2):*

The steps necessary in finding the value of a_x are the same as those used in Example 1 and are shown symbolically as follows:

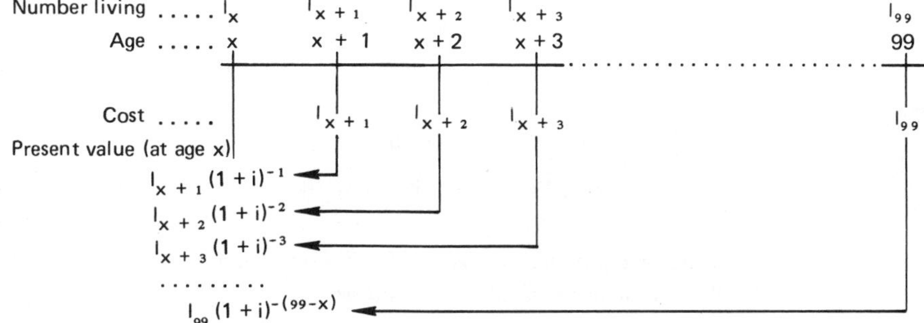

Let R = the annual payment to the annuitant
A = the net single premium for an ordinary whole life annuity that pays R per year for life

Then

$$A = Ra_x = R \cdot \frac{N_{x+1}}{D_x} \tag{19–3}$$

The values of N_x and D_x, based on an interest rate of $2\frac{1}{2}\%$ compounded annually, are listed in Table 13.

Solution of Example 1 using formula (19–3):

$R = \$1,\ x = 95$

$$A = 1 \cdot \frac{N_{95+1}}{D_{95}} = \frac{N_{96}}{D_{95}} = \frac{11{,}610.1087}{9{,}305.5630} = 1.24765, \quad \text{or} \quad \$1.25$$

NOTE: The division N_{96}/D_{95} may also be performed by using logarithms:

$$\begin{aligned} \log N_{96} &= 4.064\ 8363 \quad \text{(Table 14)} \\ (-)\ \log D_{95} &= 3.968\ 7427 \\ \hline \log a_{95} &= \ \ .096\ 0936 \end{aligned}$$

Find the antilog by interpolation from Table 2.

$a_{95} = 1.24765$

---

[4] *Proof (continued)*

Total present value of the costs $= l_{x+1}(1+i)^{-1} + l_{x+2}(1+i)^{-2} + l_{x+3}(1+i)^{-3} + \cdots + l_{99}(1+i)^{-(99-x)}$

Let $v = (1+i)^{-1}$

The present value $= vl_{x+1} + v^2l_{x+2} + v^3l_{x+3} + \cdots + v^{99-x}l_{99}$

Let a_x = the net single premium, or the present value of an ordinary whole life annuity of \$1 payable at the end of each year for a person whose age now is x years

$$a_x = \frac{\text{Total present value of the costs}}{\text{Number of annuitants at age } x \text{ on the purchase date}}$$

$$= \frac{vl_{x+1} + v^2l_{x+2} + v^3l_{x+3} + \cdots + v^{99-x}l_{99}}{l_x}$$

Multiply both the numerator and the denominator by v^x. Then

$$a_x = \frac{v^{x+1}l_{x+1} + v^{x+2}l_{x+2} + v^{x+3}l_{x+3} + \cdots + v^{99}l_{99}}{v^xl_x}$$

According to Section 19.3 (footnote 3), $D_x = v^xl_x$. Thus,

$$a_x = \frac{D_{x+1} + D_{x+2} + D_{x+3} + \cdots + D_{99}}{D_x}$$

Let $N_x = D_x + D_{x+1} + D_{x+2} + \cdots + D_{99}$ Then
$N_{x+1} = D_{x+1} + D_{x+2} + \cdots + D_{99}$ and

$$a_x = \frac{N_{x+1}}{D_x} \tag{19–2}$$

EXAMPLE 2

A person aged 35 wishes to purchase an ordinary whole life annuity that will pay \$1,000 at the age of 36 and the same amount at the end of each year thereafter for life. Find the net single premium of the annuity.

Since the first payment is to be made one year after the date of purchase, the contract is an ordinary whole life annuity. The interest rate is assumed to be $2\frac{1}{2}\%$.

$x = 35,\ R = \$1{,}000$

Substituting the above values in formula (19–3),

$$A = R \cdot \frac{N_{x+1}}{D_x} = R \cdot \frac{N_{35+1}}{D_{35}} = 1{,}000 \cdot \frac{N_{36}}{D_{35}}$$

$$= 1{,}000 \cdot \frac{89{,}956{,}987.56}{3{,}949{,}851.09} = \$22{,}774.78 \quad \text{(Table 13)}$$

EXAMPLE 3

A person aged 25 has \$50,000. If the money is used to purchase an ordinary whole life annuity with the first payment payable one year from the purchase date, what is the size of each annual payment?

The net single premium of the annuity is known, $\$50{,}000 = A,\ x = 25,\ R = ?$

Substituting the above values in formula (19–3),

$$50{,}000 = R \cdot \frac{N_{25+1}}{D_{25}} = R \cdot \frac{N_{26}}{D_{25}}$$

$$R = 50{,}000 \cdot \frac{D_{25}}{N_{26}} = 50{,}000 \cdot \frac{5{,}165{,}007.95}{134{,}674{,}488.96} = \$1{,}917.59 \text{ (per year)}$$

EXERCISE 19–3 REFERENCE: SECTION 19.4A

1. A person aged 20 wishes to purchase an ordinary whole life annuity that will pay \$3,000 at age 21 and the same amount at the end of each year thereafter. What is the net single premium of the annuity?
2. A person aged 32 wants to buy an annuity that will pay \$2,500 annually for life with the first payment to be made one year after the purchase date. What is the purchase price (the net single premium)?
3. Find the net single premium for an ordinary whole life annuity of \$2,500 per year for a person now aged 60.
4. What is the net single premium for an ordinary whole life annuity of \$1,000 per year for a person now aged 30?
5. Find the net single premium for an ordinary whole life annuity of \$2,000 payable at the end of each year for a person now aged 45.
6. Compute the net single premium for an ordinary whole life annuity of \$3,000 per year if the annuity is bought by a person now aged 40.
7. What is the net single premium for an ordinary whole life annuity of \$4,000 per year for a person now aged 50?
8. Find the net single premium for an ordinary whole life annuity of \$5,000 payable at the end of each year for a person now aged 55.
9. If the net single premium of an ordinary whole life annuity for a person now aged 30 is \$20,000, what is the size of each annual payment?
10. Refer to Problem 9. What is the size of each annual payment if the annuity is purchased by a person aged 22?

11. A person aged 27 has \$120,000. If the money is used to buy an ordinary whole life annuity with the first payment to be made one year from the purchase date, what is the size of each annual payment?
12. A person aged 48 paid \$70,000 for an ordinary whole life annuity with the first payment to be made in one year. Find the size of the annual payment.

B. Whole Life Annuity Due

The first payment of an ordinary whole life annuity is made one year after the date of purchase, whereas the first payment of a whole life annuity *due* is made at the *time of purchase*. Thus, if the annual payment is \$1, the net single premium of a whole life annuity due on the purchase date is *\$1 more* than the net single premium of an ordinary whole life annuity.

Let $\ddot{a}_x$ = the net single premium, or the present value, of a whole life annuity due of \$1 payable now and each year hereafter for life for a person now aged x years

Then

$$\ddot{a}_x = 1 + a_x, \quad \text{or}$$

$$\ddot{a}_x = \frac{N_x}{D_x} \qquad \textbf{(19–4)}^5$$

Let $A(\text{due})$ = the net single premium or the present value of a whole life annuity due that will pay R per year for life

$$A(\text{due}) = R\ddot{a}_x = R \cdot \frac{N_x}{D_x} \qquad \textbf{(19–5)}$$

EXAMPLE 4

A person aged 35 wishes to purchase a whole life annuity that will pay \$1,000 now and the same amount at the end of each year thereafter for life. Find the net single premium of the annuity.

$x = 35$, $R = \$1{,}000$. Since the first payment is made now, this is a whole life annuity due problem. The net single premium is

$$A(\text{due}) = R\ddot{a}_x = 1{,}000 \cdot \frac{N_{35}}{D_{35}} = 1{,}000 \cdot \frac{93{,}906{,}838.64}{3{,}949{,}851.09}$$

$$= \$23{,}774.78$$

[5] *Proof–Formula (19–4):*

$$\ddot{a}_x = 1 + a_x = 1 + \frac{N_{x+1}}{D_x} = \frac{D_x + N_{x+1}}{D_x}$$

$$= \frac{D_x + (D_{x+1} + D_{x+2} + \cdots + D_{99})}{D_x} = \frac{N_x}{D_x} \qquad (19–4)$$

The above result may also be obtained by a method similar to that used in obtaining the ordinary whole life annuity [formula (19–2)].

NOTE: Example 4 is identical to Example 2, except that the first payment in Example 4 is made at the time of purchase. Since the annuitant receives $1,000 at the time of purchase, the cost is also $1,000 higher than the cost in Example 2. Thus, the difference between the two purchase prices in Examples 4 and 2 is $1,000, or $23,774.78 − $22,774.78.

EXAMPLE 5 A person aged 25 owes a life insurance company $50,000. If the company allows that person to discharge the obligation by annual payments payable for life, with the first payment due now, what is the size of the annual payment?

The present value of the annuity A(due) is known.

$A(\text{due}) = \$50{,}000,\ x = 25,\ R = ?$ (annual payment)

Substituting the values in formula (19–5),

$$A(\text{due}) = R\ddot{a}_x = R \cdot \frac{N_x}{D_x} = R \cdot \frac{N_{25}}{D_{25}}$$

Thus,

$$50{,}000 = R \cdot \frac{N_{25}}{D_{25}}$$

$$R = 50{,}000 \cdot \frac{D_{25}}{N_{25}} = 50{,}000 \cdot \frac{5{,}165{,}007.95}{139{,}839{,}496.91} = \$1{,}846.76$$

NOTE: The concept of finding the annual payments of a whole life annuity due is important in finding the *annual* premiums payable for life for a life insurance policy. (See Section 20.2B.)

★C. Deferred Whole Life Annuity

The first payment of a deferred whole life annuity begins after a period of more than one year has elapsed from the date of purchase. The period of deferment may be expressed in two ways:

1. It is the period from the date of purchase to the date of the first payment. The payments thus form a whole life annuity *due* with the term beginning on the date of the first payment.
2. It is the period from the date of purchase to the date that is one year prior to the date of the first payment. The payments thus form an *ordinary* whole life annuity.

For convenience in this chapter, the period of deferment is expressed from the date of purchase to the date of the first payment (item 1 above). For example, if a person aged 60 buys a whole life annuity with the first payment to be made at 65 years of age, the period of deferment is considered to be five years. The annuity is a deferred whole life annuity *due*, with the term beginning at age 65.

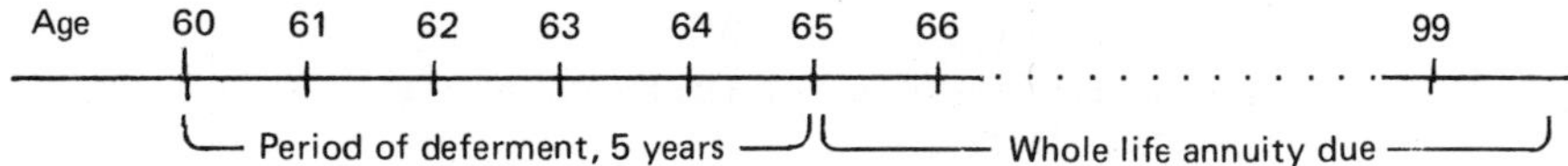

Let k = the period of deferment in years

${}_{k|}\ddot{a}_x$ = the net single premium, or the present value, of a deferred annuity of $1 per year for life, with the first payment at the end of the deferment period, k years, for a person now aged x years

Then

$$ {}_{k|}\ddot{a}_x = \frac{N_{x+k}}{D_x} \qquad \textbf{(19–6)}^{6} $$

Let A(defer.) = the net single premium, or the present value, of a whole life annuity that will pay R per year after k years

Then

$$ \textbf{A(defer.)} = R \cdot {}_{k|}\ddot{a}_x = R \cdot \frac{N_{x+k}}{D_x} \qquad \textbf{(19–7)} $$

EXAMPLE 6

A person aged 25 wishes to purchase a whole life annuity that will pay $3,000 a year for life. The first payment is due at age 65. Find the net single premium of the annuity.

The period of deferment $k = 65 - 25 = 40$ (years), $x = 25$, $R = \$3,000$

Substituting the values in formula (19–7),

$$ A(\text{defer.}) = 3{,}000 \cdot \frac{N_{25+40}}{D_{25}} = 3{,}000 \cdot \frac{N_{65}}{D_{25}} $$

$$ = 3{,}000 \cdot \frac{15{,}077{,}832.60}{5{,}165{,}007.95} = \$8{,}757.68 $$

EXAMPLE 7

A 14-year-old boy inherited $50,000. If he uses the money to purchase a whole life annuity with the first payment due at age 25, what will be the size of each payment?

---

[6]*Proof—Formula (19–6):*

The value of ${}_{k|}\ddot{a}_x$ is obtained as follows:

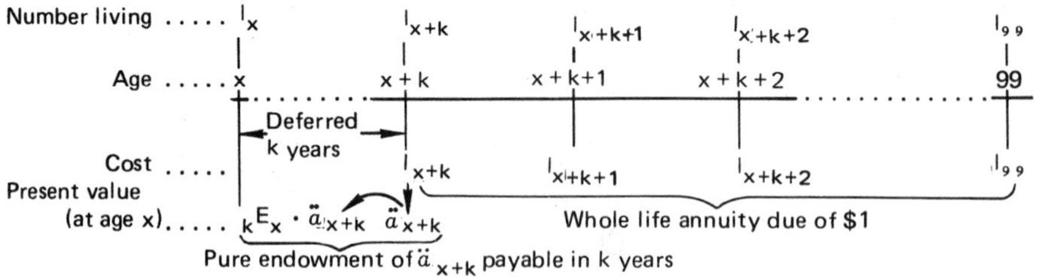

Number living ..... l_x l_{x+k} l_{x+k+1} l_{x+k+2} l_{99}

Age ..... x $x+k$ $x+k+1$ $x+k+2$ 99

Deferred k years

Cost ..... l_{x+k} l_{x+k+1} l_{x+k+2} l_{99}

Present value (at age x)..... ${}_kE_x \cdot \ddot{a}_{x+k}$ $\ddot{a}_{x+k}$ Whole life annuity due of $1

Pure endowment of $\ddot{a}_{x+k}$ payable in k years

The following result is obtained from the above diagram:

$$ {}_{k|}\ddot{a}_x = {}_kE_x \cdot \ddot{a}_{x+k} = \frac{D_{x+k}}{D_x} \cdot \frac{N_{x+k}}{D_{x+k}} = \frac{N_{x+k}}{D_x} \qquad \text{(19–6) [See formulas (19–1) and (19–4).]} $$

Note: Formula (19–6) may also be proved by using a method similar to that used in proving formula (19–2).

$A(\text{defer.}) = \$50{,}000,\ x = 14,\ k = 25 - 14 = 11$ (years),
$x + k = 14 + 11 = 25,\ R = ?$ (per year)

Substituting the values in formula (19–7),

$$50{,}000 = R \cdot \frac{N_{25}}{D_{14}}$$

$$R = 50{,}000 \cdot \frac{D_{14}}{N_{25}} = 50{,}000 \cdot \frac{6{,}905{,}108.16}{139{,}839{,}496.91} = \$2{,}468.94$$

EXERCISE 19–4 REFERENCE: SECTION 19.4B and C

1. Refer to Problem 1 of Exercise 19–3. What is the net single premium if the annuity pays $3,000 annually starting at age 20?
2. Refer to Problem 2 of Exercise 19–3. If the first payment is made on the purchase date, what is the purchase price?
3. A person aged 45 wishes to buy a whole life annuity that will pay $1,000 now and the same amount at the end of each year thereafter for life. What is the net single premium of the annuity?
4. Find the net single premium of a whole life annuity of $2,000 per year for someone aged 30. Assume that the first $2,000 is payable to the annuitant on the purchase date.
5. What is the net single premium of a whole life annuity due of $3,000 per year for a person aged 18?
6. What is the net single premium of a whole life annuity due of $4,000 per year for a person aged 70?
7. If the net single premium of a whole life annuity due is $20,000, what is the size of the annual payment for a person now aged 30?
8. Refer to Problem 7. If the person is 22 years old now, what is the size of the annual payment?
9. A person, aged 55, purchases a life insurance policy. The net single premium (purchase price) of the policy is $2,000. If the insurance company allows the premium to be paid by equal annual payments for life, with the first payment due now (on the purchase date), find the size of the annual payment.
10. A person, who is the beneficiary of a $10,000 insurance policy, decides to use the money to purchase a whole life annuity with the first payment due now. If the person is 26 years old, what will be the size of each annual payment?

★11. Find the net single premium of a whole life annuity of $1,000 per year for a person now aged 36 if the first payment is to be made 10 years from now.

★12. A person aged 42 wishes to buy a whole life annuity of $500 payable at the beginning of each year. The first payment is due at age 55. What is the net single premium of the annuity?

★13. Refer to Problem 3. What is the net single premium of the annuity if the first payment is to be made at age 50?

★14. Refer to Problem 4. What is the net single premium of the annuity if the first payment is to be made at age 38?

★15. Refer to Problem 10. If the first payment is to be made at age 40, what will be the size of each annual payment?

★16. A young man aged 20 has $15,000. If he wishes to use the money to buy a whole life annuity with the first payment to be made at age 35, what is the size of each payment?

19.5 TEMPORARY LIFE ANNUITIES

When the payments of a life annuity cease at the end of a certain number of years, even though the annuitant is still living, the annuity is called a *temporary life annuity*. Like whole life annuities, temporary life annuities may be classified as ordinary, due, and deferred, depending upon the date of the first payment.

A. Ordinary Temporary Life Annuity (Immediate Temporary Life Annuity)

The first annual payment of an *ordinary temporary life annuity* is made one year after the date of purchase. Thus, if a person now aged x purchases an ordinary temporary life annuity, the first annual payment will be made to him at $x + 1$ years of age.

Let n = the number of payments

$a_{x:\overline{n}|}$ = the net single premium, or the present value, at age x of an ordinary temporary life annuity of $1 payable each year for n annual payments

Then

$$a_{x:\overline{n}|} = \frac{N_{x+1} - N_{x+n+1}}{D_x} \qquad \textbf{(19–8)}^7$$

Let A(tem.) = net single premium, or present value, of an ordinary temporary life annuity that will pay R per year

---

[7] *Proof–Formula (19–8):*

The value of $a_{x:\overline{n}|}$ is obtained as follows:

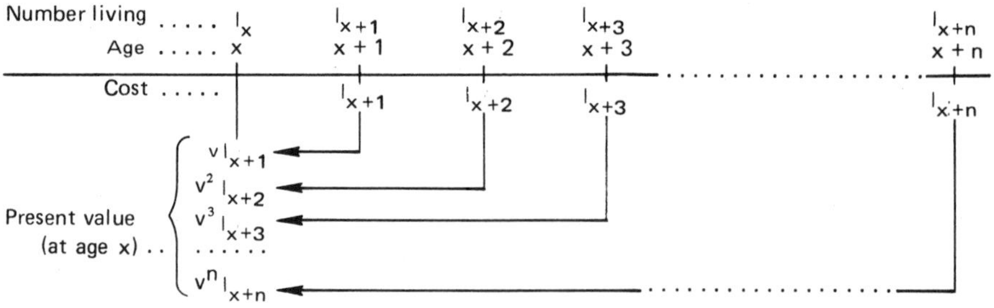

Number living	l_x	l_{x+1}	l_{x+2}	l_{x+3}	...... l_{x+n}
Age	x	$x+1$	$x+2$	$x+3$	...... $x+n$
Cost		l_{x+1}	l_{x+2}	l_{x+3}	...... l_{x+n}

Present value (at age x) ..
- $v l_{x+1}$
- $v^2 l_{x+2}$
- $v^3 l_{x+3}$
- ......
- $v^n l_{x+n}$

The net single premium to each annuitant at the present time (age x) is

$$a_{x:\overline{n}|} = \frac{vl_{x+1} + v^2 l_{x+2} + v^3 l_{x+3} + \cdots + v^n l_{x+n}}{l_x}$$

Then

$$A(\text{tem.}) = Ra_{x:\overline{n}|} = R \cdot \frac{N_{x+1} - N_{x+n+1}}{D_x} \tag{19–9}$$

EXAMPLE 1

What is the net single premium of a five-year ordinary temporary life annuity of $2,000 per year for a person aged 20 if the first payment is to be made at age 21?

$x = 20,\ n = 5,\ R = \$2{,}000$

$$A(\text{tem.}) = Ra_{x:\overline{n}|} = 2{,}000 \cdot \frac{N_{20+1} - N_{20+5+1}}{D_{20}} = 2{,}000 \cdot \frac{N_{21} - N_{26}}{D_{20}}$$

$$= 2{,}000 \cdot \frac{161{,}928{,}780.91 - 134{,}674{,}488.96}{5{,}898{,}264.97}$$

$$= 2{,}000 \cdot \frac{27{,}254{,}291.95}{5{,}898{,}264.97} = \$9{,}241.46$$

B. Temporary Life Annuity Due

The first payment of a *temporary life annuity due* is made on the date of purchase. If the periodic payment is $1, the present value of the first payment is also $1. The remaining payments form an ordinary temporary life annuity. Let n = the number of payments. The number of the remaining payments is $n - 1$, and the present value of the remaining payments of $1 each is $a_{x:\overline{n-1}|}$.

Let $\ddot{a}_{x:\overline{n}|}$ = the net single premium, or the present value, at age x, of a temporary life annuity *due* of $1 payable each year for n annual payments

Then

$$\ddot{a}_{x:\overline{n}|} = 1 + a_{x:\overline{n-1}|}, \quad \text{or}$$

$$\ddot{a}_{x:\overline{n}|} = \frac{N_x - N_{x+n}}{D_x} \tag{19–10}$$[8]

The net single premium of a temporary life annuity due of R per year for n payments is

$$A(\text{tem. due}) = R\ddot{a}_{x:\overline{n}|} = R \cdot \frac{N_x - N_{x+n}}{D_x} \tag{19–11}$$

---

[7]*Proof (continued)*

Multiply both the numerator and the denominator by v^x, and substitute commutation symbols:

$$a_{x:\overline{n}|} = \frac{D_{x+1} + D_{x+2} + D_{x+3} + \cdots + D_{x+n}}{D_x}$$

Since $N_{x+1} = D_{x+1} + D_{x+2} + D_{x+3} + \cdots + D_{x+n} + D_{x+n+1} + \cdots + D_{99}$, and
$N_{x+n+1} = D_{x+n+1} + \cdots + D_{99}$,

the difference between N_{x+1} and N_{x+n+1} equals the numerator in the fraction on the right side in the above equation. Thus, the equation may be written in the following simple manner:

$$a_{x:\overline{n}|} = \frac{N_{x+1} - N_{x+n+1}}{D_x} \tag{19–8}$$

EXAMPLE 2

What is the net single premium for a six-year temporary life annuity of $2,000 per year for a person aged 20 if the first payment is due now?

$x = 20,\ n = 6,\ R = \$2{,}000$

$$A(\text{tem. due}) = 2{,}000 \cdot \frac{N_{20} - N_{20+6}}{D_{20}} = 2{,}000 \cdot \frac{N_{20} - N_{26}}{D_{20}}$$

$$= 2{,}000 \cdot \frac{167{,}827{,}045.88 - 134{,}674{,}488.96}{5{,}898{,}264.97}$$

$$= \frac{2{,}000(33{,}152{,}556.92)}{5{,}898{,}264.97} = \$11{,}241.46$$

NOTE: The difference between the answers in Example 1 and Example 2 is $2,000, which is the value of the first payment on the date of purchase.

EXAMPLE 3

The purchase price (or the net single premium) of a life insurance policy issued to a person aged 25 is $339.65. That person will pay the premium by making equal annual payments for 20 years or for life, whichever is the shorter of the two periods. If the first payment is due now (the purchase date), what is the size of the annual payment?

$A(\text{tem. due}) = \$339.65,\ x = 25,\ n = 20,\ R = ?$

Substituting the above values in formula (19–11),

$$339.65 = R \cdot \frac{N_{25} - N_{25+20}}{D_{25}}$$

$$R = 339.65 \cdot \frac{D_{25}}{N_{25} - N_{45}}$$

$$= 339.65 \cdot \frac{5{,}165{,}007.95}{139{,}839{,}496.91 - 58{,}927{,}803.08}$$

$= \$21.68$ (annual payment)

NOTE: The concept of finding the annual payments of a temporary life annuity due is important in finding the annual premiums payable for a limited number of payments for a life insurance policy. (See Example 3, Section 20.2B.)

★C. Deferred Temporary Life Annuity

The first annual payment of a *deferred temporary life annuity* is made after a period of k (more than 1) years, or at age $x + k$ of the annuitant, if then still living. The n annual payments form a temporary life annuity *due*.

---

[8] *Proof–Formula (19–10):*

$$\ddot{a}_{x:\overline{n}|} = 1 + a_{x:\overline{n-1}|} = 1 + \frac{N_{x+1} - N_{x+(n-1)+1}}{D_x} = \frac{D_x + N_{x+1} - N_{x+n}}{D_x}$$

Since $D_x + N_{x+1} = N_x$ (see Section 19.4B), then $$\ddot{a}_{x:\overline{n}|} = \frac{N_x - N_{x+n}}{D_x} \qquad (19–10)$$

Let ${}_{k}|\ddot{a}_{x:\overline{n}|}$ = the net single premium, or the present value, at age x, of a deferred temporary life annuity due of \$1 per year for n annual payments with the first payment at the end of k years, or at age $x + k$

Then

$$ {}_{k}|\ddot{a}_{x:\overline{n}|} = \frac{N_{x+k} - N_{x+k+n}}{D_x} \quad \textbf{(19–12)}^{9} $$

The net single premium of a deferred temporary life annuity of R per year is

$$ \textbf{A(tem. defer.)} = R \cdot \frac{N_{x+k} - N_{x+k+n}}{D_x} \quad \textbf{(19–13)} $$

EXAMPLE 4

What is the net single premium for an eight-year temporary life annuity of \$1,000 per year for a person aged 25 if the first payment is due at age 45?

$x = 25,\ k = 45 - 25 = 20,\ n = 8,\ R = \$1,000$

$$ \begin{aligned} A(\text{tem. defer.}) &= 1{,}000 \cdot \frac{N_{25+20} - N_{25+20+8}}{D_{25}} = 1{,}000 \cdot \frac{N_{45} - N_{53}}{D_{25}} \\ &= 1{,}000 \cdot \frac{58{,}927{,}803.08 - 37{,}504{,}037.97}{5{,}165{,}007.95} \\ &= \$4{,}147.87 \end{aligned} $$

EXERCISE 19–5 REFERENCE: SECTION 19.5

1. What is the net single premium of a 10-year ordinary temporary life annuity of \$5,000 per year for a person aged 30 if the first payment is to be made at age 31?
2. Find the net single premium of an ordinary temporary life annuity of 15 payments of \$1,500 each for a person aged 45 if the first payment is to be made one year after the purchase date.
3. How much would a person aged 40 have to pay for a 20-year ordinary temporary life annuity of \$2,000 each year if the first payment is to be made at age 41?
4. What is the net single premium of a five-year ordinary temporary life annuity of \$1,200 per year for a person aged 24 if the first payment is to be made at age 25?
5. A person aged 42 has \$8,000. If the money is used to buy a 10-year ordinary temporary life annuity, what is the size of the annual payment to that individual?

---

[9]*Proof–Formula (19–12):*

The value of ${}_{k}|\ddot{a}_{x:\overline{n}|}$ may be obtained by a method similar to the proof for formula (19–6), in Section 19.4C, as follows:

$$ {}_{k}|\ddot{a}_{x:\overline{n}|} = {}_{k}E_{x} \cdot \ddot{a}_{x+k:\overline{n}|} = \frac{D_{x+k}}{D_x} \cdot \frac{N_{x+k} - N_{x+k+n}}{D_{x+k}} = \frac{N_{x+k} - N_{x+k+n}}{D_x} \quad (19–12) $$

Note: The value of $\ddot{a}_{x+k:\overline{n}|}$ is the net single premium of a temporary life annuity due of \$1 payable for n annual payments for a person now aged $x + k$. The value of ${}_{k}|\ddot{a}_{x:\overline{n}|}$ is equal to the present value (age x) of the pure endowment of $\ddot{a}_{x+k:\overline{n}|}$ payable in k years. [See formulas (19–1) and (19–10).]

6. A person aged 20 owes a life insurance company $1,500. The company allows the debt to be paid by 18 equal annual payments or for life, whichever period is the shorter. If the first payment is due at age 21, what is the size of the annual payment?
7. Find the cost of an ordinary temporary life annuity of $1,000 per year for 15 payments for a person aged 40 if the first payment is due now.
8. What is the net single premium of a 10-year ordinary temporary life annuity of $3,000 per year for a person aged 35 if the first payment is made on the date of purchase?
9. Refer to Problem 1. What is the net single premium if the first payment of the life annuity is made at age 30?
10. Refer to Problem 2. What is the net single premium if the first payment of the life annuity is made at age 45?
11. Refer to Problem 5. If that person buys a 10-year temporary life annuity due, what is the size of the annual payment?
12. Refer to Problem 6. If the first of the 18 annual payments is due at age 20, find the size of the annual payment.
★13. Find the net single premium for a 20-year temporary life annuity of $500 per year for a person aged 28 if the first payment is due at age 40.
★14. What is the net single premium for a 15-year temporary life annuity of $2,000 per year for a person now aged 32 if the first payment is to be made at age 50?
★15. Refer to Problem 5. If a 10-year temporary life annuity is bought with the first payment to be made to the individual at age 50, what is the size of the annual payment?
★16. A person aged 20 paid $1,500 to buy a 12-year temporary life annuity with the first payment to be made to him at age 36. What will be the size of each annual payment?

19.6 SUMMARY OF LIFE ANNUITY FORMULAS

Symbols: a = net single premium (present value) of a life annuity of $1 per year
A = net single premium (present value) of a life annuity of R per year
x = age of the annuitant on the purchase date
$D_x = v^x l_x$
$N_x = D_x + D_{x+1} + D_{x+2} + \cdots + D_{99}$

D_x and N_x are commutation symbols. Values of the two symbols at the interest rate $2\frac{1}{2}\%$ are tabulated in Table 13. Logarithms of the values of D_x and N_x are tabulated in Table 14 (computed from Table 13).

Application	*Formula*	*Formula Number*	*Reference Page*
Pure Endowment	$_nE_x = \frac{D_{x+n}}{D_x}$	(19–1)	548

n = number of years from purchase date to payment date
E = net single premium of a $1 pure endowment contract

Whole Life Annuities

Ordinary (Immediate)– First Payment at Age $x + 1$:	$a_x = \frac{N_{x+1}}{D_x}$	(19–2)	551
	$A = Ra_x = R \cdot \frac{N_{x+1}}{D_x}$	(19–3)	552
Due–First Payment at Age x:	$\ddot{a}_x = 1 + a_x$, or $\ddot{a}_x = \frac{N_x}{D_x}$	(19–4)	554
	$A(\text{due}) = R\ddot{a}_x = R \cdot \frac{N_x}{D_x}$	(19–5)	554
Deferred–First Payment at Age $x + k$ (k = Number of Years of Deferment)	$_{k\|}\ddot{a}_x = \frac{N_{x+k}}{D_x}$	(19–6)	556
	$A(\text{defer.}) = R \cdot {}_{k\|}\ddot{a}_x = R \cdot \frac{N_{x+k}}{D_x}$	(19–7)	556

In general, for whole life annuities:

$$\text{Net single premium (present value) of an annuity of \$1 per year} = \frac{N_{\text{age on first payment date}}}{D_{\text{age on purchase date}}}$$

Temporary Life Annuities

n = number of payments

Ordinary (Immediate)– First Payment at Age $x + 1$, for n Payments, and Last Payment at Age $x + n$:	$a_{x:\overline{n}\|} = \frac{N_{x+1} - N_{x+n+1}}{D_x}$	(19–8)	558
	$A\ (\text{tem.}) = Ra_{x:\overline{n}\|} = R \cdot \frac{N_{x+1} - N_{x+n+1}}{D_x}$	(19–9)	559
Due–First Payment at Age x, for n Payments, Last Payment at Age $x + n - 1$:	$\ddot{a}_{x:\overline{n}\|} = 1 + a_{x:\overline{n-1}\|}$, or $\ddot{a}_{x:\overline{n}\|} = \frac{N_x - N_{x+n}}{D_x}$	(19–10)	559
	$A(\text{tem. due}) = R\ddot{a}_{x:\overline{n}\|} = R \cdot \frac{N_x - N_{x+n}}{D_x}$	(19–11)	559
Deferred–First Payment at Age $x + k$, Last Payment at Age $x + k + n - 1$, for a Total of n Payments:	$_{k\|}\ddot{a}_{x:\overline{n}\|} = \frac{N_{x+k} - N_{x+k+n}}{D_x}$	(19–12)	561
	$A\ (\text{tem. defer.}) = R \cdot \frac{N_{x+k} - N_{x+k+n}}{D_x}$	(19–13)	561

In general, for temporary life annuities:

$$\text{Net single premium (present value) of an annuity of \$1 per year} = \frac{N_{\text{age on first payment date}} - N_{\text{age on first payment date} + \text{number of payments}}}{D_{\text{age on purchase date}}}$$

EXERCISE 19–6 REVIEW OF CHAPTER 19

1. Define: (a) l_4, (b) l_{50}, (c) d_{29}, (d) d_{62}, (e) q_{35}, (f) q_{46}.
2. Define: (a) l_{10}, (b) l_{15}, (c) d_{40}, (d) d_{53}, (e) q_{28}, (f) q_{25}.
3. Find the net single premium of a \$2,500 pure endowment contract payable in 16 years to a person now aged 20.
4. What is the net single premium of a \$4,000 pure endowment contract payable in 24 years to a person now aged 43?
5. A life insurance company collected \$500 for a 20-year pure endowment contract from a person aged 26. How much will that person receive at age 46 if then alive?
6. A person aged 36 pays \$200 for a 15-year pure endowment contract. How much will that person receive from the insurance company if alive at the end of the 15-year period?
7. A person aged 24 wishes to buy a whole life annuity of \$3,000 per year. What is the net single premium if the first payment of the annuity is made at (a) age 24, and (b) age 25?
8. A whole life annuity of \$1,000 per year is bought by a person aged 38. What is the net single premium if the first payment of the annuity is made at (a) age 39, and (b) age 38?

★9. Refer to Problem 7. What is the net single premium if the first payment of the annuity is made at age 30?

★10. Refer to Problem 8. Find the net single premium if the first payment of the annuity is made at age 50.

11. A person aged 20 paid \$10,000 to a life insurance company for a whole life annuity. What is the size of each annual payment if that person receives the first payment at (a) age 20, and (b) age 21?
12. A person aged 31 owes a life insurance company \$1,000. The company allows the debt to be paid by annual payments payable for life. What is the size of the annual payment if the first payment is due at (a) age 32, and (b) age 31?

★13. Refer to Problem 11. What is the size of the annual payment if the first payment is made at age 33?

★14. Refer to Problem 12. Find the size of the annual payment if the first payment is due at age 40.

15. A person aged 29 wishes to buy a 12-year temporary life annuity of \$1,000 per year. What is the net single premium if the first payment is made to that person at (a) age 30, and (b) age 29?
16. What is the net single premium of a 24-year life annuity of \$600 per year for a person aged 46 if the first payment is made at (a) age 46, and (b) age 47?

★17. Refer to Problem 15. Find the net single premium if the first payment is made at age 37.

★18. Refer to Problem 16. What is the net single premium if the first payment is made at age 58?

19. A person aged 28 paid \$4,000 to a life insurance company for a 10-year temporary life annuity. What is the size of each annual payment if the first payment is made at (a) age 28, and (b) age 29?

20. The purchase price of a life insurance policy issued to a person aged 40 is $700. The company allows the premium to be paid by 15 annual payments or by an annual payment for life, whichever period is shorter. What is the size of the annual payment if the first payment is due at (a) age 41, and (b) age 40?

★21. Refer to Problem 19. What is the size of the annual payment if the first payment is made at age 35?

★22. Refer to Problem 20. Find the size of the annual payment if the first payment is due at age 48.

20 LIFE INSURANCE

The basic concept of life insurance was introduced in the previous chapter. This chapter explains life insurance contracts in detail. The basic types of life insurance contracts are discussed first (Sections 20.1 to 20.4). Next, other related topics are presented: deferred life insurance (Section 20.5), natural premium and level premium (Section 20.6), and terminal reserves (Section 20.7).

20.1 BASIC TYPES OF LIFE INSURANCE

Life insurance companies have made available many types of life insurance contracts (policies) to meet individual needs. However, there are only three basic types of life insurance contracts: (1) whole life insurance, (2) term insurance, and (3) endowment insurance. Every life insurance contract is one of these three kinds or is a combination of them. The protection offered by any type of life insurance contract may also be deferred to a future date. Thus, in addition to the three basic types of insurance, a discussion of deferred life insurance is included in this chapter.

20.2 WHOLE LIFE INSURANCE

A *whole life insurance* contract provides that the insurance company will pay the face value of the policy to the beneficiary upon the death of the insured, regardless of when the death occurs. The premium for a whole life insurance policy (simply called a whole life policy) may be paid by a single amount or in periodic payments. When a premium is payable periodically, there are two plans under which the premium may be paid. Under the *straight life* plan, premiums are payable until death, while under the *limited payment life* plan, premiums are payable for a specified number of years. *Net premiums are computed at a nominal interest rate of* $2\frac{1}{2}\%$ *in all of the life insurance problems in this chapter,* as explained in Section 19.1.

A. Finding the Net Single Premium

The following example is used to illustrate the method of finding the net single premium for a whole life policy.

EXAMPLE 1

A $1,000 whole life policy is issued to a man aged 40. Find the net single premium. First, find the net single premium for a $1 whole life policy. The cost of the $1 policy and its present value (at age 40) are diagrammed numerically and symbolically as follows:

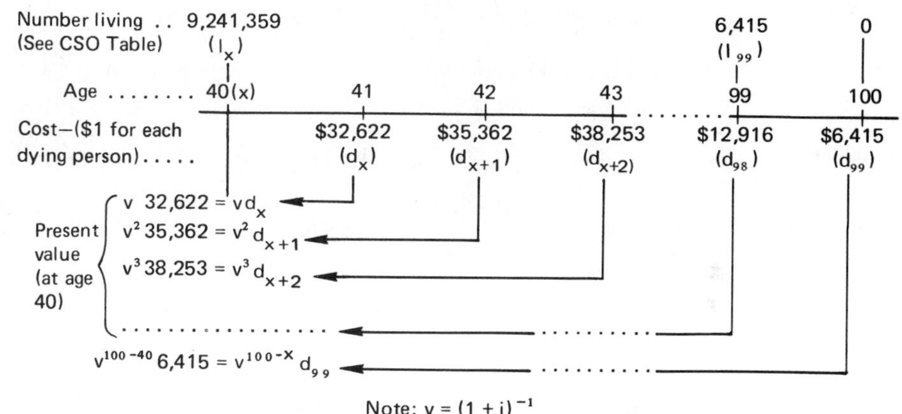

The cost in each year depends on the number of persons who die that year. According to the 1958 CSO table, 32,622 persons will die between ages 40 and 41. For simplicity in this chapter, *the cost is computed with the assumption that all death benefits are paid at the end of the year of death*. Therefore, $32,622 is required for the death benefits one year after the policies are issued (at the end of age 40 or the beginning of age 41).

The present value of the total cost is distributed among the people who are living at age 40. The cost of each policy, or the net single premium to each person at age 40, is denoted by A_{40} and is computed as follows:

$$A_{40} = \frac{v(32{,}622) + v^2(35{,}362) + v^3(38{,}253) + \cdots + v^{100-40}(6{,}415)}{9{,}241{,}359}$$
$$= .467128 \; (i = 2\tfrac{1}{2}\%)$$

The answer above may be calculated by using Table 6 (where $v^n = (1 + i)^{-n}$), but the calculation is quite laborious. However, it can be simplified by using the following formula and the commutation columns in Table 13.

Let A_x = the net single premium (or present value) of a $1 whole life insurance policy, issued at age x

NOTE:

The symbol A has a subscript, such as A_x, when it is used to represent the net single premium of a $1 life insurance policy. When the symbol A has no subscript, it represents the net single premium of a life annuity of R per payment, such as A and A(due). (See Chapter 19.)

Then the following formula can be obtained by a method similar to that followed in the above illustration:

$$A_x = \frac{M_x}{D_x} \qquad \textbf{(20–1)}^1$$

The values of M_x and D_x are listed in Table 13 (at a $2\frac{1}{2}\%$ interest rate).

The value of A_{40} in Example 1 may be computed by using the above formula, as follows:

$$A_{40} = \frac{M_{40}}{D_{40}} = \frac{1{,}607{,}743.17}{3{,}441{,}765.06} = .467128$$

For a \$1,000 whole life policy, the net single premium is

$.467128 \times 1{,}000 = \$467.13$

NOTE: The division M_{40}/D_{40} may also be performed by using logarithms:

$\log M_{40} = 6.206\ 2167$	$= 16.206\ 2167 - 10$	
$(-) \log D_{40}$	$= 6.536\ 7812$	(Table 14)
$\log A_{40}$	$= 9.669\ 4355 - 10$	

Find the antilog by interpolation from Table 2.

$A_{40} = .4671274$

B. Finding the Net Annual Premium

STRAIGHT LIFE (ALSO CALLED ORDINARY LIFE)

Under the straight life plan, premiums are payable periodically until death.

Let P_x = the net annual premium that is payable to the insurance company for a \$1 policy each year for life, beginning at age x

---

[1] *Proof–Formula (20–1):*

The value of A_x is obtained as follows (see the diagram in Example 1):

$$A_x = \frac{vd_x + v^2d_{x+1} + v^3d_{x+2} + \cdots + v^{100-x}d_{99}}{l_x}$$

Multiply both the numerator and the denominator by v^x. Then

$$A_x = \frac{v^{x+1}d_x + v^{x+2}d_{x+1} + v^{x+3}d_{x+2} + \cdots + v^{100}d_{99}}{v^x l_x}$$

Let the commutation symbol $C_x = v^{x+1}d_x$. The above equation may be written

$$A_x = \frac{C_x + C_{x+1} + C_{x+2} + \cdots + C_{99}}{D_x}$$

Let the commutation symbol $M_x = C_x + C_{x+1} + C_{x+2} + \cdots + C_{99}$

The above equation may be further simplified as follows: $A_x = \dfrac{M_x}{D_x}$ (20–1)

The following formula can be obtained:

$$P_x = \frac{M_x}{N_x} \qquad \textbf{(20–2)}^2$$

EXAMPLE 2

Refer to Example 1. If the man wishes to pay the net premium annually, with the first annual premium payable at the date of purchase (at age 40), what should be the size of the net annual premium?

$x = 40$. Substituting the x value in formula (20–2),

$$P_{40} = \frac{M_{40}}{N_{40}} = \frac{1{,}607{,}743.17}{75{,}194{,}899.17} = \$.021381$$

The annual premium for a $1,000 policy is

$.021381 \times 1{,}000 = \$21.381$, or $21.38

LIMITED PAYMENT LIFE

Under the limited payment life plan, premiums are payable periodically for a specified number of years. A whole life policy with a limited number of payments provides protection during the lifetime of the insured, but the premiums are payable for only a specified number of years. Some examples are the 20-payment life, 30-payment life, and life paid up at age 65.

Let ${}_nP_x$ = the net annual premium, beginning at age x, for an n payment life policy of $1

The following formula can be obtained:

$${}_nP_x = \frac{M_x}{N_x - N_{x+n}} \qquad \textbf{(20–3)}^3$$

---

[2] *Proof–Formula (20–2):*

The insurance company collects only the annual premiums from the insured who is living. Thus, the annual premiums (P_x) form a *whole life annuity due*. The present value of the annual premiums can be obtained by using formula (19–5).

$A(\text{due}) = R\ddot{a}_x$, or
$A(\text{due}) = P_x\ddot{a}_x$

The present value must be equal to the net single premium A_x, or $A(\text{due}) = A_x$. Substituting the value in the above equation,

$$A_x = P_x\ddot{a}_x, \qquad P_x = A_x \div \ddot{a}_x = \frac{M_x}{D_x} \div \frac{N_x}{D_x} = \frac{M_x}{D_x} \cdot \frac{D_x}{N_x} = \frac{M_x}{N_x}, \quad \text{or} \quad P_x = \frac{M_x}{N_x} \qquad (20\text{–}2)$$

Note: This is identical to the type of problem of finding the unknown annual payment when the present value of a whole life annuity due is known. (See Example 5, page 555.)

[3] *Proof–Formula (20–3)*

The n annual premiums (${}_nP_x$) form a *temporary life annuity due*. The present value of the annual premiums can be obtained by using formula (19–11).

$A(\text{tem. due}) = R\ddot{a}_{x:\overline{n}|}$, or

EXAMPLE 3 A \$1,000 whole life policy is issued to a man aged 25. Find (a) the net single premium, (b) the net annual premium if the policy is a straight life policy, (c) the net annual premium if the policy is a 20-payment life policy.

(a) $x = 25$

Substituting the value in formula (20–1),

$$A_{25} = \frac{M_{25}}{D_{25}} = \frac{1{,}754{,}288.51}{5{,}165{,}007.95} = \$.339649$$

The net single premium for a \$1,000 policy is

$$.339649 \times 1{,}000 = \$339.649, \quad \text{or} \quad \$339.65$$

(b) $x = 25$

Substituting the value in formula (20–2),

$$P_{25} = \frac{M_{25}}{N_{25}} = \frac{1{,}754{,}288.51}{139{,}839{,}496.91} = \$.0125450145$$

The net annual premium for the \$1,000 policy is

$$.012545 \times 1{,}000 = \$12.545, \quad \text{or} \quad \$12.55$$

(c) $n = 20,\ x = 25$

Substituting these values in formula (20–3),

$$_{20}P_{25} = \frac{M_{25}}{N_{25} - N_{25+20}} = \frac{M_{25}}{N_{25} - N_{45}} = \frac{1{,}754{,}288.51}{139{,}839{,}496.91 - 58{,}927{,}803.08}$$

$$= \$.02168152$$

The net annual premium for the \$1,000 policy for 20 payments is $.02168 \times 1{,}000 = \$21.68$. (Also see Example 3, Section 19.5.)

---

[3] *Proof (continued)*

$$A(\text{tem. due}) = {}_nP_x \cdot \ddot{a}_{x:\overline{n|}}$$

The present value must be equal to the net single premium A_x, or $A(\text{tem. due}) = A_x$. Substituting the value in the above equation, then, $A_x = {}_nP_x\ddot{a}_{x:\overline{n|}}$.

Since

$$A_x = \frac{M_x}{D_x} \quad \text{and} \quad \ddot{a}_{x:\overline{n|}} = \frac{N_x - N_{x+n}}{D_x}$$

then

$$\frac{M_x}{D_x} = {}_nP_x \cdot \frac{N_x - N_{x+n}}{D_x}$$

Solve for ${}_nP_x$.

$$_nP_x = \frac{M_x}{D_x} \cdot \frac{D_x}{N_x - N_{x+n}} = \frac{M_x}{N_x - N_{x+n}} \qquad (20\text{–}3)$$

NOTE: ***In order to simplify mathematical operations, round the decimals of the values in the commutation columns (Table 13) when computing the problems in the exercises in this chapter.*** Examples:

C_{20} = 10,300.1828, rounded to 10,300
M_{25} = 1,754,288.5116, rounded to 1,754,289

EXERCISE 20–1 REFERENCE: SECTION 20.2

A. For each of the following whole life policies, find (a) the net single premium, and (b) the net annual premium:

	Face Value of Policy	*Age of Insured on Purchase Date*	*Payment Plan*
1.	$4,000	26	straight life
2.	4,000	28	5-payment life
3.	2,000	34	10-payment life
4.	2,000	42	straight life
5.	1,000	50	straight life
6.	1,000	55	15-payment life
7.	1,000	65	20-payment life
8.	1,000	75	straight life

B. Statement problems:

9. Find the net single premium of a whole life policy of $1,000 issued to someone aged (a) 10, (b) 30, (c) 60, (d) 85.
10. Find the net single premium of a whole life policy of $1,000 issued to someone aged (a) 4, (b) 24, (c) 44, (d) 64.
11. A $1,000 whole life policy is issued to a person aged 35. Find the net single premium.
12. What is the net single premium of a $2,000 whole life policy issued to a person aged 45?
13. Refer to Problem 11. If the policy is a straight life policy, what is the net annual premium?
14. Refer to Problem 12. Find the net annual premium if the policy is a straight life policy.
15. Refer to Problem 11. If the policy is a 15-payment life policy, what is the net annual premium?
16. Refer to Problem 12. Find the net annual premium if the policy is a 10-payment life policy.

20.3 TERM INSURANCE

A *term insurance* policy provides that the insurance company will pay the face value of the policy to the beneficiary upon the death of the insured, if the insured dies during the term covered in the policy. The insurance company has no obligation for payment if the insured outlives the term. For example, if a five-year term policy is issued to someone aged 20, the insurance company is liable for payment of the policy if the insured dies within the five-year period, from the date of issuance until age 25.

A. Finding the Net Single Premium

Let n = the term in years

$A^{1}_{x:\overline{n|}}$ = the net single premium for a \$1, n-year term policy issued to a person aged x

The following formula can then be obtained:

$$A^{1}_{x:\overline{n|}} = \frac{M_x - M_{x+n}}{D_x} \qquad \textbf{(20–4)}^{4}$$

---

[4] *Proof—Formula (20–4):*

The cost of a \$1, n-year term policy and its net single premium (present value at age x) are diagrammed and derived as follows:

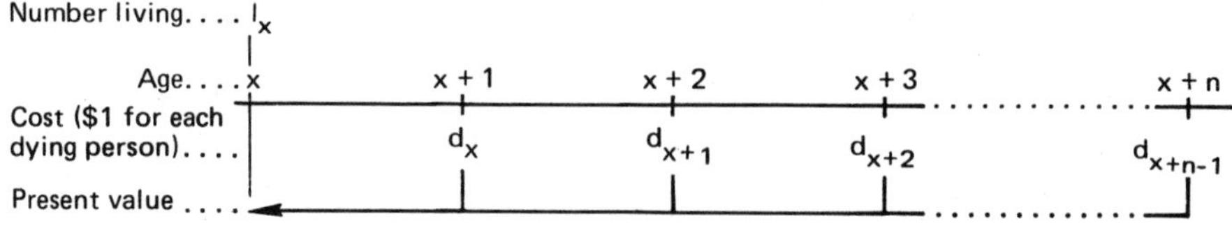

The present value of the cost at age x is divided by the number of persons living at age x, as follows:

$$A^{1}_{x:\overline{n|}} = \frac{vd_x + v^2d_{x+1} + v^3d_{x+2} + \cdots + v^n d_{x+n-1}}{l_x}$$

Multiply both the numerator and the denominator by v^x, and substitute the commutation symbols. Then

$$A^{1}_{x:\overline{n|}} = \frac{C_x + C_{x+1} + C_{x+2} + \cdots + C_{x+n-1}}{D_x}$$

Since $M_x = C_x + C_{x+1} + C_{x+2} + \cdots + C_{x+n-1} + C_{x+n} + \cdots + C_{99}$,

and $M_{x+n} = C_{x+n} + \cdots + C_{99}$,

the difference between M_x and M_{x+n} equals the numerator in the above equation. Thus, the equation may be written in the following manner:

$$A^{1}_{x:\overline{n|}} = \frac{M_x - M_{x+n}}{D_x} \qquad (20–4)$$

B. Finding the Net Annual Premium

Let $P^1_{x:\overline{n}|}$ = the net annual premium for an n year term policy of \$1 issued at age x

The following formula can be obtained:

$$P^1_{x:\overline{n}|} = \frac{M_x - M_{x+n}}{N_x - N_{x+n}} \qquad \textbf{(20–5)}^5$$

In formula (20–5), it is assumed that the number of years in the term of the policy is the same as the number of the annual premium payments. If the term (n) is larger than the number of payments (y), the letter y should replace the letter n in the denominator of the fraction:

$$_yP^1_{x:\overline{n}|} = \frac{M_x - M_{x+n}}{N_x - N_{x+y}} \qquad \textbf{(20–6)}^6$$

EXAMPLE 1 A \$1,000, five-year term policy is issued to a man aged 20. Find (a) the net single premium, and (b) the net annual premium.

$x = 20$, $n = 5$, $x + n = 25$

(a) Substituting the values in formula (20–4),

---

[5] *Proof–Formula (20–5):*

The n annual premiums ($P^1_{x:\overline{n}|}$) form a temporary life annuity due. The present value of the annual premiums can be obtained by using formula (19–11).

$A(\text{tem. due}) = R\ddot{a}_{x:\overline{n}|}$, or

$$A(\text{tem. due}) = P^1_{x:\overline{n}|}\,\ddot{a}_{x:\overline{n}|} = P^1_{x:\overline{n}|} \cdot \frac{N_x - N_{x+n}}{D_x} \quad \text{(See Section 19.5B.)}$$

The present value must be equal to the net single premium $A^1_{x:\overline{n}|}$, or

$$A(\text{tem. due}) = A^1_{x:\overline{n}|} = \frac{M_x - M_{x+n}}{D_x}$$

Substituting the value in the above equation,

$$P^1_{x:\overline{n}|} \cdot \frac{N_x - N_{x+n}}{D_x} = \frac{M_x - M_{x+n}}{D_x}$$

$$P^1_{x:\overline{n}|} = \frac{M_x - M_{x+n}}{N_x - N_{x+n}} \qquad (20\text{–}5)$$

[6] *Proof–Formula (20–6):*

Here the y annual premiums ($_yP^1_{x:\overline{n}|}$) form a temporary life annuity due. Thus,

$$A(\text{tem. due}) = {}_yP^1_{x:\overline{n}|} \cdot \frac{N_x - N_{x+y}}{D_x} = \frac{M_x - M_{x+n}}{D_x}$$

$$_yP^1_{x:\overline{n}|} = \frac{M_x - M_{x+n}}{N_x - N_{x+y}} \qquad (20\text{–}6)$$

$$\text{The net single premium} = 1{,}000A^{1}_{x:\overline{n}|} = 1{,}000 \cdot \frac{M_{20} - M_{25}}{D_{20}}$$

$$= 1{,}000 \cdot \frac{1{,}804{,}922.42 - 1{,}754{,}288.51}{5{,}898{,}264.97}$$

$$= 1{,}000 \cdot \frac{50{,}633.91}{5{,}898{,}264.97} = 1{,}000(.0085845)$$

$$= \$8.5845, \quad \text{or} \quad \$8.58$$

(b) Since the number of annual premium payments is not indicated in the problem, the number of years in the term of the policy is assumed to be the same as the number of payments.

Substituting the x and n values in formula (20–5),

$$\text{The net annual premium} = 1{,}000P^{1}_{x:\overline{n}|} = 1{,}000 \cdot \frac{M_{20} - M_{25}}{N_{20} - N_{25}}$$

$$= 1{,}000 \cdot \frac{1{,}804{,}922.42 - 1{,}754{,}288.51}{167{,}827{,}045.88 - 139{,}839{,}496.91}$$

$$= 1{,}000 \cdot \frac{50{,}633.91}{27{,}987{,}548.97} = 1{,}000(.0018091584)$$

$$= \$1.8091584, \quad \text{or} \quad \$1.81$$

EXAMPLE 2

Refer to Example 1. Assume that the net premium is payable in three equal annual payments. Find the net annual premium.

$x = 20$, $n = 5$ (years, the term of the policy), $y = 3$ (annual payments), $x + n = 25$, $x + y = 23$

Substituting the values in formula (20–6),

$$\text{The net annual premium} = 1{,}000\,{}_{y}P^{1}_{x:\overline{n}|} = 1{,}000 \cdot \frac{M_{20} - M_{25}}{N_{20} - N_{23}}$$

$$= 1{,}000 \cdot \frac{50{,}633.91}{167{,}827{,}045.88 - 150{,}590{,}926.74}$$

$$= 1{,}000(.002937663) = \$2.94$$

EXERCISE 20–2 REFERENCE: SECTION 20.3

A. For each of the following term insurance policies, find (a) the net single premium, (b) the net annual premium:

	Face Value of Policy	*Age of Insured on Purchase Date*	*Term of Policy*	*Payment Plan*
1.	$1,000	30	5 years	5 payments
2.	1,500	25	10 years	10 payments
3.	2,000	35	15 years	15 payments
4.	2,000	40	20 years	20 payments
5.	3,000	26	12 years	12 payments
6.	3,000	38	16 years	16 payments
7.	4,000	45	10 years	6 payments
8.	4,000	22	18 years	10 payments

B. Statement problems:

9. Find the net single premium and the net annual premium for a 10-year, \$5,000 term policy issued to someone aged (a) 18, (b) 28, (c) 50.
10. Find the net single premium and the net annual premium for a 20-year, \$10,000 term policy issued to someone aged (a) 16, (b) 36, (c) 56.
11. A \$1,000, 25-year term policy is issued to a person aged 24. Find (a) the net single premium, (b) the net annual premium.
12. A \$2,000, 30-year term policy is issued to a person aged 32. Find (a) the net single premium, (b) the net annual premium.
13. Refer to Problem 11. If the policy specifies that the net premium is payable in 20 equal annual payments, find the size of the net annual premium.
14. Refer to Problem 12. If the policy specifies that the net premium is payable in 15 equal annual payments, what is the size of the net annual premium?

20.4 ENDOWMENT INSURANCE

An *endowment insurance* policy combines the features of a pure endowment and a term insurance policy. The provisions of the combination are that (a) if the insured is living at the end of the term of the policy, the face value of the policy will be payable to the policyholder; and (b) if the insured dies during the term of the policy, the face value of the policy will be payable to the designated beneficiary. Thus, an n-year endowment insurance policy may be treated as a combined policy consisting of an n-year pure endowment and an n-year term insurance policy.

A. Finding the Net Single Premium

Let $A_{x:\overline{n|}}$ = the net single premium of an n-year endowment insurance policy of \$1, issued at age x

Then the value of $A_{x:\overline{n|}}$ is the sum of the net single premium of a \$1, n-year pure endowment policy and the net single premium of a \$1, n-year term insurance policy, which may be written as follows:

$$A_{x:\overline{n|}} = {}_nE_x + A^1_{x:\overline{n|}} = \frac{D_{x+n}}{D_x} + \frac{M_x - M_{x+n}}{D_x}, \quad \text{or}$$

$$A_{x:\overline{n|}} = \frac{M_x - M_{x+n} + D_{x+n}}{D_x} \qquad \textbf{(20–7)}$$

B. Finding the Net Annual Premium

Let $P_{x:\overline{n|}}$ = the net annual premium of an n-year endowment insurance policy of \$1, issued at age x

Then the following formula may be obtained:

$$P_{x:\overline{n|}} = \frac{M_x - M_{x+n} + D_{x+n}}{N_x - N_{x+n}} \qquad \textbf{(20–8)}[7]$$

In formula (20–8), it is assumed that the number of years in the term of the policy is the same as the number of the annual premium payments. If the term (n) is larger than the number of payments (y), the letter y should replace the letter n in the denominator of the fraction:

$$ {}_yP_{x:\overline{n}|} = \frac{M_x - M_{x+n} + D_{x+n}}{N_x - N_{x+y}} \qquad \textbf{(20–9)}^{8} $$

EXAMPLE 1 A \$1,000, 20-year endowment insurance policy was bought by someone aged 40. Find (a) the net single premium, (b) the net annual premium.

$x = 40,\ n = 20,\ x + n = 60$

(a) The net single premium is computed by using formula (20–7), as follows:

$$ A_{x:\overline{n}|} = A_{40:\overline{20}|} = \frac{M_{40} - M_{60} + D_{60}}{D_{40}} = \frac{1{,}607{,}743.17 - 1{,}187{,}445.15 + 1{,}749{,}787.72}{3{,}441{,}765.06} $$

$$ = \frac{2{,}170{,}085.74}{3{,}441{,}765.06} = \$.630515 $$

The net single premium of the 20-year endowment insurance of \$1,000 is

$.630515 \times 1{,}000 = \$630.515$, or \$630.52

(b) Since the number of annual premium payments is not indicated in the problem, the number of years in the term of the policy is assumed to be the same as the number of payments.

---

[7] *Proof–Formula (20–8):*

The n annual premiums ($P_{x:\overline{n}|}$) form a temporary life annuity due. The present value of the annual premiums can be obtained by using formula (19–11).

$$ \text{A(tem. due)} = R\ddot{a}_{x:\overline{n}|}, \quad \text{or} $$

$$ A(\text{tem. due}) = P_{x:\overline{n}|} \cdot \ddot{a}_{x:\overline{n}|} = P_{x:\overline{n}|} \cdot \frac{N_x - N_{x+n}}{D_x} $$

The present value must be equal to the net single premium $A_{x:\overline{n}|}$, or

$$ A(\text{tem. due}) = A_{x:\overline{n}|} = \frac{M_x - M_{x+n} + D_{x+n}}{D_x} \quad \text{[See formula (20–7).]} $$

Thus,

$$ P_{x:\overline{n}|} \cdot \frac{N_x - N_{x+n}}{D_x} = \frac{M_x - M_{x+n} + D_{x+n}}{D_x} $$

$$ P_{x:\overline{n}|} = \frac{M_x - M_{x+n} + D_{x+n}}{N_x - N_{x+n}} \qquad (20–8) $$

[8] *Proof–Formula (20–9):*

Here, the y annual premiums (${}_yP_{x:\overline{n}|}$) form a temporary life annuity due. Thus,

$$ A(\text{tem. due}) = {}_yP_{x:\overline{n}|} \cdot \frac{N_x - N_{x+y}}{D_x} = \frac{M_x - M_{x+n} + D_{x+n}}{D_x} $$

$$ {}_yP_{x:\overline{n}|} = \frac{M_x - M_{x+n} + D_{x+n}}{N_x - N_{x+y}} \qquad (20–9) $$

Substituting the x and n values in formula (20–8),

$$\text{Net annual premium} = 1{,}000P_{40:\overline{20|}} = 1{,}000 \cdot \frac{M_{40} - M_{60} + D_{60}}{N_{40} - N_{60}}$$

$$= 1{,}000 \cdot \frac{2{,}170{,}085.74}{75{,}194{,}899.17 - 23{,}056{,}044.97}$$

$$= 1{,}000(.04162) = \$41.62.$$

EXAMPLE 2 Refer to Example 1. Assume that the net single premium is payable in 15 equal annual payments. Find the size of the annual premium payment.

$x = 40$, $n = 20$, $y = 15$, $x + n = 60$, $x + y = 55$

Substituting the values in formula (20–9),

$$\text{Net annual premium} = 1{,}000\,{}_{15}P_{40:\overline{20|}} = 1{,}000 \cdot \frac{M_{40} - M_{60} + D_{60}}{N_{40} - N_{55}}$$

$$= \frac{1{,}000(2{,}170{,}085.74)}{75{,}194{,}899.17 - 32{,}978{,}578.86} = \$51.40$$

EXERCISE 20–3 REFERENCE: SECTION 20.4

A. For each of the following endowment insurance policies, find (a) the net single premium, (b) the net annual premium:

	Face Value of Policy	*Age of Insured on Purchase Date*	*Term of Policy*	*Payment Plan*
1.	$1,000	30	5 years	5 payments
2.	1,500	25	10 years	10 payments
3.	2,000	35	15 years	15 payments
4.	2,000	45	20 years	20 payments
5.	3,000	22	25 years	25 payments
6.	3,000	32	18 years	18 payments
7.	4,000	50	20 years	15 payments
8.	5,000	20	10 years	8 payments

B. Statement problems:

9. A $1,000, 30-year endowment insurance policy was purchased by someone aged 28. Find (a) the net single premium, (b) the net annual premium.
10. A $1,500, 45-year endowment insurance policy was bought by someone aged 20. Find (a) the net single premium, (b) the net annual premium.
11. Refer to Problem 9. If the policy were purchased by a person aged 35, what would be the answers to (a) and (b)?
12. Refer to Problem 10. If the policy were purchased by a person aged 25, what would be the answers to (a) and (b)?
13. Refer to Problem 9. Assuming that the net single premium is payable in 25 equal annual payments, what is the size of the net annual premium?
14. Refer to Problem 10. What should be the size of the net annual premium if the premium of the policy were payable in 30 equal annual payments?

★20.5 DEFERRED LIFE INSURANCE

Life insurance may be deferred for a specified period of time. When the insurance is deferred for k years, the insurance protection does not begin at the time the policy is issued, but only after k years have passed. Thus, a 10-year deferred whole life insurance policy issued to someone aged 20 does not provide insurance protection until the age of 30. However, insurance premiums are paid beginning at the age of 20, or on the purchase date. An insurance company seldom sells a deferred insurance policy. More often, the company sells a combined insurance policy that includes a deferred provision.

The net single premium for an insurance policy may be derived by the same reasoning as in the preceding sections. However, the following methods involve less computation.

A. Deferred Whole Life Insurance

Let $_{k|}A_x$ = the net single premium for a whole life insurance policy of \$1 deferred k years, issued at age x

Then the value of $_{k|}A_x$ *equals* the net single premium for a \$1 whole life insurance policy *minus* the net single premium for a \$1, k-year term insurance policy. Thus,

$$_{k|}A_x = A_x - A^{1}_{x:\overline{k}|} = \frac{M_x}{D_x} - \frac{M_x - M_{x+k}}{D_x}, \quad \text{or}$$

$$_{k|}A_x = \frac{M_{x+k}}{D_x} \tag{20–10}$$

B. Deferred Term Insurance

Let $_{k|}A^{1}_{x:\overline{n}|}$ = the net single premium for an n-year term insurance policy of \$1 deferred k years, issued at age x

Then the value of $_{k|}A^{1}_{x:\overline{n}|}$ *equals* the net single premium for a \$1, $k + n$ term insurance policy *minus* the net single premium for a \$1, k-year term insurance policy. Thus,

$$_{k|}A^{1}_{x:\overline{n}|} = A^{1}_{x:\overline{k+n}|} - A^{1}_{x:\overline{k}|} = \frac{M_x - M_{x+k+n}}{D_x} - \frac{M_x - M_{x+k}}{D_x}, \quad \text{or}$$

$$_{k|}A^{1}_{x:\overline{n}|} = \frac{M_{x+k} - M_{x+k+n}}{Dx} \tag{20–11}$$

C. Deferred Endowment Insurance

Let $_{k|}A_{x:\overline{n}|}$ = the net single premium for an n-year endowment insurance policy of \$1 deferred k years, issued at age x.

Then the value of $_{k|}A_{x:\overline{n}|}$ *equals* the net single premium for a $k + n$ year pure endowment policy of \$1 *plus* the net single premium for an n-year term insurance policy of \$1 deferred k years. Thus,

$$_{k|}A_{x:\overline{n}|} = {}_{k+n}E_x + {}_{k|}A^{1}_{x:\overline{n}|} = \frac{D_{x+k+n}}{D_x} + \frac{M_{x+k} - M_{x+k+n}}{D_x}, \quad \text{or}$$

$$_{k|}A_{x:\overline{n}|} = \frac{M_{x+k} - M_{x+k+n} + D_{x+k+n}}{D_x} \tag{20–12}$$

EXAMPLE 1

A policy issued to someone aged 20 provides the following: (a) \$1,000 if the insured dies in 30 years, (b) \$3,000 if the insured dies after 30 years. Find the net annual premium for life.

The policy actually combines two types of insurance: (a) 30-year term insurance of \$1,000, and (b) whole life insurance of \$3,000 deferred for 30 years.

The net single premium for type (a) is $1{,}000A^{1}_{20:\overline{30|}}$ [formula (20–4)].

The net single premium for type (b) is $3{,}000 \cdot {}_{30|}A_{20}$ [formula 20–10)].

Let P = the annual premium of the policy payable for life.

The annual premiums (P) form a whole life annuity due. The present value of the annuity is $P\ddot{a}_x$ or $P\ddot{a}_{20}$ [formula (19–5)].

The present value of the annuity must be equal to the two net single premiums, or

$$P\ddot{a}_{20} = 1{,}000A^{1}_{20:\overline{30|}} + 3{,}000 \cdot {}_{30|}A_{20}$$

$$P \cdot \frac{N_{20}}{D_{20}} = 1{,}000 \cdot \frac{M_{20} - M_{20+30}}{D_{20}} + 3{,}000 \cdot \frac{M_{20+30}}{D_{20}}$$

$$P = \frac{D_{20}}{N_{20}} \cdot \frac{1{,}000(M_{20} - M_{50}) + 3{,}000M_{50}}{D_{20}} = \frac{1{,}000M_{20} + 2{,}000M_{50}}{N_{20}}$$

$$= \frac{1{,}000(1{,}804.922.42) + 2{,}000(1{,}454{,}100.51)}{167{,}827{,}045.88} = \$28.08$$

EXAMPLE 2

A policy, issued to a boy aged 10, promises to pay (a) \$1,000 if he dies before reaching age 25, (b) \$2,000 if he dies after reaching 25 but before 37, and (c) \$5,000 if he dies after reaching 37 but before 65, or if he is alive at 65. Find the net annual premium if the policy is a 20-payment policy.

The policy consists of the following types of insurance benefits: (a) a 15-year term insurance of \$1,000, (b) a 12-year term insurance of \$2,000, deferred 15 years – from age 10 to age 25, and (c) a 28-year endowment insurance of \$5,000, deferred 27 years – from age 10 to age 37.

As of the purchase date:

The net single premium for type (a) is $1{,}000A^{1}_{10:\overline{15|}}$ [formula (20–4)].

The net single premium for type (b) is $2{,}000 \cdot {}_{15|}A^{1}_{10:\overline{12|}}$ [formula (20–11)].

The net single premium for type (c) is $5{,}000 \cdot {}_{27|}A_{10:\overline{28|}}$ [formula (20–12)].

The 20 annual premiums (P) form a temporary life annuity due. The present value of the annuity is $P\ddot{a}_{x:\overline{n|}}$ *or* $P\ddot{a}_{10:\overline{20|}}$ [formula (19–11)].

The present value of the annuity must be equal to the three net single premiums, or

$$P\ddot{a}_{10:\overline{20|}} = 1{,}000A^{1}_{10:\overline{15|}} + 2{,}000 \cdot {}_{15|}A^{1}_{10:\overline{12|}} + 5{,}000 \cdot {}_{27|}A_{10:\overline{28|}}$$

$$P \cdot \frac{N_{10} - N_{30}}{D_{10}} = 1{,}000 \cdot \frac{M_{10} - M_{25}}{D_{10}} + 2{,}000 \cdot \frac{M_{25} - M_{37}}{D_{10}} + 5{,}000 \cdot \frac{M_{37} - M_{65} + D_{65}}{D_{10}}$$

$$P(N_{10} - N_{30}) = 1{,}000(M_{10} - M_{25}) + 2{,}000(M_{25} - M_{37}) + 5{,}000(M_{37} - M_{65} + D_{65})$$

$$P = \frac{1{,}000M_{10} + 1{,}000M_{25} + 3{,}000M_{37} - 5{,}000M_{65} + 5{,}000D_{65}}{N_{10} - N_{30}}$$

$$= \$86.19$$

★EXERCISE 20–4 REFERENCE: SECTION 20.5

1. Find the net single premium for a whole life insurance policy of $5,000 deferred 15 years, issued to someone now aged 25.
2. Find the net single premium for a whole life insurance policy of $3,000 deferred 22 years, issued to someone now aged 18.
3. What is the net single premium for a five-year term insurance policy of $1,000 deferred three years, issued to a person who is 30 years of age?
4. What is the net single premium for a 12-year term insurance policy of $2,000 deferred eight years, issued to a person who is 40 years of age?
5. Find the net single premium for a 20-year endowment insurance policy of $3,000 deferred 10 years, issued to someone who is 20 years of age.
6. What is the net single premium for a 30-year endowment insurance policy of $2,500 deferred 20 years, issued to someone now aged 35?
7. A policy issued to a person aged 25 provides the following: (a) $2,000 if the insured dies within 20 years, (b) $5,000 if the insured dies after 20 years. Find the net annual premium for life.
8. A policy issued to a person aged 30 provides the following: (a) $2,500 if the insured dies within 10 years, (b) $3,500 if the insured dies after 10 years. Find the net annual premium for life.
9. A policy issued to a child at age 8 promises to pay: (a) $1,000 if the insured dies before age 20, (b) $3,000 if death occurs after age 20 but before 25, and (c) $6,000 if death occurs after age 25 but before 50, or if the insured is living at age 50. Find the net annual premium if the policy is a 30-payment policy.
10. A policy issued to a woman aged 22 provides that the insurance company will pay: (a) $2,000 if she dies before age 40, (b) $4,000 if she dies after reaching age 40 but before 65, and (c) $1,000 if she dies after reaching age 65 but before 80, or if she is alive at age 80. What is the net annual premium if the policy is a 40-payment policy?
11. Refer to Problem 9. If item (c) reads: "$6,000 if the insured dies after reaching age 25," what is the net annual premium?
12. Refer to Problem 10. Find the net annual premium if item (c) reads: "$1,000 if she dies after reaching age 65."

20.6 NATURAL PREMIUM AND LEVEL PREMIUM

A. Computing the Natural Premium

The net single premium of a one-year term insurance policy is called the *natural premium*. According to the 1958 CSO Table, the death rate decreases from birth until age 10 and increases after the age of 10. Thus, if a person, aged 10, purchases a one-year term policy every year, the natural premium would increase from year to year. The natural premium for a particular age may be computed by using the following term insurance formula:

$$A^{1}_{x:\overline{n|}} = \frac{M_x - M_{x+n}}{D_x}. \quad \text{Here } n = 1. \text{ Thus,}$$

$$A^{1}_{x:\overline{1|}} = \frac{M_x - M_{x+1}}{D_x} = \frac{C_x}{D_x}, \quad \text{or it may be written}$$

$$c_x = \frac{C_x}{D_x} \qquad \textbf{(20–13)}^9$$

The values of C_x based on $2\frac{1}{2}\%$ interest are given in Table 13.

The value of c_x is called the natural premium at age x, or the net single premium for a $1, one-year term policy issued at age x.

EXAMPLE 1

Find the net single premium for a $1,000, one-year term policy if the policy is issued at age (a) 20, (b) 21, (c) 22, (d) 23, (e) 24.

Since the policy is a one-year term policy, the natural premium formula is used to compute the value of the net single premium for each age as follows.

(a) $x = 20$

Substituting the value in formula (20–13), the natural premium for a $1 policy is

$$c_x = \frac{C_x}{D_x} = \frac{C_{20}}{D_{20}} = \frac{10{,}300.18}{5{,}898{,}264.97} = .0017463$$

The natural premium (or the net single premium) for a $1,000 policy is

$.0017463 \times 1{,}000 = \$1.7463$, or $1.75

(b) $x = 21$

$$c_{21} = \frac{C_{21}}{D_{21}} = .0017853$$

Total net single premium $= .0017853 \times 1{,}000 = \$1.7853$, or $1.79

(c) $x = 22$

$$c_{22} = \frac{C_{22}}{D_{22}} = .0018146$$

Total net single premium $= .0018146 \times 1{,}000 = \$1.8146$, or $1.81

(d) $x = 23$

$$c_{23} = \frac{C_{23}}{D_{23}} = .0018439$$

Total net single premium $= .0018439 \times 1{,}000 = \$1.8439$, or $1.84

(e) $x = 24$

$$c_{24} = \frac{C_{24}}{D_{24}} = .0018634$$

Total net single premium $= .0018634 \times 1{,}000 = \$1.8634$, or $1.86

NOTE: The division C_x/D_x may also be performed by using logarithms. The division in (a), for example, is computed as follows:

---

9 *Proof–Formula (20–13):*

$$\begin{aligned} M_x &= C_x + C_{x+1} + C_{x+2} + \cdots + C_{99} \\ M_{x+1} &= \qquad\;\; C_{x+1} + C_{x+2} + \cdots + C_{99} \\ \hline M_x - M_{x+1} &= C_x \end{aligned}$$

Also see the proof for formula (20–1) for the value of C_x.

$$\begin{array}{rcl} \log C_{20} = 4.012\ 8449 & = & 14.012\ 8449 - 10 \\ (-)\ \log D_{20} & = & 6.770\ 7243 \quad \text{(Table 14)} \\ \hline \log c_{20} & = & 7.242\ 1206 - 10 \end{array}$$

Find the antilog by interpolation from Table 2.

$c_{20} = .0017463$

B. Checking Natural Premium Against Cost

The natural premium represents the net cost of the death claim. The premium is collected by the insurance company at the beginning of each age and is invested at $2\frac{1}{2}\%$. The total amount at the end of each age should be enough to pay the death claim. The answer to (a) in Example 1 may be checked as follows:

At age 20, there are l_{20} or 9,664,994 persons living. The total premium collected from the group at the beginning of age 20 is

$1.7463 \times 9{,}664{,}994 = \$16{,}877{,}979.02$

The interest on the total premium for one year at $2\frac{1}{2}\%$ is

$16{,}877{,}979.02 \times 2\frac{1}{2}\% = \$421{,}949.48$

The total amount at the end of age 20 is

$16{,}877{,}979.02 + 421{,}949.48 = \$17{,}299{,}928.50$

There are d_{20} or 17,300 persons dying during the period from the beginning of age 20 to the end of age 20. The death claim against the total amount for each death is

$$\frac{17{,}299{,}928.50}{17{,}300} = \$999.996, \quad \text{or} \quad \$1{,}000 \text{ (policy value)}$$

C. Comparing Natural Premium with Level Premium

The answers in Example 1 indicate that the net cost of the death benefits (net single premium) to the insurance company for a $1,000, one-year term policy is $1.75 if the policyholder is 20 years old, $1.79 if the policyholder is 21 years old, $1.81 if the policyholder is 22 years old, and so on. The natural premium increases from year to year as the policyholder grows older. However, an insurance company usually sells policies having a term of more than one year and collects equal annual premiums for each policy. Since the net annual premium is a fixed amount for every year during the policy term, it is called a *level premium*.

EXAMPLE 2 A $1,000, five-year term policy is issued to a person aged 20. (a) Find the natural premium for each age during the term of the policy. (b) Find the level premium (net annual premium). (c) Construct a chart of the natural premiums and the level premium.

(a) The natural premium for each age is as follows:

Age 20: $1.7463
Age 21: $1.7853

Age 22: $1.8146
Age 23: $1.8439
Age 24: $1.8634 (See Example 1.)

(b) The level premium is

$$1{,}000P^{1}_{20:\overline{5}|} = 1{,}000 \cdot \frac{M_{20} - M_{25}}{N_{20} - N_{25}} = \$1.8092$$ [see Example 1(b), Section 20.3, page 574].

(c) Chart (see below):

Level Premium for a Five-Year Term Policy Issued at Age 20 and Natural Premiums for Ages 20 through 24 (Policy Face Value: $1,000)

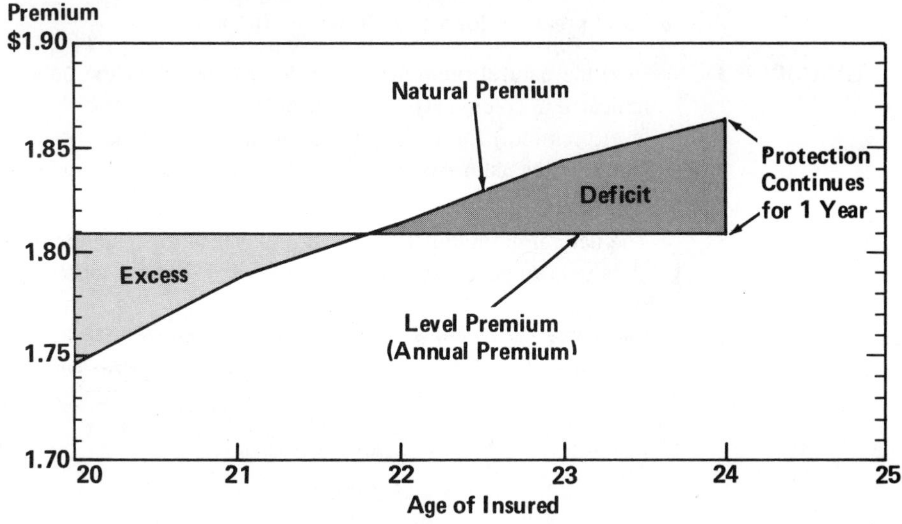

The answers in Example 2 are also tabulated in the following schedule:

Comparison of Level Premium and Natural Premium

(1) *Age*	*(2)* *Natural Premium*	*(3)* *Excess (or Deficit) of Level Premium over Natural Premium: $1.8092 − (2)*
20	$1.7463	$0.0629
21	1.7853	0.0239
22	1.8146	−0.0054
23	1.8439	−0.0347
24	1.8634	−0.0542

In Example 2, during the first year the insurance company collects $.06 (or $1.8092 − $1.7463) more than the net cost of the insurance. [See column (3) in the above schedule.] The company usually deposits the excess premium, \$.06, in a *reserve fund*, which is invested to earn interest to meet future needs. (See Section 20.7.) On the other hand, when the policy holder reaches age 24, the insurance company collects \$.05 (or \$1.8092 − \$1.8634) less than the net cost to the company. The company usually makes up the deficit premium from the reserve fund.

In general, for every insurance policy, the level premium is greater than the natural premium (the net cost to the company) in the earlier policy years. On the other hand, in the later policy years the level premium is less than the natural premium. If the policyholder wishes to cancel the contract before the entire amount of the reserve fund has been used, it is possible to recover a *cash surrender value*, which is paid by the life insurance company when the policyholder surrenders the policy to the company.

The following example illustrates the relationship between the natural premiums and the level premium for a straight whole life policy.

EXAMPLE 3

Find the natural premiums for a \$1,000 policy if the policy is issued at the ages indicated in column (1) of the schedule below. Also find the net annual premium (the level premium) for a \$1,000 straight whole life policy issued to a person aged 50. Compare the natural premiums with the level premium and show the excess or deficit premiums.

The natural premiums for the required ages are computed by using formula (20–13) and are arranged, respectively, in column (2) of the following schedule.

Level Premium for a \$1,000, Straight Whole Life Policy Issued at Age 50 and Natural Premiums for Various Ages

(1) Age (x)	*(2) Natural Premium:* $1{,}000 \cdot \frac{C_x}{D_x}$	*(3) Excess (or Deficit) of Level Premium over Natural Premium: \$32.38 − (2)*
50	\$ 8.12	\$ 24.26
55	12.68	19.70
60	19.84	12.54
65	30.98	1.40
70	48.58	− 16.20
75	71.58	− 39.20
80	107.30	− 74.92
85	157.21	−124.83
90	222.58	−190.20
95	342.67	−310.29
99	975.61	−943.23

The net annual premium (the level premium) is

$$1{,}000P_{50} = 1{,}000 \cdot \frac{M_{50}}{N_{50}} = \$32.38$$

The comparison between the natural premiums and the level premium is shown in column (3) of the schedule.

Example 3 is diagrammed in the following chart, which covers a portion of the information presented in the schedule on page 584.

Level Premium for a $1,000 Straight Whole Life Policy for a Person Aged 50 and Natural Premiums for Various Ages

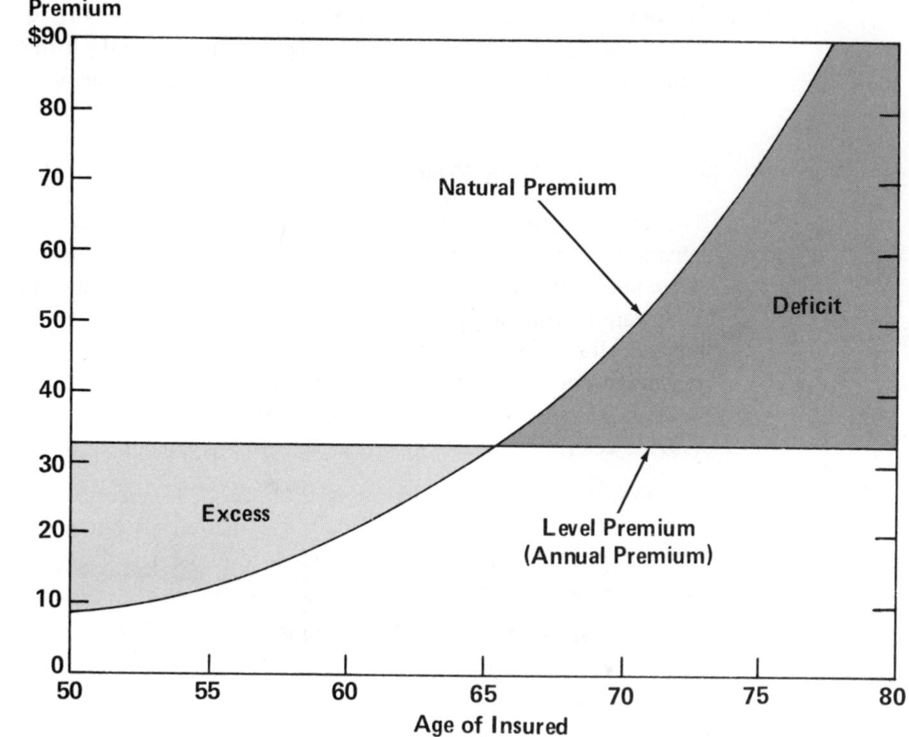

EXERCISE 20–5 REFERENCE: SECTION 20.6

1. Find the net single premium for a $1,000, one-year term policy if the policy is issued at age (a) 8, (b) 9, (c) 10, (d) 11, (e) 12.
2. Find the net single premium for a $2,000, one-year term policy, if the policy is issued at age (a) 30, (b) 31, (c) 32, (d) 33, (e) 34.
3. Refer to the checking method described on page 582. Use this method to check whether the natural premium obtained in Problem 1(a) is sufficient to pay the net cost of the death claim.
4. Refer to the checking method described on page 582. Use this method to check whether the natural premium obtained in Problem 2(a) is sufficient to pay the net cost of the death claim.
5. A $1,000, five-year term policy is issued to someone aged 25. Construct a chart of the natural premiums and the level premium for the policy.
6. A $1,000, five-year term policy is issued to someone aged 40. Construct a chart of the natural premiums and the level premium for the policy.

★20.7 TERMINAL RESERVE

A. General Computation

Terminal reserve is the value accumulated from the excess premiums and the interest on the premiums. It represents the value of an insurance policy at the end of any policy year; the premium then due is not included. For example, the fourth terminal reserve for an insurance policy is the value of the policy at the end of the fourth year after the policy is issued, but it does not include the net annual premium for the fifth year. The value of the terminal reserve at the end of a particular policy year may be obtained in various ways. Two methods are illustrated below.

RETROSPECTIVE METHOD

The *retrospective method* is based on the premiums collected in the *past* and the death benefits paid in the *past*. Premiums are collected by the insurance company at the *beginning* of each policy year and are invested at a given interest rate for accumulation. The death benefits are paid from this accumulated sum. It is assumed here, as in the previous discussion, that the death benefits are paid at the *end* of the year of death. The remaining part (premiums and interest less death benefit payments) is the terminal reserve, which is divided by the number of surviving policyholders in the 1958 CSO Table to determine the terminal reserve per policyholder for the year.

EXAMPLE 1 The CSO Table shows that $l_{20} = 9{,}664{,}994$. Assume that each of the 9,664,994 persons aged 20 is issued a $1,000, five-year term insurance policy and the annual premiums are invested at $2\frac{1}{2}\%$. Find the terminal reserve per surviving policyholder at the end of each policy year.

The terminal reserves are computed in the following table:

(1) Policy Year	*(2) Surviving Policy-holders at Beginning of Year*	*(3) Premiums Paid at Beginning of Year: (2) × 1.8091584**	*(4) Reserve Fund at Beginning of Year: (3) + (7)***	*(5) One Year's Interest for the Reserve Fund: (4) × $2\frac{1}{2}\%$*	*(6) Death Claims at End of Year: $1,000 Each (of d_x)*	*(7) Reserve Fund at End of Year: (4) + (5) − (6)*	*(8) Terminal Reserve per Survivor: (7) ÷ (2)****
1	9,664,994	$17,485,505	$17,485,505	$437,138	$17,300,000	$622,643	$.064538
2	9,647,694	17,454,207	18,076,850	451,921	17,655,000	873,771	.090734
3	9,630,039	17,422,266	18,296,037	457,401	17,912,000	841,438	.087539
4	9,612,127	17,389,860	18,231,298	455,782	18,167,000	520,080	.054209
5	9,593,960	17,356,993	17,877,073	446,927	18,324,000	−0−	−0−

*Net annual premium. See Section 20.6, Example 2(b).

**Of the preceding year. For example, $18,076,850 = 17,454,207 + 622,643.

***Of the succeeding year. For example, $.064538 = 622,643 ÷ 9,647,694.

The preceding method may be used to compute the terminal reserves for any type of insurance. As shown below, the procedure used in this method may also be expressed symbolically to obtain a formula. The formula can then be used to find the terminal reserve per surviving policyholder at the end of any given policy year without constructing a table.

Let P = the net annual premium (or level premium) for a policy of $1
t = the number of years the policy is in force: the terminal reserve is desired at the end of the tth policy year
V = tth terminal reserve per surviving policyholder for a $1 policy
V' = $V \times$ Policy value = the total tth terminal reserve per surviving policyholder

If the tth terminal reserve is on a date that is before or on the date of the last payment of the n annual premiums, the formula for the value of V is as follows:

$$V = \frac{P(N_x - N_{x+t}) - (M_x - M_{x+t})}{D_{x+t}}, \quad \text{where} \quad t \leq n \qquad \textbf{(20–14)}^{10}$$

---

10 *Proof–Formula (20–14):*

The number of years that the policy has been in force (t) is smaller than or equal to the number of annual premium payments (n) (or, $t \leq n$).

Let age $x + t$ be the comparison date and i be the interest rate compounded annually. The accumulated values of the *past* annual premiums and the *past* death benefits at age $x + t$ are diagrammed respectively as follows:

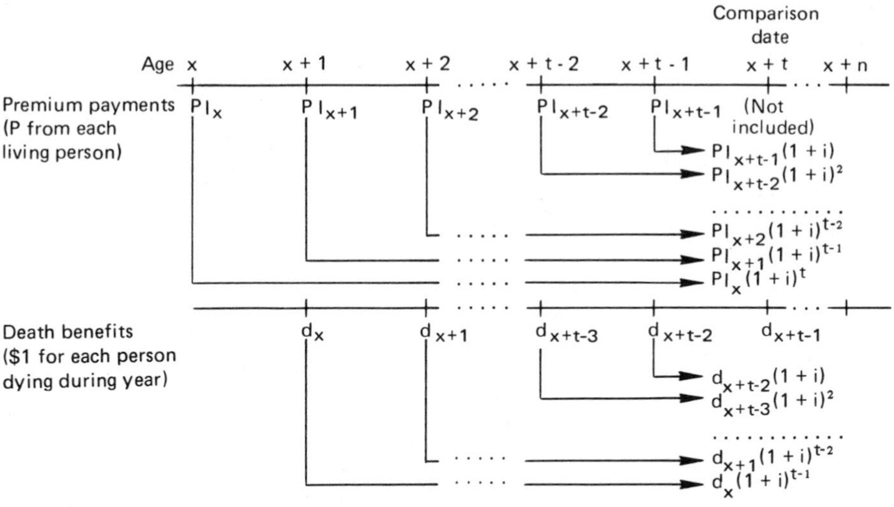

Comparison date
Age x | x + 1 | x + 2 | ..... | x + t - 2 | x + t - 1 | x + t | ... | x + n

Premium payments (P from each living person): Pl_x, Pl_{x+1}, Pl_{x+2}, ..., Pl_{x+t-2}, Pl_{x+t-1}, (Not included)
$Pl_{x+t-1}(1+i)$
$Pl_{x+t-2}(1+i)^2$
....
$Pl_{x+2}(1+i)^{t-2}$
$Pl_{x+1}(1+i)^{t-1}$
$Pl_x(1+i)^t$

Death benefits ($1 for each person dying during year): d_x, d_{x+1}, ..., d_{x+t-3}, d_{x+t-2}, d_{x+t-1}
$d_{x+t-2}(1+i)$
$d_{x+t-3}(1+i)^2$
....
$d_{x+1}(1+i)^{t-2}$
$d_x(1+i)^{t-1}$

At the end of the tth policy year, the comparison date, the total accumulated annual premiums (not considering the payments of the death benefits) are

$$Pl_x(1+i)^t + Pl_{x+1}(1+i)^{t-1} + \cdots + Pl_{x+t-1}(1+i) \qquad \text{(I)}$$

If the tth terminal reserve is on a date that is after the last payment of the n annual premiums [this may occur in a limited payment life insurance policy as in Example 5(b) below], the formula for the value of V is as follows:

$$V = \frac{P(N_x - N_{x+n}) - (M_x - M_{x+t})}{D_{x+t}}, \quad \text{where} \quad t > n \qquad \textbf{(20–15)}$$[11]

EXAMPLE 2 What is the third terminal reserve for a \$1,000, five-year term policy issued to a person aged 20?

$P = .0018091584$ [for a \$1 policy, see Section 20.6, Example 2(b)],
$x = 20, n = 5, t = 3, x + t = 23$

Since t is smaller ($<$) than n, the above values are substituted in formula (20–14) as follows:

$$V = \frac{.0018091584(N_{20} - N_{23}) - (M_{20} - M_{23})}{D_{23}} = .000087539$$

---

[10]*Proof (continued)*

The total accumulated annual death benefits (if they had been withheld and invested by the insurance company) at the end of the tth policy year are

$$d_x(1 + i)^{t-1} + d_{x+1}(1 + i)^{t-2} + \cdots + d_{x+t-1} \qquad \text{(II)}$$

The total accumulated annual death benefits are subtracted from the total accumulated annual premiums to obtain the total terminal reserve at the end of the tth policy year. The total terminal reserve is divided by the l_{x+t} policyholders who are living at age $x + t$. The result is the terminal reserve per surviving policyholder and is as follows:

$$V = \frac{\text{(I)} - \text{(II)}}{l_{x+t}}, \quad \text{or}$$

$$V = \frac{P[l_x(1 + i)^t + l_{x+1}(1 + i)^{t-1} + \cdots + l_{x+t-1}(1 + i)] - [d_x(1 + i)^{t-1} + d_{x+1}(1 + i)^{t-2} + \cdots + d_{x+t-1}]}{l_{x+t}}$$

Substitute v for $(1 + i)^{-1}$, or $v^{-1} = (1 + i)$.

$$V = \frac{P[l_x v^{-t} + l_{x+1}v^{-(t-1)} + \cdots + l_{x+t-1}v^{-1}] - [d_x v^{-(t-1)} + d_{x+1}v^{-(t-2)} + \cdots + d_{x+t-1}]}{l_{x+t}}$$

Multiply both the numerator and the denominator of the fraction by v^{x+t}.

$$V = \frac{P(v^x l_x + v^{x+1}l_{x+1} + \cdots + v^{x+t-1}l_{x+t-1}) - (v^{x+1}d_x + v^{x+2}d_{x+1} + \cdots + v^{x+t}d_{x+t-1})}{v^{x+t}l_{x+t}}$$

Substitute the appropriate commutation symbols.

$$V = \frac{P(D_x + D_{x+1} + \cdots + D_{x+t-1}) - (C_x + C_{x+1} + \cdots + C_{x+t-1})}{D_{x+t}}$$

$$= \frac{P(N_x - N_{x+t}) - (M_x - M_{x+t})}{D_{x+t}}, \quad \text{where} \quad t \leq n \qquad \text{(20–14)}$$

The third terminal reserve for a \$1,000 policy is

$V' = 1{,}000V = 1{,}000(.000087539) = \$.087539$

The answer may be compared with that given in column (8) of the table in Example 1 of this section.

EXAMPLE 3 Find the seventh terminal reserve for a 10-year endowment policy of \$1,000 issued to a man aged 20.

$x = 20,\ n = 10,\ t = 7,\ x + t = 27,\ t$ is smaller than n

The net annual premium of a 10-year endowment policy of \$1 issued to a man aged 20 is:

$$P = P_{20:\overline{10}|} = \frac{M_{20} - M_{30} + D_{30}}{N_{20} - N_{30}} = .087980555 \quad \text{[formula (20–8)]}.$$

---

[11] *Proof–Formula (20–15):*

The number of years that the policy has been in force (t) is larger than the number of annual premium payments (n), (or $t > n$).

If the tth terminal reserve is on a date after the last payment of the n annual premiums is made, the total accumulated annual premiums at the end of the tth policy year (the comparison date) would be

$$\begin{aligned} &Pl_x(1 + i)^t + Pl_{x+1}(1 + i)^{t-1} + \cdots + Pl_{x+n-2}(1 + i)^{t-(n-2)} + Pl_{x+n-1}(1 + i)^{t-(n-1)} \\ &\quad = P(l_xv^{-t} + l_{x+1}v^{-(t-1)} + \cdots + l_{x+n-2}v^{-[t-(n-2)]} + l_{x+n-1}v^{-[t-(n-1)]}) \\ &\quad = P(l_xv^{-t} + l_{x+1}v^{-t+1} + \cdots + l_{x+n-2}v^{-t+n-2} + l_{x+n-1}v^{-t+n-1}) \qquad \text{(IA)} \end{aligned}$$

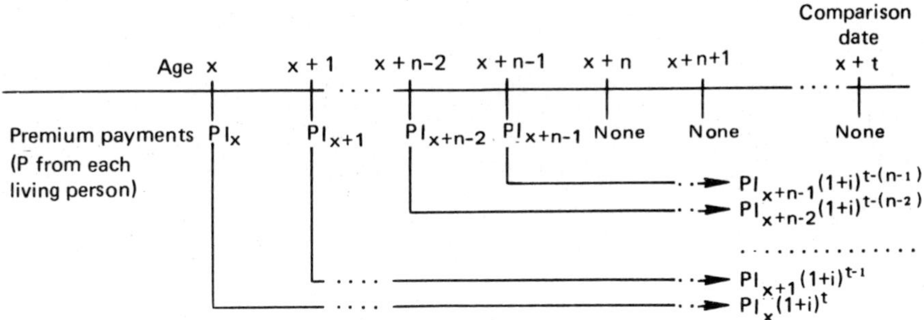

The total accumulated annual death benefits are the same as shown in the diagram for equation (II) in the proof of formula (20–14). Thus, the terminal reserve per surviving policyholder is as follows:

$$V = \frac{(IA) - (II)}{l_{x+t}}$$

Multiply both the numerator and the denominator of the fraction by v^{x+t}, and substitute the appropriate commutation symbols, as was done in the proof of formula (20–14). Then

$$V = \frac{P(N_x - N_{x+n}) - (M_x - M_{x+t})}{D_{x+t}}, \quad \text{where} \quad t > n \qquad \text{(20–15)}$$

Substituting the above values in formula (20–14),

$$V = \frac{.087980555(N_{20} - N_{27}) - (M_{20} - M_{27})}{D_{27}} = .67169$$

The seventh terminal reserve for the $1,000 policy is

$V' = 1{,}000V = 1{,}000(.67169) = \$671.69$

EXAMPLE 4 Find the tenth terminal reserve for a $1,000 straight whole life policy issued to a person aged 25.

$P = .0125450145$ [for a $1 policy, see Example 3(b), Section 20.2], $x = 25, t = 10,$ $x + t = 35$; t is smaller than the number of payments (n), since the premiums are payable until the death of the insured.

Substituting the values in formula (20–14),

$$V = \frac{.0125450145(N_{25} - N_{35}) - (M_{25} - M_{35})}{D_{35}} = .12187$$

The tenth terminal reserve for the $1,000 policy is

$V' = 1{,}000V = 1{,}000(.12187) = \$121.87$

EXAMPLE 5 A $1,000 whole life policy is issued to a person aged 25. If the policy is a 20-payment life policy, find the (a) 15th and (b) 30th terminal reserves.

The net annual premium for a policy of $1 is $.02168152 [see Section 20.2, Example 3(c)], or $P = .02168152$

(a) $x = 25; n = 20; t = 15$, which is smaller than the value of n;
$x + t = 25 + 15 = 40$

The 15th terminal reserve is computed by using formula (20–14) as follows:

$$V = \frac{P(N_x - N_{x+t}) - (M_x - M_{x+t})}{D_{x+t}}$$

$$= \frac{.02168152(N_{25} - N_{40}) - (M_{25} - M_{40})}{D_{40}} = .36465$$

The terminal reserve for a $1,000 policy is

$V' = 1{,}000V = 1{,}000(.36465) = \$364.65$

(b) $x = 25; n = 20; t = 30$, which is greater ($>$) than the value of n;
$x + n = 25 + 20 = 45; x + t = 25 + 30 = 55$

Substituting the values in formula (20–15),

$$V = \frac{P(N_x - N_{x+n}) - (M_x - M_{x+t})}{D_{x+t}}$$

$$= \frac{.02168152(N_{25} - N_{45}) - (M_{25} - M_{55})}{D_{55}} = .62455$$

The terminal reserve for a $1,000 policy is

$V' = 1{,}000V = 1{,}000(.62455) = \$624.55$

★EXERCISE 20–6 REFERENCE: SECTION 20.7A

1. A 15-year term insurance policy of \$1,000 was issued to a person aged 25. Find (a) the 5th and (b) the 15th terminal reserves.
2. What are (a) the 8th and (b) the 12th terminal reserves for a 20-year term insurance policy of \$2,000 issued to a person aged 30?
3. Find (a) the 6th and (b) the 25th terminal reserve for a 25-year endowment policy of \$1,000 issued to someone aged 22.
4. A 15-year endowment policy of \$2,000 was issued to someone aged 35. Find (a) the 4th and (b) the 10th terminal reserves.
5. What are (a) the 12th and (b) the 50th terminal reserves for a \$1,000 straight life policy issued to a person aged 30?
6. A \$1,000 straight life policy was issued to a person aged 20. Find (a) the 15th and (b) the 65th terminal reserves.
7. A \$1,000 whole life policy is issued to someone aged 26. If the policy is a 25-payment life policy, find (a) the 10th and (b) the 34th terminal reserves.
8. A \$1,000 whole life policy is issued to someone aged 30. If the policy is a 15-payment life policy, find (a) the 5th and (b) the 25th terminal reserves.

PROSPECTIVE METHOD

The *prospective method* is based on the annual premiums to be collected in the *future* and the annual death benefits to be paid in the *future*.

Let age $x + t$ be the comparison date. Values at age $x + t$ may be written as follows:

$$\begin{bmatrix}\textbf{\textit{t}th terminal}\\ \textbf{reserve } (\textbf{\textit{V}}')\end{bmatrix} = \begin{bmatrix}\textbf{Present value}\\ \textbf{(at age } x + t\textbf{) of}\\ \textbf{future death}\\ \textbf{benefits}\end{bmatrix} - \begin{bmatrix}\textbf{Present value}\\ \textbf{(at age } x + t\textbf{) of}\\ \textbf{future net annual}\\ \textbf{premiums}\end{bmatrix} \qquad \textbf{(20–16)}$$

At age $x + t$, the present value of the future death benefits is the net single premium for the benefits. The present value (at age $x + t$) of the future net annual premiums is the present value of a life annuity due formed by the future annual premiums.

EXAMPLE 6

Find the third terminal reserve for a \$1,000, five-year term policy issued to a person aged 20.

$x = 20$, $t = 3$, $x + t = 20 + 3 = 23$. The future or remaining term from age $x + t$, or 23, is $(5 - 3) = 2$ (years).

At age 23, the future death benefits of the policy are equal to a two-year term insurance policy of \$1,000. The present value, or the net single premium, of the two-year policy is

$1{,}000A^{1}_{23:\overline{2}|}$

The net annual premium of the five-year term policy is computed as follows:

$1{,}000P^{1}_{20:\overline{5}|} = 1.8091584$ [See Section 20.6, Example 2(b).]

At age 23, the two future annual premium payments of \$1.8091584 per year form a two-year life annuity due. The present value of the annuity is

$A(\text{tem. due}) = 1.8091584\ddot{a}_{23:\overline{2}|}$ [formula (19–11)]

Thus,

$$V' = 1{,}000A^{1}_{23:\overline{2}|} - 1.8091584\ddot{a}_{23:\overline{2}|}$$

$$= 1{,}000 \cdot \frac{M_{23} - M_{23+2}}{D_{23}} - 1.8091584 \cdot \frac{N_{23} - N_{23+2}}{D_{23}}$$

$$= \$.087539$$

The above answer may be compared with that given in Section 20.7, Example 2.

Example 6 is diagrammed as follows:

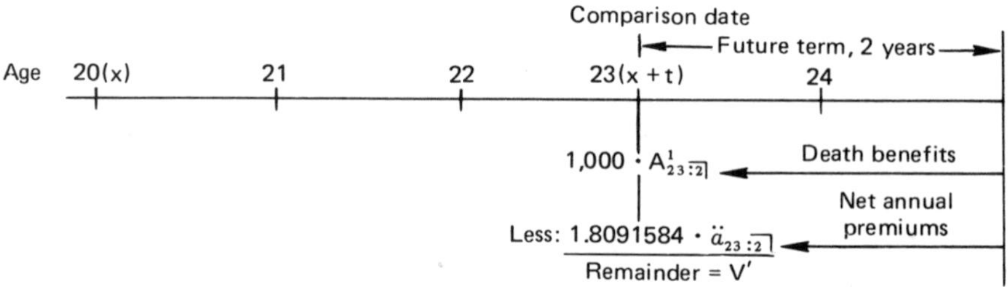

EXAMPLE 7 Find the seventh terminal reserve for a 10-year endowment policy of \$1,000 issued to a person aged 20.

$x = 20, t = 7, x + t = 20 + 7 = 27$. The future (remaining term) $= 10 - 7 = 3$ (years).

The future death benefits of the policy at age 27 are equivalent to a three-year endowment insurance policy of \$1,000 for a person aged 27. The present value, or net single premium, of the three-year policy is

$1{,}000A_{27:\overline{3}|}$

The net annual premium of the 10-year endowment policy is

$1{,}000P_{20:\overline{10}|} = 1{,}000(.087980555) = \$87.980555$ (See Section 20.7, Example 3.)

The future net annual premiums at age 27 form a three-year temporary life annuity due of \$87.980555 per year. The present value of the annuity at age 27 is

$87.980555\ddot{a}_{27:\overline{3}|}$

Thus,

$$V' = 1{,}000A_{27:\overline{3}|} - 87.980555\ddot{a}_{27:\overline{3}|}$$

$$= 1{,}000 \cdot \frac{M_{27} - M_{27+3} + D_{27+3}}{D_{27}} - 87.980555 \cdot \frac{N_{27} - N_{30}}{D_{27}}$$

$$= \$671.69$$

The above answer may be compared with that given in Section 20.7, Example 3.

EXAMPLE 8 Find the tenth terminal reserve for a \$1,000 straight whole life policy issued to a person aged 25.

$x = 25; t = 10; x + t = 35$; the future (remaining term) = age 35 to 99 (the end of the CSO Table)

The future death benefits of the policy at age 35 are equivalent to a whole life policy of \$1,000 for a person aged 35. The net single premium (present value) of the new whole life policy is

$1{,}000A_{35}$

The net annual premium of the original whole life policy is

$1{,}000P_{25} = \$12.545$ [See Example 3(b), Section 20.2.]

The future net annual premiums at age 35 form a whole life annuity due of \$12.545 per year. The present value of this annuity is

$12.545\ddot{a}_{35}$

Thus,

$$V' = 1{,}000A_{35} - 12.545\ddot{a}_{35} = 1{,}000 \cdot \frac{M_{35}}{D_{35}} - 12.545\frac{N_{35}}{D_{35}}$$

$$= \$121.87$$

The above answer may be compared with that given in Example 4.

EXAMPLE 9 Find the 30th terminal reserve for a \$1,000, 20-payment life policy issued to a person aged 25.

$x = 25; t = 30; x + t = 55$; the future (remaining term of the life policy) = age 55 to 99 (the end of the CSO Table)

The future death benefits of the policy at age 55 are equivalent to a whole life policy of \$1,000 for age 55. The net single premium of the policy for a person aged 55 is

$$1{,}000A_{55} = 1{,}000 \cdot \frac{M_{55}}{D_{55}} = \$624.55$$

There are no future net annual premiums at age 55, since the original policy is paid up in 20 annual premium payments. Thus,

$V' = 624.55 - 0 = \$624.55$

The above answer may be compared with that given in Example 5(b).

★EXERCISE 20–7 REFERENCE: SECTION 20.7A

Use the prospective method to compute the following problems:

1. A life insurance policy was issued to a person aged 30. The value of future death benefits at age 40 is \$467.13. Find the tenth terminal reserve by assuming that the net annual premium is \$14.80 payable for life.
2. A life insurance policy was issued to a person aged 20. The value of future death benefits at the end of the 18th policy year is \$895.72. If the net annual premium is \$21.51 payable for life, what is the 18th terminal reserve?

3. Compute Problems 1, 3, 5, and 7 in Exercise 20–6.
4. Compute Problems 2, 4, 6, and 8 in Exercise 20–6.

B. Uses of the Terminal Reserve

The value of an insurance policy in any policy year is based on the terminal reserve. A policyholder may use the reserve for any one of the following purposes:

1. The policyholder may surrender the policy to the insurance company and receive the cash value of the reserve.
2. A policyholder who has no intention of surrendering the policy may borrow money on the reserve at a low interest rate from the insurance company, the reserve being regarded as security for the loan.
3. The policyholder may also use the reserve as a single premium payment to extend the original policy for a period of time, or to convert the original policy to a reduced amount of paid-up insurance. In fact, if a person stops paying the annual premium and fails to do anything about the policy, the company usually continues to keep the policy in force for an extended period of time based on the amount of the terminal reserve.

EXAMPLE 10

The annual premium payment on a $1,000 straight whole life policy issued to a person aged 25 is discontinued at age 35. The policyholder wishes to use the reserve as the premium payment. Find (a) the extended term of the policy with the original face value ($1,000), and (b) the new policy face value for the same type of policy (whole life policy).

First, find the tenth terminal reserve of the original policy. In Example 4 of this section, the tenth terminal reserve for a $1,000 straight life policy issued to a person aged 25 is $121.87.

(a) The net single premium on a $1,000, n-year term policy issued at age 35 is now equal to the tenth terminal reserve, or

$$1{,}000A^{1}_{35:\overline{n}|} = 121.87$$

$$A^{1}_{35:\overline{n}|} = \frac{121.87}{1{,}000} = .12187$$

Thus,

$$A^{1}_{35:\overline{n}|} = \frac{M_{35} - M_{35+n}}{D_{35}} = .12187$$

$$\frac{1{,}659{,}440.36 - M_{35+n}}{3{,}949{,}851.09} = .12187$$

$$M_{35+n} = 1{,}178{,}072.01$$

The following nearest values are obtained from Table 13:

$$M_{60} = 1{,}187{,}445.15$$
$$M_{35+n} = 1{,}178{,}072.01$$
$$M_{61} = 1{,}152{,}722.42$$

When the interpolation method is used, the value of 1,178,072.01 is found to be $M_{60.26994}$, as follows:

	x(age)	M_x	
	60	1,187,445.15	(1)
	35 + n	1,178,072.01	(2)
	61	1,152,722.42	(3)
(2) − (3)	$(35 + n) - 61$	25,349.59	(4)
(1) − (3)	−1	34,722.73	(5)

$$\frac{(35+n)-61}{-1} = \frac{25{,}349.59}{34{,}722.73}$$

Solve for n from the proportion formed by the differences on lines (4) and (5).

$$(35 + n) - 61 = (-1) \cdot \frac{25{,}349.59}{34{,}722.73}$$

$$35 + n = -.73006 + 61 = 60.26994$$

$$n = 60.26994 - 35$$

$$= 25.26994, \quad \text{or 25 years and 99 days}$$

$$[.26994 \times 365 \text{ (days a year)} = 99 \text{ days}]$$

(b) The net single premium of a \$1 whole life policy at age 35 is

$$A_{35} = \frac{M_{35}}{D_{35}} = \$.420127$$

The face value of the new whole life policy at age 35 is

$$\frac{121.87}{.420127} = \$290.08$$

★EXERCISE 20–8 REFERENCE: SECTION 20.7B

1. A 15-year term insurance policy of \$1,000 was issued to a person at age 25. The policyholder stopped making annual premium payments at age 30. (a) What is the term of the new policy if the policyholder wishes to use the reserve to buy a term insurance policy with the same face value? (b) What is the amount of the new policy if the policyholder wishes to use the reserve to buy a 10-year term insurance policy? (Also see Problem 1, Exercise 20–6.)
2. Refer to Problem 1. Assume that the policyholder stopped making annual premium payments at age 32. What is the answer to (a)? What is the answer to (b) if the policyholder now wishes to use the reserve to buy a five-year term insurance policy?
3. A person now aged 28 is unable to maintain the annual premium payments on a \$1,000, 25-year endowment insurance policy, which was issued at age 22. If the policyholder wishes to use the reserve as the premium payment, find (a) the term of the new policy for a term insurance policy with a face value of \$1,000, and (b) the face value of the new policy for a 15-year endowment insurance policy. (Also see Problem 3, Exercise 20–6.)
4. Refer to Problem 3. If the policyholder is now 35 and is unable to maintain the annual premium payments, what is the answer to (a)? What is the answer to (b) for a 10-year endowment insurance policy?
5. A straight life policy of \$1,000 issued to someone aged 30 is discontinued at age 42. (a) Find the term of the new policy if the policyholder wishes to use the reserve to purchase an extended insurance policy of the same face value. (b) Find the amount of

the new policy if the policyholder wishes to keep the same type of policy, the whole life policy. (Also see Problem 5, Exercise 20–6.)

6. Refer to Problem 5. Find the answers to (a) and (b) if the policy is discontinued at age 50.

20.8 SUMMARY OF LIFE INSURANCE FORMULAS

Symbols:

A = the net single premium (or present value) of a $1 life insurance policy (see note for symbol A on page 567).
P = the net annual premium of a $1 life insurance policy
V = terminal reserve for tth policy year of a $1 life insurance policy
V' = total terminal reserve for tth policy year of a life insurance policy
x = age of the insured on the date the policy is issued
n = number of net annual premium payments, also number of years in the length of a term or an endowment insurance policy
y = number of net annual premium payments for a term insurance or an endowment insurance policy; y is used only when the number of premium payments (y) does not equal the number of years in the length of a policy (n), or $y \neq n$
k = number of years that a life policy is deferred
$D_x = v^x l_x$
$N_x = D_x + D_{x+1} + D_{x+2} + \cdots + D_{99}$
$C_x = v^{x+1} d_x$
$M_x = C_x + C_{x+1} + C_{x+2} + \cdots + C_{99}$

Application	*Formula*	*Formula Number*	*Reference Page*
Whole Life Insurance			
Net Single Premium	$A_x = \dfrac{M_x}{D_x}$	(20–1)	568
Net Annual Premium	$P_x = \dfrac{M_x}{N_x}$	(20–2)	569
	${}_nP_x = \dfrac{M_x}{N_x - N_{x+n}}$	(20–3)	569
Term Insurance			
Net Single Premium	$A^1_{x:\overline{n}\mid} = \dfrac{M_x - M_{x+n}}{D_x}$	(20–4)	572
Net Annual Premium	$P^1_{x:\overline{n}\mid} = \dfrac{M_x - M_{x+n}}{N_x - N_{x+n}}$	(20–5)	573
	${}_yP^1_{x:\overline{n}\mid} = \dfrac{M_x - M_{x+n}}{N_x - N_{x+y}}$	(20–6)	573

Application	*Formula*	*Formula Number*	*Reference Page*
Endowment Insurance			
Net Single Premium	$A_{x:\overline{n}\rvert} = \dfrac{M_x - M_{x+n} + D_{x+n}}{D_x}$	(20–7)	575
Net Annual Premium	$P_{x:\overline{n}\rvert} = \dfrac{M_x - M_{x+n} + D_{x+n}}{N_x - N_{x+n}}$	(20–8)	575
	${}_yP_{x:\overline{n}\rvert} = \dfrac{M_x - M_{x+n} + D_{x+n}}{N_x - N_{x+y}}$	(20–9)	576
Deferred Life Insurance			
Deferred Whole Life Insurance	${}_{k\rvert}A_x = \dfrac{M_{x+k}}{D_x}$	(20–10)	578
Deferred Term Insurance	${}_{k\rvert}A^1_{x:\overline{n}\rvert} = \dfrac{M_{x+k} - M_{x+k+n}}{D_x}$	(20–11)	578
Deferred Endowment Insurance	${}_{k\rvert}A_{x:\overline{n}\rvert} = \dfrac{M_{x+k} - M_{x+k+n} + D_{x+k+n}}{D_x}$	(20–12)	578
Natural Premium	$A^1_{x:\overline{1}\rvert} = c_x = \dfrac{C_x}{D_x}$	(20–13)	581

In general (either the insurance protection beginning on the date the policy is issued or deferred for a number of years), the above formulas may be summarized in the following manner:

The *net single premium*
of a $1 whole life or term insurance policy is

$$A = \frac{M_{\text{age when insurance protection begins}} - M_{\text{age when insurance protection ends}}}{D_{\text{age on the policy date}}}$$

of a $1 endowment insurance policy is

$$A = \frac{M_{\text{age when insurance protection begins}} - M_{\text{age when insurance protection ends}} + D_{\text{age when insurance protection ends}}}{D_{\text{age on the policy date}}}$$

The *net annual premium*
of a $1 whole life or term insurance policy is

$$P = \frac{M_{\text{age when insurance protection begins}} - M_{\text{age when insurance protection ends}}}{N_{\text{age on the policy date}} - N_{\text{age when annual premium payment ends}}}$$

of a $1 endowment insurance policy is

$$P = \frac{M_{\text{age when insurance protection begins}} - M_{\text{age when insurance protection ends}} + D_{\text{age when insurance protection ends}}}{N_{\text{age on the policy date}} - N_{\text{age when annual premium payment ends}}}$$

The value of M, D, and N for the age larger than the highest age (99) given in Table 13 is zero. Thus, the first and third general formulas above are also valid for whole life insurance policies.

Application	*Formula*	*Formula Number*	*Reference Page*
Terminal Reserves			
Retrospective Method	$V = \dfrac{P(N_x - N_{x+t}) - (M_x - M_{x+t})}{D_{x+t}}, \quad (t \le n)$	(20–14)	587
	$V = \dfrac{P(N_x - N_{x+n}) - (M_x - M_{x+t})}{D_{x+t}}, \quad (t > n)$	(20–15)	588
Prospective Method			
	$\begin{bmatrix} t\text{th terminal} \\ \text{reserve } (V^t) \end{bmatrix} = \begin{bmatrix} \text{Present value (at age } x + t) \\ \text{of future death benefits} \end{bmatrix} - \begin{bmatrix} \text{Present value (at age } x + t) \text{ of} \\ \text{future net annual premiums} \end{bmatrix}$	(20–16)	591

EXERCISE 20–9 REVIEW OF CHAPTER 20

1. A \$2,000 whole life policy is issued to a person aged 32. Find (a) the net single premium, (b) the net annual premium if the policy is a straight life policy, and (c) the net annual premium if the policy is a 25-payment life policy.
2. A \$1,000 whole life policy is issued to a person at age 20. What are (a) the net single premium, (b) the net annual premium if the policy is a straight life policy, and (c) the net annual premium if the policy is a 30-payment life policy?
3. Refer to Problem 1. If the policy is issued to someone at age 22, what are the answers to (a), (b), and (c)?
4. Refer to Problem 2. If the policy is issued to a child at age 10, what are the answers to (a), (b), and (c)?
5. A \$1,000, 15-year term policy is issued to someone aged 30. Find (a) the net single premium, (b) the net annual premium if the policy is a 15-payment policy, and (c) the net annual premium if the policy is a 10-payment policy.
6. A \$1,000, 20-year term policy is issued to someone aged 24. Find (a) the net single premium, (b) the net annual premium if the policy is a 20-payment policy, and (c) the net annual premium if the policy is a 15-payment policy.
7. Refer to Problem 5. Assuming that the policy is issued at age 40, what are the answers to (a), (b), and (c)?
8. Refer to Problem 6. Assuming that the policy is issued at age 14, what are the answers to (a), (b), and (c)?
9. A \$1,000, 40-year endowment insurance policy was bought by a person aged 25. Find (a) the net single premium, (b) the net annual premium if the policy is a 40-payment policy, and (c) the net annual premium if the policy is a 35-payment policy.
10. A \$1,000, 25-year endowment insurance policy was issued to a person at age 30. Find (a) the net single premium, (b) the net annual premium if the policy is a 25-payment policy, and (c) the net annual premium if the policy is a five-payment policy.

11. Refer to Problem 9. If the policy is bought by a person at age 18, what are the answers to (a), (b), and (c)?
12. Refer to Problem 10. If the policy is issued to a person aged 35, what are the answers to (a), (b), and (c)?
★13. A policy issued to a man at age 22 promises that the insurance company will pay \$1,000 if the insured dies before reaching age 40, \$2,000 if he dies after reaching 40 but before 50, \$3,000 if he dies after reaching 50 but before 65 or if he is alive at 65, and \$1,000 if he dies after 65. Find the net annual premiums if (a) the premium of the policy is payable annually for life, and (b) the premium is payable in 15 equal annual payments.
★14. Refer to Problem 13. Assume that the policy is issued to a boy at age 12. (a) What is the annual premium if the premium of the policy is payable annually for life? (b) What is the annual premium if the premium of the policy is payable in 25 equal annual payments?
15. A \$1,000, 10-year term policy is issued to a woman aged 30. (a) What is the level premium? (b) What are the natural premiums for ages 30, 33, 36, and 39?
16. A \$1,000, 15-year term policy is issued to a woman at age 50. (a) What is the level premium? (b) Find the natural premiums for ages 50, 55, 60, and 64.
★17. Find the 15th terminal reserve for a \$1,000 policy issued at age 22. Assume that the policy is (a) a 25-year term insurance policy, (b) a 20-year endowment insurance policy, (c) a straight life policy, (d) a 40-payment life policy.
★18. Find the 10th terminal reserve for a \$1,000 policy issued at age 28. Assume that the policy is (a) a 30-year term insurance policy, (b) a 25-year endowment insurance policy, (c) a straight life policy, (d) a 30-payment life policy.
★19. Refer to Problem 17. Suppose that the insured stops paying the annual premium at age 37 but wishes to buy a new term insurance policy of \$1,000. What is the term of the new policy if the insured buys the policy with the reserve obtained from assumption (a)? (b)? (c)? (d)?
★20. Refer to Problem 18. Suppose that the insured is unable to maintain the annual premium payment at age 38, but wants to buy a new term insurance policy of \$1,000. What is the term of the new policy if the insured buys the policy with the 10th terminal reserve obtained from assumption (a)? (b)? (c)? (d)?
★21. Refer to Problem 17. Suppose that the insured stops paying the annual premium at age 37 but wishes to buy a new policy of reduced face value. What is the face value of the new policy if the reserve obtained from assumption (a) is used to buy a 10-year term insurance policy? from assumption (b) is used to buy a five-year endowment insurance policy? from assumption (c) is used to buy a whole life insurance policy? from assumption (d) is used to buy a whole life insurance policy?
★22. Refer to Problem 18. Suppose that the insured is unable to maintain the annual premium payment at age 38, but wants to buy a new policy of reduced face value. What is the face value of the new policy if the reserve obtained from assumption (a) is used to buy a 20-year term insurance policy? from assumption (b) is used to buy a 15-year endowment insurance policy? from assumption (c) is used to buy a whole life insurance policy? from assumption (d) is used to buy a whole life insurance policy?

APPENDIX TABLES

The tables included in this book are designed primarily for the text, *Mathematics for Management and Finance*. However, the coverage in the tables is complete enough for most practical business problems involving logarithms, compound interest, annuity, and life insurance. The special features of the tables are summarized below.

The tables of logarithms include six-place and seven-place mantissas (Tables 2 and 3). The difference between any two adjacent mantissas may be easily found by using the guide printed in the column headed *D*. The value in the *D* column on each line is the *greatest* difference between adjacent mantissas on the line.

The compound interest and annuity tables (Tables 5 through 11) include the most commonly used periodic interest rates on the investment market today. The rates are:

$\frac{1}{4}\%$, $\frac{1}{3}\%$, $\frac{5}{12}\%$, $\frac{11}{24}\%$, $\frac{1}{2}\%$, $\frac{13}{24}\%$, $\frac{7}{12}\%$, $\frac{5}{8}\%$, $\frac{2}{3}\%$, $\frac{3}{4}\%$, $\frac{7}{8}\%$, 1% (from 1 to 240 periods);

$1\frac{1}{8}\%$, $1\frac{1}{4}\%$, $1\frac{3}{8}\%$, $1\frac{1}{2}\%$, $1\frac{5}{8}\%$, $1\frac{3}{4}\%$, $1\frac{7}{8}\%$, 2%, $2\frac{1}{4}\%$, $2\frac{1}{2}\%$, $2\frac{3}{4}\%$, 3%, $3\frac{1}{4}\%$, $3\frac{1}{2}\%$, $3\frac{3}{4}\%$, 4%, $4\frac{1}{2}\%$, 5%, $5\frac{1}{2}\%$, 6%, $6\frac{1}{2}\%$, 7%, $7\frac{1}{2}\%$, 8%, $8\frac{1}{2}\%$, 9%, $9\frac{1}{2}\%$, 10% (from 1 to 100 periods).

The selection of the above periodic rates is based on the nominal annual rates from $2\frac{1}{2}\%$ to 10%, at an interval of $\frac{1}{2}\%$, compounded (or converted) monthly, quarterly, semiannually, and annually. Table 4 summarizes the periodic rates and thus serves as a convenient guide to the use of Tables 5 through 11. Table 4 also presents the periodic rates converted to decimal fractions.

The values in Tables 5 through 11 have been computed and compiled by the author and have been checked with various sources, especially the tables in the third edition of this book. The author is grateful to Dale H. Shao and Lenzo H. Chavis for their help in obtaining the values by computer.

The insurance mortality tables include: Table 12 – the Commissioners 1958 Standard Ordinary Mortality Table, Table 13 – Commutation Columns, based on the 1958 CSO Table, and Table 15 – the Commissioners 1980 Standard Ordinary Mortality Table, which is the latest issue. The author wishes to express his appreciation to the Society of

Actuaries for permission to reprint the three insurance tables. Table 14 provides logarithms of the values in Table 13. This table is computed solely by the author for figuring the answers in the examples and problems in Chapters 19 and 20 by the use of logarithms.

TABLE 1 THE NUMBER OF EACH DAY OF THE YEAR

Day of Month	Jan.	Feb.	Mar.	Apr.	May	June	July	Aug.	Sept.	Oct.	Nov.	Dec.	Day of Month
1	1	32	60	91	121	152	182	213	244	274	305	335	1
2	2	33	61	92	122	153	183	214	245	275	306	336	2
3	3	34	62	93	123	154	184	215	246	276	307	337	3
4	4	35	63	94	124	155	185	216	247	277	308	338	4
5	5	36	64	95	125	156	186	217	248	278	309	339	5
6	6	37	65	96	126	157	187	218	249	279	310	340	6
7	7	38	66	97	127	158	188	219	250	280	311	341	7
8	8	39	67	98	128	159	189	220	251	281	312	342	8
9	9	40	68	99	129	160	190	221	252	282	313	343	9
10	10	41	69	100	130	161	191	222	253	283	314	344	10
11	11	42	70	101	131	162	192	223	254	284	315	345	11
12	12	43	71	102	132	163	193	224	255	235	316	346	12
13	13	44	72	103	133	164	194	225	256	286	317	347	13
14	14	45	73	104	134	165	195	226	257	287	318	348	14
15	15	46	74	105	135	166	196	227	258	288	319	349	15
16	16	47	75	106	136	167	197	228	259	289	320	350	16
17	17	48	76	107	137	168	198	229	260	290	321	351	17
18	18	49	77	108	138	169	199	230	261	291	322	352	18
19	19	50	78	109	139	170	200	231	262	292	323	353	19
20	20	51	79	110	140	171	201	232	263	293	324	354	20
21	21	52	80	111	141	172	202	233	264	294	325	355	21
22	22	53	81	112	142	173	203	234	265	295	326	356	22
23	23	54	82	113	143	174	204	235	266	296	327	357	23
24	24	55	83	114	144	175	205	236	267	297	328	358	24
25	25	56	84	115	145	176	206	237	268	298	329	359	25
26	26	57	85	116	146	177	207	238	269	299	330	360	26
27	27	58	86	117	147	178	208	239	270	300	331	361	27
28	28	59	87	118	148	179	209	240	271	301	332	362	28
29	29	*	88	119	149	180	210	241	272	302	333	363	29
30	30		89	120	150	181	211	242	273	303	334	364	30
31	31		90		151		212	243		304		365	31

* For leap years, February has 29 days, and the number of each day from March 1 is one greater than the number given in the table.

TABLE 2 LOGARITHMS OF NUMBERS 1,000 TO 1,499

SIX-PLACE MANTISSAS

N	0	1	2	3	4	5	6	7	8	9	D#
100	00 0000	0434	0868	1301	1734	2166	2598	3029	3461	3891	434
01	4321	4751	5181	5609	6038	6466	6894	7321	7748	8174	430
02	00 8600	9026	9451	9876	*0300	*0724	*1147	*1570	*1993	*2415	426
03	01 2837	3259	3680	4100	4521	4940	5360	5779	6197	6616	422
04	01 7033	7451	7868	8284	8700	9116	9532	9947	*0361	*0775	418
05	02 1189	1603	2016	2428	2841	3252	3664	4075	4486	4896	414
06	5306	5715	6125	6533	6942	7350	7757	8164	8571	8978	410
07	02 9384	9789	*0195	*0600	*1004	*1408	*1812	*2216	*2619	*3021	406
08	03 3424	3826	4227	4628	5029	5430	5830	6230	6629	7028	402
09	03 7426	7825	8223	8620	9017	9414	9811	*0207	*0602	*0998	399
110	04 1393	1787	2182	2576	2969	3362	3755	4148	4540	4932	395
11	5323	5714	6105	6495	6885	7275	7664	8053	8442	8830	391
12	04 9218	9606	9993	*0380	*0766	*1153	*1538	*1924	*2309	*2694	388
13	05 3078	3463	3846	4230	4613	4996	5378	5760	6142	6524	385
14	05 6905	7286	7666	8046	8426	8805	9185	9563	9942	*0320	381
15	06 0698	1075	1452	1829	2206	2582	2958	3333	3709	4083	377
16	4458	4832	5206	5580	5953	6326	6699	7071	7443	7815	374
17	06 8186	8557	8928	9298	9668	*0038	*0407	*0776	*1145	*1514	371
18	07 1882	2250	2617	2985	3352	3718	4085	4451	4816	5182	368
19	5547	5912	6276	6640	7004	7368	7731	8094	8457	8819	365
120	07 9181	9543	9904	*0266	*0626	*0987	1347	*1707	*2067	*2426	362
21	08 2785	3144	3503	3861	4219	4576	4934	5291	5647	6004	359
22	6360	6716	7071	7426	7781	8136	8490	8845	9198	9552	356
23	08 9905	*0258	*0611	*0963	*1315	*1667	*2018	*2370	*2721	*3071	353
24	09 3422	3772	4122	4471	4820	5169	5518	5866	6215	6562	350
25	09 6910	7257	7604	7951	8298	8644	8990	9335	9681	*0026	347
26	10 0371	0715	1059	1403	1747	2091	2434	2777	3119	3462	344
27	3804	4146	4487	4828	5169	5510	5851	6191	6531	6871	342
28	10 7210	7549	7888	8227	8565	8903	9241	9579	9916	*0253	339
29	11 0590	0926	1263	1599	1934	2270	2605	2940	3275	3609	337
130	3943	4277	4611	4944	5278	5611	5943	6276	6608	6940	334
31	11 7271	7603	7934	8265	8595	8926	9256	9586	9915	*0245	332
32	12 0574	0903	1231	1560	1888	2216	2544	2871	3198	3525	329
33	3852	4178	4504	4830	5156	5481	5806	6131	6456	6781	326
34	12 7105	7429	7753	8076	8399	8722	9045	9368	9690	*0012	324
35	13 0334	0655	0977	1298	1619	1939	2260	2580	2900	3219	322
36	3539	3858	4177	4496	4814	5133	5451	5769	6086	6403	319
37	6721	7037	7354	7671	7987	8303	8618	8934	9249	9564	317
38	13 9879	*0194	*0508	*0822	*1136	*1450	*1763	*2076	*2389	*2702	315
39	14 3015	3327	3639	3851	4263	4574	4885	5196	5507	5818	312
140	6128	6438	6748	7058	7367	7676	7985	8294	8603	8911	310
41	14 9219	9527	9835	*0142	*0449	*0756	*1063	*1370	*1676	*1982	308
42	15 2288	2594	2900	3205	3510	3815	4120	4424	4728	5032	306
43	5336	5640	5943	6246	6549	6852	7154	7457	7759	8061	304
44	15 8362	8664	8965	9266	9567	9868	*0168	*0469	*0769	*1068	302
45	16 1368	1667	1967	2266	2564	2863	3161	3460	3758	4055	300
46	4353	4650	4947	5244	5541	5838	6134	6430	6726	7022	297
47	16 7317	7613	7908	8203	8497	8792	9086	9380	9674	9968	296
48	17 0262	0555	0848	1141	1434	1726	2019	2311	2603	2895	293
49	3186	3478	3769	4060	4351	4641	4932	5222	5512	5802	292
N	**0**	**1**	**2**	**3**	**4**	**5**	**6**	**7**	**8**	**9**	**D**

* Prefix first two places on next line.

Example: The mantissa for number (N) 1072 is *03* 0195.

\# The *highest difference* between adjacent mantissas on the *individual line.* It is also the *lowest difference* between adjacent mantissas on the *preceding line* in many cases.

TABLE 2 LOGARITHMS OF NUMBERS 1,500–1,999

SIX-PLACE MANTISSAS

N	0	1	2	3	4	5	6	7	8	9	D
150	17 6091	6381	6670	6959	7248	7536	7825	8113	8401	8689	290
51	17 8977	9264	9552	9839	*0126	*0413	*0699	*0986	*1272	*1558	288
52	18 1844	2129	2415	2700	2985	3270	3555	3839	4123	4407	286
53	4691	4975	5259	5542	5825	6108	6391	6674	6956	7239	284
54	18 7521	7803	8084	8366	8647	8928	9209	9490	9771	*0051	282
55	19 0332	0612	0892	1171	1451	1730	2010	2289	2567	2846	280
56	3125	3403	3681	3959	4237	4514	4792	5069	5346	5623	278
57	5900	6176	6453	6729	7005	7281	7556	7832	8107	8382	277
58	19 8657	8932	9206	9481	9755	*0029	*0303	*0577	*0850	*1124	275
59	20 1397	1670	1943	2216	2488	2761	3033	3305	3577	3848	273
160	4120	4391	4663	4934	5204	5475	5746	6016	6286	6556	272
61	6826	7096	7365	7634	7904	8173	8441	8710	8979	9247	270
62	20 9515	9783	*0051	*0319	*0586	*0853	*1121	*1388	*1654	*1921	268
63	21 2188	2454	2720	2986	3252	3518	3783	4049	4314	4579	266
64	4844	5109	5373	5638	5902	6166	6430	6694	6957	7221	265
65	21 7484	7747	8010	8273	8536	8798	9060	9323	9585	9846	263
66	22 0108	0370	0631	0892	1153	1414	1675	1936	2196	2456	262
67	2716	2976	3236	3496	3755	4015	4274	4533	4792	5051	260
68	5309	5568	5826	6084	6342	6600	6858	7115	7372	7630	259
69	22 7887	8144	8400	8657	8913	9170	9426	9682	9938	*0193	257
170	23 0449	0704	0960	1215	1470	1724	1979	2234	2488	2742	256
71	2996	3250	3504	3757	4011	4264	4517	4770	5023	5276	254
72	5528	5781	6033	6285	6537	6789	7041	7292	7544	7795	253
73	23 8046	8297	8548	8799	9049	9299	9550	9800	*0050	*0300	251
74	24 0549	0799	1048	1297	1546	1795	2044	2293	2541	2790	250
75	3038	3286	3534	3782	4030	4277	4525	4772	5019	5266	248
76	5513	5759	6006	6252	6499	6745	6991	7237	7482	7728	247
77	24 7973	8219	8464	8709	8954	9198	9443	9687	9932	*0176	246
78	25 0420	0664	0908	1151	1395	1638	1881	2125	2368	2610	244
79	2853	3096	3338	3580	3822	4064	4306	4548	4790	5031	243
180	5273	5514	5755	5996	6237	6477	6718	6958	7198	7439	241
81	25 7679	7918	8158	8398	8637	8877	9116	9355	9594	9833	240
82	26 0071	0310	0548	0787	1025	1263	1501	1739	1976	2214	239
83	2451	2688	2925	3162	3399	3636	3873	4109	4346	4582	237
84	4818	5054	5290	5525	5761	5996	6232	6467	6702	6937	236
85	7172	7406	7641	7875	8110	8344	8578	8812	9046	9279	235
86	26 9513	9746	9980	*0213	*0446	*0679	*0912	*1144	*1377	*1609	234
87	27 1842	2074	2306	2538	2770	3001	3233	3464	3696	3927	232
88	4158	4389	4620	4850	5081	5311	5542	5772	6002	6232	231
89	6462	6692	6921	7151	7380	7609	7838	8067	8296	8525	230
190	27 8754	8982	9211	9439	9667	9895	*0123	*0351	*0578	*0806	229
91	28 1033	1261	1488	1715	1942	2169	2396	2622	2849	3075	228
92	3301	3527	3753	3979	4205	4431	4656	4882	5107	5332	226
93	5557	5782	6007	6232	6456	6681	6905	7130	7354	7578	225
94	28 7802	8026	8249	8473	8696	8920	9143	9366	9589	9812	224
95	29 0035	0257	0480	0702	0925	1147	1369	1591	1813	2034	223
96	2256	2478	2699	2920	3141	3363	3584	3804	4025	4246	222
97	4466	4687	4907	5127	5347	5567	5787	6007	6226	6446	221
98	6665	6884	7104	7323	7542	7761	7979	8198	8416	8635	220
99	29 8853	9071	9289	9507	9725	9943	*0161	*0378	*0595	*0813	218
N	0	1	2	3	4	5	6	7	8	9	D

TABLE 2 LOGARITHMS OF NUMBERS 2,000–2,499

SIX-PLACE MANTISSAS

N	0	1	2	3	4	5	6	7	8	9	D
200	30 1030	1247	1464	1681	1898	2114	2331	2547	2764	2980	217
01	3196	3412	3628	3844	4059	4275	4491	4706	4921	5136	216
02	5351	5566	5781	5996	6211	6425	6639	6854	7068	7282	215
03	7496	7710	7924	8137	8351	8564	8778	8991	9204	9417	214
04	30 9630	9843	*0056	*0268	*0481	*0693	*0906	*1118	*1330	*1542	213
05	31 1754	1966	2177	2389	2600	2812	3023	3234	3445	3656	212
06	3867	4078	4289	4499	4710	4920	5130	5340	5551	5760	211
07	5970	6180	6390	6599	6809	7018	7227	7436	7646	7854	210
08	31 8063	8272	8481	8689	8898	9106	9314	9522	9730	9938	209
09	32 0146	0354	0562	0769	0977	1184	1391	1598	1805	2012	208
210	2219	2426	2633	2839	3046	3252	3458	3665	3871	4077	207
11	4282	4488	4694	4899	5105	5310	5516	5721	5926	6131	206
12	6336	6541	6745	6950	7155	7359	7563	7767	7972	8176	205
13	32 8380	8583	8787	8991	9194	9398	9601	9805	*0008	*0211	204
14	33 0414	0617	0819	1022	1225	1427	1630	1832	2034	2236	203
15	2438	2640	2842	3044	3246	3447	3649	3850	4051	4253	202
16	4454	4655	4856	5057	5257	5458	5658	5859	6059	6260	201
17	6460	6660	6860	7060	7260	7459	7659	7858	8058	8257	200
18	33 8456	8656	8855	9054	9253	9451	9650	9849	*0047	*0246	200
19	34 0444	0642	0841	1039	1237	1435	1632	1830	2028	2225	199
220	2423	2620	2817	3014	3212	3409	3606	3802	3999	4196	198
21	4392	4589	4785	4981	5178	5374	5570	5766	5962	6157	197
22	6353	6549	6744	6939	7135	7330	7525	7720	7915	8110	196
23	34 8305	8500	8694	8889	9083	9278	9472	9666	9860	*0054	195
24	35 0248	0442	0636	0829	1023	1216	1410	1603	1796	1989	194
25	2183	2375	2568	2761	2954	3147	3339	3532	3724	3916	193
26	4108	4301	4493	4685	4876	5068	5260	5452	5643	5834	192
27	6026	6217	6408	6599	6790	6981	7172	7363	7554	7744	191
28	7935	8125	8316	8506	8696	8886	9076	9266	9456	9646	191
29	35 9835	*0025	*0215	*0404	*0593	*0783	*0972	*1161	*1350	*1539	190
230	36 1728	1917	2105	2294	2482	2671	2859	3048	3236	3424	189
31	3612	3800	3988	4176	4363	4551	4739	4926	5113	5301	188
32	5488	5675	5862	6049	6236	6423	6610	6796	6983	7169	187
33	7356	7542	7729	7915	8101	8287	8473	8659	8845	9030	187
34	36 9216	9401	9587	9772	9958	*0143	*0328	*0513	*0698	*0883	186
35	37 1068	1253	1437	1622	1806	1991	2175	2360	2544	2728	185
36	2912	3096	3280	3464	3647	3831	4015	4198	4382	4565	184
37	4748	4932	5115	5298	5481	5664	5846	6029	6212	6394	184
38	6577	6759	6942	7124	7306	7488	7670	7852	8034	8216	183
39	37 8398	8580	8761	8943	9124	9306	9487	9668	9849	*0030	182
240	38 0211	0392	0573	0754	0934	1115	1296	1476	1656	1837	181
41	2017	2197	2377	2557	2737	2917	3097	3277	3456	3636	180
42	3815	3995	4174	4353	4533	4712	4891	5070	5249	5428	180
43	5606	5785	5964	6142	6321	6499	6677	6856	7034	7212	179
44	7390	7568	7746	7923	8101	8279	8456	8634	8811	8989	178
45	38 9166	9343	9520	9698	9875	*0051	*0228	*0405	*0582	*0759	178
46	39 0935	1112	1288	1464	1641	1817	1993	2169	2345	2521	177
47	2697	2873	3048	3224	3400	3575	3751	3926	4101	4277	176
48	4452	4627	4802	4977	5152	5326	5501	5676	5850	6025	175
49	6199	6374	6548	6722	6896	7071	7245	7419	7592	7766	175
N	0	1	2	3	4	5	6	7	8	9	D

TABLE 2 LOGARITHMS OF NUMBERS 2,500–2,999

SIX-PLACE MANTISSAS

N	0	1	2	3	4	5	6	7	8	9	D
250	39 7940	8114	8287	8461	8634	8808	8981	9154	9328	9501	174
51	39 9674	9847	*0020	*0192	*0365	*0538	*0711	*0883	*1056	*1228	173
52	40 1401	1573	1745	1917	2089	2261	2433	2605	2777	2949	172
53	3121	3292	3464	3635	3807	3978	4149	4320	4492	4663	172
54	4834	5005	5176	5346	5517	5688	5858	6029	6199	6370	171
55	6540	6710	6881	7051	7221	7391	7561	7731	7901	8070	171
56	8240	8410	8579	8749	8918	9087	9257	9426	9595	9764	170
57	40 9933	*0102	*0271	*0440	*0609	*0777	*0946	*1114	*1283	*1451	169
58	41 1620	1788	1956	2124	2293	2461	2629	2796	2964	3132	169
59	3300	3467	3635	3803	3970	4137	4305	4472	4639	4806	168
260	4973	5140	5307	5474	5641	5808	5974	6141	6308	6474	167
61	6641	6807	6973	7139	7306	7472	7638	7804	7970	8135	167
62	8301	8467	8633	8798	8964	9129	9295	9460	9625	9791	166
63	41 9956	*0121	*0286	*0451	*0616	*0781	*0945	*1110	*1275	*1439	165
64	42 1604	1768	1933	2097	2261	2426	2590	2754	2918	3082	165
65	3246	3410	3574	3737	3901	4065	4228	4392	4555	4718	164
66	4882	5045	5208	5371	5534	5697	5860	6023	6186	6349	163
67	6511	6674	6836	6999	7161	7324	7486	7648	7811	7973	163
68	8135	8297	8459	8621	8783	8944	9106	9268	9429	9591	162
69	42 9752	9914	*0075	*0236	*0398	*0559	*0720	*0881	*1042	*1203	162
270	43 1364	1525	1685	1846	2007	2167	2328	2488	2649	2809	161
71	2969	3130	3290	3450	3610	3770	3930	4090	4249	4409	161
72	4569	4729	4888	5048	5207	5367	5526	5685	5844	6004	160
73	6163	6322	6481	6640	6799	6957	7116	7275	7433	7592	159
74	7751	7909	8067	8226	8384	8542	8701	8859	9017	9175	159
75	43 9333	9491	9648	9806	9964	*0122	*0279	*0437	*0594	*0752	158
76	44 0909	1066	1224	1381	1538	1695	1852	2009	2166	2323	158
77	2480	2637	2793	2950	3106	3263	3419	3576	3732	3889	157
78	4045	4201	4357	4513	4669	4825	4981	5137	5293	5449	156
79	5604	5760	5915	6071	6226	6382	6537	6692	6848	7003	156
280	7158	7313	7468	7623	7778	7933	8088	8242	8397	8552	155
81	44 8706	8861	9015	9170	9324	9478	9633	9787	9941	*0095	155
82	45 0249	0403	0557	0711	0865	1018	1172	1326	1479	1633	154
83	1786	1940	2093	2247	2400	2553	2706	2859	3012	3165	154
84	3318	3471	3624	3777	3930	4082	4235	4387	4540	4692	153
85	4845	4997	5150	5302	5454	5606	5758	5910	6062	6214	153
86	6366	6518	6670	6821	6973	7125	7276	7428	7579	7731	152
87	7882	8033	8184	8336	8487	8638	8789	8940	9091	9242	152
88	45 9392	9543	9694	9845	9995	*0146	*0296	*0447	*0597	*0748	151
89	46 0898	1048	1198	1348	1499	1649	1799	1948	2098	2248	151
290	2398	2548	2697	2847	2997	3146	3296	3445	3594	3744	150
91	3893	4042	4191	4340	4490	4639	4788	4936	5085	5234	149
92	5383	5532	5680	5829	5977	6126	6274	6423	6571	6719	149
93	6868	7016	7164	7312	7460	7608	7756	7904	8052	8200	148
94	8347	8495	8643	8790	8938	9085	9233	9380	9527	9675	148
95	46 9822	9969	*0116	*0263	*0410	*0557	*0704	*0851	*0998	*1145	147
96	47 1292	1438	1585	1732	1878	2025	2171	2318	2464	2610	147
97	2756	2903	3049	3195	3341	3487	3633	3779	3925	4071	147
98	4216	4362	4508	4653	4799	4944	5090	5235	5381	5526	146
99	5671	5816	5962	6107	6252	6397	6542	6687	6832	6976	146
N	0	1	2	3	4	5	6	7	8	9	D

TABLE 2 LOGARITHMS OF NUMBERS 3,000–3,499

SIX-PLACE MANTISSAS

N	0	1	2	3	4	5	6	7	8	9	D
300	47 7121	7266	7411	7555	7700	7844	7989	8133	8278	8422	145
01	47 8566	8711	8855	8999	9143	9287	9431	9575	9719	9863	145
02	48 0007	0151	0294	0438	0582	0725	0869	1012	1156	1299	144
03	1443	1586	1729	1872	2016	2159	2302	2445	2588	2731	144
04	2874	3016	3159	3302	3445	3587	3730	3872	4015	4157	143
05	4300	4442	4585	4727	4869	5011	5153	5295	5437	5579	143
06	5721	5863	6005	6147	6289	6430	6572	6714	6855	6997	142
07	7138	7280	7421	7563	7704	7845	7986	8127	8269	8410	142
08	8551	8692	8833	8974	9114	9255	9396	9537	9677	9818	141
09	48 9958	*0099	*0239	*0380	*0520	*0661	*0801	*0941	*1081	*1222	141
310	49 1362	1502	1642	1782	1922	2062	2201	2341	2481	2621	140
11	2760	2900	3040	3179	3319	3458	3597	3737	3876	4015	140
12	4155	4294	4433	4572	4711	4850	4989	5128	5267	5406	139
13	5544	5683	5822	5960	6099	6238	6376	6515	6653	6791	139
14	6930	7068	7206	7344	7483	7621	7759	7897	8035	8173	139
15	8311	8448	8586	8724	8862	8999	9137	9275	9412	9550	138
16	49 9687	9824	9962	*0099	*0236	*0374	*0511	*0648	*0785	*0922	138
17	50 1059	1196	1333	1470	1607	1744	1880	2017	2154	2291	137
18	2427	2564	2700	2837	2973	3109	3246	3382	3518	3655	137
19	3791	3927	4063	4199	4335	4471	4607	4743	4878	5014	136
320	5150	5286	5421	5557	5693	5828	5964	6099	6234	6370	136
21	6505	6640	6776	6911	7046	7181	7316	7451	7586	7721	136
22	7856	7991	8126	8260	8395	8530	8664	8799	8934	9068	135
23	50 9203	9337	9471	9606	9740	9874	*0009	*0143	*0277	*0411	135
24	51 0545	0679	0813	0947	1081	1215	1349	1482	1616	1750	134
25	1883	2017	2151	2284	2418	2551	2684	2818	2951	3084	134
26	3218	3351	3484	3617	3750	3883	4016	4149	4282	4415	133
27	4548	4681	4813	4946	5079	5211	5344	5476	5609	5741	133
28	5874	6006	6139	6271	6403	6535	6668	6800	6932	7064	133
29	7196	7328	7460	7592	7724	7855	7987	8119	8251	8382	132
330	8514	8646	8777	8909	9040	9171	9303	9434	9566	9697	132
31	51 9828	9959	*0090	*0221	*0353	*0484	*0615	*0745	*0876	*1007	132
32	52 1138	1269	1400	1530	1661	1792	1922	2053	2183	2314	131
33	2444	2575	2705	2835	2966	3096	3226	3356	3486	3616	131
34	3746	3876	4006	4136	4266	4396	4526	4656	4785	4915	130
35	5045	5174	5304	5434	5563	5693	5822	5951	6081	6210	130
36	6339	6469	6598	6727	6856	6985	7114	7243	7372	7501	130
37	7630	7759	7888	8016	8145	8274	8402	8531	8660	8788	129
38	52 8917	9045	9174	9302	9430	9559	9687	9815	9943	*0072	129
39	53 0200	0328	0456	0584	0712	0840	0968	1096	1223	1351	128
340	1479	1607	1734	1862	1990	2117	2245	2372	2500	2627	128
41	2754	2882	3009	3136	3264	3391	3518	3645	3772	3899	128
42	4026	4153	4280	4407	4534	4661	4787	4914	5041	5167	127
43	5294	5421	5547	5674	5800	5927	6053	6180	6306	6432	127
44	6558	6685	6811	6937	7063	7189	7315	7441	7567	7693	127
45	7819	7945	8071	8197	8322	8448	8574	8699	8825	8951	126
46	53 9076	9202	9327	9452	9578	9703	9829	9954	*0079	*0204	126
47	54 0329	0455	0580	0705	0830	0955	1080	1205	1330	1454	126
48	1579	1704	1829	1953	2078	2203	2327	2452	2576	2701	125
49	2825	2950	3074	3199	3323	3447	3571	3696	3820	3944	125
N	**0**	**1**	**2**	**3**	**4**	**5**	**6**	**7**	**8**	**9**	**D**

TABLE 2 LOGARITHMS OF NUMBERS 3,500–3,999

SIX-PLACE MANTISSAS

N	0	1	2	3	4	5	6	7	8	9	D
350	54 4068	4192	4316	4440	4564	4688	4812	4936	5060	5183	124
51	5307	5431	5555	5678	5802	5925	6049	6172	6296	6419	124
52	6543	6666	6789	6913	7036	7159	7282	7405	7529	7652	124
53	7775	7898	8021	8144	8267	8389	8512	8635	8758	8881	123
54	54 9003	9126	9249	9371	9494	9616	9739	9861	9984	*0106	123
55	55 0228	0351	0473	0595	0717	0840	0962	1084	1206	1328	123
56	1450	1572	1694	1816	1938	2060	2181	2303	2425	2547	122
57	2668	2790	2911	3033	3155	3276	3398	3519	3640	3762	122
58	3883	4004	4126	4247	4368	4489	4610	4731	4852	4973	122
59	5094	5215	5336	5457	5578	5699	5820	5940	6061	6182	121
360	6303	6423	6544	6664	6785	6905	7026	7146	7267	7387	121
61	7507	7627	7748	7868	7988	8108	8228	8349	8469	8589	121
62	8709	8829	8948	9068	9188	9308	9428	9548	9667	9787	120
63	55 9907	*0026	*0146	*0265	*0385	*0504	*0624	*0743	*0863	*0982	120
64	56 1101	1221	1340	1459	1578	1698	1817	1936	2055	2174	120
65	2293	2412	2531	2650	2769	2887	3006	3125	3244	3362	119
66	3481	3600	3718	3837	3955	4074	4192	4311	4429	4548	119
67	4666	4784	4903	5021	5139	5257	5376	5494	5612	5730	119
68	5848	5966	6084	6202	6320	6437	6555	6673	6791	6909	118
69	7026	7144	7262	7379	7497	7614	7732	7849	7967	8084	118
370	8202	8319	8436	8554	8671	8788	8905	9023	9140	9257	118
71	56 9374	9491	9608	9725	9842	9959	*0076	*0193	*0309	*0426	117
72	57 0543	0660	0776	0893	1010	1126	1243	1359	1476	1592	117
73	1709	1825	1942	2058	2174	2291	2407	2523	2639	2755	117
74	2872	2988	3104	3220	3336	3452	3568	3684	3800	3915	116
75	4031	4147	4263	4379	4494	4610	4726	4841	4957	5072	116
76	5188	5303	5419	5534	5650	5765	5880	5996	6111	6226	116
77	6341	6457	6572	6687	6802	6917	7032	7147	7262	7377	116
78	7492	7607	7722	7836	7951	8066	8181	8295	8410	8525	115
79	8639	8754	8868	8983	9097	9212	9326	9441	9555	9669	115
380	57 9784	9898	*0012	*0126	*0241	*0355	*0469	*0583	*0697	*0811	115
81	58 0925	1039	1153	1267	1381	1495	1608	1722	1836	1950	114
82	2063	2177	2291	2404	2518	2631	2745	2858	2972	3085	114
83	3199	3312	3426	3539	3652	3765	3879	3992	4105	4218	114
84	4331	4444	4557	4670	4783	4896	5009	5122	5235	5348	113
85	5461	5574	5686	5799	5912	6024	6137	6250	6362	6475	113
86	6587	6700	6812	6925	7037	7149	7262	7374	7486	7599	113
87	7711	7823	7935	8047	8160	8272	8384	8496	8608	8720	113
88	8832	8944	9056	9167	9279	9391	9503	9615	9726	9838	112
89	58 9950	*0061	*0173	*0284	*0396	*0507	*0619	*0730	*0842	*0953	112
390	59 1065	1176	1287	1399	1510	1621	1732	1843	1955	2066	112
91	2177	2288	2399	2510	2621	2732	2843	2954	3064	3175	111
92	3286	3397	3508	3618	3729	3840	3950	4061	4171	4282	111
93	4393	4503	4614	4724	4834	4945	5055	5165	5276	5386	111
94	5496	5606	5717	5827	5937	6047	6157	6267	6377	6487	111
95	6597	6707	6817	6927	7037	7146	7256	7366	7476	7586	110
96	7695	7805	7914	8024	8134	8243	8353	8462	8572	8681	110
97	8791	8900	9009	9119	9228	9337	9446	9556	9665	9774	110
98	59 9883	9992	*0101	*0210	*0319	*0428	*0537	*0646	*0755	*0864	109
99	60 0973	1082	1191	1299	1408	1517	1625	1734	1843	1951	109
N	0	1	2	3	4	5	6	7	8	9	D

TABLE 2 LOGARITHMS OF NUMBERS 4,000–4,499

SIX-PLACE MANTISSAS

N	0	1	2	3	4	5	6	7	8	9	D
400	60 2060	2169	2277	2386	2494	2603	2711	2819	2928	3036	109
01	3144	3253	3361	3469	3577	3686	3794	3902	4010	4118	109
02	4226	4334	4442	4550	4658	4766	4874	4982	5089	5197	108
03	5305	5413	5521	5628	5736	5844	5951	6059	6166	6274	108
04	6381	6489	6596	6704	6811	6919	7026	7133	7241	7348	108
05	7455	7562	7669	7777	7884	7991	8098	8205	8312	8419	108
06	8526	8633	8740	8847	8954	9061	9167	9274	9381	9488	107
07	60 9594	9701	9808	9914	*0021	*0128	*0234	*0341	*0447	*0554	107
08	61 0660	0767	0873	0979	1086	1192	1298	1405	1511	1617	107
09	1723	1829	1936	2042	2148	2254	2360	2466	2572	2678	107
410	2784	2890	2996	3102	3207	3313	3419	3525	3630	3736	106
11	3842	3947	4053	4159	4264	4370	4475	4581	4686	4792	106
12	4897	5003	5108	5213	5319	5424	5529	5634	5740	5845	106
13	5950	6055	6160	6265	6370	6476	6581	6686	6790	6895	106
14	7000	7105	7210	7315	7420	7525	7629	7734	7839	7943	105
15	8048	8153	8257	8362	8466	8571	8676	8780	8884	8989	105
16	61 9093	9198	9302	9406	9511	9615	9719	9824	9928	*0032	105
17	62 0136	0240	0344	0448	0552	0656	0760	0864	0968	1072	104
18	1176	1280	1384	1488	1592	1695	1799	1903	2007	2110	104
19	2214	2318	2421	2525	2628	2732	2835	2939	3042	3146	104
420	3249	3353	3456	3559	3663	3766	3869	3973	4076	4179	104
21	4282	4385	4488	4591	4695	4798	4901	5004	5107	5210	104
22	5312	5415	5518	5621	5724	5827	5929	6032	6135	6238	103
23	6340	6443	6546	6648	6751	6853	6956	7058	7161	7263	103
24	7366	7468	7571	7673	7775	7878	7980	8082	8185	8287	103
25	8389	8491	8593	8695	8797	8900	9002	9104	9206	9308	103
26	62 9410	9512	9613	9715	9817	9919	*0021	*0123	*0224	*0326	102
27	63 0428	0530	0631	0733	0835	0936	1038	1139	1241	1342	102
28	1444	1545	1647	1748	1849	1951	2052	2153	2255	2356	102
29	2457	2559	2660	2761	2862	2963	3064	3165	3266	3367	102
430	3468	3569	3670	3771	3872	3973	4074	4175	4276	4376	101
31	4477	4578	4679	4779	4880	4981	5081	5182	5283	5383	101
32	5484	5584	5685	5785	5886	5986	6087	6187	6287	6388	101
33	6488	6588	6688	6789	6889	6989	7089	7189	7290	7390	101
34	7490	7590	7690	7790	7890	7990	8090	8190	8290	8389	100
35	8489	8589	8689	8789	8888	8988	9088	9188	9287	9387	100
36	63 9486	9586	9686	9785	9885	9984	*0084	*0183	*0283	*0382	100
37	64 0481	0581	0680	0779	0879	0978	1077	1177	1276	1375	100
38	1474	1573	1672	1771	1871	1970	2069	2168	2267	2366	100
39	2465	2563	2662	2761	2860	2959	3058	3156	3255	3354	99
440	3453	3551	3650	3749	3847	3946	4044	4143	4242	4340	99
41	4439	4537	4636	4734	4832	4931	5029	5127	5226	5324	99
42	5422	5521	5619	5717	5815	5913	6011	6110	6208	6306	99
43	6404	6502	6600	6698	6796	6894	6992	7089	7187	7285	98
44	7383	7481	7579	7676	7774	7872	7969	8067	8165	8262	98
45	8360	8458	8555	8653	8750	8848	8945	9043	9140	9237	98
46	64 9335	9432	9530	9627	9724	9821	9919	*0016	*0113	*0210	98
47	65 0308	0405	0502	0599	0696	0793	0890	0987	1084	1181	97
48	1278	1375	1472	1569	1666	1762	1859	1956	2053	2150	97
49	2246	2343	2440	2536	2633	2730	2826	2923	3019	3116	97
N	**0**	**1**	**2**	**3**	**4**	**5**	**6**	**7**	**8**	**9**	**D**

TABLE 2 LOGARITHMS OF NUMBERS 4,500–4,999

SIX-PLACE MANTISSAS

N	0	1	2	3	4	5	6	7	8	9	D
450	65 3213	3309	3405	3502	3598	3695	3791	3888	3984	4080	97
51	4177	4273	4369	4465	4562	4658	4754	4850	4946	5042	97
52	5138	5235	5331	5427	5523	5619	5715	5810	5906	6002	97
53	6098	6194	6290	6386	6482	6577	6673	6769	6864	6960	96
54	7056	7152	7247	7343	7438	7534	7629	7725	7820	7916	96
55	8011	8107	8202	8298	8393	8488	8584	8679	8774	8870	96
56	8965	9060	9155	9250	9346	9441	9536	9631	9726	9821	96
57	65 9916	*0011	*0106	*0201	*0296	*0391	*0486	*0581	*0676	*0771	95
58	66 0865	0960	1055	1150	1245	1339	1434	1529	1623	1718	95
59	1813	1907	2002	2096	2191	2286	2380	2475	2569	2663	95
460	2758	2852	2947	3041	3135	3230	3324	3418	3512	3607	95
61	3701	3795	3889	3983	4078	4172	4266	4360	4454	4548	95
62	4642	4736	4830	4924	5018	5112	5206	5299	5393	5487	94
63	5581	5675	5769	5862	5956	6050	6143	6237	6331	6424	94
64	6518	6612	6705	6799	6892	6986	7079	7173	7266	7360	94
65	7453	7546	7640	7733	7826	7920	8013	8106	8199	8293	94
66	8386	8479	8572	8665	8759	8852	8945	9038	9131	9224	94
67	66 9317	9410	9503	9596	9689	9782	9875	9967	*0060	*0153	93
68	67 0246	0339	0431	0524	0617	0710	0802	0895	0988	1080	93
69	1173	1265	1358	1451	1543	1636	1728	1821	1913	2005	93
470	2098	2190	2283	2375	2467	2560	2652	2744	2836	2929	93
71	3021	3113	3205	3297	3390	3482	3574	3666	3758	3850	93
72	3942	4034	4126	4218	4310	4402	4494	4586	4677	4769	92
73	4861	4953	5045	5137	5228	5320	5412	5503	5595	5687	92
74	5778	5870	5962	6053	6145	6236	6328	6419	6511	6602	92
75	6694	6785	6876	6968	7059	7151	7242	7333	7424	7516	92
76	7607	7698	7789	7881	7972	8063	8154	8245	8336	8427	92
77	8518	8609	8700	8791	8882	8973	9064	9155	9246	9337	91
78	67 9428	9519	9610	9700	9791	9882	9973	*0063	*0154	*0245	91
79	68 0336	0426	0517	0607	0698	0789	0879	0970	1060	1151	91
480	1241	1332	1422	1513	1603	1693	1784	1874	1964	2055	91
81	2145	2235	2326	2416	2506	2596	2686	2777	2867	2957	91
82	3047	3137	3227	3317	3407	3497	3587	3677	3767	3857	90
83	3947	4037	4127	4217	4307	4396	4486	4576	4666	4756	90
84	4845	4935	5025	5114	5204	5294	5383	5473	5563	5652	90
85	5742	5831	5921	6010	6100	6189	6279	6368	6458	6547	90
86	6636	6726	6815	6904	6994	7083	7172	7261	7351	7440	90
87	7529	7618	7707	7796	7886	7975	8064	8153	8242	8331	90
88	8420	8509	8598	8687	8776	8865	8953	9042	9131	9220	89
89	68 9309	9398	9486	9575	9664	9753	9841	9930	*0019	*0107	89
490	69 0196	0285	0373	0462	0550	0639	0728	0816	0905	0993	89
91	1081	1170	1258	1347	1435	1524	1612	1700	1789	1877	89
92	1965	2053	2142	2230	2318	2406	2494	2583	2671	2759	89
93	2847	2935	3023	3111	3199	3287	3375	3463	3551	3639	88
94	3727	3815	3903	3991	4078	4166	4254	4342	4430	4517	88
95	4605	4693	4781	4868	4956	5044	5131	5219	5307	5394	88
96	5482	5569	5657	5744	5832	5919	6007	6094	6182	6269	88
97	6356	6444	6531	6618	6706	6793	6880	6968	7055	7142	88
98	7229	7317	7404	7491	7578	7665	7752	7839	7926	8014	88
99	8101	8188	8275	8362	8449	8535	8622	8709	8796	8883	87
N	**0**	**1**	**2**	**3**	**4**	**5**	**6**	**7**	**8**	**9**	**D**

TABLE 2 LOGARITHMS OF NUMBERS 5,000–5,499

SIX-PLACE MANTISSAS

N	0	1	2	3	4	5	6	7	8	9	D
500	69 8970	9057	9144	9231	9317	9404	9491	9578	9664	9751	87
01	69 9838	9924	*0011	*0098	*0184	*0271	*0358	*0444	*0531	*0617	87
02	70 0704	0790	0877	0963	1050	1136	1222	1309	1395	1482	87
03	1568	1654	1741	1827	1913	1999	2086	2172	2258	2344	87
04	2431	2517	2603	2689	2775	2861	2947	3033	3119	3205	86
05	3291	3377	3463	3549	3635	3721	3807	3893	3979	4065	86
06	4151	4236	4322	4408	4494	4579	4665	4751	4837	4922	86
07	5008	5094	5179	5265	5350	5436	5522	5607	5693	5778	86
08	5864	5949	6035	6120	6206	6291	6376	6462	6547	6632	86
09	6718	6803	6888	6974	7059	7144	7229	7315	7400	7485	86
510	7570	7655	7740	7826	7911	7996	8081	8166	8251	8336	86
11	8421	8506	8591	8676	8761	8846	8931	9015	9100	9185	85
12	70 9270	9355	9440	9524	9609	9694	9779	9863	9948	*0033	85
13	71 0117	0202	0287	0371	0456	0540	0625	0710	0794	0879	85
14	0963	1048	1132	1217	1301	1385	1470	1554	1639	1723	85
15	1807	1892	1976	2060	2144	2229	2313	2397	2481	2566	85
16	2650	2734	2818	2902	2986	3070	3154	3238	3323	3407	85
17	3491	3575	3659	3742	3826	3910	3994	4078	4162	4246	84
18	4330	4414	4497	4581	4665	4749	4833	4916	5000	5084	84
19	5167	5251	5335	5418	5502	5586	5669	5753	5836	5920	84
520	6003	6087	6170	6254	6337	6421	6504	6588	6671	6754	84
21	6838	6921	7004	7088	7171	7254	7338	7421	7504	7587	84
22	7671	7754	7837	7920	8003	8086	8169	8253	8336	8419	84
23	8502	8585	8668	8751	8834	8917	9000	9083	9165	9248	83
24	71 9331	9414	9497	9580	9663	9745	9828	9911	9994	*0077	83
25	72 0159	0242	0325	0407	0490	0573	0655	0738	0821	0903	83
26	0986	1068	1151	1233	1316	1398	1481	1563	1646	1728	83
27	1811	1893	1975	2058	2140	2222	2305	2387	2469	2552	83
28	2634	2716	2798	2881	2963	3045	3127	3209	3291	3374	83
29	3456	3538	3620	3702	3784	3866	3948	4030	4112	4194	82
530	4276	4358	4440	4522	4604	4685	4767	4849	4931	5013	82
31	5095	5176	5258	5340	5422	5503	5585	5667	5748	5830	82
32	5912	5993	6075	6156	6238	6320	6401	6483	6564	6646	82
33	6727	6809	6890	6972	7053	7134	7216	7297	7379	7460	82
34	7541	7623	7704	7785	7866	7948	8029	8110	8191	8273	82
35	8354	8435	8516	8597	8678	8759	8841	8922	9003	9084	82
36	9165	9246	9327	9408	9489	9570	9651	9732	9813	9893	81
37	72 9974	*0055	*0136	*0217	*0298	*0378	*0459	*0540	*0621	*0702	81
38	73 0782	0863	0944	1024	1105	1186	1266	1347	1428	1508	81
39	1589	1669	1750	1830	1911	1991	2072	2152	2233	2313	81
540	2394	2474	2555	2635	2715	2796	2876	2956	3037	3117	81
41	3197	3278	3358	3438	3518	3598	3679	3759	3839	3919	81
42	3999	4079	4160	4240	4320	4400	4480	4560	4640	4720	81
43	4800	4880	4960	5040	5120	5200	5279	5359	5439	5519	80
44	5599	5679	5759	5838	5918	5998	6078	6157	6237	6317	80
45	6397	6476	6556	6635	6715	6795	6874	6954	7034	7113	80
46	7193	7272	7352	7431	7511	7590	7670	7749	7829	7908	80
47	7987	8067	8146	8225	8305	8384	8463	8543	8622	8701	80
48	8781	8860	8939	9018	9097	9177	9256	9335	9414	9493	80
49	73 9572	9651	9731	9810	9889	9968	*0047	*0126	*0205	*0284	80
N	**0**	**1**	**2**	**3**	**4**	**5**	**6**	**7**	**8**	**9**	**D**

TABLE 2 LOGARITHMS OF NUMBERS 5,500–5,999

SIX-PLACE MANTISSAS

N	0	1	2	3	4	5	6	7	8	9	D
550	74 0363	0442	0521	0600	0678	0757	0836	0915	0994	1073	79
51	1152	1230	1309	1388	1467	1546	1624	1703	1782	1860	79
52	1939	2018	2096	2175	2254	2332	2411	2489	2568	2647	79
53	2725	2804	2882	2961	3039	3118	3196	3275	3353	3431	79
54	3510	3588	3667	3745	3823	3902	3980	4058	4136	4215	79
55	4293	4371	4449	4528	4606	4684	4762	4840	4919	4997	79
56	5075	5153	5231	5309	5387	5465	5543	5621	5699	5777	78
57	5855	5933	6011	6089	6167	6245	6323	6401	6479	6556	78
58	6634	6712	6790	6868	6945	7023	7101	7179	7256	7334	78
59	7412	7489	7567	7645	7722	7800	7878	7955	8033	8110	78
560	8188	8266	8343	8421	8498	8576	8653	8731	8808	8885	78
61	8963	9040	9118	9195	9272	9350	9427	9504	9582	9659	78
62	74 9736	9814	9891	9968	*0045	*0123	*0200	*0277	*0354	*0431	78
63	75 0508	0586	0663	0740	0817	0894	0971	1048	1125	1202	78
64	1279	1356	1433	1510	1587	1664	1741	1818	1895	1972	77
65	2048	2125	2202	2279	2356	2433	2509	2586	2663	2740	77
66	2816	2893	2970	3047	3123	3200	3277	3353	3430	3506	77
67	3583	3660	3736	3813	3889	3966	4042	4119	4195	4272	77
68	4348	4425	4501	4578	4654	4730	4807	4883	4960	5036	77
69	5112	5189	5265	5341	5417	5494	5570	5646	5722	5799	77
570	5875	5951	6027	6103	6180	6256	6332	6408	6484	6560	77
71	6636	6712	6788	6864	6940	7016	7092	7168	7244	7320	76
72	7396	7472	7548	7624	7700	7775	7851	7927	8003	8079	76
73	8155	8230	8306	8382	8458	8533	8609	8685	8761	8836	76
74	8912	8988	9063	9139	9214	9290	9366	9441	9517	9592	76
75	75 9668	9743	9819	9894	9970	*0045	*0121	*0196	*0272	*0347	76
76	76 0422	0498	0573	0649	0724	0799	0875	0950	1025	1101	76
77	1176	1251	1326	1402	1477	1552	1627	1702	1778	1853	76
78	1928	2003	2078	2153	2228	2303	2378	2453	2529	2604	76
79	2679	2754	2829	2904	2978	3053	3128	3203	3278	3353	75
580	3428	3503	3578	3653	3727	3802	3877	3952	4027	4101	75
81	4176	4251	4326	4400	4475	4550	4624	4699	4774	4848	75
82	4923	4998	5072	5147	5221	5296	5370	5445	5520	5594	75
83	5669	5743	5818	5892	5966	6041	6115	6190	6264	6338	75
84	6413	6487	6562	6636	6710	6785	6859	6933	7007	7082	75
85	7156	7230	7304	7379	7453	7527	7601	7675	7749	7823	75
86	7898	7972	8046	8120	8194	8268	8342	8416	8490	8564	74
87	8638	8712	8786	8860	8934	9008	9082	9156	9230	9303	74
88	76 9377	9451	9525	9599	9673	9746	9820	9894	9968	*0042	74
89	77 0115	0189	0263	0336	0410	0484	0557	0631	0705	0778	74
590	0852	0926	0999	1073	1146	1220	1293	1367	1440	1514	74
91	1587	1661	1734	1808	1881	1955	2028	2102	2175	2248	74
92	2322	2395	2468	2542	2615	2688	2762	2835	2908	2981	74
93	3055	3128	3201	3274	3348	3421	3494	3567	3640	3713	74
94	3786	3860	3933	4006	4079	4152	4225	4298	4371	4444	74
95	4517	4590	4663	4736	4809	4882	4955	5028	5100	5173	73
96	5246	5319	5392	5465	5538	5610	5683	5756	5829	5902	73
97	5974	6047	6120	6193	6265	6338	6411	6483	6556	6629	73
98	6701	6774	6846	6919	6992	7064	7137	7209	7282	7354	73
99	7427	7499	7572	7644	7717	7789	7862	7934	8006	8079	73
N	0	1	2	3	4	5	6	7	8	9	D

TABLE 2 LOGARITHMS OF NUMBERS 6,000–6,499

SIX-PLACE MANTISSAS

N	0	1	2	3	4	5	6	7	8	9	D
600	77 8151	8224	8296	8368	8441	8513	8585	8658	8730	8802	73
01	8874	8947	9019	9091	9163	9236	9308	9380	9452	9524	73
02	77 9596	9669	9741	9813	9885	9957	*0029	*0101	*0173	*0245	73
03	78 0317	0389	0461	0533	0605	0677	0749	0821	0893	0965	72
04	1037	1109	1181	1253	1324	1396	1468	1540	1612	1684	72
05	1755	1827	1899	1971	2042	2114	2186	2258	2329	2401	72
06	2473	2544	2616	2688	2759	2831	2902	2974	3046	3117	72
07	3189	3260	3332	3403	3475	3546	3618	3689	3761	3832	72
08	3904	3975	4046	4118	4189	4261	4332	4403	4475	4546	72
09	4617	4689	4760	4831	4902	4974	5045	5116	5187	5259	72
610	5330	5401	5472	5543	5615	5686	5757	5828	5899	5970	72
11	6041	6112	6183	6254	6325	6396	6467	6538	6609	6680	71
12	6751	6822	6893	6964	7035	7106	7177	7248	7319	7390	71
13	7460	7531	7602	7673	7744	7815	7885	7956	8027	8098	71
14	8168	8239	8310	8381	8451	8522	8593	8663	8734	8804	71
15	8875	8946	9016	9087	9157	9228	9299	9369	9440	9510	71
16	78 9581	9651	9722	9792	9863	9933	*0004	*0074	*0144	*0215	71
17	79 0285	0356	0426	0496	0567	0637	0707	0778	0848	0918	71
18	0988	1059	1129	1199	1269	1340	1410	1480	1550	1620	71
19	1691	1761	1831	1901	1971	2041	2111	2181	2252	2322	71
620	2392	2462	2532	2602	2672	2742	2812	2882	2952	3022	70
21	3092	3162	3231	3301	3371	3441	3511	3581	3651	3721	70
22	3790	3860	3930	4000	4070	4139	4209	4279	4349	4418	70
23	4488	4558	4627	4697	4767	4836	4906	4976	5045	5115	70
24	5185	5254	5324	5393	5463	5532	5602	5672	5741	5811	70
25	5880	5949	6019	6088	6158	6227	6297	6366	6436	6505	70
26	6574	6644	6713	6782	6852	6921	6990	7060	7129	7198	70
27	7268	7337	7406	7475	7545	7614	7683	7752	7821	7890	70
28	7960	8029	8098	8167	8236	8305	8374	8443	8513	8582	70
29	8651	8720	8789	8858	8927	8996	9065	9134	9203	9272	69
630	79 9341	9409	9478	9547	9616	9685	9754	9823	9892	9961	69
31	80 0029	0098	0167	0236	0305	0373	0442	0511	0580	0648	69
32	0717	0786	0854	0923	0992	1061	1129	1198	1266	1335	69
33	1404	1472	1541	1609	1678	1747	1815	1884	1952	2021	69
34	2089	2158	2226	2295	2363	2432	2500	2568	2637	2705	69
35	2774	2842	2910	2979	3047	3116	3184	3252	3321	3389	69
36	3457	3525	3594	3662	3730	3798	3867	3935	4003	4071	69
37	4139	4208	4276	4344	4412	4480	4548	4616	4685	4753	69
38	4821	4889	4957	5025	5093	5161	5229	5297	5365	5433	68
39	5501	5569	5637	5705	5773	5841	5908	5976	6044	6112	68
640	6180	6248	6316	6384	6451	6519	6587	6655	6723	6790	68
41	6858	6926	6994	7061	7129	7197	7264	7332	7400	7467	68
42	7535	7603	7670	7738	7806	7873	7941	8008	8076	8143	68
43	8211	8279	8346	8414	8481	8549	8616	8684	8751	8818	68
44	8886	8953	9021	9088	9156	9223	9290	9358	9425	9492	68
45	80 9560	9627	9694	9762	9829	9896	9964	*0031	*0098	*0165	68
46	81 0233	0300	0367	0434	0501	0569	0636	0703	0770	0837	68
47	0904	0971	1039	1106	1173	1240	1307	1374	1441	1508	68
48	1575	1642	1709	1776	1843	1910	1977	2044	2111	2178	67
49	2245	2312	2379	2445	2512	2579	2646	2713	2780	2847	67
N	0	1	2	3	4	5	6	7	8	9	D

TABLE 2 LOGARITHMS OF NUMBERS 6,500–6,999

SIX-PLACE MANTISSAS

N	0	1	2	3	4	5	6	7	8	9	D
650	81 2913	2980	3047	3114	3181	3247	3314	3381	3448	3514	67
51	3581	3648	3714	3781	3848	3914	3981	4048	4114	4181	67
52	4248	4314	4381	4447	4514	4581	4647	4714	4780	4847	67
53	4913	4980	5046	5113	5179	5246	5312	5378	5445	5511	67
54	5578	5644	5711	5777	5843	5910	5976	6042	6109	6175	67
55	6241	6308	6374	6440	6506	6573	6639	6705	6771	6838	67
56	6904	6970	7036	7102	7169	7235	7301	7367	7433	7499	67
57	7565	7631	7698	7764	7830	7896	7962	8028	8094	8160	67
58	8226	8292	8358	8424	8490	8556	8622	8688	8754	8820	66
59	8885	8951	9017	9083	9149	9215	9281	9346	9412	9478	66
660	81 9544	9610	9676	9741	9807	9873	9939	*0004	*0070	*0136	66
61	82 0201	0267	0333	0399	0464	0530	0595	0661	0727	0792	66
62	0858	0924	0989	1055	1120	1186	1251	1317	1382	1448	66
63	1514	1579	1645	1710	1775	1841	1906	1972	2037	2103	66
64	2168	2233	2299	2364	2430	2495	2560	2626	2691	2756	66
65	2822	2887	2952	3018	3083	3148	3213	3279	3344	3409	66
66	3474	3539	3605	3670	3735	3800	3865	3930	3996	4061	66
67	4126	4191	4256	4321	4386	4451	4516	4581	4646	4711	65
68	4776	4841	4906	4971	5036	5101	5166	5231	5296	5361	65
69	5426	5491	5556	5621	5686	5751	5815	5880	5945	6010	65
670	6075	6140	6204	6269	6334	6399	6464	6528	6593	6658	65
71	6723	6787	6852	6917	6981	7046	7111	7175	7240	7305	65
72	7369	7434	7499	7563	7628	7692	7757	7821	7886	7951	65
73	8015	8080	8144	8209	8273	8338	8402	8467	8531	8595	65
74	8660	8724	8789	8853	8918	8982	9046	9111	9175	9239	65
75	9304	9368	9432	9497	9561	9625	9690	9754	9818	9882	65
76	82 9947	*0011	*0075	*0139	*0204	*0268	*0332	*0396	*0460	*0525	65
77	83 0589	0653	0717	0781	0845	0909	0973	1037	1102	1166	65
78	1230	1294	1358	1422	1486	1550	1614	1678	1742	1806	64
79	1870	1934	1998	2062	2126	2189	2253	2317	2381	2445	64
680	2509	2573	2637	2700	2764	2828	2892	2956	3020	3083	64
81	3147	3211	3275	3338	3402	3466	3530	3593	3657	3721	64
82	3784	3848	3912	3975	4039	4103	4166	4230	4294	4357	64
83	4421	4484	4548	4611	4675	4739	4802	4866	4929	4993	64
84	5056	5120	5183	5247	5310	5373	5437	5500	5564	5627	64
85	5691	5754	5817	5881	5944	6007	6071	6134	6197	6261	64
86	6324	6387	6451	6514	6577	6641	6704	6767	6830	6894	64
87	6957	7020	7083	7146	7210	7273	7336	7399	7462	7525	64
88	7588	7652	7715	7778	7841	7904	7967	8030	8093	8156	64
89	8219	8282	8345	8408	8471	8534	8597	8660	8723	8786	63
690	8849	8912	8975	9038	9101	9164	9227	9289	9352	9415	63
91	83 9478	9541	9604	9667	9729	9792	9855	9918	9981	*0043	63
92	84 0106	0169	0232	0294	0357	0420	0482	0545	0608	0671	63
93	0733	0796	0859	0921	0984	1046	1109	1172	1234	1297	63
94	1359	1422	1485	1547	1610	1672	1735	1797	1860	1922	63
95	1985	2047	2110	2172	2235	2297	2360	2422	2484	2547	63
96	2609	2672	2734	2796	2859	2921	2983	3046	3108	3170	63
97	3233	3295	3357	3420	3482	3544	3606	3669	3731	3793	63
98	3855	3918	3980	4042	4104	4166	4229	4291	4353	4415	63
99	4477	4539	4601	4664	4726	4788	4850	4912	4974	5036	63
N	**0**	**1**	**2**	**3**	**4**	**5**	**6**	**7**	**8**	**9**	**D**

TABLE 2 LOGARITHMS OF NUMBERS 7,000–7,499

SIX-PLACE MANTISSAS

N	0	1	2	3	4	5	6	7	8	9	D
700	84 5098	5160	5222	5284	5346	5408	5470	5532	5594	5656	62
01	5718	5780	5842	5904	5966	6028	6090	6151	6213	6275	62
02	6337	6399	6461	6523	6585	6646	6708	6770	6832	6894	62
03	6955	7017	7079	7141	7202	7264	7326	7388	7449	7511	62
04	7573	7634	7696	7758	7819	7881	7943	8004	8066	8128	62
05	8189	8251	8312	8374	8435	8497	8559	8620	8682	8743	62
06	8805	8866	8928	8989	9051	9112	9174	9235	9297	9358	62
07	84 9419	9481	9542	9604	9665	9726	9788	9849	9911	9972	62
08	85 0033	0095	0156	0217	0279	0340	0401	0462	0524	0585	62
09	0646	0707	0769	0830	0891	0952	1014	1075	1136	1197	62
710	1258	1320	1381	1442	1503	1564	1625	1686	1747	1809	62
11	1870	1931	1992	2053	2114	2175	2236	2297	2358	2419	61
12	2480	2541	2602	2663	2724	2785	2846	2907	2968	3029	61
13	3090	3150	3211	3272	3333	3394	3455	3516	3577	3637	61
14	3698	3759	3820	3881	3941	4002	4063	4124	4185	4245	61
15	4306	4367	4428	4488	4549	4610	4670	4731	4792	4852	61
16	4913	4974	5034	5095	5156	5216	5277	5337	5398	5459	61
17	5519	5580	5640	5701	5761	5822	5882	5943	6003	6064	61
18	6124	6185	6245	6306	6366	6427	6487	6548	6608	6668	61
19	6729	6789	6850	6910	6970	7031	7091	7152	7212	7272	61
720	7332	7393	7453	7513	7574	7634	7694	7755	7815	7875	61
21	7935	7995	8056	8116	8176	8236	8297	8357	8417	8477	61
22	8537	8597	8657	8718	8778	8838	8898	8958	9018	9078	61
23	9138	9198	9258	9318	9379	9439	9499	9559	9619	9679	61
24	85 9739	9799	9859	9918	9978	*0038	*0098	*0158	*0218	*0278	60
25	86 0338	0398	0458	0518	0578	0637	0697	0757	0817	0877	60
26	0937	0996	1056	1116	1176	1236	1295	1355	1415	1475	60
27	1534	1594	1654	1714	1773	1833	1893	1952	2012	2072	60
28	2131	2191	2251	2310	2370	2430	2489	2549	2608	2668	60
29	2728	2787	2847	2906	2966	3025	3085	3144	3204	3263	60
730	3323	3382	3442	3501	3561	3620	3680	3739	3799	3858	60
31	3917	3977	4036	4096	4155	4214	4274	4333	4392	4452	60
32	4511	4570	4630	4689	4748	4808	4867	4926	4985	5045	60
33	5104	5163	5222	5282	5341	5400	5459	5519	5578	5637	60
34	5696	5755	5814	5874	5933	5992	6051	6110	6169	6228	60
35	6287	6346	6405	6465	6524	6583	6642	6701	6760	6819	60
36	6878	6937	6996	7055	7114	7173	7232	7291	7350	7409	59
37	7467	7526	7585	7644	7703	7762	7821	7880	7939	7998	59
38	8056	8115	8174	8233	8292	8350	8409	8468	8527	8586	59
39	8644	8703	8762	8821	8879	8938	8997	9056	9114	9173	59
740	9232	9290	9349	9408	9466	9525	9584	9642	9701	9760	59
41	86 9818	9877	9935	9994	*0053	*0111	*0170	*0228	*0287	*0345	59
42	87 0404	0462	0521	0579	0638	0696	0755	0813	0872	0930	59
43	0989	1047	1106	1164	1223	1281	1339	1398	1456	1515	59
44	1573	1631	1690	1748	1806	1865	1923	1981	2040	2098	59
45	2156	2215	2273	2331	2389	2448	2506	2564	2622	2681	59
46	2739	2797	2855	2913	2972	3030	3088	3146	3204	3262	59
47	3321	3379	3437	3495	3553	3611	3669	3727	3785	3844	59
48	3902	3960	4018	4076	4134	4192	4250	4308	4366	4424	58
49	4482	4540	4598	4656	4714	4772	4830	4888	4945	5003	58
N	**0**	**1**	**2**	**3**	**4**	**5**	**6**	**7**	**8**	**9**	**D**

TABLE 2 LOGARITHMS OF NUMBERS 7,500–7,999

SIX-PLACE MANTISSAS

N	0	1	2	3	4	5	6	7	8	9	D
750	87 5061	5119	5177	5235	5293	5351	5409	5466	5524	5582	58
51	5640	5698	5756	5813	5871	5929	5987	6045	6102	6160	58
52	6218	6276	6333	6391	6449	6507	6564	6622	6680	6737	58
53	6795	6853	6910	6968	7026	7083	7141	7199	7256	7314	58
54	7371	7429	7487	7544	7602	7659	7717	7774	7832	7889	58
55	7947	8004	8062	8119	8177	8234	8292	8349	8407	8464	58
56	8522	8579	8637	8694	8752	8809	8866	8924	8981	9039	58
57	9096	9153	9211	9268	9325	9383	9440	9497	9555	9612	58
58	87 9669	9726	9784	9841	9898	9956	*0013	*0070	*0127	*0185	58
59	88 0242	0299	0356	0413	0471	0528	0585	0642	0699	0756	58
760	0814	0871	0928	0985	1042	1099	1156	1213	1271	1328	58
61	1385	1442	1499	1556	1613	1670	1727	1784	1841	1898	57
62	1955	2012	2069	2126	2183	2240	2297	2354	2411	2468	57
63	2525	2581	2638	2695	2752	2809	2866	2923	2980	3037	57
64	3093	3150	3207	3264	3321	3377	3434	3491	3548	3605	57
65	3661	3718	3775	3832	3888	3945	4002	4059	4115	4172	57
66	4229	4285	4342	4399	4455	4512	4569	4625	4682	4739	57
67	4795	4852	4909	4965	5022	5078	5135	5192	5248	5305	57
68	5361	5418	5474	5531	5587	5644	5700	5757	5813	5870	57
69	5926	5983	6039	6096	6152	6209	6265	6321	6378	6434	57
770	6491	6547	6604	6660	6716	6773	6829	6885	6942	6998	57
71	7054	7111	7167	7223	7280	7336	7392	7449	7505	7561	57
72	7617	7674	7730	7786	7842	7898	7955	8011	8067	8123	57
73	8179	8236	8292	8348	8404	8460	8516	8573	8629	8685	57
74	8741	8797	8853	8909	8965	9021	9077	9134	9190	9246	57
75	9302	9358	9414	9470	9526	9582	9638	9694	9750	9806	56
76	88 9862	9918	9974	*0030	*0086	*0141	*0197	*0253	*0309	*0365	56
77	89 0421	0477	0533	0589	0645	0700	0756	0812	0868	0924	56
78	0980	1035	1091	1147	1203	1259	1314	1370	1426	1482	56
79	1537	1593	1649	1705	1760	1816	1872	1928	1983	2039	56
780	2095	2150	2206	2262	2317	2373	2429	2484	2540	2595	56
81	2651	2707	2762	2818	2873	2929	2985	3040	3096	3151	56
82	3207	3262	3318	3373	3429	3484	3540	3595	3651	3706	56
83	3762	3817	3873	3928	3984	4039	4094	4150	4205	4261	56
84	4316	4371	4427	4482	4538	4593	4648	4704	4759	4814	56
85	4870	4925	4980	5036	5091	5146	5201	5257	5312	5367	56
86	5423	5478	5533	5588	5644	5699	5754	5809	5864	5920	56
87	5975	6030	6085	6140	6195	6251	6306	6361	6416	6471	56
88	6526	6581	6636	6692	6747	6802	6857	6912	6967	7022	56
89	7077	7132	7187	7242	7297	7352	7407	7462	7517	7572	55
790	7627	7682	7737	7792	7847	7902	7957	8012	8067	8122	55
91	8176	8231	8286	8341	8396	8451	8506	8561	8615	8670	55
92	8725	8780	8835	8890	8944	8999	9054	9109	9164	9218	55
93	9273	9328	9383	9437	9492	9547	9602	9656	9711	9766	55
94	89 9821	9875	9930	9985	*0039	*0094	*0149	*0203	*0258	*0312	55
95	90 0367	0422	0476	0531	0586	0640	0695	0749	0804	0859	55
96	0913	0968	1022	1077	1131	1186	1240	1295	1349	1404	55
97	1458	1513	1567	1622	1676	1731	1785	1840	1894	1948	55
98	2003	2057	2112	2166	2221	2275	2329	2384	2438	2492	55
99	2547	2601	2655	2710	2764	2818	2873	2927	2981	3036	55
N	0	1	2	3	4	5	6	7	8	9	D

TABLE 2 LOGARITHMS OF NUMBERS 8,000–8,499

SIX-PLACE MANTISSAS

N	0	1	2	3	4	5	6	7	8	9	D
800	90 3090	3144	3199	3253	3307	3361	3416	3470	3524	3578	55
01	3633	3687	3741	3795	3849	3904	3958	4012	4066	4120	55
02	4174	4229	4283	4337	4391	4445	4499	4553	4607	4661	55
03	4716	4770	4824	4878	4932	4986	5040	5094	5148	5202	54
04	5256	5310	5364	5418	5472	5526	5580	5634	5688	5742	54
05	5796	5850	5904	5958	6012	6066	6119	6173	6227	6281	54
06	6335	6389	6443	6497	6551	6604	6658	6712	6766	6820	54
07	6874	6927	6981	7035	7089	7143	7196	7250	7304	7358	54
08	7411	7465	7519	7573	7626	7680	7734	7787	7841	7895	54
09	7949	8002	8056	8110	8163	8217	8270	8324	8378	8431	54
810	8485	8539	8592	8646	8699	8753	8807	8860	8914	8967	54
11	9021	9074	9128	9181	9235	9289	9342	9396	9449	9503	54
12	90 9556	9610	9663	9716	9770	9823	9877	9930	9984	*0037	54
13	91 0091	0144	0197	0251	0304	0358	0411	0464	0518	0571	54
14	0624	0678	0731	0784	0838	0891	0944	0998	1051	1104	54
15	1158	1211	1264	1317	1371	1424	1477	1530	1584	1637	54
16	1690	1743	1797	1850	1903	1956	2009	2063	2116	2169	54
17	2222	2275	2328	2381	2435	2488	2541	2594	2647	2700	54
18	2753	2806	2859	2913	2966	3019	3072	3125	3178	3231	54
19	3284	3337	3390	3443	3496	3549	3602	3655	3708	3761	53
820	3814	3867	3920	3973	4026	4079	4132	4184	4237	4290	53
21	4343	4396	4449	4502	4555	4608	4660	4713	4766	4819	53
22	4872	4925	4977	5030	5083	5136	5189	5241	5294	5347	53
23	5400	5453	5505	5558	5611	5664	5716	5769	5822	5875	53
24	5927	5980	6033	6085	6138	6191	6243	6296	6349	6401	53
25	6454	6507	6559	6612	6664	6717	6770	6822	6875	6927	53
26	6980	7033	7085	7138	7190	7243	7295	7348	7400	7453	53
27	7506	7558	7611	7663	7716	7768	7820	7873	7925	7978	53
28	8030	8083	8135	8188	8240	8293	8345	8397	8450	8502	53
29	8555	8607	8659	8712	8764	8816	8869	8921	8973	9026	53
830	9078	9130	9183	9235	9287	9340	9392	9444	9496	9549	53
31	91 9601	9653	9706	9758	9810	9862	9914	9967	*0019	*0071	53
32	92 0123	0176	0228	0280	0332	0384	0436	0489	0541	0593	53
33	0645	0697	0749	0801	0853	0906	0958	1010	1062	1114	53
34	1166	1218	1270	1322	1374	1426	1478	1530	1582	1634	52
35	1686	1738	1790	1842	1894	1946	1998	2050	2102	2154	52
36	2206	2258	2310	2362	2414	2466	2518	2570	2622	2674	52
37	2725	2777	2829	2881	2933	2985	3037	3089	3140	3192	52
38	3244	3296	3348	3399	3451	3503	3555	3607	3658	3710	52
39	3762	3814	3865	3917	3969	4021	4072	4124	4176	4228	52
840	4279	4331	4383	4434	4486	4538	4589	4641	4693	4744	52
41	4796	4848	4899	4951	5003	5054	5106	5157	5209	5261	52
42	5312	5364	5415	5467	5518	5570	5621	5673	5725	5776	52
43	5828	5879	5931	5982	6034	6085	6137	6188	6240	6291	52
44	6342	6394	6445	6497	6548	6600	6651	6702	6754	6805	52
45	6857	6908	6959	7011	7062	7114	7165	7216	7268	7319	52
46	7370	7422	7473	7524	7576	7627	7678	7730	7781	7832	52
47	7883	7935	7986	8037	8088	8140	8191	8242	8293	8345	52
48	8396	8447	8498	8549	8601	8652	8703	8754	8805	8857	52
49	8908	8959	9010	9061	9112	9163	9215	9266	9317	9368	52
N	**0**	**1**	**2**	**3**	**4**	**5**	**6**	**7**	**8**	**9**	**D**

TABLE 2 LOGARITHMS OF NUMBERS 8,500–8,999

SIX-PLACE MANTISSAS

N	0	1	2	3	4	5	6	7	8	9	D
850	92 9419	9470	9521	9572	9623	9674	9725	9776	9827	9879	52
51	92 9930	9981	*0032	*0083	*0134	*0185	*0236	*0287	*0338	*0389	51
52	93 0440	0491	0542	0592	0643	0694	0745	0796	0847	0898	51
53	0949	1000	1051	1102	1153	1204	1254	1305	1356	1407	51
54	1458	1509	1560	1610	1661	1712	1763	1814	1865	1915	51
55	1966	2017	2068	2118	2169	2220	2271	2322	2372	2423	51
56	2474	2524	2575	2626	2677	2727	2778	2829	2879	2930	51
57	2981	3031	3082	3133	3183	3234	3285	3335	3386	3437	51
58	3487	3538	3589	3639	3690	3740	3791	3841	3892	3943	51
59	3993	4044	4094	4145	4195	4246	4296	4347	4397	4448	51
860	4498	4549	4599	4650	4700	4751	4801	4852	4902	4953	51
61	5003	5054	5104	5154	5205	5255	5306	5356	5406	5457	51
62	5507	5558	5608	5658	5709	5759	5809	5860	5910	5960	51
63	6011	6061	6111	6162	6212	6262	6313	6363	6413	6463	51
64	6514	6564	6614	6665	6715	6765	6815	6865	6916	6966	51
65	7016	7066	7117	7167	7217	7267	7317	7367	7418	7468	51
66	7518	7568	7618	7668	7718	7769	7819	7869	7919	7969	51
67	8019	8069	8119	8169	8219	8269	8320	8370	8420	8470	51
68	8520	8570	8620	8670	8720	8770	8820	8870	8920	8970	50
69	9020	9070	9120	9170	9220	9270	9320	9369	9419	9469	50
870	93 9519	9569	9619	9669	9719	9769	9819	9869	9918	9968	50
71	94 0018	0068	0118	0168	0218	0267	0317	0367	0417	0467	50
72	0516	0566	0616	0666	0716	0765	0815	0865	0915	0964	50
73	1014	1064	1114	1163	1213	1263	1313	1362	1412	1462	50
74	1511	1561	1611	1660	1710	1760	1809	1859	1909	1958	50
75	2008	2058	2107	2157	2207	2256	2306	2355	2405	2455	50
76	2504	2554	2603	2653	2702	2752	2801	2851	2901	2950	50
77	3000	3049	3099	3148	3198	3247	3297	3346	3396	3445	50
78	3495	3544	3593	3643	3692	3742	3791	3841	3890	3939	50
79	3989	4038	4088	4137	4186	4236	4285	4335	4384	4433	50
880	4483	4532	4581	4631	4680	4729	4779	4828	4877	4927	50
81	4976	5025	5074	5124	5173	5222	5272	5321	5370	5419	50
82	5469	5518	5567	5616	5665	5715	5764	5813	5862	5912	50
83	5961	6010	6059	6108	6157	6207	6256	6305	6354	6403	50
84	6452	6501	6551	6600	6649	6698	6747	6796	6845	6894	50
85	6943	6992	7041	7090	7140	7189	7238	7287	7336	7385	50
86	7434	7483	7532	7581	7630	7679	7728	7777	7826	7875	49
87	7924	7973	8022	8070	8119	8168	8217	8266	8315	8364	49
88	8413	8462	8511	8560	8609	8657	8706	8755	8804	8853	49
89	8902	8951	8999	9048	9097	9146	9195	9244	9292	9341	49
890	9390	9439	9488	9536	9585	9634	9683	9731	9780	9829	49
91	94 9878	9926	9975	*0024	*0073	*0121	*0170	*0219	*0267	*0316	49
92	95 0365	0414	0462	0511	0560	0608	0657	0706	0754	0803	49
93	0851	0900	0949	0997	1046	1095	1143	1192	1240	1289	49
94	1338	1386	1435	1483	1532	1580	1629	1677	1726	1775	49
95	1823	1872	1920	1969	2017	2066	2114	2163	2211	2260	49
96	2308	2356	2405	2453	2502	2550	2599	2647	2696	2744	49
97	2792	2841	2889	2938	2986	3034	3083	3131	3180	3228	49
98	3276	3325	3373	3421	3470	3518	3566	3615	3663	3711	49
99	3760	3808	3856	3905	3953	4001	4049	4098	4146	4194	49
N	0	1	2	3	4	5	6	7	8	9	D

TABLE 2 LOGARITHMS OF NUMBERS 9,000–9,499

SIX-PLACE MANTISSAS

N	0	1	2	3	4	5	6	7	8	9	D
900	95 4243	4291	4339	4387	4435	4484	4532	4580	4628	4677	49
01	4725	4773	4821	4869	4918	4966	5014	5062	5110	5158	49
02	5207	5255	5303	5351	5399	5447	5495	5543	5592	5640	49
03	5688	5736	5784	5832	5880	5928	5976	6024	6072	6120	48
04	6168	6216	6265	6313	6361	6409	6457	6505	6553	6601	48
05	6649	6697	6745	6793	6840	6888	6936	6984	7032	7080	48
06	7128	7176	7224	7272	7320	7368	7416	7464	7512	7559	48
07	7607	7655	7703	7751	7799	7847	7894	7942	7990	8038	48
08	8086	8134	8181	8229	8277	8325	8373	8421	8468	8516	48
09	8564	8612	8659	8707	8755	8803	8850	8898	8946	8994	48
910	9041	9089	9137	9185	9232	9280	9328	9375	9423	9471	48
11	9518	9566	9614	9661	9709	9757	9804	9852	9900	9947	48
12	95 9995	*0042	*0090	*0138	*0185	*0233	*0280	*0328	*0376	*0423	48
13	96 0471	0518	0566	0613	0661	0709	0756	0804	0851	0899	48
14	0946	0994	1041	1089	1136	1184	1231	1279	1326	1374	48
15	1421	1469	1516	1563	1611	1658	1706	1753	1801	1848	48
16	1895	1943	1990	2038	2085	2132	2180	2227	2275	2322	48
17	2369	2417	2464	2511	2559	2606	2653	2701	2748	2795	48
18	2843	2890	2937	2985	3032	3079	3126	3174	3221	3268	48
19	3316	3363	3410	3457	3504	3552	3599	3646	3693	3741	48
920	3788	3835	3882	3929	3977	4024	4071	4118	4165	4212	48
21	4260	4307	4354	4401	4448	4495	4542	4590	4637	4684	48
22	4731	4778	4825	4872	4919	4966	5013	5061	5108	5155	48
23	5202	5249	5296	5343	5390	5437	5484	5531	5578	5625	47
24	5672	5719	5766	5813	5860	5907	5954	6001	6048	6095	47
25	6142	6189	6236	6283	6329	6376	6423	6470	6517	6564	47
26	6611	6658	6705	6752	6799	6845	6892	6939	6986	7033	47
27	7080	7127	7173	7220	7267	7314	7361	7408	7454	7501	47
28	7548	7595	7642	7688	7735	7782	7829	7875	7922	7969	47
29	8016	8062	8109	8156	8203	8249	8296	8343	8390	8436	47
930	8483	8530	8576	8623	8670	8716	8763	8810	8856	8903	47
31	8950	8996	9043	9090	9136	9183	9229	9276	9323	9369	47
32	9416	9463	9509	9556	9602	9649	9695	9742	9789	9835	47
33	96 9882	9928	9975	*0021	*0068	*0114	*0161	*0207	*0254	*0300	47
34	97 0347	0393	0440	0486	0533	0579	0626	0672	0719	0765	47
35	0812	0858	0904	0951	0997	1044	1090	1137	1183	1229	47
36	1276	1322	1369	1415	1461	1508	1554	1601	1647	1693	47
37	1740	1786	1832	1879	1925	1971	2018	2064	2110	2157	47
38	2203	2249	2295	2342	2388	2434	2481	2527	2573	2619	47
39	2666	2712	2758	2804	2851	2897	2943	2989	3035	3082	47
940	3128	3174	3220	3266	3313	3359	3405	3451	3497	3543	47
41	3590	3636	3682	3728	3774	3820	3866	3913	3959	4005	47
42	4051	4097	4143	4189	4235	4281	4327	4374	4420	4466	47
43	4512	4558	4604	4650	4696	4742	4788	4834	4880	4926	46
44	4972	5018	5064	5110	5156	5202	5248	5294	5340	5386	46
45	5432	5478	5524	5570	5616	5662	5707	5753	5799	5845	46
46	5891	5937	5983	6029	6075	6121	6167	6212	6258	6304	46
47	6350	6396	6442	6488	6533	6579	6625	6671	6717	6763	46
48	6808	6854	6900	6946	6992	7037	7083	7129	7175	7220	46
49	7266	7312	7358	7403	7449	7495	7541	7586	7632	7678	46
N	0	1	2	3	4	5	6	7	8	9	D

TABLE 2 LOGARITHMS OF NUMBERS 9,500–9,999

SIX-PLACE MANTISSAS

N	0	1	2	3	4	5	6	7	8	9	D
950	97 7724	7769	7815	7861	7906	7952	7998	8043	8089	8135	46
51	8181	8226	8272	8317	8363	8409	8454	8500	8546	8591	46
52	8637	8683	8728	8774	8819	8865	8911	8956	9002	9047	46
53	9093	9138	9184	9230	9275	9321	9366	9412	9457	9503	46
54	97 9548	9594	9639	9685	9730	9776	9821	9867	9912	9958	46
55	98 0003	0049	0094	0140	0185	0231	0276	0322	0367	0412	46
56	0458	0503	0549	0594	0640	0685	0730	0776	0821	0867	46
57	0912	0957	1003	1048	1093	1139	1184	1229	1275	1320	46
58	1366	1411	1456	1501	1547	1592	1637	1683	1728	1773	46
59	1819	1864	1909	1954	2000	2045	2090	2135	2181	2226	46
960	2271	2316	2362	2407	2452	2497	2543	2588	2633	2678	46
61	2723	2769	2814	2859	2904	2949	2994	3040	3085	3130	46
62	3175	3220	3265	3310	3356	3401	3446	3491	3536	3581	46
63	3626	3671	3716	3762	3807	3852	3897	3942	3987	4032	46
64	4077	4122	4167	4212	4257	4302	4347	4392	4437	4482	45
65	4527	4572	4617	4662	4707	4752	4797	4842	4887	4932	45
66	4977	5022	5067	5112	5157	5202	5247	5292	5337	5382	45
67	5426	5471	5516	5561	5606	5651	5696	5741	5786	5830	45
68	5875	5920	5965	6010	6055	6100	6144	6189	6234	6279	45
69	6324	6369	6413	6458	6503	6548	6593	6637	6682	6727	45
970	6772	6817	6861	6906	6951	6996	7040	7085	7130	7175	45
71	7219	7264	7309	7353	7398	7443	7488	7532	7577	7622	45
72	7666	7711	7756	7800	7845	7890	7934	7979	8024	8068	45
73	8113	8157	8202	8247	8291	8336	8381	8425	8470	8514	45
74	8559	8604	8648	8693	8737	8782	8826	8871	8916	8960	45
75	9005	9049	9094	9138	9183	9227	9272	9316	9361	9405	45
76	9450	9494	9539	9583	9628	9672	9717	9761	9806	9850	45
77	98 9895	9939	9983	*0028	*0072	*0117	*0161	*0206	*0250	*0294	45
78	99 0339	0383	0428	0472	0516	0561	0605	0650	0694	0738	45
79	0783	0827	0871	0916	0960	1004	1049	1093	1137	1182	45
980	1226	1270	1315	1359	1403	1448	1492	1536	1580	1625	45
81	1669	1713	1758	1802	1846	1890	1935	1979	2023	2067	45
82	2111	2156	2200	2244	2288	2333	2377	2421	2465	2509	45
83	2554	2598	2642	2686	2730	2774	2819	2863	2907	2951	45
84	2995	3039	3083	3127	3172	3216	3260	3304	3348	3392	45
85	3436	3480	3524	3568	3613	3657	3701	3745	3789	3833	45
86	3877	3921	3965	4009	4053	4097	4141	4185	4229	4273	44
87	4317	4361	4405	4449	4493	4537	4581	4625	4669	4713	44
88	4757	4801	4845	4889	4933	4977	5021	5065	5108	5152	44
89	5196	5240	5284	5328	5372	5416	5460	5504	5547	5591	44
990	5635	5679	5723	5767	5811	5854	5898	5942	5986	6030	44
91	6074	6117	6161	6205	6249	6293	6337	6380	6424	6468	44
92	6512	6555	6599	6643	6687	6731	6774	6818	6862	6906	44
93	6949	6993	7037	7080	7124	7168	7212	7255	7299	7343	44
94	7386	7430	7474	7517	7561	7605	7648	7692	7736	7779	44
95	7823	7867	7910	7954	7998	8041	8085	8129	8172	8216	44
96	8259	8303	8347	8390	8434	8477	8521	8564	8608	8652	44
97	8695	8739	8782	8826	8869	8913	8956	9000	9043	9087	44
98	9131	9174	9218	9261	9305	9348	9392	9435	9479	9522	44
99	99 9565	9609	9652	9696	9739	9783	9826	9870	9913	9957	44
N	**0**	**1**	**2**	**3**	**4**	**5**	**6**	**7**	**8**	**9**	**D**

TABLE 3 LOGARITHMS OF NUMBERS 10,000–10,499

SEVEN-PLACE MANTISSAS

N	0	1	2	3	4	5	6	7	8	9	D#
1000	000 0000	0434	0869	1303	1737	2171	2605	3039	3473	3907	435
1001	4341	4775	5208	5642	6076	6510	6943	7377	7810	8244	434
1002	8677	9111	9544	9977	*0411	*0844	*1277	*1710	*2143	*2576	434
1003	001 3009	3442	3875	4308	4741	5174	5607	6039	6472	6905	433
1004	7337	7770	8202	8635	9067	9499	9932	*0364	*0796	*1228	433
1005	002 1661	2093	2525	2957	3389	3821	4253	4685	5116	5548	432
1006	5980	6411	6843	7275	7706	8138	8569	9001	9432	9863	432
1007	003 0295	0726	1157	1588	2019	2451	2882	3313	3744	4174	432
1008	4605	5036	5467	5898	6328	6759	7190	7620	8051	8481	431
1009	8912	9342	9772	*0203	*0633	*1063	*1493	*1924	*2354	*2784	431
1010	004 3214	3644	4074	4504	4933	5363	5793	6223	6652	7082	430
1011	7512	7941	8371	8800	9229	9659	*0088	*0517	*0947	*1376	430
1012	005 1805	2234	2663	3092	3521	3950	4379	4808	5237	5666	429
1013	6094	6523	6952	7380	7809	8238	8666	9094	9523	9951	429
1014	006 0380	0808	1236	1664	2092	2521	2949	3377	3805	4233	429
1015	4660	5088	5516	5944	6372	6799	7227	7655	8082	8510	428
1016	8937	9365	9792	*0219	*0647	*1074	*1501	*1928	*2355	*2782	428
1017	007 3210	3637	4064	4490	4917	5344	5771	6198	6624	7051	427
1018	7478	7904	8331	8757	9184	9610	*0037	*0463	*0889	*1316	427
1019	008 1742	2168	2594	3020	3446	3872	4298	4724	5150	5576	426
1020	6002	6427	6853	7279	7704	8130	8556	8981	9407	9832	426
1021	009 0257	0683	1108	1533	1959	2384	2809	3234	3659	4084	426
1022	4509	4934	5359	5784	6208	6633	7058	7483	7907	8332	425
1023	8756	9181	9605	*0030	*0454	*0878	*1303	*1727	*2151	*2575	425
1024	010 3000	3424	3848	4272	4696	5120	5544	5967	6391	6815	424
1025	7239	7662	8086	8510	8933	9357	9780	*0204	*0627	*1050	424
1026	011 1474	1897	2320	2743	3166	3590	4013	4436	4859	5282	424
1027	5704	6127	6550	6973	7396	7818	8241	8664	9086	9509	423
1028	9931	*0354	*0776	*1198	*1621	*2043	*2465	*2887	*3310	*3732	423
1029	012 4154	4576	4998	5420	5842	6264	6685	7107	7529	7951	422
1030	8372	8794	9215	9637	*0059	*0480	*0901	*1323	*1744	*2165	422
1031	013 2587	3008	3429	3850	4271	4692	5113	5534	5955	6376	421
1032	6797	7218	7639	8059	8480	8901	9321	9742	*0162	*0583	421
1033	014 1003	1424	1844	2264	2685	3105	3525	3945	4365	4785	421
1034	5205	5625	6045	6465	6885	7305	7725	8144	8564	8984	420
1035	9403	9823	*0243	*0662	*1082	*1501	*1920	*2340	*2759	*3178	420
1036	015 3598	4017	4436	4855	5274	5693	6112	6531	6950	7369	419
1037	7788	8206	8625	9044	9462	9881	*0300	*0718	*1137	*1555	419
1038	016 1974	2392	2810	3229	3647	4065	4483	4901	5319	5737	419
1039	6155	6573	6991	7409	7827	8245	8663	9080	9498	9916	418
1040	017 0333	0751	1168	1586	2003	2421	2838	3256	3673	4090	418
1041	4507	4924	5342	5759	6176	6593	7010	7427	7844	8260	418
1042	8677	9094	9511	9927	*0344	*0761	*1177	*1594	*2010	*2427	417
1043	018 2843	3259	3676	4092	4508	4925	5341	5757	6173	6589	417
1044	7005	7421	7837	8253	8669	9084	9500	9916	*0332	*0747	416
1045	019 1163	1578	1994	2410	2825	3240	3656	4071	4486	4902	416
1046	5317	5732	6147	6562	6977	7392	7807	8222	8637	9052	415
1047	9467	9882	*0296	*0711	*1126	*1540	*1955	*2369	*2784	*3198	415
1048	020 3613	4027	4442	4856	5270	5684	6099	6513	6927	7341	415
1049	7755	8169	8583	8997	9411	9824	*0238	*0652	*1066	*1479	414
N	0	1	2	3	4	5	6	7	8	9	D

* Prefix first three places on next line.
Example: The mantissa for number (N) 10024 is *001* 0411.

The *highest difference* between adjacent mantissas on the *individual line*. It is also the *lowest difference* between adjacent mantissas on the *preceding line* in many cases.

TABLE 3 LOGARITHMS OF NUMBERS 10,500–11,009

SEVEN-PLACE MANTISSAS

N	0	1	2	3	4	5	6	7	8	9	D
1050	021 1893	2307	2720	3134	3547	3961	4374	4787	5201	5614	414
1051	6027	6440	6854	7267	7680	8093	8506	8919	9332	9745	414
1052	022 0157	0570	0983	1396	1808	2221	2634	3046	3459	3871	413
1053	4284	4696	5109	5521	5933	6345	6758	7170	7582	7994	413
1054	8406	8818	9230	9642	*0054	*0466	*0878	*1289	*1701	*2113	412
1055	023 2525	2936	3348	3759	4171	4582	4994	5405	5817	6228	412
1056	6639	7050	7462	7873	8284	8695	9106	9517	9928	*0339	412
1057	024 0750	1161	1572	1982	2393	2804	3214	3625	4036	4446	411
1058	4857	5267	5678	6088	6498	6909	7319	7729	8139	8549	411
1059	8960	9370	9780	*0190	*0600	*1010	*1419	*1829	*2239	*2649	410
1060	025 3059	3468	3878	4288	4697	5107	5516	5926	6335	6744	410
1061	7154	7563	7972	8382	8791	9200	9609	*0018	*0427	*0836	410
1062	026 1245	1654	2063	2472	2881	3289	3698	4107	4515	4924	409
1063	5333	5741	6150	6558	6967	7375	7783	8192	8600	9008	409
1064	9416	9824	*0233	*0641	*1049	*1457	*1865	*2273	*2680	*3088	409
1065	027 3496	3904	4312	4719	5127	5535	5942	6350	6757	7165	408
1066	7572	7979	8387	8794	9201	9609	*0016	*0423	*0830	*1237	408
1067	028 1644	2051	2458	2865	3272	3679	4086	4492	4899	5306	408
1068	5713	6119	6526	6932	7339	7745	8152	8558	8964	9371	407
1069	9777	*0183	*0590	*0996	*1402	*1808	*2214	*2620	*3026	*3432	407
1070	029 3838	4244	4649	5055	5461	5867	6272	6678	7084	7489	406
1071	7895	8300	8706	9111	9516	9922	*0327	*0732	*1138	*1543	406
1072	030 1948	2353	2758	3163	3568	3973	4378	4783	5188	5592	405
1073	5997	6402	6807	7211	7616	8020	8425	8830	9234	9638	405
1074	031 0043	0447	0851	1256	1660	2064	2468	2872	3277	3681	405
1075	4085	4489	4893	5296	5700	6104	6508	6912	7315	7719	404
1076	8123	8526	8930	9333	9737	*0140	*0544	*0947	*1350	*1754	404
1077	032 2157	2560	2963	3367	3770	4173	4576	4979	5382	5785	404
1078	6188	6590	6993	7396	7799	8201	8604	9007	9409	9812	403
1079	033 0214	0617	1019	1422	1824	2226	2629	3031	3433	3835	403
1080	4238	4640	5042	5444	5846	6248	6650	7052	7453	7855	402
1081	8257	8659	9060	9462	9864	*0265	*0667	*1068	*1470	*1871	402
1082	034 2273	2674	3075	3477	3878	4279	4680	5081	5482	5884	402
1083	6285	6686	7087	7487	7888	8289	8690	9091	9491	9892	401
1084	035 0293	0693	1094	1495	1895	2296	2696	3096	3497	3897	401
1085	4297	4698	5098	5498	5898	6298	6698	7098	7498	7898	401
1086	8298	8698	9098	9498	9898	*0297	*0697	*1097	*1496	*1896	400
1087	036 2295	2695	3094	3494	3893	4293	4692	5091	5491	5890	400
1088	6289	6688	7087	7486	7885	8284	8683	9082	9481	9880	399
1089	037 0279	0678	1076	1475	1874	2272	2671	3070	3468	3867	399
1090	4265	4663	5062	5460	5858	6257	6655	7053	7451	7849	399
1091	8248	8646	9044	9442	9839	*0237	*0635	*1033	*1431	*1829	398
1092	038 2226	2624	3022	3419	3817	4214	4612	5009	5407	5804	398
1093	6202	6599	6996	7393	7791	8188	8585	8982	9379	9776	398
1094	039 0173	0570	0967	1364	1761	2158	2554	2951	3348	3745	397
1095	4141	4538	4934	5331	5727	6124	6520	6917	7313	7709	397
1096	8106	8502	8898	9294	9690	*0086	*0482	*0878	*1274	*1670	396
1097	040 2066	2462	2858	3254	3650	4045	4441	4837	5232	5628	396
1098	6023	6419	6814	7210	7605	8001	8396	8791	9187	9582	396
1099	9977	*0372	*0767	*1162	*1557	*1952	*2347	*2742	*3137	*3532	395
1100	041 3927	4322	4716	5111	5506	5900	6295	6690	7084	7479	395
N	**0**	**1**	**2**	**3**	**4**	**5**	**6**	**7**	**8**	**9**	**D**

TABLE 4 INTEREST RATE PER CONVERSION PERIOD

FOR NOMINAL RATES FROM $2\frac{1}{2}\%$ TO 10% AND SELECTED RATES (FROM 12% TO 120%)

Nominal Rate (Annual)	Interest Rate Per Period If Nominal Rate Is Compounded		
	Monthly	Quarterly	Semiannually
$2\frac{1}{2}\%$ (= .025)	*$\frac{5}{24}\%$ (= .00208$\dot{3}$)	$\frac{5}{8}\%$ (= .00625)	$1\frac{1}{4}\%$ (= .0125)
3% (= .03)	$\frac{1}{4}\%$ (= .0025)	$\frac{3}{4}\%$ (= .0075)	$1\frac{1}{2}\%$ (= .015)
$3\frac{1}{2}\%$ (= .035)	*$\frac{7}{24}\%$ (= .00291$\dot{6}$)	$\frac{7}{8}\%$ (= .00875)	$1\frac{3}{4}\%$ (= .0175)
4% (= .04)	$\frac{1}{3}\%$ (= .00$\dot{3}$)	1% (= .01)	2% (= .02)
$4\frac{1}{2}\%$ (= .045)	*$\frac{3}{8}\%$ (= .00375)	$1\frac{1}{8}\%$ (= .01125)	$2\frac{1}{4}\%$ (= .0225)
5% (= .05)	$\frac{5}{12}\%$ (= .0041$\dot{6}$)	$1\frac{1}{4}\%$ (= .0125)	$2\frac{1}{2}\%$ (= .025)
$5\frac{1}{2}\%$ (= .055)	$\frac{11}{24}\%$ (= .00458$\dot{3}$)	$1\frac{3}{8}\%$ (= .01375)	$2\frac{3}{4}\%$ (= .0275)
6% (= .06)	$\frac{1}{2}\%$ (= .005)	$1\frac{1}{2}\%$ (= .015)	3% (= .03)
$6\frac{1}{2}\%$ (= .065)	$\frac{13}{24}\%$ (= .00541$\dot{6}$)	$1\frac{5}{8}\%$ (= .01625)	$3\frac{1}{4}\%$ (= .0325)
7% (= .07)	$\frac{7}{12}\%$ (= .0058$\dot{3}$)	$1\frac{3}{4}\%$ (= .0175)	$3\frac{1}{2}\%$ (= .035)
$7\frac{1}{2}\%$ (= .075)	$\frac{5}{8}\%$ (= .00625)	$1\frac{7}{8}\%$ (= .01875)	$3\frac{3}{4}\%$ (= .0375)
8% (= .08)	$\frac{2}{3}\%$ (= .00$\dot{6}$)	2% (= .02)	4% (= .04)
$8\frac{1}{2}\%$ (= .085)	*$\frac{17}{24}\%$ (= .00708$\dot{3}$)	*$2\frac{1}{8}\%$ (= .02125)	*$4\frac{1}{4}\%$ (= .0425)
9% (= .09)	$\frac{3}{4}\%$ (= .0075)	$2\frac{1}{4}\%$ (= .0225)	$4\frac{1}{2}\%$ (= .045)
$9\frac{1}{2}\%$ (= .095)	*$\frac{19}{24}\%$ (= .00791$\dot{6}$)	*$2\frac{3}{8}\%$ (= .02375)	*$4\frac{3}{4}\%$ (= .0475)
10% (= .10)	*$\frac{5}{6}\%$ (= .008$\dot{3}$)	$2\frac{1}{2}\%$ (= .025)	5% (= .05)
*12% (= .12)	1% (= .01)	3% (= .03)	6% (= .06)
*18% (= .18)	$1\frac{1}{2}\%$ (= .015)	$4\frac{1}{2}\%$ (= .045)	9% (= .09)
*24% (= .24)	2% (= .02)	6% (= .06)	*12% (= .12)
*30% (= .30)	$2\frac{1}{2}\%$ (= .025)	$7\frac{1}{2}\%$ (= .075)	*15% (= .15)
*120% (= 1.20)	10% (= .10)	*30% (= .30)	*60% (= .60)

*These rates are not included in the Compound Interest and Annuity Tables (5 through 11). However, approximate values for these rates in the second to fourth columns can be obtained by interpolation from the values in the tables (for rates $2\frac{1}{2}\%$ to 10%).

TABLE 5 COMPOUND AMOUNT
WHEN PRINCIPAL IS 1

$$s = (1 + i)^n$$

n	$\frac{1}{4}\%$	$\frac{1}{3}\%$	$\frac{5}{12}\%$	$\frac{11}{24}\%$	n
1	1.0025 0000	1.0033 3333	1.0041 6667	1.0045 8333	1
2	1.0050 0625	1.0066 7778	1.0083 5069	1.0091 8767	2
3	1.0075 1877	1.0100 3337	1.0125 5216	1.0138 1312	3
4	1.0100 3756	1.0134 0015	1.0167 7112	1.0184 5976	4
5	1.0125 6266	1.0167 7815	1.0210 0767	1.0231 2770	5
6	1.0150 9406	1.0201 6741	1.0252 6187	1.0278 1704	6
7	1.0176 3180	1.0235 6797	1.0295 3379	1.0325 2786	7
8	1.0201 7588	1.0269 7986	1.0338 2352	1.0372 6028	8
9	1.0227 2632	1.0304 0313	1.0381 3111	1.0420 1439	9
10	1.0252 8313	1.0338 3780	1.0424 5666	1.0467 9029	10
11	1.0278 4634	1.0372 8393	1.0468 0023	1.0515 8808	11
12	1.0304 1596	1.0407 4154	1.0511 6190	1.0564 0786	12
13	1.0329 9200	1.0442 1068	1.0555 4174	1.0612 4973	13
14	1.0355 7448	1.0476 9138	1.0599 3983	1.0661 1379	14
15	1.0381 6341	1.0511 8369	1.0643 5625	1.0710 0015	15
16	1.0407 5882	1.0546 8763	1.0687 9106	1.0759 0890	16
17	1.0433 6072	1.0582 0326	1.0732 4436	1.0808 4015	17
18	1.0459 6912	1.0617 3060	1.0777 1621	1.0857 9400	18
19	1.0485 8404	1.0652 6971	1.0822 0670	1.0907 7055	19
20	1.0512 0550	1.0688 2060	1.0867 1589	1.0957 6992	20
21	1.0538 3352	1.0723 8334	1.0912 4387	1.1007 9220	21
22	1.0564 6810	1.0759 5795	1.0957 9072	1.1058 3749	22
23	1.0591 0927	1.0795 4448	1.1003 5652	1.1109 0592	23
24	1.0617 5704	1.0831 4296	1.1049 4134	1.1159 9757	24
25	1.0644 1144	1.0867 5344	1.1095 4526	1.1211 1256	25
26	1.0670 7247	1.0903 7595	1.1141 6836	1.1262 5099	26
27	1.0697 4015	1.0940 1053	1.1188 1073	1.1314 1297	27
28	1.0724 1450	1.0976 5724	1.1234 7244	1.1365 9862	28
29	1.0750 9553	1.1013 1609	1.1281 5358	1.1418 0803	29
30	1.0777 8327	1.1049 8715	1.1328 5422	1.1470 4131	30
31	1.0804 7773	1.1086 7044	1.1375 7444	1.1522 9859	31
32	1.0831 7892	1.1123 6601	1.1423 1434	1.1575 7995	32
33	1.0858 8687	1.1160 7389	1.1470 7398	1.1628 8553	33
34	1.0886 0159	1.1197 9414	1.1518 5346	1.1682 1542	34
35	1.0913 2309	1.1235 2679	1.1566 5284	1.1735 6974	35
36	1.0940 5140	1.1272 7187	1.1614 7223	1.1789 4860	36
37	1.0967 8653	1.1310 2945	1.1663 1170	1.1843 5212	37
38	1.0995 2850	1.1347 9955	1.1711 7133	1.1897 8040	38
39	1.1022 7732	1.1385 8221	1.1760 5121	1.1952 3356	39
40	1.1050 3301	1.1423 7748	1.1809 5142	1.2007 1171	40
41	1.1077 9559	1.1461 8541	1.1858 7206	1.2062 1497	41
42	1.1105 6508	1.1500 0603	1.1908 1319	1.2117 4346	42
43	1.1133 4149	1.1538 3938	1.1957 7491	1.2172 9728	43
44	1.1161 2485	1.1576 8551	1.2007 5731	1.2228 7656	44
45	1.1189 1516	1.1615 4446	1.2057 6046	1.2284 8141	45
46	1.1217 1245	1.1654 1628	1.2107 8446	1.2341 1195	46
47	1.1245 1673	1.1693 0100	1.2158 2940	1.2397 6830	47
48	1.1273 2802	1.1731 9867	1.2208 9536	1.2454 5057	48
49	1.1301 4634	1.1771 0933	1.2259 8242	1.2511 5889	49
50	1.1329 7171	1.1810 3303	1.2310 9068	1.2568 9336	50
51	1.1358 0414	1.1849 6981	1.2362 2022	1.2626 5413	51
52	1.1386 4365	1.1889 1971	1.2413 7114	1.2684 4129	52
53	1.1414 9026	1.1928 8277	1.2465 4352	1.2742 5498	53
54	1.1443 4398	1.1968 5905	1.2517 3745	1.2800 9531	54
55	1.1472 0484	1.2008 4858	1.2569 5302	1.2859 6242	55
56	1.1500 7285	1.2048 5141	1.2621 9033	1.2918 5641	56
57	1.1529 4804	1.2088 6758	1.2674 4946	1.2977 7742	57
58	1.1558 3041	1.2128 9714	1.2727 3050	1.3037 2557	58
59	1.1587 1998	1.2169 4013	1.2780 3354	1.3097 0098	59
60	1.1616 1678	1.2209 9659	1.2833 5868	1.3157 0377	60

TABLE 5 COMPOUND AMOUNT
WHEN PRINCIPAL IS 1

$$s = (1 + i)^n$$

n	$\frac{1}{4}\%$	$\frac{1}{3}\%$	$\frac{5}{12}\%$	$\frac{11}{24}\%$	n
61	1.1645 2082	1.2250 6658	1.2887 0601	1.3217 3408	61
62	1.1674 3213	1.2291 5014	1.2940 7561	1.3277 9203	62
63	1.1703 5071	1.2332 4730	1.2994 6760	1.3338 7774	63
64	1.1732 7658	1.2373 5813	1.3048 8204	1.3399 9135	64
65	1.1762 0977	1.2414 8266	1.3101 1905	1.3461 3298	65
66	1.1791 5030	1.2456 2093	1.3157 7872	1.3523 0275	66
67	1.1820 9817	1.2497 7300	1.3212 6113	1.3585 0081	67
68	1.1850 5342	1.2539 3891	1.3267 6638	1.3647 2727	68
69	1.1880 1605	1.2581 1871	1.3322 9458	1.3709 8227	69
70	1.1909 8609	1.2623 1244	1.3378 4580	1.3772 6594	70
71	1.1939 6356	1.2665 2015	1.3434 2016	1.3835 7841	71
72	1.1969 4847	1.2707 4188	1.3490 1774	1.3899 1981	72
73	1.1999 4084	1.2749 7769	1.3546 3865	1.3962 9027	73
74	1.2029 4069	1.2792 2761	1.3602 8298	1.4026 8994	74
75	1.2059 4804	1.2834 9170	1.3659 5082	1.4091 1893	75
76	1.2089 6291	1.2877 7001	1.3716 4229	1.4155 7739	76
77	1.2119 8532	1.2920 6258	1.3773 5746	1.4220 6546	77
78	1.2150 1528	1.2963 6945	1.3830 9645	1.4285 8326	78
79	1.2180 5282	1.3006 9068	1.3888 5935	1.4351 3093	79
80	1.2210 9795	1.3050 2632	1.3946 4627	1.4417 0861	80
81	1.2241 5070	1.3093 7641	1.4004 5729	1.4483 1645	81
82	1.2272 1108	1.3137 4099	1.4062 9253	1.4549 5456	82
83	1.2302 7910	1.3181 2013	1.4121 5209	1.4616 2310	83
84	1.2333 5480	1.3225 1386	1.4180 3605	1.4683 2221	84
85	1.2364 3819	1.3269 2224	1.4239 4454	1.4750 5202	85
86	1.2395 2928	1.3313 4532	1.4298 7764	1.4818 1267	86
87	1.2426 2811	1.3357 8314	1.4358 3546	1.4886 0432	87
88	1.2457 3468	1.3402 3575	1.4418 1811	1.4954 2709	88
89	1.2488 4901	1.3447 0320	1.4478 2568	1.5022 8113	89
90	1.2519 7114	1.3491 8554	1.4538 5829	1.5091 6658	90
91	1.2551 0106	1.3536 8283	1.4599 1603	1.5160 8360	91
92	1.2582 3882	1.3581 9510	1.4659 9902	1.5230 3231	92
93	1.2613 8441	1.3627 2242	1.4721 0735	1.5300 1288	93
94	1.2645 3787	1.3672 6483	1.4782 4113	1.5370 2544	94
95	1.2676 9922	1.3718 2238	1.4844 0047	1.5440 7014	95
96	1.2708 6847	1.3763 9512	1.4905 8547	1.5514 4712	96
97	1.2740 4564	1.3809 8310	1.4967 9624	1.5582 5655	97
98	1.2772 3075	1.3855 8638	1.5030 3289	1.5653 9856	98
99	1.2804 2383	1.3902 0500	1.5092 9553	1.5725 7330	99
100	1.2836 2489	1.3948 3902	1.5155 8426	1.5797 8093	100
101	1.2868 3395	1.3994 8848	1.5218 9919	1.5870 2159	101
102	1.2900 5104	1.4041 5344	1.5282 4044	1.5942 9544	102
103	1.2932 7616	1.4088 3395	1.5346 0811	1.6016 0263	103
104	1.2965 0935	1.4135 3007	1.5410 0231	1.6089 4331	104
105	1.2997 5063	1.4182 4183	1.5474 2315	1.6163 1763	105
106	1.3030 0000	1.4229 6931	1.5538 7075	1.6237 2575	106
107	1.3062 5750	1.4277 1254	1.5603 4521	1.6311 6783	107
108	1.3095 2315	1.4324 7158	1.5668 4665	1.6386 4401	108
109	1.3127 9696	1.4372 4649	1.5733 7518	1.6461 5447	109
110	1.3160 7895	1.4420 3731	1.5799 3091	1.6536 9934	110
111	1.3193 6915	1.4468 4410	1.5865 1395	1.6612 7880	111
112	1.3226 6757	1.4516 6691	1.5931 2443	1.6688 9299	112
113	1.3259 7424	1.4565 0580	1.5997 6245	1.6765 4208	113
114	1.3292 8917	1.4613 6082	1.6064 2812	1.6842 2623	114
115	1.3326 1240	1.4662 3202	1.6131 2157	1.6919 4560	115
116	1.3359 4393	1.4711 1946	1.6198 4291	1.6997 0036	116
117	1.3392 8379	1.4760 2320	1.6265 9226	1.7074 9065	117
118	1.3426 3200	1.4809 4327	1.6333 6973	1.7153 1665	118
119	1.3459 8858	1.4858 7975	1.6401 7543	1.7231 7852	119
120	1.3493 5355	1.4908 3268	1.6470 0950	1.7310 7642	120

TABLE 5 COMPOUND AMOUNT
WHEN PRINCIPAL IS 1

$$s = (1 + i)^n$$

n	$\frac{1}{4}\%$	$\frac{1}{3}\%$	$\frac{5}{12}\%$	$\frac{11}{24}\%$	n
121	1.3527 2693	1.4958 0212	1.6538 7204	1.7390 1052	121
122	1.3561 0875	1.5007 8813	1.6607 6317	1.7469 8098	122
123	1.3594 9902	1.5057 9076	1.6676 8302	1.7549 8798	123
124	1.3628 9777	1.5108 1006	1.6746 3170	1.7630 3167	124
125	1.3663 0501	1.5158 4609	1.6816 0933	1.7711 1224	125
126	1.3697 2077	1.5208 9892	1.6886 1603	1.7792 2983	126
127	1.3731 4508	1.5259 6858	1.6956 5193	1.7873 8464	127
128	1.3765 7794	1.5310 5514	1.7027 1715	1.7955 7682	128
129	1.3800 1938	1.5361 5866	1.7098 1181	1.8038 0654	129
130	1.3834 6943	1.5412 7919	1.7169 3602	1.8120 7399	130
131	1.3869 2811	1.5464 1678	1.7240 8992	1.8203 7933	131
132	1.3903 9543	1.5515 7151	1.7312 7363	1.8287 2273	132
133	1.3938 7142	1.5567 4341	1.7384 8727	1.8371 0438	133
134	1.3973 5609	1.5619 3256	1.7457 3097	1.8455 2444	134
135	1.4008 4948	1.5671 3900	1.7530 0485	1.8539 8310	135
136	1.4043 5161	1.5723 6279	1.7603 0903	1.8624 8052	136
137	1.4078 6249	1.5776 0400	1.7676 4365	1.8710 1689	137
138	1.4113 8214	1.5828 6268	1.7750 0884	1.8795 9238	138
139	1.4149 1060	1.5881 3889	1.7824 0471	1.8882 0718	139
140	1.4184 4787	1.5934 3269	1.7898 3139	1.8968 6146	140
141	1.4219 9399	1.5987 4413	1.7972 8902	1.9055 5541	141
142	1.4255 4898	1.6040 7328	1.8047 7773	1.9142 8921	142
143	1.4291 1285	1.6094 2019	1.8122 9763	1.9230 6303	143
144	1.4326 8563	1.6147 8492	1.8198 4887	1.9318 7707	144
145	1.4362 6735	1.6201 6754	1.8274 3158	1.9407 3151	145
146	1.4398 5802	1.6255 6810	1.8350 4588	1.9496 2653	146
147	1.4434 5766	1.6309 8666	1.8426 9190	1.9585 6231	147
148	1.4470 6631	1.6364 2328	1.8503 6978	1.9675 3906	148
149	1.4506 8397	1.6418 7802	1.8580 7966	1.9765 5695	149
150	1.4543 1068	1.6473 5095	1.8658 2166	1.9856 1617	150
151	1.4579 4646	1.6528 4212	1.8735 9591	1.9947 1691	151
152	1.4615 9132	1.6583 5160	1.8814 0256	2.0038 5936	152
153	1.4652 4530	1.6638 7943	1.8892 4174	2.0130 4371	153
154	1.4689 0842	1.6694 2570	1.8971 1358	2.0222 7016	154
155	1.4725 8069	1.6749 9045	1.9050 1822	2.0315 3890	155
156	1.4762 6214	1.6805 7375	1.9129 5580	2.0408 5012	156
157	1.4799 5279	1.6861 7566	1.9209 2645	2.0502 0402	157
158	1.4836 5268	1.6917 9625	1.9289 3031	2.0596 0079	158
159	1.4873 6181	1.6974 3557	1.9369 6752	2.0690 4062	159
160	1.4910 8021	1.7030 9369	1.9450 3821	2.0785 2373	160
161	1.4948 0791	1.7087 7067	1.9531 4254	2.0880 5029	161
162	1.4985 4493	1.7144 6657	1.9612 8063	2.0976 2053	162
163	1.5022 9129	1.7201 8146	1.9694 5264	2.1072 3462	163
164	1.5060 4702	1.7259 1540	1.9776 5869	2.1168 9278	164
165	1.5098 1214	1.7316 6845	1.9858 9893	2.1265 9520	165
166	1.5135 8667	1.7374 4068	1.9941 7351	2.1363 4210	166
167	1.5173 7064	1.7432 3215	2.0024 8257	2.1461 3367	167
168	1.5211 6406	1.7490 4292	2.0108 2625	2.1559 7011	168
169	1.5249 6697	1.7548 7306	2.0192 0469	2.1658 5164	169
170	1.5287 7939	1.7607 2264	2.0276 1804	2.1757 7846	170
171	1.5326 0134	1.7665 9172	2.0360 6645	2.1857 5078	171
172	1.5364 3284	1.7724 8035	2.0445 5006	2.1957 6880	172
173	1.5402 7393	1.7783 8862	2.0530 6902	2.2058 3274	173
174	1.5441 2461	1.7843 1658	2.0616 2347	2.2159 4281	174
175	1.5479 8492	1.7902 6431	2.0702 1357	2.2260 9922	175
176	1.5518 5488	1.7962 3185	2.0788 3946	2.2363 0217	176
177	1.5557 3452	1.8022 1929	2.0875 0129	2.2465 5189	177
178	1.5596 2386	1.8082 2669	2.0961 9921	2.2568 4858	178
179	1.5635 2292	1.8142 5411	2.1049 3338	2.2671 9247	179
180	1.5674 3172	1.8203 0163	2.1137 0393	2.2775 8377	180

TABLE 5 COMPOUND AMOUNT
WHEN PRINCIPAL IS 1

$$s = (1 + i)^n$$

n	$\frac{1}{4}\%$	$\frac{1}{3}\%$	$\frac{5}{12}\%$	$\frac{11}{24}\%$	n
181	1.5713 5030	1.8263 6930	2.1225 1103	2.2880 2270	181
182	1.5752 7868	1.8324 5720	2.1313 5483	2.2985 0947	182
183	1.5792 1688	1.8385 6539	2.1402 3547	2.3090 4430	183
184	1.5831 6492	1.8446 9394	2.1491 5312	2.3196 2742	184
185	1.5871 2283	1.8508 4292	2.1581 0793	2.3302 5905	185
186	1.5910 9064	1.8570 1240	2.1671 0004	2.3409 3940	186
187	1.5950 6836	1.8632 0244	2.1761 2963	2.3516 6871	187
188	1.5990 5604	1.8694 1311	2.1851 9683	2.3624 4719	188
189	1.6030 5368	1.8756 4449	2.1943 0182	2.3732 7507	189
190	1.6070 6131	1.8818 9664	2.2034 4474	2.3841 5258	190
191	1.6110 7896	1.8881 6963	2.2126 2576	2.3950 7995	191
192	1.6151 0666	1.8944 6352	2.2218 4504	2.4060 5740	192
193	1.6191 4443	1.9007 7840	2.2311 0272	2.4170 8516	193
194	1.6231 9229	1.9071 1433	2.2403 9899	2.4281 6347	194
195	1.6272 5027	1.9134 7138	2.2497 3398	2.4392 9255	195
196	1.6313 1839	1.9198 4962	2.2591 0787	2.4504 7264	196
197	1.6353 9669	1.9262 4912	2.2685 2082	2.4617 0398	197
198	1.6394 8518	1.9326 6995	2.2779 7299	2.4729 8679	198
199	1.6435 8390	1.9391 1218	2.2874 6455	2.4843 2131	199
200	1.6476 9285	1.9455 7589	2.2969 9565	2.4957 0778	200
201	1.6518 1209	1.9520 6114	2.3065 6646	2.5071 4644	201
202	1.6559 4162	1.9585 6801	2.3161 7716	2.5186 3753	202
203	1.6600 8147	1.9650 9657	2.3258 2790	2.5301 8129	203
204	1.6642 3168	1.9716 4689	2.3355 1885	2.5417 7795	204
205	1.6683 9225	1.9782 1905	2.3452 5017	2.5534 2777	205
206	1.6725 6323	1.9848 1311	2.3550 2205	2.5651 3098	206
207	1.6767 4464	1.9914 2915	2.3648 3464	2.5768 8783	207
208	1.6809 3650	1.9980 6725	2.3746 8812	2.5886 9856	208
209	1.6851 3885	2.0047 2748	2.3845 8265	2.6005 6343	209
210	1.6893 5169	2.0114 0990	2.3945 1841	2.6124 8268	210
211	1.6935 7507	2.0181 1460	2.4044 9557	2.6244 5656	211
212	1.6978 0901	2.0248 4165	2.4145 1431	2.6364 8532	212
213	1.7020 5353	2.0315 9112	2.4245 7478	2.6485 6921	213
214	1.7063 0867	2.0383 6309	2.4346 7718	2.6607 0848	214
215	1.7105 7444	2.0451 5764	2.4448 2167	2.6729 0340	215
216	1.7148 5087	2.0519 7483	2.4550 0842	2.6851 5421	216
217	1.7191 3800	2.0588 1474	2.4652 3762	2.6974 6116	217
218	1.7234 3585	2.0656 7746	2.4755 0945	2.7098 2453	218
219	1.7277 4444	2.0725 6305	2.4858 2407	2.7222 4456	219
220	1.7320 6380	2.0794 7159	2.4961 8167	2.7347 2151	220
221	1.7363 9396	2.0864 0317	2.5065 8243	2.7472 5565	221
222	1.7407 3494	2.0933 5784	2.5170 2652	2.7598 4724	222
223	1.7450 8678	2.1003 3570	2.5275 1413	2.7724 9654	223
224	1.7494 4950	2.1073 3682	2.5380 4544	2.7852 0381	224
225	1.7538 2312	2.1143 6128	2.5486 2063	2.7979 6933	225
226	1.7582 0768	2.1214 0915	2.5592 3988	2.8107 9336	226
227	1.7626 0320	2.1284 8051	2.5699 0338	2.8236 7616	227
228	1.7670 0970	2.1355 7545	2.5806 1131	2.8366 1801	228
229	1.7714 2723	2.1426 9403	2.5913 6386	2.8496 1918	229
230	1.7758 5580	2.1498 3635	2.6021 6121	2.8626 7993	230
231	1.7802 9544	2.1570 0247	2.6130 0355	2.8758 0055	231
232	1.7847 4617	2.1641 9248	2.6238 9106	2.8889 8130	232
233	1.7892 0804	2.1714 0645	2.6348 2394	2.9022 2246	233
234	1.7936 8106	2.1786 4447	2.6458 0238	2.9155 2432	234
235	1.7981 6526	2.1859 0662	2.6568 2655	2.9288 8714	235
236	1.8026 6068	2.1931 9298	2.6678 9666	2.9423 1120	236
237	1.8071 6733	2.2005 0362	2.6790 1290	2.9557 9679	237
238	1.8116 8525	2.2078 3863	2.6901 7545	2.9693 4420	238
239	1.8162 1446	2.2151 9809	2.7013 8452	2.9829 5369	239
240	1.8207 5500	2.2225 8209	2.7126 4029	2.9966 2556	240

TABLE 5 COMPOUND AMOUNT

WHEN PRINCIPAL IS 1

$$s = (1 + i)^n$$

n	$\frac{1}{2}\%$	$\frac{13}{24}\%$	$\frac{7}{12}\%$	$\frac{5}{8}\%$	n
1	1.0050 0000	1.0054 1667	1.0058 3333	1.0062 5000	1
2	1.0100 2500	1.0108 6267	1.0117 0069	1.0125 3906	2
3	1.0150 7513	1.0163 3818	1.0176 0228	1.0188 6743	3
4	1.0201 5050	1.0218 4334	1.0235 3830	1.0252 3535	4
5	1.0252 5125	1.0273 7833	1.0295 0894	1.0316 4307	5
6	1.0303 7751	1.0329 4330	1.0355 1440	1.0380 9084	6
7	1.0355 2940	1.0385 3841	1.0415 5490	1.0445 7891	7
8	1.0407 0704	1.0441 6382	1.0476 3064	1.0511 0753	8
9	1.0459 1058	1.0498 1971	1.0537 4182	1.0576 7695	9
10	1.0511 4013	1.0555 0623	1.0598 8865	1.0642 8743	10
11	1.0563 9583	1.0612 2356	1.0660 7133	1.0709 3923	11
12	1.0616 7781	1.0669 7185	1.0722 9008	1.0776 3260	12
13	1.0669 8620	1.0727 5128	1.0785 4511	1.0843 6780	13
14	1.0723 2113	1.0785 6202	1.0848 3662	1.0911 4510	14
15	1.0776 8274	1.0844 0423	1.0911 6483	1.0979 6476	15
16	1.0830 7115	1.0902 7809	1.0975 2996	1.1048 2704	16
17	1.0884 8651	1.0961 8376	1.1039 3222	1.1117 3221	17
18	1.0939 2894	1.1021 2142	1.1103 7182	1.1186 8053	18
19	1.0993 9858	1.1080 9125	1.1168 4899	1.1256 7229	19
20	1.1048 9558	1.1140 9341	1.1233 6395	1.1327 0774	20
21	1.1104 2006	1.1201 2808	1.1299 1690	1.1397 8716	21
22	1.1159 7216	1.1261 9544	1.1365 0808	1.1469 1083	22
23	1.1215 5202	1.1322 9566	1.1431 3771	1.1540 7902	23
24	1.1271 5978	1.1384 2893	1.1498 0602	1.1612 9202	24
25	1.1327 9558	1.1445 9542	1.1565 1322	1.1685 5009	25
26	1.1384 5955	1.1507 9531	1.1632 5955	1.1758 5353	26
27	1.1441 5185	1.1570 2879	1.1700 4523	1.1832 0262	27
28	1.1498 7261	1.1632 9603	1.1768 7049	1.1905 9763	28
29	1.1556 2197	1.1695 9722	1.1837 3557	1.1980 3887	29
30	1.1614 0008	1.1759 3253	1.1906 4069	1.2055 2661	30
31	1.1672 0708	1.1823 0217	1.1975 8610	1.2130 6115	31
32	1.1730 4312	1.1887 0631	1.2045 7202	1.2206 4278	32
33	1.1789 0833	1.1951 4513	1.2115 9869	1.2282 7180	33
34	1.1848 0288	1.2016 1883	1.2186 6634	1.2359 4850	34
35	1.1907 2689	1.2081 2760	1.2257 7523	1.2436 7318	35
36	1.1966 8052	1.2146 7163	1.2329 2559	1.2514 4614	36
37	1.2026 6393	1.2212 5110	1.2401 1765	1.2592 6767	37
38	1.2086 7725	1.2278 6621	1.2473 5167	1.2671 3810	38
39	1.2147 2063	1.2345 1715	1.2546 2789	1.2750 5771	39
40	1.2207 9424	1.2412 0412	1.2619 4655	1.2830 2682	40
41	1.2268 9821	1.2479 2731	1.2693 0791	1.2910 4574	41
42	1.2330 3270	1.2546 8691	1.2767 1220	1.2991 1477	42
43	1.2391 9786	1.2614 8313	1.2841 5969	1.3072 3424	43
44	1.2453 9385	1.2683 1617	1.2916 5062	1.3154 0446	44
45	1.2516 2082	1.2751 8621	1.2991 8525	1.3236 2573	45
46	1.2578 7892	1.2820 9347	1.3067 6383	1.3318 9839	46
47	1.2641 6832	1.2890 3815	1.3143 8662	1.3402 2276	47
48	1.2704 8916	1.2960 2044	1.3220 5388	1.3485 9915	48
49	1.2768 4161	1.3030 4055	1.3297 6586	1.3570 2790	49
50	1.2832 2581	1.3100 9868	1.3375 2283	1.3655 0932	50
51	1.2896 4194	1.3171 9505	1.3453 2504	1.3740 4375	51
52	1.2960 9015	1.3243 2986	1.3531 7277	1.3826 3153	52
53	1.3025 7060	1.3315 0331	1.3610 6628	1.3912 7297	53
54	1.3090 8346	1.3387 1562	1.3690 0583	1.3999 6843	54
55	1.3156 2887	1.3459 6700	1.3769 9170	1.4087 1823	55
56	1.3222 0702	1.3532 5765	1.3850 2415	1.4175 2272	56
57	1.3288 1805	1.3605 8780	1.3931 0346	1.4263 8224	57
58	1.3354 6214	1.3679 5765	1.4012 2990	1.4352 9713	58
59	1.3421 3946	1.3753 6742	1.4094 0374	1.4442 6773	59
60	1.3488 5015	1.3828 1732	1.4176 2526	1.4532 9441	60

TABLE 5 COMPOUND AMOUNT
WHEN PRINCIPAL IS 1

$$s = (1 + i)^n$$

n	$\frac{1}{2}$%	$\frac{13}{24}$%	$\frac{7}{12}$%	$\frac{5}{8}$%	n
61	1.3555 9440	1.3903 0758	1.4258 9474	1.4623 7750	61
62	1.3623 7238	1.3978 3842	1.4342 1246	1.4715 1736	62
63	1.3691 8424	1.4054 1004	1.4425 7870	1.4807 1434	63
64	1.3760 3016	1.4130 2268	1.4509 9374	1.4899 6881	64
65	1.3829 1031	1.4206 7655	1.4594 5787	1.4992 8111	65
66	1.3898 2486	1.4283 7188	1.4679 7138	1.5086 5162	66
67	1.3967 7399	1.4361 0890	1.4765 3454	1.5180 8069	67
68	1.4037 5785	1.4438 8782	1.4851 4766	1.5275 6869	68
69	1.4107 7664	1.4517 0888	1.4938 1102	1.5371 1600	69
70	1.4178 3053	1.4595 7230	1.5025 2492	1.5467 2297	70
71	1.4249 1968	1.4674 7832	1.5112 8965	1.5563 8999	71
72	1.4320 4428	1.4754 2716	1.5201 0550	1.5661 1743	72
73	1.4392 0450	1.4834 1906	1.5289 7279	1.5759 0566	73
74	1.4464 0052	1.4914 5425	1.5378 9179	1.5857 5507	74
75	1.4536 3252	1.4995 3296	1.5468 6283	1.5956 6604	75
76	1.4609 0069	1.5076 5543	1.5558 8620	1.6056 3896	76
77	1.4682 0519	1.5158 2189	1.5649 6220	1.6156 7420	77
78	1.4755 4622	1.5240 3259	1.5740 9115	1.6257 7216	78
79	1.4829 2395	1.5322 8777	1.5832 7334	1.6359 3324	79
80	1.4903 3857	1.5405 8766	1.5925 0910	1.6461 5782	80
81	1.4977 9026	1.5489 3251	1.6017 9874	1.6564 4631	81
82	1.5052 7921	1.5573 2256	1.6111 4257	1.6667 9910	82
83	1.5128 0561	1.5657 5806	1.6205 4090	1.6772 1659	83
84	1.5203 6964	1.5742 3925	1.6299 9405	1.6876 9920	84
85	1.5279 7148	1.5827 6638	1.6395 0235	1.6982 4732	85
86	1.5356 1134	1.5913 3970	1.6490 6612	1.7088 6136	86
87	1.5432 8940	1.5999 5945	1.6586 8567	1.7195 4175	87
88	1.5510 0585	1.6086 2590	1.6683 6134	1.7302 8888	88
89	1.5587 6087	1.6173 3929	1.6780 9344	1.7411 0319	89
90	1.5665 5468	1.6260 9988	1.6878 8232	1.7519 8508	90
91	1.5743 8745	1.6349 0792	1.6977 2830	1.7629 3499	91
92	1.5822 5939	1.6437 6367	1.7076 3172	1.7739 5333	92
93	1.5901 7069	1.6526 6739	1.7175 9290	1.7850 4054	93
94	1.5981 2154	1.6616 1934	1.7276 1219	1.7961 9704	94
95	1.6061 1215	1.6706 1978	1.7376 8993	1.8074 2328	95
96	1.6141 4271	1.6796 6897	1.7478 2646	1.8187 1967	96
97	1.6222 1342	1.6887 6718	1.7580 2211	1.8300 8667	97
98	1.6303 2449	1.6979 1466	1.7682 7724	1.8415 2471	98
99	1.6384 7611	1.7071 1170	1.7785 9219	1.8530 3424	99
100	1.6466 6849	1.7163 5856	1.7889 6731	1.8646 1570	100
101	1.6549 0183	1.7256 5550	1.7994 0295	1.8762 6955	101
102	1.6631 7634	1.7350 0280	1.8098 9947	1.8879 9624	102
103	1.6714 9223	1.7444 0073	1.8204 5722	1.8997 9621	103
104	1.6798 4969	1.7538 4957	1.8310 7655	1.9116 6994	104
105	1.6882 4894	1.7633 4959	1.8417 5783	1.9236 1788	105
106	1.6966 9018	1.7729 0107	1.8525 0142	1.9356 4049	106
107	1.7051 7363	1.7825 0428	1.8633 0768	1.9477 3824	107
108	1.7136 9950	1.7921 5951	1.8741 7697	1.9599 1161	108
109	1.7222 6800	1.8018 6704	1.8851 0967	1.9721 6105	109
110	1.7308 7934	1.8116 2715	1.8961 0614	1.9844 8706	110
111	1.7395 3373	1.8214 4013	1.9071 6676	1.9968 9010	111
112	1.7482 3140	1.8313 0627	1.9182 9190	2.0093 7067	112
113	1.7569 7256	1.8412 2584	1.9294 8194	2.0219 2923	113
114	1.7657 5742	1.8511 9915	1.9407 3725	2.0345 6629	114
115	1.7745 8621	1.8612 2648	1.9520 5822	2.0472 8233	115
116	1.7834 5914	1.8713 0812	1.9634 4522	2.0600 7785	116
117	1.7923 7644	1.8814 4438	1.9748 9865	2.0729 5333	117
118	1.8013 3832	1.8916 3553	1.9864 1890	2.0859 0929	118
119	1.8103 4501	1.9018 8189	1.9980 0634	2.0989 4622	119
120	1.8193 9673	1.9121 8375	2.0096 6138	2.1120 6464	120

TABLE 5 COMPOUND AMOUNT

WHEN PRINCIPAL IS 1

$$s = (1 + i)^n$$

n	$\frac{1}{2}\%$	$\frac{13}{24}\%$	$\frac{7}{12}\%$	$\frac{5}{8}\%$	n
121	1.8284 9372	1.9225 4141	2.0213 8440	2.1252 6504	121
122	1.8376 3619	1.9329 5518	2.0331 7581	2.1385 4795	122
123	1.8468 2437	1.9434 2535	2.0450 3600	2.1519 1387	123
124	1.8560 5849	1.9539 5224	2.0569 6538	2.1653 6333	124
125	1.8653 3878	1.9645 3615	2.0689 6434	2.1788 9685	125
126	1.8746 6548	1.9751 7739	2.0810 3330	2.1925 1496	126
127	1.8840 3880	1.9858 7626	2.0931 7266	2.2062 1818	127
128	1.8934 5900	1.9966 3309	2.1053 8284	2.2200 0704	128
129	1.9029 2629	2.0074 4819	2.1176 6424	2.2338 8209	129
130	1.9124 4092	2.0183 2187	2.1300 1728	2.2478 4385	130
131	1.9220 0313	2.0292 5444	2.1424 4238	2.2618 9287	131
132	1.9316 1314	2.0402 4624	2.1549 3996	2.2760 2970	132
133	1.9412 7121	2.0512 9757	2.1675 1044	2.2902 5489	133
134	1.9509 7757	2.0624 0877	2.1801 5425	2.3045 6898	134
135	1.9607 3245	2.0735 8015	2.1928 7182	2.3189 7254	135
136	1.9705 3612	2.0848 1204	2.2056 6357	2.3334 6612	136
137	1.9803 8880	2.0961 0477	2.2185 2994	2.3480 5028	137
138	1.9902 9074	2.1074 5867	2.2314 7137	2.3627 2559	138
139	2.0002 4219	2.1188 7408	2.2444 8828	2.3774 9263	139
140	2.0102 4340	2.1303 5131	2.2575 8113	2.3923 5196	140
141	2.0202 9462	2.1418 9071	2.2707 5036	2.4073 0416	141
142	2.0303 9609	2.1534 9262	2.2839 9640	2.4223 4981	142
143	2.0405 4808	2.1651 5737	2.2973 1971	2.4374 8950	143
144	2.0507 5082	2.1768 8531	2.3107 2074	2.4527 2380	144
145	2.0610 0457	2.1886 7677	2.3241 9995	2.4680 5333	145
146	2.0713 0959	2.2005 3210	2.3377 5778	2.4834 7866	146
147	2.0816 6614	2.2124 5165	2.3513 9470	2.4990 0040	147
148	2.0920 7447	2.2244 3577	2.3651 1117	2.5146 1916	148
149	2.1025 3484	2.2364 8479	2.3789 0765	2.5303 3553	149
150	2.1130 4752	2.2485 9908	2.3927 8461	2.5461 5012	150
151	2.1236 1276	2.2607 7900	2.4067 4252	2.5620 6356	151
152	2.1342 3082	2.2730 2488	2.4207 8186	2.5780 7646	152
153	2.1449 0197	2.2853 3710	2.4349 0308	2.5941 8944	153
154	2.1556 2648	2.2977 1601	2.4491 0668	2.6104 0312	154
155	2.1664 0462	2.3101 6197	2.4633 9314	2.6267 1814	155
156	2.1772 3664	2.3226 7535	2.4777 6293	2.6431 3513	156
157	2.1881 2282	2.3352 5651	2.4922 1655	2.6596 5472	157
158	2.1990 6344	2.3479 0581	2.5067 5448	2.6762 7756	158
159	2.2100 5875	2.3606 2364	2.5213 7722	2.6930 0430	159
160	2.2211 0905	2.3734 1035	2.5360 8525	2.7098 3558	160
161	2.2322 1459	2.3862 6632	2.5508 7908	2.7267 7205	161
162	2.2433 7566	2.3991 9193	2.5657 5921	2.7438 1437	162
163	2.2545 9254	2.4121 8755	2.5807 2614	2.7609 6321	163
164	2.2658 6551	2.4252 5357	2.5957 8037	2.7782 1923	164
165	2.2771 9483	2.4383 9036	2.6109 2242	2.7955 8310	165
166	2.2885 8081	2.4515 9831	2.6261 5280	2.8130 5550	166
167	2.3000 2371	2.4648 7780	2.6414 7203	2.8306 3710	167
168	2.3115 2383	2.4782 2922	2.6568 8062	2.8483 2858	168
169	2.3230 8145	2.4916 5296	2.6723 7909	2.8661 3063	169
170	2.3346 9686	2.5051 4941	2.6879 6796	2.8840 4395	170
171	2.3463 7034	2.5187 1897	2.7036 4778	2.9020 6922	171
172	2.3581 0219	2.5323 6203	2.7194 1906	2.9202 0715	172
173	2.3698 9270	2.5460 7900	2.7352 8233	2.9384 5845	173
174	2.3817 4217	2.5598 7026	2.7512 3815	2.9568 2381	174
175	2.3936 5088	2.5737 3622	2.7672 8704	2.9753 0396	175
176	2.4056 1913	2.5876 7729	2.7834 2954	2.9938 9961	176
177	2.4176 4723	2.6016 9388	2.7996 6622	3.0126 1149	177
178	2.4297 3546	2.6157 8639	2.8159 9760	3.0314 4031	178
179	2.4418 8414	2.6299 5523	2.8324 2426	3.0503 8681	179
180	2.4540 9356	2.6442 0082	2.8489 4673	3.0694 5173	180

TABLE 5 COMPOUND AMOUNT
WHEN PRINCIPAL IS 1

$$s = (1 + i)^n$$

n	$\frac{1}{2}\%$	$\frac{13}{24}\%$	$\frac{7}{12}\%$	$\frac{5}{8}\%$	n
181	2.4663 6403	2.6585 2357	2.8655 6559	3.0886 3580	181
182	2.4786 9585	2.6729 2391	2.8822 8139	3.1079 3977	182
183	2.4910 8933	2.6874 0225	2.8990 9469	3.1272 6440	183
184	2.5035 4478	2.7019 5901	2.9160 0608	3.1469 1043	184
185	2.5160 6250	2.7165 9462	2.9330 1612	3.1665 7862	185
186	2.5286 4281	2.7313 0951	2.9501 2538	3.1863 6973	186
187	2.5412 8603	2.7461 0410	2.9673 3444	3.2062 8454	187
188	2.5539 9246	2.7609 7883	2.9846 4389	3.2263 2382	188
189	2.5667 6242	2.7759 3413	3.0020 5431	3.2464 8834	189
190	2.5795 9623	2.7909 7044	3.0195 6630	3.2667 7890	190
191	2.5924 9421	2.8060 8820	3.0371 8043	3.2871 9627	191
192	2.6054 5668	2.8212 8785	3.0548 9732	3.3077 4124	192
193	2.6184 8397	2.8365 6982	3.0727 1755	3.3284 1462	193
194	2.6315 7639	2.8519 3457	3.0906 4174	3.3492 1722	194
195	2.6447 3427	2.8673 8255	3.1086 7048	3.3701 4982	195
196	2.6579 5794	2.8829 1421	3.1268 0440	3.3912 1326	196
197	2.6712 4773	2.8985 2999	3.1450 4409	3.4124 0834	197
198	2.6846 0397	2.9142 3037	3.1633 9018	3.4337 3589	198
199	2.6980 2699	2.9300 1578	3.1818 4329	3.4551 9674	199
200	2.7115 1712	2.9458 8670	3.2004 0404	3.4767 9172	200
201	2.7250 7471	2.9618 4358	3.2190 7306	3.4985 2167	201
202	2.7387 0008	2.9778 8690	3.2378 5099	3.5203 8743	202
203	2.7523 9358	2.9940 1712	3.2567 3845	3.5423 8985	203
204	2.7661 5555	3.0102 3472	3.2757 3609	3.5645 2979	204
205	2.7799 8633	3.0265 4016	3.2948 4456	3.5868 0810	205
206	2.7938 8626	3.0429 3391	3.3140 6448	3.6092 2565	206
207	2.8078 5569	3.0594 1647	3.3333 9652	3.6317 8331	207
208	2.8218 9497	3.0759 8831	3.3528 4134	3.6544 8196	208
209	2.8360 0444	3.0926 4992	3.3723 9958	3.6773 2247	209
210	2.8501 8447	3.1094 0177	3.3920 7191	3.7003 0574	210
211	2.8644 3539	3.1262 4436	3.4118 5900	3.7234 3265	211
212	2.8787 5757	3.1431 7819	3.4317 6151	3.7467 0410	212
213	2.8931 5135	3.1602 0373	3.4517 8012	3.7701 2100	213
214	2.9076 1711	3.1773 2151	3.4719 1550	3.7936 8426	214
215	2.9221 5520	3.1945 3200	3.4921 6834	3.8173 9478	215
216	2.9367 6597	3.2118 3571	3.5125 3932	3.8412 5350	216
217	2.9514 4980	3.2292 3315	3.5330 2913	3.8652 6134	217
218	2.9662 0705	3.2467 2483	3.5536 3847	3.8894 1922	218
219	2.9810 3809	3.2643 1126	3.5743 6803	3.9137 2809	219
220	2.9959 4328	3.2819 9295	3.5952 1851	3.9381 8889	220
221	3.0109 2299	3.2997 7041	3.6161 9062	3.9628 0257	221
222	3.0259 7761	3.3176 4416	3.6372 8506	3.9875 7009	222
223	3.0411 0750	3.3356 1474	3.6585 0256	4.0124 9240	223
224	3.0563 1303	3.3536 8265	3.6798 4382	4.0375 7048	224
225	3.0715 9460	3.3718 4843	3.7013 0958	4.0628 0529	225
226	3.0869 5257	3.3901 1261	3.7229 0055	4.0881 9783	226
227	3.1023 8733	3.4084 7572	3.7446 1747	4.1137 4906	227
228	3.1178 9927	3.4269 3830	3.7664 6107	4.1394 5999	228
229	3.1334 8877	3.4455 0088	3.7884 3210	4.1653 3162	229
230	3.1491 5621	3.4641 6401	3.8105 3128	4.1913 6494	230
231	3.1649 0199	3.4829 2823	3.8327 5938	4.2175 6097	231
232	3.1807 2650	3.5017 9409	3.8551 1715	4.2439 2073	232
233	3.1966 3013	3.5207 6214	3.8776 0533	4.2704 4523	233
234	3.2126 1329	3.5398 3294	3.9002 2469	4.2971 3552	234
235	3.2286 7635	3.5590 0703	3.9229 7600	4.3239 9261	235
236	3.2448 1973	3.5782 8499	3.9458 6003	4.3510 1757	236
237	3.2610 4383	3.5976 6737	3.9688 7755	4.3782 1143	237
238	3.2773 4905	3.6171 5473	3.9920 2933	4.4055 7525	238
239	3.2937 3580	3.6367 4765	4.0153 1617	4.4331 1009	239
240	3.3102 0448	3.6564 4670	4.0387 3885	4.4608 1703	240

TABLE 5 COMPOUND AMOUNT
WHEN PRINCIPAL IS 1

$$s = (1 + i)^n$$

n	$\frac{2}{3}\%$	$\frac{3}{4}\%$	$\frac{7}{8}\%$	1%	n
1	1.0066 6667	1.0075 0000	1.0087 5000	1.0100 0000	1
2	1.0133 7778	1.0150 5625	1.0175 7656	1.0201 0000	2
3	1.0201 3363	1.0226 6917	1.0264 8036	1.0303 0100	3
4	1.0269 3452	1.0303 3919	1.0354 6206	1.0406 0401	4
5	1.0337 8075	1.0380 6673	1.0445 2235	1.0510 1005	5
6	1.0406 7262	1.0458 5224	1.0536 6192	1.0615 2015	6
7	1.0476 1044	1.0536 9613	1.0628 8147	1.0721 3535	7
8	1.0545 9451	1.0615 9885	1.0721 8168	1.0828 5671	8
9	1.0616 2514	1.0695 6084	1.0815 6327	1.0936 8527	9
10	1.0687 0264	1.0775 8255	1.0910 2695	1.1046 2213	10
11	1.0758 2732	1.0856 6441	1.1005 7343	1.1156 6835	11
12	1.0829 9951	1.0938 0690	1.1102 0345	1.1268 2503	12
13	1.0902 1950	1.1020 1045	1.1199 1773	1.1380 9328	13
14	1.0974 8763	1.1102 7553	1.1297 1701	1.1494 7421	14
15	1.1048 0422	1.1186 0259	1.1396 0203	1.1609 6896	15
16	1.1121 6958	1.1269 9211	1.1495 7355	1.1725 7864	16
17	1.1195 8404	1.1354 4455	1.1596 3232	1.1843 0443	17
18	1.1270 4794	1.1439 6039	1.1697 7910	1.1961 4748	18
19	1.1345 6159	1.1525 4009	1.1800 1467	1.2081 0895	19
20	1.1421 2533	1.1611 8414	1.1903 3980	1.2201 9004	20
21	1.1497 3950	1.1698 9302	1.2007 5527	1.2323 9194	21
22	1.1574 0443	1.1786 6722	1.2112 6188	1.2447 1586	22
23	1.1651 2046	1.1875 0723	1.2218 6042	1.2571 6302	23
24	1.1728 8793	1.1964 1353	1.2325 5170	1.2697 3465	24
25	1.1807 0718	1.2053 8663	1.2433 3653	1.2824 3200	25
26	1.1885 7857	1.2144 2703	1.2542 1572	1.2952 5631	26
27	1.1965 0242	1.2235 3523	1.2651 9011	1.3082 0888	27
28	1.2044 7911	1.2327 1175	1.2762 6052	1.3212 9097	28
29	1.2125 0897	1.2419 5709	1.2874 2780	1.3345 0388	29
30	1.2205 9236	1.2512 7176	1.2986 9280	1.3478 4892	30
31	1.2287 2964	1.2606 5630	1.3100 5636	1.3613 2740	31
32	1.2369 2117	1.2701 1122	1.3215 1935	1.3749 4068	32
33	1.2451 6731	1.2796 3706	1.3330 8265	1.3886 9009	33
34	1.2534 6843	1.2892 3434	1.3447 4712	1.4025 7699	34
35	1.2618 2489	1.2989 0359	1.3565 1366	1.4166 0276	35
36	1.2702 3705	1.3086 4537	1.3683 8315	1.4307 6878	36
37	1.2787 0530	1.3184 6021	1.3803 5650	1.4450 7647	37
38	1.2872 3000	1.3283 4866	1.3924 3462	1.4595 2724	38
39	1.2958 1153	1.3383 1128	1.4046 1843	1.4741 2251	39
40	1.3044 5028	1.3483 4861	1.4169 0884	1.4888 6373	40
41	1.3131 4661	1.3584 6123	1.4293 0679	1.5037 5237	41
42	1.3219 0092	1.3686 4969	1.4418 1322	1.5187 8989	42
43	1.3307 1360	1.3789 1456	1.4544 2909	1.5339 7779	43
44	1.3395 8502	1.3892 5642	1.4671 5534	1.5493 1757	44
45	1.3485 1559	1.3996 7584	1.4799 9295	1.5648 1075	45
46	1.3575 0569	1.4101 7341	1.4929 4289	1.5804 5885	46
47	1.3665 5573	1.4207 4971	1.5060 0614	1.5962 6344	47
48	1.3756 6610	1.4314 0533	1.5191 8370	1.6122 2608	48
49	1.3848 3721	1.4421 4087	1.5324 7655	1.6283 4834	49
50	1.3940 6946	1.4529 5693	1.5458 8572	1.6446 3182	50
51	1.4033 6325	1.4638 5411	1.5594 1222	1.6610 7814	51
52	1.4127 1901	1.4748 3301	1.5730 5708	1.6776 8892	52
53	1.4221 3713	1.4858 9426	1.5868 2133	1.6944 6581	53
54	1.4316 1805	1.4970 3847	1.6007 0602	1.7114 1047	54
55	1.4411 6217	1.5082 6626	1.6147 1219	1.7285 2457	55
56	1.4507 6992	1.5195 7825	1.6288 4093	1.7458 0982	56
57	1.4604 4172	1.5309 7509	1.6430 9328	1.7632 6792	57
58	1.4701 7799	1.5424 5740	1.6574 7035	1.7809 0060	58
59	1.4799 7918	1.5540 2583	1.6719 7322	1.7987 0960	59
60	1.4898 4571	1.5656 8103	1.6866 0298	1.8166 9670	60

TABLE 5 COMPOUND AMOUNT
WHEN PRINCIPAL IS 1

$$s = (1 + i)^n$$

n	$\frac{2}{3}\%$	$\frac{3}{4}\%$	$\frac{7}{8}\%$	1%	n
61	1.4997 7801	1.5774 2363	1.7013 6076	1.8348 6367	61
62	1.5097 7653	1.5892 5431	1.7162 4766	1.8532 1230	62
63	1.5198 4171	1.6011 7372	1.7312 6483	1.8717 4443	63
64	1.5299 7399	1.6131 8252	1.7464 1340	1.8904 6187	64
65	1.5401 7381	1.6252 8139	1.7616 9452	1.9093 6649	65
66	1.5504 4164	1.6374 7100	1.7771 0934	1.9284 6015	66
67	1.5607 7792	1.6497 5203	1.7926 5905	1.9477 4475	67
68	1.5711 8310	1.6621 2517	1.8083 4482	1.9672 2220	68
69	1.5816 5766	1.6745 9111	1.8241 6783	1.9868 9442	69
70	1.5922 0204	1.6871 5055	1.8401 2930	2.0067 6337	70
71	1.6028 1672	1.6998 0418	1.8562 3043	2.0268 3100	71
72	1.6135 0217	1.7125 5271	1.8724 7245	2.0470 9931	72
73	1.6242 5885	1.7253 9685	1.8888 5658	2.0675 7031	73
74	1.6350 8724	1.7383 3733	1.9053 8408	2.0882 4601	74
75	1.6459 8782	1.7513 7486	1.9220 5619	2.1091 2847	75
76	1.6569 6107	1.7645 1017	1.9388 7418	2.1302 1975	76
77	1.6680 0748	1.7777 4400	1.9558 3933	2.1515 2195	77
78	1.6791 2753	1.7910 7708	1.9729 5292	2.1730 3717	78
79	1.6903 2172	1.8045 1015	1.9902 1626	2.1947 6754	79
80	1.7015 9053	1.8180 4398	2.0076 3066	2.2167 1522	80
81	1.7129 3446	1.8316 7931	2.0251 9742	2.2388 8237	81
82	1.7243 5403	1.8454 1691	2.0429 1790	2.2612 7119	82
83	1.7358 4972	1.8592 5753	2.0607 9343	2.2838 8390	83
84	1.7474 2205	1.8732 0196	2.0788 2537	2.3067 2274	84
85	1.7590 7153	1.8872 5098	2.0970 1510	2.3297 8997	85
86	1.7707 9868	1.9014 0536	2.1153 6398	2.3530 8787	86
87	1.7826 0400	1.9156 6590	2.1338 7341	2.3766 1875	87
88	1.7944 8803	1.9300 3339	2.1525 4481	2.4003 8494	88
89	1.8064 5128	1.9445 0865	2.1713 7957	2.4243 8879	89
90	1.8184 9429	1.9590 9246	2.1903 7914	2.4486 3267	90
91	1.8306 1758	1.9737 8565	2.2095 4496	2.4731 1900	91
92	1.8428 2170	1.9885 8905	2.2288 7848	2.4978 5019	92
93	1.8551 0718	2.0035 0346	2.2483 8117	2.5228 2869	93
94	1.8674 7456	2.0185 2974	2.2680 5450	2.5480 5698	94
95	1.8799 2439	2.0336 6871	2.2878 9998	2.5735 3755	95
96	1.8924 5722	2.0489 2123	2.3079 1910	2.5992 7293	96
97	1.9050 7360	2.0642 8814	2.3281 1340	2.6252 6565	97
98	1.9177 7409	2.0797 7030	2.3484 8439	2.6515 1831	98
99	1.9305 5925	2.0953 6858	2.3690 3363	2.6780 3349	99
100	1.9434 2965	2.1110 8384	2.3897 6267	2.7048 1383	100
101	1.9563 8585	2.1269 1697	2.4106 7309	2.7318 6197	101
102	1.9694 2842	2.1428 6885	2.4317 6648	2.7591 8059	102
103	1.9825 5794	2.1589 4036	2.4530 4444	2.7867 7239	103
104	1.9957 7499	2.1751 3242	2.4745 0858	2.8146 4012	104
105	2.0090 8016	2.1914 4591	2.4961 6053	2.8427 8652	105
106	2.0224 7403	2.2078 8175	2.5180 0193	2.8712 1438	106
107	2.0359 5719	2.2244 4087	2.5400 3445	2.8999 2653	107
108	2.0495 3024	2.2411 2417	2.5622 5975	2.9289 2579	108
109	2.0631 9377	2.2579 3260	2.5846 7953	2.9582 1505	109
110	2.0769 4840	2.2748 6710	2.6072 9547	2.9877 9720	110
111	2.0907 9472	2.2919 2860	2.6301 0931	3.0176 7517	111
112	2.1047 3335	2.3091 1807	2.6531 2276	3.0478 5192	112
113	2.1187 6491	2.3264 3645	2.6763 3759	3.0783 3044	113
114	2.1328 9000	2.3438 8472	2.6997 5554	3.1091 1375	114
115	2.1471 0927	2.3614 6386	2.7233 7840	3.1402 0489	115
116	2.1614 2333	2.3791 7484	2.7472 0796	3.1716 0693	116
117	2.1758 3282	2.3970 1865	2.7712 4603	3.2033 2300	117
118	2.1903 3837	2.4149 9629	2.7954 9444	3.2353 5623	118
119	2.2049 4063	2.4331 0876	2.8199 5501	3.2677 0980	119
120	2.2196 4023	2.4513 5708	2.8446 2962	3.3003 8689	120

TABLE 5 COMPOUND AMOUNT

WHEN PRINCIPAL IS 1

$$s = (1 + i)^n$$

n	$\frac{2}{3}\%$	$\frac{3}{4}\%$	$\frac{7}{8}\%$	1%	n
121	2.2344 3784	2.4697 4226	2.8695 2013	3.3333 9076	121
122	2.2493 3409	2.4882 6532	2.8946 2843	3.3667 2467	122
123	2.2643 2965	2.5069 2731	2.9199 5643	3.4003 9192	123
124	2.2794 2518	2.5257 2927	2.9455 0605	3.4343 9584	124
125	2.2946 2135	2.5446 7224	2.9712 7922	3.4687 3980	125
126	2.3099 1882	2.5637 5728	2.9972 7792	3.5034 2719	126
127	2.3253 1828	2.5829 8546	3.0235 0410	3.5384 6147	127
128	2.3408 2040	2.6023 5785	3.0499 5976	3.5738 4608	128
129	2.3564 2587	2.6218 7553	3.0766 4691	3.6095 8454	129
130	2.3721 3538	2.6415 3960	3.1035 6757	3.6456 8039	130
131	2.3879 4962	2.6613 5115	3.1307 2378	3.6821 3719	131
132	2.4038 6928	2.6813 1128	3.1581 1762	3.7189 5856	132
133	2.4198 9507	2.7014 2112	3.1857 5115	3.7561 4815	133
134	2.4360 2771	2.7216 8177	3.2136 2647	3.7937 0963	134
135	2.4522 6789	2.7420 9439	3.2417 4570	3.8316 4673	135
136	2.4686 1635	2.7626 6009	3.2701 1098	3.8699 6319	136
137	2.4850 7379	2.7833 8005	3.2987 2445	3.9086 6282	137
138	2.5016 4095	2.8042 5540	3.3275 8829	3.9477 4945	138
139	2.5183 1855	2.8252 8731	3.3567 0468	3.9872 2695	139
140	2.5351 0734	2.8464 7697	3.3860 7585	4.0270 9922	140
141	2.5520 0806	2.8678 2554	3.4157 0401	4.0673 7021	141
142	2.5690 2145	2.8893 3424	3.4455 9142	4.1080 4391	142
143	2.5861 4826	2.9110 0424	3.4757 4035	4.1491 2435	143
144	2.6033 8924	2.9328 3677	3.5061 5308	4.1906 1559	144
145	2.6207 4517	2.9548 3305	3.5368 3192	4.2325 2175	145
146	2.6382 1681	2.9769 9430	3.5677 7919	4.2748 4697	146
147	2.6558 0492	2.9993 2175	3.5989 9726	4.3175 9544	147
148	2.6735 1028	3.0218 1667	3.6304 8849	4.3607 7139	148
149	2.6913 3369	3.0444 8029	3.6622 5526	4.4043 7911	149
150	2.7092 7591	3.0673 1389	3.6943 0000	4.4484 2290	150
151	2.7273 3775	3.0903 1875	3.7266 2512	4.4929 0713	151
152	2.7455 2000	3.1134 9614	3.7592 3309	4.5378 3620	152
153	2.7638 2347	3.1368 4736	3.7921 2638	4.5832 1456	153
154	2.7822 4896	3.1603 7372	3.8253 0749	4.6290 4670	154
155	2.8007 9729	3.1840 7652	3.8587 7893	4.6753 3717	155
156	2.8194 6927	3.2079 5709	3.8925 4324	4.7220 9054	156
157	2.8382 6573	3.2320 1677	3.9266 0300	4.7693 1145	157
158	2.8571 8750	3.2562 5690	3.9609 6077	4.8170 0456	158
159	2.8762 3542	3.2806 7882	3.9956 1918	4.8651 7461	159
160	2.8954 1032	3.3052 8391	4.0305 8085	4.9138 2635	160
161	2.9147 1306	3.3300 7354	4.0658 4843	4.9629 6462	161
162	2.9341 4448	3.3550 4910	4.1014 2460	5.0125 9426	162
163	2.9537 0544	3.3802 1196	4.1373 1207	5.0627 2021	163
164	2.9733 9681	3.4055 6355	4.1735 1355	5.1133 4741	164
165	2.9932 1945	3.4311 0528	4.2100 3179	5.1644 8088	165
166	3.0131 7425	3.4568 3857	4.2468 6957	5.2161 2569	166
167	3.0332 6208	3.4827 6486	4.2840 2968	5.2682 8695	167
168	3.0534 8383	3.5088 8560	4.3215 1494	5.3209 6982	168
169	3.0738 4038	3.5352 0224	4.3593 2819	5.3741 7952	169
170	3.0943 3265	3.5617 1625	4.3974 7232	5.4279 2131	170
171	3.1149 6154	3.5884 2913	4.4359 5020	5.4822 0052	171
172	3.1357 2795	3.6153 4234	4.4747 6476	5.5370 2253	172
173	3.1566 3280	3.6424 5741	4.5139 1896	5.5923 9275	173
174	3.1776 7702	3.6697 7584	4.5534 1575	5.6483 1668	174
175	3.1988 6153	3.6972 9916	4.5932 5813	5.7047 9985	175
176	3.2201 8728	3.7250 2891	4.6334 4914	5.7618 4785	176
177	3.2416 5519	3.7529 6662	4.6739 9182	5.8194 6633	177
178	3.2632 6623	3.7811 1387	4.7148 8925	5.8776 6099	178
179	3.2850 2134	3.8094 7223	4.7561 4453	5.9364 3760	179
180	3.3069 2148	3.8380 4327	4.7977 6080	5.9958 0198	180

TABLE 5 COMPOUND AMOUNT
WHEN PRINCIPAL IS 1

$$s = (1 + i)^n$$

n	$\frac{2}{3}\%$	$\frac{3}{4}\%$	$\frac{7}{8}\%$	1%	n
181	3.3289 6762	3.8668 2859	4.8397 4120	6.0557 6000	181
182	3.3511 6074	3.8958 2981	4.8820 8894	6.1163 1760	182
183	3.3735 0181	3.9250 4853	4.9248 0722	6.1774 8077	183
184	3.3959 9182	3.9544 8639	4.9678 9928	6.2392 5558	184
185	3.4186 3177	3.9841 4504	5.0113 6840	6.3016 4813	185
186	3.4414 2265	4.0140 2613	5.0552 1787	6.3646 6462	186
187	3.4643 6546	4.0441 3133	5.0994 5103	6.4283 1126	187
188	3.4874 6123	4.0744 6231	5.1440 7123	6.4925 9437	188
189	3.5107 1097	4.1050 2078	5.1890 8185	6.5575 2032	189
190	3.5341 1571	4.1358 0843	5.2344 8632	6.6230 9552	190
191	3.5576 7649	4.1668 2700	5.2802 8807	6.6893 2648	191
192	3.5813 9433	4.1980 7820	5.3264 9059	6.7562 1974	192
193	3.6052 7029	4.2295 6379	5.3730 9738	6.8237 8194	193
194	3.6293 0543	4.2612 8551	5.4201 1199	6.8920 1976	194
195	3.6535 0080	4.2932 4516	5.4675 3797	6.9609 3996	195
196	3.6778 5747	4.3254 4449	5.5153 7892	7.0305 4936	196
197	3.7023 7652	4.3578 8533	5.5636 3849	7.1008 5485	197
198	3.7270 5903	4.3905 6947	5.6123 2033	7.1718 6340	198
199	3.7519 0609	4.4234 9874	5.6614 2813	7.2435 8203	199
200	3.7769 1880	4.4566 7498	5.7109 6562	7.3160 1785	200
201	3.8020 9825	4.4901 0004	5.7609 3657	7.3891 7803	201
202	3.8274 4558	4.5237 7579	5.8113 4477	7.4630 6981	202
203	3.8529 6188	4.5577 0411	5.8621 9404	7.5377 0051	203
204	3.8786 4829	4.5918 8689	5.9134 8823	7.6130 7751	204
205	3.9045 0595	4.6263 2604	5.9652 3125	7.6892 0829	205
206	3.9305 3599	4.6610 2349	6.0174 2703	7.7661 0037	206
207	3.9567 3956	4.6959 8116	6.0700 7951	7.8437 6138	207
208	3.9831 1782	4.7312 0102	6.1231 9271	7.9221 9899	208
209	4.0096 7194	4.7666 8503	6.1767 7065	8.0014 2098	209
210	4.0364 0309	4.8024 3517	6.2308 1739	8.0814 3519	210
211	4.0633 1244	4.8384 5343	6.2853 3704	8.1622 4954	211
212	4.0904 0119	4.8747 4183	6.3403 3374	8.2438 7204	212
213	4.1176 7053	4.9113 0240	6.3958 1166	8.3263 1076	213
214	4.1451 2167	4.9481 3717	6.4517 7501	8.4095 7386	214
215	4.1727 5582	4.9852 4819	6.5082 2804	8.4936 6960	215
216	4.2005 7419	5.0226 3756	6.5651 7504	8.5786 0630	216
217	4.2285 7802	5.0603 0734	6.6226 2032	8.6643 9236	217
218	4.2567 6854	5.0982 5964	6.6805 6825	8.7510 3629	218
219	4.2851 4699	5.1364 9659	6.7390 2322	8.8385 4665	219
220	4.3137 1464	5.1750 2031	6.7979 8968	8.9269 3211	220
221	4.3424 7274	5.2138 3297	6.8574 7208	9.0162 0144	221
222	4.3714 2255	5.2529 3671	6.9174 7497	9.1063 6345	222
223	4.4005 6537	5.2923 3374	6.9780 0287	9.1974 2708	223
224	4.4299 0247	5.3320 2624	7.0390 6040	9.2894 0136	224
225	4.4594 3516	5.3720 1644	7.1006 5217	9.3822 9537	225
226	4.4891 6473	5.4123 0656	7.1627 8288	9.4761 1832	226
227	4.5190 9249	5.4528 9886	7.2254 5723	9.5708 7951	227
228	4.5492 1977	5.4937 9560	7.2886 7998	9.6665 8830	228
229	4.5795 4791	5.5349 9907	7.3524 5593	9.7632 5418	229
230	4.6100 7822	5.5765 1156	7.4167 8992	9.8608 8673	230
231	4.6408 1208	5.6183 3540	7.4816 8683	9.9594 9559	231
232	4.6717 5083	5.6604 7291	7.5471 5159	10.0590 9055	232
233	4.7028 9583	5.7029 2646	7.6131 8917	10.1596 8145	233
234	4.7342 4847	5.7456 9841	7.6798 0458	10.2612 7827	234
235	4.7658 1013	5.7887 9115	7.7470 0287	10.3638 9105	235
236	4.7975 8219	5.8322 0708	7.8147 8914	10.4675 2996	236
237	4.8295 6608	5.8759 4863	7.8831 6855	10.5722 0526	237
238	4.8617 6318	5.9200 1825	7.9521 4627	10.6779 2731	238
239	4.8941 7494	5.9644 1839	8.0217 2755	10.7847 0659	239
240	4.9268 0277	6.0091 5152	8.0919 1767	10.8925 5365	240

TABLE 5 COMPOUND AMOUNT

WHEN PRINCIPAL IS 1

$$s = (1 + i)^n$$

n	$1\frac{1}{8}\%$	$1\frac{1}{4}\%$	$1\frac{3}{8}\%$	$1\frac{1}{2}\%$	n
1	1.0112 5000	1.0125 0000	1.0137 5000	1.0150 0000	1
2	1.0226 2656	1.0251 5625	1.0276 8906	1.0302 2500	2
3	1.0341 3111	1.0379 7070	1.0418 1979	1.0456 7838	3
4	1.0457 6509	1.0509 4534	1.0561 4481	1.0613 6355	4
5	1.0575 2994	1.0640 8215	1.0706 6680	1.0772 8400	5
6	1.0694 2716	1.0773 8318	1.0853 8847	1.0934 4326	6
7	1.0814 5821	1.0908 5047	1.1003 1256	1.1098 4491	7
8	1.0936 2462	1.1044 8610	1.1154 4186	1.1264 9259	8
9	1.1059 2789	1.1182 9218	1.1307 7918	1.1433 8998	9
10	1.1183 6958	1.1322 7083	1.1463 2740	1.1605 4083	10
11	1.1309 5124	1.1464 2422	1.1620 8940	1.1779 4894	11
12	1.1436 7444	1.1607 5452	1.1780 6813	1.1956 1817	12
13	1.1565 4078	1.1752 6395	1.1942 6656	1.2135 5244	13
14	1.1695 5186	1.1899 5475	1.2106 8773	1.2317 5573	14
15	1.1827 0932	1.2048 2918	1.2273 3469	1.2502 3207	15
16	1.1960 1480	1.2198 8955	1.2442 1054	1.2689 8555	16
17	1.2094 6997	1.2351 3817	1.2613 1843	1.2880 2033	17
18	1.2230 7650	1.2505 7739	1.2786 6156	1.3073 4064	18
19	1.2368 3611	1.2662 0961	1.2962 4316	1.3269 5075	19
20	1.2507 5052	1.2820 3723	1.3140 6650	1.3468 5501	20
21	1.2648 2146	1.2980 6270	1.3321 3492	1.3670 5783	21
22	1.2790 5071	1.3142 8848	1.3504 5177	1.3875 6370	22
23	1.2934 4003	1.3307 1709	1.3690 2048	1.4083 7715	23
24	1.3079 9123	1.3473 5105	1.3878 4451	1.4295 0281	24
25	1.3227 0613	1.3641 9294	1.4069 2738	1.4509 4535	25
26	1.3375 8657	1.3812 4535	1.4262 7263	1.4727 0953	26
27	1.3526 3442	1.3985 1092	1.4458 8388	1.4948 0018	27
28	1.3678 5156	1.4159 9230	1.4657 6478	1.5172 2218	28
29	1.3832 3989	1.4336 9221	1.4859 1905	1.5399 8051	29
30	1.3988 0134	1.4516 1336	1.5063 5043	1.5630 8022	30
31	1.4145 3785	1.4697 5853	1.5270 6275	1.5865 2642	31
32	1.4304 5140	1.4881 3051	1.5480 5986	1.6103 2432	32
33	1.4465 4398	1.5067 3214	1.5693 4569	1.6344 7918	33
34	1.4628 1760	1.5255 6629	1.5909 2419	1.6589 9637	34
35	1.4792 7430	1.5446 3587	1.6127 9940	1.6838 8132	35
36	1.4959 1613	1.5639 4382	1.6349 7539	1.7091 3954	36
37	1.5127 4519	1.5834 9312	1.6574 5630	1.7347 7663	37
38	1.5297 6357	1.6032 8678	1.6802 4633	1.7607 9828	38
39	1.5469 7341	1.6233 2787	1.7033 4971	1.7872 1025	39
40	1.5643 7687	1.6436 1946	1.7267 7077	1.8140 1841	40
41	1.5819 7611	1.6641 6471	1.7505 1387	1.8412 2868	41
42	1.5997 7334	1.6849 6677	1.7745 8343	1.8688 4712	42
43	1.6177 7079	1.7060 2885	1.7989 8396	1.8968 7982	43
44	1.6359 7071	1.7273 5421	1.8237 1999	1.9253 3302	44
45	1.6543 7538	1.7489 4614	1.8487 9614	1.9542 1301	45
46	1.6729 8710	1.7708 0797	1.8742 1708	1.9835 2621	46
47	1.6918 0821	1.7929 4306	1.8999 8757	2.0132 7910	47
48	1.7108 4105	1.8153 5485	1.9261 1240	2.0434 7829	48
49	1.7300 8801	1.8380 4679	1.9525 9644	2.0741 3046	49
50	1.7495 5150	1.8610 2237	1.9794 4464	2.1052 4242	50

TABLE 5 COMPOUND AMOUNT
WHEN PRINCIPAL IS 1

$$s = (1 + i)^n$$

n	$1\frac{1}{8}\%$	$1\frac{1}{4}\%$	$1\frac{3}{8}\%$	$1\frac{1}{2}\%$	n
51	1.7692 3395	1.8842 8515	2.0066 6201	2.1368 2106	51
52	1.7891 3784	1.9078 3872	2.0342 5361	2.1688 7337	52
53	1.8092 6564	1.9316 8670	2.0622 2460	2.2014 0647	53
54	1.8296 1988	1.9558 3279	2.0905 8019	2.2344 2757	54
55	1.8502 0310	1.9802 8070	2.1193 2566	2.2679 4398	55
56	1.8710 1788	2.0050 3420	2.1484 6639	2.3019 6314	56
57	1.8920 6684	2.0300 9713	2.1780 0780	2.3364 9259	57
58	1.9133 5259	2.0554 7335	2.2079 5541	2.3715 3998	58
59	1.9348 7780	2.0811 6676	2.2383 1480	2.4071 1308	59
60	1.9566 4518	2.1071 8135	2.2690 9163	2.4432 1978	60
61	1.9786 5744	2.1335 2111	2.3002 9164	2.4798 6807	61
62	2.0009 1733	2.1601 9013	2.3319 2065	2.5170 6609	62
63	2.0234 2765	2.1871 9250	2.3639 8456	2.5548 2208	63
64	2.0461 9121	2.2145 3241	2.3964 8934	2.5931 4442	64
65	2.0692 1087	2.2422 1407	2.4294 4107	2.6320 4158	65
66	2.0924 8949	2.2702 4174	2.4628 4589	2.6715 2221	66
67	2.1160 2999	2.2986 1976	2.4967 1002	2.7115 9504	67
68	2.1398 3533	2.3273 5251	2.5310 3978	2.7522 6896	68
69	2.1639 0848	2.3564 4442	2.5658 4158	2.7935 5300	69
70	2.1882 5245	2.3858 9997	2.6011 2190	2.8354 5629	70
71	2.2128 7029	2.4157 2372	2.6368 8732	2.8779 8814	71
72	2.2377 6508	2.4459 2027	2.6731 4453	2.9211 5796	72
73	2.2629 3994	2.4764 9427	2.7099 0026	2.9649 7533	73
74	2.2883 9801	2.5074 5045	2.7471 6139	3.0094 4996	74
75	2.3141 4249	2.5387 9358	2.7849 3486	3.0545 9171	75
76	2.3401 7659	2.5705 2850	2.8232 2771	3.1004 1059	76
77	2.3665 0358	2.6026 6011	2.8620 4710	3.1469 1674	77
78	2.3931 2675	2.6351 9336	2.9014 0024	3.1941 2050	78
79	2.4200 4942	2.6681 3327	2.9412 9450	3.2420 3230	79
80	2.4472 7498	2.7014 8494	2.9817 3730	3.2906 6279	80
81	2.4748 0682	2.7352 5350	3.0227 3618	3.3400 2273	81
82	2.5026 4840	2.7694 4417	3.0642 9881	3.3901 2307	82
83	2.5308 0319	2.8040 6222	3.1064 3291	3.4409 7492	83
84	2.5592 7473	2.8391 1300	3.1491 4637	3.4925 8954	84
85	2.5880 6657	2.8746 0191	3.1924 4713	3.5449 7838	85
86	2.6171 8232	2.9105 3444	3.2363 4328	3.5981 5306	86
87	2.6466 2562	2.9469 1612	3.2808 4300	3.6521 2535	87
88	2.6764 0016	2.9837 5257	3.3259 5459	3.7069 0723	88
89	2.7065 0966	3.0210 4948	3.3716 8646	3.7625 1084	89
90	2.7369 5789	3.0588 1260	3.4180 4715	3.8189 4851	90
91	2.7677 4867	3.0970 4775	3.4650 4530	3.8762 3273	91
92	2.7988 8584	3.1357 6085	3.5126 8967	3.9343 7622	92
93	2.8303 7331	3.1749 5786	3.5609 8916	3.9933 9187	93
94	2.8622 1501	3.2146 4483	3.6099 5276	4.0532 9275	94
95	2.8944 1492	3.2548 2789	3.6595 8961	4.1140 9214	95
96	2.9269 7709	3.2955 1324	3.7099 0897	4.1758 0352	96
97	2.9599 0559	3.3367 0716	3.7609 2021	4.2384 4057	97
98	2.9932 0452	3.3784 1600	3.8126 3287	4.3020 1718	98
99	3.0268 7807	3.4206 4620	3.8650 5657	4.3665 4744	99
100	3.0609 3045	3.4634 0427	3.9182 0110	4.4320 4565	100

TABLE 5 COMPOUND AMOUNT

WHEN PRINCIPAL IS 1

$$s=(1+i)^n$$

n	$1\frac{5}{8}\%$	$1\frac{3}{4}\%$	$1\frac{7}{8}\%$	2%	n
1	1.0162 5000	1.0175 0000	1.0187 5000	1.0200 0000	1
2	1.0327 6406	1.0353 0625	1.0378 5156	1.0404 0000	2
3	1.0495 4648	1.0534 2411	1.0573 1128	1.0612 0800	3
4	1.0666 0161	1.0718 5903	1.0771 3587	1.0824 3216	4
5	1.0839 3388	1.0906 1656	1.0973 3216	1.1040 8080	5
6	1.1015 4781	1.1097 0235	1.1179 0714	1.1261 6242	6
7	1.1194 4796	1.1291 2215	1.1388 6790	1.1486 8567	7
8	1.1376 3899	1.1488 8178	1.1602 2167	1.1716 5938	8
9	1.1561 2563	1.1689 8721	1.1819 7583	1.1950 9257	9
10	1.1749 1267	1.1894 4449	1.2041 3788	1.2189 9442	10
11	1.1940 0500	1.2102 5977	1.2267 1546	1.2433 7431	11
12	1.2134 0758	1.2314 3931	1.2497 1638	1.2682 4179	12
13	1.2331 2545	1.2529 8950	1.2731 4856	1.2936 0663	13
14	1.2531 6374	1.2749 1682	1.2970 2009	1.3194 7876	14
15	1.2735 2765	1.2972 2786	1.3213 3922	1.3458 6834	15
16	1.2942 2248	1.3199 2935	1.3461 1433	1.3727 8571	16
17	1.3152 5359	1.3430 2811	1.3713 5398	1.4002 4142	17
18	1.3366 2646	1.3665 3111	1.3970 6686	1.4282 4625	18
19	1.3583 4664	1.3904 4540	1.4232 6187	1.4568 1117	19
20	1.3804 1977	1.4147 7820	1.4499 4803	1.4859 4740	20
21	1.4028 5160	1.4395 3681	1.4771 3455	1.5156 6634	21
22	1.4256 4793	1.4647 2871	1.5048 3082	1.5459 7967	22
23	1.4488 1471	1.4903 6146	1.5330 4640	1.5768 9926	23
24	1.4723 5795	1.5164 4279	1.5617 9102	1.6084 3725	24
25	1.4962 8377	1.5429 8054	1.5910 7460	1.6406 0599	25
26	1.5205 9838	1.5699 8269	1.6209 0725	1.6734 1811	26
27	1.5453 0810	1.5974 5739	1.6512 9926	1.7068 8648	27
28	1.5704 1936	1.6254 1290	1.6822 6112	1.7410 2421	28
29	1.5959 3868	1.6538 5762	1.7138 0352	1.7758 4469	29
30	1.6218 7268	1.6828 0013	1.7459 3734	1.8113 6158	30
31	1.6482 2811	1.7122 4913	1.7786 7366	1.8475 8882	31
32	1.6750 1182	1.7422 1349	1.8120 2379	1.8845 4059	32
33	1.7022 3076	1.7727 0223	1.8459 9924	1.9222 3140	33
34	1.7298 9201	1.8037 2452	1.8806 1172	1.9606 7603	34
35	1.7580 0275	1.8352 8970	1.9158 7319	1.9998 8955	35
36	1.7865 7030	1.8674 0727	1.9517 9582	2.0398 8734	36
37	1.8156 0207	1.9000 8689	1.9883 9199	2.0806 8509	37
38	1.8451 0560	1.9333 3841	2.0256 7434	2.1222 9879	38
39	1.8750 8857	1.9671 7184	2.0636 5573	2.1647 4477	39
40	1.9055 5875	2.0015 9734	2.1023 4928	2.2080 3966	40
41	1.9365 2408	2.0366 2530	2.1417 6833	2.2522 0046	41
42	1.9679 9260	2.0722 6624	2.1819 2648	2.2972 4447	42
43	1.9999 7248	2.1085 3090	2.2228 3760	2.3431 8936	43
44	2.0324 7203	2.1454 3019	2.2645 1581	2.3900 5314	44
45	2.0654 9970	2.1829 7522	2.3069 7548	2.4378 5421	45
46	2.0990 6407	2.2211 7728	2.3502 3127	2.4866 1129	46
47	2.1331 7387	2.2600 4789	2.3942 9811	2.5363 4352	47
48	2.1678 3794	2.2995 9872	2.4391 9120	2.5870 7039	48
49	2.2030 6531	2.3398 4170	2.4849 2603	2.6388 1179	49
50	2.2388 6512	2.3807 8893	2.5315 1839	2.6915 8803	50

TABLE 5 COMPOUND AMOUNT

WHEN PRINCIPAL IS 1

$$s = (1 + i)^n$$

n	$1\frac{5}{8}\%$	$1\frac{3}{4}\%$	$1\frac{7}{8}\%$	2%	n
51	2.2752 4668	2.4224 5274	2.5789 8436	2.7454 1979	51
52	2.3122 1944	2.4648 4566	2.6273 4032	2.8003 2819	52
53	2.3497 9300	2.5079 8046	2.6766 0295	2.8563 3475	53
54	2.3879 7714	2.5518 7012	2.7267 8926	2.9134 6144	54
55	2.4267 8177	2.5965 2785	2.7779 1656	2.9717 3067	55
56	2.4662 1697	2.6419 6708	2.8300 0249	3.0311 6529	56
57	2.5062 9300	2.6882 0151	2.8830 6504	3.0917 8859	57
58	2.5470 2026	2.7352 4503	2.9371 2251	3.1536 2436	58
59	2.5884 0934	2.7831 1182	2.9921 9355	3.2166 9685	59
60	2.6304 7099	2.8318 1628	3.0482 9718	3.2810 3079	60
61	2.6732 1614	2.8813 7306	3.1054 5276	3.3466 5140	61
62	2.7166 5590	2.9317 9709	3.1636 8000	3.4135 8443	62
63	2.7608 0156	2.9831 0354	3.2229 9900	3.4818 5612	63
64	2.8056 6459	3.0353 0785	3.2834 3023	3.5514 9324	64
65	2.8512 5664	3.0884 2574	3.3449 9454	3.6225 2311	65
66	2.8975 8956	3.1424 7319	3.4077 1319	3.6949 7357	66
67	2.9446 7539	3.1974 6647	3.4716 0781	3.7688 7304	67
68	2.9925 2636	3.2534 2213	3.5367 0046	3.8442 5050	68
69	3.0411 5492	3.3103 5702	3.6030 1359	3.9211 3551	69
70	3.0905 7368	3.3682 8827	3.6705 7010	3.9995 5822	70
71	3.1407 9551	3.4272 3331	3.7393 9329	4.0795 4939	71
72	3.1918 3343	3.4872 0990	3.8095 0691	4.1611 4038	72
73	3.2437 0073	3.5482 3607	3.8809 3517	4.2443 6318	73
74	3.2964 1086	3.6103 3020	3.9537 0270	4.3292 5045	74
75	3.3499 7754	3.6735 1098	4.0278 3463	4.4158 3546	75
76	3.4044 1467	3.7377 9742	4.1033 5653	4.5041 5216	76
77	3.4597 3641	3.8032 0888	4.1802 9446	4.5942 3521	77
78	3.5159 5713	3.8697 6503	4.2586 7498	4.6861 1991	78
79	3.5730 9143	3.9374 8592	4.3385 2514	4.7798 4231	79
80	3.6311 5417	4.0063 9192	4.4198 7248	4.8754 3916	80
81	3.6901 6042	4.0765 0378	4.5027 4509	4.9729 4794	81
82	3.7501 2553	4.1478 4260	4.5871 7156	5.0724 0690	82
83	3.8110 6507	4.2204 2984	4.6731 8103	5.1738 5504	83
84	3.8729 9488	4.2942 8737	4.7608 0317	5.2773 3214	84
85	3.9359 3104	4.3694 3740	4.8500 6823	5.3828 7878	85
86	3.9998 8992	4.4459 0255	4.9410 0701	5.4905 3636	86
87	4.0648 8813	4.5237 0584	5.0336 5089	5.6003 4708	87
88	4.1309 4257	4.6028 7070	5.1280 3185	5.7123 5402	88
89	4.1980 7038	4.6834 2093	5.2241 8245	5.8266 0110	89
90	4.2662 8903	4.7653 8080	5.3221 3587	5.9431 3313	90
91	4.3356 1622	4.8487 7496	5.4219 2591	6.0619 9579	91
92	4.4060 6999	4.9336 2853	5.5235 8703	6.1832 3570	92
93	4.4776 6863	5.0199 6703	5.6271 5428	6.3069 0042	93
94	4.5504 3074	5.1078 1645	5.7326 6343	6.4330 3843	94
95	4.6243 7524	5.1972 0324	5.8401 5086	6.5616 9920	95
96	4.6995 2134	5.2881 5429	5.9496 5369	6.6929 3318	96
97	4.7758 8856	5.3806 9699	6.0612 0970	6.8267 9184	97
98	4.8534 9675	5.4748 5919	6.1748 5738	6.9633 2768	98
99	4.9323 6607	5.5706 6923	6.2906 3596	7.1025 9423	99
100	5.0125 1702	5.6681 5594	6.4085 8538	7.2446 4612	100

TABLE 5 COMPOUND AMOUNT

WHEN PRINCIPAL IS 1

$$s = (1 + i)^n$$

n	$2\frac{1}{4}\%$	$2\frac{1}{2}\%$	$2\frac{3}{4}\%$	3%	n
1	1.0225 0000	1.0250 0000	1.0275 0000	1.0300 0000	1
2	1.0455 0625	1.0506 2500	1.0557 5625	1.0609 0000	2
3	1.0690 3014	1.0768 9063	1.0847 8955	1.0927 2700	3
4	1.0930 8332	1.1038 1289	1.1146 2126	1.1255 0881	4
5	1.1176 7769	1.1314 0821	1.1452 7334	1.1592 7407	5
6	1.1428 2544	1.1596 9342	1.1767 6836	1.1940 5230	6
7	1.1685 3901	1.1886 8575	1.2091 2949	1.2298 7387	7
8	1.1948 3114	1.2184 0290	1.2423 8055	1.2667 7008	8
9	1.2217 1484	1.2488 6297	1.2765 4602	1.3047 7318	9
10	1.2492 0343	1.2800 8454	1.3116 5103	1.3439 1638	10
11	1.2773 1050	1.3120 8666	1.3477 2144	1.3842 3387	11
12	1.3060 4999	1.3448 8882	1.3847 8378	1.4257 6089	12
13	1.3354 3611	1.3785 1104	1.4228 6533	1.4685 3371	13
14	1.3654 8343	1.4129 7382	1.4619 9413	1.5125 8972	14
15	1.3962 0680	1.4482 9817	1.5021 9896	1.5579 6742	15
16	1.4276 2146	1.4845 0562	1.5435 0944	1.6047 0644	16
17	1.4597 4294	1.5216 1826	1.5859 5595	1.6528 4763	17
18	1.4925 8716	1.5596 5872	1.6295 6973	1.7024 3306	18
19	1.5261 7037	1.5986 5019	1.6743 8290	1.7535 0605	19
20	1.5605 0920	1.6386 1644	1.7204 2843	1.8061 1123	20
21	1.5956 2066	1.6795 8185	1.7677 4021	1.8602 9457	21
22	1.6315 2212	1.7215 7140	1.8163 5307	1.9161 0341	22
23	1.6682 3137	1.7646 1068	1.8663 0278	1.9735 8651	23
24	1.7057 6658	1.8087 2595	1.9176 2610	2.0327 9411	24
25	1.7441 4632	1.8539 4410	1.9703 6082	2.0937 7793	25
26	1.7833 8962	1.9002 9270	2.0245 4575	2.1565 9127	26
27	1.8235 1588	1.9478 0002	2.0802 2075	2.2212 8901	27
28	1.8645 4499	1.9964 9502	2.1374 2682	2.2879 2768	28
29	1.9064 9725	2.0464 0739	2.1962 0606	2.3565 6551	29
30	1.9493 9344	2.0975 6758	2.2566 0173	2.4272 6247	30
31	1.9932 5479	2.1500 0677	2.3186 5828	2.5000 8035	31
32	2.0381 0303	2.2037 5694	2.3824 2138	2.5750 8276	32
33	2.0839 6034	2.2588 5086	2.4479 3797	2.6523 3524	33
34	2.1308 4945	2.3153 2213	2.5152 5626	2.7319 0530	34
35	2.1787 9356	2.3732 0519	2.5844 2581	2.8138 6245	35
36	2.2278 1642	2.4325 3532	2.6554 9752	2.8982 7833	36
37	2.2779 4229	2.4933 4870	2.7285 2370	2.9852 2668	37
38	2.3291 9599	2.5556 8242	2.8035 5810	3.0747 8348	38
39	2.3816 0290	2.6195 7448	2.8806 5595	3.1670 2698	39
40	2.4351 8897	2.6850 6384	2.9598 7399	3.2620 3779	40
41	2.4899 8072	2.7521 9043	3.0412 7052	3.3598 9893	41
42	2.5460 0528	2.8209 9520	3.1249 0546	3.4606 9589	42
43	2.6032 9040	2.8915 2008	3.2108 4036	3.5645 1677	43
44	2.6618 6444	2.9638 0808	3.2991 3847	3.6714 5227	44
45	2.7217 5639	3.0379 0328	3.3898 6478	3.7815 9584	45
46	2.7829 9590	3.1138 5086	3.4830 8606	3.8950 4372	46
47	2.8456 1331	3.1916 9713	3.5788 7093	4.0118 9503	47
48	2.9096 3961	3.2714 8956	3.6772 8988	4.1322 5188	48
49	2.9751 0650	3.3532 7680	3.7784 1535	4.2562 1944	49
50	3.0420 4640	3.4371 0872	3.8823 2177	4.3839 0602	50

TABLE 5 COMPOUND AMOUNT
WHEN PRINCIPAL IS 1

$$s=(1+i)^n$$

n	$2\frac{1}{4}\%$	$2\frac{1}{2}\%$	$2\frac{3}{4}\%$	3%	n
51	3.1104 9244	3.5230 3644	3.9890 8562	4.5154 2320	51
52	3.1804 7852	3.6111 1235	4.0987 8547	4.6508 8590	52
53	3.2520 3929	3.7013 9016	4.2115 0208	4.7904 1247	53
54	3.3252 1017	3.7939 2491	4.3273 1838	4.9341 2485	54
55	3.4000 2740	3.8887 7303	4.4463 1964	5.0821 4859	55
56	3.4765 2802	3.9859 9236	4.5685 9343	5.2346 1305	56
57	3.5547 4990	4.0856 4217	4.6942 2975	5.3916 5144	57
58	3.6347 3177	4.1877 8322	4.8233 2107	5.5534 0098	58
59	3.7165 1324	4.2924 7780	4.9559 6239	5.7200 0301	59
60	3.8001 3479	4.3997 8975	5.0922 5136	5.8916 0310	60
61	3.8856 3782	4.5097 8449	5.2322 8827	6.0683 5120	61
62	3.9730 6467	4.6225 2910	5.3761 7620	6.2504 0173	62
63	4.0624 5862	4.7380 9233	5.5240 2105	6.4379 1379	63
64	4.1538 6394	4.8565 4464	5.6759 3162	6.6310 5120	64
65	4.2473 2588	4.9779 5826	5.8320 1974	6.8299 8273	65
66	4.3428 9071	5.1024 0721	5.9924 0029	7.0348 8222	66
67	4.4406 0576	5.2299 6739	6.1571 9130	7.2459 2868	67
68	4.5405 1939	5.3607 1658	6.3265 1406	7.4633 0654	68
69	4.6426 8107	5.4947 3449	6.5004 9319	7.6872 0574	69
70	4.7471 4140	5.6321 0286	6.6792 5676	7.9178 2191	70
71	4.8539 5208	5.7729 0543	6.8629 3632	8.1553 5657	71
72	4.9631 6600	5.9172 2806	7.0516 6706	8.4000 1727	72
73	5.0748 3723	6.0651 5876	7.2455 8791	8.6520 1778	73
74	5.1890 2107	6.2167 8773	7.4448 4158	8.9115 7832	74
75	5.3057 7405	6.3722 0743	7.6495 7472	9.1789 2567	75
76	5.4251 5396	6.5315 1261	7.8599 3802	9.4542 9344	76
77	5.5472 1993	6.6948 0043	8.0760 8632	9.7379 2224	77
78	5.6720 3237	6.8621 7044	8.2981 7869	10.0300 5991	78
79	5.7996 5310	7.0337 2470	8.5263 7861	10.3309 6171	79
80	5.9301 4530	7.2095 6782	8.7608 5402	10.6408 9056	80
81	6.0635 7357	7.3898 0701	9.0017 7751	10.9601 1727	81
82	6.2000 0397	7.5745 5219	9.2493 2639	11.2889 2079	82
83	6.3395 0406	7.7639 1599	9.5036 8286	11.6275 8842	83
84	6.4821 4290	7.9580 1389	9.7650 3414	11.9764 1607	84
85	6.6279 9112	8.1569 6424	10.0335 7258	12.3357 0855	85
86	6.7771 2092	8.3608 8834	10.3094 9583	12.7057 7981	86
87	6.9296 0614	8.5699 1055	10.5930 0696	13.0869 5320	87
88	7.0855 2228	8.7841 5832	10.8843 1465	13.4795 6180	88
89	7.2449 4653	9.0037 6228	11.1836 3331	13.8839 4865	89
90	7.4079 5782	9.2288 5633	11.4911 8322	14.3004 6711	90
91	7.5746 3688	9.4595 7774	11.8071 9076	14.7294 8112	91
92	7.7450 6621	9.6960 6718	12.1318 8851	15.1713 6556	92
93	7.9193 3020	9.9384 6886	12.4655 1544	15.6265 0652	93
94	8.0975 1512	10.1869 3058	12.8083 1711	16.0953 0172	94
95	8.2797 0921	10.4416 0385	13.1605 4584	16.5781 6077	95
96	8.4660 0267	10.7026 4395	13.5224 6085	17.0755 0559	96
97	8.6564 8773	10.9702 1004	13.8943 2852	17.5877 7076	97
98	8.8512 5871	11.2444 6530	14.2764 2255	18.1154 0388	98
99	9.0504 1203	11.5255 7693	14.6690 2417	18.6588 6600	99
100	9.2540 4630	11.8137 1635	15.0724 2234	19.2186 3198	100

TABLE 5 COMPOUND AMOUNT
WHEN PRINCIPAL IS 1

$$s = (1 + i)^n$$

n	$3\frac{1}{4}\%$	$3\frac{1}{2}\%$	$3\frac{3}{4}\%$	4%	n
1	1.0325 0000	1.0350 0000	1.0375 0000	1.0400 0000	1
2	1.0660 5625	1.0712 2500	1.0764 0625	1.0816 0000	2
3	1.1007 0308	1.1087 1788	1.1167 7148	1.1248 6400	3
4	1.1364 7593	1.1475 2300	1.1586 5042	1.1698 5856	4
5	1.1734 1140	1.1876 8631	1.2020 9981	1.2166 5290	5
6	1.2115 4727	1.2292 5533	1.2471 7855	1.2653 1902	6
7	1.2509 2255	1.2722 7926	1.2939 4774	1.3159 3178	7
8	1.2915 7754	1.3168 0904	1.3424 7078	1.3685 6905	8
9	1.3335 5381	1.3628 9735	1.3928 1344	1.4233 1181	9
10	1.3768 9430	1.4105 9876	1.4450 4394	1.4802 4428	10
11	1.4216 4337	1.4599 6972	1.4992 3309	1.5394 5406	11
12	1.4678 4678	1.5110 6866	1.5554 5433	1.6010 3222	12
13	1.5155 5180	1.5639 5606	1.6137 8387	1.6650 7351	13
14	1.5648 0723	1.6186 9452	1.6743 0076	1.7316 7645	14
15	1.6156 6347	1.6753 4883	1.7370 8704	1.8009 4351	15
16	1.6681 7253	1.7339 8604	1.8022 2781	1.8729 8125	16
17	1.7223 8814	1.7946 7555	1.8698 1135	1.9479 0050	17
18	1.7783 6575	1.8574 8920	1.9399 2928	2.0258 1652	18
19	1.8361 6264	1.9225 0132	2.0126 7662	2.1068 4918	19
20	1.8958 3792	1.9897 8886	2.0881 5200	2.1911 2314	20
21	1.9574 5266	2.0594 3147	2.1664 5770	2.2787 6807	21
22	2.0210 6987	2.1315 1158	2.2476 9986	2.3699 1879	22
23	2.0867 5464	2.2061 1448	2.3319 8860	2.4647 1554	23
24	2.1545 7416	2.2833 2849	2.4194 3818	2.5633 0416	24
25	2.2245 9782	2.3632 4498	2.5101 6711	2.6658 3633	25
26	2.2968 9725	2.4459 5856	2.6042 9838	2.7724 6978	26
27	2.3715 4641	2.5315 6711	2.7019 5956	2.8833 6858	27
28	2.4486 2167	2.6201 7196	2.8032 8305	2.9987 0332	28
29	2.5282 0188	2.7118 7798	2.9084 0616	3.1186 5145	29
30	2.6103 6844	2.8067 9370	3.0174 7139	3.2433 9751	30
31	2.6952 0541	2.9050 3148	3.1306 2657	3.3731 3341	31
32	2.7827 9959	3.0067 0759	3.2480 2507	3.5080 5875	32
33	2.8732 4058	3.1119 4235	3.3698 2601	3.6483 8110	33
34	2.9666 2089	3.2208 6033	3.4961 9448	3.7943 1634	34
35	3.0630 3607	3.3335 9045	3.6273 0178	3.9460 8899	35
36	3.1625 8475	3.4502 6611	3.7633 2559	4.1039 3255	36
37	3.2653 6875	3.5710 2543	3.9044 5030	4.2680 8986	37
38	3.3714 9323	3.6960 1132	4.0508 6719	4.4388 1345	38
39	3.4810 6676	3.8253 7171	4.2027 7471	4.6163 6599	39
40	3.5942 0143	3.9592 5972	4.3603 7876	4.8010 2063	40
41	3.7110 1298	4.0978 3381	4.5238 9296	4.9930 6145	41
42	3.8316 2090	4.2412 5799	4.6935 3895	5.1927 8391	42
43	3.9561 4858	4.3897 0202	4.8695 4666	5.4004 9527	43
44	4.0847 2341	4.5433 4160	5.0521 5466	5.6165 1508	44
45	4.2174 7692	4.7023 5855	5.2416 1046	5.8411 7568	45
46	4.3545 4492	4.8669 4110	5.4381 7085	6.0748 2271	46
47	4.4960 6763	5.0372 8404	5.6421 0226	6.3178 1562	47
48	4.6421 8983	5.2135 8898	5.8536 8109	6.5705 2824	48
49	4.7930 6100	5.3960 6459	6.0731 9413	6.8333 4937	49
50	4.9488 3548	5.5849 2686	6.3009 3891	7.1066 8335	50

TABLE 5 COMPOUND AMOUNT

WHEN PRINCIPAL IS 1

$$s = (1+i)^n$$

n	$3\frac{1}{4}\%$	$3\frac{1}{2}\%$	$3\frac{3}{4}\%$	4%	n
51	5.1096 7263	5.7803 9930	6.5372 2412	7.3909 5068	51
52	5.2757 3700	5.9827 1327	6.7823 7003	7.6865 8871	52
53	5.4471 9845	6.1921 0824	7.0367 0890	7.9940 5226	53
54	5.6242 3240	6.4088 3202	7.3005 8549	8.3138 1435	54
55	5.8070 1995	6.6331 4114	7.5743 5744	8.6463 6692	55
56	5.9957 4810	6.8653 0108	7.8583 9585	8.9922 2160	56
57	6.1906 0991	7.1055 8662	8.1530 8569	9.3519 1046	57
58	6.3918 0473	7.3542 8215	8.4588 2640	9.7259 8688	58
59	6.5995 3839	7.6116 8203	8.7760 3239	10.1150 2635	59
60	6.8140 2339	7.8780 9090	9.1051 3361	10.5196 2741	60
61	7.0354 7915	8.1538 2408	9.4465 7612	10.9404 1250	61
62	7.2641 3222	8.4392 0793	9.8008 2272	11.3780 2900	62
63	7.5002 1651	8.7345 8020	10.1683 5358	11.8331 5016	63
64	7.7439 7355	9.0402 9051	10.5496 6684	12.3064 7617	64
65	7.9956 5269	9.3567 0068	10.9452 7934	12.7987 3522	65
66	8.2555 1140	9.6841 8520	11.3557 2732	13.3106 8463	66
67	8.5238 1552	10.0231 3168	11.7815 6709	13.8431 1201	67
68	8.8008 3953	10.3739 4129	12.2233 7586	14.3968 3649	68
69	9.0868 6681	10.7370 2924	12.6817 5245	14.9727 0995	69
70	9.3821 8999	11.1128 2526	13.1573 1817	15.5716 1835	70
71	9.6871 1116	11.5017 7414	13.6507 1760	16.1944 8308	71
72	10.0019 4227	11.9043 3624	14.1626 1951	16.8422 6241	72
73	10.3270 0540	12.3209 8801	14.6937 1774	17.5159 5290	73
74	10.6626 3307	12.7522 2259	15.2447 3216	18.2165 9102	74
75	11.0091 6865	13.1985 5038	15.8164 0961	18.9452 5466	75
76	11.3669 6663	13.6604 9964	16.4095 2497	19.7030 6485	76
77	11.7363 9304	14.1386 1713	17.0248 8216	20.4911 8744	77
78	12.1178 2582	14.6334 6873	17.6633 1524	21.3108 3494	78
79	12.5116 5516	15.1456 4014	18.3256 8956	22.1632 6834	79
80	12.9182 8395	15.6757 3754	19.0129 0292	23.0497 9907	80
81	13.3381 2818	16.2243 8835	19.7258 8678	23.9717 9103	81
82	13.7716 1734	16.7922 4195	20.4656 0754	24.9306 6267	82
83	14.2191 9491	17.3799 7041	21.2330 6782	25.9278 8918	83
84	14.6813 1874	17.9882 6938	22.0293 0786	26.9650 0475	84
85	15.1584 6160	18.6178 5881	22.8554 0691	28.0436 0494	85
86	15.6511 1160	19.2694 8387	23.7124 8467	29.1653 4914	86
87	16.1597 7273	19.9439 1580	24.6017 0284	30.3319 6310	87
88	16.6849 6534	20.6419 5285	25.5242 6670	31.5452 4163	88
89	17.2272 2672	21.3644 2120	26.4814 2670	32.8070 5129	89
90	17.7871 1159	22.1121 7595	27.4744 8020	34.1193 3334	90
91	18.3651 9271	22.8861 0210	28.5047 7321	35.4841 0668	91
92	18.9620 6147	23.6871 1568	29.5737 0220	36.9034 7094	92
93	19.5783 2847	24.5161 6473	30.6827 1603	38.3796 0978	93
94	20.2146 2415	25.3742 3049	31.8333 1789	39.9147 9417	94
95	20.8715 9943	26.2623 2856	33.0270 6731	41.5113 8594	95
96	21.5499 2641	27.1815 1006	34.2655 8233	43.1718 4138	96
97	22.2502 9902	28.1328 6291	35.5505 4167	44.8987 1503	97
98	22.9734 3374	29.1175 1311	36.8836 8698	46.6946 6363	98
99	23.7200 7034	30.1366 2607	38.2668 2524	48.5624 5018	99
100	24.4909 7262	31.1914 0798	39.7018 3119	50.5049 4818	100

TABLE 5 COMPOUND AMOUNT

WHEN PRINCIPAL IS 1

$$s = (1 + i)^n$$

n	$4\frac{1}{2}\%$	5%	$5\frac{1}{2}\%$	6%	n
1	1.0450 0000	1.0500 0000	1.0550 0000	1.0600 0000	1
2	1.0920 2500	1.1025 0000	1.1130 2500	1.1236 0000	2
3	1.1411 6613	1.1576 2500	1.1742 4138	1.1910 1600	3
4	1.1925 1860	1.2155 0625	1.2388 2465	1.2624 7696	4
5	1.2461 8194	1.2762 8156	1.3069 6001	1.3382 2558	5
6	1.3022 6012	1.3400 9564	1.3788 4281	1.4185 1911	6
7	1.3608 6183	1.4071 0042	1.4546 7916	1.5036 3026	7
8	1.4221 0061	1.4774 5544	1.5346 8652	1.5938 4807	8
9	1.4860 9514	1.5513 2822	1.6190 9427	1.6894 7896	9
10	1.5529 6942	1.6288 9463	1.7081 4446	1.7908 4770	10
11	1.6228 5305	1.7103 3936	1.8020 9240	1.8982 9856	11
12	1.6958 8143	1.7958 5633	1.9012 0749	2.0121 9647	12
13	1.7721 9610	1.8856 4914	2.0057 7390	2.1329 2826	13
14	1.8519 4492	1.9799 3160	2.1160 9146	2.2609 0396	14
15	1.9352 8244	2.0789 2818	2.2324 7649	2.3965 5819	15
16	2.0223 7015	2.1828 7459	2.3552 6270	2.5403 5168	16
17	2.1133 7681	2.2920 1832	2.4848 0215	2.6927 7279	17
18	2.2084 7877	2.4066 1923	2.6214 6627	2.8543 3915	18
19	2.3078 6031	2.5269 5020	2.7656 4691	3.0255 9950	19
20	2.4117 1402	2.6532 9771	2.9177 5749	3.2071 3547	20
21	2.5202 4116	2.7859 6259	3.0782 3415	3.3995 6360	21
22	2.6336 5201	2.9252 6072	3.2475 3703	3.6035 3742	22
23	2.7521 6635	3.0715 2376	3.4261 5157	3.8197 4966	23
24	2.8760 1383	3.2250 9994	3.6145 8990	4.0489 3464	24
25	3.0054 3446	3.3863 5494	3.8133 9235	4.2918 7072	25
26	3.1406 7901	3.5556 7269	4.0231 2893	4.5493 8296	26
27	3.2820 0956	3.7334 5632	4.2444 0102	4.8223 4594	27
28	3.4296 9999	3.9201 2914	4.4778 4307	5.1116 8670	28
29	3.5840 3649	4.1161 3560	4.7241 2444	5.4183 8790	29
30	3.7453 1813	4.3219 4238	4.9839 5129	5.7434 9117	30
31	3.9138 5745	4.5380 3949	5.2580 6861	6.0881 0064	31
32	4.0899 8104	4.7649 4147	5.5472 6238	6.4533 8668	32
33	4.2740 3018	5.0031 8854	5.8523 6181	6.8405 8988	33
34	4.4663 6154	5.2533 4797	6.1742 4171	7.2510 2528	34
35	4.6673 4781	5.5160 1537	6.5138 2501	7.6860 8679	35
36	4.8773 7846	5.7918 1614	6.8720 8538	8.1472 5200	36
37	5.0968 6049	6.0814 0694	7.2500 5008	8.6360 8712	37
38	5.3262 1921	6.3854 7729	7.6488 0283	9.1542 5235	38
39	5.5658 9908	6.7047 5115	8.0694 8699	9.7035 0749	39
40	5.8163 6454	7.0399 8871	8.5133 0877	10.2857 1794	40
41	6.0781 0094	7.3919 8815	8.9815 4076	10.9028 6101	41
42	6.3516 1548	7.7615 8756	9.4755 2550	11.5570 3267	42
43	6.6374 3818	8.1496 6693	9.9966 7940	12.2504 5463	43
44	6.9361 2290	8.5571 5028	10.5464 9677	12.9854 8191	44
45	7.2482 4843	8.9850 0779	11.1265 5409	13.7646 1083	45
46	7.5744 1961	9.4342 5818	11.7385 1456	14.5904 8748	46
47	7.9152 6849	9.9059 7109	12.3841 3287	15.4659 1673	47
48	8.2714 5557	10.4012 6965	13.0652 6017	16.3938 7173	48
49	8.6436 7107	10.9213 3313	13.7838 4948	17.3775 0403	49
50	9.0326 3627	11.4673 9979	14.5419 6120	18.4201 5428	50

TABLE 5 COMPOUND AMOUNT

WHEN PRINCIPAL IS 1

$$s=(1+i)^n$$

n	$4\frac{1}{2}\%$	5%	$5\frac{1}{2}\%$	6%	n
51	9.4391 0490	12.0407 6978	15.3417 6907	19.5253 6353	51
52	9.8638 6463	12.6428 0826	16.1855 6637	20.6968 8534	52
53	10.3077 3853	13.2749 4868	17.0757 7252	21.9386 9846	53
54	10.7715 8677	13.9386 9611	18.0149 4001	23.2550 2037	54
55	11.2563 0817	14.6356 3092	19.0057 6171	24.6503 2159	55
56	11.7628 4204	15.3674 1246	20.0510 7860	26.1293 4089	56
57	12.2921 6993	16.1357 8309	21.1538 8793	27.6971 0134	57
58	12.8453 1758	16.9425 7224	22.3173 5176	29.3589 2742	58
59	13.4233 5687	17.7897 0085	23.5448 0611	31.1204 6307	59
60	14.0274 0793	18.6791 8589	24.8397 7045	32.9876 9085	60
61	14.6586 4129	19.6131 4519	26.2059 5782	34.9669 5230	61
62	15.3182 8014	20.5938 0245	27.6472 8550	37.0649 6944	62
63	16.0076 0275	21.6234 9257	29.1678 8620	39.2888 6761	63
64	16.7279 4487	22.7046 6720	30.7721 1994	41.6461 9967	64
65	17.4807 0239	23.8399 0056	32.4645 8654	44.1449 7165	65
66	18.2673 3400	25.0318 9559	34.2501 3880	46.7936 6994	66
67	19.0893 6403	26.2834 9037	36.1338 9643	49.6012 9014	67
68	19.9483 8541	27.5976 6488	38.1212 6074	52.5773 6755	68
69	20.8460 6276	28.9775 4813	40.2179 3008	55.7320 0960	69
70	21.7841 3558	30.4264 2554	42.4299 1623	59.0759 3018	70
71	22.7644 2168	31.9477 4681	44.7635 6163	62.6204 8599	71
72	23.7888 2066	33.5451 3415	47.2255 5751	66.3777 1515	72
73	24.8593 1759	35.2223 9086	49.8229 6318	70.3603 7806	73
74	25.9779 8688	36.9835 1040	52.5632 2615	74.5820 0074	74
75	27.1469 9629	38.8326 8592	55.4542 0359	79.0569 2079	75
76	28.3686 1112	40.7743 2022	58.5041 8479	83.8003 3603	76
77	29.6451 9862	42.8130 3623	61.7219 1495	88.8283 5620	77
78	30.9792 3256	44.9536 8804	65.1166 2027	94.1580 5757	78
79	32.3732 9802	47.2013 7244	68.6980 3439	99.8075 4102	79
80	33.8300 9643	49.5614 4107	72.4764 2628	105.7959 9348	80
81	35.3524 5077	52.0395 1312	76.4626 2973	112.1437 5309	81
82	36.9433 1106	54.6414 8878	80.6680 7436	118.8723 7828	82
83	38.6057 6006	57.3735 6322	85.1048 1845	126.0047 2097	83
84	40.3430 1926	60.2422 4138	89.7855 8347	133.5650 0423	84
85	42.1584 5513	63.2543 5344	94.7237 9056	141.5789 0449	85
86	44.0555 8561	66.4170 7112	99.9335 9904	150.0736 3875	86
87	46.0380 8696	69.7379 2467	105.4299 4698	159.0780 5708	87
88	48.1098 0087	73.2248 2091	111.2285 9407	168.6227 4050	88
89	50.2747 4191	76.8860 6195	117.3461 6674	178.7401 0493	89
90	52.5371 0530	80.7303 6505	123.8002 0591	189.4645 1123	90
91	54.9012 7504	84.7668 8330	130.6092 1724	200.8323 8190	91
92	57.3718 3241	89.0052 2747	137.7927 2419	212.8823 2482	92
93	59.9535 6487	93.4554 8884	145.3713 2402	225.6552 6431	93
94	62.6514 7529	98.1282 6328	153.3667 4684	239.1945 8017	94
95	65.4707 9168	103.0346 7645	161.8019 1791	253.5462 5498	95
96	68.4169 7730	108.1864 1027	170.7010 2340	268.7590 3028	96
97	71.4957 4128	113.5957 3078	180.0895 7969	284.8845 7209	97
98	74.7130 4964	119.2755 1732	189.9945 0657	301.9776 4642	98
99	78.0751 3687	125.2392 9319	200.4442 0443	320.0963 0520	99
100	81.5885 1803	131.5012 5785	211.4686 3567	339.3020 8351	100

TABLE 5 COMPOUND AMOUNT

WHEN PRINCIPAL IS 1

$$s = (1 + i)^n$$

n	$6\frac{1}{2}\%$	7%	$7\frac{1}{2}\%$	8%	n
1	1.0650 0000	1.0700 0000	1.0750 0000	1.0800 0000	1
2	1.1342 2500	1.1449 0000	1.1556 2500	1.1664 0000	2
3	1.2079 4963	1.2250 4300	1.2422 9688	1.2597 1200	3
4	1.2864 6635	1.3107 9601	1.3354 6914	1.3604 8896	4
5	1.3700 8666	1.4025 5173	1.4356 2933	1.4693 2808	5
6	1.4591 4230	1.5007 3035	1.5433 0153	1.5868 7432	6
7	1.5539 8655	1.6057 8148	1.6590 4914	1.7138 2427	7
8	1.6549 9567	1.7181 8618	1.7834 7783	1.8509 3021	8
9	1.7625 7039	1.8384 5921	1.9172 3866	1.9990 0463	9
10	1.8771 3747	1.9671 5136	2.0610 3156	2.1589 2500	10
11	1.9991 5140	2.1048 5195	2.2156 0893	2.3316 3900	11
12	2.1290 9624	2.2521 9159	2.3817 7960	2.5181 7012	12
13	2.2674 8750	2.4098 4500	2.5604 1307	2.7196 2373	13
14	2.4148 7418	2.5785 3415	2.7524 4405	2.9371 9362	14
15	2.5718 4101	2.7590 3154	2.9588 7735	3.1721 6911	15
16	2.7390 1067	2.9521 6375	3.1807 9315	3.4259 4264	16
17	2.9170 4637	3.1588 1521	3.4193 5264	3.7000 1805	17
18	3.1066 5438	3.3799 3228	3.6758 0409	3.9960 1950	18
19	3.3085 8691	3.6165 2754	3.9514 8940	4.3157 0106	19
20	3.5236 4506	3.8696 8446	4.2478 5110	4.6609 5714	20
21	3.7526 8199	4.1405 6237	4.5664 3993	5.0338 3372	21
22	3.9966 0632	4.4304 0174	4.9089 2293	5.4365 4041	22
23	4.2563 8573	4.7405 2986	5.2770 9215	5.8714 6365	23
24	4.5330 5081	5.0723 6695	5.6728 7406	6.3411 8074	24
25	4.8276 9911	5.4274 3264	6.0983 3961	6.8484 7520	25
26	5.1414 9955	5.8073 5292	6.5557 1508	7.3963 5321	26
27	5.4756 9702	6.2138 6763	7.0473 9371	7.9880 6147	27
28	5.8316 1733	6.6488 3836	7.5759 4824	8.6271 0639	28
29	6.2106 7245	7.1142 5705	8.1441 4436	9.3172 7490	29
30	6.6143 6616	7.6122 5504	8.7549 5519	10.0626 5689	30
31	7.0442 9996	8.1451 1290	9.4115 7683	10.8676 6944	31
32	7.5021 7946	8.7152 7080	10.1174 4509	11.7370 8300	32
33	7.9898 2113	9.3253 3975	10.8762 5347	12.6760 4964	33
34	8.5091 5950	9.9781 1354	11.6919 7248	13.6901 3361	34
35	9.0622 5487	10.6765 8148	12.5688 7042	14.7853 4429	35
36	9.6513 0143	11.4239 4219	13.5115 3570	15.9681 7184	36
37	10.2786 3603	12.2236 1814	14.5249 0088	17.2456 2558	37
38	10.9467 4737	13.0792 7141	15.6142 6844	18.6252 7563	38
39	11.6582 8595	13.9948 2041	16.7853 3858	20.1152 9768	39
40	12.4160 7453	14.9744 5784	18.0442 3897	21.7245 2150	40
41	13.2231 1938	16.0226 6989	19.3975 5689	23.4624 8322	41
42	14.0826 2214	17.1442 5678	20.8523 7366	25.3394 8187	42
43	14.9979 9258	18.3443 5475	22.4163 0168	27.3666 4042	43
44	15.9728 6209	19.6284 5959	24.0975 2431	29.5559 7166	44
45	17.0110 9813	21.0024 5176	25.9048 3863	31.9204 4939	45
46	18.1168 1951	22.4726 2338	27.8477 0153	34.4740 8534	46
47	19.2944 1278	24.0457 0702	29.9362 7915	37.2320 1217	47
48	20.5485 4961	25.7289 0651	32.1815 0008	40.2105 7314	48
49	21.8842 0533	27.5299 2997	34.5951 1259	43.4274 1899	49
50	23.3066 7868	29.4570 2506	37.1897 4603	46.9016 1251	50

TABLE 5 COMPOUND AMOUNT
WHEN PRINCIPAL IS 1

$$s = (1 + i)^n$$

n	$6\frac{1}{2}$%	7%	$7\frac{1}{2}$%	8%	n
51	24.8216 1279	31.5190 1682	39.9789 7698	50.6537 4151	51
52	26.4350 1762	33.7253 4799	42.9774 0026	54.7060 4084	52
53	28.1532 9377	36.0861 2235	46.2007 0528	59.0825 2410	53
54	29.9832 5786	38.6121 5092	49.6657 5817	63.8091 2603	54
55	31.9321 6963	41.3150 0148	53.3906 9004	68.9138 5611	55
56	34.0077 6065	44.2070 5159	57.3949 9179	74.4269 6460	56
57	36.2182 6509	47.3015 4520	61.6996 1617	80.3811 2177	57
58	38.5724 5233	50.6126 5336	66.3270 8739	86.8116 1151	58
59	41.0796 6173	54.1555 3910	71.3016 1894	93.7565 4043	59
60	43.7498 3974	57.9464 2683	76.6492 4036	101.2570 6367	60
61	46.5935 7932	62.0026 7671	82.3979 3339	109.3576 2876	61
62	49.6221 6198	66.3428 6408	88.5777 7839	118.1062 3906	62
63	52.8476 0251	70.9868 6457	95.2211 1177	127.5547 3819	63
64	56.2826 9667	75.9559 4509	102.3626 9515	137.7591 1724	64
65	59.9410 7195	81.2728 6124	110.0398 9729	148.7798 4662	65
66	63.8372 4163	86.9619 6153	118.2928 8959	160.6822 3435	66
67	67.9866 6234	93.0492 9884	127.1648 5631	173.5368 1310	67
68	72.4057 9539	99.5627 4976	136.7022 2053	187.4197 5815	68
69	77.1121 7209	106.5321 4224	146.9548 8707	202.4133 3880	69
70	82.1244 6327	113.9893 9220	157.9756 0360	218.6064 0590	70
71	87.4625 5339	121.9686 4965	169.8247 4137	236.0949 1837	71
72	93.1476 1936	130.5064 5513	182.5615 9697	254.9825 1184	72
73	99.2022 1461	139.6419 0699	196.2537 1675	275.3811 1279	73
74	105.6503 5856	149.4168 4048	210.9727 4550	297.4116 0181	74
75	112.5176 3187	159.8760 1931	226.7957 0141	321.2045 2996	75
76	119.8312 7794	171.0673 4066	243.8053 7902	346.9008 9236	76
77	127.6203 1101	183.0420 5451	262.0907 8245	374.6529 6374	77
78	135.9156 3122	195.8549 9832	281.7475 9113	404.6252 0084	78
79	144.7501 4725	209.5648 4820	302.8786 6046	436.9952 1691	79
80	154.1589 0683	224.2343 8758	325.5945 6000	471.9548 3426	80
81	164.1792 3577	239.9307 9471	350.0141 5200	509.7112 2101	81
82	174.8508 8609	256.7259 5034	376.2652 1340	550.4881 1869	82
83	186.2161 9369	274.6967 6686	404.4851 0440	594.5271 6818	83
84	198.3202 4628	293.9255 4054	434.8214 8723	642.0893 4164	84
85	211.2110 6229	314.5003 2838	467.4330 9878	693.4564 8897	85
86	224 9397 8134	336.5153 5137	502.4905 8119	748.9330 0808	86
87	239.5608 6712	360.0714 2596	540.1773 7477	808.8476 4873	87
88	255.1323 2349	385.2764 2578	580.6906 7788	873.5554 6063	88
89	271.7159 2451	412.2457 7558	624.2424 7872	943.4398 9748	89
90	289.3774 5961	441.1029 7988	671.0606 6463	1018.9150 8928	90
91	308.1869 9448	471.9801 8847	721.3902 1447	1100.4282 9642	91
92	328.2191 4912	505.0188 0166	775.4944 8056	1188.4625 6013	92
93	349.5533 9382	540.3701 1778	833.6565 6660	1283.5395 6494	93
94	372.2743 6441	578.1960 2602	896.1808 0910	1386.2227 3014	94
95	396.4721 9810	618.6697 4784	963.3943 6978	1497.1205 4855	95
96	422.2428 9098	661.9766 3019	1035.6489 4751	1616.8901 9244	96
97	449.6886 7889	708.3149 9430	1113.3226 1858	1746.2414 0783	97
98	478.9184 4302	757.8970 4390	1196.8218 1497	1885.9407 2046	98
99	510.0481 4181	810.9498 3698	1286.5834 5109	2036.8159 7809	99
100	543.2012 7103	867.7163 2557	1383.0772 0993	2199.7612 5634	100

TABLE 5 COMPOUND AMOUNT

WHEN PRINCIPAL IS 1

$$s = (1 + i)^n$$

n	$8\frac{1}{2}\%$	9%	$9\frac{1}{2}\%$	10%	n
1	1.0850 0000	1.0900 0000	1.0950 0000	1.1000 0000	1
2	1.1772 2500	1.1881 0000	1.1990 2500	1.2100 0000	2
3	1.2772 8913	1.2950 2900	1.3129 3238	1.3310 0000	3
4	1.3858 5870	1.4115 8161	1.4376 6095	1.4641 0000	4
5	1.5036 5669	1.5386 2395	1.5742 3874	1.6105 1000	5
6	1.6314 6751	1.6771 0011	1.7237 9142	1.7715 6100	6
7	1.7701 4225	1.8280 3912	1.8875 5161	1.9487 1710	7
8	1.9206 0434	1.9925 6264	2.0668 6901	2.1435 8881	8
9	2.0838 5571	2.1718 9328	2.2632 2156	2.3579 4769	9
10	2.2609 8344	2.3673 6367	2.4782 2761	2.5937 4246	10
11	2.4531 6703	2.5804 2641	2.7136 5924	2.8531 1671	11
12	2.6616 8623	2.8126 6478	2.9714 5686	3.1384 2838	12
13	2.8879 2956	3.0658 0461	3.2537 4527	3.4522 7121	13
14	3.1334 0357	3.3417 2703	3.5628 5107	3.7974 9834	14
15	3.3997 4288	3.6424 8246	3.9013 2192	4.1772 4817	15
16	3.6887 2102	3.9703 0588	4.2719 4750	4.5949 7299	16
17	4.0022 6231	4.3276 3341	4.6777 8251	5.0544 7029	17
18	4.3424 5461	4.7171 2042	5.1221 7185	5.5599 1731	18
19	4.7115 6325	5.1416 6125	5.6087 7818	6.1159 0904	19
20	5.1120 4612	5.6044 1077	6.1416 1210	6.7274 9995	20
21	5.5465 7005	6.1088 0774	6.7250 6525	7.4002 4994	21
22	6.0180 2850	6.6586 0043	7.3639 4645	8.1402 7494	22
23	6.5295 6092	7.2578 7447	8.0635 2137	8.9543 0243	23
24	7.0845 7360	7.9110 8317	8.8295 5590	9.8497 3268	24
25	7.6867 6236	8.6230 8066	9.6683 6371	10.8347 0594	25
26	8.3401 3716	9.3991 5792	10.5868 5826	11.9181 7654	26
27	9.0490 4881	10.2450 8213	11.5926 0979	13.1099 9419	27
28	9.8182 1796	11.1671 3952	12.6939 0772	14.4209 9361	28
29	10.6527 6649	12.1721 8208	13.8998 2896	15.8630 9297	29
30	11.5582 5164	13.2676 7847	15.2203 1271	17.4494 0227	30
31	12.5407 0303	14.4617 6953	16.6662 4241	19.1943 4250	31
32	13.6066 6279	15.7633 2879	18.2495 3544	21.1137 7675	32
33	14.7632 2913	17.1820 2838	19.9832 4131	23.2251 5442	33
34	16.0181 0360	18.7284 1093	21.8816 4924	25.5476 6986	34
35	17.3796 4241	20.4139 6792	23.9604 0591	28.1024 3685	35
36	18.8569 1201	22.2512 2503	26.2366 4448	30.9126 8053	36
37	20.4597 4953	24.2538 3528	28.7291 2570	34.0039 4859	37
38	22.1988 2824	26.4366 8046	31.4583 9264	37.4043 4344	38
39	24.0857 2865	28.8159 8170	34.4469 3994	41.1447 7779	39
40	26.1330 1558	31.4094 2005	37.7193 9924	45.2592 5557	40
41	28.3543 2190	34.2362 6786	41.3027 4216	49.7851 8113	41
42	30.7644 3927	37.3175 3197	45.2265 0267	54.7636 9924	42
43	33.3794 1660	40.6761 0984	49.5230 2042	60.2400 6916	43
44	36.2166 6702	44.3369 5973	54.2277 0736	66.2640 7608	44
45	39.2950 8371	48.3272 8610	59.3793 3956	72.8904 8369	45
46	42.6351 6583	52.6767 4185	65.0203 7682	80.1795 3205	46
47	46.2591 5492	57.4176 4862	71.1973 1262	88.1974 8526	47
48	50.1911 8309	62.5852 3700	77.9610 5732	97.0172 3378	48
49	54.4574 3365	68.2179 0833	85.3673 5777	106.7189 5716	49
50	59.0863 1551	74.3575 2008	93.4772 5675	117.3908 5288	50

TABLE 5 COMPOUND AMOUNT

WHEN PRINCIPAL IS 1

$$s = (1 + i)^n$$

n	$8\frac{1}{2}\%$	9%	$9\frac{1}{2}\%$	10%	n
51	64.1086 5233	81.0496 9688	102.3575 9614	129.1299 3817	51
52	69.5578 8778	88.3441 6960	112.0815 6778	142.0429 3198	52
53	75.4703 0824	96.2951 4487	122.7293 1672	156.2472 2518	53
54	81.8852 8444	104.9617 0790	134.3886 0181	171.8719 4770	54
55	88.8455 3362	114.4082 6162	147.1555 1898	189.0591 4247	55
56	96.3974 0398	124.7050 0516	161.1352 9328	207.9650 5672	56
57	104.5911 8332	135.9284 5563	176.4431 4614	228.7615 6239	57
58	113.4814 3390	148.1620 1663	193.2052 4502	251.6377 1863	58
59	123.1273 5578	161.4965 9813	211.5597 4330	276.8014 9049	59
60	133.5931 8102	176.0312 9196	231.6579 1892	304.4816 3954	60
61	144.9486 0141	191.8741 0824	253.6654 2121	334.9298 0350	61
62	157.2692 3253	209.1427 7798	277.7636 3623	368.4227 8385	62
63	170.6371 1729	227.9656 2800	304.1511 8167	405.2650 6223	63
64	185.1412 7226	248.4825 3452	333.0455 4393	445.7915 6845	64
65	200.8782 8041	270.8459 6262	364.6848 7060	490.3707 2530	65
66	217.9529 3424	295.2220 9926	399.3299 3331	539.4077 9783	66
67	236.4789 3365	321.7920 8819	437.2662 7697	593.3485 7761	67
68	256.5796 4301	350.7533 7613	478.8065 7329	652.6834 3537	68
69	278.3889 1267	382.3211 7998	524.2931 9775	717.9517 7891	69
70	302.0519 7024	416.7300 8618	574.1010 5153	789.7469 5680	70
71	327.7263 8771	454.2357 9393	628.6406 5143	868.7216 5248	71
72	355.5831 3067	495.1170 1539	688.3615 1331	955.5938 1773	72
73	385.8076 9678	539.6775 4677	753.7558 5708	1051.1531 9950	73
74	418.6013 5100	588.2485 2598	825.3626 6350	1156.2685 1945	74
75	454.1824 6584	641.1908 9332	903.7721 1654	1271.8953 7140	75
76	492.7879 7543	698.8980 7372	989.6304 6761	1399.0849 0853	76
77	534.6749 5335	761.7989 0036	1083.6453 6203	1538.9933 9939	77
78	580.1223 2438	830.3608 0139	1186.5916 7142	1692.8927 3933	78
79	629.4327 2195	905.0932 7351	1299.3178 8021	1862.1820 1326	79
80	682.9345 0332	986.5516 6813	1422.7530 7883	2048.4002 1459	80
81	740.9839 3610	1075.3413 1826	1557.9146 2131	2253.2402 3604	81
82	803.9675 7067	1172.1220 3690	1705.9165 1034	2478.5642 5965	82
83	872.3048 1418	1277.6130 2022	1867.9785 7882	2726.4206 8561	83
84	946.4507 2338	1392.5981 9204	2045.4365 4381	2999.0627 5417	84
85	1026.8990 3487	1517.9320 2933	2239.7530 1547	3298.9690 2959	85
86	1114.1854 5283	1654.5459 1197	2452.5295 5194	3628.8659 3255	86
87	1208.8912 1633	1803.4550 4404	2685.5198 5938	3991.7525 2581	87
88	1311.6469 6971	1965.7659 9801	2940.6442 4602	4390.9277 7839	88
89	1423.1369 6214	2142.6849 3783	3220.0054 4939	4830.0205 5623	89
90	1544.1036 0392	2335.5265 8223	3525.9059 6708	5313.0226 1185	90
91	1675.3524 1025	2545.7239 7464	3860.8670 3395	5844.3248 7303	91
92	1817.7573 6512	2774.8391 3235	4227.6494 0218	6428.7573 6034	92
93	1972.2667 4116	3024.5746 5426	4629.2760 9538	7071.6330 9637	93
94	2139.9094 1416	3296.7863 7315	5069.0573 2445	7778.7964 0601	94
95	2321.8017 1436	3593.4971 4673	5550.6177 7027	8556.6760 4661	95
96	2519.1548 6008	3916.9118 8994	6077.9264 5844	9412.3436 5127	96
97	2733.2830 2319	4269.4339 6003	6655.3294 7199	10353.5780 1640	97
98	2965.6120 8016	4653.6830 1643	7287.5857 7183	11388.9358 1803	98
99	3217.6891 0698	5072.5144 8791	7979.9064 2016	12527.8293 9984	99
100	3491.1926 8107	5529.0407 9183	8737.9975 3007	13780.6123 3982	100

TABLE 5A SUPPLEMENT TO TABLE 5
FOR FRACTIONAL INTEREST PERIODS

$$s = (1 + i)^{\frac{1}{m}}$$

m	$\frac{1}{4}\%$	$\frac{1}{3}\%$	$\frac{5}{12}\%$	$\frac{11}{24}\%$	$\frac{1}{2}\%$	m
2	1.0012 4922	1.0016 6528	1.0020 8117	1.0022 8905	1.0024 9688	2
3	1.0008 3264	1.0011 0988	1.0013 8696	1.0015 2545	1.0016 6390	3
4	1.0006 2441	1.0008 3229	1.0010 4004	1.0011 4387	1.0012 4766	4
6	1.0004 1623	1.0005 5479	1.0006 9324	1.0007 6243	1.0008 3160	6
12	1.0002 0809	1.0002 7735	1.0003 4656	1.0003 8114	1.0004 1571	12

m	$\frac{13}{24}\%$	$\frac{7}{12}\%$	$\frac{5}{8}\%$	$\frac{2}{3}\%$	$\frac{3}{4}\%$	m
2	1.0027 0468	1.0029 1243	1.0031 2013	1.0033 2780	1.0037 4299	2
3	1.0018 0231	1.0019 4068	1.0020 7901	1.0022 1730	1.0024 9378	3
4	1.0013 5142	1.0014 5515	1.0015 5885	1.0016 6252	1.0018 6975	4
6	1.0009 0075	1.0009 6987	1.0010 3896	1.0011 0804	1.0012 4611	6
12	1.0004 5027	1.0004 8482	1.0005 1935	1.0005 5387	1.0006 2286	12

m	$\frac{7}{8}\%$	1%	$1\frac{1}{8}\%$	$1\frac{1}{4}\%$	$1\frac{3}{8}\%$	m
2	1.0043 6547	1.0049 8756	1.0056 0927	1.0062 3059	1.0068 5153	2
3	1.0029 0820	1.0033 2228	1.0037 3602	1.0041 4943	1.0045 6249	3
4	1.0021 8036	1.0024 9068	1.0028 0071	1.0031 1046	1.0034 1992	4
6	1.0014 5304	1.0016 5976	1.0018 6627	1.0020 7256	1.0022 7865	6
12	1.0007 2626	1.0008 2954	1.0009 3270	1.0010 3575	1.0011 3868	12

m	$1\frac{1}{2}\%$	$1\frac{5}{8}\%$	$1\frac{3}{4}\%$	$1\frac{7}{8}\%$	2%	m
2	1.0074 7208	1.0080 9226	1.0087 1205	1.0093 3146	1.0099 5049	2
3	1.0049 7521	1.0053 8759	1.0057 9963	1.0062 1134	1.0066 2271	3
4	1.0037 2909	1.0040 3798	1.0043 4658	1.0046 5490	1.0049 6293	4
6	1.0024 8452	1.0026 9018	1.0028 9562	1.0031 0086	1.0033 0589	6
12	1.0012 4149	1.0013 4418	1.0014 4677	1.0015 4923	1.0016 5158	12

m	$2\frac{1}{4}\%$	$2\frac{1}{2}\%$	$2\frac{3}{4}\%$	3%	$3\frac{1}{4}\%$	m
2	1.0111 8742	1.0124 2284	1.0136 5675	1.0148 8916	1.0161 2007	2
3	1.0074 4444	1.0082 6484	1.0090 8390	1.0099 0163	1.0107 1805	3
4	1.0055 7815	1.0061 9225	1.0068 0522	1.0074 1707	1.0080 2781	4
6	1.0037 1532	1.0041 2392	1.0045 3168	1.0049 3862	1.0053 4474	6
12	1.0018 5594	1.0020 5984	1.0022 6328	1.0024 6627	1.0026 6881	12

m	$3\frac{1}{2}\%$	$3\frac{3}{4}\%$	4%	$4\frac{1}{2}\%$	5%	m
2	1.0173 4950	1.0185 7744	1.0198 0390	1.0222 5242	1.0246 9508	2
3	1.0115 3314	1.0123 4693	1.0131 5940	1.0147 8046	1.0163 9636	3
4	1.0086 3745	1.0092 4598	1.0098 5341	1.0110 6499	1.0122 7223	4
6	1.0057 5004	1.0061 5452	1.0065 5820	1.0073 6312	1.0081 6485	6
12	1.0028 7090	1.0030 7254	1.0032 7374	1.0036 7481	1.0040 7412	12

TABLE 5A SUPPLEMENT TO TABLE 5
FOR FRACTIONAL INTEREST PERIODS

$$s = (1 + i)^{\frac{1}{m}}$$

m	$5\frac{1}{2}\%$	6%	$6\frac{1}{2}\%$	7%	$7\frac{1}{2}\%$	m
2	1.0271 3193	1.0295 6301	1.0319 8837	1.0344 0804	1.0368 2207	2
3	1.0180 0713	1.0196 1282	1.0212 1347	1.0228 0912	1.0243 9981	3
4	1.0134 7517	1.0146 7385	1.0158 6828	1.0170 5853	1.0182 4460	4
6	1.0089 6339	1.0097 5879	1.0105 5107	1.0113 4026	1.0121 2638	6
12	1.0044 7170	1.0048 6755	1.0052 6169	1.0056 5415	1.0060 4492	12

m	8%	$8\frac{1}{2}\%$	9%	$9\frac{1}{2}\%$	10%	m
2	1.0392 3048	1.0416 3333	1.0440 3065	1.0464 2248	1.0488 0885	2
3	1.0259 8557	1.0275 6644	1.0291 4247	1.0307 1368	1.0322 8012	3
4	1.0194 2655	1.0206 0440	1.0217 7818	1.0229 4793	1.0241 1369	4
6	1.0129 0946	1.0136 8952	1.0144 6659	1.0152 4070	1.0160 1187	6
12	1.0064 3403	1.0068 2149	1.0072 0732	1.0075 9153	1.0079 7414	12

TABLE 6 PRESENT VALUE
WHEN COMPOUND AMOUNT IS 1

$$p=(1+i)^{-n} \quad [OR,\ v^{n}=(1+i)^{-n}]$$

n	$\frac{1}{4}\%$	$\frac{1}{3}\%$	$\frac{5}{12}\%$	$\frac{11}{24}\%$	n
1	0.9975 0623	0.9966 7774	0.9958 5062	0.9954 3758	1
2	0.9950 1869	0.9933 6652	0.9917 1846	0.9908 9597	2
3	0.9925 3734	0.9900 6630	0.9876 0345	0.9863 7509	3
4	0.9900 6219	0.9867 7704	0.9835 0551	0.9818 7483	4
5	0.9875 9321	0.9834 9871	0.9794 2457	0.9773 9510	5
6	0.9851 3038	0.9802 3127	0.9753 6057	0.9729 3581	6
7	0.9826 7370	0.9769 7469	0.9713 1343	0.9684 9687	7
8	0.9802 2314	0.9737 2893	0.9672 8308	0.9640 7817	8
9	0.9777 7869	0.9704 9395	0.9632 6946	0.9596 7964	9
10	0.9753 4034	0.9672 6972	0.9592 7249	0.9553 0118	10
11	0.9729 0807	0.9640 5620	0.9552 9211	0.9509 4269	11
12	0.9704 8187	0.9608 5335	0.9513 2824	0.9466 0409	12
13	0.9680 6171	0.9576 6115	0.9473 8082	0.9422 8528	13
14	0.9656 4759	0.9544 7955	0.9434 4978	0.9379 8618	14
15	0.9632 3949	0.9513 0852	0.9395 3505	0.9337 0669	15
16	0.9608 3740	0.9481 4803	0.9356 3657	0.9294 4672	16
17	0.9584 4130	0.9449 9803	0.9317 5426	0.9252 0620	17
18	0.9560 5117	0.9418 5851	0.9278 8806	0.9209 8502	18
19	0.9536 6700	0.9387 2941	0.9240 3790	0.9167 8309	19
20	0.9512 8878	0.9356 1071	0.9202 0372	0.9126 0034	20
21	0.9489 1649	0.9325 0236	0.9163 8544	0.9084 3667	21
22	0.9465 5011	0.9294 0435	0.9125 8301	0.9042 9200	22
23	0.9441 8964	0.9263 1663	0.9087 9636	0.9001 6624	23
24	0.9418 3505	0.9232 3916	0.9050 2542	0.8960 5930	24
25	0.9394 8634	0.9201 7192	0.9012 7013	0.8919 7110	25
26	0.9371 4348	0.9171 1487	0.8975 3042	0.8879 0155	26
27	0.9348 0646	0.9140 6798	0.8938 0623	0.8838 5057	27
28	0.9324 7527	0.9110 3121	0.8900 9749	0.8798 1807	28
29	0.9301 4990	0.9080 0453	0.8864 0414	0.8758 0397	29
30	0.9278 3032	0.9049 8790	0.8827 2611	0.8718 0818	30
31	0.9255 1653	0.9019 8130	0.8790 6335	0.8678 3062	31
32	0.9232 0851	0.8989 8468	0.8754 1578	0.8638 7121	32
33	0.9209 0624	0.8959 9802	0.8717 8335	0.8599 2987	33
34	0.9186 0972	0.8930 2128	0.8681 6599	0.8560 0651	34
35	0.9163 1892	0.8900 5444	0.8645 6365	0.8521 0104	35
36	0.9140 3384	0.8870 9745	0.8609 7624	0.8482 1340	36
37	0.9117 5445	0.8841 5028	0.8574 0373	0.8443 4349	37
38	0.9094 8075	0.8812 1290	0.8538 4604	0.8404 9124	38
39	0.9072 1272	0.8782 8528	0.8503 0311	0.8366 5656	39
40	0.9049 5034	0.8753 6739	0.8467 7488	0.8328 3938	40
41	0.9026 9361	0.8724 5920	0.8432 6129	0.8290 3962	41
42	0.9004 4250	0.8695 6066	0.8397 6228	0.8252 5719	42
43	0.8981 9701	0.8666 7175	0.8362 7779	0.8214 9202	43
44	0.8959 5712	0.8637 9245	0.8328 0776	0.8177 4402	44
45	0.8937 2281	0.8609 2270	0.8293 5212	0.8140 1313	45
46	0.8914 9407	0.8580 6249	0.8259 1083	0.8102 9926	46
47	0.8892 7090	0.8552 1179	0.8224 8381	0.8066 0233	47
48	0.8870 5326	0.8523 7055	0.8190 7102	0.8029 2227	48
49	0.8848 4116	0.8495 3876	0.8156 7238	0.7992 5900	49
50	0.8826 3457	0.8467 1637	0.8122 8785	0.7956 1244	50
51	0.8804 3349	0.8439 0336	0.8089 1736	0.7919 8252	51
52	0.8782 3790	0.8410 9969	0.8055 6086	0.7883 6916	52
53	0.8760 4778	0.8383 0534	0.8022 1828	0.7847 7229	53
54	0.8738 6312	0.8355 2027	0.7988 8957	0.7811 9183	54
55	0.8716 8391	0.8327 4446	0.7955 7468	0.7776 2770	55
56	0.8695 1013	0.8299 7787	0.7922 7354	0.7740 7984	56
57	0.8673 4178	0.8272 2047	0.7889 8610	0.7705 4816	57
58	0.8651 7883	0.8244 7222	0.7857 1230	0.7670 3259	58
59	0.8630 2128	0.8217 3311	0.7824 5208	0.7635 3306	59
60	0.8608 6911	0.8190 0310	0.7792 0539	0.7600.4950	60

TABLE 6 PRESENT VALUE
WHEN COMPOUND AMOUNT IS 1

$$p = (1+i)^{-n} \quad [OR,\ v^n = (1+i)^{-n}]$$

n	$\frac{1}{4}\%$	$\frac{1}{3}\%$	$\frac{5}{12}\%$	$\frac{11}{24}\%$	n
61	0.8587 2230	0.8162 8216	0.7759 7217	0.7565 8184	61
62	0.8565 8085	0.8135 7026	0.7727 5237	0.7531 2999	62
63	0.8544 4474	0.8108 6737	0.7695 4593	0.7496 9389	63
64	0.8523 1395	0.8081 7346	0.7663 5279	0.7462 7347	64
65	0.8501 8848	0.8054 8850	0.7631 7291	0.7428 6866	65
66	0.8480 6831	0.8028 1246	0.7600 0621	0.7394 7938	66
67	0.8459 5343	0.8001 4531	0.7568 5266	0.7361 0556	67
68	0.8438 4382	0.7974 8702	0.7537 1219	0.7327 4714	68
69	0.8417 3947	0.7948 3756	0.7505 8476	0.7294 0404	69
70	0.8396 4037	0.7921 9690	0.7474 7030	0.7260 7619	70
71	0.8375 4650	0.7895 6502	0.7443 6876	0.7227 6352	71
72	0.8354 5786	0.7869 4168	0.7412 8009	0.7194 6597	72
73	0.8333 7442	0.7843 2745	0.7382 0424	0.7161 8346	73
74	0.8312 9618	0.7817 2171	0.7351 4115	0.7129 1593	74
75	0.8292 2312	0.7791 2463	0.7320 9078	0.7096 6331	75
76	0.8271 5523	0.7765 3618	0.7290 5306	0.7064 2552	76
77	0.8250 9250	0.7739 5632	0.7260 2794	0.7032 0251	77
78	0.8230 3491	0.7713 8504	0.7230 1537	0.6999 9420	78
79	0.8209 8246	0.7688 2230	0.7200 1531	0.6968 0053	79
80	0.8189 3512	0.7662 6807	0.7170 2770	0.6936 2144	80
81	0.8168 9289	0.7637 2233	0.7140 5248	0.6904 5684	81
82	0.8148 5575	0.7611 8505	0.7110 8960	0.6873 0669	82
83	0.8128 2369	0.7586 5619	0.7081 3902	0.6841 7090	83
84	0.8107 9670	0.7561 3574	0.7052 0069	0.6810 4943	84
85	0.8087 7476	0.7536 2366	0.7022 7454	0.6779 4219	85
86	0.8067 5787	0.7511 1993	0.6993 6054	0.6748 4913	86
87	0.8047 4600	0.7486 2451	0.6964 5863	0.6717 7019	87
88	0.8027 3915	0.7461 3739	0.6935 6876	0.6687 0529	88
89	0.8007 3731	0.7436 5853	0.6906 9088	0.6656 5437	89
90	0.7987 4046	0.7411 8790	0.6878 2495	0.6626 1738	90
91	0.7967 4859	0.7387 2548	0.6849 7090	0.6595 9424	91
92	0.7947 6168	0.7362 7125	0.6821 2870	0.6565 8489	92
93	0.7927 7973	0.7338 2516	0.6792 9829	0.6535 8927	93
94	0.7908 0273	0.7313 8720	0.6764 7962	0.6506 0732	94
95	0.7888 3065	0.7289 5735	0.6736 7265	0.6476 3898	95
96	0.7868 6349	0.7265 3556	0.6708 7733	0.6446 8417	96
97	0.7849 0124	0.7241 2182	0.6680 9361	0.6417 4285	97
98	0.7829 4388	0.7217 1610	0.6653 2143	0.6388 1495	98
99	0.7809 9140	0.7193 1837	0.6625 6076	0.6359 0041	99
100	0.7790 4379	0.7169 2861	0.6598 1155	0.6329 9916	100
101	0.7771 0104	0.7145 4679	0.6570 7374	0.6301 1115	101
102	0.7751 6313	0.7121 7288	0.6543 4730	0.6272 3632	102
103	0.7732 3006	0.7098 0686	0.6516 3216	0.6243 7460	103
104	0.7713 0180	0.7074 4869	0.6489 2829	0.6215 2594	104
105	0.7693 7836	0.7050 9837	0.6462 3565	0.6186 9028	105
106	0.7674 5971	0.7027 5585	0.6435 5417	0.6158 6755	106
107	0.7655 4584	0.7004 2111	0.6408 8382	0.6130 5770	107
108	0.7636 3675	0.6980 9413	0.6382 2455	0.6102 6067	108
109	0.7617 3242	0.6957 7488	0.6355 7632	0.6074 7641	109
110	0.7598 3284	0.6934 6334	0.6329 3907	0.6047 0484	110
111	0.7579 3799	0.6911 5947	0.6303 1277	0.6019 4592	111
112	0.7560 4787	0.6888 6326	0.6276 9736	0.5991 9959	112
113	0.7541 6247	0.6865 7468	0.6250 9281	0.5964 6579	113
114	0.7522 8176	0.6842 9370	0.6224 9906	0.5937 4446	114
115	0.7504 0575	0.6820 2030	0.6199 1608	0.5910 3555	115
116	0.7485 3441	0.6797 5445	0.6173 4381	0.5883 3900	116
117	0.7466 6774	0.6774 9613	0.6147 8222	0.5856 5474	117
118	0.7448 0573	0.6752 4531	0.6122 3126	0.5829 8274	118
119	0.7429 4836	0.6730 0197	0.6096 9088	0.5803 2293	119
120	0.7410 9562	0.6707 6608	0.6071 6104	0.5776 7525	120

TABLE 6 PRESENT VALUE

WHEN COMPOUND AMOUNT IS 1

$$p = (1+i)^{-n} \quad [OR,\ v^n = (1+i)^{-n}]$$

n	$\frac{1}{4}$%	$\frac{1}{3}$%	$\frac{5}{12}$%	$\frac{11}{24}$%	n
121	0.7392 4750	0.6685 3763	0.6046 4170	0.5750 3965	121
122	0.7374 0399	0.6663 1657	0.6021 3281	0.5724 1608	122
123	0.7355 6508	0.6641 0289	0.5996 3434	0.5698 0447	123
124	0.7337 3075	0.6618 9657	0.5971 4623	0.5672 0478	124
125	0.7319 0100	0.6596 9758	0.5946 6844	0.5646 1696	125
126	0.7300 7581	0.6575 0589	0.5922 0094	0.5620 4094	126
127	0.7282 5517	0.6553 2149	0.5897 4367	0.5594 7667	127
128	0.7264 3907	0.6531 4434	0.5872 9660	0.5569 2410	128
129	0.7246 2750	0.6509 7443	0.5848 5969	0.5543 8318	129
130	0.7228 2045	0.6488 1172	0.5824 3288	0.5518 5385	130
131	0.7210 1791	0.6466 5620	0.5800 1615	0.5493 3606	131
132	0.7192 1986	0.6445 0784	0.5776 0944	0.5468 2975	132
133	0.7174 2629	0.6423 6662	0.5752 1273	0.5443 3488	133
134	0.7156 3720	0.6402 3251	0.5728 2595	0.5418 5140	134
135	0.7138 5257	0.6381 0549	0.5704 4908	0.5393 7924	135
136	0.7120 7239	0.6359 8554	0.5680 8207	0.5369 1837	136
137	0.7102 9664	0.6338 7263	0.5657 2488	0.5344 6872	137
138	0.7085 2533	0.6317 6674	0.5633 7748	0.5320 3025	138
139	0.7067 5843	0.6296 6785	0.5610 3981	0.5296 0290	139
140	0.7049 9595	0.6275 7593	0.5587 1185	0.5271 8663	140
141	0.7032 3785	0.6254 9096	0.5563 9354	0.5247 8138	141
142	0.7014 8414	0.6234 1292	0.5540 8485	0.5223 8711	142
143	0.6997 3480	0.6213 4178	0.5517 8574	0.5200 0376	143
144	0.6979 8983	0.6192 7752	0.5494 9618	0.5176 3128	144
145	0.6962 4921	0.6172 2012	0.5472 1611	0.5152 6963	145
146	0.6945 1292	0.6151 6955	0.5449 4550	0.5129 1875	146
147	0.6927 8097	0.6131 2580	0.5426 8432	0.5105 7860	147
148	0.6910 5334	0.6110 8884	0.5404 3252	0.5082 4912	148
149	0.6893 3001	0.6090 5864	0.5381 9006	0.5059 3028	149
150	0.6876 1098	0.6070 3519	0.5359 5690	0.5036 2201	150
151	0.6858 9624	0.6050 1846	0.5337 3302	0.5013 2427	151
152	0.6841 8578	0.6030 0843	0.5315 1836	0.4990 3702	152
153	0.6824 7958	0.6010 0508	0.5293 1289	0.4967 6020	153
154	0.6807 7764	0.5990 0839	0.5271 1657	0.4944 9377	154
155	0.6790 7994	0.5970 1833	0.5249 2936	0.4922 3768	155
156	0.6773 8647	0.5950 3488	0.5227 5123	0.4899 9189	156
157	0.6756 9723	0.5930 5802	0.5205 8214	0.4877 5634	157
158	0.6740 1220	0.5910 8773	0.5184 2205	0.4855 3099	158
159	0.6723 3137	0.5891 2398	0.5162 7092	0.4833 1579	159
160	0.6706 5473	0.5871 6676	0.5141 2872	0.4811 1070	160
161	0.6689 8228	0.5852 1604	0.5119 9540	0.4789 1567	161
162	0.6673 1399	0.5832 7180	0.5098 7094	0.4767 3065	162
163	0.6656 4987	0.5813 3402	0.5077 5529	0.4745 5561	163
164	0.6639 8989	0.5794 0268	0.5056 4842	0.4723 9048	164
165	0.6623 3406	0.5774 7775	0.5035 5030	0.4702 3524	165
166	0.6606 8235	0.5755 5922	0.5014 6088	0.4680 8983	166
167	0.6590 3476	0.5736 4706	0.4993 8013	0.4659 5420	167
168	0.6573 9129	0.5717 4126	0.4973 0801	0.4638 2832	168
169	0.6557 5191	0.5698 4179	0.4952 4449	0.4617 1214	169
170	0.6541 1661	0.5679 4862	0.4931 8954	0.4596 0562	170
171	0.6524 8540	0.5660 6175	0.4911 4311	0.4575 0870	171
172	0.6508 5826	0.5641 8115	0.4891 0517	0.4554 2135	172
173	0.6492 3517	0.5623 0679	0.4870 7569	0.4533 4353	173
174	0.6476 1613	0.5604 3866	0.4850 5462	0.4512 7518	174
175	0.6460 0112	0.5585 7674	0.4830 4195	0.4492 1628	175
176	0.6443 9015	0.5567 2100	0.4810 3763	0.4471 6676	176
177	0.6427 8319	0.5548 7143	0.4790 4162	0.4451 2660	177
178	0.6411 8024	0.5530 2801	0.4770 5390	0.4430 9574	178
179	0.6395 8129	0.5511 9070	0.4750 7442	0.4410 7415	179
180	0.6379 8632	0.5493 5950	0.4731 0316	0.4390 6179	180

TABLE 6

TABLE 6 PRESENT VALUE
WHEN COMPOUND AMOUNT IS 1

$$p = (1+i)^{-n} \quad [OR,\ v^n = (1+i)^{-n}]$$

n	$\frac{1}{4}\%$	$\frac{1}{3}\%$	$\frac{5}{12}\%$	$\frac{11}{24}\%$	n
181	0.6363 9533	0.5475 3439	0.4711 4007	0.4370 5860	181
182	0.6348 0831	0.5457 1534	0.4691 8513	0.4350 6456	182
183	0.6332 2525	0.5439 0233	0.4672 3831	0.4330 7961	183
184	0.6316 4613	0.5420 9535	0.4652 9956	0.4311 0372	184
185	0.6300 7096	0.5402 9437	0.4633 6886	0.4291 3684	185
186	0.6284 9971	0.5384 9937	0.4614 4616	0.4271 7893	186
187	0.6269 3238	0.5367 1033	0.4595 3145	0.4252 2996	187
188	0.6253 6895	0.5349 2724	0.4576 2468	0.4232 8989	188
189	0.6238 0943	0.5331 5008	0.4557 2582	0.4213 5866	189
190	0.6222 5380	0.5313 7881	0.4538 3484	0.4194 3624	190
191	0.6207 0204	0.5296 1343	0.4519 5171	0.4175 2260	191
192	0.6191 5416	0.5278 5392	0.4500 7639	0.4156 1768	192
193	0.6176 1013	0.5261 0025	0.4482 0886	0.4137 2146	193
194	0.6160 6996	0.5243 5241	0.4463 4907	0.4118 3389	194
195	0.6145 3362	0.5226 1038	0.4444 9700	0.4099 5493	195
196	0.6130 0112	0.5208 7413	0.4426 5261	0.4080 8454	196
197	0.6114 7244	0.5191 4365	0.4408 1588	0.4062 2269	197
198	0.6099 4757	0.5174 1892	0.4389 8677	0.4043 6933	198
199	0.6084 2650	0.5156 9992	0.4371 6525	0.4025 2442	199
200	0.6069 0923	0.5139 8663	0.4353 5128	0.4006 8794	200
201	0.6053 9574	0.5122 7904	0.4335 4484	0.3988 5983	201
202	0.6038 8602	0.5105 7711	0.4317 4590	0.3970 4006	202
203	0.6023 8007	0.5088 8084	0.4299 5443	0.3952 2860	203
204	0.6008 7788	0.5071 9021	0.4281 7038	0.3934 2540	204
205	0.5993 7943	0.5055 0519	0.4263 9374	0.3916 3042	205
206	0.5978 8472	0.5038 2577	0.4246 2447	0.3898 4364	206
207	0.5963 9373	0.5021 5193	0.4228 6255	0.3880 6501	207
208	0.5949 0647	0.5004 8365	0.4211 0793	0.3862 9449	208
209	0.5934 2291	0.4988 2092	0.4193 6059	0.3845 3205	209
210	0.5919 4305	0.4971 6371	0.4176 2051	0.3827 7766	210
211	0.5904 6689	0.4955 1200	0.4158 8764	0.3810 3126	211
212	0.5889 9440	0.4938 6578	0.4141 6197	0.3792 9284	212
213	0.5875 2559	0.4922 2503	0.4124 4345	0.3775 6234	213
214	0.5860 6044	0.4905 8973	0.4107 3207	0.3758 3975	214
215	0.5845 9894	0.4889 5986	0.4090 2779	0.3741 2501	215
216	0.5831 4109	0.4873 3541	0.4073 3058	0.3724 1809	216
217	0.5816 8687	0.4857 1636	0.4056 4041	0.3707 1896	217
218	0.5802 3628	0.4841 0268	0.4039 5725	0.3690 2758	218
219	0.5787 8930	0.4824 9437	0.4022 8108	0.3673 4393	219
220	0.5773 4594	0.4808 9140	0.4006 1187	0.3656 6795	220
221	0.5759 0617	0.4792 9375	0.3989 4958	0.3639 9962	221
222	0.5744 7000	0.4777 0141	0.3972 9418	0.3623 3890	222
223	0.5730 3741	0.4761 1437	0.3956 4566	0.3606 8575	223
224	0.5716 0838	0.4745 3259	0.3940 0398	0.3590 4015	224
225	0.5701 8293	0.4729 5607	0.3923 6911	0.3574 0206	225
226	0.5687 6102	0.4713 8479	0.3907 4102	0.3557 7144	226
227	0.5673 4267	0.4698 1872	0.3891 1969	0.3541 4826	227
228	0.5659 2785	0.4682 5786	0.3875 0508	0.3525 3249	228
229	0.5645 1656	0.4667 0219	0.3858 9718	0.3509 2408	229
230	0.5631 0879	0.4651 5169	0.3842 9594	0.3493 2302	230
231	0.5617 0452	0.4636 0633	0.3827 0136	0.3477 2926	231
232	0.5603 0376	0.4620 6611	0.3811 1338	0.3461 4277	232
233	0.5589 0650	0.4605 3101	0.3795 3200	0.3445 6352	233
234	0.5575 1272	0.4590 0100	0.3779 5718	0.3429 9148	234
235	0.5561 2241	0.4574 7608	0.3763 8889	0.3414 2661	235
236	0.5547 3557	0.4559 5623	0.3748 2711	0.3398 6888	236
237	0.5533 5219	0.4544 4142	0.3732 7181	0.3383 1825	237
238	0.5519 7226	0.4529 3165	0.3717 2297	0.3367 7470	238
239	0.5505 9577	0.4514 2690	0.3701 8055	0.3352 3819	239
240	0.5492 2271	0.4499 2714	0.3686 4453	0.3337 0869	240

TABLE 6 PRESENT VALUE

WHEN COMPOUND AMOUNT IS 1

$$p = (1+i)^{-n} \quad [OR,\ v^n = (1+i)^{-n}]$$

n	$\frac{1}{2}\%$	$\frac{13}{24}\%$	$\frac{7}{12}\%$	$\frac{5}{8}\%$	n
1	0.9950 2488	0.9946 1252	0.9942 0050	0.9937 8882	1
2	0.9900 7450	0.9892 5406	0.9884 3463	0.9876 1622	2
3	0.9851 4876	0.9839 2447	0.9827 0220	0.9814 8196	3
4	0.9802 4752	0.9786 2359	0.9770 0301	0.9753 8580	4
5	0.9753 7067	0.9733 5127	0.9713 3688	0.9693 2750	5
6	0.9705 1808	0.9681 0735	0.9657 0361	0.9633 0683	6
7	0.9656 8963	0.9628 9169	0.9601 0301	0.9573 2356	7
8	0.9608 8520	0.9577 0413	0.9545 3489	0.9513 7745	8
9	0.9561 0468	0.9525 4451	0.9489 9906	0.9454 6827	9
10	0.9513 4794	0.9474 1269	0.9434 9534	0.9395 9580	10
11	0.9466 1487	0.9423 0852	0.9380 2354	0.9337 5980	11
12	0.9419 0534	0.9372 3185	0.9325 8347	0.9279 6005	12
13	0.9372 1924	0.9321 8253	0.9271 7495	0.9221 9632	13
14	0.9325 5646	0.9271 6041	0.9217 9779	0.9164 6840	14
15	0.9279 1688	0.9221 6534	0.9164 5182	0.9107 7604	15
16	0.9233 0037	0.9171 9719	0.9111 3686	0.9051 1905	16
17	0.9187 0684	0.9122 5581	0.9058 5272	0.8994 9719	17
18	0.9141 3616	0.9073 4104	0.9005 9922	0.8939 1025	18
19	0.9095 8822	0.9024 5276	0.8953 7619	0.8883 5802	19
20	0.9050 6290	0.8975 9081	0.8901 8346	0.8828 4027	20
21	0.9005 6010	0.8927 5505	0.8850 2084	0.8773 5679	21
22	0.8960 7971	0.8879 4535	0.8798 8815	0.8719 0736	22
23	0.8916 2160	0.8831 6156	0.8747 8524	0.8664 9179	23
24	0.8871 8567	0.8784 0354	0.8697 1192	0.8611 0985	24
25	0.8827 7181	0.8736 7115	0.8646 6802	0.8557 6135	25
26	0.8783 7991	0.8689 6426	0.8596 5338	0.8504 4606	26
27	0.8740 0986	0.8642 8273	0.8546 6782	0.8451 6378	27
28	0.8696 6155	0.8596 2642	0.8497 1117	0.8399 1432	28
29	0.8653 3488	0.8549 9520	0.8447 8327	0.8346 9746	29
30	0.8610 2973	0.8503 8892	0.8398 8394	0.8295 1300	30
31	0.8567 4600	0.8458 0747	0.8350 1303	0.8243 6075	31
32	0.8524 8358	0.8412 5069	0.8301 7037	0.8192 4050	32
33	0.8482 4237	0.8367 1847	0.8253 5580	0.8141 5205	33
34	0.8440 2226	0.8322 1066	0.8205 6914	0.8090 9520	34
35	0.8398 2314	0.8277 2714	0.8158 1025	0.8040 6976	35
36	0.8356 4492	0.8232 6777	0.8110 7896	0.7990 7554	36
37	0.8314 8748	0.8188 3243	0.8063 7510	0.7941 1234	37
38	0.8273 5073	0.8144 2098	0.8016 9853	0.7891 7997	38
39	0.8232 3455	0.8100 3330	0.7970 4907	0.7842 7823	39
40	0.8191 3886	0.8056 6926	0.7924 2659	0.7794 0693	40
41	0.8150 6354	0.8013 2873	0.7878 3091	0.7745 6590	41
42	0.8110 0850	0.7970 1158	0.7832 6188	0.7697 5493	42
43	0.8069 7363	0.7927 1769	0.7787 1935	0.7649 7384	43
44	0.8029 5884	0.7884 4694	0.7742 0316	0.7602 2245	44
45	0.7989 6402	0.7841 9919	0.7697 1317	0.7555 0057	45
46	0.7949 8907	0.7799 7433	0.7652 4922	0.7508 0802	46
47	0.7910 3390	0.7757 7223	0.7608 1115	0.7461 4462	47
48	0.7870 9841	0.7715 9277	0.7563 9883	0.7415 1018	48
49	0.7831 8250	0.7674 3583	0.7520 1209	0.7369 0453	49
50	0.7792 8607	0.7633 0128	0.7476 5079	0.7323 2748	50
51	0.7754 0902	0.7591 8901	0.7433 1479	0.7277 7886	51
52	0.7715 5127	0.7550 9889	0.7390 0393	0.7232 5850	52
53	0.7677 1270	0.7510 3080	0.7347 1808	0.7187 6621	53
54	0.7638 9324	0.7469 8464	0.7304 5708	0.7143 0182	54
55	0.7600 9277	0.7429 6027	0.7262 2079	0.7098 6516	55
56	0.7563 1122	0.7389 5758	0.7220 0907	0.7054 5606	56
57	0.7525 4847	0.7349 7646	0.7178 2178	0.7010 7435	57
58	0.7488 0445	0.7310 1678	0.7136 5877	0.6967 1985	58
59	0.7450 7906	0.7270 7844	0.7095 1990	0.6923 9240	59
60	0.7413 7220	0.7231 6132	0.7054 0504	0.6880 9182	60

TABLE 6 PRESENT VALUE
WHEN COMPOUND AMOUNT IS 1

$$p = (1+i)^{-n} \quad [OR,\ v^n = (1+i)^{-n}]$$

n	$\frac{1}{2}$%	$\frac{13}{24}$%	$\frac{7}{12}$%	$\frac{5}{8}$%	n
61	0.7376 8378	0.7192 6530	0.7013 1404	0.6838 1796	61
62	0.7340 1371	0.7153 9027	0.6972 4677	0.6795 7065	62
63	0.7303 6190	0.7115 3611	0.6932 0308	0.6753 4971	63
64	0.7267 2826	0.7070 0272	0.6891 8285	0.6711 5499	64
65	0.7231 1269	0.7038 8999	0.6851 8593	0.6669 8633	65
66	0.7195 1512	0.7000 9779	0.6812 1219	0.6628 4355	66
67	0.7159 3544	0.6963 2602	0.6772 6150	0.6587 2651	67
68	0.7123 7357	0.6925 7458	0.6733 3372	0.6546 3504	68
69	0.7088 2943	0.6888 4334	0.6694 2872	0.6505 6899	69
70	0.7053 0291	0.6851 3221	0.6655 4637	0.6465 2819	70
71	0.7017 9394	0.6814 4107	0.6616 8653	0.6425 1248	71
72	0.6983 0243	0.6777 6982	0.6578 4908	0.6385 2172	72
73	0.6948 2829	0.6741 1834	0.6540 3388	0.6345 5575	73
74	0.6913 7143	0.6704 8654	0.6502 4081	0.6306 1441	74
75	0.6879 3177	0.6668 7431	0.6464 6973	0.6266 9755	75
76	0.6845 0923	0.6632 8153	0.6427 2053	0.6228 0501	76
77	0.6811 0371	0.6597 0811	0.6389 9307	0.6189 3666	77
78	0.6777 1513	0.6561 5395	0.6352 8723	0.6150 9233	78
79	0.6743 4342	0.6526 1893	0.6316 0288	0.6112 7189	79
80	0.6709 8847	0.6491 0295	0.6279 3990	0.6074 7517	80
81	0.6676 5022	0.6456 0592	0.6242 9816	0.6037 0203	81
82	0.6643 2858	0.6421 2773	0.6206 7754	0.5999 5233	82
83	0.6610 2346	0.6386 6827	0.6170 7792	0.5962 2592	83
84	0.6577 3479	0.6352 2746	0.6134 9917	0.5925 2265	84
85	0.6544 6248	0.6318 0518	0.6099 4118	0.5888 4239	85
86	0.6512 0644	0.6284 0134	0.6064 0382	0.5851 8498	86
87	0.6479 6661	0.6250 1584	0.6028 8698	0.5815 5029	87
88	0.6447 4290	0.6216 4858	0.5993 9054	0.5779 3818	88
89	0.6415 3522	0.6182 9945	0.5959 1437	0.5743 4850	89
90	0.6383 4350	0.6149 6837	0.5924 5836	0.5707 8112	90
91	0.6351 6766	0.6116 5524	0.5890 2240	0.5672 3489	91
92	0.6320 0763	0.6083 5996	0.5856 0636	0.5637 1269	92
93	0.6288 6331	0.6050 8243	0.5822 1014	0.5602 1137	93
94	0.6257 3464	0.6018 2256	0.5788 3361	0.5567 3179	94
95	0.6226 2153	0.5985 8025	0.5754 7666	0.5532 7383	95
96	0.6195 2391	0.5953 5541	0.5721 3918	0.5498 3735	96
97	0.6164 4170	0.5921 4794	0.5688 2106	0.5464 2221	97
98	0.6133 7483	0.5889 5775	0.5655 2218	0.5430 2828	98
99	0.6103 2321	0.5857 8475	0.5622 4243	0.5396 5544	99
100	0.6072 8678	0.5826 2884	0.5589 8171	0.5363 0354	100
101	0.6042 6545	0.5794 8994	0.5557 3989	0.5329 7246	101
102	0.6012 5915	0.5763 6795	0.5525 1688	0.5296 6207	102
103	0.5982 6781	0.5732 6277	0.5493 1255	0.5263 7225	103
104	0.5952 9136	0.5701 7433	0.5461 2681	0.5231 0285	104
105	0.5923 2971	0.5671 0252	0.5429 5955	0.5198 5377	105
106	0.5893 8279	0.5640 4727	0.5398 1065	0.5166 2486	106
107	0.5864 5054	0.5610 0847	0.5366 8002	0.5134 1601	107
108	0.5835 3288	0.5579 8605	0.5335 6754	0.5102 2709	108
109	0.5806 2973	0.5549 7991	0.5304 7312	0.5070 5798	109
110	0.5777 4102	0.5519 8996	0.5273 9664	0.5039 0855	110
111	0.5748 6669	0.5490 1612	0.5243 3800	0.5007 7868	111
112	0.5720 0666	0.5460 5831	0.5212 9710	0.4976 6826	112
113	0.5691 6085	0.5431 1643	0.5182 7383	0.4945 7715	113
114	0.5663 2921	0.5401 9039	0.5152 6810	0.4915 0524	114
115	0.5635 1165	0.5372 8013	0.5122 7980	0.4884 5242	115
116	0.5607 0811	0.5343 8554	0.5093 0884	0.4854 1855	116
117	0.5579 1852	0.5315 0655	0.5063 5510	0.4824 0353	117
118	0.5551 4280	0.5286 4306	0.5034 1849	0.4794 0723	118
119	0.5523 8090	0.5257 9501	0.5004 9891	0.4764 2955	119
120	0.5496 3273	0.5229 6229	0.4975 9627	0.4734 7036	120

TABLE 6 PRESENT VALUE
WHEN COMPOUND AMOUNT IS 1

$$p = (1+i)^{-n} \quad [OR,\ v^n = (1+i)^{-n}]$$

n	$\frac{1}{2}$%	$\frac{13}{24}$%	$\frac{7}{12}$%	$\frac{5}{8}$%	n
121	0.5468 9824	0.5201 4484	0.4947 1046	0.4705 2955	121
122	0.5441 7736	0.5173 4257	0.4918 4138	0.4676 0700	122
123	0.5414 7001	0.5145 5539	0.4889 8895	0.4647 0261	123
124	0.5387 7612	0.5117 8324	0.4861 5305	0.4618 1626	124
125	0.5360 9565	0.5090 2601	0.4833 3361	0.4589 4784	125
126	0.5334 2850	0.5062 8364	0.4805 3051	0.4560 9723	126
127	0.5307 7463	0.5035 5605	0.4805 3051	0.4532 6433	127
128	0.5281 3396	0.5008 4315	0.4749 7300	0.4504 4902	128
129	0.5255 0643	0.4981 4486	0.4722 1839	0.4476 5120	129
130	0.5228 9197	0.4954 6111	0.4694 7976	0.4448 7076	130
131	0.5202 9052	0.4927 9182	0.4667 5701	0.4421 0759	131
132	0.5177 0201	0.4901 3692	0.4640 5005	0.4393 6158	132
133	0.5151 2637	0.4874 9631	0.4613 5879	0.4366 3262	133
134	0.5125 6356	0.4848 6993	0.4586 8314	0.4339 2062	134
135	0.5100 1349	0.4822 5770	0.4560 2301	0.4312 2546	135
136	0.5074 7611	0.4796 5955	0.4533 7830	0.4285 4704	136
137	0.5049 5135	0.4770 7539	0.4507 4893	0.4258 8526	137
138	0.5024 3916	0.4745 0515	0.4481 3481	0.4232 4001	138
139	0.4999 3946	0.4719 4876	0.4455 3585	0.4206 1119	139
140	0.4974 5220	0.4694 0615	0.4429 5197	0.4179 9870	140
141	0.4949 7731	0.4668 7723	0.4403 8306	0.4154 0243	141
142	0.4925 1474	0.4643 6193	0.4378 2906	0.4128 2229	142
143	0.4900 6442	0.4618 6019	0.4352 8987	0.4102 5818	143
144	0.4876 2628	0.4593 7193	0.4327 6541	0.4077 0999	144
145	0.4852 0028	0.4568 9707	0.4302 5558	0.4051 7763	145
146	0.4827 8635	0.4544 3554	0.4277 6031	0.4026 6100	146
147	0.4803 8443	0.4519 8728	0.4252 7952	0.4001 6000	147
148	0.4779 9446	0.4495 5220	0.4228 1311	0.3976 7453	148
149	0.4756 1637	0.4471 3025	0.4203 6100	0.3952 0451	149
150	0.4732 5012	0.4447 2134	0.4179 2312	0.3927 4982	150
151	0.4708 9565	0.4423 2541	0.4154 9937	0.3903 1038	151
152	0.4685 5288	0.4399 4239	0.4130 8968	0.3878 8609	152
153	0.4662 2177	0.4375 7221	0.4106 9396	0.3854 7686	153
154	0.4639 0226	0.4352 1479	0.4083 1214	0.3830 8259	154
155	0.4615 9429	0.4328 7008	0.4059 4414	0.3807 0320	155
156	0.4592 9780	0.4305 3800	0.4035 8986	0.3783 3858	156
157	0.4570 1274	0.4282 1848	0.4012 4924	0.3759 8865	157
158	0.4547 3904	0.4259 1146	0.3989 2220	0.3736 5332	158
159	0.4524 7666	0.4236 1687	0.3966 0864	0.3713 3249	159
160	0.4502 2553	0.4213 3464	0.3943 0851	0.3690 2608	160
161	0.4479 8560	0.4190 6471	0.3920 2172	0.3667 3399	161
162	0.4457 5682	0.4168 0700	0.3897 4819	0.3644 5614	162
163	0.4435 3912	0.4145 6146	0.3874 8784	0.3621 9244	163
164	0.4413 3246	0.4123 2802	0.3852 4060	0.3599 4280	164
165	0.4391 3678	0.4101 0661	0.3830 0640	0.3577 0713	165
166	0.4369 5202	0.4078 9717	0.3807 8515	0.3554 8534	166
167	0.4347 7813	0.4056 9963	0.3785 7679	0.3532 7736	167
168	0.4326 1505	0.4035 1393	0.3763 8123	0.3510 8309	168
169	0.4304 6274	0.4013 4000	0.3741 9841	0.3489 0245	169
170	0.4283 2113	0.3991 7779	0.3720 2824	0.3467 3535	170
171	0.4261 9018	0.3970 2722	0.3698 7066	0.3445 8172	171
172	0.4240 6983	0.3948 8825	0.3677 2560	0.3424 4146	172
173	0.4219 6003	0.3927 6079	0.3655 9297	0.3403 1449	173
174	0.4198 6073	0.3906 4480	0.3634 7272	0.3382 0074	174
175	0.4177 7187	0.3885 4021	0.3613 6475	0.3361 0011	175
176	0.4156 9340	0.3864 4695	0.3592 6902	0.3340 1254	176
177	0.4136 2528	0.3843 6497	0.3571 8544	0.3319 3792	177
178	0.4115 6744	0.3822 9421	0.3551 1394	0.3298 7620	178
179	0.4095 1984	0.3802 3461	0.3530 5445	0.3278 2728	179
180	0.4074 8243	0.3781 8610	0.3510 0691	0.3257 9108	180

TABLE 6 PRESENT VALUE
WHEN COMPOUND AMOUNT IS 1

$$p = (1+i)^{-n} \quad [OR,\ v^n = (1+i)^{-n}]$$

n	$\frac{1}{2}\%$	$\frac{13}{24}\%$	$\frac{7}{12}\%$	$\frac{5}{8}\%$	n
181	0.4054 5515	0.3761 4863	0.3489 7125	0.3237 6754	181
182	0.4034 3796	0.3741 2214	0.3469 4739	0.3217 5656	182
183	0.4014 3081	0.3721 0656	0.3449 3527	0.3197 5807	183
184	0.3994 3364	0.3701 0184	0.3429 3481	0.3177 7199	184
185	0.3974 4641	0.3681 0792	0.3409 4596	0.3157 9825	185
186	0.3954 6906	0.3661 2475	0.3389 6864	0.3138 3677	186
187	0.3935 0155	0.3641 5225	0.3370 0279	0.3118 8748	187
188	0.3915 4383	0.3621 9039	0.3350 4835	0.3099 5029	188
189	0.3895 9586	0.3602 3909	0.3331 0523	0.3080 2513	189
190	0.3876 5757	0.3582 9831	0.3311 7339	0.3061 1193	190
191	0.3857 2892	0.3563 6799	0.3292 5275	0.3042 1062	191
192	0.3838 0987	0.3544 4806	0.3273 4324	0.3023 2111	192
193	0.3819 0037	0.3525 3848	0.3254 4482	0.3004 4334	193
194	0.3800 0037	0.3506 3918	0.3235 5740	0.2985 7723	194
195	0.3781 0982	0.3487 5012	0.3216 8093	0.2967 2271	195
196	0.3762 2868	0.3468 7123	0.3198 1534	0.2948 7972	196
197	0.3743 5689	0.3450 0247	0.3179 6057	0.2930 4816	197
198	0.3724 9442	0.3431 4377	0.3161 1655	0.2912 2799	198
199	0.3706 4121	0.3412 9509	0.3142 8323	0.2894 1912	199
200	0.3687 9723	0.3394 5637	0.3124 6055	0.2876 2149	200
201	0.3669 6242	0.3376 2755	0.3106 4843	0.2858 3502	201
202	0.3651 3673	0.3358 0859	0.3088 4683	0.2840 5964	202
203	0.3633 2013	0.3339 9943	0.3070 5567	0.2822 9530	203
204	0.3615 1257	0.3322 0001	0.3052 7490	0.2805 4191	204
205	0.3597 1400	0.3304 1029	0.3035 0445	0.2787 9941	205
206	0.3579 2438	0.3286 3021	0.3017 4428	0.2770 6774	206
207	0.3561 4366	0.3268 5972	0.2999 9431	0.2753 4682	207
208	0.3543 7180	0.3250 9876	0.2982 5450	0.2736 3660	208
209	0.3526 0876	0.3233 4730	0.2965 2477	0.2719 3699	209
210	0.3508 5448	0.3216 0527	0.2948 0507	0.2702 4794	210
211	0.3491 0894	0.3198 7263	0.2930 9535	0.2685 6938	211
212	0.3473 7208	0.3181 4932	0.2913 9554	0.2669 0125	212
213	0.3456 4386	0.3164 3529	0.2897 0559	0.2652 4348	213
214	0.3439 2424	0.3147 3050	0.2880 2544	0.2635 9600	214
215	0.3422 1317	0.3130 3490	0.2863 5504	0.2619 5876	215
216	0.3405 1062	0.3113 4843	0.2846 9432	0.2603 3169	216
217	0.3388 1654	0.3096 7104	0.2830 4324	0.2587 1472	217
218	0.3371 3088	0.3080 0270	0.2814 0173	0.2571 0780	218
219	0.3354 5361	0.3063 4334	0.2797 6974	0.2555 1085	219
220	0.3337 8469	0.3046 9292	0.2781 4721	0.2539 2383	220
221	0.3321 2407	0.3030 5139	0.2765 3410	0.2523 4666	221
222	0.3304 7171	0.3014 1870	0.2749 3033	0.2507 7929	222
223	0.3288 2757	0.2997 9481	0.2733 3588	0.2492 2166	223
224	0.3271 9162	0.2981 7967	0.2717 5066	0.2476 7370	224
225	0.3255 6380	0.2965 7324	0.2701 7464	0.2461 3535	225
226	0.3239 4408	0.2949 7545	0.2686 0777	0.2446 0656	226
227	0.3223 3241	0.2933 8628	0.2670 4997	0.2430 8726	227
228	0.3207 2877	0.2918 0566	0.2655 0122	0.2415 7740	228
229	0.3191 3310	0.2902 3356	0.2639 6144	0.2400 7692	229
230	0.3175 4538	0.2886 6994	0.2624 3060	0.2385 8576	230
231	0.3159 6555	0.2871 1473	0.2609 0863	0.2371 0386	231
232	0.3143 9358	0.2855 6790	0.2593 9549	0.2356 3117	232
233	0.3128 2944	0.2840 2941	0.2578 9112	0.2341 6762	233
234	0.3112 7307	0.2824 9921	0.2563 9548	0.2327 1316	234
235	0.3097 2445	0.2809 7725	0.2549 0852	0.2312 6774	235
236	0.3081 8353	0.2794 6349	0.2534 3018	0.2298 3129	236
237	0.3066 5028	0.2779 5788	0.2519 6041	0.2284 0377	237
238	0.3051 2466	0.2764 6039	0.2504 9916	0.2269 8511	238
239	0.3036 0662	0.2749 7096	0.2490 4639	0.2255 7527	239
240	0.3020 9614	0.2734 8956	0.2476 0205	0.2241 7418	240

TABLE 6 PRESENT VALUE
WHEN COMPOUND AMOUNT IS 1

$$p=(1+i)^{-n} \quad [OR,\ v^n=(1+i)^{-n}]$$

n	$\frac{2}{3}\%$	$\frac{3}{4}\%$	$\frac{7}{8}\%$	1%	n
1	0.9933 7748	0.9925 5583	0.9913 2590	0.9900 9901	1
2	0.9867 9882	0.9851 6708	0.9827 2704	0.9802 9605	2
3	0.9802 6373	0.9778 3333	0.9742 0276	0.9705 9015	3
4	0.9737 7192	0.9705 5417	0.9657 5243	0.9609 8034	4
5	0.9673 2310	0.9633 2920	0.9573 7539	0.9514 6569	5
6	0.9609 1699	0.9561 5802	0.9490 7102	0.9420 4524	6
7	0.9545 5330	0.9490 4022	0.9408 3868	0.9327 1805	7
8	0.9482 3175	0.9419 7540	0.9326 7775	0.9234 8322	8
9	0.9419 5207	0.9349 6318	0.9245 8761	0.9143 3982	9
10	0.9357 1398	0.9280 0316	0.9165 6765	0.9052 8695	10
11	0.9295 1720	0.9210 9494	0.9086 1724	0.8963 2372	11
12	0.9233 6145	0.9142 3815	0.9007 3581	0.8874 4923	12
13	0.9172 4648	0.9074 3241	0.8929 2273	0.8786 6260	13
14	0.9111 7200	0.9006 7733	0.8851 7743	0.8699 6297	14
15	0.9051 3775	0.8939 7254	0.8774 9931	0.8613 4947	15
16	0.8991 4346	0.8873 1766	0.8698 8779	0.8528 2126	16
17	0.8931 8886	0.8807 1231	0.8623 4230	0.8443 7749	17
18	0.8872 7371	0.8741 5614	0.8548 6225	0.8360 1731	18
19	0.8813 9772	0.8676 4878	0.8474 4709	0.8277 3992	19
20	0.8755 6065	0.8611 8985	0.8400 9625	0.8195 4447	20
21	0.8697 6224	0.8547 7901	0.8328 0917	0.8114 3017	21
22	0.8640 0222	0.8484 1589	0.8255 8530	0.8033 9621	22
23	0.8582 8035	0.8421 0014	0.8184 2409	0.7954 4179	23
24	0.8525 9638	0.8358 3140	0.8113 2499	0.7875 6613	24
25	0.8469 5004	0.8296 0933	0.8042 8748	0.7797 6844	25
26	0.8413 4110	0.8234 3358	0.7973 1101	0.7720 4796	26
27	0.8357 6931	0.8173 0380	0.7903 9505	0.7644 0392	27
28	0.8302 3441	0.8112 1966	0.7835 3908	0.7568 3557	28
29	0.8247 3617	0.8051 8080	0.7767 4258	0.7493 4215	29
30	0.8192 7434	0.7991 8690	0.7700 0504	0.7419 2292	30
31	0.8138 4868	0.7932 3762	0.7633 2594	0.7345 7715	31
32	0.8084 5896	0.7873 3262	0.7567 0477	0.7273 0411	32
33	0.8031 0492	0.7814 7158	0.7501 4104	0.7201 0307	33
34	0.7977 8635	0.7756 5418	0.7436 3424	0.7129 7334	34
35	0.7925 0299	0.7698 8008	0.7371 8388	0.7059 1420	35
36	0.7872 5463	0.7641 4896	0.7307 8947	0.6989 2495	36
37	0.7820 4102	0.7584 6051	0.7244 5053	0.6920 0490	37
38	0.7768 6194	0.7528 1440	0.7181 6657	0.6851 5337	38
39	0.7717 1716	0.7472 1032	0.7119 3712	0.6783 6967	39
40	0.7666 0645	0.7416 4796	0.7057 6171	0.6716 5314	40
41	0.7615 2959	0.7361 2701	0.6996 3986	0.6650 0311	41
42	0.7564 8635	0.7306 4716	0.6935 7111	0.6584 1892	42
43	0.7514 7650	0.7252 0809	0.6875 5500	0.6518 9992	43
44	0.7464 9984	0.7198 0952	0.6815 9108	0.6454 4546	44
45	0.7415 5613	0.7144 5114	0.6756 7889	0.6390 5492	45
46	0.7366 4516	0.7091 3264	0.6698 1798	0.6327 2764	46
47	0.7317 6672	0.7038 5374	0.6640 0792	0.6264 6301	47
48	0.7269 2058	0.6986 1414	0.6582 4824	0.6202 6041	48
49	0.7221 0654	0.6934 1353	0.6525 3853	0.6141 1921	49
50	0.7173 2437	0.6882 5165	0.6468 7835	0.6080 3882	50
51	0.7125 7388	0.6831 2819	0.6412 6726	0.6020 1864	51
52	0.7078 5485	0.6780 4286	0.6357 0484	0.5960 5806	52
53	0.7031 6707	0.6729 9540	0.6301 9067	0.5901 5649	53
54	0.6985 1033	0.6679 8551	0.6247 2433	0.5843 1336	54
55	0.6938 8444	0.6630 1291	0.6193 0541	0.5785 2808	55
56	0.6892 8918	0.6580 7733	0.6139 3349	0.5728 0008	56
57	0.6847 2435	0.6531 7849	0.6086 0817	0.5671 2879	57
58	0.6801 8975	0.6483 1612	0.6033 2904	0.5615 1365	58
59	0.6756 8518	0.6434 8995	0.5980 9571	0.5559 5411	59
60	0.6712 1044	0.6386 9970	0.5929 0776	0.5504 4962	60

TABLE 6 PRESENT VALUE
WHEN COMPOUND AMOUNT IS 1

$$p = (1+i)^{-n} \quad [OR,\ v^n = (1+i)^{-n}]$$

n	$\frac{2}{3}\%$	$\frac{3}{4}\%$	$\frac{7}{8}\%$	1%	n
61	0.6667 6534	0.6339 4511	0.5877 6482	0.5449 9962	61
62	0.6623 4968	0.6292 2592	0.5826 6649	0.5396 0358	62
63	0.6579 6326	0.6245 4185	0.5776 1238	0.5342 6097	63
64	0.6536 0588	0.6198 9266	0.5726 0211	0.5289 7126	64
65	0.6492 7737	0.6152 7807	0.5676 3530	0.5237 3392	65
66	0.6449 7752	0.6106 9784	0.5627 1158	0.5185 4844	66
67	0.6407 0614	0.6061 5170	0.5578 3056	0.5134 1430	67
68	0.6364 6306	0.6016 3940	0.5529 9188	0.5083 3099	68
69	0.6322 4807	0.5971 6070	0.5481 9517	0.5032 9801	69
70	0.6280 6100	0.5927 1533	0.5434 4007	0.4983 1486	70
71	0.6239 0165	0.5883 0306	0.5387 2622	0.4933 8105	71
72	0.6197 6985	0.5839 2363	0.5340 5325	0.4884 9609	72
73	0.6156 6542	0.5795 7681	0.5294 2082	0.4836 5949	73
74	0.6115 8816	0.5752 6234	0.5248 2857	0.4788 7078	74
75	0.6075 3791	0.5709 7999	0.5202 7615	0.4741 2949	75
76	0.6035 1448	0.5667 2952	0.5157 6322	0.4694 3514	76
77	0.5995 1769	0.5625 1069	0.5112 8944	0.4647 8726	77
78	0.5955 4738	0.5583 2326	0.5068 5447	0.4601 8541	78
79	0.5916 0336	0.5541 6701	0.5024 5796	0.4556 2912	79
80	0.5876 8545	0.5500 4170	0.4980 9959	0.4511 1794	80
81	0.5837 9350	0.5459 4710	0.4937 7902	0.4466 5142	81
82	0.5799 2732	0.5418 8297	0.4894 9593	0.4422 2913	82
83	0.5760 8674	0.5378 4911	0.4852 4999	0.4378 5063	83
84	0.5722 7159	0.5338 4527	0.4810 4089	0.4335 1547	84
85	0.5684 8171	0.5298 7123	0.4768 6829	0.4292 2324	85
86	0.5647 1693	0.5259 2678	0.4727 3188	0.4249 7350	86
87	0.5609 7709	0.5220 1169	0.4686 3136	0.4207 6585	87
88	0.5572 6201	0.5181 2575	0.4645 6640	0.4165 9985	88
89	0.5535 7153	0.5142 6873	0.4605 3671	0.4124 7510	89
90	0.5499 0549	0.5104 4043	0.4565 4197	0.4083 9119	90
91	0.5462 6374	0.5066 4063	0.4525 8187	0.4043 4771	91
92	0.5426 4610	0.5028 6911	0.4486 5613	0.4003 4427	92
93	0.5390 5241	0.4991 2567	0.4447 6444	0.3963 8046	93
94	0.5354 8253	0.4954 1009	0.4409 0651	0.3924 5590	94
95	0.5319 3629	0.4917 2217	0.4370 8204	0.3885 7020	95
96	0.5284 1353	0.4880 6171	0.4332 9075	0.3847 2297	96
97	0.5249 1410	0.4844 2850	0.4295 3234	0.3809 1383	97
98	0.5214 3785	0.4808 2233	0.4258 0654	0.3771 4241	98
99	0.5179 8462	0.4772 4301	0.4221 1305	0.3734 0832	99
100	0.5145 5426	0.4736 9033	0.4184 5159	0.3697 1121	100
101	0.5111 4661	0.4701 6410	0.4148 2190	0.3660 5071	101
102	0.5077 6154	0.4666 6412	0.4112 2370	0.3624 2644	102
103	0.5043 9888	0.4631 9019	0.4076 5670	0.3588 3806	103
104	0.5010 5849	0.4597 4213	0.4041 2064	0.3552 8521	104
105	0.4977 4022	0.4563 1973	0.4006 1526	0.3517 6753	105
106	0.4944 4393	0.4529 2281	0.3971 4028	0.3482 8469	106
107	0.4911 6946	0.4495 5117	0.3936 9545	0.3448 3632	107
108	0.4879 1669	0.4462 0464	0.3902 8049	0.3414 2210	108
109	0.4846 8545	0.4428 8302	0.3868 9516	0.3380 4168	109
110	0.4814 7561	0.4395 8612	0.3835 3919	0.3346 9474	110
111	0.4782 8703	0.4363 1377	0.3802 1233	0.3313 8093	111
112	0.4751 1957	0.4330 6577	0.3769 1433	0.3280 9993	112
113	0.4719 7308	0.4298 4196	0.3736 4494	0.3248 5141	113
114	0.4688 4743	0.4266 4214	0.3704 0391	0.3216 3506	114
115	0.4657 4248	0.4234 6615	0.3671 9099	0.3184 5056	115
116	0.4626 5809	0.4203 1379	0.3640 0593	0.3152 9758	116
117	0.4595 9413	0.4171 8491	0.3608 4851	0.3121 7582	117
118	0.4565 5046	0.4140 7931	0.3577 1847	0.3090 8497	118
119	0.4535 2695	0.4109 9683	0.3546 1559	0.3060 2473	119
120	0.4505 2346	0.4079 3731	0.3515 3961	0.3029 9478	120

TABLE 6 PRESENT VALUE
WHEN COMPOUND AMOUNT IS 1

$$p = (1+i)^{-n} \quad [OR,\ v^n = (1+i)^{-n}]$$

n	$\frac{2}{3}\%$	$\frac{3}{4}\%$	$\frac{7}{8}\%$	1%	n
121	0.4475 3986	0.4049 0055	0.3484 9032	0.2999 9483	121
122	0.4445 7602	0.4018 8640	0.3454 6748	0.2970 2459	122
123	0.4416 3181	0.3988 9469	0.3424 7086	0.2940 8375	123
124	0.4387 0710	0.3959 2525	0.3395 0024	0.2911 7203	124
125	0.4358 0175	0.3929 7792	0.3365 5538	0.2882 8914	125
126	0.4329 1565	0.3900 5252	0.3336 3606	0.2854 3479	126
127	0.4300 4866	0.3871 4891	0.3307 4207	0.2826 0870	127
128	0.4272 0065	0.3842 6691	0.3278 7318	0.2798 1060	128
129	0.4243 7151	0.3814 0636	0.3250 2917	0.2770 4019	129
130	0.4215 6110	0.3785 6711	0.3222 0984	0.2742 9722	130
131	0.4187 6930	0.3757 4899	0.3194 1496	0.2715 8141	131
132	0.4159 9600	0.3729 5185	0.3166 4432	0.2688 9248	132
133	0.4132 4106	0.3701 7553	0.3138 9771	0.2662 3018	133
134	0.4105 0436	0.3674 1988	0.3111 7493	0.2635 9424	134
135	0.4077 8579	0.3646 8475	0.3084 7577	0.2609 8439	135
136	0.4050 8522	0.3619 6997	0.3058 0002	0.2584 0039	136
137	0.4024 0254	0.3592 7541	0.3031 4748	0.2558 4197	137
138	0.3997 3762	0.3566 0090	0.3005 1795	0.2533 0888	138
139	0.3970 9035	0.3539 4630	0.2979 1122	0.2508 0087	139
140	0.3944 6061	0.3513 1147	0.2953 2711	0.2483 1770	140
141	0.3918 4829	0.3486 9625	0.2927 6541	0.2458 5911	141
142	0.3892 5327	0.3461 0049	0.2902 2594	0.2434 2486	142
143	0.3866 7543	0.3435 2406	0.2877 0849	0.2410 1471	143
144	0.3841 1467	0.3409 6681	0.2852 1288	0.2386 2843	144
145	0.3815 7086	0.3384 2860	0.2827 3891	0.2362 6577	145
146	0.3790 4390	0.3359 0928	0.2802 8640	0.2339 2650	146
147	0.3765 3368	0.3334 0871	0.2778 5517	0.2316 1040	147
148	0.3740 4008	0.3309 2676	0.2754 4503	0.2293 1723	148
149	0.3715 6299	0.3284 6329	0.2730 5579	0.2270 4676	149
150	0.3691 0231	0.3260 1815	0.2706 8728	0.2247 9877	150
151	0.3666 5792	0.3235 9122	0.2683 3931	0.2225 7304	151
152	0.3642 2973	0.3211 8235	0.2660 1170	0.2203 6935	152
153	0.3618 1761	0.3187 9141	0.2637 0429	0.2181 8747	153
154	0.3594 2147	0.3164 1828	0.2614 1689	0.2160 2720	154
155	0.3570 4119	0.3140 6280	0.2591 4934	0.2138 8832	155
156	0.3546 7668	0.3117 2487	0.2569 0145	0.2117 7061	156
157	0.3523 2783	0.3094 0434	0.2546 7306	0.2096 7387	157
158	0.3499 9453	0.3071 0108	0.2524 6400	0.2075 9789	158
159	0.3476 7669	0.3048 1496	0.2502 7410	0.2055 4247	159
160	0.3453 7419	0.3025 4587	0.2481 0320	0.2035 0739	160
161	0.3430 8695	0.3002 9367	0.2459 5113	0.2014 9247	161
162	0.3408 1485	0.2980 5823	0.2438 1772	0.1994 9750	162
163	0.3385 5779	0.2958 3944	0.2417 0282	0.1975 2227	163
164	0.3363 1569	0.2936 3716	0.2396 0627	0.1955 6661	164
165	0.3340 8843	0.2914 5127	0.2375 2790	0.1936 3030	165
166	0.3318 7593	0.2892 8166	0.2354 6756	0.1917 1317	166
167	0.3296 7807	0.2871 2820	0.2334 2509	0.1898 1502	167
168	0.3274 9478	0.2849 9077	0.2314 0033	0.1879 3566	168
169	0.3253 2594	0.2828 6925	0.2293 9314	0.1860 7492	169
170	0.3231 7146	0.2807 6352	0.2274 0336	0.1842 3259	170
171	0.3210 3125	0.2786 7347	0.2254 3084	0.1824 0850	171
172	0.3189 0522	0.2765 9898	0.2234 7543	0.1806 0248	172
173	0.3167 9326	0.2745 3993	0.2215 3699	0.1788 1434	173
174	0.3146 9529	0.2724 9621	0.2196 1535	0.1770 4390	174
175	0.3126 1122	0.2704 6770	0.2177 1039	0.1752 9099	175
176	0.3105 4095	0.2684 5429	0.2158 2194	0.1735 5543	176
177	0.3084 8438	0.2664 5587	0.2139 4988	0.1718 3706	177
178	0.3064 4144	0.2644 7233	0.2120 9406	0.1701 3571	178
179	0.3044 1203	0.2625 0355	0.2102 5433	0.1684 5119	179
180	0.3023 9605	0.2605 4943	0.2084 3057	0.1667 8336	180

TABLE 6 PRESENT VALUE
WHEN COMPOUND AMOUNT IS 1

$$p = (1+i)^{-n} \quad [OR,\ v^n = (1+i)^{-n}]$$

n	$\frac{2}{3}\%$	$\frac{3}{4}\%$	$\frac{7}{8}\%$	1%	n
181	0.3003 9343	0.2586 0986	0.2066 2262	0.1651 3204	181
182	0.2984 0407	0.2566 8472	0.2048 3035	0.1634 9707	182
183	0.2964 2788	0.2547 7392	0.2030 5363	0.1618 7829	183
184	0.2944 6478	0.2528 7734	0.2012 9233	0.1602 7553	184
185	0.2925 1469	0.2509 9488	0.1995 4630	0.1586 8864	185
186	0.2905 7750	0.2491 2643	0.1978 1541	0.1571 1747	186
187	0.2886 5315	0.2472 7189	0.1960 9954	0.1555 6185	187
188	0.2867 4154	0.2454 3116	0.1943 9855	0.1540 2163	188
189	0.2848 4259	0.2436 0413	0.1927 1232	0.1524 9667	189
190	0.2829 5621	0.2417 9070	0.1910 4071	0.1509 8680	190
191	0.2810 8233	0.2399 9077	0.1893 8361	0.1494 9188	191
192	0.2792 2086	0.2382 0423	0.1877 4087	0.1480 1176	192
193	0.2773 7171	0.2364 3100	0.1861 1239	0.1465 4630	193
194	0.2755 3482	0.2346 7097	0.1844 9803	0.1450 9535	194
195	0.2737 1008	0.2329 2404	0.1828 9768	0.1436 5876	195
196	0.2718 9743	0.2311 9011	0.1813 1121	0.1422 3640	196
197	0.2700 9679	0.2294 6909	0.1797 3849	0.1408 2811	197
198	0.2683 0807	0.2277 6089	0.1781 7942	0.1394 3378	198
199	0.2665 3119	0.2260 6540	0.1766 3388	0.1380 5324	199
200	0.2647 6608	0.2243 8253	0.1751 0174	0.1366 8638	200
201	0.2630 1267	0.2227 1219	0.1735 8289	0.1353 3305	201
202	0.2612 7086	0.2210 5428	0.1720 7721	0.1339 9312	202
203	0.2595 4059	0.2194 0871	0.1705 8460	0.1326 6645	203
204	0.2578 2178	0.2177 7540	0.1691 0493	0.1313 5293	204
205	0.2561 1435	0.2161 5424	0.1676 3809	0.1300 5240	205
206	0.2544 1823	0.2145 4515	0.1661 8398	0.1287 6475	206
207	0.2527 3334	0.2129 4804	0.1647 4249	0.1274 8985	207
208	0.2510 5961	0.2113 6282	0.1633 1349	0.1262 2758	208
209	0.2493 9696	0.2097 8940	0.1618 9690	0.1249 7780	209
210	0.2477 4533	0.2082 2769	0.1604 9259	0.1237 4040	210
211	0.2461 0463	0.2066 7761	0.1591 0046	0.1225 1524	211
212	0.2444 7480	0.2051 3907	0.1577 2040	0.1213 0222	212
213	0.2428 5576	0.2036 1198	0.1563 5232	0.1201 0121	213
214	0.2412 4744	0.2020 9626	0.1549 9611	0.1189 1209	214
215	0.2396 4978	0.2005 9182	0.1536 5165	0.1177 3474	215
216	0.2380 6269	0.1990 9858	0.1523 1886	0.1165 6905	216
217	0.2364 8612	0.1976 1646	0.1509 9763	0.1154 1490	217
218	0.2349 1998	0.1961 4537	0.1496 8787	0.1142 7218	218
219	0.2333 6422	0.1946 8523	0.1483 8946	0.1131 4077	219
220	0.2318 1877	0.1932 3596	0.1471 0231	0.1120 2057	220
221	0.2302 8354	0.1917 9748	0.1458 2633	0.1109 1145	221
222	0.2287 5848	0.1903 6970	0.1445 6142	0.1098 1332	222
223	0.2272 4353	0.1889 5256	0.1433 0748	0.1087 2606	223
224	0.2257 3860	0.1875 4596	0.1420 6442	0.1076 4956	224
225	0.2242 4365	0.1861 4984	0.1408 3213	0.1065 8373	225
226	0.2227 5859	0.1847 6411	0.1396 1054	0.1055 2844	226
227	0.2212 8337	0.1833 8869	0.1383 9955	0.1044 8361	227
228	0.2198 1791	0.1820 2352	0.1371 9905	0.1034 4911	228
229	0.2183 6217	0.1806 6850	0.1360 0898	0.1024 2487	229
230	0.2169 1606	0.1793 2358	0.1348 2922	0.1014 1076	230
231	0.2154 7953	0.1779 8866	0.1336 5970	0.1004 0669	231
232	0.2140 5251	0.1766 6368	0.1325 0032	0.0994 1257	232
233	0.2126 3495	0.1753 4857	0.1313 5100	0.0984 2828	233
234	0.2112 2677	0.1740 4325	0.1302 1165	0.0974 5375	234
235	0.2098 2791	0.1727 4764	0.1290 8218	0.0964 8886	235
236	0.2084 3833	0.1714 6168	0.1279 6251	0.0955 3352	236
237	0.2070 5794	0.1701 8529	0.1268 5255	0.0945 8765	237
238	0.2056 8669	0.1689 1840	0.1257 5221	0.0936 5113	238
239	0.2043 2453	0.1676 6094	0.1246 6143	0.0927 2389	239
240	0.2029 7139	0.1664 1284	0.1235 8010	0.0918 0584	240

TABLE 6 PRESENT VALUE

WHEN COMPOUND AMOUNT IS 1

$$p=(1+i)^{-n} \quad [OR,\ v^n=(1+i)^{-n}]$$

n	$1\frac{1}{8}\%$	$1\frac{1}{4}\%$	$1\frac{3}{8}\%$	$1\frac{1}{2}\%$	n
1	0.9888 7515	0.9876 5432	0.9864 3650	0.9852 2167	1
2	0.9778 7407	0.9754 6106	0.9730 5696	0.9706 6175	2
3	0.9669 9537	0.9634 1833	0.9598 5890	0.9563 1699	3
4	0.9562 3770	0.9515 2428	0.9468 3986	0.9421 8423	4
5	0.9455 9970	0.9397 7706	0.9339 9739	0.9282 6033	5
6	0.9350 8005	0.9281 7488	0.9213 2912	0.9145 4219	6
7	0.9246 7743	0.9167 1593	0.9088 3267	0.9010 2679	7
8	0.9143 9054	0.9053 9845	0.8965 0571	0.8877 1112	8
9	0.9042 1808	0.8942 2069	0.8843 4596	0.8745 9224	9
10	0.8941 5880	0.8831 8093	0.8723 5113	0.8616 6723	10
11	0.8842 1142	0.8722 7746	0.8605 1899	0.8489 3323	11
12	0.8743 7470	0.8615 0860	0.8488 4734	0.8363 8742	12
13	0.8646 4742	0.8508 7269	0.8373 3400	0.8240 2702	13
14	0.8550 2835	0,8403 6809	0.8259 7682	0.8118 4928	14
15	0.8455 1629	0.8299 9318	0.8147 7368	0.7998 5150	15
16	0.8361 1005	0.8197 4635	0.8037 2250	0.7880 3104	16
17	0.8268 0846	0.8096 2602	0.7928 2120	0.7763 8526	17
18	0.8176 1034	0.7996 3064	0.7820 6777	0.7649 1159	18
19	0.8085 1455	0.7897 5866	0.7714 6020	0.7536 0747	19
20	0.7995 1995	0.7800 0855	0.7609 9649	0.7424 7042	20
21	0.7906 2542	0.7703 7881	0.7506 7472	0.7314 9795	21
22	0.7818 2983	0.7608 6796	0.7404 9294	0.7206 8763	22
23	0.7731 3210	0.7514 7453	0.7304 4926	0.7100 3708	23
24	0.7645 3112	0.7421 9707	0.7205 4181	0.6995 4392	24
25	0.7560 2583	0.7330 3414	0.7107 6874	0.6892 0583	25
26	0.7476 1516	0.7239 8434	0.7011 2823	0.6790 2052	26
27	0.7392 9806	0.7150 4626	0.6916 1847	0.6689 8574	27
28	0.7310 7348	0.7062 1853	0.6822 3771	0.6590 9925	28
29	0.7229 4040	0.6974 9978	0.6729 8417	0.6493 5887	29
30	0.7148 9780	0.6888 8867	0.6638 5615	0.6397 6243	30
31	0.7069 4467	0.6803 8387	0.6548 5194	0.6303 0781	31
32	0.6990 8002	0.6719 8407	0.6459 6985	0.6209 9292	32
33	0.6913 0287	0.6636 8797	0.6372 0824	0.6118 1568	33
34	0.6836 1223	0.6554 9429	0.6285 6546	0.6027 7407	34
35	0.6760 0715	0.6474 0177	0.6200 3991	0.5938 6608	35
36	0.6684 8667	0.6394 0916	0.6116 3000	0.5850 8974	36
37	0.6610 4986	0.6315 1522	0.6033 3416	0.5764 4309	37
38	0.6536 9578	0.6237 1873	0.5951 5083	0.5679 2423	38
39	0.6464 2352	0.6160 1850	0.5870 7850	0.5595 3126	39
40	0.6392 3216	0.6084 1334	0.5791 1566	0.5512 6232	40
41	0.6321 2080	0.6009 0206	0.5712 6083	0.5431 1559	41
42	0.6250 8855	0.5934 8352	0.5635 1253	0.5350 8925	42
43	0.6181 3454	0.5861 5656	0.5558 6933	0.5271 8153	43
44	0.6112 5789	0.5789 2006	0.5483 2979	0.5193 9067	44
45	0.6044 5774	0.5717 7290	0.5408 9252	0.5117 1494	45
46	0.5977 3324	0.5647 1397	0.5335 5612	0.5041 5265	46
47	0.5910 8355	0.5577 4219	0.5263 1923	0.4967 0212	47
48	0.5845 0784	0.5508 5649	0.5191 8050	0.4893 6170	48
49	0.5780 0528	0.5440 5579	0.5121 3860	0.4821 2975	49
50	0.5715 7506	0.5373 3905	0.5051 9220	0.4750 0468	50

TABLE 6 PRESENT VALUE
WHEN COMPOUND AMOUNT IS 1

$$p=(1+i)^{-n} \quad [OR,\ v^{n}=(1+i)^{-n}]$$

n	$1\frac{1}{8}\%$	$1\frac{1}{4}\%$	$1\frac{3}{8}\%$	$1\frac{1}{2}\%$	n
51	0.5652 1637	0.5307 0524	0.4983 4003	0.4679 8491	51
52	0.5589 2843	0.5241 5332	0.4915 8079	0.4610 6887	52
53	0.5527 1044	0.5176 8229	0.4849 1323	0.4542 5505	53
54	0.5465 6162	0.5112 9115	0.4783 3611	0.4475 4192	54
55	0.5404 8120	0.5049 7892	0.4718 4820	0.4409 2800	55
56	0.5344 6843	0.4987 4461	0.4654 4829	0.4344 1182	56
57	0.5285 2256	0.4925 8727	0.4591 3518	0.4279 9194	57
58	0.5226 4282	0.4865 0594	0.4529 0770	0.4216 6694	58
59	0.5168 2850	0.4804 9970	0.4467 6468	0.4154 3541	59
60	0.5110 7887	0.4745 6760	0.4407 0499	0.4092 9597	60
61	0.5053 9319	0.4687 0874	0.4347 2749	0.4032 4726	61
62	0.4997 7077	0.4629 2222	0.4288 3106	0.3972 8794	62
63	0.4942 1090	0.4572 0713	0.4230 1461	0.3914 1669	63
64	0.4887 1288	0.4515 6259	0.4172 7705	0.3856 3221	64
65	0.4832 7602	0.4459 8775	0.4116 1731	0.3799 3321	65
66	0.4778 9965	0.4404 8173	0.4060 3434	0.3743 1843	66
67	0.4725 8309	0.4350 4368	0.4005 2709	0.3687 8663	67
68	0.4673 2568	0.4296 7277	0.3950 9454	0.3633 3658	68
69	0.4621 2675	0.4243 6817	0.3897 3568	0.3579 6708	69
70	0.4569 8566	0.4191 2905	0.3844 4949	0.3526 7692	70
71	0.4519 0177	0.4139 5462	0.3792 3501	0.3474 6495	71
72	0.4468 7443	0.4088 4407	0.3740 9126	0.3423 3000	72
73	0.4419 0302	0.4037 9661	0.3690 1727	0.3372 7093	73
74	0.4369 8692	0.3988 1147	0.3640 1210	0.3322 8663	74
75	0.4321 2551	0.3938 8787	0.3590 7483	0.3273 7599	75
76	0.4273 1818	0.3890 2506	0.3542 0451	0.3225 3793	76
77	0.4225 6433	0.3842 2228	0.3494 0026	0.3177 7136	77
78	0.4178 6337	0.3794 7880	0.3446 6117	0.3130 7523	78
79	0.4132 1470	0.3747 9387	0.3399 8636	0.3084 4850	79
80	0.4086 1775	0.3701 6679	0.3353 7495	0.3038 9015	80
81	0.4040 7194	0.3655 9683	0.3308 2609	0.2993 9916	81
82	0.3995 7670	0.3610 8329	0.3263 3893	0.2949 7454	82
83	0.3951 3148	0.3566 2547	0.3219 1263	0.2906 1531	83
84	0.3907 3570	0.3522 2268	0.3175 4637	0.2863 2050	84
85	0.3863 8882	0.3478 7426	0.3132 3933	0.2820 8917	85
86	0.3820 9031	0.3435 7951	0.3089 9071	0.2779 2036	86
87	0.3778 3961	0.3393 3779	0.3047 9971	0.2738 1316	87
88	0.3736 3621	0.3351 4843	0.3006 6556	0.2697 6666	88
89	0.3694 7956	0.3310 1080	0.2965 8748	0.2657 7997	89
90	0.3653 6916	0.3269 2425	0.2925 6472	0.2618 5218	90
91	0.3613 0448	0.3228 8814	0.2885 9652	0.2579 8245	91
92	0.3572 8503	0.3189 0187	0.2846 8214	0.2541 6990	92
93	0.3533 1029	0.3149 6481	0.2808 2085	0.2504 1369	93
94	0.3493 7976	0.3110 7636	0.2770 1194	0.2467 1300	94
95	0.3454 9297	0.3072 3591	0.2732 5468	0.2430 6699	95
96	0.3416 4941	0.3034 4287	0.2695 4839	0.2394 7487	96
97	0.3378 4861	0.2996 9666	0.2658 9237	0.2359 3583	97
98	0.3340 9010	0.2959 9670	0.2622 8594	0.2324 4909	98
99	0.3303 7340	0.2923 4242	0.2587 2843	0.2290 1389	99
100	0.3266 9805	0.2887 3326	0.2552 1916	0.2256 2944	100

TABLE 6 PRESENT VALUE
WHEN COMPOUND AMOUNT IS 1

$$p = (1+i)^{-n} \quad [OR,\ v^n = (1+i)^{-n}]$$

n	$1\frac{5}{8}\%$	$1\frac{3}{4}\%$	$1\frac{7}{8}\%$	2%	n
1	0.9840 0984	0.9828 0098	0.9815 9509	0.9803 9216	1
2	0.9682 7537	0.9658 9777	0.9635 2892	0.9611 6878	2
3	0.9527 9249	0.9492 8528	0.9457 9526	0.9423 2233	3
4	0.9375 5718	0.9329 5851	0.9283 8799	0.9238 4543	4
5	0.9225 6549	0.9169 1254	0.9113 0109	0.9057 3081	5
6	0.9078 1352	0.9011 4254	0.8945 2868	0.8879 7138	6
7	0.8932 9744	0.8856 4378	0.8780 6496	0.8705 6018	7
8	0.8790 1347	0.8704 1157	0.8619 0426	0.8534 9037	8
9	0.8649 5791	0.8554 4135	0.8460 4099	0.8367 5527	9
10	0.8511 2709	0.8407 2860	0.8304 6968	0.8203 4830	10
11	0.8375 1743	0.8262 6889	0.8151 8496	0.8042 6304	11
12	0.8241 2539	0.8120 5788	0.8001 8156	0.7884 9318	12
13	0.8109 4750	0.7980 9128	0.7854 5429	0.7730 3253	13
14	0.7979 8032	0.7843 6490	0.7709 9808	0.7578 7502	14
15	0.7852 2048	0.7708 7459	0.7568 0793	0.7430 1473	15
16	0.7726 6468	0.7576 1631	0.7428 7895	0.7284 4581	16
17	0.7603 0965	0.7445 8605	0.7292 0633	0.7141 6256	17
18	0.7481 5218	0.7317 7990	0.7157 8536	0.7001 5938	18
19	0.7361 8911	0.7191 9401	0.7026 1139	0.6864 3076	19
20	0.7244 1732	0.7068 2458	0.6896 7989	0.6729 7133	20
21	0.7128 3378	0.6946 6789	0.6769 8640	0.6597 7582	21
22	0.7014 3545	0.6827 2028	0.6645 2653	0.6468 3904	22
23	0.6902 1938	0.6709 7817	0.6522 9598	0.6341 5592	23
24	0.6791 8267	0.6594 3800	0.6402 9053	0.6217 2149	24
25	0.6683 2243	0.6480 9632	0.6285 0604	0.6095 3087	25
26	0.6576 3584	0.6369 4970	0.6169 3845	0.5975 7928	26
27	0.6471 2014	0.6259 9479	0.6055 8375	0.5858 6204	27
28	0.6367 7259	0.6152 2829	0.5944 3804	0.5743 7455	28
29	0.6265 9049	0.6046 4697	0.5834 9746	0.5631 1231	29
30	0.6165 7121	0.5942 4764	0.5727 5824	0.5520 7089	30
31	0.6067 1214	0.5840 2716	0.5622 1668	0.5412 4597	31
32	0.5970 1071	0.5739 8247	0.5518 6913	0.5306 3330	32
33	0.5874 6442	0.5641 1053	0.5417 1203	0.5202 2873	33
34	0.5780 7077	0.5544 0839	0.5317 4187	0.5100 2817	34
35	0.5688 2732	0.5448 7311	0.5219 5521	0.5000 2761	35
36	0.5597 3168	0.5355 0183	0.5123 4867	0.4902 2315	36
37	0.5507 8148	0.5262 9172	0.5029 1894	0.4806 1093	37
38	0.5419 7440	0.5172 4002	0.4936 6277	0.4711 8719	38
39	0.5333 0814	0.5083 4400	0.4845 7695	0.4619 4822	39
40	0.5247 8046	0.4996 0098	0.4756 5836	0.4528 9042	40
41	0.5163 8914	0.4910 0834	0.4669 0391	0.4440 1021	41
42	0.5081 3199	0.4825 6348	0.4583 1058	0.4353 0413	42
43	0.5000 0688	0.4742 6386	0.4498 7542	0.4267 6875	43
44	0.4920 1169	0.4661 0699	0.4415 9550	0.4184 0074	44
45	0.4841 4434	0.4580 9040	0.4334 6798	0.4101 9680	45
46	0.4764 0280	0.4502 1170	0.4254 9004	0.4021 5373	46
47	0.4687 8504	0.4424 6850	0.4176 5894	0.3942 6836	47
48	0.4612 8909	0.4348 5848	0.4099 7196	0.3865 3761	48
49	0.4539 1301	0.4273 7934	0.4024 2647	0.3789 5844	49
50	0.4466 5487	0.4200 2883	0.3950 1984	0.3715 2788	50

TABLE 6 PRESENT VALUE
WHEN COMPOUND AMOUNT IS 1

$$p = (1+i)^{-n} \quad [OR,\ v^n = (1+i)^{-n}]$$

n	$1\frac{5}{8}\%$	$1\frac{3}{4}\%$	$1\frac{7}{8}\%$	2%	n
51	0.4395 1278	0.4128 0475	0.3877 4954	0.3642 4302	51
52	0.4324 8490	0.4057 0492	0.3806 1305	0.3571 0100	52
53	0.4255 6940	0.3987 2719	0.3736 0790	0.3500 9902	53
54	0.4187 6448	0.3918 6947	0.3667 3168	0.3432 3433	54
55	0.4120 6837	0.3851 2970	0.3599 8202	0.3365 0425	55
56	0.4054 7933	0.3785 0585	0.3533 5658	0.3299 0613	56
57	0.3989 9565	0.3719 9592	0.3468 5308	0.3234 3738	57
58	0.3926 1564	0.3655 9796	0.3404 6928	0.3170 9547	58
59	0.3863 3766	0.3593 1003	0.3342 0298	0.3108 7791	59
60	0.3801 6006	0.3531 3025	0.3280 5200	0.3047 8227	60
61	0.3740 8124	0.3470 5676	0.3220 1424	0.2988 0614	61
62	0.3680 9962	0.3410 8772	0.3160 8759	0.2929 4720	62
63	0.3622 1365	0.3352 2135	0.3102 7003	0.2872 0314	63
64	0.3564 2179	0.3294 5587	0.3045 5954	0.2815 7170	64
65	0.3507 2255	0.3237 8956	0.2989 5415	0.2760 5069	65
66	0.3451 1444	0.3182 2069	0.2934 5193	0.2706 3793	66
67	0.3395 9601	0.3127 4761	0.2880 5097	0.2653 3130	67
68	0.3341 6581	0.3073 6866	0.2827 4942	0.2601 2873	68
69	0.3288 2245	0.3020 8222	0.2775 4544	0.2550 2817	69
70	0.3235 6452	0.2968 8670	0.2724 3724	0.2500 2761	70
71	0.3183 9067	0.2917 8054	0.2674 2306	0.2451 2511	71
72	0.3132 9956	0.2867 6221	0.2625 0116	0.2403 1874	72
73	0.3082 8985	0.2818 3018	0.2576 6985	0.2356 0660	73
74	0.3033 6024	0.2769 8298	0.2529 2746	0.2309 8687	74
75	0.2985 0946	0.2722 1914	0.2482 7236	0.2264 5771	75
76	0.2937 3625	0.2675 3724	0.2437 0293	0.2220 1737	76
77	0.2890 3936	0.2629 3586	0.2392 1760	0.2176 6408	77
78	0.2844 1757	0.2584 1362	0.2348 1482	0.2133 9616	78
79	0.2798 6969	0.2539 6916	0.2304 9308	0.2092 1192	79
80	0.2753 9453	0.2496 0114	0.2262 5087	0.2051 0973	80
81	0.2709 9093	0.2453 0825	0.2220 8674	0.2010 8797	81
82	0.2666 5774	0.2410 8919	0.2179 9926	0.1971 4507	82
83	0.2623 9384	0.2369 4269	0.2139 8700	0.1932 7948	83
84	0.2581 9812	0.2328 6751	0.2100 4859	0.1894 8968	84
85	0.2540 6949	0.2288 6242	0.2061 8267	0.1857 7420	85
86	0.2500 0688	0.2249 2621	0.2023 8789	0.1821 3157	86
87	0.2460 0923	0.2210 5770	0.1986 6296	0.1785 6036	87
88	0.2420 7550	0.2172 5572	0.1950 0659	0.1750 5918	88
89	0.2382 0468	0.2135 1914	0.1914 1751	0.1716 2665	89
90	0.2343 9575	0.2098 4682	0.1878 9449	0.1682 6142	90
91	0.2306 4772	0.2062 3766	0.1844 3631	0.1649 6217	91
92	0.2269 5963	0.2026 9057	0.1810 4178	0.1617 2762	92
93	0.2233 3051	0.1992 0450	0.1777 0972	0.1585 5649	93
94	0.2197 5942	0.1957 7837	0.1744 3899	0.1554 4754	94
95	0.2162 4543	0.1924 1118	0.1712 2845	0.1523 9955	95
96	0.2127 8763	0.1891 0190	0.1680 7701	0.1494 1132	96
97	0.2093 8512	0.1858 4953	0.1649 8357	0.1464 8169	97
98	0.2060 3702	0.1826 5310	0.1619 4706	0.1436 0950	98
99	0.2027 4245	0.1795 1165	0.1589 6644	0.1407 9363	99
100	0.1995 0057	0.1764 2422	0.1560 4068	0.1380 3297	100

TABLE 6 PRESENT VALUE
WHEN COMPOUND AMOUNT IS 1

$$p = (1 + i)^{-n} \quad [OR,\ v^n = (1 + i)^{-n}]$$

n	$2\frac{1}{4}\%$	$2\frac{1}{2}\%$	$2\frac{3}{4}\%$	3%	n
1	0.9779 9511	0.9756 0976	0.9732 3601	0.9708 7379	1
2	0.9564 7444	0.9518 1440	0.9471 8833	0.9425 9591	2
3	0.9354 2732	0.9285 9941	0.9218 3779	0.9151 4166	3
4	0.9148 4335	0.9059 5064	0.8971 6573	0.8884 8705	4
5	0.8947 1232	0.8838 5429	0.8731 5400	0.8626 0878	5
6	0.8750 2427	0.8622 9687	0.8497 8491	0.8374 8426	6
7	0.8557 6946	0.8412 6524	0.8270 4128	0.8130 9151	7
8	0.8369 3835	0.8207 4657	0.8049 0635	0.7894 0923	8
9	0.8185 2161	0.8007 2836	0.7833 6385	0.7664 1673	9
10	0.8005 1013	0.7811 9840	0.7623 9791	0.7440 9391	10
11	0.7828 9499	0.7621 4478	0.7419 9310	0.7224 2128	11
12	0.7656 6748	0.7435 5589	0.7221 3440	0.7013 7988	12
13	0.7488 1905	0.7254 2038	0.7028 0720	0.6809 5134	13
14	0.7323 4137	0.7077 2720	0.6839 9728	0.6611 1781	14
15	0.7162 2628	0.6904 6556	0.6656 9078	0.6418 6195	15
16	0.7004 6580	0.6736 2493	0.6478 7424	0.6231 6694	16
17	0.6850 5212	0.6571 9506	0.6305 3454	0.6050 1645	17
18	0.6699 7763	0.6411 6591	0.6136 5892	0.5873 9461	18
19	0.6552 3484	0.6255 2772	0.5972 3496	0.5702 8603	19
20	0.6408 1647	0.6102 7094	0.5812 5057	0.5536 7575	20
21	0.6267 1538	0.5953 8629	0.5656 9398	0.5375 4928	21
22	0.6129 2457	0.5808 6467	0.5505 5375	0.5218 9250	22
23	0.5994 3724	0.5666 9724	0.5358 1874	0.5066 9175	23
24	0.5862 4668	0.5528 7535	0.5214 7809	0.4919 3374	24
25	0.5733 4639	0.5393 9059	0.5075 2126	0.4776 0557	25
26	0.5607 2997	0.5262 3472	0.4939 3796	0.4636 9473	26
27	0.5483 9117	0.5133 9973	0.4807 1821	0.4501 8906	27
28	0.5363 2388	0.5008 7778	0.4678 5227	0.4370 7675	28
29	0.5245 2213	0.4886 6125	0.4553 3068	0.4243 4636	29
30	0.5129 8008	0.4767 4269	0.4431 4421	0.4119 8676	30
31	0.5016 9201	0.4651 1481	0.4312 8391	0.3999 8715	31
32	0.4906 5233	0.4537 7055	0.4197 4103	0.3883 3703	32
33	0.4798 5558	0.4427 0298	0.4085 0708	0.3770 2625	33
34	0.4692 9641	0.4319 0534	0.3975 7380	0.3660 4490	34
35	0.4589 6960	0.4213 7107	0.3869 3314	0.3553 8340	35
36	0.4488 7002	0.4110 9372	0.3765 7727	0.3450 3243	36
37	0.4389 9268	0.4010 6705	0.3664 9856	0.3349 8294	37
38	0.4293 3270	0.3912 8492	0.3566 8959	0.3252 2615	38
39	0.4198 8528	0.3817 4139	0.3471 4316	0.3157 5355	39
40	0.4106 4575	0.3724 3062	0.3378 5222	0.3065 5684	40
41	0.4016 0954	0.3633 4695	0.3288 0995	0.2976 2800	41
42	0.3927 7216	0.3544 8483	0.3200 0968	0.2889 5922	42
43	0.3841 2925	0.3458 3886	0.3114 4495	0.2805 4294	43
44	0.3756 7653	0.3374 0376	0.3031 0944	0.2723 7178	44
45	0.3674 0981	0.3291 7440	0.2949 9702	0.2644 3862	45
46	0.3593 2500	0.3211 4576	0.2871 0172	0.2567 3653	46
47	0.3514 1809	0.3133 1294	0.2794 1773	0.2492 5876	47
48	0.3436 8518	0.3056 7116	0.2719 3940	0.2419 9880	48
49	0.3361 2242	0.2982 1576	0.2646 6122	0.2349 5029	49
50	0.3287 2608	0.2909 4221	0.2575 7783	0.2281 0708	50

TABLE 6 PRESENT VALUE
WHEN COMPOUND AMOUNT IS 1

$$p = (1+i)^{-n} \quad [OR,\ v^n = (1+i)^{-n}]$$

n	$2\frac{1}{4}$%	$2\frac{1}{2}$%	$2\frac{3}{4}$%	3%	n
51	0.3214 9250	0.2838 4606	0.2506 8402	0.2214 6318	51
52	0.3144 1810	0.2769 2298	0.2439 7471	0.2150 1280	52
53	0.3074 9936	0.2701 6876	0.2374 4497	0.2087 5029	53
54	0.3007 3287	0.2635 7928	0.2310 9000	0.2026 7019	54
55	0.2941 1528	0.2571 5052	0.2249 0511	0.1967 6717	55
56	0.2876 4330	0.2508 7855	0.2188 8575	0.1910 3609	56
57	0.2813 1374	0.2447 5956	0.2130 2749	0.1854 7193	57
58	0.2751 2347	0.2387 8982	0.2073 2603	0.1800 6984	58
59	0.2690 6940	0.2329 6568	0.2017 7716	0.1748 2508	59
60	0.2631 4856	0.2272 8359	0.1963 7679	0.1697 3309	60
61	0.2573 5801	0.2217 4009	0.1911 2097	0.1647 8941	61
62	0.2516 9487	0.2163 3179	0.1860 0581	0.1599 8972	62
63	0.2461 5635	0.2110 5541	0.1810 2755	0.1553 2982	63
64	0.2407 3971	0.2059 0771	0.1761 8253	0.1508 0565	64
65	0.2354 4226	0.2008 8557	0.1714 6718	0.1464 1325	65
66	0.2302 6138	0.1959 8593	0.1668 7804	0.1421 4879	66
67	0.2251 9450	0.1912 0578	0.1624 1172	0.1380 0853	67
68	0.2202 3912	0.1865 4223	0.1580 6493	0.1339 8887	68
69	0.2153 9278	0.1819 9242	0.1538 3448	0.1300 8628	69
70	0.2106 5309	0.1775 5358	0.1497 1726	0.1262 9736	70
71	0.2060 1769	0.1732 2300	0.1457 1023	0.1226 1880	71
72	0.2014 8429	0.1689 9805	0.1418 1044	0.1190 4737	72
73	0.1970 5065	0.1648 7615	0.1380 1503	0.1155 7998	73
74	0.1927 1458	0.1608 5478	0.1343 2119	0.1122 1357	74
75	0.1884 7391	0.1569 3149	0.1307 2622	0.1089 4521	75
76	0.1843 2657	0.1531 0389	0.1272 2747	0.1057 7205	76
77	0.1802 7048	0.1493 6965	0.1238 2235	0.1026 9131	77
78	0.1763 0365	0.1457 2649	0.1205 0837	0.0997 0030	78
79	0.1724 2411	0.1421 7218	0.1172 8309	0.0967 9641	79
80	0.1686 2993	0.1387 0457	0.1141 4412	0.0939 7710	80
81	0.1649 1925	0.1353 2153	0.1110 8917	0.0912 3990	81
82	0.1612 9022	0.1320 2101	0.1081 1598	0.0885 8243	82
83	0.1577 4105	0.1288 0098	0.1052 2237	0.0860 0236	83
84	0.1542 6997	0.1256 5949	0.1024 0620	0.0834 9743	84
85	0.1508 7528	0.1225 9463	0.0996 6540	0.0810 6547	85
86	0.1475 5528	0.1196 0452	0.0969 9795	0.0787 0434	86
87	0.1443 0835	0.1166 8733	0.0944 0190	0.0764 1198	87
88	0.1411 3286	0.1138 4130	0.0918 7533	0.0741 8639	88
89	0.1380 2724	0.1110 6468	0.0894 1638	0.0720 2562	89
90	0.1349 8997	0.1083 5579	0.0870 2324	0.0699 2779	90
91	0.1320 1953	0.1057 1296	0.0846 9415	0.0678 9105	91
92	0.1291 1445	0.1031 3460	0.0824 2740	0.0659 1364	92
93	0.1262 7331	0.1006 1912	0.0802 2131	0.0639 9383	93
94	0.1234 9468	0.0981 6500	0.0780 7427	0.0621 2993	94
95	0.1207 7719	0.0957 7073	0.0759 8469	0.0603 2032	95
96	0.1181 1950	0.0934 3486	0.0739 5104	0.0585 6342	96
97	0.1155 2029	0.0911 5596	0.0719 7181	0.0568 5769	97
98	0.1129 7828	0.0889 3264	0.0700 4556	0.0552 0164	98
99	0.1104 9221	0.0867 6355	0.0681 7086	0.0535 9382	99
100	0.1080 6084	0.0846 4737	0.0663 4634	0.0520 3284	100

TABLE 6 PRESENT VALUE
WHEN COMPOUND AMOUNT IS 1

$$p = (1+i)^{-n} \quad [OR,\ v^n = (1+i)^{-n}]$$

n	$3\frac{1}{4}\%$	$3\frac{1}{2}\%$	$3\frac{3}{4}\%$	4%	n
1	0.9685 2300	0.9661 8357	0.9638 5542	0.9615 3846	1
2	0.9380 3681	0.9335 1070	0.9290 1727	0.9245 5621	2
3	0.9085 1022	0.9019 4271	0.8954 3834	0.8889 9636	3
4	0.8799 1305	0.8714 4223	0.8630 7310	0.8548 0419	4
5	0.8522 1603	0.8419 7317	0.8318 7768	0.8219 2711	5
6	0.8253 9083	0.8135 0064	0.8018 0981	0.7903 1453	6
7	0.7994 1000	0.7859 9096	0.7728 2874	0.7599 1781	7
8	0.7742 4698	0.7594 1156	0.7448 9517	0.7306 9020	8
9	0.7498 7601	0.7337 3097	0.7179 7125	0.7025 8674	9
10	0.7262 7216	0.7089 1881	0.6920 2048	0.6755 6417	10
11	0.7034 1129	0.6849 4571	0.6670 0769	0.6495 8093	11
12	0.6812 7002	0.6617 8330	0.6428 9898	0.6245 9705	12
13	0.6598 2568	0.6394 0415	0.6196 6167	0.6005 7409	13
14	0.6390 5635	0.6177 8179	0.5972 6426	0.5774 7508	14
15	0.6189 4078	0.5968 9062	0.5756 7639	0.5552 6450	15
16	0.5994 5838	0.5767 0591	0.5548 6881	0.5339 0818	16
17	0.5805 8923	0.5572 0378	0.5348 1331	0.5133 7325	17
18	0.5623 1402	0.5383 6114	0.5154 8271	0.4936 2812	18
19	0.5446 1407	0.5201 5569	0.4968 5080	0.4746 4242	19
20	0.5274 7125	0.5025 6588	0.4788 9234	0.4563 8695	20
21	0.5108 6804	0.4855 7090	0.4615 8298	0.4388 3360	21
22	0.4947 8745	0.4691 5063	0.4448 9926	0.4219 5539	22
23	0.4792 1302	0.4532 8563	0.4288 1856	0.4057 2633	23
24	0.4641 2884	0.4379 5713	0.4133 1910	0.3901 2147	24
25	0.4495 1945	0.4231 4699	0.3983 7985	0.3751 1680	25
26	0.4353 6993	0.4088 3767	0.3839 8058	0.3606 8923	26
27	0.4216 6579	0.3950 1224	0.3701 0176	0.3468 1657	27
28	0.4083 9302	0.3816 5434	0.3567 2459	0.3334 7747	28
29	0.3955 3803	0.3687 4816	0.3438 3093	0.3206 5141	29
30	0.3830 8768	0.3562 7841	0.3314 0331	0.3083 1867	30
31	0.3710 2923	0.3442 3035	0.3194 2487	0.2964 6026	31
32	0.3593 5035	0.3325 8971	0.3078 7940	0.2850 5794	32
33	0.3480 3908	0.3213 4271	0.2967 5123	0.2740 9417	33
34	0.3370 8385	0.3104 7605	0.2860 2528	0.2635 5209	34
35	0.3264 7346	0.2999 7686	0.2756 8702	0.2534 1547	35
36	0.3161 9706	0.2898 3272	0.2657 2242	0.2436 6872	36
37	0.3062 4413	0.2800 3161	0.2561 1800	0.2342 9685	37
38	0.2966 0448	0.2705 6194	0.2468 6072	0.2252 8543	38
39	0.2872 6826	0.2614 1250	0.2379 3805	0.2166 2061	39
40	0.2782 2592	0.2525 7247	0.2293 3788	0.2082 8904	40
41	0.2694 6820	0.2440 3137	0.2210 4855	0.2002 7793	41
42	0.2609 8615	0.2357 7910	0.2130 5885	0.1925 7493	42
43	0.2527 7109	0.2278 0590	0.2053 5793	0.1851 6820	43
44	0.2448 1462	0.2201 0231	0.1979 3535	0.1780 4635	44
45	0.2371 0859	0.2126 5924	0.1907 8106	0.1711 9841	45
46	0.2296 4512	0.2054 6787	0.1838 8536	0.1646 1386	46
47	0.2224 1658	0.1985 1968	0.1772 3890	0.1582 8256	47
48	0.2154 1558	0.1918 0645	0.1708 3268	0.1521 9476	48
49	0.2086 3494	0.1853 2024	0.1646 5800	0.1463 4112	49
50	0.2020 6774	0.1790 5337	0.1587 0651	0.1407 1262	50

TABLE 6 PRESENT VALUE

WHEN COMPOUND AMOUNT IS 1

$$p = (1+i)^{-n} \quad [OR,\ v^n = (1+i)^{-n}]$$

n	$3\frac{1}{4}\%$	$3\frac{1}{2}\%$	$3\frac{3}{4}\%$	4 %	n
51	0.1957 0725	0.1729 9843	0.1529 7013	0.1353 0059	51
52	0.1895 4698	0.1671 4824	0.1474 4109	0.1300 9672	52
53	0.1835 8061	0.1614 9589	0.1421 1189	0.1250 9300	53
54	0.1778 0204	0.1560 3467	0.1369 7532	0.1202 8173	54
55	0.1722 0537	0.1507 5814	0.1320 2440	0.1156 5551	55
56	0.1667 8486	0.1456 6004	0.1272 5243	0.1112 0722	56
57	0.1615 3497	0.1407 3433	0.1226 5295	0.1069 3002	57
58	0.1564 5034	0.1359 7520	0.1182 1971	0.1028 1733	58
59	0.1515 2575	0.1313 7701	0.1139 4671	0.0988 6282	59
60	0.1467 5617	0.1269 3431	0.1098 2815	0.0950 6040	60
61	0.1421 3673	0.1226 4184	0.1058 5846	0.0914 0423	61
62	0.1376 6269	0.1184 9453	0.1020 3225	0.0878 8868	62
63	0.1333 2948	0.1144 8747	0.0983 4434	0.0845 0835	63
64	0.1291 3267	0.1106 1591	0.0947 8972	0.0812 5803	64
65	0.1250 6796	0.1068 7528	0.0913 6359	0.0781 3272	65
66	0.1211 3120	0.1032 6114	0.0880 6129	0.0751 2762	66
67	0.1173 1835	0.0997 6922	0.0848 7835	0.0722 3809	67
68	0.1136 2552	0.0963 9538	0.0818 1046	0.0694 5970	68
69	0.1100 4893	0.0931 3563	0.0788 5346	0.0667 8818	69
70	0.1065 8492	0.0899 8612	0.0760 0333	0.0642 1940	70
71	0.1032 2995	0.0869 4311	0.0732 5622	0.0617 4942	71
72	0.0999 8058	0.0840 0300	0.0706 0841	0.0593 7445	72
73	0.0968 3349	0.0811 6232	0.0680 5630	0.0570 9081	73
74	0.0937 8546	0.0784 1770	0.0655 9643	0.0548 9501	74
75	0.0908 3338	0.0757 6590	0.0632 2547	0.0527 8367	75
76	0.0879 7422	0.0732 0376	0.0609 4022	0.0507 5353	76
77	0.0852 0505	0.0707 2828	0.0587 3756	0.0488 0147	77
78	0.0825 2305	0.0683 3650	0.0566 1451	0.0469 2449	78
79	0.0799 2548	0.0660 2560	0.0545 6821	0.0451 1970	79
80	0.0774 0966	0.0637 9285	0.0525 9586	0.0433 8433	80
81	0.0749 7304	0.0616 3561	0.0506 9481	0.0417 1570	81
82	0.0726 1311	0.0595 5131	0.0488 6246	0.0401 1125	82
83	0.0703 2747	0.0575 3750	0.0470 9635	0.0385 6851	83
84	0.0681 1377	0.0555 9178	0.0453 9407	0.0370 8510	84
85	0.0659 6976	0.0537 1187	0.0437 5332	0.0356 5875	85
86	0.0638 9323	0.0518 9553	0.0421 7188	0.0342 8726	86
87	0.0618 8206	0.0501 4060	0.0406 4759	0.0329 6852	87
88	0.0599 3420	0.0484 4503	0.0391 7840	0.0317 0050	88
89	0.0580 4765	0.0468 0679	0.0377 6232	0.0304 8125	89
90	0.0562 2048	0.0452 2395	0.0363 9741	0.0293 0890	90
91	0.0544 5083	0.0436 9464	0.0350 8184	0.0281 8163	91
92	0.0527 3688	0.0422 1704	0.0338 1383	0.0270 9772	92
93	0.0510 7688	0.0407 8941	0.0325 9164	0.0260 5550	93
94	0.0494 6914	0.0394 1006	0.0314 1363	0.0250 5337	94
95	0.0479 1200	0.0380 7735	0.0302 7820	0.0240 8978	95
96	0.0464 0387	0.0367 8971	0.0291 8380	0.0231 6325	96
97	0.0449 4322	0.0355 4562	0.0281 2897	0.0222 7235	97
98	0.0435 2854	0.0343 4359	0.0271 1226	0.0214 1572	98
99	0.0421 5839	0.0331 8221	0.0261 3230	0.0205 9204	99
100	0.0408 3137	0.0320 6011	0.0251 8776	0.0198 0004	100

TABLE 6 PRESENT VALUE
WHEN COMPOUND AMOUNT IS 1

$$p = (1+i)^{-n} \quad [OR,\ v^n = (1+i)^{-n}]$$

n	$4\frac{1}{2}\%$	5 %	$5\frac{1}{2}\%$	6 %	n
1	0.9569 3780	0.9523 8095	0.9478 6730	0.9433 9623	1
2	0.9157 2995	0.9070 2948	0.8984 5242	0.8899 9644	2
3	0.8762 9660	0.8638 3760	0.8516 1366	0.8396 1928	3
4	0.8385 6134	0.8227 0247	0.8072 1674	0.7920 9366	4
5	0.8024 5105	0.7835 2617	0.7651 3435	0.7472 5817	5
6	0.7678 9574	0.7462 1540	0.7252 4583	0.7049 6054	6
7	0.7348 2846	0.7106 8133	0.6874 3681	0.6650 5711	7
8	0.7031 8513	0.6768 3936	0.6515 9887	0.6274 1237	8
9	0.6729 0443	0.6446 0892	0.6176 2926	0.5918 9846	9
10	0.6439 2768	0.6139 1325	0.5854 3058	0.5583 9478	10
11	0.6161 9874	0.5846 7929	0.5549 1050	0.5267 8753	11
12	0.5896 6386	0.5568 3742	0.5259 8152	0.4969 6936	12
13	0.5642 7164	0.5303 2135	0.4985 6068	0.4688 3902	13
14	0.5399 7286	0.5050 6795	0.4725 6937	0.4423 0096	14
15	0.5167 2044	0.4810 1710	0.4479 3305	0.4172 6506	15
16	0.4944 6932	0.4581 1152	0.4245 8109	0.3936 4628	16
17	0.4731 7639	0.4362 9669	0.4024 4653	0.3713 6442	17
18	0.4528 0037	0.4155 2065	0.3814 6590	0.3503 4379	18
19	0.4333 0179	0.3957 3396	0.3615 7906	0.3305 1301	19
20	0.4146 4286	0.3768 8948	0.3427 2896	0.3118 0473	20
21	0.3967 8743	0.3589 4236	0.3248 6158	0.2941 5540	21
22	0.3797 0089	0.3418 4987	0.3079 2566	0.2775 0510	22
23	0.3633 5013	0.3255 7131	0.2918 7267	0.2617 9726	23
24	0.3477 0347	0.3100 6791	0.2766 5656	0.2469 7855	24
25	0.3327 3060	0.2953 0277	0.2622 3370	0.2329 9863	25
26	0.3184 0248	0.2812 4074	0.2485 6275	0.2198 1003	26
27	0.3046 9137	0.2678 4832	0.2356 0450	0.2073 6795	27
28	0.2915 7069	0.2550 9364	0.2233 2181	0.1956 3014	28
29	0.2790 1502	0.2429 4632	0.2116 7944	0.1845 5674	29
30	0.2670 0002	0.2313 7745	0.2006 4402	0.1741 1013	30
31	0.2555 0241	0.2203 5947	0.1901 8390	0.1642 5484	31
32	0.2444 9991	0.2098 6617	0.1802 6910	0.1549 5740	32
33	0.2339 7121	0.1998 7254	0.1708 7119	0.1461 8622	33
34	0.2238 9589	0.1903 5480	0.1619 6321	0.1379 1153	34
35	0.2142 5444	0.1812 9029	0.1535 1963	0.1301 0522	35
36	0.2050 2817	0.1726 5741	0.1455 1624	0.1227 4077	36
37	0.1961 9921	0.1644 3563	0.1379 3008	0.1157 9318	37
38	0.1877 5044	0.1566 0536	0.1307 3941	0.1092 3885	38
39	0.1796 6549	0.1491 4797	0.1239 2362	0.1030 5552	39
40	0.1719 2870	0.1420 4568	0.1174 6314	0.0972 2219	40
41	0.1645 2507	0.1352 8160	0.1113 3947	0.0917 1904	41
42	0.1574 4026	0.1288 3962	0.1055 3504	0.0865 2740	42
43	0.1506 6054	0.1227 0440	0.1000 3322	0.0816 2962	43
44	0.1441 7276	0.1168 6133	0.0948 1822	0.0770 0908	44
45	0.1379 6437	0.1112 9651	0.0898 7509	0.0726 5007	45
46	0.1320 2332	0.1059 9668	0.0851 8965	0.0685 3781	46
47	0.1263 3810	0.1009 4921	0.0807 4849	0.0646 5831	47
48	0.1208 9771	0.0961 4211	0.0765 3885	0.0609 9840	48
49	0.1156 9158	0.0915 6391	0.0725 4867	0.0575 4566	49
50	0.1107 0965	0.0872 0373	0.0687 6652	0.0542 8836	50

TABLE 6 PRESENT VALUE
WHEN COMPOUND AMOUNT IS 1

$$p=(1+i)^{-n} \quad [OR,\ v^{n}=(1+i)^{-n}]$$

n	$4\frac{1}{2}$%	5 %	$5\frac{1}{2}$%	6 %	n
51	0.1059 4225	0.0830 5117	0.0651 8153	0.0512 1544	51
52	0.1013 8014	0.0790 9635	0.0617 8344	0.0483 1645	52
53	0.0970 1449	0.0753 2986	0.0585 6250	0.0455 8156	53
54	0.0928 3683	0.0717 4272	0.0555 0948	0.0430 0147	54
55	0.0888 3907	0.0683 2640	0.0526 1562	0.0405 6742	55
56	0.0850 1347	0.0650 7276	0.0498 7263	0.0382 7115	56
57	0.0813 5260	0.0619 7406	0.0472 7263	0.0361 0486	57
58	0.0778 4938	0.0590 2291	0.0448 0818	0.0340 6119	58
59	0.0744 9701	0.0562 1230	0.0424 7221	0.0321 3320	59
60	0.0712 8901	0.0535 3552	0.0402 5802	0.0303 1434	60
61	0.0682 1915	0.0509 8621	0.0381 5926	0.0285 9843	61
62	0.0652 8148	0.0485 5830	0.0361 6992	0.0269 7965	62
63	0.0624 7032	0.0462 4600	0.0342 8428	0.0354 5250	63
64	0.0597 8021	0.0440 4381	0.0324 9695	0.0240 1179	64
65	0.0572 0594	0.0419 4648	0.0308 0279	0.0226 5264	65
66	0.0547 4253	0.0399 4903	0.0291 9696	0.0213 7041	66
67	0.0523 8519	0.0380 4670	0.0276 7485	0.0201 6077	67
68	0.0501 2937	0.0362 3495	0.0262 3208	0.0190 1959	68
69	0.0479 7069	0.0345 0948	0.0248 6453	0.0179 4301	69
70	0.0459 0497	0.0328 6617	0.0235 6828	0.0169 2737	70
71	0.0439 2820	0.0313 0111	0.0223 3960	0.0159 6921	71
72	0.0420 3655	0.0298 1058	0.0211 7498	0.0150 6530	72
73	0.0402 2637	0.0283 9103	0.0200 7107	0.0142 1254	73
74	0.0384 9413	0.0270 3908	0.0190 2471	0.0134 0806	74
75	0.0368 3649	0.0257 5150	0.0180 3290	0.0126 4911	75
76	0.0352 5023	0.0245 2524	0.0170 9279	0.0119 3313	76
77	0.0337 3228	0.0233 5737	0.0162 0170	0.0112 5767	77
78	0.0322 7969	0.0222 4512	0.0153 5706	0.0106 2044	78
79	0.0308 8965	0.0211 8582	0.0145 5646	0.0100 1928	79
80	0.0295 5948	0.0201 7698	0.0137 9759	0.0094 5215	80
81	0.0282 8658	0.0192 1617	0.0130 7828	0.0089 1713	81
82	0.0270 6850	0.0183 0111	0.0123 9648	0.0084 1238	82
83	0.0259 0287	0.0174 2963	0.0117 5022	0.0079 3621	83
84	0.0247 8744	0.0165 9965	0.0111 3765	0.0074 8699	84
85	0.0237 2003	0.0158 0919	0.0105 5701	0.0070 6320	85
86	0.0226 9860	0.0150 5637	0.0100 0664	0.0066 6340	86
87	0.0217 2115	0.0143 3940	0.0094 8497	0.0062 8622	87
88	0.0207 8579	0.0136 5657	0.0089 9049	0.0059 3040	88
89	0.0198 9070	0.0130 0626	0.0085 2180	0.0055 9472	89
90	0.0190 3417	0.0123 8691	0.0080 7753	0.0052 7803	90
91	0.0182 1451	0.0117 9706	0.0076 5643	0.0049 7928	91
92	0.0174 3016	0.0112 3530	0.0072 5728	0.0046 9743	92
93	0.0166 7958	0.0107 0028	0.0068 7894	0.0044 3154	93
94	0.0159 6132	0.0101 9074	0.0065 2032	0.0041 8070	94
95	0.0152 7399	0.0097 0547	0.0061 8040	0.0039 4405	95
96	0.0146 1626	0.0092 4331	0.0058 5820	0.0037 2081	96
97	0.0139 8685	0.0088 0315	0.0055 5279	0.0035 1019	97
98	0.0133 8454	0.0083 8395	0.0052 6331	0.0033 1150	98
99	0.0128 0817	0.0079 8471	0.0049 8892	0.0031 2406	99
100	0.0122 5663	0.0076 0449	0.0047 2883	0.0029 4723	100

TABLE 6 PRESENT VALUE
WHEN COMPOUND AMOUNT IS 1

$$p=(1+i)^{-n} \quad [OR,\ v^n=(1+i)^{-n}]$$

n	$6\frac{1}{2}\%$	7 %	$7\frac{1}{2}\%$	8 %	n
1	0.9389 6714	0.9345 7944	0.9302 3256	0.9259 2593	1
2	0.8816 5928	0.8734 3873	0.8653 3261	0.8573 3882	2
3	0.8278 4909	0.8162 9788	0.8049 6057	0.7938 3224	3
4	0.7773 2309	0.7628 9521	0.7488 0053	0.7350 2985	4
5	0.7298 8084	0.7129 8618	0.6965 5863	0.6805 8320	5
6	0.6853 3412	0.6663 4222	0.6479 6152	0.6301 6963	6
7	0.6435 0621	0.6227 4974	0.6027 5490	0.5834 9040	7
8	0.6042 3119	0.5820 0910	0.5607 0223	0.5402 6888	8
9	0.5673 5323	0.5439 3374	0.5215 8347	0.5002 4897	9
10	0.5327 2604	0.5083 4929	0.4851 9393	0.4631 9349	10
11	0.5002 1224	0.4750 9280	0.4513 4319	0.4288 8286	11
12	0.4696 8285	0.4440 1196	0.4198 5413	0.3971 1376	12
13	0.4410 1676	0.4149 6445	0.3905 6198	0.3676 9792	13
14	0.4141 0025	0.3878 1724	0.3633 1347	0.3404 6104	14
15	0.3888 2652	0.3624 4602	0.3379 6602	0.3152 4170	15
16	0.3650 9533	0.3387 3460	0.3143 8699	0.2918 9047	16
17	0.3428 1251	0.3165 7439	0.2924 5302	0.2702 6895	17
18	0.3218 8969	0.2958 6392	0.2720 4932	0.2502 4903	18
19	0.3022 4384	0.2765 0833	0.2530 6913	0.2317 1206	19
20	0.2837 9703	0.2584 1900	0.2354 1315	0.2145 4821	20
21	0.2664 7608	0.2415 1309	0.2189 8897	0.1986 5575	21
22	0.2502 1228	0.2257 1317	0.2037 1067	0.1839 4051	22
23	0.2349 4111	0.2109 4688	0.1894 9830	0.1703 1528	23
24	0.2206 0198	0.1971 4662	0.1762 7749	0.1576 9934	24
25	0.2071 3801	0.1842 4918	0.1639 7906	0.1460 1790	25
26	0.1944 9579	0.1721 9549	0.1525 3866	0.1352 0176	26
27	0.1826 2515	0.1609 3037	0.1418 9643	0.1251 8682	27
28	0.1714 7902	0.1504 0221	0.1319 9668	0.1159 1372	28
29	0.1610 1316	0.1405 6282	0.1227 8761	0.1073 2752	29
30	0.1511 8607	0.1313 6712	0.1142 2103	0.0993 7733	30
31	0.1419 5875	0.1227 7301	0.1062 5212	0.0920 1605	31
32	0.1332 9460	0.1147 4113	0.0988 3918	0.0852 0005	32
33	0.1251 5925	0.1072 3470	0.0919 4343	0.0788 8893	33
34	0.1175 2042	0.1002 1934	0.0855 2877	0.0730 4531	34
35	0.1103 4781	0.0936 6294	0.0795 6164	0.0676 3454	35
36	0.1036 1297	0.0875 3546	0.0740 1083	0.0626 2458	36
37	0.0972 8917	0.0818 0884	0.0688 4729	0.0579 8572	37
38	0.0913 5134	0.0764 5686	0.0640 4399	0.0536 9048	38
39	0.0857 7590	0.0714 5501	0.0595 7580	0.0497 1341	39
40	0.0805 4075	0.0667 8038	0.0554 1935	0.0460 3093	40
41	0.0756 2512	0.0624 1157	0.0515 5288	0.0426 2123	41
42	0.0710 0950	0.0583 2857	0.0479 5617	0.0394 6411	42
43	0.0666 7559	0.0545 1268	0.0446 1039	0.0365 4084	43
44	0.0626 0619	0.0509 4643	0.0414 9804	0.0338 3411	44
45	0.0587 8515	0.0476 1349	0.0386 0283	0.0313 2788	45
46	0.0551 9733	0.0444 9859	0.0359 0961	0.0290 0730	46
47	0.0518 2848	0.0415 8746	0.0334 0428	0.0268 5861	47
48	0.0486 6524	0.0388 6679	0.0310 7375	0.0248 6908	48
49	0.0456 9506	0.0363 2410	0.0289 0582	0.0230 2693	49
50	0.0429 0616	0.0339 4776	0.0268 8913	0.0213 2123	50

TABLE 6 PRESENT VALUE
WHEN COMPOUND AMOUNT IS 1

$$p=(1+i)^{-n} \quad [OR,\ v^n=(1+i)^{-n}]$$

n	$6\frac{1}{2}$ %	7 %	$7\frac{1}{2}$ %	8 %	n
51	0.0402 8747	0.0317 2688	0.0250 1315	0.0197 4188	51
52	0.0378 2861	0.0296 5129	0.0232 6804	0.0182 7952	52
53	0.0355 1982	0.0277 1148	0.0216 4469	0.0169 2548	53
54	0.0333 5195	0.0258 9858	0.0201 3460	0.0156 7174	54
55	0.0313 1638	0.0242 0428	0.0187 2986	0.0145 1087	55
56	0.0294 0505	0.0226 2083	0.0174 2312	0.0134 3599	56
57	0.0276 1038	0.0211 4096	0.0162 0756	0.0124 4073	57
58	0.0259 2524	0.0197 5791	0.0150 7680	0.0115 1920	58
59	0.0243 4295	0.0184 6533	0.0140 2493	0.0106 6592	59
60	0.0228 5723	0.0172 5732	0.0130 4644	0.0098 7585	60
61	0.0214 6218	0.0161 2834	0.0121 3623	0.0091 4431	61
62	0.0201 5229	0.0150 7321	0.0112 8951	0.0084 6695	62
63	0.0189 2233	0.0140 8711	0.0105 0187	0.0078 3977	63
64	0.0177 6745	0.0131 6553	0.0097 6918	0.0072 5905	64
65	0.0166 8305	0.0123 0423	0.0090 8761	0.0067 2134	65
66	0.0156 6484	0.0114 9928	0.0084 5359	0.0062 2346	66
67	0.0147 0877	0.0107 4699	0.0078 6381	0.0057 6247	67
68	0.0138 1105	0.0100 4392	0.0073 1517	0.0053 3562	68
69	0.0129 6812	0.0093 8684	0.0068 0481	0.0049 4039	69
70	0.0121 7664	0.0087 7275	0.0063 3006	0.0045 7443	70
71	0.0114 3346	0.0081 9883	0.0058 8842	0.0042 3558	71
72	0.0107 3565	0.0076 6246	0.0054 7760	0.0039 2184	72
73	0.0100 8042	0.0071 6117	0.0050 9544	0.0036 3133	73
74	0.0094 6518	0.0066 9269	0.0047 3995	0.0033 6234	74
75	0.0088 8750	0.0062 5485	0.0044 0925	0.0031 1328	75
76	0.0083 4507	0.0058 4565	0.0041 0163	0.0028 8267	76
77	0.0078 3574	0.0054 6323	0.0038 1547	0.0026 6914	77
78	0.0073 5751	0.0051 0582	0.0035 4928	0.0024 7142	78
79	0.0069 0846	0.0047 7179	0.0033 0165	0.0022 8835	79
80	0.0064 8681	0.0044 5962	0.0030 7130	0.0021 1885	80
81	0.0060 9090	0.0041 6787	0.0028 5703	0.0019 6190	81
82	0.0057 1916	0.0038 9520	0.0026 5770	0.0018 1657	82
83	0.0053 7010	0.0036 4038	0.0024 7228	0.0016 8201	83
84	0.0050 4235	0.0034 0222	0.0022 9979	0.0015 5742	84
85	0.0047 3460	0.0031 7965	0.0021 3934	0.0014 4205	85
86	0.0044 4563	0.0029 7163	0.0019 9009	0.0013 3523	86
87	0.0041 7430	0.0027 7723	0.0018 5124	0.0012 3633	87
88	0.0039 1953	0.0025 9554	0.0017 2209	0.0011 4475	88
89	0.0036 8031	0.0024 2574	0.0016 0194	0.0010 5995	89
90	0.0034 5569	0.0022 6704	0.0014 9018	0.0009 8144	90
91	0.0032 4478	0.0021 1873	0.0013 8621	0.0009 0874	91
92	0.0030 4674	0.0019 8012	0.0012 8950	0.0008 4142	92
93	0.0028 6079	0.0018 5058	0.0011 9953	0.0007 7910	93
94	0.0026 8619	0.0017 2952	0.0011 1585	0.0007 2138	94
95	0.0025 2224	0.0016 1637	0.0010 3800	0.0006 6795	95
96	0.0023 6831	0.0015 1063	0.0009 6558	0.0006 1847	96
97	0.0022 2376	0.0014 1180	0.0008 9821	0.0005 7266	97
98	0.0020 8804	0.0013 1944	0.0008 3555	0.0005 3024	98
99	0.0019 6060	0.0012 3312	0.0007 7725	0.0004 9096	99
100	0.0018 4094	0.0011 5245	0.0007 2303	0.0004 5459	100

TABLE 6 PRESENT VALUE
WHEN COMPOUND AMOUNT IS 1

$$p = (1+i)^{-n} \quad [OR,\ v^n = (1+i)^{-n}]$$

n	$8\frac{1}{2}\%$	9%	$9\frac{1}{2}\%$	10%	n
1	0.9216 5899	0.9174 3119	0.9132 4201	0.9090 9091	1
2	0.8494 5529	0.8416 7999	0.8340 1097	0.8264 4628	2
3	0.7829 0810	0.7721 8348	0.7616 5385	0.7513 1480	3
4	0.7215 7428	0.7084 2521	0.6955 7429	0.6830 1346	4
5	0.6650 4542	0.6499 3139	0.6352 2767	0.6209 2132	5
6	0.6129 4509	0.5962 6733	0.5801 1659	0.5644 7393	6
7	0.5649 2635	0.5470 3424	0.5297 8684	0.5131 5812	7
8	0.5206 6945	0.5018 6628	0.4838 2360	0.4665 0738	8
9	0.4798 7968	0.4604 2778	0.4418 4803	0.4240 9762	9
10	0.4422 8542	0.4224 1081	0.4035 1419	0.3855 4329	10
11	0.4076 3633	0.3875 3285	0.3685 0611	0.3504 9390	11
12	0.3757 0168	0.3555 3473	0.3365 3526	0.3186 3082	12
13	0.3462 6883	0.3261 7865	0.3073 3813	0.2896 6438	13
14	0.3191 4178	0.2992 4647	0.2806 7410	0.2633 3125	14
15	0.2941 3989	0.2745 3804	0.2563 2337	0.2393 9205	15
16	0.2710 9667	0.2518 6976	0.2340 8527	0.2176 2914	16
17	0.2498 5869	0.2310 7318	0.2137 7651	0.1978 4467	17
18	0.2302 8450	0.2119 9374	0.1952 2969	0.1798 5879	18
19	0.2122 4378	0.1944 8967	0.1782 9195	0.1635 0799	19
20	0.1956 1639	0.1784 3089	0.1628 2370	0.1486 4363	20
21	0.1802 9160	0.1636 9806	0.1486 9744	0.1351 3057	21
22	0.1661 6738	0.1501 8171	0.1357 9675	0.1228 4597	22
23	0.1531 4965	0.1377 8139	0.1240 1530	0.1116 7816	23
24	0.1411 5176	0.1264 0494	0.1132 5598	0.1015 2560	24
25	0.1300 9378	0.1159 6784	0.1034 3012	0.0922 9600	25
26	0.1199 0210	0.1063 9251	0.0944 5673	0.0839 0545	26
27	0.1105 0885	0.0976 0781	0.0862 6185	0.0762 7768	27
28	0.1018 5148	0.0895 4845	0.0787 7795	0.0693 4335	28
29	0.0938 7233	0.0821 5454	0.0719 4333	0.0630 3941	29
30	0.0865 1828	0.0753 7114	0.0657 0167	0.0573 0855	30
31	0.0797 4035	0.0691 4783	0.0600 0153	0.0520 9868	31
32	0.0734 9341	0.0634 3838	0.0547 9592	0.0473 6244	32
33	0.0677 3586	0.0582 0035	0.0500 4193	0.0430 5676	33
34	0.0624 2936	0.0533 9481	0.0457 0039	0.0391 4251	34
35	0.0575 3858	0.0489 8607	0.0417 3552	0.0355 8410	35
36	0.0530 3095	0.0449 4135	0.0381 1463	0.0323 4918	36
37	0.0488 7645	0.0412 3059	0.0348 0788	0.0294 0835	37
38	0.0450 4742	0.0378 2623	0.0317 8802	0.0267 3486	38
39	0.0415 1836	0.0347 0296	0.0290 3015	0.0243 0442	39
40	0.0382 6577	0.0318 3758	0.0265 1156	0.0220 9493	40
41	0.0352 6799	0.0292 0879	0.0242 1147	0.0200 8630	41
42	0.0325 0506	0.0267 9706	0.0221 1093	0.0182 6027	42
43	0.0299 5858	0.0245 8446	0.0201 9263	0.0166 0025	43
44	0.0276 1160	0.0225 5455	0.0184 4076	0.0150 9113	44
45	0.0254 4848	0.0206 9224	0.0168 4087	0.0137 1921	45
46	0.0234 5482	0.0189 8371	0.0153 7979	0.0124 7201	46
47	0.0216 1734	0.0174 1625	0.0140 4547	0.0113 3819	47
48	0.0199 2382	0.0159 7821	0.0128 2692	0.0103 0745	48
49	0.0183 6297	0.0146 5891	0.0117 1408	0.0093 7041	49
50	0.0169 2439	0.0134 4854	0.0106 9779	0.0085 1855	50

TABLE 6 PRESENT VALUE
WHEN COMPOUND AMOUNT IS 1

$$p = (1+i)^{-n} \quad [OR,\ v^n = (1+i)^{-n}]$$

n	$8\frac{1}{2}\%$	9%	$9\frac{1}{2}\%$	10%	n
51	0.0155 9852	0.0123 3811	0.0097 6967	0.0077 4414	51
52	0.0143 7651	0.0113 1937	0.0089 2207	0.0070 4013	52
53	0.0132 5024	0.0103 8474	0.0081 4801	0.0064 0011	53
54	0.0122 1221	0.0095 2728	0.0074 4111	0.0058 1829	54
55	0.0112 5549	0.0087 4063	0.0067 9553	0.0052 8935	55
56	0.0103 7372	0.0080 1892	0.0062 0597	0.0048 0850	56
57	0.0095 6104	0.0073 5681	0.0056 6755	0.0043 7136	57
58	0.0088 1201	0.0067 4937	0.0051 7584	0.0039 7397	58
59	0.0081 2167	0.0061 9208	0.0047 2680	0.0036 1270	59
60	0.0074 8541	0.0056 8081	0.0043 1671	0.0032 8427	60
61	0.0068 9900	0.0052 1175	0.0039 4220	0.0029 8570	61
62	0.0063 5852	0.0047 8142	0.0036 0018	0.0027 1427	62
63	0.0058 6039	0.0043 8663	0.0032 8784	0.0024 6752	63
64	0.0054 0128	0.0040 2443	0.0030 0259	0.0022 4320	64
65	0.0049 7814	0.0036 9214	0.0027 4209	0.0020 3927	65
66	0.0045 8815	0.0033 8728	0.0025 0419	0.0018 5389	66
67	0.0042 2871	0.0031 0760	0.0022 8694	0.0016 8535	67
68	0.0038 9743	0.0028 5101	0.0020 8853	0.0015 3214	68
69	0.0035 9210	0.0026 1560	0.0019 0733	0.0013 9285	69
70	0.0033 1069	0.0023 9963	0.0017 4185	0.0012 6623	70
71	0.0030 5133	0.0022 0150	0.0015 9073	0.0011 5112	71
72	0.0028 1228	0.0020 1972	0.0014 5273	0.0010 4647	72
73	0.0025 9196	0.0018 5296	0.0013 2669	0.0009 5134	73
74	0.0023 8891	0.0016 9996	0.0012 1159	0.0008 6485	74
75	0.0022 0176	0.0015 5960	0.0011 0647	0.0007 8623	75
76	0.0020 2927	0.0014 3082	0.0010 1048	0.0007 1475	76
77	0.0018 7030	0.0013 1268	0.0009 2281	0.0006 4978	77
78	0.0017 2377	0.0012 0430	0.0008 4275	0.0005 9070	78
79	0.0015 8873	0.0011 0486	0.0007 6963	0.0005 3700	79
80	0.0014 6427	0.0010 1363	0.0007 0286	0.0004 8819	80
81	0.0013 4956	0.0009 2994	0.0006 4188	0.0004 4381	81
82	0.0012 4383	0.0008 5315	0.0005 8620	0.0004 0346	82
83	0.0011 4639	0.0007 8271	0.0005 3534	0.0003 6678	83
84	0.0010 5658	0.0007 1808	0.0004 8889	0.0003 3344	84
85	0.0009 7381	0.0006 5879	0.0004 4648	0.0003 0313	85
86	0.0008 9752	0.0006 0440	0.0004 0774	0.0002 7557	86
87	0.0008 2720	0.0005 5449	0.0003 7237	0.0002 5052	87
88	0.0007 6240	0.0005 0871	0.0003 4006	0.0002 2774	88
89	0.0007 0267	0.0004 6670	0.0003 1056	0.0002 0704	89
90	0.0006 4762	0.0004 2817	0.0002 8362	0.0001 8822	90
91	0.0005 9689	0.0003 9282	0.0002 5901	0.0001 7111	91
92	0.0005 5013	0.0003 6038	0.0002 3654	0.0001 5555	92
93	0.0005 0703	0.0003 3063	0.0002 1602	0.0001 4141	93
94	0.0004 6731	0.0003 0333	0.0001 9728	0.0001 2855	94
95	0.0004 3070	0.0002 7828	0.0001 8016	0.0001 1687	95
96	0.0003 9696	0.0002 5530	0.0001 6453	0.0001 0624	96
97	0.0003 6586	0.0002 3422	0.0001 5026	0.0000 9659	97
98	0.0003 3720	0.0002 1488	0.0001 3722	0.0000 8780	98
99	0.0003 1078	0.0001 9714	0.0001 2531	0.0000 7982	99
100	0.0002 8644	0.0001 8086	0.0001 1444	0.0000 7257	100

TABLE 7 AMOUNT OF ANNUITY

WHEN PERIODIC PAYMENT IS 1

$$s_{\overline{n}|i} = \frac{(1+i)^n - 1}{i}$$

n	$\frac{1}{4}$%	$\frac{1}{3}$%	$\frac{5}{12}$%	$\frac{11}{24}$%	n
1	1.0000 0000	1.0000 0000	1.0000 0000	1.0000 0000	1
2	2.0025 0000	2.0033 3333	2.0041 6667	2.0045 8333	2
3	3.0075 0625	3.0100 1111	3.0125 1736	3.0137 7101	3
4	4.0150 2502	4.0200 4448	4.0250 6952	4.0275 8412	4
5	5.0250 6258	5.0334 4463	5.0418 4064	5.0460 4388	5
6	6.0376 2523	6.0502 2278	6.0628 4831	6.0691 7159	6
7	7.0527 1930	7.0703 9019	7.0881 1018	7.0969 8862	7
8	8.0703 5110	8.0939 5816	8.1176 4397	8.1295 1649	8
9	9.0905 2697	9.1209 3802	9.1514 6749	9.1667 7677	9
10	10.1132 5329	10.1513 4114	10.1895 9860	10.2087 9116	10
11	11.1385 3642	11.1851 7895	11.2320 5526	11.2555 8146	11
12	12.1663 8277	12.2224 6288	12.2788 5549	12.3071 6954	12
13	13.1967 9872	13.2632 0442	13.3300 1739	13.3635 7740	13
14	14.2297 9072	14.3074 1510	14.3855 5913	14.4248 2713	14
15	15.2653 6520	15.3551 0648	15.4454 9896	15.4909 4092	15
16	16.3035 2861	16.4062 9017	16.5098 5520	16.5619 4107	16
17	17.3442 8743	17.4609 7781	17.5786 4627	17.6378 4996	17
18	18.3876 4815	18.5191 8107	18.6518 9063	18.7186 9011	18
19	19.4336 1727	19.5809 1167	19.7296 0684	19.8044 8410	19
20	20.4822 0131	20.6461 8137	20.8118 1353	20.8952 5466	20
21	21.5334 0682	21.7150 0198	21.8985 2942	21.9910 2457	21
22	22.5872 4033	22.7873 8532	22.9897 7330	23.0918 1677	22
23	23.6437 0843	23.8633 4327	24.0855 6402	24.1976 5426	23
24	24.7028 1770	24.9428 8775	25.1859 2053	25.3085 6018	24
25	25.7645 7475	26.0260 3071	26.2908 6187	26.4245 5775	25
26	26.8289 8619	27.1127 8414	27.4004 0713	27.5456 7030	26
27	27.8960 5865	28.2031 6009	28.5145 7549	28.6719 2129	27
28	28.9657 9880	29.2971 7062	29.6333 8622	29.8033 3426	28
29	30.0382 1330	30.3948 2786	30.7568 5866	30.9399 3288	29
30	31.1133 0883	31.4961 4395	31.8850 1224	32.0817 4090	30
31	32.1910 9210	32.6011 3110	33.0178 6646	33.2287 8222	31
32	33.2715 6983	33.7098 0154	34.1554 4090	34.3810 8080	32
33	34.3547 4876	34.8221 6754	35.2977 5524	35.5386 6076	33
34	35.4406 3563	35.9382 4143	36.4448 2922	36.7015 4628	34
35	36.5292 3722	37.0580 3557	37.5966 8268	37.8697 6171	35
36	37.6205 6031	38.1815 6236	38.7533 3552	39.0433 3145	36
37	38.7146 1171	39.3088 3423	39.9148 0775	40.2222 8005	37
38	39.8113 9824	40.4398 6368	41.0811 1945	41.4066 3217	38
39	40.9109 2673	41.5746 6322	42.2522 9078	42.5964 1256	39
40	42.0132 0405	42.7132 4543	43.4283 4199	43.7916 4612	40
41	43.1182 3706	43.8556 2292	44.6092 9342	44.9923 5783	41
42	44.2260 3265	45.0018 0833	45.7951 6547	46.1985 7281	42
43	45.3365 9774	46.1518 1436	46.9859 7866	47.4103 1626	43
44	46.4499 3923	47.3056 5374	48.1817 5357	48.6276 1355	44
45	47.5660 6408	48.4633 3925	49.3825 1088	49.8504 9011	45
46	48.6849 7924	49.6248 8371	50.5882 7134	51.0789 7152	46
47	49.8066 9169	50.7902 9999	51.7990 5581	52.3130 8347	47
48	50.9312 0842	51.9596 0099	53.0148 8521	53.5528 5177	48
49	52.0585 3644	53.1327 9966	54.2357 8056	54.7983 0234	49
50	53.1886 8278	54.3099 0899	55.4617 6298	56.0494 6123	50
51	54.3216 5449	55.4909 4202	56.6928 5366	57.3063 5459	51
52	55.4574 5862	56.6759 1183	57.9290 7388	58.5690 0872	52
53	56.5961 0227	57.8648 3154	59.1704 4502	59.8374 5001	53
54	57.7375 9252	59.0577 1431	60.4169 8854	61.1117 0499	54
55	58.8819 3650	60.2545 7336	61.6687 2600	62.3918 0030	55
56	60.0291 4135	61.4554 2194	62.9256 7902	63.6777 6272	56
57	61.1792 1420	62.6602 7334	64.1878 6935	64.9696 1913	57
58	62.3321 6223	63.8691 4092	65.4553 1881	66.2673 9655	58
59	63.4879 9264	65.0820 3806	66.7280 4930	67.5711 2212	59
60	64.6467 1262	66.2989 7818	68.0060 8284	68.8808 2310	60

TABLE 7 AMOUNT OF ANNUITY

WHEN PERIODIC PAYMENT IS 1

$$s_{\overline{n}|i} = \frac{(1+i)^n - 1}{i}$$

n	$\frac{1}{4}\%$	$\frac{1}{3}\%$	$\frac{5}{12}\%$	$\frac{11}{24}\%$	n
61	65.8083 2940	67.5199 7478	69.2894 4152	70.1965 2687	61
62	66.9728 5023	68.7450 4136	70.5781 4753	71.5182 6095	62
63	68.1402 8235	69.9741 9150	71.8722 2314	72.8460 5298	63
64	69.3106 3306	71.2074 3880	73.1716 9074	74.1799 3073	64
65	70.4839 0964	72.4447 9693	74.4765 7278	75.5199 2207	65
66	71.6601 1942	73.6862 7959	75.7868 9183	76.8660 5505	66
67	72.8392 6971	74.9319 0052	77.1026 7055	78.2183 5780	67
68	74.0213 6789	76.1816 7352	78.4239 3168	79.5768 5861	68
69	75.2064 2131	77.4356 1243	79.7506 9806	80.9415 8588	69
70	76.3944 3736	78.6937 3114	81.0829 9264	82.3125 6815	70
71	77.5854 2345	79.9560 4358	82.4208 3844	83.6898 3408	71
72	78.7793 8701	81.2225 6372	83.7642 5860	85.0734 1249	72
73	79.9763 3548	82.4933 0560	85.1132 7634	86.4633 3230	73
74	81.1762 7632	83.7682 8329	86.4679 1499	87.8596 2257	74
75	82.3792 1701	85.0475 1090	87.8281 9797	89.2623 1251	75
76	83.5851 6505	86.3310 0260	89.1941 4880	90.6714 3144	76
77	84.7941 2797	87.6187 7261	90.5657 9108	92.0870 0883	77
78	86.0061 1329	88.9108 3519	91.9431 4855	93.5090 7429	78
79	87.2211 2857	90.2072 0464	93.3262 4500	94.9376 5755	79
80	88.4391 8139	91.5078 9532	94.7151 0435	96.3727 8848	80
81	89.6602 7934	92.8129 2164	96.1097 5062	97.8144 9709	81
82	90.8844 3004	94.1222 9804	97.5102 0792	99.2628 1354	82
83	92.1116 4112	95.4360 3904	98.9165 0045	100.7177 6810	83
84	93.3419 2022	96.7541 5917	100.3286 5253	102.1793 9120	84
85	94.5752 7502	98.0766 7303	101.7466 8859	103.6477 1341	85
86	95.8117 1321	99.4035 9527	103.1706 3312	105.1227 6543	86
87	97.0512 4249	100.7349 4059	104.6005 1076	106.6045 7811	87
88	98.2938 7060	102.0707 2373	106.0363 4622	108.0931 8242	88
89	99.5396 0527	103.4109 5947	107.4781 6433	109.5886 0951	89
90	100.7884 5429	104.7556 6267	108.9259 9002	111.0908 9064	90
91	102.0404 2542	106.1048 4821	110.3798 4831	112.6000 5722	91
92	103.2955 2649	107.4585 3104	111.8397 6434	114.1161 4081	92
93	104.5537 6530	108.8167 2614	113.3057 6336	115.6391 7313	93
94	105.8151 4972	110.1794 4856	114.7778 7071	117.1691 8600	94
95	107.0796 8759	111.5467 1339	116.2561 1184	118.7062 1144	95
96	108.3473 8681	112.9185 3577	117.7405 1230	120.2502 8157	96
97	109.6182 5528	114.2949 3089	119.2310 9777	121.8014 2870	97
98	110.8923 0091	115.6759 1399	120.7278 9401	123.3596 8525	98
99	112.1695 3167	117.0615 0037	122.2309 2690	124.9250 8380	99
100	113.4499 5550	118.4517 0537	123.7402 2243	126.4976 5711	100
101	114.7335 8038	119.8465 4439	125.2558 0669	128.0774 3803	101
102	116.0204 1434	121.2460 3287	126.7777 0589	129.6644 5962	102
103	117.3104 6537	122.6501 8632	128.3059 4633	131.2587 5506	103
104	118.6037 4153	124.0590 2027	129.8405 5444	132.8603 5769	104
105	119.9002 5089	125.4725 5034	131.3815 5675	134.4693 0100	105
106	121.2000 0152	126.8907 9217	132.9289 7990	136.0856 1863	106
107	122.5030 0152	128.3137 6148	134.4828 5065	137.7093 4438	107
108	123.8092 5902	129.7414 7402	136.0431 9586	139.3405 1221	108
109	125.1187 8217	131.1739 4560	137.6100 4251	140.9791 5622	109
110	126.4315 7913	132.6111 9208	139.1834 1769	142.6253 1069	110
111	127.7476 5807	134.0532 2939	140.7633 4859	144.2790 1003	111
112	129.0670 2722	135.5000 7349	142.3498 6255	145.9402 8882	112
113	130.3896 9479	136.9517 4040	143.9429 8697	147.6091 8182	113
114	131.7156 6902	138.4082 4620	145.5427 4942	149.2857 2390	114
115	133.0449 5820	139.8696 0702	147.1491 7754	150.9699 5013	115
116	134.3775 7059	141.3358 3904	148.7622 9911	152.6618 9574	116
117	135.7135 1452	142.8069 5851	150.3821 4203	154.3615 9609	117
118	137.0527 9830	144.2829 8170	152.0087 3429	156.0690 8674	118
119	138.3954 3030	145.7639 2498	153.6421 0401	157.7844 0339	119
120	139.7414 1888	147.2498 0473	155.2822 7945	159.5075 8191	120

TABLE 7 AMOUNT OF ANNUITY
WHEN PERIODIC PAYMENT IS 1

$$s_{\overline{n}|i} = \frac{(1+i)^n - 1}{i}$$

n	$\frac{1}{4}$%	$\frac{1}{3}$%	$\frac{5}{12}$%	$\frac{11}{24}$%	n
121	141.0907 7242	148.7406 3741	156.9292 8894	161.2386 5832	121
122	142.4434 9935	150.2364 3953	158.5831 6098	162.9776 6884	122
123	143.7996 0810	151.7372 2766	160.2439 2415	164.7246 4982	123
124	145.1591 0712	153.2430 1842	161.9116 0717	166.4796 3780	124
125	146.5220 0489	154.7538 2848	163.5862 3887	168.2426 6947	125
126	147.8883 0990	156.2696 7458	165.2678 4819	170.0137 8171	126
127	149.2580 3068	157.7905 7349	166.9564 6423	171.7930 1154	127
128	150.6311 7575	159.3165 4207	168.6521 1616	173.5803 9618	128
129	152.0077 5369	160.8475 9721	170.3548 3331	175.3759 7299	129
130	153.3877 7308	162.3837 5587	172.0646 4512	177.1797 7954	130
131	154.7712 4251	163.9250 3506	173.7815 8114	178.9918 5353	131
132	156.1581 7062	165.4714 5184	175.5056 7106	180.8122 3285	132
133	157.5485 6604	167.0230 2335	177.2369 4469	182.6409 5559	133
134	158.9424 3746	168.5797 6676	178.9754 3196	184.4780 5997	134
135	160.3397 9355	170.1416 9931	180.7211 6293	186.3235 8441	135
136	161.7406 4304	171.7088 3831	182.4741 6777	188.1775 6751	136
137	163.1449 9464	173.2812 0111	184.2344 7680	190.0400 4802	137
138	164.5528 5713	174.8588 0511	186.0021 2046	191.9110 6491	138
139	165.9642 3927	176.4416 6779	187.7771 2929	193.7906 5729	139
140	167.3791 4987	178.0298 0669	189.5595 3400	195.6788 6447	140
141	168.7975 9775	179.6232 3937	191.3493 6539	197.5757 2593	141
142	170.2195 9174	181.2219 8351	193.1466 5441	199.4812 8134	142
143	171.6451 4072	182.8260 5678	194.9514 3214	201.3955 7055	143
144	173.0742 5357	184.4354 7697	196.7637 2977	203.3186 3358	144
145	174.5069 3921	186.0502 6190	198.5835 7865	205.2505 1065	145
146	175.9432 0655	187.6704 2944	200.4110 1022	207.1912 4216	146
147	177.3830 6457	189.2959 9753	202.2460 5610	209.1408 6868	147
148	178.8265 2223	190.9269 8419	204.0887 4800	211.0994 3100	148
149	180.2735 8854	192.5634 0747	205.9391 1778	213.0669 7006	149
150	181.7242 7251	194.2052 8550	207.7971 9744	215.0435 2700	150
151	183.1785 8319	195.8526 3645	209.6630 1910	217.0291 4317	151
152	184.6365 2965	197.5054 7857	211.5366 1501	219.0238 6008	152
153	186.0981 2097	199.1638 3017	213.4180 1757	221.0277 1943	153
154	187.5633 6627	200.8277 0960	215.3072 5931	223.0407 6315	154
155	189.0322 7469	202.4971 3530	217.2043 7289	225.0630 3331	155
156	190.5048 5538	204.1721 2575	219.1093 9111	227.0945 7222	156
157	191.9811 1752	205.8526 9950	221.0223 4691	229.1354 2234	157
158	193.4610 7031	207.5388 7517	222.9432 7336	231.1856 2636	158
159	194.9447 2298	209.2306 7142	224.8722 0366	233.2452 2714	159
160	196.4320 8479	210.9281 0699	226.8091 7118	235.3142 6777	160
161	197.9231 6500	212.6312 0068	228.7542 0939	237.3927 9150	161
162	199.4179 7292	214.3399 7135	230.7073 5193	239.4808 4179	162
163	200.9165 1785	216.0544 3792	232.6686 3256	241.5784 6232	163
164	202.4188 0914	217.7746 1938	234.6380 8520	243.6856 9693	164
165	203.9248 5617	219.5005 3478	236.6157 4389	245.8025 8971	165
166	205.4346 6831	221.2322 0323	238.6016 4282	247.9291 8492	166
167	206.9482 5498	222.9696 4390	240.5958 1633	250.0655 2701	167
168	208.4656 2562	224.7128 7605	242.5982 9890	252.2116 6068	168
169	209.9867 8968	226.4619 1897	244.6091 2514	254.3676 3079	169
170	211.5117 5665	228.2167 9203	246.6283 2983	256.5334 8243	170
171	213.0405 3604	229.9775 1467	248.6559 4787	258.7092 6089	171
172	214.5731 3739	231.7441 0639	250.6920 1432	260.8950 1167	172
173	216.1095 7023	233.5165 8674	252.7365 6438	263.0907 8047	173
174	217.6498 4415	235.2949 7537	254.7896 3340	265.2966 1322	174
175	219.1939 6876	237.0792 9195	256.8512 5687	267.5125 5603	175
176	220.7419 5369	238.8695 5626	258.9214 7044	269.7386 5524	176
177	222.2938 0857	240.6657 8811	261.0003 0990	271.9749 5741	177
178	223.8495 4309	242.4680 0741	263.0878 1120	274.2215 0930	178
179	225.4091 6695	244.2762 3410	265.1840 1041	276.4783 5789	179
180	226.9726 8987	246.0904 8821	267.2889 4379	278.7455 5036	180

TABLE 7

TABLE 7 AMOUNT OF ANNUITY
WHEN PERIODIC PAYMENT IS 1

$$s_{\overline{n}|i} = \frac{(1+i)^n - 1}{i}$$

n	$\frac{1}{4}\%$	$\frac{1}{3}\%$	$\frac{5}{12}\%$	$\frac{11}{24}\%$	n
181	228.5401 2159	247.9107 8984	269.4026 4772	281.0231 3413	181
182	230.1114 7190	249.7371 5914	271.5251 5875	283.3111 5683	182
183	231.6867 5058	251.5696 1634	273.6565 1358	285.6096 6630	183
184	233.2659 6745	253.4081 8172	275.7967 4905	287.9187 1060	184
185	234.8491 3237	255.2528 7566	277.9459 0217	290.2383 3803	185
186	236.4362 5520	257.1037 1858	280.1040 1010	292.5685 9708	186
187	238.0273 4584	258.9607 3098	282.2711 1014	294.9095 3648	187
188	239.6224 1420	260.8239 3341	284.4472 3977	297.2612 0519	188
189	241.2214 7024	262.6933 4652	286.6324 3660	299.6236 5238	189
190	242.8245 2392	264.5689 9101	288.8267 3842	301.9969 2745	190
191	244.4315 8523	266.4508 8765	291.0301 8316	304.3810 8004	191
192	246.0426 6419	268.3390 5727	293.2428 0892	306.7761 5999	192
193	247.6577 7085	270.2335 2080	295.4646 5396	309.1822 1739	193
194	249.2769 1528	272.1342 9920	297.6957 5669	311.5993 0255	194
195	250.9001 0756	274.0414 1353	299.9361 5567	314.0274 6602	195
196	252.5273 5783	275.9548 8491	302.1858 8965	316.4667 5857	196
197	254.1586 7623	277.8747 3453	304.4449 9753	318.9172 3122	197
198	255.7940 7292	279.8009 8364	306.7135 1835	321.3789 3519	198
199	257.4335 5810	281.7336 5359	308.9914 9134	323.8519 2198	199
200	259.0771 4200	283.6727 6577	311.2789 5589	326.3362 4329	200
201	260.7248 3485	285.6183 4165	313.5759 5154	328.8319 5107	201
202	262.3766 4694	287.5704 0279	315.8825 1801	331.3390 9751	202
203	264.0325 8855	289.5289 7080	318.1986 9516	333.8577 3504	203
204	265.6926 7003	291.4940 6737	320.5245 2306	336.3879 1633	204
205	267.3569 0170	293.4657 1426	322.8600 4191	338.9296 9428	205
206	269.0252 9396	295.4439 3331	325.2052 9208	341.4831 2204	206
207	270.6978 5719	297.4287 4642	327.5603 1413	344.0482 5302	207
208	272.3746 0183	299.4201 7557	329.9251 4877	346.6251 4084	208
209	274.0555 3834	301.4182 4283	332.2998 3689	349.2138 3941	209
210	275.7406 7718	303.4229 7030	334.6844 1955	351.8144 0284	210
211	277.4300 2888	305.4343 8020	337.0789 3796	354.4268 8552	211
212	279.1236 0395	307.4524 9480	339.4834 3354	357.0513 4208	212
213	280.8214 1296	309.4773 3645	341.8979 4784	359.6878 2739	213
214	282.5234 6649	311.5089 2757	344.3225 2263	362.3363 9660	214
215	284.2297 7516	313.5472 9067	346.7571 9980	364.9971 0509	215
216	285.9403 4960	315.5924 4830	349.2020 2147	367.6700 0849	216
217	287.6552 0047	317.6444 2313	351.6570 2989	370.3551 6269	217
218	289.3743 3847	319.7032 3787	354.1222 6752	373.0526 2385	218
219	291.0977 7432	321.7689 1533	356.5977 7696	375.7624 4838	219
220	292.8255 1875	323.8414 7838	359.0836 0104	378.4846 9293	220
221	294.5575 8255	325.9209 4998	361.5797 8271	381.2194 1444	221
222	296.2939 7651	328.0073 5315	364.0863 6513	383.9666 7009	222
223	298.0347 1145	330.1007 1099	366.6033 9166	386.7265 1733	223
224	299.7797 9823	332.2010 4669	369.1309 0579	389.4990 1387	224
225	301.5292 4772	334.3083 8351	371.6689 5123	392.2842 1768	225
226	303.2830 7084	336.4227 4479	374.2175 7186	395.0821 8701	226
227	305.0412 7852	338.5441 5394	376.7768 1174	397.8929 8037	227
228	306.8038 8171	340.6726 3446	379.3467 1512	400.7166 5653	228
229	308.5708 9142	342.8082 0990	381.9273 2644	403.5532 7454	229
230	310.3423 1865	344.9509 0394	384.5186 9030	406.4028 9371	230
231	312.1181 7444	347.1007 4028	387.1208 5151	409.2655 7364	231
232	313.8984 6988	349.2577 4275	389.7338 5505	412.1413 7419	232
233	315.6832 1605	351.4219 3523	392.3577 4612	415.0303 5549	233
234	317.4724 2409	353.5933 4168	394.9925 7006	417.9325 7795	234
235	319.2661 0515	355.7719 8615	397.6383 7243	420.8481 0227	235
236	321.0642 7042	357.9578 9277	400.2951 9899	423.7769 8940	236
237	322.8669 3109	360.1510 8575	402.9630 9565	426.7193 0060	237
238	324.6740 9842	362.3515 8937	405.6421 0855	429.6750 9740	238
239	326.4857 8367	364.5594 2800	408.3322 8400	432.6444 4159	239
240	328.3019 9813	366.7746 2609	411.0336 6852	435.6273 9528	240

TABLE 7 AMOUNT OF ANNUITY

WHEN PERIODIC PAYMENT IS 1

$$s_{\overline{n}|i} = \frac{(1+i)^n - 1}{i}$$

n	$\frac{1}{2}$%	$\frac{13}{24}$%	$\frac{7}{12}$%	$\frac{5}{8}$%	n
1	1.0000 0000	1.0000 0000	1.0000 0000	1.0000 0000	1
2	2.0050 0000	2.0054 1667	2.0058 3333	2.0062 5000	2
3	3.0150 2500	3.0162 7934	3.0175 3403	3.0187 8906	3
4	4.0301 0012	4.0326 1752	4.0351 3631	4.0376 5649	4
5	5.0502 5063	5.0544 6086	5.0586 7460	5.0628 9185	5
6	6.0755 0188	6.0818 3919	6.0881 8354	6.0945 3492	6
7	7.1058 7939	7.1147 8249	7.1236 9794	7.1326 2576	7
8	8.1414 0879	8.1533 2090	8.1652 5285	8.1772 0468	8
9	9.1821 1583	9.1974 8472	9.2128 8349	9.2283 1220	9
10	10.2280 2641	10.2473 0443	10.2666 2531	10.2859 8916	10
11	11.2791 6654	11.3028 1066	11.3265 1396	11.3502 7659	11
12	12.3355 6237	12.3640 3422	12.3925 8529	12.4212 1582	12
13	13.3972 4018	13.4310 0607	13.4648 7537	13.4988 4842	13
14	14.4642 2639	14.5037 5735	14.5434 2048	14.5832 1622	14
15	15.5365 4752	15.5823 1937	15.6282 5710	15.6743 6132	15
16	16.6142 3026	16.6667 2360	16.7194 2193	16.7723 2608	16
17	17.6973 0141	17.7570 0169	17.8169 5189	17.8771 5312	17
18	18.7857 8791	18.8531 8544	18.9208 8411	18.9888 8532	18
19	19.8797 1685	19.9553 0687	20.0312 5593	20.1075 6586	19
20	20.9791 1544	21.0633 9811	21.1481 0493	21.2332 3814	20
21	22.0840 1101	22.1774 9152	22.2714 6887	22.3659 4588	21
22	23.1944 3107	23.2976 1960	23.4013 8577	23.5057 3304	22
23	24.3104 0322	24.4238 1504	24.5378 9386	24.6526 4387	23
24	25.4319 5524	25.5561 1070	25.6810 3157	25.8067 2290	24
25	26.5591 1502	26.6945 3963	26.8308 3759	26.9680 1492	25
26	27.6919 1059	27.8391 3506	27.9873 5081	28.1365 6501	26
27	28.8303 7015	28.9899 3037	29.1506 1035	29.3124 1854	27
28	29.9745 2200	30.1469 5916	30.3206 5558	30.4956 2116	28
29	31.1243 9461	31.3102 5519	31.4975 2607	31.6862 1879	29
30	32.2800 1658	32.4798 5241	32.6812 6164	32.8842 5766	30
31	33.4414 1666	33.6557 8494	33.8719 0233	34.0897 8427	31
32	34.6086 2375	34.8380 8711	35.0694 8843	35.3028 4542	32
33	35.7816 6686	36.0267 9341	36.2740 6045	36.5234 8820	33
34	36.9605 7520	37.2219 3854	37.4856 5913	37.7517 6000	34
35	38.1453 7807	38.4235 5738	38.7043 2548	38.9877 0850	35
36	39.3361 0496	39.6316 8498	39.9301 0071	40.2313 8168	36
37	40.5327 8549	40.8463 5661	41.1630 2630	41.4828 2782	37
38	41.7354 4942	42.0676 0771	42.4031 4395	42.7420 9549	38
39	42.9441 2666	43.2954 7391	43.6504 9562	44.0092 3359	39
40	44.1588 4730	44.5299 9106	44.9051 2352	45.2842 9130	40
41	45.3796 4153	45.7711 9518	46.1670 7007	46.5673 1812	41
42	46.6065 3974	47.0191 2249	47.4363 7798	47.8583 6386	42
43	47.8395 7244	48.2738 0940	48.7130 9018	49.1574 7863	43
44	49.0787 7030	49.5352 9254	49.9972 4988	50.4647 1287	44
45	50.3241 6415	50.8036 0871	51.2889 0050	51.7801 1733	45
46	51.5757 8497	52.0787 9492	52.5880 8575	53.1037 4306	46
47	52.8336 6390	53.3608 8839	53.8948 4959	54.4356 4146	47
48	54.0978 3222	54.6499 2654	55.2092 3621	55.7758 6421	48
49	55.3683 2138	55.9459 4697	56.5312 9009	57.1244 6337	49
50	56.6451 6299	57.2489 8752	57.8610 5595	58.4814 9126	50
51	57.9283 8880	58.5590 8620	59.1985 7877	59.8470 0058	51
52	59.2180 3075	59.8762 8125	60.5439 0381	61.2210 4434	52
53	60.5141 2090	61.2006 1111	61.8970 7659	62.6036 7586	53
54	61.8166 9150	62.5321 1442	63.2581 4287	63.9949 4884	54
55	63.1257 7496	63.8708 3004	64.6271 4870	65.3949 1727	55
56	64.4414 0384	65.2167 9703	66.0041 4040	66.8036 3550	56
57	65.7636 1086	66.5700 5469	67.3891 6455	68.2211 5822	57
58	67.0924 2891	67.9306 4248	68.7822 6801	69.6475 4046	58
59	68.4278 9105	69.2986 0013	70.1834 9791	71.0828 3759	59
60	69.7700 3051	70.6739 6755	71.5929 0165	72.5271 0532	60

TABLE 7

TABLE 7 AMOUNT OF ANNUITY

WHEN PERIODIC PAYMENT IS 1

$$s_{\overline{n}|i} = \frac{(1+i)^n - 1}{i}$$

n	$\frac{1}{2}\%$	$\frac{13}{24}\%$	$\frac{7}{12}\%$	$\frac{5}{8}\%$	n
61	71.1188 8066	72.0567 8487	73.0105 2691	73.9803 9973	61
62	72.4744 7507	73.4470 9245	74.4364 2165	75.4427 7723	62
63	73.8368 4744	74.8449 3087	75.8706 3411	76.9142 9459	63
64	75.2060 3168	76.2503 4091	77.3132 1281	78.3950 0893	64
65	76.5820 6184	77.6633 6359	78.7642 0655	79.8849 7774	65
66	77.9649 7215	79.0840 4015	80.2236 6442	81.3842 5885	66
67	79.3547 9701	80.5124 1203	81.6916 3580	82.8929 1046	67
68	80.7515 7099	81.9485 2093	83.1681 7034	84.4109 9115	68
69	82.1553 2885	83.3924 0875	84.6533 1800	85.9385 5985	69
70	83.5661 0549	84.8441 1763	86.1471 2902	87.4756 7585	70
71	84.9839 3602	86.3036 8994	87.6496 5394	89.0223 9882	71
72	86.4088 5570	87.7711 6826	89.1609 4359	90.5787 8882	72
73	87.8408 9998	89.2465 9542	90.6810 4909	92.1449 0625	73
74	89.2801 0448	90.7300 1448	92.2100 2188	93.7208 1191	74
75	90.7265 0500	92.2214 6872	93.7479 1367	95.3065 6698	75
76	92.1801 3752	93.7210 0168	95.2947 7650	96.9022 3303	76
77	93.6410 3821	95.2286 5710	96.8506 6270	98.5078 7198	77
78	95.1092 4340	96.7444 7900	98.4156 2490	100.1235 4618	78
79	96.5847 8962	98.2685 1159	99.9897 1604	101.7493 1835	79
80	98.0677 1357	99.8007 9936	101.5729 8939	103.3852 5159	80
81	99.5580 5214	101.3413 8702	103.1654 9849	105.0314 0941	81
82	101.0558 4240	102.8903 1954	104.7672 9723	106.6878 5572	82
83	102.5611 2161	104.4476 4210	106.3784 3980	108.3546 5482	83
84	104.0739 2722	106.0134 0016	107.9989 8070	110.0318 7141	84
85	105.5942 9685	107.5876 3941	109.6289 7475	111.7195 7061	85
86	107.1222 6834	109.1704 0579	111.2684 7710	113.4178 1792	86
87	108.6578 7968	110.7617 4549	112.9175 4322	115.1266 7928	87
88	110.2011 6908	112.3617 0495	114.5762 2889	116.8462 2103	88
89	111.7521 7492	113.9703 3085	116.2445 9022	118.5765 0991	89
90	113.3109 3580	115.5876 7014	117.9226 8367	120.3176 1310	90
91	114.8774 9048	117.2137 7002	119.6105 6599	122.0695 9818	91
92	116.4518 7793	118.8486 7794	121.3082 9429	123.8325 3317	92
93	118.0341 3732	120.4924 4161	123.0159 2601	125.6064 8650	93
94	119.6243 0800	122.1451 0901	124.7335 1891	127.3915 2704	94
95	121.2224 2954	123.8067 2835	126.4611 3110	129.1877 2408	95
96	122.8285 4169	125.4773 4812	128.1988 2103	130.9951 4736	96
97	124.4426 8440	127.1570 1709	129.9466 4749	132.8138 6703	97
98	126.0648 9782	128.8457 8427	131.7046 6960	134.6439 5370	98
99	127.6952 2231	130.5436 9893	133.4729 4684	136.4854 7841	99
100	129.3336 9842	132.2508 1064	135.2515 3903	138.3385 1265	100
101	130.9803 6692	133.9671 6919	137.0405 0634	140.2031 2836	101
102	132.6352 6875	135.6928 2469	138.8399 0929	142.0793 9791	102
103	134.2984 4509	137.4278 2750	140.6498 0877	143.9673 9414	103
104	135.9699 3732	139.1722 2823	142.4702 6598	145.8671 9036	104
105	137.6497 8701	140.9260 7780	144.3013 4253	147.7788 6030	105
106	139.3380 3594	142.6894 2738	146.1431 0037	149.7024 7817	106
107	141.0347 2612	144.4623 2845	147.9956 0178	151.6381 1866	107
108	142.7398 9975	146.2448 3273	149.8589 0946	153.5858 5690	108
109	144.4535 9925	148.0369 9224	151.7330 8643	155.5457 6851	109
110	146.1758 6725	149.8388 5928	153.6181 9610	157.5179 2956	110
111	147.9067 4658	151.6504 8644	155.5143 0225	159.5024 1662	111
112	149.6462 8032	153.4719 2657	157.4214 6901	161.4993 0673	112
113	151.3945 1172	155.3032 3284	159.3397 6091	163.5086 7739	113
114	153.1514 8428	157.1444 5868	161.2692 4285	165.5306 0663	114
115	154.9172 4170	158.9956 5783	163.2099 8010	167.5651 7292	115
116	156.6918 2791	160.8568 8431	165.1620 3832	169.6124 5525	116
117	158.4752 8704	162.7281 9244	167.1254 8354	171.6725 3310	117
118	160.2676 6348	164.6096 3681	169.1003 8220	173.7454 8643	118
119	162.0690 0180	166.5012 7235	171.0868 0109	175.8313 9572	119
120	163.8793 4681	168.4031 5424	173.0848 0743	177.9303 4194	120

TABLE 7 AMOUNT OF ANNUITY
WHEN PERIODIC PAYMENT IS 1

$$s_{\overline{n}|i} = \frac{(1+i)^n - 1}{i}$$

n	$\frac{1}{2}$%	$\frac{13}{24}$%	$\frac{7}{12}$%	$\frac{5}{8}$%	n
121	165.6987 4354	170.3453 3799	175.0944 6881	180.0424 0658	121
122	167.5272 3726	172.2378 7940	177.1158 5321	182.1676 7162	122
123	169.3648 7344	174.1708 3458	179.1490 2902	184.3062 1957	123
124	171.2116 9781	176.1142 5994	181.1940 6502	186.4581 3344	124
125	173.0677 5630	178.0682 1218	183.2510 3040	188.6234 9677	125
126	174.9330 9508	180.0327 4833	185.3199 9475	190.8023 9363	126
127	176.8077 6056	182.0079 2572	187.4010 2805	192.9949 0859	127
128	178.6917 9936	183.9938 0198	189.4942 0071	195.2011 2677	128
129	180.5852 5836	185.9904 3507	191.5995 8355	197.4211 3381	129
130	182.4881 8465	187.9978 8326	193.7172 4779	199.6550 1589	130
131	184.4006 2557	190.0162 0513	195.8472 6507	201.9028 5974	131
132	186.3226 2870	192.0454 5958	197.9897 0745	204.1647 5262	132
133	188.2542 4184	194.0857 0582	200.1446 4741	206.4407 8232	133
134	190.1955 1305	196.1370 0339	202.3121 5785	208.7310 3721	134
135	192.1464 9062	198.1994 1216	204.4923 1210	211.0356 0619	135
136	194.1072 2307	200.2729 9231	206.6851 8393	213.3545 7873	136
137	196.0777 5919	202.3578 0435	208.8908 4750	215.6880 4485	137
138	198.0581 4798	204.4539 0912	211.1093 7744	218.0360 9513	138
139	200.0484 3872	206.5613 6780	213.3408 4881	220.3988 2072	139
140	202.0486 8092	208.6802 4187	215.5853 3710	222.7763 1335	140
141	204.0589 2432	210.8105 9318	217.8429 1823	225.1686 6531	141
142	206.0792 1894	212.9524 8390	220.1136 6858	227.5759 6947	142
143	208.1096 1504	215.1059 7652	222.3976 6498	229.9983 1928	143
144	210.1501 6311	217.2711 3389	224.6949 8470	232.4358 0878	144
145	212.2009 1393	219.4480 1920	227.0057 0544	234.8885 3258	145
146	214.2619 1850	221.6366 9597	229.3299 0539	237.3565 8591	146
147	216.3332 2809	223.8372 2807	231.6676 6317	239.8400 6457	147
148	218.4148 9423	226.0496 7972	234.0190 5787	242.3390 6497	148
149	220.5069 6870	228.2741 1549	236.3841 6904	244.8536 8413	149
150	222.6095 0354	230.5106 0028	238.7630 7670	247.3840 1966	150
151	224.7225 5106	232.7591 9937	241.1558 6131	249.9301 6978	151
152	226.8461 6382	235.0199 7836	243.5626 0384	252.4922 3334	152
153	228.9803 9464	237.2930 0325	245.9833 8569	255.0703 0980	153
154	231.1252 9661	239.5783 4035	248.4182 8877	257.6644 9923	154
155	233.2809 2309	241.8760 5636	250.8673 9546	260.2749 0235	155
156	235.4473 2771	244.1862 1833	253.3307 8860	262.9016 2049	156
157	237.6245 6435	246.5088 9368	255.8085 5153	265.5447 5562	157
158	239.8126 8717	248.8441 5018	258.3007 6808	268.2044 1035	158
159	242.0117 5060	251.1920 5600	260.8075 2256	270.8806 8791	159
160	244.2218 0936	253.5526 7964	263.3288 9978	273.5736 9221	160
161	246.4429 1840	255.9260 8998	265.8649 8503	276.2835 2779	161
162	248.6751 3300	258.3123 5630	268.4158 6411	279.0102 9983	162
163	250.9185 0866	260.7115 4823	270.9816 2331	281.7541 1421	163
164	253.1731 0120	263.1237 3579	273.5623 4945	284.5150 7742	164
165	255.4389 6671	265.5489 8936	276.1581 2982	287.2932 9666	165
166	257.7161 6154	267.9873 7971	278.7690 5225	290.0888 7976	166
167	260.0047 4235	270.4389 7802	281.3952 0505	292.9019 3526	167
168	262.3047 6606	272.9038 5582	284.0366 7708	295.7325 7235	168
169	264.6162 8989	275.3820 8504	286.6935 5770	298.5809 0093	169
170	266.9393 7134	277.8737 3800	289.3659 3678	301.4470 3156	170
171	269.2740 6820	280.3788 8741	292.0539 0475	304.3310 7551	171
172	271.6204 3854	282.8976 0639	294.7575 5252	307.2331 4473	172
173	273.9785 4073	285.4299 6842	297.4769 7158	310.1533 5189	173
174	276.3484 3344	287.9760 4742	300.2122 5392	313.0918 1033	174
175	278.7301 7561	290.5359 1767	302.9634 9206	316.0486 3415	175
176	281.1238 2648	293.1096 5389	305.7307 7910	319.0239 3811	176
177	283.5294 4562	295.6973 3119	308.5142 0864	322.0178 3773	177
178	285.9470 9284	298.2990 2506	311.3138 7486	325.0304 4921	178
179	288.3768 2831	300.9148 1145	314.1298 7247	328.0618 8952	179
180	290.8187 1245	303.5447 6668	316.9622 9672	331.1122 7633	180

TABLE 7 AMOUNT OF ANNUITY
WHEN PERIODIC PAYMENT IS 1

$$s_{\overline{n}|i} = \frac{(1+i)^n - 1}{i}$$

n	$\frac{1}{2}\%$	$\frac{13}{24}\%$	$\frac{7}{12}\%$	$\frac{5}{8}\%$	n
181	293.2728 0601	306.1889 6750	319.8112 4345	334.1817 2806	181
182	295.7391 7004	308.8474 9107	322.6768 0904	337.2703 6386	182
183	298.2178 6589	311.5204 1498	325.5590 9043	340.3783 0363	183
184	300.7089 5522	314.2078 1723	328.4581 8512	343.5056 6803	184
185	303.2125 0000	316.9097 7624	331.3741 9120	346.6525 7845	185
186	305.7285 6250	319.6263 7086	334.3072 0731	349.8191 5707	186
187	308.2572 0531	322.3576 8037	337.2573 3269	353.0055 2680	187
188	310.7984 9134	325.1037 8447	340.2246 6713	356.2118 1134	188
189	313.3524 8379	327.8647 6330	343.2093 1102	359.4381 3516	189
190	315.9192 4621	330.6406 9744	346.2113 6534	362.6846 2351	190
191	318.4988 4244	333.4316 6788	349.2309 3163	365.9514 0241	191
192	321.0913 3666	336.2377 5608	352.2681 1207	369.2385 9867	192
193	323.6967 9334	339.0590 4393	355.3230 0939	372.5463 3991	193
194	326.3152 7731	341.8956 1375	358.3957 2694	375.8747 5454	194
195	328.9468 5369	344.7475 4832	361.4863 6868	379.2239 7175	195
196	331.5915 8796	347.6149 3088	364.5950 3917	382.5941 2158	196
197	334.2495 4590	350.4978 4509	367.7218 4356	385.9853 3484	197
198	336.9207 9363	353.3963 7508	370.8668 8765	389.3977 4318	198
199	339.6053 9760	356.3106 0545	374.0302 7783	392.8314 7907	199
200	342.3034 2459	359.2406 2123	377.2121 2112	396.2866 7582	200
201	345.0149 4171	362.1865 0792	380.4125 2516	399.7634 6754	201
202	347.7400 1642	365.1483 5151	383.6315 9822	403.2619 8921	202
203	350.4787 1650	368.1262 3841	386.8694 4921	406.7823 7665	203
204	353.2311 1008	371.1202 5554	390.1261 8766	410.3247 6650	204
205	355.9972 6563	374.1304 9026	393.4019 2376	413.8892 9629	205
206	358.7772 5196	377.1570 3041	396.6967 6831	417.4761 0439	206
207	361.5711 3822	380.1999 6433	400.0108 3280	421.0853 3005	207
208	364.3789 9391	383.2593 8080	403.3442 2932	424.7171 1336	208
209	367.2008 8888	386.3353 6911	406.6970 7066	428.3715 9532	209
210	370.0368 9333	389.4280 1903	410.0694 7024	432.0489 1779	210
211	372.8870 7779	392.5374 2080	413.4615 4215	435.7492 2352	211
212	375.7515 1318	395.6636 6516	416.8734 0114	439.4726 5617	212
213	378.6302 7075	398.8068 4335	420.3051 6265	443.2193 6027	213
214	381.5234 2210	401.9670 4708	423.7569 4276	446.9894 8127	214
215	384.4310 3921	405.1443 6859	427.2288 5826	450.7831 6553	215
216	387.3531 9441	408.3389 0058	430.7210 2660	454.6005 6032	216
217	390.2899 6038	411.5507 3629	434.2335 6593	458.4418 1382	217
218	393.2414 1018	414.7799 6945	437.7665 9506	462.3070 7515	218
219	396.2076 1723	418.0266 9428	441.3202 3353	466.1964 9437	219
220	399.1886 5532	421.2910 0554	444.8946 0156	470.1102 2246	220
221	402.1845 9859	424.5729 9849	448.4898 2007	474.0484 1135	221
222	405.1955 2159	427.8727 6890	452.1060 1069	478.0112 1392	222
223	408.2214 9920	431.1904 1306	455.7432 9575	481.9987 8401	223
224	411.2626 0669	434.5260 2780	459.4017 9831	486.0112 7641	224
225	414.3189 1973	437.8797 1045	463.0816 4213	490.0488 4689	225
226	417.3905 1432	441.2515 5888	466.7829 5171	494.1116 5218	226
227	420.4774 6690	444.6416 7149	470.5058 5226	498.1998 5001	227
228	423.5798 5423	448.0501 4722	474.2504 6973	502.3135 9907	228
229	426.6977 5350	451.4770 8551	478.0169 3081	506.4530 5907	229
230	429.8312 4227	454.9225 8639	481.8053 6290	510.6183 9068	230
231	432.9803 9848	458.3867 5040	485.6158 9419	514.8097 5563	231
232	436.1453 0047	461.8696 7863	489.4486 5357	519.0273 1660	232
233	439.3260 2697	465.3714 7273	493.3037 7071	523.2712 3733	233
234	442.5226 5711	468.8922 3487	497.1813 7604	527.5416 8256	234
235	445.7352 7040	472.4320 6781	501.0816 0074	531.8388 1808	235
236	448.9639 4675	475.9910 7484	505.0045 7674	536.1628 1069	236
237	452.2087 6648	479.5693 5983	508.9504 3677	540.5138 2826	237
238	455.4698 1031	483.1670 2720	512.9193 1432	544.8920 3968	238
239	458.7471 5936	486.7841 8193	516.9113 4365	549.2976 1493	239
240	462.0408 9516	490.4209 2958	520.9266 5983	553.7307 2502	240

TABLE 7 AMOUNT OF ANNUITY

WHEN PERIODIC PAYMENT IS 1

$$s_{\overline{n}|i} = \frac{(1+i)^n - 1}{i}$$

n	$\frac{2}{3}\%$	$\frac{3}{4}\%$	$\frac{7}{8}\%$	1%	n
1	1.0000 0000	1.0000 0000	1.0000 0000	1.0000 0000	1
2	2.0066 6667	2.0075 0000	2.0087 5000	2.0100 0000	2
3	3.0200 4444	3.0225 5625	3.0263 2656	3.0301 0000	3
4	4.0401 7807	4.0452 2542	4.0528 0692	4.0604 0100	4
5	5.0671 1259	5.0755 6461	5.0882 6898	5.1010 0501	5
6	6.1008 9335	6.1136 3135	6.1327 9133	6.1520 1506	6
7	7.1415 6597	7.1594 8358	7.1864 5326	7.2135 3521	7
8	8.1891 7641	8.2131 7971	8.2493 3472	8.2856 7056	8
9	9.2437 7092	9.2747 7856	9.3215 1640	9.3685 2727	9
10	10.3053 9606	10.3443 3940	10.4030 7967	10.4622 1254	10
11	11.3740 9870	11.4219 2194	11.4941 0662	11.5668 3467	11
12	12.4499 2602	12.5075 8636	12.5946 8005	12.6825 0301	12
13	13.5329 2553	13.6013 9325	13.7048 8350	13.8093 2804	13
14	14.6231 4503	14.7034 0370	14.8248 0123	14.9474 2132	14
15	15.7206 3267	15.8136 7923	15.9545 1824	16.0968 9554	15
16	16.8254 3688	16.9322 8183	17.0941 2028	17.2578 6449	16
17	17.9376 0646	18.0592 7394	18.2436 9383	18.4304 4314	17
18	19.0571 9051	19.1947 1849	19.4033 2615	19.6147 4757	18
19	20.1842 3844	20.3386 7888	20.5731 0526	20.8108 9504	19
20	21.3188 0003	21.4912 1897	21.7531 1993	22.0190 0399	20
21	22.4609 2537	22.6524 0312	22.9434 5973	23.2391 9403	21
22	23.6106 6487	23.8222 9614	24.1442 1500	24.4715 8598	22
23	24.7680 6930	25.0009 6336	25.3554 7688	25.7163 0183	23
24	25.9331 8976	26.1884 7059	26.5773 3730	26.9734 6485	24
25	27.1060 7769	27.3848 8412	27.8098 8900	28.2431 9950	25
26	28.2867 8488	28.5902 7075	29.0532 2553	29.5256 3150	26
27	29.4753 6344	29.8046 9778	30.3074 4126	30.8208 8781	27
28	30.6718 6587	31.0282 3301	31.5726 3137	32.1290 9669	28
29	31.8763 4497	32.2609 4476	32.8488 9189	33.4503 8766	29
30	33.0888 5394	33.5029 0184	34.1363 1970	34.7848 9153	30
31	34.3094 4630	34.7541 7361	35.4350 1249	36.1327 4045	31
32	35.5381 7594	36.0148 2991	36.7450 6885	37.4940 6785	32
33	36.7750 9711	37.2849 4113	38.0665 8820	38.8690 0853	33
34	38.0202 6443	38.5645 7819	39.3996 7085	40.2576 9862	34
35	39.2737 3286	39.8538 1253	40.7444 1797	41.6602 7560	35
36	40.5355 5774	41.1527 1612	41.1009 3163	43.0768 7836	36
37	41.8057 9479	42.4613 6149	43.4693 1478	44.5076 4714	37
38	43.0845 0009	43.7798 2170	44.8496 7128	45.9527 2361	38
39	44.3717 3009	45.1081 7037	46.2421 0591	47.4122 5085	39
40	45.6675 4163	46.4464 8164	47.6467 2434	48.8863 7336	40
41	46.9719 9191	47.7948 3026	49.0636 3317	50.3752 3709	41
42	48.2851 3852	49.1532 9148	50.4929 3996	51.8789 8946	42
43	49.6070 3944	50.5219 4117	51.9347 5319	53.3977 7936	43
44	50.9377 5304	51.9008 5573	53.3891 8228	54.9317 5715	44
45	52.2773 3806	53.2901 1215	54.8563 3762	56.4810 7472	45
46	53.6258 5365	54.6897 8799	56.3363 3058	58.0458 8547	46
47	54.9833 5934	56.0999 6140	57.8292 7347	59.6263 4432	47
48	56.3499 1507	57.5207 1111	59.3352 7961	61.2226 0777	48
49	57.7255 8117	58.9521 1644	60.8544 6331	62.8348 3385	49
50	59.1104 1837	60.3942 5732	62.3869 3986	64.4631 8218	50
51	60.5044 8783	61.8472 1424	63.9328 2559	66.1078 1401	51
52	61.9078 5108	63.3110 6835	65.4922 3781	67.7688 9215	52
53	63.3205 7009	64.7859 0136	67.0652 9489	69.4465 8107	53
54	64.7427 0722	66.2717 9562	68.6521 1622	71.1410 4688	54
55	66.1743 2527	67.7688 3409	70.2528 2224	72.8524 5735	55
56	67.6154 8744	69.2771 0035	71.8675 3443	74.5809 8192	56
57	69.0662 5736	70.7966 7860	73.4963 7536	76.3267 9174	57
58	70.5266 9907	72.3276 5369	75.1394 6864	78.0900 5966	58
59	71.9968 7706	73.8701 1109	76.7969 3900	79.8709 6025	59
60	73.4768 5625	75.4241 3693	78.4689 1221	81.6696 6986	60

TABLE 7 AMOUNT OF ANNUITY

WHEN PERIODIC PAYMENT IS 1

$$s_{\overline{n}|i} = \frac{(1+i)^n - 1}{i}$$

n	$\frac{2}{3}\%$	$\frac{3}{4}\%$	$\frac{7}{8}\%$	1%	n
61	74.9667 0195	76.9898 1795	80.1555 1519	83.4863 6656	61
62	76.4664 7997	78.5672 4159	81.8568 7595	85.3212 3022	62
63	77.9762 5650	80.1564 9590	83.5731 2362	87.1744 4252	63
64	79.4960 9821	81.7576 6962	85.3043 8845	89.0461 8695	64
65	81.0260 7220	83.3708 5214	87.0508 0185	90.9366 4882	65
66	82.5662 4601	84.9961 3353	88.8124 9636	92.8460 1531	66
67	84.1166 8765	86.6336 0453	90.5896 0571	94.7744 7546	67
68	85.6774 6557	88.2833 5657	92.3822 6476	96.7222 2021	68
69	87.2486 4867	89.9454 8174	94.1906 0957	98.6894 4242	69
70	88.8303 0633	91.6200 7285	96.0147 7741	100.6763 3684	70
71	90.4225 0837	93.3072 2340	97.8549 0671	102.6831 0021	71
72	92.0253 2510	95.0070 2758	99.7111 3714	104.7099 3121	72
73	93.6388 2726	96.7195 8028	101.5836 0959	106.7570 3052	73
74	95.2630 8611	98.4449 7714	103.4724 6618	108.8246 0083	74
75	96.8981 7335	100.1833 1446	105.3778 5025	110.9128 4684	75
76	98.5441 6118	101.9346 8932	107.2999 0644	113.0219 7530	76
77	100.2011 2225	103.6991 9949	109.2387 8063	115.1521 9506	77
78	101.8691 2973	105.4769 4349	111.1946 1996	117.3037 1701	78
79	103.5482 5726	107.2680 2056	113.1675 7288	119.4767 5418	79
80	105.2385 7898	109.0725 3072	115.1577 8914	121.6715 2172	80
81	106.9401 6950	110.8905 7470	117.1654 1980	123.8882 3694	81
82	108.6531 0397	112.7222 5401	119.1906 1722	126.1271 1931	82
83	110.3774 5799	114.5676 7091	121.2335 3512	128.3883 9050	83
84	112.1133 0771	116.4269 2845	123.2943 2856	130.6722 7440	84
85	113.8607 2977	118.3001 3041	125.3731 5393	132.9789 9715	85
86	115.6198 0130	120.1873 8139	127.4701 6903	135.3087 8712	86
87	117.3905 9997	122.0887 8675	129.5855 3301	137.6618 7499	87
88	119.1732 0397	124.0044 5265	131.7194 0642	140.0384 9374	88
89	120.9676 9200	125.9344 8604	133.8719 5123	142.4388 7868	89
90	122.7741 4328	127.8789 9469	136.0433 3080	144.8632 6746	90
91	124.5926 3757	129.8380 8715	138.2337 0994	147.3119 0014	91
92	126.4232 5515	131.8118 7280	140.4432 5491	149.7850 1914	92
93	128.2660 7685	133.8004 6185	142.6721 3339	152.2828 6933	93
94	130.1211 8403	135.8039 6531	144.9205 1455	154.8056 9803	94
95	131.9886 5859	137.8224 9505	147.1885 6906	157.3537 5501	95
96	133.8685 8298	139.8561 6377	149.4764 6903	159.9272 9256	96
97	135.7610 4020	141.9050 8499	151.7843 8814	162.5265 6548	97
98	137.6661 1380	143.9693 7313	154.1125 0153	165.1518 3114	98
99	139.5838 8790	146.0491 4343	156.4609 8592	167.8033 4945	99
100	141.5144 4715	148.1445 1201	158.8300 1955	170.4813 8294	100
101	143.4578 7680	150.2555 9585	161.2197 8222	173.1861 9677	101
102	145.4142 6264	152.3825 1281	163.6304 5532	175.9180 5874	102
103	147.3836 9106	154.5253 8166	166.0622 2180	178.6772 3933	103
104	149.3662 4900	156.6843 2202	168.5152 6624	181.4640 1172	104
105	151.3620 2399	158.8594 5444	170.9897 7482	184.2786 5184	105
106	153.3711 0415	161.0509 0035	173.4859 3535	187.1214 3836	106
107	155.3935 7818	163.2587 8210	176.0039 3728	189.9926 5274	107
108	157.4295 3537	165.4832 2296	178.5439 7174	192.8925 7927	108
109	159.4790 6560	167.7243 4714	181.1062 3149	195.8215 0506	109
110	161.5422 5937	169.9822 7974	183.6909 1101	198.7797 2011	110
111	163.6192 0777	172.2571 4684	186.2982 0648	201.7675 1731	111
112	165.7100 0249	174.5490 7544	188.9283 1579	204.7851 9248	112
113	167.8147 3584	176.8581 9351	191.5814 3855	207.8330 4441	113
114	169.9335 0074	179.1846 2996	194.2577 7614	210.9113 7485	114
115	172.0663 9075	181.5285 1468	196.9575 3168	214.0204 8860	115
116	174.2135 0002	183.8899 7854	199.6809 1009	217.1606 9349	116
117	176.3749 2335	186.2691 5338	202.4281 1805	220.3323 0042	117
118	178.5507 5618	188.6661 7203	205.1993 6408	223.5356 2343	118
119	180.7410 9455	191.0811 6832	207.9948 5852	226.7709 7966	119
120	182.9460 3518	193.5142 7708	210.8148 1353	230.0386 8946	120

TABLE 7 AMOUNT OF ANNUITY

WHEN PERIODIC PAYMENT IS 1

$$s_{\overline{n}|i} = \frac{(1+i)^n - 1}{i}$$

n	$\frac{2}{3}\%$	$\frac{3}{4}\%$	$\frac{7}{8}\%$	1%	n
121	185.1656 7542	195.9656 3416	213.6594 4315	233.3390 7635	121
122	187.4001 1325	198.4353 7642	216.5289 6328	236.6724 6712	122
123	189.6494 4734	200.9236 4174	219.4235 9170	240.0391 9179	123
124	191.9137 7699	203.4305 6905	222.3435 4813	243.4395 8370	124
125	194.1932 0217	205.9562 9832	225.2890 5418	246.8739 7954	125
126	196.4878 2352	208.5009 7056	228.2603 3340	250.3427 1934	126
127	198.7977 4234	211.0647 2784	231.2576 1132	253.8461 4653	127
128	201.1230 6062	213.6477 1330	234.2811 1542	257.3846 0800	128
129	203.4638 8103	216.2500 7115	237.3310 7518	260.9584 5408	129
130	205.8203 0690	218.8719 4668	240.4077 2209	264.5680 3862	130
131	208.1924 4228	221.5134 8628	243.5112 8965	268.2137 1900	131
132	210.5803 9190	224.1748 3743	246.6420 1344	271.8958 5619	132
133	212.9842 6117	226.8561 4871	249.8001 3106	275.6148 1475	133
134	215.4041 5625	229.5575 6982	252.9858 8220	279.3709 6290	134
135	217.8401 8396	232.2792 5160	256.1995 0867	283.1646 7253	135
136	220.2924 5185	235.0213 4598	259.4412 5437	286.9963 1926	136
137	222.7610 6820	237.7840 0608	262.7113 6535	290.8662 8245	137
138	225.2461 4198	240.5673 8612	266.0100 8980	294.7749 4527	138
139	227.7477 8293	243.3716 4152	269.3376 7808	298.7226 9473	139
140	230.2661 0148	246.1969 2883	272.6943 8276	302.7099 2167	140
141	232.8012 0883	249.0434 0580	276.0804 5861	306.7370 2089	141
142	235.3532 1689	251.9112 3134	279.4961 6263	310.8043 9110	142
143	237.9222 3833	254.8005 6558	282.9417 5405	314.9124 3501	143
144	240.5083 8659	257.7115 6982	286.4174 9440	319.0615 5936	144
145	243.1117 7583	260.6444 0659	289.9236 4747	323.2521 7495	145
146	245.7325 2100	263.5992 3964	293.4604 7939	327.4846 9670	146
147	248.3707 3781	266.5762 3394	297.0282 5858	331.7595 4367	147
148	251.0265 4273	269.5755 5569	300.6272 5585	336.0771 3911	148
149	253.7000 5301	272.5973 7236	304.2577 4433	340.4379 1050	149
150	256.3913 8670	275.6418 5265	307.9199 9960	344.8422 8960	150
151	259.1006 6261	278.7091 6655	311.6142 9959	349.2907 1250	151
152	261.8280 0036	281.7994 8530	315.3409 2472	353.7836 1962	152
153	264.5735 2036	284.9129 8144	319.1001 5781	358.3214 5582	153
154	267.3373 4383	288.0498 2880	322.8922 8419	362.9046 7038	154
155	270.1195 9279	291.2102 0251	326.7175 9167	367.5337 1708	155
156	272.9203 9008	294.3942 7903	330.5763 7060	372.2090 5425	156
157	275.7398 5935	297.6022 3613	334.4689 1384	376.9311 4480	157
158	278.5781 2507	300.8342 5290	338.3955 1684	381.7004 5624	158
159	281.4353 1257	304.0905 0979	342.3564 7761	386.5174 6081	159
160	284.3115 4799	307.3711 8862	346.3520 9679	391.3826 3541	160
161	287.2069 5831	310.6764 7253	350.3826 7764	396.2964 6177	161
162	290.1216 7137	314.0065 4608	354.4485 2607	401.2594 2639	162
163	293.0558 1584	317.3615 9517	358.5499 5067	406.2720 2065	163
164	296.0095 2128	320.7418 0714	362.6872 6274	411.3347 4086	164
165	298.9829 1809	324.1473 7069	366.8607 7629	416.4480 8826	165
166	301.9761 3754	327.5784 7597	371.0708 0808	421.6125 6915	166
167	304.9893 1179	331.0353 1454	375.3176 7765	426.8286 9484	167
168	308.0225 7387	334.5180 7940	379.6017 0733	432.0969 8179	168
169	311.0760 5770	338.0269 6499	383.9232 2227	437.4179 5161	169
170	314.1498 9808	341.5621 6723	388.2825 5046	442.7921 3112	170
171	317.2442 3074	345.1238 8349	392.6800 2278	448.2200 5243	171
172	320.3591 9228	348.7123 1261	397.1159 7298	453.7022 5296	172
173	323.4949 2022	352.3276 5496	401.5907 3774	459.2392 7549	173
174	326.6515 5303	355.9701 1237	406.1046 5670	464.8316 6824	174
175	329.8292 3005	359.6398 8821	410.6580 7245	470.4799 8492	175
176	333.0280 9158	363.3371 8737	415.2513 3058	476.1847 8477	176
177	336.2482 7886	367.0622 1628	419.8847 7972	481.9466 3262	177
178	339.4899 3405	370.8151 8290	424.5587 7154	487.7660 9895	178
179	342.7532 0028	374.5962 9677	429.2736 6080	493.6437 5994	179
180	346.0382 2161	378.4057 6900	434.0298 0533	499.5801 9754	180

TABLE 7 AMOUNT OF ANNUITY

WHEN PERIODIC PAYMENT IS 1

$$s_{\overline{n}|i} = \frac{(1+i)^n - 1}{i}$$

n	$\frac{2}{3}\%$	$\frac{3}{4}\%$	$\frac{7}{8}\%$	1%	n
181	349.3451 4309	382.2438 1226	438.8275 6612	505.5759 9951	181
182	352.6741 1071	386.1106 4086	443.6673 0733	511.6317 5951	182
183	356.0252 7145	390.0064 7066	448.5493 9627	517.7480 7710	183
184	359.3987 7326	393.9315 1919	453.4742 0348	523.9255 5787	184
185	362.7947 6508	397.8860 0559	458.4421 0276	530.1648 1345	185
186	366.2133 9685	401.8701 5063	463.4534 7116	536.4664 6159	186
187	369.6548 1949	405.8841 7676	468.5086 8904	542.8311 2620	187
188	373.1191 8496	409.9283 0808	473.6081 4007	549.2594 3746	188
189	376.6066 4619	414.0027 7039	478.7522 1129	555.7520 3184	189
190	380.1173 5716	418.1077 9117	483.9412 9314	562.3095 5216	190
191	383.6514 7288	422.2435 9961	489.1757 7946	568.9326 4768	191
192	387.2091 4936	426.4104 2660	494.4560 6753	575.6219 7415	192
193	390.7905 4369	430.6085 0480	499.7825 5812	582.3781 9390	193
194	394.3958 1398	434.8380 6859	505.1556 5550	589.2019 7584	194
195	398.0251 1941	439.0993 5410	510.5757 6749	596.0939 9559	195
196	401.6786 2021	443.3925 9926	516.0433 0545	603.0549 3555	196
197	405.3564 7767	447.7180 4375	521.5586 8437	610.0854 8490	197
198	409.0588 5419	452.0759 2908	527.1223 2286	617.1863 3975	198
199	412.7859 1322	456.4664 9855	532.7346 4319	624.3582 0315	199
200	416.5378 1931	460.8899 9729	538.3960 7131	631.6017 8518	200
201	420.3147 3810	465.3466 7227	544.1070 3694	638.9178 0303	201
202	424.1168 3636	469.8367 7231	549.8679 7351	646.3069 8107	202
203	427.9442 8193	474.3605 4810	555.6793 1828	653.7700 5088	203
204	431.7972 4381	478.9182 5221	561.5415 1232	661.3077 5138	204
205	435.6758 9210	483.5101 3911	567.4550 0055	668.9208 2890	205
206	439.5803 9805	488.1364 6515	573.4202 3180	676.6100 3719	206
207	443.5109 3404	492.7974 8864	579.4376 5883	684.3761 3756	207
208	447.4676 7360	497.4934 6980	585.5077 3835	692.2198 9893	208
209	451.4507 9142	502.2246 7083	591.6309 3106	700.1420 9792	209
210	455.4604 6337	506.9913 5586	597.8077 0170	708.1435 1890	210
211	459.4968 6646	511.7937 9103	604.0385 1909	716.2249 5409	211
212	463.5601 7890	516.6322 4446	610.3238 5614	724.3872 0363	212
213	467.6505 8009	521.5069 8629	616.6641 8988	732.6310 7567	213
214	471.7682 5062	526.4182 8869	623.0600 0154	740.9573 8643	214
215	475.9133 7230	531.3664 2585	629.5117 7655	749.3669 6029	215
216	480.0861 2811	536.3516 7405	636.0200 0460	757.8606 2989	216
217	484.2867 0230	541.3743 1160	642.5851 7964	766.4392 3619	217
218	488.5152 8031	546.4346 1894	649.2077 9996	775.1036 2855	218
219	492.7720 4885	551.5328 7858	655.8883 6821	783.8546 6484	219
220	497.0571 9584	556.6693 7517	662.6273 9143	792.6932 1149	220
221	501.3709 1048	561.8443 9549	669.4253 8110	801.6201 4360	221
222	505.7133 8322	567.0582 2845	676.2828 5319	810.6363 4504	222
223	510.0848 0577	572.3111 6517	683.2003 2815	819.7427 0849	223
224	514.4853 7114	577.6034 9890	690.1783 3103	828.9401 3557	224
225	518.9152 7362	582.9355 2515	697.2173 9142	838.2295 3693	225
226	523.3747 0878	588.3075 4158	704.3180 4360	847.6118 3230	226
227	527.8638 7350	593.7198 4815	711.4808 2648	857.0879 5062	227
228	532.3829 6599	599.1727 4701	718.7062 8371	866.6588 3013	228
229	536.9321 8576	604.6665 4261	725.9949 6369	876.3254 1843	229
230	541.5117 3367	610.2015 4168	733.3474 1963	886.0886 7261	230
231	546.1218 1189	615.7780 5324	740.7642 0955	895.9495 5934	231
232	550.7626 2397	621.3963 8864	748.2458 9638	905.9090 5493	232
233	555.4343 7480	627.0568 6156	755.7930 4797	915.9681 4548	233
234	560.1372 7063	632.7597 8802	763.4062 3714	926.1278 2694	234
235	564.8715 1910	638.5054 8643	771.0860 4172	936.3891 0520	235
236	569.6373 2923	644.2942 7758	778.8330 4458	946.7529 9626	236
237	574.4349 1142	650.1264 8466	786.6478 3372	957.2205 2622	237
238	579.2644 7750	656.0024 3329	794.5310 0227	967.7927 3148	238
239	584.1262 4068	661.9224 5154	802.4831 4854	978.4706 5880	239
240	589.0204 1562	667.8868 6993	810.5048 7609	989.2553 6539	240

TABLE 7 AMOUNT OF ANNUITY

WHEN PERIODIC PAYMENT IS 1

$$s_{\overline{n}|i} = \frac{(1+i)^n - 1}{i}$$

n	$1\frac{1}{8}\%$	$1\frac{1}{4}\%$	$1\frac{3}{8}\%$	$1\frac{1}{2}\%$	n
1	1.0000 0000	1.0000 0000	1.0000 0000	1.0000 0000	1
2	2.0112 5000	2.0125 0000	2.0137 5000	2.0150 0000	2
3	3.0338 7656	3.0376 5625	3.0414 3906	3.0452 2500	3
4	4.0680 0767	4.0756 2695	4.0832 5885	4.0909 0338	4
5	5.1137 7276	5.1265 7229	5.1394 0366	5.1522 6693	5
6	6.1713 0270	6.1906 5444	6.2100 7046	6.2295 5093	6
7	7.2407 2986	7.2680 3762	7.2954 5893	7.3229 9419	7
8	8.3221 8807	8.3588 8809	8.3957 7149	8.4328 3911	8
9	9.4158 1269	9.4633 7420	9.5112 1335	9.5593 3169	9
10	10.5217 4058	10.5816 6637	10.6419 9253	10.7027 2167	10
11	11.6401 1016	11.7139 3720	11.7883 1993	11.8632 6249	11
12	12.7710 6140	12.8603 6142	12.9504 0933	13.0412 1143	12
13	13.9147 3584	14.0211 1594	14.1284 7745	14.2368 2960	13
14	15.0712 7662	15.1963 7988	15.3227 4402	15.4503 8205	14
15	16.2408 2848	16.3863 3463	16.5334 3175	16.6821 3778	15
16	17.4235 3780	17.5911 6382	17.7607 6644	17.9323 6984	16
17	18.6195 5260	18.8110 5336	19.0049 7697	19.2013 5539	17
18	19.8290 2257	20.0461 9153	20.2662 9541	20.4893 7572	18
19	21.0520 9907	21.2967 6893	21.5449 5697	21.7967 1636	19
20	22.2889 3519	22.5629 7854	22.8412 0013	23.1236 6710	20
21	23.5396 8571	23.8450 1577	24.1552 6663	24.4705 2211	21
22	24.8045 0717	25.1430 7847	25.4874 0155	25.8375 7994	22
23	26.0835 5788	26.4573 6695	26.8378 5332	27.2251 4364	23
24	27.3769 9790	27.7880 8403	28.2068 7380	28.6335 2080	24
25	28.6849 8913	29.1354 3508	29.5947 1832	30.0630 2361	25
26	30.0076 9526	30.4996 2802	31.0016 4569	31.5139 6896	26
27	31.3452 8183	31.8808 7337	32.4279 1832	32.9866 7850	27
28	32.6979 1625	33.2793 8429	33.8738 0220	34.4814 7867	28
29	34.0657 6781	34.6953 7659	35.3395 6698	35.9987 0085	29
30	35.4490 0769	36.1290 6880	36.8254 8602	37.5386 8137	30
31	36.8478 0903	37.5806 8216	38.3318 3646	39.1017 6159	31
32	38.2623 4688	39.0504 4069	39.8588 9921	40.6882 8801	32
33	39.6927 9829	40.5385 7120	41.4069 5907	42.2986 1233	33
34	41.1393 4227	42.0453 0334	42.9763 0476	43.9330 9152	34
35	42.6021 5987	43.5708 6963	44.5672 2895	45.5920 8789	35
36	44.0814 3417	45.1155 0550	46.1800 2835	47.2759 6921	36
37	45.5773 5030	46.6794 4932	47.8150 0374	48.9851 0874	37
38	47.0900 9549	48.2629 4243	49.4724 6004	50.7198 8538	38
39	48.6198 5906	49.8662 2921	51.1527 0636	52.4806 8366	39
40	50.1668 3248	51.4895 5708	52.8560 5608	54.2678 9391	40
41	51.7312 0934	53.1331 7654	54.5828 2685	56.0819 1232	41
42	53.3131 8545	54.7973 4125	56.3333 4072	57.9231 4100	42
43	54.9129 5879	56.4823 0801	58.1079 2415	59.7919 8812	43
44	56.5307 2957	58.1883 3686	59.9069 0811	61.6888 6794	44
45	58.1667 0028	59.9156 9108	61.7306 2810	63.6142 0096	45
46	59.8210 7566	61.6646 3721	63.5794 2423	65.5684 1398	46
47	61.4940 6276	63.4354 4518	65.4536 4131	67.5519 4018	47
48	63.1858 7097	65.2283 8824	67.3536 2888	69.5652 1929	48
49	64.8967 1201	67.0437 4310	69.2797 4128	71.6086 9758	49
50	66.6268 0002	68.8817 8989	71.2323 3772	73.6828 2804	50

TABLE 7 AMOUNT OF ANNUITY
WHEN PERIODIC PAYMENT IS 1

$$s_{\overline{n}|i} = \frac{(1+i)^n - 1}{i}$$

n	$1\frac{1}{8}\%$	$1\frac{1}{4}\%$	$1\frac{3}{8}\%$	$1\frac{1}{2}\%$	n
51	68.3763 5152	70.7428 1226	73.2117 8237	75.7880 7046	51
52	70.1455 8548	72.6270 9741	75.2184 4437	77.9248 9152	52
53	71.9347 2332	74.5349 3613	77.2526 9798	80.0937 6489	53
54	73.7439 8895	76.4666 2283	79.3149 2258	82.2951 7136	54
55	75.5736 0883	78.4224 5562	81.4055 0277	84.5295 9893	55
56	77.4238 1193	80.4027 3631	83.5248 2843	86.7975 4292	56
57	79.2948 2981	82.4077 7052	85.6732 9482	89.0995 0606	57
58	81.1868 9665	84.4378 6765	87.8513 0262	91.4359 9865	58
59	83.1002 4923	86.4933 4099	90.0592 5804	93.8075 3863	59
60	85.0351 2704	88.5745 0776	92.2975 7283	96.2146 5171	60
61	86.9917 7222	90.6816 8910	94.5666 6446	98.6578 7149	61
62	88.9704 2966	92.8152 1022	96.8669 5610	101.1377 3956	62
63	90.9713 4699	94.9754 0034	99.1988 7674	103.6548 0565	63
64	92.9947 7464	97.1625 9285	101.5628 6130	106.2096 2774	64
65	95.0409 6586	99.3771 2526	103.9593 5064	108.8027 7216	65
66	97.1101 7672	101.6193 3933	106.3887 9171	111.4348 1374	66
67	99.2026 6621	103.8895 8107	108.8516 3760	114.1063 3594	67
68	101.3186 9621	106.1882 0083	111.3483 4761	116.8179 3098	68
69	103.4585 3154	108.5155 5334	113.8793 8739	119.5701 9995	69
70	105.6224 4002	110.8719 9776	116.4452 2897	122.3637 5295	70
71	107.8106 9247	113.2578 9773	119.0463 5087	125.1992 0924	71
72	110.0235 6276	115.6736 2145	121.6832 3819	128.0771 9738	72
73	112.2613 2784	118.1195 4172	124.3563 8272	130.9983 5534	73
74	114.5242 6778	120.5960 3599	127.0662 8298	133.9633 3067	74
75	116.8126 6579	123.1034 8644	129.8134 4437	136.9727 8063	75
76	119.1268 0828	125.6422 8002	132.5983 7923	140.0273 7234	76
77	121.4669 8487	128.2128 0852	135.4216 0695	143.1277 8292	77
78	123.8334 8845	130.8154 6863	138.2836 5404	146.2746 9967	78
79	126.2266 1520	133.4506 6199	141.1850 5429	149.4688 2016	79
80	128.6466 6462	136.1187 9526	144.1263 4878	152.7108 5247	80
81	131.0939 3960	138.8202 8020	147.1080 8608	156.0015 1525	81
82	133.5687 4642	141.5555 3370	150.1308 2226	159.3415 3798	82
83	136.0713 9481	144.3249 7787	153.1951 2107	162.7316 6105	83
84	138.6021 9801	147.1290 4010	156.3015 5398	166.1726 3597	84
85	141.1614 7273	149.9681 5310	159.4507 0035	169.6652 2551	85
86	143.7495 3930	152.8427 5501	162.6431 4748	173.2102 0389	86
87	146.3667 2162	155.7532 8945	165.8794 9076	176.8083 5695	87
88	149.0133 4724	158.7002 0557	169.1603 3375	180.4604 8230	88
89	151.6897 4739	161.6839 5814	172.4862 8834	184.1673 8954	89
90	154.3962 5705	164.7050 0762	175.8579 7481	187.9299 0038	90
91	157.1332 1494	167.7638 2021	179.2760 2196	191.7488 4889	91
92	159.9009 6361	170.8608 6796	182.7410 6726	195.6250 8162	92
93	162.6998 4945	173.9966 2881	186.2537 5694	199.5594 5784	93
94	165.5302 2276	177.1715 8667	189.8147 4610	203.5528 4971	94
95	168.3924 3776	180.3862 3151	193.4246 9886	207.6061 4246	95
96	171.2868 5269	183.6410 5940	197.0842 8847	211.7202 3459	96
97	174.2138 2978	186.9365 7264	200.7941 9743	215.8960 3811	97
98	177.1737 3537	190.2732 7980	204.5551 1765	220.1344 7868	98
99	180.1669 3989	193.6516 9580	208.3677 5051	224.4364 9586	99
100	183.1938 1796	197.0723 4200	212.2328 0708	228.8030 4330	100

TABLE 7 AMOUNT OF ANNUITY

WHEN PERIODIC PAYMENT IS 1

$$s_{\overline{n}|i} = \frac{(1+i)^n - 1}{i}$$

n	$1\frac{5}{8}$%	$1\frac{3}{4}$%	$1\frac{7}{8}$%	2%	n
1	1.0000 0000	1.0000 0000	1.0000 0000	1.0000 0000	1
2	2.0162 5000	2.0175 0000	2.0187 5000	2.0200 0000	2
3	3.0490 1406	3.0528 0625	3.0566 0156	3.0604 0000	3
4	4.0985 6054	4.1062 3036	4.1139 1284	4.1216 0800	4
5	5.1651 6215	5.1780 8939	5.1910 4871	5.2040 4016	5
6	6.2490 9603	6.2687 0596	6.2883 8087	6.3081 2096	6
7	7.3506 4385	7.3784 0831	7.4062 8801	7.4342 8338	7
8	8.4700 9181	8.5075 3045	8.5451 5591	8.5829 6905	8
9	9.6077 3080	9.6564 1224	9.7053 7759	9.7546 2843	9
10	10.7638 5643	10.8253 9945	10.8873 5342	10.9497 2100	10
11	11.9387 6909	12.0148 4394	12.0914 9129	12.1687 1542	11
12	13.1327 7409	13.2251 0371	13.3182 0675	13.4120 8973	12
13	14.3461 8167	14.4565 4303	14.5679 2313	14.6803 3152	13
14	15.5793 0712	15.7095 3253	15.8410 7169	15.9739 3815	14
15	16.8324 7086	16.9844 4935	17.1380 9178	17.2934 1692	15
16	18.1059 9851	18.2816 7721	18.4594 3100	18.6392 8525	16
17	19.4002 2099	19.6016 0656	19.8055 4534	20.0120 7096	17
18	20.7154 7458	20.9446 3468	21.1768 9931	21.4123 1238	18
19	22.0521 0104	22.3111 6578	22.5739 6617	22.8405 5863	19
20	23.4104 4768	23.7016 1119	23.9972 2804	24.2973 6980	20
21	24.7908 6746	25.1163 8938	25.4471 7606	25.7833 1719	21
22	26.1937 1905	26.5559 2620	26.9243 1062	27.2989 8354	22
23	27.6193 6699	28.0206 5490	28.4291 4144	28.8449 6321	23
24	29.0681 8170	29.5110 1637	29.9621 8784	30.4218 6247	24
25	30.5405 3966	31.0274 5915	31.5239 7886	32.0302 9972	25
26	32.0368 2343	32.5704 3969	33.1150 5347	33.6709 0572	26
27	33.5574 2181	34.1404 2238	34.7359 6072	35.3443 2383	27
28	35.1027 2991	35.7378 7977	36.3872 5998	37.0512 1031	28
29	36.6731 4927	37.3632 9267	38.0695 2111	38.7922 3451	29
30	38.2690 8795	39.0171 5029	39.7833 2463	40.5680 7921	30
31	39.8909 6063	40.6999 5042	41.5292 6197	42.3794 4079	31
32	41.5391 8874	42.4121 9955	43.3079 3563	44.2270 2961	32
33	43.2142 0055	44.1544 1305	45.1199 5942	46.1115 7020	33
34	44.9164 3131	45.9271 1527	46.9659 5866	48.0338 0160	34
35	46.6463 2332	47.7308 3979	48.8465 7038	49.9944 7763	35
36	48.4043 2608	49.5661 2949	50.7624 4358	51.9943 6719	36
37	50.1908 9637	51.4335 3675	52.7142 3940	54.0342 5453	37
38	52.0064 9844	53.3336 2365	54.7026 3138	56.1149 3962	38
39	53.8516 0404	55.2669 6206	56.7283 0572	58.2372 3841	39
40	55.7266 9261	57.2341 3390	58.7919 6146	60.4019 8318	40
41	57.6322 5136	59.2357 3124	60.8943 1073	62.6100 2284	41
42	59.5687 7544	61.2723 5654	63.0360 7906	64.8622 2330	42
43	61.5367 6805	63.3446 2278	65.2180 0554	67.1594 6777	43
44	63.5367 4053	65.4531 5367	67.4408 4315	69.5026 5712	44
45	65.5692 1256	67.5985 8386	69.7053 5895	71.8927 1027	45
46	67.6347 1226	69.7815 5908	72.0123 3443	74.3305 6447	46
47	69.7337 7634	72.0027 3636	74.3625 6571	76.8171 7576	47
48	71.8669 5020	74.2627 8425	76.7568 6381	79.3535 1927	48
49	74.0347 8814	76.5623 8298	79.1960 5501	81.9405 8966	49
50	76.2378 5345	78.9022 2468	81.6809 8104	84.5794 0145	50

TABLE 7 AMOUNT OF ANNUITY

WHEN PERIODIC PAYMENT IS 1

$$s_{\overline{n}|i} = \frac{(1+i)^n - 1}{i}$$

n	$1\frac{5}{8}\%$	$1\frac{3}{4}\%$	$1\frac{7}{8}\%$	2%	n
51	78.4767 1857	81.2830 1361	84.2124 9943	87.2709 8948	51
52	80.7519 6525	83.7054 6635	86.7914 8380	90.0164 0927	52
53	83.0641 8468	86.1703 1201	89.4188 2412	92.8167 3746	53
54	85.4139 7768	88.6782.9247	92.0954 2707	95.6730 7221	54
55	87.8019 5482	91.2301 6259	94.8222 1633	98.5865 3365	55
56	90.2287 3659	93.8266 9043	97.6001 3289	101.5582 6432	56
57	92.6949 5356	96.4686 5752	100.4301 3538	104.5894 2961	57
58	95.2012 4655	99.1568 5902	103.3132 0042	107.6812 1820	58
59	97.7482 6681	101.8921 0405	106.2503 2292	110.8348 4257	59
60	100.3366 7614	104.6752 1588	109.2425 1648	114.0515 3942	60
61	102.9671 4713	107.5070 3215	112.2908 1366	117.3325 7021	61
62	105.6403 6327	110.3884 0522	115.3962 6642	120.6792 2161	62
63	108.3570 1918	113.3202 0231	118.5599 4641	124.0928 0604	63
64	111.1178 2074	116.3033 0585	121.7829 4541	127.5746 6216	64
65	113.9234 8532	119.3386 1370	125.0663 7564	131.1261 5541	65
66	116.7747 4196	122.4270 3944	128.4113 7018	134.7486 7852	66
67	119.6723 3152	125.5695 1263	131.8190 8337	138.4436 5209	67
68	122.6170 0690	128.7669 7910	135.2906 9118	142.2125 2513	68
69	125.6095 3327	132.0204 0124	138.8273 9164	146.0567 7563	69
70	128.6506 8818	135.3307 5826	142.4304 0524	149.9779 1114	70
71	131.7412 6186	138.6990 4653	146.1009 7533	153.9774 6937	71
72	134.8820 5737	142.1262 7984	149.8403 6862	158.0570 1875	72
73	138.0738 9080	145.6134 8974	153.6498 7553	162.2181 5913	73
74	141.3175 9153	149.1617 2581	157.5308 1070	166.4625 2231	74
75	144.6140 0239	152.7720 5601	161.4845 1340	170.7917 7276	75
76	147.9639 7993	156.4455 6699	165.5123 4803	175.2076 0821	76
77	151.3683 9460	160.1833 6441	169.6157 0455	179.7117 6038	77
78	154.8281 3102	163.9865 7329	173.7959 9901	184.3059 9558	78
79	158.3440 8814	167.8563 3832	178.0546 7399	188.9921 1549	79
80	161.9171 7958	171.7938 2424	182.3931 9913	193.7719 5780	80
81	165.5483 3374	175.8002 1617	186.8130 7162	198.6473 9696	81
82	169.2384 9417	179.8767 1995	191.3158 1671	203.6203 4490	82
83	172.9886 1970	184.0245 6255	195.9029 8827	208.6927 5180	83
84	176.7996 8477	188.2449 9239	200.5761 6930	213.8666 0683	84
85	180.6726 7965	192.5392 7976	205.3369 7248	219.1439 3897	85
86	184.6086 1069	196.9087 1716	210.1870 4071	224.5268 1775	86
87	188.6085 0061	201.3546 1971	215.1280 4772	230.0173 5411	87
88	192.6733 8875	205.8783 2555	220.1616 9862	235.6177 0119	88
89	196.8043 3132	210.4811 9625	225.2897 3047	241.3300 5521	89
90	201.0024 0170	215.1646 1718	230.5139 1291	247.1566 5632	90
91	205.2686 9073	219.9299 9798	235.8360 4878	253.0997 8944	91
92	209.6043 0695	224.7787 7295	241.2579 7469	259.1617 8523	92
93	214.0103 7694	229.7124 0148	246.7815 6172	265.3450 2094	93
94	218.4880 4557	234.7323 6850	252.4087 1600	271.6519 2135	94
95	223.0384 7631	239.8401 8495	258.1413 7943	278.0849 5978	95
96	227.6628 5155	245.0373 8819	263.9815 3029	284.6466 5898	96
97	232.3623 7288	250.3255 4248	269.9311 8398	291.3395 9216	97
98	237.1382 6144	255.7062 3947	275.9923 9368	298.1663 8400	98
99	241.9917 5819	261.1810 9866	282.1672 5107	305.1297 1168	99
100	246.9241 2426	266.7517 6789	288.4578 8702	312.2323 0591	100

TABLE 7 AMOUNT OF ANNUITY

WHEN PERIODIC PAYMENT IS 1

$$s_{\overline{n}|i} = \frac{(1+i)^n - 1}{i}$$

n	$2\frac{1}{4}$%	$2\frac{1}{2}$%	$2\frac{3}{4}$%	3%	n
1	1.0000 0000	1.0000 0000	1.0000 0000	1.0000 0000	1
2	2.0225 0000	2.0250 0000	2.0275 0000	2.0300 0000	2
3	3.0680 0625	3.0756 2500	3.0832 5625	3.0909 0000	3
4	4.1370 3639	4.1525 1562	4.1680 4580	4.1836 2700	4
5	5.2301 1971	5.2563 2852	5.2826 6706	5.3091 3581	5
6	6.3477 9740	6.3877 3673	6.4279 4040	6.4684 0988	6
7	7.4906 2284	7.5474 3015	7.6047 0876	7.6624 6218	7
8	8.6591 6186	8.7361 1590	8.8138 3825	8.8923 3605	8
9	9.8539 9300	9.9545 1880	10.0562 1880	10.1591 0613	9
10	11.0757 0784	11.2033 8177	11.3327 6482	11.4638 7931	10
11	12.3249 1127	12.4834 6631	12.6444 1585	12.8077 9569	11
12	13.6022 2177	13.7955 5297	13.9921 3729	14.1920 2956	12
13	14.9082 7176	15.1404 4179	15.3769 2107	15.6177 9045	13
14	16.2437 0788	16.5189 5284	16.7997 8639	17.0863 2416	14
15	17.6091 9130	17.9319 2666	18.2617 8052	18.5989 1389	15
16	19.0053 9811	19.3802 2483	19.7639 7948	20.1568 8130	16
17	20.4330 1957	20.8647 3045	21.3074 8892	21.7615 8774	17
18	21.8927 6251	22.3863 4871	22.8934 4487	23.4144 3537	18
19	23.3853 4966	23.9460 0743	24.5230 1460	25.1168 6844	19
20	24.9115 2003	25.5446 5761	26.1973 9750	26.8703 7449	20
21	26.4720 2923	27.1832 7405	27.9178 2593	28.6764 8572	21
22	28.0676 4989	28.8628 5590	29.6855 6615	30.5367 8030	22
23	29.6991 7201	30.5844 2730	31.5019 1921	32.4528 8370	23
24	31.3674 0338	32.3490 3798	33.3682 2199	34.4264 7022	24
25	33.0731 6996	34.1577 6393	35.2858 4810	36.4592 6432	25
26	34.8173 1628	36.0117 0803	37.2562 0892	38.5530 4225	26
27	36.6007 0590	37.9120 0073	39.2807 5467	40.7096 3352	27
28	38.4242 2178	39.8598 0075	41.3609 7542	42.9309 2252	28
29	40.2887 6677	41.8562 9577	43.4984 0224	45.2188 5020	29
30	42.1952 6402	43.9027 0316	45.6946 0830	47.5754 1571	30
31	44.1446 5746	46.0002 7074	47.9512 1003	50.0026 7818	31
32	46.1379 1226	48.1502 7751	50.2698 6831	52.5027 5852	32
33	48.1760 1528	50.3540 3445	52.6522 8969	55.0778 4128	33
34	50.2599 7563	52.6128 8531	55.1002 2765	57.7301 7652	34
35	52.3908 2508	54.9282 0744	57.6154 8391	60.4620 8181	35
36	54.5696 1864	57.3014 1263	60.1999 0972	63.2759 4427	36
37	56.7974 3506	59.7339 4794	62.8554 0724	66.1742 2259	37
38	59.0753 7735	62.2272 9664	65.5839 3094	69.1594 4927	38
39	61.4045 7334	64.7829 7906	68.3874 8904	72.2342 3275	39
40	63.7861 7624	67.4025 5354	71.2681 4499	75.4012 5973	40
41	66.2213 6521	70.0876 1737	74.2280 1898	78.6632 9753	41
42	68.7113 4592	72.8398 0781	77.2692 8950	82.0231 9645	42
43	71.2573 5121	75.6608 0300	80.3941 9496	85.4838 9234	43
44	73.8606 4161	78.5523 2308	83.6050 3532	89.0484 0911	44
45	76.5225 0605	81.5161 3116	86.9041 7379	92.7198 6139	45
46	79.2442 6243	84.5540 3443	90.2940 3857	96.5014 5723	46
47	82.0272 5834	87.6678 8530	93.7771 2463	100.3965 0095	47
48	84.8728 7165	90.8595 8243	97.3559 9556	104.4083 9598	48
49	87.7825 1126	94.1310 7199	101.0332 8544	108.5406 4785	49
50	90.7576 1776	97.4843 4879	104.8117 0079	112.7968 6729	50

TABLE 7 AMOUNT OF ANNUITY

WHEN PERIODIC PAYMENT IS 1

$$s_{\overline{n}|i} = \frac{(1+i)^n - 1}{i}$$

n	$2\frac{1}{4}\%$	$2\frac{1}{2}\%$	$2\frac{3}{4}\%$	3%	n
51	93.7996 6416	100.9214 5751	108.6940 2256	117.1806 7331	51
52	96.9101 5661	104.4444 9395	112.6831 0818	121.6961 9651	52
53	100.0906 3513	108.0556 0629	116.7818 9365	126.3470 8240	53
54	103.3426 7442	111.7569 9645	120.9933 9573	131.1374 9488	54
55	106.6678 8460	115.5509 2136	125.3207 1411	136.0716 1972	55
56	110.0679 1200	119.4396 9440	129.7670 3375	141.1537 6831	56
57	113.5444 4002	123.4256 8676	134.3356 2718	146.3883 8136	57
58	117.0991 8992	127.5113 2893	139.0298 5692	151.7800 3280	58
59	120.7339 2169	131.6991 1215	143.8531 7799	157.3334 3379	59
60	124.4504 3493	135.9915 8995	148.8091 4038	163.0534 3680	60
61	128.2505 6972	140.3913 7970	153.9013 9174	168.9450 3991	61
62	132.1362 0754	144.9011 6419	159.1336 8002	175.0133 9110	62
63	136.1092 7221	149.5236 9330	164.5098 5622	181.2637 9284	63
64	140.1717 3083	154.2617 8563	170.0338 7726	187.7017 0662	64
65	144.3255 9477	159.1183 3027	175.7098 0889	194.3327 5782	65
66	148.5729 2066	164.0962 8853	181.5418 2863	201.1627 4055	66
67	152.9158 1137	169.1986 9574	187.5342 2892	208.1976 2277	67
68	157.3564 1713	174.4286 6314	193.6914 2022	215.4435 5145	68
69	161.8969 3651	179.7893 7971	200.0179 3427	222.9068 5800	69
70	166.5396 1758	185.2841 1421	206.5184 2746	230.5940 6374	70
71	171.2867 5898	190.9162 1706	213.1976 8422	238.5118 8565	71
72	176.1407 1106	196.6891 2249	220.0606 2054	246.6672 4222	72
73	181.1038 7705	202.6063 5055	227.1122 8760	255.0672 5949	73
74	186.1787 1429	208.6715 0931	234.3578 7551	263.7192 7727	74
75	191.3677 3536	214.8882 9705	241.8027 1709	272.6308 5559	75
76	196.6735 0941	221.2605 0447	249.4522 9181	281.8097 8126	76
77	202.0986 6337	227.7920 1709	257.3122 2983	291.2640 7469	77
78	207.6458 8329	234.4868 1751	265.3883 1615	301.0019 9693	78
79	213.3179 1567	241.3489 8795	273.6864 9485	311.0320 5684	79
80	219.1175 6877	248.3827 1265	282.2128 7345	321.3630 1855	80
81	225.0477 1407	255.5922 8047	290.9737 2747	332.0039 0910	81
82	231.1112 8763	262.9820 8748	299.9755 0498	342.9640 2638	82
83	237.3112 9160	270.5566 3966	309.2248 3137	354.2529 4717	83
84	243.6507 9567	278.3205 5566	318.7285 1423	365.8805 3558	84
85	250.1329 3857	286.2785 6955	328.4935 4837	377.8569 5165	85
86	256.7609 2969	294.4355 3379	338.5271 2095	390.1926 6020	86
87	263.5380 5060	302.7964 2213	348.8366 1678	402.8984 4001	87
88	270.4676 5674	311.3663 3268	359.4296 2374	415.9853 9321	88
89	277.5531 7902	320.1504 9100	370.3139 3839	429.4649 5500	89
90	284.7981 2555	329.1542 5328	381.4975 7170	443.3489 0365	90
91	292.2060 8337	338.3831 0961	392.9887 5492	457.6493 7076	91
92	299.7807 2025	347.8426 8735	404.7959 4568	472.3788 5189	92
93	307.5257 8645	357.5387 5453	416.9278 3418	387.5502 1744	93
94	315.4451 1665	367.4772 2339	429.3933 4962	503.1767 2397	94
95	323.5426 3177	377.6641 5398	442.2016 6674	519.2720 2568	95
96	331.8223 4099	388.1057 5783	455.3622 1257	535.8501 8645	96
97	340.2883 4366	398.8084 0177	468.8846 7342	552.9256 9205	97
98	348.9448 3139	409.7786 1182	482.7790 0194	570.5134 6281	98
99	357.7960 9010	421.0230 7711	497.0554 2449	588.6288 6669	99
100	366.8465 0213	432.5486 5404	511.7244 4867	607.2877 3270	100

TABLE 7 AMOUNT OF ANNUITY

WHEN PERIODIC PAYMENT IS 1

$$s_{\overline{n}|i} = \frac{(1+i)^n - 1}{i}$$

n	$3\frac{1}{4}\%$	$3\frac{1}{2}\%$	$3\frac{3}{4}\%$	4%	n
1	1.0000 0000	1.0000 0000	1.0000 0000	1.0000 0000	1
2	2.0325 0000	2.0350 0000	2.0375 0000	2.0400 0000	2
3	3.0985 5625	3.1062 2500	3.1139 0625	3.1216 0000	3
4	4.1992 5933	4.2149 4288	4.2306 7773	4.2464 6400	4
5	5.3357 3526	5.3624 6588	5.3893 2815	5.4163 2256	5
6	6.5091 4665	6.5501 5218	6.5914 2796	6.6329 7546	6
7	7.7206 9392	7.7794 0751	7.8386 0650	7.8982 9448	7
8	8.9716 1647	9.0516 8677	9.1325 5425	9.2142 2626	8
9	10.2631 9401	10.3684 9581	10.4750 2503	10.5827 9531	9
10	11.5967 4781	11.7313 9316	11.8678 3847	12.0061 0712	10
11	12.9736 4212	13.1419 9192	13.3128 8241	13.4863 5141	11
12	14.3952 8548	14.6019 6164	14.8121 1550	15.0258 0546	12
13	15.8631 3226	16.1130 3030	16.3675 6983	16.6268 3768	13
14	17.3786 8406	17.6769 8636	17.9813 5370	18.2919 1119	14
15	18.9434 9129	19.2956 8088	19.6556 5447	20.0235 8764	15
16	20.5591 5476	20.9710 2971	21.3927 4151	21.8245 3114	16
17	22.2273 2729	22.7050 1575	23.1949 6932	23.6975 1239	17
18	23.9497 1543	24.4996 9130	25.0647 8067	25.6454 1288	18
19	25.7280 8118	26.3571 8050	27.0047 0994	27.6712 2940	19
20	27.5642 4382	28.2796 8181	29.0173 8656	29.7780 7858	20
21	29.4600 8174	30.2694 7068	31.1055 3856	31.9692 0172	21
22	31.4175 3440	32.3289 0215	33.2719 9626	34.2479 6979	22
23	33.4386 0426	34.4604 1373	35.5196 9612	36.6178 8858	23
24	35.5253 5890	36.6665 2821	37.8516 8472	39.0826 0412	24
25	37.6799 3307	38.9498 5669	40.2711 2290	41.6459 0829	25
26	39.9045 3089	41.3131 0168	42.7812 9001	44.3117 4462	26
27	42.2014 2815	43.7590 6024	45.3855 8838	47.0842 1440	27
28	44.5729 7456	46.2906 2734	48.0875 4794	49.9675 8298	28
29	47.0215 9623	48.9107 9930	50.8908 3099	52.9662 8630	29
30	49.5497 9811	51.6226 7728	53.7992 3715	56.0849 3775	30
31	52.1601 6655	54.4294 7098	56.8167 0855	59.3283 3526	31
32	54.8553 7196	57.3345 0247	59.9473 3512	62.7014 6867	32
33	57.6381 7155	60.3412 1005	63.1953 6019	66.2095 2742	33
34	60.5114 1213	63.4531 5240	66.5651 8619	69.8579 0851	34
35	63.4780 3302	66.6740 1274	70.0613 8067	73.6522 2486	35
36	66.5410 6909	70.0076 0318	73.6886 8245	77.5983 1385	36
37	69.7036 5384	73.4578 6930	77.4520 0804	81.7022 4640	37
38	72.9690 2259	77.0288 9472	81.3564 5834	85.9703 3626	38
39	76.3405 1582	80.7249 0604	85.4073 2553	90.4091 4971	39
40	79.8215 8259	84.5502 7775	89.6101 0024	95.0255 1570	40
41	83.4157 8402	88.5095 3747	93.9704 7900	99.8265 3633	41
42	87.1267 9700	92.6073 7128	98.4943 7196	104.8195 9778	42
43	90.9584 1791	96.8486 2928	103.1879 1091	110.0123 8169	43
44	94.9145 6649	101.2383 3130	108.0574 5757	115.4128 7696	44
45	98.9992 8990	105.7816 7290	113.1096 1223	121.0293 9204	45
46	103.2167 6682	110.4840 3145	118.3512 2269	126.8705 6772	46
47	107.5713 1174	115.3509 7255	123.7893 9354	132.9453 9043	47
48	112.0673 7937	120.3882 5659	129.4314 9579	139.2632 0604	48
49	116.7095 6920	125.6018 4557	135.2851 7689	145.8337 3429	49
50	121.5026 3020	130.9979 1016	141.3583 7102	152.6670 8366	50

TABLE 7 AMOUNT OF ANNUITY

WHEN PERIODIC PAYMENT IS 1

$$s_{\overline{n}|i} = \frac{(1+i)^n - 1}{i}$$

n	$3\frac{1}{4}\%$	$3\frac{1}{2}\%$	$3\frac{3}{4}\%$	4%	n
51	126.4514 6568	136.5828 3702	147.6593 0993	159.7737 6700	51
52	131.5611 3832	142.3632 3631	154.1965 3405	167.1647 1768	52
53	136.8368 7531	148.3459 4958	160.9789 0408	174.8513 0639	53
54	142.2840 7367	154.5380 5782	168.0156 1298	182.8453 5865	54
55	147.9083 0616	160.9468 8984	175.3161 9847	191.1591 7299	55
56	153.7153 2611	167.5800 3099	182.8905 5591	199.8055 3991	56
57	159.7110 7421	174.4453 3207	190.7489 5176	208.7977 6151	57
58	165.9016 8412	181.5509 1869	198.9020 3745	218.1496 7197	58
59	172.2934 8885	188.9052 0085	207.3608 6386	227.8756 5885	59
60	178.8930 2724	196.5168 8288	216.1368 9625	237.9906 8520	60
61	185.7070 5063	204.3949 7378	225.2420 2986	248.5103 1261	61
62	192.7425 2977	212.5487 9786	234.6886 0598	259.4507 2511	62
63	200.0066 6199	220.9880 0579	244.4894 2870	270.8287 5412	63
64	207.5068 7850	229.7225 8599	254.6577 8228	282.6619 0428	64
65	215.2508 5205	238.7628 7650	265.2074 4912	294.9683 8045	65
66	223.2465 0475	248.1195 7718	276.1527 2846	307.7671 1567	66
67	231.5020 1615	257.8037 6238	287.5084 5578	321.0778 0030	67
68	240.0258 3168	267.8268 9406	299.2900 2287	334.9209 1231	68
69	248.8266 7120	278.2008 3535	311.5133 9872	349.3177 4880	69
70	257.9135 3802	288.9378 6459	324.1951 5118	364.2904 5876	70
71	267.2957 2800	300.0506 8985	337.3524 6935	379.8620 7711	71
72	276.9828 3916	311.5524 6400	351.0031 8695	396.0565 6019	72
73	286.9847 8144	323.4568 0024	365.1658 0646	412.8988 2260	73
74	297.3117 8683	335.7777 8824	379.8595 2420	430.4147 7550	74
75	307.9744 1991	348.5300 1083	395.1042 5636	448.6313 6652	75
76	318.9835 8855	361.7285 6121	410.9206 6597	467.5766 2118	76
77	330.3505 5518	375.3890 6085	427.3301 9094	487.2796 8603	77
78	342.0869 4822	389.5276 7798	444.3550 7310	507.7708 7347	78
79	354.2047 7404	404.1611 4671	462.0183 8835	529.0817 0841	79
80	366.7164 2920	419.3067 8685	480.3440 7791	551.2449 7675	80
81	379.6347 1315	434.9825 2439	499.3569 8083	574.2947 7582	81
82	392.9728 4132	451.2069 1274	519.0828 6761	598.2665 6685	82
83	406.7444 5867	467.9991 5469	539.5484 7515	623.1972 2952	83
84	420.9636 5357	485.3791 2510	560.7815 4296	649.1251 1870	84
85	435.6449 7232	503.3673 9448	582.8108 5083	676.0901 2345	85
86	450.8034 3392	521.9852 5329	605.6662 5773	704.1337 2839	86
87	466.4545 4552	541.2547 3715	629.3787 4240	733.2990 7753	87
88	482.6143 1825	561.1986 5295	653.9804 4524	763.6310 4063	88
89	499.2992 8359	581.8406 0581	679.5047 1193	795.1762 8225	89
90	516.5265 1031	603.2050 2701	705.9861 3863	827.9833 3354	90
91	534.3136 2189	625.3172 0295	733.4606 1883	862.1026 6688	91
92	552.6788 1460	648.2033 0506	761.9653 9204	897.5867 7356	92
93	571.6408 7608	671.8904 2074	791.5390 9424	934.4902 4450	93
94	591.2192 0455	696.4065 8546	822.2218 1027	972.8698 5428	94
95	611.4338 2870	721.7808 1595	854.0551 2816	1012.7846 4845	95
96	632.3054 2813	748.0431 4451	887.0821 9546	1054.2960 3439	96
97	653.8553 5455	775.2246 5457	921.3477 7779	1097.4678 7577	97
98	676.1056 5357	803.3575 1748	956.8983 1946	1142.3665 9080	98
99	699.0790 8731	832.4750 3059	993.7820 0644	1189.0612 5443	99
100	722.7991 5765	862.6116 5666	1032.0488 3168	1237.6237 0461	100

TABLE 7 AMOUNT OF ANNUITY

WHEN PERIODIC PAYMENT IS 1

$$s_{\overline{n}|i} = \frac{(1+i)^n - 1}{i}$$

n	$4\frac{1}{2}$%	5%	$5\frac{1}{2}$%	6%	n
1	1.0000 0000	1.0000 0000	1.0000 0000	1.0000 0000	1
2	2.0450 0000	2.0500 0000	2.0550 0000	2.0600 0000	2
3	3.1370 2500	3.1525 0000	3.1680 2500	3.1836 0000	3
4	4.2781 9112	4.3101 2500	4.3422 6638	4.3746 1600	4
5	5.4707 0973	5.5256 3125	5.5810 9103	5.6370 9296	5
6	6.7168 9166	6.8019 1281	6.8880 5103	6.9753 1854	6
7	8.0191 5179	8.1420 0845	8.2668 9384	8.3938 3765	7
8	9.3800 1362	9.5491 0888	9.7215 7300	9.8974 6791	8
9	10.8021 1423	11.0265 6432	11.2562 5951	11.4913 1598	9
10	12.2882 0937	12.5778 9254	12.8753 5379	13.1807 9494	10
11	13.8411 7879	14.2067 8716	14.5834 9825	14.9716 4264	11
12	15.4640 3184	15.9171 2652	16.3855 9065	16.8699 4120	12
13	17.1599 1327	17.7129 8285	18.2867 9814	18.8821 3767	13
14	18.9321 0937	19.5986 3199	20.2925 7203	21.0150 6593	14
15	20.7840 5429	21.5785 6359	22.4086 6350	23.2759 6988	15
16	22.7193 3673	23.6574 9177	24.6411 3999	25.6725 2808	16
17	24.7417 0689	25.8403 6636	26.9964 0269	28.2128 7976	17
18	26.8550 8370	28.1323 8467	29.4812 0483	30.9056 5255	18
19	29.0635 6246	30.5390 0391	32.1026 7110	33.7599 9170	19
20	31.3714 2277	33.0659 5410	34.8683 1801	36.7855 9120	20
21	33.7831 3680	35.7192 5181	37.7860 7550	39.9927 2668	21
22	36.3033 7796	38.5052 1440	40.8643 0965	43.3922 9028	22
23	38.9370 2996	41.4304 7512	44.1118 4669	46.9958 2769	23
24	41.6891 9631	44.5019 9887	47.5379 9825	50.8155 7735	24
25	44.5652 1015	47.7270 9882	51.1525 8816	54.8645 1200	25
26	47.5706 4460	51.1134 5376	54.9659 8051	59.1563 8272	26
27	50.7113 2361	54.6691 2645	58.9891 0943	63.7057 6568	27
28	53.9933 3317	58.4025 8277	63.2335 1045	68.5281 1162	28
29	57.4230 3316	62.3227 1191	67.7113 5353	73.6397 9832	29
30	61.0070 6966	66.4388 4750	72.4354 7797	79.0581 8622	30
31	64.7523 8779	70.7607 8988	77.4194 2926	84.8016 7739	31
32	68.6662 4524	75.2988 2937	82.6774 9787	90.8897 7803	32
33	72.7562 2628	80.0637 7084	88.2247 6025	97.3431 6471	33
34	77.0302 5646	85.0669 5938	94.0771 2207	104.1837 5460	34
35	81.4966 1800	90.3203 0735	100.2513 6378	111.4347 7987	35
36	86.1639 6581	95.8363 2272	106.7651 8879	119.1208 6666	36
37	91.0413 4427	101.6281 3886	113.6372 7417	127.2681 1866	37
38	96.1382 0476	107.7095 4580	120.8873 2425	135.9042 0578	38
39	101.4644 2398	114.0950 2309	128.5361 2708	145.0584 5813	39
40	107.0303 2306	120.7997 7424	136.6056 1407	154.7619 6562	40
41	112.8466 8760	127.8397 6295	145.1189 2285	165.0476 8356	41
42	118.9247 8854	135.2317 5110	154.1004 6360	175.9505 4457	42
43	125.2764 0402	142.9933 3866	163.5759 8910	187.5075 7724	43
44	131.9138 4220	151.1430 0559	173.5726 6850	199.7580 3188	44
45	138.8499 6510	159.7001 5587	184.1191 6527	212.7435 1379	45
46	146.0982 1353	168.6851 6366	195.2457 1936	226.5081 2462	46
47	153.6726 3314	178.1194 2185	206.9842 3392	241.0986 1210	47
48	161.5879 0163	188.0253 9294	219.3683 6679	256.5645 2882	48
49	169.8593 5720	198.4266 6259	232.4336 2696	272.9584 0055	49
50	178.5030 2828	209.3479 9572	246.2174 7645	290.3359 0458	50

TABLE 7 AMOUNT OF ANNUITY

WHEN PERIODIC PAYMENT IS 1

$$s_{\overline{n}|i} = \frac{(1+i)^n - 1}{i}$$

n	$4\frac{1}{2}$%	5%	$5\frac{1}{2}$%	6%	n
51	187.5356 6455	220.8153 9550	260.7594 3765	308.7560 5886	51
52	196.9747 6946	232.8561 6528	276.1012 0672	328.2814 2239	52
53	206.8386 3408	245.4989 7354	292.2867 7309	348.9783 0773	53
54	217.1463 7262	258.7739 2222	309.3625 4561	370.9170 0620	54
55	227.9179 5938	272.7126 1833	327.3774 8562	394.1720 2657	55
56	239.1742 6756	287.3482 4924	346.3832 4733	418.8223 4816	56
57	250.9371 0960	302.7156 6171	366.4343 2593	444.9516 8905	57
58	263.2292 7953	318.8514 4479	387.5882 1386	472.6487 9040	58
59	276.0745 9711	335.7940 1703	409.9055 6562	502.0077 1782	59
60	289.4979 5398	353.5837 1788	433.4503 7173	533.1281 8089	60
61	303.5253 6190	372.2629 0378	458.2901 4217	566.1158 7174	61
62	318.1840 0319	391.8760 4897	484.4960 9999	601.0828 2405	62
63	333.5022 8333	412.4698 5141	512.1433 8549	638.1477 9349	63
64	349.5098 8608	434.0933 4398	541.3112 7170	677.4366 6110	64
65	366.2378 3096	456.7980 1118	572.0833 9164	719.0828 6076	65
66	383.7185 3335	480.6379 1174	604.5479 7818	763.2278 3241	66
67	401.9858 6735	505.6698 0733	638.7981 1698	810.0215 0236	67
68	421.0752 3138	531.9532 9770	674.9320 1341	859.6227 9250	68
69	441.0236 1679	559.5509 6258	713.0532 7415	912.2001 6005	69
70	461.8696 7955	588.5285 1071	753.2712 0423	967.9321 6965	70
71	483.6538 1513	618.9549 3625	795.7011 2046	1027.0080 9983	71
72	506.4182 3681	650.9026 8306	840.4646 8209	1089.6285 8582	72
73	530.2070 5747	684.4478 1721	887.6902 3960	1156.0063 0097	73
74	555.0663 7505	719.6702 0807	937.5132 0278	1226.3666 7902	74
75	581.0443 6193	756.6537 1848	990.0764 2893	1300.9486 7977	75
76	608.1913 5822	795.4864 0440	1045.5306 3252	1380.0056 0055	76
77	636.5599 6934	836.2607 2462	1104.0348 1731	1463.8059 3659	77
78	666.2051 6796	879.0737 6085	1165.7567 3226	1552.6342 9278	78
79	697.1844 0052	924.0274 4889	1230.8733 5254	1646.7923 5035	79
80	729.5576 9854	971.2288 2134	1299.5713 8693	1746.5998 9137	80
81	763.3877 9497	1020.7902 6240	1372.0478 1321	1852.3958 8485	81
82	798.7402 4575	1072.8297 7552	1448.5104 4294	1964.5396 3794	82
83	835.6835 5680	1127.4712 6430	1529.1785 1730	2083.4120 1622	83
84	874.2893 1686	1184.8448 2752	1614.2833 3575	2209.4167 3719	84
85	914.6323 3612	1245.0870 6889	1704.0689 1922	2342.9817 4142	85
86	956.7907 9125	1308.3414 2234	1798.7927 0977	2484.5606 4591	86
87	1000.8463 7685	1374.7584 9345	1898.7263 0881	2634.6342 8466	87
88	1046.8844 6381	1444.4964 1812	2004.1562 5579	2793.7123 4174	88
89	1094.9942 6468	1517.7212 3903	2115.3848 4986	2962.3350 8225	89
90	1145.2690 0659	1594.6073 0098	2232.7310 1660	3141.0751 8718	90
91	1197.8061 1189	1675.3376 6603	2356.5312 2252	3330.5396 9841	91
92	1252.7073 8692	1760.1045 4933	2487.1404 3976	3531.3720 8032	92
93	1310.0792 1933	1849.1097 7680	2624.9331 6394	3744.2544 0514	93
94	1370.0327 8420	1942.5652 6564	2770.3044 8796	3969.9096 6944	94
95	1432.6842 5949	2040.6935 2892	2923.6712 3480	4209.1042 4961	95
96	1498.1550 5117	2143.7282 0537	3085.4731 5271	4462.6505 0459	96
97	1566.5720 2847	2251.9146 1564	3256.1741 7611	4731.4095 3486	97
98	1638.0677 6976	2365.5103 4642	3436.2637 5580	5016.2941 0696	98
99	1712.7808 1939	2484.7858 6374	3626.2582 6237	5318.2717 5337	99
100	1790.8559 5627	2610.0251 5693	3826.7024 6680	5638.3680 5857	100

TABLE 7 AMOUNT OF ANNUITY

WHEN PERIODIC PAYMENT IS 1

$$s_{\overline{n}|i} = \frac{(1+i)^n - 1}{i}$$

n	$6\frac{1}{2}$%	7%	$7\frac{1}{2}$%	8%	n
1	1.0000 0000	1.0000 0000	1.0000 0000	1.0000 0000	1
2	2.0650 0000	2.0700 0000	2.0750 0000	2.0800 0000	2
3	3.1992 2500	3.2149 0000	3.2306 2500	3.2464 0000	3
4	4.4071 7462	4.4399 4300	4.4729 2188	4.5061 1200	4
5	5.6936 4098	5.7507 3901	5.8083 9102	5.8666 0096	5
6	7.0637 2764	7.1532 9074	7.2440 2034	7.3359 2904	6
7	8.5228 6994	8.6540 2109	8.7873 2187	8.9228 0336	7
8	10.0768 5648	10.2598 0257	10.4463 7101	10.6366 2763	8
9	11.7318 5215	11.9779 8875	12.2298 4883	12.4875 5784	9
10	13.4944 2254	13.8164 4796	14.1470 8750	14.4865 6247	10
11	15.3715 6001	15.7835 9932	16.2081 1906	16.6454 8746	11
12	17.3707 1141	17.8884 5127	18.4237 2799	18.9771 2646	12
13	19.4998 0765	20.1406 4286	20.8055 0759	21.4952 9658	13
14	21.7672 9515	22.5504 8786	23.3659 2066	24.2149 2030	14
15	24.1821 6933	25.1290 2201	26.1183 6470	27.1521 1393	15
16	26.7540 1034	27.8880 5355	29.0772 4206	30.3242 8304	16
17	29.4930 2101	30.8402 1730	32.2580 3521	33.7502 2568	17
18	32.4100 6738	33.9990 3251	35.6773 8785	37.4502 4374	18
19	35.5167 2176	37.3789 6479	39.3531 9194	41.4462 6324	19
20	38.8253 0867	40.9954 9232	43.3046 8134	45.7619 6430	20
21	42.3489 5373	44.8651 7678	47.5525 3244	50.4229 2144	21
22	46.1016 3573	49.0057 3916	52.1189 7237	55.4567 5516	22
23	50.0982 4205	53.4361 4090	57.0278 9530	60.8932 9557	23
24	54.3546 2778	58.1766 7076	62.3049 8744	66.7647 5922	24
25	58.8876 7859	63.2490 3772	67.9778 6150	73.1059 3995	25
26	63.7153 7769	68.6764 7036	74.0762 0112	79.9544 1515	26
27	68.8568 7724	74.4838 2328	80.6319 1620	87.3507 6836	27
28	74.3325 7427	80.6976 9091	87.6793 0991	95.3388 2983	28
29	80.1641 9159	87.3465 2927	95.2552 5816	103.9659 3622	29
30	86.3748 6405	94.4607 8632	103.3994 0252	113.2832 1111	30
31	92.9892 3021	102.0730 4137	112.1543 5771	123.3458 6800	31
32	100.0335 3017	110.2181 5426	121.5659 3454	134.2135 3744	32
33	107.5357 0963	118.9334 2506	131.6833 7963	145.9506 2044	33
34	115.5255 3076	128.2587 6481	142.5596 3310	158.6266 7007	34
35	124.0346 9026	138.2368 7835	154.2516 0558	172.3168 0368	35
36	133.0969 4513	148.9134 5984	166.8204 7600	187.1021 4797	36
37	142.7482 4656	160.3374 0202	180.3320 1170	203.0703 1981	37
38	153.0268 8259	172.5610 2017	194.8569 1258	220.3159 4540	38
39	163.9736 2996	185.6402 9158	210.4711 8102	238.9412 2103	39
40	175.6319 1590	199.6351 1199	227.2565 1960	259.0565 1871	40
41	188.0479 9044	214.6095 6983	245.3007 5857	280.7810 4021	41
42	201.2711 0981	230.6322 3972	264.6983 1546	304.2435 2342	42
43	215.3537 3195	247.7764 9650	285.5506 8912	329.5830 0530	43
44	230.3517 2453	266.1208 5125	307.9669 9080	356.9496 4572	44
45	246.3245 8662	285.7493 1084	332.0645 1511	386.5056 1738	45
46	263.3356 8475	306.7517 6260	357.9693 5375	418.4260 6677	46
47	281.4525 0426	329.2243 8598	385.8170 5528	452.9001 5211	47
48	300.7469 1704	353.2700 9300	415.7533 3442	490.1321 6428	48
49	321.2954 6665	378.9989 9951	447.9348 3451	530.3427 3742	49
50	343.1796 7198	406.5289 2947	482.5299 4709	573.7701 5642	50

TABLE 7 AMOUNT OF ANNUITY

WHEN PERIODIC PAYMENT IS 1

$$s_{\overline{n}|i} = \frac{(1+i)^n - 1}{i}$$

n	$6\frac{1}{2}\%$	7%	$7\frac{1}{2}\%$	8%	n
51	366.4863 5066	435.9859 5454	519.7196 9313	620.6717 6893	51
52	391.3079 6345	467.5049 7135	559.6986 7011	671.3255 1044	52
53	417.7429 8108	501.2303 1935	602.6760 7037	726.0315 5128	53
54	445.8962 7485	537.3164 4170	648.8767 7565	785.1140 7538	54
55	475.8795 3271	575.9285 9262	698.5425 3382	848.9232 0141	55
56	507.8117 0234	617.2435 9410	751.9332 2386	917.8370 5752	56
57	541.8194 6299	661.4506 4569	809.3282 1564	992.2640 2213	57
58	578.0377 2808	708.7521 9089	871.0278 3182	1072.6451 4390	58
59	616.6101 8041	759.3648 4425	937.3549 1920	1159.4567 5541	59
60	657.6898 4214	813.5203 8335	1008.6565 3814	1253.2132 9584	60
61	701.4396 8187	871.4668 1018	1085.3057 7851	1354.4703 5951	61
62	748.0332 6120	933.4694 8690	1167.7037 1189	1463.8279 8827	62
63	797.6554 2317	999.8123 5098	1256.2814 9029	1581.9342 2733	63
64	850.5030 2568	1070.7992 1555	1351.5026 0206	1709.4889 6552	64
65	906.7857 2235	1146.7551 6064	1453.8652 9721	1847.2480 8276	65
66	966.7267 9430	1228.0280 2188	1563.9051 9450	1996.0279 2938	66
67	1030.5640 3593	1314.9899 8341	1682.1980 8409	2156.7101 6373	67
68	1098.5506 9827	1408.0392 8225	1809.3629 4040	2330.2469 7683	68
69	1170.9564 9365	1507.6020 3201	1946.0651 6093	2517.6667 3497	69
70	1248.0686 6574	1614.1341 7425	2093.0200 4800	2720.0800 7377	70
71	1330.1931 2901	1728.1235 6645	2250.9965 5160	2938.6864 7967	71
72	1417.6556 8240	1850.0922 1610	2420.8212 9296	3174.7813 9805	72
73	1510.8033 0176	1980.5986 7123	2603.3828 8994	3429.7639 0989	73
74	1610.0055 1637	2120.2405 7821	2799.6366 0668	3705.1450 2268	74
75	1715.6558 7493	2269.6574 1869	3010.6093 5218	4002.5566 2449	75
76	1828.1735 0681	2429.5334 3800	3237.4050 5360	4323.7611 5445	76
77	1948.0047 8475	2600.6007 7866	3481.2104 3262	4670.6620 4681	77
78	2075.6250 9576	2783.6428 3316	3743.3012 1506	5045.3150 1056	78
79	2211.5407 2698	2979.4978 3148	4025.0488 0619	5449.9402 1140	79
80	2356.2908 7423	3189.0626 7969	4327.9274 6666	5886.9354 2831	80
81	2510.4497 8106	3413.2970 6727	4653.5220 2666	6358.8902 6258	81
82	2674.6290 1683	3653.2278 6198	5003.5361 7866	6868.6014 8358	82
83	2849.4799 0292	3909.9538 1231	5379.8013 9206	7419.0896 0227	83
84	3035.6960 9661	4184.6505 7918	5784.2864 9646	8013.6167 7045	84
85	3234.0163 4289	4478.5761 1972	6219.1079 8369	8655.7061 1209	85
86	3445.2274 0518	4793.0764 4810	6686.5410 8247	9349.1626 0105	86
87	3670.1671 8652	5129.5917 9946	7189.0316 6366	10098.0956 0914	87
88	3909.7280 5364	5489.6632 2543	7729.2090 3843	10906.9432 5787	88
89	4164.8603 7713	5874.9396 5121	8309.8997 1631	11780.4987 1850	89
90	4436.5763 0164	6287.1854 2679	8934.1421 9504	12723.9386 1598	90
91	4725.9537 6125	6728.2884 0667	9605.2028 5966	13742.8537 0526	91
92	5034.1407 5573	7200.2685 9513	10326.5930 7414	14843.2820 0168	92
93	5362.3599 0485	7705.2873 9679	11102.0875 5470	16031.7445 6181	93
94	5711.9132 9867	8245.6575 1457	11935.7441 2130	17315.2841 2676	94
95	6084.1876 6308	8823.8535 4059	12831.9249 3040	18701.5068 5690	95
96	6480.6598 6118	9442.5232 8843	13795.3193 0018	20198.6274 0545	96
97	6902.9027 5216	10104.4999 1862	14830.9682 4769	21815.5175 9788	97
98	7352.5914 3105	10812.8149 1292	15944.2908 6627	23561.7590 0572	98
99	7831.5098 7406	11570.7119 5683	17141.1126 8124	25447.6997 2617	99
100	8341.5580 1588	12381.6617 9381	18427.6961 3233	27484.5157 0427	100

TABLE 7 AMOUNT OF ANNUITY

WHEN PERIODIC PAYMENT IS 1

$$s_{\overline{n}|i} = \frac{(1+i)^n - 1}{i}$$

n	$8\frac{1}{2}\%$	9%	$9\frac{1}{2}\%$	10%	n
1	1.0000 0000	1.0000 0000	1.0000 0000	1.0000 0000	1
2	2.0850 0000	2.0900 0000	2.0950 0000	2.1000 0000	2
3	3.2622 2500	3.2781 0000	3.2940 2500	3.3100 0000	3
4	4.5395 1413	4.5731 2900	4.6069 5738	4.6410 0000	4
5	5.9253 7283	5.9847 1061	6.0446 1833	6.1051 0000	5
6	7.4290 2952	7.5233 3456	7.6188 5707	7.7156 1000	6
7	9.0604 9702	9.2004 3468	9.3426 4849	9.4871 7100	7
8	10.8306 3927	11.0284 7380	11.2302 0009	11.4358 8810	8
9	12.7512 4361	13.0210 3644	13.2970 6910	13.5794 7691	9
10	14.8350 9932	15.1929 2972	15.5602 9067	15.9374 2460	10
11	17.0960 8276	17.5602 9339	18.0385 1828	18.5311 6706	11
12	19.5492 4979	20.1407 1980	20.7521 7752	21.3842 8377	12
13	22.2109 3603	22.9533 8458	23.7236 3438	24.5227 1214	13
14	25.0988 6559	26.0191 8919	26.9773 7965	27.9749 8336	14
15	28.2322 6916	29.3609 1622	30.5402 3072	31.7724 8169	15
16	31.6320 1204	33.0033 9868	34.4415 5263	35.9497 2986	16
17	35.3207 3306	36.9737 0456	38.7135 0013	40.5447 0285	17
18	39.3229 9538	41.3013 3797	43.3912 8265	45.5991 7313	18
19	43.6654 4998	46.0184 5839	48.5134 5450	51.1590 9045	19
20	48.3770 1323	51.1601 1964	54.1222 3267	57.2749 9949	20
21	53.4890 5936	56.7645 3041	60.2638 4478	64.0024 9944	21
22	59.0356 2940	62.8733 3815	66.9889 1003	71.4027 4939	22
23	65.0536 5790	69.5319 3858	74.3528 5649	79.5430 2433	23
24	71.5832 1882	76.7898 1305	82.4163 7785	88.4973 2676	24
25	78.6677 9242	84.7008 9623	91.2459 3375	98.3470 5943	25
26	86.3545 5478	93.3239 7689	100.9142 9745	109.1817 6538	26
27	94.6946 9193	102.7231 3481	111.5011 5571	121.0999 4192	27
28	103.7437 4075	112.9682 1694	123.0937 6551	134.2099 3611	28
29	113.5619 5871	124.1353 5646	135.7876 7323	148.6309 2972	29
30	124.2147 2520	136.3075 3855	149.6875 0218	164.4940 2269	30
31	135.7729 7684	149.5752 1702	164.9078 1489	181.9434 2496	31
32	148.3136 7987	164.0369 8655	181.5740 5731	201.1377 6745	32
33	161.9203 4266	179.8003 1534	199.8235 9275	222.2515 4420	33
34	176.6835 7179	196.9823 4372	219.8068 3406	245.4766 9862	34
35	192.7016 7539	215.7107 5465	241.6884 8330	271.0243 6848	35
36	210.0813 1780	236.1247 2257	265.6488 8921	299.1268 0533	36
37	228.9382 2981	258.3759 4760	291.8855 3369	330.0394 8586	37
38	249.3979 7935	282.6297 8288	320.6146 5939	364.0434 3445	38
39	271.5968 0759	309.0664 6334	352.0730 5203	401.4477 7789	39
40	295.6825 3624	337.8824 4504	386.5199 9197	442.5925 5568	40
41	321.8155 5182	369.2918 6510	424.2393 9121	487.8518 1125	41
42	350.1698 7372	403.5281 3296	465.5421 3337	537.6369 9237	42
43	380.9343 1299	440.8456 6492	510.7686 3604	592.4006 9161	43
44	414.3137 2959	481.5217 7477	560.2916 5647	652.6407 6077	44
45	450.5303 9661	525.8587 3450	614.5193 6383	718.9048 3685	45
46	489.8254 8032	574.1860 2060	673.8987 0340	791.7953 2054	46
47	532.4606 4615	626.8627 6245	738.9190 8022	871.9748 5259	47
48	578.7198 0107	684.2804 1107	810.1163 9284	960.1723 3785	48
49	628.9109 8416	746.8656 4807	888.0774 5016	1057.1895 7163	49
50	683.3684 1782	815.0835 5640	973.4448 0793	1163.9085 2880	50

TABLE 7 AMOUNT OF ANNUITY
WHEN PERIODIC PAYMENT IS 1

$$s_{\overline{n}|i} = \frac{(1+i)^n - 1}{i}$$

n	$8\frac{1}{2}\%$	9%	$9\frac{1}{2}\%$	10%	n
51	742.4547 3333	889.4410 7647	1066.9220 6468	1281.2993 8168	51
52	806.5633 8566	970.4907 7336	1169.2796 6082	1410.4293 1984	52
53	876.1212 7345	1058.8349 4296	1281.3612 2860	1552.4722 5183	53
54	951.5915 8169	1155.1300 8782	1404.0905 4532	1708.7194 7701	54
55	1033.4768 6613	1260.0917 9573	1538.4791 4713	1880.5914 2471	55
56	1122.3223 9975	1374.5000 5734	1685.6346 6610	2069.6505 6718	56
57	1218.7198 0373	1499.2050 6251	1846.7699 5938	2277.6156 2390	57
58	1323.3109 8705	1635.1335 1813	2023.2131 0552	2506.3771 8629	58
59	1436.7924 2095	1783.2955 3476	2216.4183 5055	2758.0149 0492	59
60	1559.9197 7673	1944.7921 3289	2427.9780 9385	3034.8163 9541	60
61	1693.5129 5775	2120.8234 2485	2659.6360 1277	3339.2980 3496	61
62	1838.4615 5916	2312.6975 3309	2913.3014 3398	3674.2278 3845	62
63	1995.7307 9169	2521.8403 1107	3191.0650 7021	4042.6506 2230	63
64	2166.3679 0898	2749.8059 3906	3495.2162 5188	4447.9156 8453	64
65	2351.5091 8125	2998.2884 7358	3828.2617 9580	4893.7072 5298	65
66	2552.3874 6165	3269.1344 3620	4192.9466 6641	5384.0779 7828	66
67	2770.3403 9589	3564.3565 3546	4592.2765 9971	5923.4857 7610	67
68	3006.8193 2954	3886.1486 2365	5029.5428 7669	6516.8343 5371	68
69	3263.3989 7255	4236.9019 9978	5508.3494 4997	7169.5177 8909	69
70	3541.7878 8522	4619.2231 7976	6032.6426 4772	7887.4695 6799	70
71	3843.8398 5546	5035.9532 6594	6606.7436 9925	8677.2165 2479	71
72	4171.5662 4318	5490.1890 5987	7235.3843 5068	9545.9381 7727	72
73	4527.1493 7385	5985.3060 7526	7923.7458 6400	10501.5319 9500	73
74	4912.9570 7063	6524.9836 2203	8677.5017 2108	11552.6851 9450	74
75	5331.5584 2163	7113.2321 4801	9502.8643 8458	12708.9537 1395	75
76	5785.7408 8747	7754.4230 4134	10406.6365 0111	13980.8490 8535	76
77	6278.5288 6290	8453.3211 1506	11396.2669 6872	15379.9339 9388	77
78	6813.2038 1625	9215.1200 1541	12479.9123 3075	16918.9273 9327	78
79	7393.3261 4063	10045.4808 1680	13666.5040 0217	18611.8201 3260	79
80	8022.7588 6259	10950.5740 9031	14965.8218 8238	20474.0021 4585	80
81	8705.6933 6591	11937.1257 5844	16388.5749 6120	22522.4023 6044	81
82	9446.6773 0201	13012.4670 7670	17946.4895 8251	24775.6425 9648	82
83	10250.6448 7268	14184.5891 1360	19652.4060 9285	27254.2068 5613	83
84	11122.9496 8686	15462.2021 3382	21520.3846 7168	29980.6275 4175	84
85	12069.4004 1024	16854.8003 2587	23565.8212 1548	32979.6902 9592	85
86	13096.2994 4511	18372.7323 5520	25805.5742 3096	36278.6593 2551	86
87	14210.4848 9794	20027.2782 6716	28258.1037 8290	39907.5252 5806	87
88	15419.3761 1427	21830.7333 1121	30943.6236 4227	43899.2777 8387	88
89	16731.0230 8398	23796.4993 0922	33884.2678 8829	48290.2055 6226	89
90	18154.1600 4612	25939.1842 4705	37104.2733 3767	53120.2261 1848	90
91	19698.2636 5004	28274.7108 2928	40630.1793 0475	58433.2487 3033	91
92	21373.6160 6029	30820.4348 0392	44491.0463 3870	64277.5736 0336	92
93	23191.3734 2542	33595.2739 3627	48718.6957 4088	70706.3309 6370	93
94	25163.6401 6658	36619.8485 9054	53347.9718 3627	77777.9640 6007	94
95	27303.5495 8074	39916.6349 6368	58417.0291 6071	85556.7604 6608	95
96	29625.3512 9510	43510.1321 1041	63967.6469 3098	94113.4365 1269	96
97	32144.5061 5518	47427.0440 0035	70045.5733 8942	103525.7801 6395	97
98	34877.7891 7837	51696.4779 6038	76700.9028 6142	113879.3581 8035	98
99	37843.4012 5853	56350.1609 7682	83988.4886 3325	125268.2939 9838	99
100	41061.0903 6551	61422.6754 6473	91968.3950 5341	137796.1233 9822	100

TABLE 7A SUPPLEMENT TO TABLE 7
FOR FRACTIONAL INTEREST PERIODS

$$s_{\overline{1/m}|i} = \frac{(1+i)^{\frac{1}{m}} - 1}{i}$$

m	$\frac{1}{4}$%	$\frac{1}{3}$%	$\frac{5}{12}$%	$\frac{11}{24}$%	$\frac{1}{2}$%	m
2	.4996 8789	.4995 8403	.4994 8025	.4994 2839	.4993 7656	2
3	.3330 5594	.3329 6365	.3328 7144	.3328 2537	.3327 7932	3
4	.2497 6597	.2496 8811	.2496 1032	.2495 7146	.2495 3261	4
6	.1664 9332	.1664 3566	.1663 7805	.1663 4927	.1663 2050	6
12	.0832 3800	.0832 0629	.0831 7461	.0831 5879	.0831 4297	12

m	$\frac{13}{24}$%	$\frac{7}{12}$%	$\frac{5}{8}$%	$\frac{2}{3}$%	$\frac{3}{4}$%	m
2	.4993 2474	.4992 7295	.4992 2118	.4991 6943	.4990 6600	2
3	.3327 3329	.3326 8728	.3326 4129	.3325 9532	.3325 0345	3
4	.2494 9379	.2494 5498	.2494 1619	.2493 7742	.2492 9994	4
6	.1662 9175	.1662 6301	.1662 3429	.1662 0558	.1661 4821	6
12	.0831 2716	.0831 1136	.0830 9557	.0830 7978	.0830 4824	12

m	$\frac{7}{8}$%	1%	$1\frac{1}{8}$%	$1\frac{1}{4}$%	$1\frac{3}{8}$%	m
2	.4989 1101	.4987 5621	.4986 0161	.4984 4719	.4982 9297	2
3	.3323 6581	.3322 2835	.3320 9109	.3319 5401	.3318 1712	3
4	.2491 8385	.2490 6793	.2489 5218	.2488 3660	.2487 2118	4
6	.1660 6226	.1659 7644	.1658 9075	.1658 0518	.1657 1975	6
12	.0830 0099	.0829 5381	.0829 0671	.0828 5968	.0828 1273	12

m	$1\frac{1}{2}$%	$1\frac{5}{8}$%	$1\frac{3}{4}$%	$1\frac{7}{8}$%	2%	m
2	.4981 3893	.4979 8509	.4978 3143	.4976 7797	.4975 2469	2
3	.3316 8042	.3315 4390	.3314 0758	.3312 7143	.3311 3548	3
4	.2486 0593	.2484 9084	.2483 7592	.2482 6117	.2481 4658	4
6	.1656 3445	.1655 4927	.1654 6423	.1653 7931	.1652 9452	6
12	.0827 6585	.0827 1904	.0826 7231	.0826 2565	.0825 7907	12

m	$2\frac{1}{4}$%	$2\frac{1}{2}$%	$2\frac{3}{4}$%	3%	$3\frac{1}{4}$%	m
2	.4972 1870	.4969 1346	.4966 0897	.4963 0522	.4960 0220	2
3	.3308 6412	.3305 9350	.3303 2362	.3300 5447	.3297 8604	3
4	.2479 1789	.2476 8985	.2474 6247	.2472 3573	.2470 0963	4
6	.1651 2531	.1649 5662	.1647 8843	.1646 2073	.1644 5354	6
12	.0824 8611	.0823 9345	.0823 0108	.0822 0899	.0821 1719	12

m	$3\frac{1}{2}$%	$3\frac{3}{4}$%	4%	$4\frac{1}{2}$%	5%	m
2	.4956 9993	.4953 9838	.4950 9757	.4944 9811	.4939 0153	2
3	.3295 1834	.3292 5136	.3289 8510	.3284 5470	.3279 2714	3
4	.2467 8417	.2465 5935	.2463 3516	.2458 8868	.2454 4469	4
6	.1642 8684	.1641 2064	.1639 5492	.1636 2496	.1632 9692	6
12	.0820 2568	.0819 3445	.0818 4349	.0816 6243	.0814 8248	12

TABLE 7A SUPPLEMENT TO TABLE 7

FOR FRACTIONAL INTEREST PERIODS

$$s_{\overline{1/m}|i} = \frac{(1+i)^{\frac{1}{m}} - 1}{i}$$

m	$5\frac{1}{2}\%$	6%	$6\frac{1}{2}\%$	7%	$7\frac{1}{2}\%$	m
2	.4933 0780	.4927 1690	.4921 2880	.4915 4348	.4909 6090	2
3	.3274 0237	.3268 8037	.3263 6113	.3258 4460	.3253 3076	3
4	.2450 0317	.2445 6410	.2441 2746	.2436 9321	.2432 6135	4
6	.1629 7080	.1626 4657	.1623 2422	.1620 0372	.1616 8505	6
12	.0813 0362	.0811 2584	.0809 4914	.0807 7351	.0805 9892	12

m	8%	$8\frac{1}{2}\%$	9%	$9\frac{1}{2}\%$	10%	m
2	.4903 8106	.4898 0392	.4892 2945	.4886 5765	.4880 8848	2
3	.3248 1960	.3243 1108	.3238 0518	.3233 0188	.3228 0115	3
4	.2428 3184	.2424 0466	.2419 7979	.2415 5721	.2411 3689	4
6	.1613 6821	.1610 5317	.1607 3991	.1604 2842	.1601 1868	6
12	.0804 2538	.0802 5286	.0800 8137	.0799 1089	.0797 4140	12

TABLE 8 PRESENT VALUE OF ANNUITY

WHEN PERIODIC PAYMENT IS 1

$$a_{\overline{n}|i} = \frac{1-(1+i)^{-n}}{i}$$

n	$\frac{1}{4}$%	$\frac{1}{3}$%	$\frac{5}{12}$%	$\frac{11}{24}$%	n
1	0.9975 0623	0.9966 7774	0.9958 5062	0.9954 3758	1
2	1.9925 2492	1.9900 4426	1.9875 6908	1.9863 3355	2
3	2.9850 6227	2.9801 1056	2.9751 7253	2.9727 0863	3
4	3.9751 2446	3.9668 8760	3.9586 7804	3.9545 8346	4
5	4.9627 1766	4.9503 8631	4.9381 0261	4.9319 7856	5
6	5.9478 4804	5.9306 1759	5.9134 6318	5.9049 1437	6
7	6.9305 2174	6.9075 9228	6.8847 7661	6.8734 1123	7
8	7.9107 4487	7.8813 2121	7.8520 5970	7.8374 8941	8
9	8.8885 2357	8.8518 1516	8.8153 2916	8.7971 6905	9
10	9.8638 6391	9.8190 8487	9.7746 0165	9.7524 7023	10
11	10.8367 7198	10.7831 4107	10.7298 9376	10.7034 1292	11
12	11.8072 5384	11.7439 9442	11.6812 2200	11.6500 1701	12
13	12.7753 1555	12.7016 5557	12.6286 0283	12.5923 0229	13
14	13.7409 6314	13.6561 3512	13.5720 5261	13.5302 8846	14
15	14.7042 0264	14.6074 4364	14.5115 8766	14.4639 9515	15
16	15.6650 4004	15.5555 9167	15.4472 2422	15.3934 4188	16
17	16.6234 8133	16.5005 8970	16.3789 7848	16.3186 4807	17
18	17.5795 3250	17.4424 4821	17.3068 6654	17.2396 3309	18
19	18.5331 9950	18.3811 7762	18.2309 0443	18.1564 1618	19
20	19.4844 8828	19.3167 8832	19.1511 0815	19.0690 1652	20
21	20.4334 0477	20.2492 9069	20.0674 9359	19.9774 5320	21
22	21.3799 5488	21.1786 9504	20.9800 7661	20.8817 4520	22
23	22.3241 4452	22.1050 1167	21.8888 7297	21.7819 1144	23
24	23.2659 7957	23.0282 5083	22.7938 9839	22.6779 7074	24
25	24.2054 6591	23.9484 2275	23.6951 6853	23.5699 4184	25
26	25.1426 0939	24.8655 3763	24.5926 9895	24.4578 4339	26
27	26.0774 1585	25.7796 0561	25.4865 0517	25.3416 9396	27
28	27.0098 9112	26.6906 3682	26.3766 0266	26.2215 1203	28
29	27.9400 4102	27.5986 4135	27.2630 0680	27.0973 1600	29
30	28.8678 7134	28.5036 2925	28.1457 3291	27.9691 2418	30
31	29.7933 8787	29.4056 1055	29.0247 9626	28.8369 5480	31
32	30.7165 9638	30.3045 9523	29.9002 1205	29.7008 2601	32
33	31.6375 0262	31.2005 9325	30.7719 9540	30.5607 5588	33
34	32.5561 1234	32.0936 1454	31.6401 6139	31.4167 6239	34
35	33.4724 3126	32.9836 6898	32.5047 2504	32.2688 6343	35
36	34.3864 6510	33.8707 6642	33.3657 0128	33.1170 7683	36
37	35.2982 1955	34.7549 1670	34.2231 0501	33.9614 2032	37
38	36.2077 0030	35.6361 2960	35.0769 5105	34.8019 1156	38
39	37.1149 1302	36.5144 1488	35.9272 5416	35.6385 6812	39
40	38.0198 6336	37.3897 8228	36.7740 2904	36.4714 0750	40
41	38.9225 5697	38.2622 4147	37.6172 9033	37.3004 4712	41
42	39.8229 9947	39.1318 0213	38.4570 5261	38.1257 0431	42
43	40.7211 9648	39.9984 7389	39.2933 3040	38.9471 9633	43
44	41.6171 5359	40.8622 6633	40.1261 3816	39.7649 4035	44
45	42.5108 7640	41.7231 8903	40.9554 9028	40.5789 5348	45
46	43.4023 7048	42.5812 5153	41.7814 0111	41.3892 5274	46
47	44.2916 4137	43.4364 6332	42.6038 8492	42.1958 5507	47
48	45.1786 9463	44.2888 3387	43.4229 5594	42.9987 7734	48
49	46.0635 3580	45.1383 7263	44.2386 2832	43.7980 3634	49
50	46.9461 7037	45.9850 8900	45.0509 1617	44.5936 4878	50
51	47.8266 0386	46.8289 9236	45.8598 3353	45.3856 3131	51
52	48.7048 4176	47.6700 9205	46.6653 9439	46.1740 0047	52
53	49.5808 8953	48.5083 9739	47.4676 1267	46.9587 7276	53
54	50.4547 5265	49.3439 1767	48.2665 0224	47.7399 6459	54
55	51.3264 3656	50.1766 6213	49.0620 7692	48.5175 9229	55
56	52.1959 4669	51.0066 3999	49.8543 5046	49.2916 7213	56
57	53.0632 8847	51.8338 6046	50.6433 3656	50.0622 2029	57
58	53.9284 6730	52.6583 3268	51.4290 4885	50.8292 5288	58
59	54.7914 8858	53.4800 6580	52.2115 0093	51.5927 8594	59
60	55.6523 5769	54.2990 6890	52.9907 0632	52.3528 3545	60

TABLE 8 PRESENT VALUE OF ANNUITY

WHEN PERIODIC PAYMENT IS 1

$$a_{\overline{n}|i} = \frac{1-(1+i)^{-n}}{i}$$

n	$\frac{1}{4}$%	$\frac{1}{3}$%	$\frac{5}{12}$%	$\frac{11}{24}$%	n
61	56.5110 7999	55.1153 5106	53.7666 7850	53.1094 1728	61
62	57.3676 6083	55.9289 2133	54.5394 3087	53.8625 4727	62
63	58.2221 0557	56.7397 8870	55.3089 7680	54.6122 4117	63
64	59.0744 1952	57.5479 6216	56.0753 2959	55.3585 1464	64
65	59.9246 0800	58.3534 5065	56.8385 0250	56.1013 8330	65
66	60.7726 7631	59.1562 6311	57.5985 0871	56.8408 6268	66
67	61.6186 2974	59.9564 0842	58.3553 6137	57.5769 6825	67
68	62.4624 7355	60.7538 9543	59.1090 7357	58.3097 1538	68
69	63.3042 1302	61.5487 3299	59.8596 5832	59.0391 1942	69
70	64.1438 5339	62.3409 2989	60.6071 2862	59.7651 9561	70
71	64.9813 9989	63.1304 9491	61.3514 9738	60.4879 5913	71
72	65.8168 5774	63.9174 3678	62.0927 7748	61.2074 2510	72
73	66.6502 3216	64.7017 6424	62.8309 8172	61.9236 0856	73
74	67.4815 2834	65.4834 8595	63.5661 2287	62.6365 2449	74
75	68.3107 5146	66.2626 1058	64.2982 1365	63.3461 8779	75
76	69.1379 0670	67.0391 4676	65.0272 6670	64.0526 1331	76
77	69.9629 9920	67.8131 0308	65.7532 9464	64.7558 1582	77
78	70.7860 3411	68.5844 8812	66.4763 1002	65.4558 1003	78
79	71.6070 1657	69.3533 1042	67.1963 2533	66.1526 1056	79
80	72.4259 5169	70.1195 7849	67.9133 5303	66.8462 3200	80
81	73.2428 4458	70.8833 0082	68.6274 0550	67.5366 8884	81
82	74.0577 0033	71.6444 8587	69.3384 9511	68.2239 9553	82
83	74.8705 2402	72.4031 4206	70.0466 3413	68.9081 6643	83
84	75.6813 2072	73.1592 7780	70.7518 3482	69.5892 1586	84
85	76.4900 9548	73.9129 0146	71.4541 0936	70.2671 5805	85
86	77.2968 5335	74.6640 2139	72.1534 6991	70.9420 0719	86
87	78.1015 9935	75.4126 4591	72.8499 2854	71.6137 7737	87
88	78.9043 3850	76.1587 8330	73.5434 9730	72.2824 8266	88
89	79.7050 7581	76.9024 4182	74.2341 8818	72.9481 3703	89
90	80.5038 1627	77.6436 2972	74.9220 1313	73.6107 5441	90
91	81.3005 6486	78.3823 5521	75.6069 8403	74.2703 4864	91
92	82.0953 2654	79.1186 2645	76.2891 1272	74.9269 3353	92
93	82.8881 0628	79.8524 5161	76.9684 1101	75.5805 2280	93
94	83.6789 0900	80.5838 3882	77.6448 9063	76.2311 3012	94
95	84.4677 3966	81.3127 9616	78.3185 6329	76.8787 6910	95
96	85.2546 0315	82.0393 3172	78.9894 4062	77.5234 5327	96
97	86.0395 0439	82.7634 5355	79.6575 3422	78.1651 9612	97
98	86.8224 4827	83.4851 6965	80.3228 5566	78.8040 1107	98
99	87.6034 3967	84.2044 8802	80.9854 1642	79.4399 1148	99
100	88.3824 8346	84.9214 1663	81.6452 2797	80.0729 1064	100
101	89.1595 8450	85.6359 6342	82.3023 0172	80.7030 2179	101
102	89.9347 4763	86.3481 3630	82.9566 4901	81.3302 5810	102
103	90.7079 7768	87.0579 4315	83.6082 8117	81.9546 3270	103
104	91.4792 7948	87.7653 9185	84.2572 0947	82.5761 5864	104
105	92.2486 5784	88.4704 9021	84.9034 4511	83.1948 4892	105
106	93.0161 1755	89.1732 4606	85.5469 9928	83.8107 1647	106
107	93.7816 6339	89.8736 6717	86.1878 8310	84.4237 7417	107
108	94.5453 0014	90.5717 6130	86.8261 0765	85.0340 3484	108
109	95.3070 3256	91.2675 3618	87.4616 8397	85.6415 1125	109
110	96.0668 6539	91.9609 9951	88.0946 2304	86.2462 1609	110
111	96.8248 0338	92.6521 5898	88.7249 3581	86.8481 6202	111
112	97.5808 5126	93.3410 2224	89.3526 3317	87.4473 6161	112
113	98.3350 1372	94.0275 9692	89.9777 2598	88.0438 2740	113
114	99.0872 9548	94.7118 9062	90.6002 2504	88.6375 7186	114
115	99.8377 0123	95.3939 1092	91.2201 4112	89.2286 0741	115
116	100.5862 3564	96.0736 6536	91.8374 8493	89.8169 4641	116
117	101.3329 0338	96.7511 6149	92.4522 6715	90.4026 0115	117
118	102.0777 0911	97.4264 0680	93.0644 9841	90.9855 8389	118
119	102.8206 5747	98.0994 0877	93.6741 8929	91.5659 0682	119
120	103.5617 5308	98.7701 7486	94.2813 5033	92.1435 8207	120

TABLE 8 PRESENT VALUE OF ANNUITY
WHEN PERIODIC PAYMENT IS 1

$$a_{\overline{n}|i} = \frac{1-(1+i)^{-n}}{i}$$

n	$\frac{1}{4}$%	$\frac{1}{3}$%	$\frac{5}{12}$%	$\frac{11}{24}$%	n
121	104.3010 0058	99.4387 1248	94.8859 9203	92.7186 2172	121
122	105.0384 0457	100.1050 2905	95.4881 2484	93.2910 3780	122
123	105.7739 6965	100.7691 3195	96.0877 5918	93.8608 4227	123
124	106.5077 0040	101.4310 2852	96.6849 0541	94.4280 4705	124
125	107.2396 0139	102.0907 2610	97.2795 7385	94.9926 6401	125
126	107.9696 7720	102.7482 3199	97.8717 7479	95.5547 0495	126
127	108.6979 3237	103.4035 5348	98.4615 1846	96.1141 8161	127
128	109.4243 7144	104.0566 9782	99.0488 1506	96.6711 0571	128
129	110.1489 9894	104.7076 7225	99.6336 7475	97.2254 8889	129
130	110.8718 1939	105.3564 8397	100.2161 0764	97.7773 4273	130
131	111.5928 3730	106.0031 4016	100.7961 2379	98.3266 7879	131
132	112.3120 5716	106.6476 4800	101.3737 3323	98.8735 0854	132
133	113.0294 8345	107.2900 1462	101.9489 4596	99.4178 4343	133
134	113.7451 2065	107.9302 4713	102.5217 7191	99.9596 9483	134
135	114.4589 7321	108.5683 5262	103.0922 2099	100.4990 7407	135
136	115.1710 4560	109.2043 3816	103.6603 0306	101.0359 9244	136
137	115.8813 4224	109.8382 1079	104.2260 2794	101.5704 6116	137
138	116.5898 6758	110.4699 7754	104.7894 0542	102.1024 9141	138
139	117.2966 2601	111.0996 4538	105.3504 4523	102.6320 9431	139
140	118.0016 2196	111.7272 2131	105.9091 5708	103.1592 8094	140
141	118.7048 5981	112.3527 1227	106.4655 5061	103.6840 6232	141
142	119.4063 4395	112.9761 2519	107.0196 3547	104.2064 4942	142
143	120.1060 7875	113.5974 6696	107.5714 2121	104.7264 5318	143
144	120.8040 6858	114.2167 4448	108.1209 1739	105.2440 8446	144
145	121.5003 1778	114.8339 6460	108.6681 3350	105.7593 5409	145
146	122.1948 3071	115.4491 3415	109.2130 7900	106.2722 7284	146
147	122.8876 1168	116.0622 5995	109.7557 6332	106.7828 5143	147
148	123.5786 6502	116.6733 4879	110.2961 9584	107.2911 0056	148
149	124.2679 9503	117.2824 0743	110.8343 8590	107.7970 3083	149
150	124.9556 0601	117.8894 4262	111.3703 4280	108.3006 5284	150
151	125.6415 0226	118.4944 6109	111.9040 7582	108.8019 7711	151
152	126.3256 8804	119.0974 6952	112.4355 9418	109.3010 1413	152
153	127.0081 6762	119.6984 7461	112.9649 0707	109.7977 7433	153
154	127.6889 4525	120.2974 8300	113.4920 2364	110.2922 6810	154
155	128.3680 2519	120.8945 0133	114.0169 5300	110.7845 0578	155
156	129.0454 1166	121.4895 3621	114.5397 0423	111.2744 9767	156
157	129.7211 0889	122.0825 9422	115.0602 8637	111.7622 5400	157
158	130.3951 2109	122.6736 8195	115.5787 0842	112.2477 8499	158
159	131.0674 5246	123.2628 0593	116.0949 7934	112.7311 0078	159
160	131.7381 0719	123.8499 7269	116.6091 0805	113.2122 1148	160
161	132.4070 8946	124.4351 8873	117.1211 0346	113.6911 2714	161
162	133.0744 0346	125.0184 6053	117.6309 7440	114.1678 5779	162
163	133.7400 5332	125.5997 9454	118.1387 2969	114.6424 1340	163
164	134.4040 4321	126.1791 9722	118.6443 7811	115.1148 0388	164
165	135.0663 7727	126.7566 7497	119.1479 2841	115.5850 3912	165
166	135.7270 5962	127.3322 3419	119.6493 8929	116.0531 2895	166
167	136.3860 9439	127.9058 8125	120.1487 6942	116.5190 8315	167
168	137.0434 8567	128.4776 2251	120.6460 7743	116.9829 1147	168
169	137.6992 3758	129.0474 6430	121.1413 2192	117.4446 2361	169
170	138.3533 5419	129.6154 1292	121.6345 1146	117.9042 2923	170
171	139.0058 3959	130.1814 7467	122.1256 5456	118.3617 3793	171
172	139.6566 9785	130.7456 5582	122.6147 5973	118.8171 5928	172
173	140.3059 3302	131.3079 6261	123.1018 3542	119.2705 0281	173
174	140.9535 4914	131.8684 0127	123.5868 9004	119.7217 7799	174
175	141.5995 5027	132.4269 7801	124.0699 3199	120.1709 9427	175
176	142.2439 4042	132.9837 9901	124.5509 6962	120.6181 6103	176
177	142.8867 2361	133.5385 7045	125.0300 1124	121.0632 8763	177
178	143.5279 0385	134.0915 9845	125.5070 6513	121.5063 8337	178
179	144.1674 8514	134.6427 8915	125.9821 3955	121.9474 5753	179
180	144.8054 7146	135.1921 4866	126.4552 4271	122.3865 1931	180

TABLE 8 PRESENT VALUE OF ANNUITY

WHEN PERIODIC PAYMENT IS 1

$$a_{\overline{n}|i} = \frac{1-(1+i)^{-n}}{i}$$

n	$\frac{1}{4}\%$	$\frac{1}{3}\%$	$\frac{5}{12}\%$	$\frac{11}{24}\%$	n
181	145.4418 6679	135.7396 8305	126.9263 8278	122.8235 7792	181
182	146.0766 7510	136.2853 9839	127.3955 6791	123.2586 4247	182
183	146.7099 0035	136.8293 0072	127.8628 0622	123.6917 2208	183
184	147.3415 4649	137.3713 9606	128.3281 0578	124.1228 2579	184
185	147.9716 1744	137.9116 9043	128.7914 7463	124.5519 6263	185
186	148.6001 1715	138.4501 8980	129.2529 2080	124.9791 4157	186
187	149.2270 4952	138.9869 0013	129.7124 5225	125.4043 7153	187
188	149.8524 1848	139.5218 2737	130.1700 7693	125.8276 6141	188
189	150.4762 2791	140.0549 7745	130.6258 0275	126.2490 2007	189
190	151.0984 8170	140.5863 5626	131.0796 3759	126.6684 5631	190
191	151.7191 8375	141.1159 6969	131.5315 8930	127.0859 7891	191
192	152.3383 3790	141.6438 2362	131.9816 6570	127.5015 9659	192
193	152.9559 4803	142.1699 2387	132.4298 7455	127.9153 1805	193
194	153.5720 1799	142.6942 7628	132.8762 2362	128.3271 5194	194
195	154.1865 5161	143.2168 8666	133.3207 2062	128.7371 0687	195
196	154.7995 5272	143.7377 6079	133.7633 7323	129.1451 9141	196
197	155.4110 2516	144.2569 0444	134.2041 8911	129.5514 1409	197
198	156.0209 7273	144.7743 2336	134.6431 7587	129.9557 8342	198
199	156.6293 9923	145.2900 2329	135.0803 4112	130.3583 0784	199
200	157.2363 0846	145.8040 0992	135.5156 9240	130.7589 9577	200
201	157.8417 0420	146.3162 8896	135.9492 3725	131.1578 5560	201
202	158.4455 9022	146.8268 6607	136.3809 8315	131.5548 9567	202
203	159.0479 7030	147.3357 4691	136.8109 3758	131.9501 2426	203
204	159.6488 4818	147.8429 3712	137.2391 0796	132.3435 4966	204
205	160.2482 2761	148.3484 4232	137.6655 0170	132.7351 8008	205
206	160.8461 1233	148.8522 6809	138.0901 2618	133.1250 2373	206
207	161.4425 0606	149.3544 2002	138.5129 8872	133.5130 8874	207
208	162.0374 1253	149.8549 0368	138.9340 9665	133.8993 8323	208
209	162.6308 3544	150.3537 2459	139.3534 5725	134.2839 1528	209
210	163.2227 7850	150.8508 8830	139.7710 7776	134.6666 9294	210
211	163.8132 4538	151.3464 0030	140.1869 6540	135.0477 2421	211
212	164.4022 3978	151.8402 6608	140.6011 2737	135.4270 1704	212
213	164.9897 6537	152.3324 9111	141.0135 7083	135.8045 7939	213
214	165.5758 2581	152.8230 8084	141.4243 0290	136.1804 1913	214
215	166.1604 2474	153.3120 4070	141.8333 3069	136.5545 4414	215
216	166.7435 6583	153.7993 7612	142.2406 6127	136.9269 6223	216
217	167.3252 5270	154.2850 9247	142.6463 0167	137.2976 8119	217
218	167.9054 8898	154.7691 9516	143.0502 5893	137.6667 0878	218
219	168.4842 7828	155.2516 8953	143.4525 4001	138.0340 5270	219
220	169.0616 2422	155.7325 8092	143.8531 5188	138.3997 2065	220
221	169.6375 3039	156.2118 7467	144.2521 0146	138.7637 2026	221
222	170.2120 0039	156.6895 7609	144.6493 9564	139.1260 5916	222
223	170.7850 3780	157.1656 9045	145.0450 4130	139.4867 4491	223
224	171.3566 4618	157.6402 2304	145.4390 4528	139.8457 8506	224
225	171.9268 2911	158.1131 7911	145.8314 1439	140.2031 8712	225
226	172.4955 9013	158.5845 6390	146.2221 5541	140.5589 5856	226
227	173.0629 3280	159.0543 8262	146.6112 7509	140.9131 0682	227
228	173.6288 6065	159.5226 4049	146.9987 8018	141.2656 3931	228
229	174.1933 7721	159.9893 4268	147.3846 7735	141.6165 6339	229
230	174.7564 8599	160.4544 9436	147.7689 7330	141.9658 8641	230
231	175.3181 9052	160.9181 0070	148.1516 7465	142.3136 1568	231
232	175.8784 9428	161.3801 6681	148.5327 8804	142.6597 5845	232
233	176.4374 0078	161.8406 9781	148.9123 2004	143.0043 2197	233
234	176.9949 1350	162.2996 9882	149.2902 7722	143.3473 1345	234
235	177.5510 3591	162.7571 7490	149.6666 6611	143.6887 4006	235
236	178.1057 7148	163.2131 3113	150.0414 9322	144.0286 0894	236
237	178.6591 2367	163.6675 7256	150.4147 6503	144.3669 2719	237
238	179.2110 9593	164.1205 0421	150.7864 8800	144.7037 0189	238
239	179.7616 9170	164.5719 3110	151.1566 6855	145.0389 4008	239
240	180.3109 1441	165.0218 5824	151.5253 1307	145.3726 4877	240

TABLE 8 PRESENT VALUE OF ANNUITY

WHEN PERIODIC PAYMENT IS 1

$$a_{\overline{n}|i} = \frac{1-(1+i)^{-n}}{i}$$

n	$\frac{1}{2}\%$	$\frac{13}{24}\%$	$\frac{7}{12}\%$	$\frac{5}{8}\%$	n
1	0.9950 2488	0.9946 1252	0.9942 0050	0.9937 8882	1
2	1.9850 9938	1.9838 6657	1.9826 3513	1.9814 0504	2
3	2.9702 4814	2.9677 9104	2.9653 3732	2.9628 8699	3
4	3.9504 9566	3.9464 1462	3.9423 4034	3.9382 7279	4
5	4.9258 6633	4.9197 6589	4.9136 7722	4.9076 0029	5
6	5.8963 8441	5.8878 7325	5.8793 8083	5.8709 0712	6
7	6.8620 7404	6.8507 6494	6.8394 8384	6.8282 3068	7
8	7.8229 5924	7.8084 6906	7.7940 1874	7.7796 0813	8
9	8.7790 6392	8.7610 1357	8.7430 1780	8.7250 7640	9
10	9.7304 1186	9.7084 2626	9.6865 1314	9.6646 7220	10
11	10.6770 2673	10.6507 3478	10.6245 3667	10.5984 3200	11
12	11.6189 3207	11.5879 6663	11.5571 2014	11.5263 9205	12
13	12.5561 5131	12.5201 4916	12.4842 9509	12.4485 8837	13
14	13.4887 0777	13.4473 0956	13.4060 9288	13.3650 5676	14
15	14.4166 2465	14.3694 7491	14.3225 4470	14.2758 3281	15
16	15.3399 2502	15.2866 7210	15.2336 8156	15.1809 5186	16
17	16.2586 3186	16.1989 2791	16.1395 3427	16.0804 4905	17
18	17.1727 6802	17.1062 6895	17.0401 3350	16.9743 5931	18
19	18.0823 5624	18.0087 2171	17.9355 0969	17.8627 1733	19
20	18.9874 1915	18.9063 1251	18.8256 9315	18.7455 5759	20
21	19.8879 7925	19.7990 6756	19.7107 1398	19.6229 1438	21
22	20.7840 5896	20.6870 1291	20.5906 0213	20.4948 2174	22
23	21.6756 8055	21.5701 7447	21.4653 8738	21.3613 1353	23
24	22.5628 6622	22.4485 7800	22.3350 9930	22.2224 2338	24
25	23.4456 3803	23.3222 4915	23.1997 6732	23.0781 8473	25
26	24.3240 1794	24.1912 1341	24.0594 2070	23.9286 3079	26
27	25.1980 2780	25.0554 9614	24.9140 8852	24.7737 9457	27
28	26.0676 8936	25.9151 2256	25.7637 9968	25.6137 0889	28
29	26.9330 2423	26.7701 1776	26.6085 8295	26.4484 0635	29
30	27.7940 5397	27.6205 0668	27.4484 6689	27.2779 1935	30
31	28.6507 9997	28.4663 1414	28.2834 7993	28.1022 8010	31
32	29.5032 8355	29.3075 6483	29.1136 5030	28.9215 2060	32
33	30.3515 2592	30.1442 8330	29.9390 0610	29.7356 7265	33
34	31.1955 4818	30.9764 9396	30.7595 7524	30.5447 6785	34
35	32.0353 7132	31.8042 2109	31.5753 8549	31.3488 3761	35
36	32.8710 1624	32.6274 8886	32.3864 6445	32.1479 1315	36
37	33.7025 0372	33.4463 2129	33.1928 3955	32.9420 2550	37
38	34.5298 5445	34.2607 4227	33.9945 3808	33.7312 0546	38
39	35.3530 8900	35.0707 7557	34.7915 8716	34.5154 8369	39
40	36.1722 2786	35.8764 4482	35.5840 1374	35.2948 9062	40
41	36.9872 9141	36.6777 7355	36.3718 4465	36.0694 5652	41
42	37.7982 9991	37.4747 8513	37.1551 0653	36.8392 1145	42
43	38.6052 7354	38.2675 0282	37.9338 2588	37.6041 8529	43
44	39.4082 3238	39.0559 4976	38.7080 2904	38.3644 0774	44
45	40.2071 9640	39.8401 4896	39.4777 4221	39.1199 0831	45
46	41.0021 8547	40.6201 2329	40.2429 9143	39.8707 1634	46
47	41.7932 1937	41.3958 9552	41.0038 0258	40.6168 6096	47
48	42.5803 1778	42.1674 8829	41.7602 0141	41.3583 7114	48
49	43.3635 0028	42.9349 2412	42.5122 1349	42.0952 7566	49
50	44.1427 8635	43.6982 2540	43.2598 6428	42.8276 0314	50
51	44.9181 9537	44.4574 1441	44.0031 7907	43.5553 8201	51
52	45.6897 4664	45.2125 1329	44.7421 8301	44.2786 4050	52
53	46.4574 5934	45.9635 4409	45.4769 0108	44.9974 0671	53
54	47.2213 5258	46.7105 2873	46.2073 5816	45.7117 0853	54
55	47.9814 4535	47.4534 8900	46.9335 7895	46.4215 7370	55
56	48.7377 5657	48.1924 4658	47.6555 8802	47.1270 2976	56
57	49.4903 0505	48.9274 2304	48.3734 0980	47.8281 0410	57
58	50.2391 0950	49.6584 3982	49.0870 6856	48.5248 2396	58
59	50.9841 8855	50.3855 1826	49.7965 8846	49.2172 1636	59
60	51.7255 6075	51.1086 7958	50.5019 9350	49.9053 0818	60

TABLE 8 PRESENT VALUE OF ANNUITY

WHEN PERIODIC PAYMENT IS 1

$$a_{\overline{n}|i} = \frac{1-(1+i)^{-n}}{i}$$

n	$\frac{1}{2}$%	$\frac{13}{24}$%	$\frac{7}{12}$%	$\frac{5}{8}$%	n
61	52.4632 4453	51.8279 4488	51.2033 0754	50.5891 2614	61
62	53.1972 5824	52.5433 3515	51.9005 5431	51.2686 9679	62
63	53.9276 2014	53.2548 7126	52.5937 5739	51.9440 4650	63
64	54.6543 4839	53.9625 7399	53.2829 4024	52.6152 0149	64
65	55.3774 6109	54.6664 6398	53.9681 2617	53.2821 8781	65
66	56.0969 7621	55.3665 6177	54.6493 3836	53.9450 3137	66
67	56.8129 1165	56.0628 8779	55.3265 9986	54.6037 5788	67
68	57.5252 8522	56.7554 6237	55.9999 3358	55.2583 9293	68
69	58.2341 1465	57.4443 0571	56.6693 6230	55.9089 6191	69
70	58.9394 1756	58.1294 3792	57.3349 0867	56.5554 9010	70
71	59.6412 1151	58.8108 7900	57.9965 9520	57.1980 0259	71
72	60.3395 1394	59.4886 4882	58.6544 4427	57.8365 2431	72
73	61.0343 4222	60.1627 6716	59.3084 7815	58.4710 8006	73
74	61.7257 1366	60.8332 5370	59.9587 1896	59.1016 9447	74
75	62.4136 4543	61.5001 2801	60.6051 8869	59.7283 9202	75
76	63.0981 5466	62.1634 0954	61.2479 0922	60.3511 9704	76
77	63.7792 5836	62.8231 1765	61.8869 0229	60.9701 3370	77
78	64.4569 7350	63.4792 7160	62.5221 8952	61.5852 2604	78
79	65.1313 1691	64.1318 9053	63.1537 9239	62.1964 9793	79
80	65.8023 0538	64.7809 9348	63.7817 3229	62.8039 7309	80
81	66.4699 5561	65.4265 9940	64.4060 3044	63.4076 7512	81
82	67.1342 8419	66.0687 2713	65.0267 0798	64.0076 2745	82
83	67.7953 0765	66.7073 9540	65.6437 8590	64.6038 5337	83
84	68.4530 4244	67.3426 2286	66.2572 8507	65.1963 7602	84
85	69.1075 0491	67.9744 2804	66.8672 2625	65.7852 1840	85
86	69.7587 1135	68.6028 2938	67.4736 3007	66.3704 0338	86
87	70.4066 7796	69.2278 4522	68.0765 1706	66.9519 5367	87
88	71.0514 2086	69.8494 9380	68.6759 0759	67.5298 9185	88
89	71.6929 5608	70.4677 9325	69.2718 2197	68.1042 4035	89
90	72.3312 9958	71.0827 6162	69.8642 8033	68.6750 2146	90
91	72.9664 6725	71.6944 1687	70.4533 0273	69.2422 5735	91
92	73.5984 7487	72.3027 7682	71.0389 0910	69.8059 7004	92
93	74.2273 3818	72.9078 5925	71.6211 1923	70.3661 8141	93
94	74.8530 7282	73.5096 8181	72.1999 5284	70.9229 1320	94
95	75.4756 9434	74.1082 6206	72.7754 2950	71.4761 8703	95
96	76.0952 1825	74.7036 1746	73.3475 6869	72.0260 2438	96
97	76.7116 5995	75.2957 6540	73.9163 8975	72.5724 4659	97
98	77.3250 3478	75.8847 2315	74.4819 1193	73.1154 7487	98
99	77.9353 5799	76.4705 0790	75.0441 5436	73.6551 3030	99
100	78.5426 4477	77.0531 3674	75.6031 3606	74.1914 3384	100
101	79.1469 1021	77.6326 2668	76.1588 7596	74.7244 0630	101
102	79.7481 6937	78.2089 9463	76.7113 9283	75.2540 6838	102
103	80.3464 3718	78.7822 5740	77.2607 0538	75.7804 4062	103
104	80.9417 2854	79.3524 3173	77.8068 3219	76.3035 4348	104
105	81.5340 5825	79.9195 3425	78.3497 9174	76.8233 9724	105
106	82.1234 4104	80.4835 8152	78.8896 0240	77.3400 2210	106
107	82.7098 9158	81.0445 8999	79.4262 8241	77.8534 3812	107
108	83.2934 2446	81.6025 7603	79.9598 4996	78.3636 6521	108
109	83.8740 5419	82.1575 5594	80.4903 2307	78.8707 2319	109
110	84.4517 9522	82.7095 4590	81.0177 1971	79.3746 3174	110
111	85.0266 6191	83.2585 6202	81.5420 5770	79.8754 1043	111
112	85.5986 6856	83.8046 2033	82.0633 5480	80.3730 7868	112
113	86.1678 2942	84.3477 3675	82.5816 2863	80.8676 5583	113
114	86.7341 5862	84.8879 2715	83.0968 9674	81.3591 6108	114
115	87.2976 7027	85.4252 0728	83.6091 7654	81.8476 1349	115
116	87.8583 7838	85.9595 9281	84.1184 8537	82.3330 3204	116
117	88.4162 9690	86.4910 9936	84.6248 4047	82.8154 3557	117
118	88.9714 3970	87.0197 4242	85.1282 5896	83.2948 4280	118
119	89.5238 2059	87.5455 3743	85.6287 5787	83.7712 7235	119
120	90.0734 5333	88.0684 9972	86.1263 5414	84.2447 4271	120

TABLE 8 PRESENT VALUE OF ANNUITY

WHEN PERIODIC PAYMENT IS 1

$$a_{\overline{n}|i} = \frac{1-(1+i)^{-n}}{i}$$

n	$\frac{1}{2}$%	$\frac{13}{24}$%	$\frac{7}{12}$%	$\frac{5}{8}$%	n
121	90.6203 5157	88.5886 4456	86.6210 6460	84.7152 7226	121
122	91.1645 2892	89.1059 8713	87.1129 0598	85.1828 7926	122
123	91.7059 9893	89.6205 4253	87.6018 9493	85.6475 8188	123
124	92.2447 7505	90.1323 2576	88.0880 4798	86.1093 9814	124
125	92.7808 7070	90.6413 5177	88.5713 8159	86.5683 4598	125
126	93.3142 9921	91.1476 3541	89.0519 1210	87.0244 4320	126
127	93.8450 7384	91.6511 9146	89.5296 5577	87.4777 0753	127
128	94.3732 0780	92.1520 3461	90.0046 2877	87.9281 5655	128
129	94.8987 1423	92.6501 7947	90.4768 4716	88.3758 0776	129
130	95.4216 0619	93.1456 4058	90.9463 2692	88.8206 7852	130
131	95.9418 9671	93.6384 3241	91.4130 8393	89.2627 8610	131
132	96.4595 9872	94.1285 6932	91.8771 3399	89.7021 4768	132
133	96.9747 2509	94.6160 6563	92.3384 9278	90.1387 8030	133
134	97.4872 8865	95.1009 3557	92.7971 7592	90.5727 0092	134
135	97.9973 0214	95.5831 9327	93.2531 9893	91.0039 2638	135
136	98.5047 7825	96.0628 5282	93.7065 7722	91.4324 7342	136
137	99.0097 2960	96.5399 2820	94.1573 2616	91.8583 5868	137
138	99.5121 6876	97.0144 3336	94.6054 6097	92.2815 9869	138
139	100.0121 0821	97.4863 8212	95.0509 9682	92.7022 0988	139
140	100.5095 6041	97.9557 8827	95.4939 4878	93.1202 0857	140
141	101.0045 3772	98.4226 6550	95.9343 3185	93.5356 1100	141
142	101.4970 5246	98.8870 2743	96.3721 6091	93.9484 3330	142
143	101.9871 1688	99.3488 8762	96.8074 5078	94.3586 9148	143
144	102.4747 4316	99.8082 5955	97.2402 1619	94.7664 0147	144
145	102.9599 4344	100.2651 5662	97.6704 7177	95.1715 7910	145
146	103.4427 2979	100.7195 9216	98.0982 3208	95.5742 4010	146
147	103.9231 1422	101.1715 7944	98.5235 1160	95.9744 0010	147
148	104.4011 0868	101.6211 3164	98.9463 2470	96.3720 7463	148
149	104.8767 2506	102.0682 6189	99.3666 8570	96.7672 7913	149
150	105.3499 7518	102.5129 8323	99.7846 0882	97.1600 2895	150
151	105.8208 7083	102.9553 0864	100.2001 0819	97.5503 3933	151
152	106.2894 2371	103.3952 5103	100.6131 9786	97.9382 2542	152
153	106.7556 4548	103.8328 2324	101.0238 9183	98.3237 0228	153
154	107.2195 4774	104.2680 3804	101.4322 0397	98.7067 8488	154
155	107.6811 4203	104.7009 0812	101.8381 4811	99.0874 8808	155
156	108.1404 3983	105.1314 4612	102.2417 3797	99.4658 2666	156
157	108.5974 5257	105.5596 6460	102.6429 8721	99.8418 1532	157
158	109.0521 9161	105.9855 7606	103.0419 0941	100.2154 6864	158
159	109.5046 6827	106.4091 9293	103.4385 1805	100.5868 0113	159
160	109.9548 9380	106.8305 2758	103.8328 2656	100.9558 2721	160
161	110.4028 7940	107.2495 9229	104.2248 4828	101.3225 6120	161
162	110.8486 3622	107.6663 9929	104.6145 9647	101.6870 1734	162
163	111.2921 7535	108.0809 6075	105.0020 8431	102.0492 0978	163
164	111.7335 0781	108.4932 8877	105.3873 2491	102.4091 5258	164
165	112.1726 4458	108.9033 9538	105.7703 3132	102.7668 5971	165
166	112.6095 9660	109.3112 9254	106.1511 1647	103.1223 4505	166
167	113.0443 7473	109.7169 9217	106.5296 9326	103.4756 2241	167
168	113.4769 8978	110.1205 0610	106.9060 7449	103.8267 0550	168
169	113.9074 5252	110.5218 4610	107.2802 7290	104.1756 0795	169
170	114.3357 7365	110.9210 2388	107.6523 0114	104.5223 4330	170
171	114.7619 6383	111.3180 5111	108.0221 7181	104.8669 2502	171
172	115.1860 3366	111.7129 3935	108.3898 9741	105.2093 6648	172
173	115.6079 9369	112.1057 0014	108.7554 9038	105.5496 8098	173
174	116.0278 5442	112.4963 4494	109.1189 6309	105.8878 8172	174
175	116.4456 2629	112.8848 8515	109.4803 2785	106.2239 8183	175
176	116.8613 1969	113.2713 3210	109.8395 9687	106.5579 9436	176
177	117.2749 4496	113.6556 9707	110.1967 8230	106.8899 3229	177
178	117.6865 1240	114.0379 9129	110.5518 9624	107.2198 0849	178
179	118.0960 3224	114.4182 2590	110.9049 5070	107.5476 3576	179
180	118.5035 1467	114.7964 1200	111.2559 5761	107.8734 2684	180

TABLE 8 PRESENT VALUE OF ANNUITY
WHEN PERIODIC PAYMENT IS 1

$$a_{\overline{n}|i} = \frac{1-(1+i)^{-n}}{i}$$

n	$\frac{1}{2}\%$	$\frac{13}{24}\%$	$\frac{7}{12}\%$	$\frac{5}{8}\%$	n
181	118.9089 6982	115.1725 6063	111.6049 2886	108.1971 9438	181
182	119.3124 0778	115.5466 8276	111.9518 7625	108.5189 5094	182
183	119.7138 3859	115.9187 8932	112.2968 1151	108.8387 0900	183
184	120.1132 7223	116.2888 9116	112.6397 4633	109.1564 8100	184
185	120.5107 1863	116.6569 9908	112.9806 9229	109.4722 7925	185
186	120.9061 8769	117.0231 2383	113.3196 6093	109.7861 1603	186
187	121.2996 8925	117.3872 7608	113.6566 6373	110.0980 0351	187
188	121.6912 3308	117.7494 6647	113.9917 1207	110.4079 5379	188
189	122.0808 2894	118.1097 0557	114.3248 1731	110.7159 7893	189
190	122.4684 8651	118.4680 0388	114.6559 9069	111.0220 9086	190
191	122.8542 1543	118.8243 7186	114.9852 4344	111.3263 0147	191
192	123.2380 2530	119.1788 1992	115.3125 8668	111.6286 2258	192
193	123.6199 2567	119.5313 5840	115.6380 3150	111.9290 6592	193
194	123.9999 2604	119.8819 9758	115.9615 8890	112.2276 4315	194
195	124.3780 3586	120.2307 4769	116.2832 6982	112.5243 6586	195
196	124.7542 6454	120.5776 1893	116.6030 8516	112.8192 4558	196
197	125.1286 2143	120.9226 2139	116.9210 4573	113.1122 9374	197
198	125.5011 1585	121.2657 6516	117.2371 6228	113.4035 2173	198
199	125.8717 5707	121.6070 6026	117.5514 4552	113.6929 4085	199
200	126.2405 5430	121.9465 1662	117.8639 0606	113.9805 6234	200
201	126.6075 1671	122.2841 4418	118.1745 5450	114.2663 9735	201
202	126.9726 5345	122.6199 5277	118.4834 0132	114.5504 5700	202
203	127.3359 7358	122.9539 5219	118.7904 5699	114.8327 5230	203
204	127.6974 8615	123.2861 5220	119.0957 3189	115.1132 9421	204
205	128.0572 0015	123.6165 6249	119.3992 3634	115.3920 9362	205
206	128.4151 2452	123.9451 9269	119.7009 8062	115.6691 6136	206
207	128.7712 6818	124.2720 5241	120.0009 7493	115.9445 0819	207
208	129.1256 3998	124.5971 5117	120.2992 2943	116.2181 4478	208
209	129.4782 4874	124.9204 9847	120.5957 5420	116.4900 8177	209
210	129.8291 0322	125.2421 0374	120.8905 5927	116.7603 2971	210
211	130.1782 1216	125.5619 7637	121.1836 5461	117.0288 9909	211
212	130.5255 8424	125.8801 2569	121.4750 5016	117.2958 0034	212
213	130.8712 2810	126.1965 6099	121.7647 5575	117.5610 4382	213
214	131.2151 5234	126.5112 9149	122.0527 8119	117.8246 3982	214
215	131.5573 6551	126.8243 2639	122.3391 3623	118.0865 9858	215
216	131.8978 7613	127.1356 7482	122.6238 3055	118.3469 3026	216
217	132.2366 9267	127.4453 4586	122.9068 7379	118.6056 4498	217
218	132.5738 2355	127.7533 4856	123.1882 7551	118.8627 5278	218
219	132.9092 7716	128.0596 9189	123.4680 4525	119.1182 6363	219
220	133.2430 6186	128.3643 8481	123.7461 9246	119.3721 8746	220
221	133.5751 8593	128.6674 3619	124.0227 2655	119.6245 3412	221
222	133.9056 5764	128.9688 5490	124.2976 5689	119.8753 1341	222
223	134.2344 8521	129.2686 4971	124.5709 9276	120.1245 3507	223
224	134.5616 7683	129.5668 2939	124.8427 4343	120.3722 0876	224
225	134.8872 4062	129.8634 0262	125.1129 1807	120.6183 4411	225
226	135.2111 8470	130.1583 7807	125.3815 2584	120.8629 5067	226
227	135.5335 1712	130.4517 6435	125.6485 7581	121.1060 3793	227
228	135.8542 4589	130.7435 7001	125.9140 7703	121.3476 1534	228
229	136.1733 7899	131.0338 0358	126.1780 3847	121.5876 9226	229
230	136.4909 2437	131.3224 7351	126.4404 6907	121.8262 7802	230
231	136.8068 8992	131.6095 8824	126.7013 7770	122.0633 8188	231
232	137.1212 8350	131.8951 5615	126.9607 7319	122.2990 1305	232
233	137.4341 1294	132.1791 8556	127.2186 6431	122.5331 8067	233
234	137.7453 8601	132.4616 8476	127.4750 5980	122.7658 9384	234
235	138.0551 1045	132.7426 6201	127.7299 6832	122.9971 6158	235
236	138.3632 9398	133.0221 2550	127.9833 9849	123.2269 9287	236
237	138.6699 4426	133.3000 8338	128.2353 5890	123.4553 9664	237
238	138.9750 6892	133.5765 4377	128.4858 5806	123.6823 8176	238
239	139.2786 7554	133.8515 1473	128.7349 0445	123.9079 5703	239
240	139.5807 7168	134.1250 0429	128.9825 0650	124.1321 3121	240

TABLE 8 PRESENT VALUE OF ANNUITY

WHEN PERIODIC PAYMENT IS 1

$$a_{\overline{n}|i} = \frac{1-(1+i)^{-n}}{i}$$

n	$\frac{2}{3}\%$	$\frac{3}{4}\%$	$\frac{7}{8}\%$	1%	n
1	0.9933 7748	0.9925 5583	0.9913 2590	0.9900 9901	1
2	1.9801 7631	1.9777 2291	1.9740 5294	1.9703 9506	2
3	2.9604 4004	2.9555 5624	2.9482 5570	2.9409 8521	3
4	3.9342 1196	3.9261 1041	3.9140 0813	3.9019 6555	4
5	4.9015 3506	4.8894 3961	4.8713 8352	4.8534 3124	5
6	5.8624 5205	5.8455 9763	5.8204 5454	5.7954 7647	6
7	6.8170 0535	6.7946 3785	6.7612 9323	6.7281 9453	7
8	7.7652 3710	7.7366 1325	7.6939 7098	7.6516 7775	8
9	8.7071 8917	8.6715 7642	8.6185 5859	8.5660 1758	9
10	9.6429 0315	9.5995 7958	9.5351 2624	9.4713 0453	10
11	10.5724 2035	10.5206 7452	10.4437 4348	10.3676 2825	11
12	11.4957 8180	11.4349 1267	11.3444 7929	11.2550 7747	12
13	12.4130 2828	12.3423 4508	12.2374 0202	12.1337 4007	13
14	13.3242 0028	13.2430 2242	13.1225 7945	13.0037 0304	14
15	14.2293 3802	14.1369 9495	14.0000 7876	13.8650 5252	15
16	15.1284 8148	15.0243 1261	14.8699 6656	14.7178 7378	16
17	16.0216 7035	15.9050 2492	15.7323 0885	15.5622 5127	17
18	16.9089 4405	16.7791 8107	16.5871 7111	16.3982 6858	18
19	17.7903 4177	17.6468 2984	17.4346 1820	17.2260 0850	19
20	18.6659 0242	18.5080 1969	18.2747 1445	18.0455 5297	20
21	19.5356 6466	19.3627 9870	19.1075 2361	18.8569 8313	21
22	20.3996 6688	20.2112 1459	19.9331 0891	19.6603 7934	22
23	21.2579 4723	21.0533 1473	20.7515 3300	20.4558 2113	23
24	22.1105 4361	21.8891 4614	21.5628 5799	21.2433 8726	24
25	22.9574 9365	22.7187 5547	22.3671 4547	22.0231 5570	25
26	23.7988 3475	23.5421 8905	23.1644 5647	22.7952 0366	26
27	24.6346 0406	24.3594 9286	23.9548 5152	23.5596 0759	27
28	25.4648 3847	25.1707 1251	24.7383 9060	24.3164 4316	28
29	26.2895 7464	25.9758 9331	25.5151 3319	25.0657 8530	29
30	27.1088 4898	26.7750 8021	26.2851 3823	25.8077 0822	30
31	27.9226 9766	27.5683 1783	27.0484 6417	26.5422 8537	31
32	28.7311 5662	28.3556 5045	27.8051 6894	27.2695 8947	32
33	29.5342 6154	29.1371 2203	28.5553 0998	27.9896 9255	33
34	30.3320 4789	29.9127 7621	29.2989 4422	28.7026 6589	34
35	31.1245 5088	30.6826 5629	30.0361 2809	29.4085 8009	35
36	31.9118 0551	31.4468 0525	30.7669 1757	30.1075 0504	36
37	32.6938 4653	32.2052 6576	31.4913 6810	30.7995 0994	37
38	33.4707 0848	32.9580 8016	32.2095 3467	31.4846 6330	38
39	34.2424 2564	33.7052 9048	32.9214 7179	32.1630 3298	39
40	35.0090 3209	34.4469 3844	33.6272 3350	32.8346 8611	40
41	35.7705 6168	35.1830 6545	34.3268 7335	33.4996 8922	41
42	36.5270 4803	35.9137 1260	35.0204 4446	34.1581 0814	42
43	37.2785 2453	36.6389 2070	35.7079 9947	34.8100 0806	43
44	38.0250 2437	37.3587 3022	36.3895 9055	35.4554 5352	44
45	38.7665 8050	38.0731 8136	37.0652 6944	36.0945 0844	45
46	39.5032 2566	38.7823 1401	37.7350 8743	36.7272 3608	46
47	40.2349 9238	39.4861 6775	38.3990 9535	37.3536 9909	47
48	40.9619 1296	40.1847 8189	39.0573 4359	37.9739 5949	48
49	41.6840 1949	40.8781 9542	39.7098 8212	38.5880 7871	49
50	42.4013 4387	41.5664 4707	40.3567 6047	39.1961 1753	50
51	43.1139 1775	42.2495 7525	40.9980 2772	39.7981 3617	51
52	43.8217 7260	42.9276 1812	41.6337 3256	40.3941 9423	52
53	44.5249 3967	43.6006 1351	42.2639 2324	40.9843 5072	53
54	45.2234 5000	44.2685 9902	42.8886 4757	41.5686 6408	54
55	45.9173 3444	44.9316 1193	43.5079 5298	42.1471 9216	55
56	46.6066 2362	45.5896 8926	44.1218 8647	42.7199 9224	56
57	47.2913 4796	46.2428 6776	44.7304 9465	43.2871 2102	57
58	47.9715 3771	46.8911 8388	45.3338 2369	43.8486 3468	58
59	48.6472 2289	47.5346 7382	45.9319 1939	44.4045 8879	59
60	49.3184 3334	48.1733 7352	46.5248 2716	44.9550 3841	60

TABLE 8 PRESENT VALUE OF ANNUITY
WHEN PERIODIC PAYMENT IS 1

$$a_{\overline{n}|i} = \frac{1-(1+i)^{-n}}{i}$$

n	$\frac{2}{3}\%$	$\frac{3}{4}\%$	$\frac{7}{8}\%$	1%	n
61	49.9851 9868	48.8073 1863	47.1125 9198	45.5000 3803	61
62	50.6475 4836	49.4365 4455	47.6952 5846	46.0396 4161	62
63	51.3055 1161	50.0610 8640	48.2728 7084	46.5739 0258	63
64	51.9591 1749	50.6809 7906	48.8454 7296	47.1028 7385	64
65	52.6083 9486	51.2962 5713	49.4131 0826	47.6266 0777	65
66	53.2533 7238	51.9069 5497	49.9758 1984	48.1451 5621	66
67	53.8940 7852	52.5131 0667	50.5336 5039	48.6585 7050	67
68	54.5305 4158	53.1147 4607	51.0866 4227	49.1669 0149	68
69	55.1627 8965	53.7119 0677	51.6348 3745	49.6701 9949	69
70	55.7908 5064	54.3046 2210	52.1782 7752	50.1685 1435	70
71	56.4147 5230	54.8929 2516	52.7170 0374	50.6618 9539	71
72	57.0345 2215	55.4768 4880	53.2510 5699	51.1503 9148	72
73	57.6501 8756	56.0564 2561	53.7804 7781	51.6340 5097	73
74	58.2617 7573	56.6316 8795	54.3053 0638	52.1129 2175	74
75	58.8693 1363	57.2026 6794	54.8255 8253	52.5870 5124	75
76	59.4728 2811	57.7693 9746	55.3413 4575	53.0564 8638	76
77	60.0723 4581	58.3319 0815	55.8526 3520	53.5212 7364	77
78	60.6678 9319	58.8902 3141	56.3594 8966	53.9814 5905	78
79	61.2594 9654	59.4443 9842	56.8619 4762	54.4370 8817	79
80	61.8471 8200	59.9944 4012	57.3600 4721	54.8882 0611	80
81	62.4309 7549	60.5403 8722	57.8538 2623	55.3348 5753	81
82	63.0109 0281	61.0822 7019	58.3433 2216	55.7770 8666	82
83	63.5869 8954	61.6201 1930	58.8285 7215	56.2149 3729	83
84	64.1592 6114	62.1539 6456	59.3096 1304	56.6484 5276	84
85	64.7277 4285	62.6838 3579	59.7864 8133	57.0776 7600	85
86	65.2924 5979	63.2097 6257	60.2592 1321	57.5026 4951	86
87	65.8534 3687	63.7317 7427	60.7278 4457	57.9234 1535	87
88	66.4106 9888	64.2499 0002	61.1924 1097	58.3400 1520	88
89	66.9642 7041	64.7641 6875	61.6529 4768	58.7524 9030	89
90	67.5141 7591	65.2746 0918	62.1094 8965	59.1608 8148	90
91	68.0604 3964	65.7812 4981	62.5620 7152	59.5652 2919	91
92	68.6030 8574	66.2841 1892	63.0107 2765	59.9655 7346	92
93	69.1421 3815	66.7832 4458	63.4554 9210	60.3619 5392	93
94	69.6776 2068	67.2786 5467	63.8963 9861	60.7544 0982	94
95	70.2095 5696	67.7703 7685	64.3334 8066	61.1429 8002	95
96	70.7379 7049	68.2584 3856	64.7667 7141	61.5277 0299	96
97	71.2628 8460	68.7428 6705	65.1963 0375	61.9086 1682	97
98	71.7843 2245	69.2236 8938	65.6221 1028	62.2857 5923	98
99	72.3023 0707	69.7009 3239	66.0442 2333	62.6591 6755	99
100	72.8168 6132	70.1746 2272	66.4626 7492	63.0288 7877	100
101	73.3280 0794	70.6447 8682	66.8774 9683	63.3949 2947	101
102	73.8357 6948	71.1114 5094	67.2887 2052	63.7573 5591	102
103	74.3401 6835	71.5746 4113	67.6963 7722	64.1161 9397	103
104	74.8412 2684	72.0343 8325	68.1004 9786	64.4714 7918	104
105	75.3389 6706	72.4907 0298	68.5011 1312	64.8232 4671	105
106	75.8334 1099	72.9436 2579	68.8982 5341	65.1715 3140	106
107	76.3245 8045	73.3931 7696	69.2919 4885	65.5163 6772	107
108	76.8124 9714	73.8393 8160	69.6822 2935	65.8577 8983	108
109	77.2971 8259	74.2822 6461	70.0691 2451	66.1958 3151	109
110	77.7786 5820	74.7218 5073	70.4526 6370	66.5305 2625	110
111	78.2569 4523	75.1581 6450	70.8328 7604	66.8619 0718	111
112	78.7320 6480	75.5912 3027	71.2097 9037	67.1900 0710	112
113	79.2040 3788	76.0210 7223	71.5834 3531	67.5148 5852	113
114	79.6728 8531	76.4477 1437	71.9538 3922	67.8364 9358	114
115	80.1386 2779	76.8711 8052	72.3210 3020	68.1549 4414	115
116	80.6012 8589	77.2914 9431	72.6850 3614	68.4702 4173	116
117	81.0608 8002	77.7086 7922	73.0458 8465	68.7824 1755	117
118	81.5174 3048	78.1227 5853	73.4036 0312	69.0915 0252	118
119	81.9709 5743	78.5337 5536	73.7582 1871	69.3975 2725	119
120	82.4214 8089	78.9416 9267	74.1097 5832	69.7005 2203	120

TABLE 8 PRESENT VALUE OF ANNUITY
WHEN PERIODIC PAYMENT IS 1

$$a_{\overline{n}|i} = \frac{1-(1+i)^{-n}}{i}$$

n	$\frac{2}{3}\%$	$\frac{3}{4}\%$	$\frac{7}{8}\%$	1%	n
121	82.8690 2076	79.3465 9322	74.4582 4864	70.0005 1686	121
122	83.3135 9678	79.7484 7962	74.8037 1613	70.2975 4145	122
123	83.7552 2859	80.1473 7432	75.1461 8699	70.5916 2520	123
124	84.1939 3568	80.5432 9957	75.4856 8723	70.8827 9722	124
125	84.6297 3743	80.9362 7749	75.8222 4261	71.1710 8636	125
126	85.0626 5308	81.3263 3001	76.1558 7867	71.4565 2115	126
127	85.4927 0173	81.7134 7892	76.4866 2074	71.7391 2985	127
128	85.9199 0238	82.0977 4583	76.8144 9391	72.0189 4045	128
129	86.3442 7389	82.4791 5219	77.1395 2309	72.2959 8064	129
130	86.7658 3499	82.8577 1929	77.4617 3292	72.5702 7786	130
131	87.1846 0430	83.2334 6828	77.7811 4788	72.8418 5927	131
132	87.6006 0029	83.6064 2013	78.0977 9220	73.1107 5175	132
133	88.0138 4135	83.9765 9566	78.4116 8991	73.3769 8193	133
134	88.4243 4571	84.3440 1554	78.7228 6484	73.6405 7617	134
135	88.8321 3150	84.7087 0029	79.0313 4061	73.9015 6056	135
136	89.2372 1673	85.0706 7026	79.3371 4063	74.1599 6095	136
137	89.6396 1926	85.4299 4567	79.6402 8811	74.4158 0293	137
138	90.0393 5688	85.7865 4657	79.9408 0606	74.6691 1181	138
139	90.4364 4724	86.1404 9288	80.2387 1728	74.9199 1268	139
140	90.8309 0785	86.4918 0434	80.5340 4440	75.1682 3038	140
141	91.2227 5614	86.8405 0059	80.8268 0981	75.4140 8948	141
142	91.6120 0941	87.1866 0108	81.1170 3575	75.6575 1434	142
143	91.9986 8485	87.5301 2514	81.4047 4423	75.8985 2905	143
144	92.3827 9952	87.8710 9195	81.6899 5711	76.1371 5747	144
145	92.7643 7038	88.2095 2055	81.9726 9602	76.3734 2324	145
146	93.1434 1429	88.5454 2982	82.2529 8242	76.6073 4974	146
147	93.5199 4797	88.8788 3854	82.5308 3759	76.8389 6014	147
148	93.8939 8805	89.2097 6530	82.8062 8262	77.0682 7737	148
149	94.2655 5104	89.5382 2858	83.0793 3841	77.2953 2413	149
150	94.6346 5335	89.8642 4673	83.3500 2569	77.5201 2290	150
151	95.0013 1128	90.1878 3795	83.6183 6499	77.7426 9594	151
152	95.3655 4100	90.5090 2029	83.8843 7670	77.9630 6529	152
153	95.7273 5861	90.8278 1171	84.1480 8099	78.1812 5276	153
154	96.0867 8008	91.1442 2998	84.4094 9788	78.3972 7996	154
155	96.4438 2127	91.4582 9279	84.6686 4722	78.6111 6828	155
156	96.7984 9795	91.7700 1765	84.9255 4867	78.8229 3889	156
157	97.1508 2578	92.0794 2199	85.1802 2173	79.0326 1276	157
158	97.5008 2031	92.3865 2307	85.4326 8573	79.2402 1065	158
159	97.8484 9700	92.6913 3803	85.6829 5983	79.4457 5312	159
160	98.1938 7119	92.9938 8390	85.9310 6303	79.6492 6052	160
161	98.5369 5813	93.2941 7757	86.1770 1415	79.8507 5299	161
162	98.8777 7298	93.5922 3580	86.4208 3187	80.0502 5048	162
163	99.2163 3078	93.8880 7524	86.6625 3470	80.2477 7275	163
164	99.5526 4647	94.1817 1239	86.9021 4096	80.4433 3936	164
165	99.8867 3490	94.4731 6367	87.1396 6886	80.6369 6966	165
166	100.2186 1083	94.7624 4533	87.3751 3642	80.8286 8284	166
167	100.5482 8890	95.0495 7352	87.6085 6150	81.0184 9786	167
168	100.8757 8368	95.3345 6429	87.8399 6184	81.2064 3352	168
169	101.2011 0961	95.6174 3354	88.0693 5498	81.3925 0844	169
170	101.5242 8107	95.8981 9706	88.2967 5835	81.5767 4103	170
171	101.8453 1232	96.1768 7053	88.5221 8919	81.7591 4953	171
172	102.1642 1754	96.4534 6951	88.7456 6462	81.9397 5201	172
173	102.4810 1080	96.7280 0944	88.9672 0161	82.1185 6635	173
174	102.7957 0609	97.0005 0565	89.1868 1696	82.2956 1025	174
175	103.1083 1731	97.2709 7335	89.4045 2735	82.4709 0123	175
176	103.4188 5826	97.5394 2764	89.6203 4929	82.6444 5667	176
177	103.7273 4264	97.8058 8352	89.8342 9917	82.8162 9373	177
178	104.0337 8408	98.0703 5585	90.0463 9323	82.9864 2944	178
179	104.3381 9610	98.3328 5940	90.2566 4757	83.1548 8063	179
180	104.6405 9216	98.5934 0884	90.4650 7813	83.3216 6399	180

TABLE 8 PRESENT VALUE OF ANNUITY
WHEN PERIODIC PAYMENT IS 1

$$a_{\overline{n}|i} = \frac{1-(1+i)^{-n}}{i}$$

n	$\frac{2}{3}\%$	$\frac{3}{4}\%$	$\frac{7}{8}\%$	1%	n
181	104.9409 8559	98.8520 1869	90.6717 0075	83.4867 9603	181
182	105.2393 8966	99.1087 0342	90.8765 3110	83.6502 9310	182
183	105.5358 1754	99.3634 7734	91.0795 8474	83.8121 7138	183
184	105.8302 8232	99.6163 5468	91.2808 7706	83.9724 4691	184
185	106.1227 9701	99.8673 4956	91.4804 2336	84.1311 3556	185
186	106.4133 7451	100.1164 7599	91.6782 3877	84.2882 5303	186
187	106.7020 2766	100.3637 4788	91.8743 3831	84.4438 1488	187
188	106.9887 6920	100.6091 7904	92.0687 3686	84.5978 3652	188
189	107.2736 1179	100.8527 8316	92.2614 4918	84.7503 3318	189
190	107.5565 6800	101.0945 7386	92.4524 8989	84.9013 1998	190
191	107.8376 5033	101.3345 6462	92.6418 7350	85.0508 1186	191
192	108.1168 7119	101.5727 6886	92.8296 1438	85.1988 2363	192
193	108.3942 4291	101.8091 9986	93.0157 2677	85.3453 6993	193
194	108.6697 7772	102.0438 7083	93.2002 2480	85.4904 6528	194
195	108.9434 8780	102.2767 9487	93.3831 2248	85.6341 2404	195
196	109.2153 8523	102.5079 8498	93.5644 3368	85.7763 6043	196
197	109.4854 8202	102.7374 5407	93.7441 7218	85.9171 8855	197
198	109.7537 9009	102.9652 1496	93.9223 5160	86.0566 2232	198
199	110.0203 2128	103.1912 8036	94.0989 8548	86.1946 7557	199
200	110.2850 8736	103.4156 6289	94.2740 8721	86.3313 6195	200
201	110.5481 0003	103.6383 7507	94.4476 7010	86.4666 9500	201
202	110.8093 7089	103.8594 2935	94.6197 4731	86.6006 8812	202
203	111.0689 1148	104.0788 3807	94.7903 3191	86.7333 5457	203
204	111.3267 3326	104.2966 1347	94.9594 3684	86.8647 0750	204
205	111.5828 4761	104.5127 6771	95.1270 7493	86.9947 5990	205
206	111.8372 6583	104.7273 1286	95.2932 5891	87.1235 2465	206
207	112.0899 9917	104.9402 6091	95.4580 0140	87.2510 1451	207
208	112.3410 5878	105.1516 2373	95.6213 1490	87.3772 4208	208
209	112.5904 5574	105.3614 1313	95.7832 1179	87.5022 1989	209
210	112.8382 0107	105.5696 4082	95.9437 0438	87.6259 6028	210
211	113.0843 0570	105.7763 1843	96.1028 0484	87.7484 7553	211
212	113.3287 8049	105.9814 5750	96.2605 2524	87.8697 7775	212
213	113.5716 3625	106.1850 6948	96.4168 7756	87.9898 7896	213
214	113.8128 8370	106.3871 6574	96.5718 7367	88.1087 9105	214
215	114.0525 3347	106.5877 5756	96.7255 2532	88.2265 2579	215
216	114.2905 9616	106.7868 5614	96.8778 4419	88.3430 9484	216
217	114.5270 8228	106.9844 7259	97.0288 4182	88.4585 0975	217
218	114.7620 0227	107.1806 1796	97.1785 2968	88.5727 8193	218
219	114.9953 6649	107.3753 0318	97.3269 1914	88.6859 2270	219
220	115.2271 8526	107.5685 3914	97.4740 2145	88.7979 4327	220
221	115.4574 6880	107.7603 3662	97.6198 4779	88.9088 5472	221
222	115.6862 2728	107.9507 0632	97.7644 0921	89.0186 6804	222
223	115.9134 7081	108.1396 5888	97.9077 1668	89.1273 9410	223
224	116.1392 0941	108.3272 0484	98.0497 8110	89.2350 4366	224
225	116.3634 5306	108.5133 5468	98.1906 1323	89.3416 2739	225
226	116.5862 1165	108.6981 1879	98.3302 2378	89.4471 5583	226
227	116.8074 9502	108.8815 0748	98.4686 2332	89.5516 3944	227
228	117.0273 1293	109.0635 3100	98.6058 2238	89.6550 8855	228
229	117.2456 7510	109.2441 9950	98.7418 3135	89.7575 1342	229
230	117.4625 9115	109.4235 2308	98.8766 6057	89.8589 2417	230
231	117.6780 7068	109.6015 1174	99.0103 2027	89.9593 3087	231
232	117.8921 2320	109.7781 7543	99.1428 2059	90.0587 4343	232
233	118.1047 5814	109.9535 2400	99.2741 7159	90.1571 7171	233
234	118.3159 8491	110.1275 6724	99.4043 8324	90.2546 2546	234
235	118.5258 1282	110.3003 1488	99.5334 6541	90.3511 1432	235
236	118.7342 5115	110.4717 7656	99.6614 2792	90.4466 4784	236
237	118.9413 0909	110.6419 6184	99.7882 8046	90.5412 3548	237
238	119.1469 9578	110.8108 8024	99.9140 3268	90.6348 8662	238
239	119.3513 2031	110.9785 4118	100.0386 9410	90.7276 1051	239
240	119.5542 9170	111.1449 5403	100.1622 7421	90.8194 1635	240

TABLE 8 PRESENT VALUE OF ANNUITY

WHEN PERIODIC PAYMENT IS 1

$$a_{\overline{n}|i} = \frac{1-(1+i)^{-n}}{i}$$

n	$1\frac{1}{8}\%$	$1\frac{1}{4}\%$	$1\frac{3}{8}\%$	$1\frac{1}{2}\%$	n
1	0.9888 7515	0.9876 5432	0.9864 3650	0.9852 2167	1
2	1.9667 4923	1.9631 1538	1.9594 9346	1.9558 8342	2
3	2.9337 4460	2.9265 3371	2.9193 5237	2.9122 0042	3
4	3.8899 8230	3.8780 5798	3.8661 9222	3.8543 8465	4
5	4.8355 8200	4.8178 3504	4.8001 8962	4.7826 4497	5
6	5.7706 6205	5.7460 0992	5.7215 1874	5.6971 8717	6
7	6.6953 3948	6.6627 2585	6.6303 5140	6.5982 1396	7
8	7.6097 3002	7.5681 2429	7.5268 5712	7.4859 2508	8
9	8.5139 4810	8.4623 4498	8.4112 0308	8.3605 1732	9
10	9.4081 0690	9.3455 2591	9.2835 5421	9.2221 8455	10
11	10.2923 1832	10.2178 0337	10.1440 7320	10.0711 1779	11
12	11.1666 9302	11.0793 1197	10.9929 2054	10.9075 0521	12
13	12.0313 4044	11.9301 8466	11.8302 5454	11.7315 3222	13
14	12.8863 6880	12.7705 5275	12.6562 3136	12.5433 8150	14
15	13.7318 8509	13.6005 4592	13.4710 0504	13.3432 3301	15
16	14.5679 9514	14.4202 9227	14.2747 2754	14.1312 6405	16
17	15.3948 0360	15.2299 1829	15.0675 4874	14.9076 4931	17
18	16.2124 1395	16.0295 4893	15.8496 1651	15.6725 6089	18
19	17.0209 2850	16.8193 0759	16.6210 7671	16.4261 6837	19
20	17.8204 4845	17.5993 1613	17.3820 7320	17.1686 3879	20
21	18.6110 7387	18.3696 9495	18.1327 4792	17.9001 3673	21
22	19.3929 0371	19.1305 6291	18.8732 4086	18.6208 2437	22
23	20.1660 3580	19.8820 3744	19.6036 9012	19.3308 6145	23
24	20.9305 6693	20.6242 3451	20.3242 3193	20.0304 0537	24
25	21.6865 9276	21.3572 6865	21.0350 0067	20.7196 1120	25
26	22.4342 0792	22.0812 5299	21.7361 2890	21.3986 3172	26
27	23.1735 0598	22.7962 9925	22.4277 4737	22.0676 1746	27
28	23.9045 7946	23.5025 1778	23.1099 8508	22.7267 1671	28
29	24.6275 1986	24.2000 1756	23.7829 6925	23.3760 7558	29
30	25.3424 1766	24.8889 0623	24.4468 2540	24.0158 3801	30
31	26.0493 6233	25.5692 9010	25.1016 7734	24.6461 4582	31
32	26.7484 4236	26.2412 7418	25.7476 4719	25.2671 3874	32
33	27.4397 4522	26.9049 6215	26.3848 5543	25.8789 5442	33
34	28.1233 5745	27.5604 5644	27.0134 2089	26.4817 2849	34
35	28.7993 6460	28.2078 5822	27.6334 6080	27.0755 9458	35
36	29.4678 5127	28.8472 6737	28.2450 9080	27.6606 8431	36
37	30.1289 0114	29.4787 8259	28.8484 2496	28.2371 2740	37
38	30.7825 9692	30.1025 0133	29.4435 7579	28.8050 5163	38
39	31.4290 2044	30.7185 1983	30.0306 5430	29.3645 8288	39
40	32.0682 5260	31.3269 3316	30.6097 6996	29.9158 4520	40
41	32.7903 7340	31.9278 3522	31.1810 3079	30.4589 6079	41
42	33.3254 6195	32.5213 1874	31.7445 4332	30.9940 5004	42
43	33.9435 9649	33.1074 7530	32.3004 1264	31.5212 3157	43
44	34.5548 5438	33.6863 9536	32.8487 4243	32.0406 2223	44
45	35.1593 1212	34.2581 6825	33.3896 3495	32.5523 3718	45
46	35.7570 4536	34.8228 8222	33.9231 9108	33.0564 8983	46
47	36.3481 2891	35.3806 2442	34.4495 1031	33.5531 9195	47
48	36.9326 3674	35.9314 8091	34.9686 9081	34.0425 5365	48
49	37.5106 4202	36.4755 3670	35.4808 2941	34.5246 8339	49
50	38.0822 1708	37.0128 7575	35.9860 2161	34.9996 8807	50

TABLE 8 PRESENT VALUE OF ANNUITY

WHEN PERIODIC PAYMENT IS 1

$$a_{\overline{n}|i} = \frac{1-(1+i)^{-n}}{i}$$

n	$1\frac{1}{8}\%$	$1\frac{1}{4}\%$	$1\frac{3}{8}\%$	$1\frac{1}{2}\%$	n
51	38.6474 3345	37.5435 8099	36.4843 6164	35.4676 7298	51
52	39.2063 6188	38.0677 3431	36.9759 4243	35.9287 4185	52
53	39.7590 7232	38.5854 1660	37.4608 5566	36.3829 9690	53
54	40.3056 3394	39.0967 0776	37.9391 9178	36.8305 3882	54
55	40.8461 1514	39.6016 8667	38.4110 3998	37.2714 6681	55
56	41.3805 8358	40.1004 3128	38.8764 8826	37.7058 7863	56
57	41.9091 0613	40.5930 1855	39.3356 2344	38.1338 7058	57
58	42.4317 4896	41.0795 2449	39.7885 3114	38.5555 3751	58
59	42.9485 7746	41.5600 2419	40.2352 9582	38.9709 7292	59
60	43.4596 5633	42.0345 9179	40.6760 0081	39.3802 6889	60
61	43.9650 4952	42.5033 0054	41.1107 2829	39.7835 1614	61
62	44.4648 2029	42.9662 2275	41.5395 5935	40.1808 0408	62
63	44.9590 3119	43.4234 2988	41.9625 7396	40.5722 2077	63
64	45.4477 4407	43.8749 9247	42.3798 5101	40.9578 5298	64
65	45.9310 2009	44.3209 8022	42.7914 6832	41.3377 8618	65
66	46.4089 1975	44.7614 6195	43.1975 0266	41.7121 0461	66
67	46.8815 0284	45.1965 0563	43.5980 2975	42.0808 9125	67
68	47.3488 2852	45.6261 7840	43.9931 2429	42.4442 2783	68
69	47.8109 5527	46.0505 4656	44.3828 5997	42.8021 9490	69
70	48.2679 4094	46.4696 7562	44.7673 0946	43.1548 7183	70
71	48.7198 4270	46.8836 3024	45.1465 4448	43.5023 3678	71
72	49.1667 1714	47.2924 7431	45.5206 3573	43.8446 6677	72
73	49.6086 2016	47.6962 7093	45.8896 5300	44.1819 3771	73
74	50.0456 0708	48.0950 8240	46.2536 6511	44.5142 2434	74
75	50.4777 3259	48.4889 7027	46.6127 3994	44.8416 0034	75
76	50.9050 5077	48.8779 9533	46.9669 4445	45.1641 3826	76
77	51.3276 1510	49.2622 1761	47.3163 4471	45.4819 0962	77
78	51.7454 7847	49.6416 9640	47.6610 0588	45.7949 8485	78
79	52.1586 9317	50.0164 9027	48.0009 9224	46.1034 3335	79
80	52.5673 1092	50.3866 5706	48.3363 6719	46.4073 2349	80
81	52.9713 8286	50.7522 5389	48.6671 9328	46.7067 2265	81
82	53.3709 5957	51.1133 3717	48.9935 3221	47.0016 9720	82
83	53.7660 9104	51.4699 6264	49.3154 4484	47.2923 1251	83
84	54.1568 2674	51.8221 8532	49.6329 9122	47.5786 3301	84
85	54.5432 1557	52.1700 5958	49.9462 3055	47.8607 2218	85
86	54.9253 0588	52.5136 3909	50.2552 2125	48.1386 4254	86
87	55.3031 4549	52.8529 7688	50.5600 2096	48.4124 5571	87
88	55.6767 8169	53.1881 2531	50.8606 8653	48.6822 2237	88
89	56.0462 6126	53.5191 3611	51.1572 7401	48.9480 0234	89
90	56.4116 3041	53.8460 6036	51.4498 3873	49.2098 5452	90
91	56.7729 3490	54.1689 4850	51.7384 3524	49.4678 3696	91
92	57.1302 1992	54.4878 5037	52.0231 1738	49.7220 0686	92
93	57.4835 3021	54.8028 1518	52.3039 3823	49.9724 2055	93
94	57.8329 0997	55.1138 9154	52.5809 5016	50.2191 3355	94
95	58.1784 0294	55.4211 2744	52.8542 0484	50.4622 0054	95
96	58.5200 5235	55.7245 7031	53.1237 5324	50.7016 7541	96
97	58.8579 0096	56.0242 6698	53.3896 4561	50.9376 1124	97
98	59.1919 9106	56.3202 6368	53.6519 3155	51.1700 6034	98
99	59.5223 6446	56.6126 0610	53.9106 5998	51.3990 7422	99
100	59.8490 6251	56.9013 3936	54.1658 7914	51.6247 0367	100

TABLE 8 PRESENT VALUE OF ANNUITY
WHEN PERIODIC PAYMENT IS 1

$$a_{\overline{n}|i} = \frac{1-(1+i)^{-n}}{i}$$

n	$1\frac{5}{8}\%$	$1\frac{3}{4}\%$	$1\frac{7}{8}\%$	2%	n
1	0.9840 0984	0.9828 0098	0.9815 9509	0.9803 9216	1
2	1.9522 8521	1.9486 9875	1.9451 2402	1.9415 6094	2
3	2.9050 7769	2.8979 8403	2.8909 1928	2.8838 8327	3
4	3.8426 3488	3.8309 4254	3.8193 0727	3.8077 2870	4
5	4.7652 0037	4.7478 5508	4.7306 0836	4.7134 5951	5
6	5.6730 1389	5.6489 9762	5.6251 3704	5.6014 3089	6
7	6.5663 1134	6.5346 4139	6.5032 0200	6.4719 9107	7
8	7.4453 2481	7.4050 5297	7.3651 0626	7.3254 8144	8
9	8.3102 8271	8.2604 9432	8.2111 4725	8.1622 3671	9
10	9.1614 0980	9.1012 2291	9.0416 1693	8.9825 8501	10
11	9.9989 2724	9.9274 9181	9.8568 0190	9.7868 4805	11
12	10.8230 5263	10.7395 4969	10.6569 8346	10.5753 4122	12
13	11.6340 0013	11.5376 4097	11.4424 3775	11.3483 7375	13
14	12.4319 8045	12.3220 0587	12.2134 3583	12.1062 4877	14
15	13.2172 0093	13.0928 8046	12.9702 4376	12.8492 6350	15
16	13.9898 6562	13.8504 9677	13.7131 2271	13.5777 0931	16
17	14.7501 7527	14.5950 8282	14.4423 2904	14.2918 7188	17
18	15.4983 2745	15.3268 6272	15.1581 1439	14.9920 3125	18
19	16.2345 1655	16.0460 5673	15.8607 2578	15.6784 6201	19
20	16.9589 3388	16.7528 8130	16.5504 0568	16.3514 3334	20
21	17.6717 6765	17.4475 4919	17.2273 9208	17.0112 0916	21
22	18.3732 0310	18.1302 6948	17.8919 1860	17.6580 4820	22
23	19.0634 2249	18.8012 4764	18.5442 1458	18.2922 0412	23
24	19.7426 0515	19.4606 8565	19.1845 0511	18.9139 2560	24
25	20.4109 2758	20.1087 8196	19.8130 1115	19.5234 5647	25
26	21.0685 6342	20.7457 3166	20.4299 4960	20.1210 4376	26
27	21.7156 8357	21.3717 2644	21.0355 3334	20.7068 9780	27
28	22.3524 5615	21.9869 5474	21.6299 7138	21.2812 7236	28
29	22.9790 4665	22.5916 0171	22.2134 6884	21.8443 8466	29
30	23.5956 1786	23.1858 4934	22.7862 2708	22.3964 5555	30
31	24.2023 2999	23.7698 7650	23.3484 4376	22.9377 0152	31
32	24.7993 4071	24.3438 5897	23.9003 1290	23.4683 3482	32
33	25.3868 0512	24.9079 6951	24.4420 2493	23.9885 6355	33
34	25.9648 7589	25.4623 7789	24.9737 6680	24.4985 9172	34
35	26.5337 0321	26.0072 5100	25.4957 2201	24.9986 1933	35
36	27.0934 3490	26.5427 5283	26.0080 7069	25.4888 4248	36
37	27.6442 1638	27.0690 4455	26.5109 8963	25.9694 5341	37
38	28.1861 9078	27.5862 8457	27.0046 5240	26.4406 4060	38
39	28.7194 9892	28.0946 2857	27.4892 2931	26.9025 8883	39
40	29.2442 7938	28.5942 2955	27.9648 8770	27.3554 7924	40
41	29.7606 6852	29.0852 3789	28.4317 9161	27.7994 8945	41
42	30.2688 0051	29.5678 0135	28.8901 0220	28.2347 9358	42
43	30.7688 0739	30.0420 6522	29.3399 7762	28.6615 6233	43
44	31.2608 1908	30.5081 7221	29.7815 7312	29.0799 6307	44
45	31.7449 6342	30.9662 6261	30.2150 4110	29.4901 5987	45
46	32.2213 6622	31.4164 7431	30.6405 3114	29.8923 1360	46
47	32.6901 5127	31.8589 4281	31.0581 9008	30.2865 8196	47
48	33.1514 4036	32.2938 0129	31.4681 6204	30.6731 1957	48
49	33.6053 5337	32.7211 8063	31.8705 8850	31.0520 7801	49
50	34.0520 0823	33.1412 0946	32.2656 0835	31.4236 0589	50

TABLE 8 PRESENT VALUE OF ANNUITY

WHEN PERIODIC PAYMENT IS 1

$$a_{\overline{n}|i} = \frac{1-(1+i)^{-n}}{i}$$

n	$1\frac{5}{8}\%$	$1\frac{3}{4}\%$	$1\frac{7}{8}\%$	2%	n
51	34.4915 2102	33.5540 1421	32.6533 5789	31.7878 4892	51
52	34.9240 0592	33.9597 1913	33.0339 7093	32.1449 4992	52
53	35.3495 7532	34.3584 4632	33.4075 7883	32.4950 4894	53
54	35.7683 3980	34.7503 1579	33.7743 1051	32.8382 8327	54
55	36.1804 0817	35.1354 4550	34.1342 9252	33.1747 8752	55
56	36.5858 8750	35.5139 5135	34.4876 4910	33.5046 9365	56
57	36.9848 8314	35.8859 4727	34.8345 0219	33.8281 3103	57
58	37.3774 9879	36.2515 4523	35.1749 7147	34.1452 2650	58
59	37.7638 3645	36.6108 5526	35.5091 7445	34.4561 0441	59
60	38.1439 9650	36.9639 8552	35.8372 2645	34.7608 8668	60
61	38.5180 7774	37.3110 4228	36.1592 4069	35.0596 9282	61
62	38.8861 7736	37.6521 3000	36.4753 2828	35.3526 4002	62
63	39.2483 9100	37.9873 5135	36.7855 9832	35.6398 4316	63
64	39.6048 1280	38.3168 0723	37.0901 5786	35.9214 1486	64
65	39.9555 3535	38.6405 9678	37.3891 1201	36.1974 6555	65
66	40.3006 4979	38.9588 1748	37.6825 6393	36.4681 0348	66
67	40.6402 4579	39.2715 6509	37.9706 1490	36.7334 3478	67
68	40.9744 1161	39.5789 3375	38.2533 6432	36.9935 6351	68
69	41.3032 3405	39.8810 1597	38.5309 0976	37.2485 9168	69
70	41.6267 9858	40.1779 0267	38.8033 4701	37.4986 1929	70
71	41.9451 8925	40.4696 8321	39.0707 7007	37.7437 4441	71
72	42.2584 8881	40.7564 4542	39.3332 7123	37.9840 6314	72
73	42.5667 7865	41.0382 7560	39.5909 4109	38.2196 6975	73
74	42.8701 3890	41.3152 5857	39.8438 6855	38.4506 5662	74
75	43.1686 4836	41.5874 7771	40.0921 4091	38.6771 1433	75
76	43.4623 8461	41.8550 1495	40.3358 4384	38.8991 3170	76
77	43.7514 2397	42.1179 5081	40.5750 6144	39.1167 9578	77
78	44.0358 4155	42.3763 6443	40.8098 7626	39.3301 9194	78
79	44.3157 1124	42.6303 3359	41.0403 6933	39.5394 0386	79
80	44.5911 0577	42.8799 3474	41.2666 2020	39.7445 1359	80
81	44.8620 9670	43.1252 4298	41.4887 0695	39.9456 0156	81
82	45.1287 5444	43.3663 3217	41.7067 0621	40.1427 4663	82
83	45.3911 4828	43.6032 7486	41.9206 9321	40.3360 2611	83
84	45.6493 4640	43.8361 4237	42.1307 4180	40.5255 1579	84
85	45.9034 1589	44.0650 0479	42.3369 2447	40.7112 8999	85
86	46.1534 2277	44.2899 3099	42.5393 1236	40.8934 2156	86
87	46.3994 3200	44.5109 8869	42.7379 7532	41.0719 8192	87
88	46.6415 0750	44.7282 4441	42.9329 8191	41.2470 4110	88
89	46.8797 1218	44.9417 6355	43.1243 9942	41.4186 6774	89
90	47.1141 0793	45.1516 1037	43.3122 9391	41.5869 2916	90
91	47.3447 5565	45.3578 4803	43.4967 3022	41.7518 9133	91
92	47.5717 1528	45.5605 3860	43.6777 7199	41.9136 1895	92
93	47.7950 4578	45.7597 4310	43.8554 8171	42.0721 7545	93
94	48.0148 0520	45.9555 2147	44.0299 2070	42.2276 2299	94
95	48.2310 5062	46.1479 3265	44.2011 4915	42.3800 2254	95
96	48.4438 3825	46.3370 3455	44.3692 2616	42.5294 3386	96
97	48.6532 2337	46.5228 8408	44.5342 0973	42.6759 1555	97
98	48.8592 6039	46.7055 3718	44.6961 5679	42.8195 2505	98
99	49.0620 0285	46.8850 4882	44.8551 2323	42.9603 1867	99
100	49.2615 0342	47.0614 7304	45.0111 6391	43.0983 5164	100

TABLE 8 PRESENT VALUE OF ANNUITY
WHEN PERIODIC PAYMENT IS 1

$$a_{\overline{n}|i} = \frac{1-(1+i)^{-n}}{i}$$

n	$2\frac{1}{4}$%	$2\frac{1}{2}$%	$2\frac{3}{4}$%	3%	n
1	0.9779 9511	0.9756 0976	0.9732 3601	0.9708 7379	1
2	1.9344 6955	1.9274 2415	1.9204 2434	1.9134 6970	2
3	2.8698 9687	2.8560 2356	2.8422 6213	2.8286 1135	3
4	3.7847 4021	3.7619 7421	3.7394 2787	3.7170 9840	4
5	4.6794 5253	4.6458 2850	4.6125 8186	4.5797 0719	5
6	5.5544 7680	5.5081 2536	5.4623 6678	5.4171 9144	6
7	6.4102 4626	6.3493 9060	6.2894 0806	6.2302 8296	7
8	7.2471 8461	7.1701 3717	7.0943 1441	7.0196 9219	8
9	8.0657 0622	7.9708 6553	7.8776 7826	7.7861 0892	9
10	8.8662 1635	8.7520 6393	8.6400 7616	8.5302 0284	10
11	9.6491 1134	9.5142 0871	9.3820 6926	9.2526 2411	11
12	10.4147 7882	10.2577 6460	10.1042 0366	9.9540 0399	12
13	11.1635 9787	10.9831 8497	10.8070 1086	10.6349 5533	13
14	11.8959 3924	11.6909 1217	11.4910 0814	11.2960 7314	14
15	12.6121 6551	12.3813 7773	12.1566 9892	11.9379 3509	15
16	13.3126 3131	13.0550 0266	12.8045 7315	12.5611 0203	16
17	13.9976 8343	13.7121 9772	13.4351 0769	13.1661 1847	17
18	14.6676 6106	14.3533 6363	14.0487 6661	13.7535 1308	18
19	15.3228 9590	14.9788 9134	14.6460 0157	14.3237 9911	19
20	15.9637 1237	15.5891 6229	15.2272 5213	14.8774 7486	20
21	16.5904 2775	16.1845 4857	15.7929 4612	15.4150 2414	21
22	17.2033 5232	16.7654 1324	16.3434 9987	15.9369 1664	22
23	17.8027 8955	17.3321 1048	16.8793 1861	16.4436 0839	23
24	18.3890 3624	17.8849 8583	17.4007 9670	16.9355 4212	24
25	18.9623 8263	18.4243 7642	17.9083 1795	17.4131 4769	25
26	19.5231 1260	18.9506 1114	18.4022 5592	17.8768 4242	26
27	20.0715 0376	19.4640 1087	18.8829 7413	18.3270 3147	27
28	20.6078 2764	19.9648 8866	19.3508 2640	18.7641 0823	28
29	21.1323 4977	20.4535 4991	19.8061 5708	19.1884 5459	29
30	21.6453 2985	20.9302 9259	20.2493 0130	19.6004 4135	30
31	22.1470 2186	21.3954 0741	20.6805 8520	20.0004 2849	31
32	22.6376 7419	21.8491 7796	21.1003 2623	20.3887 6553	32
33	23.1175 2977	22.2918 8094	21.5088 3332	20.7657 9178	33
34	23.5868 2618	22.7237 8628	21.9064 0712	21.1318 3668	34
35	24.0457 9577	23.1451 5734	22.2933 4026	21.4872 2007	35
36	24.4946 6579	23.5562 5107	22.6699 1753	21.8322 5250	36
37	24.9336 5848	23.9573 1812	23.0364 1609	22.1672 3544	37
38	25.3629 9118	24.3486 0304	23.3931 0568	22.4924 6159	38
39	25.7828 7646	24.7303 4443	23.7402 4884	22.8082 1513	39
40	26.1935 2221	25.1027 7505	24.0781 0106	23.1147 7197	40
41	26.5951 3174	25.4661 2200	24.4069 1101	23.4123 9998	41
42	26.9879 0390	25.8206 0683	24.7269 2069	23.7013 5920	42
43	27.3720 3316	26.1664 4569	25.0383 6563	23.9819 0213	43
44	27.7477 0969	26.5038 4945	25.3414 7507	24.2542 7392	44
45	28.1151 1950	26.8330 2386	25.6364 7209	24.5187 1254	45
46	28.4744 4450	27.1541 6962	25.9235 7381	24.7754 4907	46
47	28.8258 6259	27.4674 8255	26.2029 9154	25.0247 0783	47
48	29.1695 4777	27.7731 5371	26.4749 3094	25.2667 0664	48
49	29.5056 7019	28.0713 6947	26.7395 9215	25.5016 5693	49
50	29.8343 9627	28.3623 1168	26.9971 6998	25.7297 6401	50

TABLE 8 PRESENT VALUE OF ANNUITY
WHEN PERIODIC PAYMENT IS 1

$$a_{\overline{n}|i} = \frac{1-(1+i)^{-n}}{i}$$

n	$2\frac{1}{4}\%$	$2\frac{1}{2}\%$	$2\frac{3}{4}\%$	3%	n
51	30.1558 8877	28.6461 5774	27.2478 5400	25.9512 2719	51
52	30.4703 0687	28.9230 8072	27.4918 2871	26.1662 3999	52
53	30.7778 0623	29.1932 4948	27.7292 7368	26.3749 9028	53
54	31.0785 3910	29.4568 2876	27.9603 6368	26.5776 6047	54
55	31.3726 5438	29.7139 7928	28.1852 6879	26.7744 2764	55
56	31.6602 9768	29.9648 5784	28.4041 5454	26.9654 6373	56
57	31.9416 1142	30.2096 1740	28.6171 8203	27.1509 3566	57
58	32.2167 3489	30.4484 0722	28.8245 0806	27.3310 0549	58
59	32.4858 0429	30.6813 7290	29.0262 8522	27.5058 3058	59
60	32.7489 5285	30.9086 5649	29.2226 6201	27.6755 6367	60
61	33.0063 1086	31.1303 9657	29.4137 8298	27.8403 5307	61
62	33.2580 0573	31.3467 2836	29.5997 8879	28.0003 4279	62
63	33.5041 6208	31.5577 8377	29.7808 1634	28.1556 7261	63
64	33.7449 0179	31.7636 9148	29.9569 9887	28.3064 7826	64
65	33.9803 4405	31.9645 7705	30.1284 6605	28.4528 9152	65
66	34.2106 0543	32.1605 6298	30.2953 4409	28.5950 4031	66
67	34.4357 9993	32.3517 6876	30.4577 5581	28.7330 4884	67
68	34.6560 3905	32.5383 1099	30.6158 2074	28.8670 3771	68
69	34.8714 3183	32.7203 0340	30.7696 5522	28.9971 2399	69
70	35.0820 8492	32.8978 5698	30.9193 7247	29.1234 2135	70
71	35.2881 0261	33.0710 7998	31.0650 8270	29.2460 4015	71
72	35.4895 8691	33.2400 7803	31.2068 9314	29.3650 8752	72
73	35.6866 3756	33.4049 5417	31.3449 0816	29.4806 6750	73
74	35.8793 5214	33.5658 0895	31.4792 2936	29.5928 8107	74
75	36.0678 2605	33.7227 4044	31.6099 5558	29.7018 2628	75
76	36.2521 5262	33.8758 4433	31.7371 8304	29.8075 9833	76
77	36.4324 2310	34.0252 1398	31.8610 0540	29.9102 8964	77
78	36.6087 2675	34.1709 4047	31.9815 1377	30.0099 8994	78
79	36.7811 5085	34.3131 1265	32.0987 9685	30.1067 8635	79
80	36.9497 8079	34.4518 1722	32.2129 4098	30.2007 6345	80
81	37.1147 0004	34.5871 3875	32.3240 3015	30.2920 0335	81
82	37.2759 9026	34.7191 5976	32.4321 4613	30.3805 8577	82
83	37.4337 3130	34.8479 6074	32.5373 6850	30.4665 8813	83
84	37.5880 0127	34.9736 2023	32.6397 7469	30.5500 8556	84
85	37.7388 7655	35.0962 1486	32.7394 4009	30.6311 5103	85
86	37.8864 3183	35.2158 1938	32.8364 3804	30.7098 5537	86
87	38.0307 4018	35.3325 0671	32.9308 3994	30.7862 6735	87
88	38.1718 7304	35.4463 4801	33.0227 1527	30.8604 5374	88
89	38.3099 0028	35.5574 1269	33.1121 3165	30.9324 7936	89
90	38.4448 9025	35.6657 6848	33.1991 5489	31.0024 0714	90
91	38.5769 0978	35.7714 8144	33.2838 4905	31.0702 9820	91
92	38.7060 2423	35.8746 1604	33.3662 7644	31.1362 1184	92
93	38.8322 9754	35.9752 3516	33.4464 9776	31.2002 0567	93
94	38.9557 9221	36.0734 0016	33.5245 7202	31.2623 3560	94
95	39.0765 6940	36.1691 7089	33.6005 5671	31.3226 5592	95
96	39.1946 8890	36.2626 0574	33.6745 0775	31.3812 1934	96
97	39.3102 0920	36.3537 6170	33.7464 7956	31.4380 7703	97
98	39.4231 8748	36.4426 9434	33.8165 2512	31.4932 7867	98
99	39.5336 7968	36.5294 5790	33.8846 9598	31.5468 7250	99
100	39.6417 4052	36.6141 0526	33.9510 4232	31.5989 0534	100

TABLE 8 PRESENT VALUE OF ANNUITY

WHEN PERIODIC PAYMENT IS 1

$$a_{\overline{n}|i} = \frac{1-(1+i)^{-n}}{i}$$

n	$3\frac{1}{4}\%$	$3\frac{1}{2}\%$	$3\frac{3}{4}\%$	4%	n
1	0.9685 2300	0.9661 8357	0.9638 5542	0.9615 3846	1
2	1.9065 5981	1.8996 9428	1.8928 7270	1.8860 9467	2
3	2.8150 7003	2.8016 3698	2.7883 1103	2.7750 9103	3
4	3.6949 8308	3.6730 7921	3.6513 8413	3.6298 9522	4
5	4.5471 9911	4.5150 5238	4.4832 6181	4.4518 2233	5
6	5.3725 8994	5.3285 5302	5.2850 7162	5.2421 3686	6
7	6.1719 9994	6.1145 4398	6.0579 0036	6.0020 5467	7
8	6.9462 4692	6.8739 5554	6.8027 9553	6.7327 4488	8
9	7.6961 2292	7.6076 8651	7.5207 6677	7.4353 3161	9
10	8.4223 9508	8.3166 0532	8.2127 8725	8.1108 9578	10
11	9.1258 0637	9.0015 5104	8.8797 9494	8.7604 7671	11
12	9.8070 7639	9.6633 3433	9.5226 9392	9.3850 7376	12
13	10.4669 0207	10.3027 3849	10.1423 5558	9.9856 4785	13
14	11.1059 5842	10.9205 2028	10.7396 1984	10.5631 2293	14
15	11.7248 9920	11.5174 1090	11.3152 9623	11.1183 8743	15
16	12.3243 5758	12.0941 1681	11.8701 6504	11.6522 9561	16
17	12.9049 4681	12.6513 2059	12.4049 7835	12.1656 6885	17
18	13.4672 6083	13.1896 8173	12.9204 6106	12.6592 9697	18
19	14.0118 7490	13.7098 3742	13.4173 1187	13.1339 3940	19
20	14.5393 4615	14.2124 0330	13.8962 0421	13.5903 2634	20
21	15.0502 1419	14.6979 7420	14.3577 8719	14.0291 5995	21
22	15.5450 0163	15.1671 2484	14.8026 8645	14.4511 1533	22
23	16.0242 1466	15.6204 1047	15.2315 0501	14.8568 4167	23
24	16.4883 4349	16.0583 6760	15.6448 2411	15.2469 6314	24
25	16.9378 6295	16.4815 1459	16.0432 0396	15.6220 7994	25
26	17.3732 3288	16.8903 5226	16.4271 8454	15.9827 6918	26
27	17.7948 9867	17.2853 6451	16.7972 8630	16.3295 8575	27
28	18.2032 9169	17.6670 1885	17.1540 1089	16.6630 6322	28
29	18.5988 2973	18.0357 6700	17.4978 4183	16.9837 1463	29
30	18.9819 1741	18.3920 4541	17.8292 4513	17.2920 3330	30
31	19.3529 4664	18.7362 7576	18.1486 7001	17.5884 9356	31
32	19.7122 9699	19.0688 6547	18.4565 4941	17.8735 5150	32
33	20.0603 3607	19.3902 0818	18.7533 0063	18.1476 4567	33
34	20.3974 1992	19.7006 8423	19.0393 2591	18.4111 9776	34
35	20.7238 9339	20.0006 6110	19.3150 1293	18.6646 1323	35
36	21.0400 9045	20.2904 9381	19.5807 3535	18.9082 8195	36
37	21.3463 3457	20.5705 2542	19.8368 5335	19.1425 7880	37
38	21.6429 3905	20.8410 8736	20.0837 1407	19.3678 6423	38
39	21.9302 0732	21.1024 9987	20.3216 5212	19.5844 8484	39
40	22.2084 3324	21.3550 7234	20.5509 8999	19.7927 7388	40
41	22.4779 0144	21.5991 0371	20.7720 3855	19.9930 5181	41
42	22.7388 8759	21.8348 8281	20.9850 9739	20.1856 2674	42
43	22.9916 5869	22.0626 8870	21.1904 5532	20.3707 9494	43
44	23.2364 7330	22.2827 9102	21.3883 9067	20.5488 4129	44
45	23.4735 8189	22.4954 5026	21.5791 7173	20.7200 3970	45
46	23.7032 2701	22.7009 1813	21.7630 5709	20.8846 5356	46
47	23.9256 4360	22.8994 3780	21.9402 9599	21.0429 3612	47
48	24.1410 5917	23.0912 4425	22.1111 2866	21.1951 3088	48
49	24.3496 9412	23.2765 6450	22.2757 8666	21.3414 7200	49
50	24.5517 6185	23.4556 1787	22.4344 9317	21.4821 8462	50

TABLE 8 PRESENT VALUE OF ANNUITY
WHEN PERIODIC PAYMENT IS 1

$$a_{\overline{n}|i} = \frac{1-(1+i)^{-n}}{i}$$

n	$3\frac{1}{4}$%	$3\frac{1}{2}$%	$3\frac{3}{4}$%	4%	n
51	24.7474 6911	23.6286 1630	22.5874 6330	21.6174 8521	51
52	24.9370 1609	23.7957 6454	22.7349 0438	21.7475 8193	52
53	25.1205 9669	23.9572 6043	22.8770 1627	21.8726 7493	53
54	25.2983 9873	24.1132 9510	23.0139 9159	21.9929 5667	54
55	25.4706 0410	24.2640 5323	23.1460 1599	22.1086 1218	55
56	25.6373 8896	24.4097 1327	23.2732 6842	22.2198 1940	56
57	25.7989 2393	24.5504 4760	23.3959 2137	22.3267 4943	57
58	25.9553 7427	24.6864 2281	23.5141 4108	22.4295 6676	58
59	26.1069 0002	24.8177 9981	23.6280 8779	22.5284 2957	59
60	26.2536 5619	24.9447 3412	23.7379 1594	22.6234 8997	60
61	26.3957 9292	25.0673 7596	23.8437 7440	22.7148 9421	61
62	26.5334 5561	25.1858 7049	23.9458 0665	22.8027 8289	62
63	26.6667 8510	25.3003 5796	24.0441 5099	22.8872 9124	63
64	26.7959 1777	25.4109 7388	24.1389 4071	22.9685 4927	64
65	26.9209 8573	25.5178 4916	24.2303 0430	23.0466 8199	65
66	27.0421 1693	25.6211 1030	24.3183 6559	23.1218 0961	66
67	27.1594 3529	25.7208 7951	24.4032 4394	23.1940 4770	67
68	27.2730 6081	25.8172 7489	24.4850 5440	23.2635 0740	68
69	27.3831 0974	25.9104 1052	24.5639 0786	23.3302 9558	69
70	27.4896 9467	26.0003 9664	24.6399 1119	23.3945 1498	70
71	27.5929 2462	26.0873 3975	24.7131 6741	23.4562 6440	71
72	27.6929 0520	26.1713 4275	24.7837 7582	23.5156 3885	72
73	27.7897 3869	26.2525 0508	24.8518 3211	23.5727 2966	73
74	27.8835 2416	26.3309 2278	24.9174 2854	23.6276 2468	74
75	27.9743 5754	26.4066 8868	24.9806 5402	23.6804 0834	75
76	28.0623 3175	26.4798 9244	25.0415 9423	23.7311 6187	76
77	28.1475 3681	26.5506 2072	25.1003 3179	23.7799 6333	77
78	28.2300 5986	26.6189 5721	25.1569 4631	23.8268 8782	78
79	28.3099 8534	26.6849 8281	25.2115 1451	23.8720 0752	79
80	28.3873 9500	26.7487 7567	25.2641 1037	23.9153 9185	80
81	28.4623 6804	26.8104 1127	25.3148 0518	23.9571 0754	81
82	28.5349 8115	26.8699 6258	25.3636 6764	23.9972 1879	82
83	28.6053 0862	26.9275 0008	25.4107 6399	24.0357 8730	83
84	28.6734 2239	26.9830 9186	25.4561 5806	24.0728 7240	84
85	28.7393 9215	27.0368 0373	25.4999 1139	24.1085 3116	85
86	28.8032 8538	27.0886 9926	25.5420 8326	24.1428 1842	86
87	28.8651 6743	27.1388 3986	25.5827 3086	24.1757 8694	87
88	28.9251 0163	27.1872 8489	25.6219 0926	24.2074 8745	88
89	28.9831 4928	27.2340 9168	25.6596 7158	24.2379 6870	89
90	29.0393 6976	27.2793 1564	25.6960 6899	24.2672 7759	90
91	29.0938 2059	27.3230 1028	25.7311 5083	24.2954 5923	91
92	29.1465 5747	27.3652 2732	25.7649 6466	24.3225 5695	92
93	29.1976 3436	27.4060 1673	25.7975 5630	24.3486 1245	93
94	29.2471 0349	27.4454 2680	25.8289 6993	24.3736 6582	94
95	29.2950 1549	27.4835 0415	25.8592 4812	24.3977 5559	95
96	29.3414 1936	27.5202 9387	25.8884 3192	24.4209 1884	96
97	29.3863 6258	27.5558 3948	25.9165 6089	24.4431 9119	97
98	29.4298 9112	27.5901 8308	25.9436 7315	24.4646 0692	98
99	29.4720 4951	27.6233 6529	25.9698 0544	24.4851 9896	99
100	29.5128 8088	27.6554 2540	25.9949 9320	24.5049 9900	100

TABLE 8 PRESENT VALUE OF ANNUITY
WHEN PERIODIC PAYMENT IS 1

$$a_{\overline{n}|i} = \frac{1-(1+i)^{-n}}{i}$$

n	$4\frac{1}{2}\%$	5%	$5\frac{1}{2}\%$	6%	n
1	0.9569 3780	0.9523 8095	0.9478 6730	0.9433 9623	1
2	1.8726 6775	1.8594 1043	1.8463 1971	1.8333 9267	2
3	2.7489 6435	2.7232 4803	2.6979 3338	2.6730 1195	3
4	3.5875 2570	3.5459 5050	3.5051 5012	3.4651 0561	4
5	4.3899 7674	4.3294 7667	4.2702 8448	4.2123 6379	5
6	5.1578 7248	5.0756 9207	4.9955 3031	4.9173 2433	6
7	5.8927 0094	5.7863 7340	5.6829 6712	5.5823 8144	7
8	6.5958 8607	6.4632 1276	6.3345 6599	6.2097 9381	8
9	7.2687 9050	7.1078 2168	6.9521 9525	6.8016 9227	9
10	7.9127 1818	7.7217 3493	7.5376 2583	7.3600 8705	10
11	8.5289 1692	8.3064 1422	8.0925 3633	7.8868 7458	11
12	9.1185 8078	8.8632 5164	8.6185 1785	8.3838 4394	12
13	9.6828 5242	9.3935 7299	9.1170 7853	8.8526 8296	13
14	10.2228 2528	9.8986 4094	9.5896 4790	9.2949 8393	14
15	10.7395 4573	10.3796 5804	10.0375 8094	9.7122 4899	15
16	11.2340 1505	10.8377 6956	10.4621 6203	10.1058 9527	16
17	11.7071 9143	11.2740 6625	10.8646 0856	10.4772 5969	17
18	12.1599 9180	11.6895 8690	11.2460 7447	10.8276 0348	18
19	12.5932 9359	12.0853 2086	11.6076 5352	11.1581 1649	19
20	13.0079 3645	12.4622 1034	11.9503 8248	11.4699 2122	20
21	13.4047 2388	12.8211 5271	12.2752 4406	11.7640 7662	21
22	13.7844 2476	13.1630 0258	12.5831 6973	12.0415 8172	22
23	14.1477 7489	13.4885 7388	12.8750 4239	12.3033 7898	23
24	14.4954 7837	13.7986 4179	13.1516 9895	12.5503 5753	24
25	14.8282 0896	14.0939 4457	13.4139 3266	12.7833 5616	25
26	15.1466 1145	14.3751 8530	13.6624 9541	13.0031 6619	26
27	15.4513 0282	14.6430 3362	13.8980 9991	13.2105 3414	27
28	15.7428 7351	14.8981 2726	14.1214 2172	13.4061 6428	28
29	16.0218 8853	15.1410 7358	14.3331 0116	13.5907 2102	29
30	16.2888 8854	15.3724 5103	14.5337 4517	13.7648 3115	30
31	16.5443 9095	15.5928 1050	14.7239 2907	13.9290 8599	31
32	16.7888 9086	15.8026 7667	14.9041 9817	14.0840 4339	32
33	17.0228 6207	16.0025 4921	15.0750 6936	14.2302 2961	33
34	17.2467 5796	16.1929 0401	15.2370 3257	14.3681 4114	34
35	17.4610 1240	16.3741 9429	15.3905 5220	14.4982 4636	35
36	17.6660 4058	16.5468 5171	15.5360 6843	14.6209 8713	36
37	17.8622 3979	16.7112 8734	15.6739 9851	14.7367 8031	37
38	18.0499 9023	16.8678 9271	15.8047 3793	14.8460 1916	38
39	18.2296 5572	17.0170 4067	15.9286 6154	14.9490 7468	39
40	18.4015 8442	17.1590 8635	16.0461 2469	15.0462 9687	40
41	18.5661 0949	17.2943 6796	16.1574 6416	15.1380 1592	41
42	18.7235 4975	17.4232 0758	16.2629 9920	15.2245 4332	42
43	18.8742 1029	17.5459 1198	16.3630 3242	15.3061 7294	43
44	19.0183 8305	17.6627 7331	16.4578 5063	15.3831 8202	44
45	19.1563 4742	17.7740 6982	16.5477 2572	15.4558 3209	45
46	19.2883 7074	17.8800 6650	16.6329 1537	15.5243 6990	46
47	19.4147 0884	17.9810 1571	16.7136 6386	15.5890 2821	47
48	19.5356 0654	18.0771 5782	16.7902 0271	15.6500 2661	48
49	19.6512 9813	18.1687 2173	16.8627 5139	15.7075 7227	49
50	19.7620 0778	18.2559 2546	16.9315 1790	15.7618 6064	50

TABLE 8 PRESENT VALUE OF ANNUITY
WHEN PERIODIC PAYMENT IS 1

$$a_{\overline{n}|i} = \frac{1-(1+i)^{-n}}{i}$$

n	$4\frac{1}{2}$%	5%	$5\frac{1}{2}$%	6%	n
51	19.8679 5003	18.3389 7663	16.9966 9943	15.8130 7607	51
52	19.9693 3017	18.4180 7298	17.0584 8287	15.8613 9252	52
53	20.0663 4466	18.4934 0284	17.1170 4538	15.9069 7408	53
54	20.1591 8149	18.5651 4556	17.1725 5486	15.9499 7554	54
55	20.2480 2057	18.6334 7196	17.2251 7048	15.9905 4297	55
56	20.3330 3404	18.6985 4473	17.2750 4311	16.0288 1412	56
57	20.4143 8664	18.7605 1879	17.3223 1575	16.0649 1898	57
58	20.4922 3602	18.8195 4170	17.3671 2393	16.0989 8017	58
59	20.5667 3303	18.8757 5400	17.4095 9614	16.1311 1337	59
60	20.6380 2204	18.9292 8953	17.4498 5416	16.1614 2771	60
61	20.7062 4118	18.9802 7574	17.4880 1343	16.1900 2614	61
62	20.7715 2266	19.0288 3404	17.5241 8334	16.2170 0579	62
63	20.8339 9298	19.0750 8003	17.5584 6762	16.2424 5829	63
64	20.8937 7319	19.1191 2384	17.5909 6457	16.2664 7009	64
65	20.9509 7913	19.1610 7033	17.6217 6737	16.2891 2272	65
66	21.0057 2165	19.2010 1936	17.6509 6433	16.3104 9314	66
67	21.0581 0684	19.2390 6606	17.6786 3917	16.3306 5390	67
68	21.1082 3621	19.2753 0101	17.7048 7125	16.3496 7349	68
69	21.1562 0690	19.3098 1048	17.7297 3579	16.3676 1650	69
70	21.2021 1187	19.3426 7665	17.7533 0406	16.3845 4387	70
71	21.2460 4007	19.3739 7776	17.7756 4366	16.4005 1308	71
72	21.2880 7662	19.4037 8834	17.7968 1864	16.4155 7838	72
73	21.3283 0298	19.4321 7937	17.8168 8970	16.4297 9093	73
74	21.3667 9711	19.4592 1845	17.8359 1441	16.4431 9899	74
75	21.4036 3360	19.4849 6995	17.8539 4731	16.4558 4810	75
76	21.4388 8383	19.5094 9518	17.8710 4010	16.4677 8123	76
77	21.4726 1611	19.5328 5257	17.8872 4180	16.4790 3889	77
78	21.5048 9579	19.5550 9768	17.9025 9887	16.4896 5933	78
79	21.5357 8545	19.5762 8351	17.9171 5532	16.4996 7862	79
80	21.5653 4493	19.5964 6048	17.9309 5291	16.5091 3077	80
81	21.5936 3151	19.6156 7665	17.9440 3120	16.5180 4790	81
82	21.6207 0001	19.6339 7776	17.9564 2767	16.5264 6028	82
83	21.6466 0288	19.6514 0739	17.9681 7789	16.5343 9649	83
84	21.6713 9032	19.6680 0704	17.9793 1554	16.5418 8348	84
85	21.6951 1035	19.6838 1623	17.9898 7255	16.5489 4668	85
86	21.7178 0895	19.6988 7260	17.9998 7919	16.5556 1008	86
87	21.7395 3009	19.7132 1200	18.0093 6416	16.5618 9630	87
88	21.7603 1588	19.7268 6857	18.0183 5466	16.5678 2670	88
89	21.7802 0658	19.7398 7483	18.0268 7645	16.5734 2141	89
90	21.7992 4075	19.7522 6174	18.0349 5398	16.5786 9944	90
91	21.8174 5526	19.7640 5880	18.0426 1041	16.5836 7872	91
92	21.8348 8542	19.7752 9410	18.0498 6769	16.5883 7615	92
93	21.8515 6499	19.7859 9438	18.0567 4662	16.5928 0769	93
94	21.8675 2631	19.7961 8512	18.0632 6694	16.5969 8839	94
95	21.8828 0030	19.8058 9059	18.0694 4734	16.6009 3244	95
96	21.8974 1655	19.8151 3390	18.0753 0553	16.6046 5325	96
97	21.9114 0340	19.8239 3705	18.0808 5832	16.6081 6344	97
98	21.9247 8794	19.8323 2100	18.0861 2164	16.6114 7494	98
99	21.9375 9612	19.8403 0571	18.0911 1055	16.6145 9900	99
100	21.9498 5274	19.8479 1020	18.0958 3939	16.6175 4623	100

TABLE 8 PRESENT VALUE OF ANNUITY
WHEN PERIODIC PAYMENT IS 1

$$a_{\overline{n}|i} = \frac{1-(1+i)^{-n}}{i}$$

n	$6\frac{1}{2}$%	7%	$7\frac{1}{2}$%	8%	n
1	0.9389 6714	0.9345 7944	0.9302 3256	0.9259 2593	1
2	1.8206 2642	1.8080 1817	1.7955 6517	1.7832 6475	2
3	2.6484 7551	2.6243 1604	2.6005 2574	2.5770 9699	3
4	3.4257 9860	3.3872 1126	3.3493 2627	3.3121 2684	4
5	4.1556 7944	4.1001 9744	4.0458 8490	3.9927 1004	5
6	4.8410 1356	4.7665 3966	4.6938 4642	4.6228 7966	6
7	5.4845 1977	5.3892 8940	5.2966 0132	5.2063 7006	7
8	6.0887 5096	5.9712 9851	5.8573 0355	5.7466 3894	8
9	6.6561 0419	6.5152 3225	6.3788 8703	6.2468 8791	9
10	7.1888 3022	7.0235 8154	6.8640 8096	6.7100 8140	10
11	7.6890 4246	7.4986 7434	7.3154 2415	7.1389 6426	11
12	8.1587 2532	7.9426 8630	7.7352 7827	7.5360 7802	12
13	8.5997 4208	8.3576 5074	8.1258 4026	7.9037 7594	13
14	9.0138 4233	8.7454 6799	8.4891 5373	8.2442 3698	14
15	9.4026 6885	9.1079 1401	8.8271 1974	8.5594 7869	15
16	9.7677 6418	9.4466 4860	9.1415 0674	8.8513 6916	16
17	10.1105 7670	9.7632 2299	9.4339 5976	9.1216 3811	17
18	10.4324 6638	10.0590 8691	9.7060 0908	9.3718 8714	18
19	10.7347 1022	10.3355 9524	9.9590 7821	9.6035 9920	19
20	11.0185 0725	10.5940 1425	10.1944 9136	9.8181 4741	20
21	11.2849 8333	10.8355 2733	10.4134 8033	10.0168 0316	21
22	11.5351 9562	11.0612 4050	10.6171 9101	10.2007 4366	22
23	11.7701 3673	11.2721 8738	10.8066 8931	10.3710 5895	23
24	11.9907 3871	11.4693 3400	10.9829 6680	10.5287 5828	24
25	12.1978 7673	11.6535 8318	11.1469 4586	10.6747 7619	25
26	12.3923 7251	11.8257 7867	11.2994 8452	10.8099 7795	26
27	12.5749 9766	11.9867 0904	11.4413 8095	10.9351 6477	27
28	12.7464 7668	12.1371 1125	11.5733 7763	11.0510 7849	28
29	12.9074 8984	12.2776 7407	11.6961 6524	11.1584 0601	29
30	13.0586 7591	12.4090 4118	11.8103 8627	11.2577 8334	30
31	13.2006 3465	12.5318 1419	11.9166 3839	11.3497 9939	31
32	13.3339 2925	12.6465 5532	12.0154 7757	11.4349 9944	32
33	13.4590 8850	12.7537 9002	12.1074 2099	11.5138 8837	33
34	13.5766 0892	12.8540 0936	12.1929 4976	11.5869 3367	34
35	13.6869 5673	12.9476 7230	12.2725 1141	11.6545 6822	35
36	13.7905 6970	13.0352 0776	12.3465 2224	11.7171 9279	36
37	13.8878 5887	13.1170 1660	12.4153 6952	11.7751 7851	37
38	13.9792 1021	13.1934 7345	12.4794 1351	11.8288 6899	38
39	14.0649 8611	13.2649 2846	12.5389 8931	11.8785 8240	39
40	14.1455 2687	13.3317 0884	12.5944 0866	11.9246 1333	40
41	14.2211 5199	13.3941 2041	12.6459 6155	11.9672 3457	41
42	14.2921 6149	13.4524 4898	12.6939 1772	12.0066 9867	42
43	14.3588 3708	13.5069 6167	12.7385 2811	12.0432 3951	43
44	14.4214 4327	13.5579 0810	12.7800 2615	12.0770 7362	44
45	14.4802 2842	13.6055 2159	12.8186 2898	12.1084 0150	45
46	14.5354 2575	13.6500 2018	12.8545 3858	12.1374 0880	46
47	14.5872 5422	13.6916 0764	12.8879 4287	12.1642 6741	47
48	14.6359 1946	13.7304 7443	12.9190 1662	12.1891 3649	48
49	14.6816 1451	13.7667 9853	12.9479 2244	12.2121 6341	49
50	14.7245 2067	13.8007 4629	12.9748 1157	12.2334 8464	50

TABLE 8 PRESENT VALUE OF ANNUITY
WHEN PERIODIC PAYMENT IS 1

$$a_{\overline{n}|i} = \frac{1-(1+i)^{-n}}{i}$$

n	$6\frac{1}{2}$%	7%	$7\frac{1}{2}$%	8%	n
51	14.7648 0814	13.8324 7317	12.9998 2472	12.2532 2652	51
52	14.8026 3675	13.8621 2446	13.0230 9276	12.2715 0604	52
53	14.8381 5658	13.8898 3594	13.0447 3745	12.2884 3152	53
54	14.8715 0852	13.9157 3453	13.0648 7205	12.3041 0326	54
55	14.9028 2490	13.9399 3881	13.0836 0190	12.3186 1413	55
56	14.9322 2996	13.9625 5964	13.1010 2503	12.3320 5012	56
57	14.9598 4033	13.9837 0059	13.1172 3258	12.3444 9085	57
58	14.9857 6557	14.0034 5850	13.1323 0938	12.3560 1005	58
59	15.0101 0852	14.0219 2383	13.1463 3431	12.3666 7597	59
60	15.0329 6574	14.0391 8115	13.1593 8075	12.3765 5182	60
61	15.0544 2793	14.0553 0949	13.1715 1698	12.3856 9613	61
62	15.0745 8022	14.0703 8270	13.1828 0649	12.3941 6308	62
63	15.0935 0255	14.0844 6981	13.1933 0836	12.4020 0286	63
64	15.1112 7000	14.0976 3534	13.2030 7755	12.4092 6190	64
65	15.1279 5305	14.1099 3957	13.2121 6516	12.4159 8324	65
66	15.1436 1789	14.1214 3885	13.2206 1875	12.4222 0671	66
67	15.1583 2666	14.1321 8584	13.2284 8256	12.4279 6917	67
68	15.1721 3771	14.1422 2976	13.2357 9773	12.4333 0479	68
69	15.1851 0583	14.1516 1660	13.2426 0254	12.4382 4518	69
70	15.1972 8247	14.1603 8934	13.2489 3260	12.4428 1961	70
71	15.2087 1593	14.1685 8817	13.2548 2102	12.4470 5519	71
72	15.2194 5158	14.1762 5063	13.2602 9862	12.4509 7703	72
73	15.2295 3200	14.1834 1180	13.2653 9407	12.4546 0836	73
74	15.2389 9718	14.1901 0449	13.2701 3402	12.4579 7070	74
75	15.2478 8468	14.1963 5933	13.2745 4327	12.4610 8399	75
76	15.2562 2974	14.2022 0498	13.2786 4490	12.4639 6665	76
77	15.2640 6549	14.2076 6821	13.2824 6038	12.4666 3579	77
78	15.2714 2299	14.2127 7403	13.2860 0965	12.4691 0721	78
79	15.2783 3145	14.2175 4582	13.2893 1130	12.4713 9557	79
80	15.2848 1826	14.2220 0544	13.2923 8261	12.4735 1441	80
81	15.2909 0917	14.2261 7331	13.2952 3964	12.4754 7631	81
82	15.2966 2832	14.2300 6851	13.2978 9734	12.4772 9288	82
83	15.3019 9843	14.2337 0889	13.3003 6961	12.4789 7489	83
84	15.3070 4078	14.2371 1111	13.3026 6941	12.4805 3230	84
85	15.3117 7538	14.2402 9076	13.3048 0875	12.4819 7436	85
86	15.3162 2101	14.2432 6239	13.3067 9884	12.4833 0959	86
87	15.3203 9532	14.2460 3962	13.3086 5008	12.4845 4592	87
88	15.3243 1485	14.2486 3516	13.3103 7217	12.4856 9066	88
89	15.3279 9516	14.2510 6089	13.3119 7411	12.4867 5061	89
90	15.3314 5086	14.2533 2794	13.3134 6429	12.4877 3205	90
91	15.3346 9564	14.2554 4667	13.3148 5050	12.4886 4079	91
92	15.3377 4239	14.2574 2680	13.3161 4000	12.4894 8221	92
93	15.3406 0318	14.2592 7738	13.3173 3954	12.4902 6131	93
94	15.3432 8937	14.2610 0690	13.3184 5538	12.4909 8269	94
95	15.3458 1162	14.2626 2327	13.3194 9338	12.4916 5064	95
96	15.3481 7992	14.2641 3390	13.3204 5896	12.4922 6911	96
97	15.3504 0368	14.2655 4570	13.3213 5717	12.4928 4177	97
98	15.3524 9172	14.2668 6514	13.3221 9272	12.4933 7201	98
99	15.3544 5232	14.2680 9826	13.3229 6997	12.4938 6297	99
100	15.3562 9326	14.2692 5071	13.3236 9299	12.4943 1757	100

TABLE 8 PRESENT VALUE OF ANNUITY
WHEN PERIODIC PAYMENT IS 1

$$a_{\overline{n}|i} = \frac{1-(1+i)^{-n}}{i}$$

n	$8\frac{1}{2}\%$	9%	$9\frac{1}{2}\%$	10%	n
1	0.9216 5899	0.9174 3119	0.9132 4201	0.9090 9091	1
2	1.7711 1427	1.7591 1119	1.7472 5298	1.7355 3719	2
3	2.5540 2237	2.5312 9467	2.5089 0683	2.4868 5199	3
4	3.2755 9666	3.2397 1988	3.2044 8112	3.1698 6545	4
5	3.9406 4208	3.8896 5126	3.8397 0879	3.7907 8677	5
6	4.5535 8717	4.4859 1859	4.4198 2538	4.3552 6070	6
7	5.1185 1352	5.0329 5284	4.9496 1222	4.8684 1882	7
8	5.6391 8297	5.5348 1911	5.4334 3581	5.3349 2620	8
9	6.1190 6264	5.9952 4689	5.8752 8385	5.7590 2382	9
10	6.5613 4806	6.4176 5770	6.2787 9803	6.1445 6711	10
11	6.9689 8439	6.8051 9055	6.6473 0414	6.4950 6101	11
12	7.3446 8607	7.1607 2528	6.9838 3940	6.8136 9182	12
13	7.6909 5490	7.4869 0392	7.2911 7753	7.1033 5620	13
14	8.0100 9668	7.7861 5039	7.5718 5163	7.3666 8746	14
15	8.3042 3658	8.0606 8843	7.8281 7500	7.6060 7951	15
16	8.5753 3325	8.3125 5819	8.0622 6028	7.8237 0864	16
17	8.8251 9194	8.5436 3137	8.2760 3678	8.0215 5331	17
18	9.0554 7644	8.7556 2511	8.4712 6647	8.2014 1210	18
19	9.2677 2022	8.9501 1478	8.6495 5842	8.3649 2009	19
20	9.4633 3661	9.1285 4567	8.8123 8212	8.5135 6372	20
21	9.6436 2821	9.2922 4373	8.9610 7956	8.6486 9429	21
22	9.8097 9558	9.4424 2544	9.0968 7631	8.7715 4026	22
23	9.9629 4524	9.5802 0683	9.2208 9161	8.8832 1842	23
24	10.1040 9700	9.7066 1177	9.3341 4759	8.9847 4402	24
25	10.2341 9078	9.8225 7960	9.4375 7770	9.0770 4002	25
26	10.3540 9288	9.9289 7211	9.5320 3443	9.1609 4547	26
27	10.4646 0174	10.0265 7992	9.6182 9629	9.2372 2316	27
28	10.5664 5321	10.1161 2837	9.6970 7423	9.3065 6651	28
29	10.6603 2554	10.1982 8291	9.7690 1757	9.3696 0591	29
30	10.7468 4382	10.2736 5404	9.8347 1924	9.4269 1447	30
31	10.8265 8416	10.3428 0187	9.8947 2076	9.4790 1315	31
32	10.9000 7757	10.4062 4025	9.9495 1668	9.5263 7559	32
33	10.9678 1343	10.4644 4060	9.9995 5861	9.5694 3236	33
34	11.0302 4279	10.5178 3541	10.0452 5901	9.6085 7487	34
35	11.0877 8137	10.5668 2148	10.0869 9453	9.6441 5897	35
36	11.1408 1233	10.6117 6282	10.1251 0916	9.6765 0816	36
37	11.1896 8878	10.6529 9342	10.1599 1704	9.7059 1651	37
38	11.2347 3620	10.6908 1965	10.1917 0506	9.7326 5137	38
39	11.2762 5457	10.7255 2261	10.2207 3521	9.7569 5579	39
40	11.3145 2034	10.7573 6020	10.2472 4677	9.7790 5072	40
41	11.3497 8833	10.7865 6899	10.2714 5824	9.7991 3702	41
42	11.3822 9339	10.8133 6604	10.2935 6917	9.8173 9729	42
43	11.4122 5197	10.8379 5050	10.3137 6180	9.8339 9753	43
44	11.4398 6357	10.8605 0504	10.3322 0255	9.8490 8867	44
45	11.4653 1205	10.8811 9729	10.3490 4343	9.8628 0788	45
46	11.4887 6686	10.9001 8100	10.3644 2322	9.8752 7989	46
47	11.5103 8420	10.9175 9725	10.3784 6870	9.8866 1808	47
48	11.5303 0802	10.9335 7546	10.3912 9561	9.8969 2553	48
49	11.5486 7099	10.9482 3436	10.4030 0969	9.9062 9594	49
50	11.5655 9538	10.9616 8290	10.4137 0748	9.9148 1449	50

TABLE 8 PRESENT VALUE OF ANNUITY
WHEN PERIODIC PAYMENT IS 1

$$a_{\overline{n}|i} = \frac{1-(1+i)^{-n}}{i}$$

n	$8\frac{1}{2}\%$	9%	$9\frac{1}{2}\%$	10%	n
51	11.5811 9390	10.9740 2101	10.4234 7715	9.9225 5862	51
52	11.5955 7041	10.9853 4038	10.4323 9923	9.9295 9875	52
53	11.6088 2066	10.9957 2512	10.4405 4724	9.9359 9886	53
54	11.6210 3287	11.0052 5240	10.4479 8834	9.9418 1715	54
55	11.6322 8836	11.0139 9303	10.4547 8388	9.9471 0650	55
56	11.6426 6208	11.0220 1195	10.4609 8984	9.9519 1500	56
57	11.6522 2311	11.0293 6876	10.4666 5739	9.9562 8636	57
58	11.6610 3513	11.0361 1813	10.4718 3323	9.9602 6033	58
59	11.6691 5680	11.0423 1021	10.4765 6003	9.9638 7303	59
60	11.6766 4221	11.0479 9102	10.4808 7674	9.9671 5730	60
61	11.6835 4121	11.0532 0277	10.4848 1894	9.9701 4300	61
62	11.6898 9973	11.0579 8419	10.4884 1912	9.9728 5727	62
63	11.6957 6012	11.0623 7082	10.4917 0696	9.9753 2479	63
64	11.7011 6140	11.0663 9525	10.4947 0955	9.9775 6799	64
65	11.7061 3954	11.0700 8738	10.4974 5165	9.9796 0727	65
66	11.7107 2769	11.0734 7466	10.4999 5584	9.9814 6115	66
67	11.7149 5639	11.0765 8226	10.5022 4278	9.9831 4650	67
68	11.7188 5382	11.0794 3327	10.5043 3130	9.9846 7864	68
69	11.7224 4592	11.0820 4887	10.5062 3863	9.9860 7149	69
70	11.7257 5661	11.0844 4850	10.5079 8049	9.9873 3772	70
71	11.7288 0793	11.0866 5000	10.5095 7122	9.9884 8883	71
72	11.7316 2021	11.0886 6973	10.5110 2395	9.9895 3530	72
73	11.7342 1218	11.0905 2269	10.5123 5064	9.9904 8664	73
74	11.7366 0109	11.0922 2265	10.5135 6223	9.9913 5149	74
75	11.7388 0284	11.0937 8225	10.5146 6870	9.9921 3772	75
76	11.7408 3211	11.0952 1307	10.5156 7918	9.9928 5247	76
77	11.7427 0241	11.0965 2575	10.5166 0199	9.9935 0225	77
78	11.7444 2618	11.0977 3005	10.5174 4474	9.9940 9295	78
79	11.7460 1492	11.0988 3491	10.5182 1437	9.9946 2996	79
80	11.7474 7919	11.0998 4854	10.5189 1724	9.9951 1814	80
81	11.7488 2874	11.1007 7847	10.5195 5912	9.9955 6195	81
82	11.7500 7257	11.1016 3163	10.5201 4531	9.9959 6541	82
83	11.7512 1896	11.1024 1434	10.5206 8065	9.9963 3219	83
84	11.7522 7554	11.1031 3242	10.5211 6955	9.9966 6563	84
85	11.7532 4935	11.1037 9121	10.5216 1602	9.9969 6875	85
86	11.7541 4686	11.1043 9561	10.5220 2377	9.9972 4432	86
87	11.7549 7407	11.1049 5010	10.5223 [illegible]513	9.9974 9483	87
88	11.7557 3647	11.1054 5881	10.5227 3619	9.9977 2258	88
89	11.7564 3914	11.1059 2551	10.5230 4675	9.9979 2962	89
90	11.7570 8677	11.1063 5368	10.5233 3037	9.9981 1783	90
91	11.7576 8365	11.1067 4649	10.5235 8938	9.9982 8894	91
92	11.7582 3378	11.1071 0688	10.5238 2592	9.9984 4449	92
93	11.7587 4081	11.1074 3750	10.5240 4193	9.9985 8590	93
94	11.7592 0812	11.1077 4083	10.5242 3921	9.9987 1445	94
95	11.7596 3882	11.1080 1911	10.5244 1937	9.9988 3132	95
96	11.7600 3578	11.1082 7441	10.5245 8390	9.9989 3757	96
97	11.7604 0164	11.1085 0863	10.5247 3415	9.9990 3415	97
98	11.7607 3884	11.1087 2352	10.5248 7137	9.9991 2195	98
99	11.7610 4962	11.1089 2066	10.5249 9669	9.9992 0178	99
100	11.7613 3606	11.1091 0152	10.5251 1113	9.9992 7434	100

TABLE 8A SUPPLEMENT TO TABLE 8

FOR FRACTIONAL INTEREST PERIODS

$$a_{\overline{1/m}|i} = \frac{1-(1+i)^{-\frac{1}{m}}}{i}$$

m	$\frac{1}{4}\%$	$\frac{1}{3}\%$	$\frac{5}{12}\%$	$\frac{11}{24}\%$	$\frac{1}{2}\%$	m
2	.4990 6445	.4987 5346	.4984 4291	.4982 8779	.4981 3278	2
3	.3327 7886	.3325 9451	.3324 1040	.3323 1843	.3322 2653	3
4	.2496 1011	.2494 8047	.2493 5099	.2492 8631	.2492 2167	4
6	.1664 2405	.1663 4337	.1662 6279	.1662 2270	.1661 8230	6
12	.0832 2068	.0831 8322	.0831 4580	.0831 2710	.0831 0842	12
m	$\frac{13}{24}\%$	$\frac{7}{12}\%$	$\frac{5}{8}\%$	$\frac{2}{3}\%$	$\frac{3}{4}\%$	m
2	.4979 7788	.4978 2308	.4976 6839	.4975 1381	.4972 0496	2
3	.3321 3468	.3320 4289	.3319 5116	.3318 5949	.3316 7633	3
4	.2491 5707	.2490 9251	.2490 2799	.2489 6351	.2488 3468	4
6	.1661 4210	.1661 0192	.1660 6176	.1660 2162	.1659 4143	6
12	.0830 8975	.0830 7109	.0830 5243	.0830 3379	.0829 9654	12
m	$\frac{7}{8}\%$	1%	$1\frac{1}{8}\%$	$1\frac{1}{4}\%$	$1\frac{3}{8}\%$	m
2	.4967 4249	.4962 8098	.4958 2042	.4953 6080	.4949 0213	2
3	.3314 0203	.3311 2825	.3308 5501	.3305 8228	.3303 1009	3
4	.2486 4172	.2484 4912	.2482 5688	.2480 6500	.2478 7347	4
6	.1658 2131	.1657 0141	.1655 8172	.1654 6225	.1653 4299	6
12	.0829 4075	.0828 8506	.0828 2945	.0827 7395	.0827 1854	12
m	$1\frac{1}{2}\%$	$1\frac{5}{8}\%$	$1\frac{3}{4}\%$	$1\frac{7}{8}\%$	2%	m
2	.4944 4440	.4939 8761	.4935 3176	.4930 7684	.4926 2285	2
3	.3300 3841	.3297 6725	.3294 9662	.3292 2650	.3289 5689	3
4	.2476 8230	.2474 9148	.2473 0101	.2471 1089	.2469 2113	4
6	.1652 2395	.1651 0511	.1649 8649	.1648 6807	.1647 4987	6
12	.0826 6322	.0826 0800	.0825 5287	.0824 9784	.0824 4290	12
m	$2\frac{1}{4}\%$	$2\frac{1}{2}\%$	$2\frac{3}{4}\%$	3%	$3\frac{1}{4}\%$	m
2	.4917 1765	.4908 1613	.4899 1828	.4890 2406	.4881 3346	2
3	.3284 1922	.3278 8360	.3273 5001	.3268 1843	.3262 8886	3
4	.2465 4264	.2461 6554	.2457 8981	.2454 1546	.2450 4247	4
6	.1645 1409	.1642 7915	.1640 4503	.1638 1173	.1635 7925	6
12	.0823 3331	.0822 2408	.0821 1523	.0820 0674	.0818 9862	12
m	$3\frac{1}{2}\%$	$3\frac{3}{4}\%$	4%	$4\frac{1}{2}\%$	5%	m
2	.4872 4645	.4863 6300	.4854 8311	.4837 3386	.4819 9854	2
3	.3257 6129	.3252 3570	.3247 1208	.3236 7070	.3226 3706	3
4	.2446 7084	.2443 0055	.2439 3161	.2431 9770	.2424 6905	4
6	.1633 4759	.1631 1673	.1628 8668	.1624 2897	.1619 7442	6
12	.0817 9086	.0816 8347	.0815 7643	.0813 6344	.0811 5185	12

TABLE 8A

TABLE 8A SUPPLEMENT TO TABLE 8

FOR FRACTIONAL INTEREST PERIODS

$$a_{\overline{1/m}|i} = \frac{1-(1+i)^{-\frac{1}{m}}}{i}$$

m	$5\frac{1}{2}$%	6%	$6\frac{1}{2}$%	7%	$7\frac{1}{2}$%	m
2	.4802 7696	.4785 6896	.4768 7437	.4751 9301	.4735 2474	2
3	.3216 1108	.3205 9265	.3195 8169	.3185 7811	.3175 8183	3
4	.2417 4561	.2410 2731	.2403 1409	.2396 0589	.2389 0266	4
6	.1615 2300	.1610 7468	.1606 2940	.1601 8715	.1597 4789	6
12	.0809 4167	.0807 3287	.0805 2544	.0803 1937	.0801 1463	12

m	8%	$8\frac{1}{2}$%	9%	$9\frac{1}{2}$%	10%	m
2	.4718 6939	.4702 2681	.4685 9683	.4669 7931	.4653 7411	2
3	.3165 9276	.3156 1082	.3146 3592	.3136 6799	.3127 0694	3
4	.2382 0435	.2375 1089	.2368 2223	.2361 3832	.2354 5910	4
6	.1593 1159	.1588 7820	.1584 4771	.1580 2008	.1575 9528	6
12	.0799 1123	.0797 0913	.0795 0833	.0793 0881	.0791 1057	12

TABLE 9 PERIODIC PAYMENT

WHEN PRESENT VALUE OF ANNUITY IS 1

$$\frac{1}{a_{\overline{n}|i}} = \frac{i}{1-(1+i)^{-n}} \qquad \text{Note: } \frac{1}{s_{\overline{n}|i}} = \frac{1}{a_{\overline{n}|i}} - i$$

n	$\frac{1}{4}\%$	$\frac{1}{3}\%$	$\frac{5}{12}\%$	$\frac{11}{24}\%$	n
1	1.0025 0000	1.0033 3333	1.0041 6667	1.0045 8333	1
2	0.5018 7578	0.5025 0139	0.5031 2717	0.5034 4012	2
3	0.3350 0139	0.3355 5802	0.3361 1496	0.3363 9355	3
4	0.2515 6445	0.2520 8680	0.2526 0958	0.2528 7113	4
5	0.2015 0250	0.2020 0444	0.2025 0693	0.2027 5838	5
6	0.1681 2803	0.1686 1650	0.1691 0564	0.1693 5047	6
7	0.1442 8928	0.1447 6824	0.1452 4800	0.1454 8817	7
8	0.1264 1035	0.1268 8228	0.1273 5512	0.1275 9188	8
9	0.1125 0462	0.1129 7118	0.1134 3876	0.1136 7293	9
10	0.1013 8015	0.1018 4248	0.1023 0596	0.1025 3812	10
11	0.0922 7840	0.0927 3736	0.0931 9757	0.0934 2814	11
12	0.0846 9370	0.0851 4990	0.0856 0748	0.0858 3678	12
13	0.0782 7595	0.0787 2989	0.0791 8532	0.0794 1360	13
14	0.0727 7510	0.0732 2716	0.0736 8082	0.0739 0825	14
15	0.0680 0777	0.0684 5825	0.0689 1045	0.0691 3719	15
16	0.0638 3642	0.0642 8557	0.0647 3655	0.0649 6273	16
17	0.0601 5587	0.0606 0389	0.0610 5387	0.0612 7959	17
18	0.0568 8433	0.0573 3140	0.0577 8053	0.0580 0587	18
19	0.0539 5722	0.0544 0348	0.0548 5191	0.0550 7695	19
20	0.0513 2288	0.0517 6844	0.0522 1630	0.0524 4109	20
21	0.0489 3947	0.0493 8445	0.0498 3183	0.0500 5643	21
22	0.0467 7278	0.0472 1726	0.0476 6427	0.0478 8872	22
23	0.0447 9455	0.0452 3861	0.0456 8531	0.0459 0965	23
24	0.0429 8121	0.0434 2492	0.0438 7139	0.0440 9566	24
25	0.0413 1298	0.0417 5640	0.0422 0270	0.0424 2692	25
26	0.0397 7312	0.0402 1630	0.0406 6247	0.0408 8668	26
27	0.0383 4736	0.0387 9035	0.0392 3645	0.0394 6066	27
28	0.0370 2347	0.0374 6632	0.0379 1239	0.0381 3663	28
29	0.0357 9093	0.0362 3367	0.0366 7974	0.0369 0402	29
30	0.0346 4059	0.0350 8325	0.0355 2936	0.0357 5371	30
31	0.0335 6449	0.0340 0712	0.0344 5330	0.0346 7773	31
32	0.0325 5569	0.0329 9830	0.0334 4458	0.0336 6910	32
33	0.0316 0806	0.0320 5067	0.0324 9708	0.0327 2170	33
34	0.0307 1620	0.0311 5885	0.0316 0540	0.0318 3014	34
35	0.0298 7533	0.0303 1803	0.0307 6476	0.0309 8963	35
36	0.0290 8121	0.0295 2399	0.0299 7090	0.0301 9590	36
37	0.0283 3004	0.0287 7291	0.0292 2003	0.0294 4518	37
38	0.0276 1843	0.0280 6141	0.0285 0875	0.0287 3405	38
39	0.0269 4335	0.0273 8644	0.0278 3402	0.0280 5949	39
40	0.0263 0204	0.0267 4527	0.0271 9310	0.0274 1874	40
41	0.0256 9204	0.0261 3543	0.0265 8352	0.0268 0933	41
42	0.0251 1112	0.0255 5466	0.0260 0303	0.0262 2902	42
43	0.0245 5724	0.0250 0095	0.0254 4961	0.0256 7579	43
44	0.0240 2855	0.0244 7246	0.0249 2141	0.0251 4778	44
45	0.0235 2339	0.0239 6749	0.0244 1675	0.0246 4332	45
46	0.0230 4022	0.0234 8451	0.0239 3409	0.0241 6086	46
47	0.0225 7762	0.0230 2213	0.0234 7204	0.0236 9901	47
48	0.0221 3433	0.0225 7905	0.0230 2929	0.0232 5648	48
49	0.0217 0915	0.0221 5410	0.0226 0468	0.0228 3207	49
50	0.0213 0099	0.0217 4618	0.0221 9711	0.0224 2472	50
51	0.0209 0886	0.0213 5429	0.0218 0557	0.0220 3341	51
52	0.0205 3184	0.0209 7751	0.0214 2916	0.0216 5721	52
53	0.0201 6906	0.0206 1499	0.0210 6700	0.0212 9528	53
54	0.0198 1974	0.0202 6592	0.0207 1830	0.0209 4681	54
55	0.0194 8314	0.0199 2958	0.0203 8234	0.0206 1108	55
56	0.0191 5858	0.0196 0529	0.0200 5843	0.0202 8740	56
57	0.0188 4542	0.0192 9241	0.0197 4593	0.0199 7514	57
58	0.0185 4308	0.0189 9035	0.0194 4426	0.0196 7371	58
59	0.0182 5101	0.0186 9856	0.0191 5287	0.0193 8255	59
60	0.0179 6869	0.0184 1652	0.0188 7123	0.0191 0116	60

TABLE 9 PERIODIC PAYMENT
WHEN PRESENT VALUE OF ANNUITY IS 1

$$\frac{1}{a_{\overline{n}|i}} = \frac{i}{1-(1+i)^{-n}} \qquad \text{Note: } \frac{1}{s_{\overline{n}|i}} = \frac{1}{a_{\overline{n}|i}} - i$$

n	$\frac{1}{4}\%$	$\frac{1}{3}\%$	$\frac{5}{12}\%$	$\frac{11}{24}\%$	n
61	0.0176 9564	0.0181 4377	0.0185 9888	0.0188 2905	61
62	0.0174 3142	0.0178 7984	0.0183 3536	0.0185 6578	62
63	0.0171 7561	0.0176 2432	0.0180 8025	0.0183 1091	63
64	0.0169 2780	0.0173 7681	0.0178 3315	0.0180 6407	64
65	0.0166 8764	0.0171 3695	0.0175 9371	0.0178 2487	65
66	0.0164 5476	0.0169 0438	0.0173 6156	0.0175 9298	66
67	0.0162 2886	0.0166 7878	0.0171 3639	0.0173 6806	67
68	0.0160 0961	0.0164 5985	0.0169 1788	0.0171 4980	68
69	0.0157 9674	0.0162 4729	0.0167 0574	0.0169 3792	69
70	0.0155 8996	0.0160 4083	0.0164 9971	0.0167 3215	70
71	0.0153 8902	0.0158 4021	0.0162 9952	0.0165 3222	71
72	0.0151 9368	0.0156 4518	0.0161 0493	0.0163 3789	72
73	0.0150 0370	0.0154 5553	0.0159 1572	0.0161 4893	73
74	0.0148 1887	0.0152 7103	0.0157 3165	0.0159 6513	74
75	0.0146 3898	0.0150 9147	0.0155 5253	0.0157 8627	75
76	0.0144 6385	0.0149 1666	0.0153 7816	0.0156 1217	76
77	0.0142 9327	0.0147 4641	0.0152 0836	0.0154 4263	77
78	0.0141 2708	0.0145 8056	0.0150 4295	0.0152 7748	78
79	0.0139 6511	0.0144 1892	0.0148 8177	0.0151 1656	79
80	0.0138 0721	0.0142 6135	0.0147 2464	0.0149 5971	80
81	0.0136 5321	0.0141 0770	0.0145 7144	0.0148 0677	81
82	0.0135 0298	0.0139 5781	0.0144 2200	0.0146 5760	82
83	0.0133 5639	0.0138 1156	0.0142 7620	0.0145 1207	83
84	0.0132 1330	0.0136 6881	0.0141 3391	0.0143 7004	84
85	0.0130 7359	0.0135 2944	0.0139 9500	0.0142 3140	85
86	0.0129 3714	0.0133 9333	0.0138 5935	0.0140 9602	86
87	0.0128 0384	0.0132 6038	0.0137 2685	0.0139 6379	87
88	0.0126 7357	0.0131 3046	0.0135 9740	0.0138 3461	88
89	0.0125 4625	0.0130 0349	0.0134 7088	0.0137 0837	89
90	0.0124 2177	0.0128 7936	0.0133 4721	0.0135 8497	90
91	0.0123 0004	0.0127 5797	0.0132 2629	0.0134 6432	91
92	0.0121 8096	0.0126 3925	0.0131 0803	0.0133 4634	92
93	0.0120 6446	0.0125 2310	0.0129 9234	0.0132 3092	93
94	0.0119 5044	0.0124 0944	0.0128 7915	0.0131 1800	94
95	0.0118 3884	0.0122 9819	0.0127 6836	0.0130 0749	95
96	0.0117 2957	0.0121 8928	0.0126 5992	0.0128 9932	96
97	0.0116 2257	0.0120 8263	0.0125 5374	0.0127 9342	97
98	0.0115 1776	0.0119 7818	0.0124 4976	0.0126 8971	98
99	0.0114 1508	0.0118 7585	0.0123 4790	0.0125 8813	99
100	0.0113 1446	0.0117 7559	0.0122 4811	0.0124 8862	100
101	0.0112 1584	0.0116 7734	0.0121 5033	0.0123 9111	101
102	0.0111 1917	0.0115 8103	0.0120 5449	0.0122 9555	102
103	0.0110 2439	0.0114 8660	0.0119 6054	0.0122 0187	103
104	0.0109 3144	0.0113 9401	0.0118 6842	0.0121 1003	104
105	0.0108 4027	0.0113 0320	0.0117 7809	0.0120 1998	105
106	0.0107 5082	0.0112 1413	0.0116 8948	0.0119 3165	106
107	0.0106 6307	0.0111 2673	0.0116 0256	0.0118 4500	107
108	0.0105 7694	0.0110 4097	0.0115 1727	0.0117 6000	108
109	0.0104 9241	0.0109 5680	0.0114 3358	0.0116 7658	109
110	0.0104 0942	0.0108 7418	0.0113 5143	0.0115 9471	110
111	0.0103 2793	0.0107 9306	0.0112 7079	0.0115 1435	111
112	0.0102 4791	0.0107 1340	0.0111 9161	0.0114 3545	112
113	0.0101 6932	0.0106 3518	0.0111 1386	0.0113 5798	113
114	0.0100 9211	0.0105 5834	0.0110 3750	0.0112 8190	114
115	0.0100 1626	0.0104 8285	0.0109 6249	0.0112 0717	115
116	0.0099 4172	0.0104 0868	0.0108 8880	0.0111 3376	116
117	0.0098 6846	0.0103 3579	0.0108 1639	0.0110 6163	117
118	0.0097 9646	0.0102 6416	0.0107 4524	0.0109 9075	118
119	0.0097 2567	0.0101 9374	0.0106 7530	0.0109 2110	119
120	0.0096 5607	0.0101 2451	0.0106 0655	0.0108 5263	120

TABLE 9 PERIODIC PAYMENT
WHEN PRESENT VALUE OF ANNUITY IS 1

$$\frac{1}{a_{\overline{n}|i}} = \frac{i}{1-(1+i)^{-n}} \qquad \text{Note: } \frac{1}{s_{\overline{n}|i}} = \frac{1}{a_{\overline{n}|i}} - i$$

n	$\frac{1}{4}$%	$\frac{1}{3}$%	$\frac{5}{12}$%	$\frac{11}{24}$%	n
121	0.0095 8764	0.0100 5645	0.0105 3896	0.0107 8532	121
122	0.0095 2033	0.0099 8951	0.0104 7251	0.0107 1914	122
123	0.0094 5412	0.0099 2367	0.0104 0715	0.0106 5407	123
124	0.0093 8899	0.0098 5892	0.0103 4288	0.0105 9007	124
125	0.0093 2491	0.0097 9521	0.0102 7965	0.0105 2713	125
126	0.0092 6186	0.0097 3253	0.0102 1745	0.0104 6521	126
127	0.0091 9981	0.0096 7085	0.0101 5625	0.0104 0429	127
128	0.0091 3873	0.0096 1015	0.0100 9603	0.0103 4435	128
129	0.0090 7861	0.0095 5040	0.0100 3677	0.0102 8537	129
130	0.0090 1942	0.0094 9158	0.0099 7844	0.0102 2732	130
131	0.0089 6115	0.0094 3368	0.0099 2102	0.0101 7018	131
132	0.0089 0376	0.0093 7667	0.0098 6449	0.0101 1393	132
133	0.0088 4725	0.0093 2053	0.0098 0883	0.0100 5856	133
134	0.0087 9159	0.0092 6524	0.0097 5403	0.0100 0403	134
135	0.0087 3675	0.0092 1079	0.0097 0005	0.0099 5034	135
136	0.0086 8274	0.0091 5715	0.0096 4689	0.0098 9746	136
137	0.0086 2952	0.0091 0430	0.0095 9453	0.0098 4538	137
138	0.0085 7707	0.0090 5223	0.0095 4295	0.0097 9408	138
139	0.0085 2539	0.0090 0093	0.0094 9213	0.0097 4354	139
140	0.0084 7446	0.0089 5037	0.0094 4205	0.0096 9375	140
141	0.0084 2425	0.0089 0054	0.0093 9271	0.0096 4468	141
142	0.0083 7476	0.0088 5143	0.0093 4408	0.0095 9634	142
143	0.0083 2597	0.0088 0301	0.0092 9615	0.0095 4869	143
144	0.0082 7787	0.0087 5528	0.0092 4890	0.0095 0172	144
145	0.0082 3043	0.0087 0822	0.0092 0233	0.0094 5543	145
146	0.0081 8365	0.0086 6182	0.0091 5641	0.0094 0979	146
147	0.0081 3752	0.0086 1607	0.0091 1114	0.0093 6480	147
148	0.0080 9201	0.0085 7094	0.0090 6650	0.0093 2044	148
149	0.0080 4712	0.0085 2643	0.0090 2247	0.0092 7669	149
150	0.0080 0284	0.0084 8252	0.0089 7905	0.0092 3355	150
151	0.0079 5915	0.0084 3921	0.0089 3622	0.0091 9101	151
152	0.0079 1605	0.0083 9648	0.0088 9398	0.0091 4905	152
153	0.0078 7351	0.0083 5433	0.0088 5231	0.0091 0765	153
154	0.0078 3153	0.0083 1273	0.0088 1119	0.0090 6682	154
155	0.0077 9010	0.0082 7167	0.0087 7063	0.0090 2653	155
156	0.0077 4921	0.0082 3116	0.0087 3060	0.0089 8679	156
157	0.0077 0885	0.0081 9118	0.0086 9110	0.0089 4756	157
158	0.0076 6900	0.0081 5171	0.0086 5211	0.0089 0886	158
159	0.0076 2966	0.0081 1275	0.0086 1364	0.0088 7067	159
160	0.0075 9082	0.0080 7429	0.0085 7566	0.0088 3297	160
161	0.0075 5247	0.0080 3631	0.0085 3817	0.0087 9576	161
162	0.0075 1459	0.0079 9882	0.0085 0116	0.0087 5903	162
163	0.0074 7719	0.0079 6180	0.0084 6462	0.0087 2278	163
164	0.0074 4025	0.0079 2524	0.0084 2855	0.0086 8698	164
165	0.0074 0377	0.0078 8913	0.0083 9293	0.0086 5164	165
166	0.0073 6773	0.0078 5347	0.0083 5775	0.0086 1674	166
167	0.0073 3213	0.0078 1825	0.0083 2301	0.0085 8229	167
168	0.0072 9695	0.0077 8346	0.0082 8871	0.0085 4826	168
169	0.0072 6220	0.0077 4909	0.0082 5482	0.0085 1465	169
170	0.0072 2787	0.0077 1513	0.0082 2135	0.0084 8146	170
171	0.0071 9394	0.0076 8158	0.0081 8829	0.0084 4868	171
172	0.0071 6042	0.0076 4844	0.0081 5562	0.0084 1629	172
173	0.0071 2728	0.0076 1568	0.0081 2336	0.0083 8430	173
174	0.0070 9454	0.0075 8332	0.0080 9147	0.0083 5270	174
175	0.0070 6217	0.0075 5133	0.0080 5997	0.0083 2148	175
176	0.0070 3018	0.0075 1972	0.0080 2884	0.0082 9063	176
177	0.0069 9855	0.0074 8847	0.0079 9808	0.0082 6014	177
178	0.0069 6729	0.0074 5759	0.0079 6768	0.0082 3002	178
179	0.0069 3638	0.0074 2706	0.0079 3763	0.0082 0025	179
180	0.0069 0582	0.0073 9688	0.0079 0794	0.0081 7083	180

TABLE 9 PERIODIC PAYMENT

WHEN PRESENT VALUE OF ANNUITY IS 1

$$\frac{1}{a_{\overline{n}|i}} = \frac{i}{1-(1+i)^{-n}} \qquad \text{Note: } \frac{1}{s_{\overline{n}|i}} = \frac{1}{a_{\overline{n}|i}} - i$$

n	$\frac{1}{4}$%	$\frac{1}{3}$%	$\frac{5}{12}$%	$\frac{11}{24}$%	n
181	0.0068 7560	0.0073 6704	0.0078 7858	0.0081 4176	181
182	0.0068 4572	0.0073 3754	0.0078 4957	0.0081 1302	182
183	0.0068 1617	0.0073 0838	0.0078 2088	0.0080 8462	183
184	0.0067 8695	0.0072 7954	0.0077 9253	0.0080 5654	184
185	0.0067 5805	0.0072 5102	0.0077 6449	0.0080 2878	185
186	0.0067 2947	0.0072 2281	0.0077 3677	0.0080 0134	186
187	0.0067 0120	0.0071 9492	0.0077 0936	0.0079 7420	187
188	0.0066 7323	0.0071 6734	0.0076 8226	0.0079 4738	188
189	0.0066 4557	0.0071 4005	0.0076 5546	0.0079 2085	189
190	0.0066 1820	0.0071 1307	0.0076 2895	0.0078 9463	190
191	0.0065 9112	0.0070 8637	0.0076 0274	0.0078 6869	191
192	0.0065 6434	0.0070 5996	0.0075 7681	0.0078 4304	192
193	0.0065 3783	0.0070 3384	0.0075 5117	0.0078 1767	193
194	0.0065 1160	0.0070 0799	0.0075 2580	0.0077 9258	194
195	0.0064 8565	0.0069 8242	0.0075 0071	0.0077 6777	195
196	0.0064 5997	0.0069 5711	0.0074 7589	0.0077 4322	196
197	0.0064 3455	0.0069 3208	0.0074 5133	0.0077 1894	197
198	0.0064 0939	0.0069 0730	0.0074 2704	0.0076 9492	198
199	0.0063 8450	0.0068 8279	0.0074 0300	0.0076 7116	199
200	0.0063 5985	0.0068 5852	0.0073 7922	0.0076 4766	200
201	0.0063 3546	0.0068 3451	0.0073 5569	0.0076 2440	201
202	0.0063 1131	0.0068 1074	0.0073 3240	0.0076 0139	202
203	0.0062 8741	0.0067 8722	0.0073 0936	0.0075 7862	203
204	0.0062 6375	0.0067 6393	0.0072 8655	0.0075 5609	204
205	0.0062 4032	0.0067 4089	0.0072 6398	0.0075 3380	205
206	0.0062 1712	0.0067 1807	0.0072 4165	0.0075 1174	206
207	0.0061 9416	0.0066 9548	0.0072 1954	0.0074 8990	207
208	0.0061 7141	0.0066 7312	0.0071 9766	0.0074 6829	208
209	0.0061 4890	0.0066 5098	0.0071 7600	0.0074 4691	209
210	0.0061 2660	0.0066 2906	0.0071 5456	0.0074 2574	210
211	0.0061 0451	0.0066 0736	0.0071 3333	0.0074 0479	211
212	0.0060 8264	0.0065 8587	0.0071 1232	0.0073 8405	212
213	0.0060 6098	0.0065 6459	0.0070 9152	0.0073 6352	213
214	0.0060 3953	0.0065 4351	0.0070 7092	0.0073 4320	214
215	0.0060 1828	0.0065 2264	0.0070 5053	0.0073 2308	215
216	0.0059 9723	0.0065 0198	0.0070 3034	0.0073 0316	216
217	0.0059 7638	0.0064 8151	0.0070 1035	0.0072 8344	217
218	0.0059 5573	0.0064 6123	0.0069 9055	0.0072 6392	218
219	0.0059 3527	0.0064 4115	0.0069 7095	0.0072 4459	219
220	0.0059 1500	0.0064 2126	0.0069 5153	0.0072 2545	220
221	0.0058 9492	0.0064 0156	0.0069 3231	0.0072 0649	221
222	0.0058 7503	0.0063 8205	0.0069 1327	0.0071 8773	222
223	0.0058 5531	0.0063 6272	0.0068 9441	0.0071 6914	223
224	0.0058 3578	0.0063 4356	0.0068 7573	0.0071 5073	224
225	0.0058 1643	0.0063 2458	0.0068 5723	0.0071 3251	225
226	0.0057 9725	0.0063 0578	0.0068 3891	0.0071 1445	226
227	0.0057 7824	0.0062 8716	0.0068 2076	0.0070 9657	227
228	0.0057 5941	0.0062 6870	0.0068 0278	0.0070 7886	228
229	0.0057 4075	0.0062 5042	0.0067 8497	0.0070 6132	229
230	0.0057 2225	0.0062 3230	0.0067 6732	0.0070 4395	230
231	0.0057 0391	0.0062 1434	0.0067 4984	0.0070 2673	231
232	0.0056 8574	0.0061 9655	0.0067 3252	0.0070 0969	232
233	0.0056 6773	0.0061 7892	0.0067 1536	0.0069 9280	233
234	0.0056 4988	0.0061 6144	0.0066 9836	0.0069 7606	234
235	0.0056 3218	0.0061 4412	0.0066 8151	0.0069 5949	235
236	0.0056 1464	0.0061 2696	0.0066 6482	0.0069 4307	236
237	0.0055 9725	0.0061 0995	0.0066 4828	0.0069 2679	237
238	0.0055 8001	0.0060 9308	0.0066 3189	0.0069 1067	238
239	0.0055 6292	0.0060 7637	0.0066 1565	0.0068 9470	239
240	0.0055 4598	0.0060 5980	0.0065 9956	0.0068 7887	240

TABLE 9 PERIODIC PAYMENT

WHEN PRESENT VALUE OF ANNUITY IS 1

$$\frac{1}{a_{\overline{n}|i}} = \frac{i}{1-(1+i)^{-n}} \qquad \text{Note: } \frac{1}{s_{\overline{n}|i}} = \frac{1}{a_{\overline{n}|i}} - i$$

n	$\frac{1}{2}$%	$\frac{13}{24}$%	$\frac{7}{12}$%	$\frac{5}{8}$%	n
1	1.0050 0000	1.0054 1667	1.0058 3333	1.0062 5000	1
2	0.5037 5312	0.5040 6616	0.5043 7924	0.5046 9237	2
3	0.3366 7221	0.3369 5095	0.3372 2976	0.3375 0865	3
4	0.2531 3279	0.2533 9457	0.2536 5644	0.2539 1842	4
5	0.2030 0997	0.2032 6170	0.2035 1357	0.2037 6558	5
6	0.1695 9546	0.1698 4061	0.1700 8594	0.1703 3143	6
7	0.1457 2843	0.1459 6910	0.1462 0986	0.1464 5082	7
8	0.1278 2886	0.1280 6608	0.1283 0351	0.1285 4118	8
9	0.1139 0736	0.1141 4204	0.1143 7698	0.1146 1218	9
10	0.1027 7057	0.1030 0331	0.1032 3632	0.1034 6963	10
11	0.0936 5903	0.0938 9024	0.0941 2175	0.0943 5358	11
12	0.0860 6643	0.0862 9642	0.0865 2675	0.0867 5742	12
13	0.0796 4224	0.0798 7125	0.0801 0064	0.0803 3039	13
14	0.0741 3609	0.0743 6432	0.0745 9295	0.0748 2198	14
15	0.0693 6436	0.0695 9197	0.0698 1999	0.0700 4845	15
16	0.0651 8937	0.0654 1646	0.0656 4401	0.0658 7202	16
17	0.0615 0579	0.0617 3248	0.0619 5966	0.0621 8732	17
18	0.0582 3173	0.0584 5810	0.0586 8499	0.0589 1239	18
19	0.0553 0253	0.0555 2865	0.0557 5532	0.0559 8252	19
20	0.0526 6645	0.0528 9239	0.0531 1889	0.0533 4597	20
21	0.0502 8163	0.0505 0743	0.0507 3383	0.0509 6083	21
22	0.0481 1380	0.0483 3951	0.0485 6585	0.0487 9281	22
23	0.0461 3465	0.0463 6031	0.0465 8663	0.0468 1360	23
24	0.0443 2061	0.0445 4625	0.0447 7258	0.0449 9959	24
25	0.0426 5186	0.0428 7751	0.0431 0388	0.0433 3096	25
26	0.0411 1163	0.0413 3732	0.0415 6376	0.0417 9094	26
27	0.0396 8565	0.0399 1140	0.0401 3793	0.0403 6523	27
28	0.0383 6167	0.0385 8751	0.0388 1415	0.0390 4159	28
29	0.0371 2914	0.0373 5508	0.0375 8186	0.0378 0946	29
30	0.0359 7892	0.0362 0498	0.0364 3191	0.0366 5969	30
31	0.0349 0304	0.0351 2924	0.0353 5633	0.0355 8430	31
32	0.0338 9453	0.0341 2088	0.0343 4815	0.0345 7633	32
33	0.0329 4727	0.0331 7379	0.0334 0124	0.0336 2964	33
34	0.0320 5586	0.0322 8254	0.0325 1020	0.0327 3883	34
35	0.0312 1550	0.0314 4237	0.0316 7024	0.0318 9911	35
36	0.0304 2194	0.0306 4900	0.0308 7710	0.0311 0622	36
37	0.0296 7139	0.0298 9865	0.0301 2698	0.0303 5636	37
38	0.0298 6045	0.0291 8793	0.0294 1649	0.0296 4614	38
39	0.0282 8607	0.0285 1377	0.0287 4258	0.0289 7250	39
40	0.0276 4552	0.0278 7344	0.0281 0251	0.0283 3271	40
41	0.0270 3631	0.0272 6447	0.0274 9379	0.0277 2429	41
42	0.0264 5622	0.0266 8461	0.0269 1420	0.0271 4499	42
43	0.0259 0320	0.0261 3183	0.0263 6170	0.0265 9278	43
44	0.0253 7541	0.0256 0429	0.0258 3443	0.0260 6583	44
45	0.0248 7117	0.0251 0031	0.0253 3073	0.0255 6243	45
46	0.0243 8894	0.0246 1834	0.0248 4905	0.0250 8106	46
47	0.0239 2733	0.0241 5698	0.0243 8798	0.0246 2032	47
48	0.0234 8503	0.0237 1495	0.0239 4624	0.0241 7890	48
49	0.0230 6087	0.0232 9106	0.0235 2265	0.0237 5563	49
50	0.0226 5376	0.0228 8422	0.0231 1612	0.0233 4943	50
51	0.0222 6269	0.0224 9344	0.0227 2563	0.0229 5928	51
52	0.0218 8675	0.0221 1777	0.0223 5027	0.0225 8425	52
53	0.0215 2507	0.0217 5637	0.0219 8919	0.0222 2350	53
54	0.0211 7686	0.0214 0845	0.0216 4157	0.0218 7623	54
55	0.0208 4139	0.0210 7327	0.0213 0671	0.0215 4171	55
56	0.0205 1797	0.0207 5014	0.0209 8390	0.0212 1925	56
57	0.0202 0598	0.0204 3844	0.0206 7251	0.0209 0821	57
58	0.0199 0481	0.0201 3756	0.0203 7196	0.0206 0801	58
59	0.0196 1392	0.0198 4697	0.0200 8170	0.0203 1809	59
60	0.0193 3280	0.0195 6615	0.0198 0120	0.0200 3795	60

TABLE 9 PERIODIC PAYMENT

WHEN PRESENT VALUE OF ANNUITY IS 1

$$\frac{1}{a_{\overline{n}|i}} = \frac{i}{1-(1+i)^{-n}} \qquad \text{Note: } \frac{1}{s_{\overline{n}|i}} = \frac{1}{a_{\overline{n}|i}} - i$$

n	$\frac{1}{2}$%	$\frac{13}{24}$%	$\frac{7}{12}$%	$\frac{5}{8}$%	n
61	0.0190 6096	0.0192 9461	0.0195 2999	0.0197 6709	61
62	0.0187 9796	0.0190 3191	0.0192 6762	0.0195 0508	62
63	0.0185 4337	0.0187 7762	0.0190 1366	0.0192 5148	63
64	0.0182 9681	0.0185 3136	0.0187 6773	0.0190 0591	64
65	0.0180 5789	0.0182 9275	0.0185 2946	0.0187 6800	65
66	0.0178 2627	0.0180 6144	0.0182 9848	0.0185 3739	66
67	0.0176 0163	0.0178 3711	0.0180 7449	0.0183 1376	67
68	0.0173 8366	0.0176 1945	0.0178 5716	0.0180 9680	68
69	0.0171 7206	0.0174 0817	0.0176 4622	0.0178 8622	69
70	0.0169 6657	0.0172 0299	0.0174 4138	0.0176 8175	70
71	0.0167 6693	0.0170 0366	0.0172 4239	0.0174 8313	71
72	0.0165 7289	0.0168 0993	0.0170 4901	0.0172 9011	72
73	0.0163 8422	0.0166 2158	0.0168 6100	0.0171 0247	73
74	0.0162 0070	0.0164 3838	0.0166 7814	0.0169 1999	74
75	0.0160 2214	0.0162 6013	0.0165 0024	0.0167 4246	75
76	0.0158 4832	0.0160 8663	0.0163 2709	0.0165 6968	76
77	0.0156 7908	0.0159 1771	0.0161 5851	0.0164 0147	77
78	0.0155 1423	0.0157 5317	0.0159 9432	0.0162 3766	78
79	0.0153 5360	0.0155 9287	0.0158 3436	0.0160 7808	79
80	0.0151 9704	0.0154 3663	0.0156 7847	0.0159 2256	80
81	0.0150 4439	0.0152 8430	0.0155 2650	0.0157 7096	81
82	0.0148 9552	0.0151 3575	0.0153 7830	0.0156 2314	82
83	0.0147 5028	0.0149 9084	0.0152 3373	0.0154 7895	83
84	0.0146 0855	0.0148 4944	0.0150 9268	0.0153 3828	84
85	0.0144 7021	0.0147 1141	0.0149 5501	0.0152 0098	85
86	0.0143 3513	0.0145 7666	0.0148 2060	0.0150 6696	86
87	0.0142 0320	0.0144 4505	0.0146 8935	0.0149 3608	87
88	0.0140 7431	0.0143 1650	0.0145 6115	0.0148 0826	88
89	0.0139 4837	0.0141 9088	0.0144 3588	0.0146 8337	89
90	0.0138 2527	0.0140 6811	0.0143 1347	0.0145 6134	90
91	0.0137 0493	0.0139 4809	0.0141 9380	0.0144 4205	91
92	0.0135 8724	0.0138 3073	0.0140 7679	0.0143 2542	92
93	0.0134 7213	0.0137 1594	0.0139 6236	0.0142 1137	93
94	0.0133 5950	0.0136 0365	0.0138 5042	0.0140 9982	94
95	0.0132 4930	0.0134 9377	0.0137 4090	0.0139 9067	95
96	0.0131 4143	0.0133 8623	0.0136 3372	0.0138 8387	96
97	0.0130 3583	0.0132 8096	0.0135 2880	0.0137 7933	97
98	0.0129 3242	0.0131 7788	0.0134 2608	0.0136 7700	98
99	0.0128 3115	0.0130 7694	0.0133 2549	0.0135 7679	99
100	0.0127 3194	0.0129 7806	0.0132 2696	0.0134 7864	100
101	0.0126 3473	0.0128 8118	0.0131 3045	0.0133 8251	101
102	0.0125 3947	0.0127 8625	0.0130 3587	0.0132 8832	102
103	0.0124 4610	0.0126 9321	0.0129 4319	0.0131 9602	103
104	0.0123 5457	0.0126 0201	0.0128 5234	0.0131 0555	104
105	0.0122 6481	0.0125 1259	0.0127 6328	0.0130 1687	105
106	0.0121 7679	0.0124 2489	0.0126 7594	0.0129 2992	106
107	0.0120 9045	0.0123 3889	0.0125 9029	0.0128 4465	107
108	0.0120 0575	0.0122 5452	0.0125 0628	0.0127 6102	108
109	0.0119 2264	0.0121 7174	0.0124 2385	0.0126 7898	109
110	0.0118 4107	0.0120 9050	0.0123 4298	0.0125 9848	110
111	0.0117 6102	0.0120 1078	0.0122 6361	0.0125 1950	111
112	0.0116 8242	0.0119 3252	0.0121 8571	0.0124 4198	112
113	0.0116 0526	0.0118 5568	0.0121 0923	0.0123 6588	113
114	0.0115 2948	0.0117 8024	0.0120 3414	0.0122 9118	114
115	0.0114 5506	0.0117 0615	0.0119 6041	0.0122 1783	115
116	0.0113 8195	0.0116 3337	0.0118 8799	0.0121 4579	116
117	0.0113 1013	0.0115 6188	0.0118 1686	0.0120 7504	117
118	0.0112 3956	0.0114 9165	0.0117 4698	0.0120 0555	118
119	0.0111 7021	0.0114 2263	0.0116 7832	0.0119 3727	119
120	0.0111 0205	0.0113 5480	0.0116 1085	0.0118 7018	120

TABLE 9 PERIODIC PAYMENT

WHEN PRESENT VALUE OF ANNUITY IS 1

$$\frac{1}{a_{\overline{n}|i}} = \frac{i}{1-(1+i)^{-n}} \qquad \text{Note: } \frac{1}{s_{\overline{n}|i}} = \frac{1}{a_{\overline{n}|i}} - i$$

n	$\frac{1}{2}$%	$\frac{13}{24}$%	$\frac{7}{12}$%	$\frac{5}{8}$%	n
121	0.0110 3505	0.0112 8813	0.0115 4454	0.0118 0425	121
122	0.0109 6918	0.0112 2259	0.0114 7936	0.0117 3945	122
123	0.0109 0441	0.0111 5816	0.0114 1528	0.0116 7575	123
124	0.0108 4072	0.0110 9480	0.0113 5228	0.0116 1313	124
125	0.0107 7808	0.0110 3249	0.0112 9033	0.0115 5157	125
126	0.0107 1647	0.0109 7121	0.0112 2941	0.0114 9102	126
127	0.0106 5586	0.0109 1093	0.0111 6948	0.0114 3148	127
128	0.0105 9623	0.0108 5163	0.0111 1054	0.0113 7292	128
129	0.0105 3755	0.0107 9329	0.0110 5255	0.0113 1531	129
130	0.0104 7981	0.0107 3588	0.0109 9550	0.0112 5864	130
131	0.0104 2298	0.0106 7938	0.0109 3935	0.0112 0288	131
132	0.0103 6703	0.0106 2377	0.0108 8410	0.0111 4800	132
133	0.0103 1197	0.0105 6903	0.0108 2972	0.0110 9400	133
134	0.0102 5775	0.0105 1514	0.0107 7619	0.0110 4086	134
135	0.0102 0436	0.0104 6209	0.0107 2349	0.0109 8854	135
136	0.0101 5179	0.0104 0985	0.0106 7161	0.0109 3703	136
137	0.0101 0002	0.0103 5841	0.0106 2052	0.0108 8633	137
138	0.0100 4902	0.0103 0774	0.0105 7021	0.0108 3640	138
139	0.0099 9879	0.0102 5784	0.0105 2067	0.0107 8723	139
140	0.0099 4930	0.0102 0869	0.0104 7187	0.0107 3881	140
141	0.0099 0055	0.0101 6026	0.0104 2380	0.0106 9111	141
142	0.0098 5250	0.0101 1255	0.0103 7644	0.0106 4414	142
143	0.0098 0516	0.0100 6554	0.0103 2978	0.0105 9786	143
144	0.0097 5850	0.0100 1921	0.0102 8381	0.0105 5226	144
145	0.0097 1252	0.0099 7355	0.0102 3851	0.0105 0734	145
146	0.0096 6718	0.0099 2855	0.0101 9386	0.0104 6307	146
147	0.0096 2250	0.0098 8420	0.0101 4986	0.0104 1944	147
148	0.0095 7844	0.0098 4047	0.0101 0649	0.0103 7645	148
149	0.0095 3500	0.0097 9736	0.0100 6374	0.0103 3407	149
150	0.0094 9217	0.0097 5486	0.0100 2159	0.0102 9230	150
151	0.0094 4993	0.0097 1295	0.0099 8003	0.0102 5112	151
152	0.0094 0827	0.0096 7162	0.0099 3905	0.0102 1052	152
153	0.0093 6719	0.0096 3087	0.0098 9865	0.0101 7049	153
154	0.0093 2666	0.0095 9067	0.0098 5880	0.0101 3102	154
155	0.0092 8668	0.0095 5102	0.0098 1950	0.0100 9209	155
156	0.0092 4723	0.0095 1190	0.0097 8074	0.0100 5370	156
157	0.0092 0832	0.0094 7332	0.0097 4251	0.0100 1584	157
158	0.0091 6992	0.0094 3525	0.0097 0479	0.0099 7850	158
159	0.0091 3203	0.0093 9768	0.0096 6758	0.0099 4166	159
160	0.0090 9464	0.0093 6062	0.0096 3087	0.0099 0532	160
161	0.0090 5773	0.0093 2404	0.0095 9464	0.0098 6947	161
162	0.0090 2131	0.0092 8795	0.0095 5890	0.0098 3410	162
163	0.0089 8536	0.0092 5232	0.0095 2362	0.0097 9919	163
164	0.0089 4987	0.0092 1716	0.0094 8881	0.0097 6475	164
165	0.0089 1483	0.0091 8245	0.0094 5445	0.0097 3076	165
166	0.0088 8024	0.0091 4819	0.0094 2053	0.0096 9722	166
167	0.0088 4608	0.0091 1436	0.0093 8705	0.0096 6411	167
168	0.0088 1236	0.0090 8096	0.0093 5401	0.0096 3143	168
169	0.0087 7906	0.0090 4798	0.0093 2138	0.0095 9918	169
170	0.0087 4617	0.0090 1542	0.0092 8917	0.0095 6733	170
171	0.0087 1369	0.0089 8327	0.0092 5736	0.0095 3589	171
172	0.0086 8161	0.0089 5151	0.0092 2595	0.0095 0486	172
173	0.0086 4992	0.0089 2015	0.0091 9494	0.0094 7421	173
174	0.0086 1862	0.0088 8918	0.0091 6431	0.0094 4395	174
175	0.0085 8770	0.0088 5858	0.0091 3406	0.0094 1407	175
176	0.0085 5715	0.0088 2836	0.0091 0418	0.0093 8456	176
177	0.0085 2697	0.0087 9850	0.0090 7468	0.0093 5542	177
178	0.0084 9715	0.0087 6901	0.0090 4553	0.0093 2664	178
179	0.0084 6768	0.0087 3987	0.0090 1673	0.0092 9821	179
180	0.0084 3857	0.0087 1107	0.0089 8828	0.0092 7012	180

TABLE 9 PERIODIC PAYMENT

WHEN PRESENT VALUE OF ANNUITY IS 1

$$\frac{1}{a_{\overline{n}|i}} = \frac{i}{1-(1+i)^{-n}} \qquad \text{Note: } \frac{1}{s_{\overline{n}|i}} = \frac{1}{a_{\overline{n}|i}} - i$$

n	$\frac{1}{2}\%$	$\frac{13}{24}\%$	$\frac{7}{12}\%$	$\frac{5}{8}\%$	n
181	0.0084 0979	0.0086 8262	0.0089 6018	0.0092 4238	181
182	0.0083 8136	0.0086 5451	0.0089 3241	0.0092 1498	182
183	0.0083 5325	0.0086 2673	0.0089 0497	0.0091 8791	183
184	0.0083 2547	0.0085 9927	0.0088 7786	0.0091 6116	184
185	0.0082 9802	0.0085 7214	0.0088 5107	0.0091 3473	185
186	0.0082 7088	0.0085 4532	0.0088 2459	0.0091 0862	186
187	0.0082 4404	0.0085 1881	0.0087 9843	0.0090 8282	187
188	0.0082 1752	0.0084 9261	0.0087 7257	0.0090 5732	188
189	0.0081 9129	0.0084 6670	0.0087 4701	0.0090 3212	189
190	0.0081 6537	0.0084 4110	0.0087 2174	0.0090 0722	190
191	0.0081 3973	0.0084 1578	0.0086 9677	0.0089 8260	191
192	0.0081 1438	0.0083 9075	0.0086 7208	0.0089 5828	192
193	0.0080 8931	0.0083 6601	0.0086 4767	0.0089 3423	193
194	0.0080 6452	0.0083 4154	0.0086 2355	0.0089 1046	194
195	0.0080 4000	0.0083 1734	0.0085 9969	0.0088 8696	195
196	0.0080 1576	0.0082 9341	0.0085 7610	0.0088 6374	196
197	0.0079 9178	0.0082 6975	0.0085 5278	0.0088 4077	197
198	0.0079 6806	0.0082 4635	0.0085 2972	0.0088 1807	198
199	0.0079 4459	0.0082 2321	0.0085 0691	0.0087 9562	199
200	0.0079 2138	0.0082 0032	0.0084 8436	0.0087 7343	200
201	0.0078 9843	0.0081 7768	0.0084 6206	0.0087 5148	201
202	0.0078 7571	0.0081 5528	0.0084 4000	0.0087 2978	202
203	0.0078 5324	0.0081 3313	0.0084 1818	0.0087 0832	203
204	0.0078 3101	0.0081 1121	0.0083 9661	0.0086 8709	204
205	0.0078 0901	0.0080 8953	0.0083 7526	0.0086 6610	205
206	0.0077 8724	0.0080 6808	0.0083 5415	0.0086 4535	206
207	0.0077 6571	0.0080 4686	0.0083 3327	0.0086 2482	207
208	0.0077 4440	0.0080 2587	0.0083 1261	0.0086 0451	208
209	0.0077 2330	0.0080 0509	0.0082 9217	0.0085 8442	209
210	0.0077 0243	0.0079 8454	0.0082 7194	0.0085 6455	210
211	0.0076 8178	0.0079 6419	0.0082 5194	0.0085 4490	211
212	0.0076 6133	0.0079 4407	0.0082 3214	0.0085 2545	212
213	0.0076 4110	0.0079 2415	0.0082 1256	0.0085 0622	213
214	0.0076 2107	0.0079 0443	0.0081 9318	0.0084 8719	214
215	0.0076 0125	0.0078 8492	0.0081 7400	0.0084 6836	215
216	0.0075 8162	0.0078 6561	0.0081 5502	0.0084 4973	216
217	0.0075 6220	0.0078 4650	0.0081 3624	0.0084 3130	217
218	0.0075 4297	0.0078 2758	0.0081 1766	0.0084 1306	218
219	0.0075 2393	0.0078 0886	0.0080 9926	0.0083 9502	219
220	0.0075 0508	0.0077 9032	0.0080 8106	0.0083 7716	220
221	0.0074 8642	0.0077 7197	0.0080 6304	0.0083 5949	221
222	0.0074 6794	0.0077 5381	0.0080 4520	0.0083 4200	222
223	0.0074 4965	0.0077 3583	0.0080 2755	0.0083 2469	223
224	0.0074 3154	0.0077 1802	0.0080 1008	0.0083 0757	224
225	0.0074 1360	0.0077 0040	0.0079 9278	0.0082 9061	225
226	0.0073 9584	0.0076 8295	0.0079 7566	0.0082 7383	226
227	0.0073 7825	0.0076 6567	0.0079 5871	0.0082 5723	227
228	0.0073 6083	0.0076 4856	0.0079 4192	0.0082 4079	228
229	0.0073 4358	0.0076 3162	0.0079 2531	0.0082 2452	229
230	0.0073 2649	0.0076 1484	0.0079 0886	0.0082 0841	230
231	0.0073 0957	0.0075 9823	0.0078 9257	0.0081 9247	231
232	0.0072 9281	0.0075 8178	0.0078 7645	0.0081 7668	232
233	0.0072 7621	0.0075 6549	0.0078 6048	0.0081 6105	233
234	0.0072 5977	0.0075 4935	0.0078 4467	0.0081 4558	234
235	0.0072 4348	0.0075 3337	0.0078 2902	0.0081 3027	235
236	0.0072 2735	0.0075 1755	0.0078 1351	0.0081 1511	236
237	0.0072 1137	0.0075 0187	0.0077 9816	0.0081 0009	237
238	0.0071 9554	0.0074 8634	0.0077 8296	0.0080 8523	238
239	0.0071 7985	0.0074 7097	0.0077 6790	0.0080 7051	239
240	0.0071 6431	0.0074 5573	0.0077 5299	0.0080 5593	240

TABLE 9 PERIODIC PAYMENT

WHEN PRESENT VALUE OF ANNUITY IS 1

$$\frac{1}{a_{\overline{n}|i}} = \frac{i}{1-(1+i)^{-n}} \qquad \text{Note: } \frac{1}{s_{\overline{n}|i}} = \frac{1}{a_{\overline{n}|i}} - i$$

n	$\frac{2}{3}$%	$\frac{3}{4}$%	$\frac{7}{8}$%	1%	n
1	1.0066 6667	1.0075 0000	1.0087 5000	1.0100 0000	1
2	0.5050 0554	0.5056 3200	0.5065 7203	0.5075 1244	2
3	0.3377 8762	0.3383 4579	0.3391 8361	0.3400 2211	3
4	0.2541 8051	0.2547 0501	0.2554 9257	0.2562 8109	4
5	0.2040 1772	0.2045 2242	0.2052 8049	0.2060 3980	5
6	0.1705 7709	0.1710 6891	0.1718 0789	0.1725 4837	6
7	0.1466 9198	0.1471 7488	0.1479 0070	0.1486 2828	7
8	0.1287 7907	0.1292 5552	0.1299 7190	0.1306 9029	8
9	0.1148 4763	0.1153 1929	0.1160 2868	0.1167 4036	9
10	0.1037 0321	0.1041 7123	0.1048 7538	0.1055 8208	10
11	0.0945 8572	0.0950 5094	0.0957 5111	0.0964 5408	11
12	0.0869 8843	0.0874 5148	0.0881 4860	0.0888 4879	12
13	0.0805 6052	0.0810 2188	0.0817 1669	0.0824 1482	13
14	0.0750 5141	0.0755 1146	0.0762 0453	0.0769 0117	14
15	0.0702 7734	0.0707 3639	0.0714 2817	0.0721 2378	15
16	0.0661 0049	0.0665 5879	0.0672 4965	0.0679 4460	16
17	0.0624 1546	0.0628 7321	0.0635 6346	0.0642 5806	17
18	0.0591 4030	0.0595 9766	0.0602 8756	0.0609 8205	18
19	0.0562 1027	0.0566 6740	0.0573 5715	0.0580 5175	19
20	0.0535 7362	0.0540 3063	0.0547 2042	0.0554 1531	20
21	0.0511 8843	0.0516 4543	0.0523 3541	0.0530 3075	21
22	0.0490 2041	0.0494 7748	0.0501 6779	0.0508 6372	22
23	0.0470 4123	0.0474 9846	0.0481 8921	0.0488 8584	23
24	0.0452 2729	0.0456 8474	0.0463 7604	0.0470 7347	24
25	0.0435 5876	0.0440 1650	0.0447 0843	0.0454 0675	25
26	0.0420 1886	0.0424 7693	0.0431 6959	0.0438 6888	26
27	0.0405 9331	0.0410 5176	0.0417 4520	0.0424 4553	27
28	0.0392 6983	0.0397 2871	0.0404 2300	0.0411 2444	28
29	0.0380 3789	0.0384 9723	0.0391 9243	0.0398 9502	29
30	0.0368 8832	0.0373 4816	0.0380 4431	0.0387 4811	30
31	0.0358 1316	0.0362 7352	0.0369 7068	0.0376 7573	31
32	0.0348 0542	0.0352 6634	0.0359 6454	0.0366 7089	32
33	0.0338 5898	0.0343 2048	0.0350 1976	0.0357 2744	33
34	0.0329 6843	0.0334 3053	0.0341 3092	0.0348 3997	34
35	0.0321 2898	0.0325 9170	0.0332 9324	0.0340 0368	35
36	0.0313 3637	0.0317 9973	0.0325 0244	0.0332 1431	36
37	0.0305 8680	0.0310 5082	0.0317 5473	0.0324 6805	37
38	0.0298 7687	0.0303 4157	0.0310 4671	0.0317 6150	38
39	0.0292 0354	0.0296 6893	0.0303 7531	0.0310 9160	39
40	0.0285 6406	0.0290 3016	0.0297 3780	0.0304 5560	40
41	0.0279 5595	0.0284 2276	0.0291 3169	0.0298 5102	41
42	0.0273 7697	0.0278 4452	0.0285 5475	0.0292 7563	42
43	0.0268 2510	0.0272 9338	0.0280 0493	0.0287 2737	43
44	0.0262 9847	0.0267 6751	0.0274 8039	0.0282 0441	44
45	0.0257 9541	0.0262 6521	0.0269 7943	0.0277 0505	45
46	0.0253 1439	0.0257 8495	0.0265 0053	0.0272 2775	46
47	0.0248 5399	0.0253 2532	0.0260 4228	0.0267 7111	47
48	0.0244 1292	0.0248 8504	0.0256 0338	0.0263 3384	48
49	0.0239 9001	0.0244 6292	0.0251 8265	0.0259 1474	49
50	0.0235 8416	0.0240 5787	0.0247 7900	0.0255 1273	50
51	0.0231 9437	0.0236 6888	0.0243 9142	0.0251 2680	51
52	0.0228 1971	0.0232 9503	0.0240 1898	0.0247 5603	52
53	0.0224 5932	0.0229 3546	0.0236 6084	0.0243 9956	53
54	0.0221 1242	0.0225 8938	0.0233 1619	0.0240 5658	54
55	0.0217 7827	0.0222 5605	0.0229 8430	0.0237 2637	55
56	0.0214 5618	0.0219 3478	0.0226 6449	0.0234 0824	56
57	0.0211 4552	0.0216 2496	0.0223 5611	0.0231 0156	57
58	0.0208 4569	0.0213 2597	0.0220 5858	0.0228 0573	58
59	0.0205 5616	0.0210 3727	0.0217 7135	0.0225 2020	59
60	0.0202 7639	0.0207 5836	0.0214 9390	0.0222 4445	60

TABLE 9 PERIODIC PAYMENT

WHEN PRESENT VALUE OF ANNUITY IS 1

$$\frac{1}{a_{\overline{n}|i}} = \frac{i}{1-(1+i)^{-n}} \qquad \text{Note: } \frac{1}{s_{\overline{n}|i}} = \frac{1}{a_{\overline{n}|i}} - i$$

n	$\frac{2}{3}\%$	$\frac{3}{4}\%$	$\frac{7}{8}\%$	1%	n
61	0.0200 0592	0.0204 8873	0.0212 2575	0.0219 7800	61
62	0.0197 4429	0.0202 2795	0.0209 6644	0.0217 2041	62
63	0.0194 9108	0.0199 7560	0.0207 1557	0.0214 7125	63
64	0.0192 4590	0.0197 3127	0.0204 7273	0.0212 3013	64
65	0.0190 0837	0.0194 9460	0.0202 3754	0.0209 9667	65
66	0.0187 7815	0.0192 6524	0.0200 0968	0.0207 7052	66
67	0.0185 5491	0.0190 4286	0.0197 8879	0.0205 5136	67
68	0.0183 3835	0.0188 2716	0.0195 7459	0.0203 3889	68
69	0.0181 2816	0.0186 1785	0.0193 6677	0.0201 3280	69
70	0.0179 2409	0.0184 1464	0.0191 6506	0.0199 3282	70
71	0.0177 2586	0.0182 1728	0.0189 6921	0.0197 3870	71
72	0.0175 3324	0.0180 2554	0.0187 7897	0.0195 5019	72
73	0.0173 4600	0.0178 3917	0.0185 9411	0.0193 6706	73
74	0.0171 6391	0.0176 5796	0.0184 1441	0.0191 8910	74
75	0.0169 8678	0.0174 8170	0.0182 3966	0.0190 1609	75
76	0.0168 1440	0.0173 1020	0.0180 6967	0.0188 4784	76
77	0.0166 4659	0.0171 4328	0.0179 0426	0.0186 8416	77
78	0.0164 8318	0.0169 8074	0.0177 4324	0.0185 2488	78
79	0.0163 2400	0.0168 2244	0.0175 8645	0.0183 6983	79
80	0.0161 6889	0.0166 6821	0.0174 3374	0.0182 1885	80
81	0.0160 1769	0.0165 1790	0.0172 8494	0.0180 7179	81
82	0.0158 7027	0.0163 7136	0.0171 3992	0.0179 2851	82
83	0.0157 2649	0.0162 2847	0.0169 9854	0.0177 8887	83
84	0.0155 8621	0.0160 8908	0.0168 6067	0.0176 5273	84
85	0.0154 4933	0.0159 5308	0.0167 2619	0.0175 1998	85
86	0.0153 1570	0.0158 2034	0.0165 9497	0.0173 9050	86
87	0.0151 8524	0.0156 9076	0.0164 6691	0.0172 6418	87
88	0.0150 5781	0.0155 6423	0.0163 4190	0.0171 4089	88
89	0.0149 3334	0.0154 4064	0.0162 1982	0.0170 2056	89
90	0.0148 1170	0.0153 1989	0.0161 0060	0.0169 0306	90
91	0.0146 9282	0.0152 0190	0.0159 8413	0.0167 8832	91
92	0.0145 7660	0.0150 8657	0.0158 7031	0.0166 7624	92
93	0.0144 6296	0.0149 7382	0.0157 5908	0.0165 6673	93
94	0.0143 5181	0.0148 6356	0.0156 5033	0.0164 5971	94
95	0.0142 4308	0.0147 5571	0.0155 4401	0.0163 5511	95
96	0.0141 3668	0.0146 5020	0.0154 4002	0.0162 5284	96
97	0.0140 3255	0.0145 4696	0.0153 3829	0.0161 5284	97
98	0.0139 3062	0.0144 4592	0.0152 3877	0.0160 5503	98
99	0.0138 3082	0.0143 4701	0.0151 4137	0.0159 5936	99
100	0.0137 3308	0.0142 5017	0.0150 4604	0.0158 6574	100
101	0.0136 3735	0.0141 5533	0.0149 5271	0.0157 7413	101
102	0.0135 4357	0.0140 6243	0.0148 6133	0.0156 8446	102
103	0.0134 5168	0.0139 7143	0.0147 7184	0.0155 9668	103
104	0.0133 6162	0.0138 8226	0.0146 8418	0.0155 1073	104
105	0.0132 7334	0.0137 9487	0.0145 9830	0.0154 2656	105
106	0.0131 8680	0.0137 0922	0.0145 1416	0.0153 4412	106
107	0.0131 0194	0.0136 2524	0.0144 3169	0.0152 6336	107
108	0.0130 1871	0.0135 4291	0.0143 5086	0.0151 8423	108
109	0.0129 3708	0.0134 6216	0.0142 7162	0.0151 0669	109
110	0.0128 5700	0.0133 8297	0.0141 9393	0.0150 3069	110
111	0.0127 7842	0.0133 0527	0.0141 1774	0.0149 5620	111
112	0.0127 0131	0.0132 2905	0.0140 4301	0.0148 8317	112
113	0.0126 2562	0.0131 5425	0.0139 6971	0.0148 1155	113
114	0.0125 5132	0.0130 8084	0.0138 9780	0.0147 4133	114
115	0.0124 7838	0.0130 0878	0.0138 2724	0.0146 7245	115
116	0.0124 0675	0.0129 3803	0.0137 5799	0.0146 0488	116
117	0.0123 3641	0.0128 6858	0.0136 9003	0.0145 3860	117
118	0.0122 6732	0.0128 0037	0.0136 2331	0.0144 7356	118
119	0.0121 9944	0.0127 3338	0.0135 5781	0.0144 0974	119
120	0.0121 3276	0.0126 6758	0.0134 9350	0.0143 4709	120

TABLE 9 PERIODIC PAYMENT
WHEN PRESENT VALUE OF ANNUITY IS 1

$$\frac{1}{a_{\overline{n}|i}} = \frac{i}{1-(1+i)^{-n}} \qquad \text{Note: } \frac{1}{s_{\overline{n}|i}} = \frac{1}{a_{\overline{n}|i}} - i$$

n	$\frac{2}{3}\%$	$\frac{3}{4}\%$	$\frac{7}{8}\%$	1%	n
121	0.0120 6724	0.0126 0294	0.0134 3035	0.0142 8561	121
122	0.0120 0284	0.0125 3942	0.0133 6832	0.0142 2525	122
123	0.0119 3955	0.0124 7702	0.0133 0740	0.0141 6599	123
124	0.0118 7734	0.0124 1568	0.0132 4754	0.0141 0780	124
125	0.0118 1618	0.0123 5540	0.0131 8874	0.0140 5065	125
126	0.0117 5604	0.0122 9614	0.0131 3096	0.0139 9452	126
127	0.0116 9690	0.0122 3788	0.0130 7418	0.0139 3939	127
128	0.0116 3875	0.0121 8060	0.0130 1838	0.0138 8524	128
129	0.0115 8154	0.0121 2428	0.0129 6352	0.0138 3203	129
130	0.0115 2527	0.0120 6888	0.0129 0960	0.0137 7975	130
131	0.0114 6992	0.0120 1440	0.0128 5659	0.0137 2837	131
132	0.0114 1545	0.0119 6080	0.0128 0446	0.0136 7788	132
133	0.0113 6185	0.0119 0808	0.0127 5320	0.0136 2825	133
134	0.0113 0910	0.0118 5621	0.0127 0279	0.0135 7947	134
135	0.0112 5719	0.0118 0516	0.0126 5321	0.0135 3151	135
136	0.0112 0609	0.0117 5493	0.0126 0444	0.0134 8437	136
137	0.0111 5578	0.0117 0550	0.0125 5646	0.0134 3801	137
138	0.0111 0625	0.0116 5684	0.0125 0926	0.0133 9242	138
139	0.0110 5749	0.0116 0894	0.0124 6281	0.0133 4759	139
140	0.0110 0947	0.0115 6179	0.0124 1711	0.0133 0349	140
141	0.0109 6218	0.0115 1536	0.0123 7213	0.0132 6012	141
142	0.0109 1560	0.0114 6965	0.0123 2787	0.0132 1746	142
143	0.0108 6972	0.0114 2464	0.0122 8430	0.0131 7549	143
144	0.0108 2453	0.0113 8031	0.0122 4141	0.0131 3419	144
145	0.0107 8000	0.0113 3664	0.0121 9918	0.0130 9356	145
146	0.0107 3613	0.0112 9364	0.0121 5761	0.0130 5358	146
147	0.0106 9291	0.0112 5127	0.0121 1668	0.0130 1423	147
148	0.0106 5031	0.0112 0954	0.0120 7638	0.0129 7551	148
149	0.0106 0833	0.0111 6841	0.0120 3669	0.0129 3739	149
150	0.0105 6695	0.0111 2790	0.0119 9760	0.0128 9988	150
151	0.0105 2617	0.0110 8797	0.0119 5910	0.0128 6294	151
152	0.0104 8597	0.0110 4862	0.0119 2117	0.0128 2659	152
153	0.0104 4633	0.0110 0984	0.0118 8381	0.0127 9079	153
154	0.0104 0726	0.0109 7162	0.0118 4701	0.0127 5554	154
155	0.0103 6873	0.0109 3395	0.0118 1075	0.0127 2084	155
156	0.0103 3074	0.0108 9681	0.0117 7502	0.0126 8666	156
157	0.0102 9327	0.0108 6019	0.0117 3981	0.0126 5300	157
158	0.0102 5632	0.0108 2409	0.0117 0512	0.0126 1986	158
159	0.0102 1988	0.0107 8849	0.0116 7093	0.0125 8721	159
160	0.0101 8394	0.0107 5340	0.0116 3724	0.0125 5504	160
161	0.0101 4848	0.0107 1878	0.0116 0402	0.0125 2336	161
162	0.0101 1350	0.0106 8465	0.0115 7128	0.0124 9215	162
163	0.0100 7899	0.0106 5098	0.0115 3901	0.0124 6141	163
164	0.0100 4494	0.0106 1777	0.0115 0720	0.0124 3111	164
165	0.0100 1134	0.0105 8502	0.0114 7583	0.0124 0126	165
166	0.0099 7819	0.0105 5270	0.0114 4490	0.0123 7185	166
167	0.0099 4547	0.0105 2083	0.0114 1441	0.0123 4286	167
168	0.0099 1318	0.0104 8938	0.0113 8434	0.0123 1430	168
169	0.0098 8131	0.0104 5834	0.0113 5469	0.0122 8614	169
170	0.0098 4986	0.0104 2772	0.0113 2544	0.0122 5840	170
171	0.0098 1881	0.0103 9751	0.0112 9660	0.0122 3105	171
172	0.0097 8816	0.0103 6769	0.0112 6816	0.0122 0409	172
173	0.0097 5791	0.0103 3827	0.0112 4010	0.0121 7751	173
174	0.0097 2803	0.0103 0922	0.0112 1242	0.0121 5132	174
175	0.0096 9854	0.0102 8056	0.0111 8512	0.0121 2549	175
176	0.0096 6942	0.0102 5226	0.0111 5818	0.0121 0003	176
177	0.0096 4066	0.0102 2433	0.0111 3161	0.0120 7492	177
178	0.0096 1226	0.0101 9676	0.0111 0539	0.0120 5016	178
179	0.0095 8422	0.0101 6954	0.0110 7952	0.0120 2575	179
180	0.0095 5652	0.0101 4267	0.0110 5399	0.0120 0168	180

TABLE 9 PERIODIC PAYMENT
WHEN PRESENT VALUE OF ANNUITY IS 1

$$\frac{1}{a_{\overline{n}|i}} = \frac{i}{1-(1+i)^{-n}} \qquad \text{Note: } \frac{1}{s_{\overline{n}|i}} = \frac{1}{a_{\overline{n}|i}} - i$$

n	$\frac{2}{3}\%$	$\frac{3}{4}\%$	$\frac{7}{8}\%$	1%	n
181	0.0095 2917	0.0101 1613	0.0110 2880	0.0119 7794	181
182	0.0095 0215	0.0100 8993	0.0110 0394	0.0119 5453	182
183	0.0094 7546	0.0100 6406	0.0109 7941	0.0119 3144	183
184	0.0094 4909	0.0100 3851	0.0109 5520	0.0119 0867	184
185	0.0094 2305	0.0100 1328	0.0109 3130	0.0118 8621	185
186	0.0093 9732	0.0099 8837	0.0109 0771	0.0118 6405	186
187	0.0093 7189	0.0099 6376	0.0108 8443	0.0118 4219	187
188	0.0093 4678	0.0099 3945	0.0108 6145	0.0118 2063	188
189	0.0093 2196	0.0099 1544	0.0108 3876	0.0117 9936	189
190	0.0092 9743	0.0098 9173	0.0108 1637	0.0117 7838	190
191	0.0092 7320	0.0098 6830	0.0107 9425	0.0117 5768	191
192	0.0092 4925	0.0098 4516	0.0107 7242	0.0117 3725	192
193	0.0092 2558	0.0098 2230	0.0107 5087	0.0117 1710	193
194	0.0092 0219	0.0097 9971	0.0107 2959	0.0116 9721	194
195	0.0091 7907	0.0097 7739	0.0107 0857	0.0116 7759	195
196	0.0091 5622	0.0097 5534	0.0106 8782	0.0116 5822	196
197	0.0091 3363	0.0097 3355	0.0106 6733	0.0116 3911	197
198	0.0091 1130	0.0097 1202	0.0106 4709	0.0116 2026	198
199	0.0090 8923	0.0096 9074	0.0106 2711	0.0116 0164	199
200	0.0090 6741	0.0096 6972	0.0106 0737	0.0115 8328	200
201	0.0090 4584	0.0096 4894	0.0105 8787	0.0115 6515	201
202	0.0090 2451	0.0096 2840	0.0105 6862	0.0115 4725	202
203	0.0090 0342	0.0096 0810	0.0105 4960	0.0115 2959	203
204	0.0089 8257	0.0095 8804	0.0105 3081	0.0115 1216	204
205	0.0089 6195	0.0095 6821	0.0105 1225	0.0114 9495	205
206	0.0089 4156	0.0095 4861	0.0104 9392	0.0114 7796	206
207	0.0089 2140	0.0095 2923	0.0104 7581	0.0114 6118	207
208	0.0089 0146	0.0095 1008	0.0104 5792	0.0114 4463	208
209	0.0088 8175	0.0094 9114	0.0104 4024	0.0114 2828	209
210	0.0088 6225	0.0094 7242	0.0104 2278	0.0114 1214	210
211	0.0088 4296	0.0094 5391	0.0104 0552	0.0113 9621	211
212	0.0088 2388	0.0094 3561	0.0103 8847	0.0113 8048	212
213	0.0088 0512	0.0094 1752	0.0103 7163	0.0113 6494	213
214	0.0087 8635	0.0093 9963	0.0103 5498	0.0113 4961	214
215	0.0087 6789	0.0093 8194	0.0103 3853	0.0113 3446	215
216	0.0087 4963	0.0093 6445	0.0103 2228	0.0113 1950	216
217	0.0087 3156	0.0093 4715	0.0103 0621	0.0113 0473	217
218	0.0087 1369	0.0093 3005	0.0102 9034	0.0112 9015	218
219	0.0086 9600	0.0093 1313	0.0102 7465	0.0112 7575	219
220	0.0086 7851	0.0092 9640	0.0102 5914	0.0112 6152	220
221	0.0086 6120	0.0092 7985	0.0102 4382	0.0112 4747	221
222	0.0086 4407	0.0092 6349	0.0102 2867	0.0112 3360	222
223	0.0086 2713	0.0092 4730	0.0102 1370	0.0112 1990	223
224	0.0086 1036	0.0092 3129	0.0101 9890	0.0112 0636	224
225	0.0085 9376	0.0092 1546	0.0101 8427	0.0111 9299	225
226	0.0085 7734	0.0091 9979	0.0101 6981	0.0111 7979	226
227	0.0085 6109	0.0091 8430	0.0101 5552	0.0111 6674	227
228	0.0085 4501	0.0091 6897	0.0101 4139	0.0111 5386	228
229	0.0085 2910	0.0091 5380	0.0101 2742	0.0111 4113	229
230	0.0085 1335	0.0091 3880	0.0101 1361	0.0111 2856	230
231	0.0084 9776	0.0091 2396	0.0100 9996	0.0111 1613	231
232	0.0084 8233	0.0091 0928	0.0100 8646	0.0111 0386	232
233	0.0084 6706	0.0090 9475	0.0100 7311	0.0110 9174	233
234	0.0084 5194	0.0090 8038	0.0100 5992	0.0110 7976	234
235	0.0084 3698	0.0090 6616	0.0100 4687	0.0110 6793	235
236	0.0084 2217	0.0090 5209	0.0100 3397	0.0110 5624	236
237	0.0084 0751	0.0090 3816	0.0100 2122	0.0110 4469	237
238	0.0083 9299	0.0090 2438	0.0100 0860	0.0110 3328	238
239	0.0083 7863	0.0090 1075	0.0099 9613	0.0110 2200	239
240	0.0083 6440	0.0089 9726	0.0099 8380	0.0110 1086	240

TABLE 9 PERIODIC PAYMENT

WHEN PRESENT VALUE OF ANNUITY IS 1

$$\frac{1}{a_{\overline{n}|i}} = \frac{i}{1-(1+i)^{-n}} \qquad \text{Note: } \frac{1}{s_{\overline{n}|i}} = \frac{1}{a_{\overline{n}|i}} - i$$

n	$1\frac{1}{8}\%$	$1\frac{1}{4}\%$	$1\frac{3}{8}\%$	$1\frac{1}{2}\%$	n
1	1.0112 5000	1.0125 0000	1.0137 5000	1.0150 0000	1
2	0.5084 5323	0.5093 9441	0.5103 3597	0.5112 7792	2
3	0.3408 6130	0.3417 0117	0.3425 4173	0.3433 8296	3
4	0.2570 7058	0.2578 6102	0.2586 5243	0.2594 4479	4
5	0.2068 0034	0.2075 6211	0.2083 2510	0.2090 8932	5
6	0.1732 9034	0.1740 3381	0.1747 7877	0.1755 2521	6
7	0.1493 5762	0.1500 8872	0.1508 2157	0.1515 5616	7
8	0.1314 1071	0.1321 3314	0.1328 5758	0.1335 8402	8
9	0.1174 5432	0.1181 7055	0.1188 8906	0.1196 0982	9
10	0.1062 9131	0.1070 0307	0.1077 1737	0.1084 3418	10
11	0.0971 5984	0.0978 6839	0.0985 7973	0.0992 9384	11
12	0.0895 5203	0.0902 5831	0.0909 6764	0.0916 7999	12
13	0.0831 1626	0.0838 2100	0.0845 2904	0.0852 4036	13
14	0.0776 0138	0.0783 0515	0.0790 1246	0.0797 2332	14
15	0.0728 2321	0.0735 2646	0.0742 3351	0.0749 4436	15
16	0.0686 4363	0.0693 4672	0.0700 5388	0.0707 6508	16
17	0.0649 5698	0.0656 6023	0.0663 6780	0.0670 7966	17
18	0.0616 8113	0.0623 8479	0.0630 9301	0.0638 0578	18
19	0.0587 5120	0.0594 5548	0.0601 6457	0.0608 7847	19
20	0.0561 1531	0.0568 2039	0.0575 3054	0.0582 4574	20
21	0.0537 3145	0.0544 3749	0.0551 4884	0.0558 6550	21
22	0.0515 6525	0.0522 7238	0.0529 8507	0.0537 0332	22
23	0.0495 8833	0.0502 9666	0.0510 1080	0.0517 3075	23
24	0.0477 7701	0.0484 8665	0.0492 0235	0.0499 2410	24
25	0.0461 1144	0.0468 2247	0.0475 3981	0.0482 6345	25
26	0.0445 7479	0.0452 8729	0.0460 0635	0.0467 3196	26
27	0.0431 5273	0.0438 6677	0.0445 8763	0.0453 1527	27
28	0.0418 3299	0.0425 4863	0.0432 7134	0.0440 0108	28
29	0.0406 0498	0.0413 2228	0.0420 4689	0.0427 7878	29
30	0.0394 5953	0.0401 7854	0.0409 0511	0.0416 3919	30
31	0.0383 8866	0.0391 0942	0.0398 3798	0.0405 7430	31
32	0.0373 8535	0.0381 0791	0.0388 3850	0.0395 7710	32
33	0.0364 4349	0.0371 6786	0.0379 0053	0.0386 4144	33
34	0.0355 5763	0.0362 8387	0.0370 1864	0.0377 6189	34
35	0.0347 2299	0.0354 5111	0.0361 8801	0.0369 3363	35
36	0.0339 3529	0.0346 6533	0.0354 0438	0.0361 5240	36
37	0.0331 9072	0.0339 2270	0.0346 6394	0.0354 1437	37
38	0.0324 8589	0.0332 1983	0.0339 6327	0.0347 1613	38
39	0.0318 1773	0.0325 5365	0.0332 9931	0.0340 5463	39
40	0.0311 8349	0.0319 2141	0.0326 6931	0.0334 2710	40
41	0.0305 8069	0.0313 2063	0.0320 7078	0.0328 3106	41
42	0.0300 0709	0.0307 4906	0.0315 0148	0.0322 6426	42
43	0.0294 6064	0.0302 0466	0.0309 5936	0.0317 2465	43
44	0.0289 3949	0.0296 8557	0.0304 4257	0.0312 1038	44
45	0.0284 4197	0.0291 9012	0.0299 4941	0.0307 1976	45
46	0.0279 6652	0.0287 1675	0.0294 7836	0.0302 5125	46
47	0.0275 1173	0.0282 6406	0.0290 2799	0.0298 0342	47
48	0.0270 7632	0.0278 3075	0.0285 9701	0.0293 7500	48
49	0.0266 5910	0.0274 1564	0.0281 8423	0.0289 6478	49
50	0.0262 5898	0.0270 1763	0.0277 8857	0.0285 7168	50

TABLE 9 PERIODIC PAYMENT

WHEN PRESENT VALUE OF ANNUITY IS 1

$$\frac{1}{a_{\overline{n}|i}} = \frac{i}{1-(1+i)^{-n}} \qquad \text{Note: } \frac{1}{s_{\overline{n}|i}} = \frac{1}{a_{\overline{n}|i}} - i$$

n	$1\frac{1}{8}\%$	$1\frac{1}{4}\%$	$1\frac{3}{8}\%$	$1\frac{1}{2}\%$	n
51	0.0258 7494	0.0266 3571	0.0274 0900	0.0281 9469	51
52	0.0255 0606	0.0262 6897	0.0270 4461	0.0278 3287	52
53	0.0251 5149	0.0259 1653	0.0266 9453	0.0274 8537	53
54	0.0248 1043	0.0255 7760	0.0263 5797	0.0271 5138	54
55	0.0244 8213	0.0252 5145	0.0260 3418	0.0268 3018	55
56	0.0241 6592	0.0249 3739	0.0257 2249	0.0265 2106	56
57	0.0238 6116	0.0246 3478	0.0254 2225	0.0262 2341	57
58	0.0235 6726	0.0243 4303	0.0251 3287	0.0259 3661	58
59	0.0232 8366	0.0240 6158	0.0248 5380	0.0256 6012	59
60	0.0230 0985	0.0237 8993	0.0245 8452	0.0253 9343	60
61	0.0227 4534	0.0235 2758	0.0243 2455	0.0251 3604	61
62	0.0224 8969	0.0232 7410	0.0240 7344	0.0248 8751	62
63	0.0222 4247	0.0230 2904	0.0238 3076	0.0246 4741	63
64	0.0220 0329	0.0227 9203	0.0235 9612	0.0244 1534	64
65	0.0217 7178	0.0225 6268	0.0233 6914	0.0241 9094	65
66	0.0215 4758	0.0223 4065	0.0231 4949	0.0239 7386	66
67	0.0213 3037	0.0221 2560	0.0229 3682	0.0237 6376	67
68	0.0211 1985	0.0219 1724	0.0227 3082	0.0235 6033	68
69	0.0209 1571	0.0217 1527	0.0225 3122	0.0233 6329	69
70	0.0207 1769	0.0215 1941	0.0223 3773	0.0231 7235	70
71	0.0205 2552	0.0213 2941	0.0221 5009	0.0229 8727	71
72	0.0203 3896	0.0211 4501	0.0219 6806	0.0228 0779	72
73	0.0201 5779	0.0209 6600	0.0217 9140	0.0226 3368	73
74	0.0199 8177	0.0207 9215	0.0216 1991	0.0224 6473	74
75	0.0198 1072	0.0206 2325	0.0214 5336	0.0223 0072	75
76	0.0196 4442	0.0204 5910	0.0212 9157	0.0221 4146	76
77	0.0194 8269	0.0202 9953	0.0211 3435	0.0219 8676	77
78	0.0193 2536	0.0201 4436	0.0209 8151	0.0218 3645	78
79	0.0191 7226	0.0199 9341	0.0208 3290	0.0216 9036	79
80	0.0190 2323	0.0198 4652	0.0206 8836	0.0215 4832	80
81	0.0188 7812	0.0197 0356	0.0205 4772	0.0214 1019	81
82	0.0187 3678	0.0195 6437	0.0204 1086	0.0212 7583	82
83	0.0185 9908	0.0194 2881	0.0202 7762	0.0211 4509	83
84	0.0184 6489	0.0192 9675	0.0201 4789	0.0210 1784	84
85	0.0183 3409	0.0191 6808	0.0200 2153	0.0208 9396	85
86	0.0182 0654	0.0190 4267	0.0198 9843	0.0207 7333	86
87	0.0180 8215	0.0189 2041	0.0197 7847	0.0206 5584	87
88	0.0179 6081	0.0188 0119	0.0196 6155	0.0205 4138	88
89	0.0178 4240	0.0186 8491	0.0195 4756	0.0204 2984	89
90	0.0177 2684	0.0185 7146	0.0194 3641	0.0203 2113	90
91	0.0176 1403	0.0184 6076	0.0193 2799	0.0202 1516	91
92	0.0175 0387	0.0183 5272	0.0192 2222	0.0201 1182	92
93	0.0173 9629	0.0182 4724	0.0191 1902	0.0200 1104	93
94	0.0172 9119	0.0181 4425	0.0190 1829	0.0199 1273	94
95	0.0171 8851	0.0180 4366	0.0189 1997	0.0198 1681	95
96	0.0170 8816	0.0179 4541	0.0188 2397	0.0197 2321	96
97	0.0169 9007	0.0178 4941	0.0187 3022	0.0196 3186	97
98	0.0168 9418	0.0177 5560	0.0186 3866	0.0195 4268	98
99	0.0168 0041	0.0176 6391	0.0185 4921	0.0194 5560	99
100	0.0167 0870	0.0175 7428	0.0184 6181	0.0193 7057	100

TABLE 9 PERIODIC PAYMENT

WHEN PRESENT VALUE OF ANNUITY IS 1

$$\frac{1}{a_{\overline{n}|i}} = \frac{i}{1-(1+i)^{-n}} \qquad \text{Note: } \frac{1}{s_{\overline{n}|i}} = \frac{1}{a_{\overline{n}|i}} - i$$

n	$1\frac{5}{8}\%$	$1\frac{3}{4}\%$	$1\frac{7}{8}\%$	2%	n
1	1.0162 5000	1.0175 0000	1.0187 5000	1.0200 0000	1
2	0.5122 2024	0.5131 6295	0.5141 0604	0.5150 4950	2
3	0.3442 2487	0.3450 6746	0.3459 1073	0.3467 5467	3
4	0.2602 3810	0.2610 3237	0.2618 2759	0.2626 2375	4
5	0.2098 5476	0.2106 2142	0.2113 8930	0.2121 5839	5
6	0.1762 7314	0.1770 2256	0.1777 7345	0.1785 2581	6
7	0.1522 9250	0.1530 3059	0.1537 7040	0.1545 1196	7
8	0.1343 1247	0.1350 4292	0.1357 7537	0.1365 0980	8
9	0.1203 3285	0.1210 5813	0.1217 8566	0.1225 1544	9
10	0.1091 5351	0.1098 7534	0.1105 9969	0.1113 2653	10
11	0.1000 1073	0.1007 3038	0.1014 5278	0.1021 7794	11
12	0.0923 9537	0.0931 1377	0.0938 3518	0.0945 5960	12
13	0.0859 5496	0.0866 7283	0.0873 9396	0.0881 1835	13
14	0.0804 3771	0.0811 5562	0.0818 7704	0.0826 0197	14
15	0.0756 5898	0.0763 7739	0.0770 9955	0.0778 2547	15
16	0.0714 8031	0.0721 9958	0.0729 2285	0.0736 5013	16
17	0.0677 9580	0.0685 1623	0.0692 4091	0.0699 6984	17
18	0.0645 2309	0.0652 4492	0.0659 7127	0.0667 0210	18
19	0.0615 9715	0.0623 2061	0.0630 4882	0.0637 8177	19
20	0.0589 6597	0.0596 9122	0.0604 2148	0.0611 5672	20
21	0.0565 8743	0.0573 1464	0.0580 4709	0.0587 8477	21
22	0.0544 2709	0.0551 5638	0.0558 9116	0.0566 3140	22
23	0.0524 5648	0.0531 8796	0.0539 2517	0.0546 6810	23
24	0.0506 5188	0.0513 8565	0.0521 2540	0.0528 7110	24
25	0.0489 9336	0.0497 2952	0.0504 7188	0.0512 2044	25
26	0.0474 6408	0.0482 0269	0.0489 4775	0.0496 9923	26
27	0.0460 4967	0.0467 9079	0.0475 3861	0.0482 9309	27
28	0.0447 3781	0.0454 8151	0.0462 3215	0.0469 8967	28
29	0.0435 1791	0.0442 6424	0.0450 1773	0.0457 7836	29
30	0.0423 8075	0.0431 2975	0.0438 8616	0.0446 4992	30
31	0.0413 1834	0.0420 7005	0.0428 2941	0.0435 9635	31
32	0.0403 2365	0.0410 7812	0.0418 4046	0.0426 1061	32
33	0.0393 9054	0.0401 4779	0.0409 1314	0.0416 8653	33
34	0.0385 1357	0.0392 7363	0.0400 4202	0.0408 1867	34
35	0.0376 8792	0.0384 5082	0.0392 2227	0.0400 0221	35
36	0.0369 0931	0.0376 7507	0.0384 4960	0.0392 3285	36
37	0.0361 7393	0.0369 4257	0.0377 2021	0.0385 0678	37
38	0.0354 7837	0.0362 4990	0.0370 3066	0.0378 2057	38
39	0.0348 1955	0.0355 9399	0.0363 7788	0.0371 7114	39
40	0.0341 9472	0.0349 7209	0.0357 5913	0.0365 5575	40
41	0.0336 0140	0.0343 8170	0.0351 7190	0.0359 7188	41
42	0.0330 3732	0.0338 2057	0.0346 1393	0.0354 1729	42
43	0.0325 0045	0.0332 8666	0.0340 8319	0.0348 8993	43
44	0.0319 8893	0.0327 7810	0.0335 7781	0.0343 8794	44
45	0.0315 0106	0.0322 9321	0.0330 9610	0.0339 0962	45
46	0.0310 3531	0.0318 3043	0.0326 3651	0.0334 5342	46
47	0.0305 9025	0.0313 8836	0.0321 9763	0.0330 1792	47
48	0.0301 6460	0.0309 6570	0.0317 7815	0.0326 0184	48
49	0.0297 5716	0.0305 6124	0.0313 7689	0.0322 0396	49
50	0.0293 6684	0.0301 7391	0.0309 9275	0.0318 2321	50

TABLE 9 PERIODIC PAYMENT
WHEN PRESENT VALUE OF ANNUITY IS 1

$$\frac{1}{a_{\overline{n}|i}} = \frac{i}{1-(1+i)^{-n}} \qquad \text{Note: } \frac{1}{s_{\overline{n}|i}} = \frac{1}{a_{\overline{n}|i}} - i$$

n	$1\frac{5}{8}\%$	$1\frac{3}{4}\%$	$1\frac{7}{8}\%$	2%	n
51	0.0289 9263	0.0298 0269	0.0306 2472	0.0314 5856	51
52	0.0286 3360	0.0294 4665	0.0302 7187	0.0311 0909	52
53	0.0282 8888	0.0291 0492	0.0299 3333	0.0307 7392	53
54	0.0279 5769	0.0287 7672	0.0296 0830	0.0304 5226	54
55	0.0276 3927	0.0284 6129	0.0292 9605	0.0301 4337	55
56	0.0273 3294	0.0281 5795	0.0289 9589	0.0298 4656	56
57	0.0270 3807	0.0278 6606	0.0287 0717	0.0295 6120	57
58	0.0267 5406	0.0275 8503	0.0284 2931	0.0292 8667	58
59	0.0264 8036	0.0273 1430	0.0281 6174	0.0290 2243	59
60	0.0262 1645	0.0270 5336	0.0279 0395	0.0287 6797	60
61	0.0259 6184	0.0268 0172	0.0276 5545	0.0285 2278	61
62	0.0257 1608	0.0265 5892	0.0274 1579	0.0282 8643	62
63	0.0254 7875	0.0263 2455	0.0271 8455	0.0280 5848	63
64	0.0252 4946	0.0260 9821	0.0269 6133	0.0278 3855	64
65	0.0250 2782	0.0258 7952	0.0267 4575	0.0276 2624	65
66	0.0248 1350	0.0256 6813	0.0265 3747	0.0274 2122	66
67	0.0246 0615	0.0254 6372	0.0263 3616	0.0272 2316	67
68	0.0244 0548	0.0252 6597	0.0261 4149	0.0270 3173	68
69	0.0242 1118	0.0250 7459	0.0259 5319	0.0268 4665	69
70	0.0240 2299	0.0248 8930	0.0257 7097	0.0266 6765	70
71	0.0238 4064	0.0247 0985	0.0255 9458	0.0264 9446	71
72	0.0236 6388	0.0245 3600	0.0254 2377	0.0263 2683	72
73	0.0234 9250	0.0243 6750	0.0252 5830	0.0261 6454	73
74	0.0233 2626	0.0242 0413	0.0250 9796	0.0260 0736	74
75	0.0231 6496	0.0240 4570	0.0249 4254	0.0258 5508	75
76	0.0230 0840	0.0238 9200	0.0247 9185	0.0257 0751	76
77	0.0228 5640	0.0237 4285	0.0246 4568	0.0255 6447	77
78	0.0227 0877	0.0235 9806	0.0245 0387	0.0254 2576	78
79	0.0225 6536	0.0234 5748	0.0243 6625	0.0252 9123	79
80	0.0224 2600	0.0233 2093	0.0242 3266	0.0251 6071	80
81	0.0222 9053	0.0231 8828	0.0241 0294	0.0250 3405	81
82	0.0221 5882	0.0230 5936	0.0239 7696	0.0249 1110	82
83	0.0220 3073	0.0229 3406	0.0238 5457	0.0247 9173	83
84	0.0219 0612	0.0228 1223	0.0237 3564	0.0246 7581	84
85	0.0217 8487	0.0226 9375	0.0236 2004	0.0245 6321	85
86	0.0216 6687	0.0225 7850	0.0235 0767	0.0244 5381	86
87	0.0215 5199	0.0224 6636	0.0233 9839	0.0243 4750	87
88	0.0214 4013	0.0223 5724	0.0232 9212	0.0242 4416	88
89	0.0213 3119	0.0222 5102	0.0231 8873	0.0241 4370	89
90	0.0212 2506	0.0221 4760	0.0230 8813	0.0240 4602	90
91	0.0211 2166	0.0220 4690	0.0229 9023	0.0239 5101	91
92	0.0210 2089	0.0219 4882	0.0228 9494	0.0238 5859	92
93	0.0209 2267	0.0218 5327	0.0228 0217	0.0237 6868	93
94	0.0208 2691	0.0217 6017	0.0227 1183	0.0236 8118	94
95	0.0207 3353	0.0216 6944	0.0226 2385	0.0235 9602	95
96	0.0206 4246	0.0215 8101	0.0225 3814	0.0235 1313	96
97	0.0205 5362	0.0214 9480	0.0224 5465	0.0234 3242	97
98	0.0204 6695	0.0214 1074	0.0223 7329	0.0233 5383	98
99	0.0203 8237	0.0213 2876	0.0222 9400	0.0232 7729	99
100	0.0202 9983	0.0212 4880	0.0222 1671	0.0232 0274	100

TABLE 9 PERIODIC PAYMENT

WHEN PRESENT VALUE OF ANNUITY IS 1

$$\frac{1}{a_{\overline{n}|i}} = \frac{i}{1-(1+i)^{-n}} \qquad \text{Note: } \frac{1}{s_{\overline{n}|i}} = \frac{1}{a_{\overline{n}|i}} - i$$

n	$2\frac{1}{4}\%$	$2\frac{1}{2}\%$	$2\frac{3}{4}\%$	3%	n
1	1.0225 0000	1.0250 0000	1.0275 0000	1.0300 0000	1
2	0.5169 3758	0.5188 2716	0.5207 1825	0.5226 1084	2
3	0.3484 4458	0.3501 3717	0.3518 3243	0.3535 3036	3
4	0.2642 1893	0.2658 1788	0.2674 2059	0.2690 2705	4
5	0.2137 0021	0.2152 4686	0.2167 9832	0.2183 5457	5
6	0.1800 3496	0.1815 4997	0.1830 7083	0.1845 9750	6
7	0.1560 0025	0.1574 9543	0.1589 9748	0.1605 0635	7
8	0.1379 8462	0.1394 6735	0.1409 5795	0.1424 5639	8
9	0.1239 8170	0.1254 5689	0.1269 4095	0.1284 3386	9
10	0.1127 8768	0.1142 5876	0.1157 3972	0.1172 3051	10
11	0.1036 3649	0.1051 0596	0.1065 8629	0.1080 7745	11
12	0.0960 1740	0.0974 8713	0.0989 6871	0.1004 6209	12
13	0.0895 7686	0.0910 4827	0.0925 3252	0.0940 2954	13
14	0.0840 6230	0.0855 3652	0.0870 2457	0.0885 2634	14
15	0.0792 8852	0.0807 6646	0.0822 5917	0.0837 6658	15
16	0.0751 1663	0.0765 9899	0.0780 9710	0.0796 1085	16
17	0.0714 4039	0.0729 2777	0.0744 3186	0.0759 5253	17
18	0.0681 7720	0.0696 7008	0.0711 8063	0.0727 0870	18
19	0.0652 6182	0.0667 6062	0.0682 7802	0.0698 1388	19
20	0.0626 4207	0.0641 4713	0.0656 7173	0.0672 1571	20
21	0.0602 7572	0.0617 8733	0.0633 1941	0.0648 7178	21
22	0.0581 2821	0.0596 4661	0.0611 8640	0.0627 4739	22
23	0.0561 7097	0.0576 9638	0.0592 4410	0.0608 1390	23
24	0.0543 8023	0.0559 1282	0.0574 6863	0.0590 4742	24
25	0.0527 3599	0.0542 7592	0.0558 3997	0.0574 2787	25
26	0.0512 2134	0.0527 6875	0.0543 4116	0.0559 3829	26
27	0.0498 2188	0.0513 7687	0.0529 5776	0.0545 6421	27
28	0.0485 2525	0.0500 8793	0.0516 7738	0.0532 9323	28
29	0.0473 2081	0.0488 9127	0.0504 8935	0.0521 1467	29
30	0.0461 9934	0.0477 7764	0.0493 8442	0.0510 1926	30
31	0.0451 5280	0.0467 3900	0.0483 5453	0.0499 9893	31
32	0.0441 7415	0.0457 6831	0.0473 9263	0.0490 4662	32
33	0.0432 5722	0.0448 5938	0.0464 9253	0.0481 5612	33
34	0.0423 9655	0.0440 0675	0.0456 4875	0.0473 2196	34
35	0.0415 8731	0.0432 0558	0.0448 5645	0.0465 3929	35
36	0.0408 2522	0.0424 5158	0.0441 1132	0.0458 0379	36
37	0.0401 0643	0.0417 4090	0.0434 0953	0.0451 1162	37
38	0.0394 2753	0.0410 7012	0.0427 4764	0.0444 5934	38
39	0.0387 8543	0.0404 3615	0.0421 2256	0.0438 4385	39
40	0.0381 7738	0.0398 3623	0.0415 3151	0.0432 6238	40
41	0.0376 0087	0.0392 6786	0.0409 7200	0.0427 1241	41
42	0.0370 5364	0.0387 2876	0.0404 4175	0.0421 9167	42
43	0.0365 3364	0.0382 1688	0.0399 3871	0.0416 9811	43
44	0.0360 3901	0.0377 3037	0.0394 6100	0.0412 2985	44
45	0.0355 6805	0.0372 6751	0.0390 0693	0.0407 8518	45
46	0.0351 1921	0.0368 2676	0.0385 7493	0.0403 6254	46
47	0.0346 9107	0.0364 0669	0.0381 6358	0.0399 6051	47
48	0.0342 8233	0.0360 0599	0.0377 7158	0.0395 7777	48
49	0.0338 9179	0.0356 2348	0.0373 9773	0.0392 1314	49
50	0.0335 1836	0.0352 5806	0.0370 4092	0.0388 6549	50

TABLE 9 PERIODIC PAYMENT
WHEN PRESENT VALUE OF ANNUITY IS 1

$$\frac{1}{a_{\overline{n}|i}} = \frac{i}{1-(1+i)^{-n}} \qquad \text{Note: } \frac{1}{s_{\overline{n}|i}} = \frac{1}{a_{\overline{n}|i}} - i$$

n	$2\frac{1}{4}\%$	$2\frac{1}{2}\%$	$2\frac{3}{4}\%$	3%	n
51	0.0331 6102	0.0349 0870	0.0367 0014	0.0385 3382	51
52	0.0328 1884	0.0345 7446	0.0363 7444	0.0382 1718	52
53	0.0324 9094	0.0342 5449	0.0360 6297	0.0379 1471	53
54	0.0321 7654	0.0339 4799	0.0357 6491	0.0376 2558	54
55	0.0318 7489	0.0336 5419	0.0354 7953	0.0373 4907	55
56	0.0315 8530	0.0333 7243	0.0352 0612	0.0370 8447	56
57	0.0313 0712	0.0331 0204	0.0349 4404	0.0368 3114	57
58	0.0310 3977	0.0328 4244	0.0346 9270	0.0365 8848	58
59	0.0307 8268	0.0325 9307	0.0344 5153	0.0363 5593	59
60	0.0305 3533	0.0323 5340	0.0342 2002	0.0361 3296	60
61	0.0302 9724	0.0321 2294	0.0339 9767	0.0359 1908	61
62	0.0300 6795	0.0319 0126	0.0337 8402	0.0357 1385	62
63	0.0298 4704	0.0316 8790	0.0335 7866	0.0355 1682	63
64	0.0296 3411	0.0314 8249	0.0333 8118	0.0353 2760	64
65	0.0294 2878	0.0312 8463	0.0331 9120	0.0351 4581	65
66	0.0292 3070	0.0310 9398	0.0330 0837	0.0349 7110	66
67	0.0290 3955	0.0309 1021	0.0328 3236	0.0348 0313	67
68	0.0288 5500	0.0307 3300	0.0326 6285	0.0346 4159	68
69	0.0286 7677	0.0305 6206	0.0324 9955	0.0344 8618	69
70	0.0285 0458	0.0303 9712	0.0323 4218	0.0343 3663	70
71	0.0283 3816	0.0302 3790	0.0321 9048	0.0341 9266	71
72	0.0281 7728	0.0300 8417	0.0320 4420	0.0340 5404	72
73	0.0280 2169	0.0299 3568	0.0319 0311	0.0339 2053	73
74	0.0278 7118	0.0297 9222	0.0317 6698	0.0337 9191	74
75	0.0277 2554	0.0296 5358	0.0316 3560	0.0336 6796	75
76	0.0275 8457	0.0295 1956	0.0315 0878	0.0335 4849	76
77	0.0274 4808	0.0293 8997	0.0313 8633	0.0334 3331	77
78	0.0273 1589	0.0292 6463	0.0312 6806	0.0333 2224	78
79	0.0271 8784	0.0291 4338	0.0311 5382	0.0332 1510	79
80	0.0270 6376	0.0290 2605	0.0310 4342	0.0331 1175	80
81	0.0269 4350	0.0289 1248	0.0309 3674	0.0330 1201	81
82	0.0268 2692	0.0288 0254	0.0308 3361	0.0329 1576	82
83	0.0267 1387	0.0286 9608	0.0307 3389	0.0328 2284	83
84	0.0266 0423	0.0285 9298	0.0306 3747	0.0327 3313	84
85	0.0264 9787	0.0284 9310	0.0305 4420	0.0326 4650	85
86	0.0263 9467	0.0283 9633	0.0304 5397	0.0325 6284	86
87	0.0262 9452	0.0283 0255	0.0303 6667	0.0324 8202	87
88	0.0261 9730	0.0282 1165	0.0302 8219	0.0324 0393	88
89	0.0261 0291	0.0281 2353	0.0302 0041	0.0323 2848	89
90	0.0260 1126	0.0280 3809	0.0301 2125	0.0322 5556	90
91	0.0259 2224	0.0279 5523	0.0300 4460	0.0321 8508	91
92	0.0258 3577	0.0278 7486	0.0299 7038	0.0321 1694	92
93	0.0257 5176	0.0277 9690	0.0298 9850	0.0320 5107	93
94	0.0256 7012	0.0277 2126	0.0298 2887	0.0319 8737	94
95	0.0255 9078	0.0276 4786	0.0297 6141	0.0319 2577	95
96	0.0255 1366	0.0275 7662	0.0296 9605	0.0318 6619	96
97	0.0254 3868	0.0275 0747	0.0296 3272	0.0318 0856	97
98	0.0253 6578	0.0274 4034	0.0295 7134	0.0317 5281	98
99	0.0252 9489	0.0273 7517	0.0295 1185	0.0316 9886	99
100	0.0252 2594	0.0273 1188	0.0294 5418	0.0316 4667	100

TABLE 9 PERIODIC PAYMENT

WHEN PRESENT VALUE OF ANNUITY IS 1

$$\frac{1}{a_{\overline{n}|i}} = \frac{i}{1-(1+i)^{-n}} \qquad \text{Note: } \frac{1}{s_{\overline{n}|i}} = \frac{1}{a_{\overline{n}|i}} - i$$

n	$3\frac{1}{4}\%$	$3\frac{1}{2}\%$	$3\frac{3}{4}\%$	4%	n
1	1.0325 0000	1.0350 0000	1.0375 0000	1.0400 0000	1
2	0.5245 0492	0.5264 0049	0.5282 9755	0.5301 9608	2
3	0.3552 3095	0.3569 3418	0.3586 4005	0.3603 4854	3
4	0.2706 3723	0.2722 5114	0.2738 6875	0.2754 9005	4
5	0.2199 1560	0.2214 8137	0.2230 5189	0.2246 2711	5
6	0.1861 2997	0.1876 6821	0.1892 1219	0.1907 6190	6
7	0.1620 2204	0.1635 4449	0.1650 7370	0.1666 0961	7
8	0.1439 6263	0.1454 7665	0.1469 9839	0.1485 2783	8
9	0.1299 3555	0.1314 4601	0.1329 6517	0.1344 9299	9
10	0.1187 3107	0.1202 4137	0.1217 6134	0.1232 9094	10
11	0.1095 7936	0.1110 9197	0.1126 1521	0.1141 4904	11
12	0.1019 6719	0.1034 8395	0.1050 1230	0.1065 5217	12
13	0.0955 3925	0.0970 6157	0.0985 9642	0.1001 4373	13
14	0.0900 4176	0.0915 7073	0.0931 1317	0.0946 6897	14
15	0.0852 8858	0.0868 2507	0.0883 7595	0.0899 4110	15
16	0.0811 4013	0.0826 8483	0.0842 4483	0.0858 2000	16
17	0.0774 8966	0.0790 4313	0.0806 1280	0.0821 9852	17
18	0.0742 5415	0.0758 1684	0.0773 9662	0.0789 9333	18
19	0.0713 6804	0.0729 4033	0.0745 3058	0.0761 3862	19
20	0.0687 7888	0.0703 6108	0.0719 6210	0.0735 8175	20
21	0.0664 4424	0.0680 3659	0.0696 4862	0.0712 8011	21
22	0.0643 2936	0.0659 3207	0.0675 5531	0.0691 9881	22
23	0.0624 0555	0.0640 1880	0.0656 5339	0.0673 0906	23
24	0.0606 4891	0.0622 7283	0.0639 1890	0.0655 8683	24
25	0.0590 3933	0.0606 7404	0.0623 3169	0.0640 1196	25
26	0.0575 5981	0.0592 0540	0.0608 7470	0.0625 6738	26
27	0.0561 9588	0.0578 5241	0.0595 3343	0.0612 3854	27
28	0.0549 3512	0.0566 0265	0.0582 9540	0.0600 1298	28
29	0.0537 6682	0.0554 4538	0.0571 4991	0.0588 7993	29
30	0.0526 8172	0.0543 7133	0.0560 8762	0.0578 3010	30
31	0.0516 7172	0.0533 7240	0.0551 0046	0.0568 5535	31
32	0.0507 2976	0.0524 4150	0.0541 8131	0.0559 4859	32
33	0.0498 4961	0.0515 7242	0.0533 2395	0.0551 0357	33
34	0.0490 2581	0.0507 5966	0.0525 2287	0.0543 1477	34
35	0.0482 5348	0.0499 9835	0.0517 7320	0.0535 7732	35
36	0.0475 2831	0.0492 8416	0.0510 7001	0.0528 8688	36
37	0.0468 4645	0.0486 1325	0.0504 1122	0.0522 3957	37
38	0.0462 0445	0.0479 8214	0.0497 9159	0.0516 3192	38
39	0.0455 9920	0.0473 8775	0.0492 0860	0.0510 6083	39
40	0.0450 2794	0.0468 2728	0.0486 5946	0.0505 2349	40
41	0.0444 8814	0.0462 9822	0.0481 4164	0.0500 1738	41
42	0.0439 7753	0.0457 9828	0.0476 5286	0.0495 4020	42
43	0.0434 9403	0.0453 2539	0.0471 9106	0.0490 8989	43
44	0.0430 3579	0.0448 7768	0.0467 5434	0.0486 6454	44
45	0.0426 0108	0.0444 5343	0.0463 4098	0.0482 6246	45
46	0.0421 8835	0.0440 5108	0.0459 4943	0.0478 8205	46
47	0.0417 9616	0.0436 6919	0.0455 7824	0.0475 2189	47
48	0.0414 2320	0.0433 0646	0.0452 2609	0.0471 8065	48
49	0.0410 6828	0.0429 6167	0.0448 9179	0.0468 5712	49
50	0.0407 3027	0.0426 3371	0.0445 7422	0.0465 5020	50

TABLE 9 PERIODIC PAYMENT
WHEN PRESENT VALUE OF ANNUITY IS 1

$$\frac{1}{a_{\overline{n}|i}} = \frac{i}{1-(1+i)^{-n}} \qquad \text{Note: } \frac{1}{s_{\overline{n}|i}} = \frac{1}{a_{\overline{n}|i}} - i$$

n	$3\frac{1}{4}\%$	$3\frac{1}{2}\%$	$3\frac{3}{4}\%$	4%	n
51	0.0404 0817	0.0423 2156	0.0442 7235	0.0462 5885	51
52	0.0401 0103	0.0420 2429	0.0439 8523	0.0459 8212	52
53	0.0398 0797	0.0417 4100	0.0437 1199	0.0457 1915	53
54	0.0395 2819	0.0414 7090	0.0434 5183	0.0454 6910	54
55	0.0392 6095	0.0412 1323	0.0432 0398	0.0452 3124	55
56	0.0390 0553	0.0409 6730	0.0429 6775	0.0450 0487	56
57	0.0387 6131	0.0407 3245	0.0427 4249	0.0447 8932	57
58	0.0385 2767	0.0405 0810	0.0425 2760	0.0445 8401	58
59	0.0383 0405	0.0402 9366	0.0423 2251	0.0443 8836	59
60	0.0380 8993	0.0400 8862	0.0421 2670	0.0442 0185	60
61	0.0378 8483	0.0398 9249	0.0419 3967	0.0440 2398	61
62	0.0376 8827	0.0397 0480	0.0417 6097	0.0438 5430	62
63	0.0374 9983	0.0395 2513	0.0415 9016	0.0436 9237	63
64	0.0373 1912	0.0393 5308	0.0414 2684	0.0435 3780	64
65	0.0371 4574	0.0391 8826	0.0412 7063	0.0433 9019	65
66	0.0369 7935	0.0390 3031	0.0411 2118	0.0432 4921	66
67	0.0368 1962	0.0388 7892	0.0409 7816	0.0431 1451	67
68	0.0366 6622	0.0387 3376	0.0408 4124	0.0429 8578	68
69	0.0365 1886	0.0385 9453	0.0407 1013	0.0428 6272	69
70	0.0363 7727	0.0384 6095	0.0405 8456	0.0427 4506	70
71	0.0362 4117	0.0383 3277	0.0404 6426	0.0426 3253	71
72	0.0361 1033	0.0382 0973	0.0403 4898	0.0425 2489	72
73	0.0359 8451	0.0380 9160	0.0402 3848	0.0424 2190	73
74	0.0358 6347	0.0379 7816	0.0401 3255	0.0423 2334	74
75	0.0357 4702	0.0378 6919	0.0400 3098	0.0422 2900	75
76	0.0356 3496	0.0377 6450	0.0399 3356	0.0421 3869	76
77	0.0355 2709	0.0376 6390	0.0398 4011	0.0420 5221	77
78	0.0354 2323	0.0375 6721	0.0397 5045	0.0419 6939	78
79	0.0353 2323	0.0374 7426	0.0396 6442	0.0418 9007	79
80	0.0352 2690	0.0373 8489	0.0395 8184	0.0418 1408	80
81	0.0351 3411	0.0372 9894	0.0395 0258	0.0417 4127	81
82	0.0350 4471	0.0372 1628	0.0394 2647	0.0416 7150	82
83	0.0349 5855	0.0371 3676	0.0393 5340	0.0416 0463	83
84	0.0348 7550	0.0370 6025	0.0392 8323	0.0415 4054	84
85	0.0347 9545	0.0369 8662	0.0392 1582	0.0414 7909	85
86	0.0347 1826	0.0369 1576	0.0391 5107	0.0414 2018	86
87	0.0346 4383	0.0368 4756	0.0390 8887	0.0413 6370	87
88	0.0345 7205	0.0367 8190	0.0390 2910	0.0413 0953	88
89	0.0345 0281	0.0367 1868	0.0389 7166	0.0412 5758	89
90	0.0344 3601	0.0366 5781	0.0389 1646	0.0412 0775	90
91	0.0343 7156	0.0365 9919	0.0388 6340	0.0411 5995	91
92	0.0343 0937	0.0365 4273	0.0388 1240	0.0411 1410	92
93	0.0342 4935	0.0364 8834	0.0387 6336	0.0410 7010	93
94	0.0341 9142	0.0364 3594	0.0387 1622	0.0410 2789	94
95	0.0341 3550	0.0363 8546	0.0386 7088	0.0409 8738	95
96	0.0340 8151	0.0363 3682	0.0386 2729	0.0409 4850	96
97	0.0340 2939	0.0362 8995	0.0385 8537	0.0409 1119	97
98	0.0339 7906	0.0362 4478	0.0385 4504	0.0408 7538	98
99	0.0339 3045	0.0362 0124	0.0385 0626	0.0408 4100	99
100	0.0338 8351	0.0361 5927	0.0384 6895	0.0408 0800	100

TABLE 9 PERIODIC PAYMENT

WHEN PRESENT VALUE OF ANNUITY IS 1

$$\frac{1}{a_{\overline{n}|i}} = \frac{i}{1-(1+i)^{-n}} \qquad \text{Note: } \frac{1}{s_{\overline{n}|i}} = \frac{1}{a_{\overline{n}|i}} - i$$

n	$4\frac{1}{2}\%$	5%	$5\frac{1}{2}\%$	6%	n
1	1.0450 0000	1.0500 0000	1.0550 0000	1.0600 0000	1
2	0.5339 9756	0.5378 0488	0.5416 1800	0.5454 3689	2
3	0.3637 7336	0.3672 0856	0.3706 5407	0.3741 0981	3
4	0.2787 4365	0.2820 1183	0.2852 9449	0.2885 9149	4
5	0.2277 9164	0.2309 7480	0.2341 7644	0.2373 9640	5
6	0.1938 7839	0.1970 1747	0.2001 7895	0.2033 6263	6
7	0.1697 0147	0.1728 1982	0.1759 6442	0.1791 3502	7
8	0.1516 0965	0.1547 2181	0.1578 6401	0.1610 3594	8
9	0.1375 7447	0.1406 9008	0.1438 3946	0.1470 2224	9
10	0.1263 7882	0.1295 0458	0.1326 6777	0.1358 6796	10
11	0.1172 4818	0.1203 8889	0.1235 7065	0.1267 9294	11
12	0.1096 6619	0.1128 2541	0.1160 2923	0.1192 7703	12
13	0.1032 7535	0.1064 5577	0.1096 8426	0.1129 6011	13
14	0.0978 2032	0.1010 2397	0.1042 7912	0.1075 8491	14
15	0.0931 1381	0.0963 4229	0.0996 2560	0.1029 6276	15
16	0.0890 1537	0.0922 6991	0.0955 8254	0.0989 5214	16
17	0.0854 1758	0.0886 9914	0.0920 4197	0.0954 4480	17
18	0.0822 3690	0.0855 4622	0.0889 1992	0.0923 5654	18
19	0.0794 0734	0.0827 4501	0.0861 5006	0.0896 2086	19
20	0.0768 7614	0.0802 4259	0.0836 7933	0.0871 8456	20
21	0.0746 0057	0.0779 9611	0.0814 6478	0.0850 0455	21
22	0.0725 4565	0.0759 7051	0.0794 7123	0.0830 4557	22
23	0.0706 8249	0.0741 3682	0.0776 6965	0.0812 7848	23
24	0.0689 8703	0.0724 7090	0.0760 3580	0.0796 7900	24
25	0.0674 3903	0.0709 5246	0.0745 4935	0.0782 2672	25
26	0.0660 2137	0.0695 6432	0.0731 9307	0.0769 0435	26
27	0.0647 1946	0.0682 9186	0.0719 5228	0.0756 9717	27
28	0.0635 2081	0.0671 2253	0.0708 1440	0.0745 9255	28
29	0.0624 1461	0.0660 4551	0.0697 6857	0.0735 7961	29
30	0.0613 9154	0.0650 5144	0.0688 0539	0.0726 4891	30
31	0.0604 4345	0.0641 3212	0.0679 1665	0.0717 9222	31
32	0.0595 6320	0.0632 8042	0.0670 9519	0.0710 0234	32
33	0.0587 4453	0.0624 9004	0.0663 3469	0.0702 7294	33
34	0.0579 8191	0.0617 5545	0.0656 2958	0.0695 9843	34
35	0.0572 7045	0.0610 7171	0.0649 7493	0.0689 7386	35
36	0.0566 0578	0.0604 3446	0.0643 6635	0.0683 9483	36
37	0.0559 8402	0.0598 3979	0.0637 9993	0.0678 5743	37
38	0.0554 0169	0.0592 8423	0.0632 7217	0.0673 5812	38
39	0.0548 5567	0.0587 6462	0.0627 7991	0.0668 9377	39
40	0.0543 4315	0.0582 7816	0.0623 2034	0.0664 6154	40
41	0.0538 6158	0.0578 2229	0.0618 9090	0.0660 5886	41
42	0.0534 0868	0.0573 9471	0.0614 8927	0.0656 8342	42
43	0.0529 8235	0.0569 9333	0.0611 1337	0.0653 3312	43
44	0.0525 8071	0.0566 1625	0.0607 6128	0.0650 0606	44
45	0.0522 0202	0.0562 6173	0.0604 3127	0.0647 0050	45
46	0.0518 4471	0.0559 2820	0.0601 2175	0.0644 1485	46
47	0.0515 0734	0.0556 1421	0.0598 3129	0.0641 4768	47
48	0.0511 8858	0.0553 1843	0.0595 5854	0.0638 9765	48
49	0.0508 8722	0.0550 3965	0.0593 0230	0.0636 6356	49
50	0.0506 0215	0.0547 7674	0.0590 6145	0.0634 4429	50

TABLE 9 PERIODIC PAYMENT
WHEN PRESENT VALUE OF ANNUITY IS 1

$$\frac{1}{a_{\overline{n}|i}} = \frac{i}{1-(1+i)^{-n}} \qquad \text{Note: } \frac{1}{s_{\overline{n}|i}} = \frac{1}{a_{\overline{n}|i}} - i$$

n	$4\frac{1}{2}\%$	5%	$5\frac{1}{2}\%$	6%	n
51	0.0503 3232	0.0545 2867	0.0588 3495	0.0632 3880	51
52	0.0500 7679	0.0542 9450	0.0586 2186	0.0630 4617	52
53	0.0498 3469	0.0540 7334	0.0584 2130	0.0628 6551	53
54	0.0496 0519	0.0538 6438	0.0582 3245	0.0626 9602	54
55	0.0493 8754	0.0536 6686	0.0580 5458	0.0625 3696	55
56	0.0491 8105	0.0534 8010	0.0578 8698	0.0623 8765	56
57	0.0489 8506	0.0533 0343	0.0577 2900	0.0622 4744	57
58	0.0487 9897	0.0531 3626	0.0575 8006	0.0621 1574	58
59	0.0486 2221	0.0529 7802	0.0574 3959	0.0619 9200	59
60	0.0484 5426	0.0528 2818	0.0573 0707	0.0618 7572	60
61	0.0482 9462	0.0526 8627	0.0571 8202	0.0617 6642	61
62	0.0481 4284	0.0525 5183	0.0570 6400	0.0616 6366	62
63	0.0479 9848	0.0524 2442	0.0569 5258	0.0615 6704	63
64	0.0478 6115	0.0523 0365	0.0568 4737	0.0614 7615	64
65	0.0477 3047	0.0521 8915	0.0567 4800	0.0613 9066	65
66	0.0476 0608	0.0520 8057	0.0566 5413	0.0613 1022	66
67	0.0474 8765	0.0519 7757	0.0565 6544	0.0612 3454	67
68	0.0473 7487	0.0518 7986	0.0564 8163	0.0611 6330	68
69	0.0472 6745	0.0517 8715	0.0564 0242	0.0610 9625	69
70	0.0471 6511	0.0516 9915	0.0563 2754	0.0610 3313	70
71	0.0470 6759	0.0516 1563	0.0562 5675	0.0609 7370	71
72	0.0469 7465	0.0515 3633	0.0561 8982	0.0609 1774	72
73	0.0468 8606	0.0514 6103	0.0561 2652	0.0608 6505	73
74	0.0468 0159	0.0513 8953	0.0560 6665	0.0608 1542	74
75	0.0467 2104	0.0513 2161	0.0560 1002	0.0607 6867	75
76	0.0466 4422	0.0512 5709	0.0559 5645	0.0607 2463	76
77	0.0465 7094	0.0511 9580	0.0559 0577	0.0606 8315	77
78	0.0465 0104	0.0511 3756	0.0558 5781	0.0606 4407	78
79	0.0464 3434	0.0510 8222	0.0558 1243	0.0606 0724	79
80	0.0463 7069	0.0510 2962	0.0557 6948	0.0605 7254	80
81	0.0463 0995	0.0509 7963	0.0557 2884	0.0605 3984	81
82	0.0462 5197	0.0509 3211	0.0556 9036	0.0605 0903	82
83	0.0461 9663	0.0508 8694	0.0556 5395	0.0604 7998	83
84	0.0461 4379	0.0508 4399	0.0556 1947	0.0604 5261	84
85	0.0460 9334	0.0508 0316	0.0555 8683	0.0604 2681	85
86	0.0460 4516	0.0507 6433	0.0555 5593	0.0604 0249	86
87	0.0459 9915	0.0507 2740	0.0555 2667	0.0603 7956	87
88	0.0459 5522	0.0506 9228	0.0554 9896	0.0603 5795	88
89	0.0459 1325	0.0506 5888	0.0554 7273	0.0603 3757	89
90	0.0458 7316	0.0506 2711	0.0554 4788	0.0603 1836	90
91	0.0458 3486	0.0505 9689	0.0554 2435	0.0603 0025	91
92	0.0457 9827	0.0505 6815	0.0554 0207	0.0602 8318	92
93	0.0457 6331	0.0505 4080	0.0553 8096	0.0602 6708	93
94	0.0457 2991	0.0505 1478	0.0553 6097	0.0602 5190	94
95	0.0456 9799	0.0504 9003	0.0553 4204	0.0602 3758	95
96	0.0456 6749	0.0504 6648	0.0553 2410	0.0602 2408	96
97	0.0456 3834	0.0504 4407	0.0553 0711	0.0602 1135	97
98	0.0456 1048	0.0504 2274	0.0552 9101	0.0601 9935	98
99	0.0455 8385	0.0504 0245	0.0552 7577	0.0601 8803	99
100	0.0455 5839	0.0503 8314	0.0552 6132	0.0601 7736	100

TABLE 9 PERIODIC PAYMENT
WHEN PRESENT VALUE OF ANNUITY IS 1

$$\frac{1}{a_{\overline{n}|i}} = \frac{i}{1-(1+i)^{-n}} \qquad \text{Note: } \frac{1}{s_{\overline{n}|i}} = \frac{1}{a_{\overline{n}|i}} - i$$

n	$6\frac{1}{2}\%$	7%	$7\frac{1}{2}\%$	8%	n
1	1.0650 0000	1.0700 0000	1.0750 0000	1.0800 0000	1
2	0.5492 6150	0.5530 9179	0.5569 2771	0.5607 6923	2
3	0.3775 7570	0.3810 5166	0.3845 3763	0.3880 3351	3
4	0.2919 0274	0.2952 2812	0.2985 6751	0.3019 2080	4
5	0.2406 3454	0.2438 9069	0.2471 6472	0.2504 5645	5
6	0.2065 6831	0.2097 9580	0.2130 4489	0.2163 1539	6
7	0.1823 3137	0.1855 5322	0.1888 0032	0.1920 7240	7
8	0.1642 3730	0.1674 6776	0.1707 2702	0.1740 1476	8
9	0.1502 3803	0.1534 8647	0.1567 6716	0.1600 7971	9
10	0.1391 0469	0.1423 7750	0.1456 8593	0.1490 2949	10
11	0.1300 5521	0.1333 5690	0.1366 9747	0.1400 7634	11
12	0.1225 6817	0.1259 0199	0.1292 7783	0.1326 9502	12
13	0.1162 8256	0.1196 5085	0.1230 6420	0.1265 2181	13
14	0.1109 4048	0.1143 4494	0.1177 9737	0.1212 9685	14
15	0.1063 5278	0.1097 9462	0.1132 8724	0.1168 2954	15
16	0.1023 7757	0.1058 5765	0.1093 9116	0.1129 7687	16
17	0.0989 0633	0.1024 2519	0.1060 0003	0.1096 2943	17
18	0.0958 5461	0.0994 1260	0.1030 2896	0.1067 0210	18
19	0.0931 5575	0.0967 5301	0.1004 1090	0.1041 2763	19
20	0.0907 5640	0.0943 9293	0.0980 9219	0.1018 5221	20
21	0.0886 1333	0.0922 8900	0.0960 2937	0.0998 3225	21
22	0.0866 9120	0.0904 0577	0.0941 8687	0.0980 3207	22
23	0.0849 6078	0.0887 1393	0.0925 3528	0.0964 2217	23
24	0.0833 9770	0.0871 8902	0.0910 5008	0.0949 7796	24
25	0.0819 8148	0.0858 1052	0.0897 1067	0.0936 7878	25
26	0.0806 9480	0.0845 6103	0.0884 9961	0.0925 0713	26
27	0.0795 2288	0.0834 2573	0.0874 0204	0.0914 4809	27
28	0.0784 5305	0.0823 9193	0.0864 0520	0.0904 8891	28
29	0.0774 7440	0.0814 4865	0.0854 9811	0.0896 1854	29
30	0.0765 7744	0.0805 8640	0.0846 7124	0.0888 2743	30
31	0.0757 5393	0.0797 9691	0.0839 1628	0.0881 0728	31
32	0.0749 9665	0.0790 7292	0.0832 2599	0.0874 5081	32
33	0.0742 9924	0.0784 0807	0.0825 9397	0.0868 5163	33
34	0.0736 5610	0.0777 9674	0.0820 1461	0.0863 0411	34
35	0.0730 6226	0.0772 3396	0.0814 8291	0.0858 0326	35
36	0.0725 1332	0.0767 1531	0.0809 9447	0.0853 4467	36
37	0.0720 0534	0.0762 3685	0.0805 4533	0.0849 2440	37
38	0.0715 3480	0.0757 9505	0.0801 3197	0.0845 3894	38
39	0.0710 9854	0.0753 8676	0.0797 5124	0.0841 8513	39
40	0.0706 9373	0.0750 0914	0.0794 0031	0.0838 6016	40
41	0.0703 1779	0.0746 5962	0.0790 7663	0.0835 6149	41
42	0.0699 6842	0.0743 3591	0.0787 7789	0.0832 8684	42
43	0.0696 4352	0.0740 3590	0.0785 0201	0.0830 3414	43
44	0.0693 4119	0.0737 5769	0.0782 4710	0.0828 0152	44
45	0.0690 5968	0.0734 9957	0.0780 1146	0.0825 8728	45
46	0.0687 9743	0.0732 5996	0.0777 9353	0.0823 8991	46
47	0.0685 5300	0.0730 3744	0.0775 9190	0.0822 0799	47
48	0.0683 2505	0.0728 3070	0.0774 0527	0.0820 4027	48
49	0.0681 1240	0.0726 3853	0.0772 3247	0.0818 8557	49
50	0.0679 1393	0.0724 5985	0.0770 7241	0.0817 4286	50

TABLE 9 PERIODIC PAYMENT
WHEN PRESENT VALUE OF ANNUITY IS 1

$$\frac{1}{a_{\overline{n}|i}} = \frac{i}{1-(1+i)^{-n}} \qquad \text{Note: } \frac{1}{s_{\overline{n}|i}} = \frac{1}{a_{\overline{n}|i}} - i$$

n	$6\frac{1}{2}$%	7%	$7\frac{1}{2}$%	8%	n
51	0.0677 2861	0.0722 9365	0.0769 2411	0.0816 1116	51
52	0.0675 5553	0.0721 3901	0.0767 8668	0.0814 8959	52
53	0.0673 9382	0.0719 9509	0.0766 5927	0.0813 7735	53
54	0.0672 4267	0.0718 6110	0.0765 4112	0.0812 7370	54
55	0.0671 0137	0.0717 3633	0.0764 3155	0.0811 7796	55
56	0.0669 6923	0.0716 2011	0.0763 2991	0.0810 8952	56
57	0.0668 4563	0.0715 1183	0.0762 3559	0.0810 0780	57
58	0.0667 2999	0.0714 1093	0.0761 4807	0.0809 3227	58
59	0.0666 2177	0.0713 1689	0.0760 6683	0.0808 6247	59
60	0.0665 2047	0.0712 2923	0.0759 9142	0.0807 9795	60
61	0.0664 2564	0.0711 4749	0.0759 2140	0.0807 3830	61
62	0.0663 3684	0.0710 7127	0.0758 5638	0.0806 8314	62
63	0.0662 5367	0.0710 0019	0.0757 9600	0.0806 3214	63
64	0.0661 7577	0.0709 3388	0.0757 3992	0.0805 8497	64
65	0.0661 0280	0.0708 7203	0.0756 8782	0.0805 4135	65
66	0.0660 3442	0.0708 1431	0.0756 3942	0.0805 0100	66
67	0.0659 7034	0.0707 6046	0.0755 9446	0.0804 6367	67
68	0.0659 1029	0.0707 1021	0.0755 5268	0.0804 2914	68
69	0.0658 5400	0.0706 6331	0.0755 1386	0.0803 9719	69
70	0.0658 0124	0.0706 1953	0.0754 7778	0.0803 6764	70
71	0.0657 5177	0.0705 7866	0.0754 4425	0.0803 4029	71
72	0.0657 0539	0.0705 4051	0.0754 1308	0.0803 1498	72
73	0.0656 6190	0.0705 0490	0.0753 8412	0.0802 9157	73
74	0.0656 2112	0.0704 7164	0.0753 5719	0.0802 6989	74
75	0.0655 8287	0.0704 4060	0.0753 3216	0.0802 4984	75
76	0.0655 4699	0.0704 1160	0.0753 0889	0.0802 3128	76
77	0.0655 1335	0.0703 8453	0.0752 8726	0.0802 1410	77
78	0.0654 8178	0.0703 5924	0.0752 6714	0.0801 9820	78
79	0.0654 5217	0.0703 3563	0.0752 4844	0.0801 8349	79
80	0.0654 2440	0.0703 1357	0.0752 3106	0.0801 6987	80
81	0.0653 9834	0.0702 9297	0.0752 1489	0.0801 5726	81
82	0.0653 7388	0.0702 7373	0.0751 9986	0.0801 4559	82
83	0.0653 5094	0.0702 5576	0.0751 8588	0.0801 3479	83
84	0.0653 2941	0.0702 3897	0.0751 7288	0.0801 2479	84
85	0.0653 0921	0.0702 2329	0.0751 6079	0.0801 1553	85
86	0.0652 9026	0.0702 0863	0.0751 4955	0.0801 0696	86
87	0.0652 7247	0.0701 9495	0.0751 3910	0.0800 9903	87
88	0.0652 5577	0.0701 8216	0.0751 2938	0.0800 9168	88
89	0.0652 4010	0.0701 7021	0.0751 2034	0.0800 8489	89
90	0.0652 2540	0.0701 5905	0.0751 1193	0.0800 7859	90
91	0.0652 1160	0.0701 4863	0.0751 0411	0.0800 7277	91
92	0.0651 9864	0.0701 3888	0.0750 9684	0.0800 6737	92
93	0.0651 8649	0.0701 2978	0.0750 9007	0.0800 6238	93
94	0.0651 7507	0.0701 2128	0.0750 8378	0.0800 5775	94
95	0.0651 6436	0.0701 1333	0.0750 7793	0.0800 5347	95
96	0.0651 5431	0.0701 0590	0.0750 7249	0.0800 4951	96
97	0.0651 4487	0.0700 9897	0.0750 6743	0.0800 4584	97
98	0.0651 3601	0.0700 9248	0.0750 6272	0.0800 4244	98
99	0.0651 2769	0.0700 8643	0.0750 5834	0.0800 3930	99
100	0.0651 1988	0.0700 8076	0.0750 5427	0.0800 3638	100

TABLE 9 PERIODIC PAYMENT

WHEN PRESENT VALUE OF ANNUITY IS 1

$$\frac{1}{a_{\overline{n}|i}} = \frac{i}{1-(1+i)^{-n}} \qquad \text{Note: } \frac{1}{s_{\overline{n}|i}} = \frac{1}{a_{\overline{n}|i}} - i$$

n	$8\frac{1}{2}\%$	9%	$9\frac{1}{2}\%$	10%	n
1	1.0850 0000	1.0900 0000	1.0950 0000	1.1000 0000	1
2	0.5646 1631	0.5684 6890	0.5723 2697	0.5761 9048	2
3	0.3915 3925	0.3950 5476	0.3985 7997	0.4021 1480	3
4	0.3052 8789	0.3086 6866	0.3120 6300	0.3154 7080	4
5	0.2537 6575	0.2570 9246	0.2604 3642	0.2637 9748	5
6	0.2196 0708	0.2229 1978	0.2262 5328	0.2296 0738	6
7	0.1953 6922	0.1986 9052	0.2020 3603	0.2054 0550	7
8	0.1773 3065	0.1806 7438	0.1840 4561	0.1874 4402	8
9	0.1634 2372	0.1667 9880	0.1702 0454	0.1736 4054	9
10	0.1524 0771	0.1558 2009	0.1592 6615	0.1627 4539	10
11	0.1434 9293	0.1469 4666	0.1504 3693	0.1539 6314	11
12	0.1361 5286	0.1396 5066	0.1431 8771	0.1467 6332	12
13	0.1300 2287	0.1335 6656	0.1371 5206	0.1407 7852	13
14	0.1248 4244	0.1284 3317	0.1320 6809	0.1357 4622	14
15	0.1204 2046	0.1240 5888	0.1277 4370	0.1314 7378	15
16	0.1166 1354	0.1202 9991	0.1240 3470	0.1278 1662	16
17	0.1133 1198	0.1170 4625	0.1208 3078	0.1246 6413	17
18	0.1104 3041	0.1142 1229	0.1180 4610	0.1219 3022	18
19	0.1079 0140	0.1117 3041	0.1156 1284	0.1195 4687	19
20	0.1056 7097	0.1095 4648	0.1134 7670	0.1174 5962	20
21	0.1036 9541	0.1076 1663	0.1115 9370	0.1156 2439	21
22	0.1019 3892	0.1059 0499	0.1099 2784	0.1140 0506	22
23	0.1003 7193	0.1043 8188	0.1084 4938	0.1125 7181	23
24	0.0989 6975	0.1030 2256	0.1071 3351	0.1112 9978	24
25	0.0977 1168	0.1018 0625	0.1059 5939	0.1101 6807	25
26	0.0965 8016	0.1007 1536	0.1049 0940	0.1091 5904	26
27	0.0955 6025	0.0997 3491	0.1039 6852	0.1082 5764	27
28	0.0946 3914	0.0988 5205	0.1031 2389	0.1074 5101	28
29	0.0938 0577	0.0980 5572	0.1023 6444	0.1067 2807	29
30	0.0930 5058	0.0973 3635	0.1016 8058	0.1060 7925	30
31	0.0923 6524	0.0966 8560	0.1010 6399	0.1054 9621	31
32	0.0917 4247	0.0960 9619	0.1005 0739	0.1049 7172	32
33	0.0911 7588	0.0955 6173	0.1000 0441	0.1044 9941	33
34	0.0906 5984	0.0950 7660	0.0995 4945	0.1040 7371	34
35	0.0901 8937	0.0946 3584	0.0991 3756	0.1036 8971	35
36	0.0897 6006	0.0942 3505	0.0987 6437	0.1033 4306	36
37	0.0893 6799	0.0938 7033	0.0984 2600	0.1030 2994	37
38	0.0890 0966	0.0935 3820	0.0981 1901	0.1027 4693	38
39	0.0886 8193	0.0932 3555	0.0978 4032	0.1024 9098	39
40	0.0883 8201	0.0929 5961	0.0975 8719	0.1022 5941	40
41	0.0881 0737	0.0927 0789	0.0973 5716	0.1020 4980	41
42	0.0878 5576	0.0924 7814	0.0971 4803	0.1018 5999	42
43	0.0876 2512	0.0922 6837	0.0969 5783	0.1016 8805	43
44	0.0874 1363	0.0920 7675	0.0967 8478	0.1015 3224	44
45	0.0872 1961	0.0919 0165	0.0966 2729	0.1013 9100	45
46	0.0870 4154	0.0917 4160	0.0964 8390	0.1012 6295	46
47	0.0868 7807	0.0915 9525	0.0963 5333	0.1011 4682	47
48	0.0867 2795	0.0914 6139	0.0962 3439	0.1010 4148	48
49	0.0865 9005	0.0913 3893	0.0961 2603	0.1009 4590	49
50	0.0864 6334	0.0912 2687	0.0960 2728	0.1008 5917	50

TABLE 9 PERIODIC PAYMENT
WHEN PRESENT VALUE OF ANNUITY IS 1

$$\frac{1}{a_{\overline{n}|i}} = \frac{i}{1-(1+i)^{-n}} \qquad \text{Note: } \frac{1}{s_{\overline{n}|i}} = \frac{1}{a_{\overline{n}|i}} - i$$

n	$8\frac{1}{2}\%$	9%	$9\frac{1}{2}\%$	10%	n
51	0.0863 4688	0.0911 2430	0.0959 3728	0.1007 8046	51
52	0.0862 3983	0.0910 3041	0.0958 5523	0.1007 0900	52
53	0.0861 4139	0.0909 4443	0.0957 8042	0.1006 4413	53
54	0.0860 5087	0.0908 6570	0.0957 1220	0.1005 8523	54
55	0.0859 6761	0.0907 9359	0.0956 4999	0.1005 3175	55
56	0.0858 9101	0.0907 2754	0.0955 9325	0.1004 8317	56
57	0.0858 2053	0.0906 6702	0.0955 4149	0.1004 3906	57
58	0.0857 5568	0.0906 1157	0.0954 9426	0.1003 9898	58
59	0.0856 9599	0.0905 6076	0.0954 5118	0.1003 6258	59
60	0.0856 4106	0.0905 1419	0.0954 1187	0.1003 2951	60
61	0.0855 9049	0.0904 7152	0.0953 7599	0.1002 9946	61
62	0.0855 4393	0.0904 3240	0.0953 4325	0.1002 7217	62
63	0.0855 0107	0.0903 9654	0.0953 1338	0.1002 4736	63
64	0.0854 6160	0.0903 6366	0.0952 8611	0.1002 2482	64
65	0.0854 2526	0.0903 3352	0.0952 6122	0.1002 0434	65
66	0.0853 9179	0.0903 0589	0.0952 3850	0.1001 8573	66
67	0.0853 6097	0.0902 8056	0.0952 1776	0.1001 6882	67
68	0.0853 3258	0.0902 5732	0.0951 9883	0.1001 5345	68
69	0.0853 0643	0.0903 3602	0.0951 8154	0.1001 3948	69
70	0.0852 8234	0.0902 1649	0.0951 6576	0.1001 2678	70
71	0.0852 6016	0.0901 9857	0.0951 5136	0.1001 1524	71
72	0.0852 3972	0.0901 8214	0.0951 3821	0.1001 0476	72
73	0.0852 2089	0.0901 6708	0.0951 2620	0.1000 9522	73
74	0.0852 0354	0.0901 5326	0.0951 1524	0.1000 8656	74
75	0.0851 8756	0.0901 4058	0.0951 0523	0.1000 7868	75
76	0.0851 7284	0.0901 2896	0.0950 9609	0.1000 7153	76
77	0.0851 5927	0.0901 1830	0.0950 8775	0.1000 6502	77
78	0.0851 4677	0.0901 0852	0.0950 8013	0.1000 5911	78
79	0.0851 3526	0.0900 9955	0.0950 7317	0.1000 5373	79
80	0.0851 2465	0.0900 9132	0.0950 6682	0.1000 4884	80
81	0.0851 1487	0.0900 8377	0.0950 6102	0.1000 4440	81
82	0.0851 0586	0.0900 7685	0.0950 5572	0.1000 4036	82
83	0.0850 9756	0.0900 7050	0.0950 5088	0.1000 3669	83
84	0.0850 8990	0.0900 6467	0.0950 4647	0.1000 3335	84
85	0.0850 8285	0.0900 5933	0.0950 4243	0.1000 3032	85
86	0.0850 7636	0.0900 5443	0.0950 3875	0.1000 2756	86
87	0.0850 7037	0.0900 4993	0.0950 3539	0.1000 2506	87
88	0.0850 6485	0.0900 4581	0.0950 3232	0.1000 2278	88
89	0.0850 5977	0.0900 4202	0.0950 2951	0.1000 2071	89
90	0.0850 5508	0.0900 3855	0.0950 2695	0.1000 1883	90
91	0.0850 5077	0.0900 3537	0.0950 2461	0.1000 1711	91
92	0.0850 4679	0.0900 3245	0.0950 2248	0.1000 1556	92
93	0.0850 4312	0.0900 2977	0.0950 2053	0.1000 1414	93
94	0.0850 3974	0.0900 2731	0.0950 1874	0.1000 1286	94
95	0.0850 3663	0.0900 2505	0.0950 1712	0.1000 1169	95
96	0.0850 3375	0.0900 2298	0.0950 1563	0.1000 1063	96
97	0.0850 3111	0.0900 2109	0.0950 1428	0.1000 0966	97
98	0.0850 2867	0.0900 1934	0.0950 1304	0.1000 0878	98
99	0.0850 2642	0.0900 1775	0.0950 1191	0.1000 0798	99
100	0.0850 2435	0.0900 1628	0.0950 1087	0.1000 0726	100

TABLE 10 PERIODIC PAYMENT

WHEN AMOUNT OF ANNUITY FOR FRACTIONAL INTEREST PERIOD IS 1

$$\frac{1}{s_{\overline{1/m}|i}} = \frac{i}{(1+i)^{\frac{1}{m}} - 1} \qquad \text{Note: } \frac{1}{a_{\overline{1/m}|i}} = \frac{1}{s_{\overline{1/m}|i}} + i$$

m	$\frac{1}{4}$%	$\frac{1}{3}$%	$\frac{5}{12}$%	$\frac{11}{24}$%	$\frac{1}{2}$%	m
2	2.0012 4922	2.0016 6528	2.0020 8117	2.0022 8905	2.0024 9688	2
3	3.0024 9861	3.0033 3087	3.0041 6282	3.0045 7868	3.0049 9446	3
4	4.0037 4805	4.0049 9653	4.0062 4459	4.0068 6845	4.0074 9221	4
6	6.0062 4697	6.0083 2794	6.0104 0824	6.0114 4815	6.0124 8788	6
12	12.0137 4380	12.0183 2232	12.0228 9946	12.0251 8752	12.0274 7524	12

m	$\frac{13}{24}$%	$\frac{7}{12}$%	$\frac{5}{8}$%	$\frac{2}{3}$%	$\frac{3}{4}$%	m
2	2.0027 0468	2.0029 1243	2.0031 2013	2.0033 2780	2.0037 4300	2
3	3.0054 1016	3.0058 2579	3.0062 4135	3.0066 5682	3.0074 8755	3
4	4.0081 1586	4.0087 3940	4.0093 6283	4.0099 8616	4.0112 3249	4
6	6.0135 2744	6.0145 6684	6.0156 0607	6.0166 4513	6.0187 2276	6
12	12.0297 6261	12.0320 4964	12.0343 3633	12.0366 2268	12.0411 9435	12

m	$\frac{7}{8}$%	1%	$1\frac{1}{8}$%	$1\frac{1}{4}$%	$1\frac{3}{8}$%	m
2	2.0043 6547	2.0049 8756	2.0056 0927	2.0062 3059	2.0068 5153	2
3	3.0087 3306	3.0099 7789	3.0112 2203	3.0124 6549	3.0137 0827	3
4	4.0131 0118	4.0149 6891	4.0168 3567	4.0187 0147	4.0205 6632	4
6	6.0218 3794	6.0249 5163	6.0280 6382	6.0311 7452	6.0342 8372	6
12	12.0480 4930	12.0549 0119	12.0617 5002	12.0685 9580	12.0754 3853	12

m	$1\frac{1}{2}$%	$1\frac{5}{8}$%	$1\frac{3}{4}$%	$1\frac{7}{8}$%	2%	m
2	2.0074 7208	2.0080 9226	2.0087 1205	2.0093 3146	2.0099 5049	2
3	3.0149 5037	3.0161 9179	3.0174 3253	3.0186 7260	3.0199 1199	3
4	4.0224 3021	4.0242 9314	4.0261 5513	4.0280 1615	4.0298 7623	4
6	6.0373 9144	6.0404 9767	6.0436 0242	6.0467 0569	6.0498 0748	6
12	12.0822 7822	12.0891 1488	12.0959 4851	12.1027 7911	12.1096 0670	12

m	$2\frac{1}{4}$%	$2\frac{1}{2}$%	$2\frac{3}{4}$%	3%	$3\frac{1}{4}$%	m
2	2.0111 8742	2.0124 2284	2.0136 5675	2.0148 8916	2.0161 2007	2
3	3.0223 8875	3.0248 6282	3.0273 3422	3.0298 0294	3.0322 6902	3
4	4.0335 9355	4.0373 0709	4.0410 1687	4.0447 2289	4.0484 2518	4
6	6.0560 0664	6.0621 9992	6.0683 8735	6.0745 6894	6.0807 4472	6
12	12.1232 5284	12.1368 8698	12.1505 0915	12.1641 1941	12.1777 1779	12

m	$3\frac{1}{2}$%	$3\frac{3}{4}$%	4%	$4\frac{1}{2}$%	5%	m
2	2.0173 4950	2.0185 7744	2.0198 0390	2.0222 5242	2.0246 9508	2
3	3.0347 3244	3.0371 9322	3.0396 5138	3.0445 5985	3.0494 5791	3
4	4.0521 2374	4.0558 1860	4.0595 0975	4.0668 8103	4.0742 3769	4
6	6.0869 1471	6.0930 7893	6.0992 3740	6.1115 3716	6.1238 1418	6
12	12.1913 0434	12.2048 7909	12.2184 4211	12.2455 3306	12.2725 7753	12

TABLE 10 PERIODIC PAYMENT

WHEN AMOUNT OF ANNUITY FOR FRACTIONAL INTEREST PERIOD IS 1

$$\frac{1}{s_{\overline{1/m}|i}} = \frac{i}{(1+i)^{\frac{1}{m}} - 1} \qquad \text{Note: } \frac{1}{a_{\overline{1/m}|i}} = \frac{1}{s_{\overline{1/m}|i}} + i$$

m	$5\frac{1}{2}\%$	6%	$6\frac{1}{2}\%$	7%	$7\frac{1}{2}\%$	m
2	2.0271 3193	2.0295 6301	2.0319 8837	2.0344 0804	2.0368 2207	2
3	3.0543 4565	3.0592 2313	3.0640 9043	3.0689 4762	3.0737 9477	3
4	4.0815 7981	4.0889 0752	4.0962 2091	4.1035 2009	4.1108 0514	4
6	6.1360 6860	6.1483 0059	6.1605 1031	6.1726 9791	6.1848 6355	6
12	12.2995 7585	12.3265 2834	12.3534 3533	12.3802 9715	12.4071 1409	12

m	8%	$8\frac{1}{2}\%$	9%	$9\frac{1}{2}\%$	10%	m
2	2.0392 3048	2.0416 3333	2.0440 3065	2.0464 2248	2.0488 0885	2
3	3.0786 3195	3.0834 5923	3.0882 7668	3.0930 8437	3.0978 8235	3
4	4.1180 7618	4.1253 3329	4.1325 7657	4.1398 0612	4.1470 2204	4
6	6.1970 0737	6.2091 2954	6.2212 3021	6.2333 0950	6.2453 6759	6
12	12.4338 8648	12.4606 1463	12.4872 9883	12.5139 3939	12.5405 3661	12

TABLE 11 VALUES OF j_m

(NOMINAL RATE j COMPOUNDED m TIMES PER YEAR) AND THEIR EQUIVALENT VALUES OF f (EFFECTIVE RATE)

$$j_m = m[(1+f)^{\frac{1}{m}} - 1]$$

m	$f = {}^*\frac{1}{4}\%$	$\frac{1}{3}\%$	$\frac{5}{12}\%$	$\frac{11}{24}\%$	$\frac{1}{2}\%$	m
2	j = .0024 9844	.0033 3056	.0041 6234	.0045 7809	.0049 9377	2
3	.0024 9792	.0033 2964	.0041 6089	.0045 7635	.0049 9169	3
4	.0024 9766	.0033 2917	.0041 6017	.0045 7548	.0049 9065	4
6	.0024 9740	.0033 2871	.0041 5945	.0045 7460	.0049 8962	6
12	.0024 9714	.0033 2825	.0041 5873	.0045 7373	.0049 8858	12

m	$\frac{13}{24}\%$	$\frac{7}{12}\%$	$\frac{5}{8}\%$	$\frac{2}{3}\%$	$\frac{3}{4}\%$	m
2	.0054 0935	.0058 2485	.0062 4026	.0066 5559	.0074 8599	2
3	.0054 0692	.0058 2203	.0062 3702	.0066 5191	.0074 8133	3
4	.0054 0570	.0058 2062	.0062 3540	.0066 5006	.0074 7900	4
6	.0054 0448	.0058 1921	.0062 3379	.0066 4822	.0074 7667	6
12	.0054 0327	.0058 1780	.0062 3217	.0066 4638	.0074 7434	12

m	$\frac{7}{8}\%$	1%	$1\frac{1}{8}\%$	$1\frac{1}{4}\%$	$1\frac{3}{8}\%$	m
2	.0087 3094	.0099 7512	.0112 1854	.0124 6118	.0137 0306	2
3	.0087 2460	.0099 6685	.0112 0807	.0124 4828	.0136 8746	3
4	.0087 2143	.0099 6272	.0112 0285	.0124 4183	.0136 7966	4
6	.0087 1827	.0099 5859	.0111 9763	.0124 3539	.0136 7188	6
12	.0087 1510	.0099 5446	.0111 9241	.0124 2895	.0136 6410	12

m	$1\frac{1}{2}\%$	$1\frac{5}{8}\%$	$1\frac{3}{4}\%$	$1\frac{7}{8}\%$	2%	m
2	.0149 4417	.0161 8452	.0174 2410	.0186 6292	.0199 0099	2
3	.0149 2562	.0161 6277	.0173 9890	.0186 3402	.0198 6813	3
4	.0149 1636	.0161 7182	.0173 8631	.0186 1959	.0198 5173	4
6	.0149 0710	.0161 4105	.0173 7374	.0186 0517	.0198 3534	6
12	.0148 9785	.0161 3021	.0173 6119	.0185 9077	.0198 1898	12

* Example: Nominal rate .249844% (or .00249844) compounded semiannually is equivalent to the effective rate $\frac{1}{4}\%$.

TABLE 11

TABLE 11 VALUES OF j_m

(NOMINAL RATE j COMPOUNDED m TIMES PER YEAR) AND THEIR EQUIVALENT VALUES OF f (EFFECTIVE RATE)

$$j_m = m[(1+f)^{\frac{1}{m}} - 1]$$

m	$f = 2\frac{1}{4}\%$	$2\frac{1}{2}\%$	$2\frac{3}{4}\%$	3%	$3\frac{1}{4}\%$	m
2	$j =$ .0223 7484	.0248 4567	.0273 1349	.0297 7831	.0322 4014	2
3	.0223 3333	.0247 9451	.0272 5170	.0297 0490	.0321 5414	3
4	.0223 1261	.0247 6899	.0272 2087	.0296 6829	.0321 1125	4
6	.0222 9192	.0247 4349	.0271 9009	.0296 3173	.0320 6844	6
12	.0222 7125	.0247 1804	.0271 5936	.0295 9524	.0320 2571	12

m	$3\frac{1}{2}\%$	$3\frac{3}{4}\%$	4%	$4\frac{1}{2}\%$	5%	m
2	.0346 9899	.0371 5488	.0396 0781	.0445 0483	.0493 9015	2
3	.0345 9943	.0370 4078	.0394 7821	.0443 4138	.0491 8907	3
4	.0345 4978	.0369 8390	.0394 1363	.0442 5996	.0490 8894	4
6	.0345 0024	.0369 2714	.0393 4918	.0441 7874	.0489 8908	6
12	.0344 5078	.0368 7050	.0392 8488	.0440 9771	.0488 8949	12

m	$5\frac{1}{2}\%$	6%	$6\frac{1}{2}\%$	7%	$7\frac{1}{2}\%$	m
2	.0542 6386	.0591 2603	.0639 7674	.0688 1609	.0736 4414	2
3	.0540 2139	.0588 3847	.0636 4042	.0684 2737	.0731 9942	3
4	.0539 0070	.0586 9538	.0634 7314	.0682 3410	.0729 7840	4
6	.0537 8036	.0585 5277	.0633 0644	.0680 4156	.0727 5827	6
12	.0536 6039	.0584 1061	0631 4033	.0678 4974	.0725 3903	12

m	8%	$8\frac{1}{2}\%$	9%	$9\frac{1}{2}\%$	10%	m
2	.0784 6097	.0832 6667	.0880 6130	.0928 4495	.0976 1770	2
3	.0779 5670	.0826 9933	.0874 2740	.0921 4104	.0968 4035	3
4	.0777 0619	.0824 1758	.0871 1272	.0917 9174	.0964 5476	4
6	.0774 5674	.0821 3712	.0867 9955	.0914 4420	.0960 7121	6
12	.0772 0836	.0818 5792	.0864 8788	.0910 9841	.0956 8968	12

TABLE 12 COMMISSIONERS 1958 STANDARD ORDINARY MORTALITY TABLE

Age, x	Number Living l_x	Number Dying d_x	Deaths per 1,000	Age, x	Number Living l_x	Number Dying d_x	Deaths per 1,000
0	10,000,000	70,800	7.08	50	8,762,306	72,902	8.32
1	9,929,200	17,475	1.76	51	8,689,404	79,160	9.11
2	9,911,725	15,066	1.52	52	8,610,244	85,758	9.96
3	9,896,659	14,449	1.46	53	8,524,486	92,832	10.89
4	9,882,210	13,835	1.40	54	8,431,654	100,337	11.90
5	9,868,375	13,322	1.35	55	8,331,317	108,307	13.00
6	9,855,053	12,812	1.30	56	8,223,010	116,849	14,21
7	9,842,241	12,401	1.26	57	8,106,161	125,970	15.54
8	9,829,840	12,091	1.23	58	7,980,191	135,663	17.00
9	9,817,749	11,879	1.21	59	7,844,528	145,830	18.59
10	9,805,870	11,865	1.21	60	7,698,698	156,592	20.34
11	9,794,005	12,047	1.23	61	7,542,106	167,736	22.24
12	9,781,958	12,325	1.26	62	7,374,370	179,271	24.31
13	9,769,633	12,896	1.32	63	7,195,099	191,174	26.57
14	9,756,737	13,562	1.39	64	7,003,925	203,394	29.04
15	9,743,175	14,225	1.46	65	6,800,531	215,917	31.75
16	9,728,950	14,983	1.54	66	6,584,614	228,749	34.74
17	9,713,967	15,737	1.62	67	6,355,865	241,777	38.04
18	9,698,230	16,390	1.69	68	6,114,088	254,835	41.68
19	9,681,840	16,846	1.74	69	5,859,253	267,241	45.61
20	9,664,994	17,300	1.79	70	5,592,012	278,426	49.79
21	9,647,694	17,655	1.83	71	5,313,586	287,731	54.15
22	9,630,039	17,912	1.86	72	5,025,855	294,766	58.65
23	9,612,127	18,167	1.89	73	4,731,089	299,289	63.26
24	9,593,960	18,324	1.91	74	4,431,800	301,894	68.12
25	9,575,636	18,481	1.93	75	4,129,906	303,011	73.37
26	9,557,155	18,732	1.96	76	3,826,895	303,014	79.18
27	9,538,423	18,981	1.99	77	3,523,881	301,997	85.70
28	9,519,442	19,324	2.03	78	3,221,884	299,829	93.06
29	9,500,118	19,760	2.08	79	2,922,055	295,683	101.19
30	9,480,358	20,193	2.13	80	2,626,372	288,848	109.98
31	9,460,165	20,718	2.19	81	2,337,524	278,983	119.35
32	9,439,447	21,239	2.25	82	2,058,541	265,902	129.17
33	9,418,208	21,850	2.32	83	1,792,639	249,858	139.38
34	9,396,358	22,551	2.40	84	1,542,781	231,433	150.01
35	9,373,807	23,528	2.51	85	1,311,348	211,311	161.14
36	9,350,279	24,685	2.64	86	1,100,037	190,108	172.82
37	9,325,594	26,112	2.80	87	909,929	168,455	185.13
38	9,299,482	27,991	3.01	88	741,474	146,997	198.25
39	9,271,491	30,132	3.25	89	594,477	126,303	212.46
40	9,241,359	32,622	3.53	90	468,174	106,809	228.14
41	9,208,737	35,362	3.84	91	361,365	88,813	245.77
42	9,173,375	38,253	4.17	92	272,552	72,480	265.93
43	9,135,122	41,382	4.53	93	200,072	57,881	289.30
44	9;093,740	44,741	4.92	94	142,191	45,026	316.66
45	9,048,999	48,412	5.35	95	97,165	34,128	351.24
46	9,000,587	52,473	5.83	96	63,037	25,250	400.56
47	8,948,114	56,910	6.36	97	37,787	18,456	488.42
48	8,891,204	61,794	6.95	98	19,331	12,916	668.15
49	8,829,410	67,104	7.60	99	6,415	6,415	1,000.00

TABLE 13 COMMUTATION COLUMNS—INTEREST AT $2\frac{1}{2}$%

BASED ON 1958 CSO MORTALITY TABLE

Age, x	D_x	N_x	C_x	M_x
0	10,000,000.0000	324,850,104.9680	69,073.1710	2,076,826.7172
1	9,687,024.4290	314,850,104.9680	16,632.9566	2,007,753.5462
2	9,434,122.5838	305,163,080.5390	13,990.2787	1,991,120.5896
3	9,190,031.7084	295,728,957.9552	13,090.0808	1,977,130.3109
4	8,952,794.4741	286,538,926.2468	12,228.1241	1,964,040.2301
5	8,722,205.5791	277,586,131.7727	11,487.5189	1,951,812.1060
6	8,497,981.3556	268,863,926.1936	10,778.2903	1,940,324.5871
7	8,279,935.2370	260,365,944.8380	10,178.0782	1,929,546.2968
8	8,067,807.4636	252,086,009.6010	9,681.6066	1,919,368.2186
9	7,861,350.0557	244,018,202.1374	9,279.8558	1,909,686.6120
10	7,660,329.9546	236,156,852.0817	9,042.8478	1,900,406.7562
11	7,464,449.7860	228,496,522.1271	8,957.6178	1,891,363.9084
12	7,273,432.4866	221,032,072.3411	8,940.8062	1,882,406.2906
13	7,087,090.8833	213,758,639.8545	9,126.8500	1,873,465.4844
14	6,905,108.1581	206,671,548.9712	9,364.0939	1,864,338.6344
15	6,727,326.7826	199,766,440.8131	9,582.3146	1,854,974.5405
16	6,553,663.2627	193,039,114.0305	9,846.7536	1,845,392.2259
17	6,383,971.1254	186,485,450.7678	10,090.0279	1,835,545.4723
18	6,218,174.4633	180,101,479.6424	10,252.3993	1,825,455.4444
19	6,056,259.3006	173,883,305.1791	10,280.6243	1,815,203.0451
20	5,898,264.9735	167,827,045.8785	10,300.1828	1,804,922.4208
21	5,744,104.7377	161,928,780.9050	10,255.1657	1,794,622.2380
22	5,593,749.4258	156,184,676.1673	10,150.6810	1,784,367.0723
23	5,447,165.8414	150,590,926.7415	10,044.0865	1,774,216.3913
24	5,304,263.9929	145,143,760.9001	9,883.7932	1,764,172.3048
25	5,165,007.9517	139,839,496.9072	9,725.3439	1,754,288.5116
26	5,029,306.7854	134,674,488.9555	9,617.0037	1,744,563.1677
27	4,897,023.7928	129,645,182.1701	9,507.1611	1,734,946.1640
28	4,768,076.9758	124,748,158.3773	9,442.8900	1,725,439.0029
29	4,642,339.5370	119,980,081.4015	9,420.4356	1,715,996.1129
30	4,519,691.3751	115,337,741.8645	9,392.0634	1,706,575.6773
31	4,400,062.8465	110,818,050.4894	9,401.2183	1,697,183.6139
32	4,283,343.0569	106,417,987.6429	9,402.5686	1,687,782.3956
33	4,169,468.7479	102,134,644.5860	9,437.1317	1,678,379.8270
34	4,058,337.1968	97,965,175.8381	9,502.3390	1,668,942.6953
35	3,949,851.0856	93,906,838.6413	9,672.2130	1,659,440.3563
36	3,843,840.9771	89,956,987.5557	9,900.3401	1,649,768.1433
37	3,740,188.4751	86,113,146.5786	10,217.2318	1,639,867.8032
38	3,638,747.0704	82,372,958.1035	10,685.3232	1,629,650.5714
39	3,539,311.8617	78,734,211.0331	11,222.0794	1,618,965.2482
40	3,441,765.0620	75,194,899.1714	11,853.1042	1,607,743.1688
41	3,345,966.5023	71,753,134.1094	12,535.2926	1,595,890.0646
42	3,251,822.2774	68,407,167.6071	13,229.3739	1,583,354.7720
43	3,159,280.1784	65,155,345.3297	13,962.4424	1,570,125.3981
44	3,068,262.0685	61,996,065.1513	14,727.5918	1,556,162.9557
45	2,978,698.8164	58,927,803.0828	15,547.3085	1,541,435.3639
46	2,890,500.3526	55,949,104.2664	16,440.4699	1,525,888.0554
47	2,803,559.9048	53,058,603.9138	17,395.7457	1,509,447.5855
48	2,717,784.6405	50,255,044.0090	18,427.9447	1,492,051.8398
49	2,633,069.2135	47,537,259.3685	19,523.3861	1,473,623.8951

TABLE 13 COMMUTATION COLUMNS—INTEREST AT $2\frac{1}{2}\%$

BASED ON 1958 CSO MORTALITY TABLE

Age, x	D_x	N_x	C_x	M_x
50	2,549,324.6723	44,904,190.1550	20,692.9455	1,454,100.5090
51	2,466,453.0891	42,354,865.4827	21,921.2231	1,433,407.5635
52	2,384,374.4270	39,888,412.3936	23,169.1325	1,411,486.3404
53	2,303,049.8123	37,504,037.9666	24,468.5917	1,388,317.2079
54	2,222,409.2905	35,200,988.1543	25,801.7117	1,363,848.6162
55	2,142,402.4988	32,978,578.8638	27,171.9031	1,338,046.9045
56	2,062,976.8254	30,836,176.3650	28,599.9098	1,310,875.0014
57	1,984,060.3996	28,773,199.5396	30,080.3536	1,282,275.0916
58	1,905,588.3725	26,789,139.1400	31,604.8230	1,252,194.7380
59	1,827,505.7998	24,883,550.7675	33,144.7659	1,220,589.9150
60	1,749,787.7198	23,056,044.9677	34,722.7242	1,187,445.1491
61	1,672,387.2632	21,306,257.2479	36,286.6291	1,152,722.4249
62	1,595,310.6622	19,633,869.9847	37,836.1144	1,116,435.7958
63	1,518,564.5694	18,038,559.3225	39,364.2006	1,078,599.6814
64	1,442,162.1578	16,519,994.7531	40,858.9196	1,039,235.4808
65	1,366,128.5462	15,077,832.5953	42,316.6940	998,376.5612
66	1,290,491.6985	13,711,704.0491	43,738.1310	956,059.8672
67	1,215,278.1249	12,421,212.3506	45,101.6207	912,321.7362
68	1,140,535.6099	11,205,934.2257	46,378.0358	867,220.1155
69	1,066,339.5743	10,065,398.6158	47,449.5963	820,842.0797
70	992,881.7500	8,999,059.0415	48,229.7870	773,392.4834
71	920,435.3077	8,006,177.2915	48,625.9779	725,162.6964
72	849,359.6946	7,085,741.9838	48,599.8832	676,536.7185
73	780,043.7396	6,236,382.2892	48,142.0663	627,936.8353
74	712,876.2140	5,456,338.5496	47,376.6752	579,794.7690
75	648,112.3021	4,743,462.3356	46,392.1628	532,418.0938
76	585,912.5111	4,095,350.0335	45,261.0951	486,025.9310
77	526,360.8716	3,509,437.5224	44,008.9628	440,764.8359
78	469,513.8465	2,983,076.6508	42,627.3426	396,755.8731
79	415,434,9294	2,513,562.8043	41,012.5834	354,128.5305
80	364,289.7989	2,098,127.8749	39,087.3533	313,115.9471
81	316,317.3241	1,733,838.0760	36,831.6174	274,028.5938
82	271,770.6619	1,417,520.7519	34,248.4382	237,196.9764
83	230,893.6600	1,145,750.0900	31,397.0289	202,948.5382
84	193,865.0736	914,856.4300	28,372.4430	171,551.5093
85	160,764.2229	720,991.3564	25,273.7507	143,179.0663
86	131,569.3974	560,227.1335	22,183.1949	117,905.3156
87	106,177.1855	428,657.7361	19,177.1362	95,722.1207
88	84,410.3641	322,480.5506	16,326.1748	76,544.9845
89	66,025.3978	238,070.1865	13,685.6613	60,218.8097
90	50,729.3636	172,044.7887	11,291.0955	46,533.1484
91	38,200.9638	121,315.4251	9,159.6932	35,242.0529
92	28,109.5415	83,114.4613	7,292.8738	26,082.3597
93	20,131.0686	55,004.9198	5,681.8884	18,789.4859
94	13,958.1795	34,873.8512	4,312.1729	13,107.5975
95	9,305.5630	20,915.6717	3,188.7449	8,795.4246
96	5,889.8533	11,610.1087	2,301.6880	5,606.6797
97	3,444.5103	5,720.2554	1,641.3408	3,304.9917
98	1,719.1569	2,275.7451	1,120.6380	1,663.6509
99	556.5882	556.5882	543.0129	543.0129

TABLE 14 LOGARITHMS OF VALUES IN TABLE 13

Age x	$\log D_x$	$\log N_x$	$\log C_x$	$\log M_x$	Age x
0	7.000 0000	8.511 6830	4.839 3094	6.317 4003	0
1	6.986 1904	8.498 1038	4.220 9695	6.302 7104	1
2	6.974 7016	8.484 5320	4.145 8264	6.299 0976	2
3	6.963 3170	8.470 8939	4.116 9423	6.296 0353	3
4	6.951 9586	8.457 1837	4.087 3598	6.293 1504	4
5	6.940 6263	8.443 3978	4.060 2262	6.290 4380	5
6	6.929 3157	8.429 5325	4.032 5499	6.287 8744	6
7	6.918 0269	8.415 5842	4.007 6657	6.285 4552	7
8	6.906 7555	8.401 5487	3.985 9474	6.283 1583	8
9	6.895 4972	8.387 4222	3.967 5412	6.280 9621	9
10	6.884 2475	8.373 2005	3.956 3052	6.278 8465	10
11	6.872 9978	8.358 8796	3.952 1926	6.276 7751	11
12	6.861 7394	8.344 4553	3.951 3767	6.274 7134	12
13	6.850 4680	8.329 9236	3.960 3209	6.272 6457	13
14	6.839 1705	8.315 2807	3.971 4657	6.270 5248	14
15	6.827 8425	8.300 5225	3.981 4705	6.268 3379	15
16	6.816 4841	8.285 6453	3.993 2931	6.265 0887	16
17	6.805 0909	8.270 6449	4.003 8924	6.263 7651	17
18	6.793 6629	8.255 5173	4.010 8255	6.261 3712	18
19	6.782 2045	8.240 2579	4.012 0195	6.258 9252	19
20	6.770 7243	8.224 8619	4.012 8449	6.256 4585	20
21	6.759 2224	8.209 3240	4.010 9427	6.253 9731	21
22	6.747 7030	8.193 6384	4.006 4951	6.251 4842	22
23	6.736 1706	8.177 7988	4.001 9104	6.249 0066	23
24	6.724 6251	8.161 7983	3.994 9236	6.246 5410	24
25	6.713 0710	8.145 6298	3.987 9050	6.244 1011	25
26	6.701 5081	8.129 2854	3.983 0398	6.241 6867	26
27	6.689 9322	8.112 7564	3.978 0508	6.239 2860	27
28	6.678 3433	8.096 0342	3.975 1049	6.236 8996	28
29	6.666 7369	8.079 1092	3.974 0710	6.234 5163	29
30	6.655 1088	8.061 9714	3.972 7610	6.232 1255	30
31	6.643 4589	8.044 6105	3.973 1841	6.229 7288	31
32	6.631 7828	8.027 0151	3.973 2465	6.227 3165	32
33	6.620 0807	8.009 1731	3.974 8401	6.224 8903	33
34	6.608 3481	7.991 0717	3.977 8305	6.222 4414	34
35	6.596 5807	7.972 6972	3.985 5259	6.219 9617	35
36	6.584 7654	7.954 0349	3.995 6501	6.217 4229	36
37	6.572 8935	7.935 0694	4.009 3333	6.214 8089	37
38	6.560 9519	7.915 7847	4.028 7877	6.212 0945	38
39	6.548 9188	7.896 1635	4.050 0734	6.209 2375	39
40	6.536 7812	7.876 1884	4.073 8321	6.206 2167	40
41	6.524 5216	7.855 8409	4.098 1345	6.203 0030	41
42	6.512 1268	7.835 1016	4.121 5393	6.199 5782	42
43	6.499 5882	7.813 9500	4.144 9614	6.195 9343	43
44	6.486 8925	7.792 3642	4.168 1318	6.192 0551	44
45	6.474 0266	7.770 3202	4.191 6552	6.187 9253	45
46	6.460 9731	7.747 7931	4.215 9142	6.183 5227	46
47	6.447 7099	7.724 7559	4.240 4430	6.178 8180	47
48	6.434 2150	7.701 1797	4.265 4769	6.173 7839	48
49	6.420 4623	7.677 0342	4.290 5552	6.168 3866	49

TABLE 14 LOGARITHMS OF VALUES IN TABLE 13

Age x	log D_x	log N_x	log C_x	log M_x	Age x
50	6.406 4251	7.652 2868	4.315 8224	6.162 5945	50
51	6.392 0728	7.626 9033	4.340 8648	6.156 3697	51
52	6.377 3744	7.600 8468	4.364 9098	6.149 6767	52
53	6.362 3033	7.574 0780	4.388 6090	6.142 4887	53
54	6.346 8240	7.546 5549	4.411 6485	6.134 7662	54
55	6.330 9011	7.518 2319	4.434 1200	6.126 4713	55
56	6.314 4943	7.489 0605	4.456 3646	6.117 5613	56
57	6.297 5549	7.458 9881	4.478 2829	6.107 9812	57
58	6.280 0291	7.427 9588	4.499 7534	6.097 6719	58
59	6.261 8588	7.395 9123	4.520 4149	6.086 5698	59
60	6.242 9854	7.362 7848	4.540 6138	6.074 6135	60
61	6.223 3369	7.328 5071	4.559 7466	6.061 7248	61
62	6.202 8453	7.293 0059	4.577 9065	6.047 8337	62
63	6.181 4333	7.256 2019	4.595 1014	6.032 8603	63
64	6.159 0141	7.218 0099	4.611 2868	6.016 7139	64
65	6.135 4916	7.178 3389	4.626 5117	5.999 2944	65
66	6.110 7552	7.137 0914	4.640 8602	5.980 4850	66
67	6.084 6757	7.094 1640	4.654 1922	5.960 1480	67
68	6.057 1089	7.049 4481	4.666 3123	5.938 1294	68
69	6.027 8955	7.002 8310	4.676 2325	5.914 2596	69
70	5.996 8976	6.954 1971	4.683 3154	5.888 4000	70
71	5.963 9933	6.903 4252	4.686 8683	5.860 4354	71
72	5.929 0916	6.850 3854	4.686 6352	5.830 2914	72
73	5.892 1190	6.794 9328	4.682 5247	5.797 9159	73
74	5.853 0141	6.736 9013	4.675 5646	5.763 2743	74
75	5.811 6502	6.676 0954	4.666 4446	5.726 2528	75
76	5.767 8328	6.612 2910	4.655 7250	5.686 6594	76
77	5.721 2836	6.545 2375	4.643 5411	5.644 2069	77
78	5.671 6484	6.474 6644	4.629 6883	5.598 5234	78
79	5.618 5030	6.400 2898	4.612 9171	5.549 1609	79
80	5.561 4470	6.321 8320	4.592 0362	5.495 7052	80
81	5.500 1230	6.239 0085	4.566 2208	5.437 7959	81
82	5.434 2026	6.151 5295	4.534 6408	5.375 1092	82
83	5.363 4120	6.059 0899	4.496 8886	5.307 3860	83
84	5.287 4996	5.961 3529	4.452 8968	5.234 3945	84
85	5.206 1624	5.857 9300	4.402 6697	5.155 8796	85
86	5.119 1549	5.748 3642	4.346 0241	5.071 5334	86
87	5.026 0312	5.632 1107	4.282 7838	4.981 0123	87
88	4.926 3958	5.508 5035	4.212 8844	4.883 9167	88
89	4.819 7110	5.376 7050	4.136 2658	4.779 7321	89
90	4.705 2594	5.235 6415	4.052 7361	4.667 7625	90
91	4.582 0743	5.083 9160	3.961 8809	4.547 0612	91
92	4.448 8537	4.919 6766	3.862 8987	4.416 3469	92
93	4.303 8668	4.740 4016	3.754 4927	4.273 9149	93
94	4.144 8288	4.542 4999	3.634 6962	4.117 5231	94
95	3.968 7427	4.320 4718	3.503 6198	3.944 2568	95
96	3.770 1044	4.064 8363	3.362 0464	3.748 7057	96
97	3.537 1275	3.434 6097	3.215 1988	3.519 1704	97
98	3.235 3155	3.357 1236	3.049 4653	3.221 0622	98
99	2.745 5340	2.745 5340	2.734 8101	2.734 8101	99

TABLE 15 COMMISSIONERS 1980 STANDARD ORDINARY MORTALITY TABLE

(BASED ON EXPERIENCE OF 1970–1975)

Age	Male		Female		Age	Male		Female	
	Deaths Per 1,000	Expectation of Life (Years)	Deaths Per 1,000	Expectation of Life (Years)		Deaths Per 1,000	Expectation of Life (Years)	Deaths Per 1,000	Expectation of Life (Years)
0	4.18	70.83	2.89	75.83	50	6.71	25.36	4.96	29.53
1	1.07	70.13	.87	75.04	51	7.30	24.52	5.31	28.67
2	.99	69.20	.81	74.11	52	7.96	23.70	5.70	27.82
3	.98	68.27	.79	73.17	53	8.71	22.89	6.15	26.98
4	.95	67.34	.77	72.23	54	9.56	22.08	6.61	26.14
5	.90	66.40	.76	71.28	55	10.47	21.29	7.09	25.31
6	.86	65.46	.73	70.34	56	11.46	20.51	7.57	24.49
7	.80	64.52	.72	69.39	57	12.49	19.74	8.03	23.67
8	.76	63.57	.70	68.44	58	13.59	18.99	8.47	22.86
9	.74	62.62	.69	67.48	59	14.77	18.24	8.94	22.05
10	.73	61.66	.68	66.53	60	16.08	17.51	9.47	21.25
11	.77	60.71	.69	65.58	61	17.54	16.79	10.13	20.44
12	.85	59.75	.72	64.62	62	19.19	16.08	10.96	19.65
13	.99	58.80	.75	63.67	63	21.06	15.38	12.02	18.86
14	1.15	57.86	.80	62.71	64	23.14	14.70	13.25	18.08
15	1.33	56.93	.85	61.76	65	25.42	14.04	14.59	17.32
16	1.51	56.00	.90	60.82	66	27.85	13.39	16.00	16.57
17	1.67	55.09	.95	59.87	67	30.44	12.76	17.43	15.83
18	1.78	54.18	.98	58.93	68	33.19	12.14	18.84	15.10
19	1.86	53.27	1.02	57.98	69	36.17	11.54	20.36	14.38
20	1.90	52.37	1.05	57.04	70	39.51	10.96	22.11	13.67
21	1.91	51.47	1.07	56.10	71	43.30	10.39	24.23	12.97
22	1.89	50.57	1.09	55.16	72	47.65	9.84	26.87	12.28
23	1.86	49.66	1.11	54.22	73	52.64	9.30	30.11	11.60
24	1.82	48.75	1.14	53.28	74	58.19	8.79	33.93	10.95
25	1.77	47.84	1.16	52.34	75	64.19	8.31	38.24	10.32
26	1.73	46.93	1.19	51.40	76	70.53	7.84	42.97	9.71
27	1.71	46.01	1.22	50.46	77	77.12	7.40	48.04	9.12
28	1.70	45.09	1.26	49.52	78	83.90	6.97	53.45	8.55
29	1.71	44.16	1.30	48.59	79	91.05	6.57	59.35	8.01
30	1.73	43.24	1.35	47.65	80	98.84	6.18	65.99	7.48
31	1.78	42.31	1.40	46.71	81	107.48	5.80	73.60	6.98
32	1.83	41.38	1.45	45.78	82	117.25	5.44	82.40	6.49
33	1.91	40.46	1.50	44.84	83	128.26	5.09	92.53	6.03
34	2.00	39.54	1.58	43.91	84	140.25	4.77	103.81	5.59
35	2.11	38.61	1.65	42.98	85	152.95	4.46	116.10	5.18
36	2.24	37.69	1.76	42.05	86	166.09	4.18	129.29	4.80
37	2.40	36.78	1.89	41.12	87	179.55	3.91	143.32	4.43
38	2.58	35.87	2.04	40.20	88	193.27	3.66	158.18	4.09
39	2.79	34.96	2.22	39.28	89	207.29	3.41	173.94	3.77
40	3.02	34.05	2.42	38.36	90	221.77	3.18	190.75	3.45
41	3.29	33.16	2.64	37.46	91	236.98	2.94	208.87	3.15
42	3.56	32.26	2.87	36.55	92	253.45	2.70	228.81	2.85
43	3.87	31.38	3.09	35.66	93	272.11	2.44	251.51	2.55
44	4.19	30.50	3.32	34.77	94	295.90	2.17	279.31	2.24
45	4.55	29.62	3.56	33.88	95	329.96	1.87	317.32	1.91
46	4.92	28.76	3.80	33.00	96	384.55	1.54	375.74	1.56
47	5.32	27.90	4.05	32.12	97	480.20	1.20	474.97	1.21
48	5.74	27.04	4.33	31.25	98	657.98	.84	655.85	.84
49	6.21	26.20	4.63	30.39	99	1,000.00	.50	1,000.00	.50

ANSWERS TO ODD-NUMBERED PROBLEMS

EXERCISE 1–1, PAGE 8

1. $\frac{21}{5}$
3. $\frac{91}{8}$
5. $\frac{47}{12}$
7. $\frac{48}{5}$
9. $\frac{275}{6}$
11. $\frac{40,312}{325}$
13. $4\frac{1}{2}$
15. $1\frac{3}{8}$
17. $5\frac{1}{8}$
19. $8\frac{2}{5}$
21. $6\frac{28}{31}$
23. $37\frac{29}{124}$
25. $5; \frac{1}{2}$
27. $5; \frac{2}{3}$
29. $5; \frac{4}{7}$
31. $121; \frac{7}{11}$
33. $26; \frac{3}{8}$
35. $22; \frac{14}{17}$
37. $\frac{1}{4}, \frac{1}{5}$
39. $\frac{3}{4}, \frac{5}{7}$
41. $\frac{4}{9}, \frac{7}{16}$
43. $\frac{5}{6}, \frac{3}{4}, \frac{2}{5}$
45. $\frac{3}{5}, \frac{1}{2}, \frac{2}{7}$
47. $\frac{5}{3}, \frac{9}{7}, \frac{11}{9}, \frac{13}{11}$
49. $\frac{12}{5}, \frac{12}{15}, \frac{2}{3}, \frac{3}{5}, \frac{1}{3}$

EXERCISE 1–2, PAGE 10

1. $\frac{2}{5}$
3. $1\frac{1}{3}$
5. $1\frac{5}{12}$
7. $6\frac{5}{12}$
9. $2\frac{21}{40}$
11. $17\frac{1}{8}$
13. $\frac{19}{21}$
15. $1\frac{7}{16}$
17. $\frac{97}{100}$
19. $11\frac{13}{30}$
21. $22\frac{19}{33}$
23. $67\frac{3}{20}$
25. $\frac{1}{20}$
27. $\frac{2}{21}$
29. $\frac{13}{100}$
31. $\frac{3}{7}$
33. $2\frac{1}{3}$
35. $7\frac{2}{3}$
37. $7\frac{7}{9}$
39. $5\frac{74}{99}$
41. $2\frac{1}{4}$
43. $\frac{1}{6}$
45. $\frac{3}{20}$
47. $7\frac{11}{45}$
49. $\frac{1}{12}$
51. $\frac{7}{26}$
53. $\frac{1}{3}$
55. $\frac{25}{84}$
57. $\frac{49}{225}$
59. $3\frac{21}{44}$
61. $\frac{10}{171}$
63. $\frac{2}{9}$
65. $8\frac{1}{15}$
67. $152\frac{11}{14}$
69. $3,468\frac{9}{40}$
71. 845

EXERCISE 1–3, PAGE 14

1. 3
3. $\frac{5}{4}$
5. $\frac{18}{15}$
7. $\frac{110}{339}$
9. 5
11. $\frac{39}{70}$
13. $7\frac{14}{23}$
15. $\frac{7}{9}$
17. $\frac{\text{[illegible]}}{15}$
19. $\frac{17}{18}$
21. $16\frac{2}{5}$
23. $6\frac{3}{7}$
25. $\frac{14}{15}$
27. $1\frac{1}{14}$
29. $\frac{14}{45}$
31. $\frac{25}{42}$
33. $5\frac{9}{31}$
35. $\frac{1}{8}$
37. $1\frac{5}{7}$
39. $1\frac{4}{11}$
41. $\frac{15}{32}$
43. $1\frac{1}{15}$
45. $8\frac{31}{37}$
47. $\frac{38}{51}$
49. 42.75
51. 632.44
53. 1.67
55. 7,362.06
57. 2.38
59. 43.01

EXERCISE 1–4, PAGE 18

1. .2
3. .353
5. .933
7. .553
9. 3.077
11. 4.8
13. 3.35
15. 42.438
17. $\frac{8}{25}$
19. $\frac{17}{25}$
21. $\frac{19}{500}$
23. $1\frac{41}{50}$
25. $3\frac{1}{500}$
27. $11\frac{7}{200}$
29. $4\frac{71}{200}$
31. $2\frac{3,501}{4,000}$
33. 12
35. 16
37. 4,500
39. 2,400
41. 56
43. 121
45. 200
47. 350
49. 30
51. 44
53. 600
55. 200
57. 5
59. 6
61. 1,000
63. 900
65. 156
67. 1,320
69. 3.33
71. 1.65
73. 176
75. 900
77. 1.26
79. 7
81. 2,700
83. 156
85. $.\dot{1}4285\dot{7}$
87. $.41\dot{6}$
89. $.3\dot{8}$
91. $.\dot{5}1\dot{8}$
93. $.8\dot{6}$
95. $.11\dot{3}$
97. $\frac{1}{3}$
99. $\frac{4}{15}$
101. $\frac{35}{99}$
103. $\frac{13}{300}$
105. $4\frac{7}{18}$
107. $1\frac{169}{370}$

EXERCISE 2–1, PAGE 26

1. -12
3. -30
5. -47
7. -31
9. 31
11. 45
13. 22
15. 25
17. -21.23
19. -34.37
21. 2.736
23. 23.057
25. -23
27. 7
29. -25
31. 7
33. $26a$
35. $-18c$
37. $-58et$
39. $-68f$
41. $43h$
43. $28w$
45. $2cd - 2c$
47. $9ab - a$
49. $10a + 10b + 3$
51. $7xy + 28x + 7y$
53. 27
55. 45
57. 5
59. -26
61. -37.5764
63. -31.361
65. 6.79
67. 14.83
69. -32
71. 23
73. $22xy$
75. $26ab$
77. $-5bc$
79. $-2b$
81. $-5a + 6d$
83. $12f$
85. $9h$
87. $a - b + 1$

EXERCISE 2–2, PAGE 30

1. 42
3. 90
5. 18
7. 35
9. -24
11. -72
13. -14
15. $-2,272$
17. 32
19. 15,625
21. a^6
23. c^4
25. 144
27. $(xy)^3$
29. $(mn)^a$
31. 15,625
33. p^{10}
35. y^{ab}
37. $b^{y/x}$
39. 64
41. $-18xy$
43. $35xy^2$
45. $30x^3y^2$
47. $-21p^5q^3$
49. $8a + 6$
51. $20c - 15$
53. $4ta + 4tb$
55. $-21be + 14b^2$
57. $a^2 - b^2$
59. $a^2 - 2ab + b^2$
61. $-4y^2 + 14y - 6$
63. $6t^5 - 6at^3 + 12t^2 - 12a$

EXERCISE 2–3, PAGE 34

1. -4
3. -6
5. -12
7. -21
9. 18
11. 23
13. 15
15. -14
17. 7
19. -10
21. 4
23. $\frac{1}{36}$
25. a^3
27. $\dfrac{1}{x^4}$
29. 25
31. 64
33. $(a/b)^3$
35. $(ab/c)^4$
37. $26x$
39. $21a$
41. $\dfrac{7}{4a}$
43. $\dfrac{-5}{x^3}$
45. $8b^3 - 6b$
47. $-3a^4 + (b^2/2)$
49. $-9m^2 - 2mn^7 - 3$
51. $\dfrac{-9a^2}{4} + a - b$
53. $3x + 5$
55. $(3x^2 - 2x + 1) + \dfrac{37}{8x + 5}$
57. $(5x + 3) + \dfrac{-6x - 11}{5x^2 - 2x + 3}$
59. $4x + \dfrac{14x + 4}{7x^2 - 3}$

EXERCISE 2–4, PAGE 36

1. 8
3. 4
5. 7
7. 1,152
9. 18
11. −24
13. 118
15. 39
17. 26
19. 65
21. 309
23. −8
25. $3x - 3$
27. $7x - 4$
29. $-42x + 9y$
31. $6x - 15y$

EXERCISE 2–5, PAGE 39

1. $5(2a + b)$
3. $6(x + 1)$
5. $6(-3x + y - z)$
7. $(a + 2c)(3x - y)$
9. $(a - b)(x + y)$
11. $(14c - 2d)(2a + b)$
13. $(3x + y^2)(3x - y^2)$
15. $(5x - 4y)(5x + 4y)$
17. $(x^2 + 7)(x^2 - 7)$
19. $(x + 3)^2$
21. $(2x + 6)^2$ or $4(x + 3)^2$
23. $(6y - 5)^2$
25. $(3a + 4b)^2$
27. $(x + 2)(x + 1)$
29. $(y + 1)(2y + 3)$
31. $(a + 1)(2a - 3)$
33. $(x + 3)(7x - 1)$
35. $(3b + 4)(7b - 5)$

EXERCISE 2–6, PAGE 43

1. $1\frac{1}{2}$
3. 5
5. 4
7. 4
9. 12
11. 3
13. −.6
15. .11
17. $2a$
19. $2d$
21. $(5n - d)/3c$
23. $-7a/26$
25. 24 years
27. Betty has $974
29. 20 dimes; 32 quarters
31. 64
33. 2.5 hours; 150 miles
35. 40 miles per hour
37. Cost = $240
39. 6 girls
41. 3 quarters; 9 dimes; 18 half-dollars
43. $22
45. $40; $25; $20
47. 100 units

EXERCISE 2–7, PAGE 49

1. $\frac{1}{9}$
3. $\frac{4}{1}$
5. $\frac{104}{63}$
7. $\frac{245}{913}$
9. 65 miles/hour
11. 30 dollars/day
13. 2
15. 4.4
17. 156
19. 40
21. $2\frac{2}{5}$
23. 6.4
25. $41\frac{1}{6}$
27. $\frac{1}{3}$
29. A: $\frac{13}{7}$ (higher)
    B: $\frac{4}{3}$
31. $\frac{5}{8}$; $\frac{1}{8}$; $\frac{1}{4}$
33. 60; 180
35. 108; 162; 378
37. 120; 180; 300; 420
39. 3,080; 800; 3,808
41. $18,000; $12,000; $9,000; $7,200
43. $96\frac{2}{3}$ miles
45. $75
47. $77\frac{1}{7}$ feet
49. $108
51. 100 minutes, or $1\frac{2}{3}$ hours
53. 64 men

EXERCISE 2–8, PAGE 52

1. .0031
3. .0458
5. .29
7. 2.16
9. 45
11. $\frac{3}{50}$
13. $6\frac{3}{20}$
15. $\frac{3}{250}$
17. $\frac{3}{12,500}$
19. $\frac{21}{500,000}$
21. 45%
23. 4.7%
25. .35%
27. 7,200%
29. 146%
31. 2%
33. 371%
35. 92%
37. 1,647%
39. 55%

EXERCISE 2–9, PAGE 54

1. 175
3. 24.09
5. 29.16
7. 102.50
9. 12.12
11. 20
13. 6.39
15. 6
17. 73.44
19. 44.62
21. 191.25
23. $28; 80%
25. $6,180

EXERCISE 2–10, PAGE 55

1. 75%
3. 300%
5. 14.1%
7. 130%
9. 40%
11. 8%
13. 16.7%
15. 30%
17. 25%
19. 30.6%
21. 36.5%
23. 25% increase
25. 10% (loss); $29

EXERCISE 2–11, PAGE 58

1. 800
3. 4,600
5. 7,000
7. 500
9. 80
11. 182.50
13. 200
15. 200
17. 215
19. 40
21. $50,000
23. $5
25. 180 (inches)

EXERCISE 2–12, PAGE 59

1. 1,288 (bushels)
3. 78.1 (gallons)
5. 28.5 and 47.5
7. 98; 245; 343
9. $710 (Mesk); $994 (Dean)
11. 5; 10; 22.5; 31
13. 29.75
15. 460
17. $120
19. 150%
21. $360
23. $1,980 (A); $3,168 (B); $4,224 (C)
25. $200
27. $30
29. 1,100 TV sets

EXERCISE 3–1, PAGE 64

1. $x = 11$, $y = 2$
3. $x = -1$, $y = 5$
5. $x = 3$, $y = -1$
7. $x = 2$, $y = -3$
9. $x = 5$, $y = 6$
11. $x = -4$, $y = 2$
13. $x = 10$, $y = -2$
15. $x = 10$, $y = 3$
17. $x = 5$, $y = 1$
19. $x = 2$, $y = 3$
21. $x = -3$, $y = 4$
23. $x = -2$, $y = -3$
25. $x = 2$, $y = 3$
27. $x = -1$, $y = 2$
29. $x = 4$, $y = -3$
31. $x = 2$, $y = -5$
33. $x = 4$, $y = -3$
35. $x = 5$, $y = -2$
37. Dependent
39. Inconsistent
41. Dependent
43. Inconsistent
45. x = $21.50 (hat), y = $132.00 (coat)
47. x = $7, y = $5
49. x = 35 tickets to adults, y = 5 tickets to children
51. x = 13 (girl), y = 7 (brother)
53. 98
55. x = 35 pounds at $2.70, y = 15 pounds at $3.00

EXERCISE 3–2, PAGE 70

1. $\frac{1}{5}$
3. $\dfrac{1}{2(a - b)}$
5. $\dfrac{1}{a + b}$
7. $\dfrac{1}{3x - y^2}$
9. $\dfrac{4}{x^2 - 7}$
11. $\dfrac{4}{x + 3}$
13. $\dfrac{19x}{20}$
15. $\dfrac{2\frac{1}{6}}{x}$
17. $\dfrac{2a + b}{a + b}$
19. $\dfrac{3(4x + 1)}{2(2x + 1)(3x + 1)}$
21. $\dfrac{x}{15}$
23. $\dfrac{-7}{12x}$
25. $\dfrac{c}{a + c}$
27. $\dfrac{21x - 8}{(5x - 6)(-3x + 2)}$
29. $\dfrac{3a^2b^3x}{4y^2}$
31. $\dfrac{4n^2}{3ym^2}$
33. $\dfrac{1}{xy(x + y)}$
35. $\dfrac{x(2x + 3)}{(2x - 1)(2x + 1)}$
37. $\frac{1}{2}$
39. $\dfrac{2x(6x^2 - y^2)}{(2x - y)(x - y)}$
41. $\dfrac{2x - 1}{5x - 2}$
43. $\dfrac{xy^2 + 2}{2 + x}$
45. $x = 42$
47. $x = 12$
49. 10
51. −6
53. −9
55. 7
57. $3\frac{1}{5}$
59. $S/(1 + in)$
61. $-a/4$
63. 45 and 35
65. 35 hours
67. 120 toy guns
69. 10 gallons

EXERCISE 3–3, PAGE 75

1. $x = 10; y = -2$
3. $x = 7; y = 1$
5. $x = 2; y = -4$
7. $x = 1; y = 3$
9. $x = 3, y = 2$
11. $x = -2; y = -3$
13. $x = 6; y = 2$

EXERCISE 3–4, PAGE 81

1. $\sqrt{a}$
3. $\sqrt[3]{18^2}$
5. $\sqrt[4]{x}$
7. $\sqrt[3]{x^5}$
9. $\sqrt[4]{127^3}$
11. $\sqrt[5]{a^3}$
13. $a^{3/5}$
15. $34^{5/4}$
17. $45^{3/2}$
19. $x^{5/3}$
21. $28^{1/3}$
23. $b^{2/6} = b^{1/3}$
25. $\sqrt{x^2y^3}$
27. $\sqrt{64x}$
29. $\sqrt[3]{c^3d^2}$
31. $\sqrt{46,875}$
33. $\sqrt{162t}$
35. $\sqrt{a^5b}$
37. $17\sqrt{2}$
39. $12\sqrt{3} + 2\sqrt{3} - \sqrt{3} = 13\sqrt{3}$
41. $5\sqrt{7}$
43. $30\sqrt{6}$
45. $24\sqrt{70}$
47. 2
49. $\sqrt{.625}$ or $\dfrac{\sqrt{10}}{4}$
51. $\dfrac{\sqrt[6]{648}}{3}$
53. 16
55. 32
57. 145
59. 67.4
61. 21.313 or 21.31
63. 1.0119 or 1.012

EXERCISE 3–5, PAGE 84

1. $x = \frac{9}{4}$; $x = -\frac{9}{4}$
3. $x = -\frac{4}{3}$; $x = \frac{3}{5}$
5. $x = \frac{5}{2}$; $x = -\frac{5}{2}$
7. $x = \frac{1}{4}$; $x = 1\frac{1}{2}$
9. $y = -7$ $y = 1\frac{1}{3}$
11. $y = -1\frac{2}{3}$; $y = -\frac{1}{4}$
13. $x = 3$ $x = 2$
15. $x = \frac{1}{3}$; $x = 4$
17. $x = 1\frac{1}{3}$; $x = \frac{1}{2}$
19. $x = 7$ $x = \frac{3}{4}$
21. $x = 1\frac{1}{6}$; $x = -\frac{2}{3}$
23. $x = 2\frac{1}{3}$; $x = -2\frac{1}{3}$
25. $m = 3$ $m = -\frac{2}{7}$
27. $n = 1\frac{1}{3}$; $n = \frac{3}{8}$
29. $x = 1\frac{1}{5}$; $x = \frac{3}{7}$
31. $x = \frac{1}{3}$; $x = -2\frac{1}{4}$

EXERCISE 3–6, PAGE 88

1. $x^5 + 5x^4y + 10x^3y^2 + 10x^2y^3 + 5xy^4 + y^5$
3. $x^6 + 24x^5y + 240x^4y^2 + 1{,}280x^3y^3 + 3{,}840x^2y^4 + 6{,}144xy^5 + 4{,}096y^6$
5. $1 + 7i + 21i^2 + 35i^3 + 35i^4 + 21i^5 + 7i^6 + i^7$
7. $x^6 - 12x^5y + 60x^4y^2 - 160x^3y^3 + 240x^2y^4 - 192xy^5 + 64y^6$
9. 1.061208
11. 1.1040808
13. 1.1322656
15. 1.7058475
17. .90572
19. .67392
21. 1.0032738
23. 1.0170594

EXERCISE 3–7, PAGE 93

1. log 58 = 1.763428
3. log 0.00325 = 7.511883 − 10
5. log 0.4795 = 9.680789 − 10
7. log 136 = 2.133539
9. log 0.010492 = 8.0208583 − 10
11. $10^{2.167317} = 147$
13. $10^{3.389520} = 2{,}452$
15. $10^{1.897627} = 79$
17. $10^{8.802089-10} = .0634$
19. $10^{2.0179927} = 104.23$
21. 2.454845
23. 0.582404
25. 3.636287
27. 6.596817 − 10
29. 3.375481
31. 1.0191994
33. $N = 159.1$
35. $N = 2.79$
37. $N = 0.003985$
39. $N = 49{,}100$
41. $N = 1.454$
43. $N = 0.00002796$

EXERCISE 3–8, PAGE 95

1. 8.424620 − 10
3. 9.511416 − 10
5. 0.139375
7. 9.8955 − 10
9. 2.586857
11. 1.916791
13. $N = 5{,}503.7$
15. $N = 370.04$
17. .0034377
19. 28,003
21. 2,903.31
23. .0104341

EXERCISE 3–9, PAGE 99

1. 1.06455
3. 174,605
5. 8.147
7. −3,097
9. 0.1607
11. 2,803
13. 27
15. .0008809
17. 1.495
19. 7,783,000
21. 2,025
23. −38,070
25. 17
27. 3.9
29. 2.89
31. .8071

EXERCISE 3–10, PAGE 101

1. $1\frac{1}{4}\%$
3. 2%
5. 6%
7. 2%
9. 100
11. 30

EXERCISE 4–1, PAGE 109

1. (a) Finite set
   (b) Infinite set
   (c) Empty set
   (d) Finite set
3. (a) $A = \{a, b, c, d, e, f, g, h, i, j\}$
   $A = \{x | x$ is a letter and x represents each of the first ten letters of the alphabet$\}$
   (b) $A = \{2, 3, 4, 5, 6, 7, 8\}$
   $A = \{x | x$ is an integer and $2 \le x \le 8\}$
5. 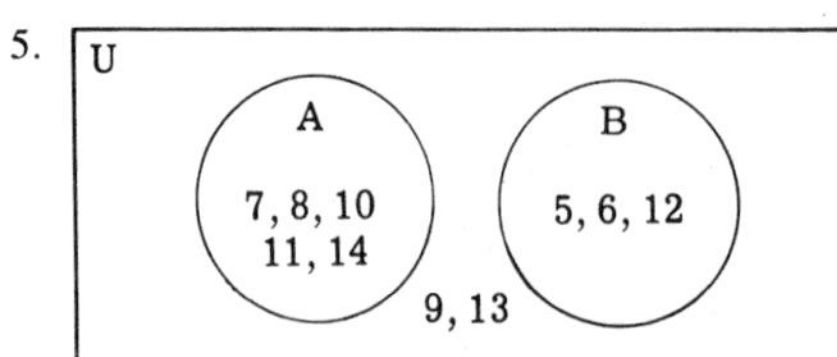

7. (a) $A \cup B' = \{7, 8, 9, 10, 11, 13, 14\}$
   (b) $A \cap B' = A = \{7, 8, 10, 11, 14\}$
   (c) $A' = \{5, 6, 9, 12, 13\}$
   (d) $B - A = B = \{5, 6, 12\}$
9. (a) $A \cup B = \{a, b, c, d, e, f, g, h, i\}$
   (b) $A \cap B = A = \{a, e\}$
   (c) $A' = \{b, d, f, j, k\}$
   (d) $A \cup A' = U = \{a, b, c, d, e, f, g, h, i, j, k\}$
   (e) $A - B = A \cap B' = \{c, g, h, i\}$
11. (a) $A \cup B = \{1, 2, 3, 4, 5, 6, 7\}$
    (b) $A - C = A \cap C' = \{1, 2, 3\}$
    (c) $A \cap B = \{3, 6\}$
    (d) $B \cap C = \{6, 7\}$
    (e) $A \cap B \cap C = \{6\}$
    (f) $(A \cup B) \cap C = \{5, 6, 7\}$
    (g) $A' \cap B' \cap C = \{8, 9, 10\}$
    (h) $A \cap B \cap C' = \{3\}$

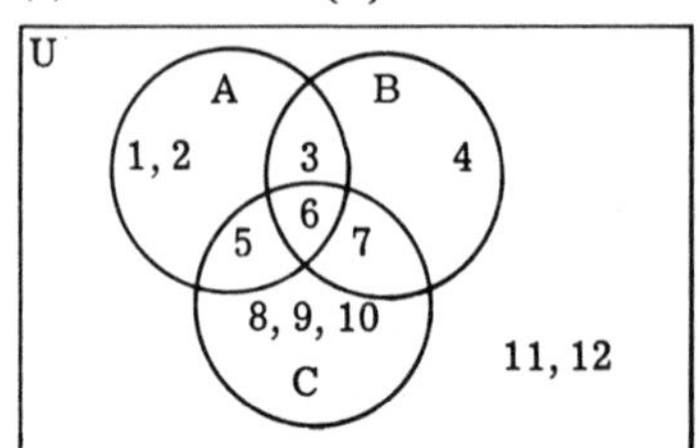

13. (a) $(A \cap B') \cup C$ (/ / / /)
    (b) $(A - B) - C$ (\ \ \ \)
    (c) $(B - C) \cap A'$ (≡)

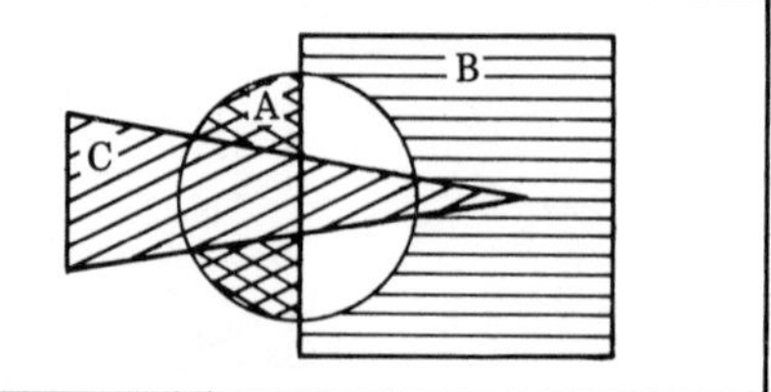

EXERCISE 4–2, PAGE 116

1. (a) 720; 1,680; 60, 720
   (b) 10; 15; 1; 44,850
3. 16
5. 24
7. (a) 24
   (b) 12
9. 6
11. 360
13. 142,506
15. (a) 1
    (b) 4
    (c) 1
17. (a) 1,320
    (b) 495
19. (a) 120
    (b) 792

EXERCISE 4–3, PAGE 124

1. (a) $\frac{6}{23}$
   (b) $\frac{17}{23}$
   (c) $\frac{17}{23}$
   (d) 1
   (e) 0
3. $\frac{33}{80}$
5. (a) $\frac{23}{35}$
   (b) $\frac{12}{35}$
   (c) $\frac{13}{35}$
   (d) $\frac{35}{35} = 1$
   (e) $\frac{18}{35}$
7. (a) $\frac{9}{64}$
   (b) $\frac{15}{64}$
   (c) $\frac{15}{32}$
   (d) $\frac{25}{64}$
   Yes. The probability of all possible ways is always equal to 1.
9. (a) $\frac{1}{8}$
   (b) $\frac{1}{4}$
11. (a) $\frac{343}{1,000}$
    (b) $\frac{441}{1,000}$
    (c) $\frac{189}{1,000}$
    (d) $\frac{27}{1,000}$
    Yes.
13. $\frac{125}{1,000} = .125$
    No, since the probability is not close to .5 (or $\frac{1}{2}$).
15. (a) .99821
    (b) .00179
17. (a) .89002
    (b) .10998

EXERCISE 5–1, PAGE 133

1. [5, 11]
3. [−3, 1]
5. $\begin{bmatrix} -2 \\ 4 \end{bmatrix}$
7. $\begin{bmatrix} 3 \\ 9 \\ 12 \end{bmatrix}$
9. [12, 72]
11. $\begin{bmatrix} 8 \\ 10 \end{bmatrix}$
13. [24, 48, 54]
15. $\begin{bmatrix} \frac{2}{5} \\ \frac{3}{5} \\ \frac{7}{5} \end{bmatrix}$
17. 56
19. 97
21. $\begin{bmatrix} 8 & 15 \\ 3 & 11 \end{bmatrix}$
23. $\begin{bmatrix} -4 & 1 \\ 1 & 2 \\ 5 & -2 \end{bmatrix}$
25. $\begin{bmatrix} 9 & 27 \\ 6 & 12 \end{bmatrix}$
27. $\begin{bmatrix} \frac{1}{4} & \frac{1}{2} \\ \frac{3}{4} & \frac{9}{4} \\ 2 & 1 \end{bmatrix}$
29. $\begin{bmatrix} 24 & 81 \\ 14 & 40 \end{bmatrix}$
31. $\begin{bmatrix} 21 & 63 & 81 \\ 12 & 32 & 38 \end{bmatrix}$
33. $\begin{bmatrix} 51 & 39 & 30 \\ 24 & 20 & 18 \end{bmatrix}$
35. $\begin{bmatrix} 46 & 74 \\ 80 & 79 \end{bmatrix}$
37. $\begin{bmatrix} 7 & 17 \\ 27 & 63 \\ 32 & 88 \end{bmatrix}$
39. $\begin{bmatrix} 70 & 68 \\ 22 & 41 \end{bmatrix}$
41. $\begin{bmatrix} 6 & 16 & 19 \\ 21 & 63 & 81 \\ 36 & 68 & 56 \end{bmatrix}$
43. $\begin{bmatrix} 12 & 10 & 9 \\ 51 & 39 & 30 \\ 36 & 44 & 60 \end{bmatrix}$
45. $\begin{bmatrix} 49 & 140 \\ 168 & 567 \\ 308 & 532 \end{bmatrix}$

EXERCISE 5–2, PAGE 138

1. (a) −22
   (b) −22
3. (a) −14
   (b) −14
5. (a) −17
   (b) −17
7. (a) 240
   (b) 240
9. (a) $8 - 2 = 6$
   (b) $-2 + 8 = 6$
11. −22
13. $168 - 60 + 132 = 240$

EXERCISE 5–3, PAGE 142

1. $\begin{bmatrix} 5 & -3 \\ 7 & 1 \end{bmatrix} \cdot \begin{bmatrix} 1 & 0 \\ 0 & 1 \end{bmatrix} = \begin{bmatrix} 5 & -3 \\ 7 & 1 \end{bmatrix}$ and $\begin{bmatrix} 1 & 0 \\ 0 & 1 \end{bmatrix} \cdot \begin{bmatrix} 5 & -3 \\ 7 & 1 \end{bmatrix} = \begin{bmatrix} 5 & -3 \\ 7 & 1 \end{bmatrix}$

3. (a) and (b) No inverse

5. (a) $\begin{bmatrix} -\frac{7}{17} & \frac{5}{17} \\ \frac{9}{17} & -\frac{4}{17} \end{bmatrix}$

(b) $-\frac{1}{17}\begin{bmatrix} 7 & -5 \\ -9 & 4 \end{bmatrix}$

7. $\frac{1}{240}\begin{bmatrix} 93 & 42 & -3 \\ -78 & -12 & 18 \\ -3 & -22 & 13 \end{bmatrix}$

EXERCISE 5–4, PAGE 146

1. (a) and (b) $x = -5$; $y = 12$
3. (a) and (b) $x = 6$; $y = 2$
5. (a) and (b) $x = 2$; $y = -3$
7. $x = 2$; $y = -3$; $z = 1$
9. $x = 1$; $y = -3$; $z = 2$

EXERCISE 5–5, PAGE 152

1. (a)

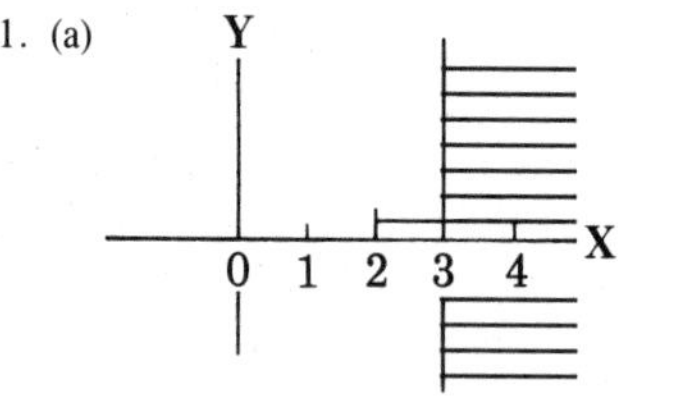

(b)

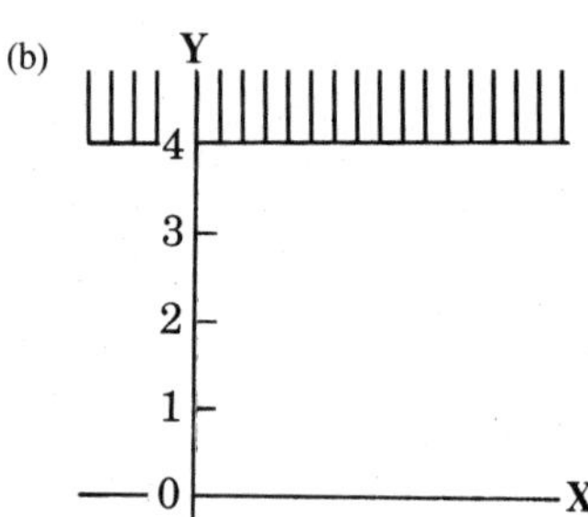

(c) (d)

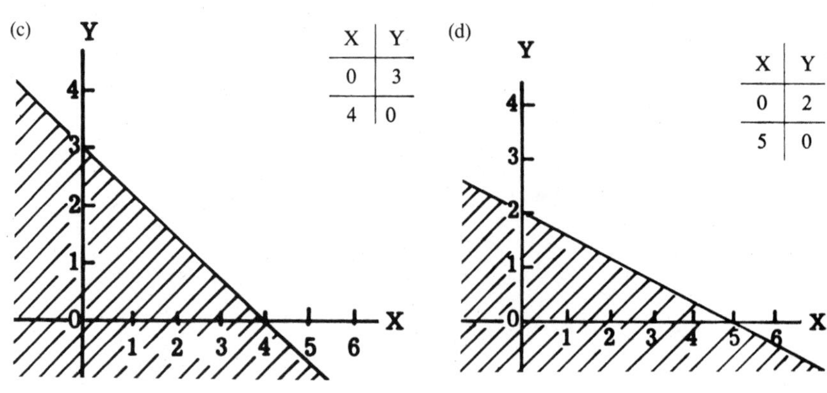

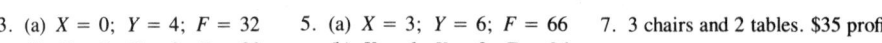

3. (a) $X = 0$; $Y = 4$; $F = 32$
   (b) $X = 5$; $Y = 2$; $F = 23$
5. (a) $X = 3$; $Y = 6$; $F = 66$
   (b) $X = 6$; $Y = 0$; $F = 96$
7. 3 chairs and 2 tables. $35 profit.

EXERCISE 5–6, PAGE 158

1. 5
3. 10
5. 23
7. 61
9. 125
11. 239
13. 1110
15. 11010
17. 101010
19. 110001
21. 1111101
23. 101010000
25. (a) 101, (b) 5
27. (a) 1001, (b) 9
29. (a) 11001, (b) 25
31. (a) 1000000, (b) 64
33. (a) 110, (b) 6
35. (a) 1001, (b) 9
37. (a) 101100, (b) 44
39. (a) 110, (b) 6
41. (a) 101010, (b) 42
43. (a) 1111000, (b) 120
45. (a) 11001000, (b) 200
47. (a) 101110100, (b) 372
49. (a) 11, (b) 3
51. (a) 100, (b) 4
53. (a) 101, (b) 5
55. (a) 1010, (b) 10
57. (a) 1100, (b) 12
59. (a) 110, (b) 6

EXERCISE 5–7, PAGE 163

1. (a) 1,200 decimeters
   (b) 12,000 centimeters
   (c) 12 decameters
   (d) 120,000 millimeters
3. (a) 1,430 decigrams, (b) 14,300 centigrams, (c) .143 kilogram
5. (a) 3,580 grams, (b) 35,800 decigrams, (c) 358 decagrams
7. (a) 13,640 centigrams, (b) 136,400,000 micrograms, (c) 13.64 decagrams
9. (a) 50 deciliters, (b) .005 kiloliter
11. (a) 12.54 meters, (b) 12,540 millimeters, (c) .1254 hectometer
13. (a) 49.21 feet, (b) 16.40 yards
15. (a) 771.60 grains, (b) 1.76 ounces
17. (a) 107,639 square feet, (b) 2.47 acres
19. (a) 93.70 inches, (b) 7.81 feet
21. (a) 21.18 ounces, (b) 1.32 pounds
23. (a) 353,147 or 353.15 cubic feet, (b) 13.08 cubic yards
25. (a) 14.189 or 14.19 bushels, (b) 56.756 or 56.76 pecks, (c) 454.048 or 454.05 quarts
27. (a) 55.06 dry liters, (b) 220.24 dry liters, (c) 352.381 or 352.38 dry liters
29. 1,360.78 kilograms
31. 18.58 square meters
33. 10.6286 or 10.63 kilometers per liter

EXERCISE 6–1, PAGE 176

1. **Personal Income By Sources**
1987 and 1988
(Billions of Dollars)

Item	*1987*	*1988*	*Increase (+) or Decrease (−)*
Wage and salary disbursements	2,248.3	2,425.0	+ 176.7
Other labor income	207.9	217.4	+ 9.5
Proprietors' income	313.0	323.0	+ 10.0
Rental income	18.4	18.2	− 0.2
Dividends	88.6	95.4	+ 6.8
Personal interest income	527.0	573.2	+ 46.2
Net transfer payments	376.8	389.6	+ 12.8
Total	3,780.0	4,041.8	+ 261.8

Source: Department of Commerce, *Survey of Current Business*, July 1988.

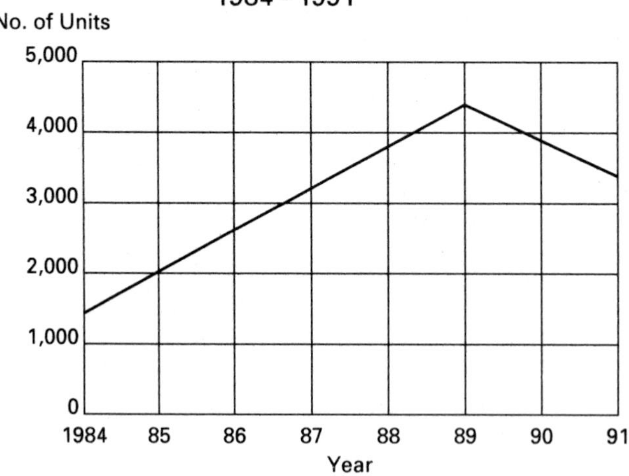

Exercise 6–1 (*continued*)

(b)

Units Shipped by Fox Distributors
1984 - 1991

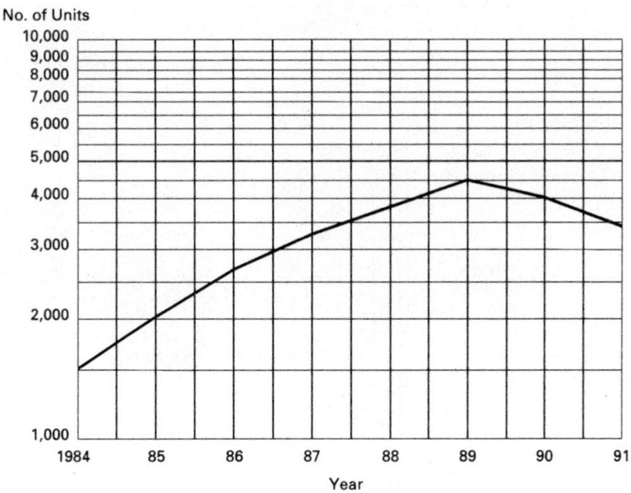

5.

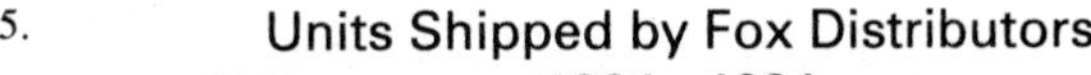

No. of Units 1984 - 1991

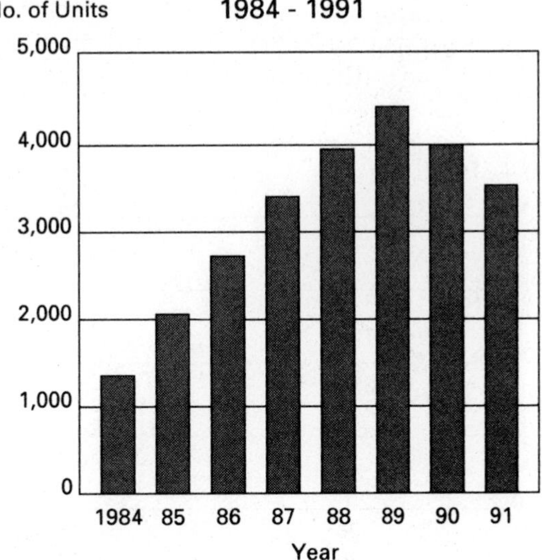

Exercise 6–1 (*continued*)

7. Types of Common Stock Owned by Bagge Investment Company

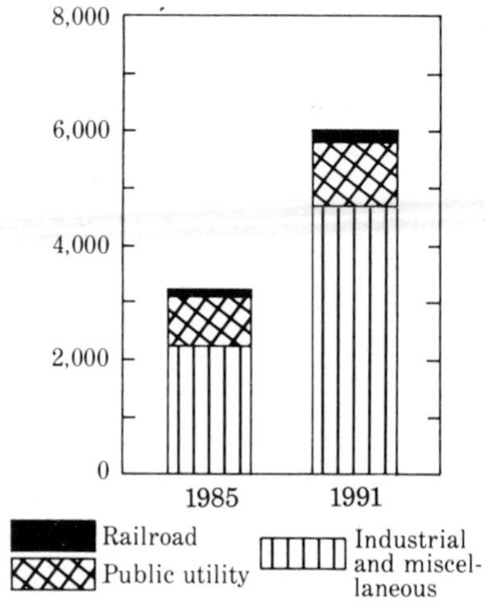

9. Types of Common Stocks Owned by Bagge Investment Company 1991

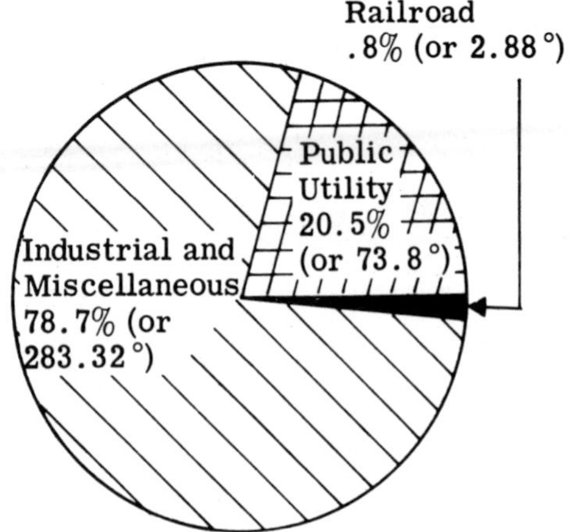

EXERCISE 6–2, PAGE 181

1. (a) 6, (b) 5, (c) 4; median is.
3. (a) 13; (b) 19

EXERCISE 6–3, PAGE 186

1. (a) 17, (b) 5
3. $8.25
5. (a) 5, (b) 5.72

EXERCISE 6–4, PAGE 189

1. (a) 11, (b) 2.86, (c) 3.38
3. (a) $2.13, (b) $2.74

EXERCISE 7–1, PAGE 198

1. $40.60
3. $16.17
5. $79.82
7. $70
9. $53.50
11. $324.50
13. $32
15. $374
17. $1,243.50
19. $14.40
21. $28.83
23. $120.34
25. (a) $29.25, (b) $94.25
27. $118.75
29. (a) $85.60, (b) $29.96
31. $35
33. (a) $7.31, (b) $2.19
35. $56
37. (a) $22.49, (b) $27.49
39. $43.20

EXERCISE 7–2, PAGE 200

1. (a) $10, (b) 20%, (c) 25%
3. (a) $16.10, (b) 34.81%, (c) 53.40%
5. (a) $0.80, (b) 9.76%, (c) 10.81%
7. (a) $23.10, (b) 26.19%, (c) 35.48%
9. (a) $42.30, (b) 32.92%, (c) 49.07%
11. (a) $460, (b) $400
13. (a) $160, (b) $104
15. (a) $69.30, (b) $52.50
17. (a) $25.42, (b) $12.71
19. (a) $2,145.82, (b) $1,384.40
21. (a) $3,291.70, (b) $2,304.19
23. (a) $600, (b) 50%, (c) 33.33%
25. (a) 31.31%, (b) 23.85%
27. (a) $14,000, (b) $19,600
29. $3,000

EXERCISE 7–3, PAGE 204

1. 13.04%
3. 24.24%
5. 32.43%
7. 39.39%
9. 44.44%
11. 60%
13. 13.64%
15. 51.52%
17. 138.10%
19. 300%
21. 900%
23. 11.11%
25. 25.93%
27. $\frac{1}{3}$, or $33\frac{1}{3}$%
29. .105, or 10.5%
31. .189, or 18.9%
33. .735, or 73.5%
35. .2647, or 26.47%
37. .8182, or 81.82%

EXERCISE 7–4, PAGE 205

1. $30
3. $46.08
5. $120
7. $3,500
9. $2.88
11. $182
13. $40.82
15. $5.50
17. $3
19. (a) 25%
    (b) $\frac{1}{3} = 33\frac{1}{3}$%
21. (a) $15
    (b) $21
23. (a) $12
    (b) $7.80
25. 25.93%
27. 20%
29. 45.5%
31. 61.29%
33. 7.06%
35. 56.7%

EXERCISE 7–5, PAGE 208

1. (a) $478.80
   (b) $221.20
   (c) 31.6%
3. (a) $100.41
   (b) $49.59
   (c) 33.06%
5. (a) $500
   (b) $500
   (c) 50%
7. (a) $6.48
   (b) $23.52
   (c) 78.4%
9. (a) $32.71
   (b) $2.79
   (c) 7.86%
11. $18.87
13. $10.20
15. $2,513.70

EXERCISE 7–6, PAGE 211

1. (a) $38.17, (b) $9.83
3. (a) $35.90, (b) $60.10
5. (a) $5.82, (b) $119.88
7. $55
9. $2,821.43
11. $620
13. 29.44%
15. 31.6%
17. 66.52%
19. (a) X Co. offered a lower price, $91.80.
    (b) The difference is $5.10.
21. $25.65
23. $800
25. $650
27. $270
29. (a) 25%, (b) 32.5%

EXERCISE 7–7, PAGE 214

1. (a) $12, (b) $588
3. (a) $10.41, (b) $510.19
5. (a) $2.19, (b) $70.65
7. (a) None, (b) $126.42
9. (a) $.59, (b) $29.06
11. $1,550.36
13. (a) $824.50, (b) $833, (c) $850
15. (a) $567.75, (b) $579
17. (a) $4, (b) $138

EXERCISE 7–8, PAGE 216

1. $3,195
3. $233.40
5. $13,742.35
7. $5.52
9. $1,800; $2,880; $2,490
11. $550
13. $22,000
15. $55,000

EXERCISE 7–9, PAGE 219

1. $.01
3. $.06
5. $.07
7. $.12
9. $.20
11. $.10
13. (a) $.22
    (b) $7.51
15. (a) $14
    (b) $.42
17. (a) $3.20
    (b) $1,020
19. (a) $11.89
    (b) $8.25

EXERCISE 7–10, PAGE 221

1. (a) 7.5%
   (b) $3,375
3. (a) 3.75%
   (b) $975
5. (a) 3.334%
   (b) $600.12
7. (a) 2.502%
   (b) $1,063.35
9. 1.8%
11. $985.28
13. (a) 1.389%
    (b) $694.44

EXERCISE 7–11, PAGE 227

1. (a) (1) $222, (2) $153.96
   (b) $1,674.04
   (c) (1) $153.96, (2) $.60, (3) $5.40
   (d) $2,209.96
   (e)

Federal income tax withheld	$ 222.00
FICA tax	307.92
Employee's net	1,674.04
FUTA tax	.60
State unempl. tax	5.40
Employer's total cost	$2,209.96

3. (a) (1) $249, (2) $115.65
   (b) $1,175.35
   (c) (1) $115.65, (2) None, (3) None
   (d) $1,655.65
   (e)

Federal income tax withheld	$ 249.00
FICA tax	231.30
Employee's net	1,175.35
Employer's total cost	$1,655.65

5. (a) (1) $1,347, (2) $751
   (b) $7,902
   (c) (1) $751, (2) $33, (3) $297
   (d) $11,081
   (e)

Federal income tax withheld	$ 1,347
FICA tax	1,502
Employee's net	7,902
FUTA tax	33
State unempl. tax	297
Employer's total cost	$11,081

Exercise 7–11 (*continued*)

7. (a) (1) $25,601.50, (2) $3,379.50
   (b) $71,019.00
   (c) (1) $3,379.50, (2) $42, (3) $378
   (d) $103,799.50
   (e)

Federal income tax withheld	$ 25,601.50
FICA tax	6,759.00
Employee's net	71,019.00
FUTA tax	42.00
State unempl. tax	378.00
Employer's total cost	$103,799.50

9. (a) (1) $348, (2) $229.81
   (b) $2,482.19
   (c) (1) $229.81, (2) None, (3) None
   (d) $3,289.81
   (e)

Federal income tax withheld	$ 348.00
FICA tax	459.62
Employee's net	2,482.19
Employer's total cost	$3,289.81

11. FICA tax = $380.01. Federal income tax withheld = $932
13. (a) $1,075, (b) $12, (c) $874
15. (a) $40,000, (b) $118,000

EXERCISE 7–12, PAGE 237

1. $1,504
3. $1,519
5. $3,287
7. $3,011
9. $5,300
11. $8,901
13. $81,200
15. (a) $7,354
    (b) $254 (tax payable)
17. (a) $8,100
    (b) $2,900 (tax refundable)
19. $122,720

EXERCISE 8–1, PAGE 241

1. $27.51
3. $21.93
5. $5.70
7. $6.30
9. $57.12
11. (a) 39 days, (b) 39 days
13. (a) 160 days, (b) 157 days
15. (a) 67 days, (b) 66 days
17. (a) 390 days, (b) 384 days
19. (a) 114 days, (b) 113 days

EXERCISE 8–2, PAGE 245

1. (a) $\frac{116}{360}$, (b) $\frac{116}{365}$
3. (a) $\frac{45}{360}$, (b) $\frac{45}{365}$
5. (a) $\frac{30}{360}$, (b) $\frac{30}{365}$
7. (a) $20.25, (b) $19.97
9. (a) $527.50, (b) $520.27
11. (a) $24.66, (b) $24.32
13. (1) $8.52, (2) $8.52
15. (1) $17.60, (2) $17.60
17. $29.20
19. $5.11
21. $6.57
23. $36.00
25. $2.88
27. $3.60

EXERCISE 8–3, PAGE 248

1. Interest = $28
   Amount = $2,828
3. Amount = $4,556.25
   Time = 75 days
5. Interest = $19.20
   Time = 4 months
7. Interest = $19
   Interest rate = 10%
9. Amount = $2,720
   Time = 2 years
11. Amount = $3,979
    Interest rate = 5%
13. (a) $47.25, (b) $5,447.25
15. Interest = $41.67
    Amount = $1,041,67
17. Interest = $129.60
    Amount = $669.60
19. (a) $997.50, (b) November 7, 1991
21. 9%
23. 5%
25. 36.73%
27. 3 months
29. 30 days
31. $1,200 at 10%
    $3,000 at 12%

EXERCISE 8–4, PAGE 253

1. \$520
3. \$5,500
5. \$225
7. \$3,400
9. \$3,000
11. \$1,500
13. \$460
15. \$3,500
17. (a) \$877.19, (b) \$122.81
19. (a) \$1,607.14, (b) \$192.86
21. \$544.15
23. \$504.90
25. \$1,001.64

EXERCISE 8–5, PAGE 258

1. (a) \$239, (b) \$240
3. (a) \$363.20, (b) \$363.21
5. (a) \$426, (b) \$426.30
7. (a) \$1,248.34, (b) \$1,248.72
9. (a) \$879, (b) \$884.56
11. \$10,100
13. \$10,186.96
15. \$552.32
17. \$551.61

EXERCISE 8–6, PAGE 264

1. \$4,240
3. \$3,800
5. \$7,546.67
7. \$1,396.72 (each payment)
9. (a) \$1,904.76, (b) \$2,000, (c) \$2,066.67
11. \$1,517.20 (each payment)
13. \$819.67 (each payment)
15. \$4,197
17. \$4,617.50

EXERCISE 8–7, PAGE 270

1. 50 days
3. $3\frac{1}{3}$ months
5. $2\frac{1}{2}$ months
7. 125 days
9. 5 months
11. 9.22 months, or 9 months and 7 days
13. $5\frac{21}{25}$ months
15. $6\frac{2}{15}$ months
17. 30 days after June 30, or on July 30; \$1,212

EXERCISE 8–8, PAGE 273

1. (a) \$200, (b) \$12.50
3. (a) 105 days, (b) 104 days
5. (a) 513 days, (b) 506 days
7. I = \$20
   I_e = \$19.73
9. I = \$4.35
   I_e = \$4.29
11. I = \$66.00
   S = \$506.00
13. \$659.40
15. (a) \$12, (b) \$612, (c) August 29, 1991
17. 3%
19. 4%
21. 3 months
23. (a) 30 days, (b) 20 days
25. \$6,000
27. \$5,000
29. \$800; \$40
31. (a) \$818.18, (b) \$21.82
33. (a) \$2,528.83, (b) \$2,528.93
35. (a) \$571.43, (b) \$600, (c) \$612
37. \$753.47
39. \$1,974.63
41. 94 days from now
43. 44 days
45. 3 months and 14 days
47. 111 days from April 10 or on July 30, 1993

EXERCISE 9–1, PAGE 279

1. \$70; \$2,930
3. \$800; 6%
5. \$30; 45 days
7. 6%; \$8,887.50
9. \$800; \$42
11. \$900; \$39,100
13. \$3,337.25
15. \$3,000
17. 9%
19. 4 months

EXERCISE 9–2, PAGE 285

1. (a) Nov. 3, 1991
   (b) $4,210
   (c) 60 days
   (d) $126.30
   (e) $4,083.70
3. (a) June 18, 1992
   (b) $1,800
   (c) 50 days
   (d) $15
   (e) $1,785
5. (a) Feb. 5, 1993
   (b) $3,645
   (c) 20 days
   (d) $32.40
   (e) $3,612.60
7. (a) Dec. 1, 1994
   (b) $2,537.50
   (c) 30 days
   (d) $14.80
   (e) $2,522.70
9. (a) Aug. 21, 1995
   (b) $1,674
   (c) 75 days
   (d) $31.39
   (e) $1,642.61
11. $7.50, $242.50
13. $4,500
15. $6.65, $373.35
17. (a) June 4
   (b) $2,490
   (c) 80 days
   (d) $77.47
   (e) $2,412.53
19. $36.05, $2,126.95
21. $50,000

EXERCISE 9–3, PAGE 289

1. 11.65%
3. 16.98%
5. 14.81%
7. 10.34%
9. 8.28%
11. 12.37%
13. 4.96%
15. $2,450; 8.16%
17. $3,570; 5.04%
19. 5%; 5.08%

EXERCISE 9–4, PAGE 290

1. (a) $6.30, (b) $623.70
3. (a) $672, (b) $673.08
5. $300
7. $13\frac{1}{3}$%
9. $\frac{1}{5}$ year or 72 days
11. $600
13. $800.62
15. (a) $25; $1,975
   (b) $1,975.31; $24.69
   $.31 (difference)
17. 12.24%
19. 17.35%

EXERCISE 10–1, PAGE 299

1. 22
3. 41.68
5. 21
7. 67.29
9. 498.15
11. 6,691.2032
13. 4.7724089
15. 2.6285714
17. 86
19. 30.4
21. 186.75
23. 30
25. 6
27. 9.75
29. 24
31. (a) 23
   (b) 32
   (c) 50
33. (a) 24
   (b) 19
   (c) 10
35. (a) 10
   (b) 14
   (c) 12
37. (a) 48
   (b) 80
   (c) 200
39. 0.2
41. 81
43. 70
45. 2.5
47. 4
49. 307.59583

EXERCISE 10–2, PAGE 309

1. (a) 12, (b) 5.7227616; 6.1178895
3. (a) 11, (b) 3.380617; 3.4641016
5. 25, or 25% increase
7. −5, or 5% decrease
9. (a) 3.9512437, (b) 1.6486586
11. (a) 20.085537, (b) 1.1735109
13. (a) 324, (b) 625
15. (a) 5,040, (b) 3,628,800
17. (a) 0.146, (b) 65.75
19. (a) 0.04, (b) 0.0666667
21. (a) 81, (b) 32,768
23. (a) 10, (b) 4
25. (a) 16, (b) 142

EXERCISE 10–3, PAGE 321

1. BASIC Program

```
10 LET A=4
20 LET B=7
30 LET C=A+B
40 PRINT C
50 END
```

Computer Display (RUN)

```
11
```

3. BASIC Program

```
10 READ A,B
20 DATA 68, 124
30 LET C=A+B
40 PRINT C
50 END
```

Computer Display (RUN)

```
192
```

5. BASIC Program

```
10 READ A,B
20 LET C=A*B
30 PRINT "PRODUCT IS ";C
40 GOTO 10
50 DATA 5, 16, 7, 25, 8, 30
60 END
```

Computer Display (RUN)

```
PRODUCT IS 80
PRODUCT IS 175
PRODUCT IS 240
```

7. BASIC Program

```
10 READ A,B
15 IF B=0 THEN 10
20 LET C=A/B
30 PRINT "QUOTIENT IS ";C
40 GOTO 10
50 DATA 20, 4, 35, 0, 60, 12
60 END
```

Computer Display (RUN)

```
QUOTIENT IS 5
QUOTIENT IS 5
```

9. BASIC Program

```
5 REM -WAGES
10 LET S=0
20 LET C=0
30 READ G
40 IF G=0 THEN 80
50 LET S=S+G
60 LET C=C+1
70 GOTO 30
80 PRINT "SUM OF WAGES = ";S,"NUMBER
   OF WAGES = ";C,"AVERAGE WAGE = ";S/C
90 DATA 5.20, 4.10, 6.50, 12.30, 15.25, 24.81
100 DATA 0
110 END
```

Computer Display (RUN)

```
SUM OF WAGES =68.16
NUMBER OF WAGES =6
AVERAGE WAGE =11.36
```

11. BASIC Program

```
5 REM --SQUARES AND SQUARE
  ROOTS
10 FOR X=4 TO 8
20 PRINT X,X^2, SQR (X)
30 NEXT X
40 END
```

Computer Display (RUN)

```
4    16    2
5    25    2.23606798
6    36    2.44948974
7    49    2.64575131
8    64    2.82842713
```

13. BASIC Program

```
10 INPUT A,B
20 LET C=A+B
30 PRINT C
40 END
```

Computer Display
(a) (RUN)

```
? 5
??6
11
```

(b) (RUN)

```
? 9
??12
21
```

EXERCISE 10–4, PAGE 325

1. 21
3. 54
5. 72
7. 20.5
9. 1,200
11. 750.4535
13. 459.06

EXERCISE 11–1, PAGE 327

1. $220.50; $20.50
3. $3,182.70; $182.70
5. $1,728; $728
7. $15,454.52; $454.52
9. $20; $0.50
11. $180; $2.70

EXERCISE 11–2, PAGE 331

1. $5,142.86
3. $75,842.94
5. $36,564.47
7. $1,208.86
9. $1,061.52
11. $2,226.64
13. $1,061.68; $1,061.36; $1,060.90; $1,060
15. (a) $1,806.11; $806.11
    (b) $3,262.04; $2,262.04
    (c) $5,891.60; $4,891.60
17. $2,095.89
19. $134.77

EXERCISE 11–3, PAGE 334

1. $937.81
3. $2,058.36
5. $617.72
7. $1,169.41
9. $923.90
11. $3,192.05

EXERCISE 11–4, PAGE 336

1. $584.62
3. $5,118.06
5. $2,364.86
7. $3,604.70
9. $3,455.34
11. $28,757.50; $12,757.50
13. $8,269.33; $3,269.33

EXERCISE 11–5, PAGE 338

1. $753.78
3. $335.03
5. $734.04
7. $1,226.23
9. (a) $895.17; $504.83
   (b) $753.71; $646.29
11. $4,902.23
13. $2,558.45; $1,041.55
15. $2,729.03
17. $1,500

EXERCISE 11–6, PAGE 342

1. $351.05; $248.95
3. $4,410.18; $1,589.82
5. $1,860.24; $597.68
7. $2,627.73; $419.63
9. $302.87
11. $5,066.88
13. $5,051.89
15. $7,955.10
17. $5,803.83

EXERCISE 11–7, PAGE 346

1. 2%
3. 10%
5. 1.06%
7. 4.26%
9. 6.38%
11. 4%, 4.04%
    4.06%, 4.07%
13. H – 19.56%
    B – 21% (Better)

EXERCISE 11–8, PAGE 348

1. 30
3. 10
5. 14
7. 10
9. 10 months
11. 5 years
13. $1,665.07; July 1, 1996

EXERCISE 11–9, PAGE 353

1. $19,204.08; $15,204.08
3. $600; $816.70
5. $3,580.11
7. $1,405.03
9. $2,881.76
11. Method A–$7,094.58; $2,094.58
    Method B–$7,092.28; $2,092.28
13. $222.20; $427.80
15. $565.53; $178.54
17. Method A–$618.87; $181.13
    Method B–$618.86; $181.14
19. 5.14%
21. 5%; 5.06%; 5.09%; 5.12%
23. A–5.61%
    P–6% (higher)
25. 41 months (or 3 years and 5 months)

EXERCISE 12–1, PAGE 359

1. $5,375.67
3. .328%
5. $197.32
7. 83.88
9. $7,555.35
11. (a) 1.2336498 (most accurate)
    (b) 1.2336699 (least accurate)
    (c) 1.2336506 (next accurate)

EXERCISE 12–2, PAGE 364

1. $1,498.38
3. $3,829.01
5. $1,652.35
7. $6,171.69
9. (a) $3,726.18
   (b) $4,200
   (c) $5,026.06
11. $3,576.91
13. $2,470.79
15. $1,175.06

EXERCISE 12–3, PAGE 367

1. 23.6952 (or 5 years and 333 days)
3. 15.7426 (or 7 years and 314 days)
5. 5.76266 (or 5 years and 275 days)
7. (a) 21.75 (or 5 years and 158 days)
   (b) 25.5882 (or 6 years and 143 days)
9. 14.6029 (or 7 years and 109 days)
11. 1.2672 (or 1 year and 96 days)
13. 2.2239 (or 2 years and 81 days)

EXERCISE 12–4, PAGE 373

1. 6.4%
3. 18.69%
5. 6.94%
7. (a) 5.13%, (b) 22.14%
9. 4.60%
11. (a) $1,040.81; $40.81
    (b) $1,083.29; $83.29

EXERCISE 12–5, PAGE 375

1. (a) 4,813.18, (b) 352.48, (c) 5.47%, (d) 19.54
3. (a) $245.72, (b) $348.44
5. $491.20
7. $1,718.15
9. $2,356.63
11. 46.275 (or 3 years and 308 days)
13. 4.91%
15. 6.9%
17. (a) 7.25%; (b) 5.65%
19. (a) $11,051.71; $1,051.71
    (b) $12,214.03; $2,214.03

EXERCISE 13–1, PAGE 380

1. \$8,060.20; \$60.20
3. \$1,672, \$72
5. \$12,364.82; \$364.82
7. \$6,556.20

EXERCISE 13–2, PAGE 383

1. \$20,043.46
3. \$96,774.11
5. \$40,455.10
7. \$10,460.50
9. \$7,444.52
11. \$568.91
13. \$1,445.81
15. \$12,285.11

EXERCISE 13–3, PAGE 385

1. \$7,900.99
3. \$520.66
5. \$2,284.63
7. \$5,062.59

EXERCISE 13–4, PAGE 388

1. \$60,091.22
3. \$25,302.64
5. \$32,144.64
7. \$5,975.19
9. \$4,868.77
11. \$2,736.77
13. \$596.71
15. \$6,656.88

EXERCISE 13–5, PAGE 393

1. \$10,897.91; \$8,829.43 (Method A)
   \$10,897.58; \$8,828.98 (Method B)
3. \$8,273.80; \$4,978.58 (Method A)
   \$8,273.90; \$4,978.50 (Method B)
5. \$609,985.50
7. \$75,153.78
9. \$294,315.22; \$153.77

EXERCISE 13–6, PAGE 396

1. \$818.99
3. \$41.79
5. \$620.90
7. \$88.70
9. \$384
11. \$542.72
13. \$274.69
15. \$724.32

EXERCISE 13–7, PAGE 400

1. $9\frac{1}{2}\% < i < 10\%$, nominal rate $= i$
3. $\frac{1}{2}\% < i < \frac{13}{24}\%$, nominal rate: between 6% and $6\frac{1}{2}\%$
5. $\frac{7}{8}\% < i < 1\%$, nominal rate: between $3\frac{1}{2}\%$ and 4%
7. $i = 1.636\%$, nominal rate = 3.27%
9. $i = 3.068\%$, nominal rate = 6.14%
11. $i = 1.747\%$, nominal rate = 6.99%
13. No. 5.76% (rate on debt)

EXERCISE 13–8, PAGE 402

1. 9 years
3. 24 months
5. 45 quarters
7. 15 semiannual periods, or $7\frac{1}{2}$ years
9. 20 semiannual periods, or 10 years
11. 22 years

EXERCISE 13–9, PAGE 413

1. \$16,894.12
3. (a) \$2,696.10; (b) \$1,684.94
5. \$4,946.19
7. \$51,434.74
9. \$1,352.45; \$1,064.51
11. \$7,865.70; \$2,274.96
13. \$33,290.34; \$7,451.26
15. \$460.44
17. \$75.85
19. 4.83%
21. 6%
23. 4.95%
25. 9%
27. 18 (quarters), or $4\frac{1}{2}$ years
29. \$15,278.57

EXERCISE 14–1, PAGE 420

1. \$4,798.51; \$2,807.56
3. \$6,868.09; \$5,039.33
5. \$34,871.41; \$18,737.77
7. \$53,965.98; \$14,151.70
9. \$26,564.90
11. \$11,634.29
13. \$29,625.14
15. \$694.54

EXERCISE 14–2, PAGE 423

1. $16\frac{1}{2}$%–18%
3. 13%–14%
5. 20 (semiannual periods or 10 years)
7. \$2,219.73
9. \$340.15
11. 25 (months or 2 years and 1 month)
13. \$49.95
15. \$1,413.78
17. $4\frac{1}{2}$%–$5\frac{1}{2}$%
19. $5\frac{1}{2}$%–6%
21. 43 months, or 3 years and 7 months
23. 18 semiannual payments, or 9 years

EXERCISE 14–3, PAGE 428

1. \$9,647.84; \$4,848.68
3. \$433.23
5. 25
7. \$9,270.23; \$6,294.68
9. \$6,854.19; \$1,460.13
11. \$11,084.71
13. 18
15. \$4,675.16

EXERCISE 14–4, PAGE 434

1. \$23,291.06; \$18,908.83
3. \$1,062.02; \$584.59
5. \$24,969.92; \$8,877.68
7. \$4,827.33; \$2,994.20
9. (a) \$13,541.26; \$11,697.45
   (b) \$13,563.67; \$11,678
11. \$116,782.69
13. \$4,440.20

EXERCISE 14–5, PAGE 437

See answers to problems of Exercise 14–4.

EXERCISE 14–6, PAGE 441

1. \$354.16
3. \$164.56
5. \$116.43
7. \$117,034.73; \$95,014.56
9. \$1,127.36; \$620.55
11. \$41,712.84; \$18,684.56
13. \$25,962.54; \$703.53
15. \$1,846.10; \$719.52
17. \$17,998.65; \$8,336.86
19. \$471.48
21. \$92.41
23. \$8,605.02; \$6,378.73
25. \$4,505.61; \$2,826.88

EXERCISE 14–7, PAGE 452

1. \$6,860.38; \$2,826.38
3. \$6,660.56; \$2,744.06
5. (a) \$6,693.13; \$2,733.42
   (b) \$6,613.61; \$2,759.63
7. (a) \$5,806.02; \$3,192.76
   (b) \$5,774.25; \$3,206.24
9. \$1,243.84
11. \$950.48
13. \$2,338.73
15. \$110,985.86
17. \$2,788.67; \$2,070.50
19. \$420.05
21. (a) \$418.36
    (b) \$439.76
23. \$23.18
25. \$23.16
27. $5\%-5\frac{1}{2}\%$
29. $5\%-5\frac{1}{2}\%$
31. 30
33. 41
35. \$2,589.43; \$1,075.96
37. \$618.31
39. 46
41. (a) \$5,101.01
    (b) \$4,901.97
    (c) \$4,853.43
    (d) \$4,710.69

EXERCISE 15–1, PAGE 459

1. \$152.46; \$1,166.58
3. \$1,101.96; \$1,059.58
5. \$562.89; \$5,799.31
7. \$50.09; \$129.09
9. R = \$1,614.16

(1)	(2) (2) − (5)	(3) (2) × 3%	(4)	(5) (4) − (3)
1	\$6,000.00	\$180.00	\$1,614.16	\$1,434.16
2	4,565.84	136.98	1,614.16	1,477.18
3	3,088.66	92.66	1,614.16	1,521.50
4	1,567.16	47.01	1,614.17	1,567.16
Total		\$456.65	\$6,456.65	\$6,000.00

11. R = \$955.57

(1)	(2) (2) − (5)	(3) (2) × 2%	(4)	(5) (4) − (3)
1	\$7,000.00	\$140.00	\$ 955.57	\$ 815.57
2	6,184.43	123.69	955.57	831.88
3	5,352.55	107.05	955.57	848.52
4	4,504.03	90.08	955.57	865.49
5	3,638.54	. . .	. . .	. . .
Total		\$460.82	\$3,822.28	\$3,361.46

EXERCISE 15–2, PAGE 463

1. (a) 26
   (b) \$1,084.32
   (c) \$21.69 (interest)
   \$178.31 (principal)
   (d) \$159.49
   \$5,159.49
3. (a) 6
   (b) \$2,245.64
   (c) \$44.91
   \$955.09
   (d) \$322.69
   \$5,322.69
5. (a) 34
   (b) \$1,178.53
   (c) \$11.79
   \$38.21
   (d) \$.72
   \$1,650.72

Exercise 15–2 (*continued*)

7.

(1)	*(2)* *(2) − (5)*	*(3)* *(2) × 3%*	*(4)*	*(5)* *(4) − (3)*
1	$8,000.00	$240.00	$2,500.00	$2,260.00
2	5,740.00	172.20	2,500.00	2,327.80
3	3,412.20	102.37	2,500.00	2,397.63
4	1,014.57	30.44	1,045.01	1,014.57
Total		$545.01	$8,545.01	$8,000.00

EXERCISE 15–3, PAGE 467

1. (a) $54.00 (higher monthly payment), (b) $52.15
3. 11.04% compounded monthly
5.

(1)	*(2)* *(2) − (5)*	*(3)* *(2) × 5%*	*(4)* *34,646.22 − (3)*	*(5)* *Multiple of $500, close to (4)*	*(6)* *(3) + (5)*
1	$150,000	$ 7,500	$27,146.22	$ 27,000	$ 34,500
2	123,000	6,150	28,496.22	28,500	34,650
3	94,500	4,725	29,921.22	30,000	34,725
4	64,500	3,225	31,421.22	31,500	34,725
5	33,000	1,650	32,996.22	33,000	34,650
Total		$23,250		$150,000	$173,250

EXERCISE 15–4, PAGE 470

1. (a) $120
   (b) $259.47
   (c) $1,616.38
   (d) $4,383.62
   (e) $24.25
3. (a) $300
   (b) $1,144.67
   (c) $6,016.76
   (d) $3,983.24
   (e) $150.42
5. (a) $31.50
   (b) $73.71
   (c) $243.98
   (d) $206.02
   (e) $24.40

7.

(1)	*(2)* *2% × (5)*	*(3)*	*(4)* *(2) + (3)*	*(5)* *(4) + (5)*	*(6)* *Book Value $5,000 − (5)*
1	...	$1,213.12	$1,213.12	$1,213.12	$3,786.88
2	$ 24.26	1,213.12	1,237.38	2,450.50	2,549.50
3	49.01	1,213.12	1,262.13	3,712.63	1,287.37
4	74.25	1,213.12	1,287.37	5,000.00	...
Total	$147.52	$4,852.48	$5,000.00		

Exercise 15–4 (*continued*)

9.

(1)	(2)	(3)	(4) (2) − (3)	(5) 1,213.12 + (4)	(6) (3) + (5)
1	. . .	. . .	. . .	$1,213.12	$1,213.12
2	$24.26	$ 24.26	. . .	1,213.12	1,237.38
3	49.01	73.52	−$24.51	1,188.61	1,262.13
4	74.25	111.38	− 37.13	1,175.99	1,287.37
Total		$209.16		$4,790.84	$5,000.00

2,450.50 × 3% = 73.52
3,712.63 × 3% = 111.38

EXERCISE 15–5, PAGE 474

1. $2,069.61, $21,157.26

3. R = $768.84

(1)	(2)	(3) (2) × 1%	(4)	(5)
1	$3,000.00	$30.00	$ 768.84	$ 738.84
2	2,261.16	22.61	768.84	746.23
3	1,514.93	15.15	768.84	753.69
4	761.24	7.61	768.85	761.24
Total		$75.37	$3,075.37	$3,000.00

5.

(1)	(2)	(3) (2) × 5%	(4)	(5)
1	$10,000.00	$ 500.00	$ 2,000.00	$ 1,500.00
2	8,500.00	425.00	2,000.00	1,575.00
3	6,925.00	346.25	2,000.00	1,653.75
4	5,271.25	263.56	2,000.00	1,736.44
5	3,534.81	176.74	2,000.00	1,823.26
6	1,711.55	85.58	1,797.13	1,711.55
		$1,797.13	$11,797.13	$10,000.00

7. $9,474.97
9. $47.37, $52.63
11. (a) $105
    (b) 10.8% compounded monthly

13.

(1)	(2) (2) − (5)	(3) (2) × 10%	(4) 79,139.24 − (3)	(5)	(6) (3) + (5)
1	$300,000	$30,000	$49,139.24	$49,000	$ 79,000
2	251,000	25,100	54,039.24	54,000	79,100
3	197,000	19,700	59,439.24	59,000	78,700
4	138,000	13,800	65,339.24	65,000	78,800
5	73,000	7,300	71,839.24	73,000	80,300
Total		$95,900		$300,000	$395,900

Exercise 15–5 (*continued*)

15. (a) $150
    (b)

(1)	(2) (5) × 2%	(3)	(4) (2) + (3)	(5)	(6) Book Value $5,000 − (5)
1	. . .	$ 960.79	$ 960.79	$ 960.79	$4,039.21
2	$ 19.22	960.79	980.01	1,940.80	3,059.20
3	38.82	960.79	999.61	2,940.41	2,059.59
4	58.81	960.79	1,019.60	3,960.01	1,039.99
5	79.20	960.79	1,039.99	5,000.00	. . .
	$196.05	$4,803.95	$5,000.00		

17. (a) $1,060.79
    (b) $1,060.79

19.

(1)	(2)	(3)	(4) (2) − (3)	(5)	(6) (3) + (5)
1	. . .	. . .	. . .	$ 960.79	$ 960.79
2	$19.22	$ 19.22	. . .	960.79	980.01
3	38.82	58.22	−$19.40	941.39	999.61
4	58.81	88.21	− 29.40	931.39	1,019.60
5	79.20	158.40	− 79.20	881.59	1,039.99
		$324.05		$4,675.95	$5,000.00

21. (a) $5,842.74
        $9,157.26
    (b) $262.92

EXERCISE 16–1, PAGE 480

1. $517.16
3. $1,740.56
5. $737.94
7. $4,983.86
9. (a) $11,449.83
   (b) $11,553.91
11. (a) $1,856.59
    (b) $1,712.93

EXERCISE 16–2, PAGE 483

1. (a) $4,277.59
   (b) $100
   (c) $4,177.59
3. (a) $4,537.18
   (b) $41.67
   (c) $4,495.51
5. (a) $953.14
   (b) $9.75
   (c) $943.39
7. (a) $9,218.51
   (b) $325
   (c) $8,893.51
9. (a) $2,904.13
   (b) $2,866.63
11. $7,515.15
13. (a) $2,000
    (b) $54.17
    (c) $2,054.17

EXERCISE 16–3, PAGE 487

1. (a) $617.74 (premium), (b) $8,617.74
3. (a) $483.17 (discount), (b) $4,516.83
5. (a) $56.44 (premium), (b) $956.44
7. (a) $1,379.86 (discount), (b) $8,620.14
9. (a) $195.83 (discount), (b) $2,804.17
11. (a) 0, (b) $3,000

EXERCISE 16–4, PAGE 491

1. $4,094.27

(1)	(2) 4,000 × $2\frac{1}{2}$%	(3) (5) × 2%	(4) (2) − (3)	(5) (5) − (4)
0	...	...	...	$4,094.27
1	$100	$ 81.89	$18.11	4,076.16
2	100	81.52	18.48	4,057.68
3	100	81.15	18.85	4,038.83
4	100	80.78	19.22	4,019.61
5	100	80.39	19.61	4,000.00
	$500	$405.73	$94.27	

3. $3,819.40

(1)	(2) 4,000 × $2\frac{1}{2}$%	(3) (5) × $3\frac{1}{2}$%	(4) (3) − (2)	(5) (5) + (4)
0	...	...	...	$3,819.40
1	$100	$133.68	$ 33.68	3,853.08
2	100	134.86	34.86	3,887.94
3	100	136.08	36.08	3,924.02
4	100	137.34	37.34	3,961.36
5	100	138.64*	38.64	4,000.00
	$500	$680.60	$180.60	

*138.65 − 1¢ for correction.

5. $8,229.82

EXERCISE 16–5, PAGE 494

1. 11.964%
3. 13.169%
5. 4.671%
7. 4.956%
9. 6.250%
11. 3.830%

EXERCISE 16–6, PAGE 497

1. $197.93
3. $2,937.96
5. $481.26
7. 12.50% < ? < 12.60%
9. 12.50% < ? < 12.60%
11. $1,950.52
13. (a) $3,949.64
    (b) $200
    (c) $4,149.64
15. 13.04%

EXERCISE 16–7, PAGE 500

1. (a) $9,623.78
   (b) $4,315.81
3. (a) $10,399.42
   (b) $4,476.44
5. $17,328.15
7. $15,654.04

EXERCISE 16–8, PAGE 501

1. (a) \$956.24
   (b) \$979.67
   (c) \$932.80

3. (a) \$964.21
   (b) \$6.67
   (c) \$957.54

5. (a) \$1,920
   (b) \$13.33
   (c) \$1,933.33

7. (a) \$475.22
   (b) \$7,475.22

9. (a) \$6,560.36
   (b) \$7,000

11. (a) \$5,888.49
    (b)

(1)	*(2)* 6,000 × $2\frac{1}{2}$%	*(3)* (5) × 3%	*(4)* (3) − (2)	*(5)* (5) + (4)
0	. . .	. . .	. . .	\$5,888.49
1	\$150	\$176.65	\$ 26.65	5,915.14
2	150	177.45	27.45	5,942.59
3	150	178.28	28.28	5,970.87
4	150	179.13	29.13	6,000.00
	\$600	\$711.51	\$111.51	

13. (a) \$6,231.26
    (b)

(1)	*(2)* 6,000 × $2\frac{1}{2}$%	*(3)* (5) × $1\frac{1}{2}$%	*(4)* (2) − (3)	*(5)* (5) − (4)
0	. . .	. . .	. . .	\$6,231.26
1	\$150	\$ 93.47	\$ 56.53	6,174.73
2	150	92.62	57.38	6,117.35
3	150	91.76	58.24	6,059.11
4	150	90.89	59.11	6,000.00
	\$600	\$368.74	\$231.26	

15. 3.738%
17. 7.755%
19. \$7,835.52
21. \$10,315.00
23. 12.642%
25. (a) \$9.790.15
    (b) \$3,944.98
27. \$20,275.82

EXERCISE 17–1, PAGE 508

1. \$299,500
3. \$480

(1)	*(2)*	*(3)*	*(4)*
0	. . .	. . .	\$2,650
1	\$ 480	\$ 480	2,170
2	480	960	1,690
3	480	1,440	1,210
4	480	1,920	730
5	480	2,400	250
Total	\$2,400		

5. \$440; \$592; \$496; \$464; \$408

Exercise 17–1 (*continued*)

(1)	*(2)*	*(3)*	*(4)*
0	. . .	. . .	$2,650
1	$ 440	$ 440	2,210
2	592	1,032	1,618
3	496	1,528	1,122
4	464	1,992	658
5	408	2,400	250
Total	$2,400		

7. $840

EXERCISE 17–2, PAGE 514

1. $900; $750; $600; $450; $300; $150

(1)	*(2)*	*(3)*	*(4)*
0	. . .	. . .	$3,350
1	$ 900	$ 900	2,450
2	750	1,650	1,700
3	600	2,250	1,100
4	450	2,700	650
5	300	3,000	350
6	150	3,150	200
	$3,150		

3. $639.13; $593.48; $547.83; $502.17; $456.52; $410.87
5. (a) $33\frac{1}{3}$% or $\frac{1}{3}$ (rate)

(1)	*(2)* *(4)* $\times \frac{1}{3}$	*(3)*	*(4)*
0	. . .	. . .	$3,350.00
1	$1,116.67	$1,116.67	2,233.33
2	744.44	1,861.11	1,488.89
3	496.30	2,357.41	992.59
4	330.86	2,688.27	661.73
5	220.58	2,908.85	441.15
6	147.05	3,055.90	294.10
	$3,055.90		

(b) .374831 (rate)

(1)	*(2)* *(4) × .374831*	*(3)*	*(4)*
0	. . .	. . .	$3,350.00
1	$1,255.68	$1,255.68	2,094.32
2	785.02	2,040.70	1,309.30
3	490.77	2,531.47	818.53
4	306.81	2,838.28	511.72
5	191.81	3,030.09	319.91
6	119.91	3,150.00	200.00
	$3,150.00		

EXERCISE 17–3, PAGE 517

1. $607.23; $607.23; $607.23; $607.21

(1)	(2)	(3) (6) × 5%	(4) (2) − (3)	(5)	(6) 2,400 − (5)
0	...	...	...	...	$2,400.00
1	$ 607.23	$120.00	$ 487.23	$ 487.23	1,912.77
2	607.23	95.64	511.59	998.82	1,401.18
3	607.23	70.06	537.17	1,535.99	864.01
4	607.21	43.20	564.01	2,100.00	300.00
	$2,428.90	$328.90	$2,100.00		

3. $487.23; $511.59; $537.17; $564.01

(1)	(2)	(3) (5) × 5%	(4) (2) + (3)	(5)	(6) 2,400 − (5)
0	...	...	...	...	$2,400.00
1	$ 487.23	...	$ 487.23	$ 487.23	1,912.77
2	487.23	$ 24.36	511.59	998.82	1,401.18
3	487.23	49.94	537.17	1,535.99	864.01
4	487.21	76.80	564.01	2,100.00	300.00
	$1,948.90	$151.10	$2,100.00		

5. $864.01

EXERCISE 17–4, PAGE 520

1. (a) 10.33%, (b) 9.25 (years) 3. (a) 10.59%, (b) 8.66 (years) 5. 9.2303 (years)

EXERCISE 17–5, PAGE 524

1. (a) $28,000
   (b) $.07
   (c) $7,000
   (d) $2,000
3. (a) $6,692.76
   (b) $2,307.24
   (c) 7.69%
5. (a) $7,170.81
   (b) $1,829.19
   (c) 6.1%
7. $55,630.58
9. $55,497.07

EXERCISE 17–6, PAGE 527

1. (a) $540
   (b) $900; $720; $540; $360; $180
   (c) 1 − $1,200; $720; $432; $259.20; $155.52
   2 − $1,107.17; $698.55; $440.76; $278.09; $175.43
   (d) $658.97

Exercise 17–6 (*continued*)

(1)	(2)	(3) (6) × 6%	(4) (2) − (3)	(5) from (4)	(6) Book Value
0	...	...	...	...	$3,000.00
1	$ 658.97	$180.00	$ 478.97	$ 478.97	2,521.03
2	658.97	151.26	507.71	986.68	2,013.32
3	658.97	120.80	538.17	1,524.85	1,475.15
4	658.97	88.51	570.46	2,095.31	904.69
5	658.97	54.28	604.69	2,700.00	300.00
	$3,294.85	$594.85	$2,700.00		

(e) $478.97; $507.71; $538.17; $570.46; $604.69

(1)	(2)	(3) (5) × 6%	(4) (2) + (3)	(5) from (4)	(6) Book Value
0	...	...	...	...	$3,000.00
1	$ 478.97	...	$ 478.97	$ 478.97	2,521.03
2	478.97	$ 28.74	507.71	986.68	2,013.32
3	478.97	59.20	538.17	1,524.85	1,475.15
4	478.97	91.49	570.46	2,095.31	904.69
5	478.97	125.72	604.69	2,700.00	300.00
	$2,394.85	$305.15	$2,700.00		

3. $88 (first year); $80 (second year)
5. 8.96%
7. (a) $496,000; $124,000
   (b) $41,000
9. (a) $115,077.87
   (b) $49,922.13
   (c) 9.98%
11. $554,564.76
13. $554,062.11

EXERCISE 18–1, PAGE 533

1. $20,000
3. $3,250.97
5. $17,850
7. $20,435.98
9. (a) $50,000
   (b) $51,000
11. (a) $49,751.24
    (b) $50,751.24
13. $16,666.67
15. $16,213.29

EXERCISE 18–2, PAGE 537

1. (a) $2,000
   (b) $1,533.60
3. $395,061.73
5. $12,400
7. $12,141.29
9. $34,900.18
11. $36,555.75
13. $4,393.60

EXERCISE 18–3, PAGE 539

1. $28,116.60 ($15,000 type is cheaper)
3. $27,852.99 ($17,500 type is cheaper)
5. $1,126.20
7. $200.64

EXERCISE 18–4, PAGE 541

1. $10,000
3. $10,150
5. $3,316.72
7. $3,366.72
9. (a) $16,666.67
   (b) $24,875.62
11. $126,472.24
13. $129,413.60
15. $25,479.28
17. X (K = $1,044.94)
19. $1,013.48
21. $213.48

EXERCISE 19–1, PAGE 546

1. (a) 9,896,659
   (b) 9,664,994
   (c) 9,439,447
   (d) 9,000,587
   (e) 3,221,884
   (f) 6,415
3. (a) 14,449
   (b) 17,300
   (c) 21,239
   (d) 56,910
   (e) 254,835
   (f) 6,415
5. (a) 1.23
   (b) 1.79
   (c) 14.21
   (d) 49.79
7. (a) 45,175
   (b) 376

EXERCISE 19–2, PAGE 549

1. $875.06
3. $1,508.26
5. $1,896.06
7. $4,037.64
9. $668.64
11. $610.14
13. $682.83
15. $731.37

EXERCISE 19–3, PAGE 553

1. $82,360.89
3. $30,441.20
5. $37,566.13
7. $66,456.60
9. $815.70
11. $4,710.63

EXERCISE 19–4, PAGE 557

1. $85,360.88
3. $19,783.07
5. $86,891.17
7. $783.73
9. $129.93
11. $14,555.52
13. $15,075.10
15. $668.84

EXERCISE 19–5, PAGE 561

1. $43,216.36
3. $29,314.54
5. $940.81
7. $12,265.89
9. $44,408.84
11. $912.19
13. $5,467.49
15. $1,190.70

EXERCISE 19–6, PAGE 564

1. (a) 9,882,210
   (b) 8,762,306
   (c) 19,760
   (d) 179,271
   (e) .00251
   (f) .00583
3. $1,629.23
5. $869.97
7. (a) $82,090.80
   (b) $79,090.80
9. $65,233.03
11. (a) $351.45
    (b) $364.25
13. $577.50
15. (a) $10,109.25
    (b) $10,388.50
17. $8,309.58
19. (a) $450.08
    (b) $462.41
21. $545.25

EXERCISE 20–1, PAGE 571

1. (a) $1,387.52
   (b) $51.82
3. (a) $822.48
   (b) $92.80
5. (a) $570.39
   (b) $32.38
7. (a) $730.81
   (b) $69.54
9. (a) $248.08
   (b) $377.59
   (c) $678.62
   (d) $890.62
11. $420.13
13. $17.67
15. $33.86

EXERCISE 20–2, PAGE 574

1. (a) $10.43
   (b) $2.20
3. (a) $103.97
   (b) $8.38
5. (a) $68.55
   (b) $6.59
7. (a) $273.12
   (b) $49.09
9. (a) $80.42; $9.03
   (b) $100.45; $11.30
   (c) $522.99; $61.02
11. (a) $54.78
    (b) $2.98
13. $3.49

EXERCISE 20–3, PAGE 577

1. (a) $884.35
   (b) $186.51
3. (a) $1,394.82
   (b) $112.43
5. (a) $1,651.03
   (b) $89.55
7. (a) $2,625.94
   (b) $224.44
9. (a) $498.91
   (b) $24.28
11. (a) $513.23
    (b) $25.72
13. $27.27

EXERCISE 20–4, PAGE 580

1. $1,556.38
3. $10.78
5. $1,425.06
7. $58.16
9. $102.31
11. $63.59

EXERCISE 20–5, PAGE 585

1. (a) $1.20
   (b) $1.18
   (c) $1.18
   (d) $1.20
   (e) $1.23
3. Yes, natural premium equals cost of death claim, $1,000.
5. Level 1,000 $P^{1}_{25:\overline{5}|} = 1.94733$
   1,000 $c_{25} = 1.88286$, 1,000 $c_{26} = 1.91219$
   1,000 $c_{27} = 1.94138$, 1,000 $c_{28} = 1.98046$
   1,000 $c_{29} = 2.02915$

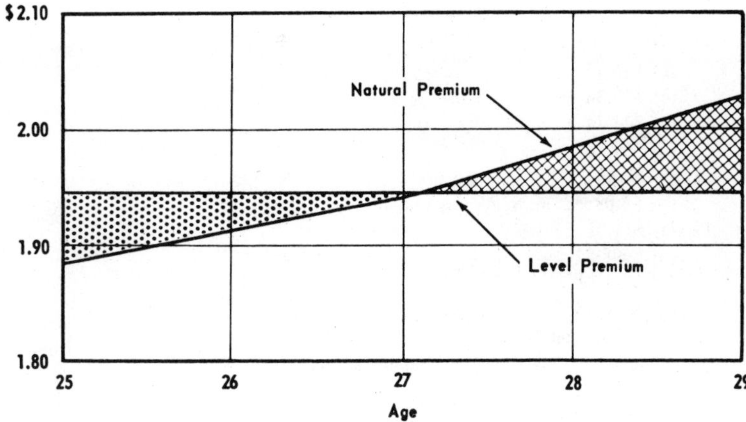

EXERCISE 20–6, PAGE 591

1. (a) $1.73
   (b) 0
3. (a) $184.46
   (b) $1,000
5. (a) $175.65
   (b) $774.30
7. (a) $195.18
   (b) $678.62

EXERCISE 20–7, PAGE 593

1. $143.78
3. See Exercise 20–6 for answers to Problems 1, 3, 5, and 7.

EXERCISE 20–8, PAGE 595

1. (a) 304 days
   (b) $79.11
3. (a) 40 years and 168 days
   (b) $265.35
5. (a) 22 years and 242 days
   (b) $360.74

EXERCISE 20–9, PAGE 598

1. (a) $788.07
   (b) $31.72
   (c) $43.47
3. (a) $637.99
   (b) $22.85
   (c) $34.61
5. (a) $36.54
   (b) $2.93
   (c) $4.11
7. (a) $78.36
   (b) $6.39
   (c) $8.90
9. (a) $410.85
   (b) $17.01
   (c) $18.17
11. (a) $398.65
    (b) $16.17
    (c) $17.38
13. (a) $44.48
    (b) $99.15
15. (a) $2.46
    (b) $2.08, $2.26, $2.58, $3.17
17. (a) $11.31
    (b) $698.32
    (c) $175.41
    (d) $206.18
19. (a) 3 years and 313 days
    (b) a whole life policy of $1,000 and a cash value of $259.87
    (c) 28 years and 126 days
    (d) 30 years and 353 days
21. (a) $324.35
    (b) $789.48
    (c) $400.07
    (d) $470.25

INDEX

A

B

C

D

E

F

G

H

I

K

L

M

N

O

P

Q

R

S

T

U

V

W

X

Y

Z